Macmillan Education LaunchPad — SOCIAL PSYCHOLOGY

LaunchPad for SOCIAL PSYCHOLOGY

Available May 2015 at **http://www.macmillanhighered.com/launchpad/greenberg1e**

Each chapter in **LaunchPad** for **SOCIAL PSYCHOLOGY** features a collection of activities carefully chosen to help master the major concepts. The site serves students as a comprehensive online study guide, available anytime, with opportunities for self-quizzing with instant feedback, exam preparation, and further exploration of topics from the textbook. For instructors, all units and activities can be instantly assigned, and students' results and analytics are collected in the Gradebook.

FOR STUDENTS

- Full e-Book of **SOCIAL PSYCHOLOGY**
- LearningCurve Quizzing
- Student Video Activities
- Interactive Flashcards
- PsychSim 6.0 activities
- *Scientific American* Newsfeed
- *The Science of Everyday Life* Online Activities and Experiments
- Interactive Data Visualization Activities

FOR INSTRUCTORS

- Test Bank and Gradebook
- Presentation Slides
- Electronic Figures, Photos, and Tables
- Videos
- Resource Manual with Lecture Notes and Suggested Activities

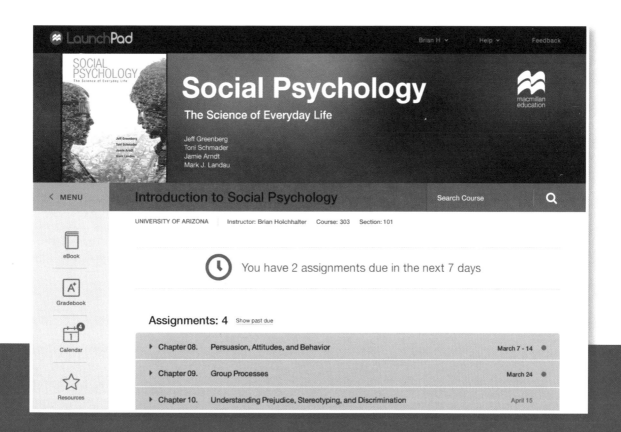

Social Psychology

Social Psychology

The Science of Everyday Life

Jeff Greenberg
University of Arizona

Toni Schmader
University of British Columbia

Jamie Arndt
University of Missouri

Mark Landau
University of Kansas

WORTH
PUBLISHERS

A Macmillan Education Imprint
New York

Vice President, Editing, Design, and Media Production:
Catherine Woods

Publisher: Rachel Losh

Associate Publisher: Jessica Bayne

Senior Acquisitions Editor: Christine Cardone

Senior Development Editor: Valerie Raymond

Executive Marketing Manager: Katherine Nurre

Marketing Assistant: Allison Greco

Assistant Editor: Catherine Michaelsen

Associate Media Editor: Anthony Casciano

Art Director: Diana Blume

Cover Designer: Kevin Kall

Text Designer: Marsha Cohen, Parallelogram Graphics

Director of Editing, Design, and Media Production:
Tracey Kuehn

Managing Editor: Lisa Kinne

Senior Project Editor: Jane O'Neill

Photo Editor: Cecilia Varas

Photo Researcher: Teri Stratford

Art Manager: Matt McAdams

Studio Art: Precision Graphics

Anatomical Art: Jeremy Mack

Composition: TSI evolve

Production Manager: Sarah Segal

Printing and Binding: C.O.S. Printers Pte Ltd - Singapore

Front cover and title page image: Jasper James/Getty Images

Back cover image: Michael Sugrue/Getty Images

Library of Congress Preassigned Control Number:
2015930043

ISBN-13: 978-0-7167-0422-5

ISBN-10: 0-7167-0422-6

© 2015 by Worth Publishers

Worth Publishers
41 Madison Avenue
New York, NY 10010
www.macmillanhighered.com

ABOUT THE AUTHORS

[Jeff Greenberg]

Jeff Greenberg, Ph.D. is a professor of psychology and a College of Science Fellow at the University of Arizona. As a small child growing up in the Bronx, he was very curious about the human propensities for vanity and prejudice. Jeff majored in psychology at the University of Pennsylvania, but it wasn't until he took social psychology in his final semester that he found a field where people where asking the questions he thought should be asked. Soon after starting a master's program in social psychology at Southern Methodist University, he knew this was what he wanted to spend his life studying and teaching. After receiving his M.A., Jeff completed his Ph.D. at University of Kansas in 1982 under the mentorship of Jack Brehm. He has since received numerous research and teaching awards. His research has contributed to understanding self-serving biases, how motivation affects cognition, the effects of ethnic slurs, the role of self-awareness in depression, cognitive dissonance, and how concerns about death contribute to prejudice, self-esteem striving, and many other aspects of social behavior. Jeff has also coauthored or coedited six prior books, including the *Handbook of Experimental Existential Psychology* and *In the Wake of 9/11: The Psychology of Terror.*

[UBC Department of Psychology]

Toni Schmader, Ph.D. is a Canada Research Chair in Social Psychology at the University of British Columbia. She received her B.A. from Washington & Jefferson College in Pennsylvania before completing her Ph.D. at the University of California, Santa Barbara. Before moving to Canada in 2009, Toni taught at the University of Arizona for 10 years. At the University of British Columbia, she was awarded the Killam Prize for excellence in research, and at the University of Arizona she received the Magellan Prize for excellence in teaching. Toni is currently a member of the executive committee of the Society for Personality and Social Psychology and an associate editor at the *Journal of Personality and Social Psychology.* She was drawn to research in social psychology for its ability to take a systematic empirical approach to examining important social issues and to teaching for the opportunity to share those insights with others. Her research examines how individuals are affected by and cope with tarnished identities and negative stereotypes. Toni has published work on topics of social identity threat, stigma and identity, stereotyping and prejudice, self-conscious emotion, and gender roles.

[Jamie Arndt]

Jamie Arndt, Ph.D. is the 2012 Frederick A. Middlebush Professor of Psychological Sciences at the University of Missouri (MU). After attending Skidmore College in the eastern United States for his B.A., and the University of Arizona in the west for his Ph.D., he settled in the middle, accepting a position at MU in 1999. During his time at MU, he has received the Robert S. Daniel Junior Faculty Teaching Award, the Provost's Junior Faculty Teaching Award, the International Society for Self and Identity Early Career Award, and the University of Missouri Chancellor's ffor Outstanding Research and Creative Activity in the Social and Behavioral Sciences. Jamie is a founding member of the Social Personality and Health Network and former Chair of the Society for Personality and Social Psychology Training Committee, and has served on the editorial boards of various journals in the field. He has authored or coauthored scholarly works pertaining to the self, existential motivation, psychological defense, and their implications for many topics, most notably health decision making, creativity, and legal judgment.

[Omri Gillath]

Mark J. Landau, Ph.D. is an associate professor of psychology at the University of Kansas. Mark received his B.A. from Skidmore College, where he became very interested in the fusion of experimental psychology and existential philosophy. He continued his research and education at the University of Colorado, Colorado Springs, and then at the University of Arizona, where he received his Ph.D. in 2007. Mark's research explores how existential motives influence social perceptions and behavior, and how people use conceptual metaphors to construct meaning. He has received a number of awards recognizing his research, including the Theoretical Innovation Prize from the Society for Personality and Social Psychology and the Outstanding Early Career Award from the International Society for Self and Identity. Mark has taught social psychology for over 14 years. He enjoys showing students that research, much like an inspiring novel or movie, affirms our common humanity—reminding us that we are not alone in our strivings, insecurities, and foibles—and thereby sharpens our ethical awareness.

C O N T E N T S

Chapter 2

[Gandee Vasan/Getty Images]

Fundamentals of Social Behavior   37

Chapter 3

[Colin Anderson/Getty Images]

The Core Elements of Social Cognition   81

The "Why" of Social Cognition: The Motives Behind Thinking   82

The "How" of Social Cognition: Two Ways to Think About the Social World   84

The "What" of Social Cognition: Schemas as the Cognitive Building Blocks of Knowledge   93

Chapter 4

[Tooga/Getty Images]

Thinking About People and Events   117

Chapter 5

[Hugh Kretschmer/ Getty Images]

The Nature, Origins, and Functions of the Self   153

Chapter 6

The Key Self-motives: Consistency, Esteem, Presentation, and Growth   189

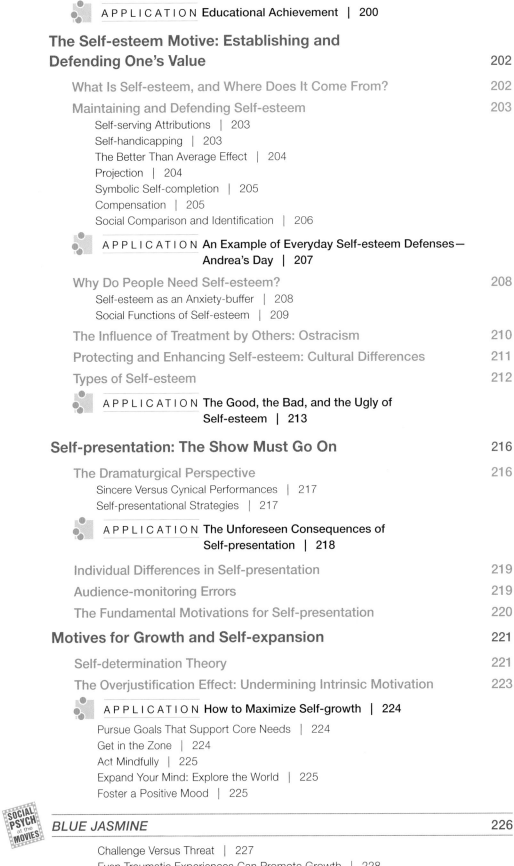

Chapter 7

[Mike Powell/Getty Images]

Chapter 8

[Travelif/Getty Images]

Persuasion, Attitudes, and Behavior 271

Chapter 9

[Tim Klein/Getty Images]

Chapter 10

Understanding Prejudice, Stereotyping, and Discrimination   349

Chapter 11

[CURTO DE LA TORRE/AFP/Getty Images]

Chapter 12

[Colin Anderson/
Getty Images]

Interpersonal Aggression   425

Chapter 13

[Stephen Simpson/Getty Images]

Chapter 14

[alex grabchilev/evgeniya bakanova/Getty Images]

Interpersonal Attraction 507

Chapter 15

[Ira Block/National Geographic/Getty Images]

PREFACE

Since our own days as undergrads, we've been excited by how the science of social psychology helps us understand everyday life. Our goal in this book is to generate this same kind of excitement for a new generation of students. How? By presenting the best, brightest, and most current ideas and findings the field has to offer in a conceptually coherent and lively narrative. We want students to appreciate that social psychology is, first and foremost, the science of all of us. And so we have aimed to write a book that all students, regardless of their backgrounds, social identities, and career interests, will find enriching and enjoyable.

There's only one good reason to spend many years bringing a new social psych text into the world: to present the field's body of knowledge in a more compelling and appealing way than any of the texts that are currently available. We have tried to do this primarily through a lot of hard work, digging into literatures both from within the traditional bounds of the field and from related disciplines, thinking creatively, staying abreast of the latest developments, and discussing and debating what to present and how best to do it. Indeed, every chapter involved a close collaboration among the four of us, resulting in a consistent voice that conveys our collective knowledge, experience, and insight.

Connecting Theory, Research, and Application

These nuts and bolts are very important, but so is the architectural plan, the overarching vision that provides coherent structure both within and across chapters. Our vision is to present social psychology in a more coherent and integrative way than prior texts have done. As teachers of introductory social psychology, we have long been struck by the tendency of textbooks to treat each topic as a distinct form of human behavior—essentially presenting students with a few topic-focused theories, some clever studies, and closely related phenomena. The result can seem, across chapters, like analyses of entirely different beings: One being is prone to confirmation bias, another to prosocial behavior, yet another to aggression, and so forth. Of course, all of these are elements of human behavior, so in our book we emphasize the core human motivations, cognitive processes, emotions, and cultural and situational forces that contribute to the varied ways we act, think, and feel.

In our teaching, we find that what sticks with students is rarely a single experiment or definition picked from the field's vast array of concepts and findings. Instead, students most value learning the broader theories in the field, theories that often have implications for understanding diverse social phenomena. For instance, Kevin, one of our former students who is now in finance, notes that he has benefited from theories in social cognition that explain how people's habits of thought can bias their judgments and decisions. Anna, now a graduate student, still gains insight from existential theories of the motives behind people's quest for meaning and self-worth. Among the theories we cover in greater depth than most texts are action identification, attachment, cognitive dissonance, conceptual metaphor, construal level, ego depletion, objectification, reactance, regulatory focus, self-affirmation, self-determination, self-perception, social learning, symbolic self-completion, system justification, terror management, and thought suppression.

We believe that theories and research discoveries have their greatest value when they are applied to everyday experiences, important social issues, and contemporary events. We want students to easily see the intimate connections among theory, research, and applications. To accomplish this, we weave together theory; findings; personal, historical, and media examples; and applications throughout the narrative flow of the text. We also created specially designated application sections that translate findings to health, law, politics, social justice, fashion, and a variety of other topics that matter to students' lives. These applications are seamlessly integrated throughout the text (rather than being covered in separate applied chapters at the end of the text) and are indicated visually with descriptive icons. For convenient reference, the icons also appear next to each application heading in the detailed Table of Contents.

APPLICATION
Can the Unconscious Help Us Make Better Health Decisions?

There is a big push in the health care field to assist patients in making more informed medical decisions. You or someone you know may have encountered some of these

so-called decision aids like the one shown in the photo on the left. In addition to providing information about the disease and treatment options, they guide you through a series of rational and deliberate questions so that you can arrive at a more educated understanding of the choices you can make for your treatment. In short, they rely strongly on the conscious processing system.

But is conscious reasoning always the best way to make these decisions? Recent research suggests that perhaps even medical decisions can benefit from some input from the intuitive processing system (de Vries et al., 2013). One reason for this may be that the intuitive system is better able to integrate feelings and emotions that can play a key role in treatment adherence. Although the potential benefits of intuitive processing by no means suggest that we should avoid information or careful reasoning in health and other important decisions, it does highlight the possibility that complex decisions may best be made by integrating conscious and unconscious processes (Nordgren et al., 2011).

To reinforce further how social psychological knowledge can illuminate the world we all live in, we also highlight in feature boxes how the field's knowledge can be applied to understand real historical and personal events (Social Psych Out in the World):

SOCIAL PSYCH out in the WORLD

Food for Body, Mind, and Soul

One of the ways that culture influences you in your everyday life is the food you eat. Think about what you have eaten so far today. How would the food you eat be different if you had grown up in Chicago, Berlin, Tokyo, Marrakech, or Chang Mai? Not only do cultural adaptations dictate how we obtain sustenance but all cultures have particular ways of preparing and serving foods that embody their unique identity as groups and help to define the social environment. Whether it's hot dogs in the United States, schnitzel in Germany, sushi in Japan, tagines in Morocco, or panang curry in Thailand—you get the idea, and we're getting hungry!—specific food preparations help define a culture. People in that culture are especially likely to eat those foods at times when they want to commemorate particular past events that serve to affirm their cultural identity. Just as most Americans eat turkey on Thanksgiving, other cultures also have specific dishes that are eaten on days of particular historical and symbolic importance. As a result, food is a delicious representation of a culture.

Cultures also specify ritualistic ways in which meals are to be consumed. This includes prayers ("Thank you, Lord, for this food we are about to share") and other utterances that precede meals ("Bon appetit!"), utensils that should be used (forks, chopsticks, fingers), rules for exactly how the utensils should be held, and customs for the order in which different courses are served. If you have ever watched the culinary explorer Anthony Bourdain on television, perhaps you've caught a glimpse of some of the food customs of far-flung places around the world.

The echoes of cultural adaptation on how we eat don't stop at the social environment; they extend to the metaphysical. The physical necessity of eating is transformed into an

Anthony Bourdain has built a reputation for hosting television programs that introduce viewers to the food and eating customs of far-flung cultures.
[Tannis Toohey/*Toronto Star* via Getty Images]

Culture and the arts are mirrors to our inner nature as well as the major issues facing society. So each chapter also includes a feature box that connects theories and findings to human behavior as portrayed on film. These boxes reinforce key concepts by bringing them to life using vivid examples from classic and contemporary films (Social Psych at the Movies):

SOCIAL PSYCH at the MOVIES

Milk: Charismatic Leadership Style

Milk (Jinks et al., 2008) is a moving biopic about Harvey Milk, an influential figure in the movement for gay civil rights. In depicting Milk's rise to leadership, the movie illustrates a number of features of an effective leadership style. The story begins in the Castro district of San Francisco in the early 1970s. Milk, played by Sean Penn, has just moved from New York, and although he is enamored of his neighborhood's charm, he is outraged by everyday acts of disc[...] his new city. Police harassment an[...] are common, and Milk is told that [...] join the neighborhood merchant's [...] his "unholy" lifestyle.

Fed up, Milk stands on top [...] announces to his neighbors that [...] begins his rise into the political sp[...] activist—referred to by his neighbo[...] Street—to being one of the first o[...] major public office in America. In [...] he was on the Board of Supervisor[...] being fatally shot, he made major [...] What made him an effective leader[...]

To answer this question, let's [...] *charisma*, introduced as one of th[...] leader. Charisma is that special [...]

seen in larger-than-life celebrities and leaders, but it is difficult to define. According to Ernest Becker (1975), a charismatic leader is one who with great self-confidence offers people a heroic vision, a grand mission to triumph over evil and bring about a better future.

Early in his career, Milk was a *relationship-oriented* leader who focused on making sure that his staff members felt included and enjoyed their work on his campaign. But his career really took off after he followed the advice given to him by another politician: If you want to win over the people, you have to give them hope for a better life and a better tomorrow. Eventually Milk embodies charisma. His heroic vision can be seen in three messages that he gave to the American people.

legacy that will make a mark on history. For example, he says to members of his campaign, "If there should be an assassination, I would hope that five, ten, one hundred, a thousand would rise. I would like to see every gay lawyer, every gay architect come out—If a bullet should enter my brain, let that bullet destroy every closet door.... And that's all. I ask for the movement to continue." This message is attractive to people because, as we've noted in this chapter, they join groups in part to cope with the fear of death. Belonging to a group means that one's life does not end with death but continues on so long as the group survives.

A third message in Milk's heroic vision is that there is a clear enemy out there who is holding society back from progress. In 1978, Anita Bryant, a former singer and model, started advocating for a proposition that would ban gays from teaching in schools. Armed with moral rhetoric and the support of the Christian community, she got this legislation passed in Florida and was gaining traction in other states. Milk initially feels defeated by Anita Bryant's success, but when he walks into the street, he finds that it is exactly what was needed to bring the gay community's anger to the boiling point. Now hundreds of citizens are ready to take action. Milk seizes the moment, grabs a bullhorn, and says, "I know you're angry. I'm angry. Let's march the streets of San Francisco and share our anger."

He leads the march to the steps of City Hall, where he gives the people the enemy they want: "I am here tonight to say that we will no longer sit quietly in the closet. We must fight. And not only in the Castro, not only in San Francisco, but everywhere the Anitas go. Anita Bryant cannot win tonight.

Anita Bryant brought us together! She is going to create a national gay force!"

Because of Milk's charismatic leadership style, he is remembered today as a major figure in the continuing struggle for equal human rights.

Guided by the charismatic leadership of Harvey Milk (portrayed by Sean Penn in the movie *Milk*), gay rights supporters felt united in a grand mission to overcome discrimination.
[Focus Features/Photofest]

Think ABOUT

[nmedia/Shutterstock]

Why might humans have evolved the ability to experience moods in the first place? For one thing, moods may inform the person about the status of things in the immediate environment. Think about this from the evolutionary perspective.

To help students relate concepts to their own lives, we engage them in the narrative by asking specific questions throughout the text, often highlighted as *Think About* features. Here is one such question, in blue type and accompanied by a photo, asked directly to the student.

Overarching Perspectives

A final aspect of this textbook's overarching integrative vision is to utilize five broad perspectives that serve as recurring motifs throughout the book: culture, evolution, social cognition, cognitive neuroscience, and existential psychology. These themes provide some sense of continuity both within and across chapters. Of course, social psychology is a diverse field that is not constrained by one single perspective or one small set of perspectives. Instead, the field's accumulated knowledge has benefited from researchers' seeking to understand behavior from many different points of view and levels of analysis. We think that's one of the most exciting aspects of our field. Although each of the five broad perspectives is noted in the context of presenting particular theories and research findings, it was important to us not to use them in a restricting, rigid, or imperialistic way.

Both across and within chapters, there is no one perfect way to organize the vast array of theories and research programs generated by social, personality, cultural, and evolutionary psychologists, as well as researchers in related disciplines. We believe that, whatever the topic and approach to organization, the coverage has to convey the classic and contemporary discoveries that are most revealing in answering important questions. With this goal in mind, we have ensured that our organization of each chapter is not guided in a formulaic way by the five perspectives but by our desire to provide a conceptually coherent, comprehensible, and memorable discussion of the best and most useful theories and findings pertinent to that topic.

Overview of the Text's Organization

Chapter 1 begins with a brief consideration of the roots and history of social psychology. We then lay out the five perspectives and the core assumptions of the field. The second half of the chapter is devoted to introducing students to the scientific methods used by social psychologists to investigate human behavior, with a focus on the cyclical interplay of theory and research, correlational and experimental methods, and strengths and limitations of theory and methods. We conclude with a consideration of ethics in research.

Chapter 2 considers cultural and evolutionary perspectives in more detail. Our treatment aims to give equal weight to both perspectives, each of which helps set the stage for understanding the fundamental motivations and cognitive architecture that underlies human behavior. Culture profoundly influences human experience. It's not just something to discuss to explain gender roles or differences in prevalence of the fundamental attribution error. In our view, culture reveals as much about how people are similar as it does about how they are different. Thus, we carefully consider in Chapter 2 how cultures are structured and the psychological functions they serve. Similarly, the evolution of our species didn't merely produce domain-specific adaptations that may help explain individual phenomena such as sex differences in aggression or attraction. More clearly, evolution produced the basic sociability, cognitive capacities, potential for learning and growth, motivations, and emotions that underlie all of our experiences and behaviors. By explaining the joint roles of culture and evolution in shaping the core proclivities of our species, we aim to provide students with a richer and more balanced framework for understanding and evaluating subsequent theory and evidence regarding human behavior.

Following up on these broad aspects of human behavior, Chapters 3 and 4 review the important insights that have come from understanding social cognition, including cutting-edge research from social neuroscience that examines brain regions and processes associated with particular aspects of thought, emotion, and judgment. Typically, traditional topics in social cognition, such as heuristics and biases, are presented in a listlike, piecemeal fashion. We instead begin with the motives that guide perception, memory, and decision making. Part of the motivational frame is provided by the fifth perspective we present, an existential perspective that emphasizes how social life is shaped by core aspects of the human experience, including the needs for meaning, belonging, security, and growth.

After covering how we view others and the world around us, we focus on the self in Chapters 5 and 6. These chapters cover the structure and functioning of the self and set the stage for subsequent chapters by illustrating the mutual constitution of self and social reality. The self-concept is largely the product of social and cultural influences; at the same time, individuals' self-regulatory capacities and motives for consistency, esteem, self-presentation, and growth inform their construal of self, other people, and social events.

The next three chapters, 7 through 9, focus on the rich topics of social influence, persuasion, and group processes. Together, these chapters show how individuals' motives, beliefs, attitudes, and behavior influence, and are themselves influenced by, interactions with other people. But in addition to covering classic theories and research, these chapters describe recent developments, such as social priming and mimicry, regulatory focus, implicit attitudes, and system justification.

Having examined the person's core needs, desires, cognitive capacities, self-motives, and relations to the social world, we proceed in the final six chapters to focus on specific forms of social thought and behavior. The first three cover the darker side of human behavior. Chapters 10 and 11 examine prejudice, stereotyping, and discrimination—their determinants and consequences, as well as potential ways to counteract them. Chapter 12 takes up the equally complex problem of interpersonal aggression. We discuss the consequences of aggression, its distal and proximal causes, and practical ways to move toward less violent societies.

In contrast to these negative proclivities, the final three chapters focus on the more positive aspects of human experience: prosocial behavior, interpersonal attraction, and close relationships. We choose to end with these topics for three main reasons. First, they cast a hopeful, upbeat light on human behavior. Second, researchers have made great strides in understanding these topics in the last decade. And finally, although all the topics in social psychology are relevant to everyday life, none are more pertinent to students' own experiences than those concerning the human desire for and experience of community and close relationships.

We have worked long and hard to write a text that truly conveys our field in a coherent, engaging, and up-to-date manner that works very well for both instructors and students. Of course, it's up to all of you to decide if we have succeeded, so please let us know how we did, one way or the other. We would love to hear from you. Here are our email addresses:

Jeff:	jeff@u.arizona.edu
Toni:	tschmader@psych.ubc.ca
Jamie:	arndtj@missouri.edu
Mark:	mjlandau@ku.edu

Multimedia to Support Teaching and Learning

LaunchPad

Developed with extensive feedback from instructors and students, Worth Publishers' breakthrough online course space offers:

- Prebuilt units for each chapter, curated by experienced educators, with relevant media organized and ready to be assigned or customized to suit your course
- One location for all online resources, including an interactive e-Book, Learning-Curve's adaptive quizzing (see below), flashcard activities, and more

- Intuitive and useful analytics, with a gradebook that lets you track how students in the class are performing individually and as a whole
- A streamlined and intuitive interface that lets you build an entire course in minutes
- **Videos and activities** to enhance the learning process

  - *The Science of Everyday Life Activities and Experiment* provides interactive online activities that offer students insights into research in social psychology and how it applies to everyday life. After reading a short introduction, students participate in trials or answer questions related to an actual social psychology experiment or research study. Students will later see their responses as compared to the original study. A closing short quiz tests what students learned.
  - **Student Video Activities** include engaging video modules that instructors can assign for student assessment.

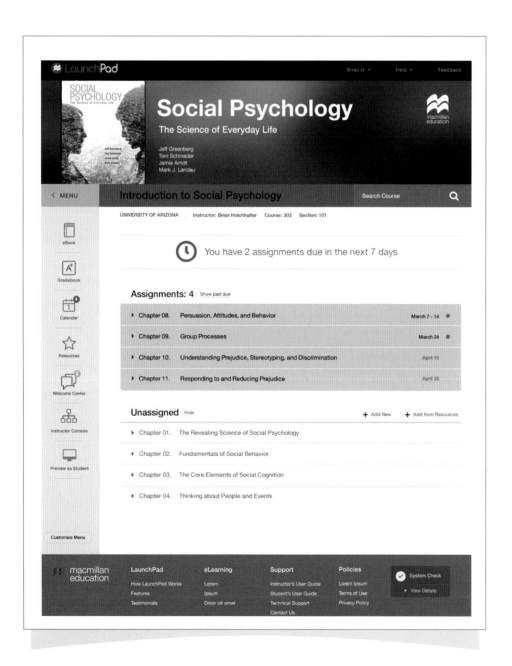

– **PsychSim 6 Activities** provide interactive simulations that immerse students in the world of psychological research, placing them in the role of scientist or subject in activities that highlight important concepts, processes, and experimental approaches.

– **Online Data Activities** help students develop quantitative reasoning skills by asking them to evaluate information and data from published research.

• A full suite of instructor resources including **Lecture Slides, Illustration Slides, Chapter Figures, Photos, and Tables, Computerized Test Bank, and Instructor's Resource Manual.**

• **An Instructor's Resource Manual** containing a rich offering of in- and out-of-class discussion topics, assignments, and activities as well as chapter outlines and learning objectives.

LearningCurve

In a gamelike format, LearningCurve's adaptive and formative quizzing provides an effective way to get students involved in the coursework. It offers:

• A unique learning path for each student, with quizzes shaped by each individual's correct and incorrect answers.

• A Personalized Study Plan, to guide students' preparation for class and for exams.

• Feedback for each question with live links to relevant e-Book pages, guiding students to the resources they need to improve their areas of weakness.

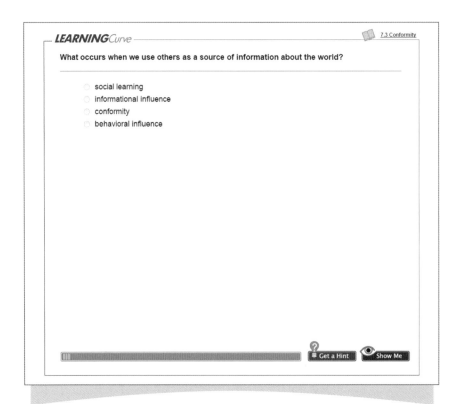

Course Management

Worth Publishers supports multiple Course Management Systems with enhanced cartridges for upload into Blackboard, WebCT, Angel, Desire2Learn, Sakai, and Moodle. Cartridges are provided free on adoption of *Social Psychology: The Science of Everyday Life* and can be downloaded from Worth's online catalog at www.worthpublishers.com.

Assessment

The **Computerized Test Bank,** powered by Diploma, includes a full assortment of test items. Each chapter features over 100 multiple-choice, true/false, and essay questions to test students at several levels of Bloom's taxonomy. All the questions are matched to the outcomes recommended in the 2013 APA Guidelines for the Undergraduate Psychology Major. The accompanying gradebook software makes it easy to record students' grades throughout a course, sort student records, view detailed analyses of test items, curve tests, generate reports, and add weights to grades.

ACKNOWLEDGMENTS

The production of this book, spanning over a decade, was very much a large-scale team effort, including not just the four of us, but many colleagues in our field and an entire team of talented people at Worth. If it takes a village to raise a child, it takes a small city to write a textbook!

First, we would like to thank the leader of the Worth team, Chris Cardone, Worth's Senior Acquisitions Editor for Psychology. We greatly appreciate her passion for this project, her dedication to making it a success, and her wise guidance throughout the process. Although Chris has overseen the bulk of development and production of this book, we also owe a debt of gratitude to prior editors Marge Byers, who energetically first set us on the path toward this book, and Erik Gilg, who kept the ball rolling until Chris took over.

A critical moment in the progress of this book occurred when Valerie Raymond graciously agreed to become our development editor. She enthusiastically embraced our vision for this book and has in our view done a great job helping to turn our presentations of the field's knowledge into a pedagogically sound textbook. Valerie was a sheer pleasure to work with, and we wouldn't have wanted anyone else helping us cut our chapter drafts in half!

We have worked extensively with a number of other helpful, pleasant, and hardworking people at Worth who have had a hand in sculpting this textbook. Thanks to the very talented copy editor Barbara Curialle for improving our sentences, catching our typos, and generally polishing our writing. Thanks to Senior Project Editor Jane O'Neill for overseeing the transformation from Word documents into beautifully laid out textbook pages. Thanks to Photo Editor Cecilia Varas and Photo Researcher Teri Stratford for the great work they have done assisting with the visual highlights of the book.

Beyond these individuals, with whom we worked directly, many other people at Worth have helped with the production or marketing of the book. Thus, our thanks go out to Production Manager Sarah Segal, Digital Development Manager Adam Feil, Senior Tech Advisor Gayle Yamazaki, Associate Publisher Jessica Bayne, Executive Media Editor Rachel Comerford, Associate Media Editor Anthony Casciano, Director of Rights and Permissions Hilary Newman, Permissions Manager Jennifer MacMillan, Executive Marketing Manager Kate Nurre, Cover Designer Kevin Kall, Art Manager Matt McAdams, Assistant Editor Catherine Michaelsen, Stephanie Ellis and Carlise Stembridge in Market Development, Director of Advertising Todd Elder, Promotions Manager Iris Elam, and National Sales Specialist Kari Ewalt.

In our professional lives, our efforts in writing this book have been supported and improved by many people along the way. This book's emphasis on conceptual organization and the fundamental motives that guide human behavior reflects the influence of Jack Brehm. Our vision for the book, especially the first two chapters, was helped substantially by the input of our colleagues Sheldon Solomon and Tom Pyszczynski. Many thanks also to current graduate student Uri Lifshin for his excellent work helping us to put together the massive reference section. Sincere thanks as well to Josh Hicks, Liz Pinel, Clay Routledge, Lyra Stein, Daniel Sullivan, and Meg Kozak Williams for their high-quality help with supplementary materials to accompany the text. Many others, too numerous to mention here—mentors, collaborators, faculty colleagues, and our own graduate students—have contributed to our understanding and knowledge of social psychology, and have enhanced our careers and our ability to produce this book. Thanks to all of them for the positive impact they have had on this textbook.

In addition, we would like to thank the faculty and staff at the institutions that provided the foundation of our development as social psychologists, and the schools that currently support our work (in alphabetical order): Skidmore College; Southern Methodist University; the State University of New York at Buffalo; the University of Arizona; the University of British Columbia; the University of California, Santa Barbara; the University of Colorado, Colorado Springs; the University of Kansas; the University of Missouri; the University of Pennsylvania; and Washington and Jefferson College.

And before we entered the halls of colleges and universities, the loving support and encouragement of our parents were instrumental for each of us in our pursuit of scholarly careers. So we wish to express our deep and sincere thanks to Murray and Edith Greenberg, Mary Alice and Len Schmader, Charles and Melinda Arndt, and Sara Landau.

Next, we would like to thank the faculty who reviewed our manuscript at various stages:

Karen Altendorf, *Oklahoma State University*
Kristin Anderson, *University of Houston, Downtown*
Shane Bench, *Washington State University*
Brooke Bennett-Day, *Wesleyan College*
John Bickford, *University of Massachusetts Amherst*
Ryan Brunner, *Westminster College*
Keith Campbell, *University of Georgia*
Clara Cheng, *Carlow University*
Kelly Charlton, *The University of North Carolina, Pembroke*
Florette Cohen, *College of Staten Island*
Traci Craig, *University of Idaho*
Alex Czopp, *Western Washington University*
Keith Davis, *University of South Carolina*
Danielle Dickens, *University of Georgia*
Robert Dushay, *Morrisville State College*
Scott Eidelman, *University of Arkansas*
Yuna Ferguson, *Truman State University*
Eli Finkel, *Northwestern University*
Dennis Fox, *University of Illinois, Springfield*
Madeleine Fugere, *Eastern Connecticut State University*
Laura C. Garza, *Texas A&M University, Kingsville*
Kathleen Geher, *State University of New York at New Paltz*
Bryan Gibson, *Central Michigan University*
Peter Glick, *Lawrence University*
Jonathan Gore, *Eastern Kentucky University*
Lisa Harrison, *California State University, Sacramento*
William Hart, *University of Alabama*
Brian Harward, *Palomar College*
Elaine Hatfield, *University of Hawaii*
Mahzad Hojjat, *University of Massachusetts*
Alisha Janowsky, *University of Central Florida*
Stephen Kilianski, *Rutgers University*
Robin Kowalski, *Clemson University*

Daniel Lassiter, *Ohio University*
Jennifer Leszczynski, *Eastern Connecticut State University*
David A. Lopez, *California State University, Northridge*
Jill Lorenzi, *Virginia Tech*
Keith Maddox, *Tufts University*
Lynda Mae, *Arizona State University*
Molly Maxfield, *University of Colorado*
Christopher Mazurek, *Columbia College*
Kathleen C. McCulloch, *Idaho State University*
Jared McGinley, *Virginia Tech*
James McNulty, *Florida State University*
Kristin Mickelson, *Kent State University*
Lisa Molix, *Tulane University*
Matt Motyl, *University of Illinois at Chicago*
Paige Muellerleile, *Marshall University*
Matt Newman, *Research Now Group, Inc.*
Charles Nichols, *Loyola University, New Orleans*
Kathryn Oleson, *Reed College*
Karyn Plumm, *University of North Dakota*
Heather Price, *University of Regina*
Anila Putcha-Bhagavatula, *California State University, Long Beach*
Alan Roberts, *Indiana University*
Laura Scherer, *University of Missouri*
Brandon Schmiechel, *St. Louis University*
Dylan Selterman, *University of Maryland*
Nicole Shelton, *Princeton University*
Margaret L. Signorella, *Pennsylvania State University*
Curt Sobolewski, *The Pennsylvania State University*
Mark Stewart, *American River College*
Michael Strube, *Washington University in St. Louis*
Heather Terrell, *University of North Dakota*
Margaret Thomas, *Earlham College*
Carol Toris, *College of Charleston*
John Updegraff, *Kent State University*
Anre Venter, *University of Notre Dame*
Matthew Vess, *Ohio University*
Ruth Warner, *St. Louis University*
Todd Williams, *Grand Valley State*

The following instructors graciously participated in Worth's focus groups. We are very grateful for the feedback they provided:

Danny Axsom, *Virginia Tech*
Lauren Brewer, *Stephen F. Austin State University*
Ryan P. Brown, *The University of Oklahoma*
Amy Canevello, *University of North Carolina, Charlotte*
Don Carlston, *Purdue University*
Corey L. Cook, *Skidmore College*
Kathleen Cook, *Seattle University*
Cinnamon Danube, *University of California, Merced*
Dorothee Dietrich, *Hamline University*
Christopher Downing, *Virginia Tech*
Miriam Eisenberg, *National Institutes of Health*

Sally Farley, *University of Baltimore*
Samuel Fung, *Austin Peay State University*
Amber Garcia, *The College of Wooster*
Donna Garcia, *California State University, San Bernardino*
Jonathan Gerber, *Gordon College*
James Gire, *Virginia Military Institute*
AnaMarie Guichard, *California State University, Stanislaus*
Tamara Hamai, *Mount St. Mary's College*
Lisa Harrison, *California State University, Sacramento*
Robert Haynes, *Rowan University*
Dawn Howerton, *Marshall University*
Jaime Kurtz, *James Madison University*
Justin J. Lehmiller, *Harvard University*
Dana Leighton, *Hendrix College*
Mercedes A. McCormick, *Pace University NYC*
Abigail Mitchell, *Nebraska Wesleyan University*
Matt Newman, *Research Now Group, Inc.*
Wade Rowatt, *Baylor University*
Marc Setterlund, *Alma College*
Ryan Smith, *Virginia Tech*
Lyra Stein, *Rutgers University*
Elena Stepanova, *The University of Southern Mississippi*
Ronald Stoffey, *Kutztown University of Pennsylvania*
Laura E. VanderDrift, *Syracuse University*
Todd Williams, *Grand Valley State University*
Monica Wilson, *National University*
Jennifer Zimmerman, *DePaul University*

We would also like to thank the following professors who class tested sample chapters:

Catherine Cottrell, *New College of Florida*
Lauren Coursey, *University of Texas at Arlington*
Karen Douglas, *San Antonio College*
Michael Ekema-Agbaw, *Virginia Tech*
Heather LaCost, *Waubonsee Community College*
Paige Muellerleile, *Marshall University*
Elena Reigadas, *Los Angeles Harbor College*
Amy Smith, *University of Nebraska, Lincoln*
Stephanie Smith, *Ohio University*
Melissa Streeter, *University of North Carolina at Wilmington*
Lora Vasiliauskas, *Virginia Western Community College*

Most sincerely,
Jeff, Toni, Jamie, and *Mark*

The Revealing Science of Social Psychology

TOPIC OVERVIEW

New knowledge can be both liberating and useful. It broadens our appreciation of our life experiences and gives us more information for better decisions. However, such newfound knowledge also comes at a cost. This theme is central to the classic sci-fi film *The Matrix* (Silver et al., 1999). In the film, the prophet Morpheus offers the protagonist, Neo, the choice between a blue pill and a red pill. If Neo takes the blue pill, he will stay inside a safe and familiar world, a computer program created for him that is the only reality he has ever known. But if he takes the red pill, Neo will be pulled out of that virtual reality into a more authentic and complex view of himself and the world around him.

Learning about social psychology will be like swallowing that red pill. As a blue-piller, you live day to day, absorbed in a world of classes, jobs, relationships, sports, parties, Facebook, YouTube, Instagram, and Twitter. When you think of the future, perhaps you're thinking about grad school or starting your career. Maybe you're involved in student government or environmentalism, or supporting the troops, or helping fight poverty. This is the "programmed" world in which we all live, established by our culture and internalized by us through the socialization process. Though each of us plays a unique role within this reality, we're both part of it and constrained by it. Social psychology, like the red pill, can take you outside the ordinary reality you live in to a more enlightened and sometimes more disturbing vantage point, one that reveals

In the film *The Matrix*, Morpheus offers Neo the choice of either the blue pill, which maintains his current view of reality, or the red pill, which like social psychology, provides a more revealing and complex view. Which would you choose? Why?

[© Warner Bros/Photofest]

Social psychology The scientific study of the causes and consequences of people's thoughts, feelings, and actions regarding themselves and other people.

that each of us is a complex but fragile and vulnerable animal with certain propensities and capacities, striving to satisfy basic needs and desires within the cultural matrix. Although no one can live for long outside the comfort of their culturally constructed reality, by taking an occasional foray beyond it, we can better comprehend many of the events we care about within the ordinary reality in which we generally reside.

Social psychology is the scientific study of the causes and consequences of people's thoughts, feelings, and actions regarding themselves and other people. It is a set of concepts and discoveries that can fundamentally expand and enrich your understanding of yourself, of those in your social sphere, and of events in the world around you. In this first chapter, we'll start with the historic origins of the field and some broad perspectives and core assumptions social psychologists utilize to study human behavior in a social context. We'll then consider the ways in which all of us, as intuitive scientists, flip through our encyclopedic knowledge of culture to draw inferences about human behavior. However, because this intuitive approach can be limited and biased, we'll turn to the discerning eye and sharp tools of science to isolate and understand human behavior.

The Roots of Social Psychology

Every human being has wondered, at one time or another, about him- or herself and the social world, so we are all amateur social psychologists at heart. Although social psychology is a relatively young field, the concerns this science addresses go back to the dawning days of humankind. The very earliest discovered written texts, such as the 5,000-year-old Sumerian *Epic of Gilgamesh*, focused on basic questions about what it means to be human and how humans come to behave the way they do. Since then, philosophers, poets, playwrights, and novelists all have attempted to delineate the psychological forces responsible for human social behavior. However, it wasn't until the twentieth century that these questions were put under the lens of scientific inquiry.

Although modern social psychology is sometimes characterized in textbooks and elsewhere as a field full of hundreds of small, largely disconnected theories about various aspects of social behavior, the field's origins were influenced by several broad perspectives. Let's briefly consider these influential ideas.

An Instinct-based View of Human Behavior

In 1855, the British sociologist Herbert Spencer extended Charles Darwin's theory of evolution by natural selection from the biological to the social realm. Spencer argued that social behavior is the result of the same evolutionary processes that produce physical characteristics such as body size and eye color. For example, Spencer felt that societies evolve just as organisms do, becoming larger, more complex, and more differentiated over time. Spencer's evolutionary view of human activity heavily influenced William McDougall when he published the very first social psychology textbook, *An Introduction*

Webs created by spiders and humans: How much behavior is instinctual?
[Left: Maryna Pleshkun/Shutterstock; right: © Joe Baraban/Alamy]

to Social Psychology, in 1908. This textbook proposed that most human behavior was instinctively determined, just as it is for spiders that spin webs and beavers that build dams, and consequently unlearned and uninfluenced by experience. McDougall's (1923) conception of instinctual human behavior stood in sharp contrast to what would become the two most dominant schools of thought in academic psychology during the first half of the 20th century: psychoanalysis and behaviorism.

Psychoanalytic Theory: The Hidden Desires That Guide Behavior

Inspired partly by Darwin's concept of the "struggle for existence," Sigmund Freud claimed that human behavior was directed primarily by aggressive and sexual drives (Freud, 1920/1961a). Aggressive behavior is critical for warding off predators and effectively competing for scarce resources; sexual behavior is critical for reproducing and perpetuating genes. But, because unbridled aggression and sexuality undermine the communal order necessary for very social human animals to survive, Freud proposed that human beings' desires for sex and aggression are kept unconscious by repression, until they are transformed in ways that allow them to be consciously expressed in a socially acceptable fashion. This is the basis for Freud's psychoanalytic theory that human behavior is directed by bodily desires excluded from consciousness to appease social forces. Consequently, a substantial proportion of human mental activity is unconscious, and what we are conscious of is rarely a direct reflection of the motivational underpinnings of what we're doing, because the true intent of our behavior is generally hidden from us.

Behaviorism: Behavior Is Shaped by Experience

In direct opposition to psychoanalysis, early behaviorists such as John Watson (1930) argued that only overt behavior can be directly observed and measured and that phenomena such as feelings, wishes, unconscious processes, and consciousness are unobservable fictions that psychologists had invented to explain behavior. The behaviorists also argued that most of the supposedly instinctual behaviors studied by McDougall and his colleagues were substantially modified by experience, suggesting the possibility that they might be learned, rather than innate, responses. The behaviorists also bemoaned the difficulty of deciding what qualified as an instinct and were incredulous when at one point the list of alleged instincts exceeded 6,000! Behaviorists instead proposed that human behavior is predominantly determined by the nature of experiences in response to the demands of the environment. In simplified form, the argument of these theorists was that, in a particular environment, behaviors followed by desirable outcomes would be likely to reoccur, whereas behaviors that are followed by undesirable outcomes would not. As John Watson (1930) put it: "Give me a dozen healthy infants, well formed, and my own specified world to bring them up in and I'll guarantee to take any one at random and train him to become any type of specialist I might select—doctor, lawyer, artist, merchant—chief, and yes, even beggar-man and thief, regardless of his talents, penchants, tendencies, abilities, vocations and race of his ancestors" (p. 82). These behaviorist ideas persuaded many early 20th-century research psychologists to confine their investigations to readily observable behavior.

The Emergence of Modern Social Psychology

So what, then, causes human behavior? Is it instinct, as the McDougalls of the world argued? Is it the unconscious drives emphasized by Freud and his psychoanalyst disciples? Or is it experience via responses to the environment, as Watson avowed? And how do we sort out the role, if any, of unconscious and conscious mental processes in all of this? Social psychology emerged as a new field that would come to address these very questions. Its birth was sparked by two important and integrative books published in the 1920s.

In 1922, John Dewey published *Human Nature and Conduct: An Introduction to Social Psychology*, a seminal work that set the agenda for a mature social psychology. Dewey felt strongly that human behavior is determined by both instinct (nature) and experience (nurture) and that the key is to identify the complex interaction between nature and nurture. He also insisted that both unconscious and conscious processes are important determinants of human activity. Further, Dewey optimistically asserted that understanding the psychological underpinnings of human behavior would allow humans to influence what happens to us in the future by injecting informed reason into the mix of human instinct and environmentally determined experience. He thus saw humankind as a work in progress into which we can have at least some conscious input that may have monumental effects on human evolution. Dewey also stressed the uniquely existential concerns of human beings: How do self-conscious, finite creatures find meaning in an unfathomably large universe of seemingly infinite possibilities?

The other influential book of the 1920s was Floyd Allport's *Social Psychology*, published in 1924. Allport tried to integrate into the study of consciousness the experimental techniques of behaviorism, the advances learned from psychoanalysis, and the ideas from evolutionary theory. Like Dewey, Allport was interested in how humans can apply what we learn about ourselves to promote constructive individual and social change. *Social Psychology* became the classic text in the field for decades and inspired a burst of empirical research that culminated in the 1931 publication of *Experimental Social Psychology*, by Gardner and Lois Murphy. Besides promoting the promise of experimental approaches to studying social psychological phenomena, this husband-and-wife team stressed the fundamental role of culture in determining human activities and emphasized the need for social psychologists to investigate carefully the nature and function of culture.

Another important development in social psychology stemmed from World War II and the desire to understand how individuals in a society could nearly annihilate a portion of their population. Events on the scale of the Holocaust demanded explanation, and social psychologists began testing theories of power and social influence, an interest that would also be fueled by the political activism that dominated the late 1960s. As research in social psychology grew in the 1950s and sixties, the field's concern with understanding important social problems and unsavory forms of behavior contributed to a shift in focus from broad conceptions of human social behavior to relatively specific, topic-based theories about particular phenomena, an emphasis still prominent today.

During the 1970s and eighties, a cognitive revolution took hold in most of psychology. Social psychology was also swept up in this shift toward understanding the mental processes that underlie behavior. Most social psychologists began to embrace the metaphor of the human being as an information processor, a concept from which the social cognition perspective emerged. **Social cognition** is the way that an individual understands his or her own social world. The **social cognition perspective** focuses on how people perceive, remember, and interpret events and individuals in their social world, including themselves. This focus remains strong to the present day and has expanded to include newer techniques to measure the neural underpinnings of thought and emotion.

Toward an Integrated Perspective on Human Behavior

Since the early 1990s, four trends that hark back to the roots of the field have combined forces with the *social cognition perspective*, leading to a renewed focus on answering the core questions from the field's origins.

The first, the **evolutionary perspective**, is a reinvigorated effort to view humans as a species of animal and their social behavior as a consequence of particular evolutionary adaptations. The evolutionary perspective emphasizes that humans are animals and as such, subject to the same physical laws and evolutionary processes as all other forms of life. This suggests that a proper understanding of human activity

Social cognition The way an individual understands his or her own social world.

Social cognition perspective A view that focuses on how people perceive, remember, and interpret events and individuals, including themselves, in their social world.

Evolutionary perspective A view that humans are a species of animal and that their social behavior is a consequence of particular evolved adaptations.

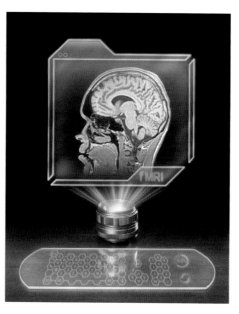

There are five influential perspectives in social psychology: cognitive, evolutionary, cultural, neuroscience, and existential (depicted clockwise from top left).

Cultural perspective A view that focuses on the influence of culture on thought, feeling, and behavior.

Cultural animals Humans are animals who view reality through a set of symbols provided by the culture in which they are raised.

Existential perspective A view that focuses on the cognitive, affective, and behavioral consequences of basic aspects of the human condition such as the knowledge of mortality, the desire for meaning, and the precarious nature of identity.

Neuroscience perspective The study of the neural processes that occur during social judgment and behavior. Neuroscience involves assessments of brain waves, brain imaging, and cardiovascular functioning.

requires recognizing uniquely human adaptations in addition to those we share with other creatures.

The second, the cultural perspective, is a rediscovery of the importance of culture as a determinant of thinking and behavior. It emphasizes the central role of culture in just about everything people do. Social psychologists, perhaps not surprisingly given the "social" in social psychology, have always viewed humans as fundamentally social creatures biologically constructed to exist in proximity to, and to coordinate with, other members of their own species. Dogs, bees, ants, termites, and many other life forms are also social creatures, but humans stand apart. Unlike any other species, humans are cultural animals: Only humans create their own symbolic conception of reality. This creation is *culture*. Culture gives meaning to life, and it is taken to be an absolute representation of reality by those who share the same cultural background despite the fact that it is often clear, even to the casual observer, that people from different cultures can have radically different beliefs about the nature of reality.

The third, the existential perspective, is a return to examining basic questions about existence and human nature, regarding matters such as meaning, identity, the body, and free will. Social psychologists are increasingly using an existential perspective to examine human behavior, devoting considerable attention to understanding the basic nature of the self and the core human motives; the needs for meaning and social connections; and the ways in which people cope with the often harsh realities of mortal life, the limits of the physical body, the possibilities of trauma and loss, and the inevitability of death.

The fourth, the social neuroscience perspective, is gaining increased momentum as technological advances enable us to understand better what is going on inside the brain when people engage in social thought and behavior. Social neuroscience utilizes assessments of brain-wave amplitudes after exposure to specific events and the flow of oxygen to different areas of the brain to examine the neural processes that occur during social judgment and behavior. In so doing, researchers can enhance knowledge of the role of various cognitive, emotional, and motivational processes in social phenomena.

SECTION review | The Roots of Social Psychology

Social psychology is a relatively young science, though humans have long been amateur social psychologists at heart.

Roots

- In the mid-1880s, Herbert Spencer extended Darwin's theory of evolution by natural selection to argue that social behavior of humans is the result of the same evolutionary processes.
- Freud claimed that human behavior is driven by aggressive and sexual drives that are largely hidden from our conscious experience.
- Behaviorists argued that only overt behavior can be directly observed and measured. They discounted the study of such things as feelings, wishes, and consciousness.
- The stage for modern social psychology was set by the integrative efforts of John Dewey, Floyd Allport, and Gardner and Lois Murphy.

Perspectives of modern social psychology

- The social cognition perspective focuses on how we perceive, remember, and interpret events and people.
- The evolutionary perspective is a reinvigorated view of humans as a species of animal and of social behavior as a consequence of evolutionary adaptations.
- The cultural perspective underscores the effect of culture on thinking and behavior.
- The existential perspective focuses on basic human concerns such as mortality, meaning, and connection.
- The neuroscience perspective focuses on understanding how biological systems influence, and are influenced by, social processes.

The Four Core Assumptions of Social Psychology

I am human and let nothing human be alien to me.

—Terence, ancient Roman playwright (195/185–159 BC)

The central question that social psychologists attempt to answer is, *Why do people behave the way they do?* From this very general question, we can derive more specific ones that focus on problems we would like to remedy. Why can't people get along with each other better? Why do people care so much about what others think of them? Why do people sometimes conform but other times struggle to stand out from the crowd? Why do people so often make bad choices? How is it possible that the same species that created the Sistine Chapel, the Taj Mahal, *Moby Dick*, penicillin, the Underground Railroad, democracy, and the Red Cross also produced slavery, the Crusades, concentration camps, the bombing of Hiroshima, and the events of September 11, 2001?

Typically, social psychologists try to answer these broad questions by focusing on more specific inquiries into aspects of human behavior. Where do stereotypes of groups come from? How do stereotypes affect the ways people who believe them view members of the stereotyped group? What information do people use to infer the causes of another person's behavior? How well does a person's image of herself match the image that others have of her? Does violent content in the mass media encourage violent behavior in viewers? If so, how? Does the nature of people's attachment to their parents play a role in their adult romantic relationships? Political scientists, sociologists, anthropologists, economists, philosophers, poets, and novelists all attempt to address some of these questions. However, each discipline approaches them from a particular perspective based on some core assumptions. Such assumptions help define a particular field and distinguish it from others. Contemporary social psychology is based on four core assumptions.

1. Behavior Is a Joint Product of the Person and the Situation

One core assumption is based on an idea proposed by Kurt Lewin (1936), who is generally considered the father of modern social psychology: Any given behavior is determined by the combined influences of individual features of the person and specific aspects of the situation.

To grasp Lewin's idea fully, we first need to appreciate that a person's immediate environment profoundly influences how he or she thinks, feels, and acts in social life. This idea of the power of the situation—sometimes referred to as the "great lesson of social psychology" (Jones & Nisbett, 1971)—means that certain situations elicit pretty much the same behavior from people, regardless of how those people differ from each other. Look around at the other students in your social psych class. Some of them are very extraverted and talkative, whereas others are quieter and more reserved. And yet all of them are quiet while the instructor lectures. Why? Because the situation tells them, in a classroom, this is how you behave. In fact, situations can be so powerful that they lead people to do things they normally would never do. This was vividly demonstrated in Stanley Milgram's (1974) famous studies of obedience. As we'll discuss in more detail in chapter 7, participants in these studies were remarkably compliant when ordered by an authoritative experimenter to administer what appeared to be potentially lethal electrical shocks to an innocent victim.

And yet, each of us is a unique individual, with a constellation of personality traits, values, attitudes, and beliefs about the world that sets us apart from every other person. Because of the unique genetic makeup that we inherit from our biological parents and even more because of the lessons we have learned from the vast array of experience we have had over the course of our lives, we develop

Dispositions Consistent preferences, ways of thinking, and behavioral tendencies that manifest across varying situations and over time.

dispositions: consistent preferences, ways of thinking, and behavioral tendencies that manifest across varying situations and over time.

The field of personality psychology is focused largely on describing traits and documenting their influence on behavior. And the field finds, in fact, that people show a good deal of consistency in behavior across diverse situations that reflect their unique ways of adapting to the world. There is also a high level of consistency in behavior and traits across the lifespan. For example, Costa and McCrae (1994) have shown that behavior observed in the first years of life is associated with related behavioral tendencies in early, middle, and late adulthood. Dispositions powerfully guide how we think, feel, and act in social life. If we go back to your social psych class, chances are that one or two students *are* talking while the instructor lectures—their dispositional extraversion overrides the power of the situation. And even in the classic Milgram study, 35 percent of the participants refused to continue shocking the victim prior to the final command to do so.

Now that we've recognized the power of the situation and the influence of the person's dispositions, we might be tempted to argue about which is more important than the other in determining people's behavior. And indeed, for many years psychologists have debated the relative importance of the roles played by individual differences in personality, attitudes, and values on the one hand and situational forces on the other. But following Lewin's lead, most social psychologists focus on understanding how personality dispositions and situational factors *interact* to determine our thoughts, feelings, and actions. In other words, the focus is on what types of situations lead particular types of persons to behave in specific ways. Therefore, throughout this book, we'll consider the influence of the person's situation, his or her unique personality, attitudes, and values, and the ways in which these factors interact.

2. Behavior Depends on a Socially Constructed View of Reality

A second assumption of social psychology is that virtually all human thoughts, feelings, and actions involve and are influenced by other people and thus are social in nature. Throughout life, we routinely encounter and interact with other people. But even when we're completely alone, people routinely occupy and consequently help to shape our thoughts. As a result, our view of reality is shaped by our connections to others.

Imagine, for example, a student named Carly who lives alone and is startled from sleep by the piercing sound of her alarm clock. She awakens to thoughts of the Western civilization class she has in an hour and what a bore Professor Drone is. She worries a bit about an upcoming exam and whether she is smart enough to do well in the class. Gazing at the clock, Carly thinks of her younger sister Jen, who gave it to her the day she left for college. Then she wonders why she let her friend Megan talk her into taking an 8 a.m. class with her. As she gets out of bed, Carly notices the Monet painting of a bridge in a garden on the calendar hanging from her closet door. She opens Pandora on her tablet and hears an old Kanye West song. Then Carly lays out her clothes, thinking about what would be the right look for her lunch date with Dwayne. She jumps in the shower and starts singing the new Miley Cyrus single—quietly, so Nick, her neighbor in the next apartment, won't be disturbed. So in the course of a mere half hour alone with her thoughts, Carly's inner world has been populated by internal representations of eight other people: Professor Drone, her sister Jen, her friend Megan, Claude Monet, Kanye West, her lunch date Dwayne, Miley Cyrus, and her neighbor Nick.

These and many other people fundamentally shape the way Carly views the world and her place in it. Take, for example, her insecurity about her Western civilization class. How does she know if she is smart enough? Certainly her current grade in the class provides some information. But that grade is feedback from the instructor. In addition, on receiving a grade, most students wonder how everyone else did.

In 1954, Leon Festinger pointed out that looking to others—our social comparisons—is essential to how we understand ourselves. We get a sense of the right or wrong way to act, what is good or bad, and what is true or not true by examining what other people do or say. Whether it's Carly's aptitude for history or her choice of appropriate attire for a lunch date, her knowledge and consequent behavior are products of the social reality in which she lives.

Are you tall? For many judgments we make about ourselves, we rely on social comparisons with others.
[Zurjeta/Shutterstock]

3. Behavior Is Strongly Influenced by Our Social Cognition

If our very view of reality is shaped by our social connections with others, then the third assumption, that *social cognition* shapes behavior, should come as no surprise. This assumption is based on the work of another pioneering figure in social psychology, Fritz Heider (1958), who emphasized the important role people's causal explanations of others' actions play in determining their behavior. For example, in March 2003, President George W. Bush launched an invasion of Iraq. Some Americans believed he did this to avert a terrorist threat or to promote freedom in the Middle East. Others believed Bush wanted to gain access to Iraqi oil or seek revenge against Saddam Hussein. Each individual American's understanding of the president's motives for this action likely played a significant role in how each American felt about Bush and voted in the 2004 election. Because people—the president; our parents, friends, or lovers; or even the salespeople who try to sell us products— play such a major role in our daily existence, we spend a great deal of time and energy thinking about them, trying to understand them, and struggling to make sense of what they say and do. The way each individual understands other people, whether the understanding is accurate or not, has a powerful influence on that individual's social behavior.

4. The Best Way to Understand Social Behavior Is to Use the Scientific Method

The final core assumption of social psychology, also inspired by Kurt Lewin, is that science is the best way to understand the causes and consequences of the thoughts, feelings, and behaviors of social life. As we noted earlier, many fields attempt to understand human affairs, including anthropology, economics, sociology, history, humanities, philosophy, and sociology. Social psychology can be distinguished most clearly from these other pursuits by greater emphasis on the scientific method, and especially the use of experiments, as a way of developing, testing, and refining theories to understand the determinants of social behavior. The field developed as a way of refining intuitive thinking, to help us get closer to the truth by providing more accurate conceptions of the way the world really is. The scientific method provides the basis for how social psychologists accumulate knowledge regarding the determinants of human thoughts, feelings, and actions. However, before we describe the specifics of the scientific method, we need a brief overview of how people intuitively come to comprehend the world around them and the people who inhabit that world. These insights are important because they help to explain why social psychologists rely so heavily on the scientific method for understanding the causes and consequences of social behavior.

Scientific method The process of developing, testing, and refining theories to understand the determinants of social behavior.

SECTION review   The Four Core Assumptions of Social Psychology

Social psychology is based on four core assumptions.

Behavior is determined by the combined influence of specific aspects of the person and the situation.	Virtually all human thoughts, feelings, and actions involve other people and are social in nature.	To understand behavior, we must learn how people think about themselves and their social world.	The scientific method offers the best route to accurately understanding social behavior.

Attribution theory The view that people act as intuitive scientists when they observe other people's behavior and infer explanations as to why those people acted the way they did.

Causal attributions Explanations of why an individual engaged in a particular action.

Cultural Knowledge: The Intuitive Encyclopedia

How do we know what we know? According to Heider's (1958) attribution theory, people are intuitive scientists. Like scientists, ordinary people have a strong desire to understand what causes other peoples' actions. Heider suggested that we act as intuitive scientists when we observe other people's behavior and apply logical rules to figure out why they acted the way they did. Heider labeled these explanations causal attributions. These attributions are based largely on cultural knowledge, a vast store of information accumulated within a culture that explains how the world works and why things happen as they do. This process of observing and explaining is such an integral part of our daily lives that we usually don't even notice that we are doing it.

Think ABOUT

[© Colin Hawkins/ cultura/Corbis]

Cultural knowledge A vast store of information, accumulated within a culture, that explains how the world works and why things happen as they do.

Think about the last time you caught a cold. What explanations of how you caught it did you consider? You probably tried to remember whether any of your recent contacts showed any signs of sneezes or sniffles, because our culture, informed by medical science, tells us that colds are transmitted by viruses or germs carried by other people suffering from colds. But the explanations provided by cultures vary over time, and different cultures explain things in different ways. Your grandparents probably would have thought back to instances in which they were caught in the rain or experienced a draft or a rapid change in temperature. Someone living in ancient Greece might have wondered about whether the various humors of her body were out of balance. And members of many traditional cultures would consider the possibility that they had offended the spirits.

Such cultural wisdom is passed down across generations and shared by individuals within cultures. Sometimes, when the answers we seek aren't part of our readily available cultural cupboard of knowledge, we consult experts: wise men, priestesses, or shamans in ancient times; physicians, ministers, psychotherapists, or online bloggers in modern times. In other words, a good deal of our understanding of the world comes from widely shared cultural belief systems and the words of authority figures who interpret that knowledge for us.

Asking Questions About Behavior

When trying to explain the specific actions of specific people, expert opinions are not always helpful. In these circumstances, you might think that the best way to explain a person's behavior is simply to ask them for their motives. How many times have you asked someone, "Why did you do that?" or, "What were you thinking?" How many times have you fielded similar questions from others?

We've all acquired valuable insights about people's behavior by asking them to explain themselves. After all, people can reveal things about themselves that no one else can know. Similarly, we can ask ourselves about the causes of our own behavior and draw on sources of information to which only we have access. We all have rich memories of our personal histories and awareness of our thoughts, feelings, and other private experiences to which no one else is privy. Unfortunately, people's explanations for their own behavior can be misleading. Here are a couple of reasons why.

People Don't Always Tell the Truth

We do not deal much in fact when we are contemplating ourselves.

—Mark Twain, "Does the Race of Man Love a Lord?" (1902)

Often, people are not honest about why they acted a certain way. Because we depend on other people for so many of the things we need in life, we care a great deal about the impressions they form of us. So although people may be forthright when asked to report their hometown or college major, they may be less candid when answering questions about their weight, age, GPA, or sexual proclivities. As we'll see in later chapters on the self and interpersonal relations, people have a variety of motives for not telling the truth.

People Often Don't Really Know What They Think They Know

Our accounts of our own behavior are often inaccurate, even when we believe we are telling the truth. Sometimes, powerful psychological forces may block awareness of our motives. Erich Fromm (1941) described a clinical example of such repression in the case of a young medical student who seemed to have lost interest in his classes. When Fromm suggested that the student's interest in medicine seemed to be wavering, the student protested that he had always wanted to be a doctor. Several months later, however, the student recalled an incident from childhood when he was playing with building blocks and happily announced to his physician father that he wanted to be a great architect when he grew up. Upset that his son didn't want to follow in his own footsteps, his father ridiculed architecture as a childish profession and insisted that his son would grow up to be a doctor as he was. So the future medical student repressed his desire to practice architecture, and decades later sincerely believed he was in medical school because he wanted to be there.

When are you not honest with yourself? For many weight-conscious people, it may be when they are weighing themselves.

[Bodrov Kirill/Shutterstock]

The prevalence of this kind of repression continues to be debated, but social psychological research has shown that even without repression, people often can't explain their own actions and feelings because they simply do not know why they do what they do or feel the way they feel. People are routinely inaccurate even when explaining their most mundane and innocuous activities. In a classic paper published in 1977, Richard Nisbett and Tim Wilson proposed that when people are asked why they have certain preferences or are in the mood they are in, they usually generate answers quite readily, but such explanations are often based either on a priori (i.e., preexisting) causal theories acquired from their culture or on factors that are particularly prominent in their conscious attention at that moment. These sources of information often lead us to inaccurate explanations.

A priori causal theories Preexisting theories, acquired from culture or factors that are particularly prominent in conscious attention at the moment.

To test these ideas, Nisbett and Wilson designed a series of studies that revealed participants' reasons for their preferences, then compared them with participants' own accounts of their behavior. We'll go over more of these studies in chapter 5, but here is one example, conducted in the lingerie section of a large American department store. Individual female shoppers were shown four pairs of stockings arrayed in a row across a table, asked to select their favorite, and then explain why they preferred it over the others. In fact, the stockings were identical except for slight differences in scent. After each individual participated in the study, the stockings were shuffled and put back on the table so that the particular position of each pair of stockings varied randomly. As it turned out, the only factor that had any impact on the shoppers' choices was where they were placed on the table. As marketing experts know, all other things being equal, people are likely to pick products that are placed at the end of a table (or an aisle in a grocery store). In this study, 71% of the participants chose the stockings on the right side of the table, regardless of which pair of stockings was in that position (presumably because people looked at the stockings from left to right, just as when they are reading in English). The women in the study were quite confident in the explanations they provided to justify their choices, such as perceived differences in color or texture, but not a single one of them suggested that her choice was determined primarily by where the stockings were positioned on the table. Yet this was clearly the most influential determinant of most of the women's choices!

Research with both men and women has shown similar inaccuracies regarding what factors do and do not affect them in a variety of domains. For instance, people are inaccurate even in judging what determines their day-to-day mood fluctuations (Wilson et al., 1982). Although our moods are influenced by many factors, our explanations for our feelings tend to be biased toward factors that our intuitive theories of mood tell us are most likely to influence our feelings, for example, the weather or how much sleep we've recently had.

Why are people so likely to give inaccurate explanations of their preferences and feelings? Nisbett and Wilson argued that the human capacity for introspection—looking inward and observing our own thought processes—is actually quite limited.

[Sam Diephuis /Getty Images]

Think
ABOUT

Although we generally have clear access to the *products* of these processes, we typically have little or no access to the *processes* themselves.

To get an intuitive sense of this, think of a time you had a craving for some food, say a burrito from your favorite Mexican take-out restaurant. You are clearly aware of the thought, "A burrito sure would taste good about now," but where did that thought come from? How did it come to you? And why is it a burrito rather than a slice of pizza you crave? Complete mysteries, right?

Explaining Others' Behavior

If people often don't even know why they do and feel things, it's not surprising they are also limited in their knowledge of why other people do and feel things. Indeed, we generally don't go through all that much effort in thinking about why people behave the way they do. For the most part, we tend to be a bit lazy when it comes to thinking and reasoning, a tendency that has led some social psychologists to suggest that people are cognitive misers who avoid expending effort and cognitive resources when thinking and prefer to seize on quick and easy answers to the questions they ask. If we think an explanation makes sense, we tend to accept it without much thought or analysis.

However, when events are important to us or occur unexpectedly, we more carefully scrutinize our environment and the people in it to make inferences about how the world works and why the people around us are behaving the way they are. We might even go to the trouble of verifying our inferences with other people. Having decided what caused an event or another person's actions, we then use these causal

Cognitive misers A term that conveys the human tendency to avoid expending effort and cognitive resources when thinking and to prefer seizing on quick and easy answers to questions.

attributions to direct our own behavior. But even when we put the effort in, some major pitfalls in intuitively observing and reasoning can lead us to accept faulty conclusions about ourselves, other people, and reality in general.

Our Observations Come From Our Own Unique and Limited Perspective

One problem occurs when we make inferences based on observation of only part of an event or of an event viewed from a limited perspective. Imagine that you are a clinical psychologist doing a psychological assessment of a new client. You drive up to your client's house to meet him for the first time and observe him in a rather ferocious verbal dispute with a man in his front yard. From this observation you infer that your client is a hostile and aggressive man. However, suppose that minutes before you arrived, the normally docile and peaceful client happened to discover this man running from the house with the client's laptop under his arm. Seeing a broader range of your client's behavior would almost certainly alter your judgment of his personality.

Thus, sometimes our judgments are based on incomplete observations, and we would make very different inferences if we could observe the entire event in question. For a historical example, consider the 6th-century BC Greek philosopher Thales, who confidently proclaimed after careful observation that the earth is flat and floating on a large body of water. For most of human history, this idea fitted with what the average person observed of the world and made a good deal of sense. Of course, we now know this theory to be incorrect for a variety of reasons, including the fact that the earth, viewed from a space shuttle, appears spherical in shape. Our limited perspectives as observers thus profoundly influence our observations. What appears obvious from one perspective can seem ludicrous when seen from a different point of view.

Our Reasoning Processes May Be Biased to Confirm What We Set Out to Assess

A more fundamental problem is that we rarely are objective observers and interpreters of the world around us. One of the great lessons of social psychology is that everything we observe, through all of our senses, is influenced by our desires, prior knowledge and beliefs, and current expectations. This is confirmation bias, and put simply, it means our views of events and people in the world are biased by how we want and expect them to be.

> **Confirmation bias** The tendency to view events and people in ways that fit how we want and expect them to be.

The tendency to reach conclusions that are consistent with our expectations and desires was demonstrated by Charles Lord and colleagues in 1979. They asked introductory psychology students to report their attitudes about some important issues so they could identify a subset who had strong feelings either in favor of, or opposed to, capital punishment. A few weeks later, this subset of students was recruited to participate in a laboratory study of how people evaluate factual information, although they were unaware of being selected because of their extreme feelings about capital punishment. The students then read summaries of two studies on capital punishment as a crime deterrent, one of which concluded that capital punishment reduced crime and the other that capital punishment is ineffective as a deterrent to crime. After reading the two studies, the students were asked to evaluate how well or poorly each study had been conducted and how convincing the studies' conclusions were. Finally, everyone in the study reported his or her current attitude about capital punishment.

If perception is a direct reflection of reality, then all the students in the study should have pretty much agreed about the quality of the research they read, because they all were exposed to exactly the same materials. But this was not the case. Students originally in favor of capital punishment found the study demonstrating its effectiveness for reducing crime more convincing, whereas

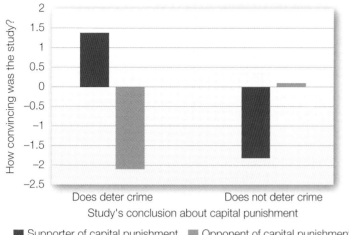

Figure 1.1

Confirmation Bias

When presented with evidence for and against capital punishment, people were more convinced by the evidence that supported their initial attitude.

[Data source: Lord et al. (1979)]

Confederate A supposed participant in a research study who actually is working with experimenters, unknown to the real participants.

opponents of capital punishment were much more convinced by the research showing the ineffectiveness of capital punishment (see **FIGURE 1.1**). Regardless of their position on the issue, they found the study that confirmed their belief to be of higher scientific quality. In addition, students who favored capital punishment became even more favorable toward capital punishment after reading both studies, whereas those who opposed capital punishment became even more opposed to it after reading the same two studies. In other words, the students' judgments of the same "reality" (the two studies) were dependent on their initial attitudes (for or against capital punishment), and the same "reality" caused them to change their attitudes in different directions (becoming more supportive of or opposed to capital punishment).

The Act of Observing May Change the Behavior We Seek to Explain

One final problem is that when people are being observed, the presence of the observer causes them to alter their behavior, sometimes knowingly but often unconsciously. What is observed, then, is the result, to some extent, of the presence of the observer. Consider a personnel manager for a large company who is reluctant to hire a job candidate who appeared fidgety at her interview. Examining a clever study by Tanya Chartrand and John Bargh (1999), we might question whether the personnel officer's own inability to sit still actually made the job candidate seem so jittery. People in this study were asked to spend 10 minutes in two different sessions with one other participant. During each session, the pair looked at a picture and discussed whether it should be included in a psychological test. However, the supposed other participant in each session, unknown to the real participants, was a **confederate**, someone working with the experimenters. One confederate rubbed his or her head throughout the session; the other confederate tapped his or her foot repeatedly during the other session. Videotapes of the naive participants during the sessions were then shown to impartial judges with no foreknowledge of the study. The impartial judges found that the real participants tapped their feet more when they were in the room with the confederate with the happy feet, and rubbed their heads more when they were with the confederate with the itchy scalp (**FIGURE 1.2**). No one in the study realized that the person in the room with them during the sessions was influencing his or her behavior. This is just one example of many studies that have

Figure 1.2

The Subtle Influence of Others

Number of times participants rubbed their heads and shook their foot per minute when with a confederate who engaged in one or the other behavior.

[Data source: Chartrand & Bargh (1999) © 1999 American Psychological Association. Reprinted by permission]

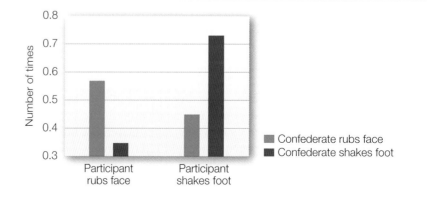

shown how observers unwittingly can be directly responsible for eliciting what they observe in others.

This all boils down to a simple conclusion: Basing psychological inferences on one's own observations is a tenuous proposition. Sometimes we have a limited perspective and don't see enough of an event to make a complete judgment. Sometimes our desires, prior beliefs, and expectations bias our perception. Sometimes our observations match reality reasonably well, but we're partly responsible for what we've observed. Does this mean we should abandon observation as a way to learn about ourselves and the world around us? Quite the contrary: Careful observation is an essential aspect of scientific inquiry. We should take great pains to focus on what is happening in the world around us, but we can become better observers by understanding when and how our observations might be suspect and by using the scientific methods that have been developed to minimize the influence of these biases.

People often imitate each other without even realizing it.
[Getty Images/Flickr RF]

SECTION review | Cultural Knowledge: The Intuitive Encyclopedia

People's intuitive understanding of much of what happens in the world is derived from cultural knowledge.

Asking questions has limitations.	**The intuitive mode of observing and reasoning is faulty.**
• People don't always tell the truth. • People often don't know the truth.	• We often prefer quick and easy answers. • Our inferences often are based on our own limited perspective and preexisting expectations. • We may be biased to confirm what we prefer to believe. • Observation itself may change a person's behavior.

The Scientific Method: Systematizing the Acquisition of Knowledge

Research Methods
Video on LaunchPad

SCIENCE: We must recognize that there are many ways of knowing, but . . . in the entire course of prehistory and history only one way of knowing has encouraged its own practitioners to doubt their own premises and to systematically expose their own conclusions to the hostile scrutiny of nonbelievers.

— Marvin Harris, American anthropologist (1927–2001), *Cultural Materialism*

Over thousands of years, humans have refined everyday thinking to sharpen it and make it less susceptible to the many biases that limit it; the result is the scientific method. Science is a method for answering questions about the nature of reality that reduces the impact of the human biases we have just reviewed.

Theory An explanation for how and why variables are related to each other.

Research The process whereby scientists observe events, look for patterns, and evaluate theories proposed to explain those patterns.

Just like everyone else, scientists make observations, look for patterns in what they observe, and then generate explanations for how or why things happen as they do. These explanations are called theories. Research is the process whereby scientists observe events in the world, look for consistent patterns, and evaluate theories proposed to explain those patterns. Research and theory are simply scientific refinements of the observations and explanations we all make every day to help us get through life. However, whereas ordinary intuitive thinking typically leads us to accept explanations relatively uncritically (especially if they are consistent with our expectations and desires), generating a plausible account of our observations is just the beginning of scientific inquiry.

The Cycle of Theory and Research in Social Psychology

As the social psychologist Kurt Lewin put it, "There is nothing so practical as a good theory" (1952, p. 169). Theories tell us about causal factors that influence particular kinds of behavior. This knowledge can help us alter behavior in beneficial ways. For example, if theories specify factors that lead to bad things such as child abuse and good things such as charitable giving, we can design ways to alter these factors to reduce the occurrence of the bad behaviors and increase the occurrence of good behaviors. And research tells us whether our theories provide the right explanations. The concept of theory is often misunderstood: In grade school, many of us were taught to distinguish theories from facts. This probably gave a lot of people the idea that the difference between a theory and a fact lies in the level of certainty we have about its truth, as if a theory is a sort of weaker version of a fact that shouldn't be taken all that seriously. But in scientific thinking, the concepts of fact and theory are entirely different from one another. They serve different functions and play different roles in the process of doing science. A fact is the *content* of research observations that have been replicated, that is, verified by multiple observers. A theory, on the other hand, is an *explanation* for the facts. Although a theory may be our current best explanation for how or why things happen as they do, it is not—and is not expected to be—an entirely complete or accurate explanation in any absolute sense. The history of science shows us that a theory accepted as useful scientific truth in one era often is viewed as a quaint but misguided *mis*understanding centuries or even decades later. Scientific knowledge is continually evolving, moving toward a more and more useful understanding of reality.

Hypothesis An "if-then" statement that follows logically from a theory and specifies how certain variables should be related to each other if the theory is correct.

To assess the validity of a theory, a scientist starts by deriving testable hypotheses from the theory (see **FIGURE 1.3**). A hypothesis is an "if-then" statement that follows logically from the theory and specifies how certain variables (characteristics that vary and that can be measured) should be related to each other if the theory is correct. Hypotheses are the bridges that scientists use to move from a theory, which explains how or why something happens as it does, to research, in which new observations are made and checked to see if they correspond with what is predicted by a hypothesis.

Typically, a theory generates numerous hypotheses. Once they are tested, either the theory is accepted as it is or is revised or replaced in light of the research findings. The reformulated theory (or the new theory) is then used to generate additional hypotheses, which are then tested, and the cycle continues. In this way, through the ongoing interplay between theory and research, the process spirals toward more sophisticated theories that provide increasingly accurate explanations of reality and programs of research that probe increasingly refined questions about these processes. Let's consider the cycle of theory and research using the example of the development of stereotype threat theory, a topic we will cover more fully in chapter 11.

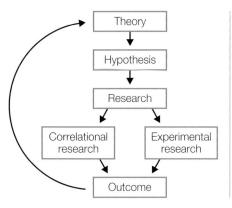

Figure 1.3

The Cycle of Theory and Research

Theories lead to hypotheses that are then tested. The outcomes of these tests influence views and revisions of the theory.

Stereotype Threat: Case Study of a Theory

To illustrate the ongoing interplay between theory and research, let's focus on some influential findings in social psychology that address the question of why people who are members of stereotyped groups sometimes perform poorly on standardized tests of their abilities. This work was inspired by the fairly consistent observation that members of stigmatized groups (groups within a culture that are viewed negatively in some way), such as African Americans and women, tend, on average, to perform less well in certain academic areas—specifically, general scholastic aptitude and mathematics, respectively—than their nonstigmatized peers. Although it is clear that there is wide variability in the performance of people of all races and genders and that it is impossible to predict accurately a person's performance from simple demographic information such as race or gender, these race and gender gaps in test scores beg for some explanation. No one disputes that these average differences between groups exist, but as you might expect, the theories that attempt to explain why they are there have been extremely controversial. They range from locating a cause in nature (the most contentious being a presumption of genetic inferiority) to pointing to systemic inequalities in environment (patterns of poverty or discrimination within American society).

In 1995, Claude Steele and Josh Aronson proposed a creative new theoretical explanation for poor performance by members of stigmatized groups, which they labeled *stereotype threat theory*. The basic idea is that if you are a member of a group about which there are negative stereotypic beliefs, engaging in behavior that is relevant to those negative beliefs puts you in a doubly threatening situation. Not only will you be judged as an individual but your performance also will be taken as evidence of the ability of your entire group. So in the context of a test of verbal intelligence, unlike a White male, whose performance is typically taken as indicative of only his own ability, an African American male might worry that a low score will be viewed as evidence of his entire race's alleged deficiencies in intelligence. Likewise, a woman who misses too many math questions could be seen as confirming the stereotypes of women's inability to do math. Steele proposed that this resulting experience of *stereotype threat* is at least part of the reason members of stigmatized groups tend to perform less well in areas relevant to negative stereotypes concerning their group. Steele further posited that, because of the prevailing negative stereotypic beliefs about the group, the situation itself—having to take a test—arouses stereotype threat and reduces stigmatized students' ability to perform up to their potential. Stereotype threat theory thus proposes that conditions that bring the stereotype to mind contribute to poor performance among members of various stigmatized groups.

This, of course, is a very different explanation from one that assumes that differences in the abilities and potential of particular groups result from *either* genetic inferiority or a lifetime of experience with poverty or discrimination. If true, stereotype threat theory would also be a nice example of how understanding basic social psychological processes can shed new light on important personal and social issues. But to have any scientific credibility, this theoretical explanation must be tested. How would a social psychologist use the scientific method to assess the validity of the stereotype threat theory? To do so, the social psychologist will have to generate hypotheses from the theory, and then test those hypotheses with research. Consider these two hypotheses that have been generated from the theory of stereotype threat:

1. The more a person is conscious of the negative stereotype of his or her group, the worse that person will perform in areas related to the stereotype.
2. Situations that make a negative stereotype of a person's group prominent in the person's mind will lead to worse performance than situations that do not.

Hypothesis 1 proposes an association between two variables that can be assessed with correlational research. Hypothesis 2 posits that one variable has a causal influence on the other and can be assessed only through experimental research. We will discuss each of these two primary approaches to research in social psychology and how they were used to test these hypotheses derived from stereotype threat theory.

Research: The Correlational Method

Correlational method Research in which two or more variables are measured and compared to determine to what extent if any they are associated.

One of the most widely used approaches to doing research is the **correlational method**, whereby two or more preexisting characteristics (the variables) of a group of individuals are measured and compared to determine whether and/or to what extent they are associated. If the variables are associated, then knowing a person's standing on one variable predicts, beyond chance levels, his or her standing on the other variable; if this is the case, we can say that the variables are correlated. To test stereotype threat hypothesis 1, we might: (1) measure the extent to which particular members of a given group are conscious of their stereotyped status; and (2) assess each person's performance on stereotype-related dimensions.

Liz Pinel and colleagues (Pinel et al., 2005) tested this very hypothesis. They first measured the *stigma consciousness*—the tendency to be highly conscious of one's stereotyped status and to believe that these stereotypes have a big effect on how one is viewed by others—of academically stigmatized students (specifically, African Americans and Hispanic Americans) and nonacademically stigmatized students (specifically, European Americans and Asian Americans). Then, they obtained information about their participants' GPAs. To assess whether stigma consciousness is correlated with GPA, the researchers computed **correlation coefficients**. Pinel and colleagues found a moderate negative correlation between stigma consciousness and GPA. Let's briefly consider what this statistic can tell us about how two variables are related.

Correlation coefficient A positive or negative numerical value that shows the direction and the strength of a relationship between two variables.

The Correlation Coefficient

The correlation coefficient (typically indicated by *r*)gives us two vital pieces of information about a relationship: both the direction and the strength of the relationship (**FIGURE 1.4**).

- The sign, positive (+) or negative (−), tells us the *direction* of the relationship. A positive correlation occurs when a high level of one variable tends to be accompanied by a corresponding high level of another variable. A negative correlation exists when a high level of one variable is accompanied by a low level of the other variable. If Pinel and colleagues had found that the higher a person scores on stigma consciousness, the better her GPA, they would have found a positive correlation. The negative correlation that they actually found tells us that the *higher* a person's level of stigma consciousness the *lower* that person's GPA. This negative correlation provides some evidence for stereotype threat hypothesis 1.

- The numerical value tells us the *strength* of the relationship. The strength of a correlation refers to how closely associated the two variables are, how much knowing a person's standing on one variable tells us about, or enables us to predict, the person's standing on the other variable. If knowing a person's level of stigma consciousness enables us to predict his test performance with absolute certainty, the two variables are perfectly correlated, and the correlation coefficient equals −1.0 (or +1.0 if it were a positive relationship). Perfect correlations are virtually nonexistent in the behavioral sciences. When they do occur, it typically means that the two variables are different measures of the same underlying conceptual variable. For example, temperature as measured on Fahrenheit and

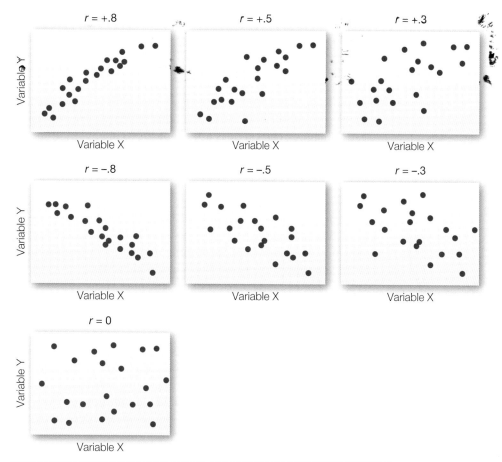

Figure 1.4

Correlation Coefficient

The correlation coefficient (signified by the letter r) is a measure of the relationship between two variables. These graphs represent the three kinds of correlations between Variables X and Y: positive, negative, and no correlation. The sign of r (+ or −) tells us whether the relationship is positive or negative. The absolute value of r tells us the strength of the relationship. The stronger the correlation, the more confidently we can predict the value of one variable from the value of the other.

Celsius thermometers will be perfectly correlated (as long as the thermometers are operating correctly). On the other hand, we would find a correlation of 0 if the two variables are completely unrelated. This means that knowing something about a person's standing on one variable tells you nothing whatsoever about where she stands on the other. For example, according to stereotype threat theory, knowing a person's level of stigma consciousness should only relate to his GPA if he is not a member of an academically stigmatized group. Sure enough, Pinel and colleagues observed no correlation between stigma consciousness and GPA for nonacademically stigmatized groups.

It's important to be clear that although the sign of a correlation coefficient tells you whether two variables are positively or negatively correlated, it tells you nothing at all about the strength of that relationship. Thus, a correlation of −0.60 reflects a stronger relationship than a correlation of +0.35.

Pinel and colleagues' finding of a moderate negative correlation between stigma consciousness and GPA tells us that knowing how sensitive a person is to stereotypes about his or her group gives us some basis for predicting how well he or she is likely to score on measures of academic performance, although we couldn't predict the person's performance with absolute certainty or precision. Clearly, many variables other than stigma consciousness influence college GPA. And imperfections in our two measures would also reduce the size of any correlation we observe. Nonetheless, the negative correlation between stigma consciousness and test performance tells us that these two variables are indeed related, which is consistent with the hypothesis deduced from stereotype threat theory.

Correlation Does Not Imply Causation

Scientists usually are interested in understanding why variables are correlated. But finding a negative correlation between stigma consciousness and test performance does not allow us to conclude that fear of confirming stereotypes about one's group *causes* poorer performance. Correlation does not imply causality. There must be a correlation between the two variables if one variable causes the other, but there are two major reasons that correlation does not enable us to infer causation.

THE FAMILY CIRCUS. By Bil Keane

"I wish they didn't turn on that seatbelt sign so much! Every time they do, it gets bumpy."

[FAMILY CIRCUS © 1998 Bil Keane, Inc. Dist. by King Features Synd.]

First, although it is certainly possible that stereotype threat causes poorer test performance, it is also possible that the causal relationship runs in the other direction: Doing poorly on tests makes a person especially sensitive to the stereotypes about his or her group, and perhaps fearful that he or she might be contributing to these stereotypes. This is known as the reverse causality problem: Correlations tell us nothing about which of two inter-related variables is the cause and which is the effect.

The second major reason that we cannot draw causal inferences from correlations is referred to as the third variable problem: The two variables are correlated, but it is still possible that neither exerts a causal influence on the other. It may be that some third variable—for example, a general tendency to be self-conscious and anxiety prone—is responsible for the correlation found between stigma consciousness and performance. Being self-conscious and nervous might make a person concerned about how others view his or her group and at the same time may interfere with test performance. Such correlations between anxiety proneness and stigma consciousness, and between anxiety proneness and test performance, would create a correlation between stigma consciousness and test performance even if there were no causal relationship between the latter two variables. Taken together, the reverse causality and third variable problems make it impossible to be conclusive about causality from correlational findings.

Reverse causality problem A correlation between variables *x* and *y* may occur because one causes the other, but it is often impossible to determine if *x* causes *y* or *y* causes *x*.

Third variable problem The possibility that two variables may be correlated but do not exert a causal influence on one another; rather, both are caused by some additional variable.

Longitudinal studies Studies in which variables are measured in the same individuals over two or more periods of time, typically over months or years.

Longitudinal Studies

In longitudinal studies two variables are measured at multiple points in time. By examining correlations between one variable at time 1 and another variable at time 2, such studies can make us more confident about likely causal order. For example, one classic study of aggression (see Huesmann et al., 1984) found that amount of violent television watched in childhood correlated positively with amount of aggressive behavior in adulthood. In contrast, aggressiveness in childhood did not correlate with amount of violent television watching in adulthood. The result of this longitudinal study suggests that childhood television watching affected later aggression, rather than childhood aggressiveness affecting later television viewing. However, such studies are not definitive about causation because the third variable problem remains. For example, it could be that neglectful parents both allow their children to watch a lot of violence, and for other reasons produce adult offspring with aggressive tendencies.

Research: The Experimental Method

Fortunately, there is an approach to research that lets us draw conclusions about cause and effect: the experimental method. As a consequence, this method is extremely popular among social psychologists. An experiment is a study in which the researcher takes active control and manipulates one variable, referred to as the independent variable, measures possible effects on another variable, referred to as the dependent variable, and tries to hold all other variables constant. The independent variable is manipulated because it is being investigated as the possible cause. The dependent variable is the one that is then measured to assess the effect. An experiment can tell us if the dependent variable *depends* on the independent variable. An experiment would be needed to test hypothesis 2: that conditions which increase the individual's awareness of the negative stereotype of that person's group (and thereby increase stereotype threat) will reduce the person's test performance. Such an experiment must involve:

1. Manipulating our research participants' awareness of the negative stereotype of their group, creating two or more conditions differing in the level of the independent variable: stereotype threat
2. Assessing participants' performance on a test that is relevant to that negative stereotype, providing a measurement of the dependent variable
3. Holding everything else constant within the setting

When all the requirements of the experimental method are met, the study has internal validity, which means that it is possible to conclude that the manipulated independent variable caused the change in the measured dependent variable. Let's translate that into a real example.

Steele and Aronson (1995) conducted a series of experiments that provided the first evidence that stereotype threat caused reduced performance among members of stigmatized groups. In one study, African American and White college students were given a challenging test of verbal ability that consisted of sample items from the verbal portion of the Graduate Record Exam. Performance on the test was the dependent measure. To manipulate stereotype threat, the researchers simply asked half of the participants to indicate their race on the answer form prior to beginning the test; this simple act of indicating race was meant to bring to mind the stereotypes about how each participant's group was supposed to perform on such tests. The other half of the participants, the control group, took the test with no mention being made of race, so they were much less likely to be thinking about stereotype-related issues while taking the test. Whether or not race was mentioned was the independent variable. The racial identity of the participants was the second variable that the experimenters expected to play a causal role. We should note that demographic variables such as race, age, or gender are commonly treated as independent variables, even though the experimenter cannot manipulate them. The caveat to interpreting these variables is to keep in mind that there are lots of different ways that Blacks and Whites might differ from each other (e.g., cultural beliefs, socioeconomic status) that could underlie any racial differences observed.

As stereotype threat hypothesis 2 predicts, when participants were reminded of their race, there was a significant drop in the performance of African American students but not in the performance of White students (see **FIGURE 1.5**). This pattern of results is referred to as an interaction, which occurs when the effect of one independent variable on the dependent variable depends on the level of a second variable. In this study, the effect of the reminder of race depended on whether the participant's racial identity was African American or White. Because African American students are stereotyped in the United States as being less intelligent, for them, the reminder of racial identity led to lower performance; for White students, however, it had no effect. Thus, even though we cannot randomly assign a person to his or her race, the fact that a reminder of race influenced Blacks and Whites differently suggests that racial identity is what mattered here.

How Experiments Make Causal Inference Possible

The experimental method overcomes the limitations of the correlational method so that causal inferences are possible. As we previously noted, the first major obstacle to drawing causal inferences from correlational studies is the reverse causality problem,

The experimental method A study in which a researcher manipulates a variable, referred to as the independent variable, measures possible effects on another variable, referred to as the dependent variable, and tries to hold all other variables constant.

Internal validity The judgment that for a particular experiment it is possible to conclude that the manipulated independent variable caused the change in the measured dependent variable.

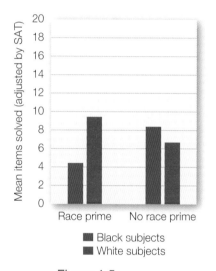

Figure 1.5

Stereotype Threat

Black students performed more poorly on a test when reminded of their race. White students were unaffected by such a reminder.

[Data source: Steele & Aronson (1995) © 1995 American Psychological Association. Reprinted by permission]

Interaction A pattern of results in which the effect of one independent variable on the dependent variable depends on the level of a second independent variable.

because you typically can't tell which variable is the cause and which is the effect. In an experiment, because the researcher determines whether a participant is exposed to the experimental condition (race reminder) or the control condition (no race reminder) and subsequently measures performance, it is impossible for the participant's poor test performance to have caused him or her to be reminded of his or her race. Causes must come before effects. Consequently, the causal sequence problem is eliminated.

What about the third variable problem? Recall that in an experiment, the only thing that differs between conditions is the independent variable. Everything else is held constant. The researcher treats participants in the various conditions in identical ways: the same instructions are given; the physical setting is the same; and any written, audio, and video materials are identical, except for what is to be manipulated between conditions (the independent variable). All this is done so that if there is a difference between conditions, we can be confident that the cause is the independent variable. By holding everything constant across the various conditions in the experiment except the independent variable, the experimenter solves the third variable problem.

Controlling the Impact of Individual Differences by Random Assignment

But how do we know that the participants in the experimental group and the control group didn't simply differ on the dependent measure to begin with? And how do we know that differences between the two samples on some other dimension that existed prior to manipulation of the independent variable were not responsible for the differences in test performance that occurred? The potential problem of preexisting differences among participants in the various experimental conditions is solved by **random assignment**, in which participants are assigned to conditions in such a way that each person has an equal chance of being in either condition (**FIGURE 1.6**). Deciding which treatment to give each participant can be done by tossing a coin, pulling names from a hat, or using a random number generator to put individuals into treatment conditions.

Random assignment is an essential component of all experiments in which participants are put in different conditions. It ensures that, if a sufficiently large sample is used, no systematic average differences will exist among the participants in the various experimental conditions. This is because random assignment evenly distributes people, and all the ways they may vary, across all the conditions of

Random assignment
A procedure in which participants are assigned to conditions in such a way that each person has an equal chance of being in any condition of an experiment.

Figure 1.6

Random Assignment

Even though individuals differ from each other, when they are randomly assigned to groups, the groups' averages will be largely the same.

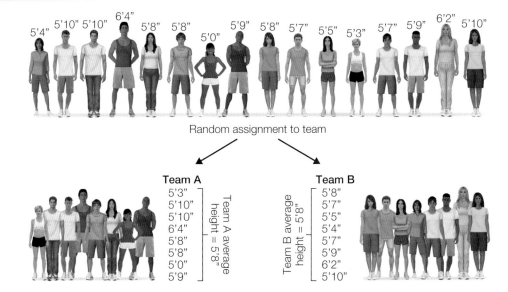

the experiment. For example, if a sample of 100 people was randomly divided into two groups of 50, the mean height, weight, level of self-esteem, and verbal GRE performance of the two groups would be virtually identical. Random assignment thereby controls for individual differences that might otherwise vary between the experimental and control groups, and is thus essential for eliminating the third variable problem. Because the experimental method eliminates both the causal sequence and third variable problems, it provides internal validity and causal inferences can be made.

Experimental and Correlational Research in Concert

Because the experimental method enables us to infer causes for behavior, it is generally the preferred way to conduct research in social psychology, but in some situations experimental methods cannot be applied. Many of the variables that social psychologists are interested in cannot be manipulated. There are many important questions about the effect of variables like gender, age, race, and sexual preference, but people can't be randomly assigned to be male or female, old or young, Black or White, or straight or gay. Furthermore, many of the questions of interest to social psychologists deal with long-standing personality dispositions, attitudes, values, and other individual differences. Correlational methods that examine relationships between preexisting differences among people are the only way questions such as these can be addressed. Correlational methods also have the advantage of examining the relationship between variables as they naturally occur in the real world. Experimental methods, by definition, involve observing the effects of variables that are created by researchers; consequently there is always some question as to how well these experimentally created variables mirror the forces that operate on us in real life. For all these reasons, correlational methods have been, and will continue to be, important tools for social psychologists.

In fact, the correlational method and the experimental method provide complementary information about how or why people behave the way they do. Let's go back to the example of research testing hypotheses derived from stereotype threat theory. The experimental research by Steele and Aronson (1995) provides compelling evidence that stereotype threat is at least one of the factors that cause poorer performance by members of stigmatized groups; on the other hand, the correlational research by Pinel and colleagues (2005) suggests that some students will be more vulnerable to these effects. When applied together, these two research strategies enable social psychologists to document the role that both individual differences and situational forces play in leading people to behave the way they do. Such evidence fits the first core assumption of social psychology: that behavior is a function of a combination of the features of the person and the situation.

Field Research and Quasi-experimental Methods

Because social psychologists ultimately want to understand the forces that operate on us in real life, another important type of research is field research. This type of research occurs outside the laboratory, for example, in schools, office buildings, medical clinics, football games, or even in shopping malls or on street corners. Field research is not wedded to an experimental or correlational approach. It can be either. It also often utilizes quasi-experimental designs. In a quasi-experimental design, groups of participants are compared on some dependent variable, but for practical or ethical reasons, the groups are not formed on the basis of random assignment. Note that the stereotype threat study described earlier can be considered partly quasi-experimental because participants are not randomly assigned to race.

We can also use research on stereotype threat to highlight an example of field research. One goal of a field study might be to see if we can use stereotype threat

Field research Research that occurs outside the laboratory, for example, in schools, office buildings, medical clinics, football games, or even in shopping malls or on street corners.

Quasi-experimental designs Type of research in which groups of participants are compared on some dependent variable, but for practical or ethical reasons, the groups are not formed on the basis of random assignment.

to design interventions that reduce racial differences in students' actual academic achievement. This is exactly what researchers such as Greg Walton and Geoff Cohen have done (Walton & Cohen, 2007, 2011). They reasoned that for many if not most college students, the transition to college can be stressful. These students have to adjust to a more rigorous type of study than you had in high school. They might also be living away from family for the first time and trying to make new friends. When we add feelings of stereotype threat, perhaps from not seeing many other faculty or students who share their racial background, students from minority backgrounds might be at greater risk for feeling that they don't belong, and this might impair their academic performance. In the context of the transition to university, Walton and Cohen wanted to see if shoring up feelings of belonging at college would reduce stereotype threat and improve academic performance for racial minorities.

To do this, they randomly assigned a sample of White and Black first-year college students to one of two conditions. In the intervention condition, students read testimonials the researchers had compiled from more senior students. They each sounded something like this:

> Freshman year even though I met large numbers of people, I didn't have a small group of close friends. . . . I was pretty homesick, and I had to remind myself that making close friends takes time. Since then . . . I have met people some of whom are now just as close as my friends in high school were. (WALTON & COHEN, 2007, P. 88)

These testimonials from students of different racial, gender, and ethnic backgrounds send the message that stress is a pretty normal and understandable part of *all* students' experience. Those students in the control condition read similar testimonials about how students' political attitudes had changed. Then the researchers proceeded to follow both groups of students for the next three years (**FIGURE 1.7**).

Among students in the control group, Black students earned GPAs that were significantly lower than those of their White peers. But for those students who

Figure 1.7

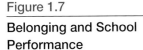

Belonging and School Performance

A racial gap in achievement observed between European American and African American students was reduced when first-year students received an intervention to bolster feelings of belonging.

[Data source: Walton & Cohen (2011) © 2011 by the American Association for the Advancement of Science. Reprinted by permission]

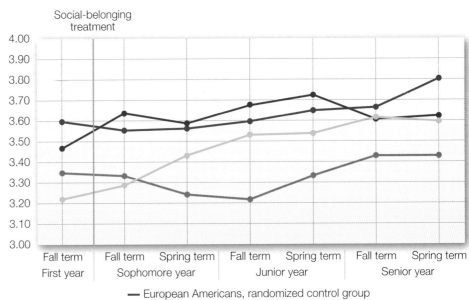

Social-belonging treatment

Legend:
— European Americans, randomized control group
— European Americans, social-belonging treatment
— African Americans, randomized control group
— African Americans, social-belonging treatment

received the intervention and learned that stress is a part of everyone's experience at university, this racial gap in achievement was cut in half over the next three years. Whereas learning about how stressed other students are did not matter too much for White students, it significantly boosted how Black students performed in their courses, and it did so by helping students see that their experience of stress and adversity at college in no way meant that they didn't belong there.

One of the strengths of field research like this study is that it tries to capture social behavior as it occurs out in the world. This is important because, as you well know, the world is a complex place and researchers need to study that complexity. The chief weakness, though, is that researchers often lose a lot of the control they have in the laboratory in terms of what participants are exposed to, and thus don't always have the clearest manipulation or measurement of the variables they want to study.

Quasi-experimental designs have an additional weakness. Because the researchers are not randomly assigning participants to the levels of the independent variable, there is a greater chance that participants may differ on some other potentially important characteristic. So although the researchers may be able to overcome the reverse causality problem of correlational designs, it is more difficult to overcome the third variable problem. None of these methods is perfect, but each has its own strengths and weaknesses, and each plays a useful role in helping social psychologists understand human behavior.

What Makes for a Good Theory in Social Psychology?

The ultimate function of a good theory is to be *useful* by moving this ongoing cyclical process of science forward. It should advance our understanding of how and why people behave the way they do, facilitating efforts to make the world a better place. Our experiences in applying our newfound knowledge to issues of real human importance ultimately come back to tell us how well our theoretical understanding fits the world in which we live. A useful theory has the following characteristics.

Organizes Observations

First, a theory should organize the observations, or facts, that come out of the research process. Theories create order out of chaos and simplify the bewildering array of facts that we observe in the world around us. Theories provide a more abstract and general way of describing the nature of reality than the complex and sometimes messy observations that theories seek to explain. For example, Steele's stereotype threat theory summarizes and simplifies results from other studies that have shown that members of stigmatized groups perform worse when very few other members of their group are present, when the person administering a test is from a different ethnic group, and when the test is presented as one on which their group tends to perform poorly. This rather disparate set of facts coheres within the broader theory that performance is impaired when conditions make it likely that people will think of a relevant negative stereotype about their group. Generally speaking, the broader the range of observations that a theory can make sense of, the better. Theories that are able to account for a wide variety of observations are said to have conceptual power.

Explains Observations

Theories do much more than simplify and organize knowledge. A good theory should also give us insight into how or why things happen. To do this effectively, a theory must be conceptually coherent and logically consistent. It should specify clear relationships between variables that help us understand the processes through which particular events in the world occur. To be truly useful, a theory should provide us with understanding that goes beyond what we already know. It should shed new light on what we observe happening within and around us, giving us a sort of "aha, now I get it" experience. Stereotype threat theory provides an entirely new way of thinking about group differences in academic achievement, and it does this in a coherent and logically consistent way. It is also a relatively simple idea that fits well with our understanding of basic psychological processes. In this sense, stereotype threat theory is highly *parsimonious*—it explains a wide range of observations with a relatively small number of basic principles. Einstein's theory of relativity and Darwin's theory of evolution are two of the most parsimonious theories in the history of science in that both explain extremely diverse sets of observations with just a few relatively simple principles.

Provides Direction for Research

Third, a good theory should inspire research. It should enable us to deduce clear and novel hypotheses that follow logically from its propositions, hypotheses that in turn lead to research that tells us how well the theory fits with reality. Stereotype threat theory has inspired a great deal of research that has both supported its core propositions and led to refinements in our understanding of how stereotype threat undermines performance. Many potentially interesting ideas about why people behave the way they do have been discussed over the millennia; some of these ideas might be quite accurate. But unless a theory produces hypotheses that can be used to assess its fit with reality, it is not scientifically useful. That's not to say that a useful theory must be easy to test, or that it must be testable immediately on its development. Indeed, some of the most influential and important theories in the history of science could not be tested directly for many years after they were proposed. For example, the theory that physical matter is made up of tiny particles moving about in space could not be tested until suitable techniques were developed to enable physicists to assess the nature and movement of atomic particles. An intriguing new theory that seems at first to defy scientific testing often provides the impetus for the development of new technologies that can be used to test the theory's core propositions.

Generates New Questions

Fourth, in addition to inspiring research, a good theory should shed light on phenomena beyond what the theory was originally designed to explain. In other words, a good theory should be generative, providing new theoretical insights in other domains. When we combine a good theory with other ideas, new ideas should spill out. Stereotype threat theory has been generative in the sense that it has led to new ideas about performance deficits in a wide range of areas and among a wide variety of different groups of people. It has also led to finer-grained ideas about the processes through which fear of confirming negative stereotypes of one's group undermines successful performance (more on this to follow).

Has Practical Value

A good theory should have practical applications that help us solve pressing problems and improve the quality of life. In recent years, stereotype threat theory has begun to inform interventions applied in schools and on college campuses (Walton & Spencer, 2009). For example, the theory implies that remedial programs to help negatively stereotyped minority-group students may backfire because they continually remind the students of the negative stereotype of their group. Typically, practical applications of social psychological theories take time to emerge. One of the earliest theories about how to reduce prejudice, developed by Gordon Allport in his classic book *The Nature of Prejudice* (1954), led to what is known as the *contact hypothesis*.

The idea is that specific forms of contact between groups can break down stereotypes and negative feelings and thus reduce prejudice and intergroup conflict. In 1961, Muzafer Sherif and colleagues (Sherif et al., 1961) conducted a famous study at a Boy Scout camp in Oklahoma that supported this hypothesis and led to myriad practical applications. For example, Elliot Aronson (1978) used ideas from Allport and supported by the Sherif study to reduce interracial conflict in Austin, Texas, public schools that had recently been desegregated. His jigsaw classroom technique promotes the kind of contact that Sherif and colleagues had found effective in their summer-camp study. We'll cover all these examples in greater depth later in the text, and we'll highlight examples of practical applications of theories throughout.

Assessing Abstract Theories with Concrete Research

Theories deal with the world of abstract conceptual variables, such as attitudes, self-esteem, anxiety, attraction, and conflict. They specify relationships among these variables in attempts to explain important aspects of human behavior. For example, one explanation for why stereotype threat undermines performance is that it creates anxiety that people try to regulate and control, saddling minority students with an extra cognitive task that nonstigmatized students don't have to worry about (Schmader et al., 2008). Anxiety is a conceptual variable that most psychologists define as a vague, undifferentiated feeling of unease, tension, or fear. Anxiety can involve various psychological and bodily reactions: a feeling of dread, a vague sense of impending doom, sweaty palms, racing heart, butterflies in the stomach, fidgeting, nailbiting, or a desire to change the topic or flee the situation. Different people experience anxiety in somewhat different ways and exhibit a rather wide range of symptoms or signs that they are experiencing it. The abstract concept of anxiety refers to the essential underlying phenomenon that is indicated by these various signs and symptoms. So how would a scientist conduct research on—that is, make observations of—something so abstract and diffuse as the concept of anxiety?

These people are reacting to the terrorist bombings at the Boston Marathon, April 15, 2013. Social psychologists assess anxiety by self-report, facial expressions, overt behavior, and physiological measures.

[Bill Green/*The Boston Globe* via Getty Images]

To conduct research on any conceptual variable, we first must develop an operational definition of that concept. Defining a concept operationally involves moving from the abstract world of concepts to the more concrete world of specific instances. An **operational definition** entails finding a specific, concrete way to measure or manipulate a conceptual variable. Ideally, an operational definition will capture a typical instance of the conceptual variable that illustrates its core meaning or essence. In reality, any conceptual variable can be operationalized in a variety of ways, so that no single operational definition is likely to provide the perfect or only instance of the concept.

Operational definition A specific, concrete method of measuring or manipulating a conceptual variable.

Measuring and Manipulating What We Intend

Let's first examine this issue with regard to a dependent variable. Operationalizing a dependent variable refers to specifying precisely how it will be measured in a particular study. For example, a researcher might operationalize the conceptual variable anxiety in the following ways:

1. Scores on a self-report survey of the subjective feeling of anxiety (e.g., tension, apprehension, uneasiness, butterflies in the stomach)

2. Overt behaviors that are thought (on the basis of a theoretical conception) to be indicators of anxiety (e.g., chewing on the fingernails, rapidly tapping one's foot, twitching eyelids)

3. Physiological measures that assess bodily symptoms or signs that are thought (again, on the basis of a theoretical conception) to be indicators of anxiety (e.g., rapid heart rate, sweaty palms, exaggerated startle response)

These various operationalizations tap into different aspects of the concept of anxiety. It's important that multiple operationalizations of a given conceptual variable are highly correlated with each other, so that we can be confident that the various operationalizations are all tapping into the same underlying conceptual variable. Construct validity is the degree to which the dependent variable measures what it intends to measure or the independent variable manipulates what it intends to manipulate. Often researchers assess the construct validity of an independent variable by including a manipulation check, which is a measure that directly assesses whether the manipulation created the change that was intended. For dependent variables, if different operationalizations of a given conceptual variable are not strongly related to each other, we may actually be tapping into two different conceptual variables. Poor construct validity is one of the primary potential problems in the research process. If it is not clear that an operationalization of a dependent variable measures what it was intended to measure, then we can't draw any clear conclusion from an experiment using that operationalization. An experiment that lacks construct validity for either the independent or the dependent variable does not have internal validity. No clear conclusions can be drawn from the results of such an experiment.

Problems with the construct validity of independent variables are particularly common in social psychological research. Operationalizations of the manipulation of any one specific conceptual independent variable might also inadvertently alter several other conceptual variables. For example, if we manipulate stereotype threat by informing our research participants that it is widely believed that their group performs poorly on a particular task, this may well be increasing their concern that their poor performance might confirm a negative stereotype, just as our conceptual definition of stereotype threat would suggest. But it may also be doing other things. Maybe it's just creating a general increase in fear of failure that has little to do with concerns about stereotypes. It might even be creating anger at the thought that some people view one's group as inferior.

How can we know if the effect of our independent variable is due to concerns about stereotypes, performance anxiety, anger, or any number of other possible consequences of our manipulation? This is a crucial question for determining whether a study has internal validity. When more than one conceptual variable differs across conditions in an experiment, the independent variable is confounded. Confounds cloud the interpretation of research results because a variable other than the conceptual variable we intended to manipulate may be responsible for the effect on the dependent variable, making alternative explanations possible. Alternative explanations make it unclear which conceptual variable really is responsible for the changes in the dependent variable that occur. Confounds and alternative explanations are thus a major problem in social psychological research, and in all of science. Much of the controversy and disagreement among scientists results from the confounding of variables.

Researchers do their best to avoid confounds in their studies. Ideally, the researcher carefully considers potential confounds and alternative explanations when planning the study and includes control groups that expose participants to these possible confounding alternative causal variables without exposing them to the variable that is being investigated as a possible cause. To control for possible confounds in experiments on the effect of stereotype threat on test performance, we might include control conditions in which participants are threatened,

Construct validity The degree to which the dependent measure assesses what it intends to assess or the manipulation manipulates what it intends to manipulate.

Confound A variable other than the conceptual variable intended to be manipulated that may be responsible for the effect on the dependent variable, making alternative explanations possible.

distracted, or angered in ways unrelated to stereotypes of the groups to which they belong. If the experimental stereotype threat induction group shows worse performance than any of these other groups, we can confidently rule out performance anxiety, distraction, and anger as alternative explanations for our findings, which would increase our confidence that stereotype threat is, in fact, causing the poorer performance.

The problem of confounding can also be minimized by replicating our studies with different operationalizations of the crucial variables, a process known as conceptual replication. If different studies, each flawed in one way or another, with possible confounds operating, yield consistent results, the probability that an alternative explanation is responsible for the results is reduced. Science is thus a cumulative process, and scientific knowledge depends heavily on ongoing conceptual replications of findings to rule out any confounds that might be affecting our results.

Conceptual replication The repetition of a study with different operationalizations of the crucial variables but yielding similar results.

Can the Findings Be Generalized?

As you can see, establishing the construct validity of an experiment's independent and dependent variables is essential to the internal validity of the experiment. If a study has high internal validity, we may know, for instance, that stereotype threat undermined performance by a group of African American students at a university in California in the early 1990s. This is important because it supports a hypothesis derived from stereotype threat theory and thereby increases confidence in the theory. And even if this finding comes from a unique sample, it demonstrates that the effect *can* occur. Once internal validity has been established, we can then ask, What does this tell us about other people, in other settings, at other times? This is the basic question regarding external validity, the ability to generalize one's findings. Can we generalize beyond the group of people studied at a particular time and place?

Social psychology studies rely heavily on readily available college-student samples. But how can we know if findings from such studies can be generalized?
[Diego Cervo/Shutterstock]

External validity The judgment that a research finding can be generalized to other people, in other settings, at other times.

In the case of stereotype threat, one external validity question would be whether these effects are limited to African Americans or extend to other stigmatized groups, and even farther, to majority-group members in domains in which they are negatively stereotyped. For example, would the performance of American women be worsened by reminding them of the stereotype that women supposedly have poor mathematical ability? Would the athletic performance of American White males be diminished by reminding them of the stereotype that "White men can't jump"? Research suggests that the answer to both questions is yes. For instance, one study (Spencer et al., 1999) showed that leading women participants to believe that women typically perform poorly on the math test they were about to take led to poorer math performance among the women.

Another study (Stone et al., 1999) had White and Black participants engage in a task akin to miniature golf. Half the participants were told that the task measured sports intelligence, and the other half were told that it measured athletic ability. The researchers reasoned that Whites would feel stereotype threat when they were led to believe that the task measured athletic ability, but Blacks would experience stereotype threat when the task was framed as a measure of sports intelligence. These hypotheses were supported: Whites performed poorly when the

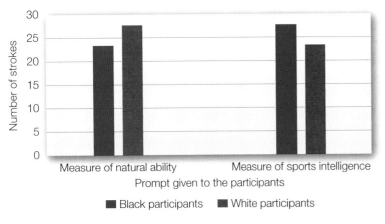

Figure 1.8

Stereotype Threat in Blacks and Whites

Any group that is negatively stereotyped—and that is any group!—can be affected by stereotype threat. In this study, White participants needed more strokes to sink a golf putt when they thought their natural ability was being assessed, but Black participants needed more strokes when they thought their sports intelligence was being assessed.

[Data source: Stone et al. (1999)]

task was described as a measure of athletic ability, and Blacks performed poorly when it was described as a measure of sports intelligence (**FIGURE 1.8**). Over the years, the results of many studies have shown that the problem of stereotype threat is indeed a general one that, depending on the performance domain, can affect members of any group that is negatively stereotyped—that is, virtually everyone!

These examples illustrate that if we are really to have confidence in the external validity of the findings of psychological research, the research needs to be replicated with other types of operationalizations and other participants from varying cultures, geographical regions, and socioeconomic levels. Social psychological research has been criticized for its heavy use of college students as research participants and for participants who might be described as WEIRD (that is, from countries that are Western, educated, industrialized, rich, and democratic [Heinrich et al., 2010]). This is not surprising, because most of the research has been conducted by scientists who are themselves WEIRD. However, some have wondered whether we are simply piling up knowledge about the middle class in WEIRD nations but are learning little about other North Americans, Europeans, and Australians, let alone people from other continents. This narrow choice of participants is a problem, because if culture does exert a powerful role in shaping our view of ourselves and the world around us, then building a science of human behavior largely drawn from only a limited slice of human diversity is likely to skew the conclusions we draw. The ideal solution to this problem would be to sample people randomly from the entire population of the earth. Of course, such random sampling is never possible. Although the rare cross-national survey study might be able to recruit samples that are broadly representative of people from diverse racial, ethnic, national, geographic, and economic constituencies, they are still not representative of people they cannot reach or those who are unwilling to fill out the survey. Most studies that take place in laboratories are forced to rely on samples of convenience, typically college students much like yourself. How, then, can we hope that the findings from such research will inform us about why people in general do the things they do?

One important point to remember is that scientific progress is made in the aggregate. Every study that scientists carry out contains some limitation or weakness; only by conducting multiple studies, using a diverse set of procedures and with a diverse array of samples, can we learn the more general patterns of the human condition. According to this logic, a good, internally valid experiment teaches us what is possible and lends support to a broader theory, even when it doesn't capture the effect as it actually occurs among people in general. For example, Steele and Aronson's (1995) demonstration that merely marking one's race on a cover sheet to a test can lead Black but not White students to underperform doesn't apply only to the rare occurrences when students fill out demographic information in a testing context. It tells us something conceptual about how reminding people of their group identity can lead to subtle but profound shifts in behavior.

A second answer to the problem of nonrepresentative samples is the increasingly global nature of psychology. Social psychologists can currently be found on every populated continent. Although research from North America and western Europe still dominates the field, the broadening reach of social psychology as a science will continue to fuel efforts to replicate key findings in other cultural and geographic settings. Although these true tests of generalizability will sometimes confirm the universal nature of phenomena, they might also reveal important cultural differences in how we think and feel about ourselves and others. Throughout this text, we'll highlight some of the research that has already revealed such interesting cultural variations.

The Limitations of Science

The scientific method has helped improve our lives in many ways. By providing a way of assessing the merits of competing claims about the nature of reality, science has greatly enhanced our understanding of the world we live in, ourselves, and how we fit into that world. By applying the knowledge gained from scientific inquiry, humankind has solved many of the problems that have plagued us for millennia, greatly reducing our vulnerability to disease, providing improved means of meeting our basic needs, and giving us control over aspects of life that our ancestors never dreamed possible. But the knowledge science has given us has also created problems our ancestors could have never imagined, such as the potential to kill each other by the millions and to use up or poison the natural resources we rely on for survival. These are very real problems that must be faced. Social psychology can help us grapple with them by providing the knowledge needed to get people to look beyond their immediate personal benefits to see the long-term consequences of their decisions for others and to put aside age-old ethnic and religious rivalries and realize that our mutual survival depends on our ability to coexist peacefully with each other. However, there are some things that the science of social psychology, no matter how far it progresses, cannot help us with. Despite its enormous utility, science has some important limitations.

First, *there are aspects of reality that we humans cannot know.* Our knowledge of the world originates in the information provided to us by our sense organs. Unfortunately, human sense organs are capable of registering only a tiny fraction of the things that are actually happening in the world. For example, our hearing is limited to a relatively narrow range of sound frequencies. Our dogs can hear many sounds we have no hope of perceiving; bats live in an even more highly differentiated world of sound that we can't even imagine. Although we often use the knowledge that science gives us to develop technologies that enable us to assess things that our raw sense organs cannot perceive, the fact that we are capable of perceiving only part of what is happening in the world makes a complete understanding of all aspects of reality an elusive goal.

Second, *although the scientific method may be objective, the human beings who apply it are not.* The scientific method was developed to provide a more objective way of answering questions and evaluating the validity of competing claims about how the world works. But science remains a human endeavor. Scientists may try their best to put their biases aside and be objective, but human nature makes a complete elimination of individual bias impossible. This is part of the reason that controversies continue to rage in all active areas of scientific inquiry. Scientists, social psychologists included, often stake their reputations, careers, and ultimately their self-esteem on the ideas they espouse. It is a rare occurrence for a scientist to gleefully greet new findings that disconfirm important claims he or she has made; more often, egos get involved, and even highly trained scientists committed to the pursuit of truth muster their best arguments to try to convince the scientific community of flaws in the competing point of view and to show that their own ideas were right all along. Fortunately, the scientific method, and the communal nature of the scientific enterprise, typically weeds out these biases in the long run. But it is important to realize that scientists are human beings subject to the same needs, desires, and expectations that produce bias in all humans.

Third, *not all questions can be answered scientifically*. Many of the most pressing crises facing us today involve questions of values, morality, and ethics. Although social psychology can fruitfully employ the scientific method to understand how values develop, change, and influence human behavior, science cannot tell us which values are the right ones to invest in. Is safety more important than freedom? Are the rights of the individual more important than the welfare of the group? Should scientific knowledge be used to restrict behaviors that are injurious to the people who engage in them? These are important questions we all will be facing in the years to come, and although science can help us understand the consequences of different courses of action, it cannot tell us which consequences are more important than others and which values we should use to guide our decisions.

Fourth, *human values exert a powerful influence on the way science is conducted*. The questions we choose to ask—or perhaps more important, choose not to ask—are often determined by nonscientific political, religious, and/or economic factors. For example, studies of the genetic underpinnings of behavior were actively discouraged or prohibited outright in the Soviet Union during most of the 20th century because communist ideology claimed that all differences among individuals are the result of environmental influences of the state and society; why bother studying genes when we already know that they're irrelevant? Similarly, questions pertaining to women's contributions to science and politics are unlikely to arise in cultural milieus where females are regarded as uneducable subordinates. Scientists, like all human beings, live in a world of values, morals, and ethics. Sometimes these values limit the search for truth that is the ultimate goal of the scientific method. But human values also direct scientific inquiry toward questions that serve our highest aspirations and steer scientific research away from practices that would violate these values.

SECTION review | The Scientific Method: Systematizing the Acquisition of Knowledge

Science is a method for answering questions that reduces the impact of human biases. Theory and research have a cyclical relationship: Research provides systematic observations; theory provides the basis for predicting and explaining these observations; research then tests hypotheses derived from the theory to assess its validity, refine it, or generate alternate theories.

Correlational Method	Experimental Method
• Two or more variables are measured and compared to determine whether or not they are related. • A relationship between variables does not mean that one caused the other.	• This process seeks to control variables so that cause and effect can be determined. • The independent variable is manipulated, and its effect on the dependent variable is observed. • Participants must be randomly assigned to conditions to reduce possible confounds.

Features of a Good Theory	Internal and External Validity	Limitations of Science
• Organizes the facts. • Explains observations. • Inspires new research. • Generates new questions. • Has practical applications.	• Abstract ideas need to be made specific and quantifiable to be manipulated and measured properly. • Studies should be able to be replicated using different operationalizations of variables.	• Human knowledge is limited. • Humans are biased. • Some questions are outside the scope of science. • Human values influence the questions asked.

Ethical Considerations in Research

The ultimate goal of psychological research is to advance our understanding of the human condition in order to make life better for people, so we certainly wouldn't want to undermine the quality of life for the participants in our research. Accordingly, social psychologists devote considerable attention to ethical concerns. Because many of the issues of interest to social psychologists pertain to the dark and distressing side of human nature and behavior, social psychologists are compelled to include these unpleasant aspects of existence in their research. To study fear, it is often necessary to make people afraid; to study egotism and prejudice, people must be put in situations where these unbecoming characteristics become manifest. Social psychologists must continually ask whether the value of the research findings is worth the distress or discomfort that participants might experience because of their studies.

Harming Research Participants

Obviously, some practices are ethically unacceptable under any circumstances. Clear examples of inhumane treatment that could never be justified under any circumstances are the horrible experiments conducted by Nazi Germany in the concentration camps during World War II: studying the behavioral and psychological effects of starvation and freezing; infecting children with hepatitis to learn how the liver functions; injecting pregnant women with toxic substances to refine abortion and sterilization techniques (Lifton, 1986). The Tuskegee syphilis experiment, conducted between 1932 and 1972 by the United States Health Service, in which African Americans infected with syphilis were not told that they had the disease and were not given penicillin in order to study the progression of the disease was also heinous (Jones, 1981). In general, anything that could cause permanent, long-term damage to human participants is clearly out of bounds for research purposes; virtually all scientists support such limitations.

But what about experiments that produce temporary discomfort and stress? Perhaps Milgram's (1974) classic studies of obedience to authority, in which participants believed they were giving a middle-aged man extremely painful and potentially lethal electric shocks, is the most famous example of social psychological research that put participants in an extremely stressful situation. Some observers thought Milgram's studies were ethically unacceptable, but it would be hard to argue that this research did not produce important findings; indeed, they are some of the best known and most influential in the history of social psychology. But was the stress that participants endured worth it? One could argue that no one was really hurt by the shocks that participants thought they were giving, and that the participants themselves decided to deliver the shocks. Critics argued that the problem with this study was that participants were forced to face some very upsetting truths about themselves: They were capable of causing great pain to and potentially killing another human being when ordered to do so by an experimenter.

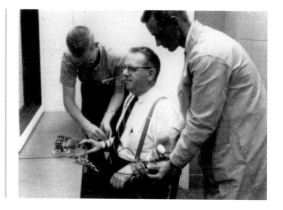

The Milgram studies sparked a debate about ethics in social psychological research.

[Stanley and Alexandra Milgram]

Debate about the ethics of the Milgram studies will probably continue for years, and we will discuss these studies in greater detail in chapter 7. Currently, the American Psychological Association (APA) does not allow researchers at American colleges to replicate these studies exactly as they were originally done. At the same time, the results of these studies are considered highly valuable and are taught in virtually every college in North America and in those of many other countries as well. Whether the value of what we learned about obedience to authority outweighed the risks to participants is ultimately a personal judgment that we must all make for ourselves. Regardless of where you stand on this issue, the Milgram research illustrates the conflict that social psychologists often face when deciding whether their research is ethically acceptable.

Deceiving Research Participants

Another ethical issue of particular concern to social psychologists is the use of deception in research. Social psychologists often mislead the participants in their studies about the true purpose of their research. They do this to create the psychological states they wish to study. Indeed, social psychologists use deception in their research more than any other scientists do. In his obedience studies, Milgram told participants they were in a study of learning and that their role was to deliver increasingly high voltage electric shocks to another participant with a heart condition. In fact, the purpose of the study was to investigate obedience; no shocks were actually delivered, and the apparently suffering "other participant" was a confederate of the experimenter acting according to a prearranged script. This was a powerful deception, and as already noted, one that many people believe stepped beyond ethical bounds.

Most social psychological experiments involve some level of deception, but the vast majority of these studies use relatively minor deception by offering a **cover story**, an explanation of the purpose of the study that is different from the true purpose. Many of the studies we will be discussing have gone further than that, though. Some researchers have staged emergencies, told participants they did poorly on intelligence tests, frustrated participants, threatened them with electric shocks, and given them false information about their personalities.

There are two primary reasons for the use of deception in social psychological research. First, if participants know the true purpose of the research, their responses are likely to be affected by their knowledge of that purpose. But participants need not even be accurate in their suspicions about the purposes of a study for those suspicions to taint the study's findings. A substantial body of research has shown that if people know (or think they know) the purpose of a study, it puts a demand on them to behave in a certain way (Orne, 1962). For example, if people knew the purpose of Milgram's research, they probably would have disobeyed very quickly. Aspects of a study that give away a purpose of the study are called **demand characteristics**. Studies with demand characteristics are inconclusive because the possibility that the participants were affected by their knowledge of the purpose introduces an alternative explanation for the results of the study. One source of demand characteristics can be an experimenter's expectations of how participants are supposed to behave. As we noted, researchers are people with their own desires and biases, and these can affect how they treat participants even if the researchers are not aware of it. This is known as **experimenter bias**. To eliminate this bias whenever possible, experiments should be designed so that the researchers are "blind" to experimental conditions; that is, they won't know which condition a particular subject is in. That way there is no way for them to systematically treat any participant differently depending on what condition the participant is in.

Second, researchers often use deception to create the conditions necessary to test a hypothesis. For example, if the hypothesis is that frustration leads to aggression, a social psychologist might manipulate level of frustration and then measure aggression to test this hypothesis. The manipulation of the independent variable, frustration, would require staging some sort of frustrating experience. For example, one study (Geen, 1968) tested the frustration-aggression hypothesis by having participants try unsuccessfully to solve a puzzle that was rigged to be impossible.

Cover story An explanation of the purpose of the study that is different from the true purpose.

Demand characteristics Aspects of a study that give away its purpose or communicate how the participant is expected to behave.

Experimenter bias The possibility that the experimenter's knowledge of the condition a particular participant is in could affect her behavior toward the participant and thereby introduce a confounding variable to the independent variable manipulation.

Think
ABOUT

[jcjgphotography/Shutterstock]

Although it is clear that deception is a useful practice for conducting research, the question remains whether this kind of deliberate misrepresentation is justified or not. Some argue that deception is never defensible because it betrays the trust that should exist between the researcher and the research participant. Others argue that deception often is the only way to study many important psychological states and that the knowledge gained through the use of deception in research justifies the potential distress. Where do you stand? We, like the vast majority of social psychologists, embrace the latter position. So do the APA and other legal and professional organizations that govern research in the countries where social psychology flourishes.

Ethical Safeguards

To provide guidance on these matters, the APA established a Code of Ethics that all psychological researchers in the United States must abide by. First, the ethical implications of all studies must be carefully considered and approved, both by the investigators conducting the research and by ethical review boards at their institutions. These ethical review boards judge whether the potential benefits of the research outweigh the research's potential costs and risks to the participants. Second, participants must give their informed consent to take part in any study, after they are provided with a full disclosure of all the procedures they are to undergo and the potential risks that participation might entail. Participants must also have the right to ask questions and to withdraw from the study at any time, even after the study begins. Finally, participants must be assured that the information they provide will be treated confidentially, that adequate steps will be taken to protect their confidentiality, and that their identities will not in any way be linked to their responses without their explicit consent.

These safeguards are very important, but when deception is used, the informed consent cannot be fully informing. To minimize any potential negative effects of deception, at the conclusion of a study experimenters conduct a debriefing. In this debriefing, the experimenter probes for suspicion about the true purpose of the study, gently reveals any deceptions, clarifies the true purpose of the study, and explains why the deception was necessary to achieve the goals of the research. For example, in Milgram's studies of obedience, all participants were fully debriefed, and many were quite relieved to meet and shake hands with the person whom they believed they had been shocking. When properly done, the debriefing should be informative, comforting, and educational, not only alleviating any negative feelings and misconceptions the participant had about the study or their actions in the study, but also providing a peek behind the curtain of social psychological research. Research shows that properly done debriefings do indeed achieve these goals (Sharpe & Faye, 2009).

Debriefing At the end of a study, the procedure in which participants are assessed for suspicion and then receive a gentle explanation of the true nature of the study in a manner that counteracts any negative effects of the study experience.

SECTION review | Ethical Considerations in Research

Any research involving human participants must be conducted in accordance with ethical principles based on a cost-benefit analysis.

Harm	Deception	Ethical Safeguards
No lasting physical or psychological harm must be caused.	The use of deception must be justified in any study and its potential for any harm minimized.	• The APA has established a Code of Ethics. An ethical review board assesses whether each study meets these ethical standards. • Informed consent is an important protection, though limited in studies using deception. • Debriefings that are reassuring and educational are crucial to ensure the ethicality of deception research.

CONNECT ONLINE:

Check out our videos and additional resources located at:
www.macmillanhighered.com/launchpad/greenberg1e

Fundamentals of Social Behavior

TOPIC OVERVIEW

Human beings are the result of a lengthy, improbable, and by no means inevitable historical process that began with the earth's original life forms. Humans have inherited a set of biological, behavioral, and psychological characteristics that have evolved over billions of years of evolution by natural selection. Think about it: Trillions of life forms have struggled for billions of years to survive and reproduce in inhospitable and often hostile environments, and the fruit of their labor is, well, *you*. The time frame and true nature of this process are virtually impossible to fathom. Consider this: The time between the extinction of Stegosaurus and the appearance of Tyrannosaurus rex was much longer than the time between the extinction of Tyrannosaurus rex and this very moment (over 80 million years vs. about 65 million years).

Many of our inherited characteristics also can be found in other species, yet the human mind works in ways that set our species apart from all other life forms. Perhaps most notable, the unique evolution of the human brain has enabled humans to construct and maintain *culture*. This was an enormous leap because culture allows us to use our evolved minds to create styles of living that are unprecedented on the world's stage.

As outlined in chapter 1, the evolutionary and cultural influences on social life are two of the perspectives we'll explore throughout this book. This chapter sets the stage by discussing how, at a fundamental level, evolution and culture make us humans the types of creatures that we are. First we'll trace the evolutionary origins of uniquely human mental

[Gandee Vasan/Getty Images]

capacities, motives, and emotions, and we'll see how these evolved tendencies continue to influence how we modern humans think, feel, and act in everyday life. Then we'll explore the nature and functions of culture and its profound influence on all of our lives.

Evolution: How Living Things Change Over Time

Probably all the organic beings which have ever lived on this earth have descended from some one primordial form, into which life was first breathed. . . . [W]hen we regard every production of nature as one which has had a history . . . every complex structure and instinct as the summing up of many contrivances, each useful to the possessor . . . how far more interesting . . . will the study of nature become! . . .

In the distant future I see open fields for far more important researches. Psychology will be based on a new foundation.

—Charles Darwin, *The Origin of Species*

To get to the roots of human nature, let's begin, well, at the beginning. Planet Earth arrived on the galactic scene roughly 4.6 billion years ago. Within a billion years after that, conditions were ripe for the appearance of a completely unique and unprecedented form of matter—**LIFE!** To stay alive, these fledgling single-celled creatures had to have the capacity and motivation to approach that which was good for them and avoid that which was bad for them. Given that every individual life form was of finite duration, to keep life "breathing" (to borrow Darwin's term) over time, there had to be a way for these early pilgrims to reproduce. Primeval reproduction was by fission, a simple process of splitting that resulted in offspring identical to the parental cells. How could these very simple original life forms lead to the fantastic variety of creatures that have and continue to inhabit our planet? **Evolution**, the idea that species change over time and are descended from common ancestors, goes back at least to the ancient Greek philosopher Anaximander (610–546 BC). Charles Darwin's genius was to propose the theory of natural selection to explain the *process* through which evolution occurs.

Evolution The concept that different species are descended from common ancestors but have evolved over time, acquiring different genetic characteristics as a function of different environmental demands.

Natural selection The process by which certain attributes are more successful in a particular environment and therefore become more represented in future generations.

Natural Selection

Perfectly self-replicating life forms never could evolve; they would continue to produce exact copies of themselves as offspring. But nothing about life is perfect, so mistakes in this most basic reproduction process sometimes occurred, and slightly different variations of the "primal creature" resulted. Some single-cell protozoans began to reproduce by fusion in addition to fission; for example, paramecia lying close to each other exchanged genetic material before dividing into multiple new organisms. This process eventually led to the prevalence of species that rely on sex for reproduction. These processes of reproduction cause *variability*, the first ingredient in the recipe for evolution by natural selection. There are two primary sources of such variability:

1. *Mutation*: Random mistakes in DNA replication that caused variations. Most were maladaptive, leading to an almost immediate end to the organism's life. However, some were adaptive, which means that they actually improved the resulting organism's chances of surviving and reproducing.
2. *Sexual recombination*: When a new creature is produced, it does not have the exact same genetic makeup as the creatures that produced it but has a combination of its parents' genes.

The second key ingredient for evolution by natural selection is *competition*. In a world of limited food, mating partners, and other resources, even infinitesimally small variations might help an individual compete more effectively, at first with other "primal creatures" and eventually with other species vying for the same resources in the same environments.

Variability and competition in particular environments determine which genes are passed along to subsequent generations through reproduction. These genes influence each individual organism's physical and behavioral attributes. Those creatures that possess attributes that improve their prospects for survival, reproduction, and survival of their offspring are more successful in passing along their genes, which, in turn, leads to the widespread representation of those attributes in future generations. These attributes are known as adaptations. Over time, individuals with the most successful adaptations outnumber and eventually replace less well-adapted versions of the creature.

Adaptations Attributes that improve an individual's prospects for survival and reproduction.

Survival of the Fittest: Yes, but What Is Fittest?

The process of evolution by natural selection has often been characterized as the *survival of the fittest*. (Darwin himself never used this term; it was coined by Darwin's contemporary Herbert Spencer in 1864.) However, "fittest" does not mean strongest or most aggressive. If it did, *Tyrannosaurus rex* would still be roaming the planet instead of merely posing in fossilized form for museum patrons. What is "fittest" depends entirely on the natural environments in which particular organisms reside. Creatures adapted for warmth would not be fit in cold environments, and vice versa, which is why you don't find alligators and iguanas in Alaska or polar bears and penguins in Panama (except in zoos!).

Once new variants on a life form emerge, with new ways of exploiting an environmental niche for survival and reproduction, attributes that were once adaptive may become less adaptive. If these less useful attributes aren't harmful, they may remain as harmless vestiges of early ancestors. Other attributes that might have been utterly useless to past generations may now acquire tremendous adaptive value. For example, if mutations cause individuals of an aquatic species to develop new ways of obtaining oxygen so that they can survive on dry land, what was functional for their ancestors (e.g., gills) may become utterly worthless. However, new variations—such as body protuberances that make it possible to move around on land (rudimentary legs)—may now become especially advantageous. So the process of evolution is highly dependent on changes in both the external environment and the characteristics of the organisms in the local environment.

Depictions of evolution in popular culture often describe "Mother Nature" as calling the shots, encouraging one species to realize its full potential while neglecting or punishing another species. But this is false. The process of natural selection just happens—it has no intention and strives toward no goal. Rather, variability and competition are simply facts of life, and so organisms evolve by a gradual refinement of previous adaptations. A fairly random mixture of characteristics of environments and organisms determines which attributes are adaptive and which are maladaptive. For example, bipedalism (standing up on two legs) gave early humans significant benefits, such as freeing up their hands for using tools, but it has its downsides, including slipped disks, fallen arches, and shin splints. Like much of life, evolution is a series of trade-offs where even those attributes that were beneficial enough to be passed down over generations can also come with certain costs. Keeping this in mind, we'll want to avoid making the naturalistic fallacy, whereby we assume (quite incorrectly) that the way things *are* is necessarily how they *ought* to be (Ismail et al., 2012).

New species of amphibians evolved from fish as random mutations allowed for movement and survival out of the water.

Naturalistic fallacy A bias toward believing that biological adaptations are inherently good or desirable.

SECTION review | Evolution: How Living Things Change Over Time

Evolution occurs through the process of natural selection, which is a consequence of variability and competition.	The process of evolution leads to adaptations that improve the organism's prospects for survival and reproduction in its current environment.	What is adaptive depends on the interaction between the physical environment and the attributes of the organism.	Adaptations are trade-offs. Evolution is not guided by any purpose or goal. Do not infer that an attribute is "more natural" or "better" just because it evolved.

General Adaptations of the Cultural Animal

With an overview of evolutionary theory in place, we can ask what adaptations characterize human beings. Evolutionary psychologists tend to focus on what are known as domain-specific adaptations, attributes that evolved to meet a particular challenge but that are not particularly useful when dealing with other types of challenges (Barkow et al., 1992). For example, photosensitive cells in our eyes evolved because they helped us to see color, but they are useless when it comes to, say, digesting proteins. Focusing on domain-specific adaptations may be useful in considering specific aspects of behavior, such as dating preferences (Neuberg et al., 2010), as we'll discuss in chapter 14.

In contrast, domain-general adaptations are attributes that are useful for dealing with various challenges across different areas of life. For example, the human capacity for learning can help you to build a shelter, find food, and avoid a saber-toothed tiger. According to the archaeologist Stephen Mithen (1996, 1998), the flexibility of these domain-general adaptations is what most clearly distinguishes humans from other primate species and accounts for humans' ability to proliferate across the earth's diverse natural environments, from tropical forest to frozen tundra. Next we'll see how four of these domain-general adaptations shape virtually all forms of human behavior.

Domain-specific adaptations Attributes that evolved to meet a particular challenge but that are not particularly useful when dealing with other types of challenges.

Domain-general adaptations Attributes that are useful for dealing with various challenges across different areas of life.

Humans Are Social Beings

As you'll recall from chapter 1, the second core assumption of social psychology is that *behavior depends on a socially constructed view of reality.* Therefore, human sociability and social sensitivity should not be surprising. From birth on, human beings cannot survive without extensive relationships with other human beings. As infants we need caretakers to feed, protect, and comfort us; as adults virtually everyone desires and depends on friends and lovers, as well as the extended communities that help us meet our basic needs. Except for the very rare hermit, people spend their entire lives enmeshed in a complex web of connections with other human beings. In fact, most hermits are not as removed from the social world as they appear: Even Henry David Thoreau, the American writer who famously wrote of his solitary time at Walden Pond "seeking the great facts of his existence," hung out with his friend Ralph Waldo Emerson and brought his mother his dirty laundry!

Darwin recognized that in many species, the prospects for survival and gene perpetuation are vastly improved for those who get along well with other members of their species. Because of the adaptive value of social sensitivity, the human brain has evolved several tools that help individuals react appropriately to and get along with one another. For example, there is an area in the brain called the fusiform face area, which functions specifically to recognize human faces (**FIGURE 2.1**) (Kanwisher et al., 1997). This ability is useful, because faces convey important information. Most obvious, each face is unique, making it possible not only to recognize individuals and recall information about them (*"that's* the guy who lent me an ax") but also to interpret what they might be thinking and feeling.

Another feature of the human brain that supports sociability is that it is very quick to pick up on the experience of being socially rejected or excluded. When rejection or exclusion occurs, it triggers a strong negative reaction in the brain. In fact, social exclusion activates an area of the brain responsible for generating feelings of physical pain (Eisenberger et al., 2003). So we generally try hard to fit in to minimize experiencing such aversive feelings.

The brain also contains an inborn readiness to categorize people in ways that increase the likelihood that social interactions will go smoothly. Both humans and other primates share a universal tendency to categorize and behave toward others along at least two distinct dimensions (Boehm, 1999; de Waal, 1996).

Figure 2.1

Fusiform Face Area

The fusiform face area allows us to recognize the faces of the people we know.

[Research from: Farshad A. Mansouri, Keiji Tanaka & Mark J. Buckley (2009). *Nature Reviews Neuroscience 10*(2), 141–152.]

- *Closeness* or *solidarity*: People quickly categorize others as friend or foe, which tells them immediately whether they can expect good things or bad things from them.
- *Status* or *hierarchy*: People categorize others' power or rank within the group so that they can determine the most appropriate way to interact with them. In both human and other primate groups, individuals respect these status hierarchies the vast majority of the time, thus averting direct confrontations and violence.

The social nature of the human animal is also reflected in a more fundamental fact of human psychology: that it is shaped by socialization. This term refers to the lifelong process of learning from others what is desirable and undesirable conduct in various specific situations. This learning occurs in our relationships with our parents, siblings, friends, teachers, and many others with whom we have significant relationships over the course of our lives.

Socialization Learning from parents and others what is desirable and undesirable conduct in a particular culture.

The socialization process has a profound influence on people's thought and behavior because, compared with almost all other species, humans are particularly immature when they are born. Whereas a baby turtle or spider can be zipping around the same day it is born, human infants are born in a profoundly helpless state and require years of care if they are to have any chance of survival. This extended period of immaturity and helplessness allows children to learn how to function well in the specific environment in which they develop. In so doing, our relative immaturity provides added flexibility to our species and helps to account for the incredible diversity that we see among people.

Humans Are Very Intelligent Beings

All living things are intelligent in the broad sense that they have their own ways of detecting external conditions and responding accordingly to stay alive and reproduce. In this respect, cockroaches are pretty smart—they have been around since before the dinosaurs.

Imagination: The Possibility of Possibilities

Nevertheless, humans have the greatest intelligence in terms of their capacities for learning, symbolic thought, and imagination, and consequently, for altering their surroundings the better to meet their needs and desires. That's why *there are* iguanas in Alaska and penguins in Panama. As the philosopher Søren Kierkegaard put it, by virtue of our unique form of consciousness, we humans have the "the possibility of possibilities." (1844/1980; p. 42). Take a scene in the movie *Casino* (De Fina & Scorsese, 1995) in which Sam "Ace" Rothstein (played by Robert De Niro) looks out at an empty desert and says, essentially, "*This* is where Las Vegas will go." No other species is capable of such audacity! Imagine a squirrel looking out on to a grassy field and saying, "*This* is where my acorn castle will go."

In the movie *Casino*, the human ability to imagine new possibilities enabled Sam Rothstein to envision building a series of large casinos on what was a dusty desert landscape. Although the movie may not have the facts right on Las Vegas's history, it nicely illustrates the power of human imagination.

[© Universal/Courtesy Everett Collection]

The capacity to imagine a future unlike anything we have experienced firsthand provides the basis for a uniquely human form of control over the world in which we live. An especially important component of this capacity, making it possible to transform our wishes into reality, is the capacity to think and communicate with symbols.

Symbolic Thought and Language: The Great Liberators

What does a red light have to do with stopping, other than being a socially agreed-on symbol for "Stop"? Most symbols bear no obvious relation to the objects or ideas they represent. Nonetheless, this connection of specific meanings to arbitrary symbols enables humans to consider a wide variety of concepts and to communicate these ideas to other humans.

The most important result of our symbolic thinking is that it makes language possible. Language is a tool for learning and sharing systems of symbols, which can be combined to convey a virtually infinite number of meanings. The emergence of language allowed a quantum leap in the flexibility and adaptability of the human species. It enables people to think and communicate about other people, objects, and events that are not in their current environment. Language vastly increases the sources of information that people can use to make decisions and plan action. To illustrate: Coyotes coordinate attacks on prey through the use of a variety of barks, yips and howls, but only humans can sit back and discuss their plans, recount prior military actions, and debate on nationwide call-in talk shows the pros and cons of a future attack. To paraphrase the philosopher Suzanne Langer (1967, 1972, 1982), symbols allowed humans to escape the confines of animal intelligence, which is stuck in the "here and now"—and to transcend the boundaries of time and space. Language, the use of symbols, and abstract thought are involved in another remarkable human adaptation: the self.

The Self

And then an event did occur, to Emily, of considerable importance. She suddenly realized who she was.

—Richard Hughes, *A High Wind in Jamaica* (1929/2010, p. 135)

Being able to think about the external world by using symbols is a powerful adaptation, but humans' ability to think about the *self* by using symbols is more than just a variation on that same theme. People not only experience life but also experience the fact that they are experiencing it: *I am, and I know that I am, and I know that I know that I am.* Being able to represent the self symbolically as an "I" or "me" enables people to think about the meaning of their experiences. A deer confronted by a pack of wolves may experience fear, but only humans can consciously contemplate the fact that *I am very afraid right now* and ponder the meaning of this feeling. Only humans can feel foolish or embarrassed about their fears or even fear that they might become afraid. Only humans can fear things that don't exist (e.g., ghosts, witchcraft) or that may or may not happen in the future, such as a relationship falling apart or a nuclear holocaust destroying the planet.

Having a self also makes it possible to evaluate one's actions, feelings, thoughts, or overall sense of identity in light of one's values, ambitions, and principles ("Am I the person I aim to be?"), and then to modify one's thought and behavior to bring them in line with those standards. Can you think of a time when your actions didn't match your sense of self? For example, you may have been aware that a sarcastic remark toward a friend conflicted with the value you place on being kind and considerate of other people's feelings. This awareness is likely to lead you to try to adjust your behavior toward that person, or people in general, in the future.

Think
ABOUT

[Joshua Blake/ Getty Images]

Being able to think about the self symbolically also enables people to mentally simulate future events and to imagine various possibilities for their lives. In this way, people can delay a habitual response to a situation and consider alternative responses, to ponder the past and anticipate the future, and to ask "why?" and "what if?" questions. In a nutshell, having a concept of self that connects past, present, and future is adaptive because it vastly improves our ability to monitor and change our behavior, ultimately increasing our chances that things will go our way. Having a self gives humans freedom and flexibility in their behavior unlike that found in any other known living thing.

Conscious and Nonconscious Aspects of Thinking

Although humans are quite capable of being self-aware, this does not mean that all human behavior is the result of conscious processes under our intentional control. Just as shoppers automatically might be drawn to prefer the product they most recently evaluated (remember the study involving shoppers choosing stockings in chapter 1?), much of our behavior is the result of nonconscious processes. You don't have to think about sweating when the temperature gets high; you don't have to think about moving when a car is coming toward you unexpectedly; you don't have to think of smiling when you recognize a familiar face in a crowd. And very often people are not consciously aware of the factors affecting their behavior. Indeed, research shows that people's judgments can be influenced by exposure to subliminal stimuli they are not even aware they have seen. For example, super quick (28-millisecond) subliminal flashes of words associated with aggressiveness can lead people to judge others as more aggressive (Todorov & Bargh, 2002).

Of course, the idea that human behavior is the result of nonconscious processes is not new. It is a central tenet of Freud's psychoanalytic theory and also figured in the work of William James (1890), a prominent American psychologist whose ideas laid much of the groundwork for contemporary social psychology. James also pointed out that consciously controlled behavior can *become* nonconscious and automatic. An action can become habitual, such that conscious thought is no longer needed to perform it. For example, learning to play a musical instrument requires rigorous conscious attention over long hours of repetitive practice. Once musical skills have been acquired, however, playing the instrument becomes quite automatic. In fact, once these skills become habits, consciously thinking about them (for example, thinking about each finger's placement on a flute) can interfere with smooth action (Beilock, 2011)!

The process by which a task no longer requires conscious attention is referred to as *automatization*. Can you see how automatization would be quite adaptive? For one thing, it allows people to get stuff done without actively thinking about the actions they are performing, freeing their minds to concentrate on other tasks. As a result of automatization, many human responses result from unconscious **automatic processes**, while responses to more novel, complex and challenging situations involve more conscious, **controlled processes**. Any given human behavior may be a result of one or the other, or a combination of both types of processes.

We'll talk more about these two processes in chapter 3; for now, we can note that humans are thought to have two mental systems that generally operate simultaneously (Epstein, 1980). One is an *experiential* system of thought and decision making that relies on emotions, intuitions, and images that are processed in the brain's evolutionarily older regions, including the limbic system. Automatic processes often happen within this system (**FIGURE 2.2**). The other is a *rational* system that is logical, analytic, and primarily linguistic; this system involves greater activity from the more recently evolved frontal lobes of the cerebrum, and supports controlled processes (Figure 2.2). It takes over when the person has sufficient time, motivation, and cognitive resources to think carefully about her situation and herself.

People are exceptionally intelligent creatures not so much because of any single specific cognitive capacity but rather because of the whole package of verbal, nonverbal, conscious, nonconscious, experiential, and rational proclivities at their disposal. Keep in mind, too, that the mighty intellect of human beings would all be for naught without voluntary control of sensory motor systems (e.g., eye-hand coordination

Automatic processes Human thoughts or actions that occur quickly, often without the aid of conscious awareness.

Controlled processes Human thoughts or actions that occur more slowly and deliberatively, and are motivated by some goal that is often consciously recognized.

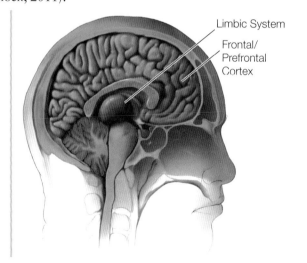

Limbic System

Frontal/
Prefrontal
Cortex

Figure 2.2

Limbic System and Frontal Cortex

Our experiential and rational systems take place in different regions of the brain that support different types of thought processes. Yet these systems are neurally connected and work together in producing thought and behavior.

and kinesthetic awareness and balance) and especially fine motor control of the hands. Indeed, the Greek philosopher Anaxagoras (500–428 BC) claimed that "man is the most intelligent of animals because he has hands." Humans' intellectual and manual capacities evolved hand in hand (so to speak) because each facilitated the adaptive value of the other. Dolphins are rather intelligent, but alas, not very handy, which limits their ability to manipulate objects in the world and express themselves symbolically. Maybe that's why we go to watch them at SeaWorld instead of Flipper and the family coming to see us at PeopleWorld!

Humans Are Motivated, Goal-Striving Beings

The process of natural selection resulted in systems that energize, direct, and regulate behaviors that help people survive and prosper. In psychology, the concept of motivation refers broadly to generating and expending energy toward achieving or avoiding some outcome. Motivation can vary in strength (low to high) and in direction (toward one end state or another). Strength and direction of motivation vary from individual to individual and from situation to situation. For example, some people are motivated to lose weight, whereas others are not; among those who want to lose weight, some are highly motivated and others much less so. An upcoming high school reunion may increase a person's motivation to lose weight much more than a pie-baking competition at next summer's county fair.

Motivation The process of generating and expending energy toward achieving or avoiding some outcome.

Needs and Goals

Humans direct their behavior toward the satisfaction of needs and goals. Needs are what is necessary for the individual to survive and prosper. Psychologists have proposed a variety of psychological needs that go beyond the minimal physical requirements for sustaining life. For example, Ed Deci and Rich Ryan's self-determination theory (Deci & Ryan, 2000) argues that the needs for *competence* (being able to do things successfully), *relatedness* (having close connections with other people), and *autonomy* (being in control of one's life) are basic prerequisites for human well-being, and that psychological functioning deteriorates when these needs are not met.

Needs Internal states that drive action that is necessary to survive or thrive.

Goals, on the other hand, are what people strive for to meet their needs. For example, to meet your need for nutrition, you may decide to pursue the goal of getting a pizza. To meet your need for relatedness to other people, you might choose the goal of striking up a conversation with the person sitting across from you.

Goals Cognitions that represent outcomes that we strive for in order to meet our needs and desires.

Earlier, we mentioned that human intellectual capacities operate beneath conscious awareness. The same holds for motivation: People are not always aware that their behavior is directed toward a particular goal, or what underlying need their current goals ultimately serve. Right now you are probably not consciously thinking about the goal that reading this book is serving (at least not until we just brought it up).

Hedonism: Approaching Pleasure, Avoiding Pain

Earlier, we noted that for a life-form to survive and reproduce into future generations, it must be inclined to approach what is good for it and avoid what is bad for it. In humans, these inclinations are greatly facilitated by evolved tendencies to experience displeasure, pain, and negative emotions in response to harmful stimuli; and pleasure, satisfaction, and positive emotions in response to beneficial stimuli. These basic tendencies gave rise to one of the most basic aspects of human motivation: hedonism, the motivation to approach pleasure and avoid pain.

Hedonism The human preference for pleasure over pain.

Hedonism was adaptive in the environments in which our ancestors evolved because things that brought pleasure were generally good for our ancestors and things that brought pain were generally bad for them. Like simpler forms of life, we humans generally try to avoid what's bad for us—what could kill us or otherwise interfere with our prospering—and generally seek out what is good for us.

But this doesn't mean that everything that appeals to people is necessarily good for them. Because hedonistic tendencies evolved over many thousands of years in environments different from those that modern humans inhabit, many things that were good for humans back then are not good for them now. Fortunately, we have the mental flexibility to step back temporarily, consider what is good and bad for us in the long run, and in this way override our evolved preferences. For example, most people innately find pleasure in sweet and fatty foods because humans' ancient ancestors lived in harsh environments where the more calories they could get, the better. However, because of evidence that too much calorie-rich food can be harmful over the long run, many people who are lucky enough to live amid a ready surplus of such foods now consciously try to avoid them, in some cases paying *more* for foods made with *fewer* calories. Imagine how bizarre that would have been a million years ago!

The Two Fundamental Psychological Motives: Security and Growth

The concept of hedonism suggests it can be useful to think of two basic motivational orientations that guide human behavior: *security* (avoiding the bad) and *growth* (approaching the good). Neuroscience research supports the distinction between these motivational systems: Avoidance motivation involves more right-hemisphere activity, whereas approach motivation tends to involve primarily left-hemisphere activity (Harmon-Jones & Allen, 1998; Harmon-Jones, 2003).

Back in the 1930s, Otto Rank (Rank, 1932/1989; Menaker, 1982), a theorist mentored by Freud, studied how security and growth motives develop and interact over the course of the life span to influence a person's thinking and behavior. He noted that children frequently are distressed and anxious and seek relief from these negative feelings through the nourishment, safety, and comfort provided by their parents. This means that children avoid negative emotions by establishing and sustaining a secure relationship with their loving and protective parents. This desire for security is one side of Rank's analysis of human motivation.

The other side emerges when children are able to maintain that sense of security and as a result, begin to actively and playfully explore their surroundings in ways that expand their physical, cognitive, emotional, and interpersonal capabilities. This is the growth-oriented side of human motivation. Think of a curious toddler running around a room, opening closet doors, pulling out whatever looks interesting, and trying to play with anyone who offers a smile. Rank suggested that these exploratory tendencies lead to *individuation*, the emergence of the child's own personality as a unique human being. Over the years, other theorists have echoed these ideas, proposing that, throughout their lives, people simultaneously seek to feel secure while also seeking stimulation and growth (Lewin, 1935; Scholer & Higgins, 2013).

Whenever we want to understand why people behave the way they do, regardless of the specific social context, it is informative to consider the influence of these two motivational orientations. For example, people want careers that provide financial security, stability, and prestige, but at the same time are interesting and challenging. Similarly, people seek relationships with those they can trust and rely on, but whom they also find exciting and fun. We even want cars that are safe and dependable *and* that provide pure driving excitement!

To make sense of behavior it also helps to consider how these motivational orientations interact with each other. Rank noted that there is a complex interplay between security and growth tendencies, such that they can at times pull the person in opposite directions. In childhood, authentic desires for stimulation and new experiences often conflict with what a child's security-providing parents demand. Hence, toddlers throw fits during the "terrible twos," and teenagers rebel against their parents as they seek to create their own adult identity. In adulthood, we often feel a tension between competing desires to fit in with our group, which strengthens security, and to stand out and assert our uniquely creative self, which supports growth. Should you choose the safe, reliable job, car, and relationship partner? Or should you look for more exciting and challenging alternatives?

Rank's analysis suggests two broad tendencies that have been highly supported by social psychological research over the last 60 years, much of which we will describe over the course of this book:

- To sustain security-providing feelings of acceptance and self-worth, people are inclined to follow the crowd, obey authority, and accept the values espoused within their own cultural milieu.
- However, as part of their striving for growth, people exhibit a need for uniqueness, want to express their personal views and preferences, and assert their personal freedoms when they are threatened.

The Hierarchy of Goals: From Abstract to Concrete

How do we turn our abstract goals into tangible actions? To answer these questions, we need to understand that any specific activity can be thought of as simultaneously serving many interrelated goals that can be arranged hierarchically (Carver & Scheier, 1981; Powers, 1973). This means that any goal can be understood as helping the person to achieve another, more abstract goal at a higher level in the hierarchy of standards. For example, think about a young woman who is tying her shoe; let's call her Rita. Why is Rita doing that? Well, one obvious possibility is that she just noticed that her shoe was untied and wanted to avoid tripping on the laces. So that's why Rita tied her shoe, and perhaps that's all there is to it (see **FIGURE 2.3**).

But why is Rita concerned about tripping? Let's suppose that Rita tied her shoe in order to run faster in a 5K race that day. She wanted to win the race to get a college scholarship in order to have better job prospects than her immigrant parents, who had to work right out of high school. And Rita wanted to attend college mainly so she could go into politics in the hope of changing the immigration laws, so people like her parents would have more productive and dignified lives. She even

Figure 2.3

Rita

Goals, and the actions of which they are composed, can be represented hierarchically in terms of being more or less concrete or abstract. This figure shows how the act of tying a shoe can be connected to both coordinated muscle activity and to being remembered for societal contributions.

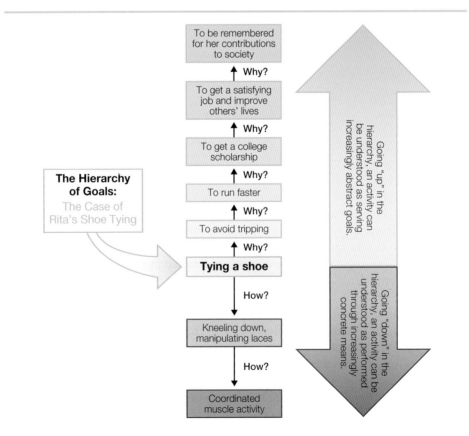

had hopes of becoming the first female president and winning a Nobel Peace Prize for her efforts to improve the lives of others and ultimately be remembered for hundreds or, better yet, thousands of years. So that's why Rita tied her shoe: to win the race to go to college on an athletic scholarship to avoid working at Wal-Mart to initiate legislation favorable to newcomers to America to become president and win the Nobel Prize and make the world a better place and be remembered by others for a *very long time*! The point is, each goal Rita pursues is a means to the end of achieving another, more abstract goal. This hierarchy of goals ultimately connects to her motive of maintaining a sense of personal value, identity, and purpose in life.

If low-level and high-level descriptions of a person's goals are equally valid, what determines the level at which people prefer to describe what they are doing? One factor influencing people's preferred level of action description is the time frame in which they are thinking. People tend to use relatively low-level identifications when they think about immediately impending tasks but more abstract higher-order goals when contemplating tasks well in the future (Trope & Liberman, 2003).

In addition, Robin Vallacher and Dan Wegner's (1987) action identification theory suggests that the challenges people face in the moment also affect how they are likely to describe their actions. For example, you may describe your goal at this moment as getting your social psych reading assignment done, rather than describing it more concretely as moving your eyes across the page or more abstractly as progressing toward a professional career. But when action bogs down because of challenges, people often shift to lower levels of action description. For example, if Rita fumbles with getting her shoe tied, her action identification shifts to lower levels so that she can make the appropriate adjustments to her shoe-tying behavior rather than be distracted by grandiose visions of a Nobel Prize. It is interesting to note, however, that if the challenge becomes too daunting—for example, if Rita does poorly in the race—she may shift upward in the hierarchy, considering the higher-order goals that running is serving, and begin to wonder if track is really her thing and if maybe she should consider another route to funding her college education.

Hierarchy of goals The idea that goals are organized hierarchically from very abstract goals to very concrete goals, with the latter serving the former.

Humans Are Very Emotional Beings

A key component of the motivational system is emotion. Darwin (1872) asserted that emotions signal important changes in bodily states and environmental circumstances. Consequently, both the experience and anticipation of emotions play a critical role in motivating behavior; they both energize and direct the actions that people pursue.

Positive emotions reinforce one's own successful actions and the actions of others that benefit the self. Positive emotions (such as happiness) and the expectation of them also provide motivation and energy directed toward improving one's efforts to learn, achieve, help others, and grow (Fredrickson, 2001). Negative emotions (such as fear) and the expectation of them motivate a person to avoid actions and others that could be harmful. In addition, perceiving that the self has fallen short of an important goal or standard generates negative emotion, spurring the individual to engage in actions to alleviate that negative emotion. In these basic ways, emotions serve the important function of motivating action by kicking the person into gear when something needs to be done to reach his or her goals and, ultimately, satisfy physical and psychological needs.

The internal experience of emotion is accompanied by external displays. These expressions arise automatically and help to prepare the body to act appropriately. For example, scrunching the nose and mouth in disgust limits air intake, which can be important if dangerous airborne germs are afloat (Chapman et al., 2009). But in humans these displays take on the added function of communicating our feelings to others (Shariff & Tracy, 2011). In humans, emotional displays are most prominently communicated by facial expressions, but posture, vocalizations, and other cues also convey our feelings.

What Is Emotion?
Video on LaunchPad

How do we know that these nonverbal displays of emotion are partly meant to communicate feelings to others? One piece of evidence is that they are typically more prominent when they can be witnessed by others than when they cannot. Consider adults at a bowling alley. Research shows that when they get a strike, they rarely smile while they face down the alley at the pins, but they smile frequently when they turn around to face their friends sitting behind them (Kraut & Johnston, 1979). This finding suggests that emotions are not merely private matters; rather, they help others understand a person's current mental state and plan an appropriate response. In this way, emotions support the social nature of humans, which we discussed earlier.

The Wide-Ranging Palette of Emotions

What emotions do humans experience? What triggers these emotions? Contemporary emotion researchers generally distinguish several categories of emotions. For example, the neurologist Antonio Damasio (1999) proposed a three-part division of emotions: *background emotions, primary emotions,* and *secondary emotions,* all of which can occur at varying levels of consciousness, from complete unconsciousness to dim awareness to profound domination of our conscious experience.

Background Emotions: Background emotions make up an individual's general affective tone at a given moment. As the term implies, these emotions are in the psychological background and provide what some German writers call *Lebensgefühl,* or "sense of life" (Langer, 1982). Another way to think about background emotions is that, for an emotionally unimpaired person, there's never a waking moment in which he or she has no feelings or emotions. People always feel something, even if only vaguely, making it fairly likely that they'll experience other, more specific emotions. These background feelings are what we typically refer to when we say we are in a good or bad mood.

Primary Emotions: Whereas mood tends to be a diffuse general feeling that is often not the focus of our attention, at other times we are acutely aware of feeling a specific emotion. Research suggests that there are six primary emotions: happiness, sadness, fear, anger, surprise, and disgust. All humans seem to be born with the capacity to experience these basic emotions. Three sets of findings support this conclusion. First, for people around the world, these emotions tend to be triggered by the same types of stimuli in the physical and social environments (Lazarus, 1991; Mesquita & Frijda, 1992; Rozin & Fallon, 1987). For example, humans typically experience sadness when a loved one dies and disgust when confronted with a rotting animal carcass.

Second, the experience of these emotions involves brain structures, such as the amygdala and the anterior cingulate cortex, that developed very early in human evolution (Ekman & Cordaro, 2011; Lindquist et al., 2012). Third, these emotions are associated with distinctive facial expressions that are recognized easily by people the world over (Ekman, 1980; Izard, 1977). For example, members of geographically isolated tribes in New Guinea, who have never before encountered Americans, can accurately recognize primary emotions conveyed by the facial expressions of an American; and Americans with no experience with New Guineans are equally adept at interpreting the facial expressions of members of these isolated tribes (**FIGURE 2.4** shows the pictures of emotional expressions used in this research). The clearest interpretation of these findings is that these emotions are innate, at least to a large degree.

Secondary Emotions: We often experience secondary emotions that are variations on the six primary emotions. For example, joy, ecstasy, and delight are variations of happiness; gloom, misery, and wistfulness are variations of sadness; panic, anxiety, and

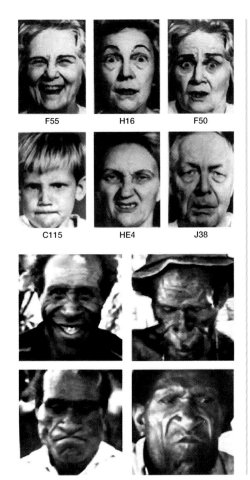

F55   H16   F50

C115   HE4   J38

Figure 2.4

Cultural Similarities in Emotional Expression

Evidence that people across diverse cultures recognize the same emotional expressions suggests that at least some emotions are universally experienced.

[Paul Ekman, Ph.D./Paul Ekman Group, LLC]

terror are variations of fear. Another group of secondary emotions includes the social emotions, which depend on even more recent brain structures, specifically the frontal lobes (see Figure 2.2). These include sympathy, embarrassment, shame, guilt, pride, jealousy, envy, gratitude, admiration, indignation, and contempt. These emotions also appear similarly across diverse cultures.

Social emotions regulate social behavior by: (1) drawing the person's attention to socially inappropriate behavior; (2) reinforcing appropriate social behavior; and (3) helping to repair disrupted social relationships. So we feel proud of the good things we do and guilty about the bad things. Those feelings of guilt provoke attempts to apologize to people we have hurt (Tracy & Robins, 2004).

Emotions and Facial Expression Video on LaunchPad

How Cognitions Influence Emotions

Primary emotions involve rather general and diffuse activation of specific bodily systems, including specific brain regions, the autonomic nervous system, and facial muscles (Lazarus 1991; Lazarus & Folkman, 1984; Mandler, 1984; Schachter & Singer, 1962). However, the various subtle shades of emotional experience depend on higher-level cognitive processes and interpretations. Cognitive appraisal theory (Lazarus, 1991) proposes that people's subjective experience of emotions is determined by a two-step process involving a very fast primary appraisal that is often followed by a more careful and thoughtful secondary appraisal (**FIGURE 2.5**). The primary appraisal process often takes place before people are consciously aware of what happened in the outside world to produce it; it signals whether something good or bad is happening. This process involves evolutionarily older brain structures in the limbic system, particularly the thalamus, which responds to the environment with physiological arousal and an initial experience of emotion (LeDoux, 1996) (see Figure 2.2).

Once we experience arousal and an initial emotional response, we are likely to engage in a secondary appraisal process to assess the environment further. This secondary appraisal often leads to a refinement, a modification, or even a change in the nature of the emotion people experience. At this point, the rational processing system (Epstein, 1980, 2013) gets involved as we consider memories, cultural influences, and thoughts of future ramifications. This can lead to a very different emotional response than we experienced from the primary appraisal process. This secondary appraisal involves activity in the prefrontal lobes, a part of the brain associated with consciousness and high-level cognitive functioning (LeDoux, 1996).

Cognitive appraisal theory The idea that our subjective experience of emotions is determined by a two-step process involving a primary appraisal of benefit or harm, and a secondary appraisal providing a more differentiated emotional experience.

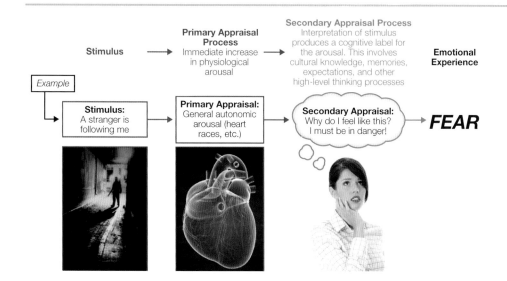

Figure 2.5

Lazarus's Cognitive Appraisal Theory of Emotions

Lazarus's theory of emotions explains how our appraisals of a stimulus help to determine the specific emotion that we feel. How would the woman's emotion change if the secondary appraisal revealed that it was her best friend following her?

[Photos, left to right: Tony Hutchings/ Getty Images; Sebastian Kaulitzki/ Shutterstock; Edyta Pawlowska/ Shutterstock]

Discovering that someone is in your apartment will elicit an immediate jolt of arousal, but the realization that it's a surprise party for your birthday will engage a secondary and more positive emotional response.

[ollyy/Shutterstock]

One of our colleagues recently experienced this two-step appraisal process rather vividly. He walked into a dark room, and the lights were suddenly turned on and a host of people were screaming at him. The primary appraisal initially led to arousal and a mixed state of surprise and fear. When the secondary appraisal process sized up the situation, he recognized that the screaming people were his friends. It was a surprise birthday party, which resulted in an outburst of unmitigated joy. On the other hand, if the secondary appraisal process yielded the recognition that these were Charles Manson family members recently released from prison dropping by for an unexpected visit, intense fear would have been the resulting emotional reaction.

How Emotions Affect Cognition

Just as cognition influences emotions, emotions also affect cognitions. In examining this influence, researchers have focused primarily on the impact of background emotion—how our being in a positive or negative mood affects our cognitive processes.

A variety of experimental procedures have been developed to put people in temporary good or bad moods, such as showing people funny or sad videos. When positive moods are triggered, people make more positive judgments about themselves, other people, and events; they make more optimistic predictions about the future; and they find it easier to recall positive memories. In contrast, bad moods lead people to view most things more negatively, to recall more negative memories, and to have more negative expectancies (Bower & Forgas, 2000; Isen, 1987). In addition, people in a good mood don't analyze things too much but rely instead on their preexisting knowledge in making judgments. In contrast, people in negative moods think more intensely about themselves and their environment in an attempt to understand what they are experiencing. Presumably, this occurs because whereas a positive mood signals that everything is fine, a bad mood signals that something is not right and needs to be rectified.

Specific primary and secondary emotions can also influence cognition by directing attention, memory, and interpretation in particular ways—indeed, far too many to enumerate here. But we will provide just a few examples: sadness and depression focus people on themselves (Smith & Greenberg, 1981); anxiety increases sensitivity to threatening thoughts about the self (Abdel-Khalek, 1998; Loo, 1984); surprise leads people to put extra effort into understanding the causes of an event (Pyszczynski & Greenberg, 1981; Wong & Weiner, 1981); anger makes it difficult to consider the big picture before responding (Zillmann et al., 1975).

Emotions also influence cognitions in a less obvious manner. Emotions are typically viewed as impediments to rational thought. How many times have all of us been told to stop being so emotional and be "reasonable"? Indeed, strong emotions can at times makes it impossible to think logically. Nevertheless, emotions are utterly necessary for rationality and good decision making, especially in matters pertaining to complex social judgments. Recall that the frontal lobes are important for the social emotions described previously (see Figure 2.2). In *Descartes' Error*, Antonio Damasio (1994) describes studies of people with frontal-lobe damage who are unable to make complex social judgments, especially in complex situations that involve long-term planning. Thus, higher-order cognition depends on adequate functioning of emotions, suggesting that our more intuitive experiential system is important and works in concert with our more rational cognitive system. Emotions provide us with important information about how a given situation affects our needs and desires.

SECTION review | General Adaptations of the Cultural Animal

Over the course of evolution, human beings inherited four domain-general adaptations. Each is important for understanding human thought and behavior.

	Humans are:		
Social Beings	**Very Intelligent Beings**	**Motivated, Goal-Striving Beings**	**Very Emotional Beings**
• People seek connection and avoid exclusion. • People quickly decide whether and how to interact with others. • People are profoundly shaped by socialization throughout their lives.	• People have an unprecedented capacity to: imagine things that do not exist; think about the world using symbols and language; contemplate why things happen; and conceive of themselves and their experiences across time. • People think using two systems: an experiential system (intuitive, nonconscious, automatic) and a controlled system (rational, conscious, effortful).	• Needs are necessary for survival; striving for goals is how people meet their needs. Both can influence behavior without awareness. • Hedonism is the motivation to approach pleasure and avoid pain. It is reflected in two fundamental human motivations: growth and security. • Humans can arrange goals hierarchically, allowing flexibility in self-regulation and planning.	• Emotions help people self-regulate to achieve goals and to communicate internal states to other people. • Humans have background, primary, and secondary emotions. • The experience of emotions is influenced by an initial rapid physiological response, followed by a secondary appraisal of the situation. • Emotions and cognitions affect each other.

Culture: The Uniquely Human Adaptation

Culture and history and religion and science [are] different from anything else we know of in the universe. That is fact. It is as if all life evolved to a certain point, and then in ourselves turned at a right angle and simply exploded in a different direction.

—Julian Jaynes (1920–97), *The Origin of Consciousness in the Breakdown of the Bicameral Mind* (1976, p. 9).

Our depiction of human beings up to this point is already fairly complex, but it is a one-dimensional depiction of three-dimensional beings. Every individual has three primary psychological dimensions—the *universal*, the *individual*, and the *cultural*. So far we have focused on the universal dimension—the evolved characteristics shared by all human beings. A second dimension of the person is the individual dimension: a person's personality, values, attitudes, beliefs that result from that person's unique genetic makeup and life experiences and that help distinguish him or her from all others.

The third dimension is the cultural, which includes those aspects of each person that have been shaped by the particular culture within which she or he was socialized and that he or she currently inhabits. To round out our psychological depiction of humankind, we now turn to this profoundly influential aspect of human life—the cultural dimension which makes us uniquely *cultural animals*.

What Is Culture?

The scheme of things is a system of order. . . . It is self-evidently true, is accepted so naturally and automatically that one is not aware of an act of acceptance having taken place. It comes with one's mother's milk, is chanted in school, proclaimed from the White House, is insinuated by television, validated at Harvard. Like the air we breathe, the scheme of things disappears, becomes simply reality, the way things are.

—Allen Wheelis (1915–2007), *The Scheme of Things* (1980, p. 69)

Consider the present moment, right now, as you read this sentence. This is a moment of your conscious experience of life. It is a moment you will never experience again (perhaps thankfully). Now it's gone, and you are on to another fleeting moment. Your conscious life consists of a continual sequence of such moments, interspersed with sleep, until your death. But is that generally how you conceive of time? Probably not.

Instead, we think of time in terms of minutes, hours, days, years, and so forth. Perhaps right now it's 9:00 p.m. Well, there is another 9:00 p.m. every day. And perhaps it's Tuesday—there'll be another one next week, and maybe you make a plan to meet up with a friend by saying, "See you next Tuesday." This is our culture at work, giving people a convenient and comforting scaffolding for their stream of consciousness. Someone raised in a different culture may experience time in a distinctly different manner. People in India, for example, recognize elaborate cosmic cycles called *yugas* which consist of 12,000-year *mahayugas*; there are a thousand *mahayugas* in a *kalpa* and 14 *kalpas* in a *manvantara*, after which a new *yuga* is initiated (Eliade, 1959). Take away culture, and there is no "next Tuesday" or "next *kalpa*"—merely a sequence of lived moments. This is just one of many basic ways that culture determines how we think about the world in our day-to-day lives.

Think
ABOUT

[Shutterstock]

What sets humans apart from other animals is that they spend the bulk of their waking hours (and even some of their time sleeping) embedded in a world of ideas and values that gives life meaning, significance, purpose, and direction. Think about what really matters to you, the things you aspire to, dream about, and probably sometimes worry about. For some it's making the grade in school; for others it's that new car that would feel so incredibly cool to drive. Some are obsessed with music, movies, or the arts, whereas others are wrapped up with nightlife and the club scene. Maybe spiritual values and the fate of the soul capture your attention, or the crazy goings-on in Washington and internationally and how they are affecting the future of the world. All of these uniquely human concerns are rooted in culture.

Culture A set of beliefs, attitudes, values, norms, morals, customs, roles, statuses, symbols, and rituals shared by a self-identified group, a group whose members think of themselves *as* a group.

Culture is a set of beliefs, attitudes, values, norms, morals, customs, roles, statuses, symbols, and rituals that is shared by a self-identified group—a group whose members think of themselves *as* a group. Cultures are perpetuated when they are passed from generation to generation, yet they continually change in response to influences from the environment, the needs of their members, and contact with other cultures.

The Common yet Distinctive Elements of Culture

All cultures have certain basic elements, and yet each culture's version of these features is unique. The similarities among cultures are not surprising, given that, as we have noted, people everywhere have the same basic motivations, emotions, and cognitive capabilities, and must contend with the same basic realities of life on this planet. At the same time, different groups inhabit different physical environments and different cultural histories. As a result, each culture's version of the basic elements is unique. These differences are what make meeting and learning about various groups of people from other parts of the world so interesting but also sometimes confusing or disturbing. Let's briefly consider each of these elements and how they are similar and different across cultures.

● *Beliefs* are accepted ideas about some aspect of reality. The idea that the earth revolves around the sun is a belief. Within a culture, many beliefs are virtually never disputed; these ideas are so unquestioned that they are often referred to as *cultural truisms*. In Western cultures, the aforementioned sun-earth relationship is one; that brushing your teeth is good for you is another (McGuire & Papageorgis, 1961). Some beliefs seem self-evidently true to one culture but may be vigorously disputed or rejected outright in another. For example, in some cultures, belief in an afterlife is widely accepted, whereas in others, it is not.

Beliefs are generally taken on faith and based on learning from parents, teachers, and other cultural authorities rather than being derived through specific personal experience. After all, if we relied only on personal experience, all but a few scientists and astronauts would believe that the sun revolves around the earth, as the vast majority of people once did. Similarly, how many people have seen the supposed proof that brushing teeth is good for us? The fact that we hold these and thousands of other beliefs on *faith* is a perfect example of how culture helps people in a group to create a shared sense of reality.

● Members of a culture tend to share similar *attitudes*, which are preferences, likes and dislikes, and opinions about what is good and bad. Attitudes are closely linked to beliefs, but they refer more specifically to how people evaluate something as good or bad. For example, a group of people may share the belief that abortion is legal in the United States, but their attitude toward the legalization of abortion could be favorable or unfavorable.

● A culture's *values* reflect its members' guiding principles and shared goals. Although cultures differ in their values, Shalom Schwartz and colleagues (e.g., Schwartz, 1992) has shown that cultures around the world recognize 10 core values (**Table 2.1**). These values can be viewed as stemming from the two basic motivational orientations mentioned earlier in this chapter: security and growth. The values of *security*,

Table 2.1 **Ten Cross-cultural Values, Ranked by Importance**

1. **Benevolence**. Preserving and enhancing the welfare of those with whom one is in frequent personal contact; being helpful, honest, forgiving, and responsible.

2. **Self-direction**. Independent thought and action; choosing one's own goals; the freedom to create and explore.

3. **Universalism**. Understanding, appreciation, tolerance, and protection of the welfare of all people and of nature. Advocating for justice, peace, and respect for other people and the environment.

4. **Security**. Safety, harmony, and stability of society, of relationships, and of self. Maintaining social order; establishing trust and reciprocation with others.

5. **Conformity**. Restraint of actions, inclinations, and impulses likely to upset or harm others and violate social expectations or norms. Obeying authorities, being polite. Self-discipline; honoring parents and elders.

6. **Achievement**. Personal success through demonstrating competence according to social standards. Being ambitious and feeling competent.

7. **Hedonism**. Pleasure and sensuous gratification for oneself. Enjoying life.

8. **Stimulation**. Excitement, novelty, and challenge in life.

9. **Tradition**. Respect, commitment, and acceptance of the customs and ideas that traditional culture or religion provide the self. Accepting one's role and observing cultural norms, customs, and rituals. Being devout and humble; accepting one's portion in life.

10. **Power**. Social status and prestige, control or dominance over people and resources. Seeking authority, wealth, and public esteem.

tradition, conformity, benevolence, and *universalism* reflect a desire to sustain safety, order, harmony, meaning, connection, and approval. In contrast, the values of *self-direction, stimulation, hedonism, achievement,* and *power* involve freedom, choice, excitement, enjoyment, accomplishment, and influence over others.

Across over 50 different cultures there is remarkable agreement in the importance people give each of these value types. *Benevolence,* the desire to be a good person ranked first; *self-direction,* the desire for personal freedom, and *universalism,* the desire for a just, meaningful, and peaceful world, were a close second and third. Presumably, the high level of consensus regarding these values reflects their psychological importance in serving the basic motives of security and growth. Nevertheless, cross-cultural differences in values also play an important role in various aspects of life (Schwartz, 1992; Schwartz et al., 2013).

● Values have a broad influence in a wide range of situations; in contrast, *norms* are shared beliefs about what is appropriate or expected behavior in particular situations. For example, many cultures have highly specific norms regarding who sits where during a social gathering, who sits down first, and who passes through a door first. In every culture, some situations involve very clear norms. In the United States, court proceedings and religious services are examples of such situations. These are known as *strong situations,* because norms strongly influence and constrain behavioral options (Mischel, 1977). In contrast, *weak situations* involve norms that are less clear or strict, so that almost anything goes. In the United States, hanging around with your friends would be an example of a relatively weak situation.

Food for Body, Mind, and Soul

One of the ways that culture influences you in your everyday life is the food you eat. Think about what you have eaten so far today. How would the food you eat be different if you had grown up in Chicago, Berlin, Tokyo, Marrakech, or Chang Mai? Not only do cultural adaptations dictate how we obtain sustenance but all cultures have particular ways of preparing and serving foods that embody their unique identity as groups and help to define the social environment. Whether it's hot dogs in the United States, schnitzel in Germany, sushi in Japan, tagines in Morocco, or panang curry in Thailand—you get the idea, and we're getting hungry!—specific food preparations help define a culture. People in that culture are especially likely to eat those foods at times when they want to commemorate particular past events that serve to affirm their cultural identity. Just as most Americans eat turkey on Thanksgiving, other cultures also have specific dishes that are eaten on days of particular historical and symbolic importance. As a result, food is a delicious representation of a culture.

Cultures also specify ritualistic ways in which meals are to be consumed. This includes prayers ("Thank you, Lord, for

this food we are about to share") and other utterances that precede meals ("Bon appetit!"), utensils that should be used (forks, chopsticks, fingers), rules for exactly how the utensils should be held, and customs for the order in which different courses are served. If you have ever watched the culinary explorer Anthony Bourdain on television, perhaps you've caught a glimpse of some of the food customs of far-flung places around the world.

The echoes of cultural adaptation on how we eat don't stop at the social environment; they extend to the metaphysical. The physical necessity of eating is transformed into an

Anthony Bourdain has built a reputation for hosting television programs that introduce viewers to the food and eating customs of far-flung cultures.

[Tannis Toohey/*Toronto Star* via Getty Images]

- *Morals* are beliefs about what good and bad behavior is. Three basic moral domains, abbreviated as CAD, have been proposed (Shweder et al., 1997). *Community morals* concern social role obligations, respect for authority, and loyalty to the group. *Autonomy morals* concern harming other individuals or infringing on their rights and freedoms. *Divinity morals* pertain to what is considered sacred and pure in the culture. Transgressions against each of these morals are associated with distinct emotions: Violations of community morals usually evoke feelings of contempt; violations of autonomy morals evoke anger; and violations of divinity morals evoke disgust (Rozin et al., 1999).

  All cultures specify community, autonomy, and divinity morals but vary in the extent to which they emphasize each moral domain. A culture that places high value on conformity (e.g., China) is likely to emphasize morals concerning community; a culture that values self-direction highly (e.g., the United States) is likely to emphasize morals concerning autonomy; and a culture that highly values tradition (e.g., Yemen) is likely to emphasize morals concerning divinity (Shweder et al., 1997). Each culture's laws and prescribed punishments are likely to reflect these value-driven moral emphases.

  Jonathan Haidt and colleagues (e.g., Haidt & Kesebir, 2010) more recently developed moral foundations theory by expanding Shweder's CAD to five basic moral domains: harm/care and fairness/reciprocity (based on autonomy); ingroup/loyalty and authority/respect (based on community), and purity/sanctity (based on divinity). They have found that in the United States, individuals near the

event of not just social significance (e.g., the business lunch) but also spiritual significance, whether it is the Jewish Seder, the wedding rehearsal dinner, or the Irish wake. Further, all cultures imbue life-sustaining food substances with spiritual power or group identity. In many cultures, certain foods are deemed sacred and others unclean. Whereas devout Jews and Muslims refuse to eat pork because it is viewed as unclean and insulting to their conception of God, Hindus avoid beef because cows are viewed as sacred and killing them as immoral. Many vegetarians and vegans eschew all animal meat and/or products because their belief that animals are intelligent make it disgusting and immoral even to consider eating them (Ruby & Heine, 2012). By infusing the very basic biological need for nutrition with sacred meaning, cultures elevate the animal activity of eating to a uniquely human level that separates humans from all other living creatures and thus proclaims our importance in the cosmic scheme of things.

Finally, because we associate food with different cultures, we can realize our desire to adapt to or affiliate with a culture by embracing the food customs we associate with that culture. So if you emigrated from China to the United States and you want to become acculturated quickly, you'll not only start learning the language and adopting the clothing styles but you also will start eating what seems like American food. The problem, from a health point of view, is that you might also begin gaining too much weight, because American food is typically high in fat and sugar. In one clever study, when Asian American college students were told by an experimenter that they didn't look American, they were more likely to choose American food for their lunch. The meal they chose had 182 calories more than the meal chosen by Asian American participants whose identity as Americans was not called into question (Guendelman et al., 2011). People use the food they eat to signal to themselves and others their cultural identity.

We are what we eat. When we eat food, we express our cultural identity through the food choices we make.
[Getty Images/Blend Images]

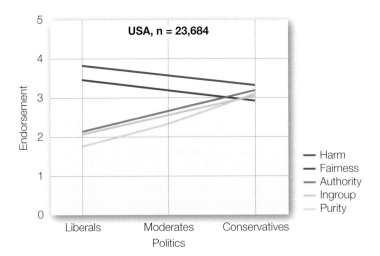

Figure 2.6

Moral Foundations

In the United States, individuals near the liberal end of the political spectrum value care and fairness above other possible moral foundations, whereas those near the conservative end emphasize all five moral domains.

[Data source: Graham et al. (2009)]

liberal end of the political spectrum focus mainly on harm/care and fairness/reciprocity, whereas those near the conservative end emphasize all five moral domains equally (**FIGURE 2.6**; Graham et al., 2009).

- *Customs* are specific patterns or styles of dress, speech, and behavior that, within a given culture, are deemed appropriate in particular contexts (**FIGURE 2.7**). For example, in the United States, it is customary to clap after watching actors perform an enjoyable play; in Japan it is customary to burp after an enjoyable meal. In Navajo culture, the first person who sees a baby smile, which typically doesn't happen until about six weeks after birth, is expected to throw a party to celebrate it. It is interesting that people are just as likely to try to avoid that honor as to try to be the lucky host: customs are widely followed, but not always happily.

- All cultures have *social roles*, positions within a group that entail specific ways of acting and dividing labor, responsibility, and resources. The enactor of the role is someone who has met the culture's requirements for taking on that role and has implicitly or explicitly agreed to do so. He or she usually communicates that role through certain forms of conduct, appearance, and demeanor that are recognized by other group members. Some roles, such as those defined by gender, can inform the person's thought and action across a very wide range of situations. Other roles, such as orchestra conductor, dictate how a person acts in a particular situation. Roles help define the self-concept. For example, a person's self-definition may begin, "I am an American citizen, a mother, and a professor." The privileges, responsibilities, and norms of a social role may be flexible or rigid. In the United States, the role of parent allows a certain latitude in how a person treats a child as long as that person takes care of the child's basic needs.

- *Cultural symbols* represent either the culture as a whole or beliefs or values prevalent in the culture. In cultures where members share a nationality, flags are often used to symbolize the culture's meaning, history, and values. Cultures defined around religious beliefs often create and recognize sacred symbols and artifacts, such as crucifixes and masks. Because symbols are seen as embodiments of cherished beliefs, ideals, and other aspects of cultural identity, they often are treated with great care, and in some cases only by select individuals. As a demonstration, try seeing if you can borrow the original U.S. Constitution for the weekend.

- Cultural symbols are central aspects of a culture's *rituals*, which are patterns of actions performed in particular contexts that reinforce cultural beliefs, values, and morals, and that often signal a change associated with the end of or

beginning of something of biological, historical, or cultural significance (e.g., birth, puberty, marriage, the founding of one's nation, annual holidays). Funerals, weddings, tea ceremonies, puberty-related ceremonies (e.g., confirmations, bar and bat mitzvahs, *quinceañeras*), birthday parties, and bridal showers are typical rituals. Another common ritual in universities and colleges is the commencement ceremony (**FIGURE 2.8**).

Culture as Creative Adaptation

Culture provides a uniquely advantageous means for adapting to environmental change. Cultural innovations can accumulate far more rapidly than genetic mutations, and good ideas can spread horizontally across populations as well as vertically between generations. This strategy of cultural adaptation, more than anything else, has enabled our species to transform itself from a relatively insignificant large African mammal to the dominant life form on Earth.

—Richard Klein, *The Dawn of Human Culture* (2002, p. 26).

Figure 2.7

Ornamentation

All cultures share certain elements but put a distinctive mark on them. For example, people in virtually every culture use jewelry, tattooing, and other techniques to adorn their bodies and advertise their status. The particular style of ornamentation, however, differs greatly from culture to culture.

[Left to right: Getty Images/photosindia; Angelo Giampiccolo/Shutterstock; Will Oliver/AFP/Getty Images; Frederick M. Brown/Getty Images]

Figure 2.8

Rituals

Universities and colleges around the world hold a commencement ceremony—a ritual that marks the beginning of the graduate's entrance into the "real world." Like many rituals, commencement ceremonies vary in distinctive ways from one institution to another. At the University of Kansas, for example, graduates walk through the doors of a large bell tower and down a big hill to the stadium where the formal ceremony takes place. At the University of Hawaii at Mānoa, graduates are ushered into the ceremony by selected male and female students, each carrying a *ko'o*, or ceremonial wand, that symbolizes complementary male and female energies.

[Left: Andrew Locke]

Cultural evolution The process whereby cultures develop and propagate according to systems of belief or behavior that contribute to the success of a society.

Culture is a creative adaptation that a group develops to serve its needs and desires in its particular environment. According to the anthropologist Weston La Barre (1954), cultural evolution can occur quickly, as a group develops new technologies and revises belief systems to provide flexible adaptation in meeting the demands of a changing environment. Through such cultural evolution, people can avoid getting locked into specific environmental niches. This capacity is the reason humans can be found almost everywhere on our planet and, over the last few decades, even in outer space and on the moon. Indeed, cultures can change within a single generation and sometimes almost virtually overnight. Just think of how much music, fashion, politics, and social norms have changed in the very few years that you've been alive. It seems unimaginable, but when your parents were growing up, there was no Internet! How did people back then get information and music? How did they socialize?

Cultural Diffusion: Spreading the Word

Cultural diffusion The transfer of inventions, knowledge, and ideas from one culture to another.

Once a component of culture develops, it is picked up and used by others. Generally, the more adaptive it is, the more readily it spreads. The transfer of inventions, knowledge, and ideas from one culture to another, a process that the anthropologist Ralph Linton (1936) labeled cultural diffusion, is made possible by the human capacity for communication and learning, combined with the urge to explore and grow. This diffusion often occurs through friendly contact, business and trade, mass communication, and immigration, but also commonly results from conquest and colonization. For example, many aspects of Roman culture were diffused throughout Europe as the Roman empire spread its domination across Europe and beyond, often by means of extreme violence.

Through cultural diffusion, a culture doesn't have to depend solely on the ingenuity of its own members to meet the adaptive challenges of the environment; rather, it can benefit from knowledge, skills, and inventions developed by other cultures. For example, when the inhabitants of Tasmania arrived there over 20,000 years ago, they had a culture that was equivalent to that of Europe at the time in its material development. But because the Tasmanians were isolated from outside influence, by the time Europeans first visited them in the eighteenth century, European culture was far more technologically advanced (Linton, 1936). Europe's location and sea-travel-friendly coastlines allowed its evolving cultures to benefit extensively from cultural diffusion in terms of technological innovation and development (Diamond & Bellwood, 2003).

Historical examples of ideas that have diffused in this manner include the belief in one deity (monotheism), knowledge that the earth revolves around the sun, and the idea that women should have equal rights with men. And the easier travel and communication became around the globe, the more quickly cultural diffusion occurred. Under such conditions, inventions are especially likely to spread rapidly, as can be seen with radio, television, computers, the Internet, and cell phones.

Of course, as this diffusion occurs, other cultures typically adapt these influences for their own purposes. When Marco Polo brought the technology for making pasta back from the Far East, the Italians developed their own forms and uses for it; those of us who enjoy Italian restaurants are glad of that. But these modifications are not always so unambiguously beneficial. The Internet has led to development of web sites devoted to things such as music and comic books in some cultures, but it has led to web sites devoted to racism and spreading terrorism in others.

An oft-overlooked consequence of cultural diffusion is that all but the most isolated and technologically primitive of cultures are actually hybrid products of many cultures (Linton, 1936). To mention a few examples: Americans often think of horses and cows as prototypical symbols of the American West, but they were first domesticated in Southwest Asia. Windmills and wooden shoes, so closely associated with Holland, originally appeared in Persia (now Iran). The use of eggs to symbolize the Christian Easter celebration dates back to pagan fertility ceremonies as well as to Egyptian traditions 5,000 years ago. The general point is that much of what people consider central characteristics of their own culture are actually elements borrowed from other cultures and subsequently elaborated on. Thus, cultures are amazingly complex and useful adaptations, best viewed as cumulative collaborative products of the ingenuity of the entire human species, and hence should be sources of pride for us all rather than only for members of particular groups.

Cultural Transmission

How do we do it? Cultural innovation and diffusion across generations requires a specific kind of social interaction between experienced teachers and youngsters amenable to learning by formal instruction or imitation. The developmental psychologist Peter Hobson (2004) makes a strong case for the role of education as a defining feature of our species. Although other animals, especially higher primates, clearly learn a great deal by observing the behavior of others, human adults routinely engage in cultural transmission: explicit efforts to teach children knowledge and skills, largely with the help of language. And human children, regardless of the extent of their formal schooling, spend a considerable proportion of their early years as beneficiaries of direct efforts to inculcate them into the cultural universe of their compatriots.

Cultural transmission The process whereby members of a culture learn explicitly or implicitly to imitate the beliefs and behaviors of others in that culture.

SECTION review | Culture: The Uniquely Human Adaptation

Culture is a set of psychological and social elements shared by members of a group and passed from generation to generation.

Elements of Culture	Cultural Evolution
All culture have the same basic elements, yet each culture's version of them is unique.	Culture enables people to flexibly and rapidly adapt their biological and psychological capacities to thrive in diverse and changing environments. This flexibility is made possible by the transmission of cultural elements among cultures and over generations within a culture.

How Culture Helps Us Adapt

What does culture *do* for individuals and groups? One insightful answer comes from the social anthropologist W. Lloyd Warner (1959), who proposed that culture helps people adapt to three aspects of their environment:

- The *physical environment*, through the development of skills and tools that help people meet their basic biological goals of survival and reproduction
- The *social environment*, via the development of social roles, relationships, and order
- The *metaphysical environment*, through the development of cultural worldviews that provide answers to the big questions that have concerned humans throughout time: *Who am I? Where did we come from? Why are we here? What makes for a good life? What happens to us after death?*

The nature of cultural adaptations to each of these environments is simultaneously affected by adaptations to each of the other environments, but for ease of presentation we will first consider cultural adaptations to each environment one at time.

Culture and the Natural Environment

Imagine what life would be like if you had to sleep outdoors and nourish and defend yourself with your bare hands, fortified by an occasional rock or stick! Yet our primate ancestors made do with this state of affairs for millions of years until the development of the first stone tools some 2 million or so years ago, followed a few hundred thousand years later by hand axes, control of fire, and basic shelters. These momentous developments marked the earliest beginnings of our history as the cultural animal. At this point, survival became increasingly dependent on learning how to do things that were first invented or discovered by others. The result of this entirely new form of adaptation—the emergence of a rudimentary precultural mode of living—was that our hominid ancestors were able to live in larger groups and extend their range of exploitable habitats.

Living in groups had many advantages. As group size increased, the number of protohumans available to learn from, and to teach, increased in kind, providing a richer array of knowledge. This promoted more rapid development, initially of tools and later of other aspects of culture. The expanded range of habitats brought more challenges to be solved with the increasing intellect that was emerging in our ancestors. These factors made increases in cognitive sophistication even more adaptive and provided a fertile ground for cultural knowledge to expand.

The Varieties of Ways to Adapt to the Physical Environment

Throughout human history, all cultures have developed means of meeting basic human needs, and hominid groups exploited the natural environments in which they lived to produce unique solutions to problems of survival. Groups living in areas with rich supplies of plants were especially likely to develop technologies for harvesting fruits and nuts; those in areas with large concentrations of animals developed effective means of hunting and trapping; those living near water developed techniques for fishing. In this way, the physical environment that groups inhabited shaped the sorts of technologies they developed.

Yet culturally developed adaptations are only partially determined by the character of specific environments. If the physical environment were the sole determinant of adaptation, then groups in similar environments should adapt to their surroundings in similar ways, but this is often not the case. Because of their different histories and traditions, groups that occupy the same territory often have radically different and mutually incompatible ways of extracting a living from it. A particularly tragic example can be found in Sudan. A vicious and genocidal civil war has been raging over an area known as the Darfur region between two groups of occupants: Arab herders and African farmers. In the American West, conflicts between herders and farmers over the same land were also prevalent in the 19th century.

Culture, Cognition, and Perception

How a given culture adapts to its physical surroundings has a profound and, in some cases surprising, influence on people's basic perceptions and thought processes. For example, people from hunter-gatherer cultures are especially strong in visual and spatial abilities (Berry, 1966; Kleinfeld, 1971), presumably because they must be able to visually organize and recall the vast amounts of natural territory they explore. Consider the Inuit of Canada and Alaska—in order to hunt, they must navigate a white-dominated terrain by using only the subtlest of visual cues (Nelson, 1962). And the vocabulary of the Eskimo language reflects and reinforces these spatial abilities by including words that make very elaborate spatial and geometric distinctions (Berry, 1966).

Although spatial location is critical for survival in such cultures, the ability to quantify things precisely is less important. For example, although traditional Australian Aborigines do very well in spatial memory tasks, they do not do well in quantitative tasks. Indeed, when speaking their native language, traditional Aborigines generally refer to quantities greater than five simply as "many" (Dasen, 1994). In contrast, people from predominantly sedentary agricultural cultures, such as the Baoule of Côte d'Ivoire (the Ivory Coast) in West Africa, are not so skilled in visual-spatial tasks but are stronger in quantitative tasks (Dasen, 1994).

Culture affects not only the development of cognitive skills but also susceptibility to tricks of visual perception. Consider the well-known Müller-Lyer illusion, depicted in **FIGURE 2.9**. Does the line on the right with the closed-angle arrowhead ends look shorter to you than the line on the left with the open-angle ends? In fact, the lines are same the same length, as a ruler clearly shows.

This illusion was once considered a universal "bug" of the human perceptual system (Gregory, 1966). But cross-cultural research has shown that the more a culture relies on the cultural innovation of carpentry (with extensive use of straight edges and right angles), the more its members fall prey to this illusion (Segall et al., 1963; Stewart, 1973). People inhabiting a physical environment containing many straight lines and angular line intersections interpret the lines three-dimensionally (Gregory, 1968). This leads them to view the right line as an "outside" corner protruding toward them, and the left line as an "inside" corner farther away. If two lines seem the same length on the retina, but the brain unconsciously interprets one as closer, the assumed closer line will be viewed as shorter. Yet some cultural groups, such as rural Zambians from the Zambezi Valley, inhabit environments that have less carpentered structures, and so they are rarely exposed to straight lines and sharp angles. Members of these cultures tend to view the lines as two-dimensional patterns. This eliminates the illusion that one line is farther away than the other. As a result, members of these latter cultures judge the relative lengths of the two lines more accurately than do members of highly carpentered cultures such as the United States.

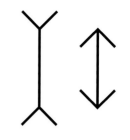

FIGURE 2.9

Müller-Lyer Illusion

Is one line longer than the other? Your ability to answer this question correctly depends on the culture in which you were raised.

Culture and the Social Environment

All groups of people, if they are to prosper, have to get along with each other, cooperate to achieve mutual goals, and minimize disruptive conflicts within the group. As societies grew in size from small bands of 100 or so people to thousands of people living in close proximity, a number of challenges of social organization arose. What were those big challenges? How do cultures differ in their solutions to them?

The Uncertainties of Group Living

One problem people in all cultures face lies in knowing what they *should* do and what they are *allowed* to do. In most modern societies, people interact on a daily basis with strangers. Because they cannot always be sure that the strangers view the world exactly as they do, they can be uncertain about what they should do in a situation, where they fit in, and how they should treat others. Consider your own awkward moments of wondering, for example, if you should call your friend's mom by her first name.

Michael Hogg's (2007) *uncertainty identity theory* explains how, to reduce this uncertainty, people identify with culturally defined groups that have clear guidelines for behavior. For example, your current author is a member of a culturally defined group of professors, and this group gives him a certain role to play. That role entails how he should act, and also how other groups (e.g., students) should act toward him. Supporting this theory are studies showing that when people are led to feel uncertain about who they are, they are more likely to identify with their cultural group, especially if that group has a clear sense of boundaries, expectations, and cohesion (Hogg et al., 2007).

How Individuals Relate to Each Other: Individualism/Collectivism

A second problem that people in all cultures face is figuring out how to orient themselves toward their relationships—that is, how to think about the relationship between self and other. Through study of cultures around the world, Alan Fiske (1990) proposed that there are four basic patterns of social relations:

1. *Community sharing*, in which cooperation and self-sacrifice are prevalent and, as in a family, "What's mine is yours."
2. *Authority ranking*, in which one person gives orders and the other follows them, like a sergeant and a private in the army.
3. *Equality matching*, in which everyone is treated equally and has the same rights, as is typical in friendship.
4. *Market pricing*, in which relationships follow economic principles, as is typical in business relationships.

All four of these relationship patterns can be found in every known culture, but their prevalence varies considerably across cultures. The cross-cultural psychologist Harry Triandis (1994) noted that more traditional, ethnically homogenous cultures stress community sharing and authority ranking, and can be characterized as collectivistic. In collectivistic cultures, the emphasis is on interdependence, cooperation, and the welfare of the group over that of the individual. People in such cultures—for example Korea, Japan, and Pakistan—are expected to fit in with the group, obey authority figures, be part of the whole, and be especially sensitive to how their actions affect others within the group.

More ethnically heterogeneous cultures—such as the United States, Australia, and Germany—emphasize equality matching and market pricing and are referred to as individualistic. In individualistic cultures, individual initiative, achievement, and creativity are highly encouraged, and people look primarily after their own interests and those of their immediate families. **Table 2.2** displays the primary distinguishing characteristics of collectivistic and individualistic cultures.

As the value categories displayed in Table 2.1 on p. 53 clearly show, both individualism and collectivism reflect core human values. Consequently, all cultures encourage some collectivistic and some individualistic tendencies. Members within

Collectivistic culture A culture in which the emphasis is on interdependence, cooperation, and the welfare of the group over that of the individual.

Individualistic culture A culture in which the emphasis is on individual initiative, achievement, and creativity over maintenance of social cohesion.

Table 2.2 **Characteristics of Individualism and Collectivism**

High levels of collectivism in a culture are associated with . . .	High levels of individualism in a culture are associated with . . .
Valuing group membership.	Valuing independence, uniqueness, and autonomy.
Valuing group harmony, even if it means silencing one's personal views.	General encouragement to express one's personal views, even at the cost of disrupting social harmony.
Tolerance for inconsistencies in descriptions of the self across different role contexts.	Preference for consistency of the self across different role contexts.
Fostering of an *interdependent self-construal* that defines the self in relation to others versus evaluating the self in comparison to others.	Fostering of an *independent self-construal* that defines and evaluates the self as distinct from others.
A clear distinction between ingroup and outgroup, coupled with a marked preference for the ingroup over the outgroup.	A tendency to regard others as individuals, not members of groups, and to treat people the same regardless of group membership.
Cognition that tends toward a holistic style that looks for relations between parts; sensitivity to connection and context.	Cognition that tends toward an analytical style that looks for parts of the whole; sensitivity to separation and contrast.

Here are a few of the many excellent papers on the extensive implications of this cultural difference: Cross et al., 2010; Gardner et al., 2004; Markus & Kitayama, 1991; Morelli & Rothbaum, 2007; Shweder et al., 1997; Singelis et al., 1995; Suh, 2002.

cultures vary considerably in how much they embrace individualistic and collectivistic concerns. Thus, it would be inaccurate to portray members of cultures such as Japan and China as mindless automatons expressing only the collective will of the group. And it would be similarly misguided to portray members of cultures such as the United States and Great Britain as self-absorbed nonconformers with no concern for their relationships and groups. Nevertheless, the broad distinction between individualistic and collectivistic cultures does help account for a variety of interesting psychological differences among typical members of the two types of cultures.

The Nature of the Self

Hazel Markus and Shinobu Kitayama (1991) point out that in collectivist cultures, people tend to have a more **interdependent self-construal**. They view themselves primarily in terms of how they relate to others and contribute to the greater whole. Indeed, in their research, Markus and Kitayama showed that when asked to complete the sentence "I am____," members of collectivistic cultures tend to fill in the blank with responses indicating their social relationships (e.g., a daughter) and group identifications (e.g., Malaysian).

In contrast, people inhabiting individualistic cultures exhibit a more **independent self-construal**. They view themselves as unique individuals who should stand out from the crowd and "do their own thing." Thus, when asked to complete the sentence "I am____," they tend to fill in personal traits (e.g., honest) and feelings (e.g., happy).

Interdependent self-construal Viewing self primarily in terms of how one relates to others and contributes to the greater whole.

Independent self-construal Viewing self as a unique active agent serving one's own goals.

Fitting in and Sticking out

In collectivistic cultures, behaving in a manner that fits expectations and sustains social harmony is more important than expressing one's personal attitudes or preferences, or outperforming others. It is not that members of collectivistic cultures don't have personal opinions; they just don't view them as important relative to adherence to norms of appropriate behavior. In individualistic cultures, in contrast, people value freedom of speech highly and are generally encouraged to express their personal views, even if they cause debate or dissension (Gardner et al., 1999; Triandis, 1994).

Emotion

Individualistic and collectivistic cultures also differ in the way members experience and display their emotions. The collectivistic emphasis on harmony prioritizes social harmony over the freedom to broadcast one's emotional reactions. In a study exploring this tendency (Ekman et al., 1972), American and Japanese students displayed the same negative facial expressions in response to a graphic film of a circumcision ritual when viewing it alone, but the Japanese participants inhibited such negative expressions when viewing the film in the presence of an experimenter, suggesting that individuals raised in collectivistic cultures feel less comfortable displaying their emotional reactions.

In addition to differences in emotional displays, different cultures view particular emotions as more or less desirable. For example, compared with Australians and Americans, Chinese participants judge *pride* to be less desirable and *guilt* more desirable (Eid & Diener, 2001). This fits with *pride* being associated with individual accomplishment, which we would expect to be a priority among members of individualistic cultures. In contrast, *guilt* signals a harm done to others and motivates efforts to repair the threatened relationship (Baumeister et al., 1994; Rank, 1936b; Tangney & Dearing, 2002). Thus, the differential values placed on pride and guilt support the idea that collectivist cultures place greater emphasis on social obligations and maintaining social bonds. These cultural differences in emotional norms and displays have important implications, particularly when people from different cultures interact. For example, in medical contexts, differences in cultural norms for

In 2012, three members of the Russian punk-protest band Pussy Riot were arrested and sent to prison after they gave an unauthorized performance at Moscow's Cathedral of Christ the Saviour. Although they were convicted of being hooligans motivated by religious hatred, some people believe they were punished for publicly speaking out against political policies and social oppression.

[Aleshkovsky Mitya/ITAR-TASS/Landov]

emotion might lead American doctors to view Asian patients as less excited about, and thus receptive to, medical treatment (Tsai, 2007).

A third psychological difference refers to how people generally draw a distinction between the ingroup and the outgroup, with members of outgroups treated very differently from fellow ingroup members. In collectivistic cultures, people are less constrained in expressing negative feelings regarding outgroup members. Indeed, treating outgroup members differently is considered the right thing to do. In contrast, members of individualistic cultures tend to view others as individuals rather than as group members and thus try to adhere to the norm of treating people the same regardless of their group membership (Triandis, 1994).

Modernization and Cultural Values

The spectrum between individualism and collectivism is one general way to characterize a culture's norms and values, and to understand how that value profile governs social relations and provides social order. An important factor that influences how cultures evolve to meet these needs is modernization. Over the last 500 years, there has been a general trend toward increased *socioeconomic development*; industrial, technological and economic advancements; and *democratization*. How might these changes have influenced the values that people hold?

One consequence of these changes is that we live in increasingly diverse societies because social policies allow for immigration, and technology makes it easier to travel far from home while still maintaining connections with family. Triandis (1989) proposed that as cultures become more heterogeneous, they tend to become more individualistic and less collectivistic. Consider that a recent analysis of pronoun use in American books published between 1960 and 2008 revealed a 10% decrease in the use of words such as "we" and "us" alongside a 42% increase in "I" and "me" (Twenge et al., 2013). Even the already individualistic United States might be becoming even more individualistic over time.

This rise in individualism might result from the increasing mobility that people have. Shigehiro Oishi and colleagues have argued that as people move around from place to place, forgoing their roots in a single, long-standing community to increase their personal opportunities in a new place, they adopt more individualistic values (Oishi, Lun, & Sherman, 2007; Oishi et al., 2009). Those who have moved around a lot see their social group memberships as being less central to how they view themselves and feel less obligation to their friends (Oishi, 2010). They are even more likely to be fair-weather fans of their local baseball team, only coming to games when the team is winning (Oishi & Kisling, 2009; Oishi, Rothman et al., 2007)! In contrast, collectivism tends to foster stability and community loyalty. For example, Chinese participants in a study perceived themselves to have less job mobility than U.S. participants. This perception positively correlates with their belief that, in order to succeed, an individual must conform to the normatively fixed expectations of her role in the workplace (Chen et al., 2009).

In cities such as Miami that have fewer lifelong residents, fans are less likely to remain loyal when their team is having a losing season. The Miami Marlins, for example, have shown considerable variability in their attendance over the years.

[AP Photo/J. Pat Carter]

As those within societies become more mobile, societies become increasingly diverse and tend to value that diversity as well as other progressive belief systems. Schwartz and Sagie (2000) examined socioeconomic development, cultural values, and political characteristics of 42 countries from 1988 to 1994. They found that as cultures modernized or embraced democracy, they increasingly prioritized new ideas, individual initiative, personal worth, equality, and status judgments based on achievement rather than on tradition. As socioeconomic development increased, so did the importance of the values of self-direction, stimulation, universalism, benevolence, and hedonism. At the same time, socioeconomic development was associated with decreased emphasis on the past, traditional bases of status, and decreased concern for personal safety. This research shows how economic and political features of a culture relate to the psychological values held dear by members of that culture. Of course, it is likely that both causal directions help account for the relationships between these variables; a culture's value profile contributes to how receptive it is to modernization, and modernization then reinforces those pro-modernization value priorities.

Culture and the Metaphysical Environment

Happy the hare at morning, for she cannot read
The hunter's waking thoughts, lucky the leaf
Unable to predict the fall, lucky indeed
The rampant suffering suffocating jelly
Burgeoning in pools, lapping the grits of the desert.
But what shall man do, who can whistle tunes by heart,
Knows to the bar when death shall cut him short like the cry of the shearwater,
What can he do but defend himself from his knowledge?

—W. H. Auden (1907–73),
"The Cultural Presupposition"

In addition to helping people adapt to their physical and social environments, culture helps them to adapt to their metaphysical environment, by which we mean our understanding of the nature of reality and the significance of our lives within the cosmic order of things. But why are people the world over preoccupied with understanding their place in the metaphysical environment? To answer this question we have to recognize that humans' sophisticated intellectual abilities are a mixed blessing. On the one hand, our ability to think symbolically about time and space is tremendously adaptive; as we've seen in this chapter, it allows us to imagine possibilities and communicate with each other in complex ways. But this intelligence has some problematic consequences. According to the cultural anthropologist Ernest Becker, writing in books such as *The Birth and Death of Meaning* (1971) and *The Denial of Death* (1973), the most chilling result of our species' vast intelligence is the awareness that the only truly certain thing about life is that it will end someday. We know that death is inevitable and inescapable, and that it could come at any moment from any number of causes. Awareness of the fragility of life and the inevitability of death in an animal that seeks survival creates the potential for paralyzing terror. Becker proposed that such terror simply would be too much for a self-conscious animal to bear, leaving us quivering piles of biological protoplasm quaking in fear and unable to act effectively, unless we do something to manage this potential terror.

In the mid-1980s, Sheldon Solomon, Tom Pyszczynski, and Jeff Greenberg synthesized Becker's ideas into **terror management theory**, or TMT (Greenberg et al., 1986; Solomon et al., 1991). Terror management theory proposes that humans have fashioned a partial solution to this existential dread, using the same cognitive abilities that made them aware of mortality to manage this terror. As our hominid ancestors' cognitive capacities increased, they began to wonder how the world works, how to do the things necessary to survive, and eventually, to ask more difficult questions about where they came from, what happened when they died, and what life is all about. In order to feel secure in a threatening world, each cultural group has created answers to these questions. We call these answers **cultural worldviews**—human-constructed symbolic conceptions of reality. The more effective a cultural worldview was at helping individuals manage their mortality fears, the more likely it was to be accepted and transmitted among members of that culture and from one generation to the next.

In this way, cultural worldviews emerged that gave life meaning, order, value, and promises that life will continue in some manner beyond the point of physical death. To

Terror management theory To minimize fear of mortality, humans strive to sustain faith that they are enduringly valued contributors to a meaningful world and therefore transcend their physical death.

Cultural worldview Human-constructed shared symbolic conceptions of reality that imbue life with meaning, order, and permanence.

specify, all cultural worldviews consist of: (1) a theory of reality that provides answers to basic questions about life, death, the cosmos, and one's place in it; (2) institutions, symbols, and rituals that reinforce components of that worldview; (3) a set of standards of value that prescribe what is good and bad, and what it means to be a good human being; and (4) the promise of actual or symbolic immortality to those who believe in the worldview and live up to the standards of value that are part of it.

By imposing meaning on the subjective experience of reality and creating a sense of enduring significance for the self, cultural worldviews help people maintain the belief that they are more than transient animals in a purposeless universe, fated only to die. A person can view him- or herself as a unique person with a rich history, family heritage, group memberships, and social roles that give life value. We identify as students, professors, doctors, lawyers; as Malaysians, Guatemalans, Americans, Italians; as members of the Communist Party or the local bowling club. All of these identifications support the belief that our lives are part of something bigger and longer lasting than our mere biological existence. We cling to these cultural worldviews every day to feel secure in the world. Rarely do we stop to realize that the cultural worldview is ultimately of our own collective creation!

Although all cultural worldviews address basic existential concerns, they vary considerably in the specific beliefs and values they employ. In the following sections, we will consider both the similarities and the differences among cultures in the aspects of their worldviews central to terror management: creation stories, cultural institutions, symbols and rituals, bases of self-worth, and modes of striving for immortality.

Creation Stories

Where did we come from? How did life begin? How do we humans fit into the grand scheme of things?

- In Mali in West Africa, the Fulani (**FIGURE 2.10a**) believe the world was created from a giant drop of milk, from which the god Doonari emerged and created stone. The stone created iron, iron created fire, fire created water, and water created air.
- The Aztecs' world was initiated when Coatlicue (**FIGURE 2.10b**), the Lady of the Skirt of Snakes, was created in the image of the unknown. She was impregnated by an obsidian knife and gave birth to female and male offspring who became the moon and the stars.
- In the Judeo-Christian tradition that has dominated much of the Western world for the past three millennia, God created the universe in six days and rested on the seventh. Shortly thereafter he made Adam, the first man (**FIGURE 2.10c**). Because Adam was lonely, God took a rib from his body while he was sleeping to create the first woman, Eve, who became his companion. Eve was tempted by a serpent and convinced Adam to disobey God's command. After eating the forbidden fruit of the Tree of Knowledge, Adam and Eve were expelled from the idyllic Garden of Eden and became mortal.

These examples were gleaned from David and Margaret Leeming's (1994) *Dictionary of Creation Myths*. The Leemings acknowledge the tremendous variation in the details but note the common themes:

> The basic creation story, then, is that of the process by which chaos becomes cosmos, no-thing becomes some-thing. In a real sense this is only story we have to tell. . . .
> It lies behind our attempts to "make something" of our lives, that is, to make a difference. (P. VIII)

Questions concerning the origins of life have had great importance for human-kind since the earliest days of our species and continue to fascinate. Perhaps it has occurred to you that the big bang theory of the origin of the universe and the theory of evolution by natural selection are contemporary examples of creation stories.

(a)

(b)

(c)

Figure 2.10

Creation Stories

All cultures have stories about the creation of the world and the people in it: (a) members of the Fulani tribe from West Africa; (b) figurine of Coatlicue, the Aztec goddess; (c) *The Expulsion from Paradise*, 1740, painting depicting the Judaeo-Christian God with Adam and Eve.

[Left to right: ©AfriPics.com/Alamy; DEA/G. Dagli Orti/Getty Images; © The Metropolitan Museum of Art/Art Resource, NY]

Institutions, Symbols, and Rituals: Worldview Transmission and Maintenance

Cultural worldviews must be transmitted from generation to generation and must be continually reinforced so people can sustain faith in them and avoid the realization that they are essentially fictional accounts of reality. For example, in the United States, the elaborate public education system teaches children the history of the United States in terms of names, events, and dates. But it also teaches mythical stories, such as the honesty of George Washington and the steadfastness of Betsy Ross in sewing the first American flag. Similar names, events, and dates might be taught in another culture, but the tone of those lessons might be quite different, conveying that particular culture's current view of those historical people and events. For example, although Americans view the December 7, 1941 attack on Pearl Harbor as an unjustified, egregious sneak attack, the Japanese view it quite differently. In the context of their worldview, the United States had acted aggressively toward Japan by imposing an embargo that threatened its national security. The embargo blocked Japan's access to the South Pacific's oil and natural resources, which were critical to the survival of the Japanese way of life.

Similarly, in a culture's primary language classes, children learn the cherished poems, stories, and novels of that culture, and the cultural morals and values they convey. Science classes convey certain attitudes and values regarding the environment, animals, other people, and appropriate goals toward which the society should strive. In addition, churches, mosques, and synagogues teach the religious aspects of the worldview. These aspects of the culture are further reinforced throughout people's lives by a wide variety of clubs and organizations, such as the Girl Scouts and the Lions Club; and by many rituals, such as first communions, bar mitzvahs, weddings, and funerals; and even by playing the Star Spangled Banner before major sporting events (e.g., Super Bowl).

Holidays celebrating culturally significant events and values, such as Independence Day, Cinco de Mayo and Eid al Fitr (the end of Ramadan) also play a key role in maintaining faith in the dominant cultural worldview. And of course, people in every culture are surrounded by cherished symbols of their cultural beliefs, including totem poles, flags, murals, coins, or artwork.

Think
ABOUT

[Chris Hill/ Shutterstock]

What are some of your own cherished cultural symbols?

Bases of Self-worth: Standards, Values, Social Roles, and Self-esteem

Beyond providing and maintaining a meaningful explanation of reality, all cultures give their members standards of value, specifying which personal characteristics and

Self-esteem A person's evaluation of his of her value or self-worth.

behaviors are good and which are bad. Living up to these cultural standards of value provides a sense of **self-esteem**, which refers to the person's evaluation of his or her self-worth. Someone with a high level of self-esteem views him- or herself as a valuable member of a meaningful universe and thus has a protective shield against the potential for terror inherent in the human condition. Self-esteem is thus one of the most basic psychological mechanisms by which culture fulfills its anxiety-managing function (Pyszczynski et al., 2004).

All cultures provide a wide range of benefits to those who meet or exceed the cultural standards of value, for example, money, better health care, awards and prizes, and good mating prospects. These benefits contribute to individuals' hope that they will continue, in some way, beyond physical death. Reinforcing the connection between goodness and good outcomes, all cultural worldviews convey that good things will happen to the worthy and bad things will happen to the unworthy. Melvin Lerner labeled these ideas **just world beliefs** and, with colleagues, has shown that people are highly motivated to maintain faith in such beliefs (e.g., Lerner & Simmons, 1966). For example, people look for ways to believe that victims of misfortune must have done something to deserve their fates (Hafer & Bègue, 2005).

Just world beliefs The idea that good things will happen to the worthy and bad things will happen to the unworthy.

Although the need for self-esteem is universal, the standards that one must meet to attain self-esteem are specified by one's cultural worldview (Sedikides et al., 2003). Most cultures share some of these standards, probably because they have adaptive value in helping the group function effectively. For example, most (but not all) cultures value strength, speed, intelligence, honesty, sharing, and cooperation. However, standards of value and achievement, and what it means to be good and/or right, often vary greatly across cultures, just as basic views of reality do. For example, according to the anthropologist Walter Goldschmidt (1990):

- A heroic accomplishment for a Crow Indian warrior is to gallop into an enemy camp and touch one enemy warrior without injuring him.
- Tlingit Indians are valued in proportion to how many blankets and other objects they have accumulated and then either given away or destroyed.

We would add to this list:

Gender Development
Video for LaunchPad

- American men are highly valued if they can hit a spherical object with a wooden stick effectively 3 out of every 10 times that such an object is hurled at them.

Status Symbols. Standards for self-esteem vary across and within cultures. Some American men base their self-esteem on the ability to afford a sweet ride and a nice house.
[Digital Vision/Getty Images]

Standards for obtaining self-esteem also vary considerably for individuals within each culture, depending on family, gender, and age. In the United States, a small waistline and ability to do cheerleading routines might garner self-esteem for a teenage girl, whereas a pot-bellied middle-aged male might base his self-worth on his ability to afford a Jaguar and a large house in the suburbs. In a traditional tribal culture, one person might acquire self-worth as a shaman, another as a warrior, another as a skilled pot maker.

Striving for Immortality

Recognizing the inevitability of death is a terrifying prospect for an animal that shares with all life forms a basic biological imperative to survive. A cultural worldview provides a theory of reality and standards through which individuals can attain self-esteem. For those who attain that sense of value, it also provides the prospect of either literal or symbolic immortality. Literal immortality is afforded by aspects of the cultural worldview that reassure a person that physical death is not the end of life and promise some form of life after death to those who are worthy. Symbolic immortality is the sense that, by being part of something greater and more enduring than one's individual self, some part of the self will live on after the body dies.

Even a passing glance at past and current cultures the world over reveals that the hope of literal immortality has been central to most cultures and organized religions. Archeological excavations reveal that elaborate ritual burials begin abruptly and appear regularly with the emergence of modern humans, suggesting that concerns about death have been with us from the earliest days of our species (Mithen, 1996; Tattersall, 1998). Indeed, the oldest known written story—the Sumerian *Epic of Gilgamesh*—concerns the protagonist's fear of the prospect of his own death and his quest to obtain immortality. This quest was also central to ancient Egyptian, Chinese, and Greek cultures.

Virtually all major contemporary religions promise some form of afterlife. Recent surveys suggest that most people around the world believe in some form of afterlife: 51% say yes, 26% say probably but not certain, 23% say no. Confidence in the afterlife is even higher in the United States: 69% say absolutely yes, and only 11% say that you simply cease to exist after death (Ipsos/Reuters, 2011).

Consider different cultures' contemporary conceptions of the afterlife (Panati, 1996). Many Jews believe that the righteous are resurrected in Olam Ha-Ba, the World to Come. Christians believe that everyone has the gift of eternal life. The body dies, but the soul lives forever. Heaven is also central to Muslim conceptions of the hereafter. Hindus believe there is an eternal, changeless core of the self, the *atman*, entrapped in the world of *samsara*, an endless cycle of death and rebirth. For traditional Australian Aborigines, death marks only the end of the physical life, with the spirit released to rejoin those of ancestors and become a part of the land itself. In sum, a central component of cultural worldviews in almost all times and places has been the prospect of physical immortality.

In addition to the prospect of literal immortality, cultures can offer routes to symbolic immortality. In symbolic immortality, humans transcend death by being part of, or by contributing something to, an entity greater than the self that will continue after physical death. The psychohistorian Robert Jay Lifton (1979) proposed that cultures provide (in varying degrees) four different modes of symbolic immortality: biosocial, creative, natural, and experiential. Research supports the idea that the more people have a sense of symbolic immortality, the less afraid they are of death (Florian & Mikulincer, 1998).

Biosocial immortality is obtained by having children and identifying with larger collectives such as nations. Some aspect of parents will live on through their children and their children's children and so on in perpetuity; nations are presumed to continue indefinitely.

Creative immortality results from contributions to one's culture. Examples include heroic acts or noteworthy leadership, helping others by using one's knowledge and skills for the betterment of humankind and passing them on, and highly regarded scientific and artistic accomplishments.

Natural immortality results from strongly identifying with nature—a sense of being one with the universe—and the coincident recognition that an eternal part of one's self will persist over time.

Finally, *experiential immortality* results from "peak experiences," described by Abraham Maslow (1964) as quasi-mystical experiences characterized by sudden feelings of intense well-being, a heightened sense of control over the body

Literal immortality A culturally shared belief that there is some form of life after death for those who are worthy.

Symbolic immortality A culturally shared belief that, by being part of something greater and more enduring than our individual selves, some part of us will live on after we die.

One way to feel immortal is to have children, because your genes as well as your lasting influence will live on in them for future generations. Jim Bob and Michelle Duggar have 19 kids.

[Doug Meszler/Splash News/Newscom]

According to Abraham Maslow, peak experiences can allow us to transcend our mortal selves.

[Blend Images/Masterfile]

and emotions, and a wider sense of awareness that fills the individual with a timeless (no time = no death!) sense of wonder and awe. Experiential transcendence is often aided by altered states of consciousness and found in combination with one of the other modes of transcendence, such as a grandpa down on the floor playing with a grandchild, a musician lost in her performance, or a hiker communing with nature at the summit of Pike's Peak.

These various forms of immortality are found in all cultures. The fact that these elements of culture are universal suggests that they reflect a basic human desire to minimize the terror of mortality by feeling transcendent over death. The fact that cultures vary so much in how they explain the origins of life; their institutions, symbols, and rituals; what makes for a good and valuable life; and what happens after death is a testament to human creativity. It shows that, although probably not just any set of beliefs and values will do, there are many ways to fulfill this desire.

The Essential Role of Social Validation

TMT proposes that people protect themselves from the uniquely human fear of death by immersing themselves in the world of symbols and ideas provided by their culture. This might seem a rather flimsy defense against the biological reality of death. In a sense, it *is* flimsy. But people work very hard to sustain unwavering faith in the absolute validity of their cultural worldview and their sense of self-worth within it to defend against that reality.

Confidence in the absolute correctness of our own beliefs and values, and of our own value, is bolstered primarily through *social consensus* and *social validation*. The idea that people rely on others to help them verify the validity of their own perceptions and beliefs has a long history in social psychology that we briefly touched on in chapter 1. According to Festinger's *social comparison theory* (1954), people constantly compare themselves, their performance, and their attitudes with those of others around them. When other people share the same beliefs or values, it implies that those beliefs and values are correct; when other people hold different beliefs and values, it raises the possibility that someone is mistaken. When cultures collide, worldviews are threatened.

The Threat of Other Cultures: A Root Cause of Prejudice

As we have seen, cultures vary greatly in their beliefs about human origins, bases of self-esteem, and beliefs about spirituality and transcending death. Therefore, learning about another culture, especially one with very different versions of these beliefs, suggests that perhaps our views, even though socially validated within our culture, may not be absolutely true. People must therefore minimize this threat to their cultural worldview posed by alternative cultural worldviews. From a TMT perspective, the efforts to do so play a central role in prejudice and intergroup conflict. This idea was a primary focus of early research to test hypotheses derived from TMT.

Empirical Tests of TMT

Research to assess TMT has focused primarily on cultural worldviews and self-esteem. Here we will focus on the cultural worldview-related research; we will cover self-esteem research later, in chapter 6. One basic hypothesis derived from TMT was: *If cultural worldviews function to alleviate anxiety associated with the awareness of death, then reminding people of their mortality* (mortality salience) *should increase their need for the protection provided by such beliefs.* The strategy for testing this hypothesis was to get people to think about their own death, and then make judgments about others who either violate or uphold important aspects of their cultural worldviews. If cultural worldviews really do function to protect the person from

Mortality salience The state of being reminded of one's mortality.

concerns about mortality, thinking about death should make people especially prone to derogate those who violate important cultural ideals and to venerate those who uphold them; a general tendency called worldview defense.

Punishing Villains and Rewarding Heroes

In the initial test of the mortality salience hypothesis (Rosenblatt et al., 1989), municipal court judges were told they were participating in a study examining the relationship among personality traits, attitudes, and bond decisions. (A bond is a sum of money that a defendant must pay after arrest to be released from prison prior to the trial date.) Embedded in the questionnaire packets for half of the judges, who were chosen by random assignment, was a "new personality assessment" that asked for short responses to the following questions: "*Please briefly describe the emotions that the thought of your own death arouses in you,*" and "*Jot down, as specifically as you can, what you think will happen to you as you physically die and once you are physically dead.*" The other judges were the control group and did not receive this questionnaire.

All of the judges were then presented with a hypothetical legal case brief that provided information about the defendant, who was charged with prostitution, and the circumstances of her arrest. The information was followed by a form asking the judges to set bond for the defendant. Because prostitution violates a moral stance in the judges' worldviews, the hypothesis was that reminders of mortality would motivate the judges to uphold their worldview by being especially punitive toward the prostitute, in the form of setting an especially high bond. As shown in **FIGURE 2.11**, the results supported this hypothesis. This is a shockingly large difference, given that all judges reviewed exactly the same materials, except for the presence or absence of the mortality reminder.

Many follow-up studies have corroborated this initial finding and have furthermore shown that the effects depend on the individual's version of the cultural worldview. For example, if people are not morally opposed to prostitution, then a prostitute does not threaten their worldview. As a result, thoughts of death do not affect the way such people judge prostitutes. It is also important to note that heightened awareness of mortality does not lead only to negativity toward those who violate one's worldview. It also leads to more positive responses toward those who uphold important cultural values. For example, reminders of death led to larger recommendations of monetary reward to a hypothetical person who behaved heroically by risking personal injury to report a suspected mugger to the police (Rosenblatt et al., 1989).

The Safety of a National Identity

Research has also examined how thoughts of death affect reactions to people and ideas that more directly support or challenge one's worldview. For example, when reminded of death (vs. a control topic), American participants gave especially positive evaluations to essays and authors that praised America and especially negative evaluations to those that were critical of America. Presumably, being reminded of death increased participants' need for faith in their American worldview and as a result, they were especially attracted to people who helped them view their nation in a positive light and especially repulsed by those whose comments conflicted with such a rosy view. Studies conducted in other countries similarly show that mortality salience intensifies nationalistic bias. For example, Germans interviewed at a cemetery expressed a greater preference for German culture over other European cultures in terms of features such as travel destinations, cars, and cuisine compared with those interviewed away from a cemetery (Jonas et al., 2005). And after a reminder of mortality, people are especially reluctant to treat cultural symbols such as flags and crosses inappropriately (Greenberg et al., 1995).

Worldview defense The tendency to derogate those who violate important cultural ideals and to venerate those who uphold them.

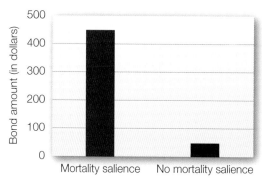

FIGURE 2.11

Worldview Defense after Mortality Reminders

According to terror management theory, cultural worldviews protect people against mortality fears. Consequently, people primed to think about their deaths—that is, in a state of mortality salience—adhere more closely to their cultural worldview. In this study, after being reminded of death, judges imposed more punitive judgments on a prostitute, because prostitution violates the cultural worldview's standards for good and bad behavior.

[Data source: Rosenblatt et al. (1989)]

The Protective Shield of Cultural Beliefs

The studies on villains and heroes, national identities, and cultural symbols show-case just a few of the ways that reminders of mortality influence people's judgment and behavior. When particularly aware of their mortality, people cling more tena-ciously to that which supports their cultural worldview. This provides protection from thoughts of death. So what might happen when these cultural beliefs are com-promised or one's faith in their validity is undermined? If you've been following the logic of TMT, you might suspect that when cultural beliefs are undermined—when the existential shield is weakened—thoughts of death would leak through into a per-son's conscious mind. This is known as the *death thought accessibility hypothesis*: Threats to people's terror management resources increase how accessible thoughts of death are to consciousness.

Many studies have supported this idea (Hayes et al., 2010). The typical study has an individual read a criticism of her worldview and then asks her to complete a series of word stems such as coff_ _. Reading a criticism of their worldview makes it more likely that people will complete such word stems with "coffin" instead of the more common "coffee." The more death-related word stems a person completes, the higher death thought accessibility is. Whereas worldview threat increases death thought accessibility, bolstering one's worldview reduces it.

Consider one particularly chilling example of this process (Hayes et al., 2008). When Christian participants read about how Muslims are gaining dominance in Nazareth, the childhood home of Jesus Christ, thoughts of death became more accessible. But when participants were later exposed to a news story describing how a plane full of Muslims had crashed and all aboard had died, thoughts of mortality were no longer close to awareness (Hayes et al., 2008). This study thus illustrates not only how threats to one's culture can "unleash the beast of mortality awareness," but that this beast can be recaged through the annihilation of the worldview threat.

Is Death the Factor Responsible for These Findings?

Such findings are also important because they help to highlight the direct connection between awareness of death and cultural beliefs. Not only do reminders of death increase investment in culture, but threatening that culture increases awareness of death. Of course, death is not the only psychological threat that leads, for example, to more extreme reactions to those who are different. Other threats can and indeed do produce important psychological responses. We have touched on some of these already, such as the threat of uncertainty (Hogg, 2007), and we will discuss others in later chapters. At the same time, thoughts of death do produce unique effects in hu-man judgments and decisions that are not produced by other unpleasant, uncertain, or anxiety-provoking events (Burke et al., 2010). The overall body of evidence pro-vides strong support for the idea that faith in cultural worldviews assuages people's concerns specifically about their own mortality.

Culture as a Synthesis of Human-Created Adaptations

Table 2.3 lists the three human environments we have discussed and summarizes how culture helps people to adapt to each of them. However, it is important to recognize that each of these domains of cultural adaptation simultaneously influences, and is influenced by, adaptations to the other two domains.

For example, the demands of the *physical environment*, such as how specific groups extract a living from it, greatly influence a culture's *social environment*, such as roles and norms. Hunting cultures are generally more individualistic, because hunting is a relatively individual activity. In contrast, agricultural cultures are generally collectivis-tic because large-scale agriculture requires more coordinated actions of larger groups of individuals. The *metaphysical environment* also affects adaptation to the physical environment. Consider that the earliest tools often contain an aesthetic dimension (e.g., ornamental marks on hand axes) that may have lent prestige to the tool maker or owner and enhanced the tool with ritual significance and coincident supernatural power (Kingdon, 1993).

To appreciate more fully how a synthesis of adaptations to the physical, social, and metaphysical environments determines the character of a culture, let's look at culture's influence on people's thinking styles.

The physical, social, and metaphysical worlds interact to influence some basic aspects of thinking. The most widely studied broad cultural difference in style of thinking about the world concerns East Asian versus Western cultures. In his book *Geography of Thought: How Asians and Westerners Think Differently—and Why*, R. E. Nisbett (2003) makes a strong case for the idea that the East Asian collectivism and European/ American individualism are rooted in

Table 2.3 **Cultural Adaptation**

Environments	Human Adaptations
The Physical Environment: How do people in groups manage the physical environments in which they live?	Technology (skills and tools).
The Social Environment: How do people in large groups of (mostly) strangers get along with each other?	Shared beliefs systems (e.g., norms, roles, and interaction customs) that reduce uncertainty about the self and one's actions; orient the self toward relationships with others; and establish and maintain social order.
The Metaphysical Environment: How do people in groups manage the awareness of threatening realities inherent to our existence, most notably the fact that it ends in death?	Faith in a meaning-providing cultural worldview, combined with a feeling of self-esteem, ensures psychological equanimity in the face of death.

an even more fundamental cultural difference in the way members of these respective cultures tend to think. Specifically, East Asians tend to think holistically, attending to balance, context, and the complex relations among things, whereas Westerners tend to think analytically, focusing on stable categories, classification, and logical, linear relationships.

Nisbett argues that these differences reflect very different metaphysical traditions of philosophical thought that emerged in ancient China, a great influence in the Far East, and ancient Greece, a central influence on Western culture. Ancient China was a relatively ethnically homogeneous, large culture that gave rise to the philosophies of Taoism and Confucianism, which in turn led to a focus on the yin and yang, multiple sides to truth and life, balance, social cohesion and obligation, and harmony with nature. This Chinese tradition encouraged social practices that promoted holistic thinking, which focuses on overall context and relations among contiguous elements. This type of thinking then reinforced a collectivistic worldview and its associated social practices, as we discussed earlier in this chapter.

Ancient Greece, in contrast, was composed of small, contentious city-states with easy access to the sea in a region of the world where travel and exposure to people of many widely varying cultures was prevalent. In this physical and social environment, a tradition of thought promoted by Aristotle and other philosophers developed. This ancient Greek tradition encouraged social practices that promoted analytic thinking, which focuses on classification of discrete objects and their properties, logic, debate, and individuality. This type of thinking, in turn, reinforced an individualistic worldview and its associated social practices.

Although Nisbett's historical analyses of the genesis of East–West differences is plausible and thought provoking, it cannot be proven definitively. However, a substantial set of research findings do provide clear support for the idea that East Asians are more holistic in their thinking and Westerners are more analytic. For example, one aspect of the holistic versus analytic distinction is a focus on relationships as contrasted with categories. Chinese and American students were presented with sets of three words such as *panda*, *monkey*, and *banana* and asked which two are most closely related (Ji et al., 2004). The Americans generally chose category-based pairs such as panda and monkey (animal), whereas the Chinese students generally chose relationship-based pairs such as monkey and banana; (monkeys eat bananas).

One more example might help to illustrate further the cultural difference between holistic and analytical thinking. Holistic thinking involves seeing multiple sides to an issue and sustaining contradictions, known as dialectical thinking, whereas analytic thinking involves choosing one view over another. To assess this difference, Chinese and American graduate students were asked to read and analyze stories about conflicts between people (Peng & Nisbett, 1999). The Chinese students tended to attribute the cause of the conflict to both individuals and emphasize the need for compromise—a holistic, dialectical approach. The American students, in contrast, tended to take the side of one person or the other—a linear, analytic approach.

SECTION review | How Culture Helps Us Adapt

Culture simultaneously helps people adapt to the physical, social, and metaphysical environment in which they live.

Culture and the Physical Environment

- Human adaptation to the natural environment was facilitated by technological innovations and group living, which encouraged more flexible means of solving problems. In a given culture, adaptation to the physical environment takes particular forms, depending on the challenges of local environments and the unique needs and values of the groups that occupy them.

Culture and the Social Environment

People in every culture must adapt to their social environment in terms of:
- Uncertainty about what one can and should do.
- Orienting the self toward one's relationships and personal goals.

Cultures differ in how they solve these problems.
- Cultures provide clearly defined roles and norms.
- Collectivistic cultures emphasize cooperation and group welfare. Individualistic cultures emphasize values such as individual achievement. This distinction has implications for how people conceptualize themselves, experience and display emotions, and form attitudes about outgroup members.

Modernization has a range of consequences that determine which values are most important to members of a culture.

Culture and the Metaphysical Environment

- Cultural worldviews help people understand why they are alive, what they should be doing while they are alive, and what will happen to them once they are dead.
- Both faith in the cultural worldview and the maintenance of self-esteem manage the potential for anxiety stemming from the awareness of mortality. Because these are symbolic constructs, maintaining faith in them depends primarily on social consensus and validation. As a result, people defend them vehemently when threatened by others who challenge their views.
- Tests of terror management theory support the hypothesis that reminding people of their mortality increases protection of their worldviews, and that undermining the worldview increases thoughts about death.

Culture as a Synthesis of Human-Created Adaptations

Humans adapt to each of the three environments simultaneously because each is heavily influenced by adaptations in the other two domains.
- Cultures can be defined as either holistic or analytical on the basis of different metaphysical traditions.
- Many aspects of a given culture reflect its adaptation to all three environments.

Culture in the Round: Central Issues

There is no domain of human thought or activity that is not influenced by a culture's particular rich synthesis of adaptation to the physical, social, and metaphysical world. To conclude this chapter, we consider some important, broad questions about culture.

Does Culture Illuminate or Obscure Reality?

Culture is a uniquely human form of adaptation. Some theorists (Harris, 1979/2010) view it as a body of knowledge that developed to provide *accurate* information to people that helps them adjust to the many demands of life, whether that means obtaining food and shelter, defending against rival outgroups, and so on. Culture also tells us how groups of people work together to achieve mutually beneficial goals, and how to live our lives so that others will like and accept us—and maybe even fall in love with us. So if adaptation to physical and social environments were all that cultures were designed to facilitate, perhaps cultures would always strive toward an accurate understanding of the world.

However, adaptation to the metaphysical environment suggests that people do not live by truth and accuracy alone. Sometimes it is more adaptive for cultural worldviews to distort the truth about life and our role in it. Some things about life are too emotionally devastating to face head on, such as the inevitability of death. Because overwhelming fear can get in the way of many types of adaptive action, it sometimes is adaptive for cultures to provide "rose-colored glasses" with which to understand reality and our place in it. From the existential perspective, the adaptive utility of accurate worldviews is tempered by the adaptive value of anxiety-buffering illusions. As you will see throughout this textbook, compromise between accurate and pleasing perceptions of ourselves and the world pervades many aspects of everyday social life.

Cultural traumas Tragic historical examples of cultural disruptions, some of which have led to complete cultural disintegration.

Is Culture a Good or Bad Thing?

Culture is a necessary part of being human. Building on generations of accumulated wisdom and innovation culled from many cultural influences, our own culture helps us enjoy our lives, answer our toughest questions, and keep our deepest fears at bay. It provides tried and true forms of cuisine, entertainment, and technology. It gives us ways to feel connected, protected, and valuable. A human lacking or stripped of culture would be psychologically (and probably physically) naked, fearful, hard pressed to survive, and barely recognizable as a member of our species.

Cultures other than one's own are important as well, because through cultural diffusion, cultures share innovations that mutually enhance people's lives, offering them novel cuisines, technologies, music, and art. Imagine if you visited Oslo, Prague, Rio, or Beijing and all you found was strip malls full of the same fast-food restaurants and big-box stores you have in your hometown!

Although we can't go about stripping an individual of his or her culture in a laboratory experiment to assess these functions of culture directly, anthropologists and psychologists have detailed many tragic historical examples of cultural disruptions, some of which have led to complete cultural disintegration. The documented effects of these cultural traumas seem to provide clear evidence of the psychological importance of culture.

A dramatic and sudden example of cultural trauma befell the inhabitants of Bikini Island in the South Pacific. The Bikinians were removed from the island by the U.S. government, which used the island to conduct 67 nuclear tests between 1945 and 1958 (**FIGURE 2.12**). The result was severe demoralization and stress among the Bikinian people, problems with which their descendants are still coping today. In a similar finding, research on children displaced by war or natural disaster consistently

Figure 2.12

Cultural Trauma

Culture makes us human, providing us with a basis for making meaningful sense of our lives and feeling valuable. Forcibly stripping a group of their cultural heritage—as in, for example, the forcible removal of the people living on Bikini Island for the purpose of conducting nuclear testing—has had severe negative consequences for the Bikinians' psychological functioning and health.

[Associated Press]

shows that those children whose cultural base has been disrupted by traumatic events are likely to develop posttraumatic stress disorder, whereas those who retain a strong cultural base cope much better (Beauvais, 2000).

Over the course of history, cultural traumas have been experienced by indigenous tribal cultures throughout the world, as their ways of life and belief systems have been abruptly or gradually altered, and sometimes completely undermined, by intrusions from more technologically advanced cultures. The best-documented cases of these cultural traumas were set in motion by European explorers, missionaries, traders, and armies. The cross-cultural counseling psychologist Mike Salzman (Salzman & Halloran, 2004) has argued that the long-term consequences of such traumas have been remarkably similar around the globe, even though the victimized groups were often genetically, geographically, and culturally quite different. Many of the descendants of these traumatized cultures, largely stripped of their traditional ways and beliefs and not embraced by or able to embrace the dominant colonizer culture, have had difficulty sustaining a sense that they are valuable contributors to any meaningful world. Consequently, they suffer a high prevalence of debilitating anxiety, resulting in poverty, physical health problems, anxiety disorders, depression, and abuse of alcohol and other drugs. All of these unfortunate phenomena, taken together, make a strong case for the positive psychological value of an intact, functioning culture.

On the other hand, even cultures that are working well for their members have their negative side. Each culture limits the way its people think about themselves and the world and creates divides between its people and others within and outside the culture. We humans have great potential for freedom of thought and choice

Black Robe

Black Robe, directed by Bruce Beresford (Eberts et al., 1991) with the help of Native American consultants, is a fictionalized but realistic account of historical events. In the 1600s, Jesuit priests traveled from France to what is now Québec to help convert the Huron tribe to Christianity. Algonquin tribe members are given gifts such as metal tools in exchange for helping Father LaForgue and his assistant Daniel reach the Huron mission. The film emphasizes both the commonalities and the differences between the French and Algonquin cultures.

Early in the movie, we see the Algonquin chief, Chomina, and Samuel de Champlain, the leader of the French, getting dressed in garb that connotes their high status. Every culture uses clothes and ornaments for this purpose. Both the French and Algonquin play music and dance. They both ingest consciousness-altering substances, tobacco for the Algonquin, alcohol for the French. At first, La Forgue doesn't

realize that the Algonquin have a viable worldview of their own. As the film progresses, we see clearly that, consistent with terror management theory, each culture has a belief in an afterlife and the members of both strive for self-esteem. The Algonquin men try to maintain their value as warrior and hunters. As Chomina approaches death, he questions whether he has been a great enough warrior. La Forgue sees his mission as a heroic effort to bring the Huron from outer darkness to

[Samuel Goldwyn Company/Photofest]

because of our reduced reliance on instinctual patterns of behavior and our flexible intelligence. But culture imposes preferred beliefs, attitudes, values, norms, morals, customs, and rituals on us, often leading us to internalize these worldviews long before we have the cognitive or physical capabilities or independence to question them or develop and institute alternative ways of thinking and behaving. Indeed, Becker (1971) argued that each culture is like a shared neurosis, a particular, peculiar, and limited way of viewing the world and acting in it. Consequently, those outside the culture are likely to view the behavior of those within it as odd, if not outright crazy.

Culture affects how people treat those of lower status within the culture as well as those outside the culture. This has contributed greatly to social problems within cultures and egregious conflicts between cultures, often leading to the tragic cultural traumas we have already noted. This aspect of culture is what makes James Joyce's (1961, pp. 22–23) pronouncement that "History . . . is a nightmare from which I am trying to awake" so apt.

[Chris Hondros/Getty Images]

Think ABOUT

All these very real negatives notwithstanding, culture is with us and in us and always will be, at least in some form. As we proceed through this textbook, we will continually consider the specific ways cultures contribute both positively and negatively to human functioning.

We will leave it to you to ponder whether some cultures and aspects of culture provide a better ratio of benefits to costs than others.

---

qualification for the protection and salvation of Jesus. Daniel eventually betrays La Forgue so that he can be with Annuka, Chomina's daughter, with whom he has fallen in love. But when faced with the prospect of death at the hands of the Iroquois tribe, he shifts his loyalty back to Christianity, La Forgue, and his heroic quest.

We also see what seem, from outside each culture's respective worldview, very strange behaviors. La Forgue self-flagellates with a tree branch after he has lustful thoughts about Annuka. The Algonquin don't understand La Forgue's commitment to celibacy and wonder if he is some sort of demon. In order to decide what to do about La Forgue, Chomina travels out of his way to consult a dwarf covered in face paint who claims to be a shaman from the underworld. La Forgue sees this as one of numerous signs that the Algonquin are being controlled by the devil.

The cultures are different in two principal ways. First, the French culture is more individualistic, the Algonquin more collectivistic. The Algonquin share everything without question and have no sense of private property (communal sharing). They also obey Chomina and the other tribal elders (authority ranking). The French are oriented more toward market pricing,

wanting to trade tobacco for other things rather than sharing it. And there is more of a sense of equality matching between LaForgue and Daniel. Daniel has no problem disobeying La Forgue and at one point is willing to abandon him to be with Annuka and the Algonquin. Annuka has no thought of ever abandoning her tribe.

Second, French culture is more technologically advanced, an advantage that helped many European nations colonize indigenous tribal cultures. La Forgue eventually reaches the Huron mission and finds the Huron plagued by a deadly disease and desperate. He converts them and holds a large-scale baptism ceremony. In this way, the film depicts the process described by Salzman (2001) whereby Europeans, who had developed immunity to the germs they carried, infected indigenous tribes around the globe when they came into contact with them, leading to the death of up to half the local populations. These mass epidemics led the tribal peoples to question their own worldviews and often to convert to Christianity in the hope of gaining protection from further death. In the case of the Huron tribe depicted in the film, a few decades after converting to Christianity, they were wiped out by rival tribes.

Is There Just One Culture? Beyond a Monolithic View

For presentational purposes in this chapter, we have generally treated culture as a single, largely static entity. However, as we noted at the outset of this chapter, cultures actually are continually evolving. In addition, cultures are often very heterogeneous, consisting of many subcultures. It is important to recognize that members of such subcultures are profoundly influenced by both their subculture and its relationship to the dominant culture.

The tone of this chapter could be taken to suggest that because people are deeply embedded in their cultures, they are mere helpless pawns of their cultural upbringing. But clearly within cultures, people vary greatly in their traits, beliefs, values, preferences, and behaviors. So how much of the person is determined by his or her culture as opposed to universal or unique characteristics? Although there is no basis for putting a number on how much, one way to examine this issue is to consider research on immigrants, people who move from one culture to another. How much do they keep? How much do they change? How easily can they adapt to the norms and customs of a very different culture? Fortunately, there is a body of theory and research on acculturation—the process whereby individuals change in response to exposure to a new culture—that can help answer such questions.

Acculturation The process whereby individuals adapt their behavior in response to exposure to a new culture.

One of our wives has worked with the International Rescue Committee (IRC) to help refugees allowed into the United States to settle into life in America; she found this to be an incredibly eye-opening experience. In the last decade, many refugees have fled from Sudan, Somalia, and other parts of Africa, where civil war, ethnic cleansing, and genocide have killed many and left many more homeless. Traditional African tribal cultures are generally very collectivistic and technologically primitive, and polygamy, with associated limits on women's rights, is prevalent. For people from these regions, the shift to American culture is a radical one. When they arrive, many of these individuals don't know, for example, what a doorknob or a toilet is, or how they work. Many have never walked on a paved road.

Refugees from war-torn nations not only must cope with the stress of upheaval and loss but also must learn quickly to adapt to life in a new and unusual culture.

[Mary Elizabeth Greenberg]

Imagine the adjustment to American culture! One caseworker found a group of Somali women sitting in a modern American apartment in a circle on the kitchen floor, cleaning chicken together. This is very odd when seen through American eyes—why aren't they being hygienic and using the counter? But it's not so strange if we consider that they had never seen a kitchen counter before and didn't know what it was for—and more important, that preparing food in this way was a long-standing traditional communal activity in their culture. Yet, despite the radical cultural shift and the steep learning curve necessary to learn new ways, many African refugees have adapted quite successfully—a testament to the flexibility of human intelligence and the capacity to move beyond the limits of one particular cultural worldview.

Systematic research confirms that, although some level of *acculturative stress* is not uncommon, most immigrants succeed in growing accustomed to their new culture (Berry, 2006; Furnham & Bochner, 1986). Some people gradually shift almost entirely from their traditional culture to the beliefs and ways of the new culture, a process known as assimilation. As people assimilate, they not only embrace the new culture's ways of dressing, eating, and so on but also begin thinking in ways promoted by the new culture (Berry, 1997; Church, 1982; Kitayama & Markus, 2000).

Assimilation The process whereby people gradually shift almost entirely from their former culture to the beliefs and ways of the new culture.

Most immigrants retain aspects of their former culture while adapting to the new culture, a process known as integration. Immigrants who have achieved integration are referred to as *bicultural* because they identify with two cultures simultaneously. It is interesting to note that research on bicultural individuals suggests that they can think and act like members of either culture, depending on which culture's language

Integration The process whereby people retain aspects of their former culture while internalizing aspects of a new host culture.

they are using or which culture's symbols are prominent in their minds. Consider a study set in Hong Kong (Hong et al., 1997), a city of people primarily of Chinese descent and under Chinese control since 1997, but heavily influenced by Western culture because of 100 prior years of British rule. Researchers showed participants a cartoon of one fish swimming in front of a group of other fish. If shown pictures of a cowboy and Mickey Mouse first, they explained the lead fish's behavior in terms of the characteristics of the fish, much as Westerners typically do. However, if first shown pictures of a Chinese dragon and temple, they explained the fish's behavior in terms of the situation the fish was in, as Easterners typically do. This phenomenon further attests to the ability of people to transcend the perspective of one particular cultural worldview and shift to another when exposed to that worldview as well.

Whether individuals with a background in one culture but living in another ends up assimilating, integrating, or becoming marginalized depends in part on their own choices, the strength of their initial cultural identification, and the compatibility of the two cultures. But it also depends on the attitude of the current culture toward immigrants and those with sub-cultural identifications (Berry, 2001). Some cultures promote a melting pot viewpoint that assumes that all people will converge toward the mainstream culture; this orientation more or less forcefully encourages assimilation. Other cultures value cultural diversity and promote multiculturalism, or cultural pluralism, encouraging integration (Allport, 1954).

In historical terms, American culture could be characterized as having generally had a melting pot orientation with regard to European immigrants, while simultaneously having a discriminatory orientation, fostering marginalization, with regard to African Americans, Native Americans, and Hispanic Americans. Currently, the cultural diversity movement, which primarily targets societal orientations toward blacks, Native Americans, and Hispanics, is attempting to move American culture toward a multicultural orientation. If it succeeds, it may eventually help shift members of these groups from marginalization to integration (Moghaddam, 1988).

Melting pot An ideological view holding that diverse peoples within a society should converge toward the mainstream culture.

Multiculturalism (cultural pluralism) An ideological view holding that cultural diversity is valued and that diverse peoples within a society should retain aspects of their traditional culture while adapting to the host culture.

SECTION review | Culture in the Round: Central Issues

Social psychologists consider broad issues about culture.			
Cultures strike a balance between human needs for accurate information and for comforting beliefs that often obscure reality.	Culture serves many vital functions that promote happiness and well-being. Culture also contributes to a variety of social ills in creating divides between people within and outside a culture. Theory and research on cultural traumas reveal the psychological harm that results when one's culture has disintegrated.	Culture is not a single, blanket entity but contains important subcultural differences and influences.	People coming to a new culture can struggle, but they can assimilate to and integrate aspects of the new culture.

CONNECT ONLINE:

Check out our videos and additional resources located at:
www.macmillanhighered.com/launchpad/greenberg1e

The Core Elements of Social Cognition

Think back to your first kiss. You probably remember who you were with and how you felt. But do you remember the day of the week or what you were wearing? Most people would like to think that their memories are like snapshots of the past (maybe with a little Instagram filtering to give them a warm glow), yet recollections of even distinctive events lack a lot of detail. Moreover, people often remember events in ways that differ from how they actually occurred.

Like memory, ordinary sensory perception captures only a thin slice of the objective world. For example, the human eye sees only a portion of the electromagnetic spectrum, whereas bees and other insects can detect ultraviolet light. Everyday perception is also riddled with inaccuracies, some persistent. As just one example, it seems perfectly obvious to see the sun as "rising" and "setting" as it traverses the sky, yet we know that the sun remains stationary while the earth revolves around it. Our window into reality is not only small, it's dirty.

Most of us normally take it for granted that our understanding of the world is a straightforward reflection of reality as it exists outside of us. We assume—if we reflect on the source of our knowledge at all—that we take in sensations from our environment and add them to a big pile of knowledge in our head. The whole (that is, understanding) is the sum of its parts (impressions of stimuli). But as the examples above suggest, this conventional wisdom breaks down on closer inspection.

Figure 3.1

Figure and Ground

Do you see a vase or two faces? The mind plays an active part in how we construct reality.

In the mid-20th century, psychologists in the *Gestalt* school, such as Kurt Koffka and Max Wertheimer, proposed that people *construct* an understanding of reality. Just as builders construct a house not by simply piling bricks together but by arranging them in orderly ways, the mind actively selects which pieces of information it takes in and organizes those pieces into a network of knowledge. Gestalt psychologists devised a number of visual perception exercises to demonstrate the different ways that the mind actively constructs meaning. One of the most popular and compelling of these exercises is depicted in **FIGURE 3.1**.

After thinking about that first kiss, you might see the image in Figure 3.1 as two faces looking at each other. Look again, and you'll notice that the same image can be seen as a dark vase against a white background. When most people stare at this image, these two interpretations pop back and forth in their mind's eye. The fact that the *same* physical stimulus can be viewed in more than one way shows that the perceiver has an active role in what is perceived. The whole is *more* than the sum of its parts.

The insights of the Gestalt school had a monumental influence on social psychology. If the mind constructs an understanding of even simple stimuli like the image in Figure 3.1, then certainly it must take an active role in shaping how a person makes sense of the people, ideas, and events that he or she encounters in everyday life. But how? What are the specific mental processes through which we construct a meaningful understanding of the social world? The research area known as *social cognition* emerged in the 1970s with the goal of answering this question. Its penetrating discoveries are at the heart of the social cognitive perspective and also the topic of this and the next chapter.

The "Why" of Social Cognition: The Motives Behind Thinking

When you gaze at the image in Figure 3.1, what is your visual system doing? In essence, it is making a choice between which of two visually meaningful interpretations it prefers. In a similar way, our everyday thinking about the social world is largely a matter of choices, many of which are made without our conscious awareness. The difference is that, in our social life, the choices are much more challenging and the consequences are often more important.

> Sidney likes action movies, but doesn't like them to be too gory or violent. She has a bit of an anticorporate vibe, so maybe she'd prefer an independent film. She spent last semester in France, so maybe even something subtitled. But I don't really want to have to read the whole time; it's more fun to be able to talk during the movie. And something funny—it should be funny, not sad. There's that newish movie that is supposed to be Tom Cruise's comeback film. Oh, but Sidney hates Tom Cruise. But maybe it would be fun to make fun of the movie the whole time. Wait, *Sharknado* would be perfect for that! Oh, but that might be too gory...

Figure 3.2

Information Overload

Even simple decisions, such as which movie to watch, require an ability to sort through and reason about a complex web of information.

[Konstantin Sutyagin/Shutterstock]

A major challenge that we all face in making sense of the social world is the sheer *quantity* of information that is available at any given moment. To illustrate, imagine that a friend is coming over soon to watch a movie, and she's asked you to go on Netflix and find a "good one." Yikes. Now you're scanning through hundreds of movie titles, most of which you've never heard of. You could learn about each one if you read the plot summary and dozens of customer reviews. You might also want to consider your friend's tastes in movies, the nature of your relationship with this person, how long the movie is and what else you'd like to do tonight, and so on. If you were to weigh all of the relevant pieces of information, you would be so immersed in thought that you would die of starvation before you selected a movie (**FIGURE 3.2**).

What's important in this example is not the choice of a movie per se, but something more fundamental: the choice of when to stop thinking and reach a conclusion that feels certain . . . or certain *enough*. We make this same basic choice every moment that we navigate our social world. Whether we are forming an impression of a stranger or figuring out how we feel about a political issue, there is always more information that we *could* consider, but eventually we have to reach a conclusion and move on. According to Arie Kruglanski's *theory of lay epistemology* (1989, 2004), three motives influence this choice:

The Need for Accurate Knowledge: This refers to a motivation to achieve an accurate, truthful understanding of a given person, idea, or event. For example, if an employer is looking over a job application, she might be motivated to know for sure whether an applicant is qualified for a job, and so she will invest a lot of time and energy in thinking about the applicant's résumé. The motive to be accurate may even drive her to stay extra hours at work to gather additional information about the applicant. Most of us would like to believe that if any force is driving the way we think, it is the motivation to be rational and accurate—to strive for the truth rather than folly. But thinking carefully takes time and energy, resources that are in short supply. Further, we often want to reach a particular conclusion. Thus, people are also motivated toward nonspecific and specific forms of closure.

The Need for Nonspecific Closure: We reach *closure* when we stop the thought process and grab the first handy judgment or decision, quickly and without extensive effort. By *nonspecific*, we mean that the person does not have a strong preference for one conclusion over another; rather, she desires *a* conclusion—*any* conclusion. Why? Because feeling uncertain, confused, or ambivalent can at times feel unpleasant and even frightening. Choosing *a* movie in the end might be more important than choosing *the best* movie.

The Need for Specific Closure: This is the motive to reach a conclusion that fits well with the specific beliefs and attitudes that one already prefers. Often these are beliefs and attitudes that enable us to see the world as meaningful and ourselves as valuable. If you held the attitude that *The Hangover: Part II* is the greatest movie of all time, and you read just one customer review praising the movie, chances are you'll halt the thinking process right there and confidently declare, "Yup, just as I thought: it's a great movie." In contrast, if you hated that movie and read the same review, you would be more likely to continue reading reviews until you found one that affirms your belief that it stinks.

Which of these three motives influences how a person thinks? It depends on his or her situation at the time. The need for accuracy is often active when there is a risk that a false judgment or a poor decision would have negative consequences for the self or others. Returning to our movie choice example, if you were intent on impressing your friend with your fine taste in films, and you felt that a poor movie choice would embarrass you, you would think long and hard about the relevant information until you felt confident that you were making the right choice. Or, to take another example, if during a presidential election season, one candidate advocates aggressive military responses, whereas the other promises peace, you might be particularly motivated to gain an accurate impression of each candidate before voting, because you believe that going to war would affect you and the people you care about.

The need for nonspecific closure usually takes priority in situations where thinking involves a lot of effort or is otherwise unpleasant. If we feel that we are under time pressure to make a decision, if we have a lot of things on our mind, or if we are simply exhausted from a long day at work, we will be more inclined to terminate the thinking process early and reach closure on a "good enough" conclusion. The first recommended movie that pops up might be the one you choose to watch.

The need for specific closure comes into play when our prior beliefs and values are brought to mind, when those beliefs are central to our sense of meaning in life or personal worth, or perhaps especially when we feel that our beliefs are being challenged by contradictory information. For example, although the potential costs of going to war might activate the need for accurate knowledge, people's need for specific closure might nudge them to take military action because doing so aligns with their deeply held political views. This can lead them to dismiss strong evidence brought to light by a political opponent.

Which motive influences a person's thinking also depends on his or her personality traits. Some people have a high need for nonspecific closure, meaning that they seek and prefer simple and clear knowledge and feel especially uncomfortable when confronted with ambiguous or confusing situations (Thompson et al., 2001). By contrast, other people are more tolerant of complexity and ambiguity and are willing to gather more information and deliberate before arriving at a conclusion. In fact, they may view novelty, surprise, and uncertainty to be the very spice of life.

Keep these three motives in mind as you read the rest of this chapter—and indeed, this entire textbook—because you'll see how they influence social thought and behavior in various ways across a wide range of situations.

SECTION review | The "Why" of Social Cognition

WHY: Three basic motives influence thinking about the social world.

The need for accurate knowledge	The need for nonspecific closure	The need for specific closure
• A desire to achieve an accurate understanding. • Activated when being inaccurate could result in undesired outcomes.	• A desire for a simple, clear-cut understanding as opposed to confusion and ambiguity. • Activated when thinking is effortful or unpleasant (e.g., when under time pressure).	• A desire to understand something in a way that fits well with previously held beliefs and values. • Activated when prior beliefs and values are brought to mind, central to one's sense of meaning in life or personal worth, or threatened by contradictory information.

The "How" of Social Cognition: Two Ways to Think About the Social World

As we humans evolved, we developed neocortical structures in the brain that allow for high-level thought processes: consciousness, self-awareness, language, logic, and rationality. Yet we also have older brain structures, such as the limbic system, that we share with birds and reptiles. The result of having a hybrid brain is that social cognition is governed by two systems of thinking: a rational, and controlled way of thinking—the **cognitive system**; and an unconscious, intuitive, and automatic way of thinking—the **experiential system** (Epstein, 1994; Kahneman, 2011; Sloman, 1996). Depending on the individual and the circumstances, a person's thought and action can be produced primarily by one or the other system. The rise and fall of facilitated communication as a treatment for autism provides an example.

Cognitive system A conscious, rational, and controlled system of thinking.

Experiential system An unconscious, intuitive, and automatic system of thinking.

The Strange Case of Facilitated Communication

In the fall of 1991, Mark and Laura Storch were informed that their 14-year-old daughter, Jenny, had accused her father of repeated sexual abuse that her mother had ignored. Their daughter was promptly removed from their home while her parents spent the next 10 months fighting the charges, which turned out to be false (Berger, *New York Times*, February 1994). Her stunned parents were not only shocked by the specific allegations; they were also dumbfounded because their daughter was severely autistic and had little ability to communicate with others verbally! With no ability to share whatever thoughts she had, how had her teachers and aides tapped into Jenny's inner world? Jenny had apparently told of a history of abuse by using a technique known as facilitated communication, which allows individuals with severe forms of autism to spell out their internal thoughts with the help of an assistant. The assistant, called the facilitator, steadies the autistic person's arm to allow the individual to hunt and peck at letter keys. When first introduced in the United States in the early 1990s, facilitated communication seemed a revolutionary way to unlock the inner world of loved ones who could not otherwise communicate their thoughts.

Although it initially seemed to provide severely autistic children with a method for communicating with others, facilitated communication was eventually discredited after it was discovered that the adult facilitators were unconsciously shaping the messages that the children typed out.

[© Krista Kennell/Corbis]

Facilitated communication quickly aroused skepticism, however, as children such as Jenny began sharing horrific stories of sexual abuse (Gorman, 1999). When the scientific community investigated the technique, study after study suggested that the thoughts being typed out were not those of the autistic child, but rather were those of the facilitator. In one experiment, two autistic middle schoolers were shown pictures of common objects and asked to type out what they saw (Vázquez, 1994). The experimenter could not see the pictures on the cards, and in half the trials, the facilitator was also prevented from seeing the cards. But in the other half of trials, the facilitator could see what was shown to the child. When their facilitator knew what the card depicted, both children typed out correct answers on all 10 of the trials. However, when the picture was shown only to the children and not to their facilitator, one child was unable to identify any of the pictures correctly, and the other got only 2 out of 10 correct. On the basis of this kind of evidence, the American Psychological Association passed a resolution in 1994 denouncing the validity of facilitated communication.

The rise and fall of this controversial technique was fraught with heartache and dashed hopes. But it also illuminated something rather interesting about human psychology. In practically all of the cases where communicated messages were deemed written by the facilitator and not the child, the facilitators adamantly and fervently believed that they had not and could not have constructed the thoughts that had been typed out on paper. But the research clearly suggests that they had played an integral role. Although their conscious, cognitive system produced the belief that they were merely helping their pupil control his or her muscles, their unconscious, experiential system was likely guiding their pupil's finger toward each letter to spell out meaningful words, phrases, and ideas.

Dual Process Theories

The core idea that thinking is governed by two systems of thought that operate relatively independently of one another forms the basis for a number of theories that you'll encounter in this textbook. These theories are often referred to as dual process theories because they posit two ways of processing information. They have been developed to explain wide-ranging phenomena, from the attitudes we hold to the inferences we make about why other people act the way they do.

Dual process theories Theories that are used to explain a wide range of phenomena by positing two ways of processing information.

To appreciate the gist of these theories, let's analyze what you are doing right now. You made a conscious intention to read your social psych textbook, and you're following through with it, pushing distracting thoughts about other matters out of your mind. You are able to consciously think about the concepts and ideas that you're reading about, and perhaps you are going further to *elaborate* on that information—that is, think it over, critique it, and compare it with your prior knowledge and experience. In each case, you are using the cognitive system to consciously direct your attention, guide your behavior, and make deliberate decisions.

At the same time that your cognitive system is busy with rational thinking, your experiential system operates in the background, controlling your more automatic thoughts and behaviors. You might read a sentence about a lazy black dog yawning and lying down, and might find yourself yawning involuntarily, even though you don't feel the slightest bit tired. Or your favorite song might come on and, before you are consciously aware of it, you find yourself in a better mood. It is because these two systems can operate independently of each other that well-intentioned facilitators could guide their pupils' hands without being aware of doing so, but it's also why your unconscious mind can interpret your environment at the same time that your conscious focus is on your textbook.

The two systems have different ways of organizing information. The cognitive system uses a system of rules to fit ideas into logical patterns. Much as your intuitive understanding of English grammar tells you that something is wrong with the statement "Store Jane to the goes," your cognitive system uses a type of grammar to detect when ideas fit and don't fit. In this way, it can think critically, plan behavior, and make deliberate decisions. By contrast, the experiential system is guided by automatic associations among stimuli, concepts, and behaviors that have been repeatedly associated through our personal life history of learning. Because of the vast array of information in the world, our brains have evolved to learn from repetition. After repeatedly observing that dark clouds in the sky are often followed by rain, we automatically form an association between clouds and rain. The experiential system organizes these associations into an elaborate network of knowledge.

Heuristics Mental short cuts, or rules of thumb, that are used for making judgments and decisions.

Because the experiential system stores a large collection of well-learned associations, it can be used to make rapid, "good enough" judgments and decisions at times when using the cognitive system would be too slow and effortful (Epstein, 1990). These mental short cuts, or rules of thumb, are called heuristics. One simple heuristic that people utilize automatically is that "more is better."

Think ABOUT

[© 2014 Macmillan, photo by Cecilia Varas]

Imagine that you could win money by closing your eyes and picking a red marble from a jar filled with many colored marbles. Let's say you can choose to draw a marble from either a small jar with one red marble and nine marbles of other colors or from a large jar with 10 red marbles and 90 marbles of other colors. Which jar would you choose? Intuitively, it seems as if the chances are better with more possible winning marbles, even though statistically, and therefore rationally, this is not true: The chances of winning the money are equal for the two jars. Yet a large majority of people choose the large jar with 10 red marbles rather than the small jar with one (Kirkpatrick & Epstein, 1992).

The marble-choice scenario helps us to see the intuitive appeal of heuristics, but it raises an important question: Do heuristics influence judgment when the real-world stakes are high? The answer is "yes." For example, imagine that a deadly disease is threatening a small town of 600 people, and public health officials are considering two different treatment plans. If Treatment A is adopted, 200 lives will be saved. If Treatment B is adopted, there's a 1/3 probability that all 600 people will be saved, and a 2/3 probability that no one will be saved. Which would you choose?

If you are like most participants asked this question by the Nobel Prize winner Daniel Kahneman and his collaborator, Amos Tversky (Tversky & Kahneman, 1981), you would probably choose Treatment A. But now consider the following version of the same problem: If Treatment A is adopted, 400 people will die. If Treatment B is adopted, there is a 1/3 probability that nobody will die and a 2/3 probability that all 600 people will die. Would you now prefer Treatment B? If you take a close look at these two framings of the issue, they are statistically identical choices. But people's preferences change dramatically when they are cued to think about what would be lost compared with what might be gained. When the question is framed the second way, in terms of lives lost, the vast majority of people prefer to take the chance with Treatment B where there is some chance of avoiding any loss of life. Our experiential minds are more readily swayed by thinking about what we might lose than by thinking about what we might gain. It takes a much closer and more rational consideration of the odds to realize that these choices are the same.

APPLICATION

Two Routes to Engaging in Risky Health Behavior

Dual process theories have enabled us to understand a number of important decisions that people make, including those that affect their physical health. The decision, for example, to engage in risky behavior such as smoking or unprotected sex can be influenced by our conscious intentions ("No way would I have unprotected sex!"), but unfortunately, in the heat of the moment, these conscious intentions can fall by the wayside. Rather, it is often people's experientially derived *willingness* to engage in risky behavior that better predicts whether they will do so (Gerrard et al., 2008). These experiential feelings of willingness are strongly influenced by the images and associations that people have developed for a given behavior. For example, if adolescents' experiential system associates smokers with a cool rebel image, they are more willing to try smoking should the opportunity arise, even if they consciously report having little intention of lighting up (Gerrard et al., 2005).

If an adolescent's experiential system associates smoking as something that is cool, they are more likely to try it even if they are consciously aware of the dangers.
[© Bubbles Photolibrary/Alamy]

Implicit and Explicit Attitudes

Attitudes are emotional reactions to people, objects, and ideas. If we have two systems for thinking, does that mean we have two ways of evaluating something as good or bad? The answer is "yes" according to dual process theories of attitudes (Gawronski & Bodenhausen, 2006; Nosek, 2007). According to these theories, implicit attitudes are based on automatic associations that make up the experiential system. Some automatic associations can be passed on genetically through evolution (such as an automatic fear response to snakes; Öhman & Mineka, 2003), but most are learned from our culture (such as a negative attitude toward eating pork or fried ants). By contrast, explicit attitudes are often reported consciously through the cognitive system.

Because we have no direct conscious access to our experiential system, measuring people's implicit attitudes requires a bit of cleverness. One popular task developed by Tony Greenwald and colleagues is the *implicit association test* (Greenwald et al., 1998). We'll be describing this task in more detail in chapter 8, where we look more closely at how attitudes are formed and change. We'll also return to it in chapter 10 because the study of implicit attitudes has been extremely important in our understanding of prejudice. For now, the point to remember is that this task measures the degree to which a person mentally associates two concepts (e.g., "flowers"

Implicit attitudes Automatic associations based on previous learning through the experiential system.

Explicit attitudes Attitudes people are consciously aware of through the cognitive system.

and "pleasant"), essentially by measuring how quickly she or he can lump together examples of Concept 1 (rose, petunia, tulip) alongside examples of Concept 2 (happy, lucky, freedom). If you are like the average person (and not an entomologist), you'd probably be quicker to throw these flower and pleasant words in the same mental file folder than to group the same pleasant words with insect names such as *flea*, *locust*, and *maggot*. It's this difference in speed that tells us something about your implicit attitude toward flowers relative to insects, which may or may not be the same as what you would report explicitly on a questionnaire.

If the cognitive and experiential systems can both produce attitudes, and if these two systems operate independently of one another, does that mean that the same person can have different attitudes toward the same thing? The answer, again, is "yes." To illustrate, when volunteers in one study (Nosek, 2005) were asked whether they prefer dogs or cats, what they consciously *said*—that is, their explicit attitude—was that they prefer dogs. But their responses on a reaction-time measure revealed that, at an implicit level, they associated cats with *good* more than dogs with *good* (perhaps because cats seldom have a bad reputation as dangerous animals). People's explicit attitudes toward dogs and cats were correlated positively with their implicit attitudes, but only moderately so, suggesting that implicit and explicit attitudes can coexist at different levels of consciousness. Not only can they coexist, they can kick in under certain circumstances to influence how we act. Your explicit attitude might dictate which kind of pet you choose to adopt from the local humane society (a very conscious decision), but it's your implicit attitude that probably accounts for the automatic startle response you might have if you encounter a German Shepherd, rather than a tabby cat, in a dark alley.

As shown in **FIGURE 3.3**, some attitudes are pretty similar when assessed implicitly or explicitly (Nosek, 2007). For example, in a study on judging political parties, the correlation of about .75 suggests that people's reported party preferences on a questionnaire correlate quite strongly with their automatic evaluations of Republicans and Democrats. Other attitudes can be quite distinct, so the preference people *say* they have for family versus career might be only weakly correlated (about .30) with their implicit attitude for one over the other. Our implicit and explicit attitudes are more likely to align when we feel strongly about the issue in question, have given it a lot of thought, and feel comfortable expressing our attitudes (Nosek, 2007). On the other hand, when we are explicitly undecided about an issue, our implicit attitudes predict our later explicit preferences (Galdi et al., 2008). It seems that our experiential system is a bit of a backseat driver at times, whispering directions when our cognitive system is not sure which way to turn.

Automaticity and Controlled Processes

The example of the German Shepherd in the dark alley illustrates how the experiential system guides simple behaviors such as automatic reactions to the environment. But this system guides behavior in more sophisticated ways, as well. In particular, it can control the behaviors necessary to reach our goals. By building up mental associations through routine interactions with the physical and social environment, we can *automatize* certain behaviors, meaning that we can perform those behaviors without devoting much conscious attention to what we are doing. It is as though we were on autopilot. Think about how you can brush your teeth, drive home from work, or go through the grocery checkout lane without much thought. Such automatization of behaviors is highly adaptive, because it allows us to accomplish goals while saving our mental energy.

But what happens when we encounter a novel challenge that our automatized routine is not prepared to handle? Imagine that you are brushing your teeth with your electronic toothbrush, just as you've done every day for the past few years, and all of a sudden the toothbrush stops working. Your experiential system probably won't be able to handle this situation, because it does not have a set of well-learned

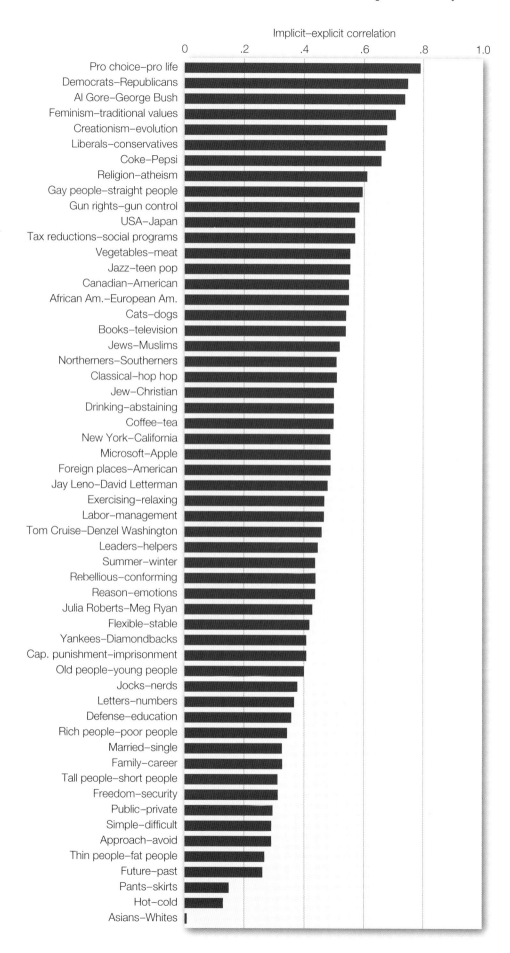

Implicit–explicit correlation

Pro choice–pro life	
Democrats–Republicans	
Al Gore–George Bush	
Feminism–traditional values	
Creationism–evolution	
Liberals–conservatives	
Coke–Pepsi	
Religion–atheism	
Gay people–straight people	
Gun rights–gun control	
USA–Japan	
Tax reductions–social programs	
Vegetables–meat	
Jazz–teen pop	
Canadian–American	
African Am.–European Am.	
Cats–dogs	
Books–television	
Jews–Muslims	
Northerners–Southerners	
Classical–hop hop	
Jew–Christian	
Drinking–abstaining	
Coffee–tea	
New York–California	
Microsoft–Apple	
Foreign places–American	
Jay Leno–David Letterman	
Exercising–relaxing	
Labor–management	
Tom Cruise–Denzel Washington	
Leaders–helpers	
Summer–winter	
Rebellious–conforming	
Reason–emotions	
Julia Roberts–Meg Ryan	
Flexible–stable	
Yankees–Diamondbacks	
Cap. punishment–imprisonment	
Old people–young people	
Jocks–nerds	
Letters–numbers	
Defense–education	
Rich people–poor people	
Married–single	
Family–career	
Tall people–short people	
Freedom–security	
Public–private	
Simple–difficult	
Approach–avoid	
Thin people–fat people	
Future–past	
Pants–skirts	
Hot–cold	
Asians–Whites	

Figure 3.3

Implicit and Explicit Attitudes

On some issues, such as those at the top of this graph, people's implicit and explicit attitudes are highly related; for other issues, the two types of attitudes are quite distinct.

[Data source: Nosek (2007)]

associations about toothbrush malfunction. Fortunately, the cognitive system is designed to override the experiential system in these situations, applying controlled processes of reasoning and decision making to solve unexpected problems and help you reach your goals. However, three conditions must be met in order for the cognitive system to successfully override the experiential system:

- We are *aware* that controlled processes are necessary either to get the job done or to counteract automatic processes that are not working as they should. For example, you consciously have to remind yourself to stop by the drugstore to pick up a new toothbrush battery because your automatic tendency will be to drive straight home.

- We are *motivated* to exert control over our thoughts and behaviors. You need to care enough about getting your toothbrush fixed to change your usual habit of driving home.

- We have the *ability* to consider our thoughts and actions at a more conscious level, because controlled processes require more mental effort. Sometimes we do not have enough cognitive resources to engage controlled ways of thinking. In these cases, the need for nonspecific closure kicks in, usually leading us to think and act in ways that are familiar and automatic. For example, after a long, exhausting day studying at the library, you may be more likely to fall back on unconscious routines and habits (such as driving straight home) rather than working toward new, consciously chosen goals (such as getting that new toothbrush battery) even if you're aware that you need to remind yourself and are motivated to do so.

By knowing that these three conditions must be in place for the cognitive system to operate, researchers have a powerful way of testing dual process theories in the laboratory. If the cognitive system's style of deliberate, effortful thinking requires awareness, motivation, and ability, then when people are put into situations where one or more of these conditions is missing, the cognitive system will lose its control over thinking and behavior. For example, if people are asked to memorize a long series of numbers, they lose the ability to focus attention on difficult decisions. In these situations, the experiential system will take over, because it can operate automatically without awareness, motivation, and ability; hence, people will tend to think and act more on the basis of automatic associations, heuristics, and gut-level attitudes. Throughout this book we will see how researchers have used this reasoning to test dual process theories of diverse phenomena.

The Smart Unconscious

Although it is tempting to view the conscious, rational cognitive system as the entire basis of human intelligence, and the experiential unconscious as more primitive, in actuality the unconscious is quite smart in at least five ways (**FIGURE 3.4**). For one, the basic motives that we said earlier guide social cognition—the needs for accurate knowledge, clear knowledge, and preferred knowledge—are largely unconscious. People rarely seem to be aware that these motivations are influencing their judgments and behavior. Second, during sleep, our cognitive system shuts down, but our

Figure 3.4

The Smart Unconscious

There are five ways the unconscious is smart.

Five ways the unconscious is smart

1. The motives that guide thinking often operate unconsciously
2. Memory consolidation occurs during sleep
3. Unconscious mind wandering can help generate creative ideas
4. Intuition can facilitate sound decisions
5. Unconscious emotional associations can promote beneficial decisions

unconscious stays busy *consolidating* memories—that is, organizing and solidifying what we've learned and experienced (Diekelmann & Born, 2010). Third, studies of ground-breaking artists and scientists indicate that after these individuals engage in extensive conscious deliberation on some problem or issue, an incubation period in which conscious attention is shifted to more mundane matters tends to precede moments of creative insight, which seem to just pop into consciousness out of nowhere, or more precisely, out of the unconscious (Cattell, 1971; Csikszentmihalyi, 1996; Wallas, 1926).

Fourth, intuition plays a critical role in good decision making. It was long believed that successful decision making relies on a conscious, systematic, and deliberative process of weighing costs and benefits. In choosing a college, you might have been encouraged to weigh the pros and cons of each school, scrupulously comparing features such as the availability of student aid and the student-to-faculty ratio. A sense of how a campus *feels* to you when you visit might seem irrelevant, and you might be encouraged to ignore it and focus instead on the facts. But research is beginning to show that unconscious, intuitive processes can steer us toward the best decisions in an automatic way. For example, our unconscious can intuitively sense when information is logically coherent, and it responds with a burst of positive affect (Topolinski & Strack, 2009; Winkielman & Cacioppo, 2001; Winkielman et al., 2007).

In many cases, though, we fail to listen to our unconscious feelings when forming attitudes and making decisions. One reason for this is that we often have difficulty verbalizing—that is, putting into words—why we like or dislike something. In chapter 1 (pp. 11–12) we described a study by Nisbett and Wilson (1977) that made this point by revealing the factors that influenced shoppers' stocking preferences without their conscious awareness. Because we have so little internal access to what actually determines our emotional reactions, when we are deciding things such as what fruit jam or poster we prefer or even how we feel about a relationship partner or a college, a conscious consideration of what we like or don't like will lead us to focus on factors that are easy to verbalize. And yet those factors may not reflect our feelings deep down.

In fact, when we think consciously about why we hold an attitude toward something, we often come up with a story that *sounds* reasonable but that does a poorer job than our gut feelings at predicting later behavior (Wilson et al., 1989). In one study (Wilson & Kraft, 1993), some participants were first asked to analyze the reasons that they felt the way they did about their current romantic relationship, and were then asked to rate their overall satisfaction with the relationship. Another group of participants did not do a reasoned analysis; they just rated their overall satisfaction on the basis of their gut feelings. You might think that the people led to analyze their reasons would figure out how they really felt about the relationship, so that their satisfaction ratings would predict whether their relationship stayed together or not. But the results revealed the exact opposite. It was the people asked to rate their satisfaction based on their gut feelings whose satisfaction ratings predicted whether they were still dating that partner several months later. As for the people asked to think hard about why they felt what they felt, their satisfaction ratings did not predict the outcome of their relationship.

A fifth way that the unconscious is smart is that our unconscious evaluations are essential for good judgment. According to Damasio's (2001) somatic marker hypothesis, there are certain somatic (i.e., bodily) changes that people experience as an emotion. These somatic changes become automatically associated with the positive or negative contexts for that emotion. When people encounter those contexts again, the somatic changes become a marker or a cue for what will happen next, helping to shape their decisions even without any conscious understanding of what they are doing. We can see this when we compare the decisions made by healthy adults with those made by adults who have suffered damage to areas of the brain responsible for social judgments, particularly the ventromedial sector of the prefrontal cortex.

Somatic marker hypothesis The idea that changes in the body, experienced as emotion, guide decision making.

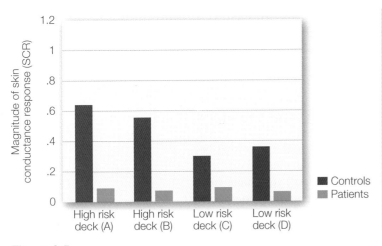

Figure 3.5

Somatic Markers of Risk

After playing a gambling game with both a high-risk and a low-risk deck of cards, most people (the controls) exhibit higher arousal just before selecting from the risky deck. Over time they learn to avoid these risky choices. Patients with ventromedial damage to the prefrontal cortex do not show this arousal and do not learn to avoid the risk.

[Data source: Bechara et al. (1996)]

Here's an example of a typical study. Participants are given a gambling task in which their choice of cards from four different decks can either win or lose them money. Two of the decks are risky; they can give big payouts, but choosing from them repeatedly over the course of the game is a losing strategy. The other two decks give more modest payouts, but the losses are milder as well, and a normal participant eventually learns to stick to these less risky options. Patients with ventromedial damage to the prefrontal cortex, however, don't learn to avoid the risky decks. Why do these people continue to make high-risk decisions that will lose them money in the end? Part of the reason is that they don't show any fear that their choices will have negative consequences. Bechara and colleagues (1996) assessed participants' skin conductance as a measure of arousal just before deciding which deck to choose from. Normal participants showed elevated arousal prior to each pick (**FIGURE 3.5**). They were anticipating that their choice could be a bad one, and as such, were more likely to learn from their mistakes. Ventromedial patients did not show evidence of this increased arousal, and without that somatic marker to warn them against the riskier decks, they chose from them over and over again as their money dwindled away!

We don't need to be consciously aware of how our brain is interpreting our emotional associations for those emotions to aid our decision making. In one study (Bechara et al., 1997), 30% of normal participants were unable to explain why they chose cards from one deck more or less than from another. They had no conscious understanding of the patterns that had shaped their decision making over the course of the task, yet they showed the same pattern of improved performance as the participants who had developed a clear hunch that two of the decks were riskier than the others.

APPLICATION

Can the Unconscious Help Us Make Better Health Decisions?

There is a big push in the health care field to assist patients in making more informed medical decisions. You or someone you know may have encountered some of these

Medical decision aids use a rational approach to guide people through medical treatment options, but some research suggests that the intuitive system can better integrate the role of emotion in decision making.

[© Sonda Dawes/The Image Works]

so-called decision aids like the one shown in the photo on the left. In addition to providing information about the disease and treatment options, they guide you through a series of rational and deliberate questions so that you can arrive at a more educated understanding of the choices you can make for your treatment. In short, they rely strongly on the conscious processing system.

But is conscious reasoning always the best way to make these decisions? Recent research suggests that perhaps even medical decisions can benefit from some input from the intuitive processing system (de Vries et al., 2013). One reason for this may be that the intuitive system is better able to integrate feelings and emotions that can play a key role in treatment adherence. Although the potential benefits of intuitive processing by no means suggest that we should avoid information or careful reasoning in health and other important decisions, it does highlight the possibility that complex decisions may best be made by integrating conscious and unconscious processes (Nordgren et al., 2011).

SECTION review | The "How" of Social Cognition

Social cognition is governed by two systems of thinking: a *cognitive system* that is conscious, rational, and controlled; and an *experiential system* that is unconscious, intuitive, and automatic.

The two ways of thinking influence attitudes and behavior

- Implicit attitudes are unconscious, automatic, and based on learned associations (often called *heuristics*). Conscious, explicit attitudes are relatively independent of implicit attitudes. Hence, the same person can hold opposing implicit and explicit attitudes toward the same thing.
- Routine behaviors can become automatic, but in novel situations, the cognitive system takes over to make deliberate, reasoned judgments and decisions.
- The cognitive system requires awareness, motivation, and ability. If these conditions are not met, the cognitive system is interrupted, whereas the experiential system is relatively unimpeded.

The unconscious can be smart

The unconscious does "smart" things such as consolidating memories and guiding decision making.

The "What" of Social Cognition: Schemas as the Cognitive Building Blocks of Knowledge

So far we've outlined the broad motives and systems that guide our thinking about the social world. Let's turn now to consider some of the more specific thought processes that people use to understand the world. The first thing to notice is how quickly and effortlessly the mind classifies stimuli into categories. Categories are like mental containers into which people place things that are similar to each other. Or, more precisely, even if two things are quite different from one another (two unique individuals, for instance), when people place them in the same category ("frat boys"), they think about those two items *as though* they were the same. This makes life easier.

Categories Mental "containers" in which people place things that are similar to each other.

To appreciate what categories can do, stop and look around your surroundings. What do you see? As for this author, I'm sitting at the dining room table in my house. I see my laptop in front of me and a stack of books nearby, along with my half-eaten lunch. There are pictures hanging on the walls, a plant in a corner of the room, and our pet dog near my feet (probably hoping for some of the lunch). Just within this 4-foot radius of my world, things are already pretty complex. I don't have the mental capacity to attend to and process every aspect of the environment, so I group stimuli together into broad categories. For example, although each of these books is unique, for now I lump them into the category *books*; in fact, for added convenience I can lump the books along with those pens and used tea bags under the broader category *things on my desk that I don't have to deal with at the moment*. If people didn't group things into categories of objects and ideas, they would be utterly and hopelessly overwhelmed by what William James called the "blooming, buzzing confusion" that they first experience as newborn infants before they develop categories (James, 1890, p. 462).

Think
ABOUT

[Dag Sundberg/ Getty Images]

Categorization is an interesting process in its own right, but it is just the starting point of our mind's active meaning making. That's because as soon as people classify

Schema A mental structure, stored in memory, that is based on prior knowledge.

a stimulus as an instance of a category, their minds quickly access knowledge about that category, including beliefs about the category's attributes, expectations about what members of that category are like, and plans for how to interact with it, if at all. All of this knowledge is stored in memory in a mental structure called a schema. For example, if you are at the library and you categorize a person behind the desk as a librarian, you instantly access a schema for the category *librarian* that contains beliefs about which traits are generally shared by members of that group (e.g., intelligence), theories about how librarians' traits relate to other aspects of the world (e.g., librarians probably do not enjoy extreme sports), and examples of other librarians you have known. Bringing to mind schemas allow the person to "go beyond the information given" (Bruner, 1957), elaborating on the information that strikes their senses with what they already know (or think they know). We can demonstrate this with a simple example. Read the following paragraph:

> The procedure is quite simple. First, you arrange things into different groups. Of course, one pile may be sufficient, depending on how much there is to do. If you have to go somewhere else due to lack of facilities, that is the next step; otherwise you are pretty well set. It is important not to overdo things. That is, it is better to do too few things at once than too many. At first the whole procedure will seem complicated. Soon, however, it will become just another facet of life (BRANSFORD & JOHNSON, 1973, P. 400).

You might be scratching your head right now, wondering what these instructions are referring to. If you close your textbook and five minutes later try to remember all of the points in the paragraph, you will probably run into difficulty. What if we tell you that the paragraph is about laundry? Now, reread the paragraph and you will see that the information makes much more sense to you than it did initially. After five minutes, you might do a reasonable job of remembering each of the steps described. The mere mention of the word *laundry* activated your schema of this process and made it a template for understanding the information you were reading.

Schemas are given special names depending on the type of knowledge that they represent. Schemas that represent knowledge about events are called scripts. These types of schemas (like the laundry example) always involve a temporal sequence, meaning that they describe how events unfold over time (first you sort, then you put one pile into the machine, then you add the soap, and so on). Scripts make coordinated action possible. Playing a game of tennis requires that both you and your partner have a schema of the game, so that you can coordinate your actions and follow the rules of the game, even though you are playing against one another. They also allow you to fill in missing information. If I told you that I got a sandwich at the student union, I don't need to tell you, for example, that I paid for it. You can fill that detail in because you have the same basic "getting food at a restaurant" script as I do. Our reliance on scripts becomes embarrassingly apparent when we find ourselves without a script for a new situation. Imagine being invited to a Japanese tea ceremony but not knowing where to sit, what to say and when to say it, and how to sip the tea—when everyone else in attendance seems thoroughly acquainted with this very complex ritual of great importance for maintaining respectful social relations.

Scripts Schemas about an event that specify the typical sequence of actions that take place.

Impressions Schemas people have about other individuals.

Schemas that represent knowledge about other people are called impressions. Your schema of the cyclist Lance Armstrong might include physical characteristics (athletic, good looking), personality traits (charismatic, courageous), and other beliefs about him (philanthropist, cancer survivor, stripped of titles after doping scandal). Similarly, we can also have a schema for a category of people (e.g., sports superstars), called a *stereotype*. You can see that your impression of Armstrong contains many traits (e.g., wealthy, athletic, courageous) that are also part of your stereotype for sports superstars. Finally, as we will discuss in chapter 5, we also have a schema about ourselves—our self-concept.

Regardless of their type, the content of our schemas consists of a pattern of learned associations. These patterns of associations can change and expand over time. You first might have learned about Lance Armstrong as an incredible athlete and cancer survivor and only later had to update this positive view of him after repeatedly encountering media reports about his use of performance-enhancing drugs, which eventually led to his being stripped of his seven Tour de France titles. Some of our associations with Armstrong might be stronger than others, because we more frequently think about or hear about Armstrong in terms of those aspects. The learned associations stored in our schemas profoundly shape our perception, judgment, and behavior.

But it's also important to realize that schemas are not passively filled up with information from the outside. Because of our need for specific closure—again, the motive to maintain particular beliefs and attitudes—we often tailor our schemas to include only some pieces of knowledge. Think about it this way: On your computer you probably have file folders that contain documents, pictures, and sound files that are related in some way, and you label those file folders accordingly, such as "Social Psychology Class" and "Summer Vacation." The schemas stored in your long-term memory are like those file folders in the sense that they contain all the bits of knowledge you have about a given category, from *Nazis* and *pedophiles* to *doorknobs* and *stickers*. But the similarities end there. Computer file folders usually don't magically acquire or lose documents, and they never insist that you open *this* picture and get nervous if you open up *that* picture. But that is exactly what schemas do, even without our conscious awareness. For example, if you are the president of the Lance Armstrong fan club, your schema for Lance likely will emphasize the bits of knowledge that flatter the athlete (great cyclist, charity sponsor) and will downplay anything that casts him in a negative light.

Your schema of Lance Armstrong might include aspects of his physical characteristics (athletic), personality traits (courageous), and beliefs about his life experiences (cancer survivor, stripped of Tour de France titles after doping scandal).
[Bryn Lennon/Getty Images]

Self-concept A schema people have about themselves.

Where Do Schemas Come From? Cultural Sources of Knowledge

Let's take a closer look at where we acquire the knowledge that makes up our schemas. The example of Lance Armstrong pointed to various sources of knowledge. In some cases, we come into direct contact with people, events, and ideas and form concepts on the basis of that personal experience. But looking at this from the cultural perspective, we also learn a great deal about our social world indirectly, from parents, teachers, peers, books, newspapers, magazines, television, movies, and the Internet. A lot of our general knowledge comes during childhood from the culture in which we are raised. As children learn language and are told stories, they are taught concepts such as *honesty* and *courage*, *good* and *evil*, *love* and *hate*. From this learning, people develop ideas about what people in the world are like, the events that matter in life, and the meaning of their own thoughts and feelings, among other fundamental lessons.

A considerable amount of our cultural knowledge is transmitted to us by our parents, but also by peers, teachers, and mass media sources. For most children in industrialized nations, television and movies provide scripts of situations (workplace interactions: *Mad Men*; romance: the *Twilight* series), schemas of types of people (villain, hero, *femme fatale*, nerd, ingénue) and stereotypes of groups of people (gay men are effeminate; grandmothers are kind; Asians are martial artists) before the child has firsthand experience with such situations, people, and groups. And children intuitively sense that television and books provide a preview of the next steps in their lives: Grade school kids tend to like shows and books about middle school, and middle school kids tend to like shows and books about high school.

Finally, the basic way that we categorize information and build schemas is thought to be culturally universal, but as we have described it here, the content of those schemas and how they are organized is shaped by our cultural experiences. This can result in cultural differences in the meaning that concepts can sometimes have. For example, kids who grow up in a rural Native American culture—which values connections with nature—have a concept of "animal" that is most closely linked to those species that become part of their daily lives (Winkler-Rhoades et al., 2010). In contrast, urban-dwelling European American kids asked to list animals bring to mind exotic species such as elephants and lions that populate their picture books. Here we see the both groups develop a schema for the same general category, but the content of that schema differs in important ways, depending on the physical and social environment in which people carry out their daily lives.

Rumors and Gossip

Rumors and gossip are two other common sources of knowledge contained in our schemas. Much of what we learn about other people or events comes from news passed from one person to another. But beware. When information is passed from person to person to person before you get it, it tends to be distorted in various ways.

For one, as people perceive and relay information, it is altered a bit as it is filtered by each person's schemas and motive for specific closure. Specifically, transmitted information can be biased by processes called *sharpening* and *leveling*. Think about how you tell a story to a friend. You're probably going to emphasize the main features of the story, which is called sharpening, and leave out a lot of details, which is called leveling. The main features are more memorable than the details, and they also make for a more interesting tale. An unfortunate consequence of this bias is that people hearing about a person or event, rather than gaining knowledge firsthand, will tend to form an oversimplified, extreme impression of that person or event (Baron et al., 1997; Gilovich, 1987).

For example, Robert Baron and colleagues (1997) had a participant watch a videotape in which a young man described unintentionally getting drunk at a party, getting involved in a fight, and getting into a subsequent car accident. The man noted this was uncharacteristic of him, that he was egged on by friends, and that he regretted his actions. The participant rated the man on various positive and negative traits. Then the participant, now in the role of storyteller, was asked to speak into a tape recorder to describe the man's story. Listeners then heard the audiotape and rated the man on the same traits. The listeners rated the man more negatively than the teller did. These effects seem to result both from a tendency of storytellers to leave out mitigating factors and complexities and a tendency of listeners to attend only to the central aspects of the stories they hear.

In addition to this tendency to tell simplified stories, our stereotypes of groups can also make us biased in our recall and retelling of information. Gordon Allport and Joseph Postman (1947) demonstrated this back in the 1940s in a study involving White American participants. They briefly showed a person a picture depicting a scene on the New York subway involving a White man standing, holding a razor, and pointing his finger at a Black man (**FIGURE 3.6**). They then had that person describe the scene to another person who had not seen the picture. That second person then described the scene to a third person, and so on, until the information had been conveyed

Figure 3.6

Spreading Rumors

People talked about the event depicted in this picture to others, who in turn told the story to still others, and so on. Over the course of several retellings, people's memories of the event became more consistent with racial stereotypes: Eventually the man holding the razor was remembered as Black, not White.

[G. W. Allport and L. J. Postman, *The Psychology of Rumor*. New York: Henry Holt, 1947]

to a seventh person. More than half the time, that seventh person reported that the scene involved the Black man, rather than the White man, holding the razor. So when we get our information filtered through lots of people, it's pretty likely that prevalent schemas (such as stereotypes about a person's group) have biased the information.

Mass Media Biases

Of course, we don't get information only from having it told to us directly by others; we also learn a great deal from the stories we see and hear in the media. Just as rumors and gossip can distort the truth, media portrayals seldom are realistic accounts of what life is like, although they do provide vivid portrayals of possible scenarios. Think about your own schemas or scripts about dating and romantic love. Your earliest ideas about such matters probably came from fairy tales, television shows, the Internet, and movies. Unfortunately, these media offer biased views of many of these matters. For example, they tend to portray romantic relationships and love in oversimplified ways; to portray men, women, and ethnic groups in stereotypic ways; and to show a lot of violence (Dixon & Linz, 2000). The latter feature may explain why people who watch a lot of television think that crime and violence are far more prevalent in the world than they actually are (Shanahan & Morgan, 1999).

News programming is based on reality, and so people tend to assume it paints a fairly realistic, accurate, and less biased picture of events and people. But the news is created at least as much as it is reported. Those who produce the news choose which events and people to report about, and what perspective on the events to provide. These decisions are heavily influenced by concerns with television ratings and newspaper sales, and by the political and social preferences of those who own and sponsor the television programs, radio shows, newspapers, and magazines that report the news. And just as Allport and Postman showed over six decades ago, racial stereotypes can play a role as well. Just consider the two different descriptions of similar actions by people dealing with the aftermath of Hurricane Katrina's devastation of New Orleans in 2005 (**FIGURE 3.7**). Both images show people leaving a grocery store and wading through floodwaters with food and supplies; the White people are described as "finding" food, whereas the Black individual is described as "looting."

Figure 3.7

Media Biases

After Hurricane Katrina, both of these images appeared in different news sources. Whereas the media described the White people as *finding* food in grocery stores, they described this Black individual as having *looted* a grocery store.

[Left: Chris Graythen/Getty Images; right: AP Photo/Dave Martin]

How Do Schemas Work? Accessibility and Priming of Schemas

We now have a sense of how important schemas are in helping us to acquire and organize information about the people, ideas, and events that we encounter. But which of the many schemas stored in a person's memory will be activated and shape thought and action at any given moment?

The person's current situation plays a major role in activating particular schemas. If the characteristics of a social gathering across the street—loud music, alcohol in abundance—lead Yana to categorize it as a *party*, she will access her *party* schema, which gives her information she can use to figure out how else to think about this event, what inferences to make ("This ongoing noise will likely interfere with my social psych reading"), and what actions to take ("I should go to the library"). Of course, the more fine grained a person's categories are, the more specific will be the schemas activated. Returning to the example, if Yana has different categories for a *game-day keg party* and a *standard keg party*, she can access different schemas in order to fine-tune her understanding of the event and her response to it. ("It's a game-day keg party, so if our team loses the party will probably be over by 8 o'clock.")

Accessibility refers to the ease with which people can bring an idea into consciousness and use it in thinking. When a schema is highly accessible, the salience of that schema is increased: it is activated in the person's mental system, even if she is not consciously aware of it, and it tends to color her perceptions and behavior (Higgins, 1996). We just saw that the characteristics of the person's current situation can increase the salience of a schema, making it more accessible for thinking and acting.

Priming occurs when something in the environment activates an *idea* that increases the salience of a schema. This happens because the information that we store in memory is connected in associative networks (**FIGURE 3.8**). These networks are tools that psychologists use to describe how pieces of information stored in a

Accessibility The ease with which people can bring an idea into consciousness and use it in thinking.

Salience The aspect of a schema that is active in one's mind and, consciously or not, colors perceptions and behavior.

Priming The process by which exposure to a stimulus in the environment increases the salience of a schema.

Associative networks Models for how pieces of information are linked together and stored in memory.

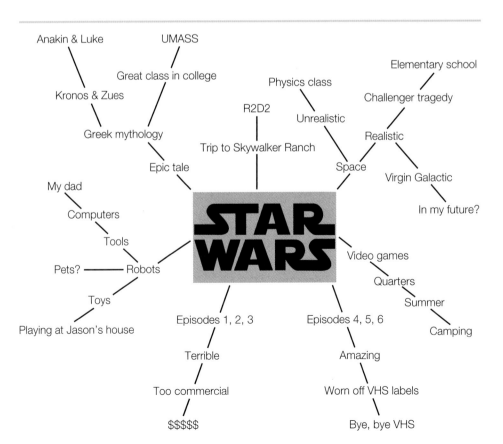

Figure 3.8

Associative Networks

Information is organized in associative networks in which closely related concepts are cognitively linked. Bringing one concept to mind can prime other concepts connected to it, sometimes without the person's conscious awareness.

[Reprinted by permission of Joseph Herda.]

person's memory are linked to other bits of information (Anderson, 1996; Collins & Loftus, 1975). These links result from semantic associations and experiential associations. **Semantic associations** result when two concepts are similar in meaning or belong to the same category. The words *nice* and *kind*, for example, have similar meanings; the words *dog* and *cat* both refer to household pets. Thus, we might expect them to be linked in a person's associative network. **Experiential associations** occur when one concept has been experienced close in time or space to another concept. For example, for many people who consume their fair share of television or live in high-crime areas, guns are experientially associated with violence. Through these two kinds of mental links, priming, or "turning on," one idea will bring to mind other ideas that are closely linked in a person's associative network, but will be less likely to bring to mind ideas that are not strongly linked.

In addition to the immediate environment and priming, the person's personality determines how accessible certain schemas are. **Chronically accessible schemas** are those that represent information that is important to an individual, relevant to how they think of themselves, or used frequently (Higgins, 2012; Markus, 1977). Such schemas are very easily brought to mind by even the most subtle reminder. For example, Mary is really interested in environmental issues, whereas Wanda is attuned to contemporary fashion. Mary is more likely to notice a hybrid car in the parking lot or express disdain over the plethora of plastic cups lying around at a party. Meanwhile, Wanda has her fashion radar working and her associated constructs chronically accessible, so she may dislike the tacky cups and be more likely than Mary to notice that Cynthia arrived in last season's designer shoes. Even though they are in the same situation, the differences in what schemas are chronically accessible for Mary and Wanda lead to very different perceptions and judgments of the scene.

People are also likely to interpret others' behavior in terms of their own chronically accessible schemas (Higgins et al., 1982). If you read a biography of Herman Melville and if *honesty* is a chronically accessible trait for you, you would be likely to have a good memory for incidents in Melville's life that pertain to honesty, and your overall impression of Melville will be largely colored by how honest he appears to have been. On the other hand, if *kindness* is chronically accessible for you, his incidents of kindness or unkindness would be particularly memorable and influence your attitudes.

Situational and chronic influences on schema accessibility also can work together to influence our perceptions of the world. For example, after witnessing a fellow student smile as a professor praises her class paper, students in one study were more likely to rate her as conceited if they had very recently been primed with words related to the schema *arrogance*, but this effect was most pronounced for students who showed high chronic accessibility for the schema *conceitedness* (Higgins & Brendl, 1995). In other words, a certain situation or stimulus may prime particular schemas for one person but not for another, depending on which ideas are chronically accessible to each (Bargh et al., 1986).

Priming and Social Perception

Now that we have some understanding of how schemas operate, let's examine in a bit more detail the consequences that schemas have for social perception and behavior. Imagine that you recently met a fellow named Donald. You learn that Donald is the type of person you might see in an energy-drink commercial with a penchant for extreme activities—skydiving, kayaking, demolition derby—and who is now thinking of mountain climbing without a harness. What do you think your impression of him would be? Would you see him as reckless or adventurous?

Semantic associations Mental links between two concepts that are similar in meaning or that are parts of the same category.

Experiential associations Mental links between two concepts that are experienced close together in time or space.

Chronically accessible schemas Schemas that are easily brought to mind because they are personally important and used frequently.

This man is free climbing without a safety harness. Would you describe him as adventurous or reckless? Because of priming, your impression might be influenced by what you were thinking about just before meeting him.

[James Balog/Getty Images]

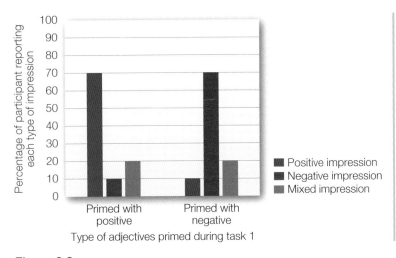

Figure 3.9

Forming Impressions

In this experiment, people's impressions of a man named Donald were influenced by adjectives that had previously been primed. If they had just read several positive words, they formed a more positive impression than if they had just read several negative words.

[Data source: Higgins et al. (1977)]

A study by Higgins and colleagues (1977) suggests that your impression will depend on the traits that are accessible to you before you met him. Participants in this study were told they would be completing two unrelated studies on perception and reading comprehension, but in actuality the tasks were related. In the "first" study, participants performed a task in which they identified colors while reading words (commonly referred to as a *Stroop task*). In this task, you might see the word *bold* printed in blue letters, and your job would be to identify the color blue. This task gives the researchers a way to make certain ideas accessible for some participants but not for others. Half of the participants were randomly assigned to read words with negative implications (e.g., *reckless*). The other half of the participants read words with positive implications (e.g., *adventurous*). In the "second" study, participants were asked to read information about a person named Donald who takes part in various high-risk activities, and to answer some questions about their impression of Donald. You can see from **FIGURE 3.9** that the words participants were primed with during task 1 had a dramatic effect on the impressions they formed of Donald. Those participants who had previously read negative words pertaining to recklessness were likely to form more negative impressions of Donald, whereas those participants who had previously read positive words pertaining to adventurousness tended to view Donald more positively. Their impressions differed despite the fact that they were presented with identical information about Donald! What led to these different impressions, of course, were the different ideas that were primed in the participants before they read about him. This finding suggests that our impressions of others are shaped by salient schemas.

Priming and Behavior

Just like impressions, social behavior can be influenced by recently primed schemas without the person being consciously aware of their influence. Consider this scenario. You show up to participate in a psychology study, thinking that it concerns language proficiency. You are asked to complete a task in which you try to unscramble words to make sentences. You're told to use four of the five words presented. You start on the task and are presented with *they/her/bother/see/usually*. So you start scribbling something like "they usually bother her" and then proceed to the next set of words. Unknown to you, you have been randomly assigned to be in a condition in which words related to the schema *rudeness* have been primed (notice the word *bother*). Other participants were presented with neutral words or words related to the schema *politeness* (e.g., *respect*).

After completing a series of such sentences, you take your packet to the experimenter to find out what you need to do next. The problem is that the experimenter is stuck in conversation with another person, and the conversation doesn't seem likely to end anytime soon. Think about a time when you are in a hurry but have to wait your turn. Would you wait patiently or try to interrupt others so that you can get on your way? Would other thoughts in your mind influence your behavior?

Study results suggest that they would (Bargh et al., 1996). When no category was primed, 38% of participants interrupted within a 10-minute time frame. But among those primed with rudeness, 64% were too impatient to wait that long, whereas only 17% of those primed with politeness-related words interrupted. Schemas that are primed in one context can shape behavior in a different context.

The Role of the Unconscious

Why are priming studies useful? They illustrate how our experiential system can operate behind the scenes, influencing our everyday thought and behavior outside of our awareness. Indeed, psychologists from Freud (1923/1961b) to Wilson (2002) have made the point that consciousness is the mere tip of an iceberg: We are continually influenced by features of the environment and mental processes without being aware of them.

Of course, this idea is not completely new in popular culture. Over the years there have been a number of controversial media accounts of subliminal priming. For example, in 1957, a movie theater proprietor claimed to have boosted popcorn and soda sales at concession stands by presenting subliminal messages encouraging patrons to visit the snack bar. This was later discovered to be false because no such messages were actually presented, but it certainly raised the ire of many moviegoers at the time. In 1990, the heavy metal band Judas Priest was sued over purportedly presenting subliminal messages in one of their songs that encouraged a young man to commit suicide.

Although these examples turned out to be groundless, subliminal priming is a reality. It's just that now we understand how and when subliminal primes are likely to influence thought and behavior. Part of this development is owing to advances in technology, because we now have the means to present information (such as words and pictures) precisely long enough to activate them in the mind without bringing them into conscious attention. (In most experiments, exposures range from 10 to 100 milliseconds.)

We can see the effect of such subliminal priming in a study by Bargh and Pietromonaco (1982). They had participants read about a person named Donald (no relation to the earlier mountain climber) who refused to pay his rent until the landlord painted the apartment. Prior to reading about Donald, participants completed a computer task in which they were asked to identify where on the screen a brief flash appeared. Unknown to participants, directly following the flash a word was presented for 100 milliseconds to the periphery of their visual focus, followed by a string of "XXX"s that served to cover (or mask) the stimulus. Participants were shown 100 flashes. If participants were exposed to a lot of words related to *hostility* (*curse*, *punch*), they judged Donald to be more aggressive than did participants exposed to only a few or no hostility-related words. Yet no participant reported being aware of having seen the words, which suggests the power of subliminal priming.

We now also have a much better theoretical grasp of how subliminal priming works, and therefore when it will—and will not—be likely to influence thought and behavior. We now know that subliminal primes do not lead people automatically and robotically to do whatever it is they are told to do, such as buy a soda or commit suicide. Rather, the concept of accessibility that we've been discussing suggests that subliminal priming makes some ideas more accessible than others, but they still are only one factor that determines thought and behavior. Other factors include the ideas and goals made salient by the environment and those that are chronically accessible for the person (Strahan et al., 2002). This means that a primed schema will be more likely to tip interpretation of an ambiguous event one way or another, rather than reverse long-standing attitudes. With regard to behavior, a primed schema might subtly nudge a person to respond more aggressively to a stressful situation. But it will not transform a normally peaceful individual into a total jerk.

Assimilation and Contrast

The priming effects described so far are known as assimilation effects. This is because the judgment of the person or event is assimilated in, or changes in the direction of, the primed idea. For instance, priming the schema *reckless* increased the perception of mountain climbing Donald as reckless. But primes sometimes have

Assimilation effects Occur when priming a schema (e.g., reckless) changes a person's thinking in the direction of the primed idea (e.g., perceiving others as more reckless).

Contrast effects Occur when priming a schema (e.g., reckless) changes a person's thinking in the opposite direction of the primed idea (e.g., perceiving others as less reckless).

the opposite consequence, leading to **contrast effects.** For example, in some studies, priming the schema *hostility* led people to view a person as *less* hostile (Lombardi et al., 1987; Martin, 1986). Although there are some complexities to determining when assimilation effects and when contrast effects are likely to occur (Higgins, 1996), contrast effects seem to emerge under a few conditions. The first is when people are very aware of the primed information and that it might affect their subsequent judgments. Accordingly, assimilation effects are consistently found for subliminal and subtle primes, but contrast effects are common when the primes and their relation to the subsequent judgment are very obvious. In these situations, people's conscious cognitive system often tries to counteract the potential influence of the prime by shifting their judgment or behavior in the direction opposite of that implied by the prime (Wegener & Petty, 1995).

Two other conditions in which contrast can occur are when the prime is extreme or when it evokes a specific example of a category (Dijksterhuis et al., 1998; Herr, 1986; Schwarz & Bless, 1992). For example, when rating oneself after being primed with an extreme example, it may be harder to view oneself as consistent with the category. And when primed with a specific person who fits the category, the individual is more likely to compare the self with that specific person. In one study (Dijksterhuis et al.,

When primes create contrast effects: People can assimilate the concept *intelligence* and perform better when primed with the category *professors* rather than the category *supermodels.* Yet if primed with the specific person *Albert Einstein,* instead of the specific supermodel *Claudia Schiffer,* they tend to show a contrast effect and perform worse intellectually.

[Left: Getty Images/Photo Researchers RM; right: William Stevens/Gamma-Rapho via Getty Images]

1998), when students were asked to think about *professors in general*, they performed better on a test of general knowledge than students asked to think about *supermodels in general* (an assimilation effect). However, when participants were asked to think about specific exemplars of those categories (Albert Einstein as a professor and Claudia Schiffer as a supermodel), the specific exemplars caused participants to compare themselves with the exemplars, leading to a contrast effect in which those primed with Albert Einstein did worse than those primed with Claudia Schiffer. After all, it's rather difficult to think of oneself as smart when compared with Einstein!

Confirmation Bias: How Schemas Alter Perceptions and Shape Reality

Schemas and the expectations and interpretations that they produce are generally quite useful. Your *party* schema tells you what to expect there, how to dress, and so forth. Your *mom* schema helps you predict and interpret things your mom will say and do. And the schemas that become active in particular situations are usually the ones most relevant to that situation. However, once we have a schema, we tend to view new information in such a way as to confirm what we already believe or feel. This is known as *confirmation bias*. In chapter 1 (pp. 13–14) we saw how this bias influenced students' evaluations of an article on capital punishment (Lord et al., 1979). Confirmation bias helps people preserve their worldview by sustaining a stable, consistent set of beliefs and attitudes about the world. In this way, it provides the individual with psychological security. However, confirmation bias also often leads to inaccurate interpretations of new information.

This effect happens for a number of reasons. First, once we have a schema of a person or situation, that schema guides us to look for certain kinds of information and ignore other kinds of information. We see this demonstrated in a study by Snyder and Frankel (1976). Participants watched a silent videotape of a woman being interviewed. They were told that the interview was about either sex or politics. Participants were told to watch the videotape to assess the woman's emotional state. When participants thought the interview was about sex, they rated her as more anxious than when they thought the interview was about politics. The videotape was the same in both cases, but when participants thought the topic was sex, they *expected* the woman to be anxious over discussing such a personal topic, and therefore they watched more closely for nonverbal signs of anxiety. You've heard the expression "Seeing is believing"; studies such as these suggest that the converse holds true as well: "Believing is seeing"!

Second, a salient schema leads us to interpret ambiguous information in a schema-confirming manner. In one study, trained therapists watched a videotaped interview with a man. Half the therapists were told it was a job interview, and the other half were told it was an interview with a mental patient (Langer & Abelson, 1974). Although everyone listened to the same interview, therapists who thought the man was a mental patient saw more signs of mental illness than those who thought he was a job applicant. When the interviewee described conflicts with his bosses in past jobs, those who thought he was a mental patient tended to interpret his actions as stemming from his defensiveness, repression, and aggressive impulses. Those who thought it was a job interview interpreted the same actions as signs of perceptiveness and a realistic perspective.

The Ironic Biasing Influence of Objective Information

Could this insidious schema-based confirmation bias actually cause objective information to do more harm than good? To find out, Darley and Gross (1983) had participants watch one of two versions of a videotape about a nine-year-old fourth grader named Hannah, showing her playing in a playground, along with scenes of her neighborhood and school. The videotapes made it clear that Hannah had either an upper-class or lower-class background. Darley and Gross reasoned that participants shared the common schema of upper-class kids as academically successful and the common schema of lower-class kids as unsuccessful.

Half the participants (the no-performance group) were then simply asked to rate Hannah's academic abilities on a scale ranging from kindergarten to sixth-grade level. The other half (the performance group) were shown a second videotape, which was the same whether Hannah was earlier depicted as upper or lower class, before being asked to rate Hannah. This videotape showed Hannah performing on an oral achievement test, answering questions ranging from easy to hard, doing well on some and not well on others.

Which group do you think was especially likely to be influenced in their ratings by Hannah's socioeconomic status—the no-performance group or the performance group? We might expect participants given only class-based schemas to rate Hannah higher if they thought she was upper rather than lower class. However, one would hope that participants provided with objective evidence of Hannah's academic abilities would rely on that information and ignore the class-based schemas.

And yet the opposite occurred, as we see in **FIGURE 3.10**. The objective evidence *increased* the bias rather than decreasing it. The group that didn't have the opportunity to see Hannah perform estimated her math abilities to be the same regardless of whether she was upper or lower class. They seemed to realize that they didn't have much basis for prejudging her abilities after only seeing her on a playground. However, the group that observed Hannah take an oral achievement test rated her much better if she was upper rather than lower class. These participants saw Hannah's performance and rated

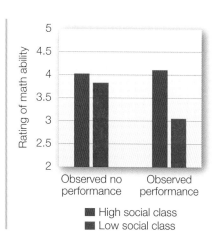

Figure 3.10

Schemas Bias Interpretation

When rating the math ability of a little girl, participants were not biased by her social class if they had no opportunity to observe her taking an achievement test. However, those who watched a video of her taking an oral test interpreted her performance more negatively if they believed that she attended a lower-class elementary school.

[Data source: Darley & Gross (1983)]

her abilities in line with what they expected from a student of her social class. The point is that the participants didn't interpret the so-called objective evidence objectively; instead, they interpreted it as confirming what they already believed they knew about Hannah's ability.

Biased Information Gathering

People's schemas, even when tentative, can also lead to biased efforts to gather additional information, efforts that tend to confirm their preexisting schemas. Participants in one study had a brief discussion with a conversation partner who was described to them as being an extravert or an introvert (Snyder & Swann, 1978). Their job was to assess whether this was true, and they were given a set of questions to choose from to guide their conversation. Participants tended to ask the conversation partner questions that already assumed the hypothesis was true and would lead to answers confirming the hypothesis. For example, a participant wanting to determine if the partner was an extravert chose to ask questions such as, "What kinds of situations do you seek out if you want to meet new people?" and "In what situations are you most talkative?" However, if they wanted to determine if the partner was an introvert, they chose questions such as, "What factors make it hard for you to really open up to people?" and "What things do you dislike about loud parties?" What's important to note here is that these are leading questions: When answering a question about how she livens up a party, for example, a person is very likely to come across as extraverted, even if she is not; likewise, even an extravert will look introverted when talking about what he dislikes about social situations. This study shows that people tend to seek evidence that fits the hypothesis they are testing rather than also searching for evidence that might not fit that hypothesis.

These effects could have important implications for how clinical psychologists diagnose disorders. In one series of studies, participants were shown a set of drawings of a human figure along with a psychological symptom of the person who drew each picture (Chapman & Chapman, 1967). After viewing all of the pictures, participants were asked to draw conclusions about whether people who share the same symptoms have a tendency to draw certain features of a person in a distinctive way. In a sense, they were given the opportunity to play amateur therapists who use drawings to uncover people's psychological issues. And their responses showed a great deal of convergence: Participants often concluded that people with paranoid tendencies drew unusual eyes in their pictures, and men who were worried about their masculinity drew images with broader shoulders and more muscular physiques. However, unknown to the participants, the researchers had randomly paired each symptom with a picture so that there was no true correlation between these aspects of the drawings and the mental issues they imagined for the artists. Rather, they saw in the pictures what they expected to see given their expectations for paranoid or worried types. Follow-up studies showed that these biases are present even among experienced clinicians (Chapman & Chapman, 1969). When people do not try to actively disconfirm their expectancies for others, they run the risk of seeing only what they already believe.

The Self-fulfilling Prophecy

Self-fulfilling prophecy The phenomenon whereby initially false expectations cause the fulfillment of those expectations.

Another vivid testament to the power of schemas is evidence that they not only bias our perceptions of social reality, but can also *create* the social reality that we expect. More specifically, people's initially false expectations can cause the fulfillment of those expectations, a phenomenon that Robert Merton (1948) labeled the self-fulfilling prophecy. To investigate this idea, Robert Rosenthal and Lenore Jacobson (1968) went to an elementary school in 1964 and administered some tests to the students. After scoring the tests, they gave the teachers the names of some kids in their class who, according to the Harvard Test of Inflected Acquisition, were on the verge of experiencing a substantial leap forward in their general learning abilities. The teachers were told that these kids were "late bloomers" who were about to display an "intellectual growth spurt."

Two years later, the kids labeled as late bloomers actually scored substantially higher than their classmates did on a test of general abilities. However, unknown to the teachers, the list of kids originally labeled late bloomers was a random selection from the class rosters. So the only reason they experienced a dramatic intellectual growth spurt was that the teachers were led to expect they would!

Self-fulfilling Prophecy Video on LaunchPad

What accounts for this self-fulfilling prophecy? Years of additional research have revealed that although such effects don't always occur, when they do, it is because teachers' expectations affect their behavior toward the students in ways that improve the students' learning (Rosenthal, 2002). For example, kids expected to do well are given more attention and more nods and smiles, are challenged more, and are given more positive reinforcement for their successes (e.g., Harris & Rosenthal, 1985; Jussim, 1986). Students tend to respond to such behavior with more engagement and more effort, and consequently, more learning. One study also showed that these expectations can work in the opposite direction: If students expect a teacher to be excellent, the teacher performs better (Feldman & Prohaska, 1979).

Through a process known as the self-fulfilling prophecy, teachers' positive expectations for their students can shape how well those students actually perform.

[Darrin Henry/Shutterstock]

Since that classic study on teachers and students, self-fulfilling prophecies have been demonstrated in many other contexts as well (e.g., Snyder et al., 1977). If you expect someone to be friendly and sociable, you are likely to act in ways that elicit such behavior. If you expect someone to be unpleasant and annoying, you are likely to act in ways that provoke that kind of behavior. One study found that army platoon leaders led to expect their platoon to be made up of exceptional recruits actually produced better soldiers (Eden, 1990). Mere expectations won't turn a serial killer such as Jeffrey Dahmer into a humanitarian such as Nelson Mandela, but most of us are capable of being pleasant or unpleasant, industrious or indifferent. Within a moderate range of variability, it seems quite clear that perceivers' expectations about others often shift people's behavior toward confirming those expectations.

Limits on the Power of Confirmation Biases

We have beaten the drum for confirmation bias very loudly in this section, and the large body of evidence warrants doing so. However, confirmation biases do not always occur. If people's observations clearly conflict with their initial expectations, they will revise their view of particular people and events. This is especially likely if the gap between what people expect and what they observe is very extreme. For example, if you play chess with a nine-year-old and don't expect the child to show much skill, and then the kid beats you, you will likely revise your opinion of the child's chess ability. In fact, because your expectation was so different from the outcome, you might even overrate the child's ability.

It is interesting, though, that even in such cases, people usually grant the exception but keep the underlying schema. In the chess example, you'd probably think, "This kid's a genius, but most nine-year-olds stink at chess." Of course, if enough nine-year-olds whip you in chess, the schema eventually would give way to the data.

In addition, as we noted in the section on priming effects, when people are aware of and concerned about being biased, their cognitive system may kick in to correct the feared bias. Another way to think about this correction is to say that people's need for accuracy trumps their need for closure, leading them to think more carefully—or at least to respond in a way that is opposite to what they think is a biased judgment. However, the evidence suggests that this correction process tends to be inexact and sometimes leads people to bend over backward in the opposite direction. Finally, in the context of self-fulfilling prophecies, if the target of your expectation knows you think a certain way about him or her, the person may go out of the way to try to disconfirm your expectation (Hilton & Darley, 1985).

Beyond Schemas: Metaphor's Influence on Social Thought

So far we've focused on people's use of schemas. It makes intuitive sense that people think about a thing by applying their accumulated knowledge about other things that are like it. But do people ordinarily use other cognitive devices to make meaningful sense of the social world? To find out, listen to how people commonly talk about the abstract ideas that matter in their daily lives:

I can *see* your point (*understanding is seeing*)
I'll *keep* that *in* mind (*the mind is a container*)
Christmas is *fast approaching* (*events are moving objects*)
That is a *heavy* thought (*thoughts are objects with weight*)
I feel *down* (*feelings are vertical locations*)
I *devoured* the book, but I'm still *digesting* its claims (*ideas are food*)
Her arguments are *strong* (*arguments are muscle force*)
I'm moving *forward* with the chapter (*progress is forward motion*)
The economy *went from* bad *to* worse (*states are locations*)

These are *metaphoric* expressions because they compare things that, on the surface, are quite different. (These comparisons are reflected in the statements in parentheses.) That is why these expressions do not make sense if taken literally. For example, feelings do not have an actual vertical location, and arguments cannot have muscle strength.

SOCIAL PSYCH out in the WORLD

A Scary Implication: The Tyranny of Negative Labels

In a 2013 episode of the radio program *This American Life*, Ira Glass (Glass, 2013) described the murder case of Vince Gilmer. In 2006, Gilmer was sentenced to life in prison and described by the judge as a "cold-blooded killer." The evidence was irrefutable and showed that Vince was guilty of strangling his elderly father to death and dumping the body on the side of the road in another state, after chopping off the fingers to make the body harder to identify. Although Vince didn't deny his role in ending his father's life, he maintained that his crime was not the act of a cold-blooded killer. Representing himself in court, he laid out a rather incoherent case for his insanity built around the idea his brain was destabilized by low levels of serotonin after he went cold turkey from his antidepressants. Although Vince showed some unusual twitching behavior, severe mood swings, and cognitive problems in the lead-up to his trial, law enforcement officials, a psychiatrist, the judge, and the jury all assumed he was faking these symptoms. After all, isn't this exactly what you would expect from a cold-blooded killer trying to avoid doing time for his crime?

The good news about human nature is that extremely negative behavior such as Vince's is actually rare. But be-

cause it's so harmful or disruptive to society when people do bad or unusual things, we are quick to slap a negative label on those who commit crimes or who exhibit other abnormal tendencies and we are very reluctant to peel these labels off. Once someone is labeled a psychopath, as Vince was, his or her every action is interpreted as evidence of psychopathic tendencies. Negative or unusual behaviors seem fitting for a psychopath, but of course anything positive or exculpatory might also seem like a cunning attempt to charm and manipulate others. If the label is accurate, we tend not to stress about the mental straitjackets we apply to people. But these labels not only leave little room for people to grow beyond or redeem themselves from past wrongs, they also make it nearly impossible for those who have been mislabeled to break free of these binds.

In Vince's case, it took someone who was willing to construct an impression or schema of him built around more positive associations to provide a different interpretation of what had happened to Vince. You see, before Vince killed his father, he was a beloved and compassionate doctor. The physician who took over Vince's clinic learned about the close and caring relationships he had with his patients and dug into Vince's case in more detail. Eventually, he discovered that Vince had tested positive for Huntington's disease, a degenerative condition that could explain every one of the unusual behaviors, mood changes, and violent actions that Vince had been displaying over the past few years. Although Huntington's is a terminal illness with no

According to many philosophers and psychologists, such metaphoric expressions are more than merely colorful figures of speech; instead, they offer a powerful window into how people make sense of abstract ideas.

From this perspective, metaphors are cognitive tools that people use to understand abstract ideas by applying their knowledge of *other types* of ideas that are more concrete and easier to understand (Kövecses, 2010; Lakoff & Johnson, 1980). For example, when Lisa says, "Christmas is fast approaching," she may be using her knowledge about *moving objects* to conceptualize *time*. Why? Because Lisa may find it difficult to get a clear image of time in her mind (not surprising, since physicists aren't sure what time is!). Yet she has a concrete schema for physical objects moving around, and this schema tells her that objects tend to be more relevant as they draw closer. By using her *objects* schema to think about time, Lisa can make sense of what an "approaching" event means for her (time to buy gifts!), even though there is no such thing as an event moving toward her.

How does this perspective enhance what we know about social cognition? It suggests that people's everyday efforts to construct meaning draw on metaphors as well as schemas. Whereas schemas organize knowledge about a given idea, metaphors connect an idea to knowledge of a *different type of thing*. Often, we construct metaphors around things that are connected to our bodily experiences. For instance, people understand *morality* partly by using a schema that might contain memories of moral and immoral individuals and behaviors. But people also understand morality metaphorically

Metaphor A cognitive tool that allows people to understand an abstract concept in terms of a dissimilar, concrete concept.

---

cure, and Vince Gilmer remains locked up in a psychiatric facility, Vince could finally feel vindicated that the label of cold-blooded killer might not be the best explanation for his behavior.

Stories like Vince's reveal the power of schemas to influence a person's perceptions and lead to confirmation biases that justify whatever label she or he has already decided on. Of course, in Vince's case, he had committed an unspeakable crime and was, in fact, exhibiting unusual and dangerous behavior.

Can negative labels be just as confining when inaccurately applied to sane and healthy people? Imagine the following horror film scenario: You wake up one day in a psychiatric institution and have been labeled a schizophrenic. How easy do you think it would be to convince the staff you were not schizophrenic and get them to release you?

In 1973, David Rosenhan set out to examine this very question in a provocative and controversial study. Rosenhan and seven other normal people checked themselves into San Francisco–area mental hospitals. Once admitted, they tried to convince the staff they were normal and should be released. These pseudopatients first checked into the hospital reporting that they had heard a voice in their heads saying the words "hollow, empty, thud." Other than that one misleading symptom, they gave otherwise honest information about their names and backgrounds. Every pseudopatient was admitted, and seven of the eight were diagnosed as schizophrenic. They were kept an average of 19 days and during that time,

they behaved completely normally and never again reported having any symptoms diagnostic of schizophrenia. Even so, their normal behavior was sometimes interpreted through the lens of their diagnosis. For example, writing in a journal was noted as evidence of "obsessive writing behavior" by one psychiatrist. None of the pseudopatients were ever judged as fakes by the psychiatrists, and on their release the seven originally diagnosed as schizophrenic were released as "schizophrenic in remission." No amount of positive, normal, sane behavior was enough to wipe away the original label they had received.

This study caused an uproar, partly because of qualms about whether it was ethical, but mainly because it illustrated that mental-health diagnostic labels become schemas that once attached to a person are very hard to disconfirm! As a topper, Rosenhan informed another hospital in the area that over the next three months he would send in one or more pseudopatients and challenged the staff to detect these imposters. Now armed with such an expectation, members of the staff suspected 41 of the 193 new patients who were admitted during that period of being Rosenhan's pseudopatients. Once again, expectations led mental health professionals astray; however, this time Rosenhan didn't actually send any pseudopatients in. Most of the time, people's tendencies to use schemas to categorize and understand other people are helpful, but in cases such as these, labels can become perceptual prisons.

in terms of their bodily experiences with physical cleanliness and contamination (Zhong & House, 2013). This metaphor is reflected in common expressions such as, "Your *filthy* mind is stuck in the *gutter*; think *pure* thoughts with a *clean* conscience," and it operates at a conceptual level to shape how we make judgments about morality.

Researchers have tried to go beyond analyzing language to learn more directly whether people use metaphor to think about abstract ideas. In one procedure, participants are primed with a bodily experience, such as tasting something, seeing something, or feeling something's texture. Then, in an apparently unrelated task, they are asked to make judgments or decisions about an abstract idea. The researchers reason that if people in fact use a bodily experience to understand an abstract idea, then the prime should produce parallel changes in those judgments and decisions. To illustrate, if people understand *love* metaphorically as a *journey* ("Our relationship is *moving forward*"), then priming them with the bodily experience of journeying over rocky terrain (versus smooth terrain) should lead them to expect to encounter conflicts as their love relationships progress. Alternatively, if people do *not* use the metaphor *love is a journey*, then we wouldn't expect that priming experiences of physical journeys would influence their judgments and decisions about love.

Williams and Bargh (2008) used this procedure to examine the metaphorical link between physical and interpersonal warmth. They built on prior evidence that people commonly refer to interactions with others by using the concepts *warm* and *cold* (Asch,

Because metaphors connect seemingly unrelated concepts together, holding a warm cup of coffee might actually make you perceive other people as more warm and trustworthy.

[Africa Studio/Shutterstock]

1946; Fiske et al., 2007), as when one receives a *warm* welcome or a *cold* rejection. To determine whether this metaphor influences social perceptions, they had the experimenter—who apparently needed a free hand—ask participants to hold her coffee cup. Depending on condition, the cup was either warm or cold. Afterward, all participants were asked to read a brief description of another person and rate that person's friendliness and trustworthiness—that is, the person's interpersonal warmth. As predicted, participants who simply held a warm (versus a cold) beverage perceived a target individual as friendlier and more trustworthy, suggesting that conceptual metaphors can influence social perceptions even when people are not prompted to use metaphoric language.

Similar effects have now been found in dozens of published studies (see Landau et al., 2010; Landau et al., 2013). Subtle primes of bodily experience influence how people perceive, remember, and make judgments and decisions related to a wide range of abstract social concepts. To mention just a few surprising findings: Weight manipulations influence perceived importance; smooth textures promote social coordination; hard textures result in greater strictness in social judgment; priming closeness (vs. distance) increases felt attachment to one's hometown and families; groups and individuals are viewed as more powerful when they occupy higher regions of vertical space.

These findings highlight an important fact about the way we make sense of the world: We construct an understanding of abstract ideas by drawing on our knowledge of the sensory and motor experiences we have had from the earliest moments of life (Mandler, 2004; Williams et al., 2009).

APPLICATION

Moral Judgments and Cleanliness Metaphors

Let's look, for example, at how schemas and metaphors are applied in moral judgment. Your friend says her boyfriend lied to her and then asks you, "Wasn't that wrong of him?" She is asking you to make a moral judgment—that is, to evaluate an action as *right* or *wrong*. How do we make these judgments? Some have argued that they are based on internalized moral rules that we follow in a rational manner. If you believe stealing is immoral, then an act of stealing is wrong and a thief is immoral.

But metaphor research suggests that our understanding of right and wrong, good and evil, may be affected by bodily concepts, particularly those related to disgust, physical filth, and cleanliness. Consider a study by Schnall and colleagues (2008). Participants were asked to read about individuals who committed various kinds of moral violations, such as not returning a found wallet to its rightful owner or falsifying a resume, and to rate how morally wrong those actions are. Half the participants made their judgments in a dirty work space: on the desk were stains and the dried-up remains of a smoothie, and next to the desk was an overflowing trash can; the other participants made their judgments in a clean work space (**FIGURE 3.11**). As expected, the mere presence of filth led participants to condemn moral violations more severely, even though it didn't change their overall mood. Intrigued by these findings, and guided by the field's growing interest in replication, Johnson and colleagues (2014) re-did this study but did not find that physical cleanliness affected the severity of moral judgments. The inconsistency in these results across labs creates an exciting opportunity to take a closer look at the methods used by the two research teams. Because researchers are actively trying to understand how priming affects behavior, there is still a lot we can learn about when such metaphoric associations affect judgments and when they do not.

Figure 3.11

Moral Metaphors

When participants made moral judgments in a dirty work space, they judged moral violations more harshly than if the work space was clean.

[Data source: Schnall et al. (2008)]

SECTION review | The "What" of Social Cognition

The mind typically classifies a stimulus into a category, then accesses a schema, a mental structure containing knowledge about a category. Schemas allow people to "go beyond the information given" to make inferences, judgments, and decisions about a given stimulus. Although generally helpful, schemas can produce false beliefs and limit a person's interpretation of reality.

Sources	Accessibility and Priming	Confirmation bias	Metaphor
• Schemas come from multiple sources and are heavily influenced by culture. They are also shaped by the need for closure.	• Salient schemas are highly accessible and color thinking and behavior. • Priming occurs when activating an idea increases a schema's salience. • When primed, schemas can influence the impressions we form of others as well as our own behavior. • Often these effects operate outside of conscious awareness. • Priming can have contrast effects, leading to schema-opposing perceptions and behaviors.	• People tend to interpret information in a way that confirms their prior schemas. • Objective information may be skewed to fall in line with expectations. • Schema-inconsistent information may be overlooked. • Our expectations may shift another's behavior toward confirming those expectations. • We may revise our views for exceptional cases but retain the underlying schema.	• People use metaphor to understand an abstract concept in terms of another type of idea that is more concrete and easier to grasp.

Returning to the "Why": Motivational Factors in Social Cognition and Behavior

So far, we have focused on the automatic processes involved in how we perceive people and events in the environment. We have not said too much about motivation. This doesn't mean that motivational factors have little influence on when, what, and how we apply schemas to our understanding of the world. As we noted at the outset of this chapter, motivational factors are linked to cognitive processes. They are the engine that puts this cognitive machinery into action (Kruglanski, 1996; Kunda, 1990; Pyszczynski & Greenberg, 1987b).

Priming and Motivation

To see how motivation plays a role, think back to the study in which people primed with *rudeness* were quicker to interrupt an experimenter's conversation (Bargh et al., 1996). Did the prime directly trigger the rude behavior? Probably not. In that study, participants were motivated from the outset to get the experimenter's attention, so although the prime increased their tendency to interrupt a conversation, it did not trigger the behavior without some motivation to engage in it. Other research more directly reveals that primed ideas influence thought and behavior, particularly when they are compatible with the person's preexisting motivation. For example, subliminally priming the idea *thirst* can lead a person to drink more, but only when that person is thirsty; without this motivation to satisfy thirst, the prime has no effect on beverage consumption (Strahan et al., 2002).

In addition, because our motivations are intertwined with many of the objects, events, and people we encounter, priming such contexts and cues often activates specific motives and goals that are associated with them (Gollwitzer & Bargh, 2005). If we're looking for someone to date and we see an attractive person, this motivation activates not only schemas pertaining to beauty but also the goal of meeting that person.

Cesario and colleagues (Cesario et al., 2006) illustrated this point using a priming procedure developed by Bargh and associates (1996). In the original study, participants had to rearrange sets of scrambled words to form grammatical sentences. Embedded within this sentence-unscrambling task were some words related to college students' concept of the elderly (compared to only neutral words in a no-prime condition). After completing the sentence-unscrambling task, participants were told they could leave. Little did they know that the experimenter measured how long it took them to walk down the hallway to the elevator. Participants primed with the *elderly* schema walked more slowly than those who did not have this schema primed. This was originally interpreted as an "automatic activation" effect in which the *elderly* schema was salient (as a result of being primed) and automatically influenced participants' behavior.

However, Cesario and colleagues argued that being exposed to the prime didn't just make the *elderly* schema accessible but also activated participants' feelings about and motivation to interact with elderly individuals. Some people have positive attitudes about old people, and others have more negative attitudes. For those who have positive attitudes toward the elderly, when the *elderly* schema is activated, so too is the motivation to interact positively with such people. These participants might unconsciously adjust their behavior to have a smoother interaction with an elderly person; this could include walking more slowly, as Bargh and his team had shown.

But when the same schema is primed for those who have negative attitudes toward the elderly, so too is the motivation to avoid them. Therefore, the researchers hypothesized, these participants should walk faster to avoid the elderly and leave them in the dust. This was exactly what they found. When participants had positive attitudes about the elderly, they responded to the *elderly* prime by walking more slowly. However, when participants had negative attitudes about the elderly, they responded to the prime by walking faster! These results support the point that primes do not influence behavior in a simple manner, but rather interact with the person's motivation to determine what she or he thinks and does in a given context (Cesario et al., 2010).

Priming helps people prepare to act. When primed with the concept of "elderly," for example, people who have positive attitudes toward older adults walk more slowly, perhaps because doing so would allow them to interact with an elderly person more easily.

[Lisa F. Young/Shutterstock]

Motivated Social Cognition

Clearly, people are not simply automatons, blindly controlled by whatever schemas happen to be accessible in their minds. Indeed, the tools that we use to think serve our needs and goals. As a result, we do not think about the world "out there" as though we were video cameras; rather, our everyday thinking is significantly shaped by the motives and needs that we have in the moment. What are those motives and needs? Some stem from our bodies, of course. A hungry person is more likely to think about food than sex and will likely look for, and notice, a restaurant faster than an attractive person who happens to be walking by.

Other motives have to do with the kinds of thoughts we want to have about the people, ideas, and events that we encounter in our social environment. Specifically, *what* we think about, and *how* we think about it, are continually influenced by three psychological motives that we introduced earlier in this chapter: to be *accurate*, to be *certain*, and to maintain *particular beliefs and attitudes* that fit with our worldview (Kruglanski, 1980, 2004). These motives are constantly at work, sometimes below our conscious radar, filtering which bits of information get into our minds, how we interpret and remember them, and which we bring to mind to justify what we want to believe.

For one, the motive for accuracy can lead people to set aside their schemas and focus on the objective facts. For example, when a person is motivated to understand who another person really is, perhaps because he is going to work with her on a task, he may be motivated to look past the convenient stereotypes he has for her group and put more thought into her individual personality (Fiske & Neuberg, 1990).

What about the need for nonspecific closure? When people are motivated to gain a clear, simple understanding of their surroundings, they tend to see events in a way that wraps up the world in a neat little package. We mentioned at the beginning of the chapter that this need can become active when the situation makes thinking unpleasant. In a study demonstrating this motivation for nonspecific closure (Kruglanski & Freund, 1983), participants told that they had to form an impression of someone in a limited amount of time tended to reach a conclusion based on the first bits of information they received, failing to take into account relevant information that they encountered later (known as the *primacy effect*). In contrast, participants not under time pressure felt more comfortable considering all the relevant information before reaching a conclusion about what the person was like.

Mental laziness is not the only reason people seek closure on simple, consistent interpretations of the world. Sure, sometimes thinking takes effort and so we stick to familiar, simple conclusions. Yet another benefit of maintaining well-structured knowledge is that the opposite states of mind—uncertainty, ambiguity, and complexity—can be very unsettling. According to the *meaning maintenance model*, even brief exposure to stimuli that seem out of place or inconsistent with expectations can put people on the alert to make sense of their environment or to affirm other moral convictions (Heine et al., 2006; Proulx & Heine, 2008, 2009). In one study, after simply viewing nonsensical word pairs such as "turn-frogs" and "careful-sweaters" (compared with sensible word associations), participants were more eager to reaffirm a sense of meaning by acting in line with their moral beliefs (Randles et al., 2011). When unexpected events occur, people have an automatic tendency to restore a sense of meaning, even in unrelated areas of life.

Why, deep down, are inconsistent states of mind threatening? From the existential perspective, maintaining clear, simple interpretations of reality provides people with a psychological buffer against the threatening awareness of their mortality (Landau et al., 2004) and a broader sense of meaning (Heine et al., 2006). If the world appears fragmented, chaotic, or vague, people may have difficulty sustaining faith that there is anything bigger than themselves—anything that they can rely on to give their life meaning and significance—and so they are left with the possibility that they will simply die and be forgotten. Conversely, the sense that the world is ordered—that people act in consistent ways, for example, and that people generally get what they deserve—buttresses people's faith that they can establish some meaning and personal value that will be remembered after they die. In studies supporting this idea, participants reminded of their mortality were more likely to show primacy effects in impression formation, and they showed particularly strong dislike of someone who acted inconsistently from one situation to the next. Thoughts of mortality not only increase the tendency to think of members of other groups in simplified, stereotypic ways but also increase preference for outgroup members who confirm rather than call into question such stereotypes (Schimel et al., 1999).

Let's turn to the need for specific closure. In many cases, people want more than mere certainty: they want to reach conclusions that support their preferred views of the social world, including events, other people, and themselves. Mac users want to think Macs are better than PCs; most people want to believe their country is great; and we all want to think our friends are good people. In the sections above we reviewed a number of research studies that demonstrate the ways in which people filter and manipulate reality in order to maintain their preferred beliefs and attitudes.

Let's consider one more example of such motivated social cognition: how people interpret an athletic event when they attach their feelings of self-worth to the success

Pi

π (*Pi*), a surrealist psychological thriller directed by Darren Aronofsky and released in 1998 (Watson & Aronofsky, 1998), dramatically illustrates schemas' power over people's lives. The movie centers on Max Cohen (Sean Gullette), a genius mathematician who lives like a hermit in his apartment, into which he's crammed a sprawling, home-built supercomputer. Max is obsessed with the idea that reality can be understood in terms of numbers. He can state his entire worldview in three assumptions: "1. Mathematics is the language of nature. 2. Everything around us can be represented and understood through numbers. 3. If you graph the numbers of any system, patterns emerge."

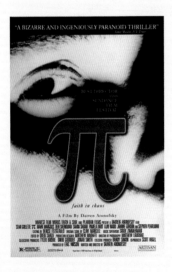

[Harvest Film Works/Album/Newscom]

For the past 10 years, Max has been trying to uncover the hidden numerical pattern beneath the stock market, a notoriously chaotic system. Max's supercomputer crashes under the strain of his research, but the answer it spits out just before crashing—a 216-digit number—fascinates Max. He starts to believe that this number provides the key to unlock not just the stock market but the very nature of the cosmos and existence.

Let's focus on three aspects of Max's life that connect with ours, albeit usually in less extreme forms.

1. Max sees elusive mathematical patterns everywhere. For him, they pop out of the environment, just as faces or a vase can pop out of Figure 3.1. For example, when we see a city street through Max's eyes, passersby appear as a jittery, undifferentiated mass of bodies, whereas the stock market numbers displayed on a building's LCD monitor are crystal clear. Later, when Max becomes obsessed with spirals (a representation of the mysterious Golden Ratio in math), he sees them in his coffee, the newspaper, and the smoke rolling off a cigarette. He is hunting for order in nature, and he sees it everywhere . . . or does he?

Sol Robeson (Mark Margolis), Max's elderly mentor and only friend, warns Max about his obsession: "You have to slow down. You're losing it. . . . Listen to yourself. You want to find the number 216 in the world, you will be able to find it everywhere. Two hundred and sixteen steps from your street corner to your front door. Two hundred and sixteen seconds you spend riding on the elevator. When your mind becomes obsessed with anything, you will filter everything else out and find that thing everywhere!"

Max is clearly extreme in the way he filters reality through his schemas, but even supposedly normal people like the rest of us prefer interpretations of reality that confirm our schemas.

of one of the teams. If you've ever watched a game with another person and you were each rooting for a different team, you probably noticed that you have very different perceptions of what is happening in the game. With a close play at the plate in the bottom of the ninth, do you think Red Sox and Yankees fans see the attempted tag of the runner in the same way?

Consistent with your likely intuition, a study of fans' impressions of a particularly rough football game between Princeton University and Dartmouth College back in 1951 indicates that they would not. Following the game, Albert Hastorf and Hadley Cantril (1954) showed students from both schools a film of it and then asked them how many penalties each team had committed. Princeton students saw Dartmouth players committing many more penalties than Princeton players, whereas Dartmouth students saw their team only commit half the number of penalties that the Princeton students attributed to them. But of course, students from both schools watched the same film! Our motivations—in this example our investment in our sports team—affect the way in which we perceive events unfolding. We look for what we want to find and come up with justifications to our conclusions ("See—look at that! The receiver was mugged before the ball got there!").

When people watch competitive sports, their interpretation of controversial plays and penalties is often biased by which team they want to win.

[AP Photo/Mel Evans]

As we've seen, this is the *confirmation bias*. Perhaps the only difference is that Max's schemas are idiosyncratic: No one else seems to share them—and Max is perfectly fine with that. The rest of us tend to use schemas that we share with other members of our culture.

2. Just as powerfully as Max's schemas make some features of the environment salient, they downplay whatever does not fit within his precise mathematical worldview. When Max is approached by Devi (Samia Shoaib), his friendly neighbor bearing gifts and offering affection, he resists her. Why? For one thing, Max lacks a *script* for interacting with others—that is, he lacks knowledge of how the give-and-take of normal social interactions unfolds in time. As a result, social interactions are too uncertain and unpredictable for him to manage; hence, they end awkwardly.

But looking deeper, we also see the *self-fulfilling prophecy* at work. Schemas that other people impose on us alter how they treat us and consequently how we behave. Schemas that we impose on *ourselves* can similarly constrain us. In Max's case, he seems to have convinced himself that he lacks the capacity to establish emotional intimacy; therefore, he doesn't.

3. Finally, Max's character illustrates a simple but important point: People do not simply like order; they actually *need* order because they are threatened by the opposite: disorder and chaos. Sol tries to convince Max that the world is extremely complex and chaotic, but Max's search for order is unrelenting. Driven by purpose, he becomes more restless, disheveled, and paranoid. He is beset with debilitating migraine headaches, hallucinations, and blackout attacks.

Is Max that different from the rest of us? As we've noted in this chapter, people certainly differ in how much they prefer well-structured knowledge to unstructured knowledge. Yet within all of us lies a pit of fear that drives us to search for patterns in the environment, piece things together in coherent and predictable ways, and react negatively toward anything that threatens to unravel the order underlying our experience. We see these tendencies every day: gambling, betting, religious quests, the creation of conspiracy theories, scapegoating a "bad guy" for a hazardous outcome, or simply turning our noses up in disgust at a visually chaotic artwork, such as the movie *Pi* itself!

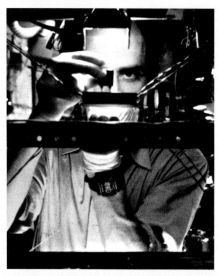

Max's search for mathematical order highlights some aspects of reality and obscures others. The rest of us may not be so fanatical, yet we all use schemas to filter our perception of the social world.

[Live Entertainment/Photofest]

Since this classic study, researchers across the globe have shown in myriad studies the many ways in which people's cognitions are biased by their motivation to maintain preferred beliefs and attitudes. Of course, there are limits to the influence of motives on people's thinking. For people to function effectively in the world, their cognitions must be generally accurate representations of external and social reality. If one's favorite college basketball team doesn't win a game all season, believing they are the best team in the nation would be too discrepant with reality and therefore unsustainable. One would have to also believe in a mass conspiracy or that everyone else was crazy. As a result, the person's understanding of reality is the product of a compromise among three motivations: desire to be accurate, to be certain, and to hold on to valued beliefs (Heine et al., 2006; Kunda, 1990).

Mood and Social Judgment

In addition to psychological motives, moods can play an important role in shaping social judgment about a given event or person. A *mood* is a generalized state of affect that persists longer than the experience of an emotion. For example, the happiness a person experiences after finding a dollar bill on the ground lasts a couple of minutes, but moods can continue to resonate for much longer. This points to another unique characteristic of moods: Unlike with emotions, often the person does not know why she or he is in a given mood. Sometimes we just find ourselves feeling bad or good, and we cannot quite put our finger on why.

Think
ABOUT

[nmedia/Shutterstock]

Why might humans have evolved the ability to experience moods in the first place? For one thing, moods may inform the person about the status of things in the immediate environment. Think about this from the evolutionary perspective. Being in a positive mood is a signal that everything is okay, that there are no immediate threats to be concerned with. Negative moods, on the other hand, signal that something is wrong and might be deserving of one's attention. In fact, over the course of our species' evolution, positive moods might have promoted exploring the environment, expanding hunting territories, and trying unfamiliar foods—behaviors that, when well attuned to cues in the environment, would have facilitated the success of the species. Likewise, negative moods might have promoted greater vigilance against attack, protection of the tribe, and more conservative eating habits—behaviors that would also increase the chance for survival when the threat of danger is real. As a result of these evolutionary pressures, people today may be oriented to use their *mood as information* in their judgments (Schwarz & Clore, 1983; 2003). Whether they realize it or not, they are listening to their moods when making decisions and forming judgments.

By this logic, mood states should affect both the content of a person's social judgments and how motivated the person is to engage in effortful processing of information. If people are feeling good while considering whether they like a person or an event such as a party, they are more likely to view each of them positively. If they are feeling lousy, that will color their view of such things negatively. Also, the more thought people put into such judgments, the more their moods color them (Forgas, 1995). The reason is that the more thinking a person does, the more his mood infuses his evaluations of the various aspects of the person or event he is evaluating.

Mood also affects how motivated people are to think extensively about people and events occurring around them. Because positive moods signal that things are okay, individuals feeling good rely on more heuristic or automatic forms of processing when making judgments about people, events, and issues (Bless et al., 1996; Forgas, 1998; Mackie & Worth, 1989). In other words, they rely more on the experiential system of cognition that we introduced at the beginning of this chapter. For instance, people in good moods are more likely to rely on stereotypes when judging people (Bodenhausen et al., 1994).

On the other hand, negative moods tell the person that something is wrong. Therefore they lead the person to think more carefully to figure out what is bothering her. Studies show, in fact, that participants experiencing a negative mood focus on relevant details before making a judgment, rather than settling on a quick and dirty judgment (Bless et al., 1990; Forgas et al., 2005; Gasper & Clore, 2002).

As a demonstration of this idea, Herbert Bless and his colleagues (Bless et al., 1990) had students recall a very happy or a very sad event in their lives, a manipulation that reliably induces a positive or negative mood. In a supposedly unrelated study, participants listened to an essay that argued for an increase in student fees at the university. For half of the sample, the arguments in the essay were rather weak, but for the other half, the arguments in the essay were quite strong—that is, its claims were logical and built on solid evidence. Because most college students are likely to be opposed to a fee increase, the default, or heuristic, response is to pay little attention to how good the arguments are and maintain one's negative attitude toward the proposal. However, if you are processing the information in the essay carefully, paying attention to details, then strong arguments for the proposal could sway your opinion. Results showed that the students who were in a happy mood processed the essay more heuristically. Their attitude toward a tuition increase was negative, even when the arguments for the increase were strong. In contrast, participants who were in a negative mood really thought carefully about the essay, so they were persuaded by the strong arguments to believe that the fee increase would be a good idea.

Our intuition might lead us to think that if a friend is in a bad mood, it is not a good time to try to change her opinion on some issue. However, according to this line of research, if your arguments are strong, it is actually the best time to do so!

The Next Step Toward Understanding Social Understanding

In this chapter, we focused primarily on how we process and are affected by information as it unfolds—how we seek knowledge, how we organize the knowledge that we have, how that knowledge can be activated by features of the situations we encounter, and how motivation affects the processing of information. But social understanding involves more than merely processing incoming information. Our cognitive system is highly attuned to rely on memories, infer causation, form impressions of people, and imagine alternative possible outcomes to make sense of people and events. In chapter 4 we will turn to these central aspects of understanding the social world.

SECTION review | Returning to the "Why"

Motivation plays a role in shaping which schemas are activated as well as when and how those schemas affect behavior and judgment.

Primed ideas influence thinking and behavior when they are compatible with the person's preexisting motivation.	The three psychological motives introduced in the first part of this chapter—to be accurate, to be certain, and to maintain particular beliefs and attitudes—are constantly at work, sometimes subconsciously, influencing which schemas come to mind and how powerfully they influence thinking and behavior.	Mood affects how motivated we will be to expend effort on processing information.

CONNECT ONLINE:

Check out our videos and additional resources located at:
www.macmillanhighered.com/launchpad/greenberg1e

Thinking About People and Events

TOPIC OVERVIEW

SOCIAL PSYCH AT THE MOVIES
Casablanca   134

SOCIAL PSYCH OUT IN THE WORLD
"Magical" Attributions   136

Imagine a scenario in which you are driving in your car, happy that your classes have just ended and listening to your favorite song. As you make a left-hand turn at an intersection, a red sports car in the oncoming lane of traffic comes straight toward you at a fairly high speed and hits the back side of your car.

With your mood now substantially ruined, you get out of your car, relieved that no one was hurt but upset and confused by this turn of events. The other driver jumps out of his car and is adamant that you cut him off. You claim that he was speeding and that you would have had plenty of room if he had been going the speed limit. It's a classic case of one person's word against the other's. The police are called to investigate what happened.

Although we hope that car crashes are not a routine part of your day, this situation and the subsequent crime-scene investigation would involve four essential ways people typically make sense of the world and that will be the focus of this chapter:

- We rely on our ability to recall events from the past (memory).
- We make inferences about what causes other people's behavior (casual attributions).
- We form impressions of other people, often on the basis of limited information (person perception).
- We imagine alternatives to the events we experience (counterfactual thinking).

[Tooga/Getty Images]

When we try to figure out who was at fault in a fender bender, we rely on basic ways of making sense of the world.

[Yellow Dog Productions/Getty Images]

An investigation of the fender bender would involve retrieving memories for what happened, making determinations of what or who caused the accident, forming an impression of those involved in the accident, and considering how things might have happened differently.

We use these same cognitive processes every day to make sense of the world around us. And, unlike a police detective, our cognitive system often engages these processes automatically and without any taxpayer expense!

Remembering Things Past

To make sense of the world, we count on our ability to remember events, people, and objects that we have encountered in the past. Through the use of our senses, we take in information from the world around us. Imagine *hearing* the fire alarm going off in your building. You look out into the hallway, and *see* people rushing from their rooms. In the case of an actual fire, you might also *smell* the acrid odor of smoke, *taste* the salty flavor of sweat on your upper lip as you hurry through the heat, and *feel* your way along a darkened stairwell to navigate to the outside world. Each of your senses is providing you with information to help you understand the situation and engage in the appropriate behavior. In this situation, it's quite clear how these sensory processes help us to perceive the demands of the situation (fire!) and engage in a certain sequence of behaviors that accomplishes an important goal (escape!). But we don't just perceive and then act. We are also equipped with the important ability to lay down traces of memory that allow us to build a record of things that have happened in the past.

This record of memory is really quite useful. Not only does it help us make sense of the world we're currently experiencing but it also allows us to learn from past experience so that we might better predict what will happen in the future. In our everyday understanding of memory, we think about memories as the past record of personal experiences that we have had (*that time when I narrowly escaped a burning building*) or information we have learned (*when you spray an aerosol can of cooking spray at a lit barbecue, it acts like a flame thrower*). But memory is really much more than that; in fact, there are different types of memory, and a sequence of processes that underlie how memories get formed and are recalled. Let's consider how memories are formed so we can then understand how they are influenced by various social factors.

How Are Memories Formed?

Studying for a test is one of those rare occasions where we actively try to store information in memory, but most of the time laying down memories happens automatically, with little effort on our part. How does this process of memory formation happen?

First, we can make a distinction between **short-term memory** (information and input that is currently activated) and **long-term memory** (information from past experience that may or may not be currently activated). At every moment, you are attending to some amount of sensory stimulation in your environment, and some of that information will be *encoded* or represented in *short-term memory*. Information that is actively rehearsed or is otherwise distinctive, goal relevant, or emotionally salient gets *consolidated* or stored into our long-term memory for later *retrieval*.

When you are at a party, embarrassed by the fact that you cannot for the life of you remember the name of your roommate's significant other, you can take some comfort in knowing that there are a lot of places where the process of remembering can break down. Maybe your roommate never mentioned the name (lack of sensory information to begin with), or perhaps you were very distracted when the name was mentioned (lack of attention needed to encode sensory information). Even if you were paying attention, you might not have been motivated to consolidate the name

Short-term memory
Information and input that is currently activated.

Long-term memory
Information from past experience that may or may not be currently activated.

into long-term memory (maybe you didn't think you would meet again). And finally, you could have the name stored somewhere in memory but are temporarily experiencing an inability to retrieve it.

How Do We Remember?

Retrieving information from long-term memory often seems like a fairly objective process. We experienced some event and then try to retrieve that event from the storage chest of information in our mind. However, like our perceptions and encoding of the social world, retrieval is a process that is colored by many of the factors discussed in chapter 3: our biases, our schemas, our motives, and our goals. As the psychologist John Kihlstrom (1994, p. 341) puts it, "[M]emory is not so much like reading a book as it is like writing one from fragmentary notes." As this quote implies, when we seek to remember an event, we often have to build that memory from the recollections that are available to us. When used in this way, memory is often referred to as a reconstructive process. Returning to our investigator metaphor, we reconstruct an idea of what happened by bringing to mind bits of evidence in much the same way as an investigator might interview several sources and gather several pieces of evidence to pull together a coherent picture of what happened.

In trying to gather this information together, we may intend to seek accurate knowledge. But the need for closure, and the tendency to reach conclusions that fit with what we expect or desire, often crash the party. Indeed, among the more potent tools that we use to reconstruct our memories are our schemas. As you might expect from our discussion of schemas in chapter 3, when we try to recall information about an event, our schemas guide what comes to mind. Just as an investigator could be biased in the search for evidence (e.g., interviewing only observers likely to support an early interpretation of the events), we often remember information that matches our preexisting schemas, and we ignore or discount information that conflicts with our schemas.

Memory for Schema-Consistent and Inconsistent Information

In one study illustrating how schemas shape memory (Cohen, 1981), participants watched a videotape of a woman they believed was a librarian or a waitress. The woman in the videotape explained that she liked beer and classical music. When participants were later asked what they remembered about the woman, those who believed she was a librarian were more likely to recall that she liked classical music. Those who believed she was a waitress were more likely to remember that she liked beer. The reason for this difference is that the schema of the woman led the participants to look for, and therefore tend to find and encode into long-term memory, characteristics she displayed that fit their schema of her. Participants exhibited such schema-consistent memory even when interviewed a week later, suggesting that our tendency to recall information consistent with our expectations can have a long shelf life!

Although most of the time we find it easier to remember information that is consistent with our schemas, sometimes information that is highly inconsistent with one of our schemas also can be very memorable (Hamilton et al., 1989). Such information is often attention grabbing and forces us to think about how to make sense of it. If you go to a funeral and someone starts tap-dancing on the coffin, it would violate your script for such an event, and you'd probably never forget it.

Whether schema-inconsistent information leads to better recall depends on whether that information is very salient, whether we are motivated to make sense of it, and whether we have the cognitive resources to notice and think about it (Moskowitz, 2005). When we are very busy or unmotivated, we primarily attend to and encode in memory information that fits our currently activated schemas.

However, if the discrepant information grabs our attention, and we have the resources to think about it, then inconsistent new information is likely to be especially memorable. If you have a generally proper and reserved grandmother, and one time she had a few too many margaritas at a wedding and started dancing wildly with a stranger, you'd probably remember that quite well (unless your resources were also quite limited, perhaps by sharing in said margaritas).

Our discussion so far concerns what happens when we try to recall information about which we have a preexisting schema. The story is quite different if our schema emerges only later on, after we've been exposed to a particular piece of information. If you take in specific information about a person or event and then are given a particular schema about it afterward, the memory is primarily consistent with the new schema, and recall of the memory reinforces the new schema.

In a study assessing the effects of schemas that develop both before and after learning specific information about a person, participants were asked to listen to an audiotape of 36 events in the life of a female college student (Pyszczynski et al., 1987). The events included some positive and some negative social behaviors on her part (e.g., "irons her roommate's skirt for her"; "criticizes her boyfriend"). However, either before or after listening to the tape, participants were given background information that created a strong schema of the student that was either positive (including such traits as modesty and kindness to others) or negative (conceit and contempt for others). Participants were later asked to recall information from the list of events that they heard.

When the schema came *before* the list of behaviors, participants mainly recalled behaviors that were highly *inconsistent* with the schema. For example, if participants had initially formed a negative schema about the person, they easily remembered that person's positive behaviors. This fits the idea presented earlier that when information is highly inconsistent with our schemas, we tend to process it more thoroughly and encode it into memory. However, if the strong general schema was formed *after* the listing of behaviors, participants were better able to recall those events that were *consistent* with the positive or negative schemas they had formed. For example, forming a negative schema after hearing the list of behaviors improved memory for negative behaviors. Because these participants did not have a schema when they were initially presented with the person's behavior, the inconsistent behaviors did not seem inconsistent at the time of encoding and thus were not processed more thoroughly. But after exposure, when participants were given a schema to work with, that schema helped to guide their recall of the behaviors that were consistent with that schema.

This last finding demonstrates that how we think about things *now* (our current schemas) is a potent guide to what we recall from the past. Another study (McFarland & Ross, 1987) demonstrated how present experiences can create expectations that guide our recollections. For the sake of illustration, let's imagine the participants Frank and Mike, each of whom has just started a dating a new partner. In the study, Frank and Mike are asked how in love they are at the beginning of their relationships. Both indicate being moderately in love. Then, two months later, Frank and Mike are questioned again. This time they are asked how in love they currently are with their partners, but also how in love they had been during the initial stages of their relationship.

Note that this second round of questioning allows the researchers to compare Frank's and Mike's memories of how in love they were with their actual ratings two months earlier. As it turns out, Mike's relationship has been going quite well, and he reports being very much in love with his partner. Frank, on the other hand, is now having lukewarm feelings. What about their memories of their initial feelings of love? Mike's estimates of how in love he was two months ago are now higher than Frank's, even though back then they were equally in love with their partners. This is exactly the pattern of results that the actual study found with real participants. Our present perceptions can create a schema that biases how we recall (or actually, reconstruct) events from the past.

Although a schema can color memory in either a positive or negative light, people have a general tendency to show a rosy recollection bias and to remember events more positively than they actually were (Mitchell et al., 1997). This is especially true if people feel positively about their current experience. More broadly, people tend to exhibit *mood-congruent memory*. That is, we are more likely to remember positive information when we are in a positive mood, and more likely to remember negative information when we are in a negative mood. Shoppers, for instance, tend to recall more positive attributes of their cars and TVs when they have previously been given a free sample (such as a paper notepad) that puts them in a good mood (Isen et al., 1978). Such mood-congruent memory effects help explain why depressed persons seem to have such difficulty extracting positive feelings from events they experienced in the past. Because they are typically in negative moods, they tend to recall more negative information from the past (Barnett & Gotlib, 1988).

One caveat to keep in mind during our discussion of this tendency to attend to and remember schema-consistent information is that there are cultural differences in these processes. Recall from chapter 2 that there is variation across cultures in underlying orientations toward analytical versus holistic ways of thinking. In individualistic cultures, people prefer to have well-defined concepts that are distinct from each other and stable over time. In collectivist cultures, people tend to think of concepts, including other people, as embedded within a broader context, which means that collectivist cultures have more tolerance for inconsistency and change over time and situation. Theorists talk about this as a preference for *dialecticism*—a way of thinking that acknowledges and accepts inconsistency (Spencer-Rodgers et al., 2010). These culturally based differences in ways of thinking, in turn, influence how people's memory biases construct stable and consistent schemas of the world and the people in it—including themselves. For example, when asked to recall aspects of themselves, Chinese participants are likely to remember aspects that imply more inconsistent self-descriptions than are European American participants (Spencer-Rodgers et al., 2009).

The Misinformation Effect

Clearly our memories are biased by our current way of understanding the world. Sometimes these biases can even lead us to remember things that didn't actually happen. The process is best captured by Elizabeth Loftus's work on the misinformation effect. The misinformation effect is the process by which cues that are given after an event can plant false information into memory. In a classic study by Loftus and colleagues (1978), all participants watched the same video depicting a car accident (**FIGURE 4.1**). After watching, some participants were asked, "How fast was the car going when it *hit* the other car?" Other participants were asked, "How fast was the

Misinformation effect The process by which cues that are given after an event can plant false information into memory.

Figure 4.1

Misinformation Effect

Loftus and her colleagues illustrated how the phrasing of a question can lead someone to remember seeing something, like broken glass, that actually wasn't there.

car going when it *smashed into* the other car?" You might not be surprised to learn that participants asked the question with the word *smashed* estimated that the car was going faster than did participants who were asked the question with the word *hit*. Even a simple word such as *smashed* can prime a schema for a severe car accident that rewrites our memory of what happened in the video.

Perhaps more interesting, however, is what happened when participants were later asked if there was broken glass at the scene of the accident. Those participants who had earlier been exposed to the word *smashed* were more than twice as likely to say "yes" than were participants previously exposed to the word *hit* (even though there was no broken glass at the scene). Thus, this study illustrates how our memories can be susceptible to misinformation. The way in which the question was asked created an expectation that led people to remember something that actually was not there!

APPLICATION
Eyewitness Testimony

Eyewitness Testimony Video on LaunchPad

The misinformation effect demonstrates not just how the metaphorical investigator in our head becomes biased in its interpretive processes but also how real-life investigations can be biased. In fact, this process has been applied to a number of controversial cases, particularly in the areas of eyewitness testimony and false memories. Eyewitness testimony is the single most influential piece of evidence in a trial, and thousands of cases are decided on the basis of such evidence. This can be disturbing when we consider how our recollection of events can be influenced by the way in which we are asked about them. Leading questions by police investigators, and exposure to information after the event took place, are capable of influencing witnesses to remember events in certain ways—ways that may not necessarily be accurate. For example, Loftus (2013) describes the case of *Al Megrahi v. Her Majesty's Advocate*, in which Abdelbaset al-Megrahi was convicted of setting explosives on Pan Am flight 103 in 1988. The airplane exploded over the Scottish town of Lockerbie, killing all 259 passengers and crew as well as 11 Lockerbie residents who were struck by falling debris (**FIGURE 4.2**). As Loftus notes, the case raised a number of concerns. The trial and al-Megrahi's conviction occurred

Figure 4.2

Al-Megrahi v. Her Majesty's Advocate

The trial of Abdelbaset al-Megrahi, accused of setting explosives on Pan Am flight 103 in 1988, is an example of judicial reliance on eyewitness testimony. But is such testimony always reliable?

[Left: Manoocher Deghati/AFP/Getty Images; right: © Martin Cleaver/AP/Corbis]

over 12 years after the event and hinged on the testimony of a shopkeeper who initially was quite tentative about his ability to identify al-Megrahi as the man who purchased clothes thought to be packed in a suitcase along with the explosives. But the shopkeeper became more certain over time, after he was exposed to considerable interrogation and media coverage after the event that included images linking al-Megrahi to the crime. Although we can't be sure that the shopkeeper was led to have a false memory, it's not often that people become more certain of their memories over time.

Similarly, vigorous debate continues about repressed memories of childhood sexual abuse. Although unfortunately, such abuse surely does occur, some researchers have suggested that some reports of such memories "recovered" during psychotherapy sessions (often involving hypnosis) may be false. How could this happen? Such dramatic reconstruction in memory may be possible because of a combination of a few different factors. First, the person who is led to believe that such events happened generally might be someone who is more susceptible than most to suggestion. Second, the person has sought help from a therapist presumably because he or she is suffering from psychological difficulties and is motivated to understand and get past those problems. Third, the person may find him- or herself working with a therapist who believes in repressed memories; in the course of therapy, the seeds of such memories can be planted by leading questions from the therapist. Note that this remains a controversial issue, and although a number of experts suggest that such dramatic false memories are possible (Kunda, 1999; Schacter, 1996), it is not clear how often false memories might occur.

In contrast, there is clear evidence that childhood sexual abuse does occur, as the highly publicized scandals in the Catholic Church and at Penn State University demonstrated. All reported memories of such abuse should be taken very seriously. Although it is conceivable that such shocking events could be falsely recalled, it seems more likely that real memories of such horrific experiences will be dismissed because they don't fit the schema most of us have of how adults—whether coaches, priests, or parents—treat children. It is interesting to note that some of Freud's early patients reported being sexually abused by their parents. Although he initially believed his patients, the idea of this happening was so shocking at the time that he later decided that these reports must have reflected fantasy wishes rather than real memories. In retrospect, it seems possible that Freud's first inclination may have been correct.

The Availability Heuristic and Ease of Retrieval

Clearly, the content of the memories people recall, whether true or false, greatly influences their judgments. But people's judgments can also be affected by how readily memories can be brought into consciousness. Try to make the following judgment as quickly as possible. Which of the two word fragments listed below could be completed by more words?

(1) _ _ _ _ I N G   or   (2) _ _ _ _ _ N _

If your first inclination was to choose option 1, you just exhibited what is referred to as the availability heuristic (Tversky & Kahneman, 1973). This is our tendency to assume that information that comes easily to mind (or is readily available) is more frequent or common. It's relatively easy to think of four letter words that you can add "ing" to, but it is more of a struggle to come up with seven-letter words with N in the sixth position. If we compare the relative difficulty in recalling such words, it's easy to conclude that option 1 could be completed with more words. Of course, on closer examination, you can readily see that option 2 has to be the correct answer. Any word that you could think of that would fit in option 1 would also fit in option 2, and some words, such as *weekend*, fit only in option 2.

The availability heuristic has the power to distort many of our judgments. If you were planning to visit Israel, you would probably be worried about possible suicide

Jerry Sandusky (the coach on the right) faced charges of sexually preying on adolescent boys. Sometimes the schemas we have of how certain people are supposed to act don't mesh with how they are accused of acting.
[Centre Daily Times/MCT via Getty Images]

Availability heuristic The tendency to assume that information that comes easily to mind (or is readily available) is more frequent or common.

bombings. When such attacks occur, they make the news. But actually, Israel has a very high fatality rate from car accidents, so that, when in Israel, you are far more likely to die in a car accident than in a suicide bombing. Similarly, people generally are more afraid of flying in an airplane than of driving their car, yet according to the National Safety Council (2014), the lifetime risk of dying in a motor vehicle accident is 1 in 112, whereas the lifetime risk of dying during air travel is 1 in 8,357. But every airplane accident attracts national media attention, whereas most car fatalities are barely covered at all. Because airplane crashes are so easily recalled, using the availability heuristic makes it seem that they are more prevalent than they really are. If the media covered each of the safe landings or each fatal car accident with as much intensity, the airline industry would probably enjoy a large increase in ticket sales!

Inspired by research on the availability heuristic, Norbert Schwarz and colleagues (1991) discovered a related phenomenon known as the ease of retrieval effect. With the availability heuristic, people rely on what they can most readily retrieve from memory to judge the frequency of events. With the ease of retrieval effect, people judge how frequently an event occurs on the basis of how easily they can retrieve a certain number of instances of that event. To demonstrate this, Schwarz and colleagues asked college students to recall either 6 instances when they acted assertively or 12 instances when they acted assertively. You might expect that the more assertive behaviors you remember, the more assertive you feel. But the researchers found the exact opposite pattern: participants asked to recall 12 instances of assertiveness rated themselves as *less* assertive than those asked only to recall 6 instances.

Ease of retrieval effect Process whereby people judge how frequently an event occurs on the basis of how easily they can retrieve examples of that event.

Think ABOUT

[wavebreakmedia/ Shutterstock]

Take a few moments and try to think about 12 distinct times when you behaved assertively. If you are like most people, coming up with 12 distinct episodes is actually pretty difficult, much more difficult than only recalling 6 times. So what do people draw from the *process* of doing this task? People seem to make the following inference: If I'm finding it difficult to complete the task that is asked of me (recalling 12 acts of assertiveness), then I must not act assertively much, and so I must not be a very assertive person. Some studies suggest that this ease of retrieval effect occurs only if the person puts considerable cognitive effort into trying to retrieve the requested number of instances of the behavior (e.g., Tormala et al., 2002). Only then do they attend to the ease or difficulty of retrieval and use it to assess how common the recalled behavior is.

APPLICATION
What Is Your Risk of Disease?

Much as we might like to think that people objectively determine their estimated risk for disease by considering their actual risk factors, this is not always the case. Peoples' judgments about health risk are strongly influenced by many of the cognitive and motivational factors covered throughout this textbook. One factor is the ease with which people can recall information that makes them feel more or less vulnerable. For example, the ease of retrieval effect we have been describing also occurs in judgments of the risk of getting HIV and other health risks (e.g., Raghubir & Menon, 1998). The more easily students could recall behaviors that increase risk of sexually transmitted diseases, regardless of the number of actual risk behaviors they remembered, the more at risk they felt. Similarly, asking participants to recall three behaviors that increase the risk of heart disease increased judgments of perceived risk more than did asking them to recall eight such behaviors (Rothman & Schwarz, 1998).

But there is an important caveat here as well as reason for optimism that, at least in certain situations, we will adopt a more thoughtful approach to estimating risk. When Rothman and Schwarz (1998) asked participants who had a family history of heart disease, and thus for whom the condition was quite relevant, to think of *personal* behaviors that increase risk, they estimated themselves to be at higher risk when asked to come up with more, rather than fewer, risky behaviors. This suggests that with greater personal relevance, people's judgments are less reliant on an ease of retrieval effect. ●

SECTION review | Remembering Things Past

We rely on our memory to make sense of the world.

Forming Memories	Remembering
Memories are formed when we encode information and consolidate it into long-term memory for retrieval.	• Our memories are often reconstructions rather than objective facts and are subject to bias. These reconstructed memories are influenced by our schemas, which generally guide us to remember information that is consistent with the most salient schema. • The misinformation effect is an example of reconstructed memory, because leading questions plant expectations that influence us to remember events differently than they actually occurred. • We often base our judgments on how readily information comes to mind (the availability heuristic) and the ease with which we can retrieve it.

Inferring Cause and Effect in the Social World

Now that we have a sense of the role of memory in how we understand people and events, we can move on to a second core process we use to gain understanding. This is the process by which we look for relationships of cause and effect. In our fender-bender example, the investigator involved is charged not only with obtaining a (let's hope accurate) record of what happened but also with identifying what factors *caused* the outcome. In our own interpretation of events, we similarly seek to pair effects with their causes, so that we will know how to act and better predict outcomes in the future. When you see that your friend is really upset, you want to know what caused those feelings so that you can effectively console your friend, maybe help fix the problem, and know how to avoid the situation in the future. Fritz Heider pioneered this line of inquiry beginning back in the 1930s. At that time, the two dominant views of what causes humans to behave the way we do—psychoanalysis and behaviorism—placed little emphasis on our conscious thoughts. But Heider argued that to understand why people behave the way they do, we have to examine how they come to comprehend their social surroundings. To this end, Heider (1958) developed a common sense, or naive, psychology: an analysis of how ordinary people like you and me think about the people and events in our lives.

Common Sense Psychology

Working from a Gestalt perspective, Heider assumed that the same kinds of rules that influence the organization of visual sensations also guide most people's impressions of other people and social situations. In one early study (Heider & Simmel, 1944), people watched a rather primitive animated film in which a disk, a small triangle, and a larger triangle moved in and out of a larger square with an opening. The participants were then asked to describe what they saw (**FIGURE 4.3**). People tended to depict the actions of the geometric objects in terms of causes, effects, and intentions, for example, "The larger triangle chased the smaller triangle out of the room [the larger square]."

    This tendency led Heider to propose that people organize their perceptions of action in the social world in terms of causes and effects. He subsequently listened to how people talked about their social lives in ordinary conversation and obtained

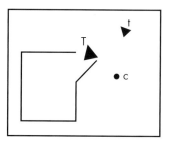

Figure 4.3

Seeing Intention

People tend to perceive actions in the world in terms of cause and effect. In viewing these shapes, subjects perceived the scene as one triangle pushing the other out of the room.

[Heider & Simmel (1994) © 1944 by the Board of Trustees of the University of Illinois. Used with permission of the University of Illinois Press]

Causal attribution The explanation that people use for what caused a particular event or behavior.

Heider Video on LaunchPad

Locus of causality Attribution of behavior to either an aspect of the actor (internal) or to some aspect of the situation (external).

further support for this proposition. Specifically, people tend to explain events in terms of particular causes. Heider referred to such explanations as causal attributions.

Because causal attributions help people make sense of, and find meaning in, their social worlds, they are of great importance. When someone is bumped into in a bar, whether he attributes the bumping to malicious intent or mere clumsiness can be a matter of life or death. When an employee is late, whether the employer attributes that behavior to the person's laziness or to her tough circumstances can determine whether she is fired or not. After a car accident, determining who was responsible can have profound financial consequences for the parties involved. If a woman shoots her abusive husband, a jury may have to decide if she did it because she feared for her life or because she wanted to collect on his life insurance. Whenever the economy is shaky, considerable debate arises over which political party's policies are most responsible for the current economic gloom. In pretty much every domain of life, from bar jostling to jurors' decision making to whom one votes for on election day, causal attributions play a significant role.

Basic Dimensions of Causal Attribution

Heider (1958) observed that causal attributions vary on two basic dimensions. The first dimension is locus of causality, which can be either *internal* to some aspect of the person engaging in the action (known as the actor), or *external* to some factor in the person's environment (the situation). For example, if Justin failed his physics exam, you could attribute his poor performance to a lack of intelligence or effort, factors internal to Justin. Or you could attribute Justin's failure to external factors, such as a lousy physics professor or an unfair exam.

The second basic dimension is *stability*: attributing behavior to either stable or unstable factors. If you attribute Justin's failure to a lack of intelligence, that's a stable internal attribution, because people generally view intelligence as relatively immutable. On the other hand, if you attribute Justin's failure to a lack of effort, that is an unstable internal attribution. You would still perceive Justin as responsible for the failure, but you would recognize that his exertion of effort can vary from situation to situation. Stable attributions suggest that future outcomes in similar situations, such as the next physics test, are likely to be similar. In contrast, unstable attributions suggest that future outcomes could be quite different; if Justin failed because of a lack of effort, he might do a lot better on the next test if he exerted himself a bit more.

External attributions can also be stable or unstable. If you attribute Justin's failure to a professor who always gives brutal tests or who is an incompetent teacher, you are likely to think that Justin will not do much better on the next test. But if you attribute Justin's failure to external unstable factors such as bad luck or his girlfriend's having broken up with him right before the test, then you're more likely to think Justin may improve on the next exam.

As poor Justin's example suggests, how we attribute a behavior—to internal or external, stable or unstable factors—affects both the impressions we form of the actor and the predictions we make about the actor's future behavior. An internal attribution for a poor performance or a negative action reflects poorly on the actor, whereas an external attribution tends to let the actor off the hook. On the other hand, an internal attribution for a positive behavior generally leads to a positive impression of the actor, whereas an external attribution for a positive action undermines the benefit to the actor's image. Attributions to stable factors lead to strong expectations of similar behavior in similar situations, whereas attributions to unstable factors do not.

 APPLICATION

School Performance and Causal Attribution

These attributional processes don't just affect how we perceive others. They can also influence how we perceive ourselves. The psychologist Carol Dweck (1975) investigated the causal attributions that elementary-school boys and girls made for their own poor performances in math courses. Dweck found that boys tended to attribute their difficulties to the unstable internal factor of lack of effort on their part or to external factors such as a bad teacher, whereas girls tended to attribute their difficulties to a stable internal cause: lack of math ability. She reasoned that once girls attributed poor math performance to a lack of math ability, they were likely to give up trying to get better at math. What's the point of trying if you simply don't have the ability? But of course, if you don't try, you won't succeed. Accordingly, Dweck concluded that the most productive causal attribution for poor performance is to an internal but unstable factor: lack of sufficient effort. This attribution implies that one can improve by working harder. So Dweck

Getting children, including girls, to attribute math performance to effort rather than natural ability can improve math performance.

[Blend Images/Ariel Skelley/Getty Images]

and colleagues (1978) developed an attributional retraining program that encourages grade-school children to attribute their failures to a lack of effort. She found that doing so led to substantial improvement in subsequent math performance.

Entity and Incremental Theorists

Inspired by her early work on achievement, Dweck and colleagues (Dweck, 2012; Hong et al., 1995) proposed that intelligence and other attributes need not be viewed as stable entities. Rather, they could be viewed as attributes that change incrementally over time. Dweck says that when we take the perspective of an *entity* theorist, we view an attribute as a fixed trait that a person can't control or change. For example, we may see an attribute such as intelligence as a stable and enduring quality. But when we take the perspective of an *incremental* theorist, we believe an attribute is a malleable ability that can increase or decrease. For example, we may see an attribute such as shyness as a quality that, with the right motivation and effort, people can change (Beer, 2002). Take a moment to think about which attributes you think are fixed entities and beyond your control, and which attributes you think are changeable.

Think ABOUT

[Lisa Peardon/ Getty Images]

These theories have implications for how an individual interacts with, and responds to, the social world. Dweck and colleagues find that entity theorists, both children and adults, make more negative stable attributions about themselves in response to challenging tasks, and then tend to perform worse and experience more negative affect in response to such tasks. Moreover, they tend to eschew opportunities to change that ability even when the ability is crucial to their success. For instance, one study measured peoples' theories about achievement and intelligence. Exchange students who had stronger entity theories expressed less interest in remedial English courses when their English was poor and improving would facilitate their academic goals (Hong et al., 1999). In contrast, incremental theorists view situations that implicate that ability more as opportunities to improve, to develop their skills and knowledge. This affects not just what we do for ourselves, but also how we treat others. When business managers had stronger incremental theories, they were more willing to provide mentorship to their employees and thus help their employees to improve (Heslin & Vanderwalle, 2008).

Although people generally have dispositional tendencies to hold either entity or incremental theories about human attributes, these views can be changed (Dweck, 2012; Heslin & Vanderwalle, 2008; Kray & Haselhuhn, 2007). For example, research has shown that convincing students that intelligence is an incremental attribute rather than a stable entity encourages them to be more persistent in response to failure, adopt more learning-oriented goals, and make fewer ability attributions for failure (Bergen, 1991; Burnette et al., 2012; Dweck, 2012).

Automatic Processes in Causal Attribution

How do people arrive at a particular attribution for a behavior they observe? Like most products of human cognition, casual attributions sometimes result from quick, intuitive, automatic processes, and sometimes from more rational, elaborate, thoughtful processes.

Whenever you ask people why some social event occurred, they can usually give an opinion. However, research has shown that people often don't put much effort into thinking about causal attributions. People make a concentrated effort primarily when they encounter an event that is unexpected or important to them (Jaynes, 1976; Pyszczynski & Greenberg, 1981; Wong & Weiner, 1981). Such events are more likely to require some action on our part and are more likely to have a significant impact on our own lives, so it is more important to arrive at an accurate causal attribution.

Let's imagine that when you were a kid, your mom always had coffee in the morning, and you came into the kitchen one morning and saw your mom put on a pot of coffee. If a friend dropped by and asked you why your mom was doing that, you would readily respond, "She always does that" or "She loves coffee in the morning"—the same knowledge that led you to expect her to do exactly what she did. However, if one morning she was brewing a pot of herbal tea, this would be unexpected, and you'd likely wonder why she was doing that instead of brewing her usual coffee. You would be even more likely to think hard about a causal attribution for her behavior if one morning she was making herself a martini.

Most events in our daily lives are expected; consequently, we don't engage in an elaborate process to determine a causal attribution. According to Harold Kelley (1973), when events readily fit existing causal schemas, we rely on them rather than engage in much thought about why the events occurred. These causal schemas come from two primary sources. Some are based on our own personal experience, as in the mom-making-coffee example. Others are based on general cultural knowledge. If an American watches another person in a restroom passing a thin, waxed piece of thread between her teeth, little or no thought about *why* is generated, because it is a culturally normative accepted form of hygiene known as flossing. But consider our discussion in chapter 2 of cultural differences and think about how people garner prestige and self-worth from the cultural perspective. In the same way we might think little of someone flossing in a restroom, a Trobriand Islander wouldn't blink an eye

Think
ABOUT

[© Albrecht G. Schaefer/Corbis]

at a man building up a large pile of yams in front of his sister's house and leaving them to rot. In that culture, this behavior is a way that people enhance their status and would not require any explanation. But if the Trobriander saw someone flossing, or if the American saw someone "yamming," then a more elaborate process of determining an attribution would almost certainly ensue.

When an event we observe isn't particularly unexpected or important to us but doesn't readily fit an obvious causal schema, we are likely to base our causal attribution on whatever plausible factor is either highly visually salient or highly accessible from memory. This "top of the head phenomenon" was illustrated in a set of studies by Shelley Taylor and Susan Fiske (Taylor & Fiske, 1975; Fiske & Taylor, 1991) in which participants heard a group discussion at a table. One particular member of each group was made visually salient. One way they accomplished this was by having only one member of the group be of a particular race or gender. Participants were asked how much each individual was responsible for the direction of the discussion. For instance, when the group included only one woman, she was viewed as most causally responsible for the discussion. Similar effects have been found if salience is achieved by having the person sitting at the apparent head of a table or if lighting is specifically focused on the person (McArthur & Post, 1977).

The Fundamental Attribution Error

This reliance on visual salience was anticipated by Heider, who proposed that people are likely to attribute behavior to internal qualities of the person, because when a person engages in an action, that actor tends to be the observer's salient focus of attention. Edward Jones and Keith Davis (1965) carried this notion further by proposing that when people observe an action, they have a strong tendency to make a **correspondent inference**, meaning that they attribute an attitude, desire, or trait that corresponds to the action to the person. For example, if you watch Ciara pick up books dropped by a fellow student leaving the library, you will automatically think of Ciara as helpful. These correspondent inferences are generally useful because they give us quick information about the person we are observing.

Correspondent inferences are most likely under three conditions (e.g., Jones, 1990). First, the individual seems to have a choice in taking an action. Second, a person has a choice between two courses of action and there is only one difference between one choice and the other. For example, if Sarah must choose between two colleges that are very similar except one is known to be more of a party school, and she chooses the party school, you may conclude Sarah is into partying. But you would be less likely to do so if the school she chose was more of a party school, but was also closer to her home, in a warmer climate, was known to be better in science, and was less expensive. Third, a correspondent inference is more likely when someone has a particular social role and acts inconsistent with that role. If a contestant in a game show such as *The Price is Right* wins a car but barely cracks a smile and simply says "Thank you," you would be likely to infer she is not an emotionally expressive person. But if she jumps up and down excitedly after she wins the new car, you would not be as certain what she is like, because most people in that role would be similarly exuberant.

Although all three of these factors increase the likelihood of a correspondent inference, this tendency is so strong that we often jump to these correspondent inferences without sufficiently considering external, situational factors that may also have contributed to the behavior witnessed (e.g., Jones & Harris, 1967). Research has found that people's tendency to attribute behavior to internal or dispositional qualities of the actor, and consequently underestimate the causal role of situational factors, is so pervasive that it is known as the **fundamental attribution error**, or FAE for short. The initial demonstration of the FAE was provided by Ned Jones and Victor Harris (1967) (**FIGURE 4.4**). Participants read an essay that was either strongly in favor of Fidel Castro (the long-time dictator of Cuba) or strongly against Castro. Half the participants were told that the essay writer chose his position on the essay. When asked what they thought the essay writer's true attitude toward Castro was, participants, not surprisingly, judged the true attitude as pro-Castro when the essay was pro-Castro and anti-Castro when the essay was anti-Castro. However, the other half of the participants were told that the writer didn't have a choice in whether to advocate for or against Castro; instead, the experimenter had assigned what side the writer should take. Logic would suggest that the lack of choice would make the position advocated by the essay a poor basis for guessing the author's true attitude. However, these participants, despite knowing the essay writer had no choice, also rated his attitudes as corresponding to the position he took in the essay.

Correspondent inference The tendency to attribute to the actor an attitude, desire, or trait that corresponds to the action.

Fundamental attribution error (FAE) The tendency to attribute behavior to internal or dispositional qualities of the actor and consequently underestimate the causal role of situational factors.

Figure 4.4

The Fundamental Attribution Error

Participants inferred that the author's true attitude matched the position advocated in the essay, even when told the author had no choice in what position he took for the essay.

[Data source: Jones & Harris (1967)]

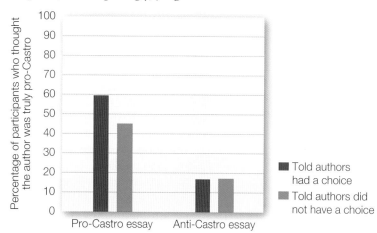

Many experiments have since similarly shown that despite reasons for attributing behavior largely, if not entirely, to situational factors, people tend to make dispositional attributions instead. One of the most compelling demonstrations was a study by Lee Ross and colleagues (1977), inspired by early precursors, which date back to the 1950s, to the present plethora of reality TV shows: quiz shows. Participants were randomly assigned the role of questioner, contestant, or observer, which ensured that the groups of students assigned to each role were equally knowledgeable. The questioners were asked to generate difficult questions that the contestants then had to answer. It is pretty obvious that coming up with tough questions from your own store of knowledge is a lot easier than answering difficult questions made up by someone else. Yet, both the observers and the contestants themselves concluded that the questioners were more knowledgeable than the contestants. Clearly these participants did not take sufficiently into account the influence of the situation—questioner and contestant roles—in making these judgments.

A compelling example of the FAE from everyday life is the tendency to think that actors are like their characters. Actors who play evil characters on soap operas have even been verbally abused in public! Leonard Nimoy, who played Mr. Spock in the original *Star Trek* television show and in subsequent movies, got so tired of being viewed as Spock when the series was at the height of its popularity that he wrote a book called *I Am Not Spock*. Similarly, slapstick comics such as Will Farrell have expressed frustration that people expect them to be wacky loons in real life. On the one hand, these errors make sense because we know these people only as their fictional characters. On the other hand, they are great examples of the FAE because we know that most of the time actors are saying lines written for them by someone else and are being directed with regard to their appearance, movements, and nonverbal behaviors.

The FAE has implications for how people judge others—for example, defendants in court—and for how they judge social issues pertinent to individuals and groups. If people are likely to make internal attributions to drug addicts, homeless people, and welfare recipients, they are probably more supportive of treating such people harshly and less likely to entertain ways to change environmental factors that contribute to these problems. Linda Skitka and colleagues (2002) found that, consistent with this reasoning, American political conservatives seem to be more susceptible to the FAE than liberals and are therefore less sympathetic to those low on the socioeconomic ladder. Likewise, conservatives judging wealthy people are led by the FAE toward attributions to those people's abilities and initiative, rather than to their trust funds, connections, or lucky breaks.

How Fundamental Is the FAE?

Although the FAE is common when people make attributions for the behavior of others, this is not the case when making attributions for oneself. And if you think about visual salience, you should be able to (literally) see why. When we are observers, the other person is a salient part of our visual field, but when we ourselves are acting in the world, we are usually focused on our surroundings rather than on ourselves. This leads to what has been labeled the **actor-observer effect**: As observers we are likely to make internal attributions for the behavior of others, but as actors we are likely to make external attributions for our own behavior (Jones & Nisbett, 1971). When observing others, we attend primarily to them and not to their situation. In contrast, when acting ourselves, we are usually reacting to someone or something in our environment. When that is the case, such external factors are likely to be more salient.

Nisbett and colleagues (1973) asked people either why their roommates had chosen their majors or why they had chosen their own. Participants made internal attributions for the roommate's choice: "Chris chose psychology because she loves analyzing people." But when explaining their own choice, they emphasized

Actor-observer effect The tendency to make internal attributions for the behavior of others and external attributions for our own behavior.

attributes of the major: "Criminal justice is a fascinating field, and it allows me to consider a wide range of fields: police work, the FBI, law school, or teaching." It is interesting that the actor-observer effect can be reversed by shifting the individual's visual perspective. For instance, Storms (1973) replicated the actor-observer effect by showing that when pairs of participants sat across from one another and had a conversation, they generally thought that their partners were determining the things they talked about. They attributed the direction that the conversation took to the person they could see—their partner. Then he demonstrated that if shown a video playback of the conversation from the discussion partner's perspective (now the actor was watching him- or herself talk!), participants were more likely to think that they were the ones steering the direction of the conversation.

The actor-observer effect has clear implications for interpersonal and intergroup relations. It suggests that when things are going badly in a relationship, whether it is a friendship, a marriage or an alliance between two countries, each actor is likely to view the external situation that is salient as responsible for the problems. This means that the friend, the marriage partner, or the other country is seen as the cause of the problem. And this, of course, can create and intensify finger-pointing and hostility between individuals and groups. Storms's work suggests that one way to combat this cognitively based conflict intensifier is to make the other party's perspective on the issues salient. This might defuse tensions by fostering greater consensus among different people regarding the causes of their problems.

There are, however, important qualifications to the actor-observer effect. For one, we are much more likely to make internal attributions for our successes ("I aced the test because I studied really hard") but external attributions for our failures ("I bombed the test because the instructor is so awful he could not teach someone to tie their shoe") (Campbell & Sedikides, 1999). We will discuss this tendency at greater length when we talk about self-esteem biases in chapter 6. Because of this tendency, the actor-observer difference is stronger for negative behaviors (Malle, 2006). In addition, research indicates that classic actor-observer asymmetries are even stronger in what we construe as unintentional behavior (Malle et al., 2007). When people have a strong intention for their behavior, they may be just as likely to make an internal attribution for their own actions as for someone else's.

The actor-observer effect can contribute to relational struggles when each partner thinks the other is the cause of an argument or problem. The flip side is that such struggles can be reduced when each partner considers the other perspective.

[Monkey Business Images/Shutterstock]

Does the FAE Occur Across Cultures?

Some social psychologists have proposed that the FAE is a product of individualistic cultural worldviews, which emphasize personality traits and view individuals as fully responsible for their own actions (Watson, 1982; Weary et al., 1980). In fact, the original evidence of the FAE was gathered in the United States and other relatively individualistic cultures. And it does seem clear, as we noted in chapter 2, that people in more collectivistic cultures are more attentive to the situational context in which behavior occurs. They also are more likely to view people as more influenced by, and indeed part of, the larger groups to which they belong. In fact, when directed to explain behavior, rather than focusing on an individual, people from more collectivistic cultures (e.g., China) generally give more relative weight to external, situational factors than do people from more individualistic cultures (Choi & Nisbett, 1998; Miller, 1984; Morris & Peng, 1994). Such research suggests that socialization in a collectivist culture might sensitize people to contextual explanations of behavior. More recent research also has suggested a weaker tendency to commit the fundamental attribution error among those of lower socioeconomic status (Varnum et al., 2011) and among Catholics compared with Protestants (Li et al., 2012).

Evidence of cross-cultural variation in attributional biases doesn't necessarily mean that individuals raised in collectivist settings don't form impressions of people's traits and personalities by observing their behavior. Douglas Krull and colleagues (1999) found that when participants are asked to judge another person's attitudes or traits on the basis of an observed behavior, people from collectivist cultures such as China are just as susceptible to the FAE as people from more individualistic cultures such as the United States. Around the globe, when the goal is to judge a person, we judge people by their behavior. But when the goal is to judge the cause of a behavior, there is cultural variation in how much the behavior is attributed to the person or the situation.

Dispositional Attribution: A Three-Stage Model

Although the FAE is very common and sometimes automatic, even people from individualistic cultures often take situational factors into account when explaining behavior. In the original Jones and Harris (1967) study, for example, participants who knew that the essay writer had no choice were less confident that the essay represented the writer's true opinions. When might people consider these situational factors before jumping to an internal attribution?

To answer this question, Dan Gilbert and colleagues (1988) proposed a model in which the attribution process occurs in a temporal sequence of three stages.

1. A behavior is observed and labeled: "That was a pro-Castro statement," or "That was helpful behavior."
2. Observers automatically make a correspondent dispositional inference.
3. If observers have sufficient accuracy motivation and cognitive resources available, they modify their attributions to take salient situational factors into account.

This model predicts that people will be especially likely to ignore situational factors and to make the FAE when they are cognitively challenged and thus have limited attention and energy to devote to attributional processing.

Putting this model to the test, Gilbert and colleagues (1988) had participants watch a videotape of a very fidgety woman discussing various topics. The participants were asked to rate how anxious a person she generally was. The videotape was silent, ostensibly to protect the woman's privacy, but participants were shown one- or two-word subtitles indicating the topic she was currently discussing. The videotape was always the same, but the subtitles indicated either very relaxing topics such as vacation, travel, and fashion, or very anxiety-provoking topics such as sexual fantasies, personal failures, and secrets.

If observers have sufficient resources, they should initially jump to an internal attribution for the fidgety behavior and view the woman as anxious, but in the condition in which the topics are anxiety provoking, they should make a correction and view the woman as less anxious. Indeed, as **FIGURE 4.5** shows, this is what happened under normal conditions. But half the observers were given a second, cognitively taxing task to do while viewing the videotape. Specifically, they were asked to memorize

---

Figure 4.5

On Second Thought

People who are cognitively strained are less likely to correct their dispositional judgments of others. In this study, participants under normal conditions did not perceive an anxious-looking woman as being an anxious person if they knew she was talking about something anxiety provoking. But under cognitive strain, participants did not correctly take into account the topic and simply assumed she was a dispositionally anxious person.

[Data source: Gilbert et al. (1988)]

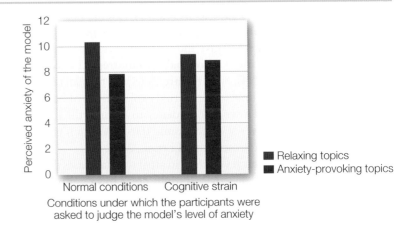

Conditions under which the participants were asked to judge the model's level of anxiety

the words in the subtitles displayed at the bottom of the screen. Under such a high cognitive load, these participants lacked the resources to correct for the situational factor (the embarrassing topics) and therefore judged the anxious-looking woman to be just as anxious if she was discussing sex and secrets as if she was discussing travel and fashion.

This three-stage model of attribution also helps us to understand how individual differences in the motivation to focus on possible situational causes can influence the kind of attributions people make. For example, Skitka and colleagues (2002) found that liberals generally are less likely than conservatives to view an AIDS victim as an irresponsible person. However, when cognitively busy, the liberal viewed the AIDS patient just as irresponsible as conservatives did. So when people have the motivation and resources, they often correct their initial leap to internal dispositional attributions, but when cognitively busy, they generally are not able make this correction.

Elaborate Attributional Processes

So far, we have discussed primarily the relatively quick, automatic ways people arrive at causal attributions: relying on salience, jumping to a correspondent inference, and then perhaps making a correction. But what happens when we encounter very unexpected or important events? As we noted earlier, when people are sufficiently surprised or care enough, they put effort into gathering information and thinking carefully before making a causal attribution. Imagine a young woman eager about a first date with a young man she met in class and really liked; they were going to meet at a restaurant at 7:00 p.m. But he's not there at 7:00, or 7:05, or 7:15. She would undoubtedly begin considering casual explanations for this unexpected, unwelcome event: Did he change his mind? Was he in a car accident? Is he always late?

Causal Hypothesis Testing

Putting conscious effort into making an attribution is like testing a hypothesis (Kruglanski, 1980; Pyszczynski & Greenberg, 1987; Trope & Liberman, 1996). First, we generate a possible *causal hypothesis* (a possible explanation for the cause of the event). This could be the interpretation we'd prefer to make, the one we fear the most, or one based on a *causal schema* (a theory we hold about the likely cause of that specific kind of event). A large paw print seems more likely caused by a bear than by a rabbit (Duncker, 1945). The causal hypothesis could also be based on a salient aspect of the event or a factor that is easily accessible from memory. Finally, causal accounts can also be based on close temporal and spatial proximity of a factor to the event, particularly if that co-occurrence happens repeatedly (Einhorn & Hogarth, 1986; Kelley, 1973; Michotte, 1963). If Frank arrives late to a party and soon after a fight breaks out, it is likely you'll entertain the hypothesis that Frank caused the melee, especially if the co-occurrence of Frank's arrival and fights happens repeatedly. The tendency of the co-occurrence of a potential causal factor (Frank's arrival) and an outcome (a fight) to lead to a causal hypothesis (Frank causes fights) is called the **covariation principle** (Kelley, 1973).

Once we have an initial causal hypothesis, we gather information to assess its plausibility. How much effort we give to assessing the validity of that information depends on our need for closure versus our need for accuracy. If the need for closure is high and the need for accuracy is low, and if the initial information seems sound and fits the hypothesis, we may discount other possibilities. But if the need for accuracy is higher than the need for closure, we may carefully consider competing causal attributions, and then decide on the one that seems to best fit the information at our disposal. What kinds of information would we be most likely to use to inform our causal attributions?

Covariation principle The tendency to see a causal relationship between an event and an outcome when they happen at the same time.

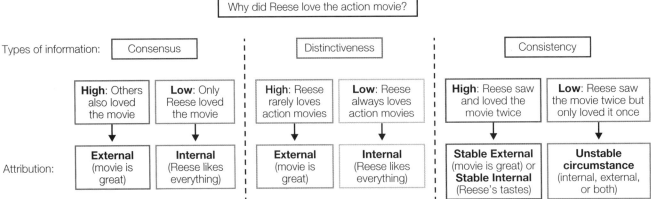

Figure 4.6

The Covariation Model

When an attribution is high in consistency, consensus, and distinctiveness, we attribute the behavior (Reese's love of the movie) to an external cause. (The movie must be great!)

Three Kinds of Information: Consistency, Distinctiveness, and Consensus

Harold Kelley (1967) described three sources of information for arriving at a causal attribution when accuracy is important: consistency (across time), distinctiveness (across situations), and consensus (across people) **(FIGURE 4.6)**.

Imagine that a few years from now, Reese, an acquaintance of yours, goes to see Sylvester Stallone's anxiously anticipated new film *Rocky 9*. (New regulations in boxing have made it legal to bring a walker into the ring.) Reese tells you, "You have to see this flick; it's an unprecedented cinematic achievement." By this time, it costs $30.00 to see a film, so you want to think hard before shelling out that kind of cash. Ultimately, you want to know if *Rocky 9* is indeed a must-see. Or was it something about Reese, or the particular circumstances when she saw the movie? In other words, why did Reese love the movie?

Maybe there was a special circumstance when Reese saw the movie that led her to love it. So if she saw it a second time and didn't like it much, Kelley would label the

Casablanca

The 1942 Hollywood classic *Casablanca*, directed by Michael Curtiz, illustrates the ways specific causal attributions affect people. It's the middle of World War II, and the Nazis are beginning to move in on Casablanca, the largest city in Morocco, a place where refugees from Nazi rule often come to make their way to neutral Portugal and then perhaps the United States. We meet the expatriate American Rick Blaine (Humphrey Bogart), the seemingly self-centered, cynical owner of Rick's Café Américain, where exit visas are often sold to refugees. A well-known anti-Nazi Czech freedom fighter, Victor Lazslo (Paul Henried), and his wife, the Norwegian Ilsa Lund (Ingrid Bergman), arrive in Casablanca with the Nazis on their trail. Victor and Ilsa hope that Rick can obtain letters of transit that would help get them out of Morocco, so they won't be captured by the Nazis. Rick is highly resistant, and it turns out,

quite bitter toward Ilsa. We then see a flashback that explains why. It turns out that Rick was not self-centered or cynical a few years earlier, but happy and optimistic. Ilsa and he had fallen in love in Paris and agreed to meet at a train scheduled to leave the city just days after the Nazis marched into the

[Warner Bros. Pictures/Photofest]

outcome low in *consistency*, and you would probably conclude there was something unique about the first time she saw it that caused her reaction. Maybe she is ultra-sensitive to variations in popcorn flavoring, and there was a delectable extra dash of butter and salt on her popcorn. This would be an attribution to an unstable factor that might be very different each time Reese saw the movie. However, if Reese saw the movie three times and loved it each time, Kelley would label the outcome high in *consistency across time*, and you would then be likely to entertain either a stable internal attribution to something about Reese, or a stable external attribution to something about the movie. Two additional kinds of information would help you decide.

First, you could consider Reese's typical reaction to other movies. If Reese always loves movies in general, or always loves boxing movies or Sly Stallone movies, then her reaction to *Rocky 9* is low in *distinctiveness*. This information would lead you to an internal attribution to something about Reese's taste in these kinds of movies rather than the quality of the movie. On the other hand, if Reese rarely likes movies, or rarely likes boxing or Stallone movies, then her reaction is high in *distinctiveness*, which would lead you more toward an external attribution to the movie.

Finally, how did other people react to the movie? If most others also loved the movie, there is high *consensus*, suggesting that something about the movie was responsible for Reese's reaction. However, if most other people didn't like the movie, you would be most likely to attribute Reese's reaction to something about her. In short, when a behavior is high in consistency, distinctiveness, and consensus, the attribution tends to be external, whereas when a behavior is high in consistency but low in distinctiveness and consensus, an internal attribution is more likely. Research has generally supported Kelley's model, although people often don't seek all three types of information, and they more reliably use distinctiveness information than consensus information (e.g., McArthur, 1972).

The presence of other potential causes also can influence the weight that we assign to a particular causal factor. For example, not too long ago, most of the baseball-watching world was in awe of players such as Barry Bonds, Mark McGwire,

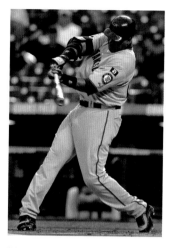

Many people now discount Barry Bonds's home-run-hitting ability, attributing at least part of his accomplishments to the use of performance-enhancing drugs.

[Doug Pensinger/Getty Images]

French capital. However, Ilsa instead sends him a note indicating she can never see him again. So he leaves alone on the train in despair, thinking that she has betrayed him. This event and his (as it turns out) incorrect attribution for it have made him defensively self-centered and cynical.

As the movie progresses, Rick learns that Ilsa thought that her husband, Victor, had died trying to escape a concentration camp, but found out that day in Paris that he was ill but alive and went to meet him. As Rick shifts his causal attribution for her not meeting him, his cynicism gradually lifts, and he ends up trying to help Victor escape. He arranges a meeting with his friend, the corrupt chief of police, Captain Louis Renault (Claude Rains), ostensibly to have Victor captured so he can have Ilsa for himself, a causal attribution quite plausible to Renault because of his own manipulative, womanizing ways. But Rick has a different reason for calling Renault to his café: to force him to arrange transport out of Casablanca for Victor. In case you haven't seen the film, we won't tell you how things turn out.

The film illustrates the importance of causal attributions not only in altering Rick's outlook on life but in other ways

as well. Major Heinrich Strasser of the Gestapo suspiciously interrogates Rick, asking him why he came to Casablanca. Rick offers an external attribution : "I came to Casablanca for the waters." Strasser points out that there are no waters in Casablanca. Rick replies, "I was misinformed," thus hiding his true attribution—to forget Paris and get away from the Nazis while helping others escape from them. Victor also suspects Rick wasn't always dispositionally the politically indifferent, self-centered character he seems to be, because he knows Rick had helped fight imperialism in Ethiopia and fascism in the Spanish civil war. Victor therefore judges Rick's current behavior to be high in distinctiveness and thus doesn't attribute it to Rick's disposition. Rather, he comes to realize that Rick's resistance to helping him had to do with his feelings for Ilsa and what happened in Paris, not self-centered indifference. In one more example of attribution from the film, when Renault, an unrepentant gambler, is ordered by the Nazis to shut down Rick's café, in order to justify doing so, he uses a convenient external attribution: "I'm shocked, shocked to find that gambling is going on in here!" he exclaims as a croupier hands him his latest winnings.

and Alex Rodriguez, attributing their remarkable accomplishments to their incredible skills and effort. However, when allegations of steroid use surfaced, many fans' discounted the players' skills, attributing some of their accomplishments to an alternative causal factor: performance-enhancing drugs. The same process applied to Lance Armstrong, as we discussed in chapter 3. This tendency is called the discounting principle, whereby the importance of any potential cause of another's behavior is reduced to the extent that other potential causes exist (Kelley, 1971; Kruglanski et al., 1978).

Discounting principle The tendency to reduce the importance of any potential cause of another's behavior to the extent that other potential causes exist.

Motivational Bias in Attribution

What makes causal attributions so intriguing to social psychologists—and we hope to you as well—is that they are both important and ambiguous. They are important because they play such a large role in the judgments and decisions we make about other people and about ourselves. They are ambiguous because we can't really see or measure causality; our causal attributions are based on guesswork because we rarely if ever have direct evidence that proves what caused a given behavior.

Magical thinking The tendency to believe that simply having thoughts about an event before it occurs can influence that event.

And if we did, it would probably tell us that the behavior was caused by a complex interaction of internal and external factors. For instance, any performance on a test is likely to be determined by a combination of the individual's inherent aptitude, physical and mental health, amount of studying prior to the test, and other events in the person's life commanding attention, as well as the particular questions on the test, the amount of time allotted for each question, and the quality of instruction in

"Magical" Attributions

Imagine that it is time for U.S. citizens to choose another president. Zach is at home on election night, watching as news channels tally up the votes from each state. He hopes and wishes and prays for his preferred candidate to emerge the victor. A couple hours later, Zach's preferred candidate is declared the president-elect. Zach believes that his hoping and wishing and praying played a role in determining the election outcome.

This is an example of **magical thinking**—believing that simply having thoughts about an event before it occurs can influence that event. Magical thinking is a type of attribution. It's a way of explaining what caused an event to happen. But it's a special type of attribution because it goes beyond our modern, scientific understanding of causation. Returning to our example, we know that the election outcome is determined by myriad factors that are external to Zach, and not by his wishes transmitting signals to election headquarters. And yet, however unrealistic or irrational magical thinking is, many of us have an undeniable intuition that we can influence outcomes with just our minds. To see this for yourself, try saying out loud that you wish someone close to you contracts a life-threatening disease. Many people find this uncomfortable because some intuitive part of them feels that simply saying it can make it happen.

[Jose Luis Pelaez Inc./Getty Images]

Why is magical thinking so common? Freud (1913/1950) proposed that small children develop this belief because their thoughts often do in fact seem to produce what they want. If a young child is hungry, she will think of food and perhaps cry. Behold! The parent will often provide that food. Although as we mature, we become more rational about causation, vestiges remain of this early sense that our thoughts affect outcomes. As a result, even adults often falsely believe they control aspects of the environment and the world external to the self. Ellen Langer's classic research on the illusion of control demonstrated that people have an inflated sense of their ability to control random or chance outcomes, such as lotteries and guessing games (Langer, 1975). For example, participants given the opportunity to choose a lottery ticket believed they had a greater chance of winning than participants assigned a lottery ticket.

the course. And yet we typically either jump on the most salient attribution, or do a little thinking and information gathering, and then pick a single attribution, or at most two contributing factors, discounting other possibilities (Kelley, 1967).

As Heider (1958) observed, because causal attributions are often derived from complex and ambiguous circumstances, there is plenty of leeway for them to be influenced by motivations other than a desire for an accurate depiction of causality. Often the intention is to preserve positive images of those we like and negative views of those we dislike. We are likely to attribute a friend's success to the friend's good qualities; if an enemy does well, we're likely to attribute it to dumb luck or cheating. Similarly, people generally believe that their country's foreign policies are motivated by noble goals such as spreading freedom and prosperity rather than ignoble goals such as greed and revenge.

If we just want closure, we grab the simplest, most readily available attribution. One explanation of the FAE is that we want to attribute people's behavior to stable traits so we can feel that we'll be able to predict their behavior in the future (Gilbert & Malone, 1995). In fact, people attribute the behavior of another person more to that individual's personality than to some other cause if they expect to have to interact with that person in the future (e.g., Miller et al., 1978). If we can believe we know what others are like, we will be more confident that we can get what we want from them.

Our attributions are also biased by our preferred views of the way the world works—our desire to maintain specific beliefs. Recall that people generally prefer to believe that the world is just, that good things happen to good people, and that bad things

Research by Emily Pronin and her colleagues have pushed this phenomenon even further (Pronin et al., 2006). In one study, people induced to think encouraging thoughts about a peer's performance in a basketball shooting task ("You can do it, Justin!") felt a degree of responsibility for that peer's success. In another study, people asked to harbor evil thoughts about someone—by placing a voodoo hex on them—believed they actually caused harm to that person when he or she later complained of a splitting headache.

Magical thinking is not only something that individuals do. We see the same type of causal reasoning in popular cultural practices. In religious rituals such as prayer or the observance of a taboo, or when people convene to pray for someone's

benefit or downfall, there is the belief that thoughts by themselves can bring about physical changes in the world. Keep in mind, though, that a firm distinction between these forms of magical thinking and rational scientific ideas about causation may be peculiar to Western cultural contexts. Some cultures, such as the Aguaruna of Peru, see magic as merely a type of technology, no more supernatural than the use of physical tools (Brown, 1986; Horton, 1967). But people in Western cultures are not really all that different. Many highly popular self-help books and videos such as *The Secret* (see www.thesecret.tv) extol the power of positive thinking, and many Americans believe at least in some superstitions.

Although magical thinking stems partly from our inflated sense of control, it can also be a motivated phenomenon—something that people *desire* to be true. Magical thinking helps people to avoid frightening thoughts about randomness and chaos. People may feel threatened by the awareness that they are limited in their ability to anticipate and control the hazards lurking in their environment. They realize that their well-being—and even their *being* at all—is subject to random, uncaring forces beyond their control. To avoid this distressing awareness, people apply magical thinking to restore a sense of control. Supporting this account, research has shown that superstitious behavior is displayed more often in high-stress situations, especially by people with a high desire for control (Keinan, 1994, 2002). This is a good example of a broader point we discuss in the main text: People's motivation to cling to specific beliefs about the world and themselves can bias how they perceive and explain the world around them.

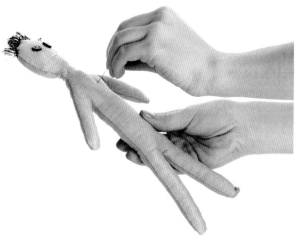

[Africa Studio/Shutterstock]

happen to bad people (Lerner, 1980). One way we preserve this belief is to view people as responsible for the outcomes they get. When people's motivations are particularly high to believe the world is just, they are especially likely to blame people who have had bad things happen to them. This has been shown regarding people who have contracted STDs, rape victims, battered spouses, and poor people (e.g., Borgida & Brekke, 1985; Furnham & Gunter, 1984; Hafer & Begue, 2005; Summers & Feldman, 1984).

SECTION review | Inferring Cause and Effect in the Social World

People tend to explain events in terms of particular causes, referred to as causal attributions.

Dimensions of Causal Attributions	Fundamental Attribution Error	A Three-Stage Model	Effort for Unexpected or Important Events
• Locus of causality refers to whether attributions are made to an internal attribute of the actor or to some external factor in the person's environment. • Stability refers to whether a causal factor is presumed to be changeable or fixed. • People who believe that attributes can change are more likely to seek opportunities to improve in areas related to that attribute.	• We tend to attribute the behavior of others to internal qualities. • We generally attribute our own behavior to the situation. • Although the FAE occurs across different cultures, collectivist cultures often emphasize situational factors more than individualistic cultures do.	• A behavior is observed and labeled. • An internal attribution is made. • Situational factors will be considered if there is a motivation for accuracy and if cognitive resources are available.	• When motivated, we make and test hypotheses for causes of the event. • We consider the consistency, distinctiveness, and consensus information regarding the event. • Motivational biases can lead us to adjust our attributions to support our own preferred beliefs.

Forming Impressions of People

Let's return to the scene of the accident with which we began this chapter. As the investigator, you show up and see the two cars in the intersection and the two drivers engaged in animated debate about who was at fault. Very quickly you'll begin to form impressions of each of them. What are the factors that influence the perceptions of the drivers that you'll form? Perhaps it's their appearance and manner of dress, the ethnic group(s) they apparently are members of, or even your first glimpse of their demeanor. Obviously the causal attribution processes we just explored will strongly affect the way in which you perceive them, but much of the time we do not engage in this kind of extensive thought. Instead, we use a variety of other processes to form an impression of each driver. We have already seen in chapter 3 that we humans have an elaborate psychological toolbox for making sense of others, one that includes schemas and metaphors. In this section, we examine some of the more specific processes that guide our perception.

Beginning With the Basics: Perceiving Faces, Physical Attributes, and Group Membership

When we encounter another person, one of the first things we recognize is whether that person is someone we already know or a total stranger. At first glance, it might seem that we identify other people in the same way that we recognize any kind of familiar object, such as our car, our house, or our dog. But there is something unique about perceiving people. As we mentioned in chapter 2, a region in the temporal lobe of the brain called the fusiform face area (FFA) helps us recognize the people we know (Kanwisher et al., 1997). The essential role of the fusiform face area has been made clear from studies of people who suffer damage to this neural region of the brain. Such individuals suffer from prosopagnosia, the inability to recognize familiar faces, even though they are quite capable of identifying other familiar objects. It seems that the ability to recognize the people we know was so important to human evolution that our brains have a region specifically devoted to this task. Research is beginning to suggest that those with autism show less activation in this brain region, consistent with the notion that autism impairs social perception (**FIGURE 4.7**) (Schultz, 2005).

Our brains are also highly attuned to certain physical characteristics of other people. In our daily interactions, we might use a range of observable characteristics to form judgments about other people, from their hair color and dress to the bumper stickers on their car. But some characteristics are perceived and interpreted so quickly, and become so integral to the impression of another person, that researchers have proposed that we have innate systems designed to detect them (Messick & Mackie, 1989). These include a person's age and sex and whether we are related to him or her (Lieberman et al., 2008). Think about the last time you bought a cup a coffee or went through the grocery-store checkout line. What do you remember about the cashier? In these kinds of quick interactions, it wouldn't be surprising if all you can remember is that the cashier was an older woman or a man in his twenties.

People may have evolved to detect these cues automatically because they are useful for efficiently distinguishing allies from enemies, potential mates, and close relatives (Kurzban et al., 2001). Our ability to recognize these characteristics quickly makes sense from the evolutionary perspective. The idea is that to survive, our ancestors had to avoid dangerous conflicts with others and to avoid infection from people who were carrying disease. Those individuals who could quickly size up another person's age, sex, and other physical indicators of health, strength, and similarity most likely had better success in surviving and reproducing than those who made these judgments less quickly or accurately. For example, recent work

Fusiform face area A region in the temporal lobe of the brain that helps us recognize the people we know.

Prosopagnosia The inability to recognize familiar faces.

Think
ABOUT

[Tyler Olson/Shutterstock]

Healthy Control vs Autism FFA activation

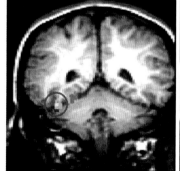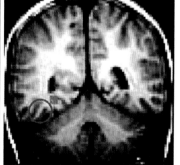

| Healthy Control | Person with Autism |

Notes:
1. Areas in red show brain areas that are significantly more active during perception of faces; areas in blue show brain areas that are more active during perception of nonface objects.
2. The right side of the brain is shown on the left side of the image, as if you were looking at the person face on.

Figure 4.7

Autism and Social Perception

The fusiform face area (FFA) underlies our ability to recognize people, an ability that is somewhat impaired in those who are autistic.

[Robert T. Schultz (2005). Developmental deficits in social perception in autism: the role of the amygdala and fusiform face areas, *International Journal of Developmental Neuroscience* 23(2–3), 125–141.]

suggests that merely viewing pictures of people who are sick triggers physiological reactions designed to cue the immune system to prepare to fend off potential disease (Schaller et al., 2010).

Because we are a highly social species, our ability to survive and thrive has depended not just on avoiding disease but even more on our ability to successfully coordinate behaviors within our social groups, whether they are families, tribes, clubs, or communities. As a result, we tend immediately to recognize features of other people that indicate that they are likely to be cooperative group members or, alternatively, to pose a threat to our group functioning. Of course, that doesn't mean that such judgments are correct, especially as they pertain to our functioning in the modern world, only that the brain may have evolved to make such judgments automatically.

Impression Formation

Think back to when you first arrived at college. You moved into your new dorm or apartment and met the person with whom you would be sharing your living space for the next nine months. You were probably thinking, Who is this person? What will he or she be like as a roommate? Once we have made an initial determination of a person's basic characteristics, such as gender, the next step in person perception is to form an impression of that person's personality. What traits, preferences, and beliefs make your roommate the unique person he or she is? Knowing what people are like is useful because it guides how you act toward them. If you think someone is likely to be friendly, you might be more likely to smile at him or her and act friendly yourself, whereas if you think someone is likely to be hostile, you might avoid him or her altogether.

How do we form impressions of others? There are generally two ways: one from the bottom up, the other from the top down. Let's look at each in detail.

Building an Impression from the Bottom Up: Decoding the Behaviors and Minds of Others

We build an impression from the bottom up when we watch what a person does and says, then, on the basis of those observations, form an impression in our minds of who the person is. We call this building from the bottom up because we gather individual observations of a person to form an overall impression of who that person is. To grasp this concept, imagine that a friend takes a trip to a city you've never been to, and she posts new pictures of the city every day on Facebook. Even though you have no prior knowledge of that city, by looking at these pictures you would eventually build up an impression of the city—from the bottom up. Later we'll contrast this with forming an impression from the top down.

Brief Encounters: Impressions from Thin Slices

We are quite accurate at forming impressions of individuals by observing what they say and do. In fact, we can often decode certain personality characteristics based on very thin slices of a person's behavior. A meta-analysis of over three dozen studies found that perceivers were reasonably accurate at forming an impression of an individual's personality that corresponded to how that person might describe him- or herself, even after watching only 30 seconds of that person's behavior (Ambady & Rosenthal, 1992). Having more time to observe the person did not seem to increase people's overall accuracy. For example, in one study a small sample of college students gave their impression of a lecturer whom they saw on video for only 30 seconds. The students' impressions were strongly correlated with the end-of-term teaching evaluations made by students who were actually in the lecturer's course.

In fact, people can accurately perceive the personality traits of others without ever seeing or meeting them, having only evidence of everyday behaviors, such as how they decorate their dorm rooms, what they post on Facebook, or the music they listen to (Gosling et al., 2002; Rentfrow & Gosling, 2006; Vazire & Gosling, 2004). Some personality traits, such as conscientiousness and openness to new experiences, can be accurately perceived merely by seeing people's office space or bedrooms (Gosling et al., 2002). Check out the exercise in **FIGURE 4.8** to get a sense of what we mean.

Likewise, when college students were randomly paired and given time to get to know one another, music was one of the most discussed topics of conversation, and such discussions helped them form accurate judgments of each other's personality (Rentfrow & Gosling, 2006). For example, a preference for music with vocals was found to be diagnostic of someone who is socially extraverted.

Theory of Mind

Not only can we learn about a person's personality on the basis of minimal information but we are also pretty good at reading peoples' minds. No, we are not telepathic. But we do have an evolved propensity to develop a theory of mind—a set of ideas about other people's thoughts, desires, feelings, and intentions, given what we know about them and the situation they are in (Malle & Hodges, 2005). This capacity is highly valuable for understanding and predicting how people will behave, which helps us cooperate effectively with some people, compete against rivals, and avoid those who might want to do us harm.

For example, we use others' facial expressions and tone of voice to make inferences about how they are feeling. If your new roommate comes home with knit eyebrows, pursed lips, clenched fists, and a low and tight voice, you might reasonably assume that your roommate is angry about something. Most children develop a theory of mind around the age of four (Cadinu & Kiesner, 2000). We know this because children around this age figure out that their own beliefs and desires are separate from others' beliefs and desires. (Before that, they assume that if they know something, everyone else knows it as well.) However, people with certain disorders, such as autism, never develop the ability to judge accurately what others might be thinking (Baron-Cohen et al., 2000). Even those with high-functioning forms of autism, who live quite independently and have successful careers, showed an impaired ability to determine a person's emotions on the basis of the expression in their eyes or the tone of their voice (Baron-Cohen et al., 2001; Rutherford et al., 2002). As a result, these individuals often have difficulty with the social tasks that most of us take for granted, such as monitoring social cues indicating that our own behavior might offend or step outside behavioral norms.

Research has begun to uncover the brain regions involved in this kind of mindreading. Neuroscientists have focused on a brain region labeled the medial prefrontal cortex (Frith & Frith, 1999). Some researchers believe that this region contains mirror neurons, which respond very similarly both when one does an action oneself and when one simply observes another person perform that same action (**FIGURE 4.9**) (Uddin et al., 2007). When seeing your roommate's expressions

Figure 4.8

Clues to Personality

What's your impression of the person who lives in the room on the left? What about the person living in the room on the right? Think about how you make these judgments without even seeing or knowing the person.

[Sam Gosling]

Theory of mind A set of ideas about other peoples' thoughts, desires, feelings, and intentions based on what we know about them and the situation they are in.

Mirror neurons Certain neurons that are activated both when one performs an action oneself and when one simply observes another person perform that action.

Figure 4.9

Mirror Neurons

Mirror neurons in the frontal parietal regions of the right hemisphere are activated both when we think about ourselves and when we think about or observe others. Researchers speculate that these mirror neurons underlie our ability to imagine what others are thinking and feeling.

[Image from Uddin, Iacoboni, Lange, & Keenan (2007)]

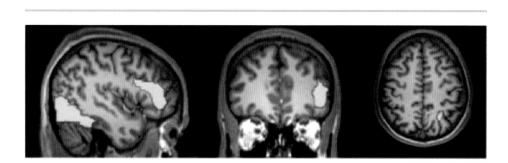

of anger as described above, you might have found yourself imitating these same facial displays. But even if your own facial expression didn't change, mirror neurons in your brain were firing that allowed you to simulate your roommate's emotional state, helping you to understand what your roomate is thinking and feeling (Iacoboni, 2009).

Building an Impression from the Top Down: Perceiving Others Through Schemas

Bottom-up processes exemplify the ways in which we build our impressions of others by observing their individual actions and expressions and drawing inferences about who they are or what they are thinking. Sometimes, however, our impressions of others are based instead on the schemas we have about people *like* them. Building an impression from the top down is a way of forming impressions that are based on our own preconceived ideas.

Transference

Transference A process whereby we activate schemas of a person we know and use the schemas to form an impression of someone new.

We often automatically perceive certain basic characteristics about a person and then infer that that individual will share the features that we associate with other people like him or her. Sometimes this quick inference might result from the person's reminding us of another person we already know. Let's suppose your roommate arrives at the dorm and your first thought is that she bears some resemblance to your favorite cousin. Research by Susan Andersen and colleagues (Andersen et al., 1996) suggests that because of this perceived similarity, you might be more likely to assume that your roommate's resemblance to your cousin lies not just in appearance but extends to her personality as well. This process was first identified by Freud (1912/1958) and labeled **transference**. Transference is a complex process in psychoanalytic theory, but in the context of social psychological research it has been more narrowly defined as forming an impression of and feelings for an unfamiliar person using the schema one has for a familiar person who resembles him or her in some way.

If you meet someone who reminds you of Will Smith, you're likely to transfer some of your feelings about this famous actor to the new person.
[Photo by Petroff/Dufour/Getty Images]

Andersen and her collaborators (1996) tested this process in one experiment by having participants first describe the characteristics of two people who they knew well, one whom they liked and one whom they disliked. Two weeks later, these same participants arrived at what they thought was a completely unrelated study of impression formation. Participants were asked to form an impression of a stranger with whom they would later be partnered only on the basis of a list of attributes that the person had used to describe him- or herself. Unknown to each participant, this attribute list had been preassembled to include some of the characteristics of the liked or disliked person that participant had nominated in the earlier session. In other words, participants in this condition were forming an impression of someone who should remind them of a person they already knew and liked (or disliked). A control group of participants were randomly assigned to form an impression of the same set of target individuals, so that for this group, their partners would not have any systematic resemblance to people they already knew. When coders rated the facial expressions people were making while reading about the stranger, an interesting pattern emerged. People were rated as having a more pleasant expression on their faces while reading about a person who resembled someone they already liked than those who read about someone they already disliked. Participants in the control group did not show this bias. This study demonstrates how, in forming an impression, we sometimes transfer the schematic knowledge we have about a person we are close with onto a new person who might have only a passing resemblance.

False Consensus

False consensus A general tendency to assume that other people share our own attitudes, opinions, and preferences.

Even when a person we meet doesn't remind us of someone specific, we often project onto him or her those attitudes and opinions of the person we know the best—ourselves! **False consensus** is a general tendency to assume that other people share the attitudes, opinions, and preferences that we have (Mullen et al., 1985; Ross et al.,

1977). As we mentioned earlier in our discussion of theory of mind, most of us can understand that other people do not view the world exactly as we do, and yet many times we assume they do anyhow. People who are in favor of gun control think most people agree with them. People who are against gun control think they are in the majority. We are more likely to assume false consensus among members of our ingroups than with members of outgroups (Krueger & Zeiger, 1993). After all, our ingroups are more likely to remind us of ourselves, and it is our own self-salience that leads us to assume that others share our opinions.

False consensus stems from a number of processes (Marks & Miller, 1987). For one, our own opinions and behaviors are what are most salient to us and therefore most cognitively accessible. So they are most likely to come to mind when we consider what other people think and do. Second, false consensus can be amplified by motivated processes. It is validating for our worldview and self-worth to believe that others agree with us. For example, when we feel under attack, we'd prefer to think of others as sharing our viewpoint and validating our beliefs (Sherman et al., 1984). Think of the teenager caught smoking behind the school who explains his actions by saying, "But everybody does it!" Research suggests that this isn't just a cliché—teenagers who engage in behaviors that might be bad for their health actually do overestimate the degree to which their friends are engaging in these same behaviors (Prinstein & Wang, 2005).

Finally, we might also fall prey to false consensus because we tend to like and associate with people who are in fact similar to us. We'll get into this "birds of a feather flocking together" idea more in chapter 14. If our group of friends really do like to smoke and drink, then in our own narrow slice of the world, it does seem as if *everyone does it*, because we forget to adjust for the fact that the people we affiliate with are not very representative of the population at large. In the present day, we see this happening on the Internet, where our group of Facebook friends or Twitter followers might only seem to validate and share our opinions, and the news outlets we seek out package news stories in ways that seem to confirm what we already believe. One of the benefits of having a diverse group of friends and acquaintances and a breadth of media exposure might be to disabuse us of our false consensus tendencies.

Implicit Personality Theories

As Heider (1958) suggested, we are all intuitive psychologists trying to make sense of people's behavior on a daily basis. With two or more decades of practice under our belt, we develop our own theories about how different traits are related to each other. Consequently, one way we use our preexisting schemas to form impressions of a person is to rely on our *implicit personality theories*. These are theories that we have about which traits go together and how they combine.

Asch (1946) found that people tend to combine traits in a way that forms a coherent overall depiction of a person, even when some of the traits seem to be contradictory. For example, a sociable, lonely person might be viewed as someone with lots of superficial acquaintances but no close relationships (Asch & Zukier, 1984). Asch also found that some traits are more central than others, and the more central traits affect our interpretation of other traits that we attribute to a person. Think about a guy named Bob who is described as "intelligent, skillful, industrious, warm, determined, practical, and cautious." Asch's participants viewed someone like Bob as generous, wise, happy, sociable, popular, and altruistic. Now imagine a guy named Jason, described as "intelligent, skillful, industrious, cold, determined, practical, and cautious." Asch's participants viewed someone like Jason as ungenerous, shrewd, unhappy, unsociable, irritable, and hard headed.

The only difference in the descriptions of the two guys was that *warm* was included in the list of traits for Bob and was replaced with *cold* for Jason. Yet changing that one trait—which is a metaphor, not a literal description of a person (Bob doesn't radiate more heat than Jason)—greatly altered the overall impressions of them. Combined with "warm," "intelligent" was viewed as "wise." Combined with "cold," "intelligent" was viewed as "shrewd." Warmth and coldness are therefore considered central traits that help organize overall impressions and transform interpretation of other traits ascribed to a person. When Asch replaced "warm" and "cold" with "polite" and "blunt," he did not find similar effects, suggesting that these are not central traits.

Another implicit personality theory is that similar traits go together. Having already decided that your roommate is neat and organized, you might also infer that your roommate will be a conscientious student, one who always attends class, takes clear notes, and studies hard. Such a theory seems reasonable. Why shouldn't a person who is conscientious with living habits also be conscientious with schoolwork?

Although as social perceivers we make such assumptions all the time, in fact, people often are more complicated than we realize. One study made repeated observations of conscientious behaviors in a sample of college students (Mischel & Peake, 1982). Measured behaviors included class attendance, assignment neatness, and neatness in students' dorm rooms. Peers and parents also rated the conscientiousness of these students. Interestingly, the raters tended to agree with each other about how conscientious a given person was, even though the person's own conscientious behaviors were uncorrelated across different situations. In other words, your roommate's closest friends and relatives might, like you, assume that your roommate's conscientiousness in the dorm will be reflected in conscientiousness in the classroom, but the two types of behaviors might in fact be unrelated. Rather, each of you might be relying on the same implicit personality theory to make your judgment.

This example concerning conscientiousness is an implicit personality theory about semantically similar traits being correlated with each other (tidy = organized = prompt). Another type of implicit personality theory assumes that traits of the same positive or negative type tend to go together. For example, people who are more attractive are also perceived to be more personable, happier, and more successful, a finding that has come to be known as the "what is beautiful is good" stereotype (Dion et al., 1972). But this effect is most likely reflective of a broader **halo effect** (Thorndike, 1920; Nisbett & Wilson, 1977a), whereby social perceivers' assessments of an individual on a given trait are biased by their more general impression of the individual. If the general impression is good, then any individual assessment of the person on friendliness, attractiveness, intelligence, and so on, is likely to be more positive. The same halo effect negatively biases our perceptions of the people we dislike. If you've had a strong negative reaction to your neatnik of a roommate, you might start forming assumptions that your roommate will possess many other negative qualities that will bolster your impression. Wouldn't life be simpler if people either had all good qualities or all bad ones?

Halo effect The tendency of social perceivers' assessments of an individual on a given trait to be biased by the perceivers' more general impression of the individual.

Stereotyping

The process just described involves applying a schema that we have of a type of person, "attractive people," to judge an individual whom we initially have categorized as being attractive. This is what we do when we *stereotype* others. Stereotyping is a cognitive shortcut or heuristic, a quick and easy way to get an idea of what a person might be like. Think about when you learn that your new roommate is a political science major planning for a future career in politics. Might you use whatever prior schema you have about politicians to make a judgment of what she is like as a person? Some of those impressions might later prove to be accurate (e.g., an abiding interest in current events), others might not (e.g., a knack for talking eloquently without saying anything of substance), but in both cases, they helped you size up your new living partner quickly.

We will go into much greater depth regarding the processes underlying stereotyping and its consequences for social prejudices and intergroup conflict in chapter 11. For now, we want to underscore the point that stereotyping is an application of schematic processing. Forming a completely accurate and *individualized* impression of a person (i.e., one that is unbiased by stereotypes) is an effortful process. We often fall back on mental shortcuts when the stakes are low ("Does it really matter if I falsely assume that Tom is an engineer?") or we aren't especially motivated to be accurate. But even when the stakes are high and our judgments matter, we can still be biased by our stereotypes when we are tired or fatigued. For example, when participants are asked to judge the guilt or innocence of a defendant on the basis of ambiguous evidence, their decisions are more likely to be biased in stereotypical ways when they are in the off-cycle of their circadian rhythm: for example, a person who is normally at his or her cognitive peak in the evening but makes their decision at 8:00 a.m. (Bodenhausen, 1990). In such situations, our tendency toward stereotyping may be cognitively functional, but it can clearly have very damaging social costs.

In this way, general stereotypes about a group of people are often employed to form an impression of individual members of that group. In addition, sometimes we take a bit of information we might know about a person and erroneously assume that that person is part of a larger category merely because he or she seems to map onto your schema of that category. For example, imagine you've been given the following description of a person chosen from a pool of 100 professionals:

> Jack is a 45-year-old man. He is married and has four children. He is generally conservative, careful, and ambitious. He shows no interest in political and social issues and spends most of his free time on his many hobbies, which include home carpentry, sailing, and mathematical puzzles.

If this is all you knew about Jack, do you think it's more likely that Jack is an engineer or a lawyer? If you are like most of the participants who were faced with this judgment in a study carried out in 1973, you'd stake your bet on engineer. But what if you were also told that of the 100 professionals, 70 are lawyers and 30 are engineers? Would that make you less likely to guess engineer? According to research by Amos Tversky and the Nobel Prize winner Daniel Kahneman (1973), the answer is no. As long as the description seems more representative of an engineer than a lawyer, participants guess engineer regardless of whether the person was picked out of a pool of 70% lawyers or 70% engineers!

This is because people fall prey to what Kahneman and Tversky called the **representativeness heuristic,** a tendency to overestimate the likelihood that a target is part of a larger category if it has features that seem representative of that category. In this case, "lacking interest in political issues and enjoying mathematical puzzles" seems more representative of an engineer than of a lawyer. But this conclusion depends heavily on the validity of these stereotypes and involves ignoring statistical evidence regarding the relative frequency of particular events or types of people. Even when the statistical evidence showed that far more people in the pool were lawyers than engineers (that is, a 70% base rate of lawyers), the pull of the heuristic was sufficiently powerful to override this information. Although the representativeness heuristic applies to much more than just social perception, it is part of the reason stereotypes are so sticky—we adhere quite strongly to our schemas of types or groups of people when we go about forming impressions of people around us.

Changing First Impressions

No doubt you have heard the old adage that you have only one chance to make a first impression. The research reviewed above suggests that we do form impressions of others quite quickly. As we've already seen, once we form a schema, it becomes very resistant to change and tends to lead us to assimilate new information into what we already believe. What we learn early on seems to color how we judge subsequent information. This **primacy effect** was first studied by Asch (1946) in another of his simple but elegant experiments on how people form impressions. In this study, Asch gave participants information about a person named John. In one condition, John was described as "intelligent, industrious, impulsive, critical, stubborn, and envious." In a second condition, he was described as "envious, stubborn, critical, impulsive, industrious, and intelligent." Even though participants in the two conditions were given the same exact traits to read, the order of those traits had an effect on their

Is this your stereotypical billionaire? Mark Zuckerberg, the cofounder and CEO of Facebook, is estimated to be worth over $30 billion.
[AP Photo/Paul Sakuma]

Representativeness heuristic The tendency to overestimate the likelihood that a target is part of a larger category if it has features that seem representative of that category.

Primacy effect The idea that what we learn early colors how we judge subsequent information.

global evaluations of John. They rated him more positively if they were given the first order, presumably because the opening trait of "intelligent" led people to put a more positive spin on all of the traits that followed it. When it comes to making a good impression, you really do want to put your best foot forward.

But if we do form such quick judgments of people, what happens if we later encounter information that disconfirms those initial impressions? There is some suggestion that our initial impressions can be changed. Recall our earlier discussion of memory for information that is highly inconsistent with a preexisting schema. In fact, when people do things that are unexpected, our brain signals that something unusual and potentially important has just happened (Bartholow et al., 2001). A broad network of brain areas appears to be involved in this signaling process, spurred by the release of the neurotransmitter norepinephrine in the locus coeruleus (Nieuwenhuis et al., 2005). Because of this increased processing of information, we are usually better at remembering highly unexpected information about a person (Hastie & Kumar, 1979). However, this seems to be particularly true when someone we expect good things from does something bad.

Negativity Bias

Research suggests that we are particularly sensitive to detecting the negative things in our environment (Ito et al., 1998). Life in both the physical and social world is fraught with danger; consequently, our capacity to live long and prosper depends on heightened vigilance against potential threats. Neglecting to notice a beneficial person or event can cost us valuable resources but is unlikely to cause irreparable harm, but failing to attend to a dangerous person or event can be lethal. Thus, the process of evolution seems to have biased us toward attending most carefully to negative information, which may help explain rubbernecking when we see car accidents and the popularity of violence in entertainment. It also may explain why negative information weighs more heavily in our impressions of other people than does positive information (Pratto & John, 1991).

This doesn't mean that we are inclined to see the worst in others; it simply means that when we do encounter people doing bad things, it's pretty useful to pay attention to it and factor it into our impressions. Most of the time, people follow the norms and conventions of good behavior, so bad behaviors might seem more surprising because they are relatively rarer. But they also seem more diagnostic of who a person is, given that person's apparent willingness to shirk social norms that keep most people from engaging in such bad behavior. As a consequence, we are particularly likely to remember when someone we thought was good does a bad thing, but we easily ignore and forget when people we expect bad things from do something good (Bartholow et al., 2003; Bartholow, 2010).

Stereotypes and Individuation

In addition to salient and unexpected negative behavior, impressions may also change as we get to know a person and view him or her more as an individual than as a member of a stereotyped group. When do people rely on the top-down process (applying a stereotype, or schema for someone's group, to see that person solely as a member of that group) and when do they use the bottom-up process (perceiving the person as a unique individual)?

Because it takes more mental energy to process inconsistent or unexpected information (Bartholow et al., 2003), we tend to truly perceive a person as an individual unique from his or her social groups only when we are motivated to understand who that person is (Fiske & Neuberg, 1990). This might happen when we need to work together on a project (Neuberg & Fiske, 1987) or are made to feel similar to them is some way (Galinsky & Moskowitz, 2000). Otherwise, we lazily apply the schemas we have about a group to make a quick judgment about the individual. However, as we learn new information, we might set aside those stereotypes to pay more attention to the person (Kunda et al., 2002). Learning more information about a person's individual experience can reduce our reliance on our stereotypes to understand who he or she is.

SECTION review | Forming Impressions of People

As social beings, we are highly attuned to other people.

The Basics

- A region in the temporal lobe, the fusiform face area, helps us recognize faces.
- We have evolved to quickly size up physical indicators of health, strength, and similarity, perhaps for survival reasons.

Decoding Minds and Behavior

- We build an impression from the bottom up when we gather individual observations of a person's actions to draw an inference about who he or she is.
- Our impressions are often quite accurate, even with minimal information.
- We are also pretty good at understanding what people are thinking.

Perceiving Through Schemas

- We build an impression from the top down when we use a preexisting schema to form an impression of another.
- These preexisting schemas are often heuristics that include transferring an impression we have of one person to another, assuming that similar traits go together, and relying on stereotypes.
- Such heuristics can lead us to make biased judgments.

Changing First Impressions

- Initial impressions can change when people act in unexpected ways.
- We are more likely to change an initially positive impression of someone when he or she does negative things than we are to change an initially negative impression when the person does positive things.

What If, If Only: Counterfactual Thinking

As investigators of the world around us, we gain a more coherent and often more accurate understanding of events not only through memories, assigning causes for the outcomes that do happen, and forming impressions of those involved, but by also imagining alternative outcomes. In fact, one of the most remarkable properties of the mind afforded by the evolution of the human neocortex is the capacity to fantasize—to imagine events that have *not* happened and people who do *not* exist. Fantasy and science fiction writers such as J. K. Rowling of Harry Potter fame and Philip K. Dick, whose stories were the basis for films such as *Blade Runner* and *Total Recall*, provide particularly vivid examples of this capacity because they imagine entire alternative universes.

Although most of us aren't quite that creative, we all use our imaginations every day. Indeed, every thought we have of the future is a fantasy because it requires imagining something that does not yet exist and may never exist in the way we imagine it. And as we have seen from the work on memory reconstruction, every recall of an event from the past involves using one's imagination to fill in the details: Not only is the future never exactly as we imagined it, but neither is the past!

A less obvious but equally important use of our imaginations is thinking about how things that happen a certain way could have turned out differently. These alternatives that run counter to what actually happened are known as *counterfactuals*. Just as assigning causal attributions helps us make sense of the world, so does our ability to think about alternative outcomes. Counterfactuals are so deeply ingrained in how we react to events that occur, they often affect us without our conscious awareness that they are doing so. In fact, the research we are about to present will demonstrate that counterfactual thoughts routinely influence how we judge and respond emotionally to events in our lives. However, we are also more likely to imagine counterfactual outcomes in some situations than in others. By examining these patterns of what counterfactual outcomes come easily to mind and when, research has revealed the important role that they play in our lives.

The More Easily We Can Mentally Undo an Event, the Stronger Our Reaction to It

Consider the following story, based on Kahneman and Tversky (1982), which we'll call Version A: Carmen always wanted to see the Acropolis, so after graduating from Temple University, using a travel agent, she arranged to fly from Philadelphia to Athens. She originally booked a flight in which she had to switch planes in Paris, with a three-hour layover before her flight from Paris to Athens. But a few days before her departure date, her travel agent e-mailed her that a direct flight from Philly to Athens had become available. Carmen figured, "Why not?" and so she switched to the direct flight. Unfortunately, her plane suffered engine failure and came down in the Mediterranean, leaving no survivors. How tragic would you judge this outcome for Carmen?

Well, if you are like the students who participated in Kahneman and Tversky's classic study, you would say very tragic. But what if you read Version B? Carmen always wanted to see the Acropolis, so after graduating from Temple University, using a travel agent, she arranged to fly from Philadelphia to Athens. She booked a flight in which she had to switch planes in Paris, with a three-hour layover before her flight from Paris to Athens. Unfortunately, her plane from Paris to Athens suffered engine failure and came down in the Mediterranean, leaving no survivors.

How tragic does that seem? Well, Kahneman and Tversky's research showed that people who read stories like Version B don't think they are nearly as tragic as do those who read stories like Version A. Given that the outcome is really the same in both versions—Carmen died young without ever seeing the Acropolis—why does Version A seem more tragic? Kahneman and Tversky explained that it is because of the ease with which counterfactuals to what actually occurred could be generated. With Version A, it's very easy to imagine a counterfactual in which Carmen made it safely to Greece—all she had to do was stick with her original flight plan! However, with Version B, no such obvious counterfactual is available. Rather, we would have to think for a while about ways that her tragic death might have been avoided. The general principle is that if something bad happens and the easier it is to imagine how the bad outcome could have been avoided, the more tragic and sad the event seems. And, as this example illustrates, it is generally easier mentally to undo bad outcomes if they are caused by an unusual action, such as switching flight plans.

Here's another example based on Kahneman and Tversky (1982) that illustrates the pervasive influence of counterfactual thinking on emotional reactions. Imagine you are going to fly to Las Vegas. The flight is scheduled to leave at 9:30 a.m., and you know that to be allowed to board, you have to get to the check-in counter a half hour before the flight departs. You are running late, and you hop in a cab at 8:00. Luckily it is only

Think
ABOUT

[Dave and Les Jacobs/ Getty Images]

a 20-minute ride to the airport. However, there is a major accident on the freeway to the airport, your cab is stuck in horrendous traffic, and you don't get dropped off at the airport until 9:35. So you've missed your chance to get on the flight by 35 minutes. You'd be fairly upset, no doubt. But what if when you rushed to the counter you found out that the flight was delayed and was rescheduled to take off at 10:00, so you missed being allowed to board by only 5 minutes. How upset would you be? You would probably be even more upset, because you missed making your flight by 5 minutes instead of 35! Yet in both cases, the pragmatic outcome is the same: You missed the flight and have to reschedule.

So why is the close miss more agonizing? Kahneman and Tversky explained that the close miss is more upsetting because it is much easier to imagine a counterfactual in which you would have saved 5 minutes and made the flight than a scenario in which you would have saved 35 minutes and made it. For example, maybe you would have made it if when packing you had been a little faster in deciding which shoes to bring, or finding your guide to winning blackjack. In other words, it is easier to undo mentally the close miss than the not-so-close miss, just as it was easier to undo mentally the tragic fate of Carmen if she had changed flight plans than if she had simply taken the flight she had planned to take all along. Now you can explain why if your favorite basketball team loses on a last second buzzer-beater, it is more emotionally devastating than if the team loses by 15 points: It is much easier mentally to undo the close loss: "If only that last shot had clanked off the back of the rim."

Counterfactual thinking has serious consequences in a variety of important areas of life. Consider the legal domain, where we'd like to think that jury decisions are based on a rational consideration of the facts at hand. In a series of studies, Miller and McFarland (1986) showed how this phenomenon of viewing the negative event that seems easier to undo as more unfortunate could influence trial outcomes. In one study they described a case in which a man was injured during a robbery. Half the participants read that the injury occurred in a store the victim went to regularly, whereas the other half were told it occurred in a store that the victim did not usually go to. All other details were identical, yet participants recommended over $100,000 more in compensation for the injury if the victim was injured at the store he rarely went to, because the unfortunate injury was easier mentally to undo in this version: "If only he had gone to the store where he usually shops!" To summarize, negative outcomes resulting from unusual actions or actions that were almost avoided are easier to undo mentally and therefore arouse stronger negative emotional reactions. Because our attention is drawn to causal factors that could have been undone more easily, perhaps we will know better how to avoid repeating our past mistakes in future situations.

Upward Counterfactuals

A handy term for a counterfactual that is better than what actually happened is upward counterfactual, with "upward" denoting a better alternative than what happened. All the examples we have considered so far have involved the effects of upward counterfactuals. When bad things happen, people often generate such upward counterfactuals, and the more easily they do so, the worse the negative outcomes that actually occurred seems.

So far we have also focused on how we react emotionally to the fortunes of others, but we also generate upward counterfactuals for our own less than desired outcomes: "If only I had studied harder"; "If only I hadn't had that last tequila shot"; "If only I had told her how much I care about her"; and so on. Upward counterfactuals generally make us feel worse about what actually happened. In particularly traumatic cases, for example, if a person causes a car accident by driving drunk, that individual may get caught in a recurring pattern of "if only I had" upward counterfactuals that fuel continued regret and guilt over the incident (Davis et al., 1995; Markman & Miller, 2006).

Interestingly though, studies (e.g., Gilovich & Medvec, 1994) have found that when older people look back over their lives, they tend not to regret actions they did but actions they didn't do: "If I had only gone back to school and gotten that masters degree"; "If I had only had spent more quality time with my kids"; "If I had only asked Jessica out when I had the chance." A broad survey of Americans found that their regrets about inaction are most commonly about decisions in the domain of one's love life rather than in other aspects of their lives (Morrison & Roese, 2011). This may be something to keep in mind while you are young. But research suggests that one reason that we regret actions we didn't do in our distant past is that we no longer recall the more concrete pressures and difficulties that kept us from taking that alternative course of action. For example, when Tom Gilovich and colleagues (1993) asked current Cornell students how much they would be affected by adding a challenging course to their workload, the students focused on the negative impact, such as lower grades, less sleep, and less time for socializing. However, when they asked Cornell alumni how adding a challenging course would have affected them in a typical semester back in the day, the alumni thought the negative impact would have been minor. Still, research on regret suggests that sometimes those fears and difficulties so salient in the present may not be so daunting as to warrant forgoing a path that offers greater rewards down the road.

Upward counterfactual
Imagined alternative where the outcome is better than what actually happened.

If upward counterfactuals, whether contrasted with things we did or with things we didn't do, tend to lead to such negative feelings about the past, why do people so commonly engage in them? Neal Roese and colleagues (e.g., Roese, 1994; Epstude & Roese, 2008) proposed that by making us consider what we could have done differently, upward counterfactuals serve an important function: They can provide insight into how to avoid a similar bad outcome in the future. Supporting this point, Roese found that students encouraged to think about how they could have done better on a past exam reported greater commitment to attending class and studying harder for future exams. Thus, although upward counterfactuals can make us feel worse about what transpired, they better prepare us to avoid similar ills in the future.

Downward Counterfactuals

Downward counterfactuals Imagined worse alternative outcomes to something that actually happened.

We often also generate downward counterfactuals, thoughts of alternatives that are worse than what actually happened. These counterfactuals don't help us prepare better for the future, but they help us feel better about the past (Roese, 1994). By making salient possible outcomes that would have been worse than what actually happened, downward counterfactuals allow us to feel better about what happened. They have more of a consolation function. After a robbery, you might conclude that although they took your television, at least they didn't get your laptop. When visiting a friend in the hospital who broke both her legs in a car accident, people often offer consoling comments such as, "You were lucky—you could have had spine damage and been paralyzed for life."

It is worth considering how people use counterfactuals to reframe such bad events. While visiting Los Angeles once, a football player from one of our schools was shot in the leg by a random bullet. The bullet missed the bone, so the newspaper emphasized how lucky the player was, because if the bullet had hit the bone it would have caused more serious, potentially permanent damage. That makes sense, but the player would have been even luckier if he hadn't been shot at all! So whether he was lucky or not depends on whether you focus on the upward counterfactual of not being shot at all, or on the downward counterfactual of the bullet's shattering a bone. When people want to put a positive spin on an outcome, they choose the downward counterfactual.

Retail stores often take advantage of how making a downward counterfactual salient can place actual outcomes in a more positive light. Imagine that you come upon a pair of athletic shoes with a sign indicating a price of $60.00. You may think, "That's not a bad price." But what if the sign indicated that the shoes were reduced 50% from $120.00 to $60.00. The sign is essentially making salient a downward counterfactual— the shoes could have cost $120.00! Does this downward counterfactual make paying $60.00 for the shoes more enticing? Of course, this can be harder to pull off for some items than others. It might be tough to generate a downward counterfactual for the jazzed-up version of Lebron James's new shoe, rumored to be close to $300.00 But when those puppies go on sale for a mere $199.00, they'll fly off the shelves.

Upward and Downward Counterfactuals and Personal Accomplishments: The Thrill of Victory, the Agony of Defeat

Counterfactuals also affect how we feel about our own achievements. Subjective, emotional reactions of satisfaction or regret are not determined so much by what you did or did not accomplish, but rather by the counterfactuals you generate about those outcomes. In one clever demonstration of this phenomenon, researchers asked participants to judge the happiness of athletes at the 1992 Barcelona Summer Olympics who had won either the silver or the bronze medal by watching silent videotapes of them at the awards ceremony (Medvec et al., 1995). The silver medal, which means the person was the second best in the world at the event, is obviously a greater achievement than the bronze medal, which means the person was the third best in the world. However, on the basis of an analysis of which counterfactuals are most likely for silver- and bronze-medal winners, the researchers predicted that the bronze-medal winners would actually be happier than the silver-medal winners. They reasoned that for silver-medal winners, the most salient counterfactual is likely to be the upward counterfactual that

"If only I had gone X seconds faster, or trained a little harder, I could have won the ultimate prize, the gold medal!" In contrast, bronze-medal winners are likely to focus on the downward counterfactual that "If I hadn't edged out the fourth-place finisher, I would have gone home with no medal at all!" In support of this reasoning, Medvec and colleagues found that bronze-medal winners were rated as appearing happier on the awards stand than silver-medal winners. Furthermore, in televised interviews, bronze medalists were more likely to note that at least they received a medal, whereas the silver medalists were more likely to comment on how they could have done better.

Is It Better to Generate Upward or Downward Counterfactuals?

This work on counterfactual thinking illustrates how the human capacity for imagining "if only" alternatives to events that have already occurred plays a central role in our emotional reactions to those events. Now, in light of all this, you might be wondering, is it better to generate upward counterfactuals? Or is it better to generate downward counterfactuals? Well, that depends on a few factors. If you're down in the dumps and just want to feel better about what happened, downward counterfactuals and imagining a worse outcome can improve how you feel. But that's not always the most productive response. Sometimes we can learn a lot from that which bums us out. Indeed, if the outcome pertains to an event that is likely to reoccur in the future, upward counterfactuals can give you a game plan for improvement or avoiding the bad outcome. But it also depends on whether you're able to exert any control over the outcome that you experienced or that you might face in the future (Roese, 1994). Say that you get into a car accident, because—shame on you—you were texting while driving. In this case, assuming you're reasonably okay, it would be more productive to generate an upward counterfactual such as "If I only I had not been texting, I would not have hit the stop sign." This teaches you to avoid texting while driving, and seeing as how you're likely to be driving again, this is a good lesson to learn! But say you were attentively driving when someone ran a stop sign and nailed your rear fender. In this case the outcome is out of your control, and so you're better off generating a downward counterfactual and thanking your lucky stars that it was just a fender bender and you're all right.

In sum, counterfactuals, our processes of remembering, of forming impressions of others, and of generating causal attributions all have important implications for the way we feel toward the past and act in the future. This can help or hinder our efforts to regulate our actions to achieve our desired goals, a theme we will pick up, along with much of what we have discussed regarding perceiving others, in the next set of chapters, where we focus on the self.

Most people would be pretty thrilled to win a silver medal at the Olympics. So why does the American gymnast McKayla Maroney look so glum? Her reaction exemplifies research on Olympic medalists, which finds that athletes who win a silver ("What mistakes did I make that kept me from winning a gold?") are usually less happy than those who win a bronze ("At least I won something!").

[Ronald Martinez/Getty Images]

SECTION review | What If, If Only: Counterfactual Thinking

Counterfactual thoughts routinely influence how we judge and respond emotionally to events in our lives and those of others.

Easily Undone	If Only...	At Least...
A close miss is more upsetting, because it's easier to imagine a better counterfactual.	Upward counterfactuals—"if onlys"—make us feel worse but prepare us to avoid similar ills in the future. They are best applied when we have the possibility of exerting control over future outcomes.	Downward counterfactuals—"It could have been worse: at least..."—are best applied when there is no possibility of future action, or we're unable to exert control over outcomes.

CONNECT ONLINE:

Check out our videos and additional resources located at:
www.macmillanhighered.com/launchpad/greenberg1e

The Nature, Origins, and Functions of the Self

TOPIC OVERVIEW

In the last two chapters, we explored how people understand others and events in the world around them. Our understanding of the external world has a considerable effect on our behavior, but so too does the world inside our minds. Humans have the unique ability to focus attention on their own thoughts, feelings, and desires— in short, we have a sense of *self*. In some ways, the self is private. Only you know what it's like from your point of view. Yet the self is also a thoroughly *social* thing. People's cultural and social environments profoundly influence how they understand and experience the self, and the self significantly influences how they think, feel, and act in the social world.

A useful starting point for understanding the self is a distinction proposed by William James in his groundbreaking *Principles of Psychology* (1890). James noted that, in one sense, the self is all the knowledge you have about your life and experiences. James labeled this the *Me,* but today we call it the **self-concept**. In another sense, the self is the controlling voice in your head that contemplates, makes decisions, and chooses what courses of action to take—what James and Freud

Self-concept A person's knowledge about him- or herself, including one's own traits, social identities, and experiences.

[Hugh Kretschmer/ Getty Images]

Ego The aspect of self that directs one's thoughts and actions.

labeled the *I*. Freud originally wrote in German, and his early English translators used the Latin word for "I," **ego**, and that has become the most common term for the aspect of self that directs one's actions. James noted that these two aspects of the self make it a unique topic to study: It is simultaneously *doing* the thinking, and it is what is being thought *about*. It's like using your eyes to look at your eyes!

This chapter builds on James's distinction to examine how the self and the social world relate to each other. We first explore how people's cultural and social environments shape the self-concept by determining *what* they know about themselves and *how* they come to acquire that knowledge. We then examine how the ego regulates a person's thoughts, feelings, and behavior. Finally, we'll look at people's everyday efforts to regulate their actions and thoughts, and we'll consider why they sometimes succeed and other times fall short.

External Influences on the Self-concept

What knowledge makes up the self-concept? Each individual has unique knowledge about him- or herself, accumulated over years of personal experience. These experiences are heavily influenced by culture, gender, and the social situation.

The Influence of Culture on the Self-concept

As we noted when we introduced the cultural perspective in chapter 2, people's self-concept emerges as they are socialized into the prevailing cultural worldview conveyed by parents, teachers, and the mass media. Culture shapes virtually all the ways that people describe themselves. When you are asked the question "Who are you?" your first response is usually your name. If you're like me, your name seems somehow meaningful and not at all arbitrary: I'm Jeff. I can't think of myself any other way. But your name is not an inherent part of you. It's a label given to you at birth that reflects various cultural influences, such as famous movie stars (in Jeff's case) and the Bible (in Mark's case). In some cultures, such as the Native American Nez Perce culture in Idaho, people's names often change over the course of their lives (Cash Cash, 2006). After you give your name, other ways of describing yourself might come to mind: *I am a student, woman, friend of Susan's, American citizen, psychology major, honest person, shy person, amateur photographer, Gemini, daughter, Jew, Midwesterner*. This list illustrates the various ways in which culture shapes people's self-concept. Across the person's lifespan, culture offers a set of socially acknowledged identities (e.g., *woman, American*), roles (e.g., *student, friend of Susan*), traits (*honest, shy*), and interests and hobbies (e.g., *photography*). If you are raised in Canada, your self-concept may very well include *hockey player*, but this is rather unlikely if you are raised in equatorial Africa.

Even within a geographic region, culture influences the self-concept. According to **social identity theory** (Tajfel & Turner, 1979), people define themselves largely in terms of the social groups with which they identify. People come to know what characteristics they have by thinking of themselves in terms of family, race, nationality, and other important group memberships. Thus, two people raised in the same geographic region may define themselves in very different ways depending on the groups with which they identify (Smith & Henry, 1996; Tropp & Wright, 2001).

In a study to demonstrate this tendency (Schmader & Major, 1999), college students were asked to complete an artistic-preference task for which they made subjective judgments of abstract paintings. They were then informed that analysis of

Social identity theory The theory that people define and value themselves largely in terms of the social groups with which they identify.

artistic preferences reveals that some individuals have a "figure" orientation whereas others have a "ground" orientation. In fact, each student was randomly told she or he was a part of either the figure or ground group. The students were next asked to complete a questionnaire measuring a new personality trait called *surgency*. Without learning their own score on the measure, students were told that both groups tend to be equal in surgency, that figures tend to be higher in surgency, or that grounds tend to be higher in surgency (**FIGURE 5.1**). Although the participants didn't know what surgency was (no one does, it's a fictitious trait!), they assumed that if their ingroup scored higher on surgency, then they probably were high in surgency as well, and furthermore, that surgency was a pretty important trait to have!

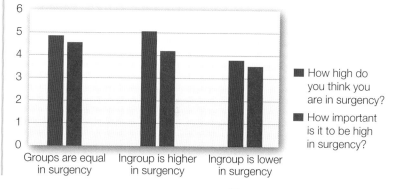

Figure 5.1

Groups and Self-definition

Students told their group is high in a trait they have never heard of assumed themselves to be high in that trait. People define themselves in terms of their social groups.

In addition to defining the identities, roles, and traits with which people describe themselves, cultures differ in whether they promote an understanding of the self as an independent or an interdependent entity. As we noted in chapter 2, in relatively individualistic cultures—for example, in North America, Australia, and Europe—people are socialized to view themselves as unique individuals, relatively independent from others. The person's repertoire of attributes, abilities, thoughts, and feelings (I am artistic and compassionate; I want to excel in school) are most central to one's self-concept. By contrast, people socialized in collectivist cultures—for example, China, Japan, India, and Mexico—tend to view themselves as interdependent, defined primarily in relation to other people (I am a daughter; I am a Buddhist) (Markus & Kitayama, 1991).

The Influence of Gender on the Self-concept

The biological differences between males and females are obvious. For example, men are physically bigger and stronger on average, and only women have the capability to bear children. We often assume that these biological differences lead men and women to have very different experiences, beliefs, and outlooks. Yet the differences between the sexes are not so substantial as we might think. In a thorough review of the research on sex differences, Janet Hyde (2005) concluded that men and women are much more similar to one another than they are different. Women rate themselves as more trusting, more anxious, and somewhat more conscientious, whereas men rate themselves as more assertive and a little more open to new experiences, but most of these differences are statistically small, and other factors such as gregariousness, impulsivity, and life satisfaction show virtually no difference at all. For example, an American stereotype holds that women talk more than men. Matthias Mehl and colleagues (2007) put this stereotype to the test. They had female and male college students wear a device called the electronically activated recorder (or EAR!), which recorded ambient sound at random times throughout the day for more than a week. Contrary to the stereotype, men and women talked virtually the same amount—about 1,600 words a day.

Not only do we imagine and exaggerate differences between men and women; we also tend to be mistaken about the origin of the differences that do exist. We commonly assume that those differences are *essential* to men and women because they are biologically or genetically based (Hyde, 2005). But people also *learn* from their culture what behaviors and self-views are appropriate for their gender. Freud (1921/1955b) noted this when he argued that children tend to identify strongly with the same-sex parent and emulate that parent's traits and qualities. Research

The electronically activated recorder (EAR; worn by the woman on the right) is a device that enables researchers to record snippets of people's everyday conversations, revealing a great deal about how people actually interact with each other.

[Dr. Matthias Mehl]

supports the idea that children model their behavior in sex-specific ways (Bussey & Bandura, 1999). When children see other members of their sex consistently perform a behavior, they are more likely to model that behavior themselves (Perry & Bussey, 1979).

In fact, adopting sex-specific behavior doesn't even require that the person observe others perform an action. Simply knowing that something is appropriate for boys or girls is enough. For example, when preschoolers are told that some unfamiliar toys are for boys and others for girls, they tend to like the toys described as appropriate for their sex and dislike the toys that are said to be for the opposite sex (Martin et al., 1995). Through this kind of sex-role socialization, most individuals (although clearly not all) come to develop a sense of themselves and their role in life that is consistent with their culture's sex roles.

Social role theory The theory that gender differences in behavior, personality, and self-definition arise because of a long history of role distribution between the sexes.

Of course, once we say that sex differences are at least partly learned as people engage with their culture over the course of their development, we're faced with broader questions: Why do cultures promote different roles for females and males? Why do women and men typically conform to gender-appropriate behaviors and preferences? How do gender roles shape people's self-concepts? To address these questions, Alice Eagly developed **social role theory** (1987), which proposes that gender differences in self-concepts arise because of a long history of role distribution between the sexes. The biological differences between the sexes in physical strength and childbearing ability have meant that, across history and culture, men have traditionally taken on physically demanding efforts to acquire food and shelter and fend off predators, while women have had more control over child rearing and managing communal relationships. Eagly acknowledges that men and women are, to some extent, genetically predisposed to succeed at these different tasks. But she suggests an additional possibility: By observing males and females engage in these specific roles, people may infer that women do more socially oriented and caregiving kinds of behaviors *because that is what they are intrinsically good at*, and that men find themselves in more roles associated with leadership and power *because that is what they are intrinsically good at*. From this perspective, men's and women's social roles shape their self-concepts, pushing them toward more gender-consistent self-perceptions.

Are these women satisfying their "natural" role? Social role theory says that people often falsely infer that men and women take on gender-specific roles because they are inherently suited to those roles.

[Left: Lana K/Shutterstock; right: Goodluz/Shutterstock]

Stable and Malleable Aspects of the Self-concept

Does the self-concept remain pretty much the same as people move from one social situation to another? Or does it change? Research supports both possibilities. Some aspects of the self-concept are relatively stable and unchanging. Often they are the attributes the person views as most important for defining his or her sense of self. A person might view his intelligence or his athletic ability, for example, as most central to who he is as a person, whereas other attributes are descriptive but not so self-defining. Take a moment to think about your own self-defining attributes. What aspects are central to who *you* are?

According to Hazel Markus (1977), people are likely to have a lot of knowledge about self-defining attributes. This knowledge is mentally organized as a **self-schema**: an integrated set of memories, beliefs, and generalizations about an attribute that is central to one's self-concept. A self-schema for *compassion*, for example, may include memories of specific events ("Last week I helped a duck get out of the road") and more general beliefs about how one typically behaves in various situations ("I always give change to homeless people"). Markus and colleagues have found

Think ABOUT

[Ann Hermes/*The Christian Science Monitor* via Getty Images]

Self-schema An integrated set of memories, beliefs, and generalizations about an attribute that is part of one's self-concept.

that people process information about a self-defining attribute very quickly, remember a lot of specific behaviors that reflect that attribute, and are reluctant to believe information that conflicts with their belief about how much of that attribute they possess.

Although central aspects of the self-concept remain stable, people's immediate social situation can also highlight different aspects of their self-concepts, changing how they think and act. At a party, you might be more conscious of your identity as Susan's friend (since you came to the party with her), that you are shy (when feeling awkward talking to people), and that you enjoy photography (when admiring several photographs hanging in the house). This portion of your self-schema that is currently activated and influencing your thoughts, feelings, and action is known as the working self-concept (Markus & Kunda, 1986). Which aspects of your total self-concept are active in your working self-concept at any given moment can be determined by your social situation, information you've been primed with, and your motivation to think or act in particular ways. When you're in class, for example, situational cues such as books and computers, as well as your motivation to succeed, will likely bring aspects of your "student self" (e.g., *intelligent, industrious*) to the forefront of your consciousness, whereas those same aspects are less likely to be active and shape your thoughts and behavior in a different context, as when you're playing Frisbee in the park.

Another situational factor is the people around you. People tend to define themselves in terms of attributes that distinguish them from other people in their current environment. To illustrate, imagine how you might see yourself if you showed up for a social gathering and realized that you were the only student in a group of elderly family members, or were the only girl in a group of young boys. When you have this sense of solo status, your unique attribute in relation to the group becomes more prominent in your working self-concept. In one study, when children were asked to consider who they are, they tended to mention characteristics such as age, gender, and ethnicity if they differed on those characteristics from the majority of their classmates (McGuire et al., 1978).

Working self-concept The portion of one's self-schema that is currently activated and strongly influences thoughts, feelings, and action.

Solo status A sense that one is unique in some specific manner in relation to other people in the current environment.

The brightly dressed woman might view attributes such as spontaneity and cheerfulness as central to her self-concept. But that might be a temporary result of her solo status among the suits.

[Greg Ceo/Getty Images]

SECTION review | External Influences on the Self-concept

People's self-concept is shaped by their cultural and social environments.

Cultural Influences	Gender Influences	Situational Influences
• Culture shapes virtually all the ways people describe themselves. • People define themselves in terms of the social groups with which they identify.	• Men and women are more similar than they are different. • Children learn from adults and the broader culture how men and women behave. • Social role theory proposes that gender roles in society, although often assumed to be "natural," are the product of history.	• The self-concept is stable from one occasion to another because people have self-schemas for the attributes that are important to them. • At the same time, the self-concept is malleable. Features of the social situation, such as solo status, highlight different self-knowledge, changing the contents of one's working self-concept at any given moment.

How Do We Come to Know the Self?

Know then thyself, presume not God to scan;
The proper study of mankind is Man.

—Alexander Pope (English poet, 1688–1744), *An Essay on Man*

Although our cultural and social environments shape the types of knowledge we have about the self, the self-concept is also influenced by our actual personality and physical attributes. Studies of identical twins reared apart indicate that some of these attributes are likely to be influenced by a person's genetic makeup (e.g., Plomin et al., 1990). Some people like to be the life of the party; other people like to blend into the background. Some people are gifted athletes; others are gifted in math.

How do people discover which attributes define who they are and what sets them apart from others? Next we consider three ways that people learn about themselves over the course of their everyday social interactions: the appraisals they get from others, their social comparisons, and their self-perceptions. We'll see that, like any means of acquiring knowledge, these processes are imperfect. Our social cognitions can lead us down a path of mistakes. That means that although it may appear that we know ourselves very well, we nevertheless make errors in how we think about and experience our traits, qualities, and emotions.

Symbolic interactionism The perspective that people use their understanding of how significant people in their lives view them as the primary basis for knowing and evaluating themselves.

Looking glass self The idea that significant people in our lives reflect back to us (much like a looking glass, or mirror) who we are by how they behave toward us.

Appraisals What other people think about us.

Reflected Appraisals: Seeing Ourselves Through the Eyes of Others

Two 20th-century sociologists, Charles Cooley (1902) and George Herbert Mead (1934), examined the social origin of the self-concept from a perspective known as symbolic interactionism. The central idea is that people use their understanding of how significant people in their lives view them as the primary basis for knowing and evaluating themselves. Cooley coined the term looking glass self to refer to the idea that significant people in a person's life reflect back to her (much like a looking glass, or mirror) who she is by how they behave toward her. People come to know themselves first by observing how others view them, or others' appraisals of them, and then incorporating those appraisals into their self-concept.

People use others' appraisals not only to know their attributes but also to evaluate themselves and their actions as good or bad. For example, a person might feel bad about the pile of laundry on the floor because she imagines Mom's voice saying, "You are such a slob!" Because people internalize others' appraisals, they evaluate themselves as if those other people were in their heads, observing them act. Cooley also pointed out that a person's self-concept is more likely to develop and change in response to the appraisals of people who are close or admired than in response to the appraisals of strangers.

Research supports many of Mead's and Cooley's insights. In fact, Baldwin and colleagues (1990) hypothesized that even unconscious reminders of approval and disapproval from significant others would influence self-evaluations. In one study, social psychology graduate students evaluated their own research ideas after being subliminally primed with a picture of a highly respected faculty member scowling with disapproval or, in the control condition, a picture of a less prominent figure with an approving expression. In a second study, the researchers first had Catholic participants read a description of a sexual dream, then subliminally presented them

Charles Cooley (left) and George Herbert Mead (right) developed the idea that people learn about and judge themselves on the basis of how other people perceive them.

[Left: Photographer unknown, c. 1902; right: The Granger Collection, NYC. All rights reserved.]

with the scowling face of either the pope or an unfamiliar other, also with a disapproving expression, and finally had them rate themselves on dimensions such as morality, intelligence, and talent. Both groups of participants rated themselves less positively (graduate students saw their ideas as less important and original; Catholics viewed themselves as less competent and worthy) after being exposed to the disapproving face of a significant authority figure, but not following exposure to the disapproving face of an unfamiliar person, even though these faces were presented to participants below the level of their conscious awareness. Even at an unconscious level, people carry with them the knowledge of how significant others view them, and they use those appraisals to judge themselves.

Mead went beyond Cooley's emphasis on appraisals of particular significant others to propose that people also internalize an image of a *generalized other*, a mental representation of how people, on average, appraise the self. This generalized other becomes the internal audience or perspective by which people view and judge themselves. A study consistent with this idea showed that overweight people are significantly less happy if they live in a society that stigmatizes obesity and values thinness than if they live in a society in which obesity is common and accepted (Pinhey et al., 1997). These findings suggest that people can think poorly about themselves because they take the perspective of a generalized other who views them negatively.

If you consider Pope Francis to be a significant figure in your life, how do you think being exposed to this image of his scowling expression would make you feel about yourself? What if you had just been engaging in some questionable activity?

[Filippo Monteforte/AFP/Getty Images]

Although this research suggests that the self-concept is highly influenced by others' direct or indirect feedback, other studies show that people's views of themselves are sometimes very different from the views that others hold of them. Does this mean that Cooley's and Mead's analyses are wrong? Not really. Remember that Cooley said that people first assess how others view them, and then they change their self-concept to bring it in line with those internalized views. But we shouldn't assume that people *accurately* judge what others think about them—in fact, they often misread the appraisals others are reflecting back onto them (Carlson et al., 2011). What matters, though, is that people base their self-views on how they *think* others view them. That is, reflected appraisals—what we *think* other people think about us—do play a significant role in shaping our self-concept, as Cooley and Mead proposed, but these reflected appraisals can be very different from the *actual appraisals* that people have of us (Ichiyama, 1993; Shrauger & Schoeneman, 1979).

Reflected appraisals What we *think* other people think about us.

This point is readily apparent when we consider people's perceptions of their physical attractiveness. If you ask Person A how physically attractive she or he is, and then you ask Person A's romantic partners and close friends to rate Person A's attractiveness, you will find that those ratings do not match up entirely. Indeed, the average correlation between the ratings is only about .24 (Feingold, 1988). That means that some people overrate their attractiveness; other people underrate it. In both cases, people's perceptions of themselves are derived from factors other than the appraisals they receive from others.

The gap between reflected appraisals and actual appraisals is partly due to distortions in the feedback that senders provide to us: People often try to be tactful, softening their feedback to others (e.g., DePaulo & Kashy, 1998). But people also selectively interpret the feedback they are given. In one study, O'Connor and Dyce (1993) interviewed members of bar bands, asking band members to rate the ability of others in the band (actual appraisals of band mates), what feedback they gave to others in the band about their abilities, and how those individuals perceived their own ability. The researchers found that band members were pretty honest with their band mates, just a little more positive in their feedback then their private evaluations of them would suggest. However, each individual seemed to think his band mates appreciated his musical ability less than they actually did and less than the feedback he got from them would suggest. So each band member seemed to let his own insecurities color how he was perceived by others, creating a gap between reflected appraisals and actual appraisals.

Social Comparison: Knowing the Self Through Comparison With Others

Social comparison theory The theory that people come to know themselves partly by comparing themselves with similar others.

Downward comparison Comparing oneself with those who are worse off.

Upward comparison Comparing oneself with those who are better off.

A second way in which people learn who they are is by comparing themselves with others. Leon Festinger (1954) first described this process in his social comparison theory. He pointed out that people often don't have an objective way of knowing where they stand on an attribute. Therefore, many, if not most, of their beliefs about themselves are on dimensions that can be assessed only relative to others. Consider, for example, whether you are a fast runner. Well, compared with a four-year-old, you probably are. Festinger called this comparison of the self with those who are worse off a downward comparison. But how does your running speed compare with that of an Olympic runner? Not so well. People engage in upward comparison when they compare themselves with those who are better off. Festinger pointed out that we generally compare ourselves with people to whom we feel similar because those people provide the most informative indication of our traits, skills, and abilities. So if you think you're fast, you're probably making that judgment relative to other people similar in age who also play the same sports you do, rather than to four-year-olds or to Olympic runners. What's more, people are more likely to compare themselves with individuals in their local environment than with large groups, national averages, or other entities that lie outside their familiar day-to-day experience (Zell & Alicke, 2010). Festinger further suggested that people are particularly likely to make these comparisons when they lack objective indicators of how they're doing and are uncertain of where they stand.

Does Self-Confidence Intimidate Others? Video on LaunchPad

Consider, for example, a job interview situation where one is likely to be uncertain about one's standing on certain characteristics. One study (Morse & Gergen, 1970) used this context to demonstrate how social comparisons can influence people's views of themselves. College-student participants came to the lab in response to an advertisement for a data-entry position. On arriving, each student and another person were asked to wait in a room and complete some initial personnel questionnaires. In one condition, the other candidate (who was actually a confederate of the research team) was dressed in a suit and carried a briefcase, giving off an air of competence and dependability. In the other condition, the confederate was dressed in wrinkled clothing, his hair was unkempt, and he carried an unorganized stack of papers. Among the questionnaires participants completed was a measure of self-esteem. According to social comparison theory, downward comparison with the person who seems like a worse candidate for the job than yourself would make you puff up with pride, whereas upward comparison with the more impressive candidate would be more likely to leave you feeling down in the dumps. This is exactly what the researchers found: Participants rated themselves more positively when they sat in the room with Mr. Sloppy compared to when they sat in the room with Mr. Neat.

Just as reflected appraisals sometimes are a poor match to what people really think of themselves, the self-knowledge people gain through social comparison is not always accurate. In fact, people consistently make errors in their use of social comparisons to judge their own attributes. These errors can come from over- or underestimating one's own attributes or from over- or underestimating the attributes of those with whom one compares oneself.

Better than average effect The tendency to rank oneself higher than most people on positive attributes.

One particularly well-documented social comparison error is the better than average effect, people's tendency to rank themselves higher than most people on positive attributes (Alicke, 1985). In two of the many demonstrations of this effect, 42% of engineers thought their work ranked in the top 5% of their peers (Zenger, 1992), and 94% of college professors thought they did above-average work (Cross, 1977). Even people in prison think they are kinder and more moral than the average person (Sedikides et al., 2014). Of course, if you think about it, many of these individuals can't be accurate. It's statistically impossible for most people to be above average—instead, the average response should be average! As we will discuss in detail in the next chapter, this and other biases in self-perception are caused in large part by the need to maintain a positive sense of self-worth.

But why else do people make this common error? To find out, Dave Dunning and colleagues (2003) reviewed evidence from various studies that examined which people are most likely to overestimate their abilities and knowledge in a variety of domains, including performance in psychology, reading comprehension, grammar, and logic tests, sense of humor, debating ability, hunters' knowledge of firearms, medical residents' interviewing skills, and medical lab technicians' problem-solving ability. In an ironic twist, the researchers found in each case that many of the same people who rated themselves as above average were the worst performers. Even when offered money for being accurate, poor performers did not become more accurate in making these judgments, suggesting that they couldn't assess themselves accurately even when highly motivated to do so (Ehrlinger et al., 2008).

Dunning and colleagues offer a simple but interesting explanation for this phenomenon. If you ask people how good they are as writers, most people would rate themselves as better than average. But why would the worst writers do this? Because they lack the knowledge of writing—of grammar, composition, and so on—to realize how bad their writing is! If they had this knowledge, they would probably be better writers! Dunning and colleagues (2003, p. 83) characterize this as a double curse: "The skills needed to produce correct responses are virtually identical to those needed to evaluate the accuracy of one's responses."

This finding raises an important question: Can people be trained to assess their weaknesses accurately, so that they know what they need to do to improve? To find out, Kruger and Dunning (1999) had participants take a test of logic. Poor performers greatly overestimated their performance. Then they trained some of these poor performers in how to distinguish correct from incorrect answers and gave them their tests to look over. Their self-ratings now became more accurate. In another ironic twist, they now rated their own logical reasoning ability lower than they did before being trained, even though the training probably strengthened that ability!

Thus, ignorance of ignorance is one source of inaccuracy in evaluating the self in comparison to others. As people get smarter and become aware of their own ignorance, they tend to become more accurate about themselves. As Dunning and colleagues (2003) note, although knowledge of your deficiencies can be humbling, it is often better than remaining blissfully unaware, because you won't be motivated to take steps to improve until you realize you have deficiencies in skills or knowledge.

Self-perception Theory: Knowing the Self by Observing One's Own Behavior

According to **self-perception theory** (Bem, 1965), we often discover who we are in the same way that we form impressions of other people. In chapter 4, we talked about how you might form an impression of your new college roommate by observing her behavior. When her behavior cannot be explained by factors in the situation, you

Self-perception theory The theory that people sometimes infer their attitudes and attributes by observing their behavior and the situation in which it occurs.

infer that it was caused by some internal disposition she possesses. In the same way, we sometimes form impressions of ourselves by observing our own behavior and making attributions for what we do. If behavior can be explained by factors in the situation, we attribute our behavior to those external factors. However, if there is no salient external factor to account for our behavior, we attribute our behavior to an internal attitude or trait.

We are most likely to learn about ourselves through this self-perception process when we find ourselves in new or unusual situations. Imagine that a friend invites you to go spelunking with him. You've never been spelunking, but you like the idea of exploring caves and trying something new. You are 30 feet into the cave and navigating a tight corridor when your heart starts racing, your palms start sweating, and you start backing out of the cave. Your friend is perfectly calm, and you had only a single cup of coffee this morning, so what could possibly be causing your behavior? You realize for the first time in your life that you are claustrophobic. This is the sort of self-knowledge that you gain only through self-perception, that is, by finding yourself in a new situation where the best explanation for your behavior is something about who you are and the traits (or in this case, phobias) you possess.

In a less dramatic way, we often find ourselves relying more on self-perception processes when we come to transition points in our life. A freshman who just showed up on campus doesn't really know what kind of college student she is yet. If asked whether she is a punctual student, she can remember back to her most recent class and think, "Yeah, I did show up on time to chemistry and was actually 20 minutes early to my Spanish class, so maybe I am punctual." Or she might think about whether she is punctual in other domains, such as her job, and generalize from that. In either case, she can make this judgment about whether she is a punctual college student, but not without first engaging in a self-perception process of consulting recent or more tangentially related examples of her own behavior. By her senior year, enough of this experience should have built up so that now when asked if she is a punctual college student, she gives an immediate "yes," without having to think about recent times when she demonstrated that trait (Klein et al., 1996).

We don't use self-perception processes just to determine our personality traits and abilities; we also use them to determine how we are currently feeling. Imagine going for a routine visit to your doctor, who asks, "So how are you feeling today?" To answer that question, you probably rely on the evidence coming from your internal physiological and psychological states. If your head is throbbing, you will likely respond that you aren't feeling so great. In this situation, your physical states clearly inform who you are (i.e., a person with a headache) in that moment. But our physical states also inform our emotions and attitudes in ways that are less obvious.

Using One's Feelings to Know the Self

Lift your chin up, and then down, and repeat this motor movement. This is a pretty basic physical act. Taking it on its own, we might not imagine that it would have any power to influence our judgment. But think about when we usually engage the muscles in our head and neck in this way. Often it is when we are signaling our agreement with something. Could this mean that our brain unconsciously uses this same sequence of muscular movements to infer agreement? Research suggests that the answer is yes.

For instance, Wells and Petty (1980) had participants listen to an audio recording that included an editorial advocating tuition increases. Under the guise of testing the durability of the headphones, participants were asked to move their chins up and down or from side to side while listening to the tape. Afterward, participants were asked how much they thought tuition should be. Those who had been nodding their heads the entire time reported tuition numbers that were about 38% higher than those who had been shaking their heads!

Another example comes from work on the facial feedback hypothesis. We become so accustomed to expressing our emotional states through our facial expressions that

Facial feedback hypothesis
The idea that changes in facial expression elicit emotions associated with those expressions.

changes in our facial movements become a signal of the emotion we might be feeling. In the first test of this hypothesis, James Laird (1974) attached electrodes to participants' faces and asked them to evaluate a series of cartoons. Before showing the participants each cartoon, he gave them instructions to contract their facial muscles or squeeze their eyebrows together in certain ways, such as, "Use your cheek muscles to pull the corners of your lips outward." Participants were told that the electrodes were measuring the activity of their facial muscles, but in reality Laird was subtly inducing them to make either a smiling expression or a frown. Those induced to make the smiling face rated the cartoons as funnier and reported feeling happier than those induced to frown. You can try this out at home without the fancy electrodes. Try putting a pen or pencil between your teeth as shown in the photo on the left. This activates your zygomaticus major muscles, forcing your lips to draw back as they do when you smile. Now hold the pen or pencil with your lips as shown in the photo on the right. This activates your corrugator supercilii muscles, which you use when you are

frowning. In one study using this technique, participants who (unknowingly) "smiled" rated cartoons as more humorous than did participants in the control condition, whereas participants who held a marker with their lips (the "frowners") found them less amusing (Strack et al., 1988). Participants seemed unconsciously to infer, "If I am smiling (or frowning), I must be amused (or turned off)."

Facial movements provide signals as to what emotions we might be feeling.
[Mark Landau]

The basic idea of self-perception is that we often lack a strong internal feeling about who we are or how we feel, so we look to our own behavior to make inferences about what we are like. Because we don't have conscious access to the processes underlying our preferences and actions, we often lack insight into why we do the things we do. As a consequence, our inferences about ourselves often can be wrong.

One of the reasons we can be wrong is that we aren't very good at accurately judging how situations influence our thoughts and behaviors. We underestimate the effects of some situational factors and overestimate the effects of others. For example, Nisbett and Wilson (1977b) showed that people liked a movie less if it was out of focus part of the time but were unaffected by a loud noise outside the room where the movie was showing. However, when the researchers asked participants about the factors that influenced their enjoyment, the participants thought the focus problems *did not* affect their liking (underestimating the effect) and that the loud noise *did* (overestimating the effect).

In much the same way as our memory is not a verbatim record of the past (see chapter 4) but is instead reconstructed online, our conscious experience of ourselves is constructed online. As a result it is susceptible to error and bias. This doesn't mean our beliefs about why we feel and behave the way we do are always wrong, but rather that they are often, if not always, based on an imperfect inference process that sometimes leads to inaccurate or incomplete understanding. If you just found out a close friend died, and you felt very sad, you would probably be right in inferring that this news made you sad. But so would an objective observer who witnessed you learning of this news but did not have access to your internal feelings. At other times, the cause of negative feelings may not be so obvious. You might erroneously attribute them to particular reasons, such as lack of sleep, when they are really due to something else. In fact, studies comparing daily fluctuations in mood with other things going on in people's day-to-day lives show that people are not very accurate in their beliefs about the factors that affect their moods (e.g., Stone et al., 1985). For example, one study found that college students thought their moods were affected by amount of sleep the prior night and the weather, but they actually were affected by neither (Wilson et al., 1982).

Using the Self to Know One's Feelings

Self-perception processes can also play an important role in the emotions we feel. Stan Schachter's (1964) **two-factor theory of emotion** proposed that people's level of arousal determines the intensity of the emotion, but the specific type of emotion they experience is determined by the meaning that is assigned to that arousal based on contextual or environmental cues. Thus, from this perspective:

$$\text{emotion} = \text{arousal} \times \text{cognitive label}$$

One startling implication of this theory is that the same arousal could be attributed to one or another emotion, depending on the self-perception process of interpreting cues present in one's environment. **FIGURE 5.2** shows an example of how the two-step process can elicit different emotions.

In the first experiment to test this idea, Schachter and Singer (1962) gave participants an injection of epinephrine (also known as adrenaline), which causes arousal in the sympathetic nervous system. However, they told participants that the study concerned the effects of a drug that influences memory and that the injection was a dose of the memory-enhancing drug. In the critical conditions of the study, participants were told that the injection would have no side effects. They were then asked to wait for the drug to take effect in a room with a confederate who was either happily shooting balls of paper into a trash can or voicing his anger over what he saw as intrusive questions on a survey he was filling out. Why did Schachter and Singer put participants in the room with different confederates? They wanted to determine if they could alter the participants' emotions by varying the salience of a label for that arousal. Thus, participants were later asked how they felt during the study. Those who witnessed the happy confederate reported being happy, whereas those who spent time with the angry confederate reported being angry themselves. Other participants, who also were given the injection but were told to expect symptoms of physiological arousal as a side effect, were much less likely to experience these emotions. This is because they already had a cognitive label for their arousal: it was a side effect of the injection. Only participants without a ready cognitive label for the arousal attributed that arousal to an emotion. Equally important, the emotion to which they attributed their arousal

Two-factor theory of emotion The theory that people's emotions are the product of both their arousal level and how they interpret that arousal.

Figure 5.2

Misattribution of Arousal and Emotion

When we observe our own behavior to figure out why we feel aroused, we can make mistakes about where that arousal came from. As a result, we can experience emotions that are fueled by something else entirely.

Correct Attribution

Why do I feel this way?

I'm pretty amped up on caffeine, that's why.

Misattribution

Well, this game IS pretty intense—I guess I'm really excited about who wins!

was vastly different—either happiness or anger—depending on the cues provided by the confederate.

This phenomenon has become known as misattribution of arousal, which occurs when we ascribe arousal resulting from one source (in the case of the first study, an injection) to a different source, and therefore experiencing emotions that we wouldn't normally feel in response to a stimulus. Although certain emotions do induce very specific and differentiated physiological responses (e.g., Barrett et al., 2007; Reisenzein, 1983), initial arousal states often are subjectively ambiguous; thus, people's emotions can be greatly influenced by their interpretation of the circumstances of the arousal. This research shows how self-perception processes influence not only how we think about the self but also how the self experiences emotions.

Understanding how people use self-perception to label their emotions can be rather useful. Consider a psychological problem such as insomnia. Storms and Nisbett (1970) asked insomniacs to take a placebo pill described as causing arousal right before they went to bed: a seemingly paradoxical form of treatment for insomnia! The researchers reasoned that insomniacs have trouble falling asleep in part because they experience anxiety about their lives and, specifically, about being able to fall asleep. But if they could be led to misattribute some of their arousal to a pill, they would feel less anxious and consequently would be able to fall asleep faster. This is precisely what happened. Studies have similarly used placebo pills to reduce self-perception of a variety of emotions, including fear, anger, sexual attraction, and guilt, and to assess the role of such emotional reactions in various kinds of behavior (e.g., Dienstbier et al., 1980; Nisbett & Schachter, 1966).

Of course, outside the confines of social psychology labs, rarely are people unwittingly given injections of adrenaline or placebo pills. This led Dolf Zillmann (e.g., Zillmann et al., 1972) to wonder: Under what conditions does misattribution of arousal occur in everyday life? According to his excitation transfer theory, misattribution happens when an individual is physiologically aroused by an initial stimulus and then a short time later encounters a second, potentially emotionally provocative, stimulus. Leftover or residual excitation caused by the first event becomes misattributed or, using Zillmann's terminology, transferred, to the reaction to the second stimulus, resulting in an intensified emotional response to that second stimulus.

In one study demonstrating this phenomenon (Zillmann et al., 1972), half the participants were asked to exercise by riding a stationary bike vigorously for two and a half minutes. The other participants were seated comfortably at a table and asked to pass thread through discs with holes (not particularly arousing!). In the second part of the study, participants were provoked with insults or not provoked by another participant (in actuality, a confederate). Participants were then given an opportunity to punish the other participant by delivering painful electric shocks.

As you see in **FIGURE 5.3**, the unprovoked participants were not very aggressive, regardless of whether they exercised. Provoked participants, however, were more aggressive if they exercised than if they did not, suggesting that they misattributed arousal as anger in response to the provocation, thus producing anger-motivated aggression. Other studies show that residual arousal, whether from exercise or viewing sexually arousing media, can intensify various other emotion-based responses later on—such as prosocial behavior

Misattribution of arousal Ascribing arousal resulting from one source to a different source.

Excitation transfer theory The idea that leftover arousal caused by an initial event can intensify emotional reactions to a second event.

Figure 5.3

Excitation Transfer

Physiological arousal created in one context can be misattributed, intensifying emotional reactions to a subsequently encountered stimulus in an unrelated context.

[Data source: Zillmann et al. (1972)]

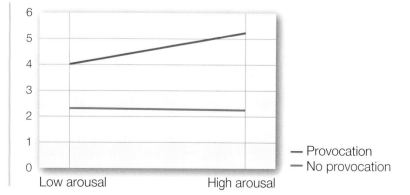

— Provocation
— No provocation

(Mueller & Donnerstein, 1981), the enjoyment of music (Cantor & Zillmann, 1973), and laughter (Cantor et al., 1974). It is critical to note that these effects occur primarily when participants are not aware of the leftover arousal from the first event. If participants are put in another emotion-provoking context immediately after being aroused, they don't misattribute their arousal because they can easily connect that arousal to the prior inducing source ("My heart is racing because I was just on the exercise bike!"; Zillmann, 1978). Also, if people have their attention focused inward toward the self, they become more aware of the residual arousal and don't misattribute their arousal or show intensified emotional reactions to the later situation (Reisenzein & Gattinger, 1982).

These findings show how the misattribution of arousal, leading to intensified emotional reactions, can happen in the course of daily events. Here's just one of many examples of how this process can affect people: Imagine a typical teenage boy getting off an intense roller-coaster ride with his date. If a few minutes later he gazes into his date's eyes, he is likely to experience stronger attraction toward her because of residual arousal from the roller-coaster ride (Meston & Frohlich, 2003).

The Self Lost or Found in *Black Swan*

The 2010 film *Black Swan*, directed by Darren Aronofsky (Medavoy et al., 2010) is a dark parable of how the influence of cultural values can distort our perceptions of ourselves.

The film is set in the intense subculture of ballet, which idealizes perfection in physical movement and form, especially for women. In this way, the ballet world is a distillation of broader cultural tendencies to view the female body as an object and to mask the physicality of the body with an idealized veneer of beauty and grace (e.g., Goldenberg, 2013). (We will discuss these ideas further in chapter 14). This subculture takes a toll

[Fox Searchlight Pictures/Photofest]

on women's health: The prevalence of eating disorders is estimated to be 25 times higher in ballerinas than in other women similar in age and backgrounds (Dunning, 1997).

The film's protagonist, Nina, played by Natalie Portman, is a somewhat uptight and self-conscious ballerina who has attained great technical skill but is being pushed by her director to be more carnal and less repressed both on and off stage. Only if she can properly lose herself in her role will she be ready for the lead in *Swan Lake*. Nina struggles either to find or lose herself within a world where she is defined by the people around her. In one sense, Nina's view of herself is a construction of how others see her, shaped by reflected appraisals. Her overbearing mother, played by Barbara Hershey, resents that she was forced to give up a dancing career to be a mother. She tries to rediscover her own identity either by driving her daughter's dancing ambitions or by obsessively painting her self-portrait. But she also tries to protect the innocence of her little girl, fawning over her and blocking her transition to adulthood. As a result, Nina lacks self-clarity. Nina's director, played by Vincent Cassel, sees her only as an object of art and of desire. To him, the two roles of the White Swan and the Black Swan represent two categories that women can occupy: the virgin or the whore. Reflecting a way in which people often buy into the stereotypical roles that society offers, Nina seems to accept this duality. Rather than expressing any unique perspective of her own, she simply struggles to find the darker drives that will enable her to embody the Black Swan role. And when she is given the role she so desperately wants, she calls her mother and says, "He picked me, mommy!" These four words capture the ways in which men's definitions of how women should be become the

Reflections, comparisons, and self-perceptions are three important ways that people learn about themselves during the course of their everyday social interactions.

Reflection	Comparison	Self-Perception
• People learn about the self by assessing how significant others behave toward them. • Others serve as a mirror, or "looking glass." • Nevertheless, people do not always perceive accurately what others think of them.	• People learn about the self by comparing themselves with others. • Upward and downward social comparisons have diverging effects on self-esteem. • Comparisons are often biased in the self's favor.	• People learn about the self by observing their own behavior and making inferences about their traits, abilities, and values. • However, these inferences can be wrong. • A self-perception process also guides the experience of emotions based on one's levels of physiological arousal and labeling of the current situation.

Self-regulation: Here's What the "I" Can Do for You

Now that we've discussed the self-concept (what James called the *Me*), it's time to turn to the ego, the part of the self that drives and controls behavior (what James

standards to which women aspire. And women themselves, just like Nina's mom, often police these roles and ideals.

In addition to defining herself through these reflected appraisals, Nina is also quite intensely caught up in social comparison. The arrival of Lily, a dancer played by Mila Kunis, marks the beginning of Nina's dark descent into negative self-focus and paranoid delusions. In contrast to Nina's technically perfect but repressed style, Lily is a free spirit who refuses to internalize the constraints that a career in ballet might place on her social life. Nina becomes obsessed with the thought that Lily might take her role, an obsession depicted by disturbing visual imagery. Nina's sense of self is defined in an incredibly narrow manner (success in dancing). Thus, she fixates on that one particular goal, as we might expect on the basis of self-regulatory perseveration theory, which is discussed later in this chapter. Perhaps because of this focus, Nina's grip on her own identity and reality disintegrates. Losing herself in her role leads her to hallucinate that she is sprouting the feathers of a swan. Nina's intense social comparison with her understudy manifests itself in visions and dreams that Lily is trying to sabotage her performance.

These cinematic devices not only create a visceral tension to the film but also capture nicely how molding oneself to the values of others alters one's view of reality. Some film critics have complained that Nina's own motivation for ballet is never really conveyed (Stevens, D., Dec. 2, 2010, Nutcracked, *Slate*). Perhaps that's because she really had none of her own; her motivations were those of others. As a consequence, she has failed to develop an authentic sense of self (Deci & Ryan, 1995; La Guardia, 2009).

Part of what drives motivation toward any goal is self-awareness of a discrepancy between what we are now and what we would like to become. Throughout the film, when Nina sees her own reflection, she often confronts an image that looks or behaves quite differently than it should. These disturbing moments on screen symbolize how it can be to see oneself carry out actions seemingly out of step with one's internal motivation.

Of course, mirrors also symbolize our own vanity. In the final scenes of the movie (spoiler alert!), Nina's obsession with living up to ideals of perfection reaches the breaking point. Her grasp on reality finally is lost when she imagines pushing her rival, Lily, into a mirror and shattering it during an intermission in the ballet performance. Although she envisions her competitor being destroyed, it is revealed in the next scene—after she dances the Black Swan role perfectly—that her attempt to pursue an ideal imposed on her by others leads only to self-destruction. The shard of glass she imagined having plunged into Lily backstage is actually impaled in her own body.

[Fox Searchlight Pictures/Photofest]

Self-regulation The process of guiding one's thoughts, feelings, and behavior to reach desired goals.

called the *I*). We'll explore self-regulation—how people decide what goals to pursue and how they attempt to guide their thoughts, feelings, and behavior to reach those goals.

The ability to self-regulate is fundamentally based on three key capacities of the human mind that emerged as the hominid cerebral cortex evolved. First, we are self-aware, able to assess our thoughts, feelings, and behavior in relation to the world around us. Second, we're able to think about overarching goals, such as curing cancer or winning an Olympic gold medal, and about abstract symbols and concepts such as kindness or honesty. Third, we are able to mentally travel in time, to pop out of the here and now to reach back to our past and envision hypothetical realities in the future.

These three capacities provide our species with a tremendous degree of flexibility and choice, a freedom to respond to a given situation in a much wider range of ways than is possible for any other animal on the planet. This means we humans can accomplish great things, such as developing, or at least conceiving of, societies in which fundamental rights are granted to all citizens, and getting some control over the effects of harmful viruses, such as HIV. On the other hand, these components of mental freedom can also lead to great evil, because we can use them to plan and execute large-scale acts of violence and create technology that threatens our future survival. Let's examine in more detail the mental capacities for self-regulation that make possible these magnificent and horrific facets of our species.

The Role of Self-awareness in Self-regulation

Self-awareness theory The theory that aspects of the self—one's attitudes, values, and goals—will be most likely to influence behavior when attention is focused on the self.

Although it's fairly easy to ask people about themselves and thereby study the self-concept, investigating the ego—the behind-the-scenes executive function of the self—is more difficult. Discussion of the regulatory function of the ego goes as far back in psychology as the 19th century, but the first major breakthrough in studying self-regulation came in 1972, when Shelley Duval and Bob Wicklund developed self-awareness theory.

Duval and Wicklund start with the idea that self-regulation requires the ability to think about the self. At any given moment, your attention is focused either inward on some aspect of self—things you need to get done today, your social life, whether you're ready for your midterms—or outward on some aspect of the environment—a building, a dog catching a Frisbee, a new tune on your iPhone, and so forth. Also, your situation focuses attention on specific aspects of the self, such as attitudes and goals. In the voting booth, for instance, self-awareness would bring to mind your attitudes about political issues, but while taking an exam in class, you might find that your academic standards and aspirations come to mind.

We saw in chapter 4 how information that is salient significantly influences behavior. Duval and Wicklund make the same point regarding the self. They propose that aspects of the self—one's attitudes, values, and goals—will be most likely to influence behavior when attention is focused in on the self, that is, when some aspect of the self is salient. The theory also asserts that when self-focused, people tend to compare their current behavior with those salient attitudes, values, and goals. In other words, self-awareness helps us become mindful of the gap between what we are doing and what we aspire to or feel we should be doing. In Freud's terminology, directing attention onto the self activates the *superego*—the internal judge that compares how one currently is with internalized standards for how one should be or wants to be. Self-awareness theory further posits that if this comparison suggests that a person is falling short of internalized standards, that person experiences negative feelings and becomes motivated to get rid of those feelings.

Self-awareness theory specifies two basic ways to cope with a negative discrepancy and feel better. One is to distract yourself from self-focus, so that you stop

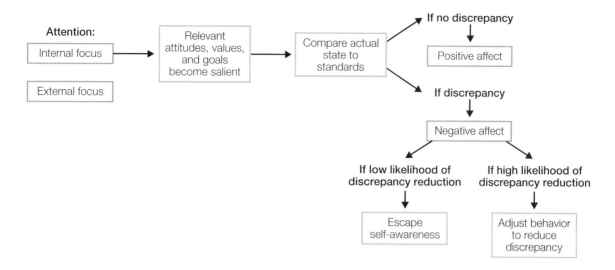

Figure 5.4

Self-awareness Theory

According to self-awareness theory, an internal focus of attention leads relevant standards to become salient. If a discrepancy is perceived when comparing one's current state to the standard, negative affect results and motivates the person to either reduce the discrepancy or escape self-focus.

thinking about the discrepancy between how you are and how you want to be. For example, if you found out you bombed on your first social psych test, you might go to a movie or hang out with friends as a distraction from dwelling on your failure. The other, generally more constructive, way is to commit to doing better. So to reduce the negative discrepancy, you would commit to studying harder, taking better notes, getting a tutor, and so on.

What determines whether you will avoid self-focus or commit to doing better? If you think your chances of successfully reducing the discrepancy are good, or if it's easy enough to change your behavior, you'll take that route. But if you think your chances are slim and the discrepancy can't be reduced with a simple act, you're more likely to take the distraction route or perhaps even give up on the goal entirely (Carver et al., 1979). This process is summarized in **FIGURE 5.4**.

Self-awareness Promotes Behaving in Line With Internal Standards

Self-awareness theory proposes a fairly elaborate process going on inside our own heads. So how could researchers test this theory? To do so, they needed a way to increase and decrease self-awareness and observe the consequences. This is a tricky problem because people tend to shift spontaneously in and out of self-focus from moment to moment.

Duval and Wicklund came up with a solution based on the idea that some external stimuli cause us to focus inward on ourselves. For example, seeing an image of ourselves in a mirror, particularly in contexts in which we don't expect to, is likely to make us think of ourselves. Can you think of an example of this for yourself, say, a time when you were unexpectedly sitting next to a mirror at a coffee shop? In fact, exposing people to mirrors has been the most common way that psychologists have increased self-awareness. They've also had people hear their names or their own voices on an audio recording, pointed video cameras at people, and asked them to write an essay in which they have to use first-person pronouns such as *I*, *me*, and *mine*.

[Getty Images]

Think
ABOUT

When researchers began randomly assigning people to be in situations that evoke high or low self-awareness, they found that, as the theory proposes, high self-awareness leads people to behave in line with their internal standards. In one classic study, Chuck Carver (1975) recruited participants who earlier had expressed either

This trick-or-treater may be more likely to do the right thing and take one piece of candy if he catches his reflection in the window.

[Jeff Greenberg]

favorable or unfavorable attitudes toward using physical punishment as a teaching tool. Once they arrived at his lab, participants were given the role of teacher and asked to use electric shock to punish another student (in reality a confederate) when they made errors on a learning task. The participants were allowed to choose the intensity of the shock they would use as the punishment. To test the role of self-awareness, Carver had half the participants deliver shocks while they were in front of a mirror, whereas the other participants delivered shocks with no mirror present. Without the self-focusing mirror, participants' prior attitudes about the use of physical punishment did not at all predict the intensity level of the shocks they chose to administer. In contrast, in the presence of the mirror, those opposed to physical punishment chose very low shock levels, whereas those in favor of physical punishment chose to administer high levels of shock. In this study, people's behavior was guided by their personal attitudes only when they were made self-aware.

In another study, Beaman and colleagues (1979) showed that a mirror can even make Halloween trick-or-treaters more likely to follow the instruction of taking only one treat from an unattended candy bowl. Fully aware of this study, one of your authors similarly left an unattended bowl outside his door with instructions while escorting his own son around the neighborhood. But he forgot the mirror, so the bowl was quickly emptied!

These studies, and many others like them, demonstrate that our internalized attitudes, values, and goals guide our behavior only to the extent that we are self-aware. Of course, as we have discussed in earlier chapters, our attitudes and values are largely taught to us by our culture. Self-awareness thus plays a crucial role in civilizing us; it brings our behavior more in line with the morals and goals we learn from our culture. Indeed, one lab study showed that heightened self-awareness reduced student cheating on a test from 71 percent to 7 percent (Deiner & Wallbom, 1976).

APPLICATION
Escaping from Self-awareness

We've seen that focusing on ourselves can lead us to behave in line with how we want to be. What happens when we perceive ourselves as falling short of our standards, but feel incapable of changing our behaviors? Self-awareness theory predicts that under these conditions, people try to escape from self-awareness. In fact, research shows that failure experiences initially direct attention to the self, but if no constructive action seems possible, people avoid self-focusing stimuli such as mirrors (Duval & Wicklund, 1972) and distract themselves with activities like watching TV (Moskalenko & Heine, 2003). A recent set of studies suggests that people may even choose unpleasant activities like shocking themselves over extended minutes of self-awareness with no external distractions (Wilson et al., 2014). Of course, when feeling positive about the self or hopeful about the future, escape from self-awareness is not needed. For example, Steenbarger and Aderman (1979) demonstrated that if participants delivered a speech poorly, they didn't subsequently avoid self-awareness if they thought it was easy to improve their speaking abilities. However, they did avoid self-awareness if they thought their speaking ability is pretty much fixed for life.

The tendency to escape self-awareness in the face of failure with little hope for improvement may contribute to problem behaviors such as binge eating and drug and alcohol abuse (Heatherton & Baumeister, 1991). This is because, as research shows, these activities tend to reduce self-focus and, therefore, any unpleasant thoughts that the self is falling short of its standards. But does everyone make equal use of this avoidance strategy? It seems likely that people who are generally high in self-awareness—who tend to think about their attitudes and feelings a lot—would be more likely to seek ways of escaping self-awareness than those individuals who are less likely to introspect.

Hull and Young (1983) examined this possibility by looking at whether people high in private self-consciousness, the trait of being generally high in self-awareness, would use alcohol as a way to escape from self-awareness. They recruited participants to take part in what they thought were two unrelated studies, one on personality and the other on alcohol preferences. (In reality the studies were related.) Participants first completed the private self-consciousness scale, indicating how much they agreed with statements such as "I'm always trying to figure myself out" (Fenigstein et al., 1975). Then they were told they did either really well or really poorly on an intelligence test. In this way, the researchers introduced a negative discrepancy between participants' standards of success and their current performance. Believing that the first study was now complete, they walked down the hall to participate in a study on wine-tasting preferences. They were asked to taste a number of different wines and rate their preferences over a 15-minute period. Did their experiences in the earlier study affect how much alcohol they consumed? Yes: Those participants who were high in private self-consciousness and received failure feedback consumed more wine than the other participants. They were, in effect, "drinking their troubles away."

This tendency to avoid unpleasant self-awareness by drowning one's problems in booze has also been documented outside the laboratory. For example, Hull and colleagues (1986) found that among alcoholics who were attending a treatment program at a veterans' hospital, those who were higher in private self-consciousness and experienced failures over the next few months were more likely to relapse. These findings, in conjunction with the experimental results, suggest that people with a generally high level of self-awareness may try to avoid confronting their own failures and inadequacies by consuming harmful levels of alcohol.

What Feelings Does Self-awareness Arouse?

At a general level, the emotions we feel when we focus internally help to keep the self on track toward meeting goals. If we sense that we are living up to our standards or making rapid progress toward a goal (such as getting an A on a midterm exam), we experience positive emotions that are reinforcing. But when we judge ourselves as falling short or making inadequate progress toward a goal, we experience anxiety, guilt, or disappointment. As we just saw, these emotions can motivate us to do better, if that seems possible, or to escape from self-awareness if change seems unlikely.

Tory Higgins's (1989) self-discrepancy theory provides a more refined understanding of the different types of emotions that self-awareness is likely to evoke. Higgins built on the Freudian notion of the superego, which posits that during childhood, we internalize a set of standards and goals regarding ourselves. Freud proposed that these internalized standards form two clusters. The first cluster is a conscience, which focuses on how you should be. Higgins refers to this as the *ought self*. The second cluster is an ego-ideal, which focuses on how you want to be or what you would like to accomplish. Higgins refers to this as the *ideal self*.

As children, when we fall short of achieving the ought self, we anticipate that our parents might become angry and punish us or withdraw love and protection, and we feel anxious as a result. Imagine being caught gorging on cookies right before dinner. You might feel anxious in anticipation of punishment. Of course, if you refrain from eating the cookies, you would feel calm and secure instead (albeit a little hungry perhaps).

In contrast, when we fall short of the ideal self, we anticipate letting our parents down and so feel discouraged and dejected. Imagine that your parents are watching you as a child playing Little League or Bobbysox, and you strike out to end the

Self-discrepancy theory The theory that people feel anxiety when they fall short of how they *ought* to be, but feel sad when they fall short of how they ideally *want* to be.

game with your team down one and the bases loaded. No matter what your parents say, you'll hear disappointment in their voices and see it in their faces. On the other hand, if you hit a game-winning double, they will be proud and you will feel elation and satisfaction.

Higgins argued that these same feelings arise throughout our lives when we fall short of meeting oughts and ideals. Failing to live up to the ought self elicits anxiety and guilt, because in those situations we have become used to expecting punishment. In contrast, failing to live up to the ideal self elicits dejection and sadness, because in those situations our parents reacted with disappointment.

Research on self-discrepancy theory has provided support for these ideas (Higgins, 1989). When college students were led to compare who they were at the time (the actual self) with the person they thought they should be (the ought self), they felt calmly secure if the discrepancy was small or nonexistent, but anxious and guilty if the discrepancy was large. When students were led to compare the actual self with the ideal self, small discrepancies were associated with feelings of satisfaction, but large discrepancies generated feelings of rejection and discouragement. These studies have also shown that although we all have both oughts and ideals, some people are more focused on their oughts and others more on their ideals. These distinctions, in turn, influence the types of emotions people generally experience when they fall short of their standards.

Another important factor is whether people attribute their shortcomings to something specific they did or to the type of person they are. People tend to feel guilty if they conclude that they engaged in a *bad behavior*, but they feel shame if they conclude they are *bad persons*. These attributions affect our emotional well-being. The psychologist Otto Rank (1930/1998) proposed that guilty feelings signal to us that an important social relationship is in trouble, and as a result, they motivate us to take action to repair the damage we have done. A wide range of findings support this idea (Baumeister et al., 1994). For instance, people who are likely to experience guilt about their self-discrepancies also feel more empathy for others (Tangney, 1991) and are more motivated to make up for their past mistakes by apologizing to those who are harmed and offering to make the situation better somehow (Tangney et al., 1996). On the other hand, people who tend to feel ashamed of themselves when they do something wrong show higher levels of depression (Tangney et al., 1992b) and are also more likely to turn to drugs and alcohol as a means of escaping painful feelings of self-awareness (Dearing et al., 2005). Furthermore, people who feel chronically ashamed of themselves also tend to be more angry, hostile, and suspicious of others (Tangney et al., 1992a).

Staying on Target: How Goals Motivate and Guide Action

Now that we have seen how self-awareness activates our concerns with meeting goals, and the basic distinction between oughts and ideals, let's focus more closely on how goals help us keep our behavior on target. When we wake up in the morning, we're likely to think about our short-term goals for the day—make breakfast, call Mom, and so forth—and we might also think about more long-term, abstract goals, such as "I've got to get my life together," "Do I really want to go to law school?" and "How am I going to get out of this relationship?" In this section, we'll consider which goals we choose to pursue, how hard we strive for them, how those goals get activated, and how goal pursuit is affected by the way we interpret our own behavior.

Pursuing Goals

Two basic components of self-regulation are choosing which goals to pursue and how much energy to direct toward pursuing a particular goal. Goals are what we strive for in order to meet our needs. They guide and energize behavior. They are associated with maintaining or approaching positive feelings or alleviating or avoiding negative feelings. People's goals generally serve either basic survival needs or the core human psychological motivations for security or growth.

What determines the amount of our available energy that we are willing to expend on achieving a particular goal? According to expectancy-value theory (Feather, 1982), effort is based on the value or desirability of the goal multiplied by the person's assessment of how likely it is that she will be able to attain the goal. If two goals are equally attainable, we will more strenuously pursue the more valued of the two. If two goals are equally valued, we will devote more effort to the one we perceive as more likely to be reached. If a given goal is highly valued but seems very unlikely to be attained, people won't direct much energy toward pursuing that goal. People also consider the difficulty of achieving a particular goal (Brehm & Self, 1989). Two goals may be equally attainable, but one may require more effort than the other. If a person is committed to both goals, he will devote more energy to attain the harder goal and view it as the more desirable goal. Although people can become more energized by difficult goals they think they can attain, if they perceive that goal attainment involves more difficulty than the goal is worth, or if they come to perceive it as simply impossible, generally they will abandon the goal, reduce how attracted they are to the goal, and cease to devote further energy to it.

Expectancy-value theory The theory that effort is based on the value or desirability of the goal, multiplied by the person's assessment of how likely it is that she will be able to attain the goal.

The children's story *The Little Engine That Could* captures the idea that expecting success energizes us to achieve our goals.

[© Universal Images Group Limited/Alamy]

Activating Goals: Getting Turned On

Once goals are activated, they can influence thought and behavior by bringing to mind other beliefs, feelings, and past knowledge. For instance, the goal "make coffee" may seem simple enough, but it actually involves cuing up a vast amount of knowledge about kitchen faucets, electrical appliances, and cleanliness, not to mention your feelings about coffee and the belief that it will help you focus on that paper you need to write. You can imagine that more complex goals, such as ending a romantic relationship, are linked to an even larger set of associations.

We can activate goals either by consciously bringing them to mind or by being unconsciously cued by the environment. It is probably easy to think of times when you have activated a goal by self-selection, that is, when you have consciously set a goal for yourself by making a commitment to achieve some desired end state (e.g., "I'm going to get that term paper finished today"). More interesting, perhaps, is that we often pursue goals without any conscious awareness that we are doing so. Surely you are reading this book in part to move toward getting a degree and perhaps toward a career in psychology or some other field. But we suspect you are not continually consciously thinking about such long-term goals at the moment; indeed, doing so would probably interfere with learning the material and thereby work against accomplishing the very goals the activity is serving. But then what initiates our goal pursuits when we are not consciously thinking of our goals?

Bargh's auto-motive theory (Chartrand & Bargh, 2002) proposes that goals are strongly associated with the people, objects, and contexts in which the person pursues them. This means that even subtle exposure to goal-related stimuli in the environment can automatically activate the goal and guide our behavior without our even knowing this is happening. For example, Sandy's goal to improve her dancing skills is associated with, among other things, her dancing shoes. In a hurry one day, she runs by a store window in which those same shoes are displayed. Without her being aware of why, the goal of improving her dancing may be activated, making it more likely that Sandy will choose to rehearse rather than give in to the temptation to sit on the couch and watch TV.

Goals are also strongly associated with other people. From early childhood, we internalize the standards and values of our parents and the broader culture, and throughout adulthood these social influences are like internal voices that shape the goals we choose and how we pursue them. Perhaps your goal to achieve in school is

Auto-motive theory The theory that even subtle exposure to goal-related stimuli can automatically activate the goal and guide behavior.

linked to your mother, who has very high expectations for you, or your grandmother, who worked tirelessly despite hardship to help pay your college tuition. If this is the case, then being reminded of these individuals, even without your realizing it, might actually make you work harder to achieve the high expectations they have for you. In one test of this idea (Shah, 2003), participants were subliminally primed with the name of a significant other who, prior to the experiment, they reported had either high or low expectations of them. They were then asked to solve a series of anagrams, or word puzzles. Those primed with someone who had high expectations of them worked for almost twice as long on the task and ended up solving almost twice as many anagrams as those primed with someone who had low expectations of their academic performance (see also Fitzsimons & Bargh, 2003). This finding, and many others like it, demonstrates just how subtly other people can influence our behavior: Our mothers pester us even when we don't realize we're thinking of them!

Does this mean that goals are represented in our minds just like every other piece of knowledge? No, goals are unique because they send urgent messages to the ego to act. In fact, whereas simple bits of knowledge—like the fact that a typical golf ball has 336 dimples—tend to fade from your memory at a constant rate, goals continue to demand attention at a constant and, in some cases, increasing rate until the end state is attained (Lewin, 1936; McClelland et al., 1953). In fact, when goal-directed action is interrupted, memory of the goal and a state of tension remain strong until the goal is attained, a substitute goal is pursued, or the goal is completely abandoned (Lewin, 1927; Zeigarnik, 1938).

Defining Goals as Concrete or Abstract

There is an old story of a man who comes across three bricklayers busy at work. He asks the first bricklayer, "What are you doing?" and the bricklayer replies, "What does is look like I'm doing? I'm laying brick." He comes to the second bricklayer and asks him, "What are you doing?" This man replies, "I'm building a wall." Still somewhat unsatisfied, the man approaches the third bricklayer and repeats his question, to which the bricklayer replies, "I am building a cathedral."

This story illustrates how the same action can take on different meaning depending on how it connects to goals. This idea is central to action identification theory (Vallacher & Wegner, 1987), which was introduced briefly in chapter 2. Action identification theory explains how people conceive of action—either their own or others'—in ways that range from very concrete to very abstract. As the story above illustrates, the three bricklayers conceive of their actions in different ways, ranging from the concrete level of stacking bricks layered with mortar to the more abstract end state of building a cathedral. One way to understand the differences in their responses is to realize that concrete conceptions specify *how* the action is accomplished, and more abstract conceptions specify *why* the action is performed. Thus, we can say that each bricklayer is building a wall *by* laying bricks (more concrete) and is doing so *because* he wants to build a cathedral (more abstract). Moreover, we refer to the organization of these representations as a hierarchy, because at each level of representation, we can either move up the hierarchy to broader, more comprehensive conceptions of a particular action, or down the hierarchy to increasingly concrete specifications of how the action is accomplished.

Being able to identify our actions at different levels in the goal hierarchy is very handy. For example, when we run into difficulty in attaining an abstract goal, we can shift to a lower-level identification that allows us to focus more attention on specific concrete actions. This is demonstrated in a study (Wegner et al., 1983) in which American participants were asked to perform the fairly routine task of eating the cheesy snack known as Cheetos. However, although some participants were asked to eat the Cheetos in the usual manner (with their hands), other participants were asked to eat the Cheetos with a pair of chopsticks (see **FIGURE 5.5**).

Action identification theory The theory that explains how people conceive of action—their own or others'—in ways that range from very concrete to very abstract.

Figure 5.5

Action Identification Theory

Ever try eating Cheetos with chopsticks? Unless you're accomplished at using these utensils, chances are the difficulty you encounter will lead you to consider the concrete goal of getting food into your mouth.

[Mark Landau]

For all but the most adept chopstick users, this presents some difficulty. (Chopsticks are certainly not the utensil of choice for most Americans who have the munchies.) Participants were then asked to describe what they were doing. Participants using their hands, who were not surprisingly performing the task rather well, were more likely to agree with fairly abstract definitions of their actions (e.g., "eating," "reducing hunger"). However, participants using the chopsticks, who were having considerably more difficulty, were more likely to endorse concrete descriptions of their action (e.g., "chewing," "putting food in my mouth"). When our action bogs down, we shift attention toward lower levels of abstraction, focusing on more concrete actions.

Although considering actions in concrete terms can be effective when we encounter problems, there are also benefits to interpreting actions at higher, more abstract levels of identification. For one, it provides a way for us to make sense of our experience with the world. For example, when you think that you are reading this textbook as one step in the larger endeavor of trying to complete your degree requirements, this helps to make sense of your (we hope not too dull) activity of staring at words on pages. And by making sense of the nitty-gritty details of our daily experience by framing them in terms of abstract goals, we also stay motivated to achieve those goals (Wegner et al., 1986).

The Benefits of Time Travel: The Role of Imagining the Future in Self-regulation

As you think about what courses to take, how much do you think about how interesting the topic is versus the amount of writing that will be involved? Do the factors that influence your decision differ if the course starts next week or next fall? According to Yaacov Trope and Nira Liberman's construal level theory (Liberman & Trope, 1998; Trope & Liberman, 2003), when people imagine events in the distant future, they focus more on the abstract meaning of those events than on the concrete details. In contrast, when thinking about events in the near future, people focus more on the concrete details. Why? We tend to have more concrete information available for events that are closer in time. For example, you probably have more information about your entertainment options for this Saturday night than for a Saturday night three months from now. So we get accustomed to having details available for near-future events but only general, abstract ideas available for more distant future events. An association forms between concrete thinking and temporally close events and between abstract thinking and temporally distant events. This association then becomes part of your routine way of thinking about future events.

Because temporal construal affects whether we focus on concrete or abstract features of future possibilities, it affects our decision making. When we are thinking about the short-run, pragmatic concerns such as ease of a task matter most. When we are thinking about the more distant future, more abstract concerns such as learning and growing as a person matter more. In one study supporting this hypothesis (Liberman & Trope, 1998), students expected to do an assignment either the next week or in nine weeks. In each case, they had to choose either a difficult but interesting assignment or an easy but uninteresting one. When thinking about next week, the students preferred the easy assignment. But when thinking about nine weeks from now, they preferred the interesting assignment.

The main point here is that when we judge what we want to do in the future, the factors that we consider vary depending on how far away that future event is. When it's close, we're more influenced by concrete details. When it's farther off, we are more influenced by our understanding of how that event is connected to our long-term goals.

Construal level theory
The theory that people focus more on concrete details when thinking about the near future, but focus more on abstract meaning when thinking about the distant future.

Another context where imagining future events shapes our thinking is when we predict how a course of action will make us feel. Imagine that Saturday night is approaching and you have two options: Are you going to check out that new band at the local club? Or are you going to the party at Maria's house? You'll probably base your plans on some mental calculation of whether you will have more fun at the club or at Maria's. The same thought process lies behind your decisions about what college to attend, what car to buy, whom to date, or even whether to get Captain Crunch or Cookie Crisp cereal for breakfast: How will the different options available to you make you feel down the road? This is a sensible strategy insofar as your predictions or "forecasts" are accurate, but how accurate are they? Although our ability to project ourselves into the future greatly enhances our capacity to predict and control our lives, research on affective forecasting—predictions of our emotional reactions to potential future events—reveals that our forecasts are often off base, like those of a pretty lousy meteorologist (Wilson & Gilbert, 2005).

Affective forecasting Predicting what one's emotional reactions to potential future events will be.

Dunn, Wilson, and Gilbert (2003) studied the accuracy of affective forecasting by taking advantage of a unique, naturally occurring experiment that happens on campuses throughout the United States every year: the random assignment of students to dorms and other housing options. In the spring of their freshman year, the researchers presented college students with a list of dorm and housing options and asked the students to predict, before being randomly assigned to a housing location, how happy they would be if they were assigned to a desirable housing location or an undesirable housing location. As you might expect, students indicated that they would be much happier if they were assigned to one of the more desirable houses. However, one year later, students did not differ in their level of happiness. Their earlier predictions had been inaccurate. Students in the desirable houses had overestimated how happy they would be, and students in the undesirable houses overestimated how miserable they would be.

Why do these affective forecasting errors happen? One explanation is that we often overestimate the impact of a salient factor, such as where a given dorm is located on campus or how big the rooms are. In so doing, we don't think about the other factors that might actually play a much larger role in our emotional lives, such as whom we are paired to room with or critical life events that could swamp any small inconvenience of geography (Schkade & Kahneman, 1998; Wilson et al., 2000).

Overestimating future negative reactions may stop us from taking chances for fear they might not work out. For example, we might not ask someone out because of the anticipated pain of being rebuffed. This is because when we forecast our affect, we tend to underestimate how successful we are at coping with negative emotions that arise. Whether we suffer a social slight or our favorite sports team loses an important game, we anticipate that the painful sting of these unpleasant events will be greater than it is and last longer than it does (e.g., Gilbert et al., 2004). Can we do anything to increase the accuracy of our affective forecasting? Asking people to think broadly about the future events that can influence their affective reactions, rather than narrowly on just one anticipated event, is a good place to start. For example, college football fans at the University of Virginia and Virginia Tech were asked to predict how happy they would be for a week after their team won or lost a game between the two schools (Wilson et al., 2000). A subset of these participants was also asked to make a diary planner of their upcoming week (the week after the game) and indicate how much time they would spend on different activities. Students who did not make a diary planner overestimated the duration of their happiness with a win and the extent of their misery with a loss. In contrast, students who had been asked to indicate their activities over the coming week did not commit this forecasting error. Instead, because they listed all the activities that would be keeping them busy, they were more aware of how these other events would make them feel, and as a result, minimized their focus on the outcome of the football game.

SECTION review | Self-regulation: Here's What the "I" Can Do For You

The ability to self-regulate is fundamentally based on three key capacities of the human mind.

We are self-aware.	**We are able to think about overarching goals.**	**We can mentally time-travel.**
• Self-regulation requires the ability to think about the self and to compare what we do with what we aspire to do.	• Goals motivate and guide our behavior.	• When an action is thought about as far in the future, we tend to focus on its abstract meaning. When it's in its near future, we focus on the concrete details.
• When what we do conflicts with what we aspire to do, but we feel we can reach the goal, we may commit to doing better.	• The amount of effort we will put into reaching a goal depends on how easily attainable and valuable it is.	• We are often poor at predicting our emotional reactions to future events, which can lead to decisions we may regret.
• If what we aspire to do seems impossible, we may seek to escape self-awareness, which may contribute to food, drug, and alcohol abuse.	• Goals can be brought to mind consciously or cued unconsciously by the environment.	
• Our ought self is the internalized idea of who we should be; our ideal self who we want to be. These different self-representations can lead to different types of affect.	• Goals can be thought about at concrete levels or more abstract levels.	

Self-regulatory Challenges

What factors make self-regulation difficult? And what are the consequences of poor self-regulation? Or, to put the matter more concretely, suppose you sat down one Sunday for a long and productive day of schoolwork, but at the end of the day, all you achieved was making a turkey sandwich and taking a nap. In this section, we'll examine some reasons that your day didn't turn out as planned. We'll also examine the causes and consequences of more serious problems in self-regulation and what you can do to overcome them.

Willpower: Running Hot and Cool

One of the keys to effective self-regulation is the capacity for what psychologists variously call effortful control, impulse control, ego control, or ego strength, and what everyone else typically calls willpower. Willpower is essentially the capacity to overcome the many temptations, challenges, and obstacles that could impede pursuit of one's long-term goals. For a dieter, the problem may be a chocolate cake; for a premed student, it might be opportunities to party or a tough organic chemistry class; for a loyal spouse it might be an attractive new acquaintance or a partner's annoying habits.

Walter Mischel and various colleagues have been studying willpower over the last 40 years (Mischel & Ayduk, 2004). To understand how people successfully use willpower to self-regulate, they built on Freud's concepts of the id and the ego, distinguishing between *hot* processes, which are driven by strong emotions, and *cool* processes, which rely more on level-headed reason. Mischel and colleagues proposed that the hot system is essential to providing the direction and energy to seek out goals. In other words, our felt and anticipated emotions lead us to desire strongly those outcomes that bring us pleasure and that help us avert or minimize pain and anxiety. But the cool system is essential to keep us on track in pursuit of such goals as we traverse a minefield of temptations and difficulties. When our hot system predominates, we tend to be impulsive, caving into these challenges and stalling or completely derailing our progress toward our long-term goals. However, when the cool system rules, we leap over these hurdles rather than being tripped up by them.

If you ever thought that some people seem to have more willpower than others, you were right. Mischel and Ebbesen (1970) studied people's varying abilities to use their

Neurological Underpinnings of Self-regulation

It was in the late summer of 1848 that Phineas Gage was busy laying railroad track in Vermont, a job that required drilling a hole in a rock and filling it with explosive powder, then running a fuse to it and covering the powder with densely packed sand (Fleischman, 2002). Gage had a custom-made tamping iron, a rod that he used to pack the sand. One day, a spark set off by his tamping iron hit the powder and set off a massive explosion. Gage lay on the ground, blood pouring from a hole where his cheek used to be and another on the top of his head. The tamping rod had shot through Gage's head, tearing through his skull and brain tissue. Surprisingly, Gage was not only alive but (after a few minutes of convulsive twitching) was conscious and quite alert!

With a doctor's help, the wound eventually healed, but the reason Gage's case has become so interesting to psychologists is that his personality changed in very specific ways. Although Gage's intellectual capacities were essentially intact and his motor functioning unimpaired, his personality was radically transformed. Before the accident, Gage had a reputation as an honest, hard-working citizen with a sharp mind. After the accident, he became impatient and susceptible to angry outbursts. He would shout a constant stream of loosely organized ideas, his speech laced with profanity and sexually inappropriate remarks. Further, he had difficulty following any coherent plan of action and had a difficult time planning or controlling his behavior. As one of his peers remarked, "Gage was no longer Gage."

There are a couple of lessons we can take away from the case of Phineas Gage. One of the big lessons is that the brain is involved not only in the way we move our limbs and process visual information but also in those aspects of our self and personality that make us who we are, including the choices we make, the impression we give to others, and the future plans that we form to give our lives coherence and meaning.

Let's take a closer look at some of these brain areas. Gage's case offers exciting clues about one of the specific brain regions responsible for self-regulation. Using brain imaging techniques and analyzing Gage's skull fractures, a reconstruction (Damasio et al., 1994) of Gage's lesions showed that the rod destroyed the very front of the frontal cortex in the left and right hemispheres, in a brain region known as the *ventromedial prefrontal cortex* (VPFC) (see figure at right).

Phineas Gage
[Collection of Jack and Beverly Wilgus]

This region of the brain is particularly important for how we process emotional information (Banfield et al., 2004). Following damage to the VPFC, people often have unimpaired intellectual abilities, but they lose the ability to process emotion, and because emotion plays a role in goal pursuit, these individuals also have difficulty forming and carrying through the coherent plans of action needed to accomplish goals.

The ventromedial prefrontal cortex is just one of the regions that are important to social and emotional aspects of self-regulation. Others include:

- The *orbitofrontal cortex* is an area that lies just behind the eye sockets. Jennifer Beer and colleagues (2003) have

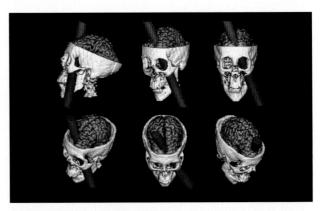

A reconstruction of Gage's injury.
[Patrick Landmann/Science Source]

examined how damage to the orbitofrontal cortex impairs people's ability to regulate their social behavior. Imagine that you are a participant in a study and asked to come up with a nickname for the experimenter, whose initials, you are told, are L.E. If you are a middle-aged man and the experimenter is an attractive, young woman, something like "lovely and enticing" might easily come to mind. This response meets the criterion and fulfills the goal of the task. But you might reject this nickname for fear of offending the experimenter or coming across as a dirty old man. You decide to play instead on her short stature and obvious intelligence and reply, "Little egghead." Still a tease, for sure, but without the sexist overtones.

This seemingly simple task actually relied on some complex mental processes. You had to generate meaningful word pairs that allowed you to achieve your goal of seeming clever but that also satisfied the goal of remaining within the bounds of social decorum. If a sexual response springs to mind, your social monitoring system flags it as inappropriate, and it is consciously suppressed.

But what would happen if your social monitoring system were damaged—something that happens to people who suffer injury to the orbitofrontal region of the brain? These individuals, it turns out, do blurt out the inappropriate nickname (Beer et al., 2003). If you did that, you probably would respond by feeling embarrassed. But orbitofrontal patients respond by feeling proud of how clever they are. Not only are they unable to monitor their thoughts ahead of time and screen out potentially offensive comments but they also aren't able to monitor the negative social feedback they get afterward.

- The *dorsolateral prefrontal cortex* (DLPFC) is not an anatomical structure but rather an area of the frontal lobes that is responsible for many executive functions. For example, it is involved in planning, inhibition, and regulation of behavior toward an abstract goal (Banfield et al., 2004). As you might imagine, people with damage to this area have difficulty carrying out even simple everyday tasks (Shallice & Burgess, 1991). Consider the case of one frontal-lobe patient, who attempted to purchase soap and discovered that the store didn't carry her favorite brand. From our discussion of hierarchies of goals and subgoals, we know that most people in this situation would find an alternative means of achieving the goal, such as purchasing another brand of soap. But the frontal-lobe patient instead gave up altogether on the goal of buying soap.
- The *anterior cingulate cortex* (ACC) (Banfield et al., 2004). This region lies on the medial (inner) surface of the frontal

lobes and interacts with areas of the prefrontal cortex. One primary function of the ACC is to signal when some behavior or outcome is at odds with your goals. The ACC helps draw your attention to conflicts between what you want and what has just happened. It then communicates with the DLPFC, which steps in to switch plans or change behavior to get you back on track.

Cunningham and colleagues (2004) looked at how the ACC and the DLPFC allow people to monitor and regulate their social biases. Cunningham presented White participants with pictures of White and Black faces and neutral gray squares while he scanned their brain activity using **functional magnetic resonance imagery (fMRI)**, a technique that provides information about activity in the brain when people perform certain cognitive or motor tasks. Some of the pictures were presented very quickly (30 ms) so that he could capture people's immediate and automatic affective response, and some were presented more slowly (525 ms) so that people would have time potentially to regulate whatever their immediate reaction had been. What did Cunningham find? First, patterns of neurological activity showed increased activation in the *amygdala,* a region implicated in fear processing, when people were presented very quickly with a Black as opposed to a White face. This neurological signature of an automatic fear response was particularly strong for participants with more negative implicit racial biases. When people had a bit longer to look at a Black face, they showed increased activation in both the ACC and the dorsolateral prefrontal cortex, but no longer showed increased amygdala activation. The level of ACC and DLPFC activity was the strongest for those people who had not only strong implicit biases but also the goal of being nonprejudiced. The implication is that after an initial fear response, the ACC in these individuals might have signaled that this was not the response they wanted to have to Blacks, and perhaps their DLPFC kicked in to reduce and regulate that immediate, knee-jerk reaction.

Although research that links neurological processes to social behaviors is still in its infancy, results such as these are beginning to shed light on the complex array of cognitive systems that are involved in helping us formulate, enact, monitor, and follow through on our goals and intentions.

Functional magnetic resonance imagery (fMRI) A scanning technique that provides information about the activity of regions of the brain when people perform certain cognitive or motor tasks.

cool system to overrule their hot system, working with children as young as four years old. The core idea was to pit an attractive short-term temptation against a more desired delayed goal that can be attained only if the short-term temptation is resisted. The original task was very simple. A child was told that when the experimenter returned in about 20 minutes, she would get *two* cookies. However, if she didn't want to wait for the two cookies, she could ring a bell, and the experimenter would return and give her *one* cookie. Two cookies are better than one, so if the child delayed gratification, she would get the preferred reward. The measure of the capacity for delay of gratification is the amount of time the child waits before ringing the bell. The highest score was obtained by waiting the full 20 minutes for the experimenter to return with the two cookies.

In an amazing finding, performance on this delay of gratification task at age four predicts a variety of indicators of self-regulatory success up to 30 years later! Specifically, the more time a four-year-old can wait to get the bigger reward, the better that person's subsequent scores as an adolescent and an adult on the SAT, level of education achieved, self-esteem, tolerance of frustration, coping with stress, and interpersonal functioning (Ayduk et al., 2000; Mischel & Ayduk, 2002; Shoda et al., 1990). The determinants of this stable individual difference are not fully understood, but studies suggest that children as young as 18 months show differences in their ability to distract themselves in order to keep tempting thoughts from derailing their self-regulation (Sethi et al., 2000). The early appearance of these differences suggests that a person's level of willpower is probably based on differences in temperament and intelligence that result from some combination of genetic predispositions and prenatal and early postnatal experiences (Rothbart et al., 2004).

These findings paint a fairly fatalistic picture, but the ceiling on one's capacity for willpower is not entirely fixed early in life. Generally, factors that keep the cool system active help the person delay gratification. But beware the factors that block the cool system and activate the hot system, such as high levels of stress, being under cognitive load (Hamilton et al., 2007; Hull & Slone, 2004; Metcalfe & Mischel, 1999), alcohol and other recreational drugs, and exposure to temptations such as cookies fresh out of the oven.

Does this mean that we should focus only on our cold process and disregard our hot desire for long-term goals? Probably not. If you never remind yourself once in a while about how great it will be to have a degree and a well-paying job down the road, for example, the hot system may turn off completely, depriving you of the motivation necessary to achieve your goals. On the other hand, if you keep reminding yourself about how great the long-term goal, such as a luxury car, will be, you're more likely to give up on the goal and blow your cash on a quick substitute, a more mediocre car, rather than wait for the payoff later. The optimal strategy lies somewhere between these two extremes of cold and hot processes. People are most successful at achieving their long-term goals if they occasionally remind themselves about the enjoyment they'll get from those goals, just to keep the juices flowing, but focus more coolly on the concrete steps necessary to achieve those goals.

Trying Too Hard: Ironic Process Theory

Sometimes, something in a situation brings to mind thoughts that distract us from what we are trying to do. When unwanted thoughts absorb our attention, we often

Think
ABOUT

[Iakov Filimonov/Shutterstock]

try to shift focus away from these thoughts and back onto the tasks that more directly relate to the central goal of the day (such as mastering statistics). As agents with free will, we should find this a piece of cake, right? Surely, I should have some say over what I think about! However, mind control—even of our own minds—is not nearly so straightforward. Try closing your eyes for one minute and NOT thinking about white bears.

How did you do? Perhaps this task wasn't too difficult, and you were able to focus your attention elsewhere. Many people, however, are surprised to discover that even though they try to keep white bears out of consciousness, the bears keep popping up. This is an example of what Dan Wegner (1994) calls ironic processing, whereby the more we try *not* to think about something, the more those thoughts enter our mind and distract us from other things. In laboratory studies, students who first spent five minutes trying to suppress thoughts of white bears reported having more than twice as many thoughts of white bears by the end of a subsequent five-minute period, compared to students who didn't first try to push thoughts of white bears out of their minds. If it's hard to sustain pushing away the thought of cute polar bears, you can imagine how difficult it must be to push away highly troubling thoughts about the low grade you just got on an exam or how badly your date went last weekend!

Yet we are continually trying to suppress thoughts. But how do we do it, and why is it often so difficult? Wegner (1994) describes two mental processes that we use to control our thoughts. One process acts as a monitor that is on the lookout for signs of the unwanted thought; in order to do such monitoring, such thoughts must be accessible, that is, close to consciousness. The second process is an operator that actively pushes any signs of the unwanted thought out of consciousness. The best way to do this is through distraction, filling consciousness with thoughts of other things.

When asked to suppress a thought, people can generally employ these two processes and suppress successfully. However, once people stop trying to suppress the thought, typically a *rebound effect* occurs: The unwanted thought becomes even more accessible than it was before suppression. Although there is still some debate about the cause of this rebound effect, one likely explanation is that the monitoring process has to keep the unwanted thought close to consciousness in order to watch for it, and so once the operator stops actively providing alternative thoughts, the unwanted thought becomes more likely to come to mind than if no effort to suppress had been initiated in the first place. For instance, participants who were asked to *not* think about a particular person in their lives right before they went to bed were more likely to dream about the person than were participants who did not receive this request (Wegner et al., 2004)!

Wegner argues that monitoring is an automatic process: It searches for signs of an unwanted thought without demanding too much mental energy. The operator, in contrast, is a controlled process, requiring more mental effort and energy to carry out. This leads to a testable prediction about the two components of thought suppression. We would expect that when a person is cognitively busy or dreaming, the automatic monitoring process will continue searching for instances of an unwanted thought, but the controlled operator process responsible for focusing attention away from that thought will be disabled. Consequently, the undesired thought kept accessible by the monitoring process will become especially likely to pop into consciousness or our dreams.

Wegner and colleagues have applied ironic process theory to many contexts in which people try to suppress a thought or a behavior. They consistently find that when people are under stress, distraction, or time urgency, efforts at thought suppression generally backfire (Wegner, 1994). Here are a couple of examples: If people reminisce about sad events and then try to suppress sad feelings, they are generally successful when cognitive load is low, but trying to suppress sadness backfires when people are asked to remember a string of nine numbers at the same time (Wegner et al., 1993). When people are listening to mellow, new age music, they can follow directions to ignore distracting thoughts and go to sleep quickly, but if their heads are filled with booming marching-band music, instructions to fall asleep quickly make it that much more difficult to fall asleep (Ansfield et al., 1996).

There are two basic ways to minimize ironic processing. One is to keep distraction, stress, and time urgency to a minimum when regulating our thought and behavior. We can, for example, work in a quiet room or start projects far in advance of their deadline. Of course, we can't always avoid mental stressors. The second strategy is simply to stop trying to control your thoughts when cognitive strain is

Ironic processing The idea that the more we try *not* to think about something, the more those thoughts enter our mind and distract us from other things.

Monitor The mental process that is on the lookout for signs of unwanted thoughts.

Operator The mental process that actively pushes any signs of the unwanted thoughts out of consciousness.

likely to be present. Under such circumstances, disengaging from effortful control can eliminate the ironic process. In fact, a form of psychotherapy called paradoxical intervention involves telling the client to stop trying to get rid of their problem. You can't sleep when you go to bed? Stop trying to! It seems to work, at least for some people, some of the time (Shoham & Rohrbaugh, 1997).

Insufficient Energy, or Ego Depletion

Our lack of success with trying to suppress unwanted thoughts highlights the more general point that goal pursuit is often an effortful process, and therefore our goals compete for a limited supply of mental energy. Perhaps you are a strong environmentalist and value recycling, but one day you come home from a long day of work and studying. You barely have enough energy to make yourself dinner. You look at the mess of recyclables and nonrecyclables, say "Forget this!" and toss them all in the trash. Why would you give up so easily on a cherished value?

Muraven, Tice, and Baumeister (1998) argue that the ego is like a muscle. We have a certain amount of ego strength that allows us to regulate and control our behavior. But just as our quadriceps ache after we've run five miles, our ego strength becomes depleted by extended bouts of self-control. This mental fatigue, or ego depletion, can make it harder to continue to regulate our behavior, even when the two types of tasks are very different. For example, in one study participants watched a film about environmental disasters that included graphic scenes of sick and dying animals. Some participants were instructed to suppress the emotions they naturally felt in response to the movie, whereas others were instructed to deliberately amplify or exaggerate the emotions they felt. A third group received no instructions about regulating their emotions. Afterward, participants were asked to squeeze a handgrip for as long as they could. Compared with those who had received no instructions, participants who had regulated their emotions—either suppressing or amplifying them—showed a significant decrease in how long they could squeeze the handgrip. Even though controlling emotions and controlling a physical action are very different things, this research suggests that they both rely on a limited supply of self-regulatory energy or strength.

Ego depletion can even explain why people sometimes engage in risky behaviors. In another study (Muraven et al., 2002), participants first had to engage in the effortful task of suppressing their thoughts (or not). Afterward, they were asked to sample different types of beer before taking a driving test. Because these participants knew that their driving skills would be measured, they should have been motivated to limit how much alcohol they drank. But despite this motivation, participants who had engaged in the effortful control of their thoughts beforehand drank more beer than those who were not cognitively depleted.

The good news is that our ego strength can be exercised and replenished. Research suggests that spending just two weeks focusing on improving your posture or monitoring and detailing what you eat can strengthen your ability to self-control your behavior on a completely unrelated task (like the handgrip task just described; Muraven et al., 1999). These findings might even suggest that it is better to start small and to gradually build your ego strength over time than to try to change a well-ingrained habit, an effort that might just leave you fatigued.

Recent research is even beginning to uncover the biological mechanisms that underlie self-control. When we engage in difficult self-control, we use a lot of glucose, the fuel that allows our prefrontal cortex to sustain self-regulation. With our blood glucose levels depleted, we literally run out of energy (Gailliot & Baumeister, 2007). No wonder you get exhausted after hours of reading or studying! Consuming that sugary Kool-Aid or a high-fat milkshake actually helps to restore glucose levels and increase mental energy (Gailliot et al., 2007). So when you are studying late at night and trying to fight off the urge to sleep, that candy bar might really help you refocus

Ego depletion The idea that ego strength becomes depleted by extended bouts of self-control.

attention on your notes. Of course if you are trying to control your intake of sweets, then this information isn't nearly so helpful!

Together, these findings support the hypothesis that self-control is a limited resource that can be depleted and replenished. However, researchers have made discoveries that cast doubt on this idea. For example, people's personal beliefs about willpower can change the ego depletion effect: If people merely believed that willpower is an unlimited resource, they did not show the typical ego depletion effect (Job et al., 2010). In another study (Schmeichel & Vohs, 2009), expressing one's core values in life (such as benevolence, tradition, or achievement) counteracted the depletion of self-control strength. If self-control is a limited resource tied to biological changes in glucose, then why would personal beliefs about willpower or affirming a core value instantly restore that limited resource?

These findings spurred Inzlicht and Schmeichel (2012) to dig deeper into the process behind ego depletion. They explored why self-control seems limited—why exercising self-control on one task leads to failures of self-control on a second task. They propose that initial acts of self-control shift people's motivation away from further restraint or impulse control and toward gratification. Put more simply, engaging in self-control is hard work; it takes deliberation and attention. After people have done this work, they are less motivated to do any further work. They feel like they are "owed" a break, and that they are justified in slacking off. It's as though our minds say: "I've put in the effort, and now I choose not to control myself any further. In fact, it's time for a reward!" Whereas the limited resource model says that exercising self-control zaps a limited resource, making it so that people cannot regulate afterwards, this account says that expending initial effort makes people choose not to regulate.

Getting Our Emotions Under Control

A specific example of self-regulation happens when we try to regulate or control our emotions. Imagine that your romantic partner of several months takes you out to dinner. You are expecting a quiet, romantic evening when, over your corn chowder, your partner blurts out that your relationship is now over. Ouch. To maintain your dignity, you try to choke back your surprise, your anger, and your crushing disappointment. But how successful are you likely to be? If you consider what you've just learned about people's attempts to push their thoughts out of mind and the ego depletion that results from such active efforts of control, you'll probably realize that attempting to control your emotions by suppressing them is likely to be ineffective.

But if suppressing your emotions is not a good way to control your feelings, is there another strategy that will work better? Building on cognitive appraisal theory of emotion, introduced in chapter 2, James Gross (2001) proposed that an alternative to emotional suppression is cognitive reappraisal—reexamining the situation so that you don't feel such a strong emotional reaction in the first place. In the example of being dumped, you might excuse yourself to go to the restroom and use that time to think about all of your partner's annoying habits that actually drove you crazy, or about the fact that you are planning to move to Ghana next year with the Peace Corps and won't have the time for a relationship anyway. With these cognitions in mind, this sudden break up can seem a little more like a blessing than a curse.

But can the mind really control the heart through reappraisal? Research suggests that it can (Gross, 2002). A typical experiment uses a method similar to that previously described in research by Muraven and colleagues (1998). Specifically, Gross (1998) showed people a disturbing film of an arm amputation. He instructed one group of participants simply to watch the film (the control condition). Another third of the participants were told to suppress their emotional response so that someone watching them wouldn't be able to tell how they were feeling. A third group was instructed to reappraise the film, for example, by imagining that it was staged rather than real. Compared with the people in the control condition, people who suppressed

Cognitive reappraisal The cognitive reframing of a situation to minimize one's emotional reaction to it.

their emotion did make fewer disgust expressions, but they showed increased activation of the sympathetic nervous system and still reported feeling just as disgusted. In contrast, participants who reappraised the film showed no increase in their physiological signs of arousal and reported lower levels of disgust than participants in the control condition. The effect of reappraisal on reducing negative emotions has been replicated in other research using more sensitive physiological measures of negative affect, such as activation of the amygdala (Goldin et al., 2008).

These findings suggest that reappraisal can be an effective way to avoid feeling strong negative emotions. Certainly the consequences are better than suppression, which can actually have the ironic effect of exacerbating your negative feelings. But we also have learned from Muraven's research that suppressing emotions has cognitive costs. Do the benefits of reappraisal come at the price of cognitive resources? The answer seems to be no. In a study by Richards and Gross (2000), participants were asked to suppress, reappraise, or simply view a series of negative images. Later they were tested on verbal information that had been presented with each picture. Participants who suppressed their emotions did worse on this memory task than those who just viewed the images, but the people who were instructed to reappraise their emotions did not show these same memory impairments. Taken together, these findings suggest that probably the best strategy for dealing with a difficult situation is to reappraise it in a cooler, more objective way so as to avoid fully feeling negative emotions that would be costly and difficult to suppress.

APPLICATION

What Happened to Those New Year's Resolutions? Implementing Your Good Intentions

What about times when we believe we can achieve our goals and yet we have difficulty actually getting started? Peter Gollwitzer (1999) points out that because our attention usually is absorbed in our everyday activities, we often make it through our days without ever seizing opportunities to act on our goals. Imagine you wake up on New Year's Day, look in the mirror, and make a resolution: "I'm going to be a better friend from now on!" Sounds great, but throughout the day your attention is absorbed in your usual tasks, and as you fall asleep that night you think to yourself: "Hey! I never got a chance to be a better friend!" The problem is that the goal still is a broad vision, and you haven't yet specified how you will implement your goal. Gollwitzer claims that we'll be more successful if we create implementation intentions, mental rules that link particular situational cues to goal-directed behaviors: "IF *Situation X* arises, THEN I will perform *Action Y*." In the example of the New Year's resolution to be friendlier, an implementation intention might be something like, "IF I see Stephen, THEN ask him how his kids are." Now, rather than taking the time and energy to decide when to get started on a goal and what to do, the person programs herself to respond to certain aspects of the situation automatically with goal-directed behaviors. This makes it more likely that effective self-regulation will proceed even in the presence of stressful situations or cognitive distraction.

Forming implementation intentions helps people reach all sorts of goals. For instance, it can encourage people to pursue their exercise goals, as demonstrated in a study by Milne, Orbell, and Sheeran (2002). College students were reminded of their vulnerability to heart disease and the benefits of exercising to reduce their risk. They had the goal of exercising more, but they had not formed any implementation intentions. This intervention was mildly successful, increasing the percentage of students who exercised regularly from 29% to 39%. In another condition, this intervention was coupled with instructions to form implementation intentions, that is, specific rules for when and where to exercise. ("As soon as I get up, I'll go for a 3-mile run.") In this condition, 91% of the participants exercised regularly! A similar study encouraging women to get early-detection screening for cervical cancer

Implementation intentions
Mental rules that link particular situational cues to goal-directed behaviors.

found that instructions to form implementation intentions increased the percentage of women who got screenings from 69% to 92% (Sheeran & Orbell, 2000). These studies illustrate the practical value of forming implementation intentions. We often fall short of our goals because we don't know when to initiate goal-directed actions, and because we have to cope with tempting distractions, bad habits, and competing goals. But we have a much better chance of achieving our goals if we create implementation intentions that link specific situational opportunities to specific goal-directed behaviors, thereby making goal pursuit automatic.

Identifying Goals at the Wrong Level of Abstraction

Throughout this chapter, we've seen how humans regulate their behavior in ways that make us very different from any other species, past or present. Unlike dogs and cats, we often devote huge chunks of our lives to attaining or avoiding what are essentially abstract ideas, such as "being a good friend" or "financial failure." If we are successful at achieving these goals, it's because we can think in flexible ways about our own actions, sometimes viewing them as steps toward broader goals and other times breaking them down into smaller, more concrete goals. So far, so good; but as you may remember from chapter 2, people generally prefer to identify their actions at a moderately abstract level so that those actions seem meaningful. For example, a football player heading onto the field will prefer, all things being equal, an abstract interpretation of his action, such as "playing to win" or "impressing the coaches," to more concrete interpretations, such as "stepping onto the field and shifting my balance forward."

What levels of abstraction help us achieve our goals? Research on this issue has revealed two basic findings (Vallacher & Wegner, 1987). First, people perform easy tasks best when they identify them at relatively abstract levels. Second, people perform difficult tasks best when they identify them at low levels of abstraction. Parenting is a particularly daunting task: Trust us, or better yet, recall—from your parents' perspective—your own childhood shenanigans while growing up! A study found that the more moms and dads thought about parenting at relatively concrete levels, the more they enjoyed their kids and the less their kids got into trouble (Wegner et al., 1982). These findings have an important implication for a variety of difficult goals, from academic excellence to maintaining a healthy romantic relationship. Although it may be useful to *begin* an action with an abstract goal in mind, and even bring that goal to mind from time to time for inspiration, we are more likely to succeed if we break difficult abstract goals down into smaller concrete actions, even though those actions may sometimes seem tedious or removed from the loftier abstract goal.

When We Can't Let Go: Self-regulatory Perseveration and Depression

There are times, however, when a person is having a difficult time and would benefit from viewing goals in more abstract terms. Moving up the hierarchy to more abstract identifications is particularly valuable when attempts to meet a goal continue to be unsuccessful. In such cases, attention will shift upward in the hierarchy to allow the person to consider his or her goals more broadly. This is useful because it allows the person to search for alternative lower-level goals that may help him or her achieve the same higher-level goal.

For instance, you may choose the goal of signing up online for a philosophy class that would help you complete your degree requirements. But what happens if the online sign-up system doesn't allow you to enroll because you don't meet the prerequisites? Although you have not met your goal, you probably won't spend the rest of the day mindlessly clicking the "Enroll" icon over and over. Rather, you'd probably consider the higher-order goal of getting enough credits to graduate. Once you do that, you'd stop fixating on getting in that one course and consider other courses you could take to get the credits you need. People can be quite flexible at compensating for blocked goal pursuit by finding substitute means of satisfying the more abstract goal.

Self-regulatory perseveration theory of depression The theory that one way in which people can fall into depression is by persistent self-focus on an unattainable goal.

But sometimes people persist in pursuing a goal long after it's no longer beneficial to do so. The self-regulatory perseveration theory of depression (Pyszczynski & Greenberg, 1987; 1992) proposes that this is one way that people can fall into depression. This theory builds on research on self-awareness. Recall that self-awareness theory claims that directing attention to the self leads people to compare their current state with their ideal state. If they notice a discrepancy and they feel they have the means to reduce it, they will alter their behavior to bring it more closely in line with their ideal. But if the chances of reducing this discrepancy are unlikely— for example, if the task is very difficult—the person will disengage, or let go of the goal and divert attention away from the self. And although giving up on goals and avoiding self-awareness can lead to destructive behaviors such as excessive alcohol consumption, letting go of unattainable goals is generally an adaptive response. If you drop a pencil down a gutter, it's pointless to sit all day by the gutter, fishing around with a coat hanger and hoping that your pencil will magically reappear.

Getting dumped is brutal. How do you get out of the doldrums and avoid being depressed? Self-regulatory perseveration theory suggests one answer.
[Getty Images/Blend Images]

But not all goals are so easily abandoned as your favorite pencil. If a goal is a central source of self-esteem, and the person has few other ways of deriving self-esteem, he or she may have great difficulty in letting go of that goal even after it becomes evident that the goal is lost or probably will never be attained. Pyszczynski and Greenberg proposed that this persistent focus on an unattainable goal results in many of the common symptoms of depression, including elevated negative emotion, a tendency to blame oneself for shortcomings, and decreased motivation and performance in other areas of life. Supporting this theory is evidence that lost and limited bases of self-esteem are precursors of depression, that depressed people tend to be high in self-awareness, and that reducing self-awareness in depressed people tends to reduce their symptoms (Pyszczynksi & Greenberg, 1992).

The reason for this escalating pattern of problems is that excessive inward focus on the self magnifies negative feelings, promotes attributing one's problems to oneself, and interferes with attention to the external world, leading to further failures. The spiral of misery and self-recrimination culminates in a negative self-image. Many of us, for example, have had the misfortune of being dumped by a romantic partner. When this happens, if the relationship was really important to us, we may become depressed as we continually think about how much we wish we were still with that person, what we did wrong, why we're unworthy of love, and so on. We obsess about getting that person back. But it's just not going to happen. We may eventually think that without that person, who previously provided us with such joy, self-worth, and meaning, life really . . . well . . . sucks. A similar negative spiral can begin with other losses in the realms of love and work: the death of a spouse, parent, or child; being laid off; or failing to get a promotion or an opportunity to pursue a desired career.

The positive spiral of recovery begins by identifying the abstract goal that the now unattainable goal was serving. In this way, the person can find alternative means of satisfying that abstract goal (**FIGURE 5.6**). As he or she invests time and energy in those alternative means, self-focus on the unattainable goal is reduced. Let's illustrate this positive spiral in the case of a failed relationship. The mourning partner recognizes that the concrete goal of being in a relationship served the more abstract goal of feeling loved and valued. This realization opens up the possibility

Figure 5.6

The Positive Spiral of Recovery

According to self-regulatory perseveration theory, recovery from depression after a loss involves moving up the goal hierarchy to consider the higher-order goal no longer being served, and then considering alternative pathways to achieve that goal.

of other means of establishing personal value. That person may consider other romantic prospects, or recognize that family, friends, or career goals provide a sense of worth. After becoming more involved in those alternative goals, the unattainable relationship seems less important, and no longer is a constant reminder of personal shortcomings.

Maintaining a state of optimal well-being, then, requires a delicate balance between self-focused pursuit of some goals and at the same time letting go of goals that are beyond our means. This idea is reflected in the well-known "Serenity Prayer" written by theologian Reinhold Niebuhr and employed by Alcoholics Anonymous:

> God grant me the serenity to accept the things I cannot change;
>
> courage to change the things I can;
>
> and wisdom to know the difference.

SECTION review | Self-regulatory Challenges

Research has discovered numerous factors that make self-regulation difficult. These findings point to some concrete strategies that people can employ to improve self-regulation and achieve their goals.

- Strengthen willpower by activating the hot system and avoiding factors that block the cool system, such as stress, cognitive overload, alcohol, or freshly baked cookies.
- Minimize ironic processing—the intrusion of thoughts we are trying to suppress—by keeping distractions and stress to a minimum when regulating thoughts and behavior or relaxing efforts to suppress thoughts.
- Strengthen your self-control by building ego strength gradually.
- Reappraise difficult situations as a way to avoid feeling strong negative emotions.
- Form "if–then" rules to program yourself to respond to situational cues with specific goal-directed behaviors.
- Start with abstract goals in mind, but break them down into smaller, concrete actions to make difficult tasks more easily attainable.
- Maintain a balance between self-focused pursuit of some goals and letting go of goals that are beyond reach.

CONNECT ONLINE:

Check out our videos and additional resources located at:
www.macmillanhighered.com/launchpad/greenberg1e

The Key Self-motives: Consistency, Esteem, Presentation, and Growth

TOPIC OVERVIEW

Your sense of self—*who you are*—is not something that exists solely in your own head. Instead, it is an active force that interacts with the social world to achieve certain goals. Put simply, the self *wants* certain things. Four self-motives have been particularly important to people across cultures and historical periods. People want to view themselves as a coherent whole; to see themselves in a positive light; to control how others perceive them; and to grow, learn, and improve.

The Motive to Maintain a Consistent Self

People want to perceive consistency among the specific things they believe, say, and do—what we'll call the *micro* level of day-to-day experience. But it's virtually impossible to be consistent all the time. For example, you probably believe in the value of energy and water conservation, but have you ever taken a long, hot shower? Have you ever had a professor urge you to do the assigned readings prior to each lecture, agree this is a good idea, and still not do it? Cognitive dissonance theory explains how people react to these micro-level inconsistencies in their thoughts and behavior. We begin this section by outlining the theory and research supporting it. Afterward we'll consider people's motivation to maintain consistency at the *macro* level of their lives as a whole.

Self-consistency at the Micro Level: Cognitive Dissonance Theory

Cognitive dissonance theory
The idea that people have such distaste for perceiving inconsistencies in their beliefs, attitudes, and behavior that they will bias their own attitudes and beliefs to try to deny inconsistencies.

According to Leon Festinger's (1957) **cognitive dissonance theory**, people have such distaste for perceiving inconsistencies in their beliefs, attitudes, and behavior that they will bias their own attitudes and beliefs to try to deny those inconsistencies. The basic idea is that when two cognitions (e.g., beliefs, attitudes, or perceived actions) are inconsistent or contradict one another, people experience an uncomfortable psychological tension known as dissonance. The more important the inconsistent cognitions are to the person, the more intense the feeling of dissonance and the stronger the motivation to get rid of that feeling. There are three primary ways to reduce dissonance:

1. Change one of the cognitions.
2. Add a third cognition that makes the original two cognitions seem less inconsistent with each other.
3. Trivialize the cognitions that are inconsistent.

Let's consider, as Festinger did back in the 1950s, the example of a cigarette smoker. Sally the smoker has two cognitions: (1) she knows cigarettes are bad for her health; and (2) she knows that she smokes cigarettes. From the cognition "Smoking is bad for me" follows the opposite cognition "I smoke." As a result, Sally often feels tense and conflicted about her smoking—that is, she experiences dissonance. To reduce the dissonance, Sally could change one of the two dissonant cognitions. However, cognitions can be difficult to change. For Sally to decide that smoking is not bad for her, she would have to call into question the judgment of the entire medical community, and this would likely conflict with a host of other beliefs she has, such as the trustworthiness of cultural authorities. Alternatively, Sally could change the cognition "I smoke" by quitting. Most smokers do in fact try to quit, and many eventually succeed, but behaviors are often hard to change once they become habits (Wood & Neal, 2007), particularly if engaging in them creates positive feelings (e.g., a nicotine high) and giving them up creates negative feelings (e.g., withdrawal symptoms).

"I finally kicked the fire breathing habit; now I'm stuck on mints and I'm gaining weight."

[Park W. B./Cartoonstock]

Think
ABOUT

[Aubord Dulac/Shutterstock]

When it's hard to change either of the dissonant cognitions, people usually add a third cognition that resolves the inconsistency between the original two cognitions. Take a minute to think of any additional cognitions that smokers use to try to reduce their dissonance. Now look at the bottom of the page and review the list in **FIGURE 6.1**. How many of these rationalizations did you come up with? These added cognitions help to reduce dissonance, but they also make it easier to avoid the difficult but healthy change of quitting.

A third way to reduce dissonance is to *trivialize* one of the inconsistent cognitions (Simon et al., 1995). Let's illustrate this with an example. Suppose you buy a

Figure 6.1

Smoking and Dissonance

Smokers often are experts at generating additional cognitions to reduce the dissonance created by doing something they know is bad for their health. How many of these have you heard before, or used yourself if you're a smoker?

- "I've only been smoking for a short time. I will quit soon."
- "My grandma smoked and lived to be 80, so my genes will protect me."
- "If I don't smoke, I'll get fat and die from that."
- "We'll all die of something. I'd rather live a shorter but more enjoyable life."
- "I prefer to take the suspense out of what kills me."
- "It's just not possible for me to quit."
- "I've cut back to 12 a day."
- "I only smoke at parties or when I'm stressed."

plasma TV, knowing that they use more energy than LED TVs. If you were to reduce dissonance by trivializing one of the cognitions, you could think to yourself, "With all the energy use in the United States, the extra electricity my new TV will use is a tiny drop in the bucket."

To understand more about the conditions that arouse dissonance and the ways people reduce it, researchers have come up with a number of laboratory situations, or *dissonance paradigms*. Two such situations are the *free choice paradigm* and the *induced compliance paradigm*.

The Free Choice Paradigm

The free choice paradigm (Brehm, 1956) is based on the idea that any time people make a choice between two alternatives, there is likely to be some dissonance. This is because all of the bad aspects of the alternative people chose, and all of the good aspects of the alternative they rejected, are inconsistent with their choice. The harder the choice, the more of these inconsistent elements there will be, and so the more dissonance there will be after the choice is made.

How do people cope with this dissonance? They do so by *spreading the alternatives*: After the choice is made, people generally place more emphasis on the positive charac-teristics of the chosen alternative and the negative aspects of the rejected alternative. For example, if you chose a fuel-efficient small car over a gas-guzzling luxury car, you could spread the alterna-tives by focusing on the value of being green as well as the extravagance and repair costs of the luxury car. But if you had instead chosen the luxury car, you might spread the alternatives by focusing on its comfort and the small car's lousy sound system.

To test this idea, Brehm (1956) asked one group of participants to choose between two con-sumer items (e.g., a stop watch, a portable radio) that they liked a lot (**FIGURE 6.2**). This was a diffi-cult decision. The other group was asked to choose between an item they liked a lot and one that they didn't like, which is an easy decision. After partici-pants chose the item they wanted, they were again asked to rate how much they liked them. Brehm reasoned that when the choice was easy, participants would not feel much dissonance, and so they would rate the items pretty much as they had before their deci-sion. But the participants who made a difficult decision would feel dissonance because their cognition "I made the right choice" is inconsistent with their cognition "The item I chose has some negative aspects, and the one I didn't choose has some attractive aspects." Brehm expected these participants to spread the alternatives on their second rating, exaggerating their chosen item's attractiveness and downplaying the other item's value. This is exactly what he found. Related research shows that people also spread the alternatives following a difficult choice by searching for information that supports their choice and avoiding information that calls their choice into question (e.g., Frey, 1982).

The Induced Compliance Paradigm

Dissonance is aroused whenever people make difficult choices. And many of our diffi-cult choices result from our being pulled in opposite directions, as when we're induced to say something we don't truly believe. For example, when your professor asks you whether you liked today's sleep-inducing lecture, you are likely to say, "Oh, it was very interesting." Could the dissonance aroused in these situations change our beliefs? Festinger and Carlsmith (1959) endeavored to find out. They had participants engage in an hour of boring tasks, such as turning wooden square pegs one quarter turn at a time. One third of the participants, those in the control condition, were then simply

Free choice paradigm
A laboratory situation in which people make a choice between two alternatives, and after they do, attraction to the alternatives is assessed.

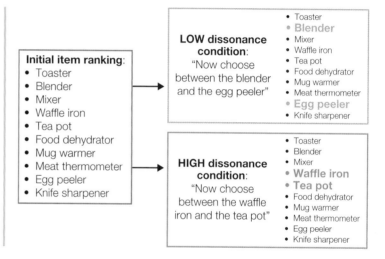

Figure 6.2

Brehm's Free Choice Paradigm

In the free choice paradigm (Brehm, 1956), participants in the high dissonance condition are asked to make a difficult choice between two similarly attractive options. Participants in the low dissonance condition make an easy choice between one attractive and one unattractive option. After making their choices, participants in the high dissonance condition increase their liking for what they chose and decrease their liking for what they didn't choose, a spreading of alternatives.

[Research from Brehm (1956)]

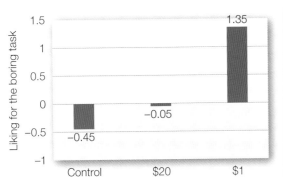

Figure 6.3

Support for Dissonance Theory Using the Induced Compliance Paradigm

When participants told another person that they liked a boring task, those who received $1.00 later reported liking the task more than those who received $20.00 and those who did not say they liked the task. Lacking sufficient justification for lying, participants in the $1.00 condition reduced dissonance by bringing their attitude in line with their behavior.

[Data source: Festinger & Carlsmith (1959)]

Induced compliance paradigm
A laboratory situation in which participants are induced to engage in a behavior that runs counter to their true attitudes.

asked how much they liked the tasks. As **FIGURE 6.3** indicates, these participants rated the tasks negatively. The other two thirds were told that the purpose of the study was to investigate the effects of expectations on performance and that they had been given no prior expectations because they were in the control condition. They were also told that the next participant was supposed to be given the expectation that the tasks would be very interesting, but the assistant who usually tells this to the next participant was running late. So the real participants were asked if they would go in the waiting room and tell the waiting participant (actually an experimental confederate) that the tasks were very interesting.

Half of these participants were offered $1.00 to say the boring tasks were interesting; the other half were offered $20.00 to do so. All of these participants agreed. Participants in these two conditions had the potential to experience dissonance, because they told the confederate something that was inconsistent with their attitude about the tasks. However, receiving $20.00 provided an added cognition that justified the action and thereby reduced the overall level of dissonance. Therefore, when later asked about their true attitudes, these participants saw the tasks for what they really were—a boring waste of time. In contrast, $1.00 is not sufficient to justify saying that a boring task is interesting and so does not reduce the dissonance. How, then, did the people in this condition reduce the dissonance they felt? They actually changed their attitude to bring it in line with their statement, rating the tasks more positively than did the participants in the other conditions.

The situation that Festinger and Carlsmith created to arouse dissonance in the lab has become known as the induced compliance paradigm. This is because the participants are induced to comply with a request to engage in a behavior that runs counter to their true attitudes.

Factors That Affect the Magnitude of Dissonance

Will people always experience dissonance when their behavior is inconsistent? Festinger argued that virtually any action a person engages in will be inconsistent with some cognition the person holds, but he did not think actions will always lead to strong feelings of dissonance. Much of the time people think or act in inconsistent ways without even being aware that they're doing so. Research shows that people feel dissonance primarily when the inconsistent cognitions are salient or highly accessible to consciousness (Newby-Clark et al., 2002; Swann & Pittman, 1975; Zanna et al., 1973). The level of dissonance that is aroused when inconsistent cognitions are salient or accessible depends on a number of factors.

Weak External Justification

Dissonance will be high if you act in a way that is counter to your attitudes with only weak external justification to do so. On the other hand, if the external justification is very strong, dissonance will be low. As we saw in the Festinger and Carlsmith study, $1.00 was a weak justification, so participants changed their attitude to reduce dissonance; $20.00 was a strong external justification, so participants maintained their original attitude. External justification doesn't have to come in the form of money; it can also be praise, grades, a promotion, or pressure from loved ones or authority figures. All of these can provide added cognitions that reduce overall dissonance.

Choice

As the work on the free choice paradigm might suggest, a key factor in creating dissonance in the induced compliance paradigm is perceived choice (Brehm & Cohen, 1962). Just as $20.00 is an added cognition that reduces the overall dissonance, so too is a lack of choice. If some twisted character held a gun to your head and told you to say your mom is an evil person, you'd probably do it and not feel too much dissonance about it. But neither would you feel you had much choice in the matter, because although the statement would be inconsistent with your love for your mom, it is quite consistent with wanting to stay alive. To study the role of perceived choice, Brehm and Cohen (1962) developed what has become the most common method for creating dissonance through induced compliance. It involves asking participants to write a counterattitudinal essay, that is, an essay that is inconsistent with their beliefs. One study using this method (Linder et al., 1967) showed that when an experimenter simply ordered students to write an essay in favor of an unpopular position—banning controversial speakers from campus—the cognition "I didn't have a choice; I was just doing what I was told" kept the dissonance low. This is known as a *low choice condition*. On the other hand, when the experimenter asked students to write the counterattitudinal essay to help the experiment but emphasized that it was up to them whether or not to do so, the students were no longer able to justify their behavior by saying, "I didn't have a choice." In this *high choice condition*, the students experienced dissonance and actually shifted their attitude toward supporting the ban on speakers.

Commitment

When people's freely chosen behavior conflicts with their attitudes, the more committed they are to the action, the more dissonance they experience. If the action can be taken back or changed easily, that reduces the extent to which the action is dissonant with one's attitude. After all, if you can just take it back, why change your attitude? A study by Davis and Jones (1960) illustrates this point. They induced participants to help the experimenter by insulting another person, and either gave participants a sense of choice in doing so (high choice condition) or did not (low choice condition). In addition, half of the participants thought they would be able to talk to the person later and explain that they didn't really mean what they said and were just helping the experimenter (low commitment—the behavior could be taken back). The other half thought they would not be able to explain themselves later to the other person (high commitment to the behavior).

If you're having a rough day and happen to treat someone badly and can't take it back, you might reduce your dissonance by deciding the person deserves the insult. And this is just what happened in the high choice, high commitment condition: The participants rated the person they insulted negatively. This did not occur in the low choice condition, and it also didn't occur in the high choice condition if the insult could be taken back. A clever field experiment at the track by Knox and Inkster (1968) also supported the role of commitment. They showed that horse-race bettors are more confident their horse will win after they have placed their bets than they are just before doing so. The higher the commitment to a chosen course of action, the more dissonance, and consequently, the more one's beliefs and attitudes are likely to change to justify the actions.

Foreseeable Aversive Consequences

The more aversive the foreseeable consequences of an action are, the more important the inconsistent cognitions are, and thus, the more dissonance. Imagine you wrote an essay arguing that smoking cigarettes is a good thing to do (it's a legal way to get a buzz, it makes you look cool) and either: (*a*) threw it away; or (*b*) read it to your 10-year-old cousin. In which case do you think you would experience more dissonance? The cognition "I wrote an essay in favor of smoking that no one read" is inconsistent with your beliefs about smoking, but it has no unwanted consequences and so arouses minimal dissonance. But encouraging a 10-year-old to smoke has foreseeable bad consequences indeed, so more dissonance will be aroused. In fact, research shows that action *b* would lead to a more positive view of smoking than would action *a* (Cooper & Fazio, 1984).

Cultural Influences

Although a consistent sense of self is an important aspect of being human, different situations may arouse dissonance for people who are from different cultures. For East Asians and people from other collectivistic cultures that value interdependence, *public* displays of inconsistency should arouse more dissonance, because harmonious connections with others are so important to them. To test this idea, Kitayama and colleagues (2004) had Western and East Asian students engage in a free-choice task either in private or with a reminder that others could see them. Whereas Westerners displayed the most spreading of alternatives (emphasizing the positive aspects of the chosen alternative and the negative aspects of the rejected alternative) when they completed the task in private, East Asians displayed the most spreading of alternatives when they thought about how others could be watching them. Note that both groups of participants were motivated to reduce dissonance, but they differed in which situations kicked that motivation into gear.

Applications of Dissonance Theory

Induced Hypocrisy

Outside the social psychology lab, it would be tricky to get people to engage in counterattitudinal actions and still feel they had a choice. So if you wanted to use

Induced hypocrisy paradigm
A laboratory situation in which participants are asked to advocate an opinion they already believe in, but then are reminded about a time when their actions ran counter to that opinion, thereby arousing dissonance.

Think
ABOUT

[La India Piaroa/Shutterstock]

what you've learned about dissonance to change people's attitudes and behavior for the sake of public health or the environment, how could you pull that off?

To achieve this goal, in the early 1990s, Elliot Aronson, Jeff Stone, and their colleagues came up with an **induced hypocrisy paradigm**. In this situation, people are asked to publicly advocate a position they already believe in but, to arouse dissonance, the experimenters remind them of a time when their actions ran counter to that position. In one study the researchers asked one group of sexually active students to make a short, videotaped speech for high-school students about the importance of using condoms to prevent AIDS (Stone et al., 1994). Another group was asked to think about such a speech but did not actually prepare one. Then, some participants from both groups were asked to think about times they failed to use condoms. Those participants who both advocated the use of condoms and who were reminded of times they didn't use them were in the induced hypocrisy condition and therefore were expected to experience dissonance. The researchers predicted that, to reduce this dissonance, these participants would be motivated to engage in behaviors consistent with the belief they had just advocated. After receiving $4.00 for taking part in the study, participants were told that the campus health

Dissonance Can Make for Better Soldiers

The motive to maintain consistency in the self can have lasting effects on commitment to important life choices. Consider the situation that many young American men were in during the Vietnam War. When they turned 18, they would find out their draft lottery number, from 1 to 365, based randomly on their birthdate. A low number meant a good chance of having to fight in Vietnam. A high number meant they would not be drafted. But they could avoid the draft lottery entirely if they

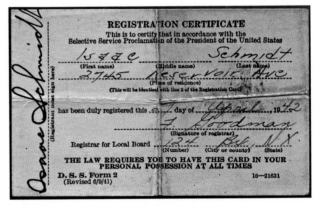

[© Bettmann/Corbis]

center had made it possible for them to purchase condoms. As the experimenters predicted, 83% of the induced hypocrisy participants purchased at least one condom, whereas participants who either didn't make a pro-condom speech or didn't think about prior failures to use condoms purchased condoms less than 50% of the time. The participants who made a very public declaration of their beliefs but then were reminded of times when they had failed to live up to them felt more dissonance, which they then reduced by reasserting their commitment to safe-sex behaviors. Inducing hypocrisy has also been shown to promote conservation of water and electricity, safe driving, exercising, and volunteering (Dickerson et al., 1992; Fointiat, 2004; Fried & Aronson, 1995; Kantola et al., 1984, Stone & Fernandez, 2008).

Effort Justification: Loving What We Suffer For

One implication Festinger drew from dissonance theory is that "people come to believe in and to love the things they suffer for." In other words, when people choose a course of action that involves unpleasant effort, suffering, and pain, they experience dissonance because of the costs of that choice. Because they usually can't go back and change their behavior, they reduce dissonance by convincing themselves that what they suffered for is actually quite valuable; this phenomenon is known as effort justification.

Elliot Aronson and Jud Mills (1959) tested this idea in a study that was inspired by fraternity initiation practices. They proposed that people who go through these initiations reduce their dissonance in the face of the effort and humiliation that is sometimes involved by becoming fonder of and more committed to those organizations. If this is true, then all other things being equal, the more severe the initiation to gain inclusion in the group, the more the group should be liked.

To test this hypothesis, they asked female students if they wanted to join a group that met regularly to discuss sexual matters. But depending on what condition the students were assigned to, gaining entry into the group required different levels of severity of initiation. In a control condition, the young women were immediately added to the group. In the mild initiation condition, participants had to read some mildly sexual words, such as *virgin*, in front of the male experimenter to join the

[Scott Adams/Universal UClick]

Effort justification The phenomenon whereby people reduce dissonance by convincing themselves that what they suffered for is actually quite valuable.

committed to six years of Reserve Officers Training Corps (ROTC) service before the draft lottery numbers for their year were announced. This would mean military service, but they would remain in the United States rather than going to war.

The researcher Barry Staw (1974) studied men who chose the ROTC and how dissonance affected satisfaction with their choice. He reasoned that men who chose to join the ROTC, only to learn that they would not have been drafted anyway because of their high lottery number, would experience a lot of dissonance about their six-year commitment to the ROTC. After all, they would not have been drafted to fight in Vietnam even though they had joined the ROTC. In contrast, guys who later learned that they would have been drafted had they entered the lottery should experience little dissonance. They knew that their decision to join the ROTC kept them on U.S. soil.

How did the guys in the first situation reduce the dissonance they felt? Staw predicted that the men who found out their lottery numbers would have been high would reduce their dissonance by liking the ROTC more. In support of this hypothesis, he found that these men increased the value they placed on their ROTC training and became better soldiers (as judged by their commanding officers) than the men who knew that the ROTC kept them from combat in Vietnam. The men who could not justify their commitment to the ROTC by saying, "Well, it's better than going to war" had to find some other way to justify their decision. They did this by becoming happier and better soldiers. Because the draft-lottery numbers randomly assigned these men to low- and high-dissonance conditions, this study provides particularly compelling evidence of the impact of dissonance and its reduction on people's responses to major life decisions.

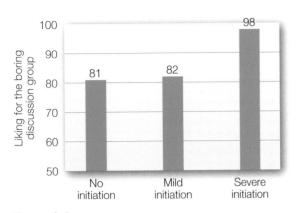

Figure 6.4

The Severity of Initiation Study: Evidence of Effort Justification

Participants expressed particularly high liking for a group if they had to go through a severe initiation to join the group. According to cognitive dissonance theory, they did this to justify the effort of having gone through the severe initiation.

[Data source: Aronson & Mills (1959)]

group. In the severe initiation condition, they had to read some sexually explicit terms and then read a passage of explicit pornography in front of the experimenter. Imagine how difficult and embarrassing that would have been to young female college students back in 1959.

Once accepted into the group, participants were told that the group discussion was about to start but that as new members getting acclimated, they would just listen in. The women were ushered to private rooms and given headphones, then listened to what turned out to be a dreadfully boring discussion of the sex habits of insects. The women were then asked how much they liked the group discussion and how committed they were to the discussion group. As the graph in **FIGURE 6.4** shows, the women who had to go through nothing or only a mild initiation were not impressed with the discussion and also were not highly committed to the group. In contrast, the severe initiation group, who had to go through a lot to get accepted, justified their effort by rating the discussion and their commitment to the group much more positively. These findings and others like them have clear implications for organizational practices and group loyalty. Could this be why so many organizations go out of their way to put new recruits through the wringer?

Might effort justification also play a role in the outcome of psychotherapy? Joel Cooper (1980) investigated whether a sense of choice would make an effortful therapy more effective. He gave participants with a severe snake phobia either a real form of therapy or a bogus one involving exercise, and he gave them either a high or low sense of choice. Compared with those who were not given a choice, participants who felt they freely chose the effortful therapy actually showed reduced phobia: They were able to move 10 feet closer to a snake than those who had the therapy without a sense of having chosen to participate in it. And the bogus therapy worked just as well as the real one; the only thing that mattered was the participants' sense of having chosen to go through the effort. In a sense, to justify the effort, the participants made themselves improve.

Although neither Cooper nor we are suggesting that dissonance reduction is the only reason that psychotherapy can work, it may be one way patients can help themselves. The practical implication is that the client's choice in participating in the therapy may help motivate positive change. This may explain why court-ordered programs to address such problems as drug addiction and anger management often don't work.

Minimal Deterrence: Advice for Parenting

In the course of raising children, parents inevitably have to stop them from acting on many of their natural impulses, usually to deter them from doing things that are harmful or socially inappropriate. ("Don't put that in your mouth!" "Stop sitting on your sister!") A typical strategy that parents use to deter a child from misbehaving is to threaten with negative consequences such as spanking and grounding from video games. In these cases the child has a strong external justification for not doing the behavior ("I don't want to get spanked!"), but this doesn't mean that the child loses the *desire* to do the behavior. A better way to deter the behavior would be to use the minimal level of external justification necessary—that is, to use *just enough* inducement or threat of punishment to prevent the behavior, while allowing the child to feel that she or he *freely chose* not to do that behavior. In these cases the child has the dissonant cognitions "I'm not doing what I enjoy" and "The punishment for doing it is pretty mild." To reduce this

Parents try to deter a lot of their children's behaviors, in this case, pulling the dog's tail.

[Ron Nickel/Getty Images]

dissonance, the child may change his attitudes, coming to believe that he is not doing the behavior because he didn't really enjoy it in the first place.

To test this idea, Aronson and Carlsmith (1963) developed a way to study the effects of minimal deterrence. They had four-year-olds at the Harvard Preschool play with five toys and rank them in order of liking. Each child's second-favorite toy was then placed on a table. In the *no-threat* condition, the experimenter told the kids he had to leave for a while, picked up the second favorite toy to take with him, and told them they could play with any of the remaining toys while he was gone. In the *mild-threat* condition, the experimenter said that while he was gone, they could play with any toy except the one on the table: "I don't want you to play with the [toy on the table]. If you played with it, I would be annoyed." In the *severe-threat* condition, he said: "I don't want you to play with the [toy on the table]. If you play with it, I would be very angry. I would have to take all of my toys and go home. . . ."

During this temptation period, the children were watched through a one-way mirror. None of the children in the mild- and severe-threat conditions played with the forbidden toy. In the no-threat condition, they couldn't, because the experimenter took it with him. When the experimenter returned (with the second-favorite toy in the no-threat condition), he asked the children to re-rank their liking for the five toys. As dissonance theory predicts, the children in the mild-threat condition now liked their formerly second favorite toy *less* than did the children in the no-threat and severe-threat conditions. Because the mild threat of annoying the experimenter was only a minimal deterrent to not playing with the attractive forbidden toy, the children in the mild-threat condition reduced their liking for that toy to justify not playing with it. The kids in the severe-threat condition also refrained from playing with the toy when forbidden to do so. But they had plenty of external justification—the threats of anger and of having all the toys taken away, so they didn't change their attitudes toward the toy. A later study (Freedman, 1965) showed that this effect was still present 40 days later! So the message for parenting is clear: Using the minimal deterrence necessary to stop a child from engaging in a behavior will make it most likely that the child will internalize that she doesn't want to engage in that behavior anyway.

Minimal deterrence Use of the minimal level of external justification necessary to deter unwanted behavior.

Dissonance as Motivation

The preceding sections showcase some of the many ways that cognitive dissonance can impact our thoughts and behavior as we strive for self-consistency. But how do we know that inconsistency truly produces negative feelings that motivate these changes in attitude and behavior? Engaging in counterattitudinal actions under high choice conditions elevates participants' ratings of discomfort, their levels of physiological arousal, and their neurological signs of motivation to exert control (Elliot & Devine, 1994; Harmon-Jones et al., 1996; Harmon-Jones et al., 2012). These indices of discomfort also predict how much people change their attitudes. Other research applies the phenomenon of *misattribution of arousal* we described in chapter 5 to support the role of negative affect as the motivator of attitude change. When participants are given an alternative explanation for why they might be experiencing tension and discomfort, they no longer adjust their attitudes after engaging in inconsistent behavior (e.g., Zanna & Cooper, 1974; Higgins et al., 1979). Taken together, this evidence provides strong support for the idea that perceived inconsistency arouses negative affect (dissonance), which then motivates attitude change (dissonance reduction). These findings support Festinger's cognitive dissonance theory, and they also provided the first compelling laboratory evidence for a more general idea introduced by Freud at the dawn of the 20th century: that psychological defenses, in this case the defense against cognitive inconsistencies, substantially influence people's thoughts and behavior.

(a)

(b)

Figure 6.5

Dorothea Lange's Classic Photo: *Migrant Mother, Nipomo, Calif.*

Dorothea Lange's photograph powerfully captures one woman's struggles during the Great Depression. Many years later, Robert Silvers replicated this iconic image in a photo-mosaic built out of Depression-era photographs of the American West. In this way, he conveys how many individual episodes and experiences make up a person's self-concept.

[Photomosaic by Robert Silvers]

Self-concept clarity A clearly defined, internally consistent, and temporally stable self-concept.

Self-verification Seeking out other people and social situations that support the way one views oneself in order to sustain a consistent and clear self-concept.

Self-consistency at the Macro Level: Sustaining a Sense of the Self as a Unified Whole

The picture on the left (**FIGURE 6.5a**) is a rendition of Dorothea Lange's classic photograph *Migrant Mother, Nipomo, Calif*. If we squint our eyes or look at the picture from a distance, we can make out a young mother with an expression of deep concern as her children huddle around her. And when we learn that this picture was taken during the Great Depression, we can imagine this woman's life struggle to care for herself and her family. But looking closer, we discover that the image is made up of hundreds of tiny photographs of assorted aspects of this woman's surroundings, such as a door and a weather vane (**FIGURE 6.5b**). Although these tiny images make up the broader image, none of them captures the emotional significance of this woman's life as clearly as the broader perspective does.

In a similar sense, the question of identity—*Who am I?*—is easy to answer from a distance. We can step back and describe ourselves with broad generalizations such as *family oriented, outgoing, ambitious,* and so on. But up close we see that our lives are made up of thousands of separate memories, behaviors, and other elements of experience that have little meaning of their own. How do we integrate these lived experiences to establish consistency at the *macro* level of our overall self-concept?

Self-consistency Across Situations

If you were to describe yourself in a personal ad right now, you might use characteristics like *ambitious, cooperative,* and *shy*. But do you always think and act in line with these broad traits? For example, you may think of yourself as *introverted*. But if you dredge up a different set of experiences—such as karaoke nights when you've been known to belt out "Sweet Home Alabama" in front of total strangers—you might come to a very different conclusion about what characteristics define you.

Despite such inconsistencies, most people prefer self-concept clarity, a clearly defined, internally consistent, and temporally stable self-concept (Campbell, 1990). In fact, individuals with high self-concept clarity may be happier and better equipped to cope with life's challenges. Why? Individuals with high self-concept clarity are less sensitive to the feedback they receive from others, such as insults or nasty looks on the street. In contrast, individuals with low self-concept clarity tend to look to other people's feedback to understand who they are. Their attitudes toward themselves are therefore more likely to fluctuate, depending on whether they perceive that others view them positively or negatively. Studies suggest that people high in social status have greater self-concept clarity than those low in social status, perhaps because they are less dependent on the social context around them (Kraus et al., 2012).

One way people sustain a clear self-concept is by seeking out diagnostic information about themselves. People often search for ways to assess their traits and abilities to have an accurate view of themselves (e.g., Sedikides & Strube, 1997; Trope, 1986). They gather others' opinions of them, take personality and ability tests, see how they do on challenging tasks, and compare themselves with others.

People also tend to seek out others and social situations that confirm the way they view themselves, a phenomenon known as self-verification. People have a propensity to seek out others who corroborate their self-image, even when that means affiliating with people who don't think all that highly of them (Swann, 1983). Most people report thinking positively of themselves and prefer others who bolster their self-esteem.

However, those with negative self-views (e.g., more depressed people) choose to interact with people who have a more negative impression of them (Swann et al., 1992). Although this preference for self-verification can help to solidify a clear and consistent sense of self, the unfortunate cost is that those with low self-esteem might avoid people who would actually help bolster and reinforce a more positive self-view.

Although self-concept clarity has benefits, to some degree we're all aware that we act differently when we find ourselves in different roles or situations. Perhaps you're laid back and even silly when hanging out with friends, but a couple hours later at the gym you're ambitious and aggressive. The poet Walt Whitman (1855/2001, p. 113) acknowledged and even celebrated contradictions in his own self-concept:

> Do I contradict myself?
> Very well then I contradict myself,
> (I am large, I contain multitudes.)

Research on **self-complexity** examines the degree to which the self-concept is made up of many distinct aspects, including social roles (e.g., student), relationships (e.g., daughter), and activities (e.g., mountain biking). One benefit of high self-complexity is that the person can cope with difficulties in one area of life by drawing strength from others (Linville, 1985). However, self-complexity contributes to stress if the many facets of the self seem to be forced on the person and cause conflicting demands (e.g., Goode, 1960; McConnell et al., 2005).

Self-complexity The extent to which an individual's self-concept consists of many different aspects.

My Story: Self-consistency Across Time

To tie together separate pieces of experience over time into a coherent whole, each person constructs a **self-narrative**, or life story, in which he or she is the protagonist in a continuously unfolding drama of life, complete with characters, setting, plot, motivation, conflicts, and their resolutions (Bruner, 1990; Erickson, 1968; Gergen & Gergen, 1988; McAdams, 1993, 2001). Self-narratives integrate these various aspects of personal history, everyday experience, roles, and envisioned future into a unified, purposeful whole: *This is what I was, how I've come to be, who I am, and what I am becoming.* Why do we need a narrative understanding of ourselves in time?

Self-narrative A coherent life story that connects one's past, present, and possible future.

A clear self-narrative provides a basis for effective action, helping us to gauge what actions we should or should not attempt and what future challenges and obstacles might arise. But making sense of experience does more than facilitate action: It also provides psychological security by connecting separate experiences together into a coherent whole that is more significant and longer lasting than a series of passing moments. For example, you might view the time you overcame a bully in grade school and the time you stood up to an oppressive boss 10 years later as fitting a theme of "standing up for myself" that summarizes an important part of your self-concept.

Dan McAdams (2006) found that middle-aged and older adults tend to structure their life stories around two story patterns. One is the contamination story in which the person first experiences good fortune but then experiences tragedy or failure and ends up in a place of bitterness or depression. But much more common is the uplifting redemption story. In this tale, people experience obstacles, challenges, sometimes even tragedies, but then turn their lives around and overcome those difficulties to feel successful in their lives. As you might guess, people who tell redemption stories report greater life satisfaction and well-being than those who tell contamination stories. Think about your mom and dad: Which kind of life stories would they tell?

Think
ABOUT

[Michael Jung/Shutterstock]

Research supports the idea that a need for psychological security motivates people to integrate their personal past and present into a coherent story. For example, Landau and colleagues (2009) showed that after a reminder of death, participants attempted to restore psychological security by seeing their past experiences as meaningfully connected to the person they are now, rather

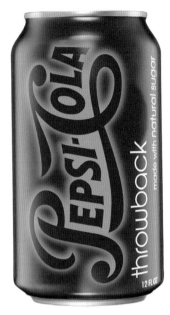

Research on nostalgia helps us understand why it can be such an effective advertising tool (Holbrook, 1993). When an advertisement conjures up positive associations of a past self, people are more favorable to that product. This is why ads often pair products with cues that were nostalgically popular among those likely to be purchasing the product (e.g., classic rock music with commercials for mini-vans) and create explicit "throwback" campaigns, like this one for Pepsi-Cola.

[PR NewsFoto/Pepsi-Cola North America]

than as isolated events. Related studies show that whereas participants typically saw life as less meaningful after being reminded of death, this was not the case for participants who were prompted to think nostalgically about the past (Routledge et al., 2008). These individuals were able to use their perceptions of the past as a psychological shield against mortality, bolstering their conception that their own life has enduring significance.

Researchers have also found that although nostalgia can be bittersweet, overall it serves a number of positive psychological functions: It generates positive moods, boosts self-esteem, enhances our feelings of being connected to others, and increases a sense of meaning in life (e.g., Routledge et al., 2011; Wildschut et al., 2006). Furthermore, nostalgic memories enable us to feel a greater sense of *self-continuity*: People who are asked about a nostalgic episode report a stronger connection between who they were in the past and who they are now (Sedikides et al., 2008).

Because self-narratives fit the past, present, and future into a consistent and meaningful structure, they can also help the person to "work through" the emotional pain caused by stressful events and experiences.

APPLICATION
Stories That Heal

The healing power of working through past traumas was emphasized by psychoanalysts such as Freud and has been supported by experimental studies by Jamie Pennebaker and colleagues. In one such study, people who wrote about an emotionally traumatic experience for four days, just 15 minutes a day, showed marked improvements in physical health (e.g., fewer physician visits for illness) many months later (Pennebaker & Beall, 1986).

How does narrating a traumatic event help with coping? Pennebaker and colleagues (1997) developed a computer program to analyze the language that individuals use while disclosing emotional topics. They found that people who narrated the trauma using words associated with seeking insight and cause-and-effect connections (e.g., *because*) showed the most pronounced health improvements. Thus, narrating can translate vague, negative feelings into a coherent explanation of why the event happened and what it means for the self, which in turn helps the person to cope with the event.

Not only do self-narratives create meaning from the past, they also allow people to view their present self as on a stable path to future selves that will make a lasting mark on the world. They may view themselves as literally continuing after their death to eternal life, or they may picture themselves as symbolically immortalized through their identification with enduring entities and causes (e.g., the nation, the corporation), memories, and cultural achievements in the sciences and arts (Greenberg et al., 2009). But a more everyday means of bolstering self-consistency is to connect current events to long-term goals. Whereas perceiving the events scheduled in the coming week (e.g., pick up business cards) as a series of separate activities offers little sense that one's actions are significant, seeing the same activities as tied to one's broader, long-term goals (e.g., advance my career) may help to sustain a meaningful conception of one's life (Landau et al., 2011).

APPLICATION
Educational Achievement

Possible selves Images of what the self might become in the future.

Personal narratives also include possible selves, vivid images of what the self might become in the future. Some possible selves are positive ("the successful designer me," "the party animal me"), whereas others are negative ("the unemployed me," "the lonely me"). Possible selves give a face to a person's goals, aspirations, fears, and insecurities. For example, your personal goal of succeeding in college probably is not some vague abstraction but more likely takes shape in your mind as a vivid image of a positive possible self, "academic star me," up on stage receiving a prestigious award as your classmates look on in admiration.

Our visions of possible selves are not just idle pictures in our minds. They also motivate and guide our behavior (Markus & Nurius, 1986). That's because thinking about a possible self can make us aware of the actions we need to take now in order to become that person in the future. In one demonstration of this, Daphna Oyserman and colleagues (2006) went into low-income urban school districts where failure in school is depressingly common. The researchers randomly assigned eighth-graders to sit in their regular homeroom period (control) or to take part in an intervention called "School-to-Jobs" twice weekly over a seven-week period. During the early part of this intervention, participants were asked to imagine academic possible selves, at one point identifying photographs of adults that fit their visions of a good future. A couple of weeks later, they were asked to describe specific strategies they need to do to realize their academic possible selves, such as attending class and completing their homework. Students in the intervention condition had fewer classroom behavior problems and better grades even a year later, suggesting that thinking about possible selves in the future, when combined with pragmatic thinking about how to get there, can motivate people to take action in the present. ●

SECTION review | The Motive to Maintain a Consistent Self

Cognitive dissonance theory explains that, at the micro level, people maintain self-consistency by minimizing inconsistences between their cognitions. To reduce dissonance, people change one of the cognitions, add a third cognition, or trivialize the inconsistent cognitions.

Free Choice Paradigm	Induced Compliance Paradigm	Factors That Affect the Magnitude of Dissonance	Cultural Influence
• Any choice creates some dissonance. • The harder the choice, the greater the dissonance. • People reduce dissonance by emphasizing the positive aspects of the chosen alternative and the negative aspects of the rejected alternative.	People induced to say or do something against their beliefs may change their beliefs to reduce dissonance if there is insufficient external justification for their behavior.	Dissonance increases with less external justification and more perceived choice, commitment, and foreseeable negative consequences.	In cultures that value interdependence, public displays of inconsistency arouse more dissonance because harmonious relationships are so valued.

Applications

• When faced with an apparent hypocrisy—a reminder of past behavior that went against a currently advocated opinion—people will reassert their commitment to the advocated opinion.
• When a course of action is difficult or unpleasant, people will convince themselves it is valuable.
• When a minimal level of external justification is used to deter behavior, people will internalize that they don't want to engage in the behavior anyway.

At the macro level, self-consistency is an important way that people make sense of their lives as a whole.

Self-concept Clarity	Self-complexity	Self-narratives
Self-concept clarity is a clear sense of *who one is* from one situation to the next. High self-concept clarity supports psychological well-being.	A complex self-concept, as defined by many distinct roles and activities, may be a buffer against stress if those aspects of self are freely chosen and controlled.	Self-narratives are coherent stories explaining how one's past, present, and future cohere into a unified whole. Threats to psychological security increase reliance on self-narratives for meaning in life.

Application: Talking or writing about a painful event can help a person cope with stressful experiences.

Application: Envisioning possible selves can help motivate people to achieve their long-term goals.

The Self-esteem Motive: Establishing and Defending One's Value

When one of your authors was growing up, his brother used to run around the house exclaiming, "I want to be special!" Although few of us may admit it so blatantly, who hasn't dreamed about becoming a world-famous scientist, an admired actor or singer, or a sports superstar? These aspirations reflect something very basic about human beings: We are driven to view ourselves as valuable, to bolster feelings of self-esteem, and to defend our positive view of ourselves when it is called into question.

What Is Self-esteem, and Where Does It Come From?

Self-esteem The level of positive feeling one has about oneself.

Self-esteem is the level of positive feeling you have about yourself, the extent to which you value yourself. Self-esteem is generally thought of as a *trait*, a general attitude toward the self ranging from very positive to very negative. Researchers have developed a number of self-report measures to assess self-esteem in both children and adults (e.g., Coopersmith, 1967; Rosenberg, 1965). Using such measures in longitudinal studies, researchers have shown that self-esteem is fairly stable over a person's life span (e.g., Trzesniewski et al., 2003).

However, self-esteem can also be viewed as a *state*, a feeling about the self that can temporarily increase or decrease in positivity in response to changing circumstances, achievements, and setbacks. In other words, someone whose trait self-esteem is pretty low can still experience a temporary self-esteem boost after getting a good grade on a test or a compliment on her appearance. Similarly, someone with normally high trait self-esteem can experience a dip in state self-esteem after being denied a promotion or having his marriage fall apart.

The fact that self-esteem can remain stable as a trait but vary as a state indicates that a number of factors influence it. One source is genetics. The stability of trait self-esteem from childhood to adulthood suggests that our self-esteem may result in part from certain inherited personality traits or temperaments (Neiss et al., 2002). This stability also suggests that, as noted in chapter 5, the reflected appraisals and social comparisons we experience as children have a lasting impact on our sense of self-worth. Research supports this idea (Harter, 1998). All else being equal, a child who better lives up to the standards of value conveyed by her parents and others is likely to receive more positive reflected appraisals and more favorable social comparisons, and therefore have greater self-esteem.

Of course, these standards are often quite different, depending on the culture in which you are raised. As we saw in chapter 4, among the Trobriand Islanders, an important symbol of self-worth is how many yams a farmer can harvest, and on certain occasions, pile in front of his home to signify his status (Goldschmidt, 1990). This type of landscaping would not be much of a source of self-esteem in front of the typical American or European home; a Lexus or Mercedes in the driveway would more likely do the trick. Bases of self-esteem generally differ between individualistic cultures such as the United States, where displaying one's personal qualities and accomplishments garners self-esteem, and more collectivistic cultures such as Japan, where displays of modesty and pleasing the family patriarch would better improve self-esteem (Markus & Kitayama, 1991; Sedikides et al., 2003).

Cultures also prescribe different standards of value for individuals at different stages of development. For example, the characteristics and achievements that made you feel valuable in grade school are likely to be different from those that gave you self-esteem in high school, and those standards continue to change throughout adulthood. In addition, because cultural worldviews offer individuals multiple paths to feeling valuable and successful, individuals raised in the same culture are likely to stake their self-esteem on different types of activities.

Crocker and Wolfe (2001) studied these differences and found that whereas one person may seek self-esteem in being physically attractive, another person's self-esteem may be tied to academic accomplishments. Other common contingencies are others' approval, virtue, and God's love. People's overall opinion of themselves increases and decreases primarily in response to achievements and setbacks in the areas of life most important to them.

Maintaining and Defending Self-esteem

Imagine this is your first couple of weeks at a new university or college. A group of students is discussing what kind of music they like, and you want to join the conversation. But you're nervous. Will they like you? How will you feel about yourself if they don't? After a while, you decide to enter in the conversation and note your fondness for the long-out-of-style pop star Barry Manilow. A painful silence in the conversation follows. Your contribution is ignored by some and ridiculed by others. Wait until they hear about your enthusiasm for ice fishing!

Think
ABOUT

[Shutterstock]

As we navigate through our social worlds, we encounter a seemingly limitless cascade of challenges and events that can potentially threaten our sense of ourselves as a person of worth. Focus on yourself for a moment. What are the soft spots in your self-esteem armor? Of course, it's never easy to admit or think about such things, but the more we understand about ourselves, ultimately the better off we are.

Some events pose a severe threat, for instance, losing one's job or being dumped by one's romantic partner. But there are also a number of other, much more minor events that can threaten self-esteem: an acquaintance on campus who doesn't say "Hi!"; asking a dumb question in class; a friend noticing a piece of toilet paper stuck to the bottom of your shoe. How can we maintain self-esteem in light of all these potential threats? It turns out that people use many strategies to defend self-esteem and enhance it when possible. We'll begin by considering strategies that focus on how we explain our own behavior and then progress to strategies that involve the self in relation to other people.

Self-serving Attributions

The self-serving attributional bias is to make external attributions for bad things that one does, but internal attributions for good things one does. In other words, people are quick to take credit for their successes and blame the situation for their failures (e.g., Snyder et al., 1976), a biased way of viewing reality that helps people maintain high levels of self-esteem (Fries & Frey, 1980; Gollwitzer et al., 1982; McCarrey et al., 1982).

What are the consequences of making self-serving attributions for our behavior? Some research suggests this bias helps support mental health. For example, self-serving attributions seem to work well for preserving self-esteem and are common among well-adjusted people. Individuals suffering from depression tend *not* to make self-serving attributions, viewing themselves as equally responsible for their successes and their failures (e.g., Alloy & Abramson, 1979). So some level of self-serving bias in attributions is probably useful for mental health (e.g., Taylor & Brown, 1988). However, this bias may interfere with an accurate understanding of poor outcomes. This is a problem because understanding the true causes of one's poor outcomes is often very helpful in improving one's outcomes in the future.

Self-handicapping

In a strategy known as self-handicapping, people set up excuses to protect their self-esteem from a failure that may happen in the future (Berglas & Jones, 1978). Suppose you decide to go out to a bar, stay out really late, and get wasted the night before

Self-handicapping Placing obstacles in the way of one's own success to protect self-esteem from a possible future failure.

an important exam. How would that be a preemptive strategy to protect your self-esteem? If you fail the test, you can say, "Well, it's because I had this killer hangover from getting plastered the night before." And if you happen to do well, this makes your success all the more remarkable. That way, even though you're doing something to hinder (handicap) your own performance, you can attribute your failure to the excuse (e.g., partying) and not your own abilities. This strategy can keep your self-esteem intact, but it's also very self-defeating because it makes poor performance more likely.

When are people most likely to self-handicap? People self-handicap when they are especially focused on the implications of their performance for self-esteem rather than on getting the rewards associated with success (Greenberg et al., 1984). In addition, Berglas and Jones (1978) showed that self-handicapping stems from uncertainty about one's competence. People who have experienced success in the past but are uncertain about whether they can succeed in the future are the most likely to self-handicap.

Self-handicapping has been used to explain a wide variety of behaviors in which individuals appear to sabotage their own success: abusing alcohol or other drugs, procrastinating, generating test anxiety, or not preparing for an exam or performance. Indeed, perhaps the most common form of self-handicapping is to simply not try one's hardest on challenging tasks. If you don't try your hardest, then you can attribute poor performance to a lack of effort rather than a lack of ability. Psychologists often attribute the lack of effort to low expectations of success, feelings of helplessness, or fear of success. But often instead what people are doing is self-handicapping. How do we know? When people who fear they will not succeed on a task are given a handy excuse should they fail (such as the presence of distracting music), they actually perform better (Snyder et al., 1981). The excuse reduces their concern with protecting their self-esteem, which frees them to put in their best effort.

Of course, not all people self-handicap to the same extent. Some individuals are generally more likely to self-handicap than others (Kimble & Hirt, 2005). There is evidence that men are more likely than women to self-handicap, suggesting that women place relatively higher value on effort (McCrea et al., 2008).

The Better Than Average Effect

Think for a moment about the percentage of the chores you do around your house or dorm. Then ask your roommate what percentage of the chores she thinks she does. We're betting the total will well exceed 100% (Allison et al., 1989). This example illustrates how people often overestimate the frequency of their own good deeds relative to those of others (Epley & Dunning, 2000). In fact, as we described in chapter 5, the average person thinks that she or he is above average on most culturally valued characteristics and behaviors (Alicke, 1985; Taylor & Brown, 1988). Clearly, we can't all be above average on these characteristics, so how do people maintain this perception that they're superior? When people perform poorly on some task, they tend to overestimate how many other people also would perform poorly. This allows people to think they are better than average even on dimensions in which they don't excel. In contrast, when people perform very well on a task, they tend to underestimate how many other people also would perform well. So people think their shortcomings are pretty common but their strengths are rather unique (Campbell, 1986).

Projection

Another way people avoid seeing themselves as having negative characteristics is to try to view others as possessing those traits which they fear they themselves possess. For example, if I fear that I'm overly hostile, I might be more likely to see others as hostile. Classic psychoanalytic psychologists such as Freud (1920/1955a), Anna Freud (1936/1966) and Carl Jung (Jung & von Franz, 1968) labeled this form of self-esteem defense projection.

Projection Assigning to others those traits that people fear they possess themselves.

In one series of studies (Schimel et al., 2003), students were given personality feedback showing that they had high or low levels of a negative trait such as repressed hostility or dishonesty. Participants then read about a person, Donald, whose behavior was ambiguously hostile (or dishonest). Those participants given an opportunity to evaluate Donald saw him as possessing more of the trait they feared they might possess (e.g., hostility). Moreover, after evaluating Donald, they were less likely to think about the trait and saw themselves as having less of that trait than participants who were not given the opportunity to rate (and thus project onto) Donald. Because they saw the feared trait in someone else, they no longer feared that they had it!

Symbolic Self-completion

In the early 1900s, Alfred Adler noted that when people feel inferior in a valued domain of life—he called that feeling an *inferiority complex*—they often compensate by striving very hard to improve in that domain (Adler, 1964). This can be a very productive kind of compensation for one's weaknesses. However, the theory of symbolic self-completion (Wicklund & Gollwitzer, 1982) suggests that people often compensate for their shortcomings in a shallower way. When people aspire to an important identity, such as lawyer or nurse, but are not there yet and worry they may not get there, they feel incomplete. To compensate for such feelings, they often acquire and display symbols that support their desired identity, even if those symbols are rather superficial.

Consider a woman who has always wanted to be a doctor, but then experiences some kind of setback, such as getting a poor MCAT score or making a mistaken diagnosis while interning. This poses a threat to her view of herself as an aspiring doctor, making her feel incomplete. She compensates by amassing symbols of competence as a premed, medical student, or doctor, perhaps prominently displaying her medical degree or wearing a lab coat and stethoscope around her neck whenever possible. In one study, male college students given feedback that they were not well suited for their career goals became very boastful regarding their relevant strengths—even when interacting with an attractive female student who they knew did not like boastful people (Gollwitzer & Wicklund, 1985). In contrast, people who are secure in their identity are more open to acknowledging their limitations and do not need to boast of their intentions or display symbols of their worth (Wicklund & Gollwitzer, 1982).

Recent research has focused on individuals who have just acquired a symbol of completeness. For instance, law students who were induced to state publicly their positive intention to study actually acted on this intention less often than students who were made to keep this intention private. Going public with their intention enhanced their symbolic completeness, thus ironically making further striving for their identity goal of becoming successful lawyers less necessary (Gollwitzer et al., 2009). This finding suggests a possible negative consequence of the growing trend of using social media to broadcast one's progress toward goals by posting, for example, calories burned or books read. These symbols might give you a premature sense of having achieved your desired identity. As a result, you may neglect to take concrete steps toward fully achieving your identity goal.

Compensation

Early personality theorists such as Gardner Murphy and colleagues (Murphy et al., 1937) and Gordon Allport (1937) noted that people possess considerable flexibility in the way they maintain self-esteem. When self-esteem is threatened in one domain, people often shore up their overall sense of self-worth by inflating their value in an unrelated domain. This is called compensation, which essentially allows a person to think, "I may be lousy in this domain, but I rule in that other one" (Greenberg &

Theory of symbolic self-completion The idea that when people perceive that a self-defining aspect is threatened, they feel incomplete, and then try to compensate by acquiring and displaying symbols that support their desired self-definition.

"I've noticed you've taken to wearing a lab coat lately. May I ask the reason why?"

[George Price/The New Yorker Collection/Cartoonbank.com]

Compensation After a blow to self-esteem in one domain, people often shore up their overall sense of self-worth by bolstering how they think of themselves in an unrelated domain.

Self-affirmation theory The idea that people respond less defensively to threats to one aspect of themselves if they think about another valued aspect of themselves.

Pyszczynski, 1985a). For example, when participants were given personality feedback that they were not very socially sensitive, they responded by viewing themselves more positively on unrelated traits (Baumeister & Jones, 1978).

This idea has been further developed by Steele's **self-affirmation theory** (Steele, 1988), which posits that people need to see themselves as having integrity and worth, but can do so in flexible ways. As a result, people respond less defensively to threats to one aspect of themselves if they bring to mind another valued aspect of themselves—that is, if they self-affirm.

For example, college students participated in a study immediately after their intramural sports team either won or lost a game (Sherman et al., 2007). As you might expect from our previous discussion of self-serving attributions, players generally were more likely to attribute the outcome to their own performance when their team won than when they lost. However, players who had self-affirmed by writing about something else they valued did not make these self-serving attributions, taking equal responsibility for their team's victory or defeat.

Self-affirmation also reduces people's defensiveness when they are faced with threatening information about their health. For example, whereas smokers tend to respond to cigarette warning labels by denying the risk or downplaying their smoking habit ("I smoke only when I party"), these defensive responses are minimized if smokers first affirm core personal values or morals (Harris et al., 2007).

When people face a self-esteem threat, do they prefer to minimize it directly, by enhancing their standing on the valued self-aspect, or indirectly, by affirming an unrelated self-aspect? To find out, Stone and colleagues (1994) induced hypocrisy regarding practicing safe sex and then gave participants a choice of purchasing condoms or donating money to a homeless shelter. Although donating money allowed participants to affirm their overall worth, most of them (78%) chose to purchase condoms instead. Thus, although self-affirmation is a powerful strategy for indirectly minimizing self-esteem threats, people generally prefer to compensate for their shortcomings directly. Consistent with symbolic self-completion theory, this is especially true when the threat pertains to an important identity goal (Gollwitzer et al., 2013).

Social Comparison and Identification

In chapter 5, we noted that social comparison plays a substantial role in how people assess their own abilities and attributes. As a consequence, comparing ourselves with others who are superior to us leads to upward comparisons that can threaten self-esteem, whereas comparing ourselves with others who are inferior leads to downward comparisons that help us feel better about ourselves. Generally, people prefer to compare themselves with others a bit less accomplished than themselves, so comparisons can bolster their self-esteem (Wills, 1981). If you're a moderately experienced tennis player, beating a similarly experienced friend in tennis in close matches feels better than either getting beaten by a pro or trouncing a novice.

Although people often prefer to compare themselves with others worse off, they also use a variant of this strategy when comparing themselves with, well, *themselves*. People tend to think they are much better in all respects now than they used to be, essentially engaging in downward comparison with their former selves (Wilson & Ross, 2001).

Basking in reflected glory Associating oneself with successful others to help bolster one's own self-esteem.

Although comparison with successful others can hurt self-esteem, affiliating with successful others can help bolster self esteem, an idea referred to as **basking in reflected glory**, or BIRGing (Cialdini et al., 1976). If you're associated with an individual or group that is successful, then that reflects positively on you. Robert Cialdini and colleagues (1976) demonstrated this with regard to college sports. Research assistants systematically observed what students wore on campus the Monday following football games for a number of weeks. Students were more likely to wear school-affiliated apparel after a win than after a loss. Thus, students were more likely to display their university allegiance when that allegiance led to association with a successful team, and less likely to do so when that allegiance led to association with an unsuccessful team. Such reactions, moreover, are especially likely to occur after people experience a threat to their self-image.

Although research on BIRGing shows that people sometimes gain self-esteem by affiliating with very successful others, other evidence suggests that people could lose self-esteem by comparing themselves with more successful others. How can other people's successes trigger opposite effects? Abe Tesser's (1988) self-evaluation maintenance model proposes that people adjust how similar they think they are to successful others, both to minimize threatening comparisons and to maximize self-esteem-bolstering identifications. When another person outperforms you in a domain (or type of activity) that is important to your self-esteem, perceiving the other person as dissimilar makes comparison less appropriate. But when the domain is not relevant to your self-esteem, comparison is not threatening, so you can BIRG by seeing yourself as similar to the successful other. For example, a math major may feel threatened by comparison with the math department's star student and so will distance from that person and see the math star as a very different person than herself. But the same person won't be threatened by a star music student and may even derive self-esteem from affiliating with that person and focusing on their similarities.

Not sold on the BIRGing idea yet? Take, then, the fact that the teams with the best-selling sports apparel traditionally are the most successful. Over the past five years in the United States, gear for the New York Yankees, the Miami Heat, and the San Francisco 49ers has been very popular in national sales for baseball, basketball, and football, respectively. Not surprisingly, these are among the winningest teams in the last five years.

[Nick Laham/Getty Images]

Closeness in age also affects self-evaluation maintenance in the context of sibling rivalry. In one study, Tesser (1980) examined relationships between brothers. They found that for males who had a more accomplished older brother, their relationship was more contentious the closer they were in age. Being farther apart in age makes comparisons less relevant, and so a younger male was likely to see himself as "just like my older brother" and could therefore gain self-esteem through identifying with him (BIRGing). When the brothers were closer in age (i.e., less than three years apart) comparison was more relevant. This self-esteem threat strained the relationship, leading to more perceptions of difference and more friction. So a key variable that determines whether people identify with or distance themselves from a successful other is whether comparison is or is not relevant. If it is relevant, people distance; if it is not, they identify. Amateur basketball players can safely admire and view themselves as generally similar to LeBron James, but if you were a fellow NBA All-Star, you'd be more likely to think you're very different from him.

Self-evaluation maintenance model The idea that people adjust their perceived similarity to successful others to minimize threatening comparisons and maximize self-esteem-supporting identifications.

APPLICATION

An Example of Everyday Self-esteem Defenses—Andrea's Day

To summarize this section on self-esteem defenses, let's consider how a fictional college student named Andrea might employ such defenses in a typical day.

Andrea wakes up and sends a text to her brother, telling him that her close friend Megan just won a poetry competition. "I don't know anything about poetry," she writes, "but I'm so proud of her!!" (*basking in reflected glory*).

Driving to work, Andrea is appalled at how bad drivers are in this town. "The majority of these people don't have a clue about how to drive," she tells herself (*the better than average effect*). She's walking to class when her mother calls her and starts yelling about how Andrea forgot to call Grandma and wish her a happy birthday yesterday. Andrea yells back, "Well, I totally would've if you had just reminded me!!" and hangs up (*self-serving attributions*).

She still has some lingering doubts about her value as a granddaughter, but she reminds herself that her job right now is to do well in school (*self-affirmation*) and that she is an excellent student (*compensation*). After class, a friend approaches Andrea and asks if she wants to come to a free ballroom dance class that evening. She agrees to come but decides to work out at the gym that afternoon. Later, as they are walking to the studio, Andrea tells her friend how tired and sore she is from working out earlier (*self-handicapping*). Andrea is stunned to see what a good dancer her friend is, and just how much more graceful her friend is than Andrea could ever hope to be. Andrea then says to herself, "My friend and I are such different people. Dancing is her thing, not mine" (*self-evaluation maintenance*).

She leaves the class to meet up with her boyfriend for dinner. At one point during dinner, Andrea looks out of the restaurant window and notices a particularly attractive guy whom she's admired a couple times. A moment later, she looks up and notices her boyfriend glancing at another woman. Instantly she starts berating her boyfriend about being loyal and keeping his eyes off other women (*projection*). That night Andrea loads her Facebook page with pictures of herself receiving an academic award and of her trips to Europe, so that everyone can see that she is educated and cosmopolitan (*symbolic self-completion*). She goes to bed, secure in the knowledge that she is a person of value.

Why Do People Need Self-esteem?

Given the wide range of ways that people defend their self-esteem, and the energy that they expend in doing so, *why* are people so driven to have high self-esteem? Do we just have an innate need to view ourselves positively? Perhaps, but our needs typically serve some function. The need for food serves the larger purpose of making sure that we get the nutrition we need for survival. But what purpose does self-esteem serve?

Self-esteem as an Anxiety-buffer

Anxiety-buffer The idea that self-esteem allows people to face threats with their anxiety minimized.

One answer to this question comes from the existential perspective of terror management theory. As we described in chapter 2, this theory starts with the idea that we humans are uniquely aware of the fact that our lives will inevitably end one day. Because this fact can create a great deal of anxiety, people are motivated to view themselves as more than merely material creatures who perish on death. According to terror management theory, this is precisely the function of self-esteem: to help the individual feel like an enduringly significant being who will continue in some way beyond death. In this way, self-esteem functions as an anxiety-buffer, protecting the individual from the anxiety stemming from the awareness of his or her mortality. The poet T. S. Eliot anticipated this idea in his eloquent ode on low self-esteem, *The Love Song of J. Alfred Prufrock* (1917/1964, p. 14):

> I have seen the moment of my greatness flicker,
> And I have seen the eternal Footman hold my coat, and snicker,
> And in short, I was afraid.

Self-esteem serves this anxiety-buffering function over the course of development. As children, we minimize our anxieties by being good, because if we are good, our parents love and protect us. As we develop and become more and more aware of our mortality and the limitations of our parents, we shift our primary source of protection from our parents to the culture at large. As adults, we therefore base our psychological security not on being good little girls or boys but on being valued citizens, lovers, group members, artists, doctors, lawyers, scientists, and so forth. We feel high self-esteem when we believe that we have or will accomplish things and fulfill roles our culture views as significant, that we are valued by the individuals and groups we cherish, and that we are making a lasting mark on the world. In this way we can maintain faith that we amount to more than mere biological creatures fated only to perish entirely.

If self-esteem protects people from death-related anxiety, then we would expect that when self-esteem is high, people will be less anxious. A large body of research examining the characteristics of high and low trait self-esteem people fits

[Excerpt from "The Love Song of J. Alfred Prufrock," from *Collected Poems* 1909–1962 by T. S. Eliot. © 1964 Thomas Sterns Eliot. Reprinted by permission of Faber and Faber Ltd. and Houghton Mifflin Harcourt Publishing Company]

this hypothesis. Compared with those low in self-esteem, high-self-esteem people are generally less anxious; less susceptible to phobias, anxiety disorders, and death anxiety; and function better under stressful circumstances (e.g., Abdel-Khalek, 1998; Loo, 1984). However, because this evidence is correlational, there are many potential explanations. It may mean that high self-esteem buffers anxiety, but it also could mean that functioning well with minimal anxiety raises people's self-esteem.

More compelling evidence that self-esteem buffers anxiety comes from experimental studies. In a study by Greenberg and colleagues (1992), half of the participants were randomly assigned to have their self-esteem boosted by receiving very positive feedback about their personality, supposedly based on questionnaires they had filled out a few weeks earlier; the other half were given more neutral personality feedback. Then participants watched a 10-minute video that was either neutral or depicted graphic scenes of death (excerpts from *Faces of Death*, Vol. 1; you might not want to watch these videos before going to bed—if ever!). Participants then reported how anxious they felt.

When the personality feedback was relatively neutral, participants reported feeling more anxiety after the threatening video than after the neutral video, as you might expect. However, if they had first received the positive personality feedback, participants who watched the threatening video did not report any more anxiety than those who watched the neutral video. The boost to self-esteem allowed them to be calm even in the face of gruesome reminders of mortality. Not only do people report less anxiety after a self-esteem boost, their bodies show fewer signs of stress. In one study, participants given self-esteem-boosting feedback showed reduced physiological arousal when they anticipated receiving electric shocks (Greenberg et al., 1992). Self-esteem accomplishes this anxiety-buffering by increasing activation of the parasympathetic nervous system, which helps to calm people and control their anxiety (Martens et al., 2008).

Another way to assess this function of self-esteem is to find out if reminding people of their own mortality leads them to strive even harder to bolster their self-esteem and to defend it against threats. In the first direct tests of this hypothesis, Israeli soldiers who reported that they either did or did not derive self-esteem from their driving ability were reminded of their mortality or not. They were then placed in a driving simulator and asked about their likelihood of engaging in risky driving behaviors on the road (Ben-Ari et al., 1999). Now, you might expect that thinking about your mortality would make you a more cautious driver, right? But this reasoning misses an important point of terror management theory, namely, that to shield ourselves from the fear of death, we strive to feel valuable. Consistent with this idea, when first reminded of their mortality, those participants who derived self-esteem from their driving ability drove especially fast and claimed they would take more driving risks when out on the road. Additional studies have shown that mortality salience also increases strivings in other self-esteem-relevant domains, such as physical and intellectual performance and displays of generosity (see Greenberg & Arndt, 2012).

If self-esteem shields us from our fear of death, then our shield should be weakened when our self-esteem is threatened, making us more likely to think about death. Across a series of studies, Hayes and colleagues (2008) found that when participants experienced a threat to their self-esteem, thoughts of death became more accessible to consciousness. In sum, a substantial body of converging evidence indicates that self-esteem provides protection from basic fears and anxieties about vulnerability and mortality.

Social Functions of Self-esteem

Our awareness of our human vulnerability and mortality is one driving force behind our striving for self-esteem. Two other perspectives place special emphasis on the social aspects of self-esteem.

First, Jerome Barkow (1989) proposed that people desire self-esteem to maximize their social status, just as monkeys try to maximize their position in a dominance hierarchy. Barkow proposed that those of our ancestors who were most focused on seeking high social status had the most access to fertile mates and resources to nurture their offspring, therefore perpetuating their genes into future generations. To the extent that desiring self-esteem serves attaining high social status, this desire would have been selected for over the course of hominid evolution.

Sociometer model The idea that a basic function of self-esteem is to indicate to the individual how much he or she is accepted by other people.

Second, according to Mark Leary and colleagues' (1995) sociometer model, a basic function of self-esteem is to indicate to the individual how much he or she is accepted by other people. According to this model, self-esteem is like the gas gauge in your car. The gas gauge is a meter that lets you know when the gas is too low and you need to fill up. Similarly, according to the model, self-esteem is like a *sociometer* that lets you know if you are currently receiving the social acceptance you need to satisfy a need to belong. Consequently, the more you perceive yourself to be liked and accepted by others, the higher your level of self-esteem. According to the sociometer model, when people appear to be motivated to maintain self-esteem, they actually are motivated to feel a sense of belongingness with others. Although both Barkow's status-maximizing perspective and Leary and Baumeister's sociometer model emphasize the social functions of self-esteem, the former emphasizes the desire to stand out and be better than others, whereas the latter emphasizes fitting in with and gaining the acceptance of others. Each perspective captures something true about self-esteem. Barkow's analysis can help explain why people often sacrifice being liked in order to be successful and gain status, whereas the sociometer model can help explain why people sometimes sacrifice status and material gain in order to fit in with the group. However, both perspectives have difficulty explaining why people are so likely to bias their judgments to preserve their self-esteem. For example, people often feel they are more worthy than other people think they are. If self-esteem were primarily an indicator of something of evolutionary value, such as social status or belonging, rather than something that buffers anxiety, why do people seem to distort their beliefs to inflate their views of themselves? It would be akin to moving the gas gauge with your fingers to convince yourself you had gas in your tank when you actually did not. Does this disconfirm the sociometer model? Or is there some way to reconcile the model or revise it to fit with the research on self-esteem defenses?

Think
ABOUT

[Winnond/Shutterstock]

The Influence of Treatment by Others: Ostracism

Despite their different emphases, terror management theory and the status and sociometer perspectives all suggest that self-esteem will be heavily influenced by how one is treated by others. Go to any schoolyard or playground, and you are likely to see this in action. Imagine seeing three kids playing a harmless game of catch, or imagine that you and two friends are outside on a sunny day tossing around a Frisbee. Typically, person A will throw to person B who will throw to person C who will throw back to person A, and so on. Well, now imagine that you are person C, and persons A and B stop throwing to you. How would you feel?

Kip Williams and colleagues set up a computerized analog of this situation that they call *cyberball* (Zadro et al., 2004). In cyberball, participants play a virtual game of catch with two other people who are presumably playing from other computer terminals. When you are a participant, your "hand" is shown at the bottom of the screen (see **FIGURE 6.6**). It catches the ball when another participant has thrown it in your direction, and you hit one of several keys to indicate which player you will throw the ball to next. In one condition, the game progresses in this way for several

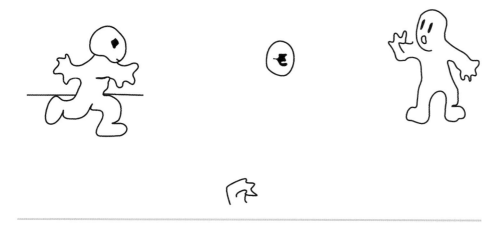

Figure 6.6

Kip Williams's Cyberball Game

In his studies of ostracism, Williams and colleagues (e.g., Zadro et al., 2004) had participants start playing this cyber game of catch with what they believed were two other participants. Soon after, the other two players' avatars stopped throwing the ball to the participant's avatar, thereby creating an intense feeling of being ostracized.

[Courtesy Professor Kipling D. Williams, Purdue University]

minutes, with everyone getting the ball an equal numbers of times. But in another condition, after a minute or so, the others players stop throwing you the ball, and your poor little virtual hand is left looking empty and lonely at the bottom of the screen while the others continue the game.

Even this simple five-minute experience of being excluded by people that a participant had never met and never would interact with significantly lowered the participant's self-esteem. In fact, even when participants were told that they were the only person playing and that the other figures were controlled by the computer, they felt lower self-esteem when the ball didn't come their way!

Looking at this from a neuroscience perspective, we find evidence that when people are excluded in a situation such as cyberball, they show activation in the *anterior cingulate cortex* (Eisenberger et al., 2003). This brain region is generally responsible for detecting when a given situation isn't meeting our goals. It also is activated when people experience physical pain, suggesting that sticks and stones might break your bones, but words—if they suggest rejection—might be perceived as just as hurtful. If even a minor slight such as exclusion from cyberball lowers self-esteem, it is not surprising that prolonged experience of social exclusion and ostracism has been linked to an increase in depression and attempted suicide (Williams & Zadro, 2001).

Protecting and Enhancing Self-esteem: Cultural Differences

As we have seen, a vast array of evidence indicates that self-esteem is of great psychological importance to people. But seen from a cultural perspective, most of this work has been conducted in relatively individualistic cultures such as the United States. Is self-esteem important in more collectivistic cultures as well?

Some social psychologists have argued it is not. They suggest that people from collectivistic cultures, such as those in East Asia, place more value on group cohesion and the self's connection with others (Markus & Kitayama, 1991). East Asian cultures also value traits such as self-criticism and emotional restraint, which are not embraced so strongly by North American culture. Does this mean that self-esteem is not a driving concern to people from East Asian cultures?

Although this question has sparked considerable debate, the weight of evidence indicates that people in all cultures strive for self-esteem (Sedikides et al., 2005). In considering this point, keep in mind our earlier discussion of how self-esteem comes from living up to cultural standards of value and fulfilling culturally sanctioned roles. Viewed this way, self-esteem is pursued universally, but the attributes, values, and roles that lead to feelings of worth vary depending on the individual's culture. Those raised in individualistic cultures tend to derive self-esteem from proving their superior skills and abilities, whereas those raised in collectivistic cultures are more likely to derive self-esteem from sustaining their honor, gracefully performing cultural rituals, and promoting group harmony. For example, one study (Sedikides et al., 2003) found that participants from the United States were more likely to see themselves as better than average on traits that are important to individualistic cultures (e.g., self-reliance), but Japanese participants were not. In contrast, participants from Japan were more likely to view themselves as better than average on traits that are important in collectivistic cultures (e.g., loyalty).

Types of Self-esteem

Up to this point, we have been talking about self-esteem as if it were a unitary construct. But is this really the case? If two people both report having high self-esteem, does this mean their feelings of worth actually are the same? Early theorists such as Karen Horney (1937) and Carl Rogers (1961) suggested that the answer is no. They pointed out that some people have more secure, authentic feelings of positive self-regard, whereas others may report the same high self-regard but are actually com-

Think
ABOUT

[Research from: Mark Landau]

pensating for feelings of inferiority. Furthermore, for some people, self-esteem is durable, but for others, it fluctuates from day to day. Take a moment to think about how you feel about yourself. Is your self-esteem generally the same as it was yesterday? And the day before that?

Mike Kernis and colleagues measured self-esteem stability by looking at how much people's responses to self-esteem measures changed over the course of a week (e.g., Kernis & Waschull, 1995). They found that self-esteem stability has a number of consequences even when people are equally high in overall levels of self-esteem. People whose self-esteem is more unstable tend to be sensitive to potential threats to their self-esteem. For example, when an acquaintance doesn't return a greeting, a person with unstable self-esteem is likely to be offended and concerned about his broader social reputation, whereas a person with stable self-esteem is more likely to ignore the same event (Kernis et al., 1998).

Why are certain feelings of self-esteem more unstable than others? One important factor is where we get our self-esteem from. As we noted previously, self-esteem can be derived from a variety of sources. Some sources, such physical appearance, are extrinsic because they provide self-esteem when we meet standards dictated by the external environment. Other sources are intrinsic because they connect feelings of self-esteem to inner qualities that seem more enduring. As a result, when people rely on extrinsic sources, their self-esteem is contingent on feedback from others. Because this feedback can vary in favorability, they have less confidence in their overall value. In contrast, when people base their self-esteem on intrinsic qualities, their feelings of value are less contingent on others' feedback. Research has found that participants reminded of extrinsic sources of self-esteem, such as social approval or personal achievements, make more downward social comparisons, are more likely to conform to the opinions of others, and are more likely to engage in self-handicapping than participants led to think about intrinsic qualities of themselves (Arndt et al., 2002; Schimel et al., 2001).

Researchers have often assumed that self-esteem is a conscious attitude about oneself, but emerging research suggests it can also be an unconscious attitude. Various methods have been developed for tapping into unconscious feelings about the self (e.g., Bosson et al., 2000). In one study, implicit self-esteem was measured as the speed at which participants could identify words such as *good* (as opposed to *bad*) after being primed with first-person pronouns such as *I*, *me*, and *myself* (as opposed to neutral primes) (Spalding & Hardin, 1999). Interestingly, these implicit signs of self-esteem are only weakly correlated with people's explicit feelings about themselves. So people's levels of explicitly reported self-esteem and implicit self-esteem are often quite different. This suggests that people can consciously report that they think they are great and have many worthwhile qualities, whereas deep inside they might harbor negative associations with their self-concept. Research suggests that this type of person is most likely to have unstable self-esteem and to exhibit narcissistic tendencies and defensive responding (Jordan et al., 2003).

APPLICATION

The Good, the Bad, and the Ugly of Self-esteem

So far we have discussed what self-esteem is, the sources of self-esteem, the many ways we maintain and defend it, and why people need self-esteem. Let's now consider four important implications of this knowledge.

1. *Self-esteem cannot be easily granted to people.* Children must internalize a meaningful worldview and clear standards for being a good and competent, and therefore valued, person. Then they must learn how to self-regulate to meet those standards of value and continue to meet them so that their value is validated throughout the life span. So school programs that give every kid a gold star and youth soccer leagues that give every player a trophy are not helping to instill secure, enduring self-esteem. And in adulthood, simply telling someone else or yourself, "You are a good, worthy person" won't do the trick either (e.g., Greenwald et al., 1991). Instead, meeting socially validated standards of self-worth provides the best basis of stable self-esteem, the kind of self-worth that best serves people's psychological needs.

"We lost!"

[Leo Cullum/The New Yorker Collection/Cartoonbank.com]

2. *People with either unstable self-esteem or low self-esteem will struggle with psychological problems such as anxiety, depression, and drug dependencies, which often result from attempts to avoid or alleviate these negative psychological feelings.* Such people are also likely to lash out at others, to express hostility, and even to resort to physical aggression. Research has clearly linked narcissism and borderline personality disorder, two psychological profiles in which unstable self-esteem and low self-esteem are prominent, to various forms of aggression (e.g., Bushman & Baumeister, 1998; Kernis et al., 1989; Salmivalli et al., 1999). The same message can be found by examining dramatic examples of school shootings, such as those at Columbine (1999) and Virginia Tech (2007). Those who engage in them often seem to be lashing out at specific people or the world in general because they do not feel valued.

3. *People pursue self-esteem in ways that fit with their cultural worldview, sometimes with harmful consequences.* Self-esteem pursuit often takes the form of trying to do good by eradicating evil in the world. Depending on one's worldview, this can lead to noble actions or ignoble ones. Those who focus on poverty or disease as evil often pursue self-esteem by helping the poor or dedicating their lives to fighting diseases such as cancer. In one study, those who reported deriving self-esteem from being altruistic were the most likely to help a stranger who they believed had been injured (Wilson, 1976).

But other people try to do good by eradicating individuals or groups they perceive to be evil, leading to aggression. Hard as it may be for Americans to believe, the people who committed the suicidal terrorist attacks on the World Trade Center and the Pentagon in 2001 did so because they thought it was the right thing to do and would prove their value. In fact, while those who commit such acts are referred to by Americans as terrorists or suicide bombers, they are often viewed as heroic martyrs by their supporters in Islamic countries. The typical Islamic suicide bomber seeks significance and eternal life in paradise by attacking evil in the name of Allah. Believing in a very different worldview, Americans have sought their own heroism by fighting in wars against symbols of evil such as Hitler, communism, and Saddam Hussein.

4. *Striving for self-esteem can have constructive or destructive consequences for the self.* For instance, young American women are socialized to derive considerable self-value from their appearance. This emphasis can lead to extreme dieting, restrictive eating, and ultimately anorexia (Geller et al., 1998). On the other hand, to the extent that the culture promotes the value of an athletic, healthy body for young women, more positive health consequences of self-esteem striving could result. Similarly, self-esteem striving will have destructive consequences for young people who are encouraged to gain self-worth through risky behaviors such as reckless driving, fighting, binge drinking, and drug use. Indeed, depending on what society defines as valuable, and the extent to which people are sensitive to these social definitions, mortality salience seems to encourage risky behaviors such as restrictive eating and excessive tanning, but also healthy behaviors such as quitting smoking (e.g., Arndt & Goldenberg, 2011). Self-esteem striving also leads people to engage in various defenses that interfere with their having an accurate view of themselves. This can lead them to choose career paths they are not suited to and to repeat mistakes rather than recognize weaknesses and work toward improving them. When people are particularly lacking in self-esteem or feel it is threatened, they are especially likely to avoid potentially useful diagnostic information about themselves (e.g., Sedikides & Strube, 1997; Strube & Roemmele, 1985).

Because self-esteem striving can be detrimental in some ways, researchers (e.g., Crocker & Park, 2004) have wondered whether people can simply stop caring about their self-worth. But the theories and research we have reviewed suggest this is both undesirable and unlikely. First, striving for personal value often leads to accomplishments that contribute positively to society. Second, if we accept the idea that self-esteem is a vital buffer against anxiety, then if we were stripped of self-worth, we would be unable to function. In this light it might not be too surprising that in societies with limited culturally embraced avenues for self-worth, we see high levels of clinical depression and dependence on chemical mood enhancers (e.g., Kirsch, 2010; Swendsen & Merikangas, 2000). We've seen the most extreme consequences of losing all sense of socially validated value with mass killings in places such as Columbine High School and Virginia Tech. Perhaps the best we can hope for is to fashion, both individually and as a society, more constructive avenues for self-esteem, open to all, without hurting others so as to lift ourselves up (e.g., Becker, 1971).

Another possibility is to cultivate **self-compassion**, an idea developed from Buddhist psychology (Brach, 2003; Neff, 2011). Compassion involves being sensitive to others' suffering and desiring to help them in some way. You feel it, for example, when you stop to consider your friend's struggle with a painful experience. Rather than judge or criticize her, you look for ways to provide comfort and care. You practice self-compassion when you take the stance of a compassionate other toward the self.

Self-compassion Being kind to ourselves when we suffer, fail, or feel inadequate, recognizing that imperfection is part of the human condition, and accepting rather than denying negative feelings about ourselves.

Self-compassion involves three elements. The first is self-kindness. When faced with painful situations or when confronting your mistakes and shortcomings, your tendency might be to beat yourself up, but with self-compassion you would respond with the same kindness toward the self that you would show to a close other. The second element is the recognition that everyone fails or makes mistakes on occasion, and that suffering and imperfection are part of the shared human experience. The third element, mindfulness, means accepting negative thoughts and emotions as they are rather than suppressing or denying them.

Self-compassion lessens the impact of negative life events and is linked to psychological well-being, including more optimism, curiosity, and creativity, and less anxiety and depression (Hollis-Walker & Colosimo, 2011; Leary et al., 2007; MacBeth & Gumley, 2012). Most of this research has used trait measures of self-compassion, but other researchers also have developed ways to increase self-compassion and look at the effects of doing so. In one study (Shapira & Mongrain, 2010), a group of volunteers wrote a self-compassionate letter to themselves every day for a week; another group wrote letters about personal memories. The self-compassion group showed higher levels of happiness as much as six months later.

Self-compassion offers a way to maintain stable high self-esteem even though you make mistakes and sometimes fall short of your own standards and goals and other people's expectations for you. This healthier approach to maintaining self-worth should make it less dependent on self-serving biases and defensiveness. By cultivating self-compassion, people can maintain self-esteem even if they fail and without having to view themselves as superior to others (e.g., Neff & Vonk, 2009).

SECTION review | The Self-esteem Motive: Establishing and Defending One's Value

Self-esteem is the level of positive feeling one has about oneself. It can be thought of as a trait (a general attitude) or a state (a temporary feeling that is changeable).

Self-serving biases to protect self-esteem	Other self-esteem defenses	Functions of self-esteem	Influence of others and culture	Stable self-esteem
• Self-serving attributions. • Self-handicapping. • Seeing self as better than average. • Projection.	• Compensating with symbols that support a desired self-definition. • Bolstering sef-views in unrelated domains. • Comparing and identifying with others.	• Buffers anxiety about vulnerability and mortality. • Indicates one's social status and how accepted one is by others.	• Influenced by how one is treated by others. • Maintained through behaviors valued by one's culture.	• Based on intrinsic factors rather than extrinsic factors. • More constant over time and more resistant to feedback from others.

Application: Five implications regarding self-esteem:

- It is not easily granted.
- Low and unstable self-esteem contributes to psychological problems.
- It depends on a person's worldview.
- Self-esteem striving can have constructive or destructive consequences for others and the self.
- Self-compassion may be one valuable route for maintaining stable high self-esteem.

Self-presentation: The Show Must Go On

Alan: I think we live our lives so afraid to be seen as weak that we die perhaps without ever having been seen at all. Denny, do you ever worry that when you die, people will never have truly known you?

Denny: I don't want them to know me, I want them to believe my version.

David E. Kelley (2008),
Boston Legal, "Tabloid Nation" April 8, 2008

We've been focusing primarily on the individual's private view of her or his own self, but the self is as much a public entity as it is a private one. Life casts people into different social roles (child, student, patient) that are part of their cultural worldview, but those people also help create their own public personas. In fact, the word *personality* derives from the Greek word *persona*, a word originally used to describe the masks that Greek actors wore on stage to represent their characters' current emotional state.

The Dramaturgical Perspective

"All the world's a stage, and all the men and women merely players."

William Shakespeare (English playwright, 1564–1616),
As You Like It, act 2, scene 7

Dramaturgical perspective
Using the theater as a metaphor, the idea that people, like actors, perform according to a script. If we all know the script and play our parts well, then like a successful play, our social interactions flow smoothly and seem meaningful, and each actor benefits.

In books such as *The Presentation of Self in Everyday Life* (1959), the sociologist Erving Goffman offered a dramaturgical perspective that uses the theater as a metaphor to understand how people behave in everyday social interactions. From this perspective, every social interaction involves self-presentation in which actors perform according to a script. If everyone involved knows the script and plays their parts well, then like a successful play, their social interactions flow smoothly and seem meaningful, and each actor benefits.

People learn their scripts and roles over the course of socialization. Parents, teachers, and the media teach children about weddings, funerals, school, parties, dates, concerts, wars, and so forth, long before they experience any of these things firsthand. Kids also learn how to be friends, teammates, students, and romantic partners. They play at various culturally valued adult roles such as astronaut, athlete, mother, doctor, teacher, or pop star. As a result of these and other socialization experiences, in every social situation there is a working consensus, an implicit agreement about who plays which role and how it should be played.

The social context defines a person's role, fellow performers, and audience. The power of the situation to define roles, perceptions, and behavior was vividly demonstrated when, in 2007, the *Washington Post* journalist Gene Weingarten persuad-

Virtuoso Joshua Bell playing a three-million-dollar violin for spare change at L'Enfant Plaza Metro Station.

[Michael Williamson/The *Washington Post*/Getty Images]

ed the internationally acclaimed violinist Joshua Bell to play for nearly an hour in a crowded Washington, DC Metro station. Three nights earlier, in the impressive setting of a sold-out concert hall, Bell took on the role of virtuoso. The listeners played their role, sitting in their seats (for which they paid $100) and stifling their coughs during the performance. But although he filled the Metro station with the same virtuosity, here Bell took on the role of the panhandler, and passersby played their part by ignoring him. Only seven people actually stopped to listen. Indeed, Bell suddenly found his very identity threatened. He said, "When you play for ticket-holders, you are already validated. I have no sense that I need to be accepted. I'm already accepted.

Here, there was this thought: *What if they don't like me? What if they resent my presence?*" (Weingarten, 2007).

Sincere versus Cynical Performances

Many of the situations people encounter are so familiar that they are not consciously aware that they're playing a role or following a script. In a classroom, for instance, you automatically take on the student role. Goffman refers to these well-practiced scripts as *sincere performances*. But when something goes awry, when someone doesn't play his or her role properly, then people become aware of the implicit rules and norms they've been following automatically all along.

In contrast to sincere performances, *cynical performances* are conscious attempts to perform in a certain way to make a particular impression. People are more likely to engage in such performances when they find themselves in unfamiliar territory or when they want to convey a specific impression. Think back to your first day of college. You probably did a lot of preparation, thinking about what to expect, how to dress, and so on. When you arrived, you were probably fairly self-conscious, thinking about how to act and what to say. Job interviews and first dates are other good examples of cynical performances. Cynical performances can turn into sincere performances as they become increasingly familiar and more rehearsed.

Are people always performing? Goffman would say yes. Even when you wish to be most genuine—for example, when offering condolences to a friend whose father has died—you still rely on scripts to express your true feelings of sympathy and offer comfort. You may end up drawing on phrases you've seen used in movies or even read in sympathy cards. So for Goffman, performing and self-presentation are not primarily done to be phony or manipulative (although sometimes they are) but simply to accomplish the goal that is important to a person in a particular social situation.

Sometimes meeting new people or being in an unfamiliar environment can be uncomfortable, if not downright painful. The premise of the *Meet the Parents* movies is based on this very idea of cynical performance. Consciously trying to play a role is never easy, yet we're forced to do it far more often than we'd probably like.
[Universal/Photofest]

Self-presentational Strategies

Honing an Image

Jones and Pittman (1982) described some common strategies we use to meet our self-presentational goals. To appear competent, we advertise our achievements through self-promotion. But self-promotion can backfire if its comes off as too boastful (e.g., Wosinka et al., 1996). Supplication involves revealing a little personal weakness, usually as a way to garner sympathy. When we simply want people to like us, we often use ingratiation, such as by flattering others, which is generally quite effective (e.g., Jones & Wortman, 1973). We also ingratiate ourselves to others by presenting ourselves as like them (Gordon, 1996). But sprinkling in a little disagreement can help us come across as more sincere and create a better impression overall (e.g., Jones, 1990; Jones et al., 1963). Finally, in certain situations, people—more often men—turn to intimidation to create an image of power and strength (Jones & Pittman, 1982).

Audience Segregation

In their everyday lives, people have to stay in character to uphold a particular public identity with a given audience. Goffman pointed out that people do so in part by keeping different audiences segregated so that they can perform consistently with each audience. If you have ever worked in a restaurant, you'd know that wait staff act very differently in the kitchen than they do out on the floor.

Similarly, at the mall with your parents, you'd probably rather not run into your friends. Your style of speaking, the words you use, the way you dress, and

Goffman (1959) pointed out that waiters have to work hard to perform in a deferential and pleasant manner to their audience, the restaurant customers. Because of the strain behaving in this manner creates, they often act very differently backstage in the kitchen area. The 2005 film *Waiting* humorously portrays this phenomenon, as exemplified here by waitress Naomi (played by Alanna Ubach), who exudes charm and patience out front with the customers but rage and contempt when back in the kitchen.

[Jeff Greenberg]

even your body posture are likely to be different when you're with your parents than when you're with your friends. How do you give two different performances at once? Faced with such a multiple audience problem, sometimes people use different communication channels to convey different self-images. For one, you may at some point find yourself flattering someone on the phone while rolling your eyes for a friend who is with you (Fleming & Rudman, 1993). A second option would be for you to adopt a compromise position on an issue when two present audiences have opposite views (e.g., Braver et al., 1977). Leaf Van Boven and colleagues (2000) investigated a third solution by asking participants to convey an image of being a nerd to one fellow student and a party animal to another. When forced to discuss college life in the presence of both students, the participants used ambiguous statements such as "Saturdays are good for one thing and one thing only." Although people use such strategies, they find multiple-audience situations very difficult, and people are not nearly so effective as they think they are at sustaining different identities simultaneously (Fleming et al., 1990; Van Boven et al., 2000).

Lying

One fundamental goal in self-presentation is to maintain *face*, a person's sense of public value. Every social encounter brings with it the risk of losing face if the person slips up or says or does the wrong thing. Fortunately, when this happens, people often tactfully work cooperatively with the person to help him or her to save face and maintain a positive self-image. Individuals often minimize threats to someone else's face out of empathy and kindness, but this tactic also helps social interactions flow smoothly and increases the likelihood that such tact will be reciprocated.

Because of the importance of protecting face, people often bend the truth. For example, you may assure someone that his presentation went well when in fact it put you to sleep. This perspective suggests that lying is pretty common and often motivated by the need to protect face—our own and others'—rather than intentionally harming or manipulating others. A study by Bella DePaulo and colleagues (1996) found considerable support for these ideas. Participants were given little notebooks and instructed over a week to record any and all lies, and the reasons for telling them.

Think ABOUT

[Kongsak/Shutterstock]

The participants lied about twice a day and lied to 38% of the people they interacted with over the week. Three quarters of the lies were about face-saving. Half the lies were told to save the participant's own face, and a quarter of them were told to protect someone else's. Women were equally likely to lie for themselves or for someone else. Men, in contrast, were more likely to save their own face than someone else's. What would you write in your notebook if you were recording any and all lies over the course of a week?

APPLICATION

The Unforeseen Consequences of Self-presentation

In 2011, among high school students who were sexually active, about 40% reported not using a condom during their last sexual encounter (U.S. Department of Health and Human Services, 2011). Why? One reason is that many people report feeling embarrassed when they buy condoms (Bell, 2009). Those who do have condoms sometimes feel that it might make the wrong impression if they suggest using one during sex (Herold, 1981). These concerns about the impression you are making on a drugstore cashier or a one-night stand can lead you to do something that could leave you with a sexually transmitted and perhaps even life-threatening disease!

Unsafe sex isn't the only risky health behavior that people might adopt for the sake of making a good impression. Those who are more concerned about the impression they make on others are also more likely to put themselves at risk for skin cancer in order to perfect their tans (Leary & Jones, 1993); use or abuse drugs and alcohol as a way to fit in with the "right" crowd (Farber et al., 1980; Lindquist et al., 1979); or engage in unhealthy dieting practices or steroid use to achieve that perfect body (Leary et al., 1994). Studies show that women eat less in front of an attractive man (Pliner & Chaiken, 1990) and when they want to present a more feminine impression (Mori et al., 1987). Based on these lines of research, interventions (e.g., for sun protection or smoking cessation) are starting to focus more on image-based concerns (Mahler et al., 2007).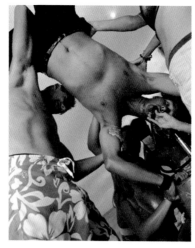

Sometimes it's difficult to determine if we're doing what we want or doing what everyone else wants us to do. Take this person, for example. How much is he really wanting to be held upside down in the midst of a large crowd to drink beer from a tap? How much is he conforming to the idea of a crazy beach party? And how much is he caving to the pressure of the group? It's often very difficult, if not impossible, to tell, but clearly people's concerns with self-presentation can sometimes lead them toward unwise actions.

[Sean Murphy/Getty Images]

Individual Differences in Self-presentation

At this point you might be thinking, "Wow, I can really see how much I self-present." Or you might think, "I don't care enough about what other people think to do this kind of stuff." Such varied reactions reflect how people differ both in their sensitivity to how others see them and how motivated they are to put effort into strategic self-presentation. This individual difference is known as self-monitoring (Snyder & Gangestad, 1986). People high in self-monitoring are social chameleons, adjusting their appearance and behavior to fit with the norms and expectations in a given situation. Those low in self-monitoring seem to march to the beat of their own drum, ignoring other people's expectations and doing what feels true to them.

People who are high in self-monitoring are better at what we called cynical performances—that is, they are able to change their expression, vocal tone, and mannerisms strategically to convey a certain character (Snyder, 1974). They also tend to have more friends, though these friendships are often less close and more short-term, but fewer long-lasting romantic relationships. Low self-monitors present themselves in a more consistent way, so their behavior stems not so much from what the situation might demand but from their own inner states and desired self-image. This means their behavior is more stable across situations. In fact, low self-monitors are more likely to choose situations where they can just be themselves.

Self-monitoring An individual difference in people's desire and ability to adjust their self-presentations for different audiences.

Audience-monitoring Errors

Does careful self-monitoring ensure that people accurately understand the impression their audience is forming of them? Unfortunately, people often have difficulty getting beyond their own subjective experience when judging how others view them. In one study, a college student wearing a Barry Manilow T-shirt was sent into a room of observers. After being in front of the observers for under a minute, the average participant in this study estimated that close to 50% of the people in the room must have noticed the shirt. In fact, reports by the observers showed that only about 25% actually did. Because the participants were acutely aware of sporting the Barry

Singer/songwriter Barry Manilow performing in the 1970s.

[Michael Ochs Archives/Getty Images]

Spotlight effect The belief that others are more focused on us than they actually are.

Illusion of transparency The tendency to overestimate another's ability to know our internal thoughts and feelings.

A chilling portrayal of the illusion of transparency can be found in Edgar Alan Poe's classic short story "The Tell-Tale Heart." In this story, the main character's paranoid fears that a detective can tell what he has buried beneath the floor give his dark secret away. In less dramatic but more everyday terms, we often doubt whether we can keep our thoughts and feelings hidden from others.

[Left: Culture Club/Getty Images; right: Print Collector/Getty Images]

Manilow attire, they falsely inferred that the rest of the world noticed as well. This is known as the spotlight effect—the belief that others are more focused on the self than they actually are (Gilovich et al., 2000). So, when we are very self-conscious of some aspect of self, we are prone to the spotlight effect. But when we are not self-conscious about some unusual aspect of self, the opposite may occur. For example, when participants wore the T-shirts for a while before entering the room of observers (so that it was no longer so salient to them), they underestimated the amount of people who would notice.

Such egocentric bias doesn't just lead people to mistake whether others notice aspects of their external appearance. It also leads people to overestimate others' ability to know their internal thoughts and feelings. Imagine a situation where you smile politely as you choke down bite after bite of a friend's new, but decidedly vile, recipe. Many of us imagine that our disgust is laid out on the table for everyone to see. According to Gilovich, Savitsky, and Medvec (1998), this is probably only an illusion of transparency, because people are often better than they think they are at hiding their internal feelings. This is something to keep in mind the next time you get nervous about giving a speech or doing something in public. In fact, even when people rate themselves as being a jittery ball of nerves, those who observe their speech often rate them as appearing less anxious (Savitsky & Gilovich, 2003).

The Fundamental Motivations for Self-presentation

Why is self-presentation so prevalent and important? We often use self-presentation to achieve specific goals such as getting a job, impressing a date, and so on. But it also serves three broader goals. One is to protect your self-image. We've discussed how influential social feedback often is to self-esteem. A second goal is to support the meaningfulness of social interactions by properly enacting the culture's scripts and roles. Finally, self-presentation also serves self-improvement and personal growth. Goffman (1959) noted that people often use idealization to convey a best-case view of oneself to others. To quote the sociologist Charles Horton Cooley (1902, p. 352), "If we never tried to seem a little better than we are, how could we improve or 'train ourselves from the outside inward?'"

SECTION review | Self-presentation: The Show Must Go On

People are motivated to manage how others view them.

Theater as a metaphor	Self-presentational strategies	Application	Self- and audience monitoring	Basic motives for self-presenting
• People self-present according to a script, like actors in a play. • Sincere performances happen automatically and unconsciously. • Cynical performances are conscious attempts to make a particular impression.	• Honing an image through self-promotion, supplication, ingratiation, and intimidation. • Audience segregation. • Lying.	Concerns about making certain impressions can lead to unhealthful behaviors.	• People high in self-monitoring are more likely to change for different audiences. • People often think others are noticing them more than they actually are and that people can tell what they are thinking and feeling more than they actually can.	• Achieving specific goals. • Supporting self-esteem. • Providing meaning. • Fostering self-improvement.

Motives for Growth and Self-expansion

All over the world, and indeed in your own community, you'll find astounding examples of people exploring new ideas, of flexible and integrative thinking, and further, of people loving, playing, and developing wisdom and maturity. These examples attest to powerful human motives for personal growth and self-expansion. Ideas about self-growth toward optimal fulfillment of one's potential have a long history in Western philosophy, dating back to the early Greek philosophers and extending to modern times (Coan, 1977). The psychoanalyst Otto Rank (1932/1989) built on this philosophical tradition, proposing that inside each person is a *life force* that urges her to break away from others and establish the self as a unique individual who determines her own actions. The developmental theorist Erik Erikson (1959, 1963) further proposed that a person progresses through eight stages of growth.

Rank's and Erikson's perspectives contributed to an influential movement in the 1960s known as humanistic psychology. One prominent theorist in this tradition, Carl Rogers (1961), posited that people are naturally motivated to expand and enrich themselves, but that conformity to society's expectations often derails this process. Abraham Maslow (e.g., Maslow et al., 1970) similarly proposed that all humans are fundamentally motivated toward self-actualization, or being all they can be, particularly if they have satisfied more immediately pressing needs such as food, shelter, and a secure sense of personal value. These ideas inspired the development of self-determination theory, the most influential contemporary perspective on growth, the factors that promote and inhibit it, and its consequences for everyday life.

Think
ABOUT

[Macmillan Archives]

Self-determination Theory

Consider for a moment why you are reading this textbook. Are you doing it because you think you have to, and it's a necessary step to completing this course? Or perhaps you would feel guilty if you didn't? Or maybe you are doing it because you truly enjoy reading and mastering this material?

Self-determination theory The idea that people function best when they feel that their actions stem from their own desires rather than from external forces.

The late singer/songwriter and philanthropist Harry Chapin illustrated the value of feeling self-determined in your actions in this anecdote about his then 88-year-old artist grandfather, who told him: "Harry there's two kinds of tired, there's good tired and there's bad tired. . . ironically enough bad tired can be a day that you won but you won other people's battles, you lived other people's days. . . other people's dreams. . . and when you hit the hay at night somehow you toss and turn you don't settle easy. . . Good tired ironically enough can be a day that you lost but. . . you knew you fought your battles, you chased your dreams. . . and when you hit the hay at night you settle easy. . . I painted and I painted and I am good tired and they can take me away."

[Text from Harry Chapin Gold Medal Collection, produced by Elektra/Asylum Records, a division of Warner; photo by Keith Bernstein/Redferns/Getty Images]

According to Ed Deci and Rich Ryan's **self-determination theory** (2000), your answers to these types of questions say a great deal about your level of self-determined motivation. People who have low levels of self-determined motivation view their action as controlled by external forces, called *extrinsic motivation*. People who have high levels of self-determined motivation view their action as originating in their own authentic desires, called *intrinsic motivation.*

To illustrate, imagine that Nick and Mikalya are in medical school. Both are going to classes, studying for tests, and so on. Nick goes to medical school purely because he feels obligated to fulfill his family's wish that he become a doctor and make lots of money. Parental expectations and financial rewards are the controlling factors, not Nick's authentic desires. Nick's behavior is an example of extrinsically motivated behavior. In contrast, Mikalya is going to medical school because being a doctor connects with her core sense of self and her value of helping others maintain their health. Although she may not enjoy all aspects of the process, such as that grueling pharmacology class, the goal of being a doctor is something she personally wants to achieve, regardless of what others expect of her. Mikalya's behavior is intrinsically motivated.

Self-determination theory proposes that people are naturally powered by curiosity to explore their environment, master new challenges, and to integrate these experiences with a core sense of who they are. However, the social world often tries to control us, moving us away from our natural tendencies for self-determination. Deci and Ryan argue that people feel self-determined in their actions when three basic needs are met:

Relatedness: being meaningfully connected with others
Autonomy: feeling a sense of authentic choice in what one does
Competence: feeling effective in what one does

When people are in social situations that allow for the satisfaction of these needs, they experience their action as more self-determined and rewarding. In fact, under these conditions, people can become intrinsically motivated to do activities that they were initially compelled to do for external reasons. However, when social situations thwart these needs, people see their actions as less self-determined, controlled instead by external forces.

Does it matter whether people feel self-determined? Yes, it makes a big difference. In our medical-school example, Nick may have a successful career as a doctor, but according to self-determination theory, he is unlikely to derive real satisfaction from his career or be as good as he could be, because he doesn't feel self-determined in his actions as a doctor. Mikalya, because she is intrinsically motivated, will be more likely to gain deep personal satisfaction from her career and will be more likely to realize her full potential as a doctor.

Research backs this up. Across a wide variety of domains—from marriage to academics to weight-loss programs—people who are more self-determined perform better and more creatively, are happier, and experience more satisfaction than those who experience controlled forms of regulation (Deci & Ryan, 2002). For instance, Sheldon and Krieger (2007) investigated students during their three years in law school, a notoriously brutal undertaking. Yet students who felt that the faculty supported their autonomy (providing a sense of choice and acknowledging their feelings) performed better on the bar exam and experienced greater life satisfaction than those who felt that their autonomy was thwarted.

In fact, when the social environment promotes our self-determined action, we may even live longer! Rodin and Langer (1977) went into nursing homes and gave some residents a pep talk about their responsibility for themselves, whereas other residents were given a talk about how the nursing staff was responsible for them. The residents encouraged to be self-reliant were also given a plant and the responsibility of caring for it. The other residents were given a plant but were informed that the staff would care for it. Eighteen months later, those residents encouraged to take responsibility for themselves and the plant were more likely still to be alive!

The power of self-determination is also seen in research on locus of control (Lefcourt, 1981, 1992). This research, initiated by Julian Rotter (1954), typically focuses on the consequences of having either an *internal* or *external* locus of control in a given situation. Individuals with a high internal locus of control feel confident that they can achieve desired outcomes. In contrast, individuals with a high external locus of control believe their outcomes in life depend primarily on external forces beyond their control. Individuals with an internal locus of control are more effective in a variety of life domains. For instance, surveying U.S. students in their senior year of college, Brown and Strickland (1972) found a positive correlation between internal locus of control and cumulative GPA. Interestingly, recent studies suggest that people lower in socio-economic status, having fewer material resources, tend to exhibit a more external locus of control (Kraus et al., 2012).

Locus of control The extent to which a person believes that either internal or external factors determine life outcomes.

Around the globe, millions of people believe that significant outcomes in their lives, including the courses of their careers and romantic relationships, are determined by the movements of celestial bodies. You may have found yourself consulting a horoscope for clues to your fate. Recalling what you have learned about self-determination theory and locus of control, how do you think belief in astrology might influence a person's motivation and ability to grow? What is the appeal of yielding control over one's life to the stars?

Think
ABOUT

[Shutterstock]

The Overjustification Effect: Undermining Intrinsic Motivation

What types of social contexts can thwart a person's sense of autonomy? Think about something that you typically enjoy doing for its own sake, such as reading, mountain climbing, or dancing. Now imagine that you started to get paid for this activity: would you enjoy it more or less? Common sense and behaviorism would suggest that if you liked it already, you'd like it even more if you received extrinsic monetary rewards for doing it. But not so fast. In a seminal study to address this question (Lepper et al., 1973), preschool children were asked to do some coloring, an activity most children find enjoyable. One group of children was promised a "good player" ribbon for their coloring; another group was promised no reward. Later, when all the children were given a free choice among a variety of activities, the children who received the promised ribbon reward were *less* interested in coloring.

Why would this happen? Self-perception theory provides the best answer. For the children offered the reward, the external inducement is so salient that they infer they are coloring *for* the reward and discount enjoyment as their reason for doing it. Consequently, when no more rewards are offered, these kids no longer saw a reason to color. Psychologists call this the overjustification effect: When external factors lead people to attribute the reason, or justification, for their action to an external incentive (such as money, candy, or affection), their intrinsic motivation and enjoyment of the task are diminished. Interestingly, the overjustification effect occurs only if the external incentive is seen as the reason for the behavior. Another group of children unexpectedly given the same ribbon *after* coloring continued to be intrinsically interested in coloring.

Overjustification effect The tendency for salient rewards or threats to lead people to attribute the reason, or justification, for engaging in an activity to an external factor, which thereby undermines their intrinsic motivation for and enjoyment of the activity.

Because extrinsic inducements are used so often in child-rearing, schools, and work settings, research on the overjustification effect has inspired a lot of controversy and interest. It turns out that this effect has been shown in everyone from preschool children to the elderly, and in collectivistic as well as individualistic cultures. Overjustification not only reduces interest in the activity but also leads to less effective, less creative performance. More self-determined kids, students, and employees will do a better job, go the extra mile, and have more satisfaction with their lives at home, in school, and at work (Deci & Ryan, 2002; Gagné & Deci, 2005).

Do rewards always undermine intrinsic motivation? If the reward is viewed as an indicator of the quality of one's efforts, rather than an inducement to engage in the activity in the first place, it often actually improves performance and intrinsic interest rather than undermining it (Eisenberger & Armeli, 1997). Rewards also can be effective as long as people aren't aware that the reward is controlling their choices. Furthermore, rewards are effective when given in an atmosphere that generally supports relatedness, autonomy, and competence. A sales manager who is friendly, caring, and appreciative, and who doesn't micro-manage and scrutinize your every move, would foster self-determined selling better than would a cold, rigid, control freak (Richer & Vallerand, 1995).

APPLICATION

How to Maximize Self-growth

Self-determination theory provides a framework for understanding the individual's motivation for self-growth. Research has also uncovered more specific types of experiences and goals that help individuals expand their capacities and enrich their enjoyment of life.

Pursue Goals That Support Core Needs

We've just seen that *why* we pursue a goal is an important factor in our growth; *what* goals we pursue also matters. Some goals strengthen a meaningful relationship or exercise a talent, helping to satisfy personal core needs (Sheldon & Elliott, 1999). Other goals, such as striving to be popular, do so less well. Indeed, people who pursue materialistic goals of fame and fortune tend to have lower levels of life satisfaction, creativity, and self-actualization than those who pursue more intrinsic goals such as good social relationships and personal growth (Kasser & Ryan, 1993; Sheldon et al., 2004). The "American dream" may not be so dreamy.

Get in the Zone

Have you ever participated in some activity where your sense of time seems to evaporate, you lose all sense of your self, and you are totally focused on the activity at hand? Maslow referred to such instances as "peak experiences," and he felt that they contribute to self-actualization. More recently, Mihaly Csikszentmihalyi (1990) labeled this experience flow. From his interviews with surgeons, mountain climbers, and others about their optimal performances, Csikszentmihalyi defines flow as a complete focus of attention on an activity and away from one's self and the passage of time. And, he argues, achieving flow can improve performance and enrich our sense of self.

Flow is achieved when the challenge of a situation, person, or task is just above our typical skill level, requiring a full engagement of all our concentration and focus. As you see depicted in **FIGURE 6.7**, when the challenge is too high, we experience anxiety, and when the challenge is too low, we experience boredom. But when skills and challenges match,

Flow The feeling of being completely absorbed in an activity that is appropriately challenging to one's skills.

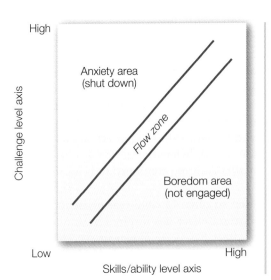

Figure 6.7

Csikszentmihalyi's Concept of Flow

When the challenge level of a task, situation, or role matches well with the person's skills and abilities, he or she experiences an enjoyable and absorbed feeling known as flow.

[Research from Csikszentmihalyi (1990)]

intrinsic motivation and flow can emerge. This idea helps explain why video games are so popular: They are designed so that once you master a given level, there's another, higher level to challenge you, so you always have a good match for your skill level (Keller & Bless, 2008). Although people cannot be in flow all the time, research suggests that even recalling past peak experiences can be beneficial and actually contributes to better physical health (Burton & King, 2004).

Skiing is one example of flow. Good skiers get the rush on the really difficult slopes, whereas novices can experience the exhilaration on much easier slopes. In both cases, though, the challenge demands a full engagement of one's skill.

[Left: Matthaeus Ritsch/Shutterstock; right: Photobac/Shutterstock]

Mindfulness The state of being and acting fully in the current moment.

Act Mindfully

The study of mindfulness, attentiveness to the present moment in which one is actively involved with one's actions and their meaning (Brown et al., 2007; Langer & Moldoveanu, 2000), grows out of traditions of contemplative thought such as Buddhism and Stoicism. According to Ellen Langer (1989), mindfulness can be understood by contrasting it with its opposite, mindlessness. When we act mindlessly, we habitually engage with our actions and the external world, and we rarely consider novel and creative approaches to life. The self becomes stagnant. But when we're mindful, we open ourselves up to consider the world and ourselves in new, more multidimensional ways. People trained in mindfulness show less anxiety and fewer symptoms when coping with medical issues (Kabat-Zinn, 1990; Shapiro et al., 1998), and in one study, were more likely than a control group to develop helpful antibodies in response to an influenza vaccine (Davidson et al., 2003). Although we still have much to learn about mindfulness, it appears that taking time out of our busy schedules to stop and smell the roses, or just be fully in the moment, might improve our creativity, concentration, and overall well-being (Brown et al., 2007).

Expand Your Mind: Explore the World

Sometimes simply exposing the self to unfamiliar environments can help a person to view the world more creatively and openly. Have you ever had a creative idea—such as a different way to approach a term paper or interpersonal dilemma—pop into your head while hiking in the woods or watching a strange foreign movie? You're not alone. Many physicists, composers, and other creative individuals have hatched their most innovative ideas while climbing mountains, looking at the stars, and taking part in other novel experiences (Csikszentmihalyi, 1996).

The idea that exposure to new environments can stimulate creativity is also one reason your university or college encourages you to study abroad, and why employers often seek to increase cultural diversity in the workplace. In fact, research shows that even brief exposure to a foreign culture can improve creativity. In one study (Leung & Chiu, 2010), Euro-American students first watched a 45-minute slide show. Some participants viewed aspects of either Chinese culture (e.g., food and architecture) or American culture. Others were shown aspects of both cultures intermixed, such as fashion that blends American and Chinese influences. Afterward, participants were asked to interpret the story of Cinderella for Turkish children, and the researchers measured how creative these interpretations were. They found that compared with participants who viewed either Chinese or American culture, those exposed to a mingling of both cultures subsequently wrote more creative Cinderella interpretations. Interestingly, exposure to only Chinese culture did not boost creativity. This suggests that people gain in creativity when they juxtapose and integrate seemingly incompatible aspects of different cultures.

Foster a Positive Mood

Positive emotions such as happiness and excitement can stimulate creative thought, in part because they tell the person that things are safe in the world and it's okay to

Figure 6.8a

Matches, Tacks, Candle

One test of creative thinking is to ask a person how to use these objects to attach the candle to a corkboard so it will burn without wax dripping onto the floor. Before turning the page, see if you can figure out the solution.

explore novel experiences (Fredrickson, 2001; Lyubomirsky et al., 2005). One way that positive mood stimulates growth is by making it more likely that the person will think in new ways and find creative solutions to problems. In an illustrative study (Isen et al., 1987), some participants were put in a positive mood by watching five minutes of a funny movie, whereas participants in the control condition watched a neutral movie. Participants were then given the objects in **FIGURE 6.8a**—a box of tacks, a candle, and a book of matches—and were told to come up with a way, using

Blue Jasmine

The 2013 film *Blue Jasmine*, written and directed by Woody Allen, illustrates a woman's struggle with dissonance, self-narrative, self-esteem, self-presentation, and growth. The protagonist, Jasmine, played by the Oscar winner Cate Blanchett, tries to regain psychological equanimity and grow as her sense of value and her grasp on reality teeter on the brink. A highly intelligent and once wealthy New Yorker who exudes elegance and was used to the "finer things in life," she arrives penniless to San Francisco to live with her very different working-class sister, Ginger, deftly played by Sally Hawkins. Jasmine takes a clerical job in a dental office, which she initially views as beneath her, and aspires to finish college through online courses so she can become an interior designer. But it's debatable whether these are genuine attempts to grow as a person or just efforts to restore the social status she was so reliant on as her basis of self-worth.

Eventually she shifts her focus toward marrying a wealthy suitor to regain her status and transform her self-narrative from a contamination story to a redemption story. As events unfold, we see flashbacks to the events that have led to her current state of low self-esteem and consequent high anxiety,

[Perdido Productions/The Kobal Collection]

and her desperate groping to turn her life around while self-medicating with alcohol and Xanax. Years ago, Jasmine quit college to marry a wealthy investment broker, Hal, played by Alec Baldwin. Hal violated the law in building their fortune and high social status; eventually he was arrested by the FBI. All their assets were seized, and Hal hanged himself while in prison.

Throughout the film, Jasmine is obsessed with trying to maintain face in light of these events. She recounts her humiliation at being seen working in a department-store shoe department by a socialite former friend. She presents herself only those objects, to attach the candle to a corkboard on the wall so that it would burn without dripping wax on the floor. After about 10 minutes, only 20% of the participants in the neutral film condition found the correct answer, but participants who had just watched a mere five minutes of funny bloopers found the correct solution 75% of the time (for the answer, please see **FIGURE 6.8b** on p. 228).

Challenge Versus Threat

Generally, negative experiences, such as feeling inadequate, unfulfilled, or threatened, motivate people to seek out security, driving them to cling to the safe and familiar parts of life and to cut off growth. Many studies show that people faced with threatening thoughts, such as their mortality or others' disapproval of them, respond with less interest in exploring new experiences (Green & Campbell, 2000; Mikulincer, 1997) and are narrower and more rigid in their thinking (e.g., Derryberry & Tucker, 1994; Fredrickson & Branigan, 2005; Landau et al., 2004; Zillman & Cantor, 1976).

Yet a popular cliché is philosopher Friedrich Nietzsche's famous line: "What doesn't kill me, makes me stronger." Indeed, Nietzsche was a strong proponent of the idea that to achieve a more freely determined and satisfying life, the person must face distressing truths and endure hardships. But given how stress and anxiety often stifles growth, how can this be? It depends on how people interpret stressful situations. According to James Blascovich and colleagues (Blascovich & Tomaka, 1996; Blascovich & Mendes, 2000), when people face stressful situations such as taking a test or giving

to her sister and others as ignorant of her husband's shady deals and blameless in his downfall. However, we eventually learn through her own memories that this is not true, and that her choices contributed to his downfall.

Part of Jasmine's current struggle stems from her inability to reduce the dissonance caused by these past actions and their foreseeable negative consequences. She feels guilt and shame both about her actions and about having been cheated on extensively by the philandering Hal. His unfaithfulness brought her to initiate his downfall with a call to the FBI. Despite his complicity in his own fate, Hal's arrest and eventual death are not easy things for Jasmine to rationalize. When she meets her eventual fiancé, her intelligence, charm, and physical attractiveness appeal greatly to him. But instead of being honest about her past and her current situation, she portrays herself as a successful designer and claims that her husband was a surgeon who died of a heart attack. When these lies come to light, her engagement and her easy path back to high social status go up in smoke.

Jasmine, stripped of self-esteem and any clear path to regaining it, becomes consumed with anxiety. She hides the broken engagement from her sister and eventually reaches out to her stepson, who rejects her. In retrospect, the viewer realizes that Jasmine's struggles were set up by her quitting college to marry the wealthy Hal and her consequent reliance on his shady successes for her social status and opportunities

for philanthropy. These became the primary bases of her self-worth, leading her to turn a blind eye to both his shady deals and his extramarital affairs.

In fairness to both the fictional Jasmine, and to real women who have made similar choices in their lives, Jasmine was in part a victim of how cultures guide people's ways of seeking and maintaining self-worth. She was raised in a patriarchal culture in which women were, and sometimes still are, reinforced for seeking self-worth through the success of a male partner, and in which successful married men often feel they have the right to "sleep around" on the sly. This point is brought home perhaps most clearly by what happens when Jasmine tries to support herself through her receptionist job with a male dentist as a way to secure an income while she pursues her online studies. Although over time Jasmine genuinely embraces this job as a way to move toward becoming the person of value she desires to be, the dentist begins sexually harassing her and eventually tries to force himself on her. Jasmine rebuffs him and promptly quits, and this precipitates her losing faith in building success and self-worth through her own intellectual development and falling back on seeking a successful suitor to restore her self-worth. Perhaps she would have built a truly stable basis of self-worth over time had she not been victimized by this problem—one that women face in the workplace in many contemporary societies.

Figure 6.8b

Solution to Question

Here is how it can be done. They key is being able to view the box containing the tacks in a different way than you usually would.

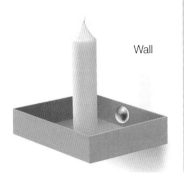

Wall

a speech, they assess whether they have the resources to meet the demands of the situation. When they conclude that their resources are inadequate, they feel threatened, but when they view their resources as meeting or surpassing the demands, they feel challenged. This feeling of challenge provides an opportunity for growth.

In fact, whether people respond to a stressor with feelings of threat or challenge is reflected in their bodies' physiological response. When people feel threatened, their heart rate increases but their veins and arteries don't expand to allow blood to flow easily through the body. People's heart rate similarly increases when they feel challenged, but here the veins and arteries dilate to improve blood flow. And feeling challenged as opposed to threatened can make a difference in performance. Blascovich and colleagues (2004) had college baseball and softball players imagine a stressful game situation at the beginning of the season while their physiological responses were being monitored. Those whose bodies signaled a challenge response actually performed better over the course of the season than those who showed a threat reaction.

Even Traumatic Experiences Can Promote Growth

When are thoughts of mortality likely to lead to defensiveness? When might they stimulate growth? Thinkers such as Seneca and Martin Heidegger argued that when people think about death in a superficial way, they are more likely to avoid their fear by clinging to conventional sources of meaning and self-esteem—just as most research on mortality salience has shown. But for people very open to new experiences and who view life holistically, brief thoughts of death can lead to appreciation of life and growth (Ma-Kellams & Blascovich, 2012; Vail et al., 2012). In addition, thinking more deeply about death can also catalyze authenticity and growth. Why? Recognition of mortality might serve as a reminder that our life spans are limited, and change what we think of as meaningful so we avoid getting mired in trivial tasks and focus on more intrinsically satisfying goals, such as lasting relationships and enjoyable activities (e.g., Carstensen et al., 1999; Kosloff & Greenberg, 2009). Indeed, research on survivors of severe traumas and near-death experiences finds that many people report growing from the experience, becoming more balanced, more accepting, and better able to appreciate life and all it has to offer (Tedeschi & Calhoun, 2004).

Elderly folks are particularly likely to think about death a great deal, in part because they have generally known more people who have died and are closer to their own end. Research shows that being close to the end has some positive consequences for the elderly (Carstensen et al., 1999). It leads them to want to maximize their enjoyment of life. Elderly people are especially interested in being with those they really care about, and they focus on the positive, how the glass of life is half full rather than half empty. Indeed, they are wise in another important way: they are consistently happier than younger people (Carstensen, 2009; Yang, 2008).

Why are older people better able to appreciate life and connect to their authentic goals? Perhaps as one approaches the loss of everything, it becomes easier to appreciate those things before one loses them. The poet W. S. Merwin (1970, p. 136) put it this way:

> and what is wisdom if it is not
> now
> in the loss that has not left this place

SECTION review | Motives for Growth and Self-expansion

People are motivated for personal growth and self-expansion.

Self-determination theory

- People thrive and grow when they feel their actions are self-determined rather than controlled by external forces.
- Intrinsic motivation is fostered by fulfillment of three basic needs: relatedness; autonomy; competence.
- An internal locus of control is generally associated with positive outcomes in life.

Overjustification effect
Initially intrinsically motivated behaviors can, if rewarded with external incentives, come to feel extrinsically motivated, with consequent decreases in interest and enjoyment.

Application: Maximize self-growth by:
- pursuing goals that support core needs.
- experiencing flow.
- acting mindfully.
- exploring novel aspects of the world.
- fostering a positive mood.
- interpreting stressful situations as opportunities for growth.

CONNECT ONLINE:

Check out our videos and additional resources located at:
www.macmillanhighered.com/launchpad/greenberg1e

Social Influence

TOPIC OVERVIEW

Over the next three chapters, we're going to focus specifically on **social influence**, the effects of other people on an individual's beliefs, attitudes, values, or behavior. In our coverage of topics such as culture, social cognition, and the development and functioning of the self, we noted many ways in which we humans are profoundly influenced by the individuals and groups around us. Our views of ourselves, our world, and other people are shaped initially by our parents and soon after by other relatives, peers, and the mass media. In a sense, the adult human is largely a product of social influences; however, we are never finished products, and we are subject to social influence throughout the life span.

In these chapters on social influence, we will delve into theories and research that specifically address how the presence, actions, and attitudes of others affect the individual's thoughts and behavior. Sometimes people influence us intentionally; other times they do so inadvertently. This chapter begins with some very basic and pervasive ways in which people learn specific behaviors and views of the world from others. Then we will focus on the formation of social norms and conformity. Conformity involves altering one's attitudes or behavior in response to the attitudes, beliefs, and behavior of other people. Generally, conformity concerns how a single individual bends beliefs or behavior to fit a majority view. But sometimes a single individual ends up influencing the

Social influence The effects of other people on an individual's beliefs, attitudes, values, or behavior.

[Mike Powell/Getty Images]

majority instead, so we will discuss minority influence as well. After that, we will describe research on compliance techniques, which are strategies one uses to get others to do what one wants them to do. Even more influential than these strategies are commands from authority figures. This rather unsubtle form of social influence compels obedience: following the explicit commands of an authority figure. Some individuals are particularly likely to emerge as authority figures under conditions of psychological threat. Thus, we will conclude the chapter with a consideration of the appeal of charismatic leaders.

Learning From Others

Like other animals, humans learn by experiencing associations between stimuli (classical conditioning), such as the bell and the food for Pavlov's dogs (Pavlov, 1927). If every time we see Tim, we have a good time, our association of Tim with good feelings may lead us to develop a positive attitude toward Tim and seek out his company. We also learn to repeat behaviors that in the past have been followed by favorable outcomes and avoid behaviors that have had unfavorable outcomes (operant conditioning). If every time we tell a joke, our friends praise us, we will become more likely to tell additional jokes. In addition to these forms of learning, we humans also learn a great deal by garnering information from others and from observing others and imitating their behaviors.

Social Learning Theory

Social learning The capacity to learn from observing others.

An old expression captures the basic idea of social learning: "Monkey see, monkey do." Plenty of animals learn this way, not just monkeys. Birds learn songs from other birds. Untrained dogs learn faster if they are taught behaviors alongside dogs who are already trained (Adler & Adler, 1977). Research in Italy has even shown that octopi are faster at learning how to open a jar to get food if they first had an opportunity to observe another octopus do it (Fiorito & Scotto, 1992). However, we humans are probably the species most reliant on social learning. The renowned teacher of psychology Henry Gleitman put it this way:

> [I]n the course of a lifetime, human beings learn a multitude of problem solutions that were discovered by those who came before them. They do not have to invent spoken language or the alphabet; they do not have to discover fire or the wheel or even how to eat baby food with a spoon. Other people show them. (GLEITMAN, 1981, P. 498)

From driving a car and hitting a tennis ball to eating sushi or doing the tango, we learn largely from watching others *model* those behaviors. In fact, we saw in chapter 4 that certain neurons, called *mirror neurons*, are activated both when one does an action oneself and when one simply observes another person perform that action (Uddin et al., 2007). As the neuroscientist Marco Iacoboni notes, "When you see me perform an action—such as picking up a baseball—you automatically simulate the action in your own brain" (Blakeslee, 2006). Albert Bandura (1965) developed social learning theory and an associated research program to better understand factors that affect how people are influenced by observing others.

In Bandura's seminal studies (Bandura et al., 1961, 1963a, 1963b), mildly frustrated nursery school children (between ages three and six) watched a film of a young woman punch and kick a large inflated Bobo doll and hit it with a mallet. Children readily imitated this behavior when they were later given an opportunity to play with the Bobo doll, punching and kicking the doll and hitting it with the mallet in a manner that was eerily similar to the model's behavior, right down to repeating the same aggressive remarks that the model had made (e.g., "Pow, right in the nose, boom, boom."). Similar results occurred whether the film showed a live-action model or a cartoon figure hitting a cartoon depiction of the doll. But observing and learning a behavior doesn't necessarily mean we will imitate it. According to social learning theory, we can either be encouraged to engage or discouraged from engaging in both new and known behaviors on the basis of whether the consequences of the actions for the model are positive or negative. Thus, children were more likely to imitate the Bobo-doll-bashing model if the model was rewarded for the actions (e.g., supplied with a 7 Up and candy), and were

Albert Bandura's classic Bobo doll studies illustrate how we learn our behaviors by watching others. Here we see that the adult's (top panel) aggressive actions are subsequently modeled by both boys and girls.

[Dr. Albert Bandura]

less likely if the model was punished for the actions (e.g., a second adult spanked the aggressive model with a rolled-up magazine) (Bandura, 1965). Learning is also influenced by our sensitivity to social cues and motivations. For example, imitation was also more likely when the model seemed likeable and similar to the children. Finally, social learning is more likely if the behavior observed is consistent with the motivational state of the observer. So frustrated kids are more likely to imitate a violent model. But rewarded models tend to be imitated regardless of the motivational state of the observer.

Does the tendency to imitation also occur in adults? The next time you find yourself at a restaurant, take a look at the people at other tables. How often do you see people mirroring each other's posture—two people both leaning in on their elbows, or a group that all have their arms folded across their chests? Tanya Chartrand and John Bargh (1999) documented this phenomenon, which they called the chameleon effect—the tendency to mimic unconsciously the nonverbal mannerisms of someone with whom you are interacting.

Chameleon effect The tendency to mimic unconsciously the nonverbal mannerisms of someone with whom you are interacting.

To document the chameleon effect, the researchers paired each participant with a partner and had them take turns telling a story about a photograph. The participants performed this task twice, with two different partners. Unknown to the participants, these partners actually were confederates of the experimenters and had been trained ahead of time either to rub their faces or shake one of their feet at certain times during the interaction. They had also been trained to smile or remain neutral during the interaction. The interactions were videotaped and later coded by judges, according to how often the participants rubbed their faces or shook a foot. As expected, when doing the task with a face-rubbing confederate, participants were more likely to rub

Like father like son? People often mirror the posture and mannerisms of those they are talking to. Sometimes mirroring conveys warmth and contentment, but other times shared animosity.

[Holloway/Getty Images]

their faces; when doing the task with a foot-shaking confederate, participants were more likely to shake a foot. They were also more likely to smile when the confederate they were paired with was smiling. None of the participants reported having any conscious awareness of the other person's mannerisms or the fact that they might have mimicked them.

Additional research shows that this kind of mimicry isn't limited to casual, nonverbal behaviors. People also automatically shift their attitudes toward what they think another person's opinions might be, especially when they are motivated to get along with that person. To show this, one study (Sinclair et al., 2005) had White participants complete an implicit association test (the IAT, which we introduced back in chapter 3) to measure their automatically activated attitudes toward African Americans in the presence of an experimenter who was wearing a T-shirt that either was blank or said "Eracism" (a play on words that suggests the eradication of racism). The researchers also had the experimenter act in either a friendly or rude way.

The researchers predicted that people would shift their attitudes toward the attitude of the experimenter, but only if they liked her. Compared with the blank T-shirt, the Eracism shirt communicated that the experimenter might have more positive attitudes toward minorities. So when the experimenter wore the latter shirt and was likeable, participants indeed exhibited more positive implicit attitudes toward African Americans in their IAT responses. But this study also demonstrated that participants did not shift their attitudes when they did not like the antiracism experimenter. Similarly, the chameleon effect occurs mainly when the other person is likeable (Cheng & Chartrand, 2003; Lakin & Chartrand, 2003).

The role of liking suggests that mimicry often may happen because most social interactions involve a general goal of trying to get along. Unless they are truly disagreeable, most people go into an interaction with a stranger with the goal of being liked. Our group-living ancestors were probably more successful at propagating their genes into the future by being able to interact with each other smoothly and thereby coordinate behavior to achieve shared goals. Given our general sociability as a species, then, we shouldn't be surprised that people have an unconscious tendency to mimic others' mannerisms and attitudes.

APPLICATION
Harmful Media-inspired Social Learning

However, this aptitude for social learning has its downside. The sociologist David Phillips (1974, 1979) discovered that media portrayals of celebrity suicides are associated with subsequent increases in suicides and car accidents among the general public. Phillips also showed that the more media coverage suicides get in a particular region of the country, the more people tried the act themselves. Feature films also often inspire unfortunate examples of social learning. The award-winning 1978 film *The Deer Hunter* showed soldiers playing the game of Russian roulette (Cimino et al., 1978). In the following weeks, many instances of teenagers playing this dangerous game were reported. In 1993 another film, *The Program*, had a scene in which teenagers were shown lying down on the median between car lanes (Goldwyn et al., 1993). Within days of the film's appearance in theaters, numerous teens tried this, sometimes with tragic consequences. We'll examine other unsavory examples of social learning in a later chapter that discusses the effects of media portrayals of aggression.

Social Priming

Observing others perform an action does much more than merely provide a model. Such exposure also communicates information about our social world. Thus, another basic way that people influence us is by priming ideas, norms, and values. For instance, watching someone engage in aggression makes aggressive concepts more accessible (Bushman, 1998). As we saw in chapter 3, when concepts are made salient or more accessible, they are more likely to influence our behavior. When other people remind us of the norm to be fair or to be charitable, for example, often we are more likely to act in accord with those norms.

Robert Cialdini's (2003) *focus theory of normative conduct* emphasizes the important role that salience plays in enhancing the influence of norms. This theory distinguishes between two different types of norms. Injunctive norms are beliefs about which behaviors are generally approved of or disapproved of in one's culture. Descriptive norms are beliefs about what most people typically do. Often the two

Injunctive norm A belief about what behaviors are generally approved of or disapproved of in one's culture.

Descriptive norm A belief about what most people typically do.

norms align. For instance, people generally think that motorists should stop at red lights and that most of them do. However, norms can also diverge. People also think that others should not litter but believe that most people do. In studies directed toward decreasing littering and increasing energy conservation and recycling, Cialdini and colleagues have found that reminding people of either type of norm regarding these behaviors, whether through exposure to another person's behavior or to a posted sign, tends to increase adherence to the norms.

APPLICATION
Using Norms to Preserve

There is a danger to using norms to change behavior. Cialdini (2003) has noted that well-intentioned efforts to get people to do the right thing, such as public service announcements, sometimes make salient a descriptive norm that turns out to be counterproductive. For instance, in 2000, visitors to the fascinating Petrified Forest National Park in Arizona were greeted by a sign saying, "Your heritage is being vandalized every day by theft losses of petrified wood of 14 tons a year, mostly a small piece at a time." Although this sign surely communicates the injunctive norm that it is wrong to take the wood, it also implies the descriptive norm that many people do take the wood. In such a case, the injunctive and descriptive norms being made salient are working at cross-purposes. Cialdini and colleagues (2006) ran a study in which they created and posted signs at two different spots in the park. One sign emphasized only the injunctive norm: "Please don't remove the petrified wood from the park." The other sign emphasized only the descriptive norm: "Many past visitors have removed the petrified wood from the park, changing the state of the Petrified Forest." The researchers were able to measure theft by tracking the disappearance of subtly marked pieces of wood placed throughout the park. Compared with the park average of just under 3% of the (specially marked) wood being stolen, the injunctive sign led to only 1.67% of the wood being stolen, but the descriptive sign led to a disturbing theft rate of 7.92%. So when you're trying to get people not to do bad things, be careful not to make salient the idea that many or most people do those bad things.

How can norms be used to reduce theft of wood from Arizona's Petrified Forest National Park?
[Getty Images/Gallo Images]

Social Contagion

The ideas of both mimicry and social priming may also help explain a phenomenon that Gustave Le Bon (1896) labeled social contagion: that ideas, feelings, and behaviors seem to spread among people like wildfires. Le Bon noted how people in crowds come to behave almost as if they were of one mind. Since his time, studies have shown that everything from yawns, laughter, and applause to moods, goals, and depression seems to be contagious, spreading easily from person to person (e.g., Aarts et al., 2004; Hatfield et al., 1993; Provine, 2004). For instance, when participants were given the goal of remembering an emotionally neutral speech, they became happier if the voice was slightly happy and sadder if the voice was slightly sad (Neumann & Strack, 2000). Even obesity seems to be contagious. The medical researchers Christakis and Fowler (2007) analyzed data on body-mass index for more than 1,200 adults over a 32-year period. They found that if a particular person becomes obese, the chances that a friend of theirs subsequently also will become obese increases by 57%.

Social contagion The phenomenon whereby ideas, feelings, and behaviors seem to spread across people like wildfire.

APPLICATION
Psychogenic Illness

One particularly remarkable form of social contagion is called mass psychogenic illness (Colligan et al., 1982). This phenomenon occurs when an individual develops physical symptoms with no apparent physical cause, which then leads other people to feel convinced that they too have the same (psychologically generated) symptoms. Instances of this phenomenon seem to date at least back to the Middle Ages (Sirois, 1982). In one fairly well-documented case that occurred in 1998, a high school teacher in Tennessee reported a gasoline smell in her classroom and developed headaches, dizziness, and nausea. As word got out, others in the school soon began reporting similar symptoms. In fact, once the idea of the gas leak and its supposed effects began to spread, over 170 students, teachers, and staff members searched internally and ultimately found such symptoms in themselves, and the entire school was evacuated. Careful investigation by the Tennessee Department of Health determined that there was no physical cause of the symptoms (Jones et al., 2000). Eventually, the authorities convinced everyone there was no gas leak, and the symptoms disappeared.

SECTION review | Learning From Others

Humans learn a great deal by observing and imitating others.

Social Learning	Social Priming	Social Contagion
• We learn to do something new from watching others model the behavior. • We unconsciously tend to mimic the nonverbal mannerisms of others. • We also shift our attitudes toward those of people we like.	• Reminders of norms and values can influence behavior. • Injunctive norms and descriptive norms can have different influences on behavior.	• Ideas, feelings, and behaviors can spread among people like wildfire.

The Social Construction of Reality

We have seen that our great reliance on social learning, and our susceptibility to concepts that are brought to mind, make us very open to social influence. Considered from the cultural perspective, these two forms of social influence play a large role in how people are socialized as children into a cultural worldview (see chapter 2). The title of sociologists Peter Berger and Thomas Luckmann's 1967 book *The Social Construction of Reality* nicely captures the point. Many of our beliefs, attitudes, values, and behaviors are taught to us in the first years of our life, when we are virtually totally dependent on our parents for sustenance, security, and knowledge. As we mature, educational, religious, and social institutions further reinforce our own culture's way of viewing the world. The version of the cultural worldview we have internalized over the course of childhood becomes a form of social influence that is both profound and largely taken for granted. The poet Samuel Taylor Coleridge put it this way:

> The great Fundamental . . . doctrines . . . are . . . taught so early, under such circumstances, and in such close and vital association with whatever makes or marks *reality* for our infant minds, that the words ever after represent sensations, feelings, vital assurances, sense of reality—rather than thoughts, or any distinct conception. Associated, *I had almost said identified*, with the parental Voice, Look, Touch,

with the living warmth and pressure of the Mother on whose lap the Child is first made to kneel, within whose palms its little hands are folded, and the motion of whose eyes its eyes follow and imitate—(yea, what the blue sky is to the Mother, the Mother's upraised Eyes and Brow are to the Child, the Type and Symbol of an invisible Heaven!)—from within and without, these great First Truths, these good and gracious Tidings, these holy and humanizing Spells, in the preconformity to which our very humanity may be said to consist, are so infused, that it were but a tame and inadequate expression to say, we all take them for granted. (COLERIDGE & FENBY, 1825/1877, p. 207).

From this cultural worldview, we learn scripts for how to behave in different situations and different social roles.

Culturally Defined Social Situations

For an illustration of the influence of culturally defined situations, think of instances in which the norm is to be quiet. You may have come up with these: a library, a tennis match, or a funeral. But this same norm doesn't apply at a playground, a hockey game, or a wedding reception. As a child, you had to learn which norms apply in which situations, but once you've internalized those rules, you don't need to decide consciously to be quiet or loud. Instead, the context itself automatically activates the norm, which then guides your behavior.

To demonstrate this, Aarts and Dijksterhuis (2003) presented participants with a picture of a library or a train station and told them they would be going to that location later in the session. A third group was shown a library but had no expectation of going to a library. Participants then had to make judgments in a lexical decision task (a task in which participants have to decide whether a presented string of letters is a word or a nonword). Only the group that expected to be going to a library showed evidence of activating the concept of silence. Specifically, they were faster than either of the other groups to recognize silence-related words as being actual words. In a second study, participants who expected to go to a library also pronounced words more softly in what they thought was an unrelated communication task. For them, the anticipation of entering a library automatically activated a norm of being quiet that then affected their speaking volume even before they left the lab!

Think
ABOUT

As you read this, what also might come to mind are the instances when people break social norms. Have you ever been studying at the library when someone walked in, talking loudly to a friend? From such casual observations, it is clear that some individuals are more likely to toe the line than others. Some seem to go out of their way to break every norm they can think of, whereas others seem to follow norms as if their very lives depended on it. Most of us fall somewhere in between. How do these tendencies end up affecting behavior? Does everyone activate the same norms, but the nonconformists merely ignore these cues? Or do they not activate the norms in the first place? Although it's probably a little of both, some research suggests that nonconformists show less automatic activation of norms. Consider the library study we just described. Aarts and colleagues (2003) followed up on this study and showed that nonconformists (those who responded on a questionnaire that adhering to social norms was not that important to them and that they didn't always try to do so) were less likely even to activate a concept of silence when expecting to visit a library. If people don't have the goal of fitting in, situations might not have the same power to activate norms that influence their behavior.

Culturally Defined Social Roles

Along with learning social situations, at an early age we also learn social roles and generalized beliefs, or stereotypes, associated with those roles. We learn about being female and being male in our society, about doctors, lawyers, nurses, firefighters, basketball players, and so forth. This knowledge is transmitted by our parents, by experiences with people in these roles, and in large part by books, television, movies, and the Internet. When we are subsequently placed in such a role, we tend to enact fairly elaborate schemas to fulfill the particular role.

This adherence to social roles was most vividly illustrated in one of the most famous of all social psychology experiments, the Stanford prison experiment. Philip Zimbardo and colleagues (Haney et al., 1973) used newspaper ads to recruit young men. The researchers created a mock prison in the basement of a building on the campus of Stanford University. They randomly assigned half the young men to be guards and the other half to be prisoners. Guards were given prison-guard-style uniforms, whistles, and nightsticks. Prisoners were dressed in loose-fitting, inmate-style clothing (see **FIGURE 7.1**). Zimbardo essentially served as prison warden and gave the "guards" some basic instructions and routines to follow in maintaining the incarceration of the "prisoners." Within days, the guards were treating the prisoners poorly, inflicting punishments that bordered on sadistic. Meanwhile, the prisoners either became rebellious or fell into bouts of depression. The effects were so powerful that this famous experiment actually never was completed! Although it was planned to last two weeks, it had to be stopped after only six days for the sake of the participants' well-being.

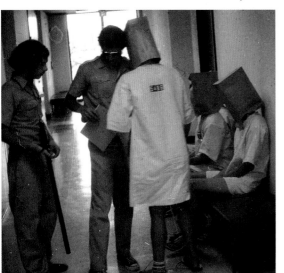

Figure 7.1

The Stanford Prison Experiment

With ordinary people randomly assigned to be prisoners or guards, the Stanford prison study provides a chilling demonstration of the power of social roles.

[Philip G. Zimbardo, Inc.]

Keep in mind that participants were randomly assigned to be guards or prisoners, meaning that we cannot conclude that the guards acted the way they did simply because they were inherently sadistic or that the prisoners were inherently submissive. Rather, their behavior was due to their assigned roles. There is no way to determine how much of this impact was a result of the self-perception and self-justifying dissonance processes activated by fulfilling the basic requirements of these roles, and how much was determined by enactment of cultural schemas for these roles. It was probably a combination of both types of processes. Regardless, the conclusion we can draw is that clearly the roles and associated trappings and routines profoundly altered the behavior of both the guards and the prisoners, attesting to the power of culturally defined roles to alter attitudes and behavior. Zimbardo (2007) and others have noted clear parallels between what he found in his experiment and phenomena such as the well-publicized abuses of detainees by American soldiers in the Iraqi detention center known as Abu Ghraib during the American occupation of Iraq.

Can the power of social roles help to explain the events at Abu Ghraib?

[AP Photo]

In light of this research and what we know from anthropology and cross-cultural psychology, it is indisputable that many of our concepts of situations and roles, beliefs about right and wrong, and views of historical and current events are influenced by the cultural milieu in which we were raised and in which we live. But does this social influence truly extend to the basic ways we perceive the world? Starting way back in the 1930s, pioneering work on how conformity influences perception suggests that it does.

SECTION review | The Social Construction of Reality

Our cultural worldview is a profound form of social influence that we often take for granted.

Culturally defined social situations	Culturally defined social roles
• Cultures prescribe particular norms for particular situations. • These norms influence our behavior as the situation activates associated schemas when and if we are motivated to fit in with others.	• Similarly, our cultures teach us the generalized beliefs that accompany particular roles. • The Zimbardo prison experiment demonstrated that these roles can contribute to particularly distasteful forms of behavior.

Conformity

Conformity is a phenomenon in which a given individual alters her beliefs, attitudes, or behavior to bring them in accordance with the behavior of others. Muzafer Sherif (1936) sought to study the possibility that even basic perceptions of events can be affected by efforts to bring one's own perceptions in line with those of others. To do so, he took advantage of a perceptual illusion first noted by astronomers. If a small, stationary point of light is shown in a pitch-black room, it appears to move. This false perception of movement is known as the autokinetic effect.

Sherif sought to determine if other people could influence an individual's perceptions of how much the point of light moves. First, he had people individually judge how much the point of light moved. He got various estimates (see **FIGURE 7.2**). Then he put two or three people together in a dark room and had them call out estimates of how much the light was moving. He made the quite remarkable finding that people started out with varying estimates, but after only a few trials they came to agree on a particular estimate of how much the light moved. He also showed that if he planted a confederate in the group who made a particularly large assessment of the distance moved, that person could move the group norm to a higher estimate. Furthermore,

Conformity The phenomenon whereby an individual alters his or her beliefs, attitudes, or behavior to bring them in accordance with those of a majority.

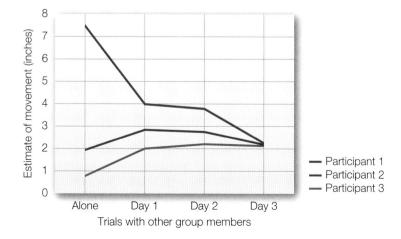

Figure 7.2

Sherif Conformity Studies on Norm Formation

The ambiguity of the estimation task reveals an informational influence on conformity and the formation of a group norm. When participants got into a group, their individual judgments converged to a common norm over the course of three days.

[Data source: Sherif (1936)]

Jacobs and Campbell (1961) showed that if the confederate was replaced by new, naïve participants, the remaining group members would sustain the group norm and bring the new participants on board with them. This "tradition" continued over five "generations" of participants.

Of course, it is reasonable to ask whether the participants' agreed-on estimate of the light's movement was just an effort to get along with others rather than a real shift in perception. Did people conform merely to agree with the group, a form of social influence called public compliance? Or did their own sense of what they were seeing actually change, a form of social influence referred to as private acceptance? Subsequent research has shown that it was the latter. One year after replicating the Sherif study, Rohrer and colleagues (1954) brought people back individually to judge the movement of the light. Those who had come to a group norm about the distance the light moved stuck to the same estimate they originally formed when part of the group: They really saw the light moving the distance the group had decided it moved, a compelling example of the social construction of reality.

This body of research demonstrated conformity to a group norm on the basis of what is called informational influence. The participants were not just trying to get along; they were trying to figure out how much the light was moving and used other people's estimates as information. Similar findings have been shown for a wide variety of tactile, perceptual, numerical, and aesthetic judgments (Sherif & Sherif, 1969). Generally, informational influence leads to private acceptance—a genuine belief that the attitude expressed or the behavior engaged in is correct. We often conform to the opinions and behavior of others for this reason. You may recall the popular television quiz show *Who Wants to Be a Millionaire?* A stumped contestant had several "lifelines": one was to contact someone who might know the right answer to a specific question; another lifeline was the opportunity to poll the studio audience. More often than not, the majority view of other people is a useful source of accurate information, often more so than single individuals. In fact, statistics show that the studio audience was able to provide the correct answer 91% of the time, whereas calling an expert—in this case, the smartest or most knowledgeable person that the contestant knew—yielded the right answer only 65% of the time (Surowiecki, 2004).

People most often seek such informational influence when they aren't sure what to think or how to behave. This was clearly the case for the ambiguous task that Sherif gave his subjects. Judging how much a point of light moves in a dark room can be tricky, especially when it's actually not moving at all! But would people be so influenced by others if the task being judged was less ambiguous? What if they could rely on their own senses to make a judgment? This is what Solomon Asch wanted to find out.

Asch Conformity Studies

Imagine that you show up to a classroom to participate in a psychology experiment on visual judgment. With you are seven other students. As you settle around a table, an experimenter explains that he will display a series of pairs of two large, white cards. On one card in each pair are three vertical lines of varying lengths labeled A, B, and C; the other card has a single vertical line (see **FIGURE 7.3**). Your task is to state out loud which line length best matches the single line. The first trial begins, and the experimenter starts with the first student to your left. The student says Line C. The next person also says Line C, and so forth, until it's your turn to respond. You respond Line C and quickly settle in to what appears to be a super boring (and totally easy) experiment. After a few such trials, however, something unexpected occurs. On presentation of the lines like those displayed in Figure 7.3, the first student responds with Line A. You probably stifle a chuckle and think this person needs to have his eyes checked. But then the next person also says Line A. And so does the

Public compliance Conforming only outwardly to fit in with a group without changing private beliefs.

Private acceptance Conforming by altering private beliefs as well as public behavior.

Informational influence Occurs when we use others as a source of information about the world.

Conformity Video on LaunchPad

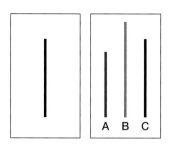

Figure 7.3

Asch Conformity Studies

The lack of ambiguity of the estimation task reveals a normative influence on conformity. Many participants went along with the group judgment even when their senses told them the judgment was incorrect.

[Photo: William Vandivert, Solomon E. Asch, "Opinions and Social Pressure," Reproduced with permission. Copyright 1955 Scientific American, Inc. All rights reserved.]

next and the person after that. All of the other seven students say Line A; you begin to think that maybe it is you who needs your eyes checked. What could be going on here? Now it is your turn. How do you think you would respond?

This is the situation students faced in one variant of Asch's (1956) classic conformity studies. In contrast to Sherif, who presented people with an ambiguous situation, Asch was interested in how people would respond in situations where there was little ambiguity about what they perceived. Indeed, when judging these line lengths alone, participants made errors on less than 1% of the trials. Thus, Asch (1956) presented each participant with two opposing forces: on the one hand, the evidence of his senses, and on the other, the unanimous opinion of a group of his peers (who actually were confederates in the experiment and instructed to respond in a set manner). This situation enabled Asch to address the question, What would people do when their physical senses indicated an answer that was in conflict with the views of the majority? Would people go with the answer they knew was correct? Or would they deny their own perceptions to agree with the group? Asch discovered that in situations such as that just described, 75% conformed to the group opinion in at least one trial, and overall, participants conformed on 37% of the trials.

What the Asch Conformity Studies Teach Us About Why People Conform

Take a moment to think about what this study teaches us beyond what we learned from Sherif's work. What did you come up with? If you started to think about *why* people conform, you're in the right ballpark. Whereas Sherif's studies show how our view of the world is shaped by information we get from other people, Asch's studies point to a different—but very potent—pressure toward conformity. Because the stimulus being judged was not ambiguous, participants had sufficient perceptual information to make a confident judgment. It is unlikely in this study that people conformed to others because they were a source of information. Rather, Asch teaches us that people will also conform to the norms of the group even if it means discounting what they know to be true. This is referred to as **normative influence** and can be contrasted with the power of *informational influence*, which we saw demonstrated in Sherif's studies (Crutchfield, 1955; Deutsch & Gerard, 1955). Normative influence occurs when we go along with the group because we want to be liked and accepted by that group, or because we want to avoid rejection. Examples of normative influence abound, as when we see teenagers dyeing their hair, getting tattoos, or pining away for the hot brand of jeans or sneakers simply because that is what everyone else is doing. (Of course, this is not to say that some people don't adorn themselves in these styles as expressions of their individuality.)

Normative influence Occurs when we use others to know how to fit in.

But the objecting reader might be thinking, "Wait a minute! How do you know that people in Asch's study were not really convinced by the group? Maybe they did think the others were informing them about the actual lengths of the lines." And indeed, in postexperimental interviews, Asch found that some participants did question their own perceptions and thought that the majority might be correct. Some questioned their viewing angle, others their eyesight. However, they were in the minority. The rest acknowledged that they made choices they didn't believe were right simply to go along with the group.

To probe this issue further, Asch conducted a number of variants of this study. He found that when people did not have to give their responses in public but could instead write down their responses privately after hearing others' judgments, they almost never went along with the group opinion. Thus, the power of having to give a *public* response played a pivotal role in participants' tendency to conform. Asch's postexperimental interviews revealed that many participants felt anxious, feared the disapproval of others, and went along with the group to avoid sticking out. When we stick out, we run the risk of looking foolish, and many people are reluctant to face that possibility (Cialdini & Goldstein, 2004).

When we stick out, we can risk ridicule and rejection from others.

[Joseph Farris/Cartoonstock]

Nonconformers may even risk social rejection and ostracism. A classic study by Stanley Schachter (1951) showed that when one confederate planted in a group stubbornly disagrees with the unanimous opinion of the group, that person is taunted, verbally attacked, and rejected. As we discussed in chapter 6, a substantial body of research shows that people find social rejection and ostracism highly upsetting. So the negative reaction that nonconformers so frequently receive helps to explain why people often submit to the norms of the group. Interestingly, Schachter also found that an initial nonconformer who subsequently steps in line is warmly received. After all, it is gratifying when someone who deviates from the rest of the group sees the light.

Although most participants in Asch's studies publicly adjusted their responses to support the group perception at least once, it was not necessarily the case that all, or even most, were blindly punting away their own individualism to succumb submissively to the group opinion. Asch recognized this as well, noting that in postexperimental interviews many subjects expressed considerable concern for the solidarity and well-being of the group. Thus, the participants' responses can also be interpreted as a result of valuing positive social relations (Hodges & Geyer, 2006). From this perspective, then, participants' conformity to the group norm despite their own perceptions can be seen as an adaptive means of productively and harmoniously coexisting with others. It is no surprise that people who come from more collectivistic cultures, which strongly value group cohesion, generally are more likely to conform than people who come from individualistic cultures, which strongly value unique self-expression (Bond & Smith, 1996).

What Personality and Situational Variables Influence Conformity?

Despite this more positive view of conformity, in many contexts, such as deciding if a defendant is guilty or if an aircraft design is safe, it would be rather alarming if individuals went along with the group despite what they know to be true from their physical perceptions. From Asch's studies, it's tempting to agree with Mark Twain, who noted, "We are discreet sheep; we wait to see how the drove is going, and then go with the drove." But we shouldn't lose sight of the fact that 25% of participants never conformed to the group. These results also provide compelling evidence that some people do resist social pressure.

Unfortunately, not a great deal is known about the personality characteristics of those who tend to conform as opposed to those who do not. Early studies found some indications that people who have such traits as a high need to achieve (McClelland et al., 1953) and a propensity to be leaders (Crutchfield, 1955) are less likely to conform. People who have a greater awareness of self and high self-esteem (Santee & Maslach, 1982) are also less likely to conform, because they are more confident in their own judgments and less in need of other people's approval. Indeed, self-esteem appears to be especially likely to help one resist conformity when those feelings of self-worth are based on who one thinks one really is, as opposed to self-esteem based on achievements that others may value (Arndt et al., 2002).

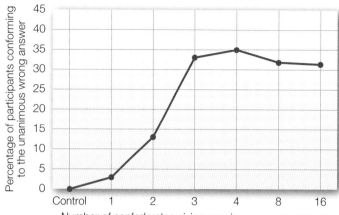

Figure 7.4

The Effect of Group Size on Conformity

Conformity is more likely as group size increases from 1 to 3 people, but then the influence starts to level off.

[Data source: Asch (1956)]

For years, psychologists also thought that women conformed more than men, but any such differences are actually quite small. It turns out that people will more readily conform on topics they don't know much about. Thus, whereas women are more likely to conform on stereotypically masculine judgments on topics such as sports or cars, men are more likely to conform on stereotypically feminine judgments on topics such as fashion or family planning (Eagly & Carli, 1981).

In addition to self-awareness, self-esteem, and gender, aspects of a situation also can influence the likelihood of conformity. In further variants of his paradigm, Asch discovered a number of factors that influence the rate of conformity. For example, larger groups of unanimous opinions elicit more conformity, but only up to a point. Asch (1956) repeated his line-judgment conformity experiment but manipulated the number of confederates who announced the incorrect answer. **FIGURE 7.4** shows the percentage of participants who conformed to the unanimous majority.

Participants were more likely to conform when three confederates gave unanimous wrong answers than when two confederates gave unanimous wrong answers. Interestingly, however, further increases in majority size above three did not lead to significantly more conformity. It appears, then, that a majority of three is quite influential.

This effect of diminishing returns for group size also is apparent with more subtle instances of conformity. Imagine walking down the street and seeing someone looking up and maybe even pointing at the sky. It's an almost reflexive response to follow that person's gaze to see what might be so interesting. Stanley Milgram and colleagues (1969) carried out a classic study to capture this simple phenomenon. On Forty-second Street in Manhattan, research confederates stopped and stared up at a sixth-floor window. The researchers varied the number of assistants, and a key finding was that the greater the number of confederates who looked up, the greater the percentage of passersby who stopped to look up as well. Forty-two percent looked up if only one confederate was gazing up at the building. This increased to about 80% with a group of five but rose to only about 85% when the number of confederates was 15. Thus, although larger numbers do increase pressure to follow the group, after a certain point, the effect of increasing numbers levels off. Perhaps this analogy will be helpful. Think of the sound of 10 people applauding. It's a lot more rousing than the sound of three

It's a bird, it's a plane, it's . . . . When we see others gazing upwards, we're likely to follow suit. Here people on the streets of Ajmer in India demonstrate this tendency.

[Getty Images/Lonely Planet Images]

people applauding. Yet the difference between 43 people and 50 people applauding is far less noticeable.

More important than the number of others is their unanimity. Even *one* dissenting voice in a group of nine confederates appears to disrupt the pressure of the majority view and decreases conformity such that participants conform to the group on less than 5% of the trials in the line-judging paradigm (Asch, 1956). Interestingly, this other dissenting voice need not indicate the correct answer or appear to be especially competent or intelligent. As long as one other person breaks from the majority view, the participant feels more empowered to express his or her own view (Allen & Levine, 1969). Knowing that one is not a lone wolf seems to bring some comfort and encouragement. Many organizations seem to understand this and deal harshly with the first person who steps out of line, so as to prevent one dissenting voice from licensing others to buck the majority view.

The study of passersby looking up by Milgram and colleagues (1969) also is interesting because it highlights the often reflexive nature of conformity. Although the people unwittingly participating in the study might briefly have had the conscious thought, "I wonder what's going on," it's also likely that they were already following the gaze of the others even as this thought was still forming in their heads. Some instances of conformity do not involve deliberative thought but rather are responsive to social cues that may influence us without our awareness (Epley & Gilovich, 1999).

Reference group A group with which an individual strongly identifies.

Another variable that contributes to conformity is the extent to which the individual identifies with the majority. When the individual strongly identifies with the larger group, that group, known as a reference group, is likely to have a substantial influence on the individual's attitudes and behavior (Turner, 1991). Reference groups are generally a source of both informational and normative influence. We trust them more than other groups, and we want their approval more. Theodore Newcomb (1943) conducted a unique longitudinal study of conformity by tracking the political and economic attitudes of new students who enrolled in Bennington College, a private college for women, back in the 1930s. The students came from wealthy, conservative backgrounds, but the staff and senior students at the college were quite liberal. He found that most of the students became increasingly liberal over their years at the college. Furthermore, a follow-up study in 1960 showed that the former students had retained the liberal attitudes they acquired in college for 25 years or more (Newcomb et al., 1967).

An interesting finding was that a minority of the young women who did not become very socially involved on campus retained their conservative attitudes throughout college. Newcomb discerned that the difference was that the young women who became liberal used the campus community as a reference group, whereas the young women who remained conservative maintained their families and friends from home as their reference group.

Neural Processes Associated With Conformity

Recent research using functional magnetic resonance imaging (fMRI) of the brain provides some insight into the neural processes that may be associated with conformity. As we noted earlier, Sherif's work suggests that a majority group opinion sometimes changes the way we actually *perceive* stimuli in our environment. Are these changes in perception reflected in how our brain processes perceptual stimuli? It appears so. Berns and colleagues (2005) scanned participants' brains while they made judgments about the spatial orientation of three-dimensional geometric figures. The procedure was somewhat similar to Asch's but participants were given feedback via computer about how other people who were purportedly in the session thought the figures were oriented. In another condition, participants were given the same type of feedback but were told it came not from other people but was computer generated. The results indicated that when participants conformed to the opinions of others, the areas of the brain implicated in spatial perception and mental rotation (the occipital-parietal areas) were more active. However, this effect did *not* occur when the feedback was said to be from the computer. Berns and colleagues argue that this suggests that peer opinion—in contrast to other forms of information—exerts an especially potent influence on how we perceive objects in our world.

Berns and colleagues also provided evidence about how the brain responds when we do go against the grain, fail to conform, and thus stick out. Specifically, when participants did not conform to group opinion, brain scans of the nonconformists showed increased activation of the amygdala in the brain's right hemisphere, an area commonly associated with fear. This study fits findings concerning rejection of deviants and the negative feelings such rejection and ostracism arouse in them, suggesting that people may conform as a way to avoid these negative feelings (Cialdini & Goldstein, 2004).

The neuroscience perspective has guided research suggesting that conformity may occur in part because people view going against the group as akin to making a mistake. In a study conducted in the Netherlands, Klucharev and colleagues (2009) had participants make judgments about how attractive they found pictures of people's faces while their brains were being scanned. After each rating, participants were informed of the average European rating of each face. About a half hour after this, participants were unexpectedly asked to re-rate the attractiveness of the faces. The results indicated that when participants learned that their ratings diverged from those of the group, areas of the brain commonly associated with detecting errors in learning tasks (the rostral cingulate cortex and the nucleus accumbens) were more active. In perhaps the most interesting finding, the more active these areas were, the more participants later changed their ratings to conform more closely to those of the group. Thus, this study suggests that people often may perceive disagreeing with the group as a mistake and seek to conform to correct what their brain registers as an error. However, in this study, the task was a relatively ambiguous and complex judgment, so it's still an open question whether going against a group judgment that is clearly wrong, as in the Asch paradigm, also would activate regions of the brain associated with error detection.

SECTION review | Conformity

People conform both to get along with others and because others are a source of information.

The Sherif and Asch conformity studies	Personality and situational influences	Neural Processes
People often conform to groups. • They want to be right: informational influence. • They want to fit in: normative influence.	People least likely to conform have: • a high need for achievement. • leadership qualities. • confidence in their own judgment. • high self-esteem. Willingness to conform also depends on: • the number of confederates. • whether or not even one other person breaks from the majority view. • how strongly the individual relates to the larger group.	fMRIs provide evidence that: • People are more sensitive to peer opinion than to other kinds of information. • Going against the group activates brain regions associated with detecting errors.

Minority Influence

Social psychologists have long considered how the numerical majority could influence people. But in the mid- to late 1960s, amid the discontent and protests surrounding the Vietnam War, and with the civil rights and other movements escalating both in the United States and abroad, open and celebrated dissent began to take root. Perhaps not surprisingly, this period also saw the dawn of research into how the voice of one could influence the views of the many. Leading this charge was Serge Moscovici (Moscovici et al., 1969; Moscovici, 1980). He pioneered work on minority influence—the process by which dissenters (or numerical minorities) produce attitude change within a group, despite the extraordinary risk of social rejection and disturbance of the status quo. It's vital to understand these processes, for without this knowledge we would have little understanding of how social change occurs.

Ralph Waldo Emerson famously wrote, "All history is a record of the power of minorities, and of minorities of one." Indeed, single individuals and small movements in philosophy, science, the arts, religion, and politics often have profoundly altered the course of history: Homer, Plato, Confucius, Moses, Jesus, Muhammad, Nicolaus Copernicus, Galileo, Karl Marx, Charles Darwin, Sojourner Truth, Thomas Edison, Susan B. Anthony, Mahatma Gandhi, Albert Einstein, Adolf Hitler, Rosa Parks, Mother Teresa, Martin Luther King Jr., César Chávez—the list could go on and on. Thus, the study of minority influence is a window into the agents of cultural and social changes through scientific or artistic achievements, technological advances, political or social movements, horrific wars, advances in racial or gender equality, or other historical trends. Toward the end of this chapter, we'll consider how individuals can influence others by holding a position of authority or rising to a leadership position. But for now, we're going to focus on how individual dissenters can influence the majority even without the advantage of being in a position of authority.

How Minorities Exert Their Influence

In Asch's classic studies on conformity, people conformed to the normative pressure of the majority, even when the majority's judgments did not appear to be correct. In their initial study of minority influence, Moscovici and colleagues (1969) developed their own perceptual judgment paradigm but with some interesting twists. Instead of confronting participants with majority pressure, Moscovici presented them with a minority view and examined how that view influenced their perceptions. In what they were told was a study of color perception, groups of six participants were asked to view slides, all varying shades of blue, and name the color in each. In the control conditions of the study, all participants indicated that they saw the slides were blue. As in the Asch studies, however, confederates were involved in the experimental conditions. In the *inconsistent* condition, each group had four actual participants and two confederates, who described two thirds of the slides as green and the other third as blue. In the *consistent* condition, the two confederates described all the slides as green. Did this minority view change what the participants reported? It did, but primarily when the minority was consistent. When the confederates were consistent in saying a slide was green, 32% of the participants indicated at least once that they too thought the slide was green, compared with only 8% in the inconsistent condition and less than 1% in the control condition.

This research indicated that a minority can indeed have an influence over the majority, a shocking finding in a field that had previously considered only how the majority could pressure the individual. Armed with these findings, Moscovici also studied the lives of historical figures such as Galileo and Freud and how they succeeded in thwarting the consensus of their times. Moscovici (1980) proposed his conversion theory to explain how and why being influenced by a minority differs from

Minority influence The process by which dissenters (or numerical minorities) produce attitude change within a group, despite the extraordinary risk of social rejection and disturbance of the status quo.

Conversion theory The explanation that people are influenced by a minority because the minority's distinctive position better captures their attention.

being influenced by the majority. According to Moscovici, because people generally want to fit in with the majority group, they often go along with the majority position without deeply considering the message the majority is delivering. They tend just to accept it. The minority position, however, is by definition more distinctive. Although Moscovici reasoned that people generally don't want to identify with the minority, the distinctiveness of the minority's position better captures their attention. As a result, they tend to consider it more thoroughly; this deeper consideration can lead to a change in attitude.

Can you think of an example where after initially reacting to a minority opinion negatively, you were eventually influenced by it?

[Buyenlarge/Getty Images]

Think
ABOUT

You may have noticed that the dual processes specified by Moscovici's conversion theory sound quite similar to the dual automatic and controlled processes we described in our presentation of social cognition (see chapter 3). If you did, you're right. Research indicates that the majority often influences us in a relatively automatic fashion. Especially when we're not invested in an issue, we tend to give the majority the benefit of the doubt and accept its position without thinking too deeply about it. But because we don't give those in the minority the benefit of the doubt, minorities often exert their influence only by provoking carefully elaborated thought (e.g., Crano & Chen, 1998; De Dreu & De Vries, 1993; Maass & Clark, 1983).

Martin and colleagues (2007) built on prior research showing that thoughtful processing tends to lead to private attitude change that better guides behavior, whereas the change in attitudes from more automatic processing tends to be more superficial, shorter lasting, and less influential in guiding behavior. Thus, Martin and colleagues reasoned that if being convinced by a minority involves more elaborate processing of the message, it should lead to a stronger and more enduring attitude that will be a more potent guide to behavior. In contrast, if one is convinced by a majority and this involves more superficial processing, the resulting attitude should be weaker and have less influence on one's behavior.

To test this idea, they presented students with arguments, attributed to either a minority or a majority, recommending that students be required to pay membership fees to join the student union. The researchers also measured how relevant students felt this issue was to them personally, because earlier research had suggested that people process information more thoroughly when it is highly relevant (Petty & Cacioppo, 1984). Consistent with this prior finding, the study showed that when personal relevance was high, all participants, regardless of minority or majority influence, processed the message thoroughly. It was when the issue was low in personal relevance that influence from a minority, rather than a majority, source made a difference. Under these conditions, participants persuaded by a minority to pay membership fees developed a stronger attitude than those who were persuaded by a majority. In fact, those who received the message from a minority source were actually more likely to sign a petition supporting membership fees than were those who received the message from a majority. Martin and colleagues explain that when the argument was attributed to the minority, it was processed more deeply; as a consequence, it led to stronger and more enduring attitudes that had a greater influence on behavior.

Part of the reason that minorities exert their influence by provoking more systematic processing of their position is that people want to understand why the minority sees a given issue so differently from the majority. Certainly, in so doing the minority group or individual courts negative reactions from others. Research consistently finds that those who adopt minority positions are generally disliked (Nemeth,

Figure 7.5

Minority Opinion

The Palazzo dei Priori (left) and the Arco Etrusco (right) are two historical landmarks in Perugia, Italy. Mucchi-Faina and colleagues (1991) showed that study participants' ideas about how to market these sites to increase tourism were more creative when participants thought that using these sites was advocated by the minority rather than the majority.

[Left: © Stuart Robertson/Alamy; right: Getty Images/DeAgostini]

Minority slowness effect
Occurs when people who hold the minority position take longer to express their opinions.

1979), and those who adopt the minority position may in fact be aware that they are flirting with such disdain. This would help to explain the minority slowness effect. When people are asked about their attitudes on various topics such as sports, politics, celebrities, and social issues, those who adopt the minority position take longer to express their opinions (Bassili, 2003).

The minority position presents a distinctive and interesting puzzle that people want to figure out. They can derive considerable benefits from trying to do so. As people think extensively about the minority's argument and why it advocates that argument, they often think about different perspectives themselves, which allows for the consideration of novel and creative possibilities (Kenworthy et al., 2008; Nemeth, 1986). In a finding consistent with this idea, Charlan Nemeth and colleagues documented that although being influenced by the majority tends to elicit conventional problem-solving solutions, being influenced by a minority increases original thinking and diversified strategies in figuring out tasks such as word completions and word compositions (e.g., Nemeth & Kwan, 1987). In one example, Mucchi-Faina and colleagues (1991) had students from Perugia, Italy, try to think of ways to enhance the international reputation of their city. The students were shown pictures of two historic landmarks in Perugia, the Palazzo dei Priori (**FIGURE 7.5, left**) and the Arco Etrusco (**FIGURE 7.5, right**) and were told that marketing these sites to enhance the city's reputation was advocated by either a majority or a minority of citizens surveyed. When students were presented with what they thought was the minority opinion on how to enhance the city's reputation (versus what they thought was the majority opinion), they offered more creative and unique ideas about how to do so.

APPLICATION

How Minorities Can Be More Influential

Earlier we noted that in addition to conforming for normative reasons, people also conform because of informational influence. We tend to trust others as sources of information. A few years ago, your current author and family were heading to a political speech by then presidential candidate Barack Obama. We did not know exactly where he was speaking but simply followed the droves of people making their way to a particular location: We assumed that these other people knew where to go and followed their lead. We used others as a source of information. Of course, we certainly would have been less likely to follow only a few people heading in a particular direction. This example illustrates the types of issues for which majorities can have greater influence. As a result of peoples' tendency to rely on others for information, minorities are not especially influential concerning issues for which there is an objective answer. We tend to trust the majority on questions of fact. In contrast, minorities tend to have their greatest potential for influence on matters of opinion. In one study, for example, minorities had less influence when Italian students were asked, "From which country *does* Italy import most of its raw oil?" than when the students were asked, "From which country *should* Italy import most of its raw oil?" (Maass et al., 1996).

Research also has identified a number of other qualities that enhance the likelihood that a minority can successfully sway the majority. These are important tips to keep in mind the next time you find yourself in a minority position and want to convince others.

- It is important for the minority to project self-confidence and be consistent in its advocacy (e.g., Moscovici et al.,1969; Wood et al., 1994). When Dr. Martin Luther King Jr. endeavored to convince a nation of the need for racial equality, he did so with unwavering consistency, even though it meant that he was hated by many.
- Although consistency and self-confidence are important, they can backfire if the minority person or group is perceived as rigid and inflexible. In these cases, the attributions will shift, and the minority position will be dismissed. ("He's just a quack with nothing important for me to consider.") Rather, studies show that a flexible and open-minded behavioral style, indicating a willingness to compromise, is an effective complement to consistency in promoting persuasion by either a minority or a majority (Moscovici et al., 1985).
- Getting members of the majority to defect, or cross over, and adopt the minority view is one of the most potent ingredients of minority influence. In fact, in studies of jury decision making, a minority is more influential when it can achieve a defection from the majority than if it starts with someone already on its side (Nemeth & Wachtler, 1974). Part of the reason that this can lead to a snowball effect and influence the rest of the majority is that it undermines an "us versus them" mentality.
- Finally, as with all forms of persuasion, the more people identify with the person attempting to persuade them, the more likely they are to be persuaded. In other words, we are more likely to be convinced if the minority (or majority) is part of *our* ingroup, because we are more likely to be influenced by those who are like us (Maass & Clark, 1984). ▶

SECTION review | Minority Influence

Despite disturbance of the status quo, minorities can produce attitude change and throughout history have been agents of cultural and social change.

How minorities exert influence

- Although people don't want to identify with a minority, the distinctiveness of the minority position better captures their attention, and they give it deeper consideration. This can lead to lasting attitude change.
- Minorities are generally disliked, so those holding a minority position may take longer to express their opinions.
- The majority finds the minority position puzzling, which may lead to original thinking and diversified strategies in figuring out solutions.

Application: When minorities are influential

- To influence opinion successfully, minority advocates need to be consistent, confident, and yet flexible.
- A minority is more influential when there is a defection from the majority and when the minority is seen as part of the ingroup.

Compliance: The Art and Science of Getting What You Want

Conformity often involves implicit pressure. But individuals also wield influence in one-on-one situations in which one person's explicit goal is simply to change the other person's behavior outright. Salespeople just want you to buy their product, parents want their kids to do the right things, and so forth. This brings us to research on the phenomena of *compliance* and *obedience*. In the case of obedience, you simply tell people what to do. It turns out this works quite well when you have authority over someone else, as you'll see in our next section. But without the power of authority over someone, what techniques can you use to gain compliance with requests?

The study of compliance has revealed a handy toolkit of methods to bring someone else's behavior in line with a request. As you learn about these methods, you'll notice how they are used all the time by advertisers, salespeople, and others who are in the business of influencing your consumer behavior. In fact, many of these methods were discovered when the social psychologist Bob Cialdini spent a few years undercover, going into car dealerships and taking other sales positions to find out which sales techniques are the most effective for getting people to pull out their credit cards (Cialdini, 2006). Of course, methods of compliance are also useful outside the marketplace for changing a range of behaviors, from getting your roommate to do the dishes to getting people to give generously to charities. Next, we review the most well-established of these methods.

12 Angry Men

The classic 1957 film *12 Angry Men* (Fonda et al., 1957), starring Henry Fonda and directed by Sidney Lumet, portrays in great detail one riveting example of minority influence while also illustrating other factors in social influence. The film opens with 12 jurors who have just heard the murder trial of a boy accused of killing his father. The jurors settle into the deliberation room, muttering that it appears to be an open-and-shut case. Soon after, an initial vote is taken by a show of hands. Ten hands rise in favor of a guilty verdict, quickly followed by another, tentative hand. Immediately, we see elements of both normative and perhaps informational social influence as the initially tentative juror looks to the others for what might be the correct verdict. When the foreman asks for votes of "not guilty," only one hand is raised.

What follows is a compelling portrayal, filmed exclusively in the confines of this one room, of the process by which one man succeeds in changing the minds of 11 other jurors. Demonstrating how art can anticipate scientific insight, the film highlights a number of factors that subsequent research has shown increase the likelihood of minority influence. Fonda's character (whose name we don't learn until the final scene of the film) takes some time to ponder his initial

[United Artists/Photofest]

Self-perception and Commitment

According to Bem's self-perception theory (discussed in chapter 5), once we freely engage in a behavior, we often adopt attitudes that are consistent with that behavior (Bem, 1967). This process explains the foot-in-the-door effect, whereby people are more likely to comply with a moderate request if they initially comply with a smaller request. This technique works remarkably well and often doubles or even triples the percentage of people who agree to a moderate request (e.g., Freedman & Fraser, 1966). How does this work? The compliance to the initial small request shifts our attitude toward being more consistent with the subsequent larger request. If you agree to let a door-to-door salesperson into your home, you may infer you have some interest in hearing about his or her product. This makes you more likely to give that product a try.

Imagine that you are participating in the following study by Burger and Caldwell (2003). In one condition, you spend time completing several questionnaires. At the end of the study, you are asked if you would be willing to volunteer a couple of hours the following weekend helping to sort food donations for a local homeless shelter. If you are like most participants, you probably would come up with some excuse for why you wouldn't have the time. In this condition, only 32% of the participants volunteered. But now rerun the simulation with the following change: At the very beginning of the session, another participant asks if you might be willing to sign a petition to increase awareness about the plight of the homeless. This is an easy enough thing to agree to, and you add your name to the list. But having done so, you now feel like a champion of the underprivileged. What happens when you

Foot-in-the-door effect
Phenomenon whereby people are more likely to comply with a moderate request after having initially complied with a smaller request.

vote but thereafter consistently advocates an open-minded consideration of the evidence. The distinctiveness, flexibility, and firmness of his views ultimately provoke a deeper and more thorough reflection in some of the other jurors, which further inspires their own creative thoughts about the issues at hand. They start to see holes in the prosecution's case that even Fonda's character did not notice. This more thoughtful and systematic consideration leads some of the jurors to more sustained attitude change. In contrast, those jurors who were simply agreeing with the majority for superficial reasons show signs of more fleeting opinions, "bouncing back and forth like a Ping-Pong ball."

Henry Fonda's character also has brief personal conversations with some of the other jurors, which helps to break down the walls between them. He no longer seems like an outcast. And as research shows, the more people identify with a minority, the more influential that minority can be.

Three of the more noteworthy performances (in the context of across-the-board stellar performances) are by Lee J. Cobb, E. G. Marshall, and Joseph Sweeney. In Lee J. Cobb's character (again, very few character names are ever revealed), we see a powerful example of personal bias and stereotypes coloring the way a person processes the information to which

he is exposed. The young defendant reminds him of his struggles with his own son, and he is unable to get beyond the bias and bitterness that seethe in him. In E. G. Marshall's character, a cool, level-headed, and (almost) always composed stockbroker, we see the ultimate example of social influence through informational routes. He rationally sticks to his vote until finally, showing his first trickle of perspiration on this stifling, hot afternoon, he admits that the accumulation of information raises a reasonable doubt. With Joseph Sweeney, an astute and rather observant older gentleman, we see the power of an initial defection. After standing alone in his insistence on continuing to go over the details of the case, Henry Fonda's character takes a gamble, asking for a vote and agreeing to abstain. If everybody else continues to vote guilty, he claims, he will go along with the verdict, adding, "But if one person votes not guilty, we stay here and talk this out." His initial success in converting a lone defector (Joseph Sweeney's character) is subsequently followed by the gradual conversion of the remaining jurors.

After the film was released, each of these tactics was subsequently examined and supported in empirical research on how and when minorities can influence numerical majorities.

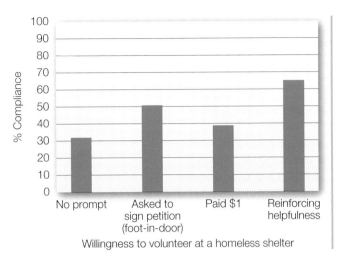

Figure 7.6

The Effect of Self-Perception Processes on Compliance

Burger and Caldwell's (2003) study shows how self-perception processes can increase compliance. When participants first agreed to a smaller request or were complimented on being thoughtful and caring, they were more likely to agree to a larger request to donate time.

[Data source: Burger & Caldwell (2003)]

Norm for social commitment Belief whereby once we make a public agreement, we tend to stick to it even if circumstances change.

Lowballing Occurs when after agreeing to an offer, people find it hard to break that commitment even if they later learn of some extra cost to the deal.

are next asked to spend your Saturday afternoon sifting through food donations? In the real experiment, 51% of the participants complied with the fairly substantial larger request if they had first complied with a smaller request (**FIGURE 7.6**). This significant increase in compliance resulted from simply carrying out an initial, smaller request.

The foot-in-the door effect happens because when a person complies with a small request, she is likely to infer that she is the type of person who helps others or is interested in the particular cause. Because of this shift in self-perception, the person becomes more receptive to the related but larger second request. Indeed, once she has this new view of herself, refusing the second request would likely arouse dissonance.

This raises an interesting possibility: If a person initially complies with a small request for extrinsic reasons, such as a monetary reward, will she be less likely to infer that she is the helping type? Perhaps yes, if she attributes her compliance to the extrinsic factor. In this case, when she is later asked to comply with a larger request, she will feel less pressure to act in ways that are consistent with her self-image. This point was also illustrated in Burger and Caldwell's (2003) study (see Figure 7.6): When participants were offered a dollar to sign a petition, they were no more willing to comply with a second, larger request to volunteer at the homeless shelter, presumably because they inferred that they signed the petition for the dollar, not because of who they were or what they believed. The role of self-perception processes is also illustrated in an additional condition in which, after signing the petition, participants were explicitly told by the requestor what caring and thoughtful people they are. Participants in this condition were much more likely to comply with the large request, because the compliment reinforced their image of themselves as thoughtful. With this strengthened self-perception, they were even more likely to act in ways that were consistent with it. This might be why we often seek to butter up a person before we ask him to do us a favor. By flattering the person for being generous or caring, for example, we validate a self-perception that he then may be more likely to uphold.

Our motivation to view ourselves as consistent also contributes to a social norm to honor our commitments. Once you make a public agreement, it is considered bad form to back out on your half of that agreement. This **norm for social commitment** underlies the strong sense of trust that is one of the building blocks of cooperative relationships. Most of the time, behaving in line with such a norm will foster healthy social bonds. Those who renege on their agreements earn a reputation for being undependable, flaky, and untrustworthy. But the norm for social commitment can get you to do things you might not otherwise want to do.

For example, this norm can make you feel trapped in a decision and forced to accept a *lowball offer*. **Lowballing** can take different forms, but the general principle is that after agreeing to an offer, people find it hard to break that commitment even if they later learn of some extra cost to the deal. Consider this technique in the context of trying to sell someone a new car. The strategy is to offer the customer what seems like a great deal and get him to commit to the idea of buying that particular new car. Then only after the customer has already mentally committed to buy the car is a certain "error in calculation" or "salesperson-manager miscommunication" revealed that raises the price. Although the customer might not have signed the deal for this new price if it had been the initial quote, he now finds it hard to say "no."

Researchers have studied lowballing in a number of real-life contexts. In one such study (Cialdini et al., 1978), researchers called participants and recruited them to take part in a psychology experiment. When participants were immediately told that the study would be taking place at 7:00 in the morning, only 24% agreed to sign up. But the compliance rate more than doubled (56%) when people were first asked if they wanted to participate in a study and only after they said "yes" were informed that it took place at 7:00 in the morning. These students were no more thrilled than the first group about having to get up so early, but even when given the chance to change their minds, none of them went back on their initial commitment. What's more, 95% of them actually showed up for the study!

Lowballing is different from the foot-in-the-door request because it requires only an initial commitment that binds one to an agreement with another person, not the enactment of any behavior that changes one's view of oneself. Because complying with an initial foot-in-the-door request leads to a change in self-view, people will comply with the second, larger request even if it comes from a different person (Freedman & Fraser, 1966). In contrast, the effect of agreeing to an initial lowball request is specific to that requestor; if someone else springs the added cost on us and asks if we will still follow through, we tend to walk away from the table (Burger & Petty, 1981). When the two strategies are compared, low-balling often gains greater compliance (Brownstein & Katzev, 1985; Cialdini et al., 1978).

Reciprocity

The age-old saying "You scratch my back, I'll scratch yours" reflects another very basic norm of social interaction: reciprocity. Humans across cultures show a very strong norm to reciprocate acts. But it is not only backs that get scratched, so to speak. Reciprocity is seen in nonhuman animals as well—apes, monkeys, even bats! After a successful night of collecting blood, vampire bats will regurgitate some of that blood to share with other bats, but not just *any* other bats: Such sharing is more likely to happen with bats who have shared their own blood in the past (Wilkinson, 1990). You cough up some of your blood, and I'll cough up some of mine.

Vampire bats also seem to follow the norm of reciprocity—though for them, it's reciprocity of blood.
[Michael Lynch/Shutterstock]

Because the norm of reciprocity is strong, it is often used to induce compliance. If you have ever donated money to an organization after it provided you with a free gift (preprinted address labels, for example), then you have felt the pull of reciprocity. But why do we reciprocate? Is it a built-in instinct, instilled over the course of evolution? Perhaps when someone does us a favor we just like that person more, or we're simply in a better mood, and these factors make us more likely to reciprocate.

A clever experiment by Regan (1971) gives us some clues to answering these questions. Each participant worked on a task alongside a confederate who came across as either very likeable or downright rude. In one condition, the confederate returned from a break halfway into the study and, as an unexpected favor, gave the participant a can of Coke. In a second condition, the participant also received a Coke, but this time from the experimenter. And in a third condition, the participant did not receive this unexpected gift. At the end of the session, the confederate asked the participant if he would be willing to help him out by purchasing lottery tickets for a fundraiser.

Regan figured that if people help others simply because they like them, then participants in this study would not help the rude confederate, even if he kindly delivered a Coke. Also, if receiving favors increases helping simply because it improves mood, then participants would be more willing to help the confederate if they had been given a free Coke, regardless of whether it came from the confederate or the experimenter. The results did not support either of these hypotheses. Instead, people bought about 75% more tickets when the confederate had given them a Coke compared with the other two conditions, regardless of whether the confederate was generally likeable or rude. This finding suggests that liking or being in a good mood are not essential ingredients of reciprocity. That is, although both positive moods and liking do tend to increase compliance, as you might expect, they were not especially influential in this context (Carlson et al., 1988; Isen et al., 1976). Rather, this experiment shows the power of reciprocity. So even if you despise your neighbor, you might still find yourself agreeing to take care of her pets if she's been bringing in your trash cans from the street.

However, reciprocation does have its limits. Simply doing someone a favor generally will not lead the person to comply with your request if you're requesting something that would violate the person's moral standards or put the person at risk, such as helping you to cheat on a test (Boster et al., 2001). So although you might take care of Rover from next door to reciprocate your neighbor's past favors, you may draw the line if he asks you to, say, help him fudge his income tax return.

Norms toward reciprocity can also play a role in negotiations. Conventional wisdom might tell you that when you approach your boss about requesting a raise, you might not want to start with a high initial request that could alienate your superior and stop the process before it starts. But such conventionality might not be so wise, because it ignores the powerful role that reciprocity can play. Although your boss might deny your request for a hefty $10,000 raise, the guilt she might experience from turning down your request could lead her to compromise at a $5,000 raise, which might have been the amount you were hoping for all along. This is called the door-in-the-face effect; it's the idea that people are more likely to comply with a moderate request after they have first been presented with and refused to agree to a much larger request. (Although this tactic isn't working for Calvin in the cartoon below, it often does!) The name draws on the nature of door-to-door sales, in which making an unreasonable request might initially get the door slammed in your face but might also open the person to considering a compromise offer.

Consider a classic study that Cialdini carried out with his research team (Cialdini et al., 1975). Members of his team approached students around campus and asked if they would be interested in volunteering their time on an upcoming Saturday chaperoning a group of juvenile delinquents on a trip to the zoo. With no financial incentive and concerns about lacking the experience, 83% of those approached refused. But the experimenters first approached another group of students with the offer of a different kind of volunteer opportunity with the same organization: spending two hours a week for two full years as counselors to delinquent kids. Not surprisingly, no one approached was willing to make this extreme commitment of time. However, when their refusal was followed by a smaller request to chaperone for one Saturday afternoon (the same request initially given to the other group of students), half of the students agreed to help out. In other words, the door-in-the-face strategy actually tripled the number of volunteers!

How is reciprocity involved here? When the person being approached with a request views the smaller compromise offer as a concession, that person can become motivated to reciprocate and do her part to maintain good faith in the exchange. This then can lead her to be more likely to accept the compromise offer. To put it simply, it is as if the person making the requests is doing you a favor by offering you the smaller request.

Door-in-the-face effect Phenomenon whereby people are more likely to comply with a moderate request after they have first been presented with and refused to agree to a much larger request.

Social Proof

During college, one of the authors of this textbook spent a summer selling educational books door to door. The job entailed trying to meet and talk to every family in a neighborhood. Whenever a family placed an order for books, its name was added to a list of buyers. The list was shown to potential customers as a sort of proof that the product was good. In one community, your author was fortunate enough to have several high school teachers and parents in the local school district purchase the books so that their names adorned the buyer sheet. When she approached the house of the high school's principal, he took just one look at this list and instantly said, "Well then, I guess I have to buy them," and pulled out his wallet without even taking a very close look at what it was he was buying!

This anecdote typifies the powerful effect that social proof has on our behavior. This technique capitalizes on our tendency to conform to what we believe others think and do. It is akin to making salient a descriptive norm but emphasizes the special value of information about what similar and respected others have done. As social comparison theory posits, we often look to similar others to provide us with information about what is good, valuable, and desirable. This makes our friends the most effective salespeople we know, and we commonly follow their recommendations for restaurants, movies, and clothing brands.

If consistency means choosing a behavior that conforms to your perception of yourself, and social proof means choosing a behavior that conforms to what others are doing, you can imagine that in some cases these two compliance strategies could pull a person in opposing directions. In fact, there can be cultural variation in which strategy is more effective. For example, in one study, students from a collectivist culture (Poland) chose to comply with a request on the basis of information about how many of their peers had complied, whereas U.S. students, who are typically more individualistic, were more influenced by considering when they had complied with similar requests in the past (Cialdini et al., 1999).

Social proof A tendency to conform to what we believe respected others think and do.

Scarcity

In the summer of 2008, record numbers of people lined up for hours, sometimes days, to buy the latest must-have gadget—the first Apple iPhone. Anticipation for the product, with its integrated camera and lightning-speed Internet connection, had been building for months. If a company such as Apple wants to sell products, why hadn't their market-research team more accurately estimated the demand for this new toy? The answer might lie in an interesting fact about human psychology: We want . . . no, *need* . . . no, *absolutely must have* things that are scarce. Perhaps because it was selected for back in prehistoric days of feast and famine, we seem to have an innate preference for anything in short supply. In one study, cafeteria food that previously had been the subject of scorn and disgust was longed for with a sense of wistful nostalgia after a fire destroyed the cafeteria (West, 1975). As the 1970s singer-songwriter Joni Mitchell once sang, "You don't know what you got, till it's gone."

Some researchers have suggested that our craving for scarce things stems from the psychological process called *reactance* (Brehm, 1966), which we will discuss in greater detail in our next chapter. When something is hard to get because it's scarce, we feel that scarcity as an insult to our basic freedom of choice, and that makes us want the object even more. But because things that are in short supply often fetch a higher price, Cialdini (1987) views scarcity as a heuristic that we have learned implicitly because we simply want what is hard to attain without giving it too much thought.

Might the initial scarcity of the original iPhone have contributed to its popularity?

[ChinaFotoPress via Getty Images]

Yet another approach proposes that things or ideas that are scarce or rare attract our attention and greater scrutiny (Brock & Brannon, 1992). As a result, our evaluations can be polarized by other information, such as strong or weak arguments for wanting the product. If at your local *taquería*, you are asked if you want a cinnamon twist that's available for only a limited time, you might comply with this attempt to sell the twists only if you are also given a good reason to do so, rather than being reminded of the fact that these tasty treats aren't even traditional to Mexican cuisine (Brock & Mazzocco, 2004).

Each of these explanations has some support, and research has not definitively favored one over the other. Regardless of the precise reason for the valuing of what's scarce, stores and manufacturers realize and exploit this little quirk of human nature. You probably have seen countless advertisements declaring that a good deal won't last: *Limited time offer! Sale ends Saturday! Limited quantity!* In fact, sometimes these offers aren't even genuine. Take the example of a Circuit City store that was going out of business and having a "liquidation sale" for a "limited time." Instead of lowering the prices on products, the company charged with orchestrating the liquidation of the store's inventory actually *raised* prices (Glass, 2009)! Many unsuspecting customers who hadn't done their homework flocked to the store and bought up electronics for more than they might have paid online or at a different vendor.

Mindlessness

A final way that we can sometimes get people to comply with requests that they might not otherwise do is to take advantage of the fact that we often go about our daily lives operating on autopilot. Think back to our discussion of schemas and how they affect behavior (see chapter 5), and you'll recall that situations bring to mind certain standard scripts of what to do and say. Once these scripts are set in motion, we sometimes fail to stop and think whether what we are actually doing seems reasonable. Imagine you are standing in line at the automated teller machine when someone approaches and wants to cut in line. Presumably, you would be more likely to comply with this request if she gives a good reason, right? Maybe not.

Ellen Langer and her colleagues did a simple study in which a confederate asked if she could cut in line at a photocopy machine (Langer et al., 1978). When the confederate explained her request by saying that she was in a rush, 94% of people agreed to let her go ahead of them, compared with only 60% when the person gave no reason whatever and simply asked to use the copy machine. But the interesting condition was one where the confederate asked to use the copy machine "because I have to make some copies." On the surface this *sounds* like a reason and probably activated a schematic impression that the requestor had a good reason, but it was really just a statement of what she planned to do. (Why else would someone use a copy machine?) Yet in a fairly mindless way, a full 93% capitulated with this request. In chapter 6, we introduced the idea that such mindlessness can stunt our creativity and lead us to behave and think in a rather rigid way. As we see here, it can also leave us vulnerable to complying with rather meaningless requests.

Of course, some situations evoke a knee-jerk reaction to say no. When a telemarketer calls during dinner, or a panhandler asks for change, our mindlessly scripted response might be to say no and go on about our business. So in these types of situations, compliance can be increased by breaking people free of their mindless response. For example, would you be more likely to give change to a panhandler who: (a) asks for a quarter or (b) asks for 37 cents? Ask almost any economists, and they would say that a rational person would answer (a), because $.25 is less than $.37. But Santos and colleagues (1994) found that when passersby were asked if they could spare any change, only 44% complied. When they were asked for a quarter, 66% complied. But in a surprise result, when they were asked for 37 cents, 75% of people dug in their pockets to fish out their coins.

Why did this last group comply? Because such a specific request breaks some people out of an automatic tendency to say no while also leading them to think there must be a good reason that the panhandler needs this exact amount. In fact, follow-up studies replicated this effect and found that the 37-cents condition was the only one in which some people asked the panhandler why he needed the money. Furthermore, the especially high compliance rate occurred only among those people who asked why. Interestingly, it didn't matter whether the reason the panhandler provided was a good one or not (Burger et al., 2007).

How often do you give money to panhandlers on the street? Would it make a difference if instead of asking for $1.00, a panhandler asked for $1.17?

[Spencer Platt/Getty Images]

In a related set of studies, the use of unusual phrasing for amounts of money (300 pennies as opposed to 3 dollars) was most effective at increasing sales when it was followed by an assertion of what a bargain that was (Davis & Knowles, 1999). The odd amount breaks down people's resistance and opens them up to the suggestion that they've been offered a good deal. The next time you are hoping to borrow money from your roommate, you might want to remember these little tricks—but don't tell your roommate where you got the tricks!

SECTION review | Compliance: The Art and Science of Getting What You Want

The study of compliance has revealed a toolkit of methods to get people to do what you want them to do.

The foot-in-the-door effect and lowballing	Reciprocity and social proof	Scarcity	Mindlessness
• People are more likely to comply with a moderate request after complying with a smaller one. • People find it hard to break a deal even if they learn later of an extra cost, because of the norm to honor commitments.	• People are likely to reciprocate favors and concessions from others. • Reciprocity contributes to the door-in-the-face effect of agreeing to a moderate request after refusing a larger one. • People often choose behaviors that conform with what respected others are doing.	• People value what is scarce.	• People may comply out of mindlessness. • When a mindless tendency to refuse is interrupted, people may comply more because they become open to suggestion.

Obedience to Authority

Obedience Any action engaged in to fulfill the direct order or command of another person.

The next set of classic studies concerns obedience—doing what someone else tells you to do. This research focuses on how obedience is sometimes behavior with much more serious consequences than being taken in by a slick roommate or an infomercial. Unlike the pressure of conformity, which can often be rather subtle, the pressure to obey is very direct and explicit. And unlike compliance techniques, which involve requests, obedience involves commands. Yet like conformity and compliance, it is a very common form of social influence. It is so common because we live in societies that have a hierarchical structuring of power (Milgram, 1974). Some people, by the nature of their roles within the culture, are given the legitimate authority to tell other people what to do in particular contexts. In families, parents have authority over children; in the classroom, teachers have authority over students; in airplanes, pilots have authority over passengers; in the army, sergeants have authority over privates; and so forth. We often even obey people who are not necessarily of higher social status, such as ushers in theaters. And generally in our society such obedience is encouraged. It is deemed good when children obey their parents, students obey their teachers, employees obey their bosses, patients obey their doctors, and citizens obey the police. But in all too many historical instances, obeying authority has led people to do great harm to themselves or others. The most dramatic example was the Nazi Holocaust, the catastrophe that inspired the seminal research on obedience.

Like many social scientists back in the early 1960s, Stanley Milgram wondered about the obedience displayed by the German people during the Nazi era. How did the demented Nazi ideology and the brutality and genocide it spawned come to be embraced by an entire nation? It is not hard to imagine that Adolf Hitler was a very

Obedience Video on LaunchPad

disturbed, hateful, narcissistic man because of some combination of genetic predispositions, childhood upbringing, and stressful life experiences. We might conclude the same of his closest Nazi allies. But how could the majority of an entire large nation participate in such egregious atrocities? Could millions of people be that deranged or evil?

Milgram did not think that Germany was filled with evildoers, but he did think that perhaps the German people were particularly prone to obedience because they were raised in an unquestioning environment that encouraged obedience to authorities. He speculated that living in this *authoritarian* society might have led citizens down the tragic path of war, genocide, and national disgrace. To understand this mass obedience, Milgram developed a laboratory situation to test people's willingness to harm another just because an authority figure told them to do so. Because of the astounding, surprising nature of the findings, these studies have become the best-known, most widely taught research produced by social psychology: the Milgram obedience studies. We refer to this research as a set of studies rather than a set of experiments because Milgram actually did not manipulate an independent variable or randomly assign participants to conditions. Rather he conducted a series of 18 demonstrations that revealed something very fundamental about human nature—something that, before this research was conducted, no one had fully realized.

In his first study, conducted at Yale University, Milgram (1963) recruited 40 ordinary men, ranging in age from 20 to 50, from the New Haven, Connecticut area to participate in a study of learning. When each man arrived at the lab, he received $4.50 and was told it was for coming to the experiment and was his no matter what happened from that point on. He and another apparent participant were greeted by an experimenter who explained that the study concerned the effects of punishment on learning. However, the apparent participant was actually a confederate working with the experimenter. The participant and the confederate chose slips of paper, ostensibly to determine randomly who would be assigned to be the teacher and who would be assigned to be the learner. This drawing was actually rigged so that the participant would always be the teacher.

The learner was then strapped into a chair and an electrode was attached to his wrist. The experimenter explained that the electrode was attached to a shock generator in the next room. The teacher's task was to read pairs of words to the learner and then test whether the learner could remember which words were paired together by choosing the correct paired word from four possible words. The learner would choose his answer by pressing one of four switches in front of him; his responses would be indicated by a light in an answer box in the adjacent room (see **FIGURE 7.7a**). The participant was then escorted into that room, which housed the shock generator and the answer box. The generator had 30 switches, labeled from 15 to 450 volts from left to right, in 15 volt increments (see **FIGURE 7.7b**). The switches for voltage levels above 180 were labeled "Very Strong Shock"; those above 240 were labeled "Intense Shock"; those above 300 were labeled "Extreme Intensity Shock"; and those above 360 were labeled "Danger: Severe Shock."

The participant was instructed to read the word pairs and then test the learner for each word pair. Whenever the learner made an error, the participant was to give a shock to the learner. With each error, he was to increase the voltage of the shock by 15 volts. Thus, the participant would administer a 15-volt shock for the first error, a 30-volt shock for the second error, a 45-volt shock for the third error, and so forth. The participant was given a sample shock of 45 volts to convince him that the shock generator was real. What the participant didn't know was that the shock generator was not connected to the electrode attached to the learner's wrist. How long the participant would continue administering escalating levels of shock before refusing to continue was the indicator of level of obedience.

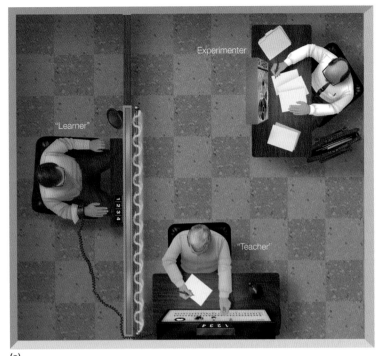

(a)

(b)

Figure 7.7

Milgram's Obedience Studies

The drawing on the left depicts the setup in one variant of Milgram's studies. Here the learner is in a private room while the teacher sits in a room with the shock generator (right) and the experimenter.

[(b) Stanley and Alexandra Milgram]

As the study proceeded, the learner used a predetermined set of three wrong answers to every correct one. In this initial study, the learner was silent when the shocks were administered, but if the participant continued to the point of delivering 300 volts, the learner pounded on the wall. In subsequent variations of the study, starting with Study 2 of the series, the learner grunted, complained, and screamed as the shocks escalated, but these reactions did not affect the level of obedience exhibited by the participants. After the 300-volt shock, the participant was confronted with silence as the learner no longer provided any answers. At this point, participants usually asked the experimenter for guidance. The experimenter told them to treat no responses after 10 seconds as a wrong answer and to continue with the appropriate level of shock. If the participant expressed unwillingness to continue, the experimenter used a set of four verbal prompts ranging from "Please continue" to "You have no other choice, you must continue." But, of course, the point is that participants *did* have a choice: Should they obey these commands, given by respected researchers at Yale University? Or should they refuse and perhaps ruin the experiment but save the learner from additional pain?

Think
ABOUT

[Claes Torstensson/Getty Images]

How do you think you would respond if you were the teacher in this study? What about other people? What percentage of participants do you think would go along with administering what they believed to be even the most dangerous shocks? Take a moment to think about it.

Milgram asked Yale senior psychology majors, graduate students, faculty, and psychiatrists to predict whether they would continue obeying all the way to 450 volts (about four times the voltage of a standard electrical outlet). He also asked people from these same groups to predict the percentage of participants in the study who would. No one predicted that they would do so themselves, and each of these groups predicted that fewer than 2% of participants would obey fully by continuing to administer shocks until the maximum voltage was reached.

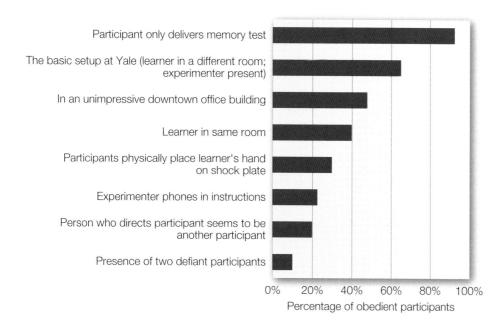

Participant only delivers memory test

The basic setup at Yale (learner in a different room; experimenter present)

In an unimpressive downtown office building

Learner in same room

Participants physically place learner's hand on shock plate

Experimenter phones in instructions

Person who directs participant seems to be another participant

Presence of two defiant participants

0%   20%   40%   60%   80%   100%
Percentage of obedient participants

Figure 7.8

Factors Affecting Obedience

Distance and legitimacy are two important factors that influence obedience. When the "teacher" is more removed from the "learner," the rate of obedience is higher. When the experimenter is more removed from the teacher, the rate of obedience is lower. When the authority is seen as more legitimate, the rate of obedience is higher.

[Data source: Milgram (1974)]

They were quite wrong in their predictions. In fact, 26 of the 40 participants, 65%, obeyed fully to the point of agreeing to deliver a dangerous 450-volt shock to the learner. Furthermore, not a single participant refused to continue until the shock level reached 315 volts. The level of obedience went far beyond what anyone predicted. As Milgram noted, this was a particularly remarkable level of obedience to engage in morally reprehensible actions because, unlike in many real-life situations, the authority figure here (the experimenter) had no real power to enforce his commands, and no significant penalty would be incurred from disobedience.

In subsequent studies, Milgram used the same shock-the-learner paradigm with one or more aspects changed each time (see **FIGURE 7.8** for rates of obedience of some of Milgram's different variations). From this series of follow-up studies, Milgram learned about variables that contributed to the high level of obedience found in the original study. The most important variable was the extent to which the person giving commands was perceived to be a legitimate authority figure. For example, if the study was run in an unimpressive-looking building in downtown New Haven rather than at the prestigious Yale University, full obedience was reduced to 47.5%. If the person directing the real participant to deliver the shocks seemed to be another participant in the study instead of the experimenter (who left, supposedly to take a telephone call), full obedience dropped to 20%.

These findings help explain why so many Germans contributed to the heinous actions during the Nazi era once Hitler became a legitimate authority figure in 1933. However, Milgram (1974) emphasized two points to make it clear that this proclivity to obey authority is a potential danger in any culture and in any era. First, he pointed out that horrific acts are not limited to dictatorships and fascist states. Once in power, duly elected officials in democracies are legitimate authorities who often demand actions that conflict with conscience. Second, he noted that the Nazi era was far from the first or the last time that obedience has led people to engage in egregious, destructive actions:

[T]he destruction of the American Indian population, the internment of Japanese Americans, the use of napalm against civilians in Vietnam, all are harsh policies that originated in the authority of a democratic nation, and were responded to with the expected obedience. . . . [W]hen lecturing . . . I faced young men who were aghast at the behavior of experimental subjects and proclaimed they would never behave in such a way, but who, in a matter of months were brought into the military and performed without compunction actions that made shocking the victim seem pallid. In this respect, they are no better and no worse than human beings of any other era who lend themselves to the purposes of authority and become instruments in its destructive processes. (1974, pp. 179–180)

Other Variables That Play a Role in Obedience

Milgram also examined the role of the physical closeness of the authority figure. If the experimenter phoned in the instructions from a distant location, full obedience was reduced to 22.5%. So the more physically distant the authority figure, the lower the percentage of obedience. This suggests that a salient authority figure will minimize disobedience, something to keep in mind when obedience is a good thing.

In addition, Milgram explored the closeness of the victim. Recall that in the original study, the victim was in a different room and could be heard but not seen. In a variation in which the victim was in the same room, full obedience dropped to 40%. And in another version of the study where participants physically had to place the learner's hand on a shock plate, obedience dropped to 30%. This is a substantial decrease in obedience, but it is also quite remarkable and disturbing that 3 in 10 participants would obey the repeated commands even when doing so meant physically compelling the shock. The plausibility of this particular variation could be called into question, however, because the confederate had to act out receiving the shocks, crying out, screaming, and so forth. Milgram (1974) did not provide enough details for us to assess this potential problem fully.

These and other variation studies indicate that the more psychologically remote the victim, the greater the obedience to doing the victim harm. It is interesting that in modern warfare, most of the killing is done very remotely. In aerial bombing, the soldiers dropping the bombs neither see nor hear their victims. The first aerial bombings occurred during the Spanish Civil War of the 1930s. Ever since then, the highest civilian casualties in war have come from this form of violence, whose victims are physically and psychologically remote.

Milgram also wondered what would happen to the level of obedience if the real participant saw two other supposed participants defy the experimenter. As Asch found with conformity, this seemed to reduce greatly the impact of social influence, because the full obedience level dropped to 10%. Those who disobey make it easier for others to disobey, something the Nazis seemed to understand. A vivid portrayal of their common response to any act of disobedience by those on the way to or in a concentration camp can be seen in the classic film *Schindler's List*: a bullet to the neck.

Thus, psychological distance from the authority, psychological closeness to the victim, and witnessing defiance all reduced obedience. But one important variation led to even more obedience than the original study. In this version, the real participant didn't physically flip the switch on the shock generator. Rather, the real participant delivered the memory test, while another supposed participant dutifully delivered shocks up to 450 volts. In this version, 92.5% of the participants obeyed fully. This is an especially chilling finding. Very few Germans actually pushed Jews and other "undesirables" into the gas chambers or shot them, but many, many people participated in indirect ways, conducting the trains, spreading hatred of Jews and other groups, arresting them, processing paperwork, building the camps, designing mobile gas chambers at the Volkswagen automobile plants, and so on.

We can see from the Milgram research that at least a minority of people will eventually disobey when they feel that their own actions are physically causing harm. But when people contribute to but are not physically causing the harm, virtually all resistance to participating in atrocities sanctioned by authorities seems to vanish. Consistent with this reluctance to be directly responsible for causing sanctioned harm, it is common practice during executions for more than one individual to pull the lever, inject the serum, flip the switch, or take aim and fire. Thus no single individual knows for sure if he or she was actually physically responsible for executing the person condemned to death. The willingness to obey when one is not certain that one is physically causing the actual harm seems virtually limitless.

The lesson here is reminiscent of the oft-quoted adage (attributed to the statesman Edmund Burke), "The only thing necessary for the triumph of evil is for good men to do nothing."

In addition, if the harm is not severe physical pain and won't occur until after the participant leaves the situation, resistance to obedience again is virtually absent. In a series of studies in the Netherlands, when participants were commanded to give negative evaluations of a job applicant's test performance that would result in the applicant's not being hired at a later date, over 90% of the participants obeyed these instructions (Meeus & Raaijmakers, 1995).

Anticipating Your Questions

No doubt you have found this set of studies both fascinating and disturbing. But the studies also may have raised some questions. Let's begin with some simple ones.

Males were used exclusively in the initial set of studies, and they are more likely to engage in extreme acts of violence. Would females show a similar level of obedience? The answer is yes. Milgram's eighth study used only females and found a similar rate of obedience.

What would levels of obedience be in other countries? Although the rate of obedience was actually a bit higher in Germany (85%; Mantell, 1971), levels of obedience similar to those in the United States were observed in a variety of other countries, ranging from relatively individualistic to relatively collectivistic ones (Blass, 2000; Milgram, 1974; Shanab & Yahya, 1978). This suggests that the explanation for obedience does not lie primarily in how authoritarian a culture is but in something about being human.

What is known about who fully obeys and who doesn't? Not much. Researchers have examined a variety of potential personality and demographic differences between the obedient and defiant participants, and most have not distinguished the two groups (Blass, 2000). But some studies have provided relevant insights regarding factors that play a small role. Burger (2009) found that people who are high in empathy for others tended to need a prod sooner than less empathetic people, but they were ultimately just as likely to be fully obedient. There is also some evidence that the defiant participants are lower in authoritarianism. *Authoritarianism* is a broad personality trait that is characterized by a "submissive, uncritical attitude toward idealized moral authorities of the ingroup" (Adorno et al., 1950, p. 228). So a submissive attitude toward authority is associated with greater obedience. Milgram (1974) also reported that more educated people and those higher in moral development were less likely to obey fully.

What about now? The original studies were done during the early 1960s, a time when people perhaps had more faith in science and authority and the civil unrest that characterized the later part of the decade had yet to arise. Would obedience levels be lower now? Well, it turns out that it's hard to answer this question definitively, because institutional review boards now generally do not allow people to use the Milgram paradigm. When Milgram published his initial research, there was quite an uproar over the ethicality of commanding study participants to engage in behaviors that they believed would seriously harm another person (e.g., Baumrind, 1964). Some critics focused on the stress that was imposed on participants; during the task, many displayed signs of stress, such as twitches and nervous laughter. Other critics contended that the most egregious ethical problem was that the study led most participants to discover something about themselves that could harm their self-image: that they were capable of seriously harming another human being simply because they were told to do so.

Milgram responded to these concerns first by noting his elaborate and thorough debriefing procedures. At the conclusion of each session, participants met the learner and saw that he was unharmed. They were fully informed of the study's purpose in examining the powerful effects of the situation on behavior. Milgram also conducted a follow-up study showing that over 83% of participants were glad that they had been in the experiment and fewer than 1% of participants were sorry they had been in it. He also had participants examined by an experienced psychiatrist one year later and found no signs that any of the participants had been harmed by the experience. Milgram and others suggested that the ethical uproar might have been a reaction to the unpleasant implications of the findings rather than to the ethicality of the procedures, and some research supports this claim (Schlenker & Forsyth, 1977). Debate regarding this matter continues.

Think
ABOUT

Replicating the Milgram Studies Video on LaunchPad

What position would you take?

Nonetheless, the American Psychological Association (APA) has judged that the potential harm of this threatening knowledge about the self could not be undone sufficiently, even by the best of debriefings. Thus, the full study cannot be replicated in the United States or other countries that adhere to the APA's judgment. However, Milgram's procedures were replicated in the Netherlands in the early 1990s and showed similarly high levels of obedience (Meeus & Raaijmakers, 1995). Moreover, in 2006, Jerry Burger (2009) obtained permission to replicate Milgram's Study 2, which originally yielded 62.5% full obedience, as long as he had the experimenter stop the study before the participant could flip the switch for 165 volts. In this way, even if the actions of the participants had resulted in actual shocks being delivered, they would not have harmed the learners greatly. Burger also carefully screened potential participants to ensure they were not especially vulnerable to psychological harm and had a trained psychologist on site to provide counseling if needed.

In Burger's voice-feedback variation, the learner began grunting in response to the 75-volt shock; after ostensibly receiving the 150-volt shock, the learner protested that he wanted to quit, was in pain, and was worried about his heart. Burger found that the percentage of participants willing to proceed past the 150-volt level was no different from what it had been over 40 years earlier. And Milgram found that 79% of those who continued past the 150-volt point were fully obedient through 450 volts. So as best we can surmise, the susceptibility to obedience to legitimate authority has not changed.

Why is this willingness to obey a part of human nature? That's a bigger question and we'll address it in the next section.

Why Do We Obey?

Milgram offered some potential answers to the question of why we obey, each of which may have some validity. First, he proposed that we humans may have an innate propensity to obey leaders. He suggested that in situations in which individuals feel that they are in the presence of a legitimate higher authority, they acquire a state of mind in which they view themselves as agents executing the wishes of that authority figure, thereby abdicating personal responsibility for their actions. Our ancestors lived in small groups, and so Milgram posited that groups with a single leader and people willing to do what they are told may have operated more effectively in obtaining food and other resources and defending the group from threats. Thus, a capacity to obey may have been selected for as part of our heritage as group-living animals.

Milgram also noted that a considerable portion of the socialization process involves teaching children to obey first their parents, then teachers, other adults, doctors, police, and a host of other legitimate authority figures within the culture. So we all have been taught to obey legitimate authority figures. And by and large we are rewarded when we do obey and punished, often severely, when we don't. Obedience is the norm in all cultures and becomes a remarkable and negative phenomenon only when authority figures tell us to do things that end up causing great harm.

Besides the innate predispositions and learning experiences we humans share, Milgram also pointed to some specific factors in the paradigm he created that may have contributed to the levels of obedience in his studies. One is the gradual increase in the severity of the actions in which the participants were commanded to engage. Fifteen volts is barely a noticeable tickle, a 30-volt shock is very tolerable, and so on. Thus, one aspect of the process was its gradual nature. Once the participant delivered 30 volts, why not proceed to 45? Once 45, why not 60? And if one has delivered 330 volts, why resist moving on to 345?

Can you think of any theories we have covered which could explain how actions once taken can increase commitment to further actions along similar lines? Recall self-perception theory (chapter 5; also covered earlier in this chapter), which suggests that we infer our attitudes from our own actions, and cognitive dissonance theory (chapter 6), which proposes that people often shift their attitudes to justify their prior actions. Either or both of these theories could help explain why someone who has delivered 315 volt shocks likely would be okay with delivering 330 volts. For both self-perception and dissonance processes to occur, though, people must have some perception of choice. Although the participants in the Milgram studies did have a choice—indeed, some chose not to continue—it is not clear if they had enough *perception* of choice for self-perception and dissonance processes to have contributed to their decision.

However, in real life, perception of choice usually is involved when we act. Self-perception and dissonance processes are likely to be involved in phenomena such as the rise of Nazism in Germany. Imagine being a non-Jewish German during the early 1930s. Perhaps a friend coaxes you into going to a Hitler rally. Once you are there, others greet you with "Heil Hitler." You find yourself following suit. Sometime later, the Nazi propaganda machine exhorts you to boycott Jewish shops. If you support that, why not support the deportation of Jews to concentration camps

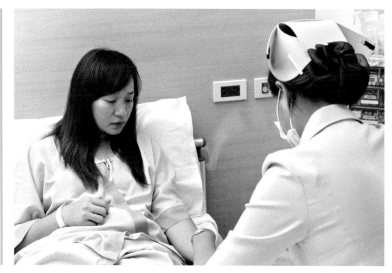

Nursing is one context in which socialization to obedience can occur. In fact, one study found that 21 of 22 nurses who received a phone call from a supposed doctor they did not know would have, without hesitation, administered an excessive level of medication (Hofling et al., 1966). Once obedience becomes routine, it can occur virtually automatically.

[Getty Images/iStockphoto]

where they will have to work for the Third Reich? The point is that historically significant atrocities often start with small acts that escalate to more severe ones over time.

Another aspect of this paradigm that Milgram noted was that, in the studies with the highest levels of obedience, the participants had to tell the authority figure to his face that they refused to continue. Milgram posited that it is very difficult to defy a legitimate authority figure in this manner. Why? Milgram based his explanation on Erving Goffman's analysis of self-presentation (1959). Defying legitimate authorities challenges the definition of the situation and disrupts the working consensus by which we all live. The participants had agreed to take part in the study, and they may have viewed their agreement as a contract they needed to honor. Thus, normative pressures worked to keep the participants on track with obeying the authority. Another, broader way to view the difficulty of defying authority is that legitimate authority figures are valued representatives of the prevailing cultural worldview (Solomon et al., 1991). In fact, the legitimacy of their authoritative position is given to them by the culture. So to defy a scientist running a study, a doctor in an examining room, a police officer who has pulled you over, or a teacher in a classroom is to go against the very worldview on which you predicate your meaningful view of the world and your own self-worth. So for this reason as well, we obey.

The Role of Charisma in the Rise to Power

So now we know that people are likely to obey beyond what our intuitions would lead us to believe. And we know some reasons why people obey. Understanding that humans have a proclivity to obey is one aspect of explaining the historical phenomenon of Nazi Germany. But another major aspect is understanding whom we obey. Obviously we obey people in various authoritative roles whom the culture tells us to obey. One important set of such individuals is the people we view as leaders. But the remaining question regarding the Nazi phenomenon is,

Death in the Voting Booth

Although research has shown that people's awareness of death can influence decisions in hypothetical elections, would reminders of death affect voting in a real political context? Landau and colleagues (2004) proposed that the dramatic spike in support for President George W. Bush and his policies following the deadly terrorist attacks of September 11, 2001 suggested that it would. On September 10, 2001, polls showed Bush's approval rating was at a dismal 49% (Pyszczynski et al., 2003). On September 13, his approval rating soared to 94%. Bush fit the characteristics of a charismatic leader in that he

exuded calm self-confidence and espoused the greatness of America and the importance of vanquishing "evil-doers." Landau and colleagues posited that the attacks heightened Americans' awareness of death on a mass scale and that people sought to avoid death-related fears by supporting Bush's message of triumphing over evil and insuring America's legacy. To assess the role of mortality threat in support for Bush, in a series of studies, Landau and colleagues examined whether reminders of death or reminders of the 9/11 attacks would increase Americans' support for President Bush and his political policies prior to the 2004 presidential election. This was exactly what they found. Moreover, these effects of mortality salience and 9/11 reminders were found among both liberal and conservative Americans, indicating that Bush's charismatic leadership quelled death concerns for Americans regardless of their political orientation.

How in the world did someone as vile as Adolf Hitler become the revered leader of Germany?

The existential perspective provides some answers. According to Ernest Becker (1973) and the terror management theory (e.g., Greenberg et al., 2008), new leaders emerge when the prevailing worldview of a culture no longer provides its members with compelling bases of meaning and self-worth. In this context, people need a more secure belief system that provides them with a sense of enduring significance, especially if death-related concerns are heightened by prevailing political or economic factors. In such circumstances, an individual who takes bold action and who very confidently espouses an alternative worldview that does seem to offer a better basis of meaning and self-worth can gain followers. A worldview that portrays the ingroup as representing the greater good and as on a heroic mission to vanquish evil is particularly suited to providing such a sense of purpose and enduring significance. A leader who exhibits these attributes—boldness, self-confidence, and a vision that inspires and meets the psychological needs of followers—is known as a **charismatic leader**.

Charismatic leader An individual in a leadership role who exhibits boldness and self-confidence and emphasizes the greatness of the ingroup.

APPLICATION

Historical Perspectives

This terror management analysis seems to fit many historical instances in which charismatic leaders, including Hitler, emerge and rise to great power. Germany was humiliated and economically devastated by the loss of World War I and the signing of the very disadvantageous Treaty of Versailles in 1919. In the wake of all these events, it did not feel good to be a German. During the early 1920s, Hitler began his crusade to oust the ruling government and rid Germany of what he called the impure evil others—Jews, communists, homosexuals, and other supposedly inferior peoples. After a bold but failed attempt to overthrow the government by violence, Hitler was tried for treason. He became a well-known figure as he confidently and eloquently attacked the government during his well-publicized trial. He was given a relatively light prison sentence despite his treasonous actions. While in prison he

In a follow-up study, Landau and colleagues posited that making mortality salient to Americans would not afford the same benefit to John Kerry, Bush's opponent in the upcoming 2004 election. Kerry did not have Bush's calm demeanor, did not emphasize the need to triumph over evil, and was painted by well-publicized political ads prior to the election as an untrustworthy waffler who continually changed his positions. Thus, Landau and colleagues predicted that whereas mortality salience would increase the appeal of Bush, it would decrease the appeal of Kerry. In a study conducted just one month prior to the election, this is precisely what happened (see **FIGURE 7.9**). This research suggests that the many reminders of the attacks of 9/11 and threats of additional terrorist attacks leading up to the election, including a video of Osama Bin Laden shown on television just one day before the polls opened, may have tipped the scales in favor of Bush, who, as you may recall, won a second term as U.S. president.

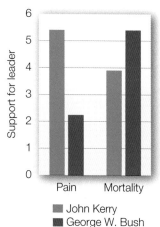

Figure 7.9

The Effects of Mortality Salience on Liking for the 2004 Presidential Candidates

Reminders of mortality increased support, and intentions to vote for George W. Bush; however, they had the opposite effect for Senator John Kerry.

[Data source: Landau et al. (2004)]

wrote *Mein Kampf* ("My Struggle"), a book in which he outlined his worldview, one which espoused the superiority of the Aryan people and his desire to lead Germany back to greatness. When he got out of prison, he organized the National Socialist Party and began gaining followers in an atmosphere of fears of economic and political instability. When Germany experienced a severe economic depression following the stock market crash of 1929, Hitler's message began to gain considerable ground. In 1933, the former fringe figure was elected chancellor as part of a coalition government. Once in office, he seized total power. The rest was a very tragic chapter in human history.

Similar contributing factors have been observed in the rise of admired leaders as well as vilified ones. For example, the Indian leader Mohandas K. ("Mahatma") Ghandi engaged in acts of nonviolent resistance and espoused a philosophy of national empowerment in his early efforts to free India from subjugation to Great Britain. He became the leader of this large nation during its process of liberation from British control without formal election to any official government position. Similar analyses can be applied to the emergence of leaders of small cults, such as the Reverend Jim Jones, and the leaders of large cults, such as the Reverend Sun Yung Moon, as well as many other religious and political leaders.

Of course, all of these historical phenomena are complex and involve many potential causal factors that are difficult to disentangle. However, social psychologists have studied the terror management analysis of the emergence of charismatic leaders by testing whether reminders of mortality increase the appeal of charismatic leaders. In a study by Cohen and colleagues (2004), half the participants were led to think about their own deaths. The other half were primed with another aversive topic, an upcoming exam. Participants then read campaign statements purportedly written by three political candidates in a hypothetical gubernatorial election. On the basis of research on leadership styles (Ehrhart & Klein, 2001), each candidate was modeled to fit the profile of either a charismatic, task-oriented, or relationship-oriented leader. The charismatic leader was bold, self-confident, and visionary, promising citizens, "You are not just an ordinary citizen, you are part of a special state and a special nation, and if we work together we can make a difference." The task-oriented candidate emphasized effectiveness at solving practical problems. The relationship-oriented candidate promised to promote positive relationships and portrayed everyone as an equal contributor to a better future for the state. Finally, participants were asked how much they admired each leader and which of the three leaders they would vote for.

Figure 7.10

The Effects of Mortality Salience and Leader Characteristics on Liking for a Leader

When reminded of mortality, participants' attitudes become much more favorable to a charismatic candidate for governor who promotes the greatness of the state.

[Data source: Cohen et al. (2004)]

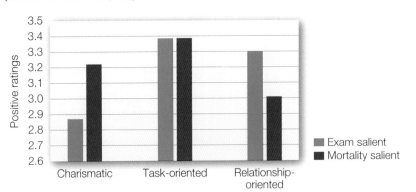

Looking at **FIGURE 7.10**, you can see that after people thought about an upcoming exam, their attitudes toward the charismatic leader were less favorable than to the other two leaders. However, after people thought about their own deaths, they were significantly more attracted to the charismatic leader. This effect was also reflected in their voting intentions. Whereas exam-primed participants gave the charismatic leader a paltry four votes (out of 94), death-primed participants gave the charismatic leader a third of the votes, significantly more. These results support the terror management analysis by showing that when people are led to think about their own deaths, rather than just any negative topic, they are especially attracted to a charismatic leader who boldly espouses the greatness of the group.

SECTION review | Obedience to Authority

In Milgram's studies, the level of obedience went far beyond what anyone predicted and made it clear that the proclivity to obey authority is a potential danger in any culture and in any era.

Variables that influence obedience	Who obeys	We obey because:	The role of charisma
• Psychological distance from the authority. • Psychological closeness to the victim. • Witnessing defiance. • Not personally causing the harm.	• Obedience does not vary according to sex or nationality. • Obedience is influenced by whether or not the participant has a submissive attitude. • More recent research suggests rates of obedience have not changed.	• We evolved a propensity to follow those in power. • We are socialized to obey authority. • Small acts may escalate such that once an action is begun, we gradually become more and more committed to continuing. • It is difficult to defy a legitimate authority.	• When the prevailing worldview no longer provides members of society with compelling bases of meaning and self-worth, charismatic leaders are likely to gain followers. • Reminders of mortality increase the appeal of charismatic leaders.

CONNECT ONLINE:

Check out our videos and additional resources located at:
www.macmillanhighered.com/launchpad/greenberg1e

WOMEN
WHERE
MAXIMUM
PERFORMANCE
LIVES
on the verge of a
NERVOUS
MEMPHIS
MUSICAL
maxell
maxell.com
LINCOLN CENTER
YOU ALREADY
KNOW
YOU'RE GONNA

Persuasion, Attitudes, and Behavior

TOPIC OVERVIEW

Having looked at some basic ways that people influence other people's behavior, let's consider a direct form of social influence called **persuasion**, referring to the ways in which people try to change someone else's mind by changing his or her attitudes. **Attitudes** are evaluations of social stimuli that range from positive to negative. People can have attitudes about pretty much anything in their social world, ranging from consumer products (e.g., air freshener) to people (e.g., themselves, presidential candidates), to social issues (e.g., global warming).

Why are people interested in persuading others? People's attitudes toward something often predict how they intend to behave toward that thing (though not always, as we'll see later on). If you have a positive attitude toward Brand X computers, for instance, then you're more likely to purchase Brand X computers than if you have a negative attitude. Thus, the goal of persuasion is to change attitudes in the hope of eventually changing behavior.

Efforts to persuade are all around us. We are exposed to them on a daily, if not an hourly, basis. Any time a person turns on the television, listens to a streaming

Persuasion Intentional effort to change other people's attitudes in order to change their behavior.

Attitude Evaluation of a stimulus; can range from positive to negative.

music station, watches a movie, surfs the Net, or browses a magazine, advertisers rush to persuade that person to prefer certain products and services. Here's an informal demonstration: In the 10 minutes it took your current author to walk to the Student Union this morning, he recorded 43 commercial messages posted on T-shirts, posters, packages, and even across people's buttocks! In fact, the president of one marketing firm suggested that whereas the average American was exposed to about 500 advertisements a day in the 1970s, today that number is closer to 5,000 (Johnson, 2009).

Everyday examples of persuasion go far beyond the commercial realm. They appear in every corner of social life, from romantic relationships to international politics. To mention just a few, teachers, writers, and filmmakers try to persuade us of particular moral messages or values about life. Our friends and other significant others may try to persuade us to eat at a new restaurant or change the way we treat someone. Psychotherapists try to get us to view aspects of ourselves and our worlds differently. Doctors try to get us to change our attitudes and behaviors toward more healthy lifestyles. Attorneys in courtrooms try to persuade judges and juries to be more favorable to their preferred positions or clients. Parents try to persuade their kids to have the right attitudes and engage in the right behaviors, whereas the kids attempt to persuade their parents to buy toys and gaming systems. On first dates, each person tries to persuade the other that he or she is attractive and relationship worthy.

As these examples convey, persuasion can have a substantial impact on people's lives. Sometimes it can change their attitudes and behaviors in ways that benefit themselves and others. For example, in 2010 an earthquake utterly destroyed Port au Prince, the capital of Haiti. News of the tragedy and donation opportunities were widely circulated on pop-up ads, social networking sites, and cell phones. As a result, millions of people donated their hard-earned money to help strangers who survived the earthquake, giving more money through private and corporate donations than any individual nation's government and even more than the World Bank emergency grant (Evans, 2010).

The flip side of the same coin, however, is that persuasion can also produce harmful changes in attitudes and behavior. For example, it often leads people to make decisions that simply don't make sense in light of the facts. Consider this: You might expect a health-conscious person deciding on a breakfast cereal to choose Kellogg's Raisin Bran over a new Scooby-Doo themed cereal probably because she associates bran with all-natural nutrition. But her attitudes toward those cereals certainly didn't come from a close examination of the nutritional data (presented in **FIGURE 8.1**), which clearly show that one cup of Raisin Bran has more calories and sugar, and less of some important vitamins, than a full cup of the Scooby-Doo cereal. Most likely her attitudes toward the cereals were created by years of commercial messages strategically designed to equate the *idea* of bran with wholesome grains and a simple, healthy lifestyle.

Because persuasion is so pervasive in everyday life, and has important consequences for people's well-being, social psychologists have focused their research on discovering what makes some attempts at persuasion more effective than others in changing attitudes. It's to this research that we now turn.

Kellogg's® Scooby-Doo!™ Cereal

Nutrition Facts
Serving Size 1 Cup (32g)

Amount Per Serving	Cereal	with ½ cup skim milk
Calories	120	160
Calories from Fat	10	10

	% Daily Value**	
Total Fat 1.5g*	**2%**	**2%**
Saturated Fat 0g	**0%**	**0%**
Trans Fat 0g		
Polyunsaturated Fat 0.5g		
Monounsaturated Fat 0.5g		
Cholesterol 0mg	**0%**	**0%**
Sodium 110mg	**5%**	**8%**
Potassium 95mg	**3%**	**8%**
Total Carbohydrate 27g	**9%**	**11%**
Dietary Fiber 3g	**13%**	**13%**
Sugars 6g		
Protein 3g		

Vitamin A	10%	15%
Vitamin C	25%	25%
Calcium	0%	15%
Iron	50%	50%
Vitamin D	10%	25%
Thiamin	25%	30%
Riboflavin	25%	35%
Niacin	25%	25%
Vitamin B$_6$	25%	25%
Folic Acid	50%	50%
Vitamin B$_{12}$	25%	35%
Zinc	10%	15%

* Amount in cereal. One half cup of skim milk contributes an additional 40 calories, 65mg sodium, 6g total carbohydrates (6g sugars), and 4g protein.

**Percent Daily Values are based on a 2,000 calorie diet. Your daily values may be higher or lower depending on your calorie needs:

	Calories	2,000	2,500
Total Fat	Less than	65g	80g
Sat. Fat	Less than	20g	25g
Cholesterol	Less than	300mg	300mg
Sodium	Less than	2,400mg	2,400mg
Potassium		3,500mg	3,500mg
Total Carbohydrate		300g	375g
Dietary Fiber		25g	30g

Ingredients: Whole grain yellow corn flour, whole wheat flour, sugar, whole grain oat flour, contains 2% or less of oat fiber, canola oil, salt, caramel color, natural and artificial flavor, annatto color, BHT for freshness.

Vitamins and Minerals: Vitamin C (ascorbic acid), reduced iron, niacinamide, zinc oxide, vitamin B$_6$ (pyridoxine hydrochloride), vitamin B$_2$ (riboflavin), vitamin B$_1$ (thiamin hydrochloride), vitamin A palmitate, folic acid, vitamin D, vitamin B$_{12}$.

CONTAINS WHEAT INGREDIENTS.

Kellogg's Raisin Bran®

Nutrition Facts
Serving Size 1 Cup (59g)

Amount Per Serving	Cereal	with ½ cup skim milk
Calories	190	230
Calories from Fat	10	10

	% Daily Value**	
Total Fat 1g*	**2%**	**2%**
Saturated Fat 0g	**0%**	**0%**
Trans Fat 0g		
Polyunsaturated Fat 0g		
Monounsaturated Fat 0g		
Cholesterol 0mg	**0%**	**0%**
Sodium 210mg	**9%**	**12%**
Potassium 390mg	**11%**	**17%**
Total Carbohydrate 46g	**15%**	**17%**
Dietary Fiber 7g	**28%**	**28%**
Sugars 18g		
Protein 5g		

Vitamin A	10%	15%
Vitamin C	0%	0%
Calcium	2%	15%
Iron	25%	25%
Vitamin D	10%	25%
Thiamin	25%	30%
Riboflavin	25%	35%
Niacin	25%	25%
Vitamin B$_6$	25%	25%
Folic Acid	25%	25%
Vitamin B$_{12}$	25%	35%
Phosphorus	20%	30%
Magnesium	20%	25%
Zinc	10%	15%

* Amount in cereal. One half cup of skim milk contributes an additional 40 calories, 65mg sodium, 6g total carbohydrates (6g sugars), and 4g protein.

**Percent Daily Values are based on a 2,000 calorie diet. Your daily values may be higher or lower depending on your calorie needs:

	Calories	2,000	2,500
Total Fat	Less than	65g	80g
Sat. Fat	Less than	20g	25g
Cholesterol	Less than	300mg	300mg
Sodium	Less than	2,400mg	2,400mg
Potassium		3,500mg	3,500mg
Total Carbohydrate		300g	375g
Dietary Fiber		25g	30g

Ingredients: Whole grain wheat, raisins, wheat bran, sugar, brown sugar syrup, contains 2% or less of salt, malt flavor.

Vitamins and Minerals: Potassium chloride, niacinamide, reduced iron, vitamin B$_6$ (pyridoxine hydrochloride), zinc oxide, vitamin B$_2$ (riboflavin), vitamin B$_1$ (thiamin hydrochloride), vitamin A palmitate, folic acid, vitamin D, vitamin B$_{12}$.

CONTAINS WHEAT INGREDIENTS.

Figure 8.1

Making the Healthy Choice

Looking at these two cereal boxes, which would you expect to be healthier? Take a closer look at the nutritional information, and you might never again judge a cereal by its name alone.

Elaboration Likelihood Model: Central and Peripheral Routes to Persuasion

In earlier chapters we made the point that people often are unwilling or unable to think deeply about every decision they make and every piece of information they encounter. As a result, they sometimes engage in controlled, deliberate thinking. At other times, they think in a more automatic and superficial manner. (For a refresher on this fundamental principle, see the section "Dual Process Theories"

Elaboration likelihood model
A theory of persuasion that proposes that persuasive messages can influence attitudes by two different routes, central or peripheral.

Central route to persuasion
A style of processing a persuasive message by a person who has both the ability and the motivation to think carefully about the message's argument. Attitude change depends on the strength of the argument.

Argument The true merits of the person, object, or position being advocated in the message.

Peripheral route to persuasion
A style of processing a persuasive message by a person who is not willing or able to put effort into thinking carefully about the message's argument. Attitude change depends on the presence of peripheral cues.

Peripheral cues Aspects of the communication that are irrelevant (that is, *peripheral*) to the true merits of the person, object, or position advocated in the message (e.g., a speaker's physical attractiveness when attractiveness is irrelevant to the position).

in chapter 3.) The elaboration likelihood model (Petty & Cacioppo, 1986), or ELM, is a theory of persuasion that builds on this distinction. This theory proposes that persuasive messages can influence attitudes in two different ways, or *routes*. Which route a person takes depends on his or her motivation and ability to elaborate on—or think carefully about—the information to which he or she is exposed.

People follow the central route to persuasion when they think carefully about the information that is pertinent, or *central*, to the true merits of the person, object, or position being advocated in the message. This information is referred to as the argument. For example, people who follow the central route while listening to a political candidate's speech will attend closely to the candidate's arguments concerning why he or she will make a good leader and they will consider whether those arguments are factual and cogent. Thus, when people follow the central route, their attitudes are influenced primarily by the strength of the argument. Strong arguments will change attitudes; weak arguments will not.

In contrast, people follow the peripheral route to persuasion when they are not willing or able to put effort into thinking carefully about the argument. In these cases, people's attitudes are influenced primarily by peripheral cues, which are aspects of the communication that are irrelevant (that is, *peripheral*) to the true merits of the person, object, or position advocated in the message. For example, people following the peripheral route while listening to a candidate's speech are not thinking carefully about the candidate's arguments. Instead, they might focus on the candidate's physical attractiveness or the smiling faces of the school children standing behind the candidate. People taking the peripheral route also tend to base their attitudes on *heuristics*—mental short cuts such as, "If a person speaks for a long time, then they must have a valid point" (see chapter 3) (Chaiken, 1987).

Note that whether people follow the central route or the peripheral route does not necessarily lead them to have more positive or more negative attitudes. In our example, a person who is diligently considering the candidate's arguments, and another person who is wowed by the surrounding pageantry, both may report the same increase or decrease in liking for the candidate. Rather, which route people follow determines which aspects of the persuasive message have the strongest influence on their attitudes. (**FIGURE 8.2** presents a summary of the two routes to persuasion.)

Why do people take one or the other route? According to the ELM, the key factors are the individual's motivation and ability to think deeply about the message. When motivation and ability to process the message are high, the person will usually take the central route. But when the person lacks either the motivation or the ability to process the message, he or she will be more likely to take the peripheral route. Next we'll look at research testing these hypotheses.

Motivation to Think

It makes sense that the more relevant a message is to a person's goals and interests, the more effort he or she will devote to thinking deeply about the message. Imagine, for example, that Jill is watching a commercial for Brand X computers. Because she relies on her laptop a lot and is in the market for a new one, this message is pertinent to Jill's goals. We would therefore expect Jill to concentrate on the commercial's *argument* and think critically about its claims ("They say this model has a big hard drive, but do I really need that?"). Bill, on the other hand, is not really into computers, and so he will be less motivated to consider the pros and cons of the advertised brand. Instead, Bill will likely take the peripheral route and base his

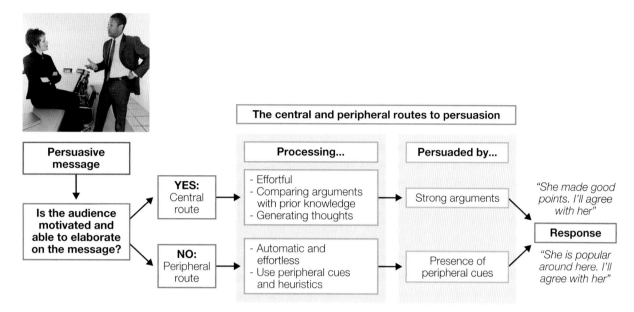

The central and peripheral routes to persuasion

Persuasive message		Processing...	Persuaded by...	

Is the audience motivated and able to elaborate on the message?

YES: Central route → - Effortful - Comparing arguments with prior knowledge - Generating thoughts → Strong arguments → *"She made good points. I'll agree with her"*

Response

NO: Peripheral route → - Automatic and effortless - Use peripheral cues and heuristics → Presence of peripheral cues → *"She is popular around here. I'll agree with her"*

Figure 8.2

The Elaboration Likelihood Model

The central and peripheral routes represent two distinct pathways of persuasion.

[Digital Vision/Getty Images]

attitudes toward Brand X on the presence of peripheral cues such as a catchy jingle or a sexy spokesperson.

An influential study by Rich Petty and colleagues (1983) demonstrates that a message's relevance to people's goals determines which persuasion route they take. Participants were asked to take part in a study on consumer attitudes. They were told that, as a reward for participating, they would be able to choose a product from among a few different brands at the end of the study. Some participants were told that they could choose from among different brands of razor blades; others were told that they could choose from among brands of toothpaste. Later, when all participants were asked to flip through some ads, they came upon an ad for Edge razor blades. You can imagine that this ad was relevant for participants expecting to choose a brand of razor blades but not for those expecting to choose a toothpaste brand.

The researchers introduced two other variables. First, half the participants read strong arguments for the Edge razor's quality, such as "Special chemically formulated coating eliminates nicks and cuts and prevents rusting." The other half read weak arguments, such as "Designed with the bathroom in mind." Second, one version of the ad featured an attractive celebrity endorsing the Edge razor, whereas the other version featured anonymous, average-looking people endorsing it.

What influenced participants' attitudes toward the Edge razor? When participants expected to choose a razor later on—that is, when the Edge ad was relevant to their decision—the most influential factor was the strength of the ad's arguments for the Edge brand's quality. If the arguments were weak, participants disliked the Edge razor; if the arguments were strong, they liked it. But a very different picture emerged among the participants who did not expect to choose a razor—that is, those to whom the ad was not relevant. They were *not* influenced by whether the ad's arguments were strong or weak. Instead, their attitudes were influenced by the spokesperson: They liked the Edge brand if it was endorsed by an attractive celebrity spokesperson, but not when it was endorsed by the Average Joe. Note, though, that among people who were motivated to think carefully about the message, the attractiveness of the spokesperson did not influence attitudes: People taking the central route to persuasion are not impressed by those kinds of peripheral cues.

Ability to Think

Let's revisit Jill, who is processing a commercial advertising Brand X computers. We mentioned that, other things being equal, Jill will be motivated to think about the commercial's central arguments because they are relevant to her goal of purchasing a new computer. But of course things are not always equal: Perhaps Jill is watching the commercial while she is hungry, hung over, or bombarded with the sounds of a nearby construction site. According to the ELM, even if people are motivated to think carefully about a message, they may be unable to do so because of distractions and other demands on their attention. Under these conditions, people will tend to take the peripheral route to persuasion.

This is demonstrated in another study by Petty and colleagues (1976). Participants listened to a recorded message arguing that the tuition at their university should be cut in half. Participants heard either strong arguments in favor of the tuition cut (such as "The currently high tuition prevents high school students from going to college") or weak arguments ("Cutting tuition would lead to increased class size"). While they listened to the message, participants repeatedly were asked to record the location of an "X" which appeared at various spots on a screen in front of them. For some participants, the Xs flashed every 15 seconds. You can imagine this would be mildly distracting. But other participants had to identify the X every 5 seconds—very distracting. As you can see in **FIGURE 8.3**, there was an interesting interaction between argument strength and level of distraction: Participants who were mildly distracted agreed with the tuition cut if they heard strong arguments for it, but not if they heard weak arguments. But participants who were highly distracted saw the tuition cut as a good idea regardless of whether the arguments in favor of it were strong or weak. With all those Xs to attend to, they were unable to discriminate between strong arguments and weak arguments.

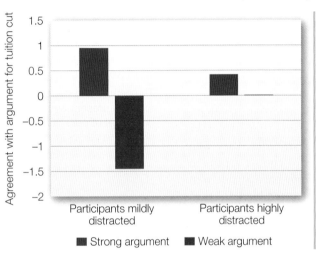

Figure 8.3

The Effects of Distraction on Persuasion

In this study, people who were only mildly distracted were persuaded through the central route; they agreed more with a planned tuition cut if the arguments they heard were strong and disagreed with it if the arguments were weak. But being highly distracted switched them to the peripheral route, and their agreement with the proposal was unaffected by the strength of the argument.

[Data source: Petty et al. (1976)]

Why It Matters

Why does it matter which route people take if either one can lead them to change their attitudes? Compared with attitudes formed through the peripheral route, attitudes formed through the central route are stronger—more durable and resistant to contrary information and more likely to determine how people behave (Petty & Cacioppo, 1986). Think about it: If you form an attitude through the central route, you are elaborating on the arguments relevant to the issue, rehearsing them in your head, and considering them in light of other evidence. The resulting attitude is therefore more likely to be supported by a range of knowledge. That means that the attitude is likely to remain in your memory even if one piece of evidence in support of that attitude is forgotten or contradicted by other evidence. Attitudes formed through the peripheral route, in contrast, are usually supported by a single, simple association or inference ("My favorite celebrity uses this product, so I do too"), and therefore may decay over time.

Consistent with this reasoning, studies show that attitudes formed through central-route processing do in fact persist longer and exert a more potent influence on behavior (Chaiken, 1980). For example, in one study students were presented with a proposal to require psychology majors to participate in research. (You might recall such experiences from your own Introduction to Psychology class.) Those who formed their attitudes through central-route processing were more likely to sustain those attitudes three weeks later, and moreover, also were more likely to engage in behavior consistent with their attitudes a month later (and actually participate in studies if they had positive attitudes) (Pierro et al., 2012). Thus, attitudes formed through the central and the peripheral routes to persuasion might be equally favorable or unfavorable immediately following a persuasive message, but which route was used influences whether a change in attitude persists over time.

To sum up, following the central or the peripheral route to persuasion orients people toward different aspects of a persuasive message. We've looked at some of those aspects, such as the attractiveness of a celebrity. Next we consider those aspects in more detail, grouping them into three categories: *Who* says *What* to *Whom*. First, we'll see how attitudes are influenced by characteristics of the individual or group communicating the message (the "*Who*," or source). Then we'll look at the characteristics of the message itself (the "*What*"). Finally, we'll *consider characteristics of the person or group receiving the message ("Whom," or the audience)*.

Source The person or group communicating the message.

Audience The person or group receiving the message.

SECTION review | Elaboration Likelihood Model

The elaboration likelihood model proposes that a persuasive message can influence attitudes by two different routes, depending on a person's motivation and ability to think carefully about the message.

Motivation	Ability	Persistence
• When people are motivated to think carefully about the message, they take the central route, basing their attitudes on argument strength. • If people are less motivated, they take the peripheral route, basing their attitudes on peripheral cues.	• When people have the mental resources to think carefully about the message, they take the central route. • If people are cognitively busy, they take the peripheral route.	• Attitude change produced by central-route processing is more durable and resistant to other influences than change produced by peripheral-route processing.

Characteristics of the Source

"What's most important is: what gets the job done. . . . I don't think that the Democratic Party has a monopoly on good ideas. I think that the Republicans have a lot to offer. And what I will do is listen and learn from my Republican colleagues, and any time they can make a case that this is something that would be good for the American people, just because Democrats didn't think of it, and Republicans are promoting it, that's not a good reason not to do it. If somebody presents to me a plan that they are ideologically wedded to, but they can't persuade me that this will actually be good for the economy, then we're not going to do it."

President-elect Barack Obama made this remark when asked about his willingness to incorporate ideas offered by the Republican Party into his plan for improving the American economy (Harwood, 2009). And technically he is correct: Logic suggests that a good argument should be persuasive regardless of who delivers it. Although this view is admirable, messages delivered by likable, attractive, powerful, and famous sources are more often met with approval than the same messages delivered by sources who lack these characteristics (Chaiken, 1979, 1980; French & Raven, 1959; Whittler & Spira, 2002).

President Barack Obama claims that he can be persuaded equally by Democrats and Republicans if the ideas are good. Research on persuasion suggests that it is often not that simple.

[Photothek via Getty Images]

Communicator Credibility

Source credibility The degree to which the audience perceives a message's source as expert and trustworthy.

Messages are especially persuasive when they are delivered by a person (or a group) perceived to have source credibility—that is, someone who is both *expert* and *trustworthy*. Consider a study by Hovland and Weiss (1951). Participants read articles that advocated various positions on different issues. For example, one article advocated that antihistamine drugs should be sold without a doctor's prescription. Half the participants were told the article was from the *New England Journal of Biology and Medicine* (an expert source), whereas the others were told it came from a popular magazine such as those you see in the supermarket (a nonexpert source). As you might expect, participants were more likely to agree with the position advocated in the articles if they thought the articles came from expert sources rather than nonexpert sources (Pornpitakpan, 2004).

Although real expertise can convey strong arguments that persuade people through central-route processing, the *appearance* of expertise often persuades through the peripheral route. For example, a commercial advertising mouthwash may feature a spokesperson wearing a white lab coat and a stethoscope around his neck, giving him the appearance of a medical expert when in reality he is most likely an actor made to look like an expert. A viewer who takes the peripheral route without paying close attention to the substantive claims being made might just assume that the mouthwash is effective because the spokesperson appears to know what he is talking about. Indeed, speakers can appear more credible, and thus be more persuasive, simply by speaking with confidence, quoting statistics, or even just by speaking quickly—none of which necessarily means that they have expert knowledge (Erickson et al., 1978; Miller et al., 1976).

Credibility Video on LaunchPad

The source of a message can also gain credibility by being perceived as trustworthy or unbiased in his or her views. Most of us are aware that other people typically have something to gain from changing our attitudes, and so we often are skeptical about whether they are telling the whole truth and nothing but the truth. In fact, if people are forewarned that another person intends to persuade them about issues they care about, they are less convinced by that person's arguments (Petty & Cacioppo, 1979).

How can the source of a persuasive message come across as trustworthy? One way is to express an opinion without the audience realizing that it is the target of persuasion. Imagine that you overhear some people at a coffee shop praising a new restaurant. You have no reason to believe that these people are biasing their opinions to influence you (they don't even know you're eavesdropping!), and so you might find their opinions more believable. In a study testing this intuition, Walster and Festinger (1962) arranged a situation so that participants were allowed to overhear a conversation between two graduate students in another room. (In actuality, they heard an audio recording.) Some participants were under the impression that the graduate students were aware that they were in the next room, whereas other participants assumed that their presence was unknown to the graduate students. Participants in the second group was more likely to change their attitudes in the direction of the graduate students' opinions, presumably because they had no reason to believe that the graduate students were purposely altering what they said.

After learning about the strategies that advertisers use to market their goods, you are right to be skeptical of some of the claims and endorsements you read or hear.

[Steve Debenport/Getty Images]

The power of overheard messages hasn't been lost on advertisers. Just think of all the commercials you've seen that attempt to portray a private conversation between two people ("Gee, Tyler, your glasses really do sparkle! What dish detergent do you use?"). In fact, advertising and public relations agencies often pay writers to masquerade online as delighted consumers, writing positive reviews of their products or services on various web sites such as Amazon.com (Dellarocas, 2006). The writers are paid to appear like average people, for example by intentionally inserting typos into their reviews. In this way, advertisers hope that the fake reviewers appear trustworthy, and thus persuasive, because the writers do not seem to have a stake in the sale of the product or service.

Another way in which a communicator gains in trustworthiness (and persuasiveness) is if he or she argues in favor of a position that seems to be *opposed* to his or her self-interest. Imagine that you heard a convicted criminal giving a speech advocating more lenient prison sentences. Even if he is making some good arguments, you might not be very persuaded because you know that he personally has something to gain from convincing you of his position. But now imagine that the same criminal is arguing for *stricter* prison sentences. Here you might conclude that, because he has nothing to gain, and perhaps something to lose, by convincing others of his point, he must believe strongly in the truth of his claims. This intuition was put to the test in another study by Walster and colleagues (1966). When participants read a statement by "Joe 'The Shoulder' Napolitano," a habitual criminal and drug dealer, arguing for more lenient court proceedings, they were completely unconvinced: Of course a convict would argue in favor of more lenient courts! But when the same alleged criminal argued for stricter court proceedings, participants were much more likely to agree with his position.

Credibility can be a peripheral cue when people are not elaborating on the persuasive message. It's a handy heuristic simply to decide, "She's an unbiased expert, I'll believe that," or "I'm not buying anything that sleazeball says." However, this kind of peripheral influence of source credibility may not last long. The decay of source effects can happen when over time, people forget the source of the message but remember the message content, a concept known as the **sleeper effect**. Suppose that you scan the front page of a sensationalistic gossip magazine while waiting on the grocery checkout line (come on, we all do it at least occasionally), and it claims that new evidence calls global warming into question. A few weeks later, the topic of global warming comes up in a conversation, and you remark that you read a story arguing that global warming may in fact not be happening, but you can't remember where you read it. Might that argument be more compelling now that you've forgotten that it came from a not-so-credible source?

Hovland and Weiss (1951) found the first evidence of the sleeper effect. Recall the experiment showing that people were more likely to agree with high-credibility sources (e.g., a medical journal) than with low-credibility sources. When the researchers again measured participants' attitudes four weeks after they were first exposed to the arguments, participants who initially had agreed with a position advocated by a high-credibility source showed less agreement, and those who disagreed with a low-

Sleeper effect The phenomenon whereby people can remember a message but forget where it came from; thus, source credibility has a diminishing effect on attitudes over time.

credibility source had come to agree with the position (see **FIGURE 8.4**). Subsequent research has clarified that such sleeper effects are most likely when people learn about the credibility of the source *after* they have been exposed to the arguments (Pratkanis, 2007). When people know in advance that an argument comes from a low-credibility source, they are better able to discount the argument.

Communicator Attractiveness

Your current author recently saw a commercial in which the actor Dennis Haysbert recommended buying insurance from Allstate Insurance Company. In this context, Haysbert is not particularly high in credibility. First, although he may be an expert actor, having appeared in many movies and television series (e.g., he played the president of the United States in the popular TV show *24*), who knows whether or not he has expert knowledge of the relative merits of different insurance companies?

Figure 8.4

The Sleeper Effect

In this study, people were more likely to change their attitude to agree with arguments if the author was an expert and therefore credible. But 4 weeks later, the credibility of the source no longer mattered, and arguments made by less credible sources were equally likely to have changed people's minds.

[Data source: Hovland & Weiss (1951)]

Second, his trustworthiness is in doubt: It is obvious that Allstate is paying him handsomely to appear in these commercials and that he is *trying* to influence us. So why is Haysbert considered an effective spokesman? If you've seen the commercials, you probably know the answer: He just seems like a likeable and straightforward guy. He is handsome and well dressed, and he looks straight at you as he asks you in his authoritative baritone voice whether you are in "good hands." This example suggests that communicators can be persuasive when they are *attractive*, even if their credibility is low.

The most obvious way that a communicator gains in attractiveness is by presenting an attractive physical appearance. Certainly you've noticed how magazines, billboards, and pretty much every other commercial medium features attractive models (some of which are computer-generated images rather than actual people). But does it work? Yes. People are more persuaded by arguments that come from communicators they consider physically attractive, even when the arguments are wholly unrelated to the communicator's attractiveness (Chaiken, 1979; Mills & Aronson, 1965).

When the communicator's attractiveness is irrelevant to the true merits of the position he or she takes, as when a supermodel graces a billboard for an energy drink, it influences the audience's attitudes through the peripheral route. It is important

Think

ABOUT

[MSPhotographic/ Shutterstock]

to note, though, that the communicator's attractiveness also can influence attitudes through the central route when it is an argument for the validity of the message (Shavitt et al., 1994). Consider an attractive, muscled spokesperson for a rather odd-looking exercise machine who says, "If you use the Abdominator for just 20 minutes every day, you will have rock-hard abs like mine." Is the spokesperson's physique relevant information for evaluating whether the exercise machine works? What if the spokesperson was sporting a bit of a belly (perhaps more of a keg than a six-pack)? What reason would you have to believe that the machine works?

Communicator Similarity

If we tend to be persuaded by those who are trustworthy, likeable, and attractive, we must also be more persuaded by people who are similar to us, right? Here the answer is a bit more complicated. In some cases, people are more easily persuaded when the source of a message is similar to themselves. In one study (Mackie et al., 1990), college students were more likely to agree with rather extreme positions (e.g., to discontinue use of the SATs in college admissions) if those positions were endorsed by a student from their own university, but not from another university.

Sometimes, however, people are influenced more by the opinions of *dissimilar* others than those of similar others. The key factor is whether the issue at hand deals primarily with subjective preference or objective facts (Goethals & Nelson, 1973). For issues dealing primarily with subjective preference—that is, when there is no "correct" answer—people are more confident in their attitude when similar others agree with them than when dissimilar others agree with them. So if you believe that Beyoncé is the greatest recording artist alive, agreement from a similar other, such as a close friend, would make you more confident in that attitude than agreement from a dissimilar other, such as a foreign exchange student.

In contrast, when people are trying to determine whether something is objectively true or factual, their attitudes are influenced more by the opinions of dissimilar others than by those of similar others. For instance, if you believe that Beyoncé sold more albums than Rihanna (which is either factually correct or incorrect), agreement from a dissimilar other would make you more confident in that belief than agreement from a similar other. Why? When similar others agree with us on matters of fact, we are often uncertain whether they agree simply because they like us, or perhaps because they have been exposed to the same faulty information that we have been exposed to. But when a dissimilar other who does not have those biases verifies our belief, we assume that the belief must be objectively true. (In case you were wondering, at least when it comes to studio albums, Beyoncé has sold more albums than Rihanna.)

SECTION review | Characteristics of the Source

The power of a message to influence attitudes depends, in part, on *who* is delivering that message, or its source.

Credibility	Attractiveness	Similarity
• Credible communicators are both expert and trustworthy. • Legitimate expertise persuades through the central route. • The *appearance* of expertise persuades through the peripheral route.	Communicators can be persuasive when they are attractive, even if their credibility is low.	• Attitudes about subjective preferences are influenced more by a similar source than by a dissimilar source. • Attitudes about objective facts are more influenced by a dissimilar source.

Characteristics of the Message

Attitudes are influenced not only by the source of the message but also by the content and style of the message itself as it appeals to both our minds and our feelings. Here we consider some characteristics of the message, including approaches you can take to enhance your own ability to persuade.

Thinking Differently: What Changes Our Minds

Argument Strength

Earlier we said that when people take the central route to persuasion, their attitudes are influenced primarily by the strength of the arguments. But what makes an argument strong or weak?

First, to be strong a message needs to be comprehensible. For example, participants in one study were more convinced by arguments arranged in a logical order than they were by the same arguments presented in a jumbled order (Eagly, 1974).

Argument strength is also influenced by the length of the message. If you want to persuade people, should you present them with a long communication that contains lots of arguments, or a short one? There is no simple answer. If the audience takes the central route, message length can either increase and decrease persuasion. On the one hand, a longer message can be more persuasive if it contains many supportive arguments rather than a few (Calder et al., 1974). On the other hand, if you try to increase the length of a message artificially by adding weak arguments or repeating the same arguments, an attentive audience may become irritated at the message and reject it (Cacioppo & Petty, 1979). Also, people's cognitive resources allow them to think about and remember only so many arguments in a given time span. The more arguments you present, the less able the audience is to think about and rehearse those arguments, and the fewer they will remember (Eagly, 1974). As a result, longer messages with arguments of varying quality can be *less* persuasive than messages containing only a few, highly convincing arguments (Anderson, 1974; Harkins & Petty, 1987). Sometimes less is more.

If the audience is taking the peripheral route, longer messages tend to be more persuasive than shorter ones (Petty & Cacioppo, 1984; Wood et al., 1985). Why? Imagine that you are reading a newspaper editorial advocating increasing the local property tax. You notice that it lists 19 bullet-pointed arguments in support of increasing the tax. Even if you didn't have the motivation or the energy to digest this long article, you might say to yourself, "If a person has that many reasons, they must have a valid point." This heuristic, or mental rule of thumb, ignores the fact that each of those 19 reasons may be totally biased, redundant, or just plain wrong. But for readers taking the peripheral route, the mere length of the message may be enough to gain their acceptance.

Confident Thoughts About the Message

We have seen that when people take the central route, they are not passively receiving a persuasive message. Rather, they are actively *elaborating* on the message, thinking carefully about its central claims and comparing that information with their prior knowledge of the topic. According to the cognitive response approach to persuasion (Greenwald, 1968), their attitudes will be influenced not only by *what* they think about the message but also by how confident those thoughts feel (Petty et al., 2002).

People often step back and think about their own thoughts—a process called *metacognition*. In doing this, they may consider how confident they are that their thoughts are correct. The more confident people feel that their thoughts about a message are correct, the more powerfully those thoughts will guide their attitudes. Some surprisingly subtle factors can influence confidence. One is simply how one moves one's body while thinking about the message. Consider how people move their heads. Usually, if you are talking and the people listening are nodding their heads up and down, it means that they agree with you, and that is likely to boost your confidence in what you are saying.

Briñol and Petty (2003) hypothesized that if people nod their *own* heads while generating thoughts about a message, those thoughts would feel more valid, and would therefore strongly guide their attitudes. To test this hypothesis, they had college students put on a pair of headphones and listen to a speech advocating that students be required to carry personal identification cards. Participants were also told that the headphones were specially designed for use during exercise and other bodily movement. Thus, to test the headphones' performance, participants were asked to move their heads while listening to the speech. Half the participants were asked to move their heads up and down (as if nodding "yes"); the other participants were asked to shake their heads from side to side (as if saying "no"). Even though this head-nodding exercise was unrelated to the persuasive communication, it had a potent effect (**FIGURE 8.5**). When presented with strong arguments for why they should carry identification cards, the head-nodding participants were more confident in their positive attitudes and more likely to agree. But when presented with weak arguments, they were more confident in the negative attitudes they formed and less likely to agree with the communication. In contrast, when participants shook their heads, they felt less confident about their positive or negative thoughts, and so those thoughts had less of an influence on whether they agreed with the message.

Statistical Trends Versus Vivid Instances

Persuasive messages often feature statistics ("Four in five dentists agree.. . .") or vivid examples ("Jared lost weight at Subway!"). Which is more persuasive? Consider this scenario: You're wondering which city to move to after graduation. After comparing statistics such as per capita crime rates and housing market trends, you tentatively decide

Cognitive response approach to persuasion Occurs when people's attitude is influenced not only by *what* they think about the message but also by their confidence in those thoughts and beliefs.

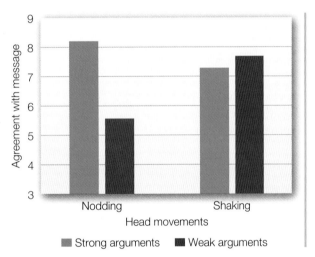

Figure 8.5

Nod If You Agree

Nodding is a subtle signal of endorsement and can magnify your response to an argument by making you more confident of your (either positive or negative) opinion. In this study, participants who were instructed to nod their heads while listening to a persuasive message were more likely to agree with the message if the arguments were strong rather than weak. But if they were instructed to shake their heads from side to side, they were not affected by the strength of the argument.

[Data source: Briñol & Petty (2003)]

on Chicago. But soon after, a friend tells you in vivid detail that her purse was stolen in Chicago, and she's not likely to return. How much will this one person's experience influence your attitudes? Rationally speaking, it shouldn't: That person's experience is one out of millions. Nevertheless, a single vivid example can have a surprisingly strong impact on attitudes, even when it conflicts with one's knowledge of what is generally or statistically true. Why? Because a vivid instance entices the audience to connect the message to their own experience and emotions (Strange & Leung, 1999). In this example, your friend's experience may trigger your own memories of times you felt unsafe in a big city or of other negative things you've heard about Chicago.

In one demonstration of this, Hamill and colleagues (1980) had participants read an article that described in vivid detail how a welfare recipient had spent the last couple years abusing the welfare system by making dishonest purchases and neglecting her adult responsibilities. After reading the article, some participants (those in the "typical" condition) were told that the woman described in the article was typical of welfare recipients and had been receiving welfare for an average length of time. In contrast, participants in the "atypical" condition were told the opposite—that the woman had been on welfare much longer than was common. The researchers also had a third group of participants who did not read about the woman's situation.

Afterward, all participants reported their attitudes toward the entire population of welfare recipients, answering questions such as, "How hard do people on welfare work to improve their situations?" As you can see in **FIGURE 8.6**, participants exposed to the vivid description of just one person abusing the welfare system reported less favorable attitudes toward the entire population of welfare recipients than did those who did not read the description. Also important, it didn't matter whether participants were told explicitly that the described woman was typical or atypical of welfare recipients. A vivid description of a single case can have a powerful influence on attitudes, even when it's not representative of a larger population of people or experiences. This is an important point to keep in mind when others attempt to persuade you: A single personal example or event can grab hold of your attention, but it's important to think about whether that single example is representative of the broader reality.

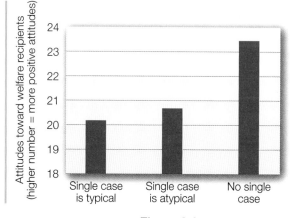

Figure 8.6

The Persuasive Power of Anecdotes

In this study, a single vivid story of a person who abuses the welfare system decreased the positivity of people's attitudes toward welfare. This striking effect occurred regardless of whether people were told that this person was typical or atypical of welfare recipients.

[Data source: Hamill et al. (1980)]

The Size of the Discrepancy

Imagine you were asked by your local newspaper to write an editorial article encouraging people to conserve natural resources. Your goal is to change people's attitudes, and, you hope, their behavior, but how extreme should your position be? You could advocate that people make large lifestyle changes such as walking to work every day rather than driving. This is a gamble: If people are persuaded, then you've successfully changed their attitudes to a significant extent, but you run the risk of turning people off completely or being dismissed as radical. On the other hand, if you advocate for smaller lifestyle changes, such as using fewer water bottles, people may be more likely to go along with you, but you will always wonder: "Could I have had a greater influence if I had pushed them outside their comfort zone a little farther than I did?"

The issue here has to do with the *discrepancy* between the position advocated in a message and the audience's preexisting attitudes. Let's consider what goes on in the audience's heads when they encounter a discrepant message. We know that people are strongly motivated to be right—to hold correct attitudes. So when they come across a message suggesting that they are misinformed or doing something wrong, it makes them uncomfortable—the greater the discrepancy, the greater the discomfort (this idea should be familiar from our discussion of cognitive dissonance in chapter 6). One way that people can reduce this discomfort is to change their attitudes to bring them closer to the position advocated in the message. With this in mind, you would be well advised to advocate a position that is highly discrepant from the audience's current attitudes, because it will produce more discomfort and thus greater attitude change. Indeed, some research has found such a linear relation between the size of the discrepancy and attitude change (Zimbardo, 1960).

However, another way that people can reduce their discomfort is to derogate the source of the message. If an audience discounts a communicator's expertise or trustworthiness, they can write off his or her message and keep their existing attitudes intact. In line with this intuition, research shows that as the size of the discrepancy increases, attitude change increases—but only up to a point. After this, people find the message so different from their own position that they dismiss it out of hand (Hovland et al., 1957).

So what gives? Should you start with a really extreme position or not? To make sense of these seemingly contradictory findings, Aronson and colleagues (1963) proposed that the key factor is the credibility of the source. If the communicator is seen as highly credible—perhaps because he or she is known to be an expert on the topic of the message—the audience will have difficulty simply derogating the source of the message. In that case, an extreme position that makes people uncomfortable is more effective. But if the communicator's credibility is in question, it is much easier for the audience to derogate the communicator and thus ignore the message. In that case, a message with a more moderate position will be more persuasive.

The Order of Presentation: Primacy Versus Recency

Imagine it is early December, with the holidays approaching, and you get a phone call in which you learn that you're one of two final applicants for a great job. The employer asks if you would like to be the first or the second person interviewed. During the interview you'll be given time to make your case as to why the employers should hire you rather than the other applicant. Other things being equal, should you opt to go first or second?

Perhaps your intuition tells you that the person who is interviewed first will be the more persuasive, because she has the chance to make the critical first impression and get the employers on her side early on. In this way, she insures that the other applicant will not only have to offer a good argument for her own candidacy but she also will have to counter-argue all the points you made in the first interview. But perhaps you sense that the person who interviews second will have the advantage, because her arguments will be fresher in the employers' memory when they make their hiring decision.

Research shows that both intuitions are correct: Arguments presented first *and* last each can provide the edge you want—and either would be better than being a middle candidate out of three or more. So what should you do? Recalling how we introduced the scenario, what question do you think you want to ask? We suggest that it would behoove you to ask the employers, "When do you plan to decide who you're going to hire—before or after the holiday break?" This is an important piece of knowledge because the timing of the overall situation makes a big difference (Miller & Campbell, 1959). Specifically, the effects of presentation order depend on (a) the amount of time between the end of the first message and the start of the second message; and (b) the amount of time between the end of the second message and the moment when the audience finally makes up its mind (see **FIGURE 8.7**).

If there is no delay separating the two messages, and if there is a considerable delay between the end of the second message and the audience's response, then the first message will be more persuasive than the second (other things being equal, of course). This is called the primacy effect. What accounts for this effect? When little time elapses between the two messages, the first message is still fresh in audience members' minds when they receive the second message. As a result, they have more difficulty learning the arguments in the second message. As we discussed earlier, arguments that are difficult to comprehend are less persuasive.

Primacy effect Occurs when initially encountered information primarily influences attitudes (e.g., the first speaker in a policy debate influences the audience's policy approval).

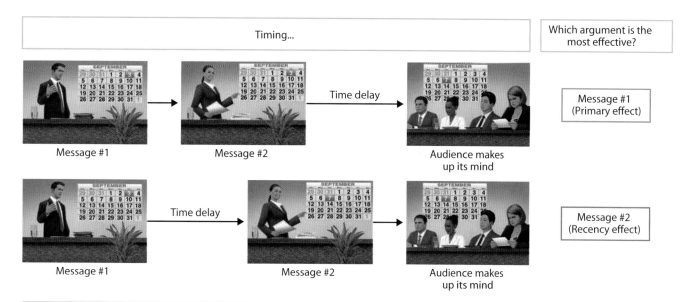

Timing...

Which argument is the most effective?

Message #1   Time delay   Message #2   Audience makes up its mind

Message #1 (Primary effect)

Time delay   Message #1   Message #2   Audience makes up its mind

Message #2 (Recency effect)

In contrast, if there is a time delay separating the two messages, and if the audience makes up its mind immediately after the second message, then the second message will be more persuasive than the first. This is called the recency effect. Under these conditions, the first message does not interfere so much with the audience's ability to learn the second argument. More important, the second argument is fresher in the audience's memory when it makes up its mind.

So the answer to which of the interview positions will have the advantage in the hiring decision is, "It depends." If the applicants are to interview back to back with no delay (i.e., before the holiday break), and if the employers are going to take some time after the second interview to think over the arguments before deciding (i.e., after the holidays), then the primacy effect will be dominant, and the first interview will be the more persuasive. But if there is to be a long break between the two interviews (i.e., one before the holiday and one after), and the employers are going to make their decision immediately after the second interview, then the recency effect will be dominant, and the second interview will be the more persuasive.

Emotional Responses to Persuasive Messages

Persuading people involves changing their thoughts, but it also involves changing how they feel about something at a deeper, "gut" level. Persuasive messages are more effective if they get the audience to associate a position or a product with positive feelings and the avoidance of negative feelings. This can be accomplished in a number of ways. Generally, this below-the-cortex approach to persuasion takes the peripheral route. Conscious deliberation about the message is not needed and might even interfere with the effectiveness of these strategies.

Repetition and Familiarity

One of the most basic ways that persuasive messages get the audience to feel positive about a position or brand is through repetition. If you have ever watched the same TV channel for more than an hour, you probably noticed that the same commercials are repeated over and over. One advantage of repeating messages is that it can help the audience to comprehend messages that might be complex. Second, even if the message is not difficult to comprehend, seeing or hearing a message over and over again increases the accessibility of a product or position in the audience's memory. This was illustrated

Figure 8.7

Getting Time on Your Side

When making a persuasive appeal, it is better to go first if the audience will be making its decision after hearing both arguments and then taking a break. But it is better to go last if the audience will make their decision immediately after hearing your presentation.

Recency effect Occurs when recently encountered information primarily influences attitudes (e.g., a commercial viewed just before shopping influences a shopper's choices).

Figure 8.8

1984

The Ministry of Truth, the governing body of the dystopian world George Orwell sets up in his book 1984, saturates its citizens with intense propaganda campaigns to indoctrinate them with officially acceptable attitudes. Which persuasion techniques does Big Brother use?

[Alamy]

Mere exposure effect Occurs when people hold a positive attitude toward a stimulus simply because they have been exposed to it repeatedly.

WAR IS PEACE

FREEDOM IS SLAVERY

IGNORANCE IS STRENGTH

He took a twenty-five cent piece out of his pocket. There, too, in tiny clear lettering, the same slogans were inscribed, and on the other face of the coin the head of Big Brother. Even from the coin the eyes pursued you. On coins, on stamps, on the covers of books, on banners, on posters, and on the wrappings of a cigarette packet—everywhere. Always the eyes watching you and the voice enveloping you. Asleep or awake, working or eating, indoors or out of doors, in the bath or in bed—no escape.

in George Orwell's dystopian novel *1984* (see **FIGURE 8.8**). In the novel, Big Brother—the ruling regime—repeated the slogan "War is peace, freedom is slavery, ignorance is strength" over and over. Sheer repetition made the message continually—and eerily—salient in the public's mind. But in our everyday experience, if we have been told our whole lives that Brawny brand paper towels are the "quicker picker-upper," then that information is going to pop up instantly when we're at the store trying to decide among 10 brands of paper towels.

Repeatedly exposing consumers to a persuasive message may have another benefit for advertisers. Research on the **mere exposure effect** shows that the more we are exposed to a novel stimulus, the more we tend to like it. Zajonc (1968) first studied this phenomenon by showing American participants pictures of Chinese characters, a novel thing for most Americans. Participants rated those characters that they viewed many times as being more aesthetically pleasing than characters that they hadn't seen or had seen only a few times. The mere exposure effect occurs even when people are unaware of having been frequently exposed to a stimulus. In fact, research suggests that the mere exposure effect actually might be strongest when exposure happens outside of awareness (Bornstein, 1989). The more often people unconsciously perceive the stimulus, the more they tend to like it, prompting Zajonc (1980) to claim that "preferences need no inferences."

The best general explanation for the mere exposure effect is that the more people are exposed to a neutral stimulus, the more familiar it feels, and people generally prefer the familiar to the unfamiliar. Debate continues regarding why the familiar is preferred, but there are two likely explanations (Chenier & Winkielman, 2007). First, as novel stimuli become familiar, they seem less strange and safer. Second, familiar stimuli are easier to perceive and grasp fully.

Think
ABOUT

[Bloomberg via Getty Images]

The mere exposure effect is one reason that corporate sponsors pay gargantuan sums for repeated presentations of their logo, spokesperson, or jingle. How many articles of clothing do you own that clearly display a specific brand name? Another subtle method of repeated exposure is product placement. As we discuss in more detail later on, this essentially involves having a product appear "naturally" in everyday contexts in movies and television shows (e.g., having various characters in a movie drinking Coca-Cola). Mere exposure effects can serve noncommercial purposes as well. For example, pink ribbons have become a ubiquitous symbol of awareness and support for those affected by breast cancer.

The mere exposure effect has been demonstrated for a host of different types of stimuli, including people, music, and geometric figures, but it has its limits. For one, the effect generally plateaus at around 20 exposures; further exposures have only minimal impact on attitudes (Chenier & Winkielman, 2007). Also, the effect does not hold for initially disliked stimuli. Furthermore, the complexity of the stimulus influences the optimal number of exposures (Cacioppo & Petty, 1979). Simpler stimuli sometimes may be liked quicker, but the liking will also turn to boredom more quickly. Think of songs that you hear on a Pandora station and initially enjoy, but after a few weeks of hearing the station playing the song all the time, you want to stuff your ears with cotton. Another exception is captured by the idea of attitude polarization (see chapter 9) (Tesser & Conlee, 1975). Research demonstrating the mere exposure effect focuses on changing people's attitudes toward something that is initially neutral. But research on attitude polarization shows that if we dislike something initially, we dislike it even more if we are exposed to it over and over.

Linking the Message to Positive Stimuli

Another way to get audience members to feel positive about a message is to get them to associate the product or position advocated in the message with stimuli that they already have positive attitudes about, even if the topic of the message and the other stimuli are not inherently related. This was seen, for example, in a recent commercial for the Dodge Charger car that depicted George Washington driving a Charger straight into a crowd of British soldiers as they cower in terror. The narrator intones, "Here are a couple things America got right: cars and freedom." In this way, the advertiser hopes to get American viewers to link the Charger with ideas that they presumably already like, including America, freedom, and masculine overpowering of sniveling weaklings: Indeed, the tongue-in-cheek subtext of the commercial is that America could never have gained its freedom if it weren't for the Dodge Charger and its power to overwhelm the British infantrymen. Of course, patriotic values are only one attractive stimulus that persuaders hope to link to their messages; they also try to associate their product or position with sexiness, cuteness, fun, or spiritual enlightenment.

Repetition also can be very useful in creating these associations. This is because repetition enhances learning, whether through classical conditioning, operant conditioning, or social learning. Classical conditioning occurs when an initially neutral stimulus (the conditioned stimulus) becomes associated with another stimulus that is inherently pleasant or unpleasant (the unconditioned stimulus). When a message repeatedly pairs an object or recommendation with an unconditioned stimulus that already triggers a positive response (e.g., sex, food, cute babies), the topic of the message will be more likely to trigger that same positive response (Staats & Staats, 1958).

In one study demonstrating the influence of classical conditioning on attitudes, Razran (1940) presented participants with slogans such as "Workers of the world, unite." These slogans were presented repeatedly while participants were either enjoying a free lunch (an unconditioned positive stimulus), inhaling unpleasant odors (an unconditioned negative stimulus), or in a neutral setting. As you might expect, participants formed more positive attitudes toward the slogans when they were paired with the free lunch and more negative attitudes toward the same slogans when they were paired with unpleasant odors. Interestingly, the participants were not consciously aware of which slogans were associated with the lunch, the odors, or the neutral conditions. This demonstrated that classical conditioning is a very basic way that people learn to associate the content of the persuasive message with positive feelings.

Operant conditioning is another form of learning that can be used to link a message with positive feelings. In this type of learning, people engage in a behavior and, if rewards follow, they are more likely to engage in that behavior again. One recent marketing trend that harnesses operant conditioning is to associate the purchase of a product with philanthropic rewards. Although these campaigns haven't always been successful, the assumption is that by buying the product, you feel better about yourself, thereby reinforcing the behavior. Some recent examples:

- Tom's Shoes: For every pair you buy, Tom's Shoes will donate a pair to children in need.
- Starbuck's Ethos Water Fund: Every bottle purchased results in a contribution to clean-water programs for children.
- Pepsi's Refresh Project: Purchases of Pepsi products helped PepsiCo give away millions in grants each month to fund philanthropic projects.

- KFC's Buckets for a Cure campaign: With every purchase of a pink bucket of fried chicken, KFC donated 50 cents to breast cancer research.
- Snickers's "Bar Hunger" program: With every purchase of a Snickers bar, the company will donate a meal to someone in need.

Social learning plays a role as well. When people watch a character in a television ad use a product and get rewarded for doing so, the observer vicariously associates the product with a good outcome and will be more likely to use the product herself. For instance, if a commercial depicts a man buying a certain brand of tequila and thereafter ten supermodels instantly focus their lustful gaze on him, the implicit message is that buying this brand of tequila produces positive attention.

Cognitive Balance and Positive Associations

Balance theory Theory proposing that the motivation to maintain consistency among one's thoughts colors how people form new attitudes and can also drive them to change existing attitudes.

The learning perspectives we just covered rely on repetition to get the audience to pair an object or position mentally with another positive stimulus or reward. Fritz Heider's balance theory gives us another way of understanding how messages can link products or positions with positive things effectively, even without repeated exposure. Heider (1946) posited that people have a strong tendency to maintain consistency among their thoughts (an idea that should be familiar after our discussion of cognitive dissonance in chapter 6). Consider this example: If it is the case that (a) you like your friend; (b) your friend likes ballroom dancing; and (c) you like ballroom dancing, then all these cognitions are consistent. But if it is the case that you hate ballroom dancing, there would be inconsistency among your thoughts, leading you to wonder about your friend, "How could someone so cool like something so lame?" To bring your cognitions back in harmony with each other—or to use Heider's term, to restore *balance*—you might convince yourself that ballroom dancing isn't that bad after all.

This perspective helps to explain why the magazine ad in **FIGURE 8.9a** might be effective. The ad assumes that you, as the magazine reader, already have a positive attitude toward Jennifer Aniston (hence the plus sign connecting you and Aniston in **FIGURE 8.9b**). The ad informs you that Aniston is positively inclined toward Smart Water. This leaves only your relation to Smart Water undetermined. According to balance theory, the audience would experience an internal pressure to evaluate Smart Water positively so that they can maintain a harmonious state in which all the elements (themselves, Aniston, Smart Water) are consistent with each other. If people were *not* naturally inclined to prefer balanced over imbalanced relations between their thoughts, then we wouldn't expect them to feel any motivation to like Smart Water, because they would be perfectly comfortable if some of the elements in this system didn't quite fit together.

Positive Mood

Another way to create positive feelings toward a message is to deliver it when people are in a good mood. In a classic study by Janis and colleagues (1965), participants read a series of persuasive messages on topics such as the armed forces and 3-D movies. Half the participants were given peanuts and soda to snack on while reading

Figure 8.9

Balance Theory

According to Heider's balance theory, if you like Jennifer Aniston and she likes Smart Water, than you are inclined to like Smart Water, too.

[Adam Nemser-PHOTOlink.net/ PHOTOlink/Newscom]

(a)

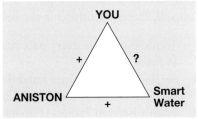
(b)

the messages, whereas the other half did not get any snacks. Participants allowed to snack were more convinced by the messages than participants who were not snacking. Since this study was conducted, research has shown that people more readily agree with messages when they experience success, hear pleasant music, or view beautiful scenery (Schwarz et al., 1991). The influence of positive mood on persuasion has not been lost on people. You probably know that businesspeople often bring clients to lunch at a fancy restaurant, or you may have experienced a salesperson opening up a conversation with a funny story. If you are in a good mood while receiving the message, you will be more likely to agree with it, even if the reason for your good mood has nothing to do with the message itself.

Negative Emotions

Of course, not all persuasive messages try to create positive emotions; some try to persuade the audience that by doing something or acquiring something, they can avoid negative consequences or punishments. For example, a message might pitch a product as providing relief from a painful or embarrassing social encounter or as reducing one's harmful impact on the environment. In these cases, the designer of the message is hoping to arouse negative emotions and then offer recommendations for assuaging your concern. Most commonly, these kinds of messages try to evoke fear in the audience. Your current author recently saw a pamphlet (and, yes, read it!) in the optometrist's office titled, "Your Eyes Are Under Attack!"

Sometimes fear works, leading to more attitude and behavioral change. Banks and colleagues (1995) found that middle-aged women were far more likely to follow a recommendation to get a mammogram if they had watched a video that framed mammography in fear-arousing terms (emphasizing how *not* getting a mammogram might result in death) than were another group of women who watched a similar video that framed mammography in more positive terms. This shows that the way a message is pitched can make a big difference. People generally are more likely to comply with a message that frames a health behavior in gain-related terms ("Use sunscreen to help your skin stay healthy") when the behavior involves prevention of a risk condition such as skin cancer. However, a message that frames a health behavior in loss-related terms ("Without regular mammograms, breast cancer can go undetected until it's too late") is often more effective for detection of a health problem such as breast cancer (Rothman & Salovey, 1997). Thus, there are different ways to use fear to effectively change attitudes.

But fear also can backfire. Janis and Feshbach (1953) found that a message was less effective at persuading the audience to practice improved oral hygiene if it used fear-arousing images of rotting gums and teeth than if it used more neutral images. Janis and Feshbach interpreted this result as showing that some fear-arousing messages are so overwhelming that the audience defensively avoids them, and so no attitude change occurs.

So what makes the difference? Leventhal (1970) proposed that arousing fear on its own is not enough to persuade people. When people are told simply that they will suffer some threatening outcome, they feel distressed or helpless, and they often tune out entirely. But if you provide them with a clear means of protecting themselves from that threatening outcome, then they are more likely to be persuaded. That is, fear-arousing messages are most effective in changing people's attitudes if, in addition to heightening fear about a threatening outcome, they provide the audience with information about what specific actions are required to mitigate or avoid that threatening outcome (Rogers & Prentice-Dunn, 1997; Witte & Allen, 2000).

In one study testing this possibility, Leventhal and colleagues (1965) found that participants were more likely to follow the recommendation of a health message and get a tetanus shot if they were exposed to a fear-arousing message about the dangers of tetanus *and* they were given a detailed set of instructions on how to get the shot. If participants only received the fear-arousing message (with no instructions on how to get the shot) *or* just the specific instructions without the fear-arousing description of tetanus, they were less likely to get the shot. These results indicate that eliciting fear is important in motivating behavior—no one in the "no fear" condition got the shot—but you also need to provide frightened people with detailed information about what actions to take to reduce the threat.

APPLICATION
Is Death Good for Your Health?

So far we've assumed that fear-arousing messages are effective because they motivate people to avoid threats to their physical health. But arousing fear may have opposite effects when it motivates people to care more about their self-images than their health. From the existential perspective of terror management theory described in chapter 2, recall that people strive to maintain self-esteem as a way of protecting themselves from concerns about death. We saw how research supports this claim by showing that people led to contemplate their own deaths make intensified efforts to bolster their standing on characteristics (e.g., physical strength) that are important to their self-esteem.

This research suggests the interesting possibility that arousing fears about death may have completely opposite effects on people's health attitudes and behavior. On the one hand, people are motivated to avoid threats to their survival, so bringing thoughts of death to mind might motivate them to avoid potentially lethal risks, such as drunk driving (Jessop et al., 2008). On the other hand, increasing people's death awareness might motivate them to enhance their self-esteem, which may mean engaging in unhealthy behaviors such as smoking, tanning, and consuming diet pills.

This Is Like That: Metaphor's Significance in Persuasion

Many times, we come across persuasive messages that, strictly speaking, make no sense. Consider the statement made by opponents of a mandatory seatbelt law being contested in California some years ago: "We don't want Governor Deukmejian sitting in our bathtub telling us to wash behind our ears."

This is an example of a *metaphoric message*, a communication that compares one type of thing with another type of thing. Beginning with Aristotle, scholars have noted metaphor's power to persuade. Returning to the bathtub metaphor above, even though people know that enacting a seat belt law does not *literally* mean having the governor in the bathtub with them, hearing the bathtub metaphor guides them to think about the seatbelt law as the same type of thing—a disgusting violation of personal privacy. In fact, study volunteers randomly assigned to read the bathtub statement evaluated the seatbelt legislation more negatively than those who didn't (Read et al., 1990).

Other common metaphoric messages try to change how people understand social problems and thus evaluate certain solutions. Many real-world problems are abstract, complex, and difficult to comprehend fully. A metaphor comparing an abstract problem with a more familiar problem suggests what solutions are more and less likely to work. For example, a recent television ad advocated cutting government spending on social programs by comparing the federal budget with a household budget. The ad aimed to get the audience thinking, "In my house we don't buy goodies that we cannot afford. Therefore, the best solution to our economic problems is to stop the government from funding programs."

Do such messages work? To find out, Thibodeau and Boroditsky (2011) asked participants to read different stories about a city with a serious crime problem. For some participants, crime was compared with a "beast" that was "preying upon" the innocent citizens of the town. For other participants it was described as a "disease" that "plagued" the town. After participants compared crime with a wild animal, they were more likely to generate solutions based on increased enforcement (e.g., calling in the National Guard, imposing harsher penalties). In contrast, participants given the virus analogy strongly preferred solutions that were more diagnostic and reform oriented (e.g., finding the root cause of the crime wave, improving the economy). In other words, the solutions that participants generated to solve the crime problem were consistent with the metaphors they read: if crime was like a beast, it must be controlled, but if it was like a disease, then it must be treated.

The question, then, is, What determines whether increasing people's awareness of their mortality increases or decreases risky but self-esteem-bolstering health behaviors?

Goldenberg and Arndt (2008) proposed that a key factor is the degree to which death-related thoughts are salient in consciousness. When people are conscious of death-related thoughts, they'll be more motivated to take practical steps to reduce or avoid threats to their physical health if they think they can do so effectively. But when death thoughts are activated outside of conscious attention, people will be motivated to enhance their self-esteem, even if it means engaging in unhealthy behaviors.

In one study supporting this analysis, undergraduates were asked to take part in a consumer marketing study (Routledge et al., 2004). All the participants had earlier indicated that having a radiant tan helped to bolster their feelings of self-esteem. The researchers had participants think about either their own deaths or dental pain (a control condition), and then indicate their intentions to protect themselves from dangerous sun exposure. Some participants indicated their tanning-related intentions immediately after being primed with death or pain, whereas others reported their intentions after completing a short task designed to distract them from thoughts of death or pain. As predicted, when concerns about death were in direct conscious attention, participants were more intent on protecting themselves from the sun, but participants distracted from thoughts of death showed the opposite response, decreasing their interest in sun protection. Thus, bringing thoughts of death to mind may prompt people to make healthy decisions, but if thoughts of death are active on the periphery of consciousness, people may be more likely to enhance their self-image, even if it means endangering their health.

 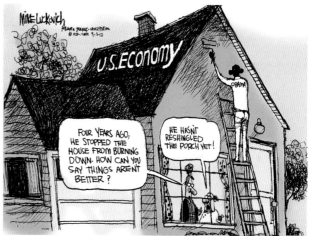

These cartoons use metaphor to compare the U. S. economy to different types of things—in one case a vehicle, in the other a house. Vehicles and houses have different qualities, and we relate to them in different ways. How might those metaphors influence people's beliefs about how the economy works and the attitudes they form toward politicians and policies?

[Left: David Horsey/Tribune Media Services; right: By permission of Mike Luckovitch and Creators Syndicate Inc.]

Metaphoric messages change attitudes, but can they change behavior? Maybe you recall seeing warning videos that are sometimes played before a movie. These videos aim to provide a lesson in the legality of downloading movies from torrent web sites on the internet. The words "You wouldn't steal a car" appear on the screen, followed by a dramatic reenactment of a car theft. Then, "You wouldn't steal a purse." After reminding you of other objects you presumably do not intend to steal, the message concludes: "Downloading pirated films is stealing." Pilfering a woman's purse and downloading a pirated film are obviously similar situations in some respects, but they differ in others (e.g., the woman is left without the purse, whereas the movie's owner still has it). Given what you've learned about social psychology research, how would you design an experiment to test whether this metaphor changes people's behavior?

SECTION review | Characteristics of the Message

Attitudes are influenced by the content and style of the message.

What changes our minds	What creates an effective emotional response	Health application
• Comprehensible messages. • Confident thoughts about the message. • Vivid instances that connect with personal experience. • A position highly discrepant from prior attitudes (given a credible source). • Order in which competing arguments are presented as they relate to the timing of the overall situation.	• Repetition and familiarity. • Learned associations with positive stimuli. • The need to maintain consistent ideas about related people or things. • Positive mood. • Use of fear to avoid negative consequences if paired with strategies to reduce the negative consequences.	• Thoughts of death can motivate people to maintain healthy behaviors. • Unconscious thoughts of death create the need to boost self-esteem and may result in unhealthy behaviors.

Characteristics of the Audience

In addition to the source of a persuasive message and the nature of the message itself, a message's impact on an audience also depends on the characteristics of the audience members. Whether a given audience member responds favorably or unfavorably to a message is determined by his or her individual age, sex, personality, socioeconomic status, education level, and habitual way of living, as well as the events and experiences of his or her life. For example, we described earlier that whether a person processes a persuasive message through the central route or the peripheral route depends in part on his or her motivation to attend to the message. So we would expect that individual differences in interests, values, and prior knowledge will determine who finds certain messages worthy of attention or not. Let's consider how audiences differ according to the following characteristics.

Persuasibility

People differ in their overall *persuasibility*, their susceptibility to persuasion. People high in persuasibility are more likely to yield to persuasive messages, whereas low-persuasibility individuals are less likely to be influenced. There are three key determinants of persuasibility.

- *Age*: Between the ages of 18 to 25, people are usually in the process of forming their attitudes, and so they are more likely to be influenced by persuasive messages. As they move into their late 20s and beyond, their attitudes tend to solidify and become more resistant to change (Koenig et al., 2008; Krosnick & Alwin, 1989).
- *Self-esteem*: People with low self-esteem are more likely to be influenced by persuasive messages than those with high self-esteem (Wood & Stagner, 1994; Zellner, 1970). People with low self-esteem are less confident and view themselves as generally less capable, so, as you might expect, they do not regard their own attitudes very highly. As a result, they are more likely to give up their current attitudes and go along with the position advocated in the message. People with high self-esteem, however, generally think highly of themselves. They are more confident in their attitudes, and they are therefore less likely to yield to influence.

● *Education and intelligence*: Audience members who are more educated and intelligent are less persuadable than those with normal to low intelligence (McGuire, 1968). We can interpret this finding in a similar way as the self-esteem finding: People who are highly intelligent are more confident in their ability to think critically and form their own attitudes.

Initial Attitudes

Another important audience characteristic is the attitude that audience members already have toward the position advocated in the message. Imagine that you are trying to persuade your parents that you should be allowed to study in Spain for a semester through a foreign exchange program. Would you be more effective if you presented only those arguments favoring a semester abroad and ignored any arguments opposed to your position—a *one-sided* message? Or would you be more persuasive if you brought up the arguments opposing the trip and then proceeded to refute them—a *two-sided* message? A two-sided message could work for you or against you. If you mention the reasons that you should not go abroad and then refute them ("One could say that this trip is too expensive, but I have some savings. . . ."), then you can show that you have thought about the issue objectively and even-handedly, and your parents might therefore be more convinced that this trip is a good idea. However, simply by mentioning those opposing arguments you run the risk of bringing them to your parents' attention and giving them more reasons to say no.

Whether a one-sided or a two-sided message is more effective depends in large part on the audience's initial attitudes toward the issue at hand. If the audience members are already leaning toward agreement with the message, they will be more persuaded by a one-sided message that ignores opposing arguments. If, however, the audience is initially leaning toward disagreement with the message, then they will be more persuaded by a two-sided message that addresses opposing arguments (Hovland et al., 1949).

Why is this the case? If audience members are initially leaning toward disagreement, they are probably aware of at least a few arguments opposing the position advocated in the message. For example, if your parents are already inclined to oppose the semester abroad, they probably have some reasons (e.g., it is too dangerous). Thus, if the message ignores the audience's opposing arguments, the audience will likely conclude that the communicator is biased, uninformed, or manipulative, and they will call into question the validity of anything he or she says.

If, however, the audience is already leaning toward agreement with the message, they are less likely to be aware of opposing arguments. Therefore, simply mentioning those opposing arguments may confuse audience members or lead them to conclude that the issue is more controversial than they initially thought. ("Hmm, I was all for the semester abroad, but now that you mention it, the trip *would* be awfully expensive.") In this case you would have been more persuasive if you had focused only on those arguments favoring your position.

When trying to convince those who might disagree with you, is it better to provide a one- or two-sided argument? It depends on how the audience is initially leaning.

[Spencer Platt/Getty Images]

Need for Cognition and Self-monitoring

Think back to the study we discussed in this chapter looking at attitudes toward Edge razor blades (Petty et al., 1983). That study showed that a person's motivation to think about a message can vary from situation to situation depending on whether

Need for cognition Differences between people in their need to think about things critically and analytically.

that message pertains to his or her current goals and interests (e.g., anticipating a choice between razors or toothpastes). But you may have noticed that, across different situations, some people are generally more interested in thinking deeply about issues, whereas others are not. According to Cacioppo and Petty (1982), individuals high in need for cognition tend to think about things critically and analytically and enjoy solving problems. They tend to agree strongly with statements such as "I really enjoy a task that involves coming up with new solutions to problems." Individuals low in need for cognition are less interested in effortful cognitive activity and agree with statements such as "I think only as hard as I have to." With your knowledge of the elaboration likelihood model (ELM), do you suspect that individuals with high need for cognition would tend to take the central route or the peripheral route to persuasion?

If you said central, you're right. This was shown in a study by John T. Cacioppo and his colleagues (1983). The researchers measured college students' need for cognition, then asked them to read an editorial, allegedly written by a journalism student, arguing that all seniors be required to pass a rigorous, comprehensive exam to graduate. Thus, in this experiment, the message is relevant to all the participants. But for half the participants, the editorial contained fairly strong arguments in favor of the exam ("The quality of undergraduate teaching has improved at schools with the exams"), whereas the other participants read fairly unconvincing arguments for the exam ("The risk of failing the exam is a challenge more students would welcome"). Overall, as you might expect, participants were more favorable toward the exam requirement when it was supported by strong rather than weak arguments. But participants with high need

Argo: The Uses of Persuasion

In 1979, Iranian militants stormed the U.S. embassy in Tehran, taking 52 Americans hostage in retaliation for what they saw as American meddling in Iran's government. Six U.S. diplomats managed to slip away and found refuge in the home of the Canadian ambassador. They feared that it was only a matter of time before they were discovered by Iranian revolutionaries and likely killed, so they could not just arrive at Tehran's airport and reveal their American identities.

Back in the United States, the CIA operative Tony Mendez came up with a plan to get the diplomats safely out of the country: convince the Iranians that the diplomats were Canadian filmmakers who were in Iran scouting exotic locations for a sci-fi adventure movie along the lines of *Star Wars*. Although all of this sounds like a crazy premise cooked up by a screenwriter dreaming of a box office smash, the movie *Argo* (Heslov et al., 2012), directed by and starring Ben Affleck in the role of Mendez, actually tells a gripping true story of rescue and persuasion.

Mendez first has to persuade the higher-ups in Washington to authorize and fund his rescue operation. He lays out the plan using strong arguments, describing the operation in detail and carefully explaining why it is the most promising

idea considered so far. But they're not convinced, because they are processing Mendez's message through the peripheral route to persuasion. Maybe they feel pressed for time, but they have difficulty getting past a simple heuristic: On the face of it, the idea of staging a fake movie sounds insane.

[Warner Bros./Photofest]

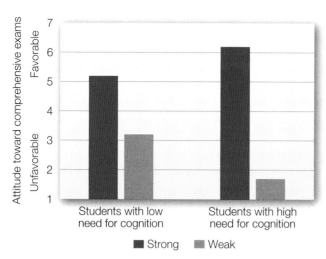

Figure 8.10

Need for Cognition

People who have a high need for cognition like to think deeply and are more persuadable through the central route. In this study, students high in need for cognition were more positive toward a proposed comprehensive exam if the arguments for it were strong than if the arguments were weak. Those low in need for cognition were less sensitive to argument strength.

[Data source: Cacioppo et al. (1983)]

for cognition were especially likely to approve of the proposal when it was supported by strong arguments and to disapprove of the proposal when it was supported by weak arguments (see **FIGURE 8.10**). So even though the message was equally relevant to all participants, some of them were inherently motivated to pay close attention to the arguments, whereas others were content merely to skim the message.

Eventually Mendez gets the green light and works with the Hollywood makeup artist John Chambers (John Goodman) and the producer Lester Siegel (Alan Arkin) to set up a phony movie-production company with the pretense of developing a sci-fi flick called *Argo*. If they are going to convince the Iranians that they are making a Hollywood movie, they need all the trappings of a film crew on a scouting mission, including a glossy poster, a script and storyboards, press releases, and an office phone if and when the Iranians decide to check things out (which they do). With all of these peripheral cues to back up their story, they create a convincing cover for the trip.

The next group that needs to be persuaded are the people whose lives are on the line. Posing as *Argo*'s producer, Mendez meets the diplomats who are in hiding and provides them with Canadian passports and fake identities. But he also gives them a crash course in the film industry and Canadian citizenship. After all, if they have any chance of making it past the authorities and getting on the plane, they need to play their roles convincingly. But they too are skeptical of Mendez's scheme and reluctant to go along with it. At first Mendez tries to persuade them by presenting himself as a trustworthy source, a powerful peripheral cue when audiences take the peripheral route. But the diplomats aren't processing information peripherally. The outcome of what happens is incredibly relevant to them, and that elicits central route processing. Shifting gears, Mendez takes the time to deliver a strong argument for why they should trust him.

He reveals his true identity and describes his training and his record of successful rescue missions. He also reminds them that he is risking his own life, too. He knows that the source of a message can gain credibility by being perceived as having nothing to gain by deception or manipulation. His willingness to risk his own life is evidence that he firmly believes that the plan can work, and the diplomats begin getting into character.

In the movie's suspenseful climax, we watch the "film crew" slowly making their way through security checkpoints in Tehran's airport. Gun-toting Iranian soldiers suspect them of being American and lock them in a room to interrogate them just as their flight is boarding. The soldiers have very strong initial attitudes of mistrust toward Americans, in large part because of being repeatedly exposed to this message by revolutionaries who give impassioned speeches on America as the enemy of Iran. As the tensions rise in the interrogation room, one of the diplomats steps in and tries a new persuasive strategy. He lays out the movie storyboards on a table and improvises a stirring synopsis of the film they are supposed to be making. He is appealing to the soldiers by applying the principle of balance. He knows that the soldiers have a very strong positive attitude toward revolution, so he's showing that the film crew is equally excited to be capturing a fictional story about a triumphant revolution on film. He's hoping that the soldiers will seek to bring those two cognitions into balance: If *we* like revolution, and *you* like revolution, then it follows that we like you. Is he persuasive? Do the Americans make it out of Iran? You'll have to watch to find out.

Just as some people are motivated to think in greater depth, other people are motivated to make a good impression and present a desired social image. Recall our discussion of self-monitoring from chapter 6. Those high in the trait of self-monitoring are social chameleons of sorts, motivated and adept at presenting themselves as the right person at the right time. If the situation calls for an outgoing individual, they can put on a gregarious face, but likewise they can portray themselves as thoughtful and quiet if the situation demands. Snyder and DeBono (1985) reasoned that because high self-monitors are concerned with projecting the right image, they should be especially influenced by ads that convey the potential for creating or enhancing a particularly desirable image. In other words, they should be more susceptible to peripheral-route cues.

In one study, not only were high self-monitors more persuaded by image-oriented ads but they also were willing to put their money where their mouths were. For example, whereas high self-monitors were willing to pay $8.24 for a bottle of Canadian Club whisky when it was accompanied by a message about quality ("Canadian Club Whisky: When it comes to great taste, everyone draws the same conclusion"), this amount rose to $9.75 when the whisky was pitched as enhancing one's status ("Canadian Club Whisky: You're not just moving in, you're moving up"). Low self-monitors, in contrast, displayed the reverse pattern. So just as certain people can be differentially motivated to think carefully about a message, others may be motivated more by the power of the images—and the peripheral cues—that a message presents.

Regulatory Focus

Earlier we noted that in certain situations, people are influenced by thinking about what they might gain, whereas in other situations they are influenced by thinking about what they could lose (Rothman, 2000). It turns out there is an additional piece to this puzzle that can further enhance our understanding of which people will be most persuaded by which type of message. Some people generally are oriented more toward the promotion of positive outcomes. Their actions are strongly driven by the *growth* motivation that we discussed in chapter 2. Consider Frank, who works out and watches what he eats so that he can look more like Ryan Reynolds. Other people are oriented more toward the prevention of negative outcomes. They are motivated to maintain *security* (see chapter 2). Consider Stephen, who works out and watches what he eats so he can avoid looking like Minnesota Fats. Note that Frank and Stephen engage in the same types of behavior, but they regulate their behavior according to two very different endpoints. We would say that Frank is high in promotion focus, whereas Stephen is high in prevention focus.

Promotion focus People's general tendency to think and act in ways oriented toward the approach of positive outcomes.

Prevention focus People's general tendency to think and act in ways oriented toward the avoidance of negative outcomes.

Why does this matter for persuasion? Because individual differences in promotion focus and prevention focus can determine which types of persuasive messages are more influential. In one study (Cesario et al., 2004) participants read an argument in favor of a new afterschool program. For some participants, the program was billed as catering to a positive end state (facilitating children's progress and graduation). For other participants, it was billed as preventing a negative end state (ensuring that fewer children failed). For participants who were promotion focused, the promotion-oriented articulation of the program was a better fit to their current motivation and, as a result, were more likely to support it. However, those who were prevention focused experienced a better fit with the avoidance message of reducing failures and thus were more likely to support the program when it was framed in prevention-oriented terms.

The regulatory fit between the characteristics of the audience and those of the message has important implications not only for changing attitudes but also for changing behavior. Let us return to the examples of Frank and Stephen. Because Frank is promotion focused, it might be easier to persuade him to *start* a weight-loss program, because signing up is itself consistent with his goal of achieving a desired end state. But although Stephen's focus on avoiding failures might not give him a leg up on starting a new diet program, it might make him more likely to *sustain* the behavior of dieting once he has started to count his calories (Fuglestad et al., 2008).

SECTION review | Characteristics of the Audience

A message's influence on attitudes and behavior depends on who receives it.

Three determinants of persuasibility	Initial attitudes	How people think and self-monitor	Regulatory style
• Age. • Self-esteem. • Education and intelligence.	• One-sided arguments obscure counterarguments, appealing to audiences leaning toward agreement. • Two-sided arguments avoid the perception of bias, appealing to audiences leaning toward disagreement.	• People with high need for cognition prefer the central route. • Those motivated to make a good impression are more susceptible to peripheral route cues.	• For audiences high in promotion focus, influential messages highlight positive outcomes. • Prevention-focused people are persuaded by messages highlighting negative outcomes.

Resistance to Persuasion

Throughout this book, we have discussed how, as motivated animals, people are far from objective consumers of information. Rather, we filter information through our own preconceptions and biases. These motivated biases give us a measure of resistance when we encounter persuasion attempts that conflict with our preexisting beliefs (Lord et al., 1979).

Further, when we're exposed to mixed evidence on a given issue, we often will focus on the information that supports, and as a consequence bolsters, our preexisting beliefs (Pyszczynski & Greenberg, 1987). This helps us to understand why it can be so hard to convince people of something they are set against. Just think about the resistance that scientists encounter when arguing to some government officials that the mounting evidence for global climate change reflects poorly on the future viability of life as we know it. Of course, in many situations, we may not have strong preexisting beliefs that arm us with skepticism about persuasive appeals. Nonetheless, resistance is not always futile. But successfully resisting persuasion depends on a few factors: We need to know what to resist, be motivated to resist it, and have strategies that will be effective.

Knowing What to Resist

In Steven Spielberg's classic film, *E.T. the Extra-Terrestrial*, a boy named Elliott tries to lure an alien from a hiding place by laying out a trail of Reese's Pieces. Shortly after the release of this blockbuster movie in 1982, sales for these delectable chocolate-covered peanut-butter snacks boomed. This is an especially popular example of the widespread advertising technique of product placement in TV shows and movies (York, 2001), which capitalizes on our tendency to be influenced by what we see in the media. If you are a fan of the TV show *American Idol*, you might recall seeing the judges drinking Coca-Cola. These famous musicians and celebrities might well be Coke fans, but their decision to consume this particular brand of soda on the show is far from a coincidence. The influence of watching celebrities or other TV or movie characters use a product extends not just to certain snack food and beverages but also to behavior that can be downright deadly. For example, the more children see movies

Television shows such as *American Idol* use product placement to advertise their corporate sponsors.
[FOX via Getty Images]

where grownups smoke, the more positive their attitudes are toward smoking and the more likely they are to start smoking (Sargent et al., 2002; Wills et al., 2008).

Product placement works for a number of reasons. These images make the product accessible and lead us to associate positive feelings with that product, particularly when we identify with the character using the product. Indeed, research on smoking finds the more people identify with the character smoking, the more likely they are to develop positive associations with smoking (Dal Cin et al., 2007). Placing particular products in movies also is an especially effective form of advertising because people most often do not realize they are being targeted with a persuasive appeal. Recall our discussion earlier in this chapter about source credibility and persuasive intent. If you are unaware that you're the target of persuasion, there is little resistance for advertisers to overcome, and so positive attitudes toward the product are free to develop.

But the effectiveness of product placement also gives us an important insight about factors opposing persuasion. If we're aware that a persuasive appeal is coming our way, we're better able to deflect its impact. In fact, such knowledge arouses motivations and cognitions that not only bolster our ability to withstand a persuasive message but can actually provoke us to do the very opposite of what the would-be persuader is trying to get us to do.

Being Motivated to Resist

As we've noted, persuasion can come from many sources. Our parents, for example, often try to persuade us to act in accord with cultural values. This socialization process is a vital ingredient in the recipe for a smooth functioning society. But sometimes our parents also impose their own idiosyncratic, maybe outdated, preferences on how we style our hair, or what we wear, or whom we date. Perhaps you've had the experience of introducing your parents to your new boyfriend or girlfriend, only to face a later barrage of "I forbid you to see that person!" comments. Did those admonitions increase or decrease your attraction to the new boyfriend? If your experiences are similar to those of many research participants, chances are that your parents' restrictions backfired. The *Romeo and Juliet effect* shows that parental opposition to a relationship partner is typically associated with deeper romantic love for that partner (Driscoll et al., 1972). The more our parents say "no way," the more we often say "yes way."

Why is forbidden fruit so much more tempting? Jack Brehm's (1966; Brehm & Brehm, 1981) seminal psychological reactance theory explains why forceful, demanding efforts to compel obedience, compliance, or persuasive attitude change can backfire. This theory is based on the assumption that people have certain *free behaviors*, a set of things they believe they have the right and the capability to do. For example, when in high school you may have felt the freedom to be able to go to college. This would be an example of a free behavior. When people sense that their freedom to pursue such a behavior is threatened, they experience an uncomfortable emotional state, called *reactance*, that they are motivated to reduce. People often try to reduce reactance by performing the threatened behavior and thus restoring their sense of freedom. In fact, the motivation to reduce reactance can be so strong that it leads people to act aggressively against the person threatening their freedom (see **FIGURE 8.11**).

Psychological reactance theory Theory proposing that people value thinking and acting freely. Therefore, situations that threaten their freedom arouse discomfort and prompt efforts to restore freedom.

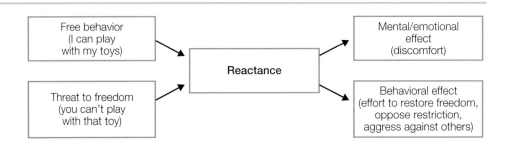

Figure 8.11

Reactance

When our freedoms are threatened, we experience reactance and engage in behavior to reassert our independence.

One of the most interesting implications of reactance theory is that even if a particular behavior doesn't much appeal to a person, if she perceives it as something she has the right to do, when her ability to engage in the behavior is threatened, her interest in engaging in that behavior increases. If you have young kids, siblings, or babysit, you can readily observe this firsthand. Pick out an action figure that has been gathering dust in the child's closet. Tell the kid that he can't play with that particular toy, and watch that neglected action figure become his favorite that he wants to play with above all else. Have you ever tried your hand at the popular notion of *reverse psychology*, whereby you tell someone to do something in the hope that they'll do the opposite? If so, you've taken advantage of reactance and how people respond to it. How did it turn out?

Think
ABOUT

[Parema/Getty Images]

In one of the first demonstrations of reactance, Brehm and colleagues (1966) invited students to participate in a study on marketing musical recordings. The students rated a few sample recordings and were told that they would receive one of the records as a gift. (Yes, if the study were done today it would likely be an iTunes download.) In one condition, participants were told that they would get to choose whichever record they wanted. In another condition, participants were also given the opportunity to choose, but the options were rigged so that the participants were told that their third-rated record inadvertently had been excluded from the shipment and was unavailable. Thus, in this condition, a restriction was placed on the participants' freedom to choose what they wanted. All subjects were then asked again to indicate their ratings of the different musical samples, and it was these changed attitudes that revealed reactance. Among subjects who were given a choice but denied the freedom to choose their third most highly rated selection, 67 percent increased their ratings of this selection, compared with 42 percent of participants' increasing their rating of this record when they had no restriction on their freedom.

So we can think about reactance as pushback against attempts to restrict our freedom to have, do, or think what we want. The amount of pushback depends on how important that freedom is to us as well as how forceful the threat is. If going to your current college or university was particularly important to you, but your parents wanted you to go to another school, there is a good chance that you may have experienced strong feelings of reactance if your parents tried to direct your decision. However, if where you went to school was not a particularly important freedom for you, then you would not have experienced much reactance if your parents tried to restrict that freedom.

Looking at reactance from the cultural perspective, we find that culture plays a big role in determining the importance people place on freedom, whose freedoms are most important, and thus how strong their reactance is. In our discussion of cultural variation in chapter 2, we saw that individual agency and a sense of personal freedom are more important to people in Western, individualistic cultures. A sense of group harmony is more important to those from collectivistic cultures, and as a result, reactance might play out differently for people from such cultures. In a study testing this idea, when European American students (who tend to value individualism) were asked to imagine trading their parking passes for a week in exchange for passes to less accessible parking locations, they showed more reactance when thinking about this limitation on their personal freedom than when thinking about the limitation on the freedom of their fellow students. In contrast, when Asian and Latin Americans (who tend to value collectivism) were presented with a similar appeal, they showed more reactance when the freedom of their fellow students was threatened than when their own freedom was (Jonas et al., 2009).

This study makes a couple of important points. It not only demonstrates the cross-cultural ubiquity of reactance but also shows how the nature of the freedom, and how much people value it, influences the amount of reactance people experience.

APPLICATION
Reactance in Jury Decision Making

This research on reactance can be applied to a fairly common occurrence in jury trials. Consider the following scenario, which you're likely to have seen in any episode of *Law and Order* or another such courtroom drama. As a witness faces intense questioning from the opposing attorney, he blurts out some off-limits comment about the defendant's prior criminal record. The judge quickly intervenes, declaring, "The jury is to disregard that testimony." When framed in terms of reactance theory, this directive can be viewed as an attempt to restrict what you are allowed to think about. And in light of what you now know about reactance, you won't be surprised to learn that such instructions often backfire and produce a boomerang effect (Lieberman & Arndt, 2000).

In an experiment by Wolf and Montgomery (1977), mock jurors were presented with a simulated trial in which specific testimony was ruled either admissible or inadmissible. An important aspect of the inadmissible conditions was that the ruling was accompanied by a weak or a strong admonition. The weak admonition simply instructed the jurors not to consider that testimony, whereas the strong admonition declared, "I want to remind you that the testimony . . . was ruled inadmissible. Therefore, it must play no role in your consideration of the case. You have no choice but to disregard it" (p. 211). After considering other testimony and arguments, the mock jurors were asked to give their verdicts. Participants receiving a strong admonition actually were more influenced by the inadmissible evidence than participants in either the weak-admonition condition or the admissible control condition. Thus, forceful instructions to ignore information may arouse reactance, leading jurors to reestablish their freedom by more heavily weighing precisely the information they have been told to disregard.

How, then, can you undermine reactance and prevent it from disrupting your efforts to persuade little Johnny that it's time to stop playing with the superhero action figure? One way to undermine reactance is through the characteristics of the person doing the persuading. In one study, researchers manipulated whether the person doing the persuading was similar to the participant by giving the persuader the same first name and birthday as half of the participants (Silvia, 2005). The other participants were faced with a persuader who did not have the same name and birthday. When the persuader was highly similar to the participants, they agreed strongly with the message that was delivered, regardless of a strong or a weak threat to their decision freedom. This occurred because the similar persuader was liked more (and therefore was viewed as less of a threat). This increased the force toward persuasion and decreased the force toward reactance.

Resisting Strategically: Attitude Inoculation

Think about what people do to protect themselves from a virus. A weak dose of a virus is administered in the form of a vaccination. The dose is strong enough to trigger the body's production of resistant antibodies but weak enough that it does not overwhelm the body's resistance. The body more effectively can marshal defenses to ward off stronger exposure to the virus that may come later.

William McGuire (1964) applied the logic of vaccination against disease in a method to increase resistance to persuasion. He was inspired by the alarming decision of nine U.S. Army prisoners to remain with their captors in the aftermath of the Korean War, and the popular theory that they must have been brainwashed. He reasoned that, prior to their capture, the soldiers had rarely if ever been exposed to anticapitalist or procommunist arguments. Therefore, they were unprepared and had no ready defenses or counterarguments when their North Korean captors launched their persuasive attack. This led McGuire to the idea of attitude inoculation as a strategy that enables people to resist persuasion. The basic idea behind attitude inoculation is that exposing people to weak forms of a persuasive argument, much like inoculating people with a small amount of a virus, should motivate them to produce the cognitive equivalent of antibodies—that is, counterarguments—against this weakly advocated position. When later exposed to strong forms of the persuasive attempt, people already possess the motivation and counterarguments to use in their defense and thus more effectively resist the persuasive appeal.

McGuire and Papageorgis (1961) initially tested the idea of attitude inoculation by studying how people fend off challenges to cultural *truisms*, beliefs that people accept without questioning them. For example, most people are told and typically unquestioningly believe that the effects of penicillin have been, almost without exception, of great benefit to humanity.

How do people respond when their truisms are called into question? The researchers inoculated some participants by exposing them to weak arguments against these truisms ("Vaccination shots can cause bleeding or infection") along with counterarguments. Two days later, these and other participants (not previously exposed to the weak arguments) were presented with stronger, logically based arguments that the truisms were not in fact true ("A substantial minority of people have potentially dangerous allergic reactions to penicillin"). Participants who had previously been exposed to the weak arguments were less persuaded by the stronger arguments than those who were not exposed to this inoculation.

Since this initial research, attitude inoculation has been widely studied across a variety of domains, such as politics, advertising, and health care, and has been shown to be a potent means of strengthening resistance to persuasion (Wan & Pfau, 2004). As McGuire originally suggested, when exposed to a weak form of an argument, people tend to generate counterarguments that act like barriers around their initial attitudes, making it harder for a stronger persuasive attempt encountered later to influence their attitudes. This occurs in part because these initial counterarguments make the opposing attitude more accessible (Pfau et al., 2003). As we'll soon see, accessible attitudes have a stronger influence on judgments and behavior.

But some forms of attitude inoculation work better than others. More specifically, the power of inoculation is greater when people play an active role in generating counterarguments (Bernard et al., 2003). In one study (Banerjee & Greene, 2007), junior high students participated in one of two workshops on resisting smoking advertisements or in a third group that did not participate in a workshop. In both of the resistance workshops, students discussed and analyzed antismoking ads. But one workshop went further, encouraging students to create their own antismoking ads. Although both workshop groups were effective in reducing students' intentions to smoke, the group of students who also created their own ads (and thus their own counterarguments) showed the lowest intentions to start smoking.

Thus, one of the catchphrases used to summarize the literature on resistance to persuasion is "Forewarned is forearmed." When we know persuasion is going to attack, we can better arm ourselves. However, a number of interesting consequences can stem from these efforts. Some bode well for our ability to process and reason about persuasion attempts more carefully; others, however, offer a less optimistic forecast.

Consequences of Forewarning

Recognizing Legitimate Appeals

Forewarnings about persuasion can improve our ability to process incoming information accurately. Whereas inoculation gives us a taste of the arguments a would-be persuader will use so that we can better resist them, other types of forewarning give us other tools to pierce the deceptions we may confront as the target of a persuasion attempt. This can help us to not only resist persuasion that relies on deceiving us but can also make us more open to legitimate appeals. This is important because sometimes people try to persuade us to do things that are good for us, and it behooves us to listen to such messages with an open mind.

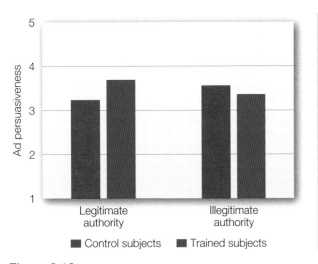

Figure 8.12

Knowledge Is Power

When participants in this study were trained to spot deceptive advertising tactics, they were less persuaded by testimonials given by actors (illegitimate authorities) than were control participants not given this training. They were also more persuaded than untrained participants by testimonials given by legitimate authorities.

[Data source: Sagarin et al. (2002)]

This receptivity is evident in research by Sagarin and colleagues (2002). They trained some of their participants to be suspicious of advertisers' manipulative intent. For example, students were taught clues to diagnose whether a spokesperson in a television commercial is an actual expert or just a model posing as an expert. ("Is that an actor pretending to be a doctor or an actual doctor promoting a brand of pain-reliever?") Other participants were not given this training. Then all subjects were presented with a series of persuasive appeals by both legitimate and illegitimate authorities and were asked to indicate how much they agreed with the position advocated by the authority presented in the commercial.

As you can see in **FIGURE 8.12**, those participants who were given the training were not only more resistant to deceptive persuasion (i.e., when the authority was not actually an authority, such as a model dressed as a stockbroker pitching the *Wall Street Journal*) but also were more likely to be persuaded by commercials by legitimate authorities (e.g., the president of a financial institution pitching an investment fund). Importantly, subsequent studies showed that these skills can last. When participants were given the training and were exposed to commercials a week later, they still were more discriminating.

This research makes two critical points. First, people are most likely to resist persuasion when (a) their motivation to resist is increased (i.e., by being told that advertisers will try to deceive them); and (b) when given the means to do so (i.e., strategies for recognizing illegitimate authorities). Second, when people are armed with the means to resist persuasion, they are also more open to appeals by legitimate authorities.

Making the Effort to Resist

Finally, as much as we might want to resist persuasion in certain contexts, we should recognize that it takes cognitive effort to do so. Recall from chapter 6 our discussion of self-regulatory depletion. People's ability to control their thoughts, desires, and intentions is a limited resource. Much like a physical muscle, this ability can be strengthened with exercise but also can be weakened with repeated use. As a form of self-control, resistance to persuasion falls prey to the processes of self-regulatory depletion.

Burkley (2008) examined this connection in a few different ways. In one study, students had to squeeze a handgrip exerciser continuously for either a short or a long time. They were then exposed to an argument for shortening summer vacation to only one month. Obviously this argument advocated a position with which most students would not agree. Yet those students who engaged in continuous hand-grip activity were more persuaded by the argument than those who did not. This shows that when people have expended their self-regulatory resources (focusing on squeezing the hand grip), they are less able to resist persuasion. Further, in another study, when all students were presented with such arguments (or not) and then asked to squeeze the hand grip, those who resisted the appeal were unable to squeeze the handgrip for as long as those who did not resist persuasion.

These findings show that although resistance to persuasion and physical exertion seem like unrelated tasks, they draw on the same supply of self-regulatory resources. When people deplete that supply by expending physical energy, they have fewer resources left over to resist persuasion, and vice versa. On a considerably more dramatic scale, we see such effects in various forms of intense indoctrination or interviewing, from police interrogation to more unsavory tactics of torture. The subjects may be deprived of basic sustenance needs such as food or sleep in an effort to wear them down, that is, to fatigue them to the point that they will be more open to the examiner's questions. This can be considered the ultimate way of breaking down resistance to persuasion, paving the way for changing someone's attitude.

| Resistance to Persuasion

Resistance is not always futile.

Awareness	Motivation	Inoculation	Consequences of Forewarning
If we're aware of a persuasive appeal, we're better able to resist it.	• Reactance theory explains why people resist persuasion attempts that infringe on their freedom. • Culture influences how much people value freedom, and thus how strongly they react to persuasion attempts.	As with a vaccine, people can build up resistance by defending themselves against weaker arguments first.	• Given the motivation and the means to resist opens people's minds to legitimate appeals. • Resistance takes cognitive effort that can be depleted.

The Relationship Between Attitudes and Behavior

Earlier we said that attempts at changing people's attitudes have the ultimate goal of changing their behavior—for example, getting them to purchase a product, go on a date, or wear their seatbelts. But how well do attitudes really predict behavior?

Consider your own experience. For instance, in anticipation of hanging out with a friend who constantly mooches off you, you might think, "The next time Sven asks to borrow my car, I'm going to tell him what I really think." Yet when Sven subsequently and predictably asks to borrow your ride, you toss him your keys with perhaps only a fleeting glance of disapproval. Some factor besides your attitude toward Sven's mooching determined your actions. It turns out that a number of factors complicate the attitude-behavior relationship.

The first hint of such complicating factors was uncovered by the sociologist Richard LaPiere back in 1934. He traveled across the United States with a young Chinese couple, visiting 251 different hotels and restaurants. At that time, there was rather strong anti-Chinese prejudice in the United States, and there were no broadly enforced laws against ethnic, racial, or gender discrimination. LaPiere was therefore curious to see how many of the places they visited would refuse service to the Chinese couple. As it turned out, they were refused service only in one case.

What makes this finding particularly surprising is that, six months later, LaPiere wrote letters to each establishment he had visited, asking if its employees would serve Chinese individuals. Of the establishments that wrote back, 92 percent said that they would not. But of course, only one actually did refuse service. Although LaPiere acknowledged a number of problems with this study (e.g., different employees might have answered his letter than those he encountered when visiting in person), the findings were striking in their total lack of support for the notion that verbal reports of attitudes guide behavior. Decades later, the relevant literature continued to reveal surprisingly limited support for the influence of attitudes on behavior (Wicker, 1969).

Why Attitudes Often Don't Predict Behavior

One reason attitudes often are poor predictors of behavior is that sometimes people do not know what their attitudes are, or at least don't know exactly why they feel the way they do. As we saw in chapter 5, people can easily verbalize the reasons that one might hold a particular attitude, but those reasons may not reflect their personal, gut-level feelings (Nisbett & Wilson, 1977); thus they can be poor predictors of behavior.

A second reason is that even when people do have a clear attitude that is relevant to a behavior, they often don't appreciate that they have *other* relevant attitudes that pull them in other directions (Fishbein & Ajzen, 1975). For example, have you ever found yourself sitting through a movie that you initially had no interest in seeing? Although you had a negative attitude toward this movie, you may have had other attitudes, such as your desire to please your significant other, who was interested in the movie. In this example, your attitudes toward your relationship won out over your attitude toward the movie to influence your movie-going behavior. As this example foreshadows, understanding why attitudes don't always predict behavior gives us important clues about when attitudes *will* predict behavior (Glasman & Albarracín, 2006).

Factors That Affect How Well Attitudes Predict Behavior

Matching the Attitude to the Behavior

One reason for LaPiere's findings is that when he asked hotel and restaurant employees whether they would serve Chinese individuals, he did not mention the specific details of his visit six months before, such as the fact that the Chinese couple was well-dressed and in the company of an American university professor. Thus, the employees' general attitude toward serving Chinese patrons may have been *too* general to predict their behavior in that specific situation. This highlights an important point: Although general attitudes are poor predictors of specific behaviors, more specific attitudes fare much better; conversely, general attitudes are better predictors of more general classes of behavior.

In a classic illustration of this point, Davidson and Jaccard (1979) asked a sample of married women about their attitudes toward birth control in general. Two years later, they interviewed the women again and asked how often they had used the birth-control pill in the preceding two years (see **FIGURE 8.13**). In the first condition, the researchers asked women, "What is your attitude toward birth control?" They found that responses correlated .08 with Pill-taking behavior. This means that there was practically no relationship between the women's attitude and their behavior.

Why do you think this relationship was so small? Obviously the question was quite general, glossing over many ways of thinking about the Pill. For example, people might have a positive attitude toward birth control in general but feel that the Pill is not the best method. Still others might be trying to get pregnant, so although they might advocate birth control for other people, they are not using birth control themselves.

In the second condition, the researchers asked a more specific question: "What is your attitude toward the birth control pill?" Here they found that the correlation between women's attitude and their behavior improved to .32. This means that women who reported more positive attitudes toward the Pill were somewhat more likely to be taking it. But the relationship between attitude and behavior still was not very strong. In the third condition women were asked about their attitudes "toward *using* birth control pills," and in the fourth condition, their attitude "about using the birth control pill in the next two years." In these conditions, the correlations increased to

Figure 8.13

Predicting Behavior

Attitudes predict behavior better when they are phrased in a very specific way. In 1979, women's use of the Pill was unrelated to their general attitudes toward birth control but was correlated with their attitudes toward the Pill and toward taking the Pill.

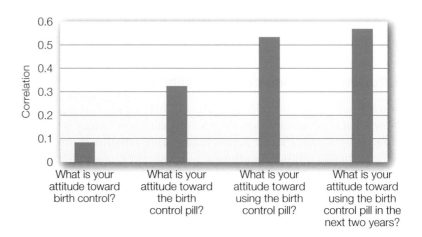

.53 and .57, respectively. These findings show that attitudes that are more specifically relevant to a behavior are better predictors of that behavior.

However, in situations where you are trying to predict a general set of behaviors, more general attitudes do a much better job. For instance, if you're trying to predict whether people will behave in environmentally friendly ways, you're better off getting their attitudes about environmental protection in general rather than one specific attitude. For example, rather than ask them how they feel about recycling soda cans, you should measure attitudes toward a range of proenvironment practices (e.g., support for hybrid cars and protecting endangered species) and combine them into an overall environmentalism attitude (Weigel & Newman, 1976).

Self-presentational Concerns

Another reason that attitudes poorly predicted behavior in LaPiere's study may be that when hotel and restaurant employees were responding in the moment to LaPiere and the couple's visit, they were probably under self-presentational pressures that they were not under when they later described in a letter what they would hypothetically do. In the lobby of a hotel, for example, the employees were most likely concerned with appearing professional and avoiding an unpleasant scene, self-presentational concerns that may have influenced their behavior more than their private attitudes toward Chinese people. In the private response to a letter sent through the mail, though, they could express their negative attitudes more freely without being concerned about public scrutiny.

The distinction between what one is willing to express in public, and what one will express in private, highlights the importance of knowing people's *true* attitudes for predicting their behavior. One technique for learning these attitudes is the *bogus pipeline* (Jones & Sigall, 1971). Imagine that you're participating in a psychology study and the researcher asks you— in front of your peers, who you know are disgusted by the proliferation of reality shows—whether you like to watch *The Voice* and *The Biggest Loser*. Even if you actually enjoy settling in on the sofa and watching the trials and tribulations of people testing their singing voices or trying to lose weight, you might be reluctant to reveal this attitude in front of the other students. In fact, you might even be reluctant to admit to this guilty pleasure if it were just you and the experimenter in the room. But now imagine that the experimenter hooks you up to a polygraph machine—that is, a "lie-detector"—and asks you the same question. Now the experimenter seems to have a pipeline, or a direct route, to your true attitudes. Under these conditions, you might be much more likely to confess your enjoyment of these shows—better that than to be caught lying!

What makes the pipeline bogus, so to speak, is that often the experimenter isn't attaching participants to a real mind-reading machine. What is important is that participants *think* that the experimenter knows exactly what they are thinking. And indeed, when people believe that there is a pipeline into their private thoughts, the attitudes they express predict their behavior better than the attitudes they express when concerned about self-presentation. The bogus pipeline is especially useful in situations where people are under strong pressures to express socially desirable attitudes, or to inhibit socially undesirable attitudes. For example, when child molesters are attached to what appears to be a lie detector, they are more likely to confess their sexual thoughts about children (Gannon et al., 2007).

Implicit Attitudes

Another approach to avoiding seeing merely what is socially desirable is to measure people's *implicit attitudes*, which we introduced in chapter 3. These are attitudes people have but are not consciously aware that they have. Implicit attitudes predict some forms of behavior better than explicit attitudes—those that people can report consciously—because they are less influenced by self-presentational concerns about how they should and should not feel. Social psychologists have developed a number of techniques to measure implicit attitudes. For example, they often present participants with a word or an image (e.g., a picture of an African American face) and then observe how quickly the subjects recognize positive or negative words. If the word or image triggers negative feelings, participants should recognize negative words more quickly.

We will talk about this work in much greater detail when we discuss prejudice in chapter 10. But as you might imagine, it often is undesirable to admit to a prejudiced attitude toward African Americans, or Hispanics, or the physically handicapped. Yet many people clearly possess these prejudiced attitudes (Devine, 1989). Indeed, because people tend to underreport their level of prejudice on explicit measures, the correlation between implicit and explicit racial attitudes is weak (Dovidio et al., 2001). Because implicit attitudes lurk beneath people's conscious awareness, they can predict subtle social behaviors that the people themselves do not recognize. For example, a person claims to have no prejudice toward African Americans, but when talking to African Americans, his body language tells a different story: He makes little eye contact, sits farther away, and interrupts the others' sentences. These behaviors are poorly predicted by his explicit attitude ("I thought the conversation went great!") but correlate highly with his implicit attitude (Dovidio et al., 2002).

Implicit attitudes are good predictors of many other types of behavior. For example, implicit attitudes toward smoking do a better job than explicit attitudes in predicting whether teens start smoking (Sherman et al., 2009), and implicit attitudes toward drinking better predict drinking behavior (Houben & Wiers, 2007). You may notice that both of these examples pertain to behaviors that are often engaged at the spur of the moment. And indeed, whereas explicit attitudes often do a better job of predicting more deliberate and reasoned behavior, implicit attitudes often fare better in predicting spontaneous behavior (Rydell & McConnell, 2006).

The Strength of the Attitude

Let's return to our example of holding a negative attitude toward a certain movie while, at the same time, holding a positive attitude toward a romantic partner who wants to see the movie. How can we determine which attitude will win out, so to speak, and exert a greater influence on your behavior? In general, whichever attitude is stronger, or held more firmly, will exert a more potent influence. So if you really detest this kind of movie or the leading actor, and your liking for your partner is not especially strong, you might be more likely to bail on the movie outing. Stronger attitudes not only influence behavior more, they are also more enduring over time and resistant to change (Petty & Krosnick, 1995). So, in this example, your partner would have a very difficult time trying to persuade you to see this movie.

What determines the strength of an attitude? There are a number of factors to consider. First, an attitude tends to be stronger when it stems from a person's own experiences rather than second-hand experiences they have heard about from others. Thus, if you see the trailer for a particular movie and think, "This stinks," your attitude toward that movie is likely to be stronger than if you heard from an acquaintance that the movie is not even worth renting.

Because attitudes stemming from firsthand experience are stronger, they do a better job of predicting behavior. This effect was shown in a study that took advantage of a severe housing shortage at Cornell University during the 1970s (Regan & Fazio, 1977). In the throes of this shortage, many first-year students had to make do with temporary accommodations, such as sleeping on a cot in a dormitory lounge. Others were fortunate enough to be assigned permanent housing. Regan and Fazio contacted students from both groups and assessed their attitudes toward the housing crisis, asking them, for example, how much they had suffered and whether they thought the university was dealing with the situation effectively. Later, the experimenters gave participants the opportunity to take action, such as signing a petition or joining a committee of students to make recommendations about the crisis. Although the two groups of students had roughly equivalent attitudes toward the housing crisis, those who had to suffer through it personally (rather than simply hearing about it) had a much stronger connection between their attitudes and their behavior. The more negative their attitudes, the more likely they were to engage in behavior to try and correct the situation. For those without the personal experience, the connection between their attitudes and their behavior was much weaker.

Another factor that contributes to attitude strength is the extent to which the individual has a vested interest in the attitude. The greater our vested interest in an attitude, the stronger the attitude, and thus the better the attitude will predict behavior. Consider, for example, the current drinking age where you live. How bummed would you be if a law were passed that raised the drinking age by a couple of years? Would you do anything to prevent such a law from passing? Do you think that it might depend on how old you currently are? Sivacek and Crano (1982) studied just this situation in Michigan in the late 1970s, when a ballot was proposed to raise the minimum drinking age from 18 to 21. The researchers assessed students' ages, their attitudes toward the proposal, and their interest in volunteering to campaign (e.g., call voters) against the proposal. Among students who were over 21, and thus had little vested interest in the drinking age issue, there was only a small relationship between their attitudes and their behavior. However, among those under 21, who would have been affected personally by the proposal, there was a much tighter relationship between their attitudes and behavior. The more against the proposal they were, the more likely they were to volunteer to work against it.

A final factor that influences attitude strength is the importance of the *attitude domain*. Two people may hold a similar attitude, but for one person the domain in question may be much more important. An avid sports fan and a casual fan may both like the Yankees. But sports are more important to the avid fan, who will have the stronger attitude about the Yankees and be more likely to purchase Yankees gear. Here's a personal example from your current author. My wife and I, though both liking Thai food in general, dislike this local Thai restaurant in our area. But whereas you couldn't drag me there with a pack of wild horses (I'd rather starve), she will concede to going there if others have already chosen that location. For me, food quality is more important, whereas for my wife, being socially amiable is more important. Our dislike is the same, but the importance of the domain (food quality vs. socializing) varies. When a domain is important to us, our attitude about it is more likely to influence our behavior. In a study of political attitudes and voting behavior, for example, Krosnick (1988) showed that the political policies that were most important to people exerted the strongest influence on their actual voting behavior.

The Accessibility of the Attitude

In situations where we have multiple attitudes that are relevant to a given behavior, the attitude that is most accessible will be the one most likely to guide behavior. We see this demonstrated in a classic study by Fazio and Williams (1986). They measured the accessibility of an attitude by measuring the speed (or *latency*) of a person's response. The basic idea is that the more quickly a person indicates her attitude when asked, the more accessible that attitude is. Fazio and Williams examined whether more accessible attitudes toward the then American presidential candidates Ronald Reagan and Walter Mondale would predict people's actual voting behavior. They assessed how quickly American citizens indicated their attitudes toward Reagan and Mondale. A few months later, after the election, they called those people and asked whom they voted for. What did the researchers find? The more quickly a participant indicated her attitude, the better that attitude predicted her voting behavior. For example, someone who more quickly said she had a positive attitude toward Reagan was more likely to vote for Reagan than someone who indicated the same positive attitude, but took longer to do so.

The fact that accessible attitudes predict behavior gives us important insights into why attitudes may at times fail to predict behavior. As we go about our daily affairs and interact with the world, we're often focused on what is happening around us, and we're not thinking of our attitudes. And unless we think about our attitudes, they are not accessible and thus have little influence on our behavior.

In a study from the 1980s, voters who were quickest to express a positive attitude toward a presidential candidate (Ronald Reagan, top; Walter Mondale, bottom) were the most likely to actually cast a vote for that candidate (Fazio & Williams, 1986).

[Dennis Oulds/Central Press/Getty Images]

Can you recall a theory that we discussed in chapter 5 that explains what kinds of situations might make our attitudes accessible and thus more likely to influence our behavior? If you came up with *self-awareness theory* (Duval & Wicklund, 1972), you hit the nail on the head. To recap, this theory explains that people's attention can be focused internally on the self or externally on the environment. When people are self-aware, they compare their current behavior with the standard, or attitude, that is relevant to their situation. If possible, they then adjust their behavior so that it matches that salient attitude.

Recall, for example, the study by Carver (1975) (see chapter 5, pp. 169–170) that initially measured participants' attitudes toward the use of punishment in teaching. When participants were not self-aware, their preexisting attitude about punishment did a poor job of predicting the level of punishment they administered when trying to teach another person a vocabulary list. Yet when participants were made self-aware by looking in a mirror, their preexisting attitudes toward punishment were much better predictors of their willingness to open up a can of punishment. The interpretation here is that self-awareness made the preexisting attitude more influential.

Think
ABOUT

[© Pixel Youth Movement 3/Alamy]

Along with heightened self-awareness, simply priming an attitude or making it salient can also make it more likely to affect behavior. In one study, Snyder and Kendzierski (1982) first measured participants' attitudes toward sex discrimination. Weeks later, they had participants read a case regarding sex discrimination and render their own verdicts. Before they did, half of them were instructed, "You may want to think about how you feel about sex discrimination before rendering your verdict." For participants not reminded to consider their attitudes, their prior attitude had virtually no influence on their verdicts. However, for those who were reminded, their prior attitude was a good predictor of their verdicts. So, if you went camping and had a great time with friends, and awoke the next morning and saw a bunch of cans and bottles on the ground, would simply reminding your friends of their pro-environment attitudes (presuming they have them) motivate them to help you clean up the camp site?

Theory of planned behavior
Theory proposing that attitudes, subjective norms, and perceived behavioral control interact to shape people's behavioral intentions.

How Attitudes Influence Behavior

But how is it that our attitudes actually guide our behavior? Do we just feel positively or negatively about something and then act accordingly? Or is there an intermediary step along the way? One influential theory proposes that our attitudes do not influence our behavior directly; rather, they do so through our *intentions*. According to the theory of planned behavior (Ajzen, 1985), attitudes are one of three ingredients in the intentions that we form (see **FIGURE 8.14**). The other two ingredients are *subjective norms* and *perceived behavioral control*. *Attitude* is your positive or negative evaluation of performing the behavior. Subjective norms are your perceptions of approval or disapproval of performing the behavior—that is, how much you perceive that others in your life think that a given behavior is a good or bad thing to do. And finally, perceived behavioral control is how much control you think you have over the behavior—whether you think you can do it or not. These three ingredients combine to shape your intentions, which in turn directly influence your behavior.

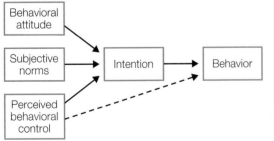

Figure 8.14

Theory of Planned Behavior

Attitudes, norms, and perceived control all shape people's intentions to engage in behavior.

APPLICATION
Understanding Risky Behavior

For an illustration of how the theory of planned behavior works, consider whether or not someone chooses to practice safe sex. If the person has a positive attitude about using condoms, thinks that others view them as important to use (a positive norm perception), and believes that he can in fact buy them and put them on (a strong sense of behavioral control), then he should have a strong intention to use condoms. This intention will be more likely to translate to behavior, and the person should in fact use a condom when having sex. But let's say, for example, that the individual's peer group or partner thinks that wearing condoms is not cool. In this case, despite the individual's positive attitude, he may develop weaker intentions and thus make the (potentially deadly) mistake of not wearing a condom during sex. Indeed, research has examined just these kinds of decisions (Albarracín et al., 2001; Sheeran & Taylor, 1999), as well as many others in a variety of different domains from health to environmental behavior to consumer purchasing.

The picture gets more complicated, though, when we recognize that many types of behaviors—particularly risky behaviors such as starting to smoke, having unsafe sex, and drinking and driving—rarely are planned in advance. Rather, these behaviors are often more reactive to the situation. People find themselves in situations where these behaviors are options that they unfortunately, and far too frequently, can't turn down (Gibbons et al., 2006). This is often especially the case with adolescent risky behavior. In these situations, intentions are not the most relevant factor to consider. Instead, it is more informative to consider people's *willingness* to engage in the behavior (Gibbons & Gerrard, 1997). As described in Rick Gibbons and Meg Gerrard's prototype/willingness model of health behavior, the distinction between willingness and intention is rather subtle but important. Like intention, willingness is influenced by one's attitudes and the norm and images of what one thinks is good to do, but willingness refers more specifically to a person's openness to being influenced by social circumstances. Thus, a young man may have no plans to drive drunk, but when drunk and with the opportunity to drive himself home, he may be more likely to do so. The point here is that attitudes often indirectly influence our behavior, and when it comes to "opportunistic" behaviors—such as risky behaviors that are often unplanned—it can be our willingness that best enables prediction about whether we will partake or not.

Prototype/willingness model of health behavior The idea that willingness refers specifically to a person's openness to being influenced by social circumstances, so that when it comes to opportunistic behaviors, one's willingness is the best predictor of behavior.

| **SECTION**
review | The Relationship Between Attitudes and Behavior |

| A number of factors complicate the attitude-behavior relationship. |

Attitudes don't always predict behavior	**Factors affecting the attitude-behavior link**	**How attitudes influence behavior**
• Attitudes may not reflect gut-level feelings. • One attitude may be trumped by other attitudes.	• Attitudes that are directly relevant are better predictors of behavior. • Self-presentation may mask the influence of attitudes on behavior. • Implicit attitudes are better predictors of subtle or spontaneous behavior. • Stronger and more accessible attitudes will most likely guide behavior.	• The theory of planned behavior proposes that attitudes, along with subjective norms and perceived behavioral control, form our intentions, which motivate behavior. • Attitudes also influence willingness to engage in a behavior, which plays a key role in decisions to engage in risky health behaviors.

CONNECT ONLINE:

Macmillan Education **LaunchPad**

Check out our videos and additional resources located at:
www.macmillanhighered.com/launchpad/greenberg1e

Group Processes

In the previous chapter, we examined how people are influenced in subtle and not so subtle ways by the behavior, requests, and commands of other individuals. In this chapter, we will explore the ways in which people are also influenced by their membership in social groups. Virtually every human on the planet identifies with at least one fundamental cultural group, whether it is a small tribe or a billion-person nation. In addition, other groups may be formed on the basis of common genes (your family), geography (neighborhood associations, gangs), ideology (Catholics, the Young Republicans), causes (MADD, Greenpeace), goals (the Senate Committee on Homeland Security, the NCAA Division I Basketball Committee), broad social interests (sororities and fraternities), shared experiences (Alcoholics Anonymous, alumni groups), and hobbies (the Garden Club of America, Hoopaholics for hula hoop enthusiasts!). Together, these groups influence people in important ways, socializing them into a worldview and validating their place within that local culture.

Let's begin with an interesting example of such a group: deadheads. In the history of rock and roll, few bands have had such devoted fans as the Grateful Dead. When

Tim Klein/Getty Images

Deadheads are more than just a collection of people who like the Grateful Dead; they are a cultural group with their own norms and rituals.
[Lynn Goldsmith/Corbis]

the band began touring in the late 1960s, die-hard fans, known affectionately as "deadheads," piled in their vans and followed along, knowing that the band's improvisational style meant that no two concerts would be the same. Over the next 30 years, a growing number of deadheads traveled with the band from city to city, some of them spending decades of their lives on the road.

To say that deadheads are a bunch of people who all like the Grateful Dead misses the strong sense of community that binds them together. Before the invention of social networking sites and blogs, deadheads shared personal stories with each other through newsletters such as the *Grateful Dead Almanac*, and they created their own economy at concerts, buying and selling veggie burritos, T-shirts, and other essentials.

As a community, deadheads expected each other to behave in certain ways and socialized newcomers to conform to those expectations. This can be seen when, following the release of the band's 1987 album *In The Dark*, concerts were flooded by younger fans whose belligerent behavior disrupted the mellow atmosphere that deadheads treasure. To restore order, a set of senior deadheads organized a mass distribution of flyers instructing everyone to "cool out." Deadheads also organized substance-abuse programs and worship services. Even today, two decades after the band's guitarist and front man Jerry Garcia died and the band stopped touring, deadheads continue to interact and help each other by sharing travel stories on fan websites and exchanging recordings of live performances free of charge. The group has become much more than a collection of people who happened to like the same band.

What Is a Group?

This question may seem strange at first, because you probably have an intuitive sense of what a group is. Are deadheads a group? You'd probably say "yes." Is a soccer team a group? Certainly. But sometimes it is difficult to say for sure whether a collection of individuals makes up a group. Are Canadians a group? Are strangers in line at the movies a group? What about the students in your social psychology class?

Most people probably would agree with your intuitive answers to these questions (Lickel et al., 2000; Lickel et al., 2001). When study volunteers were asked to rate various collections of individuals, they consistently categorized them into four types of groups: intimacy groups (such as family, romantic partners, friends), task groups (committees, orchestras, teams), social categories (women, Americans, Jews), and loose associations (people in the same neighborhood, people who like classical music).

People also share the intuition that some groups are more, well, *group-y* than others. The formal term is **entitativity**, the degree to which a collection of people feels like a cohesive group (Campbell, 1958). For example, people consider intimacy groups to be more entitative than task groups.

What features of groups makes them seem more or less cohesive? One is the presence of a *common bond*, the degree to which group members interact with and depend on each other to meet their needs and attain their goals (Johnson et al., 2006; Prentice et al., 1994; Rabbie & Horwitz, 1988; Shaw, 1981). Sometimes these interactions are based on *communal sharing*—the sense that "What's mine is yours" (Fiske, 1990). (For a refresher on this concept, go back to chapter 2, pp. 61–62, "How Individuals Relate to Each Other: Individualism/Collectivism.") You probably interact in this way when you sit around with your closest group of friends from high school. Other types of interactions are based on *market pricing*: "I will wash your back if you wash mine." This might be how you interact with classmates on an

Entitativity The degree to which a collection of people feels like a cohesive group.

assignment, for example. The point is that both types of interactions can produce a strong sense of common bond (Clark & Mills, 1979; Lickel et al., 2006).

Feeling a strong common bond in a group creates a sense of cohesion (Cartwright & Zander, 1960), but this isn't necessarily good. On the one hand, cohesive groups are more successful than less cohesive groups at reaching their goals. For instance, highly cohesive athletic teams perform better than less cohesive teams (Carron et al., 2002). However, high cohesiveness can sometimes *undermine* group performance: If group members are preoccupied with maintaining cohesion and getting along, they may be reluctant to share unpopular ideas out of fear of "rocking the boat," even when those ideas might be helpful. Later, we'll talk more about group decision making.

A second feature of groups that ups their entitativity is a *common identity*. Groups often form among individuals who share similar characteristics, and people also come to feel a certain "we-ness," or shared attachment, to groups that they belong to (Prentice et al., 1994; Rabbie & Horwitz, 1988; Turner et al., 1987). But group members may also feel a common identity when they behave similarly, and even if they simply look alike (Ip et al., 2006). Sharing the same gender, race, or even clothing style can create a sense of common identity. So, too, can having a common bond and working closely on a shared goal. For instance, a team of medical researchers might form a strong group identity as they collaborate to develop a new medicine. In fact, they might take on a team name and logo and play together in the local kickball competition.

The perception of a common identity can also come from the presence of a shared threat or common challenge (Allport, 1954; James, 1906). For instance, families often experience a renewed sense of unity in the face of adversity. School spirit reaches its peak when athletic contests with the traditional rival approach. Citizens of a nation often come together in solidarity during times of war. For example, when United Airlines Flight 93 took off for San Francisco on the morning of September 11, 2001, the 37 passengers were just a loose collection of people. But when four men on board hijacked the plane with plans to crash it into either the White House or the U.S. Capitol, the other passengers began thinking and behaving in terms of "we" instead of "I." Their coordinated assault against the hijackers successfully diverted the plane from its intended target. The group-binding power of a common enemy is so powerful that leaders sometimes invent an enemy figure—a "them"—in order to cement the perception of "us" and transform a collective into a group (Silverstein, 1992).

The feeling of being in a group can set in motion a number of psychological processes that strongly influence people's thoughts and behavior. Even loose associations, such as people standing on a street corner looking up at the sky, can elicit conformity (chapter 7). Social categories such as race, ethnicity, and gender fuel stereotyping and prejudice (chapter 10). And much of our day-to-day experience is influenced by our intimate relationships with close others (chapter 15). In this chapter, we'll stick mainly to task groups and loose connections—groups that people can choose to enter and exit. Our goal will be to understand how our attitudes and behavior changes when we are in these relatively small, face-to-face groups and collectives. But along the way, we will also make connections to other types of groups.

The movie *United 93* tells the story of how passengers on board this hijacked airliner came together as a group to thwart the terrorists' plan to fly the plane into the White House or the U.S. Capitol on September 11, 2001.

[Universal/The Kobal Collection]

SECTION review | What Is a Group?

The term *entitative* describes the degree to which a group is cohesive.

A group is cohesive when its members:

• Share a common bond as a result of interacting and depending on each other.
• Share a common identity based on similar characteristics, goals, or challenges.

Why Do People Join and Identify With Groups?

For the better part of human history, the groups into which people were born—such as family and caste—largely defined what a person could be and do, and it was not possible to voluntarily exit those groups and join different ones. Even in the most progressive of modern societies, ethnicity, social class, nationality, family, and gender are ascribed by others to people at birth and still influence how people think and behave. People don't choose their membership in these groups, yet these aspects of identity are hard to shake off. For example, the most unpatriotic person may take a strong

Think

ABOUT

[Hannah Peters/ Getty Images]

interest in her country's medal count when the summer or winter Olympic Games roll around every two years. Why should people be so proud of their country's sports success when they didn't choose where to be born and have played no direct role in their team's success? When you hear about the final count of medals from the Olympic Games, do you automatically look to see how your nation did compared with others?

Fortunately, most group memberships are not ascribed. If you are reading this textbook, chances are you have the opportunity to join any number of intramural sports teams and social clubs, committees, religious groups, and political parties. You can even move up the career ladder to join a higher social class. Of course, joining groups such as these also requires time and effort, and in some cases, entails stressful initiations and perhaps the loss of individual freedoms.

Why do people identify with groups that they are arbitrarily born into? And why join groups at all, given the commitments and personal sacrifices involved?

Promoting Survival and Achieving Goals

One answer to these questions is that belonging to groups has been crucial to the development and survival of humans as a species. Over the course of evolution, humans survived because they relied on social networks to acquire and share food, transmit information, rear children, and avoid predators and other threats (Brewer & Caporael, 2006). Within this environment, individuals with characteristics that helped them to get along with others—such as the desire for social acceptance, cooperativeness, and loyalty—had better chances of living long enough to pass on their genes to future generations. Those who lacked those characteristics had a poorer chance of survival and reproduction. Through the natural selection process, modern humans might possess an innate desire to belong to groups and to avoid being kicked out of them (Baumeister & Leary, 1995).

This evolutionary perspective on group living suggests that people will almost always identify strongly with the family and cultural groups in which they were raised. People form close bonds within kinship groups, and with non-kin in the vicinity, because people do not survive for very long without the cooperation of others (Kurzban & Neuberg, 2005). This helps us understand why people have a generally positive view of their hometown, local region, and country.

People also form and join groups to accomplish goals that they would be unlikely to accomplish on their own (Sherif, 1966). Most human achievements—from making a movie to incarcerating criminals—require the coordination of many people working in groups. For example, the textbook you are currently reading is the product of thousands of people who collaborate in a vast network of specialized groups, from lumberjacks to copy editors to truckers to ink manufacturers.

Reducing Uncertainty

Life is filled with uncertainties, from the location of your keys to the content of next week's physics exam. People generally dislike being uncertain about themselves. Nor do they like being uncertain about who other people are and how they might behave.

According to uncertainty-identity theory (Hogg, 2007), people join and identify with groups in order to reduce these negative feelings of uncertainty about themselves and others.

How does belonging to groups reduce uncertainty? Groups reinforce people's faith in their *cultural worldview* and their valued place within it. Most core beliefs can never be proven through personal experience. Even scientific facts—such as the fact that the earth revolves around the sun—are not things that people generally see firsthand. Rather, confidence in these beliefs comes from social consensus: As more people share a belief, the truer that belief will seem to be (Berger & Luckmann, 1967; Festinger, 1954). Group ceremonies (e.g., rites of passage) and group-made products (e.g., fairy tales) reinforce these beliefs, starting at the beginning of development.

A second way groups reduce uncertainty is by prescribing norms and roles. As we discussed in chapter 2, *norms* are rules for how all members of a group ought to think and behave. Most norms are unspoken agreements about what behavior is acceptable or unacceptable, but they can also be expressed formally, as when some deadheads handed out flyers instructing concertgoers to "stay cool." Whereas norms dictate how all group members should behave, *roles* are expectations for people in certain positions. When you are eating at a restaurant, you obey a norm against shouting or yelling loudly, but your server has a unique role that allows him to walk off with your credit card, even though you cannot walk off with his.

Norms and roles reduce uncertainty by providing clear guidelines for how people should think and act. As a result, people don't need to think too hard about how to conduct themselves from one situation to the next. When people feel especially uncertain about who they are, uncertainty-identity theory predicts that they will become more strongly identified with tightly knit or entitative groups that can offer a sense of self-understanding.

To test this hypothesis, Hogg and colleagues (Hogg et al., 2007) formed small groups of participants who did not previously know each other. Half of the participants were told that they and the other members of their group had all responded very similarly on a series of questionnaires and that their group was very different from other groups. In other words, they learned that their group was high in entitativity. The other participants were told that there wasn't much similarity in how the members of their group had responded, and that all the groups were fairly similar to each other. This information should have made their group seem low in entitativity.

Then, in what seemed to be an unrelated task, half the participants were asked to write about ways in which they felt uncertain about themselves, their lives, and their future, while the other half of the participants wrote about aspects of their life that made them feel certain. Finally, all of the participants were asked how much they identified with the group that they had just become part of in the study. As the researchers predicted, increasing uncertainty about the self increased group identification, but only when the group was high in entitativity (see **FIGURE 9.1**). If you think back to when you first started college or university, did you quickly identify with a new group in order to manage the uncertainty of such a major life transition?

Uncertainty-identity theory The theory that people join and identify with groups in order to reduce negative feelings of uncertainty about themselves and others.

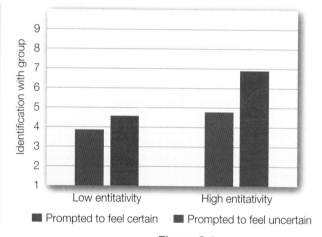

Prompted to feel certain   **Prompted to feel uncertain**

Figure 9.1

Group Identification Reduces Uncertainty

When participants were made to feel uncertain about themselves, they identified more strongly with a new group that was high in entitativity.

[Data source: Hogg et al. (2007)]

Think
ABOUT

[Robert Daly/Caiaimage/ Getty Images]

In addition to reducing uncertainty about oneself, norms and roles also reduce uncertainty about other people by making their behavior seem orderly and predictable. For example, groups usually have a norm of cooperating and agreeing with the other members of the group (Turner & Oakes, 1989). So even if you know nothing about an individual, if you know what groups she belongs to, you can expect her to behave in line with those groups' norms and roles. For example, after reading the introduction to this chapter, you may have a reasonably clear expectation of how a deadhead would act. Of course, as we will see later, such generalizations and stereotypes can also lead to errors in judgment.

Bolstering Self-esteem

Social identity theory The theory that group identities are an important part of self-definition and a key source of self-esteem.

Ingroup bias A tendency to favor groups we belong to more than those that we don't.

According to social identity theory, belonging to groups is an important source of self-esteem (Tajfel & Turner, 1979; Turner et al., 1987). As the theory maintains, personal identity—an understanding of oneself *as an individual*—is shaped by group memberships. If groups are a source of identity, and if people are motivated to view themselves in a positive light, then it follows that people would be motivated to view their groups positively as well. Indeed, people generally show a strong ingroup bias, behaving more favorably toward groups they belong to than to those that they don't (Hogg, 2006). In the next chapter we will show how ingroup bias sometimes leads people to dislike outgroups. But for now we can see that social groups satisfy the person's need for a clear and positive sense of self.

Think
ABOUT

If groups are a source of self-esteem, then you might as well identify most strongly with those groups that help enhance your self-image. You probably have a variety of group identities that may help you feel good about yourself. Try listing several things that make you the person you are. Chances are your list will include group memberships, such as "student," that you see as very positive.

People also enhance their self-esteem by identifying with successful or high-status groups. For instance, they might bask in the reflected glory of a team victory even when it is evident that they had no personal involvement in or responsibility for the group's accomplishments (see chapter 6) (Cialdini et al., 1976). By belonging to groups, people can feel good about themselves without lifting a finger!

Managing Mortality Concerns

As you'll recall from the discussion in chapter 2 on the existential perspective in social psychology, people need to cope with the threatening knowledge of their mortality. They do so by clinging to two psychological resources: faith in a cultural worldview and a sense of self-esteem. Belonging to groups strengthens these resources by allowing people to feel connected to something that is bigger and longer lasting than their personal existence. Although a person is painfully aware that she inevitably will die one day, she can take solace from the fact that because she belongs to an ancestral line, a national or religious group, a political movement, a scientific or artistic field, or some other enduring group, some part of her will live on symbolically after her body has perished. Studies in support of this idea show that people who are reminded of their death (in comparison to other negative topics) tend to view their country, religious organization, and other groups to which they belong more favorably, and as higher in entitativity and longevity (e.g., Castano & Dechesne, 2005; Sani et al., 2009).

SECTION review | Why Do People Join and Identify With Groups?

People are born into some groups and join others voluntarily. People strongly identify with both types of groups. Here is why:

Promoting survival and achieving goals	**Reducing uncertainty**	**Bolstering self-esteem**	**Managing mortality concerns**
• During human evolution, group cooperation benefitted survival and reproduction. • Hence, modern humans have an innate desire to belong to groups.	• People dislike feeling uncertain about themselves and others. • Belonging to a group reduces negative feelings of uncertainty.	• Groups are a source of self-esteem. • By viewing their group in a positive light, people feel better about themselves.	• Groups connect people to something bigger and longer lasting than their own existence. • Hence, belonging to a group eases mortality concerns.

Cooperation in Groups

The fantastic ability of humans to cooperate with each other is everywhere we look. Just marvel at how far human beings have come from their evolutionary beginnings to the construction of complex civilizations. In your own experience, your food, shelter, clothing, and physical safety, not to mention roads, electric power, waste management, intricate electronics, mass transit systems, institutions of higher education, and social welfare programs are all available to you thanks to the cooperation of many people. What's more, the big challenges facing humanity today boil down to problems of group cooperation: How do conflicting groups come to trust each other? How can groups with competing interests make compromises and reach agreements?

Social Dilemmas and the Science of Cooperation

Because cooperation is critical for groups to develop trade and build economic relationships, the psychological study of cooperation and trust is often carried out by researchers interested in behavioral economics and decision making. The method used in this research is to have participants make a decision so that researchers can measure how they weigh their own self-interest against a larger goal. These types of decisions are called *social dilemmas* because they occur in situations in which what is good for the individual (and in the short term) might not be good for the group or within a larger social context.

The Prisoner's Dilemma

The best known social dilemma is the Prisoner's Dilemma, modeled after a scene you've probably seen played out on countless television law dramas. **FIGURE 9.2** depicts a typical setup. You and your partner have been apprehended after committing a burglary and hiding your loot. The detectives are interrogating the two of you in separate

Figure 9.2

The Prisoner's Dilemma

In the Prisoner's Dilemma, you decide between cooperating and competing with a partner. Your decision depends on how much you trust your partner to cooperate with you.

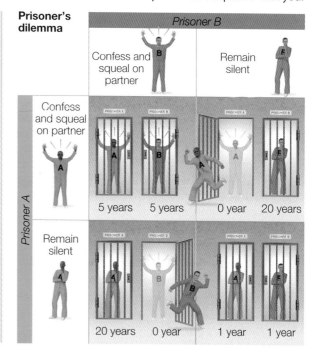

rooms. They know you did the crime, but they need to build their case. You are offered a lighter charge if you confess to the heist and rat on your friend. The dilemma is that you know that your partner is being offered the same deal. If you both remain silent (i.e., cooperate with one another), the prosecution's case will be flimsy, and you'll both get light sentences. But the best-case scenario for you personally would be to confess and squeal on your partner, assuming he's faithfully keeping quiet. By adopting this more competitive strategy (sometimes called *defection*), you walk away with a fine, whereas he does a long stretch at Sing Sing. Then again, if he's thinking the same thing, you might both end up confessing and both be locked up for five years. So maybe you should just keep your mouth shut and hope he does the same. Such a decision requires trust, and if your partner violates that trust and confesses, you'll be the one spending 20 years in the joint. What would you do?

When people are paired with partners to play this game over a series of trials, they often end up adopting a *tit-for-tat strategy*, reciprocating whatever their partners did on the last trial. A cooperative move on one trial cues the partner to make a cooperative move on the next trial. Of course, competition will also be reciprocated with competition. And generally once one player begins playing competitively, the other person responds in kind to avoid getting burned in future trials. A better strategy than tit for tat is *win-stay, lose-shift*: Stick with a strategy if it was successful on the previous trial but switch if the previous strategy resulted in failure (Nowak & Sigmund, 1993).

When Cooperation Is the Key to Economic Growth and Stability

Have you ever stopped to consider how the money we use is itself a form of cooperation? If you didn't agree to the value of your nation's currency, any purchase you made would involve an intense debate over the value of the $5.00 bill you are offering in exchange for a sandwich. Not only is it an act of cooperation to agree on the value of currency, it also can be an act of cooperation to defend it. Two national case studies make these points clear.

First, consider the case of Barbados, a former British colony. During the early 1990s, Barbados experienced an economic crisis that threatened to cripple the country. One proposed solution was to devalue the Barbadian currency, just as neighboring Jamaica had done in 1978. But the government refused and instead used persuasion techniques such as appealing to national pride to orchestrate cooperation among employers, labor unions, and the workers themselves.

The result was that employees agreed to accept a one-time 9% reduction in their wages, and businesses agreed to keep price increases at a minimum while the economy

weathered the storm and began growing again (Henry & Miller, 2009). Everyone took a temporary hit to their own economic self-interest, but in doing so they protected the value of their nation's currency, and the country quickly bounced back from its recession.

In the case of Barbados, people would not have been willing to sacrifice their own personal self-interest to preserve the value of their currency if they didn't have a strong shared belief that the currency had value. What happens when people lose that shared belief? How can they get it back?

[© Glyn Thomas/Alamy]

At the heart of the prisoner's dilemma is a very basic decision. Can I trust you or can't I? If I can't, I'd better protect myself by defecting. Once distrust is there, both sides compete with each other. This is how nations racing to have the largest armed force and weapons stockpiles end up finding it difficult to strike a new, more cooperative pact for disarmament.

Resource Dilemmas

The Prisoner's Dilemma is a scenario in which the outcome of a decision is interdependent with the choices that others make. Other social dilemmas involve competition for scarce resources. One resource dilemma is called the *commons dilemma*. The term *commons* comes from medieval times, when people would bring their herds to the town commons to graze (Hardin, 1968). Although it was in everyone's self-interest to keep the commons healthy, overgrazing by each individual farmer could easily spell the destruction of the resource, creating the "tragedy of the commons." The same dilemma arises in people's modern lives. Nearly all issues of environmental conservation are examples of the commons dilemma. It is easy for each individual to think, "Oh, if I use just a little more water than I should, not much harm will be done," or for a corporation to say, "If we cut down just a bit more rain forest than we need, no one will notice." The problem is that when many people or groups think this way, the common resources start to dry up. Solving a commons dilemma requires cooperation of self-restraint to avoid depleting a limited resource.

Twenty years ago, Brazil faced its own economic crisis. After decades of printing money, inflation skyrocketed in the early 1990s. Imagine that one day you could buy a carton of eggs for $1.00, but by the end of the year a carton of eggs would cost you $1,000.00! The rate of inflation was so high that shopkeepers increased the prices of their goods every single day. As a result, people lost all trust in their government and in the value of their currency. As you know by now, trust is the key to cooperation.

How did Brazil turn its economy around so that today it is poised to become a global leader? A group of economists formulated a scheme to create a new currency that everyone could believe in. This new currency initially existed only as a name—the *unidade real de valor*, or unit of real value (URV). It was fixed to be the equivalent of one U.S. dollar. Although people still were paying for things with the old, inflated currency, they got used to *thinking* of prices in terms of this new, more stable form of money because products and services were all labeled in URVs. On July 1, 1994, all banks across the country began using newly printed *real* notes in place of the old currency. Within six months faith in the economy was completely restored and inflation ended (Joffe-Walt, 2010).

As these two stories make clear, people can cooperate both in belief and in behavior. Trust is the linchpin to making cooperation succeed. In both examples, though, people also were cooperating with others who shared a common national identity. Their identification with their country and its currency as a symbol of cultural value might also have played a role in fostering cooperation.

Earlier in this chapter, we discussed four factors that motivate people to identify with their groups: achieving goals, reducing uncertainty, bolstering self-esteem, and managing mortality concerns. How do you think each of these factors might have played a role in facilitating cooperation in Barbados and Brazil?

[John W. Banagan/Getty Images]

Another type of resource dilemma is called the *public goods dilemma*. A valued resource can continue to exist only if everyone contributes something to it. Local blood banks, libraries, and public radio and television are all examples of public goods that endure only because enough people chip in to keep them going. Solving a public goods dilemma requires cooperation of contributions so that the resource can be maintained. Indeed, taxes are society's solution to this dilemma: Although you might not like to see those taxes come out of your weekly paycheck, they do help pay for the roads you drive on, the schooling you have received, and the parks where you vacation.

In both kinds of resource dilemmas, beware of *free riders*. These are individuals who take more than their fair share from the common pool or refuse to contribute to the public good, even while enjoying the same benefits. Free riders serve their own self-interest instead of cooperating for the larger social goal.

Taxes may be a pain, but they pay for many valued public resources that depend on everyone's chipping in.
[Kevork Djansezian/Getty Images]

Distribution Games

Researchers also study cooperation by looking at how people behave when faced with distribution games. These are called *games* because they involve somewhat artificial situations, yet they are not frivolous: They reveal the fundamental psychological processes by which people make cooperative decisions in their everyday lives. Distribution games are set up so that one person or group has the power to decide how resources get distributed. In the *ultimatum game*, one person (the decider) is given a real sum of money and told that she can decide how much to keep and how much to give to another person. The other person (the recipient) then chooses to either accept or reject this offer; but if the recipient rejects the offer, no one gets money. Researchers can look at whether people are more or less likely to distribute outcomes equally. The *dictator game* is similar, except that the recipient doesn't have the option of "punishing" the decision maker by rejecting his or her sum. This allows researchers to look at people's reactions to unfair distribution of resources.

In both games, people often distribute money equally, even though it clearly would be in their self-interest to take the whole pot and give nothing to the recipient (Camerer, 2003). People value fairness. In fact, when deciders playing the dictator game are primed with the concept of fairness and thus motivated to do the right thing, they sometimes give away more money than they keep for themselves (Jonas et al., 2013). Recipients also will punish an unfair decider by rejecting his or her offer in the ultimatum game, even when such punishment comes at a cost to themselves. If your partner offers you only $2.00 and chooses to keep $8.00 for himself, you might reject the offer and forfeit your two bucks in order to send a clear message to your partner that his unfairness is unacceptable.

When and Why Do People Cooperate?

These dilemmas and games allow researchers to study cooperation in its essence: How do people decide between what's good for other people (cooperation) and what's good for themselves (competition)? A number of factors nudge people toward either cooperation or competition. One factor is the norm that is salient in the person's immediate context. When a prisoner's dilemma was labeled the "Community Game," participants chose to cooperate on twice the number of trials than when the same dilemma was called the "Wall Street Game" (Liberman et al., 2004).

In fact, very subtle contextual cues can make a difference, although these cues often interact with people's personalities. In one study, subliminal primes of competition cued more competitive behavior in the Prisoner's Dilemma, but only among participants who generally were high in competitiveness (Neuberg, 1988). There are also interesting interactions between people's own dispositions and how their partner plays the game (Kuhlman & Marshello, 1975). Highly competitive people consistently defect regardless of the strategy their partners adopt, but highly cooperative people conform to their partner's strategy by cooperating when he cooperates, but defecting if he defects. This means that when a consistently competitive person plays with a cooperative person, competitive strategies rule the day.

Culture also plays a role in cooperative tendencies. On the surface, it might seem that individuals from collectivist cultures would generally be more cooperative. After all, what better way to achieve social harmony than through cooperation? The full picture is more complex. People from collectivist cultures do cooperate more than those from individualist cultures, but only when they are interacting with friends (Leung, 1988); when interacting with strangers, collectivists can actually be more competitive. We see this in studies that prime different cultural identities. When Chinese Americans are primed to think about their Chinese identity (rather than their American identity), they become more cooperative when playing with friends but not with strangers (Wong & Hong, 2005). To sum up, cooperative tendencies might be more or less accessible for some individuals than others, but these dispositions are also cued by who you are with and what's going on around you.

After considering factors that influence *when* people cooperate, we might wonder *why* people cooperate. Some researchers have addressed this issue by studying the neurocognitive and physiological processes that are triggered when people make decisions about social dilemmas. One line of research looks at the biological basis of trust, a prerequisite for cooperation. The hormone *oxytocin* is a biological marker of a range of prosocial behaviors including caregiving, social attachment, love, and trust (Porges, 1998). When other people place their trust in you, your levels of oxytocin rise and increase your willingness to act in a trustworthy way (Zak et al., 2005). Perceiving more trust also increases oxytocin levels, greasing the wheels of further trust and cooperation.

You can see oxytocin at work in a study by Kosfeld and colleagues (Kosfeld et al., 2005). Participants were randomly assigned to receive an injection of either oxytocin or a placebo. They then played the *trust game*, in which they decided how much money they wanted to invest with another player (called the trustee). The experimenter tripled whatever was invested, but much as in the dictator game, the trustee got to decide how much of that money she would pay back to the investor. Those who had received the boost in oxytocin were twice as likely to make the maximum investment as the placebo group.

People are not, however, blindly controlled by biochemical secretions. If the social basis for trusting others is absent, as when an interaction partner appears unreliable, an induced oxytocin boost does not increase trust (Mikolajczak et al., 2010). Oxytocin seems to signal that others are trustworthy, but it does not simply make people more gullible.

If trust influences people's tendency to be fair, what about their reactions to being treated unfairly? Take away a child's toy on the playground, and you will get a clear taste of an immediate, negative, and not to mention loud reaction to unfairness. We get a quieter indication of this negative reaction in neuroimaging studies. When people receive low offers in the ultimatum game, scans reveal activation in the anterior insula region of the brain, which is associated with an automatic emotional response. But people in these situations also exhibit increased activation of the dorsolateral prefrontal cortex, which suggests an additional cognitive deliberative response (Sanfey et al., 2003). By revealing the role of emotions, these findings contradict traditional views that decision making is a purely rational process. But they also show that when people reject an unfair offer, they override an initial impulse to take anything profitable that comes their way. In fact, if people's right dorsolateral prefrontal context is temporarily deactivated, they become more likely to accept unfair offers, even while acknowledging that they are getting the short end of the stick (Knoch et al., 2006).

Fairness Norms: Evolutionary and Cultural Perspectives

The consistent evidence of cooperation in decision-making studies points to what might be a universally evolved mechanism for fairness and prosocial behavior (Fehr & Gächter, 1998; Hoffman et al., 1998). How did these norms for fairness evolve? Treating others fairly is beneficial to each of us because people tend to reciprocate how they are treated. If I am fair with you, you likely will be fair with me. Those who are fair are treated better by others in return, thereby improving the chances that the genes associated with a propensity for fairness will be represented in future generations.

When the TV talk show host Jimmy Kimmel asked parents to videotape their children's reactions to learning that Mom or Dad had eaten all their Halloween candy, the resulting videos show people's extreme emotional reactions when others violate their trust.

[Kevin Mazur/Getty Images for SiriusXM]

Cooperation and fairness also have a strong cultural component. As we mentioned earlier, people sometimes reject offers in the ultimatum game even at a cost to themselves. By punishing these unfair offers, people enforce broader cultural norms of fairness. If this reaction were part of a biological adaptation, we might expect to see it across cultures and in our closest genetic nonhuman relatives. In fact, when chimpanzees play a version of the ultimatum game and one partner makes an unfair offer, the recipient will hiss and spit at the other chimp even while grudgingly accepting it (Proctor et al., 2013). Just like a child who is told by a parent that all the Halloween candy is gone, these close primate relatives express their outrage at having been shortchanged.

However, other research reveals that human norms of fairness vary across cultures. In large-scale industrialized societies, people playing the ultimatum game typically offer a 50-50 split of the resources. If they are in the role of recipient, they usually reject any offer below 20 or 30% (Henrich & Henrich, 2007). But when members of small-scale societies consider the same decision, they show much more variability in their responses. In some communities where almost all interaction takes place face to face, people make very low offers to others and are willing to accept even the most unbalanced proposal (Henrich et al., 2010).

At first glance, you might think that small-scale, face-to-face agrarian cultures would be more communal and more cooperative with each other than those of us living in the world of telecommuting and Facebook. But what Henrich and his colleagues (2010) argue is that once society grows beyond the reach of family and personal histories of reciprocating with others, norms of fairness and cooperation develop to help govern the needs of an expanding network of trade relationships. How could you comfortably eat that tuna-salad sandwich if you didn't implicitly trust that the farmer isn't poisoning you with contaminated lettuce and that the cannery didn't process spoiled fish? Large-scale societies such as ours can come into being and endure only if people have strong norms of fairness that dictate their own behavior and their treatment of those who violate these norms.

In tuna we trust. Large-scale societies can succeed only if people trust each other to provide quality goods and services.

[Tim Boyle/Getty Images]

At the other end of the spectrum, historical factors that erode the development of trust can also curtail economic development. Nathan Nunn (2008), an economist at Harvard, has observed that those African countries that were most affected by the slave trade have seen the least amount of economic development and also exhibit the lowest levels of trust (Nunn & Wantchekon, 2011). His theory is that because people in former African slave-trading countries worried about being tricked or sold into slavery, sometimes even by acquaintances and friends, a culture of mistrust developed that impeded later political and economic cooperation even after the slave trade ended. There is, of course, an important lesson to be learned from this theory. If individuals and groups don't develop a basis for trusting each other, it will be that much more difficult to solve the challenges that they face.

SECTION review | Cooperation in Groups

To survive and thrive, individuals in a group must cooperate, balancing their personal interests with others' interests.

Studying cooperation	Cooperation: when and why	Evolution and culture
• The Prisoner's Dilemma demonstrates how distrust escalates competition. • Resource dilemmas demonstrate how cooperation is essential to providing or maintaining valuable shared resources. • Distribution games assess whether people distribute resources fairly or unfairly and others' reactions to those decisions.	• Social norms, personality traits, and culture all play roles in determining when people will cooperate. • Oxytocin signals trust. • We respond negatively to unfairness.	• A desire for fairness and cooperation are evolved characteristics. • Norms of fairness are also promoted by cultures, although in varying ways.

Performance in a Social Context

So far, we've explained the benefits of living in groups and the cooperation needed to navigate group life. But group living also means performing actions in the presence of or alongside others. If you are like most students, you probably groan at the thought of group projects or having to give a speech to the class. If humans evolved to live in groups, why does having to perform in a group seem so unpleasant and inefficient? In this section, we explore the effects that the social context can have on performance.

Performing in Front of Others: Social Facilitation

It was 2008, and the NCAA men's basketball championship trophy was on the line. With just under 2 minutes left to play, the Memphis Tigers had a 9-point lead over the Kansas Jayhawks. That lead quickly started to vanish after a key player fouled out of the game. The Tigers' defense broke down, and the team missed several key free throws in a row that would have clinched the title for them. These gaffes and mishaps allowed the Kansas team to tie the score at the buzzer and then trounce the beleaguered Tigers in overtime. With so much on the line and so much talent on the team, why did Memphis choke?

The history of studying this and related phenomena goes back to the very beginning of social psychology and the first social psychology experiment ever published. However, this first study was concerned not with how performance is impaired by the presence of others, but with how performance can be improved by the presence of others.

Athletes have to learn to perform in front of huge crowds, but sometimes even the best players and teams can choke under pressure.

[Bill Shettle/Cal Sport Media/AP Images]

Social Facilitation Theory, Take 1: When Others Facilitate Performance

At the end of the 19th century, Norman Triplett did what most professional psychology researchers do best. He observed a phenomenon in the world, developed a theory that he thought might explain it, and went about designing experiments to test his idea. The observation was that cyclists were able to ride 20 to 30 seconds per mile faster when they were racing with other cyclists than when they were racing alone in time trials. Triplett wondered if the mere presence of other competitors helps stimulate arousal that facilitates performance.

To test his idea, Triplett asked children to reel in a cord on a fishing rod as fast as they could. Sometimes they performed this task alone, with Triplett recording their time. Sometimes they competed with each other. In support of this early version of *social facilitation theory*, the majority of the kids tested were faster at reeling in the cord when they were competing than when they were performing alone (Triplett, 1898).

Triplett's paper sparked a flurry of research exploring how an individual's performance is affected not only by a competitive environment, but also by the mere presence of other people watching. Many studies showed that performance is facilitated when an audience is watching. The problem was that other studies began showing the opposite effect—performance was impaired when others were watching. In the aftermath of World War II, interest in this phenomenon waned for several decades until, in an article in the esteemed journal *Science*, Robert Zajonc ("Zajonc" actually rhymes with "science") sought to provide an overarching framework for these mixed results.

Social Facilitation Theory, Take 2: Others Facilitate One's Dominant Response

Social facilitation theory
The theory that the presence of others increases a person's dominant response in a performance situation—the response that is most likely for that person for that particular task.

Zajonc (1965) refined social facilitation theory by suggesting that the mere presence of others does not facilitate performance but rather facilitates one's *dominant response*, that is, the response that is most likely for that person for that particular task. If that task is a simple motor task (reeling in a fishing line) or something that you've practiced very well (playing a piano sonata for the thousandth time), your dominant or automatic response is to reel fast and play accurately. In these cases, having an audience likely will enhance your performance. But if the task is a complex one (finding the logical inconsistencies in a classic philosophic text) or that you are only just beginning to learn (playing a piano sonata for the first time), the dominant response will be to make mistakes; therefore, an audience will most likely impair your performance. What is it about an audience that facilitates the dominant response?

The Role of Arousal

Zajonc thought the effect of having an audience was the byproduct of a very basic *innate arousal mechanism* whereby all animal species—humans included—experience heightened arousal in the presence of other members of their own species. Such an account would help to explain why social facilitation effects also had been found in monkeys, puppies, rats, and turtles.

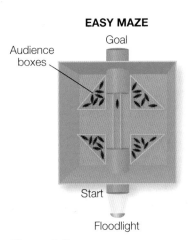
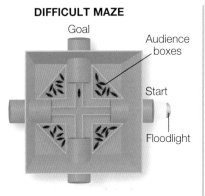

EASY MAZE   **DIFFICULT MAZE**

Goal   Goal

Audience boxes   Audience boxes

Start   Start

Floodlight   Floodlight

Figure 9.3

Do Other Species Get Aroused by an Audience?

Even cockroaches exhibit a social facilitation effect. They run an easy maze faster with other cockroaches present, but run a difficult maze more slowly with other cockroaches present, compared with when they ran the mazes in isolation.

[Research from: Visualization of Mazes used by Zajonc et al. (1969)]

To test whether this arousal effect generalizes to one of our most distant animal relatives, Zajonc carried out what is the only social psychology study performed on cockroaches (Zajonc et al., 1969). In this experiment, the cockroaches were timed as they ran a maze in order to escape a bright light for a dark corner. Two aspects of the situation were varied. First, the cockroaches either ran the maze alone or in the presence of other cockroaches placed in clear Plexiglas boxes alongside the runways. In addition, the route to the darkened goal box was either easy (just a straight shot down a runway) or relatively difficult (requiring a choice of paths and a 90-degree turn to find the goal box) (see **FIGURE 9.3**).

Just as others had found with humans, when the task was easy, the cockroaches reached their goal more quickly in the presence of other cockroaches than when they were alone. But when the task was hard, it took the cockroaches longer to reach their goal with other cockroaches lurking about. Because the psychology of a cockroach is pretty stripped down compared with our own, these findings suggest that very basic biological processes of arousal activated in the presence of others are partly responsible for social facilitation effects.

However, human psychology is more complex than cockroach psychology. Modern research reveals that the type of arousal that humans feel in the presence of others also depends on their interpretation of the situation. In chapter 6 we introduced the idea that a person's reaction to a stressful situation depends on whether she feels she has the resources to meet the demands of the task she faces (Blascovich & Tomaka, 1996). When a person believes she has the necessary resources, perhaps because she is performing a well-practiced task, she tends to show a *challenge response*: Her heart pumps harder with each beat and her arteries and veins expand to accommodate the rush of blood to vital organs and extremities (Blascovich et al., 1999). But when a person feels *threatened* because he thinks he might not have what it takes to meet the demands of the task, the physiological profile is different. His heart still beats harder, but now this is paired with a constriction of the arteries and veins that makes it more difficult to move oxygenated blood through the body. This is the pattern that people exhibit when trying to do a new and difficult task with an audience watching. Perhaps it's no surprise that their performance also suffers (Blascovich et al., 1999).

Let's return to the opening example of the NCAA championship. When Memphis's All-American Chris Douglas-Roberts approached the free-throw line with a chance to wrap up the title by sinking a couple of free throws, the stakes had changed from just a typical free throw. The additional elements of the high-pressure situation, Kansas's mounting comeback, and the fact that commentators actually had forecast that Memphis's overall weak free-throw shooting might be their undoing could have shifted the moment from a challenge to a threat, making the task much more difficult. To the Memphis fans' dismay, Chris Douglas-Roberts's performance at the free-throw line suffered.

The Role of Evaluation

The description of the NCAA championship game reveals that the social context includes more than just heightened arousal for us humans—it also carries the potential for social judgment. When all eyes are on you and a lot is at stake, the concern of social evaluation is even higher. Researchers who study responses to stressful situations use a standard laboratory paradigm called the Trier Social Stress Test, in which people give a speech and solve math problems with a panel of researchers evaluating them (Kirschbaum et al., 1993). People's stress response is strongest, meaning that they show increases in the stress hormone cortisol, when they feel that they have little control over their performance and the panel is very critical (Dickerson & Kemeny, 2004; Dickerson et al., 2008). Our physiological system has adapted to be sensitive to signs that we are socially valued and to activate a stress response when it seems that we are not.

This work reveals the physiological consequences of being judged, but what is going on mentally? When we perform in front of others, our thoughts tend to drift to what others are thinking even as we are motivated to do well ("I'd better not blow it") (Baron, 1986; Sanders & Baron, 1975). On cognitive tasks such as performing mental arithmetic, the threat of social evaluation is likely to bring distracting thoughts to mind, such as self-defeating worries, which absorb the same central cognitive resource—working memory capacity—that you need for abstract and complex forms of thought (Beilock et al., 2004; Schmader et al., 2008). With this central executive resource hijacked for the purpose of thinking about how well you are thinking, you simply have fewer cognitive resources remaining to devote to the task at hand.

Other kinds of performance don't rely on working memory resources. Becoming an expert in a domain such as basketball, piano, or whichever first-person shooter game is currently flying off the shelves means practicing to the point that certain

The comedian Jerry Seinfeld remarks on the common fear of public scrutiny: "According to most studies, people's number-one fear is public speaking. Number two is death. Death is number two. Does that sound right? This means to the average person, if you go to a funeral, you're better off in the casket than doing the eulogy."
[Theo Wargo/Getty Images Entertainment/Getty Images]

actions become automatic. When you reach this point, you no longer need to focus your conscious stream of attention on the step-by-step elements of the task at hand. When people feel the threat of social evaluation and doubts creep in, they slip out of the routine performance they have practiced and begin mentally micromanaging their movements—dooming themselves to failure (Beilock & Carr, 2001). Thus, a professional tennis player who gets nervous and thinks, "I have to remember to get my racquet back, step into my shot, shift my weight, and follow through" is likely to have found that Rafael Nadel's blistering forehand has whizzed right by him before he can set up for the shot.

So how do you go about preventing what happened to Memphis from happening to you? Perhaps we can find wisdom in the advice of the basketball legend Charles Barkley, who said, "I know I'm never as good or bad as one single performance. I've never believed in my critics or my worshippers, and I've always been able to leave the game at the arena." By disengaging his own self-evaluation from a single game, from the audience in the stands, and from the court more generally, he's less vulnerable to the disruptive evaluative pressures of being in the spotlight.

Performing With Others: Social Loafing

Research on social facilitation reveals how performance is affected when people perform in front of others. But what about performing *with* other people on a common task? Those who coach teams or manage organizations know that it can be challenging to get group performance to equal or exceed the sum of its parts. Part of the problem is simply coordinating behavior among two or more people (Latané et al., 1979). But another challenge to optimizing group performance is a phenomenon called social loafing. **Social loafing** is what happens when an individual exerts less effort when performing as a part of a collective or group than when performing as an individual.

Researchers have developed clever methods to measure social loafing in the laboratory (Latané et al., 1979). In one study, participants were asked to clap or cheer as loudly as they could as a part of an ostensible study of sound generation and perception. People had to be as loud as possible either alone, in pairs, in a group of four, or in a group of six. If the social context doesn't matter, then you should clap as loudly when you are asked to do so alone as when you are asked to clap along with a group of five others. And you can argue that maybe even clapping in a group would feel less ridiculous, so each person would clap more loudly than if clapping alone. But that's not what the researchers found. Instead, the sound generated per person was highest when people were clapping and cheering alone and decreased each time the group size was increased. The performance deficit occurred even when people were doing their clapping and shouting in individual soundproof chambers and believed that the sound they generated would be combined with the sounds of other people yelling their heads off in other chambers.

The social loafing effect has been found in domains as varied as rope pulling, swimming, cheering, brainstorming, maze solving, and vigilance tasks—basically anything in which performance is directly tied to the effort you put in. **How often have you found yourself slacking off when in a group?** People are less likely to give their all when they are part of a group. Several processes seem to be playing a role.

The Role of Accountability

The biggest reason that people slack off in groups is that they feel less accountable for their efforts. When you are solely responsible for a project, you put forth more effort than when you know your individual contribution to a group outcome will

off the mark.com   by Mark Parisi

ALL RIGHT, WHO'S *THE SLACKER THAT DESIGNED A SNOWFLAKE THAT LOOKS EXACTLY LIKE ONE FROM THE WINTER OF 1378?*

MOTHER NATURE'S SWEATSHOP

[© Mark Parisi, permission granted for use to Macmillan]

Social loafing A tendency to exert less effort when performing as part of a collective or group than when performing as an individual.

Think ABOUT

[coloroftime/ iStock/360]

not be recognized. When the clapping study was repeated so that participants believed their contribution to the total noise could be traced back to them, the social loafing effect disappeared (Williams et al., 1981).

This finding helps to explain why managers and teachers can increase productivity and performance on group projects by establishing incentives for both individual and group efforts. Is this Big Brother approach of external evaluation the only solution to social loafing? Happily, the answer is no. People are less likely to engage in social loafing merely if they have a way to monitor and evaluate their own performance (Harkins & Szymanski, 1988; Szymanski & Harkins, 1987). So raising the idea of evaluation, even if it comes from oneself, can be enough to eliminate the social loafing effect.

The Role of Expected Effort From Others

In addition to feeling less accountable in a group, people also seem to hold back effort because they believe others will do the same. After all, who wants to be the sucker who does all the work for only a piece of the credit? In studies where one's partner communicates that he or she intends to work hard for the duration of the task, participants don't socially loaf even if their own efforts are not being evaluated individually (Jackson & Harkins, 1985).

If you find yourself working in a group and are concerned that others might start slacking off, asserting the level of effort that you intend to put forth can encourage your colleagues to make a greater effort.

The Role of Perceived Dispensability

A third reason for social loafing is that people in a group can feel that their own efforts are not that important to the group outcome (Kerr & Bruun, 1983). For example, many people don't vote in elections because they feel that their one individual vote will not have much impact. However, the type of task can determine these feelings of dispensability. In some kinds of tasks, called *disjunctive tasks*, the most skilled members of the group determine the outcome. Imagine a team quiz show or a debate team in which one genius can lead to group success. On *conjunctive tasks*, the group will do only as well as the worst performer. For example, in mountain climbing, the team can get up the mountain only as fast as its slowest member. The research shows that when group tasks are disjunctive, the most skilled members of the group make the greatest effort, whereas the least skilled members slack off. On conjunctive tasks, the least skilled members exert the greatest effort, and the most skilled members slack off.

If you're leading a group and want maximum effort from everyone, you can capitalize on these effects by making your best performers view the task as disjunctive and your lesser performers perceive it to be conjunctive. In this way, all group members will believe their efforts are indispensable.

When the Value of the Group and Its Goal Are High

At the heart of the social loafing phenomenon is an assumption that people value what they can do individually more than what they can accomplish as a group. But in the real world, we freely engage in group activities ranging from team sports to community fundraisers. In these contexts, the group itself has value for us and is an extension of our own identity. When groups are cohesive or composed of friends, people are less likely to loaf (Karau & Williams, 1997). Similarly, people who value social relationships a great deal show less social loafing. For example, women and East Asians (groups that both tend to focus on maintaining relationships) are less susceptible to social loafing than more agentic and individualistic groups like American males (Karau & Williams, 1993). Also, social loafing is less likely when people feel that the task is interesting, personally meaningful, or comes with an attractive reward (Brickner et al., 1986; Zaccaro, 1984).

The twin Petronas Towers in Malaysia were constructed by workers from two different countries who competed against one another to finish their tower first.

[Martin Puddy/Stone/Getty Images]

Competition between groups probably has the same effect. When construction on the Petronas Towers in Malaysia began in 1993, they were planned to be the tallest structure in the world. Because the plan called for two identical towers to be built simultaneously, each tower was contracted to a different company, Tower One to a Korean corporation and Tower Two to a Japanese firm. Whether by design or happy accident, the pace of building soon became a matter of national pride for the construction workers, who marked their progress by comparing the heights of two flags that steadily rose higher as the build advanced. (The Korean team won the race.) With such a visible way to measure progress toward the group goal, social loafing probably was kept to a minimum. If only all construction projects could be so speedy!

Social Facilitation and Social Loafing Compared

At this point, you might be thinking that social loafing and social facilitation seem to contradict one another. According to social facilitation theory, performing in a social context heightens people's concern with being evaluated, improving their performance on an easy task and impairing performance on a difficult task. But research on social loafing has found that performing in a social context can reduce people's concern with being evaluated, leading to worse performance on an easy task and sometimes elevating performance when the task is challenging. What gives? It's important to remember that the nature of the social context in these two examples is very different. In the context of social facilitation, others stand by watching you perform, and you feel yourself in the spotlight. In the context of social loafing, others are working alongside you toward a common goal, and your own individual efforts feel anonymous.

The nature of the performance tasks studied in these two contexts also might differ in other important ways. In most studies of social loafing, performance is mostly a matter of motivation. It only takes effort to clap or cheer or pull a rope. On easy tasks such as these, being accountable or watched will increase effort and boost performance. On the other hand, performance is impaired under another's gaze on tasks for which effort doesn't guarantee success. You cannot ace your college boards merely if you are motivated enough; you still need to have the background knowledge and cognitive skills to reason through and correctly solve complex problems. The threat of being negatively evaluated can reduce performance even when motivation is high (Forbes & Schmader, 2010).

Deindividuation: Getting Caught Up in the Crowd

Deindividuation A tendency to lose one's sense of individuality when in a group or crowd.

Sometimes when individuals are in groups or crowds, they lose their sense of individuality. This psychological state is known as **deindividuation**. Deindividuation is the opposite of heightened self-awareness. As we discussed in chapter 5, when people are acutely aware of themselves as individuals, their actions tend to be guided by their personal attitudes, moral standards, and goals. When deindividuated, people feel anonymous, and their actions are more easily influenced by salient cues in their current situation. In crowds, people are more likely to do what others around them are doing, even when those actions run counter to their internalized attitudes and standards (Postmes & Spears, 1998).

People are most likely to feel deindividuated when they are overstimulated by sights and sounds, high in cognitive load, and physiologically aroused, and when there are few if any cues distinguishing them from a surrounding crowd. In this state, people often behave in more extreme ways than they otherwise would. In one study, participants who dressed identically and wore hoods over their heads were more aggressive toward a stranger than participants who could be identified at a glance (Zimbardo, 1970).

Deindividuation may help account for especially egregious actions that people sometimes engage in during wars, riots, lynchings, and incidents in which a crowd panics, leading to people being trampled to death. For example, Robert Watson (1973) found that in cultures in which warriors tend to hide their identities with paint or masks, killing, torture, and mutilating of captives is more common. A review of newspaper accounts of 60 lynchings of African-Americans in the United States between 1899 and 1946 revealed that the most savage and vicious killings were carried out by large crowds and hooded mobs (Mullen, 1986). Similarly, crowds of people are more likely to encourage a suicidal person to jump from the ledge of a building when the crowds are especially large and people's faces are obscured by the cover of darkness (Mann, 1981).

Although deindividuation likely contributes to many instances of horrifying behavior in crowds, bad behavior is not an inevitable consequence of being in a large group of people. If the salient cues in the situation are to do something positive, then deindividuation can foster prosocial behavior. In one study, female participants were asked to wear the same nurses' uniform rather than the ominous robes and hoods that participants wear in similar studies. In this case, deindividuation led to less aggression toward a stranger (Johnson & Downing, 1979). Wearing the uniform may have obscured the participants' individual identities, but it also cued them to treat others with care. In addition, whereas deindividuation can increase cheating and theft when we see others committing crimes, it can also increase donations to charity if that's what the crowd is doing (Nadler et al., 1982). Deindividuation makes it more likely that people will conform to what others around them are doing, for better or worse.

SECTION review | Performance in a Social Context

Social context influences performance.		
Social facilitation theory (individual performance with an audience)	**Social loafing (performing together)**	**Deindividuation**
• It first was thought that an audience facilitates performance on a task, but further research clarified that having an audience facilitates one's dominant response to a task. • Arousal facilitates the dominant response across species. • In humans, feeling challenged can boost performance, but feeling threatened can impair performance. • The threat of social evaluation is distracting. On cognitive tasks, it absorbs working memory, leaving fewer resources for the task at hand. • On well-learned motor tasks, negative evaluation leads people to overthink their actions, impairing performance.	The individual exerts less effort when performing as part of a group than as an individual. To avoid social loafing: • Monitor and evaluate performance. • Declare your own level of effort. • Distinguish disjunctive and conjunctive tasks. • Make the task more interesting or rewarding. • Maintain intragroup cohesion and intergroup competition.	When people feel anonymous, they are more likely to do what others around them are doing, for better or for worse.

Group Decision Making

Earlier we noted that groups are able to accomplish goals that individuals cannot accomplish on their own. These goals include maximizing performance and productivity, but another important goal of groups is to make decisions—hopefully, *good* decisions. Indeed, many important decisions are made by groups rather than individuals: the U.S. Senate, the United Nations, congressional committees, juries, political action committees, hiring committees, boards of directors, city councils, award committees, and so forth. Two (or more) heads are better than one, right?

In theory, groups have significant advantages over individuals when it comes to decision making. For instance, if four doctors are discussing a difficult medical problem, they can combine their unique knowledge and experience, consider diverse perspectives, and analyze alternative courses of action to determine which is best. Therefore, it seems like an obvious prediction that the doctors would make a better decision together than they would individually. In reality, however, the benefits of group decision making can be subverted by two psychological processes that get in the way of clear thinking: group polarization and groupthink.

Group Polarization

Imagine that, as part of a psychology experiment, you are asked to read hypothetical scenarios describing different people making decisions. One scenario describes a man deciding between taking a new job that pays a lot but may not last (a risky alternative) or keeping his current job (a conservative alternative). After reading each scenario, you are asked which alternative you personally would choose. Next, you are asked to discuss the same scenarios with a group of participants and come to a joint decision about each scenario.

When do you think you would make riskier decisions, when thinking about the scenarios alone or discussing them with others as a group? Common sense would say that, during group discussions, people will put the brakes on each other's extreme views or rash proposals, and as a result the group will make more conservative decisions. But when Stoner (1961) conducted a study like the one just described, he found the opposite result: Participants made *riskier* decisions as a group than they did on their own, a tendency that came to be known as *risky shift* (Cartwright, 1971).

The story gets more interesting, though. Researchers who followed up on these findings found that, for some decisions, groups did in fact take more conservative, middle-of-the-road positions than did individuals. Why do groups, compared to individuals, sometimes make riskier decisions and other times make less risky ones? Do you remember how research on social facilitation initially found one thing, then the opposite, and eventually resolved the paradox and arrived at a broader understanding? The same happened with research on group decision making.

Researchers eventually discovered that when people discuss their opinions with like-minded others, the discussion exaggerates their initial leanings, leading the group to take a more extreme position than any of the individual group members held initially. This broader phenomenon (which came to replace the risky shift) is known as **group polarization**, meaning that group discussion shifts group members toward an extreme position, or pole (Moscovici & Zavalloni, 1969; Myers, 1982).

Group polarization A tendency for group discussion to shift group members toward an extreme position.

This discovery reveals that group discussion amplifies the original leanings of individuals in the group. If each individual member of the group leans toward a risky alternative prior to the group discussion, they shift toward an even riskier position after group discussion. And, conversely, if each individual initially prefers a more conservative alternative, group discussion shifts them toward extreme caution (Lamm et al., 1976).

If group polarization amplifies group members' initial leanings, then we would expect group discussion to intensify initial attitudes about a variety of topics, not just decisions about risk. Numerous studies show that this is the case: When women who were moderately feminist discussed gender issues with each other, they became strongly feminist (Myers, 1975). French students who initially liked their president and disliked Americans felt stronger in both directions after group discussion (Moscovici & Zavalloni, 1969). High school students who leaned toward little racial prejudice before a group discussion became even less prejudiced after discussing racial issues with like-minded students, whereas students who initially held somewhat prejudiced attitudes became even more prejudiced after discussing racial issues together (Myers & Bishop, 1970).

Part of what makes group polarization interesting is that it seems to contradict the research on norm formation. If you look back at our discussion of conformity in chapter 7, you'll recall Sherif's (1936) finding that when individuals were put together to voice their opinions about something (in that case, the movement of a single point of light), they made middle-of-the-road judgments that canceled out their own, sometimes extreme, judgments. Group polarization research seems to show the exact opposite: Groups produce more extreme decisions, sometimes even more extreme than any of the group members' initial individual ratings. Sherif's studies are different because there was no group discussion to arrive at some consensus. This raises the question, What happens during group discussions that shifts the group toward more extreme positions? Two theories, described next, have stood the test of time (Isenberg, 1986; Myers & Lamm, 1976).

Exposure to New Persuasive Arguments

The *persuasive arguments theory* (Burnstein & Vinokur, 1977) explains group polarization through the concept of *informational influence*, which occurs when you conform to others' actions or attitudes because you believe they know something that you don't (see chapter 7). The theory assumes that people begin with at least one good argument to support their initial opinion or attitude (e.g., Mary likes Candidate X because of his immigration policy), but that they probably have not considered *all* the relevant arguments (e.g., Candidate X's environmental policy). During group discussion, group members learn new arguments from each other that reinforce the position they already preferred. As a result, the group as a whole adopts a more extreme position.

This process of polarization by persuasive arguments doesn't even require face-to-face interaction. People adopt more extreme positions than they initially held after simply overhearing a group discussion among like-minded others (Lamm, 1967) or even after merely reading a list of arguments generated by others (Burnstein et al., 1973).

How do we know that informational social influence is at work here? In one study (Liu & Latané, 1998), participants discussed a topic as a group and then were asked two weeks later how they felt about the topic. Their individual position lined up with their group's extreme position, not with the less extreme position that they endorsed prior to the discussion. This suggests that learning new arguments from the group changed how these individuals perceived the world, not just what they reported believing.

 Person A   3/10, 9:16pm
So we need to figure out where we're going for spring break. Im kinda leaning toward Austin. Just an idea.

 Person B   3/10, 11:05pm
I could see Austin working cuz the music scene

 Person C   3/11, 10:20am
yeah the music scene is obvious but it also has amazing restaurants so austin sounds great to me!

 Person B   3/11, 1:10am
oh that's good! I didn't know about the food there. Thatreminds me that the bars there are open all night :) I'm getting really excited about Austin!

 Person D   3/11, 7:30pm
what's perfect about Austin that you guys are forgetting is the shopping. I was there a couple years ago on a class trip and they've got evvvvvery thing.

 Person A   3/11, 8:47pm
oh good I've been meaning to go shopping. Austin is definitely my number one choice, no doubt about that

 Person C   3/11, 11:18pm
Grab your cowboy hats, folks—we're going to Austin!

When others add new arguments to support an opinion, the group's initial attitude becomes more extreme.

Trying to Be a "Better" Group Member

If we apply *social comparison theory* (Festinger, 1954) (see chapter 5), we can explain group polarization as the result of *normative social influence*, which occurs when you conform to others' actions or attitudes to be liked (Myers et al., 1980).

When individuals get together to make a decision, they often look around to figure out where the other group members stand on the topic at hand. Once it becomes clear what position the group is leaning toward, a cycle of comparison and amplification is set in motion: One person in the group tries to compare herself favorably with other group members. She wants to be a "better" group member, so she advocates the group's position but takes it a little further than everyone else. ("You guys seem to like this idea, but I *love* it!") Seeing this, another group member tries to present himself to the group even more favorably, so he takes the group's position even further. ("Oh yeah? I will fight tooth and nail for this idea!!")

The net effect of this cycle is that the group shifts toward a more extreme position. As we would expect from this theory, group discussion is more likely to result in polarized positions when group members are highly motivated to present themselves positively to other group members (Spears et al., 1990).

Groupthink

Most of the examples and research findings we've used to discuss group decision making deal with informal group contexts and hypothetical decisions. In these contexts, where decisions do not have earth-shattering consequences and group members are not overly concerned with being "right," it's not surprising that processes like group polarization can get in the way of clear thinking. What's more surprising is when smart people have formal discussions about important topics and still end up making really bad decisions that can result in disaster.

Consider this real-world example. On January 28, 1986, NASA launched the space shuttle *Challenger*. There was special public interest and excitement about the launch because one of the seven crew members was a private citizen and teacher, Christa McAuliffe. She was the first representative of the Teacher in Space Project, a NASA program designed to inspire students, honor teachers, and spur interest in mathematics, science, and space exploration. Consequently, students in schools around the country watched the launch on TV. However, there were warning signs that the shuttle could malfunction. Despite these warnings, NASA insisted on moving forward with the scheduled launch. The shuttle indeed broke apart 73 seconds into its flight, and all seven crew members were killed.

With so much on the line, why would smart people working together make such a bad decision? Irving Janis (1982) tried to answer this question by analyzing notoriously bad foreign policy decisions made by top U.S. officials, including the Bay of Pigs fiasco in 1961 (when President Kennedy and his inner circle launched an ill-fated attempt to overthrow the communist government of Fidel Castro in Cuba) and the decision in 1964 to escalate U.S. military involvement in Vietnam (when Congress passed the Gulf of Tonkin resolution at President Johnson's request).

Janis concluded that these bad decisions all suffered from a common problem called groupthink, a kind of faulty group thinking that occurs when group members are so intent on preserving group harmony and cohesion that they fail to analyze a problem completely (**FIGURE 9.4**). Groupthink is similar to group polarization but taken to the extreme, as if the group has become of one mind, completely unchecked by diverse opinions. Group members start to focus their attention on information that supports their position and ignore information that contradicts it, they stop testing their assumptions against reality, and they stop generating new perspectives on the problem at hand. Eventually they become convinced of the absolute truth and morality of their preferred course of action, and they never stop to think what would happen if they made an error in reasoning.

Janis described groupthink using the metaphor of a syndrome that afflicts the group, and he specified several symptoms of groupthink. One hallmark symptom is suppression of dissent: When group members express doubts about the majority's preferred position, they are harshly criticized and pressured to fall back in line with the majority view. To avoid being reprimanded or excluded, group members begin to censor themselves, meaning that they give the outward impression of agreement even though privately they think that the group is on the wrong track. This results

Groupthink was to blame for the 1986 malfunction and crash of the space shuttle *Challenger*.

[Steve Liss/Time & Life Pictures/Getty Images]

Groupthink A tendency toward flawed group decision making when group members are so intent on preserving group harmony that they fail to analyze a problem completely.

[Sidney Harris/Science Cartoons Plus]

What does groupthink feel like?

- Group members feel strong pressure to agree with the majority view.
- They feel that if they were to voice concerns about the majority view or challenge the group's assumptions, they would be criticized by other group members as stupid, weak, or evil.
- Thus, they remain silent, censoring their doubts and questions. This results in the illusion that the group is in total agreement.
- Consensual agreement without debate also gives the illusion that the group is invulnerable and morally infallible.

Why do groups fall prey to groupthink?	**How does groupthink affect decision making?**
Because group members are too focused on reaching consensus. This is more likely when: • Group members are motivated to be liked by the group or by an opinionated group leader. • They want to keep the group together, particularly if they fear that external threats or recent failures will break the group apart. • They close themselves off to new information, opinions, or perspectives.	• Group members do not gather enough information before making their decision. • They do not fully consider alternative perspectives or courses of action. • They fail to examine the risks of their preferred course of action. • As a result, they do not make adequate plans for what to do in the event that their decisions and actions turn out badly.

Figure 9.4

Harmony at All Costs?

Groupthink results in faulty group thinking.

in an illusion of unanimity: It *appears* that everyone is in agreement, although some group members may harbor serious misgivings. For example, when NASA engineers charged with understanding the safety parameters of equipment pointed out one of the shuttle's mechanical flaws, they were harshly rebuked and pressured to stay silent by those overseeing the launch (Esser & Lindoerfer, 1989; Vaughan, 1996).

Groupthink is especially likely to occur when group members view group cohesion as more important than anything else. In contrast, if group members are less concerned with reaching a consensus or being disliked by other group members, they are more likely to appraise alternative courses of action realistically and express their doubts about the majority view. Janis identified other conditions that make groupthink more likely to occur. One is the isolation of the group from outside sources of information and dissenting voices. Another is the presence of a strong leader who makes his or her opinions and preferences known to the group at the beginning of the discussion. Knowing the leader's views, the other members want to reinforce those views to win the leader's approval.

Groupthink Video on LaunchPad

APPLICATION

Improving Group Decision Making

Our discussion of group polarization and groupthink seems to suggest that making decisions as a group is often a bad idea. And sometimes it is. Yet in many cases groups do solve problems and make decisions more effectively than isolated individuals can. This is especially true when groups work together on tasks that require the contribution of different knowledge. For example, groups perform better than individuals on SAT-style analogy problems because each group member has knowledge about word meaning and other trivia that other group members do not; put everyone together and you have a very large knowledge base to draw on (Laughlin et al., 2003).

Still, the unfortunate reality is that group polarization and groupthink often force groups into an isolated universe where existing beliefs are reinforced and the status quo is justified. Fortunately, groups can use strategies to avoid these pitfalls.

Increase Group Diversity

Recall that group polarization happens when all the group members—or at least the strong majority (Van Swol, 2009)—enter the discussion already leaning toward a certain position. Also, remember that in Asch's (1956) conformity studies and Milgram's (1974) obedience studies (see chapter 7), the presence of a single nonconforming other significantly reduced conformity and obedience (Allen & Levine, 1968). In much the same way, the presence of a dissenting voice in a group discussion is a powerful antidote to group polarization. For example, when members of the same political party discuss votes, they tend to take more extreme positions than they would individually. (Democrats cast less conservative votes; Republicans cast more conservative votes.) But if just one member of the opposite party joins the discussion, group votes become less extreme (Schkade & Sunstein, 2003).

If the group cannot find someone who genuinely disagrees with the majority view, they can designate a group member to play "devil's advocate," someone who is given free license to search actively for flaws in the reasoning and plans proposed by the other members of the group. This will help the group to consider the relevant information more carefully before deciding on a course of action (Nemeth, Brown et al., 2001; Nemeth, Connell et al., 2001).

Group diversity is also a powerful safeguard against groupthink. Although we may feel more comfortable discussing decisions in groups of like-minded others, including people with diverse perspectives and opinions is likely to result in more vigorous discussion, fresh perspectives, and creative ideas (Nemeth & Ormiston, 2007; Page, 2007). In the courtroom, for example, racially diverse juries make better decisions than all-White juries (Sommers, 2006). Racially diverse jurors exchanged a wider range of information and facts and were less likely to misremember evidence as they discussed the case. It is interesting that the effects are only partly attributable to members of the minority group bringing in different kinds of information to the discussion. If members of the White majority simply expect that they'll be making a decision in a racially diverse group, they take a broader perspective on the evidence at hand (Sommers et al., 2008).

Diverse groups can make better decisions than homogeneous groups because they bring together unique viewpoints and past experiences that provide a broader framework for a problem.

[mediaphotos/E+/Getty Images]

Reinterpret Group Cohesiveness

Overemphasizing the importance of group cohesion can create a breeding ground for group polarization and groupthink. That doesn't necessarily mean, however, that improving group decision making requires squelching group cohesiveness. Rather, group members can reinterpret what it means to be a cohesive group.

Usually people interpret cohesiveness as a norm to maintain the group's unity and harmony, and to make sure that all group members get along. But groups also can be cohesive in their commitment to help group members make the best possible decisions. That is, rather than thinking of cohesiveness as pushing the group toward consensus, think about it as a promise to reach the best possible outcome and prevent the group from doing something harmful.

Studies show, in fact, that if group members think about how one of the group's norms could harm the group, the ones who are *strongly* identified with the group voice their dissent about that norm, whereas those who are weakly identified stay silent (Packer, 2009). Although we might expect that highly identified group members would be reluctant to say anything that challenges the group's majority views, in actuality they care so much about the group that they are the first to voice their dissent to protect the group from a bad decision. Groups make better decisions when they follow a norm of sharing constructive criticism than when they focus on maintaining group harmony (Postmes et al., 2001).

Encourage Individuality

Recall that according to the social comparison theory of group polarization, groups shift toward more extreme positions because group members are concerned with other group members liking them. Thus, they exaggerate their agreement with the group's position. This suggests that group polarization would be reduced if group members focused on themselves as individuals and cared less about how they are evaluated by the group. Indeed, one study showed that group discussion did not polarize group members' initial attitudes if, prior to the discussion, group members were primed to focus on their unique individual qualities (Lee, 2007).

The same holds true for groupthink, which occurs in large part because group members fail to break from the group norm and voice their doubts about ideas they perceive as wrong or harmful. If group members are led to believe that they are personally responsible for the outcome of their group's decision, they are less likely to fall victim to group-think tendencies (Kroon et al., 1991). Consider this research on groupthink and individuality side-by-side with our previous discussions of deindividuation and social loafing. What themes do they have in common?

Think
ABOUT

[Zachary Scott/Getty Images]

SECTION review | Group Decision Making

In theory, groups have more resources than do individuals for making decisions, but two psychological processes, group polarization and groupthink, can subvert good group decision making.

Group polarization	Groupthink	Groups can avoid problems of group decision making by:
Group members' initial leanings are intensified in a cycle of amplification and comparison with like-minded others.	Group members intent on preserving group harmony fail to analyze a problem completely.	• Encouraging group diversity and ensuring the presence of dissenting voices. • Focusing on achieving the best outcome rather than group harmony. • Encouraging members to take individual responsibility.

Leadership, Power, and Group Hierarchy

Most groups have leaders, individuals with extra power, status, and responsibility. Cultures have presidents, chiefs, or sovereigns. Armies have generals. Sports teams have captains. Committees have chairpersons or heads. A group leader wields power, and where there is a leader, there's a hierarchical structure.

What Makes a Leader Effective?

Conventional wisdom holds that effective leaders are those who possess certain personality traits; thus, they are effective regardless of what kind of situation they and their followers are in. There is some limited evidence that effective leaders tend to be high in the traits of extraversion, openness to experience, and conscientiousness (Judge et al., 2002), and they are more confident in their own leadership abilities (Chemers et al., 2000). However, these correlations are small, meaning that knowing a person's personality traits tells you surprisingly little about whether that person is or will become an effective leader. Indeed, Simonton (1987) analyzed 100 attributes of past U.S. presidents, including dozens of personality variables, and found no correlation between personality traits and historians' assessments of their leadership effectiveness. We need a more sophisticated picture of how leaders interact with their followers and the broader social situation.

According to one perspective, effective leaders are transformational (Bass, 1985). The three characteristics of transformational leaders are:

1. They focus on their followers' desires and abilities.
2. They are willing to challenge their followers' assumptions and behaviors.
3. They offer an inspirational visionary style.

Mother Teresa's transformational leadership style inspired her followers to commit to humanitarian action.

[RAVEENDRAN/AFP/Getty Images]

There are many examples of transformational leaders; you can probably think of a bunch on your own. Two prototypes are Dr. Martin Luther King, Jr. and Mother Teresa. You are likely familiar with the enduring effect of Dr. King's vision. Mother Teresa's vision transformed her order of nuns from a traditional group focused on prayer and contemplation to an action-focused group that had a remarkable positive impact on impoverished people living in the slums—first in Calcutta (now Kolkata), India, and then throughout the world.

However, very few leaders can achieve this high level of influence. What characteristics allow the average leader to be effective? The answer depends on the specific needs of the group members and the goals of the group. We can identify three types of leaders and the needs they satisfy (Fiedler, 1967). *Charismatic* leaders (see chapter 7) emphasize bold actions and inspire belief in the greatness of the group. *Task-oriented* leaders focus primarily on the pragmatics of achieving the group's goals. *Relationship-oriented* leaders attend

Milk: Charismatic Leadership Style

Milk (Jinks et al., 2008) is a moving biopic about Harvey Milk, an influential figure in the movement for gay civil rights. In depicting Milk's rise to leadership, the movie illustrates a number of features of an effective leadership style. The story begins in the Castro district of San Francisco in the early 1970s. Milk, played by Sean Penn, has just moved from New York, and although he is enamored of his neighborhood's charm, he is outraged by everyday acts of discrimination against gays in his new city. Police harassment and murderous gay-bashing are common, and Milk is told that his camera shop cannot join the neighborhood merchant's association on account of his "unholy" lifestyle.

Fed up, Milk stands on top of a wooden crate and announces to his neighbors that it's time to fight back. So begins his rise into the political spotlight from a grassroots activist—referred to by his neighbors as the mayor of Castro Street—to being one of the first openly gay men elected to major public office in America. In the mere 11 months that he was on the Board of Supervisors of San Francisco before being fatally shot, he made major strides for gay civil rights. What made him an effective leader?

To answer this question, let's unpack the concept of *charisma*, introduced as one of the qualities of an effective leader. Charisma is that special magnetism that we've all

seen in larger-than-life celebrities and leaders, but it is difficult to define. According to Ernest Becker (1975), a charismatic leader is one who with great self-confidence offers people a heroic vision, a grand mission to triumph over evil and bring about a better future.

Early in his career, Milk was a *relationship-oriented* leader who focused on making sure that his staff members felt included and enjoyed their work on his campaign. But his career really took off after he followed the advice given to him by another politician: If you want to win over the people, you have to give them hope for a better life and a better tomorrow. Eventually Milk embodies charisma. His heroic vision can be seen in three messages that he gave to the American people.

First, he tells people that the gay rights movement is big, a social movement on a grand scale with far-reaching implications. One way he does this is to connect the gay rights movement to the broader idea that America is a free country in which people have a fundamental right to live without bigotry. In this way he presents himself as fighting for the rights of everyone, from union workers to senior citizens to small-business owners. In one impassioned speech, he notes that the gay rights movement is "not about personal gain, not about ego, not about power... it's about the 'us's' out there. Not only gays, but the Blacks, the Asians, the disabled, the seniors, the us's. Without hope, the us's give up. I know you cannot live on hope alone, but without it, life is not worth living. So you, and you, and you... You gotta give 'em hope.... you gotta give 'em hope."

Second, he tells people that, by supporting the gay rights movement, they have an opportunity to be part of a lasting primarily to fostering equality, fairness, harmony, and participation among group members (Hogg, 2010).

None of these leadership types is more effective than the others in every context; rather, leadership effectiveness depends on a match between leadership type and the situation. Let's illustrate by looking at leaders in the context of the workplace. In some work situations, group members have clearly defined tasks and are relatively free from conflict. In these highly structured situations, people happily work toward common goals, and so a leader has less need to attend to their feelings or interpersonal dynamics. Task-oriented leaders are most effective in these types of work situations, because they can keep everyone on track toward common goals.

In other work situations, group members are confused about what they should be doing and often have a difficult time working together. Relationship-oriented leaders are the most effective in these types of situations because they can attend to people's feelings and relationships and ultimately get the group to work together more smoothly (Schriesheim et al., 1994). The broad, take-away message is that the fit of the leader to the particular demands of the situations and the goals and expectations of the group members determine that leader's appeal and effectiveness.

legacy that will make a mark on history. For example, he says to members of his campaign, "If there should be an assassination, I would hope that five, ten, one hundred, a thousand would rise. I would like to see every gay lawyer, every gay architect come out—If a bullet should enter my brain, let that bullet destroy every closet door.... And that's all. I ask for the movement to continue." This message is attractive to people because, as we've noted in this chapter, they join groups in part to cope with the fear of death. Belonging to a group means that one's life does not end with death but continues on so long as the group survives.

A third message in Milk's heroic vision is that there is a clear enemy out there who is holding society back from progress. In 1978, Anita Bryant, a former singer and model, started advocating for a proposition that would ban gays from teaching in schools. Armed with moral rhetoric and the support of the Christian community, she got this legislation passed in Florida and was gaining traction in other states. Milk initially feels defeated by Anita Bryant's success, but when he walks into the street, he finds that it is exactly what was needed to bring the gay community's anger to the boiling point. Now hundreds of citizens are ready to take action. Milk seizes the moment, grabs a bullhorn, and says, "I know you're angry. I'm angry. Let's march the streets of San Francisco and share our anger."

He leads the march to the steps of City Hall, where he gives the people the enemy they want: "I am here tonight to say that we will no longer sit quietly in the closet. We must fight. And not only in the Castro, not only in San Francisco, but everywhere the Anitas go. Anita Bryant cannot win tonight.

Anita Bryant brought us together! She is going to create a national gay force!"

Because of Milk's charismatic leadership style, he is remembered today as a major figure in the continuing struggle for equal human rights.

Guided by the charismatic leadership of Harvey Milk (portrayed by Sean Penn in the movie *Milk*), gay rights supporters felt united in a grand mission to overcome discrimination.

[Focus Features/Photofest]

Power Changes People

History is replete with scandals involving powerful people who abuse their advantages and turn a blind eye toward the suffering of others. In an oft-told (but apparently unsubstantiated) story, Marie Antoinette, the queen of France, supposedly remarked, "Qu'ils mangent de la brioche" ("Let them eat cake") on hearing of bread shortages that were threatening the underclass with starvation. The implication is that living with an abundance of resources might make it difficult to comprehend how others might be lacking. Through these cultural legends, we see the idea that power, if it doesn't corrupt, might at least make one lose sight of how the other half (or more) lives. Let's consider some of the evidence for this idea.

Loosened Inhibitions

Just as people with power have greater access to and control over resources, they also seem to have greater freedom to do as they please. In contrast, those with little power and low socioeconomic status face many constraints on what they can do and be. Dacher Keltner and colleagues (Keltner et al., 2003) argue that this creates a psychology of *behavioral approach* for those in greater power positions but a psychology of *behavioral inhibition* for those in lesser power positions. As we've emphasized throughout this textbook, *approach* and avoidance (or, to use the term employed by these researchers, *inhibition*) are general motivational orientations toward either achieving positive outcomes and reward (approach) or avoiding negative outcomes and punishments (inhibition).

According to this approach/inhibition theory of power, having an approach orientation means that you engage in goal-oriented behavior without too much concern or awareness of the obstacles that might stand in the way (Whitson et al., 2013). Even standing tall and adopting an upright or powerful posture has been shown to elevate testosterone and reduce cortisol (a stress hormone), perhaps because it prepares the person to confront and overcome challenges (Carney et al., 2010). Other research suggests that a sense of power can create a feeling of distance between the self and others, allowing for the kind of abstract thought needed to make complex decisions (Smith & Trope, 2006; Smith et al., 2008). This can make it easier for those in power to achieve more and solve thorny problems that face the group, but it can also disinhibit people from engaging in hurtful behavior toward people with less power (Galinsky et al., 2006; Guinote, 2007; Keltner et al., 2003).

For example, in one study, four members of a fraternity were brought into the lab and encouraged to tease each other (Keltner et al., 1998). In each group, two individuals were relatively new to the fraternity and thus had lower status, whereas two were higher-status members of the group. It won't surprise you that these guys had little difficulty sitting around the room teasing one another (they each took turns so that each fraternity member had the opportunity to tease every other fraternity member who took part in the study). The researchers found that the type of teasing varied depending on who was teasing whom. Higher-status fraternity brothers teased others (regardless of their status) with little concern for whether they might humiliate them or display their dominance over them. But lower-status brothers were more prosocial in the way they teased high-status brothers. They would try to tease their big brothers in ways that acknowledged their status or flattered their strengths. For example, when asked to come up with a nickname for a person using two initials, 30% of lower-status brothers gave higher-status brothers names that were essentially flattering (e.g., MM = Muscle Machine, GM = Girl Magnet). In contrast, only 7% of higher-status brothers gave these positive teases to their lower-status brothers. Most of the time these higher-status brothers gave insulting teases (e.g., PP = Pimple Party, LI = Little Impotent).

Less Empathy

We can look at this last finding in terms of subordinates having to monitor what they say around leaders, but it also raises the possibility that those in positions of power are less compassionate toward their subordinates or those who are disadvantaged. More direct evidence for this comes from studies showing that people from higher socioeconomic backgrounds (high SES) might be less generous and charitable than people from lower social classes (Piff et al., 2010). In one study, people who were simply *reminded* of how they are financially better off recommended that people give about 3 percent of their income to charity, whereas those led to think about their disadvantage in society recommended giving away almost 5 percent of one's income. This finding seems counterintuitive, because we would expect the people with more financial resources to be in a better position to give more to others. However, having lower status can make people more generous because it cues a sense of compassion and egalitarian values. Other data on charitable giving seem to support these trends (see **FIGURE 9.5**).

Related findings show that people in power positions tend to be insensitive toward less powerful others. For instance, powerful people seem to have difficulty exhibiting a concrete emotional connection to other people's suffering, sometimes even seeing them as less human (Gwinn et al., 2013; van Kleef et al., 2008). In addition, people in power are more likely to use stereotypes to form impressions of lower status individuals (Goodwin et al., 2000), devalue or take credit for the contributions of their underlings (Kipnis, 1972), and bring to mind implicit prejudices toward outgroups (Guinote et al., 2010). But those in power will be mindful of their subordinates' individuating characteristics when doing so is relevant to what they are trying to accomplish (Overbeck & Park, 2001).

Together, this research suggests that the benefits of having power can come at the cost of being less able to empathize with or be charitable to those without power.

Hierarchy in Social Groups

The fact that most groups have leaders also means that groups are often organized hierarchically, with some members having higher status than others. Although some group members have subordinate roles, they are nevertheless critical for helping the group function as a whole. For example, a beehive is a complex social structure operating in the service of one queen bee, who lays eggs. Although she might seem to have high status in this social hierarchy, the entire system would fail without swarms of female worker bees. Though sterile, the worker bees have the responsibilities of

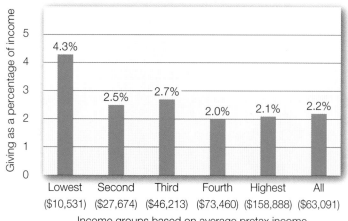

Figure 9.5

Those With Less Give More

Those who are less affluent donate a higher percentage of their income to charity.

[Data source: http://www.clearlycultural.com/geert-hofstede-cultural-dimensions/power-distance-index]

collecting honey, building the nest and caring for the larvae. The sole purpose of the male drones is to mate with a new queen once and then die. (How's that for a one-night stand?)

It's notable that the bee hierarchy is highly inflexible, with each bee having a fixed role and status. Primate societies are more flexible, but even in chimpanzee colonies, behavioral roles are largely based on biological characteristics such as age, sex, and physical strength. In human societies, although such characteristics are still influential, roles are also far more likely to be based on other socially constructed characteristics.

According to social dominance theory (Sidanius & Pratto, 1999), when human societies grow large enough to produce a surplus of food and other basic resources, the division of labor expands beyond fixed roles stemming from biological characteristics to the creation of *arbitrary sets*, groups of people distinguished by culturally defined roles, attributes, or characteristics. In addition to those who cultivate food, care for children, and offer physical security, our society includes people who specialize in providing spiritual guidance, entertaining us with music and stories, hauling away our trash, or even teaching us about the complexities of our own society. Depending on the cultural values of a society, some of these groups of people are afforded higher status, and their activities are deemed more valuable than those of groups afforded lower status. Social dominance theory proposes that to maintain stable relationships between these different groups, people generally endorse beliefs that legitimize an existing social hierarchy.

Of course, we see cross-cultural variation in the degrees of hierarchy in different societies. Hofstede and Bond (1984) refer to this variation as the power distance in a culture. They define power distance as the degree to which members of a culture or organization (especially those with less power) accept an unequal distribution of power. **FIGURE 9.6** indicates countries with high power distance in darker colors and those with low power distance in lighter colors. (Hofstede and Bond did not have relevant data for the countries shown in gray.) Countries higher in power distance have people who are more accepting of hierarchy. Although not a great deal of research has been done on cross-cultural variation in power distance, we have a few rather intuitive findings. For example, in business settings, employees from cultures with low power distance (e.g., the United States and Germany) are more committed to their company if they feel that they have some voice or ability to express their views and appeal to management. In contrast, for people from high-power-distance countries (China, Mexico, Hong Kong), employees' commitment to the organization does not depend on a sense that management cares about the employees' perspective (Brockner et al., 2001).

Social dominance theory The theory that large societies create hierarchies, and that people have a general tendency to endorse beliefs that legitimatize that hierarchy.

Power distance Variation in the extent to which members of a culture or organization (especially those with less power) accept an unequal distribution of power.

Figure 9.6

Power Distance Around the World

Countries shaded in darker colors have a higher power distance, valuing hierarchy and respect for authority. (No data were available for countries shown in gray.)

[Research from: Hofstede et al. (2010) This material is the creation and intellectual property of Kwintessential Ltd (www.kwintessential.co.uk)]

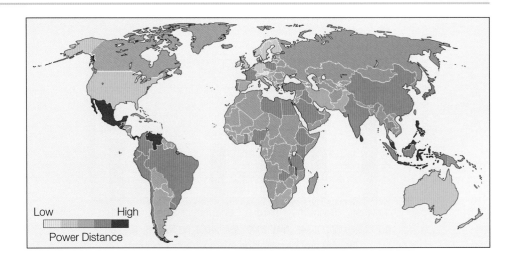

Legitimizing Hierarchy

A central idea we have touched on throughout this textbook is that much of our social reality is based on a cultural worldview that is constructed and maintained by the consensus of those who live within that reality. This means that for advantaged groups to stay in power and for group hierarchies to persist, individuals across society need to believe in the legitimacy of their leaders, the institutions that maintain them, and the social system in general. Thus, individuals generally believe that group-based social hierarchy is necessary for a functioning society. However, people vary widely in how much they value social hierarchy, or what is referred to as their *social dominance orientation* (Sidanius et al., 2001). It is not surprising that those who have greater power and enjoy higher status in society are typically higher in social dominance orientation than those who are socially disadvantaged: Once you have power, you want to keep it. In the United States, for example, Whites tend to score higher in social dominance orientation than Blacks or Latinos (Sidanius et al., 1994).

Social dominance orientation is linked to many aspects of a person's lifestyle, including the career path he or she chooses. Compared with an average cross-section of people from a community (i.e., jurors), police officers—those responsible for maintaining social order—score higher in social dominance orientation. In contrast, public defenders—those who provide a voice for the economically underprivileged— score lower in social dominance orientation (Sidanius et al., 1994). As you've now learned about correlational relationships, the causal arrow here might point both ways. That is, people's desire for social hierarchy might predict the roles and careers that appeal to them; at the same time, those roles might reinforce their beliefs about the value or vileness of group dominance. What's more, both social dominance orientation and career choice could be influenced similarly by some additional variable, such as how authoritarian one's parents were.

In chapter 2, we discussed the importance of a cultural worldview in providing structure and meaning for people's day-to-day lives as well as an understanding of their very existence. So it should come as no surprise that people are highly motivated to maintain their belief in the legitimacy of the social system, especially if they enjoy the advantages of being at the top of the heap. According to social dominance theory, individuals who are high in social dominance orientation maintain their belief in status hierarchy in part by subscribing to *legitimizing myths*. These myths include overgeneralized beliefs about the traits possessed by those who are low in social status (e.g., "Those people are all lazy"). They also include overly simplistic beliefs about why people succeed or fail in society. One such belief is that anyone can get ahead if she or he simply works hard enough.

A rather ironic consequence of believing in legitimizing myths is that the people who are advantaged in society may be more likely than underprivileged groups to claim that they are unfairly discriminated against. For example, although both Whites and Latinos can have relatively high levels of social dominance orientation, only for Whites (the more advantaged group in American society) do these beliefs predict increased perceptions that they are victims of ethnic prejudice (Thomsen et al., 2010). Consider the following experiment, in which college students were asked to role play a situation in which they were applying for a managerial position (Major et al., 2002). White participants who learned that they had been passed over for the job by a Latino manager who favored a Latino applicant were more likely to claim that they were discriminated against than were Latino participants who were passed over by a White manager who favored a White applicant. In both of these studies, we see members of the advantaged group, especially those who believe in the legitimacy of their advantaged position, crying foul when their advantaged position seems to be called into question.

System justification theory
The theory that negative stereotypes get attached to groups partly because they help to explain and justify why some individuals are more advantaged than others.

Legitimizing myths and social roles provide a framework that reinforces the rigidity and stability of the existing social hierarchy. According to **system justification theory** (Jost & Banaji, 1994), negative stereotypes get attached to groups partly because they help to explain and justify why some individuals are more advantaged than others. For example, if as a culture we label the homeless as being dim-witted, lazy, and dangerous, these traits not only provide us with an account of how a person comes to be living on the street in the first place but also validate our decision to brush off requests for spare change or to avoid voting for social programs to help them. It is more comforting to hold stereotypes that portray the world as a place where people get what they deserve and deserve what they get than to admit that random forces as well as biased systems of structural advantages might have allowed some individuals to enjoy a life of leisure, education, and abundant food while others across the globe face malnutrition, discrimination, and poor access to health care and education.

Although it's easy to understand why members of advantaged groups would want to maintain their legitimizing beliefs, the more remarkable phenomenon is that members of objectively disadvantaged groups in society often do, too. As we noted in our discussion of social identity theory earlier in this chapter, it's quite common for individuals to show *ingroup bias*, a preference for their own group over outgroups. This bias is often greater in advantaged groups than in disadvantaged groups. Conversely, some members of disadvantaged groups actually show a preference for the higher-status group over their own (Sidanius & Pratto, 1999). For instance, some studies show that Arabs living in Israel and Latinos living in Los Angeles (who both value group hierarchy and believe that the hierarchy in their respective societies is legitimate) were more favorably disposed toward the higher-status majority group than toward their own (Levin et al., 2002).

As noted in the earlier description of the concept of power distance, group hierarchies can be preserved only with some amount of buy-in from those who have lower status. The existence of **complementary stereotypes**, whereby groups are ascribed both positive and negative characteristics, are one way to get that buy-in. Kay and Jost (2003; Kay et al., 2007) have shown that people believe that the social system is fairer and more just after they are exposed to stories of those who are poor but happy or rich but dishonest than after they are exposed to stories of people who are poor and unhappy or rich and honest. We seem to like it when groups that are socially disadvantaged seem satisfied with their lives and groups that are especially well off are miserable or untrustworthy.

Complementary stereotypes
Both positive and negative stereotypes that are ascribed to a group as a way of justifying the status quo.

This might also mean that it's not so bad to be part of the working classes, living from paycheck to paycheck, if you believe that the upper classes are snobbish, cold, dishonest, and depressed. In a similar way, although most women reject stereotypes that suggest that women are less competent or intelligent than men, a large percentage still endorse the idea that women are more moral or warm (Glick & Fiske, 1996). In this way, members of disadvantaged groups who endorse positive stereotypes for their groups (e.g., when a woman proclaims that women are more caring then men) inadvertently may be promoting the very system that keeps them in their disadvantaged place.

To acknowledge instead a sense of disadvantage requires a comparison with others who are more advantaged. Karl Marx famously wrote:

> A house may be large or small; as long as the neighboring houses are likewise small, it satisfies all social requirement for a residence. But let there arise next to the little house a palace, and the little house shrinks to a hut.... [T]he occupant of the relatively little house will always find himself more uncomfortable, more dissatisfied, more cramped within his four walls" (Marx, 1847).

As Marx's quote suggests, we tend to compare ourselves with similar others or with those who are close by. Because societies tend to segregate themselves socially

People are more likely to realize that they are disadvantaged when they can compare themselves with those who are better off.
[Design Pics/Carson Ganci/ Perspectives/Getty Images]

and physically on the basis of class membership or other similarities, we most often compare ourselves with people like us—people who might be disadvantaged in the same way. This means that disadvantages can often go unnoticed, or at least fade into the background of our more salient day-to-day experience.

A classic study demonstrated this phenomenon, known as relative deprivation. When they surveyed soldiers in the U.S. Army, Stouffer and colleagues (Stouffer et al., 1949) found interesting discrepancies between the men's reported satisfaction with aspects of their jobs and the actual facts about their jobs. For example, a job in the air corps led to twice as many opportunities for promotion than did a job in the military police. But men in the military police reported much higher satisfaction with their access to promotion opportunities than did men in the air corps. Why? Because men in the air corps were more likely to come into contact with their promoted peers and feel unhappy about their own subordinate status. With fewer promoted peers in the military police, M.P.s proved that ignorance can sometimes be bliss.

Relative deprivation theory A theory stating that disadvantaged groups are less aware of and bothered by their lower status because of a tendency to compare their outcomes only with others who are similarly deprived.

Predicting Social Change

Clearly social upheaval does sometimes happen, and people in disadvantaged groups often do become disillusioned with a system that makes life difficult for them, their friends, and their families. To predict when these social changes will occur, researchers have drawn on social identity theory. This theory highlights several factors that can determine whether members of lower status groups choose to work within the system toward their own individual goals (try to increase individual mobility) or resist and try to change the status quo in the service of group goals (engage in collective action). In a nutshell, those who fight for the cause of their disadvantaged group often believe that (1) the boundaries between groups are *impermeable*; (2) the current structure is *illegitimate* but also *unstable*; and thus (3) it can be changed.

Together, these three perceptions increase identification with and loyalty to the ingroup, which promotes actions to elevate the status of that group (Tajfel & Turner, 1979). Research has supported these ideas with both experimental studies that create groups in the lab (Ellemers et al, 1988) and survey research with real-world groups (DeWeerd & Klandermans, 1999). These groups include East Germans reacting to having subordinate status to West Germans and Dutch farmers protesting against government legislation that would affect agriculture.

Individual mobility A strategy whereby individuals work within the system to achieve their own goals rather than those of the group.

Collective action Efforts by groups to resist and change the status quo in the service of group goals.

The black power movement of the 1960s was promoted by prominent and successful African Americans, such as Tommie Smith and John Carlos, medalists at the 1968 Summer Olympics.

[John Dominis/Time & Life Pictures/ Getty Images]

The permeability of group boundaries, sometimes studied as the belief in a meritocracy or the belief that one can advance one's lot in life through hard work, is particularly interesting as a predictor of collective action. During the 1960s in America, the fight for civil rights was spearheaded by the black power movement. Most of the members of this movement, however, were not the poorest and most disadvantaged Blacks but rather were members of the emerging Black middle and upper class (Caplan, 1970). Although individual mobility efforts can allow people to rise within their group, sometimes a move to collective action does not happen until relatively advantaged members of a lower-status group run up against a barrier that seems to prevent further success. It only might be at this point that the system seems rigged against them and that something in addition to their individual efforts toward individual goals is needed for further advancement.

SECTION review | Leadership, Power, and Group Hierarchy

Most groups have leaders who wield power and are at the top of a hierarchy.

Leadership style	Effects of power	Hierarchies
• Some leaders are transformational, but in general, effective leaders match their approach to the demands of the situation. • Leaders can be charismatic, task oriented, or relationship oriented.	• Power leads people to be more approach oriented and less inhibited. • People in power tend to have less empathy and can be less generous to those in need.	• As societies grow, work shifts from basic divisions of labor to culturally defined roles. • Power-distance orientation varies among cultures. • People tend to regard existing hierarchies as legitimate, even when they are disadvantaged by them. • Social change occurs when successful members of disadvantaged groups encounter barriers and act collectively to change the status quo.

Why Do People Leave and Disidentify With Groups?

Please accept my resignation. I don't want to belong to any club that will accept people like me as members.

—Groucho Marx, in a telegram to the Friars Club of Beverly Hills
(*Groucho and Me*, 1959, p. 321)

It is pretty obvious that people don't want to become members of all groups. First, most people are happy to be members of the culture in which they were raised, as opposed to the many other cultures out there. Second, in modern, large cultures, there are thousands of groups one could conceivably join. Who could keep up with that? Third, many groups aren't that appealing to most people. We'd venture to guess that our average reader doesn't have much interest in joining the Ku Klux Klan.

But it's also obvious that people are raised in groups and that they get great benefits from being members of their ascribed and chosen groups. Earlier in this chapter, we described four basic psychological needs that groups serve: promoting survival, reducing uncertainty, enhancing self-esteem, and managing the potential terror of being mortal. Given these major benefits, why would individuals ever leave or distance themselves from their groups? What groups have you left? Why?

Think
ABOUT

[Masterfile Royalty Free]

Although people leave groups for many specific reasons, they often do so because the group no longer successfully serves one or more of those four basic psychological needs. So the desire to meet those needs drives them away from, rather than toward, the group. Let's examine this possibility further.

Promoting Survival

Every year in the United States, hundreds of thousands of boys and girls as young as 12 years old join gangs (Snyder & Sickmund, 2006). But although the gang expects them to join for life, about two thirds of new initiates leave the gang after one or two years. Contrary to popular myth, those who wish to leave do not face the threat of death from fellow gang members (although they may be severely beaten). However, leaving often means facing the worst of both worlds. On the one hand, their fellow gang members reject them. On the other, because of their past criminal activities as gang members, they struggle to find legitimate employment and to be accepted by mainstream social institutions (Decker & Lauritsen, 2002). So why do they leave?

In interviews with former gang members in cities such as Rochester, Denver, and St. Louis, researchers found that the most often cited reason for their decision to leave the gang is fear of injury and death after being injured or after witnessing fellow gang members fall prey to violence (Decker & Van Winkle, 1996; Thornberry et al., 2004). Former gang members often said things such as, "Well after I got shot. . . .You know how your life just flash? It like did that so I stopped selling dope, got a job, stayed in school, just stopped hanging around cause one day I know some other gang member catch me and probably kill me" (Decker & Van Winkle, 1996, p. 269).

This is surprising because we said earlier that group members become more committed to the group when they face a common threat; we would expect, then, that the threat of violence would *strengthen* solidarity among gang members. This is indeed the case when there is a threat of violence. But when individuals experience violence themselves or observe their own friends and family being harmed, they think twice about staying in the group. Thus, young boys and girls join the gang in order to seek safety from harm, but if they realize that belonging to the gang poses risks to their lives rather than protecting them, they often leave (Decker & Van Winkle, 1996; Peterson et al., 2004). The need to survive has the power both to draw people toward groups and to push them to leave.

Reducing Uncertainty

Uncertainty-identity theory, discussed earlier in this chapter, posits that people join and identify with groups to reduce negative feelings of uncertainty. Does that mean that leaving groups always increases uncertainty about the world, the self, and other people?

No. Sometimes leaving is exactly what the person or subgroup needs to do to maintain certainty in their worldview. For example, when the individual perceives that the group has changed or has acted in a way that violates an important value or norm, the group is no longer useful in validating that individual's worldview. In fact, in this situation, belonging to the group may itself be a source of uncertainty. The individual may therefore disidentify with the group or leave it altogether in order to uphold the norm.

This can result in what are called *schisms*, which occur when a subgroup of people break away from the larger parent group and form their own group or join a different parent group. These schisms happen because the subgroup feels that the parent group has forgotten or violated its own core values (Sani & Todman, 2002). For example, in 2010, a substantial number of people left the Republican party because they felt that it was ignoring its own principle of fighting against big government. They formed the conservative tea party movement, which places more explicit emphasis on that principle. In these cases, people sacrifice the certainty of being in a group for the certainty of maintaining their values.

Bolstering Self-esteem

Earlier in this chapter, we discussed how people join and identify with groups to bolster their self-esteem. But what happens when a person feels incapable of living up to the group's standards of value? Under such circumstances, the person may seek alternative groups whose worldviews seem to provide more attainable sources of self-worth. This happens when people convert to new religions or join cults. Cults generally target poor people struggling economically and young people struggling for a positive identity and sense of purpose. People who join cults and experience religious conversions are generally under stress and have shaky self-esteem. After joining these new groups, they experience increases in self-esteem and purpose in life, as well as a reduced fear of death (e.g., Levine, 1981; Paloutzian, 1981; Ullman, 1982).

What happens when members cannot view the group positively, perhaps because a rival group is more successful? In these situations, belonging to a group threatens to *decrease* self-esteem. Do group members stick with their group through the rough times? Or do they distance themselves from the group? People are willing to disidentify with a group to protect their own self-esteem. In one study (Snyder et al., 1986), participants led to believe that their group failed a task were less interested in continuing to work with their group. They were less willing to wear a badge indicating that they were part of the group than were participants whose group succeeded on the same task or who were not given feedback on their group's performance.

People will occasionally disidentify with their group as a whole even if just one other group member does something negative (Eidelman & Biernat, 2003). Why? People assume that members of the group are similar. They share the same beliefs and engage in the same types of behaviors. Thus, when a member of your own group does something stupid or immoral, you may be afraid that you will be found guilty by association, simply because you are in the same group as that person (Cooper & Jones, 1969). When the group identity is very important, however, and the behavior is seen as being out of character for the group, another strategy is to oust the perpetrator psychologically from the group. Ruslan Tsarni, the uncle of the Tsarnaev brothers, the two men believed to be responsible for the bombings at the 2013 Boston Marathon, described them as "losers" and said that they brought shame on their family and their Chechen ethnic group. In this way, he clearly distanced not only himself, but also the rest of the family and Chechens in general, from them and their alleged misdeeds.

Ruslan Tsarni, the uncle of the suspected bombers at the 2013 Boston Marathon, reacted to the news that they might have committed the bombings by distancing himself and the rest of his family from them.

[Allison Shelley/Getty Images]

Managing Mortality Concerns

As we noted earlier, reminding people of their mortality generally increases their identification with the groups to which they belong. From the perspective of terror management theory, this happens because these groups help validate people's meaningful view of their world, their self-worth, and the sense that they are part of something larger that will continue after their death. However, when a given group identification no longer serves one of these functions, reminders of death lead people to jump ship and shift their identification to other groups that are better at providing these psychological resources.

For example, when Latinos or women are reminded of their mortality and led to think of negative aspects of the group membership (for Latinos the stereotype that Latinos tend to be drug dealers; for women, the stereotype that women are not good in math), they respond by distancing themselves from their ethnic or gender identification (Arndt et al., 2002). Latino participants, for example, disliked artwork that was attributed to Latino artists. Female participants emphasized how they were in fact different from other women.

Whether people defend or distance themselves from their group when mortality is salient depends on how permanent they consider group identity to be. When Dutch students were exposed to criticism of their university, and they were led to think that university affiliation was a permanent identification, mortality salience led them to reject that criticism as unfounded. However, if students were led to think that university affiliation was temporary and were reminded of death, they instead responded to the criticism by reducing their identification with the university (Dechesne et al., 2000).

SECTION review | Why Do People Leave and Disidentify With Groups?

The same psychological motives that drive people to join and identify with groups—promoting survival, reducing uncertainty, bolstering self-esteem, and managing mortality concerns—also can drive them to leave when group membership itself threatens to undermine those needs.

Promoting survival	Reducing uncertainty	Bolstering self-esteem	Managing mortality concerns
When people sense that belonging to a group increases the risk of being harmed or killed, they tend to break away from the group.	Subgroups may break away from a parent group when they see it as violating a core value that provides certainty.	When a group member cannot view the group positively, membership may decrease self-esteem, prompting the person to leave.	When a group no longer buffers mortality concerns by providing meaning and value, group members may disidentify, especially if they regard the group as temporary.

CONNECT ONLINE:

Macmillan Education
LaunchPad

Check out our videos and additional resources located at:
www.macmillanhighered.com/launchpad/greenberg1e

Understanding Prejudice, Stereotyping, and Discrimination

TOPIC OVERVIEW

The most persistent sound which reverberates through man's history is the beating of war drums. Tribal wars, religious wars, civil wars, dynastic wars, national wars, revolutionary wars, colonial wars, wars of conquest and of liberation, wars to prevent and to end all wars, follow each other in a chain of compulsive repetitiveness as far as man can remember his past, and there is every reason to believe that the chain will extend into the future.

—Arthur Koestler, *Janus: A summing up* (1978, pp. 2–3)

In the last three chapters, we have emphasized what social beings we humans are. We live in families, tribes, and cultures. Our groups help us survive and provide our lives with structure. They give us bases of self-worth and imbue life with meaning and purpose. All of this is great stuff. But one major problem is inherent in living within groups: It separates us from other human beings who live within other groups.

Prejudice is the all-too-common consequence of this distinction between us (the ingroup) and them (the outgroup). Virtually every known culture has been hostile to members of some other culture or oppressed certain segments of its society.

Indeed, recorded history is riddled with the bloody consequences of a seemingly endless parade of oppression, persecution, colonization, crusades, wars, and genocides. And archeological evidence suggests these problems plagued our unrecorded earlier history as well. Lethal human violence fueled by intergroup conflict has been dated back at least to between 12,000 and 10,000 BC, when evidence suggests that a battle near Jebel Sahaba, Sudan resulted in 59 well-preserved

[The Holocaust Memorial Miami Beach, Miami, Florida, USA: *The Sculpture of Love and Anguish* by Kenneth Treister. Photo @ Bildagentur-online/Schickert/Alamy]

The 1994 genocide of Tutsis by Hutus in Rwanda is one of many tragic examples of prejudice in its most extreme form.

[Evelyn Hockstein/KRT/Newscom]

casualties (Wendorf, 1968). Of course that was just an early drop in the bucket relative to what happened during the Crusades, the Spanish Inquisition, the European invasion and colonization of the Americas, the two world wars, the Nazi Holocaust, Stalin's purges, the killing fields of the Khmer Rouge, and the Hutu genocidal campaign against the Tutsi in Rwanda; the list could go on and on. The violent heritage of our species led a character from James Joyce's classic novel *Ulysses* to comment, "History . . . is a nightmare from which I am trying to awake." (Joyce, 1961, p. 28).

In this chapter and the next one, we will explore the many reasons that history has been and continues to be such a nightmare of intergroup hatred and violence. In this first chapter we will focus on the nature and causes of prejudice and how stereotyping arises and affects the way people perceive and behave toward others. In the subsequent chapter, we will consider how prejudice, stereotyping, and discrimination affect those targeted by these biases. We will also consider ways in which we might hope someday to awaken from this nightmare to an egalitarian reality in which people treat each other fairly regardless of their differences.

The Nature of Prejudice: Pervasiveness and Perspective

Prejudice probably is the most heavily studied topic in social psychology. The historical pervasiveness and destructiveness of prejudice is probably why. Virtually every person currently living on this planet has been profoundly affected by prejudice. If you are Arab American, African American, Hispanic American, Jewish American, or Native American, this is likely obvious to you. But it is equally true regardless of your ethnic background. Every ethnic and cultural group has been powerfully influenced by historical intergroup conflicts and oppression. The French have been targets of prejudice by Americans, have been involved historically in conflicts with England (including a 100-year war) and Germany. French culture has been greatly influenced by France's colonization of places such as Canada, Algeria, and Vietnam. Japan and China have exchanged many acts of hostility and violence over a long period of time. Many innocent Japanese people were killed by the atomic bombs that American pilots dropped on Nagasaki and Hiroshima during World War II. And during that war, the U.S. government forced many Japanese Americans into internment camps. Within Japan is an oppressed minority group called the Burakumin. And in most if not all cultures, women are to varying degrees targets of violence and restricted in their freedoms and opportunities. Pick a group, and you could read volumes about how that group has been affected by prejudice.

In everyday language, the word *prejudice* has a number of meanings, all based on the notion of judging something or someone prematurely from insufficient evidence. In social psychology, prejudice is defined as a negative attitude toward an individual based solely on that person's presumed membership in a particular group. Thus the person is disliked not because of her personal attributes or actions but simply because she is perceived to be in some supposedly undesirable category: physically disabled, Italian, African American, Hindu, female, lesbian, fat, old, teenager, communist.

An interesting aspect of prejudice is that, on the one hand, many if not most people seem to be prejudiced against some group. (Right now, you might be feeling some prejudice against prejudiced people!) and they usually feel that their particular

Prejudice A negative attitude toward an individual solely on the basis of that person's presumed membership in a particular group.

prejudice is justified. On the other hand, social psychologists generally assume that prejudice against a person based simply on her or his membership in a group is never justified. This assumption is based on three characteristics of prejudice.

First, prejudice involves judging an individual negatively independent of the person's actual attributes or actions. Social psychologists follow the hope famously articulated by Dr. Martin Luther King, Jr. (1992): "I have a dream that my four little children will one day live in a nation where they will not be judged by the color of their skin but by the content of their character." If someone harms you or someone you care about, you are justified in disliking that person. If a person simply practices a religion different from your own, has a different skin tone, or comes from a different country, you are not justified in disliking that person.

Second, any large category of people will include tremendous variability in virtually every possible attribute by which one might judge another person positively or negatively (Allport, 1954). There may be a group mean (what the average member of a group is like), but there also is always a normal distribution that captures the range along which most people vary from that mean. Think of members of your own extended family—siblings, parents, aunts, uncles, cousins, grandparents. Can you think of some who are generous, some who are cheap; some who are likeable, some who are unpleasant; some who are smart, some not so much; some who are honest, some who are deceitful; some who are ambitious, some who are not? If you can find variability in such a small group, imagine the variability in the many millions of people who are identified as Americans, Muslim, Hispanic, or gay. Because of this variation, assuming anything about all members of such groups will necessarily lead to many errors. To use an example where measurable data are available, consider that although the average American (male, 5'9 1/2", female, 5'4") is taller than the average Chinese person (male, 5'7"; female, 5'2 1/2") (Yang et al., 2005), literally millions of Americans are shorter than the average Chinese person, and millions of Chinese people are taller than the average American (see **FIGURE 10.1**).

Think
ABOUT

[Blend/Hill Street Studios/Getty Images]

Figure 10.1a

Human Variability

Although Americans on average are taller than Chinese people, there is great variability in the height of individuals in both groups, leading to many exceptions.

[Bill Pugliano/Getty Images]

Mean height for Chinese men — | — Mean height for American men

5' 7"   5' 9½"

Height

Figure 10.1b

Overlapping Normal Distributions of Two Groups With Different Mean Heights

The normal distribution of Chinese and American males' heights, based on the group means, might look something like this. The shaded areas represent cases in which we would be wrong if we simply assumed that American males are taller than the average Chinese male or that Chinese males are shorter than the average American male.

The third reason social psychologists judge prejudice negatively is that it has so often led to appalling acts of violence against innocent people—including babies and children—who happened to be, or were presumed to be, members of particular groups. Like Milgram in his research on obedience, many early social psychologists were inspired to focus on prejudice because of one of the most egregious examples of what prejudice can lead to: the Nazi Holocaust, which resulted in the deaths of an estimated 6 million Jews and 5 million members of other groups despised by the Nazis (e.g., Gypsies, Slavs, the physically disabled).

Stereotypes Overgeneralized beliefs about the traits and attributes of members of a particular group.

So that's the case for prejudice being a bad thing. The people who hold prejudices usually justify them with **stereotypes**: overgeneralized beliefs about the traits and attributes of members of a particular group: "African Americans are violent," "Jews are cheap," "Latinos are lazy," and so forth. Not all stereotypic traits attributed to a group are negative, but overall, stereotypes of outgroups tend to be negative. Later in this chapter, we will consider where these stereotypes come from, how they affect us, and how they are perpetuated. As we will learn, stereotypes can operate both as conscious justifications of prejudices against others and as implicit assumptions that guide how we think about groups and their members. Even when we don't acknowledge it or want it to happen, stereotypes can still sometimes bias how we think, feel, and behave toward those whom we perceive as different from us in some way.

Discrimination Negative behavior toward an individual solely on the basis of that person's membership in a particular group.

When people hold prejudices and stereotypes, either consciously or unconsciously, this often leads to **discrimination**: negative behavior toward an individual solely on the basis of membership in a particular group. Discrimination comes in many forms, ranging from cold behavior at a party to declining someone's loan application to torture and genocide. Discrimination is often the consequence of the negative attitude (prejudice) and beliefs (stereotypes) a person holds. But as you'll recall, attitudes don't always guide behavior. Because of laws, cultural norms, and competing values to be egalitarian, we can be thankful that people's behavior is not always biased by prejudice and stereotypes.

SECTION review | The Nature of Prejudice: Pervasiveness and Perspective

Prejudice is probably the most heavily studied topic in social psychology, likely because of its historical pervasiveness and destructiveness.

In social psychology, prejudice is defined as a negative attitude toward an individual based solely on that person's presumed membership in a particular group.	The people who hold prejudices usually justify them with stereotypes, overgeneralized beliefs about the traits and attributes of members of a particular group.	Prejudices and stereotypes, held either consciously or unconsciously, often lead to discrimination: negative behavior toward an individual based solely on that person's presumed membership in a particular group.

The Roots of Prejudice: Three Basic Causes

Given all the harm that has come from prejudice, stereotypes, and discrimination, why are these phenomena so prevalent? This is one of the central questions that Gordon Allport addressed in his classic book *The Nature of Prejudice* (1954). In a chapter titled "The Normality of Prejudgment," Allport proposed three basic causes of prejudice, each of which is an unfortunate consequence of some very basic aspects of human thought and feeling.

Hostile Feelings Linked to a Category

Allport viewed the first fundamental cause of prejudice to be a result of two basic human tendencies:

> First, people are likely to feel hostility when they are frustrated or threatened, or when they witness things they view as unpleasant or unjust.

Second, as we noted in our chapters on social cognition, people tend to form schemas or categories and then view new stimuli as members of these categories. Just as we routinely categorize objects (see chapter 3), we also categorize other people as members of social groups, such as *women*, *Asians*, and *teenagers*, often within milliseconds of encountering them (Fiske, 1998). For example, when someone looks at pictures of others of a different race, the brain emits electrical signals (referred to as *event-related potentials*) that are associated with increased attention and categorization. This response occurs within a few hundred milliseconds of exposure (Ito & Bartholow, 2009) and has been found both for Whites looking at pictures of Blacks and for Blacks looking at pictures of Whites (Dickter & Bartholow, 2007).

Prejudice results from the combination of these two basic tendencies: the experience of hostile feelings linked to a salient category of people. For example, in Marseilles, a Frenchman robbed at gunpoint by another a Frenchman will likely experience fear and anger, hate that man, and hope he is caught and imprisoned. A Frenchman who is robbed by an Algerian man will experience the same emotions but is more likely to direct that hate toward Algerians, a prominent immigrant group in France, and may therefore want all Algerians expelled from his country. Because what is salient to the victimized individual in the latter example is the category Algerian, his negative feelings are overgeneralized to the category rather than being applied only to the individual mugger whose actions caused his negative experience.

Allport argues that we naturally tend to jump from single experiences with a member of an outgroup to overly broad generalizations about all members of that category. The typical midwestern American who has never met a Muslim and reads about Muslims only when an act of Islamic terrorism occurs is likely to link her negative feelings about terrorism to the category Muslims. An Afghan woman whose niece was killed by an American guided missile is likely to hate Americans. A suburban European American child who knows African Americans only through television shows portraying them primarily as criminals may view the entire group as violent and dangerous. A European American kid hassled by a Mexican American in a middle-school restroom may decide he hates "Mexicans." In each of these examples, experiences with or negative information about the actions or attributes of a single individual or a small sample of individuals leads to a sweeping negative feeling that is applied to literally millions of people who are perceived to be members of the salient group. In a finding consistent with these examples, Rosenfield and colleagues (1982) showed that when White participants were asked for money by a shabbily dressed Black panhandler, they were later less willing to volunteer to help promote a racial brotherhood week than if they were initially approached by either a well-dressed Black graduate student asking them to sign a petition or by a shabbily dressed White panhandler. These two comparison conditions made it clear that only an unpleasant encounter with a Black person led to reduced support for promoting racial brotherhood.

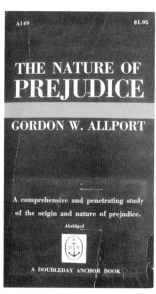

Gordon Allport's book *The Nature of Prejudice* launched more than six decades of research on the subject.

This idea of negative feelings generalized to an entire group can help explain many historical instances of increases in prejudice. A couple of very dramatic American examples concern Japanese Americans and Arab Americans. After the attack by the Japanese military on American forces at Pearl Harbor on December 7, 1941, Japanese Americans were commonly harassed. Many were removed from their homes and placed in internment camps. Similarly, after the terrorist attacks of September 11, 2001, Americans exhibited more negative attitudes and behavior toward Arab and Muslim Americans. Although these reactions were predictable, they are classic examples of prejudice—the individuals targeted had nothing to do with the attacks on the U.S. but were judged negatively because of their perceived group membership.

Realistic group conflict theory
asserts that the initial negative feelings between groups are often based on a real conflict or competition regarding scarce resources.

Realistic group conflict theory (Levine & Campbell, 1972) adds to Allport's idea by arguing that the initial negative feelings between groups are often based on a real conflict or competition over scarce resources. If individuals in one group think that their access to land, water, jobs, or other resources is being threatened or blocked by another group, the resulting sense of threat and frustration is likely to generate negative emotions about the perceived rival group. This helps explain why when new groups of immigrants arrive in a country, hostility is usually part of the dominant group's reaction, especially when economic times are tough and jobs are scarce (e.g., Dollard, 1938). Furthermore, these negative feelings are often culturally transmitted from generation to generation, so that intergroup hostilities are perpetuated even if the initial realistic conflict has become ancient history and is no longer pertinent.

Intergroup anxiety theory
Theory proposing that intergroup prejudice leads individuals to experience anxiety when they think of or interact with members of an outgroup.

Intergroup anxiety theory (Stephan & Stephan, 1985) extends realistic group conflict theory by arguing that historical conflict between different groups makes members of both groups anxious in their encounters with each other. As a result, these feelings of intergroup anxiety can be triggered even when individuals merely think about the outgroup. This anxiety can result from fear of rejection, domination, exploitation, or violence; guilt over past treatment of the group; or uncertainty about how to behave toward members of the group. This anxiety fuels prejudice because these negative feelings become associated with outgroup members.

Ingroup Bias: We Like Us Better Than Them

The second cause of prejudice that Allport identified results from a basic tendency to prefer what is familiar and what is connected to oneself to what is unfamiliar and not connected to oneself. As the mere exposure effect discussed in chapter 8 shows, the more familiar we are with a stimulus, the more we like it. We like—indeed, usually love—our own families, our own towns, our own stuff, and by the same token, our own group. We're familiar with how members of our own group look, sound, and act. In contrast, outgroups are less familiar, stranger, less known. They make us feel uneasy, anxious. They are harder to predict and understand.

Taking an evolutionary perspective, some psychologists have argued that a preference for familiar others is probably something adaptive that has been selected for (e.g., Park et al., 2003). Our ancestors, living in small groups, were probably safer if they stayed close to their own. If they ventured away from their own group and encountered other groups, they may have experienced peril, including exposure to germs. One finding consistent with this possibility is that when thoughts of disease are made salient, people become particularly negative toward ethnically different others (Faulkner et al., 2004). Allport noted that because of common backgrounds, experiences, and knowledge, it's also just easier to know what to say and how to behave around those who are members of the ingroup.

In addition to this familiarity-based preference for the ingroup over outgroups, most of us like ourselves and demonstrate a self-serving bias, as you'll recall from our coverage of self-esteem (chapter 6). So if I am great, then my group must be great also. Surely groups I am not a member of can't be as great as those to which I belong.

Indeed, research has shown that ingroup pronouns such as *us* are associated automatically with positive feelings and that outgroup pronouns such as *them* are associated automatically with negative ones (Perdue et al., 1990). So pride in one's own group and preference for one's own group over others may be a natural extension of self-serving bias. This ingroup bias can affect even political beliefs (Kosloff et al., 2010). In the lead-up to the 2008 U.S. presidential election, when undecided White voters were reminded of their race, they were more likely to believe negative reports about the African American Democratic candidate, Barack Obama. Similarly, when undecided young voters were reminded of their age, they were more likely to believe negative reports about the 65-year-old Republican candidate at the time, John McCain.

Social identity theory (see chapter 9) (Tajfel & Turner, 1986) actually looks at the relationship between self-esteem and groups the other way around, reversing the causal direction. Recall that this theory proposes that a considerable portion of our self-esteem actually derives from our group memberships. Not only is my group great because I'm in it, but I am great because I am in this group! So I gain self-esteem by thinking highly of my own group and less highly of outgroups. And sure enough, wherever you travel, you meet people who are proud of their own cultures and ethnicities and think more highly of them than they do of other cultures and ethnicities. During the World Cup and the Olympics we can see the basic truth that social identity theory captures: that people derive self-worth from their ingroup identifications.

A large body of experimental research also supports the existence of ingroup bias and the validity of social identity theory. One important line of inquiry has examined whether arbitrarily formed groups immediately exhibit ingroup bias. For example, Jonathan Swift's (1726/2001) classic satire *Gulliver's Travels* describes wars breaking out between those who believe eggs should be cracked at the big end and those who believe they should be cracked at the small end. Empirical evidence of such arbitrary forms of prejudice was found in a seminal study by Henri Tajfel. In this study, British high school students viewed a series of dots on a screen and were asked to estimate how many there were (Tajfel et al., 1971). The researchers told one random set of students that they were "overestimators" and the other set that they were "underestimators." Even in such minimal groups, researchers found bias in favor of distributing more resources to members of one's own group than to the outgroup, whether or not these groups had a history of contact with one another (Tajfel & Turner, 1986).

On which side would you crack the egg? Hundreds of years ago Jonathan Swift anticipated the finding that minimal differences can lead to ingroup bias. In *Gulliver's Travels* he describes wars breaking out between those who believe eggs should be cracked at the big end and those who believe they should be cracked at the small end.

Theory and research also suggest that in most cases the liking for the ingroup is stronger and more fundamental than the dislike of the outgroup (e.g., Allport, 1954; Brewer, 1979). Allport noted that in many contexts, people are very accepting of bias in favor of their own children and family, and pride in their own nation. However, this "love prejudice" often has negative consequences for outgroups. An African American woman who is having trouble finding employment would feel little comfort in knowing that it's not so much that White employers are biased against African Americans but just that they prefer to hire their "own kind." In addition, if we view an outgroup as threatening in some way to our beloved ingroup, our love for our own group may lead to hate for that outgroup.

A second important line of research has tested the prediction from social identity theory that ingroup bias serves self-esteem needs. From a social identity perspective, people should be especially likely to laud their own group and derogate outgroups after a threat to their personal self-esteem. In a series of studies (see **FIGURE 10.2**), Fein and Spencer (1997) gave non–Jewish American participants positive or negative feedback on a test of social and verbal skills and then had them evaluate a woman after seeing a résumé and a videotape. For half the participants, the job candidate was depicted as Italian American; for the other half she was depicted as Jewish American. Participants

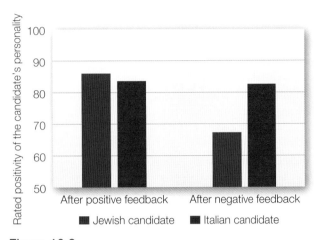

Figure 10.2

The Role of Self-Esteem Threat in Prejudice

After receiving negative feedback, American participants derogated a woman they believed was Jewish American rather than Italian American.

[Data source: Fein & Spencer (1997)]

Ethnocentrism Viewing the world through our own cultural value system and thereby judging actions and people based on our own culture's views of right and wrong and good and bad.

given self-esteem-threatening negative feedback rated the woman more negatively if they thought she was Jewish. In addition, those participants given negative feedback and who had the opportunity to derogate the Jewish American woman showed an increase in self-esteem. And the more negatively they evaluated the Jewish American woman, the more their self-esteem increased. Subsequent studies have provided further support for the role of self-esteem threat in prejudice and stereotyping, showing, for example, that threatening Whites' self-esteem brings negative stereotypes of African Americans and Asian Americans closer to mind (Spencer et al., 1998). When people feel bad about themselves, they seem to compensate through downward comparison by thinking more harshly of outgroups.

Another example of this kind of self-esteem protecting prejudice is *scapegoating*, a phenomenon whereby people who feel inferior, guilty, anxious, or unsuccessful will blame an outgroup for their troubles (Allport, 1954; Jung, 1945/1970; Miller & Bugelski, 1948). Captain Ahab blamed the white whale, the Nazis blamed the Jews, unsuccessful White Americans blame immigrants. This can explain why in tough economic times, prejudice, stereotyping, and discrimination tend to increase (e.g., Hepworth & West, 1988; Hovland & Sears, 1940). For example, recent experiments have shown that reminding people of the threat of natural disasters leads them to view outgroups as enemies with evil intentions (Landau et al., 2012; Sullivan et al., 2010). This research has also shown that such scapegoating both provides someone to blame for one's own problems and increases a sense of control over one's life (Rothschild et al., 2012).

Ethnocentrism, the Cultural Worldview, and Threat

Allport's third basic cause of prejudice stems from the fact that each of us is raised within a particular cultural worldview and therefore has specific ideas about what is right and wrong and good and bad. If the worldview that we internalize from childhood explicitly portrays particular groups negatively, we likely will to follow suit. So simply conforming to the norms and values of one's worldview can lead to prejudice. Supporting this idea, researchers have found that in places where prejudice is normative, such as the Deep South of the United States in the 1950s, the more people conform in general, the more prejudiced they tend to be (e.g., Pettigrew, 1958).

The internalized worldview contributes to prejudice in another important way. Because this worldview determines our view of what is right and good, we can't help but judge others on the basis of those cultural values. This kind of judgment is called **ethnocentrism** (Sumner, 1906) and often leads us to hold negative attitudes about others who were raised in different cultures. An American who finds out that people in culture Z believe in bathing only twice a year is going to have a hard time not judging the members of that culture negatively: "They're dirty and primitive!" By the same token, members of culture Z may observe the American tendency to bathe

Think
ABOUT

Ethnocentric biases lead people to judge others' cultural preferences and beliefs not just as different but as inferior to their own.

[Janine Wiedel Photolibrary/Alamy]

or shower virtually every day as bizarre: "They're wasteful and compulsive!" These kinds of judgments get more serious when Americans learn of cultures that practice female circumcision or believe that women should never leave the house without covering every part of their bodies. **When are right and wrong matters of mere cultural preference? When are they a legitimate basis for judging members of another group negatively? It is very hard to say, because our sense of right and wrong is so intertwined with the cultural worldview in which we were raised.**

Symbolic Racism

The theory of **symbolic racism** (Sears & Kinder, 1971) posits that the tendency to reject those groups that don't conform to one's own view of the world underlies much of the racial prejudice that European Americans have against African Americans. From this perspective, many European Americans have internalized traditional, conservative Eurocentric moral values. From their perspective, African Americans are a threat to these values and to what they consider as the American way of life.

People who exhibit signs of symbolic racism don't think they are prejudiced against Blacks or other minority groups. Rather, their negative attitudes toward these groups are expressed symbolically as opposition to policies that are seen as giving advantages to minority groups. They might deny that minorities continue to face discrimination and believe that racial disparities result from the unwillingness of people in minority groups to work hard enough. Although they recognize that disliking a group of people is indefensible, those who are high in symbolic racism feel perfectly justified in opposing social programs aimed at rectifying social inequalities that African Americans experience.

The theory of symbolic racism has been particularly useful in showing how prejudice is symbolically represented in diverging political opinions (Sears & Henry, 2005). In a typical study, participants complete questionnaires that measure symbolic racism (for example, indicating how much they agree with the statement that Blacks no longer face much discrimination). Those who score high on measures of symbolic racism—even when taking into account other factors such as political party affiliation—are more likely to support tough, punitive anti-crime policies that have been shown to discriminate against minority groups (for example, the death penalty or "three strikes and you're out" laws) (Green et al., 2006).

Symbolic racism A tendency to express negative biases held about a racial outgroup not at the group directly, but at social policies seen as benefiting that group.

Terror Management Theory

We've seen that people tend to think poorly of those who seem to live by a different set of rules and beliefs. But why can't people just leave it at "Different strokes for different folks"? According to the existential perspective of terror management theory, one reason is that people must sustain faith in the validity of their own cultural worldview so that it can continue to offer psychological security in the face of our personal vulnerability and mortality. Other cultures threaten that faith: "One culture is always a potential menace to another because it is a living example that life can go on heroically within a value framework totally alien to one's own" (Becker, 1971, p. 140).

The novelist James Baldwin summed it up this way:

> Life is tragic simply because the earth turns and the sun inexorably rises and sets, and one day, for each of us, the sun will go down for the last, last time. Perhaps the whole root of our trouble, the human trouble, is that we will sacrifice all the beauty of our lives, will imprison ourselves in totems, taboos, crosses, blood sacrifices, steeples, mosques, races, armies, flags, nations, in order to deny the fact of death, which is the only fact we have (1963, p. 105)

Basing their work on this idea, terror management researchers have tested the hypothesis that raising the problem of mortality would make people especially positive toward others who support their worldview and especially negative to others who implicitly or explicitly challenge it. In the first study testing this notion, when reminded of their own mortality, American Christian students became more positive toward a fellow Christian student and more negative toward a Jewish student (Greenberg et al., 1990). Similarly, when reminded of death, Italians and Germans became more biased toward their own cultures and against other cultures (Castano et al., 2002; Jonas et al., 2005). Reminders of mortality also increase prejudice against the physically disabled because they remind us of our own physical vulnerabilities (Hirschberger et al., 2005).

In a pair of studies particularly pertinent to the ongoing tensions in the Middle East, researchers found that when reminded of their own mortality, Iranian college students expressed greater support for suicidal martyrdom against Americans (Pyszczynski et al., 2006). The second study showed that politically conservative American college students who were reminded of their mortality similarly supported preemptively bombing countries that might threaten the United States, regardless of "collateral damage" (Pyszczynski et al., 2006). And in yet another troubling study, Hayes and colleagues (2008) found that Christian Canadians who were reminded of their mortality were better able to avoid thoughts of their own death if they imagined Muslims dying in a plane crash.

SECTION review | The Roots of Prejudice: Three Basic Causes

Gordon Allport proposed three basic causes of prejudice, each based on fundamental ways that people think and feel.

Hostility plus categorization	Ingroup bias	Threats to one's world view
• We tend to feel hostility when we are frustrated or threatened. • When negative feelings are associated with a member of an outgroup, we tend to overgeneralize those negative feelings and associated beliefs to the entire group.	• We prefer what is familiar, including people like us. • A portion of our self-esteem comes from group membership, biasing us against those in outgroups. • When our self-worth is threatened, we tend to derogate and blame members of other groups.	• Our ethnocentrism leads us to judge people from different cultures more negatively. • Ethnocentric biases are more severe when we feel vulnerable or if we see another's worldview as threatening to our own.

Is Prejudice an Ugly Thing of the Past?

The historical record shows that prejudice has been rampant in the past. But what about now? If we look around the world, surely we would conclude it's not just an ugly aspect of history. Prejudice based on ethnicity, gender, and sexual orientation continues to fuel violence and societal turmoil in many parts of the world. But what about in the United States? In the 21st century, aren't Americans past all of that? Isn't America a land of truly equal opportunity?

Although many European Americans believe that racial prejudice is a thing of the past (Norton & Sommers, 2011), African Americans are far from convinced. In a Pew survey in 2007, 67% of African Americans reported that they often encountered prejudice when applying for jobs, and 50% reported that they had experienced racism when simply shopping or dining out. In a 2013 Pew survey, 88% of African Americans said that their group still experiences "some" or a "a lot" of discrimination, compared with only 57% of European Americans who believe that African Americans still experience discrimination.

Of course there is no question that great progress has been made in improving attitudes toward and treatment of ethnic minorities; women; and gays, lesbians, bisexuals, and transgendered individuals in the United States. Dial back time about 60 years to 1954. The U.S. Supreme Court has just announced the historic decision *Brown v. Board of Education*, which struck down state laws enforcing racial segregation in the public schools. The Court ruled that "separate but equal" schools for Black and White students were inherently *un*equal. The ruling was met with stark and at times violent opposition in a number of states. President Dwight D. Eisenhower had to call in the National Guard to protect African American children heading into and out of school in Arkansas.

Contrast that situation with where America is now. About 60 years later, we have anti-discrimination laws and an African American was elected president of the United

States in 2008. In some respects at least, the United States has made tremendous strides in race relations.

Similar changes can also be seen with other prejudices—although some changes have taken longer than others. Consider prejudice and discrimination based on gender. Although the 19th Amendment guaranteed women the right to vote in 1920, it was not until 2006 that Congresswoman Nancy Pelosi became the Speaker of the House and the highest-ranking woman in U.S. political history. As of 2015, the United States has not yet had a female president, but many Democrats are enthusiastic about having Hillary Clinton on the ballot in 2016. What about prejudice against gays and lesbians? Although same-sex marriage is hotly debated, one CNN poll showed that 2010 was the first year that more than 50% of those surveyed supported same-sex marriages (CNN Political Unit, 2012). And at the end of 2010, the U.S. Senate voted to repeal the "Don't ask, don't tell" policy and struck down the ban on openly gay men and women serving in the military. In 2013, the U.S. Supreme Court decided a landmark case that opened the door for same-sex couples to qualify for federal benefits previously only extended to heterosexual couples (*U.S. v. Windsor*, 2013). There are also signs of progress toward acceptance of transgender individuals. In 2014, we saw the first openly transgender person ever to be nominated for an Emmy, Laverne Cox, for her performance in the television show *Orange is the New Black*.

Are these social, political, and legislative strides in step with the prejudices that people express? To a large extent, at least when considering more overt expressions of prejudice, the answer is yes. **FIGURE 10.3** shows the results of two polls. Looking

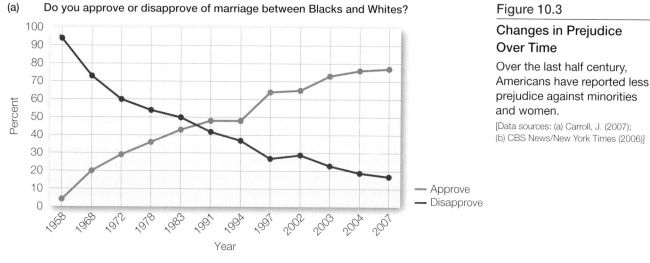

(a) Do you approve or disapprove of marriage between Blacks and Whites?

Figure 10.3

Changes in Prejudice Over Time

Over the last half century, Americans have reported less prejudice against minorities and women.

[Data sources: (a) Carroll, J. (2007); (b) CBS News/New York Times (2006)]

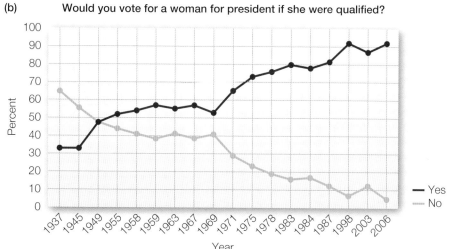

(b) Would you vote for a woman for president if she were qualified?

at **FIGURE 10.3a,** you will see that in 1958, 94% of Americans surveyed opposed interracial marriage, a number that had dropped to 17% by 2007 (Carroll, 2007). Similarly, with regard to gender attitudes, you see in **FIGURE 10.3b** that in 1937, two thirds of Americans said they would not vote for a female presidential candidate,

Think
ABOUT

[Stefanie Timmermann/ Getty Images]

but by 2006, only 5% of Americans expressed such an absolute aversion to having a woman in the Oval Office (CBS/ NY Times, 2006; Eagly, 2007). But before we conclude that problems with prejudice are all but solved, we must keep a few important points in mind.

First, yes, segregation is against the law. But how desegregated are we really as a society? Think back to high school. Did Black students sit mainly in one part of the cafeteria, Whites in another, Hispanics in another, and Asians in yet another? Did you even attend a school or live in an area that was ethnically diverse? If people are still clustering by race and ethnicity, we might wonder whether biases still exist that shape our preferences in whom to approach and whom to avoid.

Second, even if attitudes toward some groups have become more favorable over time, social and political contexts can bring about new hostilities that are simply targeted against different groups. Many Americans probably had few strong attitudes about Muslims or people from Arab nations before 2001. But

SOCIAL PSYCH out in the WORLD

Do Americans Live in a Postracial World?

History was made in 2008, when the United States elected its first African American president. Less than 50 years after Martin Luther King, Jr. spoke of his dream that his children would be judged not by the color of their skin but by the content of their character, this dream seemed much closer to reality. With a multiracial president in the White House, many Americans began to wonder, Do we now finally live in a postracial world?

Probably not. Granted, the research we've reviewed in this chapter demonstrates that racial prejudice has changed considerably over time. The election of Barack Obama certainly signaled more positive attitudes toward African Americans likely to go beyond a desire to avoid seeming racist. However, we've also learned in this chapter that in the contemporary world, prejudice is filled with ambivalence and manifests itself in subtle ways. Elections often might be a time when people try to set biases aside to weigh the more established merits of different candidates. However, among undecided voters, implicit biases seem to play a stronger role in predicting decisions at the polls (Galdi et al., 2008; see also Greenwald,

Smith et al., 2009). Such findings suggest that negative biases still lie below the surface of people's consciously held values, beliefs, and intentions.

On the other hand, the mere fact that the U.S. has had a Black president means that every American citizen now has a highly visible exemplar of a successful Black political leader. Barack Obama might in this way be able to tilt Americans' implicit associations of Blacks in a more positive direction. Indeed, there is some evidence that the election of Obama and exposure to his campaigns have helped to reduce people's implicit race bias, in part by providing a positive example of an African American that may counter many of the negative stereotypes that are so pervasive in mass media (Plant et al., 2009; Columb & Plant, 2011). When President Obama is the example that people bring to mind when they think of Black people, they are less likely to be racially prejudiced.

However, we must be careful not to look at data like these and feel that we need do no more to rectify racial inequality. There are signs that the election of Obama has in fact fostered that belief—that is, a belief that we have achieved racial equality in this country (Kaiser et al., 2009). This perception may allow people to justify keeping the status quo and not trying to change the disparities that do exist. But as you see in the figure on the next page, although everyone's income in the United States has decreased since the economic recession in 2008, the gap in income between ethnic groups in America has stayed constant (Pew Research, 2013).

the September 11, 2001 attacks on the World Trade Center and the Pentagon fueled anti-Muslim prejudice. Whereas Jews were the most salient target of religious prejudice in the United States when Allport wrote his book in 1954, today "only" about 15% of Americans surveyed report having even a little prejudice against Jews, compared with nearly 43% who report having at least some prejudice toward Muslims (Gallup, 2010). Anti-Semitism is far from gone however; it is currently quite prevalent in many European and Asian countries (Baum et al., in press). As human beings, we have the capacity to distrust and dislike those who are different, but the targets of this animosity vary according to current context and particular culture.

Third, although overt expressions of discrimination and racial injustice are certainly declining, they are far from absent. In the fall of 2014, protests cropped up throughout the U.S. in response to police killings of African Americans that many people viewed as outrageous and unwarranted (Huffington Post, 2014). The most publicized of these cases were: the shooting of Michael Brown in Ferguson, Missouri; the shooting of 12-year-old Tamir Rice, who was playing with a pellet gun in a park in Cleveland, Ohio; and the chokehold killing of Eric Garner in Staten Island, New York, who died soon after telling the five police officers holding him down "I can't breathe." As of this book's printing, the police officers involved in these actions had not been charged with any crime or fired. One reaction to these events has been to assert something that shouldn't need to be asserted, that "Black Lives Matter."

Witness to Discrimination Video on LaunchPad

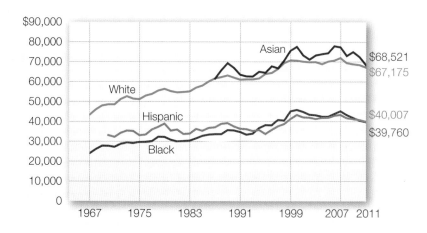

Income Disparities

Since the 1960s, Hispanic and Black Americans have not progressed in terms of income compared with White Americans. In contrast, Asian Americans have done quite well.

[Data source: Pew Research (2013)]

Endorsing Obama's election also may give Whites who are high in prejudice the moral credentials, so to speak, to think that enough has been done to improve racial equality and show stronger favoritism to Whites (Effron et al., 2009). For example, in one study participants who varied in their level of racial prejudice indicated whether they would vote for Obama or McCain in the 2008 election, or to indicate whether they would have voted for Bush or Kerry in 2004. (This condition was included to control for priming political orientation.) (Effron et al., 2009). Subsequently, participants imagined they were on a community committee with a budget surplus that could be allocated to two community organizations, one that primarily served a

White neighborhood and one that primarily served a Black neighborhood.

When participants indicated they would vote for Obama, especially those higher in prejudice turned around and allocated significantly less money to the organization that would serve the Black neighborhood and more money to the organization that would serve the White neighborhood. For people with strong racial biases, acknowledging and endorsing the success of a single outgroup member seems to come at a cost to broader policies that could benefit more people. The visible success of one person does not imply the success of the group as a whole. Clearly, more work needs to be done to fully realize Dr. King's dream.

American President Barack Obama signing the Matthew Shepard Act into law on October 28, 2009.

[© Patsy Lynch/Retna Ltd./Corbis]

Institutional discrimination Unfair restrictions on opportunities for certain groups of people through institutional policies, structural power relations, and formal laws.

But in addition to subtle and indirect forms of prejudice, extreme acts of cruelty are still evident as well. Consider the highly publicized case in 1998 in which a gay University of Wyoming student, Matthew Shepard, was beaten, tortured, and left to die (Loffreda, 2000). This horrendous crime stimulated further blatant anti-gay actions that continue to this day. A pastor and founder of the Westboro Baptist Church, the Reverend Fred Phelps, brought several of his followers from Kansas to protest at Matthew Shepard's funeral. They carried signs that read "God hates Fags" and "Fags deserve to Die." Reverend Phelps repeated such proclamations in the wake of the 2007 collapse of a bridge in Minnesota, claiming that the bridge gave way because of Minnesota's tolerance of homosexuality. Although Phelps's behavior seems to be a particularly offensive and rare exception to contemporary tolerance, hate crimes in the United States have by no means stopped. In 2011, law enforcement agencies reported over 7,700 hate-motivated offenses (Federal Bureau of Investigation, 2012). And it was not until 2009 that perceived gender, gender identity, sexual orientation, and disability were added to the federal definition of hate crimes through the Matthew Shepard Act.

Beyond these extreme acts, there is still ample evidence of discrimination, even though the majority of Americans believe otherwise. During the late 1950s, the civil rights campaign brought into public awareness the problem of **institutional discrimination**, unfair restrictions on the opportunities of certain groups of people by institutional policies, structural power relations, and formal laws (for example, a height requirement for employment as a police officer excludes most women). The more closely Americans looked at their systems of health care, criminal justice, education, and the media, the more they discovered how these systems are arranged in ways that systematically disadvantage certain groups over others. In fact, this form of discrimination is so deeply embedded in the fabric of American society that it can take place without people intending to discriminate or even their awareness that institutional practices have discriminatory effects (Pettigrew, 1958).

Despite the heightened awareness of institutional discrimination, many examples continue today. Particularly in higher-paying jobs (e.g., hospital administrator), equally qualified women may earn only about 78 cents to every dollar that men earn (Eagly & Carli, 2007; Semega, 2009). Are women paid less than men for the same jobs? Sometimes that is the case. But even when it is not, keep in mind that women are more likely to be represented in jobs that have lower earning potential (see **FIGURE 10.4**). At a broader cultural level, our society has assigned less economic value to occupations traditionally held by women (nurse, teacher, administrative assistant), with the net result that women earn less than their male contemporaries (Alksnis et al., 2008).

Clear signs of racial discrimination remain visible, whether in employment, housing, credit markets, or consumer pricing (Pager & Shepherd, 2008). For example, studies have found that pricing among fast-food chains varies according to the demographics of the patrons likely to frequent a given establishment. A Big Mac may cost a couple of dollars in a predominantly White neighborhood, but is likely to cost 15 cents more in neighborhoods with larger Black populations (Graddy, 1997; Moore & Diez Roux, 2006). Or consider how society conducts its "war on drugs." If you are caught in possession of cocaine in the United States, you could earn an all-expense-paid visit to the state penitentiary. But cocaine comes in different forms, and the Anti-Drug Abuse Act of 1986 specifies different mandatory minimum sentences, depending on the type of cocaine in your possession. Whereas 50 grams of crack cocaine will get you at least five years in prison, you would have to have 5 times that amount in powder form to get the same sentence (Sklansky, 1995). What does this have to do with prejudice? At the time this act was enacted, African Americans

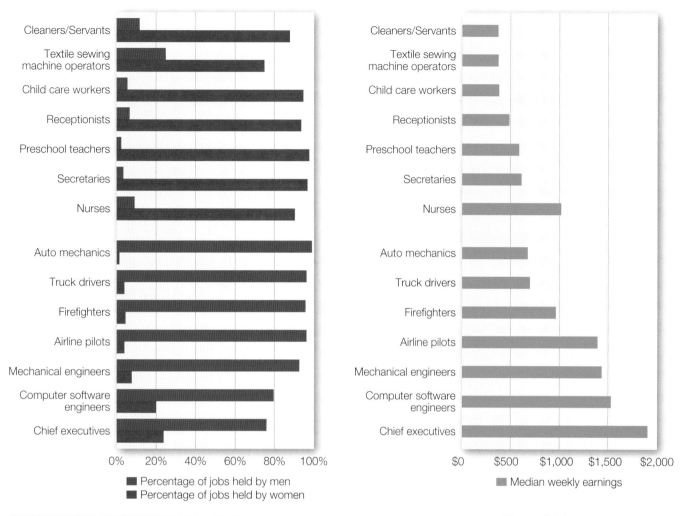

Percentage of jobs held by men
Percentage of jobs held by women

Median weekly earnings

Figure 10.4

Women Are Underrepresented in Higher-paying Jobs

Women are underrepresented in some of the highest-paid fields, which perpetuates gender inequality in overall earnings.

[Data source: U.S. Department of Labor, Bureau of Labor Statistics, 2009. Highlights of Women's Earnings in 2008. Report 1017. See http://www. bls.gov/cps/cpswom2008.pdf.]

were more likely to use crack, whereas European Americans were more likely to use powder. As a result, prison sentences for essentially the same crime were disproportionately longer for Black Americans.

Disparities that implicate prejudice run even deeper. Analyses of inmate records show that, for comparable crimes, Black males who have "Afrocentric" facial features—in other words, who are particularly likely to look like Whites' stereotypes of Blacks—receive harsher prison sentences than Black males who have less stereotypically Black facial features (Blair et al., 2004). They are also more likely to receive the death penalty for capital offenses when the victim was white (Eberhardt et al., 2006).

Despite the many encouraging declines in overt prejudice in the last few decades in the United States, these findings indicate that prejudice is still very much a problem in contemporary society. But because of progress in laws and cultural norms combating overt prejudice and discrimination, the problem has also taken on a somewhat different character. Less prevalent are the explicit signs of prejudice, such as Jim Crow laws, formerly used to mandate various forms of racial segregation, or policies that overtly prevent women from pursuing certain careers. In the contemporary world, we often see more subtle—or what are termed *modern*—forms of prejudice. Because of America's sordid history with slavery and explicit discrimination against African Americans, it is not a coincidence that the study of prejudice in the United States traditionally focused on racism in the form of prejudice against African Americans. Theories developed more recently to understand contemporary, more subtle forms of prejudice have also focused primarily on attitudes toward Blacks.

Theories of Modern Prejudice

In the early 1970s, a new understanding of prejudice emerged in social psychology. Overt demonstrations of prejudice in the United States were dissipating, yet it was clear that many people were still harboring prejudiced attitudes. Two related concepts that psychologists proposed to explain contemporary prejudice were *ambivalent racism* and *aversive racism*. Although there are some differences between these perspectives, they have much in common. Each in its own way emphasizes the need to understand how and why people might explicitly reject prejudiced attitudes but still harbor subtle biases. Let's briefly consider each of these perspectives and what they have taught us.

Ambivalent Racism

Because of changing social norms and values associated with the civil rights movement, contemporary prejudice against African Americans in the United States is often mixed with ambivalence (Katz & Hass, 1988). The term **ambivalent racism** refers to racial attitudes that are influenced by two clashing sets of values: a belief in *individualism*, that each person should be able to make it on his or her own; and a belief in *egalitarianism*, that all people should be given equal opportunities. The core idea of ambivalent racism is that many Whites simultaneously hold anti-Black and pro-Black attitudes that are linked to these contrasting values.

Consider Steve, who is White. He likes to think of himself as an accepting person and readily admits that Blacks have been disadvantaged in various ways. He supports affirmative action and votes in favor of using tax dollars for aid to the poor to help level the playing field. But while believing this, Steve also thinks that Blacks generally don't try hard enough. Social psychologists would characterize Steve as having racial ambivalence. What happens with this ambivalence?

Believing that each person should be able to make it on his or her own conflicts with trying to justify giving certain people (e.g., Blacks, women) special affirmative action opportunities. Depending on which set of values is primed, ambivalent people are likely to respond more strongly in one direction or the other. This response affirms one of the two sets of values, which at least temporarily reduces the ambivalence.

So how do you know which value people will affirm? Well, it depends on which value is currently most salient, or active (Katz & Hass, 1988). If people are thinking about values related to individualism, they tend to be more prejudiced, but if thinking about values related to egalitarianism, they tend to be less prejudiced. For example, let's take a look at **FIGURE 10.5**. When White participants were led to think about the Protestant ethic (a belief that emphasizes the individualistic value of hard work), they were more likely to report stronger anti-Black attitudes, but these individualistic thoughts did not influence their pro-Black attitudes. The pro-Black attitudes were no different from those of participants who received no priming. Thus, ambivalence remained, but the individualism prime shifted participants toward anti-Black attitudes. Conversely, when White participants were led to think about the value of humanitarianism, they were more likely to report pro-Black attitudes, but these humanitarian thoughts did not influence their anti-Black attitudes (again, as compared with the no-priming condition). Thus, again, ambivalence remained, but the humanitarian prime shifted participants toward more pro-Black attitudes.

Ambivalent racism The influence on White Americans' racial attitudes by two clashing sets of values: a belief in individualism and a belief in egalitarianism.

Figure 10.5

How Priming of Values Affects White American Attitudes Toward Black Americans

When primed to reflect on their egalitarian values, White Americans report more positive attitudes toward Blacks, but when primed with the Protestant work ethic, their attitudes become more negative.

[Data source: Katz & Hass (1988)]

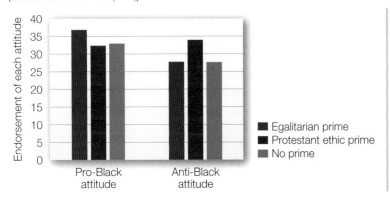

Aversive Racism

A paradox of American society—a society founded on the principles of equality and egalitarianism but built on slavery and racial injustice—is the centerpiece of another perspective on modern prejudice. Sam Gaertner and Jack Dovidio's concept of **aversive racism** (Gaertner & Dovidio, 1986) proposes that although most Whites support principles of racial equality and do not knowingly discriminate, they may at the same time possess conflicting, often nonconscious, negative feelings and beliefs about Blacks. Although they will consciously try to behave in line with their egalitarian values, in more subtle situations when decisions are complex and biases are easily rationalized, they may fall prey to the influence of prejudice, often without awareness that they are doing so.

Consider some of the earliest work on aversive racism, inspired by observations and news reports that Whites were less likely to help Black motorists in need. Gaertner and Dovidio (1977) presented White participants with what the participants thought was a situation where a Black or a White person needed help. However, the researchers varied whether a White participant thought she or he was the only person to hear the plea, or whether she or he thought others were available to help. The results of the study—shown in **FIGURE 10.6**—indicated that the White participants did not discriminate when they thought they bore sole responsibility for helping. They were equally likely to aid Black and White victims. However, if White participants thought that other people also had witnessed the emergency, they were less likely to help a Black victim than a White victim. Presumably, this occurred because, believing that others might help, they could rationalize their decision in nonracial terms (e.g., "There are plenty of people to help").

Similar results are observed in employment scenarios and college application processes. For instance, discrimination is less likely to occur when applicants have especially strong or weak records (because the applicants' records do the talking) but is more likely to occur when applicants have mixed records. That is, discrimination occurs when a gray area allows race to play a role, but it can be justified through nonracial means (Gaertner & Dovidio, 2000). For example, when a Black applicant had higher SAT scores but lower high school grades than a White applicant, high-prejudice Whites decided that high school grades were an especially important factor in college admissions decisions. But if the Black applicant had higher grades and lower SAT scores, then the high-prejudiced Whites valued those scores instead as the best indicator of future success (Hodson et al., 2002).

So prejudice is more likely to occur in situations when it can be justified by some other motive. But you might be wondering, Do all people do this? Or are particular individuals most likely to act this way? To answer this question, a number of theories about prejudice suggest that it is critical to consider not just the attitudes that people are consciously willing or able to report but also those that might reside beneath their conscious awareness. Since the 1990s, there has been an explosion of interest in this concept of *implicit prejudice*.

Implicit Prejudice

The term **implicit prejudice** refers to negative attitudes toward a group of people for which the individual has little or no conscious awareness. Some people may choose not to admit their prejudices, whereas others may not be aware of them. But as we noted in our discussion of implicit attitudes in chapter 3, measures of implicit prejudice tap into attitudes that lie beneath the surface of what people report (Nosek et al., 2011). And indeed, whereas a majority of White Americans don't report being prejudiced on explicit measures, most do show signs of having biases when their attitudes are assessed implicitly with either cognitive measures of implicit associations or physiological measures of affective responding (Dovidio et al., 2001; Cunningham et al., 2004; Hofmann et al., 2005; Mendes et al., 2002).

Aversive racism Conflicting, often nonconscious, negative feelings about African Americans that Americans may have, even though most do in fact support principles of racial equality and do not knowingly discriminate.

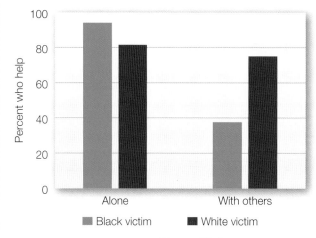

Figure 10.6

Evidence for Aversive Racism

When it was clear that they were the only ones who could help, White Americans were equally likely to help a Black or a White victim. But when they believed that others also heard the victim's cry for help, White Americans were less likely to help if the victim was Black.

[Data source: Gaertner & Dovidio (1977)]

Implicit prejudice Negative attitudes or affective reactions associated with an outgroup, for which the individual has little or no conscious awareness and which can be automatically activated in intergroup encounters.

Physiological Measures of Bias

Measures of implicit prejudice tap into people's automatic affective response to a person or a group. Some measures do this by indexing an immediate physiological reaction that people are unlikely or find difficult to control. For example, when Whites are asked to imagine working on a project with a Black or a White partner, they often report a stronger preference for working with the Black partner. But their faces tell a different story. Electrodes connected to their brows and cheeks pick up subtle movements of the facial muscles that reveal a negative attitude when they think about working with a Black partner (Vanman et al., 2004). Similarly, when Whites are actually paired up to work with a Black partner, they show a cardiovascular response that is associated with threat—their hearts pump more blood, and their veins and arteries contract (Mendes et al., 2002).

The brain also registers the threat response. The amygdala is the brain region that signals negative emotional responses, especially fear, to things in our environment. Whites who have a strong racial bias exhibit an especially pronounced amygdala response when they view pictures of Black men (Phelps et al., 2000). Interestingly, however, if given more time, this initial negative attitude tends to get downregulated by the more rational dorsolateral prefrontal cortex (Cunningham, Johnson et al., 2004; Forbes et al., 2012). This suggests that even people who acknowledge their prejudice may feel some pressure to control it. We'll discuss why and how people go about controlling their prejudiced attitudes and emotions more in our next chapter. For now, the primary point is that automatic negative bias leaks out in people's physiological responses.

Cognitive Measures of Implicit Bias

Although physiological measures provide insight into attitudes and affect, cognitive measures also tell us something about people's implicit attitudes. These measures take different forms, but they all rely on the same assumption. If you like a group, then you will quickly associate that group with good stuff. If you don't like a group, you will quickly associate that group with bad stuff. With this assumption tucked in our pocket, we can present people with members of different groups and measure how fast it takes them to identify good and bad stuff (Fazio et al., 1995; Dovidio et al., 2002).

For example, in developing one of the first studies of implicit bias, Fazio and colleagues (1995) reasoned that if Whites experience an automatic negative reaction to Blacks, then exposure to photographs of African Americans should speed up evaluations of negative words and slow down evaluations of positive words. To test this hypothesis, they presented participants with positive words (e.g., *wonderful*) and negative words (e.g., *annoying*), then asked them to indicate as fast as they could whether each was good or bad by pressing the appropriate button. Each word was immediately preceded by a brief presentation of a photograph of a Black or a White person. The results revealed substantial individual differences in White participants' automatic reactions: For many White participants, being primed with Black faces significantly sped up reactions to negative words and slowed down reactions to positive words. Other White participants did not show this pattern, and some even showed the opposite. More important, the more closely these people seemed to associate "Black" with "bad," the less friendly they were during a later 10-minute interaction with an African American experimenter.

Since the late 1990s, the most commonly used measure of implicit attitudes has been the *implicit association test*, or *IAT* (Greenwald et al., 1998), which we introduced to you in chapter 3. The basic logic of this test is that if you associate group A with "bad," then it should be pretty easy to group together instances of group A and instances of bad stuff, and relatively difficult to group together instances of group A and instances of good stuff. This basic paradigm can be used to assess implicit associations with any group you can think of, but it has most commonly been used for race, so let's take that example. You can take this and other versions of the IAT test yourself by visiting the Project Implicit web site at www.projectimplicit.com.

In the Race IAT, people are instructed to do some basic categorization tasks (**FIGURE 10.7**). The first two rounds are just practice getting used to the categories.

Hidden Prejudice: The Implicit Association Test Video on LaunchPad

For the first round, you are presented with White and Black faces one at a time, and you just need to click on one button if the face is Black and another button if the face is White. In the second round, you categorize positive ("rainbow," "present") and negative ("vomit," "cancer") words by clicking on one button if the word is positive and a different button if the word is negative. In the third round, the task becomes more complicated as you are presented with both faces and words, one at a time. Deciding as quickly as possible, you must then click one button if what you see is either a Black face or a positive word but a different button if you see either a White face or a negative word. When your cognitive network links "Black" with "bad," it's relatively hard to use the same button to categorize Black faces along with positive words without either slowing down or making lots of category errors. In contrast, if "Black" and "bad" are closely associated in your cognitive network, you should find it much easier to use the same button to indicate that you see either a Black face or negative word, the task required in a fourth round. The average difference in time it takes to make these dual category judgments (measured in milliseconds) is the measure of cognitive association.

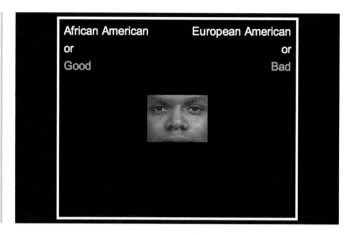

Figure 10.7

A Classic Measure of Implicit Racism

The Implicit Association Test measures the relative difficulty people can have in automatically associating Black faces with good thoughts.

[Data source: Greenwald et al. (1998)]

Research using this kind of measure has shown that most Whites and a substantial proportion of Blacks (though usually not greater than 50%) show an implicit association of "Black" with "bad." What is less clear is what this association means. Some researchers have criticized the measure for confounding the tendency to associate "Black" and "bad" with the tendency to associate "White" and "good" (Blanton & Jaccard, 2006; Blanton et al., 2006). However, other evidence suggests that IAT scores do reliably assess responses that are predictive of behavior (Greenwald et al., 2009; LeBel & Paunonen, 2011). Even if we grant that the IAT is a reliable measure, some dispute continues about what it taps into. For example, people actually show stronger racial biases when they know the measure is supposed to reveal their racial biases (Frantz et al., 2004). Anxiety about being labeled racist might actually make it more difficult for people to perform the task. In addition, some researchers have noted that an association of "Black" with "bad" could mean a variety of things, such as the acknowledgment that Blacks are mistreated and receive bad outcomes, or simply cultural stereotypes that might have little to do with one's personal attitudes (Andreychik & Gill, 2012; Olson & Fazio, 2004).

Even if we set aside the debate about the IAT in particular, a broader pattern emerges from the literature examining both implicit and explicit measures of prejudiced attitudes. Most notable, although they can be correlated, they are often quite distinct. In other words, people who have an implicit negative attitude toward a group might still explicitly report having positive feelings. But even more interesting is that people's implicit attitudes seem to predict different kinds of behavior than their explicit attitudes. Let's consider one study that has shown this most clearly.

Dovidio and colleagues (2002) had students participate in what they thought were two unrelated studies. In the first, the researchers measured implicit prejudice using a cognitive association task like the one Fazio developed in 1995. The researchers measured explicit prejudice by having White participants complete a questionnaire asking them outright how much prejudice they felt toward African Americans. After this, the participants proceeded to what they thought was an unrelated study in which they would have a brief, videotaped interaction with a Black person (actually a confederate). After the conversation, the participants were asked to judge how friendly they were toward their partners. The confederates made their own judgments of how friendly the participants seemed. Finally, the video and the audio soundtrack of the interaction were separately coded by a different group of raters whose only job was to judge how friendly the participant seemed during the interaction.

The patterns of relationships among these six variables were very telling. People's implicit "outgroup = bad" attitudes and explicit "I value being a nonprejudiced person" attitudes predicted very different things about the interaction. White students who explicitly reported being nonprejudiced were coded (only on the basis of the audio recording of what they said) as coming across in a friendly way during a discussion with a Black student, and they came away from the conversation feeling good about the interaction. But their consciously endorsed values did not predict how coders rated their nonverbal cues (on the basis of only the video without sound) or how their Black partners perceived them. Instead, Whites who had a more negative implicit association with Blacks showed more nonverbal signs of discomfort and anxiety—which was what their partners picked up on. Effects such as these pave the way for misunderstandings. Explicitly well-intentioned Whites try to say the right thing, but their body language can communicate discomfort and avoidance that turns their partners off (see also Amodio & Devine, 2006; McConnell & Liebold, 2001).

SECTION review | Is Prejudice an Ugly Thing of the Past?

Although overt discrimination is declining, modern, subtler forms of prejudice persist.

Theories of modern prejudice	Ambivalent and aversive racism	Implicit prejudice
Evidence of institutional discrimination reveals how biases can be so embedded in the structure of our society that discrimination can occur without intention.	• Ambivalent racism is the coexistence of positive and negative attitudes about Blacks resulting from clashing beliefs in individualism and egalitarianism. • Aversive racism occurs when people have nonconscious, negative feelings even when they consciously support racial equality.	• *Implicit prejudice* refers to automatically activated, negative associations with outgroups. • These associations can be revealed through physiological or cognitive measures, such as the IAT.

Stereotyping: The Cognitive Companion of Prejudice

We've explored some of the core causes of prejudice, but the social cognition perspective highlights the importance of beliefs that help promote, justify, and perpetuate prejudice. As you'll recall from chapter 3, the knowledge that we have about a given category is stored in a cognitive structure called a schema. A *stereotype* is a cognitive schema containing all knowledge about and associations with a social group (Dovidio et al., 1996; Hamilton & Sherman, 1994). For example, our stereotype of the group *librarians* may contain our beliefs about the traits shared by members of that group (librarians are smart and well read), theories about librarians' preferences and attitudes (e.g., librarians probably do not enjoy extreme sports), and examples of librarians we have known (Mr. Smith who sent me to the principal's office in ninth grade). Whether or not we care to admit it, we all probably have stereotypes about dozens of groups, including lawyers, gays, lesbians, truckers, grandmothers, goths, Russians, immigrants, and overweight individuals.

People around the globe often openly endorse certain stereotypes about various groups, but because cultures typically promote stereotypes, even people who explicitly reject the validity of stereotypic beliefs may have formed implicit associations between groups and the traits their culture attributes to those groups. At a conscious level, you might recognize that not all librarians, if any at all, fit the mold of being bookish, uptight women who wear glasses. But simply hearing the word *librarian* is still likely to bring to mind all of these associated attributes without your being aware of it.

Finally, although we commonly refer to stereotyping as having false, negative beliefs about a group or applying such beliefs to an individual, it should be clear from the librarian example that stereotypes don't have to be exclusively negative. They don't even have to be entirely false. Being well read is a pretty positive trait, and the average librarian probably has read more than your average nonlibrarian. But even if we grant this possible difference in averages of these two groups, the assertion that *all* librarians are better read than *all* nonlibrarians is certainly false. So stereotyping goes awry when we overgeneralize a belief about a group to make a blanket judgment about every member of that group.

Moreover, even though some stereotypes are positive, this doesn't mean that positive stereotyping can't have negative effects. For example, stereotypes that celebrate outgroup members' positive attributes can sometimes keep such people in a subordinate position, for example, when men celebrate women's "supportive" nature (Glick et al., 1997). Stereotypes can be benevolent on the surface but ultimately patronize the stereotyped group and allow others to justify their underprivileged status. Before we get further into the negative consequences of stereotyping, let's begin by exploring where stereotypes come from.

Where Do People's Stereotypic Beliefs Come From?

The cultural perspective provides insight into where stereotypes come from. We learn them over the course of socialization as they are transmitted by parents, friends, and the media. Even small children have been shown to grasp the prevailing stereotypes of their culture (e.g., Aboud, 1988; Williams et al., 1975). In fact, it might be best to think about stereotypes as existing within the culture as well as within individuals' minds. People who don't endorse or actively believe stereotypes about other ethnic groups can still report readily on what those cultural stereotypes are (Devine, 1989). So even if we try not to accept or endorse stereotypes ourselves, we are likely to learn cultural stereotypes through prior exposure. For example, people who watch more news programming (which tends to overreport crime by minority perpetrators) are more likely to perceive Blacks and Latinos in stereotypic ways as poor and violent (Dixon, 2008a, 2008b; Mastro, 2003). This process of social learning explains how an individual picks up stereotypes both consciously and unconsciously. But how do these beliefs come to exist in a culture in the first place?

Charles Barkley on the Media and Stereotypes Video on LaunchPad

A Kernel of Truth

Let's start with an idea Allport labeled the *kernel of truth hypothesis.* Even when stereotypes are broad overgeneralizations of what a group is like, some (but not all) stereotypes may be based on actual differences in the average traits or behaviors associated with two or more groups. This is what Allport meant by a "kernel of truth." But even though this kernel might be quite small, with much more overlap between groups than there are differences, as perceivers we tend to exaggerate any differences that might exist and apply them to all members of the group. Lee Jussim and colleagues (2009) have been particularly active in trying to distinguish stereotypes with some degree of accuracy from those with none. Stereotypes that have some accuracy tend to be those that have to do with specific facts; for example, African Americans tend to be poorer than European Americans.

But when it comes to personality traits, there is little if any support for the kernel of truth hypothesis. Consider an impressive set of studies by Robert McCrae and colleagues (Terracciano et al., 2005). They assessed the actual personalities of samples from almost 50 nations and then assessed the stereotypes about the personalities of people from those nations. There was good agreement across nations about what each nationality is like (e.g., Italians, Germans, Americans). But the researchers found no correspondence between these stereotypes and the actual personalities of the people in those nations! You might think that Germans are more conscientious than Italians, but there's no evidence from the personality data that this is actually the case.

A complicating factor with the kernel of truth hypothesis is that even when facts seem to support a stereotype about a group, those facts don't necessarily imply trait differences. For example, it may be true that a disproportionate percentage of African American males are convicted of crimes. However, this does not mean

Gender Stereotypes in Animated Films, Then and Now

What are the most memorable movies from your childhood? Have you ever stopped to think about how those stories might have laid a foundation for the gender stereotypes you hold today? Children become aware of their own gender and begin showing a preference for gender-stereotypical toys and activities between two and three years of age (Encyclopedia of Children's Health, 2013). Some of these beliefs and preferences are modeled from their parents, peers, and siblings (e.g., Tenenbaum & Leaper, 2002), but children's books, movies, and other media play a role in reinforcing cultural messages about gender.

Consider some popular children's movies. Especially for little girls, movies about princesses capture the imagination, but many parents, educators, and cultural critics have questioned the messages these movies convey about women (e.g., Shreve, 1997). In the classic 1959 film *Sleeping Beauty*, the protagonist, Aurora, pretty and kind, cannot even regain consciousness without the love and assistance of her prince (Disney & Geronimi, 1959). Snow White cheerily keeps house and cleans up after the seven dwarfs in the 1937 animated film (Disney & Hand, 1937) before her status is elevated through marriage to a prince. *Cinderella*, released in 1950, feels more obviously oppressed by the forced domestic labor and humiliation by her stepmother and stepsisters, but again she can only escape her fate through the love of a wealthy prince (Disney et al., 1950).

The common theme in these pre–women's movement films is that beauty and innocence are the qualities that a young woman should possess to achieve her Happily Ever After, which can happen only through marriage to a handsome and well-heeled man. And older, unmarried, or widowed women are cast as the villains in these stories, spurred to evil acts by jealousy of their younger rivals.

There have been some more positive trends in the princess films that have been released more recently. Reflecting cultural shifts that encourage greater agency in women, princess characters have become noticeably more assertive. Ariel, from *The Little Mermaid* (Ashman et al.,1989), is willful and adventurous, eager to explore the world beyond her ocean home. But even so, she needs the permission of her authoritative father and the love of a man to realize her dreams. Along the way, she even trades her talent (her voice)

[Elisabeth Lhomelet/Photographer's Choice/Getty Images]

it is accurate to conclude that African Americans are more violent or immoral by nature. In most cultures, minority groups that are economically disadvantaged and the targets of discrimination are more likely to get in trouble with the law. Minority-group members who are low in socioeconomic status also tend to do less well in school, but again, an attribution of intellectual inferiority is an unwarranted leap. So even in cases in which there is a kernel of truth, the stereotype leads to an unjustified jump beyond descriptive differences to assumptions about essential differences in traits and abilities.

Social Role Theory

If stereotypes don't arise from real differences in the underlying traits of different groups, where do they come from? One possibility is that they come from the roles and behaviors that societal pressures may impose on a particular group. You have read enough of this textbook so far to realize that cultural and social influences on

---

to undergo severe changes to her body (legs instead of a tail) for the opportunity to woo her love interest.

In other modern animated films, the portrayals of princesses have become more complex and counterstereotypic. First, there has been an effort to present characters from different cultures, with protagonists who are Middle Eastern (Jasmine in *Aladdin*, 1992), Native American (*Pocahontas*, 1995), Chinese (*Mulan*, 1998), African American (Tiana, *The Princess and the Frog*, 2009), and Scottish (Merida, *Brave*, 2012). Although these films provide children a broader view of human diversity, they have also been criticized for their sometimes stereotypic portrayals of people from other cultures. For example, a line in the opening song to Aladdin originally described the Middle East as a place "where they cut off your ear if they don't like your face."

Second, the modern princesses in animated films are more often cast as heroic. In *Mulan*, the protagonist disguises herself as male so that she can use her fighting skills to save and rescue the male characters in the movie. In *Tangled*, the resourceful protagonist openly mocks the outdated notion that she needs a prince to save her. Through her own wits and resources, Tiana manages to fulfill her dream of being a business owner. And most recently, *Frozen* tells the story of two strong and determined sisters. Elsa, the older sister, embraces her power to control ice even while fearing that her strength separates her from others, whereas her little sister Anna bravely risks her own life to find and save Elsa. These newer princess stories highlight autonomy, strength, and independence for young women.

Of course, before we get too encouraged by these messages of equality, we might ponder whether these modern fairy tales reflect lower levels of hostile sexism toward women (gone are the evil witches and stepmothers in these more contemporary films) but still reinforce benevolent sexist

beliefs about women. The female characters are still young, beautiful, and good, and their Happily Ever After still often involves getting the guy.

In fact, these benevolent views of women are manifested in children's movies more generally—that is, if girls and women are portrayed at all. Studies of G-rated family films have found that only about 30% of the speaking characters are female (Smith et al., 2010; Smith & Choueiti, n.d.). Female characters are more likely to wear sexy or revealing clothing than their male counterparts (Smith & Choueiti, n.d.). Although male characters are more often portrayed as having power and/or being funny, female characters are more commonly portrayed as having good motives and being attractive, although in an encouraging trend, they are also portrayed as more intelligent (Smith et al., 2010).

It's likely that these stereotypic portrayals shape our gender schemas. A meta-analysis of over 30 studies suggests that children and adults who watch more television also have more traditional views about gender (Herrett-Skjellum & Allen, 1996). Longitudinal studies suggest that the causal arrow goes from exposure to television to gender stereotypes, because the more television children watch, the more they accept gender stereotypes when they are much older (e.g., Kimball, 1986). Increasing scrutiny of these subtle ways that stereotypes are perpetuated raises questions for policy makers. Should films, television shows, and other media be rated on the basis of their stereotypic messages? The Swedish Film Institute thinks so. In 2013, Swedish theaters began employing a feminist rating system known as the Bechdel test (Rising, 2013), which awards an A rating to films that portray two female characters talking to each other about something other than a man. It's not a perfect system, but it's a start in calling needed attention to gender bias at the movies.

the big, broad stage of the world often give us a script to read from and a character to play. Given what you know about the fundamental attribution error, you should not be surprised that when people see us in a role, they jump to the conclusion that we have the traits implied by the behaviors we enact in that role. This is the basic assumption of Alice Eagly's social role theory (Eagly, 1987): We infer stereotypes that describe who people are from the roles that we see people play.

A personal anecdote illustrates this problem. Recently, your current author was driving with a friend past a construction site, and we noticed that most of the workers were Hispanic. My friend said, "Hispanic people are very hard-working people." Although there may be a kernel of truth in this assessment, social role theory suggests that the logic might be backward. Although my friend inferred that these men chose construction because of their hard-working character, in reality the large number of Hispanic men on the construction site might have little to do with their personal traits or preferences. Rather, certain aspects of society might restrict ethnic minorities from opportunities for higher education and employment into white collar positions, leading to a greater proportion of minorities in occupations involving manual and unskilled labor. Therefore, an assumption that they occupy that role because of the "way they are" is likely to be false.

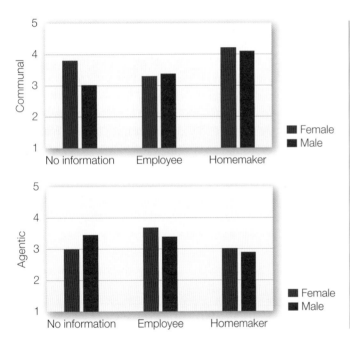

Figure 10.8

How Social Roles Can Determine Stereotypes

(a) With no other information, people assume that women are more communal than men and that (b) men are more agentic than women. But social roles might explain these stereotypes: Homemakers (either male or female) are assumed to be more communal than employees, and employees (either male or female) are assumed to be more agentic.

[Data source: Data from Eagly & Steffen (1984)]

Social role theory primarily has been used to explain the existence of strong and persistent stereotypes about men and women. Men are stereotyped to be *agentic*—assertive, aggressive, and achievement oriented. Women are stereotyped to be *communal*—warm, empathic, and emotional. Are these stereotypes supported by gender differences in behavior? Yes. Men are more likely to be the CEOs of Fortune 500 companies. Women are more likely to be the primary caregivers of children. If we look only at these statistics, we will find more than a kernel of truth to the stereotype. But does this gender segregation in the boardroom and at the playground really imply sex differences in traits? Not so fast. **FIGURE 10.8** shows what happened when people were asked to rate the traits listed in a brief description of an average man or an average woman, with either no information about the person's occupation, information that he or she was a full-time employee, or information that he or she was full-time homemaker (Eagly & Steffen, 1984). With no information, people readily applied their stereotypes, assuming that a woman is more communal than a man and that a man is more agentic than a woman. But when we size people up, occupation completely trumps anatomy. A homemaker is judged to be more communal and less agentic than an employee, regardless of that person's sex.

The moral here is that social roles play a large part in shaping our stereotypes. But because social pressures can shape the roles in which various groups find themselves, differences in stereotypes follow suit. The traditional stereotype of African Americans as lazy and ignorant was developed when the vast majority of them were slaves. At that time in the South, it was actually illegal to educate African Americans, and so it was hardly a matter of the slaves' personal preference that they would be relatively ignorant. Nor would it be surprising that they were not particularly enthused to do work that was forced on them. Similarly, Jews have been stereotyped as money hungry or cheap, a stereotype that developed in Europe at a time when Jews were not allowed to own land. As a consequence, Jews needed to become involved in trade and commerce in order to survive economically. The particular stereotypes attached to groups are often a function of these historical and culturally embedded social constraints.

The Stereotype Content Model

The stereotype content model extends the basic logic of social role theory by positing that stereotypes develop on the basis of how groups relate to one another along two dimensions (Fiske et al., 2002). The first is status: Is the group perceived as having relatively low or high status in society, relative to other groups? The second is cooperation in a very broad sense that seems to encompass likeability: In a sense, is the group perceived to have a cooperative/helpful or a competitive/harmful relationship with other groups in that society?

The answers to these questions lead to predictions about the traits that are likely to be ascribed to the group. With higher status come assumptions about competence, prestige, and power, whereas lower status leads to stereotypes of incompetence and laziness. Groups that are seen as cooperative/helpful within the society are seen as warm and trustworthy, whereas groups that are competitive/harmful within the larger society are seen as cold and conniving. These two dimensions of evaluation, *warmth* and *competence*, have long been acknowledged to be fundamental to how we view others. Within this theory, we can see how they translate into distinct stereotypes: Status determines perceived competence, whereas cooperativeness/helpfulness determines perceived warmth. Consider that these dimensions are largely independent, and we see that stereotypes can cluster together in one of four quadrants in a warmth-by-competence space (see **FIGURE 10.9**). Across cultures, higher-status groups are generally stereotyped as more competent, and cooperative groups are generally seen to be warmer (Cuddy et al., 2008).

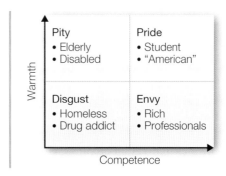

Figure 10.9

The Stereotype Content Model

According to the stereotype content model, the stereotypes we have of different groups can range along two dimensions of competence and warmth. As a result, we have different emotional reactions to different types of groups.

[Data source: Fiske et al. (2002)]

In an interesting finding, groups whose stereotypes fit into one of these quadrants tend to elicit different types of emotional responses (Cuddy, Fiske et al., 2007). Groups that are stereotyped as personally warm but incompetent (e.g., the elderly and physically disabled) elicit pity and sympathy. Groups perceived as low in warmth but high in competence (e.g., rich people, Asians, Jews, minority professionals) elicit envy and jealousy. Groups stereotyped in purely positive terms as both warm and competent tend to be ingroups or groups that are seen as the cultural norm in a society. To the degree that these groups are valued, they generally elicit pride and admiration. Finally, groups stereotyped in purely negative terms as both cold and incompetent (e.g., homeless people, drug addicts, welfare recipients) elicit disgust and scorn.

Illusory Correlations

Social role theory and the stereotype content model both assume that structural factors put groups in different roles that encourage role-consistent trait stereotypes. But in some instances, stereotypes develop from nothing more than a perceptual bias known as an **illusory correlation**. This is a faulty perception whereby people think that two things are related when in reality they are not. More specifically, an illusory correlation occurs when a person perceives that membership in a certain social group correlates—or goes hand in hand with—a certain type of behavior (Hamilton & Sherman, 1989).

These kinds of illusory correlations occur under very specific circumstances—when two things that are generally rare or distinctive co-occur in close proximity to one another. Illusory correlations are the result of the mind's seeking out relationships. When strange or unusual things happen, our attention is drawn to them because they stand out from what is familiar. And when two unusual things co-occur,

Illusory correlation A tendency to assume an association between two rare occurrences, such as being in a minority group and performing negative actions.

our mind automatically assumes a connection. For most majority-group members, minority-group members are distinctive. Also, most people, regardless of their group membership, tend to find socially undesirable behaviors distinctive. (Fortunately, most of the time, people do good things rather than bad things!) So when ingroup members see outgroup members acting negatively—for example, in news reports about Black men accused of violent crimes—two distinctive features of the situation, a minority individual and an undesirable behavior, grab their attention. This doubly distinctive perception results in an exaggerated perception of a correlation, even when the minority group is no more likely than the majority group to engage in bad behavior (Hamilton et al., 1985).

Why Do We Apply Stereotypes?

Now that we understand a little more about where stereotypes come from, we turn to the question of why we apply and maintain them. The fact that stereotypes exist and persist, even when facts seem to disconfirm them, suggests that they must serve some kind of psychological function. Indeed, research reveals that stereotypes have five primary psychological functions. Let's consider each of them.

1. Stereotypes Are Cognitive Tools for Simplifying Everyday Life

In his dialogue *Phaedrus*, Plato depicts Socrates' famous description of the human need to "carve nature at its joints." What Plato (and by extension, Socrates) meant was that simply perceiving the many varieties of things in the world is a challenge. Concepts and theories help us sort through this variety and categorize things into meaningful, if not natural, kinds. Even if we restrict our view to the social world, can we truly perceive every person we see, encounter, or interact with solely on the basis of their individual qualities, characteristics, and behaviors?

People rely on stereotypes every day because they simplify this process of social perception. Stereotypes allow people to draw on their beliefs about the traits that characterize typical group members to make inferences about what a given group member is like or how he or she is likely to act. Imagine you have two neighbors, one a librarian and the other a veterinarian. If you had a book title on the tip of your tongue, you would more likely consult the librarian than the vet—unless it was a book about animals! In other words, stereotyping is a cognitive shortcut that allows people to draw social inferences quickly and conserve scarce cognitive resources while navigating a pretty complex social environment (Taylor, 1981). If people didn't categorize others and think about them using stereotypes, they would have to spend a lot more mental energy thinking about each person as an individual. If stereotyping does in fact conserve mental resources, then people should be more likely to fall back on their stereotypes when they are stressed, tired, under time pressure, or otherwise cognitively overloaded. Many lines of research have shown that this indeed is the case (e.g., Kruglanski & Freund, 1983; Macrae et al., 1993).

And if stereotypes simplify impression formation, using them should leave people with more cognitive resources left over to apply to other tasks. To test this, researchers (Macrae et al., 1994) showed participants a list of traits and asked them to form an impression of the person being described. In forming these impressions, people were quicker and more accurate if they were also given each person's occupation. It's easier to remember that Julian is creative and emotional if you also know he is an artist, because artists are stereotyped as possessing those characteristics. But having these labels to hang your impression on also frees up your mind to focus on other tasks. In the study, this other task was an audio travelogue about Indonesia that participants were later tested on. Those who knew the occupations of the people they learned about while they were also listening to the audio travelogue not only remembered more about the people but also remembered more about Indonesia. The researchers concluded that stereotypes are "energy-saving devices" (Macrae et al., 1994, p. 37)—an empirically validated finding that has now been turned into a tongue-in-cheek slogan.

The idea that stereotypes are mental heuristics that we fall back on to save time in social perception has been turned into a tongue-in-cheek t-shirt message.

2. Stereotypes Justify Prejudices

Stereotypes aren't mere by-products of our limited cognitive capacities. People also are sometimes motivated to hang on to these beliefs to help justify their prejudices. In an extreme example, once a country has declared war on another nation, stereotypes of that nation become more negative. But in an even more general sense, encountering members of outgroups sometimes automatically elicits potent negative feelings, such as fear and disgust (e.g., Esses et al., 1993). People may have difficulty understanding why they are experiencing those negative feelings; generating a negative stereotype of the group provides a simple explanation.

According to the justification suppression model of prejudice expression (Crandall & Eshleman, 2003), people endorse and feel free to express stereotypes in part to justify their own negative affective reactions to outgroup members. In other words, stereotypes can provide people with supposedly acceptable explanations for having negative feelings about a group. If, for example, a person stereotypes all Hispanics as aggressive, then she can justify why she feels frightened around Hispanics. From this perspective, the negative feelings sometimes come first, and the stereotypes make those feelings seem acceptable, even rational.

To test this idea, Chris Crandall and colleagues (2011) set up a situation in which they induced people to have a negative feeling toward a group *prior* to forming a stereotype about that group. They did this through an affective conditioning method, which essentially involves repeatedly pairing a novel stimulus with negative words or images (e.g., sad faces) that didn't imply any specific traits associated with the group. In this way, some participants were led to have a negative affective association toward a group that they had never heard of—people from the country Eritrea. Afterward, participants were given a list of traits, such as *dangerous*, *violent*, and *unfriendly*, and asked to indicate whether those traits were descriptive of people from Eritrea. Participants who had been conditioned to have a negative affective reaction toward Eritreans were more likely than those who had not been to stereotype Eritreans as cold and threatening. After all, if the people of Eritrea are perceived as cold and threatening, then one's negative feelings suddenly seem to make sense and are justified.

3. Stereotypes Help Justify Violence and Discrimination Against Outgroups

Dehumanization

Dehumanization is the tendency to view outgroup members stereotypically as somehow less than fully human. The most extreme form of dehumanization is to compare outgroup members directly with nonhuman animals. Blatant examples of this can be seen in the way that nations portray groups they intend to kill. During World War II, Nazi propaganda portrayed European Jews as disease-carrying rats, Americans portrayed the Japanese as vermin (**FIGURE 10.10a**), and the Japanese portrayed Americans as bloodthirsty eagles mauling innocent Japanese civilians. One of our students who had served in the American military during the 1991 Persian Gulf war showed us a flyer dehumanizing Iraqi people (**FIGURE 10.10b**) that was circulated among the soldiers.

Justification suppression model The idea that people endorse and freely express stereotypes in part to justify their own negative affective reactions to outgroup members.

Dehumanization The tendency to hold stereotypic views of outgroup members as animals rather than humans.

Figure 10.10a

Dehumanizing the Outgroup

This World War II–era "Jap Trap" poster tried to garner support for the war by dehumanizing Japanese people.

[Office for Emergency Management. Office of War Information. Domestic Operations Branch. Bureau of Special Services. (03/09/1943–09/15/1945)]

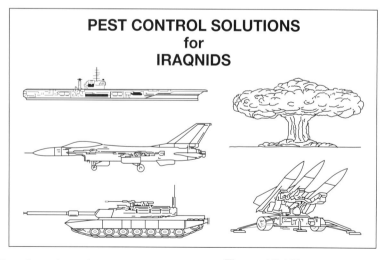

Figure 10.10b

Dehumanizing the Outgroup

This flyer, circulated among American troops during the first Persian Gulf war, dehumanized people from Iraq.

Figure 10.11

This magazine cover created controversy because of perceived similarity to this World War I poster.

[Left: De Agostini Picture Library/ Getty Images]

War enemies and prospects for genocide are not the only outgroups compared with animals. According to Goff and colleagues (2008), White Americans have for many years equated Black Americans to monkeys and apes. In **FIGURE 10.11**, the image to the left is a propaganda poster used to recruit American soldiers during World War I by portraying Germans as savage apes ruled by animal instincts for sex and aggression. The image on the right is of LeBron James, the first African American male to grace the cover of *Vogue* magazine. Notice any similarities?

Goff and colleagues proposed that, even if White Americans are not consciously aware that they associate African Americans with aggressive apes, they have learned this stereotype from their surrounding culture. In one study supporting this claim, White Americans were more likely to hold the opinion that violence against a Black crime suspect was justified if they had been primed with ape-related words beneath their conscious awareness.

The tendency to think about outgroups as nonhuman animals has likely played a role in fueling and justifying intergroup conflict across cultures and historical epochs. This is because it creates a vicious cycle of prejudice and violence against outgroup members. As we discussed in our coverage of cognitive dissonance (chapter 6), when people act in ways that fall short of their moral standards, they often attempt to seek justification for their actions. In times of extreme intergroup conflict, when innocent people are being killed, it seems reasonable to expect that the perpetrators of that violence, and even those standing by, feel that they are acting in immoral ways. One strategy to reduce or even prevent the distress and anxiety associated with a wrongful act is to regard the victims as subhuman and therefore less deserving of moral consideration. Indeed, Castano and Giner-Sorolla (2006) found that when people were made to feel a sense of collective responsibility for their ingroup's mass killing of an outgroup, they viewed members of that outgroup as less human.

Once the outgroup has been reduced to animals who do not deserve moral consideration, the perpetrators feel less inhibited about committing further violence (Kelman, 1976; Opotow, 1990; Staub, 1989). After all, it is easier to hurt or kill rats, bugs, and monkeys than to hurt and kill fellow human beings. Indeed, in one study, people were more likely to administer a higher intensity of shock to punish people described in dehumanizing (i.e., animalistic) terms than people described in distinctively human terms (Bandura et al., 1975). This perpetuates the cycle, leading ingroup members to dehumanize the victims further in order to justify their violence, thus further escalating conflict.

Infrahumanization

Infrahumanization The perception that outgroup members lack qualities viewed as unique to human beings, such as language, rational intelligence, and complex social emotions.

A more subtle form of dehumanization is **infrahumanization** (Leyens et al., 2000). When people infrahumanize outgroup members, they do not compare them directly with nonhuman animals. Rather, they perceive those outgroup members as lacking qualities viewed as unique to human beings. These qualities include language and rational intelligence, as well as complex human emotions such as hope, humiliation, nostalgia, and sympathy. People attribute these uniquely human emotions to members of their ingroup, but they are reluctant to believe that outgroup members also experience those sophisticated emotions, again because they see the outgroup as less human than their own ingroup. By contrast, people tend to attribute similar levels of the more basic emotions such as happiness, anger, and disgust to both the ingroup and the outgroup (Gaunt et al., 2002; Leyens et al., 2001).

Infrahumanization has important repercussions for people's treatment of outgroup members. Cuddy and colleagues (2007) looked at people's desire to help with relief efforts in the aftermath of Hurricane Katrina, which caused massive destruction to parts of the southeastern United States in 2005. Participants in their study were less likely to infer that racial outgroup members who suffered from the hurricane were experiencing uniquely human emotions, such as remorse and mourning, than were racial ingroup members. The more participants infrahumanized the hurricane victims in this way, the less likely they were to report that they intended to take actions to help those individuals recover from the devastation.

Sexual Objectification

Women as a group are subject to a specific form of dehumanization known as **sexual objectification**, which consists of thinking about women in a narrow way, as if their physical appearance is all that matters. Based on the work of early theorists such as the psychoanalyst Karen Horney and the philosopher Simone de Beauvoir, Barbara Fredrickson and Tomi-Ann Roberts's (1997) **objectification theory** notes that in most if not all societies women are objectified by being judged primarily on the basis of their physical appearance. Although objectification does not involve equating women with animals, it is a way of denying that women possess the psychological characteristics that make them fully human, such as a unique point of view, a complex mental life, and the capacity to make decisions.

In assessing this idea, researchers found that well-known women, but not men, were perceived more like objects—cold, incompetent, and without morality—when participants were asked to focus on the women's appearance than when they were asked to focus on the women as people (Heflick & Goldenberg, 2009; Heflick et al., 2011). For example, in studies carried out during Barack Obama's first term as president, they found that the first lady, Michelle Obama, was perceived as lower in warmth, competence, and morality when participants focused on her appearance. In contrast, focusing on President Obama's appearance did not have a similar effect on ratings of him. In addition, when the researchers examined perceptions of the Republican vice-presidential candidate, Sarah Palin, six weeks prior to the 2008 election, participants not only perceived her as less competent if they were led to focus on her appearance but also reported being less likely to vote for the Republican ticket in the upcoming presidential election.

Utilizing the neuroscience perspective, Mina Cikara and colleagues (Cikara et al., 2011) found that men who were higher in hostile sexism (expressed as a negative attitude toward women's efforts to achieve gender equality) showed decreased activation in the medial prefrontal cortex (MPFC) when viewing scantily clad and provocatively posed (and thus sexualized) female targets, but not fully clothed (nonsexualized) female targets. Because the MPFC is strongly associated with the capacity to see other people as active agents in the world with their own point of view, this study shows us how sexist men are less likely to recognize sexualized females as people with their own agency and subjectivity.

Objectification of women can help justify exploitation and poor treatment of them. Integrating objectification theory and terror management theory, Jamie Goldenberg and colleagues proposed that objectification also may help people avoid acknowledging the fact that we humans are animals and therefore mortal (e.g., Goldenberg et al., 2009). Portraying women in an idealized (often airbrushed) way and only as objects of beauty or sexual appeal reduces their connection to animalistic physicality. (After all, not too many other mammals wear makeup, use perfume, and get breast implants!) Supporting this view, Goldenberg and colleagues have shown that reminding both men and women of their mortality, or of the similarities between humans and other animals, increases negative reactions to women who exemplify the creaturely nature of the body: women who are menstruating, pregnant, or breast-feeding.

Sexual objectification The tendency to think about women in a narrow way as objects rather than full humans, as if their physical appearance is all that matters.

Objectification theory Theory proposing that the cultural value placed on women's appearance leads people to view women more as objects and less as full human beings.

In one such study, male and female participants reminded of their mortality or primed with a control topic were told to set up some chairs for an interaction task with another partner who was currently in an adjacent room either breast-feeding or bottle-feeding her baby (Cox et al., 2007). Those participants reminded of mortality and expecting to talk with the currently breast-feeding female anticipated liking her less and arranged to sit especially far from her. A similar effect was not observed when the participant was told the person was bottle-feeding her baby, suggesting something especially disturbing about the physicality of breast-feeding. In addition, men reminded of their mortality are particularly negative toward women who seem overtly sexual as opposed to wholesomely attractive (Landau et al., 2006). And when men were reminded both of their mortality and their capacity to be sexually aroused by women, they became more tolerant of a man accused of physically abusing his girlfriend. This line of research suggests that objectifying women as idealized symbols of beauty and femininity and rejecting women who seem to fall short of those ideals helps both men and women deny their own animal nature.

4. Stereotypes Justify the Status Quo

Stereotypes don't justify only our emotions and behavior, they also justify the status quo. Earlier, we talked about the stereotype content model and the finding that across cultures, the status position of a group seems to determine stereotypes about competence, whereas the cooperativeness of a group seems to determine stereotypes about warmth (Cuddy et al., 2008). Another finding from this cross-cultural comparison of stereotypes is that stereotypes about particular groups tend to be *ambivalent*—that is, to include positive traits alongside negative traits. High-status groups that are assumed to be competent are also more likely to be stereotyped as cold or immoral. Lower-status groups might be stereotyped as being less intelligent or successful but are also often seen as warm and friendly.

According to *system justification theory*, these complementary or ambivalent stereotypes help maintain the status quo (Jost & Banaji, 1994). We discussed this a bit back in chapter 9, but let's expand on it here. System justification theory proposes that people largely prefer to keep things the way they are. So from this perspective, stereotypes justify the way things are. In some ways this is the flip side of social role theory: We not only assume the traits people have by the roles they enact, but we also assert that they *should* be in those roles because they have the traits that are needed for those roles.

System justification theory suggests that those who have status and power in a society will often come to view those without power and status as being less intelligent and industrious than their own group, as a way to justify their own superior economic and political position. If advantaged members of a society didn't generate these justifications, then they would have to admit that deep injustices exist that they should all be working to rectify. Yes, disadvantaged groups would benefit from these efforts—but advantaged groups might also lose their advantages. And for everyone, the results would be massive upheaval, uncertainty, and anxiety.

This motivation to justify the system can sometimes trump people's motivations to have the best outcomes for themselves and their ingroup. Although those in higher-status positions show a stronger tendency to justify the status quo, those who are disadvantaged sometimes buy into these beliefs as well. Even if a system predictably provides you with meager outcomes, you still can prefer it to a system that is completely unpredictable. For example, when people are made to feel that the security and stability of their nation is in question, members of both lower- and higher-status ethnic groups more strongly endorse the belief that the higher-status group is relatively more competent and that the lower-status group is relatively warmer (Jost et al., 2005).

How do these complementary stereotypes play into the motivation to justify existing status differences among groups? By favoring complementary or ambivalent stereotypes, groups that are disadvantaged in terms of their status in society can still pride themselves on their warmth or morality. With that positive stereotype in your back pocket, the negative stereotypes don't seem so bad. Similarly, groups with power and status can assuage any guilt they might feel about their advantages in life by pointing to the warmth and purity of those without status. We see this most strikingly with gender. Modern theories of gender bias point to **ambivalent sexism** (Glick & Fiske, 1996). This pairs *hostile* beliefs about women (that women are incompetent or push too hard for gender equality) with *benevolent* beliefs (that women are pure and more compassionate than men). What effect do these messages have? When women are primed to think about hostile sexism, they are more motivated to engage in collective action to change gender inequality. But when they are primed with benevolent sexism, they are not (Becker & Wright, 2011).

Research also suggests that we prefer outgroup members to conform to the prevailing stereotypes. Women who are assertive and direct are often judged negatively, whereas the same actions by men lead to admiration (Rudman, 1998). In similar findings, terror management researchers (Schimel et al., 1999) have shown that reminding people of their mortality, which motivates people to want their worldviews upheld, leads white heterosexual Americans to prefer Germans, African Americans, and gay men who conform to prevailing American stereotypes of these groups over those who behave counterstereotypically.

5. Stereotypes Are Self-esteem Boosters

As described previously, self-esteem threats not only increase negative feelings about outgroup members but also lead to negative beliefs about them and make negative stereotypes of such groups more accessible to consciousness (Fein & Spencer, 1997; Spencer et al., 1998). Viewing members of outgroups as stupid, lazy, cowardly, or immoral can help people feel better about themselves. Other evidence also supports the role of stereotyping in boosting the perceiver's self-esteem. For example, if a member of a disliked outgroup praises us, we shouldn't be too motivated to apply a negative stereotype. But what happens when that person gives us negative feedback?

Research by Lisa Sinclair and Ziva Kunda (1999) shows that we selectively focus on different ways of categorizing people, depending on these self-serving motivations. In their study, White Canadian participants imagined receiving either praise or criticism from a Black or a White doctor. The researchers measured whether stereotypic knowledge was automatically brought to mind. Participants who were praised by the Black doctor activated positive stereotypes of doctors but not negative stereotypes about Blacks. However, participants who were criticized by the Black doctor activated the negative stereotype of Blacks and not the positive stereotype of doctors.

Further research suggests that once activated, these stereotypes likely bias people's judgments. For example, female and male faculty members receive similar course evaluations from students who do well in their courses, but students who receive lower grades evaluate female instructors as less competent than their male peers (**FIGURE 10.12**) (Sinclair & Kunda, 2000).

How Do Stereotypes Come Into Play?

So far, we have covered where stereotypes come from and why we tend to rely on them. But how do they actually work? Take a look at the guy in the photo. What's your impression of him? How did you form that impression? You might see the jacket, collared shirt, and neatly trimmed hair

Ambivalent sexism The pairing of *hostile* beliefs about women with *benevolent* but patronizing beliefs about them.

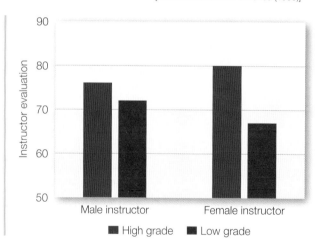

Figure 10.12

Self-esteem Threat and Gender Bias

Although student evaluations of male and female instructors are equivalent among students who perform well, students who receive a lower grade rate female instructors as less competent than male instructors.

[Data source: Sinclair & Kunda (1999)]

Think
ABOUT

[© Bettman/Corbis]

and think he's a young, attractive, professional man. You've just categorized him on the basis of age, appearance, educational level, and gender. He looks to be White, so we can throw a racial categorization in as well. From this, you are likely to activate some relevant stereotypes—intelligent, competent, well liked. Because you have no reason not to, you will probably be happy to apply these judgments to him. In general, we love sizing people up, and this guy seems approachable. If he asked you to help him load a dresser into his van, you would, right?

Unfortunately, many young women did just that. They categorized him just as you probably did. They had no way of knowing one additional group he belonged to—serial killers. The man in the photo is Ted Bundy, who brutally raped and murdered over 30 women, mostly college students, during the 1970s. It is likely that the categorizations activated by his appearance helped him carry out his heinous crimes.

Research has delved into the process by which we initially *categorize* a person as belonging to a group, *activate* stereotypes associated with that group, and then *apply* those stereotypes in forming judgments of that person. Let's learn more about how this process works.

Categorization

In the process of "carving nature at its joints," we categorize everything—*furniture, cats, cars,* and yes, *people.* The categories we attend to most readily for people are gender, age, and other cues that might signal how we should treat another (Fiske & Taylor, 1984; Kurzban et al., 2001). Kurzban and colleagues suggest that because telling friend from foe often would have meant life or death for our evolutionary ancestors, our brains might have adapted to form these categorizations on the basis of whatever cue does the job the most quickly and effortlessly. We may be particularly likely to categorize an individual as ingrouper or outgrouper by relying on cues such as accent, mode of dress, and adornment, along with other physical features such as skin tone, body shape, and hair color. But our social categories are flexible enough to be cued by a host of things, depending on what's situationally relevant. Team sports rely on the use of different-colored uniforms so that we can differentiate one team from another easily. Often we can guess someone's gender and sexual orientation merely by how they walk (Johnson & Tassinary, 2005; Johnson et al., 2007). We also can judge age, ethnicity, and gender readily from the sound of someone's voice.

But the categorization process isn't entirely objective. It's also influenced by our stereotypes and prejudices (Freeman & Ambady, 2011). For example, to the degree that people tend to stereotypically associate young Black men with anger, they are quicker to categorize an angry face as being Black if the person's race is rather ambiguous. Similarly, mixed-race individuals are more often categorized as being members of a minority and people with stronger racial prejudices are especially cautious when making these categorizations (Blascovich et al., 1997; Halberstadt et al., 2011; Ho et al., 2011).

Regardless of how we come to categorize a person as a member of an outgroup, once we do, we tend to view that person in stereotypic ways. One reason this happens is that the very act of categorizing makes us more likely to assume that all members of the outgroup category are alike. Merely by categorizing people into outgroups, we tend to view those individuals as more similar to each other—that is, more homogeneous—than they really are, and as more similar to each other than ingroup members are to each other (Linville et al., 1989; Park & Rothbart, 1982; Quattrone, 1986). This tendency is called the **outgroup homogeneity effect.** If you've ever said, or heard someone say, "Those people are all alike" or "If you've seen one, you've seen them all," you have probably witnessed this effect.

The primary explanation for the outgroup homogeneity effect is that we are very familiar with members of our own group and therefore tend to see them as

Outgroup homogeneity effect The tendency to view individuals in outgroups as more similar to each other than they really are.

unique individuals. We have less detailed knowledge about members of outgroups, so it's easier simply to assume they are all alike. In addition, we often know outgroup members only in a particular context or role. For example, a suburban White American might know African Americans mainly as sports figures, hip-hop artists, and criminals on TV. This role-restricted knowledge also encourages viewing outgroup members as less diverse than they actually are.

Let's see how this has been demonstrated in a couple of classic studies. In one demonstration, psychologists (Quattrone & Jones, 1980) asked university students to watch a video of a student from the participant's own university or from a different university make a decision (e.g., between listening to rock or classical music). The participants were then asked to estimate what percentage of people from that person's university would make the same decision. They estimated that a higher percentage of the person's fellow students would have the same musical preference when he was from a different university rather than the participants' own. So when you assume that "they are all alike," you can infer that what one likes, they all like, but you probably also like to believe that "we" are a diverse assortment of unique individuals.

I don't know officer: They all look alike to me...

[Hagen/Cartoonstock]

The outgroup homogeneity effect not only extends to the inferences we make about a person's attitudes but also leads to very real perceptual confusions. We actually do *see* outgroup members as looking more similar to each other, a phenomenon that can have very profound consequences for the accuracy of eyewitness accounts (Wells et al., 2006). This type of perceptual bias was first illustrated in a series of studies in which participant ingroup and outgroup members interacted in a group discussion (Taylor et al., 1978). When later asked to remember who said what—that is, to match a comment with a person—the participants made an interesting pattern of errors. They were more accurate at remembering ingroup statements than outgroup statements. But more telling, they were likelier to mistake one outgroup member for another. It was as if the participants thought to themselves, "I know that one of these people said that, but they are all alike, so I cannot recall which one." These confusions happen when we group other people together on the basis of visible categories, such as gender, race, age, skin tone, and attractiveness, but it even happens when we group others on the basis of nonvisible categories, such as sexual orientation and attitudes (e.g., Klauer & Wegener, 1998; van Knippenberg & Dijksterhuis, 2000).

Stereotype Activation

After we make an initial categorization, the stereotypes that we associate with that category are often automatically brought to mind. Before addressing the way in which these stereotypes can bias our subsequent judgments and behavior, let's dig a little deeper into how this activation works. In all of this work, we rely on some of the basic assumptions about schemas and schematic processing that we covered back in chapter 3.

One assumption is that stereotypes can be activated regardless of whether or not we *want* them to be activated. Sure, some folks have blatant negative beliefs about others that they are happy to bend your ear about. Others want to believe that they never ever, ever judge people on the basis of stereotypes. Most of us probably are somewhere in the middle. But regardless, individuals raised and exposed to the same cultural information all have knowledge of which stereotypes are culturally associated with which groups (Devine, 1989). This information has made it into those mental file folders in our head, even if we have tried to flag it as false and malicious. When we meet someone from Wisconsin, we mentally pull up our Wisconsin folder on the state to be better prepared for discussing the intricacies of cheese making and the Green Bay Packers. We do this unconsciously and without intending to—perhaps because most of the time its comforting to think we know what to expect from others.

Patricia Devine (1989) provided an early and influential demonstration of automatic stereotype activation. She reasoned that anything that reminds White Americans of African Americans would activate the trait *aggressive* because it is strongly associated with the African American stereotype. To test this hypothesis, she exposed White participants subliminally to 100 words. Each word was presented so briefly (for only 80 milliseconds) that participants could not detect the words and experienced them as mere flashes of light. Depending on which condition participants were in, 80 or 20% of the words—some very explicit—were related to the African American stereotype (e.g., "*lazy,*" "*ghetto,*" "*slavery,*" "*welfare,*" "*basketball,*" "*unemployed*"), while the rest of the words were neutral.

Then, as part of an apparently separate experiment, participants read a paragraph describing a person named Donald, who behaved in ways that could be seen as either hostile or merely assertive. Participants primed with the Black stereotype interpreted Donald's ambiguous behaviors as more hostile than did those who didn't get this prime. Even though *aggressive* was not primed outright, because it is part of the stereotype schema for African Americans, priming that stereotype cued people to perceive the next person they encountered as being aggressive. In later studies, this type of priming even led participants to act more aggressively toward an unsuspecting person (Bargh et al., 1996).

In an important finding, this effect was the same for those who report low and high levels of prejudice toward African Americans. However, it is important to clarify that Devine's study primed people directly with stereotypes about Blacks, not simply with the social category "Blacks" or a photo of a Black individual. Other research suggests some people are less likely to activate stereotypic biases automatically. First, Lepore and Brown (1997) showed that people with stronger prejudices activate a negative stereotype about Blacks when they are simply exposed to the category information (i.e., the word *Blacks*), whereas those who are low in prejudice don't show this activation at all.

In addition, newer research suggests that the goal of being egalitarian can itself be implicitly activated when people encounter an outgroup and can help keep negative stereotypes from coming to mind (Moskowitz, 2010; Moskowitz & Li, 2011; Sassenberg & Moskowitz, 2005). The take-away message seems to be that although low-prejudice individuals may be aware of culturally prevalent stereotypes about outgroups, they often do not activate those stereotypes.

How Do Stereotypes Contribute to Bias?

Once stereotypes are *activated*, we use them to perceive and make judgments about others in ways that confirm, rather than disconfirm, those stereotypes. Stereotypes influence information processing at various stages, from the first few milliseconds of perception to the way we remember actions years from now. And because stereotypes can be activated automatically, even people who view themselves as nonprejudiced can sometimes inadvertently view group members through the lens of negative stereotypes. Let's take a whirlwind tour of some of the ways that stereotypes color people's understanding of others. In doing so, we'll explore not just how research has examined these biases but also how they help provide insight into very real social consequences for those on the receiving end of negative stereotypes.

APPLICATION

Stereotypes Influence Perception

Just after midnight on February 4, 1999 four New York City police officers were in pursuit of a serial rapist believed to be African American. They approached a 23-year-old African immigrant, Amadou Diallo, in front of his Bronx apartment building. Assuming the police would want to see his identification, Diallo reached into his jacket and pulled out his wallet. One of the officers saw the situation differently and called out, "Gun!" The officers fired 41 bullets, 19 of which struck Diallo, killing him. Bruce Springsteen wrote a song about the incident, "American Skin (41 Shots)." The officers were acquitted of any wrongdoing by a jury in Albany, New York (about 150 miles from New York City), a decision that sparked public protest. The city eventually settled a wrongful-death lawsuit by Diallo's family for $3 million. Many factors likely played a role in the tragedy, but one thing is clear: In his hand Diallo held a wallet that was mistaken for a gun. Can research on stereotyping help us understand how this could happen?

Yes. In fact, this event inspired a line of research on what has come to be called the **shooter bias**. This bias has to do with the stereotyped association of Blacks with violence and crime (e.g., Payne, 2001; Eberhardt et al., 2004). We know that people process stereotype-consistent information more quickly than stereotype-inconsistent information, all else being equal. What is surprising is how quickly stereotypes can exert this influence on perception. In three studies (Correll et al., 2002), White American participants played a video game in which they were shown photographs of Black and White men holding an object (sample images appear in **FIGURE 10.13**), and were asked to press the "shoot" button if the individual was holding a gun and the "don't shoot" button if the individual was not holding a gun.

The experimenters predicted that White participants would be faster to shoot an armed person if he were Black rather than White. In addition, they should be faster to make the correct decision to not shoot an unarmed person if he was White rather than Black. The bar graph on the left in Figure 10.13 shows that this is just what happened. When in another study (shown in the right graph of Figure 10.13), participants were forced to make decisions under more extreme time pressure, they made

Shooter bias The tendency to mistakenly see objects in the hands of Black men as guns.

Figure 10.13

The Shooter Bias

In studies that document the shooter bias, participants play a video game in which they are instructed to shoot at anyone who is armed but to avoid shooting anyone who is unarmed.

[Photos: Bernd Wittenbrink, University of Chicago, Center for Decision Research]

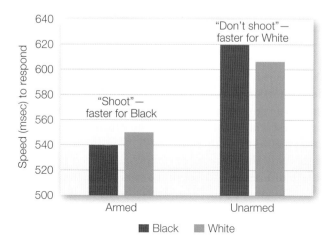

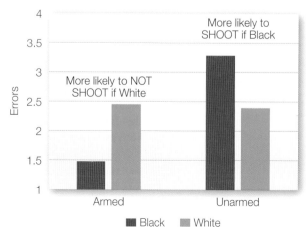

the same kind of error that the police made when they shot Diallo. That is, participants were more likely to shoot an unarmed man who was Black rather than White. Evidence from these studies suggests that these effects resulted more from the individual's knowledge of the cultural stereotype that Blacks are dangerous than from personal prejudice toward Blacks. In fact, in a follow-up study, the researchers found that even Black participants showed these same shooter biases.

Follow-up studies using the same shooter-game paradigm have revealed that the shooter bias is affected by a number of additional factors. People show a stronger shooter bias if the context itself is threatening, say, a dark street corner rather than a sunlit church (Correll et al., 2011). It's also stronger when the Blacks in the photos look more prototypically Black—in other words, they have darker skin and more typically Afrocentric features (Ma & Correll, 2010). This finding reveals part of a general tendency for stereotypes to be applied more strongly to those who seem most prototypical of a group. In fact, anything that reinforces, justifies, or increases the accessibility of a racial stereotype strengthens the likelihood that the stereotype will be applied—in the Diallo case, leading to an innocent person being killed (Correll et al., 2007).

Law-enforcement officials across the nation have become interested in this problem; many are working with researchers to understand better these kinds of biases. In one shooter-game study of police officers and community members, both were faster to shoot an armed target if he was Black rather than White. But police officers were less likely than community members to shoot an unarmed Black target (Correll et al., 2007). It is fortunate that many law-enforcement personnel receive training that has some effect in reducing these biases. Nevertheless, tragic errors resulting from such biases likely still occur.

Interpreting Behavior

If stereotypes actually can lead us to sometimes see something that isn't there, it should come as no surprise that they also color how we interpret ambiguous information and behaviors (e.g., Kunda & Thagard, 1996).

Research shows that people interpret the same behavior differently when it is performed by individuals who belong to stereotyped groups. In one study (Duncan, 1976), White students watched a videotape of a discussion between two men. They were told that whenever they heard a beep, they were to classify the behavior they had just observed into one of several categories (e.g., gives information, asks for opinion, playing around, violent behavior). Gradually, the discussion got more passionate, and at one point one of the men shoved the other. Immediately after the shove, participants heard a beep telling them to interpret that behavior. Was the shove harmless horseplay, or was it an act of aggression? If participants (who were White) watched a version of the tape in which the man delivering the shove was White, only 17% described the shove as violent, and 42% said it was playful. However, if they watched a version in which the same shove was delivered by a Black man, 75% said it was violent, and only 6% said it was playful.

In fact, stereotypes influence the interpretation of ambiguous behaviors even when those stereotypes are primed outside of conscious awareness. When police and probation officers were primed beneath conscious awareness with words related to the Black stereotype, and then read a vignette about a shoplifting incident, they rated the offender as more hostile and deserving of punishment if he was Black, but not if he was White (Graham & Lowery, 2004).

Many other studies have similarly shown that stereotypes associated with race, social class, or profession can lend different meanings to the same ambiguous behaviors (e.g., Darley & Gross, 1983; Dunning & Sherman, 1997). Some of the evidence suggests that stereotypes set up a hypothesis about a person, but because we have a general bias toward confirming our expectancies, we interpret ambiguous information as evidence supporting that hypothesis.

The Ultimate Attribution Error

Stereotypes don't only color our attention and our judgment of ambiguous information as we encounter it. They also bias our interpretation after events have played out. Recall from chapter 4 that when we make a dispositional attribution, we conclude that a person's behavior was due to some aspect of his or her character or disposition. ("That guy in the Mustang cut me off because he's a jerk!") When we make a situational attribution, we do not make reference to disposition but instead conclude that the person's behavior was due to some aspect of the situation. ("That guy in the Mustang cut me off because a dog ran onto the road.")

You might also remember that we like to make self-serving attributions for our own experiences: Good things happen because of us, bad things because of the situation. We show a similar bias when we perceive our ingroup and the exact opposite tendency in our assessments of the outgroup. This is called the **ultimate attribution error** (Hewstone, 1990; Pettigrew, 1979). When an outgroup member does something negative, or when an ingroup member does something positive, this is consistent with our automatic preference for ingroups over outgroups (Perdue et al., 1990). We infer that it's the dispositional character of the groups that caused the behaviors: *We* do good things because *we* are good people. *They* do bad things because *they* are bad people.

Of course, every now and again we might be forced to admit that an outgroup member performed well or behaved admirably and an ingroup member performed or behaved poorly. But now the attribution veers toward the situation. Not only does this error make the ingroup seem superior, it also reinforces negative stereotypes about the outgroup. It leads people to attribute stereotype-confirming information (typically the negative behaviors of outgroup members) to the outgroup's underlying disposition, thereby implying that the outgroup's bad behaviors stem from some fixed and stable "essence" of the group. ("They are unemployed because they are lazy.") In contrast, when outgroup members act in positive ways that threaten to disconfirm the stereotype, people dismiss those actions as due to situational factors that can change, such as random fluctuations in luck or temporary bursts of effort ("They performed well because they got lucky.") (e.g., Greenberg & Rosenfield, 1979; Hilton & von Hippel, 1996).

The ultimate attribution error shapes, for example, how people make attributions for men's and women's behavior (e.g., Deaux, 1984). When men succeed on a stereotypically masculine task, observers tend to attribute that success to the men's dispositional ability, but when women perform well on the same task, observers tend to attribute that success to luck or effort. Likewise, men's failures on stereotypically masculine tasks are often attributed to bad luck and lack of effort, whereas women's failures on the same tasks are attributed to their lack of ability. In this research, both men and women often exhibit this form of the ultimate attribution error: Regardless of their gender, people tend to explain men's and women's behaviors in ways that fit culturally widespread stereotypes.

The Linguistic Intergroup Bias

Group-based biases in attribution are reflected in the way people talk. Imagine that you saw someone put a dollar into a Salvation Army collection box. You could describe this behavior as "being generous," or you could describe it as "giving to charity." Both descriptions are accurate, but they differ in their implications. When you use abstract adjectives such as *generous*, you are implying that the person behaves in a similar way at different times and in different types of situations. If, however, you describe the same behavior using more concrete verbs such as *giving*, you are not im-

Ultimate attribution error The tendency to believe that bad actions by outgroup members occur *because of their internal dispositions* and good actions by them occur *because of the situation*, while believing the reverse for ingroup members.

describe the same behavior using more concrete verbs such as *giving*, you are not implying a behavioral tendency that generalizes across time and situations. Thus, you can imagine that in this case, you would prefer the abstract description if you like the person ("That's my friend, always being generous!") but the more concrete description if you dislike the person ("So my enemy gave to charity once; that doesn't mean anything."). Similarly, you can imagine that the opposite would hold true for negative behaviors: Whereas someone you like "kicked someone" (concrete verb), someone you didn't like was "aggressive" (abstract adjective).

Research by Anne Maass and colleagues bears out these intuitions. When people talk about positive behaviors performed by their ingroup, they tend to use more abstract descriptions, whereas when they talk about positive behaviors performed by outgroup members, they tend to use more concrete descriptions. Again, this is because such descriptions imply that the positive behaviors are short-lived and atypical. The opposite holds true for negative behaviors. People describe them in more concrete terms when they are performed by ingroup members than when they are performed by outgroup members. This differential pattern in language is called the **linguistic intergroup bias** (Maass et al., 1996): Stereotypic behaviors (positive ingroup and negative outgroup) are described in more abstract terms, whereas counterstereotypic behaviors (negative ingroup and positive outgroup) are described in more concrete terms.

Linguistic intergroup bias
A tendency to describe stereotypic behaviors (positive ingroup and negative outgroup) in abstract terms while describing counterstereotypic behaviors (negative ingroup and positive outgroup) in concrete terms.

Stereotypes Distort Memory

Finally, stereotypes bias how we attend to and encode information as well as what we recall or remember. Back in chapter 3, we described a study in which White participants were shown a picture of a Black man in a business suit being threatened by a young White man holding a straight razor (Allport & Postman, 1947). As that participant described the scene to another participant, who described it to another participant, and so on, the story tended to shift to the razor being in the Black man's hand and the business suit being on the White man. Rumors often can distort the facts because our stereotypes bias what we recall (and what we retell) in ways that fit our expectations. Since that initial demonstration, similar findings have also been shown even when the stereotype isn't evoked until *after* the information has been encoded, and for a wide range of stereotypes regarding ethnicity, occupation, gender, sexual orientation, and social class (e.g., Dodson et al., 2008; Frawley, 2008).

Summary: Stereotypes Tend to Be Self-confirming

The phenomena we've discussed are just a few of the many ways in which stereotypes systematically color the way we think and make judgments about other individuals and groups. A harmful consequence of this influence is that stereotypes reinforce themselves, making them relatively impervious to change (Darley & Gross, 1983; Fiske & Taylor, 2008; Rothbart, 1981). Stereotypes lead us to attend to information that fits those stereotypes and to ignore information that does not. When we do observe behaviors that are inconsistent with our stereotypes, we tend to explain them away as isolated instances or exceptions to the rule (Allport, 1954). Because stereotypes can be activated unconsciously, people may not even be aware that stereotypes are biasing what they perceive and how they explain it to themselves and to others. All they may know is that they have "seen" such and such behavior. They believe that their reactions to and interpretations of stereotyped individuals are free of prejudice because they assume that they are looking at the world objectively. The ironic fact is that the very meaning of others' attributes and behaviors has already been filtered through the lenses of their stereotypes. When it comes to stereotypes, believing is seeing.

SECTION review | Stereotyping: The Cognitive Companion of Prejudice

Stereotypes can help promote and justify prejudice, even if they are positive.

Where do stereotypes come from?

- A kernel of truth that is overblown and overgeneralized.
- Assumptions about group differences in traits inferred from group differences in social roles.
- Generalizations about a group's warmth and competence that are based on judgments of cooperativeness and status.
- Illusory correlations that make unrelated things seem related.

Why do we apply stereotypes?

- To simplify the process of social perception and to conserve mental energy.
- To justify prejudicial attitudes.
- To justify discrimination by dehumanizing, infrahumanizing, or objectifying others.
- To justify the status quo and to maintain a sense of predictability.
- To maintain and bolster self-esteem.

How do stereotypes affect judgment?

- Categorization increases the perceived homogeneity of outgroup members, thereby reinforcing stereotypes.
- Stereotypes can be activated automatically, coloring how we perceive, interpret, and communicate about the characteristics and behaviors of outgroup (and ingroup) members.
- Stereotypes influence how we perceive and interpret behavior, as well as how we remember information.
- Because of these biases, stereotypes tend to be self-perpetuating, even in the face of disconfirming information.

CONNECT ONLINE:

Check out our videos and additional resources located at:
www.macmillanhighered.com/launchpad/greenberg1e

Responding to and Reducing Prejudice

TOPIC OVERVIEW

 SOCIAL PSYCH OUT IN THE WORLD

 SOCIAL PSYCH AT THE MOVIES   420

The previous chapter focused on the causes of prejudice, stereotyping, and discrimination and the motivations and cognitions of those who hold such attitudes and act in discriminatory ways. We should not be surprised that these biases often cause physical, psychological, and economic harm to those targeted. Throughout history, this harm has often been obvious and severe, as in atrocities such as genocide, enslavement, and colonization. And these atrocities often continue to affect the targeted groups many generations after their occurrence (e.g., Salzman, 2001). Less visible forms of discrimination in economic, legal, and social realms such as hiring, career advancement, health care, legal proceedings, and loan opportunities create further problems (e.g., Nelson, 2009; Riach & Rich, 2004; Stangor, 2009). And even subtler psychological effects of feeling devalued within one's culture cause their own harm (e.g., Frable et al., 1990; Inzlicht et al., 2006). In all these ways, prejudice, stereotyping, and discrimination contribute to poverty and physical, behavioral, and mental-health problems (e.g., Anderson & Armstead, 1995; Kessler et al., 1999; Klonoff et al., 1999; Williams, 1999; Williams et al., 1999).

In this chapter we will examine what happens psychologically to people who are targeted by prejudice and the ways in which they cope. We'll look at the processes that influence how (and whether) people perceive the prejudice they experience and how they respond to it; how even subtle encounters with prejudice and stereotypes can affect one's health, behavior, and performance; and how members of stigmatized groups can remain resilient in spite of social biases and discrimination. Then we'll turn to understanding how individuals differ in their propensities for prejudice. We'll conclude by covering some promising strategies that can be used to reduce prejudice.

Prejudice From a Target's Perspective

Perceiving Prejudice and Discrimination

If you are a member of a group that is viewed or treated negatively by the larger society in which you live, your membership in that group is bound to affect you in some way (Allport, 1954). Yet, as you learned in the previous chapter, for many stigmatized groups in the United States, prejudice can be a lot subtler and harder to detect than it was 50 years ago. To an optimist, this is a sign of progress. But from a more pessimistic perspective, this makes it harder to detect when one is the target of prejudice, even when prejudice significantly affects one's thoughts and behavior. This is a dilemma that anyone who feels marginalized in society probably has faced. Take the following quote from Erving Goffman's classic 1963 book *Stigma*: "And I always feel this with straight people [people who are not ex-convicts]—that whenever they're being nice to me, pleasant to me, all the time really, underneath they're only assessing me as a criminal and nothing else" (p. 14).

Master status The perception that a person will be seen only in terms of a stigmatizing attribute rather than as the total self.

This individual's reflection reveals the **master status** that can accompany stigmatizing attributes—the perception that others will see oneself solely in terms of one aspect rather than appreciating that that aspect is only one part of a total self. As a result, individuals are persistently aware of what sets them apart in their interactions with others. For example, when asked to describe themselves, students from an ethnic-minority background are more likely to make mention of their group identity than are students from the ethnic majority (McGuire et al., 1978). Arthur Ashe, the first Black male tennis champion, expressed it this way in his autobiography: "Like many other blacks, when I find myself in a new public situation, I will count. I always count. I count the number of black and brown faces present, especially to see how many, if any, are employed by the hosts" (Ashe & Rampersad, 1994, p. 144).

The American tennis champion Arthur Ashe was very conscious of his position as the first Black man to break into a predominantly White sport.

[Focus on Sport/Getty Images]

When people are conscious of being stigmatized, they become more vigilant to signs of prejudice. In one study, women expecting to interact with a sexist man were quicker to detect sexism-related words (e.g., *harassment, hooters, bitch*) during a computer task and were more likely to judge ambiguous facial expressions as showing criticism (Inzlicht et al., 2008; Kaiser et al., 2006).

Individual Differences in Perceiving Prejudice

As you might suspect, not all minority-group members share equally the expectation of being the target of prejudice. People's sensitivity to perceiving bias and discrimination depends on the extent to which they identify with their stigmatized group. If people normally don't think about themselves as being members of disadvantaged groups, then discrimination might not seem like something that could happen to them. For these individuals, others' prejudice might have to be blatant before they acknowledge it. In contrast, people who are highly identified with their stigmatized group are more likely to recognize when prejudice and discrimination might affect their lives (Operario & Fiske, 2001; Major et al., 2003).

Stigma consciousness The expectation of being perceived by other people, particularly those in the majority group, in terms of one's group membership.

Members of minority groups also differ in their **stigma consciousness**, their expectation that other people—particularly those in the majority group—will perceive them in terms of their group membership (Pinel, 1999). Although members of stigmatized groups fall along a range of stigma consciousness, those at the higher end of this scale are more likely to expect their interactions with others to go poorly. Unfortunately, these expectations can sometimes lead to self-fulfilling prophecies. For example, when women particularly high in stigma consciousness had reason to think that a male stranger might be sexist, they evaluated an essay he had written more negatively, which then led him to evaluate *their* essays more negatively (Pinel, 2002). The negative evaluations they received might have confirmed their assumption of the man's sexism, yet his evaluations might have been more positive if they had not criticized his essay first. But as we will discuss shortly, self-fulfilling prophecies are a two-way street. They also affect how those who are nonstigmatized perceive and interact with stigmatized targets.

People differ in their perceptions of prejudice, and although they sometimes might overestimate their experience of prejudice, this is not the norm. Instead, it is more common for people to estimate that they personally experience less discrimination than does the average member of their group (Taylor et al., 1990). This effect, called the **person-group discrimination discrepancy**, has been documented in many groups, including women reporting on their experience of sexism and racial minorities reporting on their experience of racism. This effect has even been found among inner-city African American men, a group that is probably most likely to experience actual discrimination in employment, housing, and interactions with police (Taylor et al., 1994). Why is the tendency to avoid seeing prejudice and discrimination directed at oneself so pervasive?

Person-group discrimination discrepancy The tendency for people to estimate that they personally experience less discrimination than is faced by the average member of their group.

Motivations to Avoid Perceptions of Prejudice

People may fail to see the prejudice targeted at them because they are motivated to deny that prejudice and discrimination affect their lives. Why? For one thing, this denial may be part of a more general tendency to be optimistic. Experiencing discrimination, having health problems, and being at risk for experiencing an earthquake all are negative events, and people are generally overly optimistic about their likelihood of experiencing such outcomes (Lehman & Taylor, 1987; Taylor & Brown, 1988). It might be beneficial to one's own psychological health to regard discrimination as something that happens to *other* people.

Another reason is that people may be motivated to sustain their faith that the way society is set up is inherently right and good, thereby justifying the status quo (Jost & Banaji, 1994). Buying into the status quo brings a sense of stability and predictability, but it can lead stigmatized individuals to downplay their experience of discrimination. For example, in one experiment White and Latino students were put in the same situation of feeling that they had been passed over for a job that was given to someone of another ethnicity (Major et al., 2002). To what extent did they view this as discrimination? The results were quite different, depending on the students' ethnicity. Among Whites, those most convinced that the social system in America is fair, and that hard work pays off, thought it was quite discriminatory for a Latino employer to pass them over to hire another Latino. After all, if the system is fair, and Whites have been very successful in the system, an employer has no justification for choosing a minority-group member over themselves. But among Latinos, those who saw the social system as fair were least likely to feel that it was discriminatory for a White employer to pass them over in favor of a White participant. Believing the system is fair might keep people motivated to do their best, but for members of minority groups in society, it can also reduce the likelihood of recognizing discrimination when it does occur.

APPLICATION

Is Perceiving Prejudice Bad for Your Health?

Living in a society that devalues you because of your ethnicity, your sexual preferences, or religious attitudes can take a toll on both your mental and your physical health. Several studies have shown that people who report experiencing more prejudice in their daily lives also show evidence of poorer psychological health

(Branscombe et al., 1999; Schmitt et al., 2014). Negative consequences, such as increased depression and lower life satisfaction, are especially extreme when people blame themselves for their stigma or the way people treat them.

Because our culture is infused with stereotypic portrayals of various groups, these negative effects on mental health can be quite insidious. For example, there is an ongoing national debate about the use of Native American images as mascots for school and sports teams. Do these images honor the proud history of a cultural group? Or do they present an overly simplistic caricature that debases a segment of society? Research shows that when Native American children and young adults are primed with these images, their self-esteem is reduced, they feel worse about their community, and they imagine themselves achieving less in the future (Fryberg et al., 2008). One possible contributing factor is the sense many Native Americans have that they are invisible—that they are rarely represented in mainstream society except as caricatures. Yet many of these same participants in the study above didn't report that they thought Native American mascots were bad, even though their self-esteem ratings suggest that encountering these symbols erodes their mental well-being. On the basis of findings such as these, in 2014, the U.S. Patent and Trademark Office canceled the trademark that the Washington Redskins had on their football team's name and logo because both were deemed to be disparaging to Native Americans (Vargas, 2014).

Prejudice can have long-term consequences for physical health as well (Contrada et al., 2000). Like any chronic stressor, the experience of prejudice elevates the body's physiological stress response. For example, women who report being frequent targets of sexism show a greater physiological stress response (i.e., increases in cortisol, a stress-related hormone) when they believe they personally might have been targeted by bias (Townsend et al., 2011). Over time, this stress response can predict poorer cardiovascular functioning, the buildup of plaque in the arteries, and artery calcification, putting people at greater risk for coronary heart disease (Guyll et al., 2001; Lewis et al., 2006; Troxel et al., 2003).

Although perceiving frequent discrimination predicts poorer well-being, this correlation also implies that those who do not perceive frequent experiences of prejudice fare much better psychologically. Later, we will discuss how particular ways of perceiving and reacting to discrimination can also sometimes buffer people from the negative psychological consequences of prejudice (Crocker & Major, 1989).

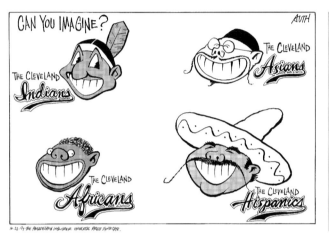

American sports leagues still have team names such as the Cleveland Indians and the Washington Redskins, with mascots to match. If the same type of ethnic mascots existed for other groups, would we more easily recognize them as being offensive?

The Harmful Impact of Stereotypes on Behavior

Although being the target of prejudice has the power to affect how people perceive themselves, it also can affect how they behave and perform. When you hold a stereotypic expectation about another person (because of their group membership, for example) you may act in a way that leads the stereotyped person to behave just as you expected. For example, you suspect that the clerk at the café is going to be rude, so you are curt with her. She responds by being curt back to you and Voilà! Your initial judgment seems to be confirmed. Yet you may be ignoring the fact that, had you approached the interaction with a different expectation in mind, she might not have acted rudely.

This was demonstrated in a classic study by Rosenthal and Jacobson (1968) in which teachers' stereotypic expectations of their students actually changed how those students performed in school. Students who were identified to the teachers as "bloomers"—that is, those who would likely experience a spurt in intellectual development—performed better over the course of the year than did students who were identified to the teachers as "non-bloomers." This result might not be surprising until you realize that the researchers labeled the students as bloomers and non-bloomers on the basis of a flip of a coin. What happened? The teachers were more attentive to and challenged the students who had been labeled as bloomers, and those students benefited from this special treatment. This shows that when a person is the target of stereotypic expectations, it can lead other people to change how they act toward that person. As a result, the target starts to act more in line with others' expectations. The other people walk away with their expectations confirmed, but they may not realize that they played a role in *causing* the target to act the way he or she did.

Teachers' expectations of students' abilities can subtly shape their interactions with those students in ways that confirm their stereotypes.

[nano/E+/Getty Images]

The Rosenthal and Jacobson study demonstrates the power of positive expectations in creating self-fulfilling prophecies. Other research shows that negative stereotypic expectations can have damaging effects. Consider how in anticipation of a job interview, you would likely spend time preparing for it, practicing answers to certain questions. But have you ever stopped to consider that how you perform in the interview might partly be a function of the expectations the interviewer holds about you? A classic demonstration of self-fulfilling prophecies shows that it is (Word et al., 1974). In the first of a pair of studies, White participants were asked to play the role of an interviewer with two different job candidates, one who happens to be White and the other Black. The researchers watched these interviews and analyzed them for differences. It turned out that when the job candidate was Black, the interviewer chose to sit farther away from him, was more awkward in his speech, and conducted a shorter interview than when the candidate was White. Something about the race of the candidate affected the way in which the interview was conducted. But does this difference in the interviewer's manner affect how the job candidate comes across during the interview?

The answer is yes. In a second study, the researchers trained their assistants to conduct an interview either using the "good interviewer" style that was more typical of the interviews with White candidates (e.g., sitting closer) or the "bad interviewer" style that was more typical of the interviews with Black candidates (e.g., sitting farther away). When the trained assistants interviewed unsuspecting White job candidates, an interesting pattern emerged. Those job candidates assigned to a "bad" interviewer came across as less calm and composed than those assigned to the "good" interviewer.

More recent research shows just how subtle these effects can be. In one set of studies, when female engineering students were paired with a male peer to work together on a project, his implicit sexist attitudes about women predicted her poorer performance on an engineering test (Logel et al., 2009). An interesting difference in this case was that the stereotype-confirming effects did not seem to result directly from negative beliefs the sexist men had about female competence in engineering. The sexist men were not more hostile or dismissive toward their female partners. Rather, they were more flirtatious with them, and in fact the women reported liking these men. Yet the men's flirtatious behavior only cued the women into acting in line with gender stereotypes, which impaired their performance on the engineering test.

Confirming Stereotypes to Get Along

Such findings point to a powerful dilemma. Stereotypes are schemas. If you return to the function of schemas we discussed in chapter 3, you'll remember that they help social interactions run smoothly. People get along better with each other when both individuals confirm the other person's expectations. This suggests that the more motivated people are to affiliate and interact positively with someone, the more likely they will be to behave in ways that are consistent with the other person's stereotypes, a form of self-stereotyping.

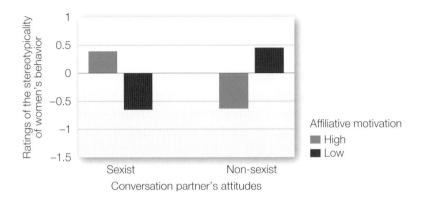

Figure 11.1

Conforming to Stereotypes

Women who were motivated to get along with others (high in affiliative motivation) acted more stereotypically during a conversation with a man the more they believed that he had sexist views about women.

[Data source: Sinclair et al. (2005)]

This is exactly what research shows. In one study (Sinclair et al., 2005), women had a casual conversation with a male student whom they were led to believe had sexist or nonsexist attitudes toward women. In actuality, he was a member of the research team trained to act in a similar way with each woman and to rate his perceptions of her afterward. Those women who generally had a desire to get along with others and make new friends (i.e., they were high in affiliative motivation) rated themselves in more gender-stereotypic ways when interacting with the guy they believed to be sexist, and as shown in **FIGURE 11.1**, he also rated their behavior to be more stereotypically feminine. Those women who were low in this general motivation to affiliate with others did just the opposite. If they thought their conversation partner would be sexist, they rated themselves as being more counterstereotypic, and the researcher also rated them as coming across in less stereotypical ways during their interaction. This study shows that when people are motivated to get along with someone who is likely to hold stereotypes of them, they tend to experience a shift in their perceptions of themselves and behave accordingly.

Objectification

Although many consequences of being stigmatized apply broadly to different forms of prejudice, some are more specific to particular identities. One important example is the objectification that can result from the strong focus in many cultures on women's bodies. The art historian John Berger (1972) wrote, "A woman must continually watch herself. She is almost continually accompanied by her own image of herself. She has to survey everything she is and everything she does because how she appears to others is of crucial importance for what is normally thought of as the success of her life" (p. 46).

In chapter 10, we discussed how the sexual objectification of women promotes certain stereotypes and prejudice against them. But Fredrickson and Robert's (1997) objectification theory also proposes that this intense cultural scrutiny of the female body leads many girls and women to view themselves as objects to be looked at and judged, a phenomenon that the researchers called **self-objectification**. Being exposed to sexualizing words or idealized media images of women's bodies, hearing other women criticizing their own bodies, or undergoing men's visual scrutiny of their bodies all prompt self-objectification, which increases negative emotions such as body shame, appearance anxiety, and self-disgust (e.g., Aubrey, 2007; Calogero, 2004; Gapinski et al., 2003; Roberts & Gettman, 2004).

Self-objectification also disrupts concentration and interferes with cognitive performance. This was first demonstrated in the now classic "that swimsuit becomes you" research (Fredrickson et al., 1998). In one of these studies, male and female college students were first asked to try on and evaluate either a swimsuit or a sweater. Then, wearing the particular garment while alone in a makeshift dressing room, they

Self-objectification

A phenomenon whereby intense cultural scrutiny of the female body leads many girls and women to view themselves as objects to be looked at and judged.

completed a short math test. Men were unaffected by what they were wearing, but women who were wearing the swimsuit were drawn to monitoring their appearance and consequently performed worse than if they were wearing a sweater.

Women who are particularly susceptible to such self-objectification experience frequent shame. The more shame they feel, the more vulnerable they are to disordered eating, depression, and sexual dysfunction (Fredrickson & Roberts, 1997). These effects of self-objectification have likely contributed to the obsession with weight that has led 73% of American women to make some serious effort at some point to lose weight, compared with only 55% of men (Saad, 2011).

Stereotype Threat

Self-fulfilling prophecies and self-stereotyping are examples of how stereotypes affect behavior of members of stereotyped groups during social interactions. Other research shows that even when a person is not interacting with someone, the immediate context can bring to mind stereotypes about his or her group, and this can interfere with the person's ability to perform at their best. This was the discovery made by the Stanford researchers Claude Steele and Joshua Aronson (1995) when they conducted pioneering work on what they called *stereotype threat*, a phenomenon you were first introduced to in chapter 1 when we covered research methods.

Stereotype threat is the concern that one might do something to confirm a negative stereotype about one's group either in one's own eyes or the eyes of someone else. Although this phenomenon has far-reaching consequences for a variety of situations, it has been studied primarily as an explanation for long-standing group differences in performance. For example, stereotype threat partly accounts for lower standardized-test scores among Blacks, Latinos, and Native Americans than for their White and Asian peers, and for why women perform less well than men on tests of mathematical ability. Traditional research has focused on whether nature (genetics, hormones, even brain size) or nurture (upbringing, educational values, access to educational resources) offers a better explanation of these performance gaps (Nisbett, 2009). Research on stereotype threat takes a different and distinctly social psychological view of this problem, noting that performance can be influenced by aspects of the situation, such as the person's experience of the classroom in which he or she is taking a test. Steele and Aronson (1995) gave Black and White undergraduates a challenging set of verbal problems to solve. The researchers varied only one thing. For half of the sample, the problems were described as a diagnostic test of verbal intelligence (the type of thing you might think when you take the SAT or GRE). For the other half, the same problems were described as a simple lab exercise. Although White students were unaffected by how the task was described, Black students performed significantly worse when the task was presented as a diagnostic test of intelligence (see **FIGURE 11.2**). They were also more likely to have stereotypes about race activated in their minds. So a single, rather small detail—how the task was framed—made a big difference. When Black students were reminded of the stereotype that their group is intellectually inferior, they performed more poorly on the test.

In addition to undermining performance on tests of math, verbal, or general intellectual ability of minorities, women, and those of lower socioeconomic status (Croizet & Claire, 1998), stereotype threat has also been shown to impair memory performance of older adults (Chasteen et al., 2005); driving performance of women (Yeung & von Hippel, 2008); athletes' performance in the face of racial stereotypes (Stone et al., 2012); men's performance on an emotional sensitivity task (Leyens et al., 2000); and women's negotiation skills (Kray et al., 2001).

Stereotype threat The concern that one might do something to confirm a negative stereotype about one's group either in one's own eyes or the eyes of someone else.

Figure 11.2

Stereotype Threat

In research on stereotype threat, Black college students performed significantly worse when a task was framed as a diagnostic test of verbal ability rather than as a nondiagnostic laboratory exercise.

[Data source: Steele & Aronson (1995)]

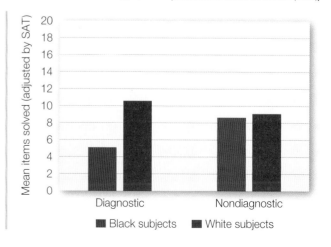

■ Black subjects   ■ White subjects

Stereotype threat is more likely to impair performance under some conditions than others (Schmader et al., 2008). The effect is strongest when:

- the stigmatized identity is made salient in the situation (e.g., being the only women in a high-level math class).
- that identity is chronically salient, due to high stigma consciousness or high identification with the group.
- the task is characterized as a diagnostic measure of an ability for which one's group is stereotyped as being inferior (as in Steele & Aronson, 1995).
- individuals are led to believe their performance is going to be compared with that of members of the group stereotyped as superior on the task.
- individuals are explicitly reminded of the stereotype.

Researchers also have learned a great deal about the processes that contribute to the deleterious effects of stereotype threat. First, it's important to point out that those who care the most about being successful feel stereotype threat most acutely (Steele, 1997). You have to be invested in doing well to be threatened by the possibility that you might not. In fact, it's partly because people are trying so hard to prove the stereotype wrong that their performance suffers (Jamieson & Harkins, 2007). When situations bring these stereotypes to mind, anxious thoughts and feelings of self-doubt are more likely to creep in (Bosson et al., 2004; Cadinu et al., 2005; Johns et al., 2008; Spencer et al., 1999). Efforts to push these thoughts away and to stay focused on the task can hijack the very same cognitive resources that people need to do well on tests and in other academic pursuits (Johns et al., 2008; Logel et al., 2009; Schmader et al., 2008). For other kinds of activities (such as trying to sink a golf putt, shoot a basket, or parallel park), becoming proficient means relying on skills that have become automatic over hours if not years of practice. When the situation reminds people of a negative group stereotype about those activities, they end up scrutinizing the behaviors that they normally do automatically; as a result, they trip themselves up (Schmader & Beilock, 2011).

Just as some people see their performance suffer in the face of negative stereotypes, others can get a boost in performance from reminders that they are positively stereotyped (Rydell et al., 2009; Shih et al., 2002; Walton & Cohen, 2003), a phenomenon known as *stereotype lift*. One caveat, however, is that when these positive stereotypes are communicated directly and explicitly ("Oh, you should do well on this math test because you're Asian"), people can also choke under the pressure of having to live up to such high expectations (Cheryan & Bodenhausen, 2000; Shih et al., 2002).

Social Identity Threat

Research on stereotype threat reveals that it's mentally taxing to cope with situations that communicate to you that you are incompetent. A more general version of this threat is called *social identity threat,* the feeling that your group simply is not valued in a domain and that you do not belong there (Steele et al., 2002). As a result, those who try to enter and excel in areas where their group has traditionally been underrepresented find themselves trying to juggle their various identities. For example, women who go into male-dominant domains find themselves having to suppress their more feminine qualities (Pronin et al., 2004; von Hippel et al., 2011). A minority student who does excel in academics can be accused of being an "Uncle Tom" or of "acting White" (Fordham & Ogbu, 1986).

On the one hand, repeated exposure to stereotype threat and social identity threat can eventually lead to disidentification, which occurs when people no longer feel that their performance in a domain is an important part of themselves, and they stop caring about being successful (Steele, 1997). This can be a serious problem if, for example, minority children disidentify with school. In fact, being the target of negative stereotypes can steer people away from certain opportunities in the first place.

For example, although women continue to be underrepresented in science, technology, engineering, and math compared with men, Figure 10.4 (PhDs Earned by

Disidentification The process of disinvesting in any area in which one's group traditionally has been underrepresented or negatively stereotyped.

Women sitting at the computer scientist's desk on the left (with the *Star Trek* poster) expressed less interest in computer science as a major than did women sitting at the computer scientist's desk on the right. The geek stereotype of computer scientists might prevent women from becoming interested in this field.

[Cheryan et al. (2010)]

Women) in the previous chapter revealed that their numbers have been steadily increasing over time. In the one exception to this trend, the number of women entering computer science has actually been decreasing over the past two decades. Research suggests why this might be: Students have a very specific stereotype of what a computer scientist is like, and women are much more likely than men to think that it isn't like them. In one study, women expressed far less interest in majoring in computer science when they completed a survey in a computer scientist's office filled with reminders of the computer-geek stereotype than did those who completed the same questionnaire in a room that did not reinforce the conventional stereotype of computer scientists (Cheryan et al., 2009). The take-away message is that even when the doors are open for women and minorities to apply and enter certain fields, the situations themselves can still communicate subtle messages that make underrepresented groups feel that they simply wouldn't fit in there.

What's a Target to Do? Coping With Stereotyping, Prejudice, and Discrimination

Given the severity of consequences associated with the existence of cultural stereotypes as well as perceiving and being the victim of prejudice, how should a targeted individual respond? People react in quite a number of ways. Some are specifically focused on protecting oneself from stereotype threat. Others focus on ameliorating other negative consequences of prejudice. Interestingly, one review of the literature revealed surprisingly little evidence that people stigmatized based on race, ethnicity, physical disability, or mental illness report lower levels of self-esteem than those who are not normally stigmatized (Crocker & Major, 1989). This seems to run counter to common sense, and to many of the theories we've covered in this book, which suggest that people's self-esteem is influenced by how others treat them.

So how do people who are devalued by society in general minimize these hits to self-esteem and remain resilient in the face of stigmatization? Research has revealed some strategies for mitigating stereotype concerns as well as coping skills that targets use to protect their self-esteem and overall sense of well-being against the daily jabs of prejudice. Let's look at a few, starting with strategies that are particularly applicable to being stereotyped and then moving to the broader experience of being the target of prejudice. Of course, as is so often the case, sometimes the solutions open the door to other problems as well.

Combating Stereotype and Social Identity Threat

We've reviewed the powerful role that prejudice and negative stereotypes can play in shaping behavior, self-perceptions, performance, and career preferences. But fortunately, research has also pointed to several ways in which these processes can be eliminated. These findings have important implications for educational and social policies.

Identification with Role Models

One set of strategies is aimed at changing or reducing the stereotype itself. When individuals are exposed to role models—people like them who have been successful—the stereotype is altered and they feel inspired to do well (Dasgupta & Asgari, 2004; Stout et al., 2011; Marx & Roman, 2002; McIntyre et al., 2003). In one study (Stout et al., 2011), college students were randomly assigned to either a female or a male calculus professor, and their performance over the course of the semester was tracked. The gender of the professor had no effect on men's attitudes or behavior. But women with a female professor participated more in class over the course of the semester and became more confident in their ability to do well.

Reappraisal of Anxiety

When stereotypes are difficult to change, targets can reinterpret what the stereotypes mean. For example, often, when people think that they are stereotyped to do poorly, they are more likely to interpret difficulties and setbacks as evidence that the stereotype is true and that they do not belong. They perform better, though, if they reinterpret difficulties and setbacks as normal challenges faced by anyone. In one remarkable study, minority college students who read testimonials about how everyone struggles and feels anxious when beginning college felt a greater sense of belonging in academics, did better academically, and were less likely to drop out of school (Walton & Cohen, 2007, 2011). Similarly, instructions to reappraise anxiety as a normal part of test-taking improves women's and minorities' performance, effects that can persist even months later when students take an actual high-stakes test such as the GRE (Jamieson et al., 2010; Johns et al., 2008). In fact, simply being able to interpret test anxiety as the result of stereotype threat improves women's performance on a math test (Johns et al., 2005).

Figure 11.3

The Power of Self-affirmation

When middle school students spent just 15 minutes at the start of the school year reflecting on their core values, the percentage of African American students who earned a D or lower at the end of the semester was dramatically reduced.

[Data source: Cohen et al. (2006)]

Self-affirmation

Another remarkably successful coping strategy is *self-affirmation*. Self-affirmation theory (for a refresher, see chapter 6) posits that people need to view themselves as good and competent. When they encounter a threat to their positive self-view in one area of life, they compensate by affirming other deeply held values. On the basis of this theory, we would expect that people who are reminded of their core values would be protected from the negative effects of stereotypes. This hypothesis was supported in a longitudinal study of middle-school students (Cohen et al., 2006; Cohen et al., 2009; Miyake et al., 2010). Students were assigned to write about either a personally cherished value or a value that others might care about but that was not central to their own lives. The researchers then tracked students' grades. This simple affirmation task had no effect on White students' academic performance. But Black students who affirmed their values were far less likely to earn low grades over the course of that semester. The positive effects on their academic performance persisted up to two years later (see **FIGURE 11.3**). Sometimes very simple psychological interventions can have very powerful effects on long-term outcomes.

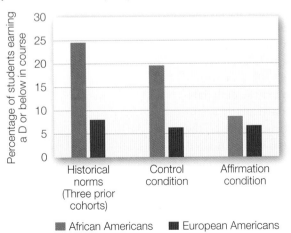

Social Strategies for Coping With Prejudice and Discrimination

Just as there are a number of ways to counter the effects of stereotype threat, there are also a number of behavioral response options for dealing with interpersonal encounters with prejudice.

Confrontation

Wanting to experience positive outcomes and to believe in fairness can make someone less likely to *perceive* discrimination. But even when people feel they have been the targets of biased attitudes or perceptions, they don't always *say* that discrimination has occurred or do anything to confront the person responsible.

Consider the following scenario: You are working on a class project in small groups, and you have to take turns choosing what kinds of people you would want with you on a deserted island. One young man in the group consistently makes sexist choices. ("Let's see, maybe a chef? No, one of the women can cook.") Would you say anything to him? In a study that presented women with this scenario, most said they would confront the guy in some way, probably by questioning his choice or pointing out how inappropriate it is (Swim & Hyers, 1999). But when women were actually put in this situation, over half of them did nothing at all.

> . . ."Fools", said I, "You do not know
> Silence like a cancer grows
> Hear my words that I might teach you
> Take my arms that I might reach you"
> But my words, like silent raindrops fell
> And echoed
> In the wells of silence
>
> — Simon & Garfunkel

This "do-nothing effect" isn't limited to targets put in the position of confronting an outgroup member. Similar silence has also been found in numerous studies in which White participants overheard a White confederate use a racial slur when referring to a Black confederate in the study (e.g., Greenberg & Pyszczynski, 1985b; Kawakami et al., 2009). Confronting those who express prejudice is a lot harder than we might imagine it to be. Being silent in these situations is particularly troubling because expressions of prejudice can rub off on the observer. In one study, White participants who heard a racial slur used to describe an African American became more negative in their evaluation of the person targeted by the slur, despite the fact that in debriefings, the participants reported being appalled by the remark (Greenberg & Pyszczynski, 1985b).

Why do racist and sexist remarks often go unchallenged? One reason is because those who do the confronting are often viewed negatively. When participants hear about a Black student who claims that his failing grade was the result of racial discrimination, they see him as a complainer (Kaiser & Miller, 2001). This kind of "blame the victim" reaction happens even when the evidence supports the student's claim that discrimination actually occurred! In other research, when Whites were confronted with the possibility that they might be biased in their treatment of others, they did try to correct their biases in the future, but they also felt angry and tended to dislike the person who confronted them (Czopp et al., 2006). Even members of your own stigmatized group can be unsympathetic when you point to the role of discrimination in your outcomes (Garcia et al., 2005). These social costs can make it difficult to address bias when it does occur, particularly if you are the person targeted by the bias and in a position of relatively little power.

Despite the costs of confrontation, real social change requires it. This raises the question, are other options available that might get a similar message across but in a way that minimizes these costs? According to the **target empowerment model**, the answer is yes (Stone et al., 2011). This model suggests that targets of bias can employ strategies that deflect discrimination, so long as those actions aren't *perceived* as confrontational. And even those that are confrontational can still be effective if they are preceded by a strategy designed to put a prejudiced person at ease.

Let's illustrate how this model works. In post–9/11 America, Arab Americans have too often been targeted by stereotypic perceptions that they endorse or are involved in terroristic activities. In a 2010 poll, 41% of Arab Americans surveyed reported experiences of discrimination based on their ethnicity (Elshinnawi, 2010). If you are an Arab American, you understandably might want others to see your perspective on the world and appreciate how hurtful these misconceptions can be. However, when prejudiced White Americans were asked by an Arab American to take his perspective, they

Target empowerment model
A model suggesting that targets of bias can employ strategies that deflect discrimination, as long as those methods aren't *perceived* as confrontational.

Think
ABOUT

[iStock/360/Getty Images]

perceived him as confrontational, stereotyped him more negatively, and reported a decreased interest in getting to know him (Stone et al., 2011). But if he first asked White perceivers to think about something they value, thereby allowing them to self-affirm, his plea for empathy worked. By getting those who are highly prejudiced to reflect on their own values or positive attributes, targets can encourage majority members to take their point of view in a less threatening manner.

When have you confronted someone who was biased against you or another person? What was the cost?

Compensation

Targets of prejudice also can cope with stigma by compensating for the negative stereotypes or attitudes they think other people have toward them. For example, when overweight women were making a first impression on a person and were led to believe that that person could see them (and thus knew their weight), they acted in a more extraverted way than if they were told that they could not be seen. They compensated for the weight-based biases they expected others to have by being extra-friendly. And it worked: those who thought they were visible were rated as friendlier by the person with whom they were interacting (Miller et al., 1995).

In a similar finding, Black college freshmen who expected others to have racial biases against them and their group reported spending more time disclosing infor-

To ease interracial tension, minority students self-disclose more to White roommates. This is effective in reducing racial biases, but does not always allow people to be themselves.

[Christine Glade/E+/Getty Images]

mation about themselves when talking with their White dormitory roommates (Shelton et al., 2005). Self-disclosure is a powerful way of establishing trust and liking, so it is not surprising that Black participants who self-disclosed a great deal were liked more by their White roommates.

Unfortunately, these kinds of compensation strategies can come with costs. In the study just mentioned, the Black participants who reported engaging in a lot of self-disclosure with a White roommate also reported feeling inauthentic in this relationship. Perhaps because they were trying to put their White roommates at ease, their efforts to compensate and find common ground left them feeling as if they had been wearing a mask of politeness rather than being true to themselves.

Another potential cost of compensation is that it can disrupt the smooth flow of social interaction. This is because the specific concerns that weigh on the mind of the target, and thus trigger their compensation, might be quite different than what weighs on the mind of the perceiver (Bergsieker et al., 2010; Shelton & Richeson, 2006). For people who belong to the more advantaged group, interactions with outgroup members can bring to mind concerns about appearing prejudiced (Vorauer et al., 1998). Assuming that they would prefer that they and their group were not seen as prejudiced jerks, we might expect them to be motivated to ingratiate themselves with others in order to come across as likeable. Thus, they will likely try to come across as warm and open, while also being careful to not let any biases pervade their judgment.

For people who belong to the disadvantaged group, the concerns for the interaction can be quite different. If you take the often-studied case of interracial interactions, a Black student having an initial conversation with her new White roommate might be most concerned about being stereotyped as incompetent. She might fear that her roommate will ask her questions that presume that she is less academically motivated or capable. To compensate for this stereotype, her impression-management goal might be to self-promote in order to boost perceptions of competence. The problem with this scenario is that interactions tend to go more smoothly when people's impression-management goals are a match or complementary in some way. If one person cracks jokes to show how warm and likeable she is while the other wants to have an intellectual conversation to bolster her perceived competence, each party might walk away from the interaction feeling a bit misunderstood and disconnected from the other. And as if this is not enough of a cost, both might feel a bit cognitively exhausted from the added effort of it all (Richeson et al., 2003; Richeson & Shelton, 2003; Richeson & Trawalter, 2005).

APPLICATION
The Costs of Concealing

When people are concerned about being discriminated against, it is not surprising that they might sometimes choose to cope by concealing their stigma, if this is an option. This strategy is common in the case of sexual orientation, which, unlike race or gender, is easily concealed. For example, Jason Collins played professional basketball in the NBA for 12 years before coming out of the closet in April 2013. In his interview with *Sports Illustrated*, he described his experience concealing his sexual orientation:

> No one wants to live in fear. I've always been scared of saying the wrong thing. I don't sleep well. I never have. But each time I tell another person, I feel stronger and sleep a little more soundly. It takes an enormous amount of energy to guard such a big secret. I've endured years of misery and gone to enormous lengths to live a lie. I was certain that my world would fall apart if anyone knew. And yet when I acknowledged my sexuality I felt whole for the first time (COLLINS & LIDZ, 2013).

When Jason Collins joined the Brooklyn Nets in the spring of 2014, he became a true trailblazer—the first openly gay male athlete actively playing a major professional sport in the United States. Yet some retired players have noted that they are sure they played with gay teammates over the years. An ESPN story from 2011 quoted the Hall of Famer and basketball analyst Charles Barkley as saying, "First of all, every player has played with gay guys." Barkley said further that any player who denied it was "a stone-freakin' idiot. It bothers me when I hear these reporters and jocks get on TV and say: 'Oh, no guy can come out in a team sport. These guys would go crazy.'. . . I'd rather have a gay guy who can play than a straight guy who can't play" (ESPN.com news services, 2011. Read the full story at: http://sports.espn.go.com/nba/news/story?id=6563128).

In some circumstances and for some people, concealment can be beneficial. In a study of HIV-positive gay men, those who were most concerned about experiencing antigay prejudice (that is, men high in rejection sensitivity) showed a faster rate of disease progression and died sooner than those less sensitive to rejection. However, for those still in the closet about their sexual orientation, being rejection sensitive did not predict the trajectory of the disease. For those who are particularly aware of and worried about how others judge them, concealment can sometimes be a beneficial way to cope (e.g., Cole et al., 1997).

But as Jason Collins's quote reveals, concealment comes with its own costs. Like the African American college students who feel inauthentic in the way they find themselves self-disclosing to their White roommates, those who conceal an important aspect of their identity might struggle with the inability simply to be themselves. Also, keeping who you are under wraps can be hard work. The effort it takes to be vigilant about what you say and how you act and to monitor whether others have figured out your secret can be emotionally and cognitively draining (Frable et al., 1990; Smart & Wegner, 1999). So although concealing a stigma might be one way to sidestep discrimination, it's often not an optimal solution.

Being involuntarily "outed" brings an additional cost: the emotional and social consequences of having one's stigmatized identity revealed to the world. A gay 18-year-old student named Tyler Clementi chose to conceal his sexual orientation when he enrolled at Rutgers University. In 2010, Tyler was publicly outed when his

When Jason Collins joined the Brooklyn Nets in the spring of 2014, he became a true trailblazer—the first openly gay male athlete actively playing a major professional sport in the United States.

[NBAE/Getty Images]

The It Gets Better Project is a campaign to provide gay and lesbian youth with positive role models of gay and lesbian adults who live happy and successful lives, even if they, too, experienced discrimination as adolescents.

[It Gets Better Project]

Rejection identification theory The idea that people can offset the negative consequences of being targeted by discrimination by feeling a strong sense of identification with their stigmatized group.

Modern travel and communication makes it easier for those who are stigmatized to find and connect with others with similar experiences. Bao Xishun (7′9″) and He Pingping (2′4″), met in 2007 when they were the world's tallest and shortest men.

[Chinatopix/Associated Press]

dormitory roommate streamed over the Internet a surreptitiously made video of an intimate encounter Tyler had with another man. The trauma of this unwanted revelation most likely was a major reason that Tyler jumped off the George Washington Bridge to his death three days later (Foderaro, 2010).

Tyler Clementi's suicide is part of a larger epidemic: Gay, lesbian, and bisexual teens are three times more likely to attempt suicide than their straight peers (Meyer, 2003), but these rates decrease as teens move into young adulthood (Russell & Toomey, 2012). Because stigma is a threat to one's very sense of identity, it might not be a coincidence that the negative consequences of prejudice are particularly high during adolescence and young adulthood, when people are still forming an identity (Erikson, 1968). The *It Gets Better* project (www.itgetsbetter.org), started by the columnist and author Dan Savage and his partner, Terry Miller, is an effort to communicate to LGBT teens that the stress of embracing their sexual identity, coming out to others, and experiencing bias will get better for them as they mature.

The Benefits of Group Identification

At the other end of the spectrum from concealment is creating and celebrating a shared identity with others who are similarly stigmatized. It's long been known that people benefit in extraordinary ways from receiving social support from others. Such support can be most helpful when it comes from someone who has "been there" and has gone through the same experience. Earlier we mentioned that those who report encountering frequent or ongoing discrimination show signs of psychological distress. But according to **rejection identification theory**, the negative consequences of being targeted by discrimination can be offset by a strong sense of identification with your stigmatized group (Branscombe et al., 1999; Postmes & Branscombe, 2002).

The old adage that there is safety in numbers applies not only to physical protection but to a less tangible sense of symbolic protection as well. Although pride in one's ethnic identity is likely supported by one's family and social circle, often such support is less readily available for those with stigmatizing identities such as homosexuality, physical deformity, and obesity. In such cases, even parents, siblings, and friends may reject the stigmatizing identity. That is why gay pride and similar movements can be so critical to a feeling of social support.

If there are psychological benefits of banding with similar others to cope with prejudice, it is easier to understand why people often self-segregate into neighborhoods, career choices, and separate areas of the cafeteria. But we also live in a unique time: It is now possible to find similar others online without ever meeting them face to face or even being on the same continent. The opportunity to make social contact is likely to be extremely beneficial for those suffering from rare genetic conditions such as dwarfism (Fernández et al., 2012) or commonly concealed stigmatizing conditions such as mental illness. Modern communications and ease of travel made it possible for the men who were once judged the tallest (Bao Xishun, 7′9″) and the shortest (He Pingping, 2′4″) on earth to meet and share their experiences of being so extremely different from the norm. We still have much more to learn about the value of online social media in helping to build and foster support networks that give a sense of psychological security to those who often are marginalized in their daily lives.

Psychological Strategies for Coping With Prejudice and Discrimination

The social strategies discussed above offer examples of how those who are stigmatized can manage their interpersonal interactions in ways that minimize their experience of bias and discrimination. Because people experience discrimination and bias in society at large as well as in interpersonal interactions, a host of psychological strategies are directed toward helping people remain resilient in the face of social devaluation.

Discounting

As we mentioned earlier, the dilemma of modern-day prejudice is that it can be so subtle. Consider an instance in which a woman is passed over for a promotion in favor of a male colleague. Is that discrimination? Or is she simply less qualified? It's often quite difficult if not impossible to know, a situation that puts those who are targeted by bias in a state of **attributional ambiguity** (Crocker et al., 1991). Crocker and her colleagues point out that the upside of attributing a negative outcome to prejudice is that it allows one to shift blame onto the biases of others and escape the negative feelings that might otherwise result. For example, if the woman in the example can dismiss the boss who rejected her as a sexist bigot, then she can maintain her opinion of herself as competent and intelligent. For instance, in one experiment, when Black college students learned that a White student was not that interested in becoming friends with them, their self-esteem was reduced when they didn't think the other person knew their race but was buffered when they believed their race was known (Crocker et al., 1991).

You might be wondering how perceiving discrimination can sometimes be psychologically beneficial after we outlined all of its negative consequences. First, attributing an isolated incident to prejudice might buffer self-esteem from negative outcomes, but perceiving that discrimination is pervasive can be harmful to well-being (Eliezer et al., 2010; McCoy & Major, 2003; Schmitt et al., 2003). Second, acknowledging that prejudice exists can reduce the shock when it happens to you. In one set of studies, women and minorities who generally believed that the world is fair (compared with those who didn't) showed a higher physiological threat response when they met and interacted with someone who was prejudiced against their group (Townsend et al., 2010).

People can also protect their self-esteem more effectively by claiming discrimination when they can be certain that discrimination did occur (Major et al., 2003). But when people blame themselves for their stigmatizing condition in the first place, they get no comfort from being the target of bias. When overweight female college students learned that a man wasn't interested in meeting them, they felt worse, not better, if they thought their weight played a factor in his evaluation (Crocker et al., 1993). Because society perceives weight as something that can be controlled, these women felt responsible for being rejected.

Devaluing

Another coping strategy that people turn to in dealing with discrimination is to devalue those areas of life where they face pervasive experiences of prejudice and discrimination. If you decide that you really don't care about working on a naval submarine, then you might be relatively unaffected by the U.S. Navy's long-standing ban (not repealed until 2010) on women serving on submarines. By the same token, getting bad grades in school might carry little weight in how you see yourself if academics take a backseat to your social calendar.

When people fail, fear rejection, or are excluded from a domain or type of activity, they can quite easily devalue that domain. This might be part of the reason that women are less likely to pursue advanced degrees in science and engineering. The tendency to devalue those areas where your group doesn't excel seems like a pretty effective strategy for managing bad outcomes. But the whole story is more complicated. It turns out that it is not so easy to devalue those domains in which higher-status groups are more accomplished. For example, on learning that women score higher on a new personality dimension described only by the name *surgency*, men readily devalue this trait as something that is not important to them personally (Schmader et al., 2001). But when women learn that men score higher in surgency, they assume that this trait is at least as valuable as when women possess it. Humans have a basic tendency to look up to those who are better off—to admire their style, covet their possessions, and aspire to take on their traits. This means that even when we repeatedly experience more negative outcomes while trying to advance our status in an area, we can find it difficult to devalue that domain.

Attributional ambiguity
A phenomenon whereby members of stigmatized groups often can be uncertain whether negative experiences are based on their own actions and abilities or are the result of prejudice.

Being socially stigmatized means that you often experience attributional ambiguity when it isn't clear if others treat you badly because of their prejudices or because of something you actually did.

[Getty Images/iStockphoto]

These pressures can leave people with a difficult choice: Continue to strive for success in arenas where they are socially stigmatized because these are the domains that society considers important or call into question the very legitimacy of that society by devaluing those domains (e.g., making the decision to drop out of school). For example, although Black and Latino college students get lower grades on average than their White and Asian peers, they report valuing education at least as much if not more (Major & Schmader, 1998; Schmader et al., 2001). However, those who regard the ethnic hierarchy in the United States as unfair and illegitimate are more likely to call into question the value and utility of getting an education (Schmader et al., 2001). If the deck is stacked against you, you might very well decide to leave the game.

Devaluing one area of life may help mitigate a setback in that area. How do groups cope with the perception that persistent discrimination creates multiple, insurmountable barriers to their success, from inferior schooling to glass-ceiling effects in the workplace? One extreme form of devaluing is to create a group identity that opposes the majority group and its characteristic behaviors, ideas, and practices, in what is labeled an *oppositional culture* (Ogbu & Simons, 1998). For example, ethnic minority students (e.g., African Americans, Mexican Americans, Native Americans) may consider doing well in school or conforming to school rules as "acting White" (Fordham & Ogbu, 1986). When students engage in these "White" behaviors, they may face opposition from their peers and from other members of the minority community. They may respond by identifying with their peers' oppositional culture and consequently devaluing any behavior or goal that seems to represent the majority culture. For example, some Black students may not put their best effort into school-related activities, or they even avoid school altogether. This strategy can increase their sense of belonging in the oppositional culture, but it also can lead them to reject opportunities for self-improvement and economic success simply because they don't want to resemble the majority culture.

One Family's Experience of Religious Prejudice

In this chapter, we are considering the scholarly evidence on how people experience, cope with, and try to deflect discrimination. But for those who are targeted by social biases, personal experience with prejudice can cut very deep. Let's examine prejudice from the perspective of one family's account told as part of the radio program *This American Life* (Spiegel, 2006, 2011).

We begin with a love story in the West Bank in the Middle East. A young Muslim American woman named Serry met and fell in love with a Muslim man from the West Bank. As they got to know one another, he told her how difficult it was for him and everyone he knew to grow up in the middle of the deep religious and political conflict between Israel and the West Bank. So when they decided to marry and make a life together, she convinced him that their children would have

a better life in the United States, a country where she spent a much happier childhood and where people from different religious backgrounds easily formed friendships.

They settled down in the suburbs of New York City, had five children, and became a very typical American family. But when terrorists attacked the World Trade Center and the Pentagon on September 11, 2001, their lives changed forever. Like everyone around them, they were horrified and deeply saddened by what had happened. But their friends, neighbors, and even strangers on the street began to treat them differently. Drivers would give Serry the finger, and someone put a note on her minivan telling her family to leave the country. The situation escalated when their fourth-grade daughter came home from school in tears on the one-year anniversary of 9/11 after the school district presented a lesson for all fourth-graders, explaining that 9/11 happened because Muslims hate Christians and Muslims hate Americans. From that day on, their once-popular daughter became the target of taunting and bullying by other kids. The situation only got worse when her teacher told the class that non-Christians and nonbelievers would burn in hell. Her nine-year-old classmates began calling her "Loser Muslim" after her teacher said

SECTION review | Prejudice From a Target's Perspective

The effects of prejudice can weigh heavily on its targets, but people can take steps to mitigate its consequences.

Perceiving prejudice	The harmful impact of stereotypes	Coping with prejudice
• Because modern prejudice is less overt, it is difficult to know if and when one is the target of prejudice. • People differ in their sensitivity to prejudice, but people commonly underestimate personal discrimination. • People may be motivated to deny discrimination out of optimism or a desire to justify the social system. • Prejudice can take a toll on a person's mental and physical health.	• Holding a stereotype can change how observers interact with targets, sometimes causing targets to act stereotypically. • Targets sometimes inadvertently act stereotypically to get along with others. • Self-objectification—viewing the self as an object to be looked at—can undermine health and performance. • Stereotype threat—the fear of confirming a negative stereotype—can undermine performance. • Social identity threat—the feeling that your group does not belong in a domain—can repel people from that domain.	• Ways to overcome stereotype threat include: identifying with role models, reappraising anxiety as normal, and self-affirmation. • To address or minimize their experience of prejudice in social interactions, stigmatized targets use confrontation, compensation, concealment, and coming together. • To minimize the negative psychological effects of social devaluation, stigmatized targets can discount negative outcomes or devalue domains where they experience discrimination. • These strategies can benefit targets in some situations, but they can also backfire or create new problems.

that she should be transferred to another classroom. Soon her younger siblings were targeted by bullying, too. Eventually even her best friend turned her back on her.

This heart-wrenching story reveals how prejudice can flare up when people feel that their worldview has been threatened. As we discussed in chapter 10, because the events of 9/11 were viewed as an attack on American values by Islamic extremists, the attacks led some Americans to view all Muslims with hate and suspicion—even those with whom they had previously been friendly. But this story also reveals how in one family, different people can respond very differently to others' prejudice.

The oldest daughter's response was to renounce her religion, to try to escape that part of her identity that her peers and her teacher so clearly devalued. When she moved to a new school, she chose to *conceal* her religious background to try to avoid further discrimination.

For Serry, the mother of the family, her religion was deeply important to her but being American was even more central to her identity. She was shocked and saddened to find that she was no longer viewed as an American, but she still believed that American values of freedom would win out in the end. As Serry explained, "I was born and raised in this country, and I'm aware of what makes this country great, and I know that what happened to our family, it doesn't speak to American values. And I feel like this is such a fluke. I have to believe this is not what America is about. I know that." In line with *system justification theory*, her belief in American values led her to minimize these events as aberrations.

But for Serry's husband, his vision of America as a land free of religious prejudice was shattered. Like every immigrant before him in the history of the United States, he had traveled to a new and different culture in the hope of making a better life for himself and his family. Once a very happy man with a quick sense of humor, he slipped into depression and eventually decided to return to the West Bank, where he died a few years later. Not much is said about his death, so it's not known how his experience with anti-Islamic prejudice might have eroded his health. But his choice was to return to his homeland, a place that is far from being free of discrimination from religious intolerance but where at least he could live among others who share the same stigmatized identity. Consistent with *rejection identification theory*, his identification as a Muslim from the West Bank seemed to offer the only source of psychological safety.

The Prejudiced Personality

Before addressing the critical question of how prejudice and stereotyping can be reduced, it's important to acknowledge that some people are more prone to being prejudiced and to employing stereotypes than others. In addition, some people are more resistant to efforts to reduce prejudice than others. Prejudice is and has been common in most if not all known cultures. However, within a culture, there is variability in both which outgroups people dislike and who exhibits these prejudices most strongly.

What accounts for these differences? One answer is that the factors that cause prejudice, which we discussed in chapter 10, vary among individuals. For example, people have different direct experiences with outgroups and are exposed to different kinds of information about them. They also vary in their level of self-esteem and the lessons they learn growing up about how groups differ and what those differences mean. However, theorists have also proposed that there may be a particular kind of person who is especially likely to be prejudiced.

Theodor Adorno was an influential theorist who advanced this perspective in response to the Nazis' rise to power in Germany and the inhumanities committed during the Holocaust. Adorno and his colleagues initially set out to explain the roots of anti-Semitism, but they discovered that individuals who express prejudice toward one group, such as an ethnic minority, also express prejudice toward other groups, such as women and the poor. More important, Adorno and colleagues found that prejudiced individuals share a cluster of personality traits: They uncritically accept authority, prefer well-defined power arrangements in society, adhere to conventional values and moral codes, and tend to think in rigid, black-and-white terms. This cluster of traits is known as the **authoritarian personality** and was originally scored by a measure know as the F scale (Adorno et al., 1950). As we might expect, people who score high on this scale tend to be prejudiced against a wide range of outgroups.

If the authoritarian personality contributes to prejudice in society, it would be useful to understand its origins. Freud (1905/1960) proposed that because of inevitable frustrations, children always develop hostile as well as loving feelings toward their parents. Building on this idea, Adorno and colleagues argued that children raised by overly strict and punitive parents are forced to stifle spontaneous impulses that are considered socially taboo or inappropriate. As a result, they suppress negative feelings of hostility toward their parents, and these feelings linger in the unconscious into adulthood. Adorno and colleagues proposed that when individuals express prejudice, they essentially are displacing these repressed feelings onto those they perceive as different or inferior to themselves and their group. They want to punish those who violate societal norms for what is "right," just as they were punished during childhood for their own "deviance."

Although research following up on the Adorno group's work has provided some refinements in how social psychologists think about and measure the prejudiced personality, most of this research has supported the general tenor of their pioneering work. Research shows, for example, that individuals with a high **need for structured knowledge**—that is, people who in general prefer to think about things in simple, clear-cut ways—tend to stereotype outgroup members more than do individuals who are relatively tolerant of ambiguity and uncertainty (Jamieson & Zanna, 1989; Kruglanski & Webster, 1996; Neuberg & Newsom, 1993). Also, people who experienced difficulties in forming secure attachments with their parents in childhood also have been shown to be particularly likely to express prejudice and hold stereotypes of outgroups (e.g., Shaver & Mikulincer, 2012).

On the basis of Adorno's pioneering work on the authoritarian personality, researchers have developed two modern measures of general proneness to prejudice: **right-wing authoritarianism** (RWA) (Altemeyer, 1981, 1998) and **social dominance orientation** (SDO), which was mentioned earlier in chapter 9 (Pratto et al., 1994; Sidanius & Pratto, 1999). Let's take a closer look at each.

Authoritarian personality
A complex of personality traits, including uncritical acceptance of authority, preference for well-defined power arrangements in society, adherence to conventional values and moral codes, and black-and-white thinking. Predicts prejudice toward outgroups in general.

Need for structured knowledge A personality trait defined as a general preference for thinking about things in simple, clear-cut ways.

Individuals high in RWA believe that the social world is inherently dangerous and unpredictable, and that the best way to maintain a sense of security in both their personal and social lives is to preserve society's order, cohesion, and tradition. More specifically, these individuals tend to display three factors:

Authoritarian submission, the tendency to submit to and comply with those they consider legitimate authority figures. For example, they strongly agree with the statement "Obedience and respect for authority are the most important virtues children should learn."

Conventionalism, conformity to traditional moral and religious norms and values. They feel that "The 'old-fashioned ways' and 'old-fashioned values' still show the best way to live."

Authoritarian aggression, the desire to punish individuals or groups that authorities label wrongdoers. They're likely to believe that "Once our government leaders and the authorities condemn the dangerous elements in our society, it will be the duty of every patriotic citizen to help stomp out the rot that is poisoning our country from within."

Because individuals high in RWA are concerned with maintaining an ordered society, they are particularly likely to express prejudice against individuals and groups seen as dangerous and thus threatening that order, such as violent criminals, as well as those who violate traditional values, such as feminists, gays, and lesbians.

Individuals high in SDO hold the belief that the world is a ruthlessly competitive jungle in which it is appropriate and right for powerful groups to dominate weaker ones. They believe that society should be structured hierarchically, with some groups having higher social and economic status than others. Hence, they agree with statements such as "Some groups of people are simply inferior to other groups." In addition to believing in a dog-eat-dog worldview, high-SDO individuals are motivated to maintain and justify their own group's power, dominance, and superiority over others. They therefore agree with statements such as "Sometimes other groups must be kept in their place." High-SDO individuals are prejudiced against groups they regard as threatening the existing group hierarchy in society, as well as lower-status groups they perceive as inferior within that hierarchy, such as physically handicapped people, unemployment beneficiaries, and homemakers (**FIGURE 11.4**).

For both high-RWA individuals and high-SDO individuals, prejudice is a response to groups that they regard as threatening cherished belief systems. Note, though, that these two types of people adhere to different sets of values and goals and therefore are likely to differ about which groups they find threatening (Duckitt, 2001). Indeed, the presence of RWA and SDO predict prejudice against

Right-wing authoritarianism (RWA) An ideology which holds that the social world is inherently dangerous and unpredictable and that maintaining security in life requires upholding society's order, cohesion, and tradition. Predicts prejudice against groups seen as socially deviant or dangerous.

Social dominance orientation (SDO) An ideology in which the world is viewed as a ruthlessly competitive jungle where it is appropriate and right for powerful groups to dominate weaker ones.

Figure 11.4

Social Dominance Orientation

These items are used to measure social dominance orientation. How would you rate your attitude toward each of them?

[Data source: Pratto et al. (1994)]

Items on the social dominance orientation scale

1. Some groups of people are simply not the equals of others.
2. Some people are just more worthy than others.
3. This country would be better off if we cared less about how equal all people were.
4. Some people are just more deserving than others.
5. It is not a problem if some people have more of a chance in life than others.
6. Some people are just inferior to others.
7. To get ahead in life, it is sometimes necessary to step on others.
8. Increased economic equality.
9. Increased social equality.
10. Equality.
11. If people were treated more equally we would have fewer problems in this country.
12. In an ideal world, all nations would be equal.
13. We should try to treat one another as equals as much as possible. (All humans should be treated equally.)
14. It is important that we treat other countries as equals.

All items are measured on a *very negative* (1) to *very positive* (7) scale. Responses to 8–14 are reverse-coded before being averaged so that higher numbers on that averaged composite imply higher levels of social dominance orientation.

specific groups. For example, RWA but not SDO predicts dislike of socially deviant groups that threaten traditional norms and values but that are not lower in the socioeconomic hierarchy, such as drug dealers and rock stars. SDO predicts dislike of disadvantaged groups, such as people who are unattractive, mentally handicapped, or obese, whereas RWA does not because high-RWA individuals are not likely to consider those groups socially deviant or dangerous (Duckitt, 2006; Duckitt & Sibley, 2007).

Although RWA and SDO predict commitment to distinct belief systems and predict dislike of different outgroups, within the United States, both variables are correlated with political conservatism (Jost et al., 2003). This does not mean that all conservatives are prejudiced or that all prejudiced people are conservatives, but it does suggest that there is a statistical tendency for measures of political conservatism, RWA, SDO, and generalized prejudice against outgroups all to correlate positively with each other (e.g., Cunningham et al., 2004).

SECTION review | The Prejudiced Personality

Building on the pioneering work of Theodor Adorno on the authoritarian personality, researchers have developed two useful measures of proneness to prejudice.

Right-wing authoritarianism	Social dominance orientation
High-RWA individuals:	High-SDO individuals:
• view the social world as dangerous.	• are competitively driven to maintain the dominance of some groups over others.
• are motivated to maintain collective security (societal order, cohesion, stability, tradition).	• are therefore prejudiced against groups that they perceive as lower in society's status hierarchy.
• are prejudiced against groups that threaten to disrupt collective security because they appear dangerous or deviant.	

Reducing Prejudice

Reducing prejudice essentially entails changing the values and beliefs by which people live. This is tricky for a number of reasons. One is that people's values and beliefs are often a long-standing basis of their psychological security. Another is that prejudice often serves specific psychological functions for people, such as allowing them to displace their hostile feelings or buttress their shaky self-esteem. A third difficulty arises because, once established, prejudiced views and stereotypes constitute schemas, and like other schemas, they tend to bias perceptions, attributions, and memories in ways that are self-perpetuating. Finally, people sometimes are not even aware of their prejudices and their influence. All of these factors make prejudice difficult to combat.

However, although there is no one-size-fits-all solution, a number of encouraging approaches are available. We will start from the top, so to speak, and examine how reducing prejudice can proceed from change at the societal or institutional level. Given that the effectiveness of such institutional change sometimes hinges on people controlling their expressions of prejudice, we will turn next to whether and when we are able to effectively do so. We will then discuss how we can go beyond controlling the expression of prejudice to actually change people's prejudiced attitudes and ease intergroup conflict.

Working From the Top Down: Changing the Culture

Remember that prejudice exists within a cultural context, legitimized (albeit subtly at times) by the laws, customs, and norms that form the fabric of the society in which people live. Thus, one of the great challenges in reducing prejudice lies in changing these laws, customs, and norms. Often such change is made by individuals within a society, but sometimes the institutional structure can help to guide people toward this goal.

For example, when the Supreme Court's 1954 decision in *Brown v. Board of Education* declared public-school segregation unconstitutional, the United States imposed a legal backbone behind reducing prejudice. Particularly in those areas of the country where this mandate was communicated with an air of inevitability, rather than as an imposition that people would avoid if they could, desegregation fostered integration and reduced prejudice (Pettigrew, 1961). As we discussed in chapter 6, a change in behavior (in this case, by law) often can lead to a change in attitude. Remember that people strive for consistency between the two. As cognitive dissonance theory teaches us, once behavior changes (e.g., more interaction with and civil behavior toward outgroups), relevant attitudes tend to fall in line (e.g., more tolerant attitudes toward outgroups).

In addition to changing the intergroup atmosphere, institutional changes can have long-term consequences for the majority group's perceptions of the disadvantaged group. The rationale behind desegregation was that separate schools for White and Black students were inherently unequal (see **FIGURE 11.5**). So what happens when the educational structure becomes (more) equal? As minorities are afforded greater opportunities, the diversity of people who emerge as success stories in our society also increases. The more such *counterstereotypic* narratives pervade the cultural landscape, the more people are exposed to examples of real people who break down preconceived ideas about certain groups. Affirmative action and improved educational and economic success for minority groups thus help to change associations and stereotypes of disadvantaged groups (Allport, 1954). The less a group is associated with poorer neighborhoods and jobs, lower academic performance, increased crime, and the like, the better. Remember the finding we noted in chapter 10 about the effect of President Obama's success: When President Obama is the example that people bring to mind when thinking of Black people, they are less likely to be prejudiced (Columb & Plant, 2011; Plant et al., 2009).

Recognizing this cycle of group images and prejudice, we see how powerfully the mass media affect how majority group members perceive minority group members. *The Jeffersons* in the 1970s and 1980s, *Murphy Brown* in the early 1990s, and *Glee* in 2010 were important in bringing into mainstream awareness the issues faced by African American families, single working moms, and gay teenagers. And research confirms that the more people are exposed to counterstereotypic fictional examples of minority groups (in *The Jeffersons*, for example, an upwardly mobile Black family), the less they show automatic activation of stereotyped associations (Blair et al., 2001; Dasgupta & Greenwald, 2001). In fact, an ambitious field experiment in Rwanda exposed people to one of two radio shows over the course of a year, either a soap opera with health messages or a soap opera with themes about reducing intergroup prejudice (Paluck, 2009). Those exposed to the show with themes about reducing prejudice showed more positive attitudes about and behavior toward interracial marriage.

Figure 11.5

Brown v. Board of Education

With their historic decision in *Brown v. Board of Education*, the Supreme Court ruled that racially segregated schools were unconstitutional.

[Kansas State Historical Society]

The popular television show *Scandal* features an intelligent, high-status African American woman as the lead character. Research suggests that counterstereotypic images in media can be very effective means of changing stereotypes.

[Shondaland/The Kobal Collection]

Connecting Across a Divide: Controlling Prejudice in Intergroup Interactions

Think

ABOUT

[Getty Images/Fuse]

Society's changing laws and less stereotypic popular portrayals of groups place responsibility on individuals within that society to control their biased attitudes and beliefs. Indeed, research finds that people are less likely to express their prejudice publicly if they believe that people in general will disapprove of such biases (Crandall et al., 2002). As students were faced with the reality of desegregation during the 1960s and 1970s, they were also faced with the reality of needing to control, at least to some extent, their prejudicial biases and stereotypic assumptions about outgroups. **To bring it closer to home, imagine that on your first day at college you move into your dorm room and meet your roommate. He is of a different race than you are, and cultural norms and your own internal attitudes say that you should not be prejudiced. But you worry that underlying uneasiness may creep into your interactions. Will you be able to set aside any prejudices you might have and avoid stereotyping?**

A Dual Process View of Prejudice

The issue of controlling prejudice takes us back to the *dual process* approach (Devine, 1989; Fazio, 1990), first introduced in chapter 3. In Process 1, stereotypes and biased attitudes are brought to mind quickly and automatically (through a *reflexive* or *experiential process*). In Process 2, people employ *reflective* or *cognitive processes* to regulate or control the degree to which those thoughts and attitudes affect their behavior and judgment.

Because prejudicial thoughts are often reinforced by a long history of socialization and cues in one's environment, they can come to mind easily and be difficult to tamp down. The success of Process 2 depends on people's motivations for controlling their thoughts. When a motivation to avoid being biased stems from an internalized goal of being nonprejudiced, people can often keep implicit biases from influencing their decisions and judgment. In many cases, though, the motivation to control prejudice stems from the perception of external pressures, such as the pressure to be politically correct or to avoid making others angry (Plant & Devine, 1998, 2009). In these cases, people may be able to control their biases, but they end up being resentful about having to censor themselves (Plant & Devine, 2001).

Given the negative consequences of extrinsically motivated efforts to suppress prejudice, how is it possible to increase people's intrinsic motivation to control prejudice? One way is to impress on them the necessity of cooperating with those with whom they are working. When people realize they need to cooperate with an outgroup person, they can be motivated to be nonbiased in their interactions with the outgroup and even show improved memory for the unique or individual aspects of that person (Neuberg & Fiske, 1987). At some level people realize that falling back on stereotypes to form impressions might not provide the most accurate assessment of another person's character and abilities. The need to work together on a common goal helps to cue this motivation to be accurate and allows people to set their biases aside.

More recent research has uncovered the neurological mechanisms that support these two processes (Lieberman et al., 2002). Bartholow and colleagues (2006) have examined specific electrical signals emitted from the brain that are indicative of efforts at cognitive control. They found that when White participants are presented with pictures of Black targets, the more of these signals that their brains emit, the lower the accessibility of stereotypic thoughts. However, this occurred only when people's cognitive-control abilities were intact. When they were impaired through the consumption of alcohol, fewer of these specific signals were emitted, and participants were less able to control their tendency to stereotype others.

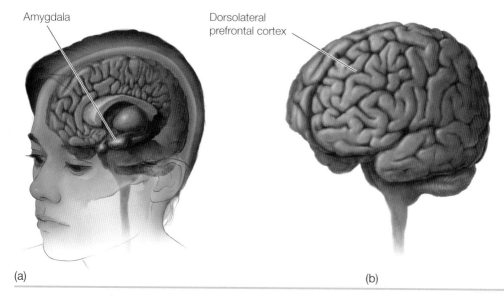

Amygdala

Dorsolateral
prefrontal cortex

(a)

(b)

Figure 11.6

Downregulating Prejudice

Social neuroscience research suggests that the immediate amygdala responses (a) that Whites sometimes exhibit to Black faces can be downregulated by the dorsolateral prefrontal cortex (DLPFC) (b).

Taking a neuroscience perspective, research shows that when White participants were exposed very briefly (for only 30 milliseconds) to pictures of Black faces, they showed increased activation in the amygdala (the fear center of the brain) to the degree that they associated "Black American" with "bad" on an implicit association test (**FIGURE 11.6**) (Cunningham et al., 2004; Phelps et al., 2000). With such a brief exposure, people can do little to override knee-jerk reactions. What is interesting is that lengthening exposure to the faces to 250 milliseconds increased activation in the dorsolateral prefrontal cortex (DLPFC), the region of the brain responsible for more effortful and controlled processes of judgment and decision making. Furthermore, the more DLPFC activation people experienced, the lower the amygdala activation they exhibited. These findings suggest that automatic negative attitudes that might have sprung to mind initially can be modified by more controlled processes (Cunningham et al., 2004).

Prejudice Isn't Always Easily Controlled

All of this research sounds pretty encouraging, but marshalling resources for mental control takes effort and energy. As a result, people face a few limitations when they attempt to control their biases.

The first limitation is that sometimes people make judgments of others when they are already aroused or upset. In these situations, cognitive control is impaired, so people likely will fall back on their prejudices and stereotypes. Consider, for example, a study in which White participants were asked to deliver shocks (that were not actually administered) to a White or Black confederate under the pretext of a behavior-modification study (Rogers & Prentice-Dunn, 1981). Half the White participants were angry about an overheard insult directed toward them by the confederate. When not angered, the White participants actually chose a less severe shock for the Black confederate than they did for the White confederate. However, after the White participants were angered, they shocked the Black confederate more strongly than his White counterpart. The arousal and negative emotion caused the participants to regress to gut-level negative attitudes.

People also can have difficulty with regulating their automatically activated thoughts when they are pressed for time, distracted, or otherwise cognitively busy. Teachers are more likely to be biased in their evaluations of students if they have to grade essays under time pressure. If instead they have ample time to make their judgments, they are better able to set aside their biases to provide fairer assessments of students' work (Kruglanski & Freund, 1983). People are also more capable of setting aside biases when they are most cognitively alert. This fact leads to the provocative idea that a tendency to stereotype might be affected by circadian rhythms, the individual differences in daily cycles of mental alertness which make some people rise bright and early and make others night owls. In a study of how circadian rhythms can affect jury decision making, Bodenhausen (1990) recruited participants to play the roles of jurors in an ambiguous case where the offense either was or was not stereotypical of the defendant's group (such as a student athlete accused of cheating on an exam). Did participants allow their stereotypes of the defendant to sway their verdicts? Not if they were participating in the study during their optimal time of day. But if morning people were participating in the evening or evening people were participating early in the morning, their verdicts were strongly colored by stereotypes.

The Downsides of Control Strategies

Even when people succeed in controlling their biases, some downstream consequences of these efforts can be negative. First, you might recall from our discussion of ego depletion in chapter 5 (Muraven et al., 1998) that exerting mental effort in one context makes it harder to exert effort afterward in another context. For example, when White college students had any kind of conversation with a Black peer, regardless of whether the conversation was even about race, they performed more poorly on a demanding computer task right afterward than when they had this conversation with another White student (Richeson et al., 2003; Richeson & Shelton, 2003; Richeson & Trawalter, 2005). In addition, trying to push an unwanted thought out of mind often has the ironic effect of activating that thought even more. As a result, the more people try not to think of a stereotypic bias, the more it can eventually creep back in, especially when cognitive resources are limited (Follenfant & Ric, 2010; Gordijn et al., 2004; Macrae et al., 1994).

Failure of control strategies can happen even when it seems that one has gotten past initial stereotypes to appreciate the outgroup person's individual qualities. In one study, participants who watched a video of a stigmatized student talking showed stereotype activation within the first 15 seconds, but after 12 minutes the stereotype was no longer active or guiding judgment (Kunda et al., 2002). This might seem to be good news, but not so fast. If participants later learned that the person in the video disagreed with them, the stereotype was reactivated. The implication is that, in our own interactions, we might often succeed in getting past initial stereotypes, but those stereotypes still might lurk just offstage, waiting to make an appearance if the situation prompts negative or threatening feelings toward that person.

We've seen that conscious efforts to control prejudice, although well intentioned, can fail or backfire completely. The implication is that reducing prejudice requires more than employing strategies to control prejudice; it also requires going to the source and changing people's prejudicial attitudes. How do we do this?

Setting the Stage for Positive Change: The Contact Hypothesis

One strategy that seems to be an intuitive way to foster more positive intergroup attitudes is to encourage people actually to interact with those who are the targets of their prejudice. In the late 1940s and the 1950s, as American society started to break down barriers of racial segregation, some interesting effects on racial prejudice were observed. For example, the more White and Black merchant marines served together in racially mixed crews, the more positive their racial attitudes became (Brophy, 1946). Such observations suggest that if people of different groups interact, prejudice should be reduced. There is certainly some truth to this. Research on the mere exposure effect (see chapters 8 and 14) shows that familiarity does increase liking, all other things being equal.

The problem with this strategy is that only rarely are all other things equal! If you look around the world and back in history, you quickly notice countless examples of people of different groups having extensive contact—yet their prejudices remain and even intensify. For example, in the American South there has long been considerable contact between Blacks and Whites, but this contact historically did not lead to decreases in prejudice (Pettigrew, 1959). Why did interracial contact in the merchant marines reduce prejudice, whereas other forms of contact do not?

In considering such questions, Allport (1954) proposed that contact between groups can reduce prejudice only if it occurs under optimal conditions. According to Allport's original recipe, four principal ingredients are necessary for positive intergroup contact:

1. *Equal status* between groups in the situation.
2. Contact that is intimate and varied, allowing people to get *acquainted*.
3. Contact involving intergroup cooperation toward a **superordinate goal**, that is, a goal that is beyond the ability of any one group to achieve on its own.
4. *Institutional support*, or contact that is approved by authority, law, or custom.

Superordinate goal A common problem or shared goal that groups work together to solve or achieve.

In the time since Allport laid out this recipe for reducing prejudice, hundreds of studies with thousands of participants have examined whether intergroup contact that meets these requirements can reduce prejudices based on such distinctions as race and ethnicity, sexual orientation, age, and physical and mental disabilities. These studies range from archival studies of historical situations to controlled interventions that manipulate features of the contact setting. Despite the diversity of methodologies, research generally finds that the more closely the contact meets Allport's requirements, the more effectively it reduces a majority group's prejudice against minorities (Pettigrew & Tropp, 2006; Tropp & Pettigrew, 2005).

To explore one of these ingredients for change in a bit more detail, let's explore a classic study by Sherif and colleagues (Harvey et al., 1961) that dramatically demonstrates the power of superordinate goals to reduce prejudice. In a unique study, Sherif and colleagues invited 22 psychologically healthy boys to participate in a summer camp in Oklahoma. Because the camp was at the former hideout of the noted Old West outlaw Jesse James, this study has come be known as the Robbers Cave study. As the boys arrived at the camp, Sherif assigned them to one of two groups, the "Rattlers" or the "Eagles." During the first week, the groups were kept separate, but as soon as they learned of each other's existence, the seeds of prejudice toward the other group began to grow (thus showing how mere categorization can breed prejudice).

During the second week, Sherif set up a series of competitive tasks between the groups. As realistic group conflict theory would predict, this competition quickly generated remarkable hostility, prejudice, and even violence between the groups as they competed for scarce prizes. In the span of a few days, the groups were stealing from each other, using derogatory labels to refer to each other (calling the rival group sissies, communists, and stinkers; the study was conducted during the 1950s!), and getting into fistfights. Was all lost at the Robbers Cave?

Prejudice Video on LaunchPad

In the Robbers Cave study, two groups of boys competing against each other at summer camp spontaneously developed prejudices against each other.

It certainly appeared that way until, during the third week, Sherif introduced different types of challenges. In one of these challenges, he sabotaged the camp's water supply by clogging the faucet of the main water tank. The camp counselors announced that there was in fact a leak and that to find the leak *all* 22 boys would need to search the pipes running from the reservoir to the camp. Thus, the campers were faced with a common goal that required their cooperation. As the Eagles and Rattlers collaborated on this and other such challenges, their hostilities disintegrated. They were no longer two groups warring with each other, but rather one united group working together. Successfully achieving common goals effectively reduced their prejudice.

Another way of looking at these challenges is that the Rattlers and Eagles faced a *shared threat*. In the example described above, it was the shared threat of going without water. Can you think of a historical example that led to a similarly cooperative spirit, only on a much grander scale? Many observers have suggested that the events of September 11, 2001, had a similar impact in reducing some types of intergroup biases in America. During and after this tragedy, the American people were confronted with the shared threat of terrorism at the hands of Osama bin Laden and al Qaeda. How did they react? In a rousing display of patriotism and goodwill, they united. Previous divisions among groups of people were set aside—at least for a time.

Research backs up the potential of shared threats to dismantle prejudices that otherwise would occur. For example, in one study testing whether people's psychological insecurity can lead to prejudice, American participants either did or did not reflect on their mortality and then evaluated an Arab student (Pyszczynski et al., 2012). As you know from our discussions of terror management theory, thinking about death tends to increase prejudice as people cling to their own group identifications. And indeed, that occurred in this study as well. However, some of the participants were first asked to think about the worldwide implications of global warming, an environmental threat that all people face. Thinking about this shared threat reduced the effect on anti-Arab prejudice of death reminders. As the researchers noted, this suggests that there may be a sunny side to global warming. As people think about the fate they share with others, this sense of common humanity can help to reduce prejudice.

The movie *Independence Day* illustrates how prejudices between racial and ethnic groups can disintegrate when members of these groups are confronted by a common threat—in this case, the threat of global annihilation by hostile extraterrestrials.

[20th Century Fox/The Kobal Collection /Barius, Claudette]

Why Does Optimal Contact Work?

Although the Robbers Cave experiment is usually described as an example of how superordinate goals can help break down intergroup biases, Allport's other key ingredients for optimal contact were present as well: The boys had equal status, the cooperative activities were sanctioned by the camp counselors, and there were plenty of activities where the boys could get to know one another. But knowing that these factors reduce prejudice doesn't tell us much about why. Other research has isolated a few key mechanisms by which optimal contact creates positive change:

> *Reducing stereotyping.* Consider that one of the most effective forms of contact involves members of different groups exchanging intimate knowledge about each other. This allows the once-different other to be *decategorized*. As a result, people are less likely to stereotype members of the outgroup (Kawakami et al., 2000).
>
> *Reducing anxiety.* Optimal contact also reduces anxiety that people may have about interacting with people who are different from themselves (Stephan & Stephan, 1985). The unfamiliar can be unsettling, so by enhancing familiarity and reducing anxiety, contact helps to reduce prejudice.
>
> *Fostering empathy.* Finally, optimal contact can lead someone to adopt the other person's perspective and increase feelings of empathy. This helps people to look past group differences to see what they have in common with others.

When Do the Effects of Contact Generalize Beyond the Individual?

An important question is, does contact reduce only prejudice toward that individual whom you get to know? Or do these effects generalize to that person's group? If Frank develops a friendship with a Muslim roommate, Ahmed, during a stay at summer camp, will this contact generalize and reduce Frank's prejudice against other Muslims when he goes back to school? Here, too, the answer is not a simple yes or no. Rather, it depends on a sequence of stages that play out over time (**FIGURE 11.7**) (Pettigrew, 1998; Pettigrew & Tropp, 2006).

In an initial stage, as two people become friends, their sense of group boundaries melts away. Perhaps you have had this experience of talking to another person and simply forgetting that he or she is from a different group. This is decategorization at work. When sharing their love of music, Frank and Ahmed are not Christian and Muslim, they are simply two roommates and friends. Their liking for each other replaces any initial anxiety they might have felt about interacting with a member of another group.

But if Frank is to generalize his positive impression of Ahmed to other Muslims, and if Ahmed is to generalize his positive impression of Frank to other Christians, those different social categories must again become salient during a second stage, after contact has been established (Brown & Hewstone, 2005). Also, Frank's overall impression of Muslims is more likely to change if he regards Ahmed as representative of the outgroup as a whole (Brown et al., 1999). If Frank views Ahmed as quite unlike other Muslims, then his positive feelings toward his new friend might never contribute to his broader view of Muslims. But if the category differences between them become salient and each considers the other to be representative of his religious group, then both Frank and Ahmed will develop more positive attitudes toward the respective religious outgroup more broadly.

You might be noticing a few rubs here. Effective contact seems to require getting to know an outgroup member as an individual, but this process of decategorization can prevent people from seeing that person as also being a representative of their group. There is a tension between focusing on people's individual characteristics and recognizing the unique vantage point of their group or cultural background. But understanding others' group identities is a key step in reducing prejudice against the group as a whole. This might be part of the reason that members of minority groups often prefer an ideology of *multiculturalism*, which endorses seeing the value of different cultural identities, over an ideology of being *colorblind*, whereby people simply pretend that group membership doesn't exist or doesn't matter (Plaut et al., 2009).

Another potential pitfall is that although this second stage of established contact might reduce intergroup prejudice, there is no guarantee that it will promote intergroup cooperation. For this reason, researchers have suggested that a stage of recategorizing outgroups into a unified group, or **common ingroup identity**, will further reduce prejudice

Common ingroup identity
A recategorizing of members of two or more distinct groups into a single, overarching group.

STAGE 1
Initial contact
Decategorization
Initial anxiety, but can lead to liking of the individual

STAGE 2
Established contact
Salient categorization
Can lessen prejudice against the outgroup

STAGE 3
Common ingroup identity
Recategorization
Maximum reduction in prejudice and fosters cooperation

Time

Figure 11.7

Stages for Intergroup Contact

Positive contact with an individual from an outgroup is most likely to generalize to the outgroup as a whole when group categorization processes are initially reduced but then reintroduced over time.

[Data source: Pettigrew (1998). Photo: mediaphotos/Getty Images]

by harnessing the biases people have in favor of their ingroups (Gaertner & Dovidio, 2000). If Frank and Ahmed see each other and other members of their respective religious groups as all part of the same camp or the same nation, then they are all in the same overarching ingroup. Perhaps this is the final dash of spice needed in the recipe of contact that will not only end intergroup prejudices but also lead to peace and cooperation.

Is this vision just pie in the sky? There are hopeful signs that having a common ingroup identity can effectively reduce some manifestations of prejudice. A few years ago a school district in Delaware instituted the Green Circle program for elementary school students. Over the course of a month, first and second graders in this program participated in exercises that encouraged them to think of their social world—which they designated their "green circle"—as getting bigger and bigger to underscore the idea that all people belong to one family, the human family. Students who participated in the program were more likely later to want to share and play with other children who were of different genders, weights, and races than students in the same school who had not yet gone through the program (Houlette et al., 2004). Studies suggest that adults also can become less prejudiced and more tolerant when the common humanity among members of different groups is made salient (Motyl et al., 2011).

Although these findings are surely encouraging, Allport (1954) was skeptical about how well people can keep salient the superordinate identity of human, as opposed to more circumscribed national, regional, and family identities. For example, some theorists suggest that we are most likely to identify with groups that provide *optimal distinctiveness* (Brewer, 1991). Such groups are large enough to foster a sense of commonality, while small enough to allow us to feel distinct from others. Geographical differences mean different languages, customs, arts, values, styles of living—all useful ways to define what feels like a shared but unique identity. Keeping salient the more abstract identity we all share is no easy chore, but superordinate goals and concerns can help. In real and ongoing interactions, even good friends from different groups probably cycle back and forth between these different identities, depending on the context.

Does Contact Increase Positive Attitudes?

It should be noted that our discussion so far has focused largely on how contact can help the majority group member foster positive intergroup attitudes toward the minority group member and his or her group. What about the other side of the coin? Does optimal contact also improve intergroup attitudes for the minority group member, such as the African American woman or the gay man put into contact with members of the majority group? A small body of research on this question shows that contact is more of a mixed bag for those in the minority (Tropp & Pettigrew, 2005). Contact situations often are framed from the perspective of reducing biases held by a majority group. The risk is that minority-group members can feel stripped of an important minority identity. Furthermore, when minority-group individuals are exposed to prejudice against their group, which is more likely to occur in the initial stages of contact, this prejudice can intensify their negative attitudes toward the majority group (Tropp, 2003). Contact situations might need to be designed specifically to reduce minority-group members' own biases against the majority.

APPLICATION

Implementing Optimal Contact in a Jigsaw Classroom

Although each of Allport's conditions can improve racial attitudes (at least among the majority group), the best recipe for success is to combine all the ingredients in the contact setting (Pettigrew & Tropp, 2006). Because the desegregation of schools seldom included all of these components for effective contact, initial evaluations of school desegregation found little success in reducing prejudice and intergroup conflict (Stephan, 1978). For example, school settings tend to emphasize competition rather than cooperation; authority figures are often mainly from the majority group

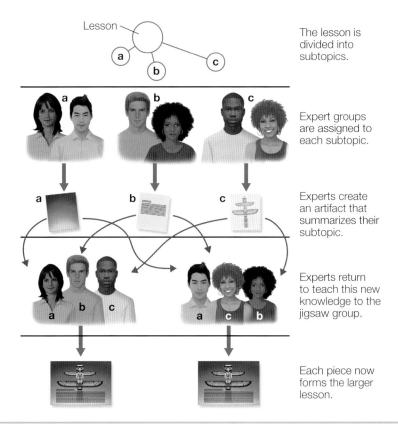

Lesson

The lesson is divided into subtopics.

Expert groups are assigned to each subtopic.

Experts create an artifact that summarizes their subtopic.

Experts return to teach this new knowledge to the jigsaw group.

Each piece now forms the larger lesson.

Figure 11.8

Jigsaw Classroom

In a jigsaw classroom assignment, a lesson is divided into different subtopics, and students in diverse groups are given the assignment of mastering one subtopic. These expert groups work together to create an artifact (e.g., a joint summary or poster). Then members of each expert group return to teach their newfound knowledge to the jigsaw group, where each member has now learned a piece that makes up the larger lesson. By giving every student equal status and encouraging cooperation toward a common goal, the jigsaw classroom is an effective way to reduce prejudice.

so that the minority students don't feel they have equal status; and ethnic groups often segregate within the school, minimizing the opportunity for intimate contact and cooperation.

How can schools do better? Consider a cooperative learning technique developed by Elliott Aronson and colleagues called the *jigsaw classroom* (**FIGURE 11.8**) (Aronson et al., 1978). In this approach, the teacher creates a lesson that can be broken down into several subtopics. For example, if the topic is the presidency of the United States, the subtopics might include influential presidents, how the executive branch relates to other branches of the government, how the president is elected, and so on. The class is also subdivided into racially mixed groups where one person in each group is given the responsibility of learning one of the subtopics of the lesson. This student meets with other students from other groups assigned to that subtopic so that they can all review, study, and become an expert in that topic, creating some kind of artifact such as a poster or a presentation to summarize their newly gained knowledge. The experts then return to their original group and take turns teaching the others what they have learned.

The power of this approach is its potential for embodying all of Allport's conditions for optimal contact. First, because the task is assigned by the teacher, it is authority sanctioned. Second, because each student is in charge of his or her own subtopic, all the kids become experts, and thus have equal status. Third, the group is graded both individually (recall our discussion from chapter 9 on accountability and social loafing) and as a group. Thus, the students share a common goal. And fourth, to do well and reach that common goal, they must cooperate in intimate and varied ways, both teaching and learning from each other. All the pieces must fit together, like the pieces in a jigsaw puzzle.

The jigsaw classroom program is generally successful, so much so that one wonders why it is not implemented more widely. One reason is that some topics in school may not lend themselves to this kind of learning approach, but still, a lot do. Compared with children in traditional classrooms, children who go through the program show increased self-esteem, intrinsic motivation for learning and, most crucial, increased peer liking across racial and ethnic groups (Blaney et al., 1977; Hänze & Berger, 2007; Slavin, 2012).

Reducing Prejudice Without Contact

As we've just seen, Allport provided us with an excellent playbook for reducing intergroup prejudices through positive and cooperative contact. But sometimes people hold prejudices about groups with which they never interact. When the opportunities for contact are infrequent, can other psychological strategies reduce intergroup biases? The answer is yes.

Perspective Taking and Empathy

Earlier, we mentioned that one of the reasons optimal contact can be so effective is that it creates opportunities to take the perspective of members of the other group

In the aftermath of the assassination of Dr. Martin Luther King, Jr., Jane Elliott taught her third-grade class about prejudice by having them feel what it is like to be targeted by negative stereotypes.

[Courtesy of Jane Elliott]

and see the world through their eyes. Direct contact isn't the only way for people to learn this lesson. To see why, let's go back in time to 1968, just a few days after Dr. Martin Luther King, Jr. was assassinated. Jane Elliott, a third-grade teacher in Riceville Iowa, was watching the news of this tragedy and dreamed up a remarkable classroom exercise to teach her all-White class of children about the injustice of racial prejudice (Peters, 1987).

Over the next couple of days, she divided the class into two groups, those that had brown eyes and those that had blue eyes. She spent one day defining one group as the privileged and the other as the downtrodden. These designations were reflected in her actions and demeanor to the class, telling them, for example, that brown-eyed individuals are special and careful, whereas blue-eyed individuals are lazy and forgetful.

What Elliott observed from this and subsequent implementations of the exercise was a remarkable, and apparently enduring, sensitivity to prejudice. Her students became acutely aware of the harmful effects that their own prejudices could have (see Peters & Cobb, 1985). It is powerful stuff, and we encourage you to search the Internet (Google or YouTube "Jane Elliott" plus "A Class Divided") to check out some video clips. In having her third graders spend a day being stigmatized for the color of their eyes, Jane Elliott implemented an impressive exercise in perspective taking.

Perspective taking is a powerful tool for reducing prejudice, because it increases empathy for the target's situation and creates a sense of connection between oneself and an outgroup. This strategy reduces prejudice against a single individual, and those positive feelings are often likely to generalize to other members of the outgroup (Dovidio et al., 2004; Galinsky & Moskowitz, 2000; Vescio et al., 2003; Vorauer & Sasaki, 2009). For example, in one study, participants who were asked to imagine vividly the experiences of a young woman who had been diagnosed with AIDS (as opposed to taking a more objective viewpoint toward her plight) felt more empathy for AIDS victims in general as well as for her (Batson et al., 1997).

The success of perspective taking is impressive. It seems to work not only for more explicit types of prejudice but also for the more implicit and subtle forms of bias we described earlier. For example, imagine that you are White and that you are asked to write about a day in the life of a young Black man (Todd et al., 2011). If you were in the perspective-taking condition, you would be told to visualize what the young man might be thinking and feeling as he went about his day. If you were in the control condition, you would be told to take a more objective approach to writing about his day. After doing your respective assignment as well as some other unrelated surveys, you are led to a different room and asked to grab two chairs from a stack and set them up for a mock-interview task between you and an assistant named either "Jake," a typical White name, or "Tyrone," a typical Black name.

Unknown to you, and to the participants who actually were in this study, the researchers measured the distance between the two chairs as an implicit measure of prejudice. They reasoned that if people had a more positive attitude toward the interviewer, they would set the chairs closer together. As you can see in **FIGURE 11.9**, participants in the control condition elected to sit farther away from Tyrone than from Jake. But if they first had to take the perspective of another young Black man during the earlier task, they sat at the same distance from the assistant regardless of his race. When we think about what it's like to walk a day in the life of someone else, our biases are often diminished. In fact, in one very clever study conducted in Barcelona, Spain, researchers used virtual reality to have light-skinned female participants see and feel what it would look like to walk around with darker skin. Participants who spent about 20 minutes inhabiting a virtual body with darker skin subsequently exhibited a weaker implicit negative attitude toward Blacks on an IAT than did participants who had a light-skinned virtual body, those who had an alien-looking, purple-skinned virtual body, or those who did not have a virtual body and merely saw a dark-skinned person walk in the background of their virtual world (Peck et al., 2013).

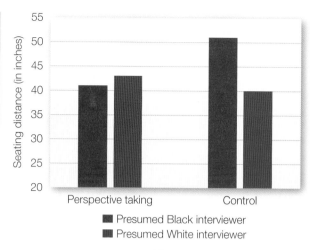

Presumed Black interviewer
Presumed White interviewer

Figure 11.9

Reducing Prejudice With Perspective Taking

Although White participants in a control condition chose to keep their distance from a Black interviewer, after having vividly imagined the day in the life of a young Black man, this implicit form of bias was eliminated.

[Data source: Todd et al. (2011)]

Reducing Prejudice by Bolstering the Self

Perspective taking reduces prejudice by changing the way people think about others. But can we also reduce prejudice by changing how people think about themselves? Because some prejudices result from people's deep-seated feelings of insecurity, when their feelings about themselves are bolstered, they often can become more tolerant and compassionate toward those who are different.

You may recall a couple of theories suggesting that people take on negative attitudes toward others to protect their positive view of themselves. For example, according to terror management theory (Solomon et al., 1991), when a person encounters someone else who holds a very different cultural worldview, it can threaten the belief system that upholds his or her sense of personal value, which can increase fears about death. When people feel that their self-esteem is threatened, or if they are reminded of their mortality, they cling more tightly to their own worldview, which can mean derogating those with a different belief system. This suggests that one remedy for prejudice is to bolster an individual's sense of self-esteem (Harmon-Jones et al., 1997; Schmeichel et al., 2009).

Research shows that bolstering self-esteem can be an effective means of reducing prejudice. In one study, participants received either positive or neutral feedback about their personalities before being reminded of their mortality. After these two experiences, they were asked to evaluate essays about the United States, presumably written by international students. One of the essays praised the United States, remarking on what a great country it is, and the other disparaged the United States, remarking on how awful it is. When participants were reminded of death and had not had their self-esteem boosted, their ethnocentric biases were revealed in their evaluations: They liked the author who praised the United States and disliked the author who disparaged the United States. However, when participants' self-esteem previously had been raised by the personality feedback, they liked the two authors equally (Harmon-Jones et al., 1997).

Self-affirmation theory (Steele, 1988) also predicts that prejudice can be a defensive reaction to feelings of personal insecurity. In the Fein and Spencer (1997) study discussed in chapter 10, participants who received negative feedback were more likely to derogate a Jewish student. However, if participants first had the chance to think about how they lived up to their own values, they showed no such pattern of discrimination.

Although bolstering a person's self-esteem can reduce prejudice, there is one caveat to this effect. If the value system being bolstered is the cultural worldview threatened by the outgroup, then the effects of self-affirmation can backfire (Arndt & Greenberg, 1999). For example, although you might be able to reduce antigay prejudice by affirming people's values and abilities in areas such as athletics or sense of humor, an affirmation of their traditional family values will do little to decrease this prejudice (Lehmiller et al., 2010; Vescio & Biernat, 2003).

Reducing Prejudice with a More Multicultural Ideology

Colorblind ideology The idea that group identities should be ignored and that people should be judged solely on their individual merits, thereby avoiding any judgment based on group membership.

Part of why bolstering how people see themselves reduces prejudice is because it makes people more open minded and less defensive (Sherman & Cohen, 2006). This leads us to consider perhaps a more straightforward strategy for reducing prejudice: reminding people of their tolerant values. Making such values salient can indeed have positive effects (e.g., Greenberg et al., 1992).

One way of encouraging tolerance is conveyed as an effort to embrace a **colorblind ideology**, which views people only on their individual merits, avoiding any judgment based on group membership. One concern with the colorblind approach is that it encourages efforts simply to control any biases or prejudices that one has

SOCIAL PSYCH at the MOVIES

Remember the Titans

Capturing the complexities of racial integration on film is no easy feat. Many movies tackle themes of racial prejudice, but the 2000 film *Remember the Titans* (Bruckheimer & Yakin, 2000) provides what might be the best cinematic example of how to reduce prejudice by applying Allport's formula for successful intergroup contact. This movie is based on the true story of separate high schools in Alexandria, Virginia that were forced to merge in 1971 as part of a rather delayed effort to desegregate Virginia's public schools. Integrating the student body also meant integrating the football teams, and the movie chronicles the growing pains of this newly diversified group and its struggle to put together a winning season.

The film centers around the head coach of the Titans, Herman Boone, played by Denzel Washington, who faces an uphill battle in training a unified team of White and Black players who previously attended separate schools, played on rival teams, and still hold deeply entrenched racial prejudices. The film clearly depicts the conflict on the football field as a microcosm of the conflict in American culture in the immediate aftermath of the civil rights movement.

The movie just as effectively portrays how Coach Boone pulls his team together to clinch the state championship in 1971.

Recall that one of the elements for effective intergroup contact is the presence of *institutional support*. In the movie, this support is established at the outset when the school board decides to give the head coaching job to the former coach of the Black high school rather than to the coach of the White high school (played by Will Patton). This decision sends a clear message to the players and their parents that the school board has good intentions to integrate not only the school and the athletic programs but also the staff. Although

[Disney Enterprises, Inc./Photofest]

toward an outgroup. Although this can sometimes be an effective way to avoid engaging in discrimination, our earlier discussion of controlling prejudice revealed that these efforts can also backfire.

Another criticism of the colorblind approach is that it can imply that everyone should conform to the status quo and act as if ethnic differences don't matter. As we alluded to above, the colorblind approach is a much more comfortable stance for the advantaged majority group than for currently disadvantaged minority groups. Allport's original formulation of the contact hypothesis largely adopted a colorblind approach. More recent research reveals that Whites in the United States tend to take this to the extreme, sometimes failing to mention a person's race, even when doing so is simply stating a descriptive fact about an individual that could help describe the person to whom they are referring (Apfelbaum et al., 2008; Norton et al., 2006).

An alternative is to embrace cultural pluralism, or a **multicultural ideology**, which acknowledges and appreciates different cultural viewpoints. This view emphasizes not just tolerating but actively embracing diversity. To understand the distinction between these two ideologies, consider the metaphors used in the United States and Canada, two countries that were formed largely as a result of immigration. The United States is typically referred to as a melting pot, a place where people of different ethnicities and former nationalities might converge and blend to form a single group. In Canada, the prevailing metaphor is the salad bowl, where citizens form an integrated collective while still maintaining their distinct ethnic heritage.

Multicultural ideology
A worldview in which different cultural identities and viewpoints are acknowledged and appreciated.

---

tensions occasionally flare among the coaches, they generally work together for successful integration.

The second element for effective contact is establishing *equal status*. Coach Boone makes his hard-as-nails coaching style crystal clear to the players' parents, to the other members of his coach staff, and to his team. But perhaps most important, he quite visibly metes out punishment equally to both Black and White players. As a result, the players quickly learn that earning a starting position on the team will have nothing to do with the color of their skin. Anyone who wants to play on the team will have to work hard.

Still, the players themselves struggle to get past their mistrust of one another. Seeing how his team continues to default to self-segregation by race, Coach Boone intervenes. When the team heads off to a training camp in two buses, he divides the players not by race but by offensive or defensive positions. To encourage contact further, he pairs White and Black players to room together for the duration of the intensive training. The overall message is that all the players, regardless of race, need to work together as a team to achieve the same *superordinate goal* of winning games.

Does this strategy of forcing players to room together work? Not at first. A White player objects to his Black roommate's iconic poster of the track and field champions Tommie Smith and John Carlos giving the raised-fist black power salute during the medal ceremony at the 1968 Olympic Games. Not surprisingly, tempers flare and a fight breaks out. Sharing

a room in the dormitory also doesn't translate into socializing during meal times. Realizing that an important ingredient is still missing, Coach Boone mandates that each player interview his roommate to further break down the barriers of misunderstanding and mistrust. As Allport would have predicted, the players finally begin to cooperate as a unified team after this final element of friendship is established.

Remember the Titans shows these important components of contact at work. If any of these components were missing, do you think that T. C. Williams High School still would have won the state championship in 1971? Why or why not? What lessons can we learn for creating more effective integration today?

[Walt Disney/Bruckheimer Films/The Kobal Collection/Bennett, Tracy]

Diversity can be described through metaphor. The melting pot depicts a colorblind approach, whereas the salad bowl emphasizes multiculturalism.

From a psychological perspective, these different ideologies suggest different ways of approaching intergroup relations. A colorblind approach suggests that we should *avoid* focusing on group identity, whereas multiculturalism suggests that we should *approach* group differences as something to be celebrated. Going into an interaction with a multicultural mind-set might sidestep all of the problems we see when people are focused on avoiding being biased. This is just what Trawalter and Richeson (2006) have found. When White participants were told to avoid being biased during an interaction with Black students, they became cognitively depleted from the effort and probably less receptive to future intergroup interactions. But when they were instead told to approach the interaction as an opportunity to have a positive interracial exchange, those effects weren't present, and the interaction went more smoothly.

In a clever application of this same idea, Kerry Kawakami and her colleagues (Kawakami et al., 2007) showed that these approach tendencies can be trained quite subtly. In one of their studies, participants completed an initial task in which they simply had to pull a joystick toward them when they saw the word *approach* displayed on a screen or push it away from them when they saw the word *avoid*. Unknown to the participants, faces were subliminally presented just before the target words appeared. Some individuals always were shown a Black face when they were cued to approach; others were shown a Black face when they were cued to avoid. After completing this task, participants had an unconscious association to approach or avoid Blacks. When they were asked to engage in an interracial interaction with a Black confederate, those in the approach condition behaved in a more friendly and open way than those in the avoid condition. These results show that our goals for interactions can be cued and created unconsciously as well as consciously and that an approach orientation toward diverse others can be quite beneficial.

Although these findings are encouraging, embracing diversity is not without its challenges. Promoting diversity also makes salient both group categories and differences between groups. And in cultural-diversity training, the line between teaching about group differences and promoting stereotyping is sometimes crossed.

Final Thoughts

Social psychology has taught us a lot, not just about where prejudice comes from and how it is activated but also about how it can be reduced. Yes, there is a long and varied list of cures, but that's because bias has many different causes and manifestations. Although our interest in being egalitarian can motivate us to control our biases, the bottom line is that seeking out common ground and understanding while also embracing the value of different viewpoints and perspectives may be the most effective way of achieving intergroup harmony.

However, encouraging tolerance assumes that people *want* to be tolerant. This is where broader changes in cultural norms can play a powerful role in helping people internalize these motivations. The more we see others behave and interact in an egalitarian way, the more we follow suit. Reducing prejudice doesn't happen overnight. All of us will suffer relapses on the way, but cultures can shift gradually toward equality. Reducing prejudice against a segment of the population can benefit everyone in the end. For example, cross-national data from the World Bank reveals a strong positive correlation between equivalent educational opportunities for both girls and boys and the economic prosperity of a country (Chen, 2004). We can all benefit from maximizing the well-being and opportunities of everyone in society.

SECTION review | Reducing Prejudice

Prejudice has no single cause. Various strategies are available to reduce it.

Changing the culture

Long-term, systematic reduction of prejudice requires changing laws, customs, and norms.

Controlling prejudice in interactions

- Individuals can prevent their automatically activated prejudices from affecting their behavior.
- However, controlling prejudice is not always easy and can backfire.

The contact hypothesis

According to Allport's conditions, optimal intergroup contact can reduce prejudice when it

- establishes equal status.
- enables people to become acquainted with outgroup members.
- encourages cooperation toward superordinate goals.
- is sanctioned by authorities.

Optimal contact
- reduces stereotyping.
- decreases intergroup anxiety.
- increases empathy for the outgroup.

Acknowledging both subgroup and superordinate identities can allow positive effects of contact to generalize.

Allport's optimal conditions for contact can reduce intergroup biases more for members of the majority than for the minority group.

The jigsaw classroom is an application of optimal contact to education.

Reducing prejudice without contact

Perspective taking increases empathy and decreases negative stereotypes.

Bolstering people's good feelings about themselves helps them feel less threatened by those who hold differing views.

Multiculturalism is perhaps the most effective ideology for reducing biases held by the majority while also valuing diverse perspectives held by minority groups.

CONNECT ONLINE:

Check out our videos and additional resources located at:
www.macmillanhighered.com/launchpad/greenberg1e

12

Interpersonal Aggression

TOPIC OUTLINE

> Nonviolence means avoiding not only external physical violence but also internal violence of spirit. You not only refuse to shoot a man, but you refuse to hate him.
>
> Martin Luther King, Jr. (1992, p. 102)

Our discussion of prejudice reveals that humans have done each other great harm because of differences in nationality, ethnicity, religion, and worldviews. If you total all the killings by all the known mass murderers over recorded history, they would make up a small drop in a very bloody bucket compared with the state-sanctioned killings that have been carried out in the name of some war or cause. In fact, laboratory research suggests that provoked individuals act more aggressively when they feel they are part of a group than when they are acting as individuals (McPherson & Joireman, 2009). Nevertheless, interpersonal aggression is also a considerable problem. Let's first consider two cases of interpersonal aggression.

On July 22, 2011, a 32-year-old Norwegian man, Anders Behring Breivik, first set off a bomb near a government building in Oslo, killing eight people, then went to a youth summer camp, where he shot and killed 69 young people and camp counselors (Mala & Goodman, 2011, July 22). Although some observers have suggested that mental-health problems contributed to Breivik's horrendous actions, many of the factors known to contribute to aggression in general likely played a role as well. He was an isolated man, full of hostile feelings who had experienced failure and frustration in his life. He was also a fan of violent electronic media and hate-filled right-wing web sites (Schwirtz & Saltmarsh, 2011).

All humans are capable of aggression, and monsters often don't look like monsters. Does this man look like a mass murderer? Maybe not, but in 2011 he set off a bomb in an office building before committing mass murder at a summer camp.

[© HO/Reuters/Corbis]

In the second case, a 14-year-old Australian girl named Chanelle Rae committed suicide after being the target of repeated cyberbullying (Dikeos, 2009, July 23). As her mother told news reporters, "Friday night she was on the internet and told me about some message that had come through, and she wanted to die because of the message. . . . I can guarantee you if she didn't go on the internet Friday night she'd be alive today." Cyberbullying can involve behaviors such as posting rumors and insults and uploading embarrassing photos, videos, and computer viruses. Because cyber socializing is so prevalent in today's world, cyberbullying is a particularly invasive form of bullying. It can follow the victim home or anywhere with Internet access. Because of repeated instances of tragedies such as this, many states have enacted laws against cyberbullying (Donnerstein, 2011).

Fortunately, extreme acts such these two tragic examples are relatively rare. On the other hand, which of us has never insulted, pushed, snapped at, or even punched or kicked another individual (or wanted to) sometime in our lives? Almost all of us have engaged in at least minor acts of aggression. Such minor acts often do not cause serious or lasting harm to their targets. But consider the following statistics (Flannery et al., 2007; Hall, 1999; Rapp-Paglicci et al., 2002; US: Federal Statistics Show, 2007):

Tina Meier gazes at a picture of her daughter, Megan Meier, who committed suicide on October 16, 2007, after being victimized by cyberbullies. Tina created the Megan Meier foundation (meganmeierfoundation.org) to teach others about the harmful effects of internet harassment.

[AP Photo/Sarah Conard]

- Reports of child abuse range between about 2 to 3 million per year in the United States.
- Twenty to 30% of American romantic partners report that acts of aggression have occurred in their relationships.
- On average, a woman in the United States is raped every 6 minutes. Over 70% of these rapes are committed by someone the woman knows. In addition, about 4% of male inmates in U.S. prisons report having been sexually assaulted.
- Some American cities average more than one murder per day.

How can we understand such interpersonal aggression? As with all human actions, we have to look to biology, culture, learning, emotion, motivation, personality, and situational factors to gain a complete picture (e.g., Berkowitz, 1993). In this chapter, we'll examine each of these factors and how they relate to different types of aggression. We will also briefly consider how to apply knowledge of the causes of aggression to reduce interpersonal violence in society.

Defining Aggression

Although people commonly use the word *aggressive* to describe everything from acts of physical violence, to vigorous scrubbing of a dirty pan, to a tenacious salesperson, social psychologists reserve the term **aggression** for any physical or verbal behavior that is intended to harm another person or persons (or any living thing). An aggressive act may be intended to cause physical harm (a punch) or psychological harm (e.g., posting hurtful comments on someone's Facebook wall) or both. We generally apply the term *violence* only to acts of aggression with more severe or lasting consequences.

Aggression Any physical or verbal behavior that is intended to harm another person or persons (or any living thing).

The Role of Intention

The definition above emphasizes the intention of the person committing the act. If a person intends to harm another person but isn't successful (e.g., throws a punch but misses), we would consider that an aggressive act. Likewise, aggression can manifest in a deliberate *failure* to act (e.g., not telling someone that he is about to embarrass himself because you want to see him humiliated). When a lifeguard applies painful pressure to someone's chest in order to help her breathe, we wouldn't call this aggression because the intention is to save a life. But intentions are not always so easily parsed. What if a woman bites her male romantic partner on the neck during a moment of intimacy? She is intending to cause pain, but whether or not it is an act of aggression depends on whether or not her intention is to harm him.

The Harm Caused by Aggression

Aggression warrants our attention because of the harm it does to those who are victimized. This harm can take many forms. When acts of aggression are physical, the most salient type of harm is immediate or lasting feelings of pain, suffering, injury, or death. Nonlethal types of physical violence, such as rape and assault, can be psychologically traumatic for the victim, leading to overgeneralized anxiety, hypervigilance, sleeplessness, nightmares, rumination, irritability, self-blame, emotional detachment (dissociation), difficulty concentrating, and humiliation. An act of violence can shatter a person's formerly security-providing view of the world as a relatively safe place (e.g., Coker et al., 2002; Janoff-Bulman & Yopyk, 2004; Winkel & Denkers, 1995). In extreme cases, posttraumatic stress disorder, or PTSD, may occur, a syndrome that can extend these reactions to trauma over many years (Keane et al., 1990). In short, many acts of violence change the victim's life forever.

As the story of Chanelle Rae's suicide reveals, verbal insults, social rejection, and cyberbullying can also have grave consequences. These acts generate feelings of frustration, humiliation, anxiety, anger, social isolation, helplessness, and despair. In children, they can result in reduced self-esteem, poorer grades, and depression (e.g., Donnerstein, 2011). These negative feelings also can lead to aggressive acts of retaliation, resulting in a vicious cycle of violence. One such incident was the shooting at Columbine High School in Colorado in 1999. The killers, Dylan Klebold and Eric Harris, felt rejected and bullied, and responded by killing 12 students and a teacher before turning their weapons on themselves (Chua-Eoan, 2007, March 1). Seung-Hui Cho, who killed 32 people at Virginia Tech University in 2009, was also the target of verbal aggression in high school and regarded the Columbine killers as heroes standing up for the oppressed. According to a student in his English class, "As soon as he started reading, the whole class started laughing and pointing and saying, 'Go back to China'" (High school classmates say gunman was bullied, 2007). People stripped of a sense of significance and value in the world, whether due to being victims of aggression or other life circumstances, sometimes perceive lashing out violently as their only recourse to enact revenge and to have a lasting impact on the world (Solomon et al., in press).

Roses lie on a balcony overlooking a vigil held in Oslo on July 25, 2011, attended by some 150,000 people holding flowers in a show of solidarity with the 77 murdered victims of the attacks in Norway.

[Odd Andersen/AFP/Getty Images]

Affective aggression Harm-seeking done to another person that is elicited in response to some negative emotion.

Instrumental aggression Harm-seeking done to another person that serves some other goal.

Acts of aggression that lead to serious harm or death also have wide-ranging effects on those who care about the victim. The grief from loss brings great suffering (e.g., Parkes & Weiss, 1983). In the case of the 2011 Norway massacre, over 10,000 people gathered outside Oslo Cathedral for a memorial service for the victims. Acts of mass murder often lead to societal changes such as stronger security measures, stricter gun laws, and sterner sentencing policies.

Finally, we should note that the collateral damage from aggression also extends to those who simply witness it (Davis & Carlson, 1987). They often experience symptoms of trauma. Those who survive attacks such as the Norway shootings also often experience survivor guilt, the haunting sense that there is something unjust in their own survival when those equally innocent did not survive (Erikson, 1968). The broad reach of aggression in harming people's lives should make us all invested in understanding its causes.

Affective and Instrumental Aggression

Social psychologists distinguish between two types of aggression (Geen, 2001). With **affective aggression**, the main goal is to harm the other person simply for the sake of doing so. Such behavior is motivated by a strong affective, or emotional, state. Affective aggression often is impulsive, as when a fight breaks out at a bar, but it can be delayed and calculated, as in the case of a premeditated plan to seek revenge by throwing a rock through someone's window. **Instrumental aggression** occurs when someone intends to inflict harm on another person to serve some other goal. A bully hits a classmate to get attention from a girl. A hit man kills for a fee. Instrumental aggression is not triggered by strong emotions, but such behavior is still intended to harm. Aggressive acts often blur the line between these two types. A robber may shoot a cashier partly to get money but also partly out of anger over things happening in his own life. A husband may punch his wife in anger but also to maintain control over her.

Although instrumental aggression certainly is important, most of the theory and research we will discuss deals with the "hot," affective type of aggression because it appears to characterize a majority of the aggressive acts committed. For example, in 2010, among those murders in the United States in which the offender could be determined, people were more likely to be killed by someone they knew than by a stranger (78% of the time). Half the murders were committed by a romantic partner, family member, or friend. For female victims, 38% of the time the killer was a current or former male romantic partner (Federal Bureau of Investigation, 2010).

Measuring Aggression

There are many statistics on different types of aggression that occur out in the world. Researchers can use these data to examine correlational relationships with potentially influential factors (e.g., watching violent TV) and how they unfold over time. But to manipulate potential causes to determine if they influence aggression, researchers have had to invent ways to measure the behavior without assaults and shootings breaking out in their labs. Fortunately, laboratory paradigms have been developed that lead participants to believe they are causing physical harm to someone else without actually doing so (Geen, 2001). For example, participants have been given opportunities to administer electric shocks to supposed other participants (e.g., Buss, 1961) or dole out a dose of painfully spicy hot sauce (e.g., Lieberman et al., 1999). Although not typical, these are forms of aggression; in fact, hot sauce has been used in numerous cases of child abuse (Koppel, 2011, August 24; Lieberman et al., 1999).

SECTION review | Defining Aggression

Aggression is any physical or verbal behavior that is intended to harm another person(s) or any living thing.

This definition emphasizes the *intention* to harm.	Harm from aggression affects not only the victim, but also loved ones, witnesses, and sometimes the broader community.	Aggression can be in either of two forms. • Affective: emotionally driven actions where the intent is to harm. • Instrumental: actions that do harm but the intent is to achieve another goal.

Biology and Human Aggression

Are we natural-born killers? When we reflect on how common aggression is in virtually every society, both past and present, it's tempting to conclude that aggressive tendencies are an inherent part of human nature. For example, before World War I, Sigmund Freud (1920/1955) maintained that people are motivated by an inborn instinct to seek pleasure and to create, which he called **eros**. But after observing how willing and even eager people were to torture, maim, and murder one another during the war, he proposed that humans are also born with an aggressive instinct, which he called **thanatos**, that seeks to destroy life. Is Freud right? Is aggressiveness biologically programmed into human nature? There is no simple answer to this question. Some evidence on the "yes" side comes from comparisons of humans with other animal species.

An Ethological Perspective

Ethology, or behavioral biology, is the study of animal behavior in its natural context. Konrad Lorenz, a Nobel Prize–winning Austrian ethologist, posited that if we observe humans and other species displaying similar aggressive behaviors under roughly similar situations, we can infer that those behaviors helped humans and other species alike to survive and reproduce (Lorenz, 1966). Such evidence would suggest a shared, innate psychological mechanism for aggression.

Ethologists draw attention to a number of interesting parallels in the aggressive behavior of humans and other animal species. For example, in species as diverse as chimpanzees, crayfish, and bald eagles, an organism will usually aggress against another organism that attempts to acquire or gain control over material resources that are necessary for survival, such as food, nesting sites, and feeding sites (Enquist & Leimar, 1983). Similarly, humans display anger and aggression when others attempt to take control of their property. Imagine that you've claimed a table at the library for yourself by setting up your laptop and books, but on returning from a quick trip to the vending machine you find that someone has taken your spot. This violation of your personal space would probably evoke anger, if not aggression (Worchel & Teddie, 1976).

Animal species also routinely exhibit threat displays and aggression when they or their offspring are attacked, tendencies that are also seen in humans. Indeed, laws in most cultures formally recognize that aggression in defense of self or others is justified. Aggression in the animal world is also commonly seen in competition over social status. In many social species such as monkeys, apes, and hyenas, members of a group are organized in a dominance hierarchy. Lower-status group members (typically males) sometimes try to achieve a higher status to gain access to more material resources, sexual partners, and control over others' behavior. Of course, high-status group members are reluctant to relinquish their dominant position and

Eros Freud's term for what he proposed is the human inborn instinct to seek pleasure and to create.

Thanatos Freud's term for what he proposed is the human inborn instinct to aggress and to destroy.

Many social species have dominance hierarchies. These animals use aggression to achieve and maintain a position of status within the group.

[Danita Delimont/Getty Images]

respond to a competitor with overt displays of anger. If the competitor doesn't back down, physical combat may ensue.

Analogously, in humans, threats to reputation are a primary trigger for aggression. From the tribal communities of Highland New Guinea (Sargent, 1974) to the Jivaro people of the western Amazon (Karsten, 1935) to the street gangs of America's inner cities (Toch, 1969), threats to one's face or status are often the trigger for violent or even homicidal aggressive acts among young men. Also consistent with the idea that anger and aggression function to maintain one's reputation, people are especially likely to retaliate against someone who insults them when they know that an audience has witnessed the insult (Brown, 1968; Felson, 1982; Kim et al., 1998).

Across species, aggression is often triggered by the perception that others are making one's life difficult, either by imposing costs (e.g., direct threats to survival, stealing resources) or denying benefits (e.g., preventing a rise in status). In addition, anger and aggression seem to have similar functions across species. Anger displays (e.g., baring one's teeth) deter others who might challenge one's status (Sell, 2011). If displays of anger are not effective at changing others' behavior, aggression is a way to reinforce the message, reducing the probability that others will repeat their harmful actions in the future (Clutton-Brock & Parker, 1995). On the basis of these parallels, it seems reasonable to conclude that the human mind has inherited from natural selection a propensity to respond to certain situations with anger and, when need be, aggression.

The Physiology of Aggression

If the human mind evolved over millions of years to respond to certain situations with anger and aggression, these adaptations should be reflected in our physiology. Research has indeed discovered physiological mechanisms involved in the detection of social threat, the experience of anger, and engaging in aggressive behavior.

Brain Regions

One region of the brain involved in the detection of social threat is the *dorsal anterior cingulate cortex*, or dACC (see **FIGURE 12.1**).

Figure 12.1

The Dorsal Anterior Cingulate Cortex (dACC)

This brain area is active when people detect actions and outcomes that interfere with their goals, including social threats.

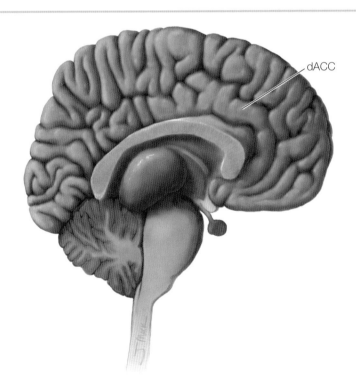

dACC

One function of the dACC is to alert us when there is a conflict between our expectations and the situation we are in (Bush et al., 2000). Imagine, for example, that you are driving in your car and the idiot driver to your left suddenly cuts in front of you, forcing you to swerve to avoid a collision. Blood rushes to your dACC to alert you that something is wrong. Suddenly your drive is not proceeding as you expected, and you need to straighten things out.

Insults and other provocations have been shown to activate the dACC because those situations create a conflict between how we feel we should be treated and how we actually are treated. The relation between the dACC and reaction to provocation is seen in a study by Denson and colleagues (2009). Participants were asked to complete difficult puzzles and to state their answers to the puzzles out loud to the experimenter. The experimenter pretended not to hear the participants and politely prompted them to speak louder. But on the third such "mishearing," the experimenter insulted the participants by saying in an irate and condescending tone, "Look, this is the third time I've had to say this! Can't you follow directions?" Relative to the baseline measure taken before the provocation, participants showed increased activation in the dACC after the insult. This activation was positively correlated with how much anger they felt toward the experimenter. Related research shows that the dACC is activated when we feel rejected by others (Eisenberger & Lieberman, 2004). Rejection is an important cause of aggressive behavior, as we will see later in this chapter. What's more, the more people show dACC activation in response to a provocation by another person, the more willing they are to retaliate against that person by subjecting him or her to blasts of painful noise (Krämer et al., 2007).

Although the dACC sounds the neural alarm when we are faced with unjustified wrongdoing, regions in the limbic system, especially the *hypothalamus* and the *amygdala* (see **FIGURE 12.2**), are involved in emotional experiences of fear and anger, which often elicit aggressive behaviors.

Driving is one situation in which our expectations can be violated, for example, when another car veers in front of us. When this happens, the dorsal anterior cingulate cortex is activated and prepares us to act, sometimes aggressively.

[Sean Murphy/Getty Images]

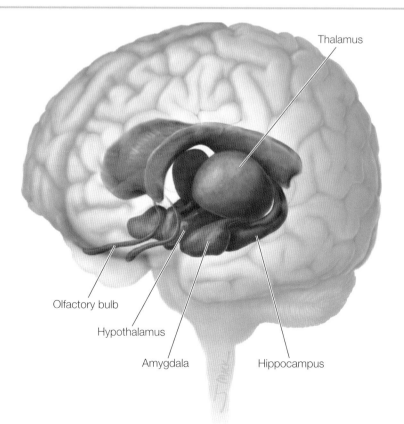

Thalamus

Olfactory bulb

Hypothalamus

Amygdala

Hippocampus

Figure 12.2

Fight or Flight

The hypothalamus and the amygdala are two brain regions that play a key role in people's emotional experiences of fear and anger and prepare them for a fight-or-flight response.

When we are faced with threat, the hypothalamus kicks into high-arousal mode, preparing our body for "fight or flight," that is, fleeing from danger or preparing to aggress against the threatening stimulus. The amygdala responds to threatening stimuli with processes generating fear or anger. When the emotion is fear, the behavior is avoidance, or "flight." When the emotion is anger, the behavior is aggression, or "fight." In experiments with cats and monkeys, a lesion to the amygdala leads them to be excessively tame, whereas stimulation to the amygdala leads them to display signs of anger such as shrieks and hisses. Neuroimaging studies with humans show that the amygdala is activated by the presentation of threatening faces (Pezawas et al., 2005), the perception of anger in others, and the experience of anger in oneself (Murphy et al., 2003). Studies also show that regions of the limbic system are activated in response to interpersonal provocations, such as unfair allocation of resources by a peer (Meyer-Lindenberg et al., 2006).

Body Chemistry

A number of hormones play a role in the experience of anger and aggressive behavior. The most widely studied is the sex hormone testosterone. The more people secrete testosterone, the more predisposed they are to aggress. For example, convicted male criminals who had committed aggressive crimes (e.g., assault) showed higher concentrations of testosterone in their blood than did males who had committed nonaggressive crimes (Dabbs et al., 1987, 1995). Of course, such correlational findings don't prove causation. What happens when testosterone levels change? One way researchers have addressed this question is by looking at individuals undergoing sex-change operations. Although testosterone level predicts aggression in both sexes (Dabbs & Hargrove, 1997; Sapolsky, 1998), males secrete more testosterone. Females transforming into males receive androgen therapy, which entails taking drugs to increase testosterone levels, whereas males transforming into females receive testosterone-reducing drugs. Female-to-male transsexuals became considerably more aggressive in the first three months of androgen therapy, whereas male-to-female transsexuals became less aggressive (Van Goozen et al., 1995).

Testosterone levels most clearly correlate with aggressiveness in situations involving provocation and interpersonal conflict. One study of Swedish boys (Olweus et al., 1980) showed that boys with higher testosterone levels were more physically and verbally aggressive, especially in response to provocations. A similar study showed that in response to mounting intensity of provocation by another participant, men with high levels of testosterone were more physically aggressive than those with lower levels of testosterone (Berman et al., 1993). These pieces of evidence have led some researchers to suggest that testosterone leads people to seek out and maintain a sense of status relative to others (Josephs et al., 2006).

Natural-born Pacifists

Before we conclude from this biological evidence that humans are born to aggress, we need to examine the other side of the biological coin. There are numerous reasons to think that both humans and other animals may have evolved not to be particularly aggressive. For one, even if an animal ends up dominating another animal in a competition, it probably will suffer injuries that will take energy to heal and that may ultimately be fatal. Also, those who are likely to aggress risk getting a bad reputation. We see this in monkeys, for example, when group members known to be overly aggressive are usually rejected by other members (Higley et al., 1994). In humans, people who are overly aggressive—either by physically attacking others or by trying to damage others' peer relationships (e.g., by spreading hateful gossip)—increase their chances of being rejected by their peers in the future, if not imprisoned (Crick & Grotpeter, 1995; Dishion et al., 1994; Dodge, 1983).

Also, although aggressing against someone who harmed us may deter them in the future, it usually damages our relationship with that person. As a result, we miss out on any benefits that might have come from that relationship. Therefore, some theorists argue that natural selection may have shaped the human mind to *forgive* valued relationship partners despite the harm they have caused us (McCullough, 2008). If ancestral humans forgave an offending relationship partner and reconciled after interpersonal conflict, they could restore relationships that, on average, would have increased their chances of surviving and reproducing. Finally, humans have evolved to be especially capable of learning, perspective-taking, empathy, imagining future events, internalizing morals, considering fairness, and controlling impulses. As we will see throughout this chapter, these capabilities often counteract inclinations to aggress.

Uniquely Human Aspects of Aggression

Two differences between humans and animals stand out when comparing aggressive behavior in humans and other species. One makes us more aggressive than other animals, the other makes us less.

Technology outstrips natural controls on aggression. When two members of the same species fight, they almost never kill each other. Over the course of evolution, these species have developed strategies to avoid unnecessary injury. For example, animals are very good at gauging each other's physical strength and fighting ability. If one animal recognizes that it will probably lose, it avoids further conflict. Also, if the animals do end up fighting, once one animal has clearly dominated the other, the loser assumes a subordinate position, such as lying on its back or baring its throat. It is as if the loser is saying to the dominant animal, "All right, you win, champ; let's both walk away." At that point the dominant animal does not go in for the kill; rather, it breaks off the combat, and in some cases even makes a friendly gesture to the subordinate animal. In this way, both animals avoid unnecessary injury (Lorenz, 1966).

If you've noticed that human aggression doesn't seem to work by these rules, you are absolutely right. Whereas other species have natural controls that restrain violence before it gets out of hand, humans seem to have far fewer qualms about killing each other. Why is this? An important part of the answer proposed by Lorenz (1966) is that our technological capacity for violence has outstripped any inhibitions against killing that we may have. The ability to pull triggers, plant bombs, and launch missiles means we can cause lethal harm so quickly and from such a distance that evolved controls over violence that might lead to less lethal actions, such as empathy and signs of submission and suffering, have no opportunity to intercede and limit the damage. Because our technological proficiency in killing is so great, we humans kill more members of our own species because of how we are different from other animals, rather than because of how we are similar to them.

The human mind specializes in self-control. Parallels between humans and other species are also limited because of the unique self-regulatory capacities afforded by our cerebral cortex. We have the ability to think abstractly and self-reflectively on our past experiences and future possibilities, reappraise emotional events, and reason about right and wrong.

Indeed, our brains are equipped with regions that allow us to inhibit aggressive responses. Earlier we saw that brain regions such as the dACC and the limbic system act as a neural alarm system that alerts us when something is wrong. In some circumstances, these regions produce an impulsive desire to retaliate aggressively to perceived hostile treatment. But obviously we don't act on every aggressive impulse that we experience. Rather, these impulses are regulated by regions of our **prefrontal cortex**, in particular the *medial prefrontal cortex*, or MPFC, and the *dorsolateral prefrontal cortex*, or DLPFC, which we discussed in chapter 11 (**FIGURE 12.3** on the next page) (Davidson et al., 2000; Raine, 2008; Siever, 2008).

These regions of the prefrontal cortex are active when we introspect, consider our morals and the consequences of our actions, reflect on our emotional responses to distressing stimuli, and control our behavior. Also, they share many neural connections with the dACC and limbic structures such as the amygdala. Through these connections, they act as an emergency brake on the aggressive impulses generated by those structures

Prefrontal cortex The region of the brain that regulates impulsive behavior.

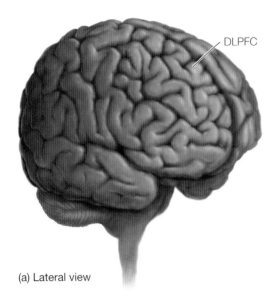

(a) Lateral view

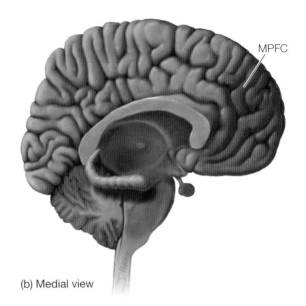

(b) Medial view

Figure 12.3

Impulse Regulation

The prefrontal cortex (PFC) is the brain area involved in controlling impulses and emotions. When our impulse is to lash out aggressively, the prefrontal cortex can help us restrain that impulse. The figure shows the dorsolateral region (a) and the medial region (b) of the PFC.

Serotonin A neurotransmitter that regulates our experience of negative affect.

(Inzlicht & Gutsell, 2007). For example, individuals who suffer injury to the prefrontal cortex become dramatically more irritable, hostile, and aggressive (Grafman et al., 1996).

What's more, our prefrontal cortex has many receptors for a neurotransmitter called **serotonin**, which damps our angry and aggressive impulses. *Neurotransmitters* are chemicals that carry messages between brain cells. Serotonin, often called the "feel-good" neurotransmitter, helps the prefrontal cortex put the brakes on impulsive responses to distressing events (Soubrié, 1986). High levels of serotonin in the nervous system of humans and other animals are correlated with low levels of aggression (Ferris et al., 1997; Suarez & Krishnan, 2006). Experimentally boosting serotonin's activity reduces aggression (Berman et al., 2009; Carrillo et al., 2009; Cleare & Bond, 1995). Reducing serotonin levels leads to more aggressive responses to distressing events such as unfair treatment by a peer (Crockett et al., 2008).

This means that if another driver cuts us off on the freeway, we may experience an aggressive impulse. Whether or not we act on that aggressive impulse will depend on a number of factors, one of which is the activation in the prefrontal cortex self-regulatory control regions of the brain. It is precisely our ability to engage in the sophisticated regulation of our emotions and control of our behavior that distinguishes human aggression from the more reactive aggression observed in other animals. As we extend our analysis, we will see how factors that impede higher-order cognitive functioning block this capacity for control, making aggressive responses more likely.

SECTION review | Biology and Human Aggression

Evidence shows that aggressiveness may be in our biology, but so is pacifism.

| There are parallels between humans and other species when it comes to using aggression to gain advantages and protect oneself and one's resources. | • The dACC region of our brains is activated when we experience injustice, insults, and other threats.
 • Regions of the limbic system help generate fight-or-flight responses to perceived threats.
 • Higher testosterone levels correlate with more aggression. | There are many advantages to being nonaggressive, and humans have many evolved cognitive and emotional capacities that often curtail aggressive impulses. | • Humans have the greatest capacity to kill because of our technology.
 • Conversely, humans also have the greatest capacity for self-control. |

Situational Triggers of Aggression: The Context Made Me Do It

We have seen how our evolutionary inheritance and biological systems give each of us a capacity for hostile feelings and aggression, a capacity that we are most likely to engage when something or someone thwarts our needs and desires. It makes sense, then, that the study of situational factors that provoke affective aggression begins by focusing on frustration. Imagine a brutal school day. You start your morning missing seemingly every traffic light as you race to campus, already late for an exam. Finally you get to class. The day that follows is filled with similar frustrations. On getting home, you open the door and trip over the dog, prompting a profanity-laced tirade at your canine companion if not an actual (hopefully off-target) kick at the four-legged bystander. If this scenario seems familiar to you, it's because we all have an intuitive sense that frustrating situations can provoke aggressive behavior. Let's take a look at how making sense of the connection between frustration and aggression has progressed, and the many different insights into aggression it has inspired.

The Frustration-Aggression Hypothesis

In 1939 a group of psychologists at Yale University first proposed the **frustration-aggression hypothesis** (Dollard et al., 1939), which posits that aggression always is preceded by frustration, and that frustration inevitably leads to aggression. Frustration is the consequence of a blockage of a desired goal. For example, when participants were prevented from obtaining a desired prize—that is, frustrated—by a bumbling partner, and then given the opportunity to shock their partner during a subsequent learning task, they chose to give this partner stronger shocks than did participants not expecting an attractive prize (Buss, 1963). Subsequent studies have found that the more frustrated people are, the more likely they are to aggress. For example, it's nearly always frustrating when someone cuts in front of you when you've been standing in line for a while. But the closer you are to the front of the line and to your goal, the more frustrating this injustice is. With increased frustration, we see a stronger aggressive response (Harris, 1974).

During the first half of the 20th century Hovland and Sears (1940) reported that the number of lynchings of African Americans by Whites in the American South correlated negatively with the value of cotton, which at the time dominated the southern economy. The researchers presumed that as the price of cotton went down, southern Whites became more frustrated at their economic misfortunes. This frustration led to more aggression against African Americans. More contemporary findings show that, across diverse cultures, aggressive behaviors (e.g., homicide, road rage, child abuse) increase with the prevalence of various sources of frustration and stressors, including shrinking workforce, unemployment, increase in population density, low economic status, and economic hardship (Geen, 1998).

Displaced Aggression

In many cases, frustration-based aggression is directed at targets that didn't cause the frustration. Dollard and colleagues (1939) labeled this phenomenon **displaced aggression**. In our opening example of your returning home from the brutal day at school, poor Rover is just lying there and did nothing to warrant being the target of aggression. Generally, people will displace aggression when something prevents them from aggressing against the original source of the frustration. The source of frustration may be something intangible, such as a downturn in the economy. Or the target is of sufficiently high status, such as one's boss or parents, that the consequences (e.g., being fired or grounded) makes one think otherwise about venting one's frustration directly on the source. In such cases, the aggressive impulse often is instead directed

Frustration-aggression hypothesis Originally the idea that aggression is always preceded by frustration and that frustration inevitably leads to aggression. Revised to suggest that frustration produces an emotional readiness to aggress.

Displaced aggression Aggression directed to a target other than the source of one's frustration.

Figure 12.4

Triggered Displaced Aggression

When rating a somewhat bumbling assistant (in the trigger condition), participants made the harshest evaluations if they had been insulted earlier by someone else. This situation illustrates triggered displaced aggression because participants derogated the assistant only if he or she did something to trigger the aggressive response.

[Data source: Pedersen et al. (2000)]

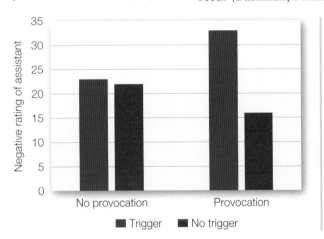

at a safer, often innocent target. But in other cases, the alternative target adds a bit to your level of frustration, leading to what is known as *triggered displaced aggression*.

Triggered displaced aggression occurs when someone does not respond to an initial frustration or provocation (i.e., the bad day at school) but later is faced with a second event that elicits a more aggressive response than would be warranted by only the relatively minor affront on its own (the dog stepping on your foot). Miller and colleagues (2003) suggest that the original provocation produces anger and aggressive thoughts. However, because the individual is prevented from retaliating, or decides not to retaliate, against the original provocation, the hostile feelings and thoughts remain. Then, when the individual is confronted with a second, actually minor, frustrating event, the preexisting hostility biases how he or she interprets and emotionally responds to that event. In the context of the bad day, your dog being in position to trip you *seems more* intentional and more painful, leading you to behave more aggressively than is warranted. The more the provoked person ruminates about the initial aversive event, the more likely triggered displaced aggression will occur (Bushman, Bonacci et al., 2005).

A study by Pedersen and colleagues (2000) provides a good illustration of how this works. Participants were initially given either insulting feedback about their performance on a task or no such feedback. The initial, insulting feedback is a provocation. Later in the study, the participants were given another task by a different assistant. In one condition, the assistant was somewhat annoying and incompetent, whereas the other participants had no such minor trigger. Participants were then given the opportunity to rate the assistant's qualifications for a job. As can be seen in **FIGURE 12.4**, in the absence of an initial provocation, participants were not especially critical of the bumbling assistant. However, when participants had initially been insulted and were then exposed to the annoying assistant, they subsequently gave her a much more negative evaluation.

What this and other studies reveal is that we don't displace our aggression against just anyone. Rather, we are most likely to lash out at targets who do something mildly annoying, are dislikable, are relatively low in social status and power, or who resemble the person with whom we actually are angry (e.g., Marcus-Newhall et al., 2000; Pedersen et al., 2008).

Think ABOUT

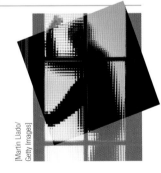

[Martin Llado/ Getty Images]

Arbitrariness of the Frustration

Although the studies we've reviewed so far support a role for frustration in aggression, other studies showed that the original hypothesis was too absolute. Although frustrated people sometimes aggress, they often do not. Can you think of times when frustration led you to aggress? What about times when you were frustrated but did not aggress? The questions for social psychologists become: When do frustrating circumstances lead to aggression? When do they not?

One factor that researchers discovered very quickly was whether the frustration seemed to be justified or arbitrary. Imagine stepping up to the refreshment counter at a movie theater and being denied a large container of buttered popcorn. If the snack-bar attendant says you can't have any because the popcorn machine is broken, your goal is frustrated but in a way that is justifiable, so you would be unlikely to aggress. But if the attendant says you can't have any but you can see plenty of popcorn behind the counter, the frustration seems to be arbitrary, and a disturbance in the theater is far more likely (e.g., Ohbuchi, 1982; Pastore, 1952). In one study (Fishman, 1965), participants were promised $2 if they succeeded on a task but then were denied the $2, either despite having succeeded (arbitrary frustration) or after being told they had failed on the task (nonarbitrary frustration). The arbitrary frustration led to participants' directing substantially more verbal aggression at the experimenter than did the nonarbitrary frustration.

Attacks, Insults, and Social Rejection

Perhaps the most reliable provocation of an aggressive response is the belief that one has or will be attacked intentionally, either physically or verbally (Geen, 2001). What could be more frustrating than being attacked or insulted? For example, in one study (Harmon-Jones & Sigelman, 2001), participants wrote an essay that an evaluator (actually a confederate) rated either positively ("I can understand why someone would think like this") or negatively ("I can't believe an educated person would think like this"). In a later part of the experiment, participants were given an opportunity to pick the type and quantity of beverage the evaluator would have to sample. When participants previously had been insulted, they were more likely to pick an unpleasant beverage (e.g., water mixed with vinegar) and to administer more of that beverage. Moreover, this aggressive reaction was related to how much each participant's brain was emitting electrical signals that typically reflect anger-related approach motivation: greater activation of the left prefrontal cortex and diminished activation of the right prefrontal cortex. Presumably the insulting evaluation elicited anger, an approach orienting emotion, which then led to the aggressive decision to have the evaluator drink more of the unpleasant beverage.

Although it is not surprising that physical attack often leads to counterattack, if only for self-defense, why aggress against someone who has insulted us? One answer is that insults threaten our self-esteem and sense of significance. When James Averill (1982, p. 174) asked participants to recall situations that made them angry, he found that a common cause was "loss of personal pride, self-esteem, or sense of personal worth." Because our sense of self-esteem and significance in the world depends so heavily on validation from others in our social sphere, insults and social rejection can arouse anger and an impulse to aggress, often in an attempt to restore wounded pride (Tangney et al., 1996). Indeed, when Leary and colleagues (2003) examined well-documented cases of school shootings between 1995 and 2001, they found that in 13 of the 15 cases, the perpetrator had been subjected to often malicious bullying, teasing, and rejection. Although a host of factors certainly contribute to the horrific acts that we see so frequently on the news, social rejection is clearly one of them.

Experimental research provides further support for the role of rejection. For example, in one study (Twenge et al., 2001), all participants had a 15-minute conversation together, then voted for the person they wanted to interact with further. The voting was rigged: Some participants were told that everyone wanted to interact with them (the accepted condition), but others were told that no one wanted to interact with them (the rejected condition). Each participant then was directed to play a computer game with another participant and told that the loser of the game would be punished by the winner by being subjected to noise blasts through a pair of headphones. Performance on the game was also rigged such that the (rejected or accepted) participant won and was thus allowed to choose the volume and duration of the unpleasant noise that the loser had to listen to. Compared with those participants who had experienced acceptance, participants who had experienced rejection opted to blast their opponents with louder and longer noises.

Of course, people don't always respond to rejection by becoming more aggressive. Sometimes, they become withdrawn and despondent. At other times, they seek acceptance (e.g., Leary et al., 2006). As with all conditions that arouse hostile feelings, other variables we will consider throughout this chapter help determine whether aggression or other responses to those feelings are more likely. But one factor particularly predictive of aggression in response to rejection is a personality trait called *rejection sensitivity*. People high in rejection sensitivity tend to expect, readily perceive, and overreact to rejection with aggressive responses (Ayduk et al., 2008).

When Do Hostile Feelings Lead to Aggression? The Cognitive Neoassociationism Model

After years of research, Berkowitz (1989) provided a particularly valuable additional answer to the "when" question in the form of his *cognitive neoassociationism model*. This model expands on the frustration-aggression hypothesis in three important ways. First, it proposes that a variety of unpleasant, stressful conditions (in addition to frustration) can make aggression more likely (although one can argue that anything unpleasant is frustrating). Second, Berkowitz hypothesized that negative affect in the form of anger or hostility is a central feature of affective aggression. Third, he specified features of situations that prime aggressive cognitions, which also make aggression more likely. Let's discuss these developments in more detail, looking first at the range of negative factors that potentially increase hostile feelings.

Physical Pain and Discomfort

It turns out that when people are hurt physically as well as emotionally, they are more likely to lash out: Physical pain triggers aggression. In one study that made this point, Berkowitz and colleagues (1981) had participants immerse one hand either in a bucket of freezing-cold ice water or in a bucket of comfortably tepid water as they were told to administer noise blasts to someone they thought was another participant in the study. Participants who experienced the pain of cold-water immersion administered a greater number of loud noise blasts to the confederate in the study.

Excessive heat can also cause discomfort, and several studies show that heat-induced discomfort can generate hostile feelings. Craig Anderson and colleagues (1989; Anderson et al., 1997; Bushman et al., 2005) have shown that as the temperature goes up, so do signs of aggression. We see this based on location, as violent crimes (but not nonviolent crimes) are more frequent in the hottest regions of countries (Anderson et al., 1996), and also with regard to time periods, as hotter years, months, and days have more violent crimes (Anderson et al., 1997). We also see this relationship in field studies. When Kenrick and MacFarlane (1986) stalled a car at a green light at an intersection in Phoenix, Arizona, they found that people were much more likely to honk the horn—often continuously and with aggressive fervor—on hotter days than on cooler days. We also find this relationship during baseball games. Looking at archival data from the 1962, 1986, 1987, and 1988 Major League Baseball seasons, Reifman and colleagues (1991) found that pitchers were more likely to hit batters on days when the temperature reached or surpassed 90 degrees Fahrenheit. Moreover, the heat did not simply distract the pitchers or reduce their accuracy. The relationship between heat and plunking the batter holds up even after the researchers took into account other indices of the pitchers' accuracy (e.g., walks, wild pitches). More recent research shows that perceived provocations intensify these effects. That is, pitchers are more likely to throw at opposing batters on hot days when one of their own teammates previously has been hit by a pitch (Larrick et al., 2011; see **FIGURE 12.5** on the next page). Whereas getting hit by a pitch is part of the game, at hotter temperatures, this potential provocation was much more likely to elicit retaliatory aggression.

The Role of Arousal in Aggression

As shown by Schachter's two factor theory of emotions (see chapter 5), under some conditions, the more arousal individuals experience, the stronger their emotional reactions will be. So when anger seems to be the appropriate response to a situation, extra sources of arousal may intensify the anger and subsequent aggression. According to Zillmann's (1971) *excitation transfer* theory (chapter 5), when people are still

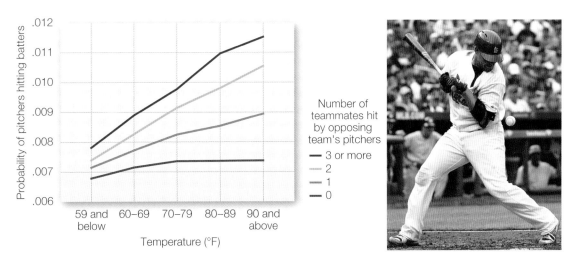

FIGURE 12.5

It's Getting Hot in Here

When temperatures are especially hot, tempers also rise. Major League Baseball pitchers were more likely to hit batters the hotter the temperature, especially if their teammates were hit earlier in the game.

[Left: Data source: Larrick et al. (2011); right: Dilip Vishwanat/Getty Images]

physiologically aroused by an initial event, but are no longer thinking about what made them aroused, this residual (or unexplained) excitation can be transferred and interpreted in the context of some new event. As a result, people who are already aroused are likely to overreact to subsequent provocations with intensified anger and aggression.

Consider the following demonstration (Zillmann & Bryant, 1974). Participants were told they would be playing a game with an opponent who was actually a confederate. Some participants were asked to ride an exercise bike, while others performed a less vigorous activity. Two minutes later a confederate either insulted them or treated them in a neutral manner. Then, about 6 minutes after the first activity when participants were still aroused by the exercise but no longer aware of it, they were given the opportunity to deliver a punishing noxious noise to the person who had previously angered them. Do you think you might be more or less aggressive after exercising? Though the idea of catharsis or "blowing off steam" might lead you to think the exercise would provide a release, purging you of aggressive inclinations, the results were quite the opposite. In accord with excitation transfer theory, those participants who engaged in exercise and were insulted actually delivered more of the noxious noise than the other participants. The excitation of exercise intensified their anger at the insulter, and thus intensified their aggressive behavior. A follow-up study (Zillmann et al., 1975) showed that when highly aroused, people are unable or unwilling to reduce their aggressive response even when apprised of mitigating circumstances for the provocation. Exercise is of course not the only source of such arousal; research shows that other sources of arousal also can exacerbate aggression in provoking situations (e.g., Zillmann, 1971).

Priming Aggressive Cognitions

Taking the social cognitive perspective, Berkowitz's cognitive neoassociationist model also proposes that hostile feelings will be especially likely to lead to aggression when hostile cognitions are primed by cues in the person's situation. What are some of the most common environmental cues that prime violence and aggression? One big category that stands out is firearms. This leads us to a discussion of one of the seminal studies of aggression—the study that introduced what is known as the **weapons effect**.

Weapons effect The tendency for the presence of firearms to increase the likelihood of aggression, especially when people are frustrated.

Imagine that you show up to take part in a study as participants did in Berkowitz and LePage (1967). You are told the study is exploring the connection between physiology and stress. You're informed that another participant (actually a confederate) will be grading ideas that you come up with for a task by administering electric shocks to you (1 shock = good answers, 7 shocks = bad answers). After generating your ideas, you get hit with 7 shocks (an outcome likely to anger most people). Other participants in the study are randomly assigned to receive just the minimal 1 shock, and likely feel less angry as a result. After this, you're brought to the room with the shock generator and given the chance to retaliate by administering electric shocks to the person who just shocked you. The second manipulation is whether people administered these shocks with a neutral object (e.g., a badminton racquet) sitting on the desk next to the shock generator, with nothing else on the desk, or—in the critical condition—with a 12-gauge shotgun and a .38-caliber revolver sitting on the desk. Participants were told that these objects were left over from a previous study, and that they should ignore them. How do you think you would respond?

Check out **FIGURE 12.6**. If participants were not previously made angry, the presence of weapons had no effect on their level of aggression. Similarly, if participants were angry but not in the presence of weapons, they were more aggressive, but not overly so. Yet a very different effect emerged when participants were both made angry and in the presence of weapons. In this condition, they administered the greatest number of intense electric shocks.

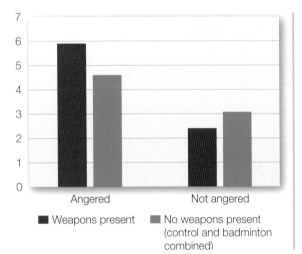

Figure 12.6

The Weapons Effect

Berkowitz and LePage's (1967) classic weapons-effect study shows that participants became the most aggressive when they were in a condition in which they were both angered and in the presence of a gun and a rifle, administering an especially large number of shocks to another person.

[Data source: Berkowitz & LePage (1967)]

You might be wondering whether something like this could happen outside the laboratory. You bet it could. In one field study, researchers got a pickup truck with a gun rack and had it stall at a traffic light (Turner et al., 1975). In one condition, there were two cues associated with violence: a military rifle in the gun rack and a bumper sticker that read "VENGEANCE." In another condition, there was one cue—the rifle—whereas the bumper sticker now read "FRIEND." In a third condition, there was neither a rifle nor a bumper sticker. Drivers behind the stalled truck were most likely to honk the horn when hostile cognitions were primed by the rifle and the "VENGEANCE" bumper sticker and least likely to honk when there were no cues priming such cognitions. This is a powerful demonstration when you consider that if participants had been thinking rationally about their behavior, someone with a rifle and a "VENGEANCE" bumper sticker would be the last person they would want to mess with.

Why does the weapons effect occur? One reason is that weapons prime aggression-related thoughts, which in turn makes it more likely an angered person will think of aggressive ways to deal with that anger. Another reason is that weapons can induce a physiological reaction that predisposes people toward more hostile actions. In one study, participants who spent 15 minutes handling a pellet gun that looks a lot like an automatic handgun, as opposed to handling the children's game Mousetrap, showed increases in their level of testosterone (Klinesmith et al., 2006). In addition, the bigger their increase in testosterone, the more aggressive they were toward another supposed participant, spiking that person's water with more hot sauce. An interesting result was that these hostile acts occurred even though these participants had not been frustrated or insulted by the person they aggressed against. The researchers suggest that because participants handled the gun for 15 minutes, their extended time with a weapon may have increased aggression even though they had not been provoked or frustrated.

Stimuli other than firearms also can become associated with violence and therefore can prime cognitions that encourage aggression. In one study, a violent film scene involving the actor Kirk Douglas led to more aggression against a provoking confederate if he was named Kirk instead of Bob (Berkowitz & Geen, 1967). In another study, Josephson (1987) showed seven- to nine-year-old children either a violent TV show in which walkie-talkies were used or a neutral show before they played a game of floor hockey. Boys who had seen the violent show and then saw walkie-talkies at the beginning of the game were the most aggressive during the game.

So stimuli other than guns can become cues that encourage aggression, but will guns always do so? It largely depends on the associations that a person has with the object. Although for many people guns have an associative history with violence and aggression, this is not the case for everyone. People who hunt for sport may see guns in a different light. As a result they don't tend to show activation of aggressive cognitions and are not more aggressive toward those who provoke them when exposed to pictures of guns; in contrast, nonhunters are (Bartholow et al., 2005). For hunters, pictures of guns actually arouse warm and pleasant cognitions (perhaps reflecting the enjoyable times with family and friends while they've hunted). But when hunters are shown pictures of assault rifles, which have no connection to recreational sport, they do show increased aggressive cognitions and behavior. Thus, the weapons effect critically depends on the person's prior learning and experiences.

Of course, most Americans are not recreational hunters. Thus these weapons-effect findings make us pause when we think about the influence that rampant exposure and accessibility of guns have on violence in this country. Consider some of the following statistics. The U.S. Bureau of Justice Statistics reports that in 2011, 11,101 persons were killed by firearm violence; 478,400 persons were victims of a crime committed with a firearm (Planty & Truman, 2013). Between 1993 and 2011, about 60 to 70% of murders in the United States were committed with firearms, especially handguns (see **FIGURE 12.7**) (Planty & Truman, 2013). Such statistics can be alarming, especially when we compare the United States with countries that ban gun ownership. Great Britain, which has one fourth the population of the United States, has one sixteenth the number of murders. Although the homes of gun owners differ in a variety of ways from non–gun owners' homes, researchers point out that people in homes with guns are 2.7 times more likely to

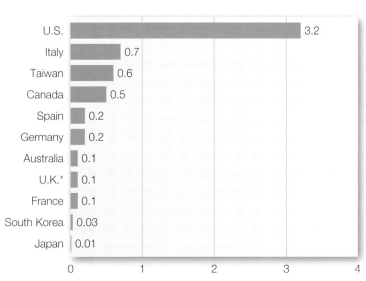

U.S.	3.2
Italy	0.7
Taiwan	0.6
Canada	0.5
Spain	0.2
Germany	0.2
Australia	0.1
U.K.*	0.1
France	0.1
South Korea	0.03
Japan	0.01

NOTE: List includes countries with a per capita GDP of more than $30,000 and a population of 20 million or more; all data for the most recent year available

* Does not include Northern Ireland

Figure 12.7

Gun-related Homicides

Gun-related homicides occur at a much higher rate in the United States than in other industrialized nations.

[Data source: United Nations Office on Drugs and Crime (2013); (http://www.unodc.org/documents/gsh/pdfs/2014_GLOBAL_HOMICI. Photo: Shutterstock]

be murdered than those in homes without guns (Kellermann et al., 1993; Wiebe, 2003). Such statistics, in conjunction with his research, prompted Berkowitz (1968, p. 22) to suggest that "the finger pulls the trigger but the trigger may also be pulling the finger."

Inhibitors of Aggression

We've covered a lot of evidence on facilitators of hostile feelings and thoughts that lead to aggression, but can you think of times you were angry and thought about acting aggressively, but did not? What factors inhibit people from acting on their hostile feelings and thoughts? Moral values that forbid hurting others, feelings of empathy for others, and consideration of possible aversive consequences for oneself, such as prison or retaliation, all play a role in whether people choose aggression or other responses, particularly when the capacity for self-control is high and not hindered by circumstances (e.g., Geen, 2001). However, as we will see in our next few sections, people differ in the strength of both facilitators and inhibitors of aggression, leading some people to be more prone to aggression than others.

SECTION review | Situational Factors in Aggression: The Context Made Me Do It

Unpleasant, frustrating experiences arouse hostile affect, which makes us prone to aggression, particularly when situational cues prime aggressive cognitions.

Frustration-aggression hypothesis	Factors that increase aggressive responses	Facilitators and inhibitors of aggression
• Frustration produces an emotional readiness to aggress. • Conditions of the situation can then trigger an aggressive response. • Displaced aggression is aggression directed at targets other than those that caused the frustration. • Triggered displaced aggression is targeted against a secondary, even minor, source of frustration.	Aggression is more likely: • if the frustration is arbitrary. • if there is an expectation of physical or verbal attack, insult, or social rejection. • in response to physical pain, heat, and discomfort. • if the individual has residual arousal from prior events.	• Stimuli that arouse hostile feelings are most likely to lead to aggression if there is a situational cue, such as a nearby weapon, that primes aggressive cognitions. • Morals, empathy, and consideration of consequences can mitigate the effects of hostile feelings and cognitions.

Learning to Aggress

One of the great adaptive features of our species is our capacity for learning, our ability to develop new responses to particular situations on the basis of our experiences in the world. But this capacity also means that much of our propensity for aggression is something that we learn. Some learning of aggression is based on operant conditioning. Beginning in early childhood, we all engage in some aggressive acts such as biting, hitting, shoving, kicking, verbal aggression, and so forth. The more these aggressive actions are reinforced in particular situations, the more frequently an individual will turn to additional aggression in similar contexts (e.g., Geen & Pigg, 1970; Geen & Stonner, 1971; Loew, 1967). In other words, if these actions garner desired attention or specific rewards, or if they alleviate negative feelings, they will become more likely (Dengerink & Covey, 1983; Geen, 2001). If Taylor hits Tim to get his lollipop, Taylor's aggression will be reinforced if the consequence is successfully enjoying a tasty lollipop. If a child is hassled and made fun of by other kids, but finds that aggressive action alleviates the hassling, the child is likely to learn that physical aggression is a way to get relief from being bothered by others. And in gang subcultures, members may win admiration for engaging in violence (Wolfgang & Ferracuti, 1967).

On the other hand, if aggressive actions do not lead to rewarding experiences, or if they lead to unpleasant experiences, the likelihood of aggression should be reduced. However, punishment does not inhibit actions nearly so well as rewards encourage them. And in some cases, attempts at punishment may actually be reinforcing because they inadvertently bring desired attention to the child. This can occur with adults as well. Throughout history, outlaws such as the bank robber John Dillinger, depicted in the movie *Public Enemies*, gained attention, publicity, and even fame for their violent actions (Brown et al., 2009).

There is another reason one's own aggressive actions tend to encourage more aggressive actions. When people act aggressively, they can feel dissonance or guilt, which leads them to shift their attitudes to justify their actions. Martens and colleagues (2007) showed that the more pill bugs participants were instructed to kill by dropping them into what they thought was a bug-killing machine (see **FIGURE 12.8**), the more such bugs they voluntarily chose to kill during a subsequent free time period. Interestingly, this escalation of killing occurred only in people who believed there was some similarity between bugs and humans and therefore were likely to feel guilty about those first bugs they killed. This process of escalating killing mirrors many historical examples in which initial acts of aggression are followed by more severe acts of aggression later (Kressel, 1996).

In addition to learning to aggress through their own actions, people also learn to aggress by watching the actions of others. Humans have a great capacity for imitation and observational learning (Bandura, 1973). Indeed, most children probably learn more about aggression from electronic media sources, from watching their parents and peers, and from their cultural upbringing than they do from their own actions. So let's take a careful look at how the electronic media, family life, and culture contribute to aggression.

Electronic Media and Aggression

A large body of research shows that exposure to violent media increases the prevalence of aggression in a society (e.g., Bushman & Huesmann, 2010). In fact, the relationship between exposure to media depictions of violence and aggressive behavior is stronger than many other relationships that are considered very well established, including, for example, the extent to which condom use predicts likelihood of contracting HIV and the extent to which calcium intake is related to bone mass (see **FIGURE 12.9**) (Bushman & Anderson, 2001). Despite this evidence, violent content is pervasive in modern television programming, films, and video games and on the Internet (Donnerstein, 2011).

Bushman and Anderson argued that one reason these research findings are largely ignored is that violent media are very popular and therefore profitable. Consequently, news media outlets, which often are connected to the businesses that gather these profits, tend to be biased in their reporting of the evidence. To illustrate the profitability of film violence, as this textbook goes to press, all of the top 10 highest-grossing films of all time worldwide feature violence and weapons: *Avatar, Titanic, Marvel's The Avengers, Harry Potter and the Deathly Hallows Part 2, Iron Man 3, Frozen, Transformers: Dark of the Moon, Lord of the Rings: The Return of the King, Skyfall,*

Sometimes the punishment for and media attention on violent actions can make them rewarding, as was the case with the bank robber John Dillinger, who was glamorized by newspapers in his day, and in the film *Public Enemies*, in which Johnny Depp played him.

[Universal Pictures/Photofest]

Figure 12.8

Does Killing Beget Killing?

When participants believed they were grinding up bugs in this modified coffee grinder, those who initially killed five bugs justified their aggression by killing even more later.

[Jeff Greenberg]

Figure 12.9

Does Media Violence Matter?

The effect of violence in the media on actual aggression seems to be just as strong as, and in many cases stronger than, a number of influences that go unquestioned in society.

[Data source: Bushman & Anderson (2001)]

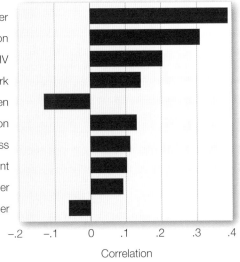

The Dark Knight Rises (Box Office Mojo, 2014). You may be thinking, "Wait, what about *Frozen*?" Well, although it may be the least graphically violent of these ten, this animated children's film features fistfights, a battle with crossbows, and a knife fight. Similarly, the most popular show on American television is *NCIS*, which typically begins with a murder and proceeds from there. The list of popular violent television shows also includes *CSI*, *Law and Order*, and their multiple spinoffs, not to mention *The Walking Dead*, *True Blood*, *Game of Thrones*, and *Breaking Bad*. The current most popular video game series include such violent offerings as *Call of Duty*, *Grand Theft Auto*, *Mortal Combat*, and *Left for Dead*. Given that the average American 12-year-old spends more time consuming media than attending school (Bushman & Huesmann, 2010) and that the average American adolescent has seen approximately 200,000 acts of violence on television (Strasburger, 2007), young people have plenty of opportunities to learn how to be aggressive.

What Is the Appeal of Media Violence?

Violence and smut are of course everywhere on the airwaves. You cannot turn on your television without seeing them, although sometimes you have to hunt around.

—Dave Barry (1966)

Why is violent entertainment so popular? From the evolutionary perspective, it's likely been adaptive for humans to be innately vigilant to viewing, and physiologically aroused by, instances of violence (e.g., Beer, 1984). As the old journalism cliché goes, "If it bleeds, it leads." If there is potential danger, we want to know what, where, how, and why. And well we should, so that we can prepare for fight or flight. The entertainment industry takes advantage of these innate tendencies. Although people don't like it directed at themselves, they do enjoy seeing violence in movies on TV or enacting it in video games—where they are not in any real danger (McCauley, 1998). This is especially true of people who are high in sensation seeking or who feel bored (Cantor, 1998; Tamborini & Stiff, 1987).

The other easy way to make viewers excited is with sexually appealing images, another feature of much popular entertainment, as Dave Barry noted. But in American culture, younger viewers are shielded much more strictly from sexual content than they are from violent content. For example, in movie ratings a single exposed penis or breast guarantees an R rating, whereas massive amounts of killing can now be found in many PG-13 movies. Back in 1985, PG-13 movies had about the same amount of gun violence as did G-rated movies; but since 2009, levels of gun violence in these adolescent-friendly PG-13 pictures now match or even exceed those in R-rated films (Bushman et al., 2013).

Another basis of the appeal of violent media is the portrayal of heroic victories over evil and injustice (e.g., Goldstein, 1998; Zillmann, 1998). One of the first violent American TV shows, *The Adventures of Superman*, expressed this very succinctly: Superman fights for "truth, justice and the American way." For American children watching that show, what could be better than that? Identifying with such heroes may provide a boost in self-esteem, a sense of control over threats, and a feeling that good triumphs in the end (Cantor, 1998). And these feelings may be especially strong when you yourself are the hero, as is typically the case for players of violent video games (Bushman & Huesmann, 2010).

The Basic Evidence for Violent Media's Contributing to Aggression

You may be thinking to yourself, "Well, I watch a lot of violent entertainment and play video games, and I don't go around hurting other people." As we noted earlier, aggression is not caused by any one factor in isolation but results from particular combinations of coexistent causal factors. Let's examine the evidence that exposure to media violence is one of those causal factors.

Research has shown clearly that the more violence an individual watches, the more aggressive that person is (e.g., Singer & Singer, 1981). Of course, this finding is merely a correlation and so could mean either that violent entertainment causally contributes to aggression or that viewers who like aggression are more likely to watch violent entertainment. Longitudinal evidence (i.e., studies that follow people over time) suggests that the former causal pathway provides the more likely explanation (e.g., Huesmann et al., 1984, 2003; Lefkowitz et al., 1977). The more violent programs an individual watches as a child, the more likely that individual is to be violent up to 22 years later as an adult. In contrast, level of aggressiveness as a child does not similarly predict interest in watching violent programs as an adult. Similar findings are emerging for violent video-game play as well (e.g., Anderson et al., 2008).

As first-person shooter games become increasingly realistic and popular, research suggests they can prime and promote aggression at least in some individuals.

[© Doug Steley A/Alamy]

The best way to assess a causal effect of exposure to violence on aggression is to conduct field studies and experiments in which some participants are randomly assigned to watch violent or nonviolent content (e.g., Berkowitz, 1965; Geen & Berkowitz, 1966). The findings of many such studies show that exposure to media violence through watching videos or playing video games increases aggression (Bushman & Huesmann, 2010; Geen, 2001). Let's consider two examples that illustrate these effects.

In a home for juvenile delinquent boys, Leyens and colleagues (1975) had boys in two of the cottages watch five nights of violent movies. Boys in two other cottages watched five nights of nonviolent movies. The boys were observed each night for frequency of hitting, slapping, choking, and kicking their cottage mates. The boys who watched the violent films engaged in more such aggressive behavior than those who watched the nonviolent films. In another study, Konijn and colleagues (2007) randomly assigned Dutch adolescent boys to play a violent or nonviolent video game for 20 minutes and then play a competitive game with another study participant. The winner got the privilege of blasting the loser with noise at a volume of their choosing, ranging from a tolerable 60 decibels to a potentially hearing-damaging 105 decibels. The adolescents who played the violent video game chose potentially harmful noise levels more often.

It's important to note that the majority of these laboratory experiments show these effects of violent media primarily when participants are frustrated or provoked (e.g., Geen & Stonner, 1973), and for viewers who are generally above average in aggressive tendencies (e.g., Anderson & Dill, 2000; Bushman, 1995). So your likely self-based observation is correct. Exposure to violent media doesn't promote aggression in all viewers or all the time. But it does so in people experiencing hostile feelings or who are generally predisposed to such feelings and to reacting to them with aggression (e.g., Geen, 2001).

How and Why Does Watching Violence Contribute to Aggression in Viewers?

Observational Learning of Aggression Video on LaunchPad

The next questions concern how and why violent media have these effects. Social learning theory and research provide some important answers (Bandura, 1973). People tend to imitate the behaviors they observe in others and learn new behaviors from them. As the Bobo doll studies showed (chapter 7), frustrated children who observed an adult model attacking a Bobo doll became more aggressive toward the doll, often in the same specific way that they saw the adult aggress. They also aggressed more if they identified with the adult model and if they observed the model being rewarded for his or her aggression.

Many subsequent experiments, with both children and adults, further support the role of social learning in the effects of observed violence in general, and violence portrayed in films and video material in particular. The more study participants identify with the character they see engaging in filmed violence, the more they are likely to aggress (e.g., Perry & Perry, 1976; Turner & Berkowitz, 1972). In addition, filmed violence is more likely to be imitated if the violence is rewarded rather than punished, if it seems justified rather than unjustified, and if the harm caused by the aggression is deemphasized or sanitized (e.g., Donnerstein, 2011; Geen & Stonner, 1972, 1973). The common

Violence on Film: *Taxi Driver*

The 1976 classic Martin Scorsese film *Taxi Driver* (Phillips et al., 1976), starring Robert De Niro as the cabbie Travis Bickle and Jodie Foster as the underage prostitute Iris, was one of the most violent films of its time. It depicts much of what we know about the causes of aggression and the kind of explosive gun violence that has become much more common since the release of the film. Paul Schrader based his screenplay in part on the diary of Arthur Bremer, who had grievously wounded a presidential candidate in an assassination attempt in 1968.

As a former marine who served in Vietnam, Travis has had training in violence (*social learning*). He is stressed by insomnia, stomach pains, and a sense of alienation and loneliness. He drinks heavily (and therefore might be more *disinhibited*) and takes amphetamines (which might elevate his *arousal*). He drives the streets of New York in his cab, witnessing aggression and violent conflict on a nightly basis (*violent cues*

and scripts). He is looking for some way to feel heroic, like a person of significance in the world (*low self-esteem with touches of narcissism*). He is deeply frustrated when he is rejected by an attractive political campaign volunteer named Betsy, whom he had viewed as an angel amid the filth and ugliness around him. One of his customers primes him with the idea of getting a .44 Magnum and avenging himself against Betsy. He subsequently attempts in vain to shoot a presidential candidate whom Betsy worked for. He eventually goes on a bloody rampage, intending to strike out at those he perceives as evil and to save Iris from a life of prostitution.

A few years after the film came out, a socially inhibited and lonely young man named John Hinckley, Jr., became obsessed with the film, watching it fifteen times and photographing himself in Travis Bickle poses. He eventually decided that he needed to save Jodie Foster, at the time an undergraduate at Yale University. He made contact with her and sent her flowers. Foster soon recognized Hinckley as an unstable stalker and cut off communication with him. He decided he needed to impress her and wrote her a letter explaining as much. His misguided effort resulted in his attempt to assassinate President Ronald Reagan in 1981. He got close enough to Reagan to wound him seriously with a pistol.

television and film scenario in which the hero uses weapons to defeat the villains fits these conditions perfectly: The likable protagonist, easy to identify with, engages in aggression that is justified and leads to a rewarding outcome. Bushman and Huesmann (2010) suggest that these conditions are even more common in violent video games in which the gamer's character is him- or herself the hero who is rewarded for aggression.

Further evidence of the effects of media violence is provided by instances in which very specific forms of violence depicted in films have been imitated in the real world. In just one of many examples, in 1971, Stanley Kubrick's disturbing, ultraviolent, dystopian science-fiction film classic *A Clockwork Orange* opened in British theaters to great controversy. After its release, the British press chronicled a series of copycat crimes, including the beating to death of a homeless man, leading Kubrick to ban the film in the United Kingdom in 1973. In one scene from the film, a gang of teens rape a woman while singing "Singin' in the Rain." Shortly after the film was banned, a gang of British teens raped a teenage girl while singing the same song (Travis, 1999). Social Psych at the Movies discusses another historically important film that inspired violence.

The sociologist David Phillips (1979, 1982) demonstrated a similar imitative tendency by examining frequencies of suicides and car accidents in communities following exposure to news coverage of real-life celebrity suicides and fictional soap opera depictions of suicides. He also examined homicides after highly publicized heavyweight boxing matches (Phillips, 1983; Phillips & Hensley, 1984). In all of these cases, he found significant increases in suicides and homicides a few days after these media depictions. The more these events were publicized in a community, the greater the increase in corresponding violent actions.

Stanley Kubrick's 1971 film *A Clockwork Orange* is one of many examples in which media violence seems to have inspired real-life violence.

[Warner Bros./Photofest]

He also wounded Reagan's press secretary James Brady, who was paralyzed by the shooting.

Hinckley's act of violence, inspired in part by *Taxi Driver*, caused great physical harm to major government officials but also eventually led to the Brady bill, which requires a three-day waiting period and a background check for anyone in the United States to purchase a firearm. The Brady Handgun Violence Prevention Act, enacted in 1993, has stopped many convicted felons and people deemed mentally unfit from purchasing such weapons, although it does not catch everyone due to inadequate resources devoted to enforcement. Seung-Hui Cho, who killed 32 people and wounded 25 others on the campus of Virginia Tech University in 2007, was able to purchase multiple weapons despite having been declared mentally ill by a judge and ordered to get treatment one year earlier.

The other major long-term effect the Hinckley shooting had was on the legal system. Hinckley eventually was found not guilty by reason of insanity, a verdict that outraged many Americans and led to changes in the insanity plea. Currently, in most states, the plea is guilty but insane rather than not guilty by reason of insanity. Meanwhile, Hinckley is still under care at a mental hospital but is allowed to leave to visit his relatives (Public Broadcasting Service, n.d.).

[Columbia Pictures/Photofest]

Another noteworthy effect of violent media is that the more violent television people watch, the more they believe that violence is common in the real world (Gerbner et al., 1980, 1982). This sense that the world is unsafe also may contribute to aggressive propensities by increasing a sense of threat and encouraging the idea that aggression is normative. Furthermore, the more children and adults watch media violence, the less they become disturbed by it and the more they become tolerant of it (Drabman & Thomas, 1974; Linz et al., 1989; Thomas et al., 1977). One recent study from the social neuroscience perspective showed that playing a violent video game leads to a reduced physiological reaction in the brain called the P3 response, which indicates a lack of surprise in response to viewing aggression. Furthermore, this neural desensitization helps explain why violent video games tend to increase aggression (Engelhardt et al., 2011). The lower participants' P3 response to violent stimuli, the more aggressive they were when administering noise blasts to an opponent.

Of course, none of these findings implies that exposure to media violence always increases aggressive tendencies, but it causes such tendencies to be more likely in the short term by making hostile feelings, violent thoughts, and scripts temporarily more accessible (Anderson & Dill, 2000; Berkowitz, 1993; Bushman, 1998; Bushman & Geen, 1990; Bushman & Huesmann, 2006). As the line of work starting with Berkowitz and LePage (1967) showed, when people experience hostile feelings along with violent thoughts, they are more likely to choose aggressive as opposed to nonaggressive ways to deal with those feelings.

In sum, both theory and research suggest the following disturbing conclusion. If 10 million people watch a violent television show or movie, play a violent video game, or listen to violent music lyrics, the majority surely won't be moved to engage in aggression. However, just as surely, a minority of them—those with hostile feelings or dispositional aggressiveness, or both—will be. And even if that minority were a mere one tenth of 1% of the viewing or gaming audience, that still would be 10,000 people moved by violent media toward engaging in aggression.

APPLICATION
Family Life and Aggression

Mass-media entertainment is not the only source of aggressive models and thoughts. Aggression is an all too common part of family life (Gelles, 2007; Green, 1998; Straus et al., 1980), whether between parents, siblings, or parents and their children. The same factors that contribute to aggression in general play a role in family violence. All relationships inevitably involve frustration at some times, and our family relationships can be especially aggravating because we are so invested in them. Raising children is very challenging, with frustration being an inevitable aspect of that experience. Moreover, family members are also closest at hand, and thus they are likely targets of displaced aggression when people are frustrated by their bosses, teachers, or other life stressors.

How does domestic aggression affect children growing up in such circumstances? Just as people who are exposed to a great deal of media violence are more likely to aggress, so are children who are exposed to a great deal of physical aggression and conflict at home (Geen, 1998; Geen, 2001; Huesmann et al., 1984; Straus et al., 1980). A violent family atmosphere generates negative affect and disrupts the psychological security that a consistently loving upbringing would provide. Sibling rivalry, conflicts between parents, lack of affection, and inconsistent discipline by parents all can increase frustration and stress in both toddlers and older children (e.g., Cummings et al., 1981, 1985).

A stressful family life also reinforces and models aggression. Aggressive parents often give children approval for responding aggressively to perceived slights and provocations. Parents who employ corporal punishment to discipline their children also are implicitly teaching that physical aggression is an appropriate way to respond to those perceived as wrongdoers and portrays violence as normative to the child. These lessons communicate that the world is a dangerous place in which most people have negative intentions, which encourages children to see hostile intent in others' actions (e.g., Dodge et al., 1990).

Stress and frustration, disrupted attachment and trust in other people, and training in and modeling of aggression in violent families have both short-term and long-term consequences (Straus et al., 1980). In the short term, these conditions of family life lead children to become more aggressive. For example, Rohner (1975) found that across 60 different cultures, rejected children are more aggressive than accepted children. In a study of American preadolescent and adolescent boys, Loeber and Dishion (1984) found that those whose family lives were characterized by marital conflict, rejection, and inconsistent discipline were especially aggressive both at home and in school.

In the long term, children who are exposed to a violent family life are more prone to become aggressive adults (Eron et al., 1991; Hill & Nathan, 2008; McCord, 1983; Olweus, 1995; Straus, 2000). Longitudinal studies find that children subjected to witnessing domestic violence or victimized by abuse are more likely as adults to become spousal abusers and child abusers themselves, creating a vicious cycle perpetuated across generations (Azar & Rohrbeck, 1986; Hotaling & Sugarman, 1990; MacEwen & Barling, 1988; Peterson & Brown, 1994; Widom, 1989). Even though only 2 to 4% of the general population of parents is physically abusive, approximately 30% of abused children grow up to be abusive parents (Gelles, 2007; Kaufman & Zigler, 1987).

Culture and Aggression

As we've considered the cultural perspective throughout this book, we've seen how culture shapes our values, beliefs, and behavior. Aggression is no exception. As we grow up, we are socialized with particular expectations and into particular roles. Along the way, we also learn how, when, and to what extent aggressive behavior is an acceptable or normative response to certain situations. Some cultures, and subcultures, may socialize us to "turn the other cheek," whereas others emphasize an "eye for an eye" or not backing down from a fight. Cultures further teach us what responses are appropriate in different situations of frustration or insult. Culture thus has a profound influence on not only the extent of aggression but also the form it can take. We see this influence when we compare national cultures as well as regions and cultural subgroups within a nation.

"When I turned the other cheek, it surprised him ... and that's when I let him have it."

[Andrew Toos/Cartoonstock]

Comparing National Cultures

Across nations, we find striking differences in prevalence of serious acts of aggression. In the United States, for example, one murder occurs every 31 seconds. This dwarfs the murder rates in other industrialized nations such as Canada, Australia, and Great Britain and is approximately double the world average (Barber, 2006). Although some countries in Eastern Europe, Africa, and Asia have higher rates, much of the violence in those nations is between groups and results from political instability, whereas violent crimes in the United States tend to be committed by individuals against other individuals. Americans have a stronger tendency than people of many other nations to resort to aggressive solutions to interpersonal conflicts (Archer & McDaniel, 1995).

As we noted earlier, the high murder rate in the United States stems in part from the ready availability of firearms (e.g., Archer, 1994; Archer & Gartner, 1984). Firearms not only prime aggression-related thoughts, they also increase the lethality of violence. People looking to aggress will use whatever is available. Aggression by firearms leads to death one in six times; aggression by knife, one in thirty times (Goldstein, 1986). Consider the Norwegian shooting spree described at the outset of this chapter. The killer would have done far less harm if he hadn't been able to obtain semiautomatic weapons.

In trying to understand how and why cultures differ in aggression, some researchers focus on individualism versus collectivism. As we first discussed in chapter 2, individualistic cultures place greater value on independence and self-reliance, whereas collectivistic cultures place greater value on cooperation and maintaining harmonious relationships with others. Perhaps as a consequence, individualistic cultures tend to have more interpersonal aggression than collectivistic cultures. For example, the United States is more individualistic than Poland, which in turn is more individualistic than China. These differences in individualism mirror the rates of aggression and violence. The United States has more aggression and violence than Poland, which in turn has more aggression and violence than China (Forbes et al., 2009). Nevertheless, there are many exceptions. Some fairly collectivistic African and Latin American cultures have homicide rates considerably higher than the more individualistic United States. There is no single or simple set of variables that can account for a given nation's record of violence.

Comparing Subcultures Within Nations

Imagine that you are walking down a narrow hallway toward your psychology classroom as another student approaches you. As you pass by, you bump shoulders. Apparently prompted by this contact, he mutters "asshole" under his breath before stepping into another room. How would you react? Do you think you might react differently if you grew up in the northern United States as opposed to the South?

Think ABOUT

[Ryan McVay/ Getty Images]

Cultures of Honor

Research on regional variations in a culture of honor suggests that the answer might be yes. In places that have a *culture of honor,* people (especially men) are highly motivated to protect their status or reputations. Daly and Wilson (1988, p. 128) describe it this way:

> A seemingly minor affront . . . must be understood within a larger social context of reputations, face, relative social status, and enduring relationships. Men are known by their fellows as "the sort who can be pushed around" or "the sort who won't take any shit," as people whose words mean action, or as people who are full of hot air, as guys whose girlfriends you can chat up with impunity or guys you don't want to mess with.

Dov Cohen and Richard Nisbett (Cohen & Nisbett, 1994; Nisbett, 1993) have documented a strong culture of honor in the southern and western United States. For example, homicide rates among White men living in rural or small-town settings in those regions are higher than corresponding rates in similar settings in other regions of the country. Southern White men are also more likely than northern White men to believe that lethal violence is justified as a means of defending life, family, property, or reputation after they perceive it as impugned. The culture of honor extends even to names of towns and businesses. More town and business names in the South conjure up images of battle and violence than in the North (Kelly, 1999). If you're driving across Delaware, New Hampshire, or New Jersey, you might happen to spot Woodlawn Kennels, Crenshaw Church, or a town called Tranquility. But in Texas and Alabama, you might drive past Battle Ax Church, Gunsmoke Kennels, or a town called Warrior.

Recall the example of someone bumping into you in a hallway and then cursing at you for being in his way. Cohen and his colleagues (1996) put unsuspecting male college students from either the North or the South in that very situation. Students from the North did not have much of a reaction to the insult, but students from the South showed comparative increases in aggressive feelings, thoughts,

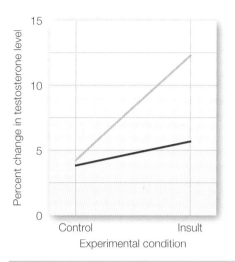

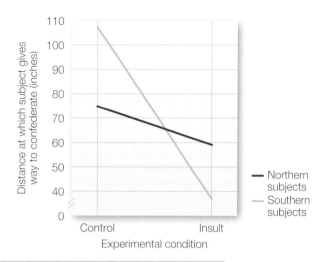

— Northern subjects
— Southern subjects

and physiology. They were more likely to think their masculine reputations were threatened and were more upset and primed for an aggressive response, as indicated by higher levels of cortisol, testosterone, and aggressive cognitions. They were also more likely subsequently to engage in dominance-affirming behavior to restore their honor after this perceived slight. In one study, they were also slower to move out of the way when walking toward another confederate in a narrow hallway through which only one person could pass at a time (see **FIGURE 12.10**). And this person was 6 feet, 3 inches tall and weighed 250 pounds—no small dude!

Why did the culture of honor develop primarily in the South and West? Cohen and Nisbett (1994; Nisbett & Cohen, 1996) theorize that the answer goes back to the environmental and economic conditions in the places the American settlers came from and in the regions where they settled. Many southern settlers came from pastoral, herding societies, such as Scotland. Other settlers, who migrated to the arid western regions of the country, became economically more dependent on cattle ranching and sheepherding than on farming. In contrast, the North largely was settled by farmers and developed a more agricultural, as opposed to herding, economy. Because people from a herding-based culture are more vulnerable to having their livelihood (e.g., livestock) rustled away, norms developed whereby men cultivated a rough, tough affect, responding harshly and violently to even the smallest threat or slight. These aggressive responses were intended to discourage theft of their means of sustenance. In contrast, because it is more difficult to steal a whole crop than a single sheep, such norms did not develop in the more agricultural North.

In addition, because much of the South and West remained frontier land with widely scattered, less effective law enforcement, it became even more important to protect one's own property. As a result, norms for retributive justice are thought to have developed in the South and West more vigorously than in the North. Similar perceptions and reactions have been observed among participants from Brazil and Chile (Vandello & Cohen, 2003; Vandello et al., 2009), whose cultures also emphasize honor and which have an economic history of herding, but not among Canadians, who are more neutral with respect to honor.

Although these economic and environmental conditions no longer apply, the culture of honor persists, reinforced by institutional norms and scripts of action that people learn through socialization processes and extending to their attitudes and behavior. People from the South have a more lenient attitude toward crimes—even murder—when they believe the perpetrator is acting to protect honor, for example, killing to defend his family (Vandello et al., 2008). Indeed, when employers were sent a job application from a fictitious applicant who admitted that he had impulsively killed a man who had an affair with his wife and then publicly taunted him about it, southern employers responded more sympathetically than those in the North (Cohen & Nisbett, 1997).

Figure 12.10

Culture of Honor

After being insulted, students from the South showed greater increases in testosterone than those from the North, and they were subsequently less likely to back down when approaching another confederate in a narrow hallway.

[Data source: Cohen et al. (1996)]

Herding cultures are associated with cultures of honor.

[Getty Images/iStockphoto]

However, no such differences emerged with respect to an applicant who admitted stealing a car because he needed the money. Not just any aggressive or criminal action is considered more acceptable, but specifically those that involve matters of honor.

Protecting One's Status

Although cultures of honor might initially develop in societies focused on herding, *low-status compensation theory* suggests that the larger status disparities—that is, an unequal distribution of wealth—found in herding societies account for the link between cultures of honor and aggressive proclivities (Henry, 2009). In other words, herding cultures tend to have greater status disparities between the haves and the have-nots, leading lower-status men to become especially sensitive to status threats (e.g., insults). People with high status are not similarly bothered by status threats because

Race and Violence in Inner-City Neighborhoods

On July 4, 2009, a 16-year-old boy was shot and killed in Englewood, an economically disadvantaged and predominantly African American neighborhood on the South Side of Chicago (Glass, 2013). It is also a neighborhood terrorized by gang violence. Presumably because of the stressors that come with poverty, poorer neighborhoods generally have high rates of violent crime and gang activity (Berkowitz, 1993; Short, 1997).

On the surface, Terrance Green's murder seems like another statistic in a larger and disturbing pattern: In the United States, violence is more prevalent in inner-city, Black neighborhoods than other American neighborhoods. For example, although African Americans are approximately 13% of the U.S. population, according to the FBI (2010), in 2010, they accounted for 53% of homicide offenders. Young Black males

are also more likely than White males to be victims of violence. You may have heard such statistics before, but let's probe further to understand what might lie beneath these cycles of violence.

When you think about gang violence, you probably think about killings between rival gangs over drugs or money. It's true that Terrance was a gang member and that he was killed by a rival gang. But although these facts about Terrance's death conform to the general beliefs people have about gang violence, many others do not. For example, children reared in fatherless homes tend to be more violent and aggressive than children in two-parent families (Lykken, 2000; Staub, 1996; Vaden-Kiernan et al., 1995), and Black kids are increasingly being raised by single moms without the help of a father (Kids Count, 2013). But although Terrance grew up in Chicago's toughest neighborhood, he came from a loving, two-parent household. He was the youngest of five kids; his oldest brother is a pastor. With such a stable and supportive home life, how did Terrance end up in a gang?

Many social psychological processes lie beneath the cycle of violence (Anderson, 2000). In a place like Englewood, students often don't join gangs by choice. Instead, the gang you end up in depends on the block you live on. By the time Terrance and his friends hit puberty, they were bullied by older kids for merely walking down a street in another gang's territory. By default, Terrance was assumed to be part of the gang in his neighborhood, even though he'd never been recruited or agreed to be a member. He was an athlete and a natural leader, so he found himself having to defend his friends as well as himself.

Without knowing what else to do, Terrance and his teenage friends banded together to protect themselves, calling themselves Yung Lyfe (Young Unique Noble Gentlemen Live Youthful and Fulfilled Everyday)—not exactly a name designed to strike fear in the minds of others. Terrance's father never realized that his son had been backed into being a gang member. And after Terrance was killed, he was shocked to

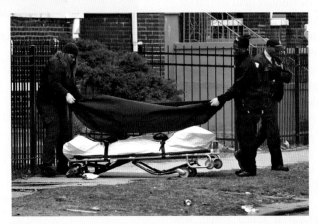

[Scott Olson/Getty Images]

they have various material signs of their status (e.g., the luxury car, the nice house). Across 92 different countries—from Mongolia to Finland—P. J. Henry found that the greater percentage of pastureland a country has, the higher the murder rate. But this relationship between pastureland and murder rates was explained by status disparities. More pastureland is associated with greater status disparities, which in turn are associated with higher murder rates. Thus the culture of honor involves protecting not only one's resources but also protecting one's status and sense of self-worth.

Gangs

The ideas of a culture of honor and the protection of tenuous self-worth can help explain gang-related violence. In 1967, Wolfgang and Ferracuti developed the very similar concept of *subcultures of violence* to explain inner-city gang-related violence.

learn that a 23-block section of his neighborhood was named TG City after his son, not just to memorialize Terrance but to establish a new and bigger gang territory for those kids who rallied together to avenge Terrance's death. In the three years after Terrance Green was murdered, at least 10 shootings and seven additional murders were part of a string of retaliatory attacks. If you want to learn more about Terrance's story and those of other teenagers in his community, check out a two-part story called "Harper High School" that was broadcast on *This American Life* in February 2013 (Glass, 2013).

Stories like Terrance's reveal the bind that teens can find themselves in when they live within a gang culture in which many people have guns and aren't afraid to use them to terrorize others and settle even the smallest of arguments. What would you do in this situation? Maybe you are thinking, Why not go to your parents, your teachers, or the police? Unfortunately, you'd be unlikely to tell them anything they don't already know. It's no secret that gang violence is a problem in these neighborhoods. What we are missing are effective solutions. A recent large-scale study of over 100 U.S. cities suggests that in cities with a greater proportion of Black residents, *fewer* arrests are made of violent Black offenders (Stucky, 2012). In such cases, the local police might lack either the resources or the motivation to bring an end to the violence. Instead, kids accept the belief voiced by one gang member: "There's no solution to the violence. Killing, killing is the solution" (Jacobson, 2012).

Breaking the cycle of violence in places like Englewood means confronting and looking beyond the racial stereotypes that feed the cycle. Gangs often form in the first place to regulate a market of illegal activities, such as drugs and prostitution. Without ready access to a good education, job training, or job opportunities, illegal behavior can seem like the only choice for survival. As one young Englewood man said in the previously cited interview with Walter Jacobson, "We've got to eat. We want to. We want money. . . . In our neighborhood, I ain't going to lie to you. [Selling drugs] . . . that's where the money comes from."

Because neither the police nor the government can regulate these illegal activities, gangs rely on a culture of honor and code of the street to police each other and enforce norms. Once people outside this life start seeing an increased prevalence of gang behavior and violence among members of a specific ethnic or racial group, a stereotyped association of Black = violent begins to form (Dixon, 2008). African Americans are more prevalent in gangs than Euro-Americans (National Gang Center, 2011). But, although any given gang member is more likely to be Black than White, television, movies, and news reporting often exaggerate this association even further (Dixon & Linz, 2000).

From learning about schematic processing in chapter 4 and stereotyping in chapter 10, we know that once such stereotypes are established, they can bias our perceptions. In a study of prison inmates convicted of violent crimes, those inmates who looked more Black (e.g., darker skin tone and more Afrocentric features) were more likely to have been sentenced to death, even when the crime was as severe as one committed by a White inmate (Blair et al., 2004; Eberhardt et al., 2006). With such strong associations of "Black" with "violence," self-fulfilling prophecies are likely to occur. For example, if Whites see a young Black (vs. White) male with a neutral expression on his face, they're more likely to think he is angry (Hugenberg & Bodenhausen, 2003). But how well will his interactions go if people assume he is angry and likely to be violent? It's hard not to feel angry when people seem to assume that you are angry anyway.

As we try to understand the disturbing cycles of violence that plague lower-income African American urban communities, social psychology has much to teach us. Although gang subcultures and fatherless homes play a role, the reasons for these situations, and the stereotypes and norms they conjure up and perpetuate also can fuel an escalating aggressive and violent lifestyle. We only hope it doesn't take too many more victims such as Terrance Green before policies and programs are developed that help to solve the problem.

The FBI's 2011 National Gang Threat Assessment estimates that approximately 1.4 million people belong to 33,000 different gangs across the United States. Perhaps due to the appeal of the sense of status and power it may offer, gang membership is particularly high among Hispanic-Americans (46% of all gang members) and African-Americans (35%) relative to Euro-Americans (11%) (National Gang Center, 2011). In some communities, gangs are estimated to perpetrate an average of 48% of violent crime and up to 90% in certain jurisdictions (Federal Bureau of Investigation, 2011). A number of factors contribute to gang-related violence, including the strain of poverty and the attempts by poor teenagers to exert some kind of control over their lives through delinquency (Goldstein, 1994). But it is also important to consider the subcultural norms and expectations that develop within economically disadvantaged inner-city neighborhoods, which sociologist Elijah Anderson (2000) has dubbed "the code of the street." In this subculture, violence and aggression are means of maintaining one's honor and status. The code of the street sets up the rules for being someone of value not to be trifled with. Social Psych Out in the World takes a closer look at an example of gang violence in the African American community.

SECTION review | Learning to Aggress

As a species, we excel at social learning, sometimes including how to aggress.

Electronic Media	**Family Life**	**Culture**
• Experimental and longitudinal research shows that watching media violence contributes to aggression. • This is especially true when the hero is easy to identify with and is triumphant. • Aggressive and frustrated people are more susceptible to the influence of media violence than are others.	• A violent family life disrupts psychological security and models aggression. • Rejected or abused children are more likely to become aggressive themselves.	• Individualistic cultures tend to have higher levels of aggression than collectivistic ones. • A culture of honor or code of the street may encourage aggression that is regarded as necessary to protect one's livelihood or status.

Individual Differences in Aggression

Clearly factors within a person, as well as the situation, influence who is more and less likely to be aggressive. In this section we briefly consider eight such individual difference variables: gender, age, trait aggressiveness, intelligence, narcissism, low and unstable self-esteem, and the ability to control one's thoughts and behavior.

Gender Differences in Aggression

Over the course of history and across the globe today, men are more likely than women to be physically aggressive (Archer, 2004; Card et al., 2008). Men commit the vast majority of violent and homicidal aggressive acts, such as murder, armed robbery, and aggravated assault (e.g., Daly & Wilson, 1988). However, women are more likely than men to engage in acts of verbal aggression by spreading malicious rumors and gossip, excluding others from desirable events and groups, and threatening to end friendships (Archer, 2004; Card et al., 2008; Crick & Grotpeter, 1995). Men and women do not differ in their overall level of aggression as much as they do in their preferred mode of aggression—physical for men, verbal for women.

Although verbal aggression does not physically harm the victims, it can be extremely harmful for emotional and psychological health, as we saw in the case of

Chanelle Rae. Victims of verbal aggression are at a high risk for depression and anxiety (Crick & Grotpeter, 1996). The distress and humiliation they experience can even lead them to take their own lives.

That said, because the consequences of physical aggression are usually more immediately apparent and severe, considerable research has sought to understand why men are more physically aggressive than women. One theory traces this gender difference back to physiological differences between men and women (Maccoby & Jacklin, 1974). Recall that testosterone level is correlated with aggressive behavior, particularly in response to provocation, and that on average men secrete more testosterone than women. Another factor is that men may be more likely than women to engage in physical aggression and do more physical harm because they are generally larger and physically stronger than women. A third factor is that men are more likely than women to interpret other people's actions as intended to provoke them, for example, by insulting their reputations (Crick & Dodge, 1994; Dodge & Coie, 1987). As we've seen, this interpretation of others' actions as provoking is the most common trigger of an aggressive response.

Another way to understand the gender difference in physical aggressiveness is to ask, Why aren't women more aggressive? According to Eagly and Steffen (1986), boys and girls are socialized with different normative expectations about what men and women should and should not do. Social norms dictate that a certain amount of physical aggression is acceptable among young boys, but not among young girls (e.g., Björkqvist et al., 1992). Compared with men, women are more likely to consider physical aggression inappropriate. As a result, they inhibit their aggressive impulses to avoid the stronger experience of guilt or anxiety that would result if they did act on their aggression (Brock & Buss, 1964; Eagly & Steffen, 1986; Wyer et al., 1965).

Such evidence suggests that when women are in situations where they feel less constrained by traditional gender-role norms, they should be less likely to inhibit themselves from physically aggressing. Some research supports this idea (e.g., Bettencourt & Miller, 1996). Thus, when asking why men are more physically aggressive than women, one area we need to look at is gender-role norms.

Aggressive Behavior Across the Life Span

Even if some people are more aggressive than others, how do these propensities change over time? Here we note some general trends in aggression levels at different phases of the life span. We'll also discuss the time line of the gender differences mentioned in the previous section.

Pint-sized Aggressors

Most of us think that children are bundles of joy during the preschool years (ages 2 to 3), but toddlers physically aggress at a level that even the most hardened criminal would find impressive: Fully 25% of preschoolers' social interactions involve some form of physical aggression, whether it is pushing other children or taking their toys (Tremblay, 2000). The level of aggression is so high partly because, at this age, children are just beginning to experiment with how much control they have over their environment. Also, their abilities to control their impulses, let alone communicate their desires, are not yet fully developed.

Learning About Self and Others

In the first few years after toddlerhood, most children's brains develop in ways that give them more control over their actions,

Words do hurt. Victims of verbal aggression are at higher risk of depression and anxiety. In some cases, they commit suicide.

[Jupiterimages/Getty Images]

As toddlers, children are still learning to control their emotions and actions. Sometimes this leads to aggression against others.

[Cresta Johnson/Shutterstock]

and they are socialized to learn that kicking and punching are often not the most effective means of getting what they want. As a result, they begin to express their desires and frustrations in nonaggressive ways. Children also develop the ability to think about other people's intentions.

Boys Get Physical, Girls Get Verbal

As children move through elementary school, gender differences in preferred mode of aggression become more noticeable. Around age 11, girls begin to engage in significantly more verbal aggression than boys, while boys start to surpass girls in physical aggression (Lagerspetz et al., 1988). Longitudinal studies provide some evidence that socialization places more pressure on girls to inhibit their aggression than it does on boys: Among those eight-year-old children nominated by their peers as high in aggressiveness, 47% of the boys continued to be high in physical aggressiveness into middle adulthood, whereas only 18% of the girls continued to be highly aggressive into middle adulthood (Huesmann et al., 2009). These findings suggest that socialization reduces physical aggressiveness in girls more than it does in boys.

The Hazards of Puberty

Gender differences in preferred mode of aggression peak in adolescence and early adulthood. Between the ages of 15 and 30, males show a dramatic spike in the rate of violent criminal offenses. For instance, collapsing over about a dozen-year period, the average homicide perpetrator in the United States is a 27-year-old male (Federal Bureau of Investigation, 2009). One reason for this spike in physical aggression in adolescence is that this is also when testosterone levels peak. In fact, differences in verbal aggression also are at their height around the same time range: 18-year-old women show higher levels of verbal aggression than men of the same age (Lagerspetz & Björkqvist, 1994).

Well-behaved Adults

After early adulthood, rates of interpersonal aggression and rates of violent criminal offenses decline, even among men. One reason is that men secrete less testosterone after they reach age 25. In addition, by adulthood both men and women are employing verbal means of aggression more often (Björkqvist et al., 1994). Of course, these developmental trends are also affected by the social norms of the society in question, but at least among middle-class, European, and North American males, physical aggression in middle and late adulthood is commonly considered acceptable only in self-defense or in defense of others (Holm, 1983).

Trait Aggressiveness

Some people are more likely to aggress than others over time and across situations. People who are high in such trait aggressiveness are susceptible to hostile thoughts, are likely to express anger, and tend to engage in physical and verbal aggression. Researchers often measure trait aggressiveness in adults by giving them questionnaires that ask how much they agree with statements such as "Once in a while I can't control the urge to strike another person" and "I sometimes feel like a powder keg ready to explode" (Buss & Perry, 1992).

Individual differences in trait aggressiveness emerge as early as age three (Olweus, 1979). These differences are stable across the life span, with trait aggressiveness in childhood correlating highly with aggressiveness as much as 40 years later (Huesmann et al., 2009). Indeed, the continuity of aggression across the life span is as stable as the continuity of IQ. Laboratory studies show that individuals who are high in trait aggressiveness engage in higher levels of aggressive behavior under both neutral and provoking conditions (Bettencourt et al., 2006; Bushman, 1995).

Why Are Some People High in Trait Aggressiveness?

A complete answer to this question would likely involve virtually all the factors we have already discussed in this chapter. But let's take a brief look at two basic influences, one nurture, the other nature.

Bad Parenting

Coercive parenting styles, inconsistent discipline, physical abuse, and exposure to family conflicts all contribute to the child's tendency to behave in an aggressive and antisocial manner later in life (Rhee & Waldman, 2002). In fact, bad parenting can set into motion a chain of aggressiveness that spans three generations (Capaldi et al., 2003; Conger et al., 2003; Hops et al., 2003; Thornberry et al., 2003).

From the social cognitive perspective, part of what children learn from more aggressive parents is not just aggressive behavior but also aggressive interpretation of social information. When a person is provoked, the degree to which he or she infers that another's actions were committed with hostile intent (a hostile attribution) strongly predicts whether the person will react aggressively (a probability of about 76%). If the same person infers that the actions were committed benignly, the probability of an aggressive behavioral reaction is much lower (about 25%) (Dodge, 1980). The link between hostile attributions and aggressive behavior persists across ages, demographic and cultural groups, and social contexts (de Castro et al., 2003). It is not surprising that children classified as highly aggressive (e.g., by their peers and teachers) are more likely than their less aggressive peers to attribute hostile intent to others' actions, even when others' intentions are benign (Dodge, 1980; Nasby et al., 1980). This has been called the **hostile attribution bias** (Crick & Dodge, 1994). In hostile family environments, children quickly learn to attribute hostile motives to others. The experience of physical and/or psychological abuse by one's parents during the first five years of life predicts a tendency toward the hostile attribution bias, which in turn predicts aggressive behavior even years later (Dodge et al., 1990; Weiss et al., 1992).

Hostile attribution bias The tendency to attribute hostile intent to others' actions, even when others' intentions are innocent.

Genetic Factors

The clearest evidence for the role of genetic influences on aggressiveness comes from studies of twins (Miles & Carey, 1997; Rhee & Waldman, 2002). In one study (Rushton et al., 1986), monozygotic twin pairs (twins who are genetically identical) were more similar in aggressiveness than were dizygotic twin pairs (those who on average share only half of their genes). In another study (Eley et al., 2003), researchers looked at over 1,000 identical and fraternal pairs of Swedish twins and had parents rate their children's aggressiveness first as children (ages 8 to 9) and then again as adolescents (ages 13 to 14). Twins' aggressiveness over time was highly correlated, particularly when they were identical, suggesting that aggressive behavior might be influenced by genetic factors.

Although there have been few successes so far in identifying any single gene that makes people aggressive, studies have found interesting links between aggressiveness and genes involved in the production of serotonin. As noted earlier, serotonin is a neurotransmitter that helps regulate stress. Low levels of serotonin are associated with high levels of aggression. For the body to metabolize and secrete serotonin, it needs an enzyme called monoamine oxidase A, or "MAO-A" for short. A rare genetic variant that causes low levels of MAO-A has been linked to violent and antisocial behavior (Brunner et al., 1993, Munafò et al., 2003), perhaps because individuals with this genetic variant have greater difficulty metabolizing serotonin to help them deal with stress (Meyer-Lindenberg et al., 2006).

It's important to keep in mind that this genetic factor—referred to by some researchers as the *warrior gene*—does not universally predict aggressive behavior. It does so largely in response to enduring and situational stressors. For example, the genetic variant causing low MAO-A levels (and thus disrupted use of stress-damping serotonin) predicts aggressive behavior only among people who had been exposed to high levels of maltreatment and stress during childhood (Caspi et al., 2002; Kim-Cohen et al., 2006). If an individual had been mistreated early in life, this genetic variant increases the risk of aggressiveness later in life. But if the individual was reared in an environment that was nurturing and supportive, this genetic variant does not predict aggressiveness.

The genetic variant indicating low MAO-A also predicts higher levels of aggression when people are currently provoked. In one experiment, participants were told that another person in the study had taken money from them (McDermott et al., 2009). Other participants were not given this provocation. All participants later had the opportunity to determine how much hot sauce that person had to consume. The researchers found that MAO-A did not predict aggression in the absence of provocation. However, when participants were told the other person had taken money from them, low levels of MAO-A predicted greater allocations of hot sauce (i.e., more aggression). Thus, we should consider this genetic factor a biological predisposition that interacts with the person's environment, rather than as a strict determinant of the person's behavior.

Intelligence

Poor intellectual functioning is linked to high aggressiveness, especially in children (e.g., Pitkanen-Pulkinen, 1979). This link is the product of a number of processes. For one, if people are less able to process the subtleties of a social situation and the intentions behind other people's actions, they may be more likely to infer automatically that other people are deliberately trying to offend them (Guerra et al., 1994).

Poor intellectual functioning also makes it more likely that people will feel frustrated in their lives. This may be especially evident in school, where students with deficits in reading comprehension and mathematical reasoning may be continually frustrated by the tasks assigned to them. Intellectual deficits may also make it difficult to understand the inappropriateness of aggression, consider future consequences, or to think of nonaggressive means of responding to frustrating situations (Geen, 2001; Slaby & Guerra, 1988).

Finally, not only does poor intellectual functioning lead to aggression, but aggression can in turn impair intellectual functioning (Huesmann, 1988). Children who tend to lash out aggressively often end up disrupting good relationships with their teachers and peers, foreclosing opportunities to learn problem-solving skills and advance intellectually. In fact, a 22-year longitudinal study showed that aggressiveness in children at age 8 predicted poor intellectual functioning at age 30 better than intellectual functioning at age 8 predicts adult aggressiveness (Huesmann & Eron, 1984).

Personality Traits and Reactivity to Provocation

We've seen that perceived provocation is a major trigger of aggressive behavior. A number of personality traits predict how strongly people react to provocation, and thus how likely they are to retaliate with anger and aggression.

Narcissism and Deficits in Self-esteem

A long-standing belief of many researchers and lay individuals alike is that low self-esteem contributes to aggression. Research backs this up. Physically abusive parents and spouses and aggressive children tend to have lower self-esteem than their non-aggressive counterparts (Anderson & Lauderdale, 1982; Burdett & Jensen, 1983; Goldstein & Rosenbaum, 1985; Tangney et al., 2011). Given that provocations are often threats to self-esteem, those who have lower self-esteem also react more emotionally than others to failure, negative social feedback, and social rejection.

More recently, researchers have focused on those who have unstable self-esteem. *Narcissists*, people who have a grandiose but fragile view of themselves (Baumeister et al., 1996; Thomaes & Bushman, 2011), tend to agree with statements such as "If I ruled the world, it would be a much better place." Nevertheless, narcissists exhibit low self-esteem when it is measured implicitly. Individuals with unstable self-esteem have views of themselves that fluctuate radically in response to social situations (Kernis et al., 1989). People who are high in narcissism or unstable self-esteem respond to provocations with higher levels of aggressive behavior than those who are comparatively low in these traits (Bushman & Baumeister, 1998). Unlike trait aggressiveness, which predicts aggressive behavior under both neutral and provocation conditions, narcissism and unstable self-esteem seem to make people particularly reactive to threats to their self-views (Bettencourt et al., 2006).

Individual Differences in Impulsivity

As we saw in the earlier section on biology and human aggression, human evolution has endowed us with sophisticated cognitive abilities. These abilities enable us to reflect on the likely consequences of our actions, allowing us to inhibit or override an aggressive impulse. However, people differ in their ability to control their thoughts and behaviors. Individuals who are high in impulsivity tend to react to situations without thinking through the consequences of their actions (Barratt, 1994). They respond affirmatively to questions such as "Do you do things on the spur of the moment?" They also tend to respond to insults, attacks, and frustrations with angry outbursts, whereas low-impulsivity individuals tend to stay calm, refrain from overt signs of anger, and inhibit their urge to behave aggressively after being provoked (Caprara et al., 2002). For example, high- and low-impulsivity individuals can experience equivalent levels of negative affect and anger in response to a provocation, but the high-impulsivity individuals are less able to resist the urge to lash out aggressively (e.g., Hynan & Grush, 1986). Consequently, high impulsivity is correlated with aggressive behaviors, and has in fact been found to be "one of the strongest known correlates of crime" (Pratt & Cullen, 2000, p. 952).

It is interesting to note that a certain subgroup of violent criminals does not fit this high-impulsivity pattern. On the one hand, studies of violent criminals reveal one group of individuals who often have a history of impulsive actions and assaults (D'Silva & Duggan, 2010; Du Toit & Duckitt, 1990; Megargee, 1966). These individuals seem to have *undercontrolled* aggressive impulses. But a second group of violent criminals often have no prior assaultive history; they seem to be low in impulsivity and have rigid inhibitions against expressing anger. Researchers suggest that these *overcontrolled* offenders allow their frustrations and hostilities to build up until they boil over into an extreme act of aggression.

The social neuroscience perspective has provided evidence regarding brain regions that may contribute to the behavior of the undercontrolled violent person (Davidson et al., 2000; Raine, 2008). As we mentioned earlier in this chapter and discussed further in chapter 5, the *prefrontal cortex* is the part of the brain that governs our ability to monitor and control our behavior. Individuals with antisocial personality disorder have an 11% to 14% deficit in prefrontal gray matter relative to matched controls and individuals with other psychiatric disorders (Raine et al., 2000). Other research showed that convicted murderers displayed less glucose metabolism in their prefrontal regions than a control group of persons of the same sex and age (Raine et al., 1997). Differences in the functioning of prefrontal regions also predict aggressive responses to provocation. Participants with weak frontal-lobe functioning tend to be more aggressive (administering painful electric shocks) toward a confederate who has previously provoked them (who had administered painful shocks to the participants themselves) than when they were not provoked. In contrast, the effect of provocation is substantially weaker among individuals with strong frontal-lobe functioning (Lau et al., 1995).

SECTION review | Individual Differences in Aggression

Individual differences affect a person's tendency toward aggression.

Gender differences	Across the life span	Trait aggressiveness	Intelligence	Personality traits
• Men and women differ more in their mode, than in their overall level, of aggression. • These differences are influenced by both social roles and biology (e.g., testosterone).	• Before learning to control their environment and impulses, toddlers are quite physically aggressive. • Socialization reduces aggression over the course of early childhood. • Aggression peaks in males between the ages of 15 and 30, after which it declines rapidly.	• Some people are high in trait aggressiveness. • Maltreatment and stress during childhood may also exacerbate genetic predispositions toward aggression.	• Frustration and misunderstanding may contribute to aggression in low-intellect individuals. • Aggression can also impair future intellectual functioning.	• Narcissists and those with low and/or unstable self-esteem are more likely to retaliate with aggression. • People with undercontrolled impulsivity also react aggressively. • People with overcontrolled impulsivity aggress when hostility boils over.

The Roles of Alcohol and Other Drugs in Aggression

In most if not all known cultures, many people have engaged in activities that alter their state of consciousness, whether through meditation, trances, or the use of mind-altering substances such as alcohol, marijuana, cocaine, opiates, MDMA (ecstasy), methamphetamine, and hallucinogens (McKenna, 1993; Rosen & Weil, 2004; Weil, 1972). Although these drugs can be appealing for a variety of reasons, both the resulting altered states and the desire for these drugs can contribute to aggression in a variety of ways.

Some theorists have argued that the criminalization of recreational drugs and the extremely ineffective "war on drugs" play a substantial role in crime and violence. These drugs generate huge profits that legitimate authorities are unable to regulate and that bankroll other illegal activities (Goldstein, 1986). Both small-time drug dealers and large-scale drug cartels must therefore devise their own means of protection. As a result, the illegal drug trade contributes to a large percentage of violent crimes, ranging from assault to homicide, in countries such as the United States (Roth, 1994) and Mexico (Miroff & Booth, 2010). For example, Mexican drug cartels hire *sicarios*, assassins who protect their turf and business interests. The book *El Sicario: The Autobiography of a Mexican Assassin* (Molloy & Bowden, 2011) tells the story of one such hit man who killed hundreds of people and was very well paid for doing so.

The effects of drugs on users also can contribute to violence. Although a common belief has it that addicts turn to crimes such as muggings and burglary to support their addiction, at least for heroin, evidence for this link is not clear (Kretschmar & Flannery, 2007). However, drugs can increase physiological arousal, heightening emotional reactions to provocations and reducing higher-order cognition and impulse control. Some drugs can create a sense of paranoia, which also intensifies feelings of being threatened. Unfortunately, experimental research on the effects of illegal drugs on aggression is rare because of the ethical and practical difficulty of giving such drugs to participants. In one of those rare experiments, participants given a high dose of cocaine gave higher-intensity shocks to an opponent in a competitive game than did those given a placebo (Licata et al., 1993). However, complementary correlational evidence on this topic has not supported a clear link between cocaine and amphetamine use and aggression. More research is needed before strong conclusions can be drawn about the direct effects of these and other stimulants on aggression (Kretschmar & Flannery, 2007; Kruesi, 2007).

The vast majority of studies on the effects of drugs on aggression have focused on alcohol (Kretschmar & Flannery, 2007; Kruesi, 2007). This is partly because alcohol is a legal recreational drug and partly because it is the most commonly used (and abused) recreational drug in the United States and most other large cultures. Imagine that you are at a sporting event, a party, or a concert, and a fight breaks out. How likely do you think it would be that at least one of the combatants is drunk? If you're like most people, you'd probably think it would be pretty likely. Correlational research strongly supports this intuition. In fact, when researchers review the literature and various crime reports, they find that alcohol is involved in about half of all violent crimes and sexual assaults worldwide (Beck & Heinz, 2013; Chermack & Giancola, 1997). Some studies show even higher rates. In one study of 882 persons arrested in Ohio for felonies, over 75% of offenders who were arrested for violent crimes, ranging from assault to murder, were legally intoxicated (Shupe, 1954). Clearly, alcohol use is positively associated with aggression. This is especially true for people with aggressive dispositions, tendencies to hostility, and low impulse control (Geen, 2001).

Experimental research further supports a causal role of alcohol use in aggression. When given an opportunity to deliver electric shocks or aversive noise to another person, participants who have consumed alcohol under conditions of threat or competition engage in more aggression than sober participants. The higher the dose of alcohol, the greater the aggression (Bushman & Cooper, 1990; Taylor & Leonard, 1983). In contrast, threatened participants who have consumed the psychoactive ingredients in marijuana generally have been found to be less rather than more aggressive than sober participants (e.g., Taylor & Leonard, 1983). Why is alcohol intoxication such a significant contributor to aggression?

One reason is that alcohol impairs higher-order thinking such as self-awareness, and therefore reduces inhibitions and impulse control (e.g., Hull et al., 1983; Ito et al., 1996). A minor slight or insult that a sober person would likely ignore or deflect is more likely to provoke aggression in a drunk person. In addition, this cognitive impairment makes it less likely that drunk people will consider the consequences of their actions (Steele & Josephs, 1990; Taylor & Leonard, 1983). Neuroscience research further shows that patterns of electrical activity in the brains of intoxicated people indicate that they are less distressed than sober participants by the mistakes they make (Bartholow et al., 2012). All these factors highlight alcohol's tendency to reduce the self-regulatory controls with which we ordinarily inhibit aggressive impulses.

A second reason that alcohol increases aggression is that we *expect* alcohol use to lead to aggression. Participants who drank a placebo beverage that they believed contained alcohol (but actually did not) showed increased behavioral signs of aggression compared with those who knew they were not drinking alcohol (Rohsenow & Bachorowski, 1984). In fact, simply exposing participants to alcohol-related pictures (e.g., a beer bottle or martini glass), or even flashing alcohol-related words on a computer screen so quickly they can't be consciously seen, increases the accessibility of aggressive cognitions, leads participants to interpret a person's behavior as more aggressive, and leads to more hostile evaluations of another person when frustrated (Bartholow & Heinz, 2006; Friedman et al., 2007). These effects tend to be stronger the more strongly people believe that alcohol use causes aggression.

Although the bulk of the experimental research has focused on the effects of aggression on perpetrators, some research suggests that victims of violent crimes are also more likely to be drunk (e.g., Chermack & Giancola, 1997). One explanation for the latter finding is suggested by research showing that when people have consumed alcohol, they become less able to read the emotions on the face of another person and other social cues (Steele & Josephs, 1990; Taylor & Leonard, 1983), a phenomenon Steele and Josephs refer to as *alcohol myopia*. So in a bar or at a party, a drunk person may, because of alcohol's disinhibiting effects, become increasingly annoying to another person, but because of their insensitivity to facial and social cues, they are insufficiently aware of how much they are angering that person. Consequently, alcohol consumption not only makes a person a more likely perpetrator of violence, but also a more likely victim of it. Worth keeping in mind!

SECTION review | The Roles of Alcohol and Other Drugs in Aggression

Altered states can contribute to aggression.	
Drugs contribute to aggression because: • Illegal business activities are often regulated through violence. • Drugs can increase arousal and create a sense of paranoia.	The most commonly used drug is alcohol, and research supports its causal role in aggression because: • It impairs higher-order thinking. • We *expect* it to lead to aggression. • It impedes a potential victim's ability to read social cues.

Violence Against Women

Some forms of male aggression are directed primarily at women. Men are on average more physically aggressive, larger in size, and have greater power and status in society, giving them a clear advantage in physical altercations. Furthermore, because women can block some of men's specific desires (or be perceived to block them), women have been common targets of male aggression in many places and times over the course of history (Brownmiller, 1975; Gelles, 2007). Thus, substantial theory and research have focused on two common forms of violence directed at women: domestic violence and sexual coercion.

Domestic Violence

You hit me once
I hit you back
You gave a kick
I gave a slap
You smashed a plate
Over my head
Then I set fire to our bed. . . .
A kiss with a fist is better than none

Florence and the Machine (2008), *"Kiss with a Fist"*

Domestic violence is violence between current or former romantic partners. Although some self-report survey research suggests that in heterosexual relationships, the frequency of physical aggression by males and females is actually the same (Straus, 2005), males clearly engage in more injurious and lethal physical aggression against their partners than females do (Gelles, 2007). Many of the causal contributors to aggression that we have already discussed also contribute to domestic violence against women (e.g., Hamberger & Hastings, 1991; MacEwen & Barling, 1988; O'Leary & Vivian, 1990). **FIGURE 12.11** provides a more detailed presentation of how some of these factors fit together. In addition, macho cultures of honor often promote attitudes that are particularly accepting of violence against women (e.g., Vandello & Cohen, 2003). Male abusers tend to hold beliefs that condone violence against women, such as the belief that marital violence is acceptable (Stith & Farley, 1993).

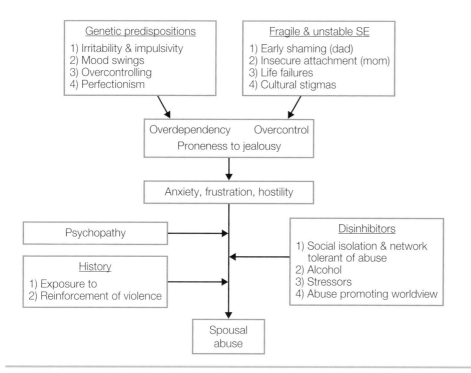

Figure 12.11

What Predicts Spousal Abuse?

Different factors contribute to male domestic violence against women.

[Research from: Jeff Greenberg]

Research on the personalities of male domestic violence offenders has revealed three types, each characterizing about a third of total offenders (Dutton, 1998; Geen, 2001). The first type, the *psychopathic abuser*, is likely to employ physical aggression both inside and outside the relationship. These men are bullies with low impulse control and often a history of violent incidents. The second type, the *overcontrolled abuser*, is a man who generally is not violent but builds up resentments from various aspects of his life and eventually uses his relationship partner as a target for his displaced aggression.

The third and perhaps best-understood type, the *borderline abuser*, is narcissistic and likely to have a borderline personality organization, which entails an uncertain, insecure sense of self, a proclivity for defensiveness, abandonment issues, anger, and impulsivity (Dutton, 2002). These men tend to have experienced disordered childhood attachment with one or both parents that involved neglect or abuse, and to have been shamed in childhood, typically by their fathers. They are overly dependent on their re-lationship partner for psychological security and consequently use jealous outbursts to control their partner. This type of offender often traps a woman in a cyclical pattern of escalating tension, hostility, and abuse, followed by contrition (e.g., "Baby, please don't leave me. I promise I'll quit drinking and never do that again.") (Dutton, 2002; Walker, 1979). The 1984 award-winning film *The Burning Bed* portrays the true story of a woman caught in this cycle who endured over 15 years of on-again, off-again abuse. Finally, as the title implies, she did something drastic about it (Avnet et al., 1984).

Sexual Coercion and Rape

Sexual coercion occurs when an individual forces sexual behavior such as kissing, fondling, or sexual penetration on another person. The most severe form of sexual coercion is rape, forcing individuals to engage in sexual intercourse against their will. Rape is generally more traumatic for the victim than are other forms of physi-cal assault (Malamuth & Huppin, 2007). The great majority of rapes of women are committed by men who know their female victims. Date rape, which occurs in the context of dating or an ongoing romantic relationship, is more common than rape by a stranger (Catanese, 2007; Malamuth & Huppin, 2007). Almost half of college women report having been sexually coerced at least once, and 6 to 15% of college women report having been raped.

Perhaps more disturbing are the data that come from men themselves. Fifteen to 30% of American college men admit having engaged in at least one act of sexual coercion (Catanese, 2007; Malamuth & Huppin, 2007). The pioneering researcher Neil Malamuth (1981) went one step further, asking men on a 1 to 5 scale (where 1 represents zero likelihood) how likely was it they would rape a woman if they knew they could get away with it. In American college student samples, 65% of males choose 1, but 35% said the likelihood was higher than zero. When you think about all the social pressures against admitting that one would carry out a felony act of violence, a man who indicates anything other than a 1 (zero likelihood) is someone to be concerned about.

Men who rape and commit other acts of sexual coercion are motivated by a combination of being turned on by the idea of dominating women and by insecurity about and hostility toward women (Malamuth & Huppin, 2007). Both convicted rapists and men who report a higher than 0% chance of raping a woman if they could get away with it report being aroused by stories of women being forced to have sex (Barbaree & Marshall, 1991; Donnerstein et al., 1987). These men also lack empathy for others, tend to be narcissistic, and believe rape myths (Burt, 1980). Such myths include the beliefs that women like to be dominated, are aroused by the idea of being raped, and bring the attacks on themselves. Table 12.1 lists some common rape myths and statements that researchers have used to measure men's endorsement of them (Payne et al., 1999).

Sexually aggressive men also associate sex with power. Indeed, when men prone to sexual aggression (but not other men) are subtly primed with power-related stimuli (e.g., words such as *influence, authority,* and *control*), they rate a female confederate as more attractive (Bargh et al., 1995). Sexually aggressive men also tend to view friendliness from a female as a sexual invitation and view female assertiveness as hostility (Murphy et al., 1986; Zurbriggen, 2000). Malamuth (2007) has labeled this combination of motivations, attitudes, perceptions, and beliefs the *hostile masculinity syndrome*. Men who have this syndrome are likely to engage in acts of sexual coercion, especially if they are sexually promiscuous. They are also likely to abuse their spouses. Convicted rapists display this syndrome, but in addition, they are more likely than other sexually aggressive males to have a general history of aggressiveness (Malamuth & Huppin, 2007).

Table 12.1 **Sample Items Used to Measure Rape Myths**

Rape Myth	Measuring Statement
She asked for it	When women go around wearing low-cut tops or short skirts, they're just asking for trouble.
It wasn't really rape	If a woman doesn't physically resist sex—even when protesting verbally—it really can't be considered rape.
He didn't mean to	Men don't usually intend to force sex on a woman, but sometimes they get too sexually carried away.
She wanted it	Although most women wouldn't admit it, they generally find being physically forced into sex a real turn-on.
She lied	Many so-called rape victims are actually women who had sex willingly and changed their minds afterward.
Rape is a trivial event	Women tend to exaggerate how much rape affects them.
Rape is a deviant event	Men from nice, middle-class homes almost never rape.

[Research from: Payne et al. (1999)]

The prevalence of this syndrome has led some evolutionary theorists to speculate that it occurs in some present-day men because it is a sexual strategy that (though abhorrent) could have been an effective means of perpetuating one's genes into future generations (Buss & Malamuth, 1996; Thornhill & Thornhill, 1992).

In contrast, more feminist and socially oriented theorists and researchers (e.g., Brownmiller, 1975; Donnerstein et al., 1987) have focused on the ways that cultural environments promote beliefs in rape myths, make domination of women seem normative, and objectify women, portraying them as mere objects of sexual pleasure for men (as we discussed in chapters 10 and 11). For example, a substantial body of research supports a strong learning component to a propensity to engage in sexual aggression. Not only do mainstream films often depict sexual coercion and sometimes even rape as pleasing to women, but participants randomly assigned to watch such films (compared with control films) report an increased belief in rape myths and acceptance of violence against women (Donnerstein et al., 1987; Malamuth & Check, 1981). In other experiments, male participants assigned to watch pornographic films that depict violence against women became more aggressive toward a female confederate who insulted them (e.g., Donnerstein et al., 1987). Although nonviolent pornography depicting consensual sex doesn't have this same effect, long-term exposure to even nonviolent sex scenes predicts greater acceptance of violence against women and increases the likelihood of sexual aggression (Donnerstein et al., 1987; Geen, 2001; Hald et al., 2010).

Taken together, the experimental and correlational research suggests that films that reinforce rape myths and portray women as victims of violence or sex objects may indeed contribute to aggression against women in the real world. Furthermore, this is especially likely for men characterized by the hostile masculinity syndrome (Vega & Malamuth, 2007).

SECTION review | Violence Against Women

Women have been targets of male aggression in many places and times over the course of history.

- Male abusers of current or former romantic partners tend to believe that marital violence is acceptable.
- There are three categories of domestic violence offenders: psychopathic, overcontrolled, and borderline.

- Men who commit acts of sexual coercion are insecure about and hostile toward women, are turned on by the idea of dominating them, and tend to believe myths about rape.
- Evidence suggests that films which portray women as targets of violence promote aggression against women and more tolerance of it.

Reducing Aggression

It would be an overstatement to say that all types of aggression are bad for individuals and for society in general. The unfortunate truth is that people occasionally intend to block others' goals or otherwise cause harm. Appropriate expressions of anger and aggression can help a person avoid being treated unjustly (DaGloria, 1984; Felson & Tedeschi, 1993). Also, in many cultures, people value a capacity for and willingness to engage in aggression in military and law-enforcement personnel and in spectator sports such as ice hockey, football, and boxing. Nevertheless, the vast majority of aggressive behavior is harmful and often has tragic consequences. How can we reduce, if not prevent, unnecessary aggression?

When this question is put to psychologists and lay people alike, a frequent answer is *catharsis*, or allowing people to "blow off steam" or otherwise vent their aggressive impulses. These ideas are generally incorrect. Catharsis—whether it is vicarious (e.g., watching a violent film) or direct (e.g., punching a pillow)—has side effects that make it not only ineffective but also likely to exacerbate aggression. These side effects include making violence seem acceptable, reinforcing aggressive scripts and actions, and increasing arousal that can get misattributed as anger in response to provocation (e.g., Bandura, 1973; Geen, 2001; Zillmann, 1979). If vicarious catharsis worked, people would be less aggressive after watching hockey, football, wrestling matches, and violent films than they are before seeing them. But quite the opposite is true: Crowds are more aggressive after such events than before them (e.g., Geen, 2001).

What does work? Because aggression has so many causes, there is no easy answer. Nonetheless, theory and research suggest a range of hopeful approaches that target societal, interpersonal, and individual factors.

Societal Interventions

1. **Reduce frustration by improving the quality of life.** One way that we can curb aggression is by reducing the prevalence and severity of aversive states that trigger frustration and hostility. We can do this by putting people in other, more uplifting emotional states of mind. In one study, insulted participants were less aggressive if they heard an uplifting song before being given the opportunity to aggress (Greitemeyer, 2011b). Of course, it's difficult to imagine people listening to uplifting music all the time. There are so many sources of frustration and pain that reducing aversive emotions is a tough challenge. Obvious starting points would be improving the economy and providing healthier and more pleasant living conditions, especially in neighborhoods that are plagued by aggression. Another approach is to teach children prone to be aggressive better problem-solving, communication, and negotiating skills. If they learn these skills, they will experience less frustration in their lives and employ more constructive approaches to dealing with the frustrations that do arise (e.g., Goldstein, 1986).

2. **Gun control.** We know that the mere presence of firearms can prime aggressive thoughts and that interacting with guns can boost testosterone, further fueling aggressive behavior. We also know that firearms make aggression more lethal. Therefore, controlling the number and kinds of weapons that are available, and who can obtain them, may not only prevent people from causing unnecessary death and pain but also make it less likely that people's thoughts turn to aggression in the first place.

3. **Punishing aggression.** In most societies, efforts to curb aggression involve punishing aggressive offenders. This can be effective. In one study (Fitz, 1976), participants were less likely to aggress against someone if they knew that they would suffer severe consequences as a result. However, many forms of punishment also model aggression and can increase the recipients' frustration, thus having the opposite of the intended effect. For example, children who are physically punished at home are more aggressive outside the home later in life (e.g., Gershoff, 2002; Lefkowitz et al., 1978). Given these conflicting findings, researchers have investigated the specific conditions under which punishment is effective (Baron, 1977; Berkowitz, 1993). To be effective, punishment must be: (1) severe (without modeling aggression); (2) delivered promptly, before the aggressors benefit from or change their behavior; (3) perceived as justified; and (4) administered consistently. The American legal system rarely meets criteria (2) and (4) (Goldstein, 1986), thereby limiting the system's deterrent value. A long process intervenes between arrest and sentencing. Laws and sentencing are often inconsistent within and between states. For example, activities such as gambling, prostitution, and marijuana consumption are legal in some states but can result in prison sentences in others.

These criteria also help explain why the death penalty has not been effective in deterring violent crime. In fact, as **FIGURE 12.12** shows, murder rates tend to be higher in states with the death penalty than in those without it. When the death penalty is introduced, the murder rate actually tends to increase (Goldstein, 1986). Capital punishment makes aggression salient and communicates the idea that killing is sometimes justified. Executions tend to happen many years after

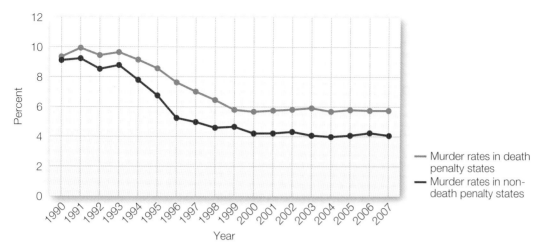

Figure 12.12

Murder Rates in States With and Without the Death Penalty

The death penalty is intended as both punishment and deterrent, but statistics show that murder rates are higher in those states with the death penalty than in those without it.

[Data source: Goldstein (1986)]

the murder that they are intended to punish. Thus, the link between the actions and the punishment is temporally remote. In addition, most murders are committed in a fit of rage when people are unlikely to be thinking of consequences.

What forms of treatment would work to decrease violence in an individual? One promising alternative approach is *multisystematic therapy* (Borduin et al., 2009; Henggeler et al., 1998), which addresses what drives individuals to aggress in specific contexts in which they are embedded, such as school and neighborhood. Courses and other training programs that focus on rehabilitation, as opposed to deterrence or retribution, also hold greater promise. But American penal institutions spend very few of their resources on rehabilitation (Goldstein, 1986), a fact that probably contributes to the high recidivism rate. Half or more of inmates released from U.S. prisons in a given year end up returning for another stint (Goldstein, 1986; Bureau of Justice Statistics, n.d.).

4. **Reduce or reframe media depictions of aggression.** With all the evidence that exposure to violence in the media can prime and model violent thoughts and actions, we might reduce aggression by minimizing people's exposure to such media depictions. Of course, censorship carries its own costs, but there is no question that American society can do a better job of limiting exposure of young children to violence in the media. Another approach is to direct people to media that model prosocial behavior or depict the negative consequences of aggression. The media frequently portray people as benefitting from aggressive behavior. Viewing such portrayals increases aggression. In contrast, exposure to scenes showing punishment of aggressive behavior inhibits viewers from aggressing (Betsch & Dickenberger, 1993). Just as playing violent video games can increase aggressive cognitions and behavior, playing prosocial video games decreases hostile attributions and aggressive cognitions (Greitemeyer & Osswald, 2009). The more children play prosocial video games, the more they also engage in prosocial behavior (Gentile et al., 2009). Thus, there is potential for reducing aggression in exposing people, and especially children, to different types of media depictions.

Another alternative approach is to educate people about how to interpret violent media depictions. Rosenkoetter and colleagues (2009) designed a 7-month media literacy program in which children were encouraged to distinguish between "pretend" aggression and aggression in the real world, and to choose prosocial models to admire and imitate. Children who took part in this program were less willing to employ aggression after being exposed to media depictions of aggression (Byrne, 2009). Incorporating media-literacy courses into school curricula may help counteract aggression-promoting media influences.

Interpersonal Interventions

1. **Improve parental care.** People can learn to be better parents. Training parents in more effective methods of raising their children often leads to a reduction in aggressive and antisocial behavior in the children (Patterson et al., 1982). Training juvenile offenders and their parents to communicate better with each other helped to reduce violent activity among the aggressive youth (Goldstein et al., 1998). Given that most children will eventually become parents, why aren't courses on appropriate parenting routinely included in school curricula?

2. **Strengthen social connections.** A greater sense of communal connection, more cooperation and less competition, and fewer experiences of social rejection would reduce aggression in society. Improving people's social skills is likely to lead to more positive social interactions and has been shown to be effective in reducing aggression in children (Pepler et al., 1995). Connecting with others, even if only briefly, helps to reduce aggression that stems from feeling rejected. For example, Twenge and colleagues (2007) gave participants the opportunity to have a short, friendly interaction with the experimenter (as opposed to a neutral interaction) after being rejected socially and found that these participants subsequently showed lower levels of aggression. This friendly interaction helped to restore the rejected participant's trust in others. The more participants trusted others, the less aggressive they were.

3. **Enhance empathy.** Aggressive behaviors such as threatening, attacking, and fighting with others seem to reflect a low awareness of or concern for the pain and suffering that other people experience. *Empathy* is the ability to take another person's point of view and to experience vicariously the emotions that he or she is feeling. Results of many studies conducted with children and adults document an inverse relationship between empathy and aggression (Richardson et al., 1994). This is true both when empathy is assessed as an individual difference variable and when empathy is experimentally induced by instructing individuals to imagine how another person feels. Programs that teach juvenile delinquents how to take other people's perspective also have been found to be beneficial (Goldstein, 1986).

Individual Interventions

1. **Improve self-awareness.** Berkowitz proposed that people can become aware of what makes them feel unpleasant or stressed and that they can choose not to let that distress trigger aggressive behavior. In addition, self-awareness tends to bring internalized morals and standards to mind and increase their influence on behavior. The effectiveness of such self-awareness is demonstrated in a study by Berkowitz and Troccoli (1990). Participants were put through an uncomfortable physical activity or not. Half the participants in each of these conditions were then distracted with an irrelevant task, whereas the remaining participants were asked to attend to their inner feelings. Immediately afterward, all participants rated another student's personality. As you can see from **FIGURE 12.13**, when participants were distracted, the more discomfort they felt, the more unfavorably they rated the target. In contrast, those participants prompted to attend to their emotional states did not verbally aggress, and even became

Figure 12.13

Self-awareness of Feelings and Aggression

If people focus their awareness on their feelings, they are less likely to view others negatively. This is one promising avenue toward reducing aggression.

[Data source: Berkowitz & Troccoli (1990)]

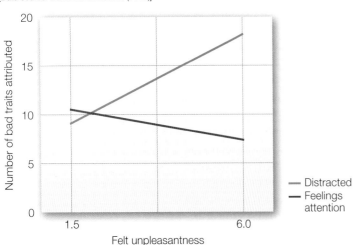

more reluctant to say negative things about the target person (perhaps in an effort to be fair and correct for the possible distorting influence of their negative mood).

2. **Increase self-regulatory strength.** If we can improve people's self-regulatory abilities, they will be better able to control their aggressive impulses. This can be facilitated by reducing the prevalence of factors that inhibit self-awareness and self-control, such as alcohol use, environmental stressors such as noise, and conditions that foster deindividuation (described in chapter 9).

    In addition, we can increase self-regulatory strength by helping people to practice controlling their behavior. In one study (Finkel et al., 2009), participants who took part in a 2-week regimen designed to bolster self-regulatory strength (e.g., by brushing their teeth with the nondominant hand or by making sure that they did not begin sentences with "I") reported a reduced likelihood of being physically aggressive toward their romantic partner.

3. **Teach how to minimize hostile attributions.** Hudley and Graham (1993) developed a 12-week program designed to prevent aggressive children from lashing out by reducing their tendency to attribute hostile intent to others. Through games, role-play exercises, and brainstorming sessions, they taught children about the basic concepts of intention in interpersonal interactions and helped them to decide when someone's actions (e.g., spilling milk on them in the lunchroom) are deliberate or accidental. Compared with boys who went through an equally intensive program that did not focus on attributions of intent, boys who received the attribution training were less likely to presume that their peers' actions (real and imagined) were hostile in intent, they were less likely to engage in verbally hostile behaviors, and they were rated as less aggressive by their teachers.

4. **Improve people's sense of self-worth and significance.** When people have high, stable self-esteem, they respond to threats with lower levels of hostility and anger (e.g., Kernis et al., 1989). One source for such a foundation is a stable, secure attachment with a close other. Indeed, studies show that, among troubled and delinquent adolescents undergoing residential treatment programs, those who formed secure attachment bonds with staff members exhibited less aggressive and antisocial behavior (Born et al., 1997). More broadly, a society that provides a wide range of attainable ways of developing and maintaining self-esteem should foster less aggressive people.

SECTION review | Reducing Aggression

Aggression has many causes, so there is no single, easy way to reduce its prevalence. However, some approaches do inspire hope.

Societal interventions	Interpersonal approaches	Individual approaches
Large-scale efforts to: • improve quality of life. • better control access to weapons. • punish aggression more effectively. • better address media violence.	Improve parental care. Strengthen social connections. Promote empathy.	Improve self-awareness and self-regulatory control. Reduce hostile attribution bias. Promote stable bases of self-worth.

CONNECT ONLINE:

Macmillan Education
LaunchPad

Check out our videos and additional resources located at:
www.macmillanhighered.com/launchpad/greenberg1e

Prosocial Behavior

TOPIC OVERVIEW

In our exploration of prejudice and aggression, we have encountered some of the darker sides of human nature. But as social animals, human beings also are drawn to help each other. Just as we can find extraordinary examples of the harm people inflict on those they do not like, we can also find examples of extraordinary acts of kindness carried out for the benefit of others. Take the example of the three men in the photo on the next page: Cody Beasley, Travis Mauldin, and Brandon Smith. They jumped into a fast-running river to save a woman from drowning in Fort Pierce, Florida. In recognition for their bravery, they were among 83 recipients of the 2011 Carnegie Hero Fund Awards, granted to individuals who risk their own lives to save others. Also shown is Christine Kerr, who received one of Canada's Caring Canadian Awards for her tireless dedication to volunteer work at hospitals and senior homes. Such individuals remind us that people sometimes go out of their way to help and care for others in need, even when that means making personal sacrifices or putting themselves in harm's way.

[Stephen Simpson/Getty Images]

People who have won the Carnegie Hero Fund Award (left) or the Caring Canadian Award (right) are honored for the ways they have put other people's needs above their own self-interest.

[Left: Scripps Treasure Coast Newspapers; right: Cpl. Issa Paré, Rideau Hall, Rideau Hall © Her Majesty The Queen in Right of Canada represented by the Office of the Secretary to the Governor General]

If people always helped others, we would not have much to cover in this chapter. But just as we can easily bring to mind uplifting stories of helping, we can also easily recollect instances when someone could have been saved from danger, or a social problem could have been alleviated, if people had intervened. Consider an incident in October 2009, when a 15-year-old girl was raped and beaten by several teenage boys in a dark alley outside their school's homecoming dance (Chen, 2009). Over 20 other students were said to have watched—some even recording the horrific event on their cellphones—yet no one called the police.

Which of these events better captures human nature? Are we the devoted volunteers and brave at heart who elevate the needs of others above our own? Or are we the apathetic bystanders who look on and do nothing as great harm is carried out? We are of course both, and one of the questions that social psychology examines is why this is the case. Why do we act with compassion and courage? When do we turn our backs on others? In this chapter, we will consider the whys and whens of our prosocial tendencies.

Prosocial behavior An action by an individual that is intended to benefit another individual or set of individuals.

Vincent van Gogh painted *The Potato Eaters* to draw attention to the struggles that ordinary people face in their daily lives.

[Art Resource, NY]

The Basic Motives for Helping

Before we begin, let's define what we mean by prosocial behavior. **Prosocial behavior** is action by an individual that is intended to benefit another individual or set of individuals. Defined in this way, many of the actions of artists such as Vincent van Gogh, actors such as Meryl Streep, entertainers such as Beyoncé, scientists such as Louis Pasteur, and political figures such as Martin Luther King, Jr. can be considered prosocial behavior. Many people have benefited from the artistic creations, scientific discoveries, and social changes initiated by such esteemed individuals whether they starred in our favorite movies, developed life-saving vaccines, or led the struggle for civil rights. Although these individuals often may be motivated by the desire for money, fame, or self-expression, they also often, if not usually, intend to produce things of value to others. For example, when Van Gogh painted *The Potato Eaters*, he not only wanted to create art that others would appreciate and enjoy but also wanted to draw attention to the difficult lives of the people he portrayed.

Although it is important to acknowledge these forms of prosocial behavior, theory and research on prosocial behavior generally have not focused on people with extraordinary talent. Instead, most of this work studies the factors that influence whether ordinary people choose to help or not help each other from day to day. Sometimes the kind of help people give is quite minor, such as stopping to help someone pick up a bag of groceries that has spilled. Other times, it can be much more dramatic, such as providing CPR to someone who has collapsed. Some instances of helping come at personal cost or physical risk. Other times, the person giving help benefits as much, if not more than, the person receiving help.

Psychologists often take it as an assumption that people's actions are motivated primarily by some degree of self-interest. This perspective is at the heart of the *functional approach*, posited by William James when he first developed psychology as a discipline in America in the late 1800s. Consequently, even though prosocial behavior is directed toward the benefit of someone else, theorists have often posited self-serving or *egoistic* motivations for helping. As Ralph Waldo Emerson claimed, "It is one of the most beautiful compensations of this life that no man can sincerely try to help another without helping himself." In terms of broad motivations that guide human behavior, helping others can enhance people's self-esteem and sense of significance within the context of their worldview. When they follow their internalized morals and social norms—that is, they do the right thing—people can feel good about themselves and their value in the larger scheme of things. Prosocial behavior also can serve more circumscribed goals, such as making the helper better liked or giving the helper a better sense of being socially accepted in a group. We might help a teacher so we can get a letter of recommendation for graduate school; an attractive individual so we can get a date; or a high-status person so we can get a job, entry into a club, or some other favor in return.

However, being social animals, we don't care only about ourselves. We also genuinely care about those with whom we form emotional attachments—our families, our relationship partners, our friends, our group members, our pets, and perhaps anyone in distress with whom we identify. The staunchest advocate of this position, the social psychologist Dan Batson (e.g., 1991), asserts that helping is often the result of altruistic motivation, a desire to help another person purely for the other person's benefit, regardless of whether there is any benefit to the self. He argues that when we feel *empathy* for another person, we help not to serve our own needs but rather to serve the needs of the other. This kind of helping is known as altruism.

Dramatic examples of altruism occur when people risk their lives to help unrelated others. During the Nazi occupation of Europe, a substantial number of non-Jewish individuals protected Jews whom the Nazis would have killed outright or sent to concentration camps. When asked in interviews why they put their own lives on the line to protect others, many of them complete strangers, these rescuers reported being motivated by either of two factors (Fogelman & Wiener, 1985). In many cases, they wanted to live up to deeply held *moral values* passed down to them by their parents and learned through their religious upbringing. In other cases, they were motivated by feelings of empathy, either because members of their own group also had been persecuted or because they had personal affection for the victims. For example, the German journalist Gitta Bauer described her experience protecting Ilse Mosle, the 17-year-old daughter of Jewish friends, by saying, "It took me nine months to deliver her to freedom, so I consider Ilse my baby" (Fogelman & Wiener, 1985, p. 233).

Human Nature and Prosocial Behavior

If you take an evolutionary perspective on human behavior, you might think that people who risk their lives to save others from the Nazis, or who throw themselves into raging rivers to save a stranger, are acting very strangely. After all, a core assumption of evolutionary theory is that species evolve new traits and behavioral tendencies when those attributes benefit the propagation of an organism's genes to the next generation. We might therefore expect people to care only about their own well-being and reproductive opportunities. But our inherited propensities are far more complicated than that and encourage prosocial behavior in a variety of ways.

Altruism The desire to help another purely for the other person's benefit, regardless of whether we derive any benefit.

Kin Selection: Hey, Nice Genes!

A propensity for helping close relatives, or *kin*, may have been selected for over the course of hominid evolution. The idea that natural selection led to greater tendencies to help close kin as opposed to those who are less genetically related is known as **kin selection** (Hamilton, 1964). The principle underlying kin selection is that because close relatives share many genes with an individual, when the individual helps close kin, those shared genes are more likely to be passed on to offspring. In this way, genes promoting the propensity for helping close kin become more prevalent in future generations. In support of this idea, people report that they are more likely to help another person the closer their genetic relationship (Burnstein et al., 1994). Regardless of whether they are risking their lives or merely lending a hand, people report being more helpful to parents and siblings than to cousins, aunts, and uncles. Also, they are more likely to help distant relatives than acquaintances or strangers. What's more, these findings hold up across very different cultures (Madsen et al., 2007).

Although the idea of kin selection is popular with evolutionary psychologists and some biologists, its role in human prosocial behavior is difficult to isolate. Cultures invariably teach people that they are obligated to help close relatives, so we don't know how much of the preference for helping close kin is innate and how much culturally learned. In addition, it is important to acknowledge that many examples of human helping cannot be explained by kin selection. These include devoted parents who raise adopted children; people from developed countries who give to charities such as CARE and UNICEF; individuals who would more readily help a good friend than a disliked first cousin; and good Samaritans, who, at great personal risk, help complete strangers and unrelated friends.

Sociability, Attachment, and Helping

Why do people like Joe Delaney (see Social Psych Out in the World) help when it clearly doesn't serve their interests to do so? One key answer is that our evolutionary history likely selected for a general proclivity to be helpful. This inherited propensity can lead to behaviors that sometimes will prevent the transmission of an individual's

Kin selection The idea that natural selection led to greater tendencies to help close kin than to help those with whom we have little genetic relation.

A Real Football Hero

During the 1980s, Joe Delaney was a star running back, jersey no. 37 for the NFL's Kansas City Chiefs. Many thought he was on his way to a Hall of Fame career. In 1983, he was the best young running back in the American Football conference. He was also happily married with three young daughters. However, his bright future was cut tragically short by his own heroic actions (Reilly, 2003; Chiefs Kingdom: Joe Delaney, Sept 28, 2013; http://www.kcchiefs.com/media -center/videos/Chiefs_Kingdom_Joe_Delaney/0cb24631 -8c8a-41fa-a2ab-ea04fc495990).

On a hot and sunny afternoon on June 29, 1983, Joe Delaney was relaxing at a park in Monroe, Louisiana. After hearing cries for help from a nearby pond, he bounded into action. Three young boys had waded into the pond to cool off in the hot Louisiana sun. The boys included two brothers, Harry and LeMarkits Holland, and their cousin Lancer Perkins, all aged 10 or 11. None of them knew how to swim, but they had unexpectedly stepped into deep water and were struggling to stay above the surface. Joe did not stop to consider if someone else should be attempting this rescue. Although he knew that his own swimming skills were weak, Joe felt an immediate obligation to try to save these children. He managed to grab LeMarkits just as water began to enter the boy's lungs, saving his life. But his attempt to save the other two failed, and the boys and Joe drowned.

genes, even though on average, across people and situations, they may have adaptive value. As we noted in chapter 2, our hominid ancestors lived in small groups in which members were successful by caring about others: emotionally attaching to them, caring for and cooperating with them, fitting in with the group, trying to be liked and to live up to internalized morals. These bonds with others are associated with an innate capacity to experience certain emotions that foster helping: sympathy, empathy, compassion, and guilt. Thus, prosocial behavior arises from our evolved proclivities for sociability and forming close attachments and the *emotions* these proclivities arouse. They are the bases for the human propensity to engage in prosocial behavior. We help because we care.

Reciprocal Helping

Evolutionary psychologists have suggested another explanation of why helping is such a prominent aspect of human behavior. Recall that we've already covered some of the surprising examples of what humans can achieve through cooperation (see chapter 9). In fact, cooperation itself can be viewed as a form of prosocial behavior. Cooperating with others for a common goal or to combat a common enemy means placing a certain amount of trust in someone else. If I help you today, you might be more likely to help me tomorrow, and that, my friends, could give me a genetic advantage over the grumpy lout who never does anything for anyone else. This pattern of *you scratch my back, I'll scratch yours* is referred to as the **norm of reciprocity**. Evolutionary theory suggests that patterns of reciprocity can provide individuals or even groups with an adaptive advantage (Trivers, 1971).

Norm of reciprocity An explanation for why we give help: if I help you today, you might be more likely to help me tomorrow.

Reciprocal helping can be found in numerous animal species, including in (as we noted in chapter 7) vampire bats, impalas, capuchin monkeys, and chimps (Brosnan & de Waal, 2002). For example, if baboon A grooms baboon B, baboon B is more likely to share food later with baboon A. In humans, feeling obligated to return favors seems to be pretty automatic. We even feel the need to reciprocate and return favors to people we don't like (Regan, 1971). Humans are also generous to others when the likelihood that they will reciprocate is low (Delton et al., 2011) and even without a tit-for-tat agreement that they will receive help in the future

The park was crowded that day with people enjoying the summer afternoon, but only this man celebrated for his speed and agility rushed into action. In a documentary on the event, Deron Cherry, Delaney's teammate, described Joe's heroic actions that day, "You ask yourself, what would you do in that situation? And if you have to think about it, then you know you are not going to do the right thing. But he never thought about it. The thing that was on his mind was, 'I need to save these kids.'" (Chiefs Kingdom, September 28, 2013).

As you will learn in this chapter, crowds of people can often immobilize people from stepping up to help. But Joe Delaney's story offers a powerful exception to the rule. People do sometimes help others at extraordinary costs to themselves. Joe even continued to help kids after his death. A foundation started in his honor, The 37 Forever Foundation, spent the next two decades offering free swimming lessons to children (Reilly, 2003).

[NFL Photos/Associated Press]

Many social species engage in reciprocal helping. If you pick the bugs out of my fur, I'll pick the bugs out of yours.

[Philippe Bourseiller/The Image Bank/Getty Images]

(de Waal, 1996). For example, it is unlikely that Joe Delaney gave his life in his efforts to save three drowning boys because he thought they might somehow pay him back—he simply saw children in need and wanted to help.

Biological Bases of Helping

If helpfulness does indeed have a genetic basis, there should be some evidence of gene-based variability in this trait. Consistent with this idea, studies have found evidence of the heritability of prosocial tendencies (Knafo & Plomin, 2006). When pairs of seven-year-old twins were rated by parents for prosocial behavior, identical twins showed correlations greater than .60, whereas fraternal twins showed correlations lower than .40. Keep in mind that identical twins share 100% of their genes and that fraternal twins share only about 50%. But both types of twins are typically raised together in the same household by the same parents and go to the same school. So when behavioral geneticists observe higher correlations among identical (monozygotic) twins than among fraternal (dizygotic twins), they conclude that the trait has some genetic component. In this case, the heritability of prosocial tendencies was estimated to be 62% for the seven-year-olds in this study. In other words, 62% in the variation in prosocial behaviors among the children in this study was attributed to genetic factors. This is suggestive evidence, but it is not definitive, because identical twins' similar levels of helpfulness could result from their being treated especially similarly by others because their other personality and physical attributes are so similar.

Other evidence suggestive of a biological basis for helpfulness can be found in the study of other social animals. Chimpanzees will help out their human caretaker by getting something that she cannot reach (Warneken & Tomasello, 2006). They will also share food with other chimps and will help other chimps who have helped them in the past or with whom they have formed friendships or alliances (Brosnan & de Waal, 2002). Such examples of helping are not confined to primates. Scientists monitoring a group of killer whales near Patagonia observed that when an elderly female had damaged her jaw and could not eat properly, she was fed and kept alive by her companions (Mountain, 2012). Similarly, in an experiment, rats who first shared a cage with another rat for a couple of weeks worked to free their cage mate when they found he was trapped behind a closed door (Bartal et al., 2011). Without any prior learning about how to open the door or any clear reward for doing so, the rats figured out how to free their buddy. If a pile of delicious chocolate chips was placed behind a second closed door, the rats were as likely to free their cage mate as free the chocolate chips. And when both doors had been opened, the two rats tended to share the chocolate. Who knew rats could make such good roommates! Of course, nonhuman animals are occasionally stingy, keeping food for themselves even when another is visibly begging for a snack (Vonk et al., 2008), but a good deal of evidence shows that species other than humans can and do engage in prosocial behavior.

As shown in laboratory research by Bartal and colleagues (2011), even rats will work to free a trapped cage mate without prior learning or obvious reward.

[Bartal et al. (2011)]

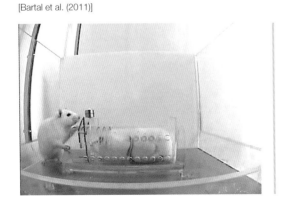

If prosocial behavior is an inherent part of our human nature, then we might see evidence of it at a very young age. In fact, babies have a pretty keen sense of who's naughty and who's nice. Infants as young as 3 months prefer others who are helpful rather than hurtful (Hamlin et al., 2007, 2010; Hamlin & Wynn, 2011). If we come into the world ready to evaluate people on the basis of their good or bad behavior, perhaps we come preequipped to carry out good behavior ourselves. Toddlers less than two years old will help an experimenter pick up something she has dropped (Warneken & Tomasello, 2006). What's more, the toddlers did not help simply because they were interested in picking stuff up when it fell. They picked up the fallen item only if it seemed to have been dropped by accident, and not when the experimenter intentionally dropped it. Young kids do not help just anyone but selectively help those who have been helpful in the past (Dunfield & Kuhlmeier, 2010). These early examples of helping also might reflect a motive to affiliate with others. Even 18-month-old toddlers are more likely to help when they are primed with affiliation by first seeing two dolls standing together (Over & Carpenter, 2009). Taken together, these examples from an emerging body of research point to an innate prosocial proclivity in our species.

Learning to Be Good

Humans are no doubt genetically predisposed toward helping, but we also are predisposed to learn and so develop helpful tendencies through the socialization process. Positive parenting practices, for example, predict greater prosocial behavior in children even after controlling for any shared genetic relationship (Knafo & Plomin, 2006). Although genes provide people with some basic inclinations, culture and learning shape when and for whom these inclinations are cued. Indeed, among the most important genetic inheritances we humans share is the enormously flexible capacity for learning and internalizing local morals and social norms (Becker, 1962; Hoffman, 1981). In this way, people's prosocial behavior is jointly influenced by both genes and environment (Eisenberg & Mussen, 1989; Knafo et al., 2011).

A learning-theory account of prosocial development suggests that people learn to be helpful in a series of stages. At a young age, they learn to be helpful to get things they want. Parents facilitate this mindset with charts that award a child a star every time she shares her toys, says "Please" and "Thank you," or makes her bed. Later in development, people learn to help because social rewards come from the approval they receive from others. A child might learn that other kids are more likely to play with her when she has helped them in the past. And finally, in stage three, people help because they adhere to internalized values (Bar-Tal, 1976; Cialdini et al., 1981). That means that they are listening to the voice of their moral conscience rather than pursuing material goodies or approval from others. Knowing that even young infants show signs of helping, as we saw earlier, we can conclude that people's propensity for prosocial behavior comes on line early in development, but these learning stages shape how this propensity is expressed and the types of situations that bring it out.

As cultural animals, people are saturated with information that can cue ways of being and behaving. These include parents, teachers, role models, and media. Some prosocial instruction is fairly explicit. At a young age, children are taught to share with siblings and playmates. They might be given chores to do around the house to teach them ways that they can help the family. In an effort to extend the prosocial orientation beyond close family and friends, many elementary and secondary schools offer programs to encourage community service or fund-raising efforts for local and international charities. In 1993, President Bill Clinton signed into law the National Community Service Act, a program that provides students the opportunity to receive academic credit, money toward college tuition, and/or job training for the time they spend volunteering with community agencies (Lee, 1993).

Just as children learn specific behaviors and acts of charity from the people around them, so too do these people influence children's emotional responses to those in need. For example, parents who display more emotional warmth themselves tend to have children who are better able to empathize with others and who are seen by others as more socially competent (Zhou et al., 2002). These relationships are present even after researchers controlled for the empathy these children displayed during a study two years previously, underscoring the causal role that parents might be playing. Children also can learn to be more prosocial if they are encouraged to integrate helpfulness into their personal identities. In one study, second graders who were labeled helpful when they shared were more likely to be helpful later than those who shared but weren't labeled helpful (Eisenberg et al., 1987).

When they are quite young, children show a desire to help others.

[Yuri Arcurs/Getty Images]

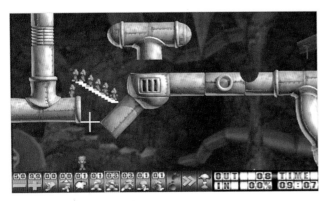

Practicing helping can make you more prosocial. Immediately after people play the video game *Lemmings*, which requires them to keep the little lemmings from leaping to their deaths, they are more helpful to other people.

[AP Photo/Sony]

People also learn prosocial tendencies from the media. Consider video games. In chapter 12 we saw that violent video games can encourage aggressive responses. Yet playing video games that reward prosocial behaviors increases prosocial behavior (Greitemeyer, 2011a). When study participants first played *Lemmings*, a video game whose primary goal is to keep your little group of lemmings alive, they were later almost three times more likely to help the experimenter pick up spilled pencils than were those who had played *Tetris*. Of course, picking up pencils poses no great sacrifice. But what about a more dangerous situation? When the experimenters constructed a scenario in which the participants witnessed the female experimenter being harassed by her hostile ex-boyfriend, 56% of those who had just played the prosocial video game *City Crisis* intervened to help her, compared with only 22% who had played *Tetris* (Greitemeyer & Osswald, 2010). In these cases, the prosocial video games primed prosocial thoughts and behavioral scripts, which remained accessible in people's minds and influenced their behavior when they interacted with others later on. If only the sales of prosocial videogames were higher than those of their more violent counterparts.

SECTION review | The Basic Motives for Helping

Prosocial behavior is an action by an individual that benefits another.

Genetic influences	Learned behavior
• People may be helpful because prosocial behavior might have been generally adaptive in the history of our species. • Although the propensity for helping is especially strong among close kin, it is not restricted to them. • Prosocial emotions contribute to helping. • Norms of reciprocity contribute to prosocial behavior, even among strangers. • Research with twins, toddlers, and nonhuman animals points to an inherited biological basis of prosocial behavior.	• Parents greatly influence prosocial behavior in children. • Children learn prosocial behavior in stages: to get things (such as gold stars), for social rewards, and to satisfy internal moral values. • Media can encourage prosocial behavior by making helping-related thoughts more accessible.

In an episode of the television show *Friends*, Phoebe is challenged by her friend Joey to find a way to help others that doesn't in some way benefit her.

[Warner Bros TV/Bright/Kauffman/Crane Pro/The Kobal Collection]

Does Altruism Exist?

The popular 1990s television show *Friends* had an episode in which the good-hearted Phoebe and her struggling actor friend Joey debate whether it is possible to engage in truly altruistic behavior (Curtis & Jensen, 1998). Phoebe claims that she constantly acts for the benefit of others. But when Joey catches Phoebe admitting that it makes her feel good to put smiles on other people's faces, it highlights a seemingly selfish side to Phoebe's benevolence. If helping makes us feel good or enhances our self-esteem, we could argue that it benefits us as well as the recipient of the help. Is Joey right? Recall the distinction we made earlier between egoistic and altruistic motivations for helping. Is every act of helping inherently egoistic in some way? Or is true altruism possible? Fortunately, we don't have to rely on sitcoms to answer this question. Researchers have developed theories and carried out studies to try to differentiate selfish from selfless acts of helping.

Social Exchange Theory: Helping to Benefit the Self

Helping others can bring material benefits. Strong reciprocity norms all but guarantee that giving a little help to others might mean that you can count on them for help down the road. A **social exchange theory** approach to helping focuses on such egoistic motivations for helping. It maintains that people provide help to someone else when the benefits of helping and the costs of not helping (either to oneself or the other person) outweigh the potential costs of helping and the benefits of not helping (Thibaut & Kelley, 1959). It may sound like the kind of theory an accountant would dream up, but it is not so difficult to imagine carrying out this kind of mental calculation in some situations. Imagine that you are driving down the highway and see a car get a flat tire and pull off the road. Would you stop to help? Sure, you might be able to help the stranded motorist change his tire (a clear benefit to helping), but if you don't stop, he will probably just call a tow truck (a rather low cost to not helping). You might feel good about yourself for helping (another benefit), but you could also end up getting pretty greasy and grimy on the side of the road (a clear cost). According to social exchange theory, the decision to help is determined by some quick mental calculations involving consideration of such benefits and costs.

To study how people weigh costs and benefits in deciding whether or not to help, researchers in one study observed whether people helped a trained research assistant who collapsed on a subway. **If you saw a stranger collapsed in a subway car or other public place, and he seemed to need help, would you come to his aid?** When he carried a cane, he was helped within one minute in nearly 90% of the trials. When he appeared to be drunk, he was helped in fewer than 20% of the trials (Piliavin et al., 1969). Piliavin and colleagues argue that the reason we help is to reduce the arousal we feel when we see someone in distress. The costs of not helping an invalid seem much higher than the costs of not helping someone who is drunk. But the fact that someone needs help also can be offset by our aversion to situations or people we find disgusting or disturbing. In another subway collapse study, people helped less, and those who did took more time, if the person who had collapsed had blood trickling out of his mouth (Piliavin & Piliavin, 1972). Although the victim's need for help was quite clear, people were reluctant to step forward when they might get bloody. Lending a hand also can cost us time, we might fear it's a trap, or we might feel embarrassed if we do the wrong thing. When it's a question of helping someone who is in physical danger, we might worry about our own welfare if we intervene to break up an argument or prevent an attack. All of these factors can weigh against helping when someone is in need.

On the other side of the scale are the possible benefits of helping. Obviously the person in need stands to benefit from what you actually do. But there are other, less tangible benefits to helping. When the Dalai Lama received the Nobel Peace Prize in 1989, he included these words of wisdom in his acceptance speech: "If you want others to be happy, practice compassion. If you want to be happy, practice compassion." Research backs up these words. People who generally feel compassion for others also feel better about themselves (Crocker et al., 2010). When people help others for intrinsic reasons, that is, reasons that align with their core values (see the discussion of self-determination theory in chapter 6), both they and the recipients of their help feel a boost to their well-being (Weinstein & Ryan, 2010). People even report feeling happier after spending money on others than spending the same amount on themselves (Dunn et al., 2008). We are particularly happy when we help someone we feel close to (Aknin et al., 2011). These are exactly the kinds of benefits that Phoebe derives from helping other people, but the question remains: Does that make her selfless acts actually selfish?

Social exchange theory
An approach that maintains that people provide help to someone else when the benefits of helping and the costs of not helping outweigh the potential costs of helping and the benefits of not helping.

[Uriel Sinai/Getty Images News/Getty Images]

Whom Do We Help?
Video on LaunchPad

According to the Dalai Lama, "If you want others to be happy, practice compassion. If you want to be happy, practice compassion."

[Toru Yamanaka/AFP/Getty Images]

Empathy: Helping to Benefit Others

Empathy-altruism model
The idea that the reason people help others depends on how much they empathize with them. When empathy is low, people help others when benefits outweigh costs; but when empathy is high, people help others even at costs to themselves.

Empathy in Adolescence
Video on LaunchPad

According to Daniel Batson's **empathy-altruism model** (Batson et al., 1981), people might very well provide help to others to get certain psychological payoffs. But this rational approach to helping applies only to situations in which people feel no real connection to another person. When your next-door neighbor is stressed out over moving, you might pitch in and pack a few boxes because you have the afternoon free and you know you would feel guilty if you didn't. But you might not skip your favorite class or switch a shift at work to load her things onto a moving van—unless, that is, you feel a true sense of empathy for her situation. When a person empathizes with another person who is suffering or in need of help, he or she takes the perspective of that person and may even vicariously experience the pain, confusion, and other negative states that person might be feeling. If your neighbor is moving out because of a difficult breakup, the type you've experienced yourself, you easily might be able to imagine what she is going through and even feel her sadness. If this is the case, your motivation for stuffing dishes into boxes of packing peanuts might be to reduce her sense of suffering. Thus, Batson has argued that the road to true altruism is paved with empathy. More precisely, the capacity for empathy allows people to understand someone else's distress, and when they empathize with another's plight, they offer to lend a hand regardless of their selfish interests.

Is this true? Research shows that empathy can be an emotionally powerful experience. When people vicariously feel another person's emotion, their brains show activation in the same areas that are activated when they themselves feel the same emotion (de Vignemont & Singer, 2006; Preston & de Waal, 2002). What's more, studies show strong correlations between empathy and helping. For example, people are particularly likely to help others whom they feel similar to and like. These are also the people with whom they find it easiest to empathize (Batson et al., 2007; Coke et al., 1978). Also, do you remember how exposure to prosocial media, such as helping-oriented video games, can promote prosocial behavior? Follow-up research points to empathy as the key factor explaining this effect (Prot et al., 2013). The more adolescents and young adults engaged with prosocial movies, TV shows, and video games, the more empathy they felt for others and, as a result, the more likely they were to help others. Indeed, this finding held true for men and women of all ages and across seven different countries.

Thus, empathy is a powerful spur to prosocial behavior. But remember that the empathy-altruism model makes a stronger claim: that empathy will encourage helping even when the costs to the helper are high. To test this, Batson and colleagues designed a series of studies testing whether people who felt empathy for another person in need would be equally likely to help regardless of the costs of helping. The researchers reasoned that in situations where it is easy not to help, but people help anyway, they help for the good of the other person, not simply to relieve their own discomfort or guilt regarding the other person's plight.

One study examined whether similarity between the self and someone in need leads to feelings of empathy and, consequently, more helping, regardless of the costs of helping (Batson et al., 1981). Imagine you are a participant in this study. You arrive at a laboratory along with another participant named Elaine. After completing an initial preference survey, you learn that the two of you either share the same tastes in magazines and other preferences or have very different tastes. Elaine is randomly assigned to complete a performance task under stressful circumstances; you are assigned to observe and form an impression of her either during the entire study or only during her first set of trials. It sounds pretty straightforward. But the stress that Elaine is exposed to consists of repeated mild but painful electric shocks. After her first round of shocks, Elaine is obviously anxious and explains that she is unusually fearful of electricity. The experimenter isn't sure what to do but after giving it some thought turns to you and suggests that perhaps you could switch places with Elaine. Would you volunteer? Would it matter whether you feel similar to or dissimilar to Elaine? Would it matter if you were not going to have to watch her take any more shocks or if the study procedure called for you to observe a second round of trials?

Look at the two bars on the left of **FIGURE 13.1**. When people didn't feel especially similar to Elaine and so were not likely to feel empathy for her, 64% volunteered to trade places with her if they would otherwise have to watch her endure another set of shocks. However, if they didn't have to watch her take any more shocks, it was easy for them simply to leave the study, and in fact only 18% stayed to help. In the absence of empathy, these participants relied on a cost-benefit analysis to decide whether or not to help, and they determined that by not helping and simply removing themselves from the situation, they wouldn't suffer costs. But now look at the two bars on the right. When participants were made to feel similar to Elaine, a situation we know can increase empathy, 80 to 90% of participants stayed and took her place regardless of whether they had an easy means to escape. This is one of many experiments in which Batson and colleagues have demonstrated that feelings of empathy lead to helping even when the cost of not helping is low—that is, even when it would be easy simply to ignore the person in need (Batson, 2011).

Feeling empathy for someone in need is an important precursor to providing help, and as we just saw, it will lead people to step up even at some cost to themselves. But sometimes, people might perceive the costs as being too high. In these cases, people will sometimes choose to avoid experiencing empathy in the first place. For example, in one study, participants were told that they could choose to listen to one of two personal appeals from a homeless man, one that would likely make them empathize with his plight or a more objective account of his situation (Shaw et al., 1994). When making this choice, some participants were aware that later they would have to decide whether to volunteer either an hour of time writing fund-raising letters on this man's behalf (a relatively small investment of time) or spend several hours providing emotional and social support to him (a much larger investment of time). When knowing they would face a decision of whether to commit a significant amount of time helping the homeless man, about two thirds opted to hear the objective account, knowing that this would elicit less empathy and sadness. In contrast, when they knew the request for help would be much smaller, only one third asked to hear the objective story, and two thirds were willing to have their heartstrings plucked by the more emotional appeal. Empathy can be such a powerful emotion that people sometimes actively avoid situations that would make them empathize with others.

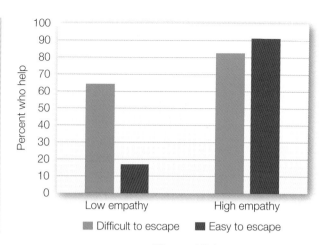

Figure 13.1

People Help When Either Empathy or the Cost of Not Helping Is High

This study by Batson and colleagues shows us that empathy is a key catalyst for helping. When people were low in empathy (on the left), they helped only if they would suffer by not helping. However, people high in empathy (on the right) helped regardless of the costs of not helping.

[Data source: Batson et al. (1981)]

Negative State Relief Hypothesis: Helping to Reduce Our Own Distress

Although Batson has been a champion of altruism, critics have argued that empathy is not always about what another person feels. They grant that when people empathize with someone in need, they feel that person's pain. But they point out that the pain becomes *their* pain, such that the motivation to help really traces back to reducing one's own pain—that is, egoistic motivation. The idea that people help to reduce their own distress has been labeled the **negative state relief hypothesis** (Cialdini et al., 1987). From this point of view, alleviating another person's sadness is merely a means to an end of alleviating our own. To test this account, Cialdini and colleagues

Negative state relief hypothesis The idea that people help in order to reduce their own distress.

recreated Batson's study in which participants observed Elaine receiving shocks. They found that even when participants were asked to take Elaine's perspective and feel her pain, they didn't volunteer to trade places with her if something else happened to improve their mood, such as receiving praise or money. In a second experiment, some participants were led to believe that nothing they could do would change how they were feeling because a "mood-fixing pill" they had taken would leave them in the same emotional state for the duration of the study. These participants, who felt incapable of making themselves feel better, also were quite unlikely to help, even though they reported a good deal of empathy for the person in need. These findings suggest that the link between empathy and helping is still ultimately about the self. After all, because taking the perspective of another leads you to include the other in your own self-concept (Aron et al., 1992; Cialdini et al., 1997), helping someone you feel connected to in some way might inevitably be motivated by a desire to help yourself, or at least what seems like a version of you.

Okay, Altruism: Yes or No?

The debate over the existence of a pure altruistic motive consumed research on prosocial behavior during the 1980s, with papers from one camp shot like cannonballs at the other side. Batson's team countered with evidence that empathy

Prosocial Behavior in *The Hunger Games*

Imagine this: You and 23 other people are competing in the biggest reality TV show ever created. The stakes are life and death, and only the strongest survive. Worse yet, you are forced to play, and there can be only one winner. What would you do?

This is the premise of the film *The Hunger Games* (Collins et al., 2012), based on the popular novel, the first of a trilogy by Suzanne Collins (2008). The time is the distant future. The Capitol government rules over the nation of Panem. To punish lower-class citizens for a past uprising, the Capitol forces each of its 12 districts to offer up a teenage boy and girl, chosen by lottery, to compete in the annual Hunger Games, a nationally televised event in which these young Tributes must fight one another to the death until a sole survivor remains. In these cutthroat circumstances, we might expect the characters to have little capacity for prosocial behavior. Yet acts of kindness and care do occur. The concepts outlined in this chapter help explain why.

The story's first remarkable prosocial act occurs when the protagonist, Katniss Everdeen (played by Jennifer Lawrence),

steps forward to take the place of her beloved 12-year-old sister, Prim (played by Willow Shields), who was initially selected to be District 12's female Tribute. Why would Katniss volunteer to be thrust into a situation in which she is almost certain to die? The idea of kin selection provides one answer, that we are innately predisposed to help those who share many of our genes.

We also witness characters who are not genetically closely related helping one another. In one scene, Katniss has been chased up a tree by an alliance of vicious, highly trained Tributes from other districts. Her goose appears to be cooked until 12-year-old Rue (played by Amandla Stenberg), a Tribute who is hiding in a nearby tree, gives her a tip: break

[Lionsgate/Photofest]

increases helping, even when people can expect that some other good event will boost their mood (Batson et al., 1989). Also, when taking another's perspective, people are most likely to help the person specifically with the problem they are confronting; people are not motivated to provide help that would be irrelevant (Dovidio et al., 1990). This, too, suggests that people can be sensitive to another's needs and work to alleviate another person's pain rather than merely to reduce their own sadness or guilt. Furthermore, isn't feeling another person's distress—allowing it to affect you—usually a sign that you really care about the other person's well-being?

When the dust from all of these studies settled, what did we learn? Researchers use meta-analysis to aggregate evidence across many studies investigating the same question. The meta-analyses on altruism did not provide a great deal of support for the negative state relief hypothesis (Carlson & Miller, 1987; Miller & Carlson, 1990). Moreover, recent neuroscience evidence suggests that there are qualitatively distinct neural responses to imagining what someone else is feeling when he or she is in pain and imagining your own experience of pain if you were in another person's place (Lamm et al., 2007). Although we might be like Joey, helping just to make ourselves feel better when we don't empathize with others, Phoebe might have been right in claiming that the primary motive behind her helpful nature was a genuine altruistic concern with the welfare for others.

---

a branch to drop a nest of poisonous wasps on the assailants. Rue also cares for Katniss after she is subsequently stung by one of the wasps. Why does Rue choose to help another competitor, knowing that it could mean her disadvantage, or death, later in the Games? Kin selection probably is not the answer: Katniss and Rue have different ethnic backgrounds, and their homelands are far apart, making it unlikely that they are close genetic relatives. More likely, Rue anticipates that Katniss will reciprocate by providing help in the future. In this case, reciprocal helping may have been stronger than the situational pressure to kill everyone in sight. And it pays off: Later, Katniss shares food with Rue and does her best to protect her. When Rue is fatally wounded, Katniss shows tremendous empathy for her, easing her dying, and paying respect to her after her death in numerous ways and at considerable risk to herself.

Another scene illustrates the power of empathy to spur altruism. Prior to entering the arena, Katniss is mentored by Haymitch Abernathy (Woody Harrelson). Later, while watching the Hunger Games on TV, Haymitch sees Katniss in agonizing pain after she is injured in battle. This prompts him to petition a sponsor from Panem's elite class to have a healing balm delivered to Katniss. Why does he take the time and energy to do this? He does not personally benefit, and Katniss had done nothing special to deserve his favor. Empathy seems to be the answer. Because Haymitch is a former victor in the Hunger Games, he can easily put himself in Katniss's shoes and feel her pain and fear. When he sees her wince in pain, he winces too. He may help simply to stop feeling bad (in keeping with the negative state relief hypothesis), but he could just as easily distract himself from Katniss's plight to do so. So his actions more likely result from empathy, a genuine concern for another's well-being.

Perhaps the most profound displays of prosocial action occur between Katniss and Peeta Mellark (Josh Hutcherson), the male Tribute from District 12. Throughout the Hunger Games, Katniss and Peeta put their own lives in great danger to help and protect one another. One basis for this may be their shared social identity of being from the same District. But beyond that, Peeta is clearly in love with Katniss. Katniss's feelings for Peeta are more ambivalent, but their affection and consequent empathy is increasingly reciprocated over the course of the Games. As the research on rescuers of Jews during the Nazi era found, affection is a common basis for empathy and helping, and this may be especially true when feelings of romantic love are involved. In addition, such feelings may signal the possibility of reproduction. If so, we may be prepared to offer help to those with whom we fall in love.

The ultimate problem for Katniss and Peeta is that there can be only one survivor of the Games. In case you are one of the few who haven't seen this film, we won't reveal how that dilemma is resolved.

SECTION review | Does Altruism Exist?

Researchers have studied whether genuine altruism exists or whether prosocial behavior is done for one's own benefit.

The social exchange theory	The empathy-altruism model	The negative state relief hypothesis
People do a quick cost-benefit analysis to determine whether or not to help someone.	People can feel empathy, and this empathy leads to genuinely altruistic acts.	Helping triggered by empathy is still egoistic because it reduces one's own pain. However, meta-analysis finds little evidence that negative state relief is the real motivation for helping those with whom we empathize.

The Social and Emotional Triggers of Helping

Our discussion of nature and nurture and the existence of altruism examines the *why* of helping—that is, the motivations that underlie prosocial behavior. Let's take a closer look at *when* and *whom* we help. By definition, helping is a social process, one that it is influenced by how we think and feel about our relationships to other people. In this section, we'll consider the social and emotional processes that trigger our prosocial tendencies.

Similarity and Prejudice

Stop and think about the last few times you helped someone else. How would you describe the person you helped? Most of the time, people help those who are close to them. If they do stop to help a stranger, it is often because they feel a sense of similarity to that person. After all, it is easier for us to imagine ourselves in the shoes of people like us, to take their perspective, and feel a sense of empathy for their situation (Krebs, 1975). In one study conducted in the 1970s, research assistants dressed either like hippies (think bell bottoms; sandals; flowered shirts; and long, flowing hair) or more conservatively (pressed slacks, polished shoes, short hair) (Emswiller et al., 1971). They positioned themselves in the campus student union, approached passing students, and asked to borrow a dime. Some of the students they asked were themselves dressed like hippies; others were dressed more conservatively. What did the researchers find? People were more likely to help if the other person dressed the way they did. When it comes to helping, birds of a feather most definitely do flock together.

[Viacheslav Nikolaenko/Shutterstock]

Think ABOUT

The notion that people are more likely to help similar others has a pleasant ring to it, but the dark underbelly of this effect is people's tendency to walk past those who are dissimilar or against whom they are prejudiced. Many studies of helping have revealed that markedly less help is given to members of socially devalued groups. In one study, researchers made phone calls to unsuspecting White participants (Gaertner, 1973). Speaking either without a distinctive accent or with a southern Black accent, the caller pretended to be someone whose car had broken down and who had just used his or her last dime to call what seemed to be a wrong number. The request: Will you please phone a garage and send out a tow truck? When participants presumed that the caller was White, they were significantly more likely to volunteer to call a tow truck than when they presumed that the caller was Black.

We know what you are thinking: This study took place 40 years ago. Surely times have changed! Maybe not. A more recent meta-analysis of similar studies (Saucier et al., 2005) found that racial discrimination in how help is given has not diminished over time. In one set of experiments published in 2008, 92% of White college students came to the aid of another White student who had fallen and seemed to be injured in the next room, compared with only 70% when the victim was Black (Kunstman & Plant, 2008). And those who did offer help to the Black victim were about a minute slower to respond. When Black participants were faced with the same situation, they were equally likely to help the victim regardless of his or her race. In follow-up studies, Whites reported that when the victim was Black, the situation seemed less severe and they felt less responsible for intervening. Indeed, according to the meta-analysis by Saucier and colleagues (2005), Whites are especially unlikely to help a Black individual when they can claim nonracial justifications for their inaction, evidence of what has been called *aversive racism*, a topic you might remember learning about in chapter 10.

Race isn't the only dimension on which prejudice plays a role in the failure to help. Even families aren't immune. Parents are less likely to pay for tuition for their overweight than for their normal-weight children (Crandall, 1991), an effect that is typical of a general prejudice against those who are overweight (Crandall, 1994). Even when people do not actively harm members of socially stigmatized groups, the tendency to withhold help and assistance can be a subtle but pervasive form of discrimination. This type of discrimination is especially likely when people have a convenient excuse for their inaction. For example, as we reviewed in chapter 10 as well, a White participant is less likely to help a Black victim if it is plausible that someone else might intervene (Gaertner & Dovidio, 1977).

The Empathy Gap

We've already described Batson's theoretical view that empathy is what drives true altruism. And one of the reasons people are more likely to help those they feel similar to is that they find it easier to empathize with their plight. More generally, however, people tend to underestimate other people's experience of physical pain (Loewenstein, 2005) as well as the pain of social rejection (Nordgren et al., 2011). Because of this **empathy gap**, people often fail to give help when help is needed. Asking people to experience pain or rejection actually can help close this gap. In one study, middle-school teachers were more favorable to antibullying programs at their school after they were first asked to imagine in vivid detail the pain of being rejected (Nordgren et al., 2011).

Another way to close the empathy gap is to take the perspective of the person in need, that is, to imagine what that person is experiencing from his or her point of view. For example, after students listened to and took the perspective of a drug addict recounting his struggles with addiction, they were more likely to support funding a campus agency that would help fight addiction. Those who merely listened objectively to the same man's experience were less willing to fund this new group (Batson et al., 2002). When people feel empathy for someone who is disadvantaged in society, they are also more likely to support policies that would help his or her group.

An interesting byproduct of empathy is that it makes people more likely to help when they focus on the suffering of a single individual than when they consider a tragedy that befalls a large group. In the aftermath of the tsunami that leveled many coastal communities in Japan in 2011, humanitarian groups rallied to raise money to meet the basic needs of the survivors and to begin to repair the massive damage that had been done. When such a disaster happens, the enormous scale of suffering is almost beyond comprehension. People can find it so emotionally overwhelming to contemplate that they actually downregulate their reaction to avoid distress (Cameron & Payne, 2011). In an ironic consequence, they are less likely to help in those situations where help is most sorely needed. This is why many fund-raising organization such as UNICEF, Save the Children, and the Animal Legal Defense Fund often feature the suffering of a representative child or animal to elicit most effectively the kinds of empathy that trigger helping.

Empathy gap The underestimation of other people's experience of physical pain as well as the pain of social rejection.

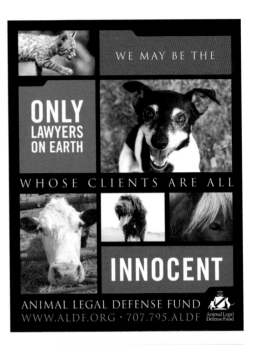

People are more likely to help when they focus on individual suffering than when they focus on tragic consequences to a large group. This is why many charitable organizations feature the experiences of individuals when soliciting donations.

The Role of Causal Attributions

One factor that often contributes to people's decision to help is whether or not they believe the person in need deserves her or his misfortune. This is where attribution theory enters the scene. You'll recall from chapter 4 that people have a tendency, especially in individualistic cultures, to make dispositional attributions. They infer that another person's condition is the result of his or her own personality or freely chosen actions, not the result of the situation. In addition, you may recall that we have a desire to believe in a just world where people generally get what they deserve. Because of these tendencies, people are quick to assume that others deserve their suffering. Even children as young as three assume that if a random bad thing happens to a person, that person must not be very nice (Olson et al., 2008). This means that if you are hoping to get some help when you find yourself in a bind, you might be fighting an uphill battle.

Thus, one key determinant of providing help to someone else is whether you think he is responsible for his current need. Is he in his present position because of something he could have controlled? If the answer is yes, we are more likely to turn our backs on him. If a classmate asks to borrow your notes from a class he missed, you are less likely to help him out if the reason for his absence was completely within his control (Weiner, 1980). On the other hand, when something uncontrollable hap-

People are less likely to offer help to the homeless if they attribute the person's need to his or her own lack of effort.

pens, our response is to feel sympathy rather than disgust or anger, and this emotional response activates our desire to help out (Reisenzein, 1986). Thinking back to the studies where a confederate collapsed in a crowded subway car, we might wonder whether attributions played a role in people's willingness to help someone who seemed disabled or their apathy about the person who seemed drunk.

The attributions people make affect their decision to help not only single individuals but also groups of people. When a group is socially stigmatized due to factors out of its control, people feel sympathy and offer their support for policies that would benefit its members (Weiner et al.,1988). For example, we might expect people to be much more supportive of charities that help those with cancer or heart disease than those suffering from obesity or drug abuse, which are viewed as being much more within a person's control. More recent evidence suggests that some groups in society that might be most in need of help, such as the homeless and drug addicts, actually elicit disgust rather sympathy. When observing these groups, people show reduced activation in areas of the brain, such as the medial prefrontal cortex, where perceptions and impressions of human beings are formed (Harris & Fiske, 2006). That is, their brains react as though they were observing objects rather than people. In fact, when people dehumanize others, they assume that those others experience a smaller range of uniquely human emotions (Leyens et al., 2000). You can imagine how this makes it particularly unlikely that they experience empathy: If you assume that another person doesn't have the capacity to experience complex negative emotions such as regret and anxiety, then viewing the world from their perspective will leave you emotionally unaffected.

Other Prosocial Feelings

We have focused on the role of empathy in helping, but other prosocial feelings also play a role in motivating a tendency to help. Among these are guilt, communal feelings, gratitude, and feeling socially secure.

Guilt

Our previous discussion of attributions focused on judging how responsible someone else is for his or her situation, but sometimes people offer help because they feel a personal responsibility for another person's plight. As we noted earlier, internalized morals play a strong role in helping. People often help because they think it is the right thing to do. Although doing the right thing boosts their self-esteem, failing to live up to their own moral standards can make people feel guilty. Usually this guilt stems from the thought that we have not treated another person or group properly. In this way, it cues the person that there is a need to repair a social relationship (Baumeister et al., 1994; Rank, 1932/1989). Guilt is a bit like a Bat-Signal beamed into the sky calling for the Caped Crusader, but instead it calls the person into action to right some wrong. Many studies have demonstrated that inducing people to feel guilty increases their tendency to help others (Cunningham et al., 1980). In one staged experiment, when shoppers at a mall were made to believe that they had broken a confederate's camera (rather than being told that the camera was malfunctioning), they later were more than three times as likely to help a passerby whose bag full of candy was spilling on the ground (Regan et al., 1972). In these situations, helping someone (even if it is not the person who was harmed) can help people alleviate guilt.

Even when people do not feel personally responsible for harm done to another person or group, they can nevertheless feel guilt about that harm, a feeling labeled *collective guilt*. For example, when people identify with a group that is socially advantaged over others, they can feel collective guilt about an outgroup that is less fortunate, especially if they see that the outgroup's disadvantaged position in society is illegitimate (Miron et al., 2006). Collective guilt motivates a desire to make reparations to victims of past injustice or otherwise support policies that level the playing field (Regan, 1971). This relationship has been found in many circumstances: among U.S. and British students reflecting on the harm to the Iraqi people during their countries' occupation of Iraq (Iyer et al., 2007); Chileans reflecting on Chile's disadvantaged indigenous people (Brown et al., 2008); South Africans reflecting on their country's history of apartheid (Klandermans et al., 2008); men reflecting on gender inequality (Gunn & Wilson, 2011); and White Americans reflecting on racial disadvantage in the United States (Iyer et al., 2003).

Although this research shows that guilt is effective at motivating helping, this effect may be short lived. Some researchers argue that when people help out of guilt—

over either personal or collective actions—they are simply engaging in negative state relief (Iyer et al., 2003). In other words, they are helping only to make themselves feel better. The problem with this kind of helping is that it sometimes leads only to token forms of help that actually reduce the likelihood of providing more significant help at a later time (Dutton & Lennox, 1974). This work leads back to the conclusion that the best forms of helping are motivated by sympathy or empathy rather than guilt.

A Communal Feeling

All this talk of guilt and empathy reminds us that one of the strongest motivators of our behavior is to form, strengthen, and maintain close relationships with others (Baumeister & Leary, 1995; Bowlby, 1973). Guilt lets us know when we might be falling down on that job and need to give a little help to restore a close relationship, but sympathy and empathy motivate lasting change. In romantic relationships, being willing to make sacrifices for your partner is a strong predictor of the health of your relationship (van Lange et al., 1997).

Communal orientation
A frame of mind in which people don't distinguish between what's theirs and what is someone else's.

In close relationships, people are more likely to adopt a **communal orientation** where they don't distinguish between what is theirs and what is someone else's. When "you and I" become a "we," the person attends to his or her partner's needs regardless of whether that partner ever will be able to reciprocate (Clark et al., 1986). People become more sensitive to the partner's sadness and more likely to help when the partner is feeling down (Clark et al., 1987). Family relationships are the prototypical communal relationship, especially the relationship between a parent and child. Think of all the ways in which your parents have helped you over the years. (Now might be a good time to send a thank-you note!) How have you returned the

Think
ABOUT

[Wong Sze Yuen/Shutterstock]

favor? But even our relationships with friends and acquaintances can take on these communal characteristics when we treat a friend to lunch without ever keeping track of whether she pays us back. In our communal relationships, helping someone else feels a lot like helping ourselves. Maybe this is why we feel the largest boost in mood when we help someone we feel communally connected to and the biggest drop in mood when we turn our back on that person (Williamson & Clark, 1989, 1992).

The Recipient's Gratitude

It is not surprising that when the people we help express their gratitude, we are more likely to help again, not just the person who thanked us but anyone else in need (Grant & Gino, 2010). This effect of gratitude on prosociality doesn't happen only because being thanked makes us feel good or cues a norm of reciprocity (Bartlett & DeSteno, 2006). Rather, people who express their gratitude to us make us feel more communal and enhance our feelings of social value. When we feel like a valued part of a community, we are more likely to keep helping that community. Before you draw the conclusion that gratitude is only about appreciating others, keep in mind that gratitude also has benefits for us. People who count their blessings feel happier, become more optimistic, exercise more, and sleep better (Emmons & McCullough, 2003). And people who score higher in gratitude are rated by their friends as engaging in more helpful behavior (McCullough et al., 2002).

Feeling Socially Secure

Evidence such as this suggests that a focus on how others help you is beneficial because it emphasizes that you are a part of a social *ecosystem*, which is a lot better for mental health than an emphasis on your own self-interested

[Mike Twohy/The New Yorker Collection/Cartoonbank.com]

"The takeaway tonight is 'Thanks.'"

egosystem (Crocker, 2011). In fact, people who suffer from feelings of insecurity in their social relationships, especially those who avoid becoming too close to others, find it more difficult to feel compassion for someone in distress and are less likely to come to that person's aid. People who are either dispositionally more secure in their relationships or who are primed with a sense of relationship security feel more compassionate and behave more prosocially toward both family members and distant acquaintances (Mikulincer et al., 2005; van Lange et al., 1997).

SECTION review | The Social and Emotional Triggers of Helping

Helping is a social process that is influenced by how we think and feel about our relationships with other people.

Similarity and prejudice	The empathy gap	Causal attributions	Other prosocial feelings
• People are most likely to help those who are similar to them. • This can lead to prejudicial behavior when people ignore the plight of those who are different.	• People tend to underestimate others' pain. • This can result in an empathy gap and less likelihood of offering help.	• Because of attributional processes and a desire to see the world as just, people may convince themselves a person bears responsibility for his troubles. • This feeling can reduce empathy and thus helping.	• People are motivated to help by feelings of guilt, communal connections, and others' gratitude. • A clear sense of one's own relational security can also facilitate helping.

Priming Prosocial Feelings and Behavior

Evolutionary perspectives on helping provide insight into how prosocial tendencies and associated emotions may have become part of human nature. Social learning perspectives provide insight into how helpfulness is learned and transmitted within a given culture or social environment. We might think of evolutionary processes as giving us the basic machinery to be helpful and of social learning as providing us with culturally specific scripts for how to be helpful. But we still need situational accounts to provide insight into when we enact these scripts and when we do not. The story of when we help is based partly on our relationships with others and partly on the emotions triggered in social situations. As we've seen in several places throughout this book, however, even very subtle situational cues can activate behavioral scripts outside our conscious awareness. The same is true of prosocial behaviors. Let's review a few of the subtle ways in which people can be primed with prosocial scripts.

Positive Affect

One of the earliest lines of studies examining what primes people to be prosocial looked at the effect of positive mood. You no doubt can recall an experience when you felt bright and cheerful, whistling as you walked down the street, quite willing to spend your time stopping to help someone pick up their spilled groceries or digging into your pockets to give your spare change to a panhandler. If your intuitions tell you that you'll be more helpful in a positive mood, research by Alice Isen suggests you are right. Whether participants' positive mood arose from succeeding in a difficult task, receiving cookies, or unexpectedly finding a dime in a pay phone (note to the perplexed: There used to be booths with phones in them that accepted coins as payment for a call), they were more likely to help afterward. They give more money to charities, offer more assistance to someone who has spilled their belongings, and are more likely to buy a stamp and mail a letter that has been left behind (Isen, 1970; Isen & Levin, 1972; Levin & Isen, 1975). Like most priming effects, these can be transient, dissipating once people's mood returns to baseline (Isen et al., 1976).

If you did have the intuition that people are more helpful when they are happy, can you spell out why that would be the case? What is it about being in a good mood that makes people more prosocial? Several processes might be in play (Carlson et al., 1988). On the one hand, good moods are inherently rewarding, making people loath to do anything that might knock them out of that mood. Consequently, when people are in a good mood they may help in order to avoid the guilt that would arise if they turned their backs on someone in need. In addition to this rather selfish influence, happy moods make people see the best in other people. With this more positive frame of reference on humanity comes a more prosocial orientation and a tendency to see the inherent good that comes from lending a helping hand (Carlson et al., 1988).

Prosocial Metaphors

Many concepts related to prosocial behavior, such as morality and fairness, are inherently abstract and difficult to grasp in their own terms. As we discussed in chapter 3, people often make sense of abstract concepts using *metaphor*. Metaphor is a mental tool that people use to think about and understand an abstract concept by using their knowledge of a different type of concept that is more concrete and easier to comprehend.

Do people use metaphor to understand concepts related to prosocial behavior? Many common expressions about these concepts suggest that they do. Take, for example, the relationship between morality and vertical height. Being moral does not mean literally being higher in space. Still, people talk about taking the "moral high ground" to refer to virtuous behavior, and when they watch or hear about heartwarming stories of altruism such as those we described at the beginning of this chapter, they talk about feeling "uplifted." In general, people organize their moral view of the world by ranking different beings along a vertical dimension, putting the most moral agents, such as god(s), at the top and animals who they think lack any moral compass at the bottom (Brandt & Reyna, 2011).

If people think about the abstract concept of morality in terms of a concrete state (e.g., being at a high altitude or clean), then situations that prime that state should change how people think about morality and thus affect their willingness to lend a hand. Height is one way to prime morality; cleanliness is another. When we behave immorally, we feel dirty. Lady Macbeth, tortured by her conscience after goading Macbeth to murder the king, cries "Out, damn'd spot!" as she compulsively washes her hands over and over again in Shakespeare's *Macbeth* (1606/1869). If we associate "dirtiness" with immoral behavior, then we might associate "cleanliness" with virtuous, prosocial behavior. After all, cleanliness is next to godliness, or so they say. Primed with the fresh scent of window cleaner, participants in one study reported a greater interest in volunteering for Habitat for Humanity, and they actually donated more money to that charity than did participants in an unscented room (Liljenquist et al., 2010). If you need to ask a favor of a friend, you might want to bring along a little Windex to seal the deal!

Priming Prosocial Roles

Social roles and relationships come with certain norms that tell us how to behave. For example, when you take the role of friend, that role carries the norm that you will help more than when you take the role of stranger or coworker. If people commit themselves to a helping profession such as teaching, nursing, or customer service, taking on that role should also prepare them to be helpful. What's more surprising are the subtle ways that these prosocial roles and relationships can be primed. In one study, people at an airport were asked to do a quick survey in which they recalled and answered a few questions about either a close friend or a coworker. Afterward, they were merely asked to rate their interest in helping the experimenter by completing a second, longer survey. Only 19% agreed when they were first primed to think of a coworker, but 53% agreed when first primed with a friend (Fitzsimons & Bargh, 2003). You might say that thinking about friendship puts us in a friendly state of mind and readies us to act in a friendly, helpful way. We might even be more likely to incorporate these subtle cues into our behavior when we otherwise feel deindividuated or disinhibited (Hirsh et al., 2011). Just as people can become more aggressive when they feel deindividuated but are primed with an aggressive role, they can become more prosocial when they feel deindividuated and are primed with a caregiving role, like being a nurse (Johnson & Downing, 1979).

Priming Mortality

A pale light . . . fell straight upon the bed; and on it . . . was the body of this man. . . . Oh cold, cold, rigid, dreadful death!. . . But of the loved, revered, and honoured head, thou canst not turn one hair to thy dread purposes. . . . It is not that the hand is heavy and will fall down when released. . .but that the hand was open, generous, and true; the heart brave, warm, and tender. . . . [S]ee his good deeds springing up from the wound, to sow the world with life immortal!"

—Charles Dickens, *A Christmas Carol* (1843/1950, pp. 115–116)

Some social roles and occupations, such as nursing, carry with them the norm to be helpful. When people take on those roles, or simply bring them to mind, they become more helpful.
[michaeljung/iStock/360/Getty Images]

Most of us are socialized to try to do the right thing. Cultural worldviews usually if not always promote helping as the way to be a good, valuable person. Consequently, helping behaviors normally contribute to our sense of significance in the world and of creating a legacy of positive impact into the future, even beyond our own lives. By applying an existential perspective, terror management theory therefore suggests that mortality salience should promote prosocial behavior. In the classic Charles Dickens tale *A Christmas Carol*, the stingy Ebenezer Scrooge is ultimately moved to become a charitable person by the ghost of Christmas Future, which shows him his fate: to be forgotten after his death. He realizes that generosity will ensure that he has a positive impact and will be remembered beyond his physical death.

Will reminders of mortality generally make people more generous? In support of this "Scrooge effect," studies by Jonas and colleagues (2002) have shown that mortality salience increases donations to valued charities. A study at a university library similarly showed that a flier reminding passersby of their mortality made them more willing to help a psychology student complete her research project (Hirschberger et al., 2008). Consistent with these experiments, real-world reminders of death, such as the terrorist attacks of September 11, 2001, generally increase charitable giving, volunteerism, and blood donations (Glynn et al., 2003; Penner et al., 2005; Yum & Schenck-Hamlin, 2005). Further research has shown that reminders of mortality are especially likely to increase social behavior when prosocial cultural values have also been primed (Gailliot et al., 2008; Jonas et al., 2008). It is interesting that these prosocial effects of reminders of mortality may be blocked or even reversed if the prosocial actions themselves remind people of death—for example, if the request is for organ donation (Hirschberger et al., 2008). Prosocial behavior can help embed us in a world that we value and thus make us better able to distance ourselves from the reality of death, but only if the charitable action does not itself conjure up thoughts of our mortality.

In the classic Charles Dickens tale *A Christmas Carol*, the stingy Ebenezer Scrooge is ultimately moved to become a charitable person by the ghost of Christmas Future, which shows him his fate: to be forgotten after his death.
[ClassicStock/Alamy]

Priming Religious Values

When it comes to priming moral behavior, some of the most potent concepts come from religion. Religion, like culture more generally, gives people a set of rules and restrictions that help regulate their behavior. Religious teachings explain what it is to be a good and moral person and almost invariably preach kindness and compassion. Indeed, the notion that we should do unto others as we would have them do unto us captures our basic prosocial norm for positive reciprocity and can be found in all of the major world religions (Batson et al., 1993). The problem is that true reciprocity only really works with people we see and interact with on an ongoing basis. When societies got big, people found themselves having more and more one-time interactions with complete strangers. These large societies function better if we expand our notion of reciprocity to people we do not know. Big religions help do this by incorporating the message of reciprocity as a general principle, a "golden rule" (Norenzayan & Shariff, 2008; Shariff et al., 2010).

Does this then imply that those who are religious act more prosocially? Not necessarily. It's true that people who report high levels of religiosity also report being more altruistic, but in laboratory settings designed to measure the likelihood of helping, religiosity is unrelated to the actual likelihood of prosocial actions (Batson et al., 1993). Other work points to competing values associated with religiosity, at least in the United States (Malka et al., 2011). On the one hand, religiosity in America is associated with conservative ideologies that tend to oppose social welfare policies. Religious individuals also tend to make dispositional attributions (Jackson & Esses, 1997), which as we discussed earlier, can make people less likely to help a person out. However, religiosity is also associated with prosocial values that predict increased support for social welfare. These competing cultural messages indicate that the relationship of religiosity to helping is not so clear cut.

Even if we can't always count on religious adherence to predict prosocial practices, the mere idea of religion can still prime more positive acts. Participants who first unscrambled sentences that primed them with concepts such as "divine" and "sacred" were more generous to a stranger than those primed with neutral concepts (Shariff & Norenzayan, 2007). This effect was present even for those who report being atheists, although it is interesting that priming people with other ways that society promotes justice ("courts" and "contracts") had the same effect. In fact, one of the ways that concepts of deities might help us keep on the moral path is by giving us the sense that someone is always watching what we do, keeping track of when we are naughty or nice (Gervais & Norenzayan, 2012).

We can also view religion as defining our cultural worldview, one we are motivated to uphold when reminded of our mortality. Although religious fundamentalism often is associated with prejudice and intolerance toward other groups, people primed with the more compassionate side of their religious ideals are in fact more likely to turn the other cheek. When reminded of their mortality and primed with compassionate values, fundamentalist Christian Americans were less supportive of using extreme military force to defend the homeland against attack (Rothschild et al., 2009). In this way, religion can play an important role in promoting prosocial behavior even toward those who do not share the same religious worldview.

SECTION review | Priming Prosocial Feelings and Behavior

Situations can trigger helping behaviors, even without our awareness. Prosocial behavior is increased by:				
Positive moods that put people in a prosocial mindset.	Physical cues (e.g., clean scents) that are linked to prosocial concepts by means of metaphor.	Friends and primes of friendship that cue a communal orientation.	Reminders of mortality that lead people to help someone who supports their worldview.	Priming religion or religious values, although the relationship between dispositional religiosity and helping is more complicated.

Why Do People Fail to Help?

We like to think of ourselves as good, moral people, capable of empathy and compassion. Prosocial behavior benefits our relatives, friends, and groups; materially benefits victims; and psychologically benefits ourselves. At this point, we might expect that being helpful will always be the norm. But we can probably think of times when we passed by a panhandler without giving him money, closed the door on a solicitor seeking donations for a local charity, or made excuses to a friend looking for a ride to the airport. The fact of the matter is that we don't always give or receive help. The flip side of looking at variables that elevate our helpful tendencies is to consider those that inhibit helping.

The Bystander Effect

We began this chapter with dramatic examples of helping. But during the Nazi era, for every rescuer who helped Jews avoid persecution, there were many, many more people who did nothing—or worse. Of course the risks of helping in such a context were high. We also considered many examples of more mundane helping in which the potential costs of helping were fairly low. Giving our spare change to a charity or helping someone pick up dropped papers takes little effort on our part, and no great harm is done if we casually walk on by. In these situations, not giving help typically goes unnoticed. But then there are high-need situations in which helping would be low cost but still doesn't happen. Every month or so in countries around the world, you can find a story in the news of a horrible tragedy that could have been prevented by a mere phone call, such as the story we noted earlier of a girl who was gang-raped outside of a homecoming dance while other students stood by and watched. When such events happen, we read about them with horror but also confusion. How could someone stand by and do *nothing* to help? Is this evidence of a callous generation of youth, desensitized to harm by hours spent playing violent video games or watching slasher movies? Probably not. The sad truth is that such events have happened for generations. In fact, social psychologists first took an interest in studying the complexities of prosocial behavior after just such an incident made headlines in 1964.

Kitty Genovese was brutally murdered in 1964. News accounts claimed that witnesses heard the attack take place but did not help, spurring researchers to study the bystander effect.

[*NY Daily News* via Getty Images]

In the early morning hours on a cold day in March, Kitty Genovese returned home after work. As she walked toward her apartment building in Queens, New York, she was attacked from behind and stabbed in the back. The perpetrator continued to assault and stab her in a brutal attack that lasted over 30 minutes. During this time, Genovese cried for help, screamed that she had been stabbed, and tried to fight off her assailant. A New York newspaper reported that 38 people had witnessed the attack from their apartment windows and yet no one called the police until after the attack had ended. Unfortunately, by then it was too late. Genovese died on the way to the hospital (Gansberg, 1964).

At the time, people took this horrific episode as evidence of the moral disintegration of New Yorkers—not just the murderer but also the witnesses who did not act. Although there has been some recent debate about whether the newspaper report exaggerated the number of witnesses (Manning et al., 2007), there were clearly more than enough witnesses to expect someone to have picked up the phone and called the police, yet no one did. This event inspired John Darley and Bibb Latané (1968) to engage in a groundbreaking set of studies documenting the **bystander effect**. The bystander effect generally refers to a phenomenon in which a person who witnesses another in need is less likely to help when there are other bystanders present to witness the event. On the surface, this idea seems ironic. Shouldn't the presence of other witnesses encourage individuals to help? The interesting fact of psychology is that sometimes the presence of others can make an individual inactive, although as we will see, this can happen for a few different reasons.

Bystander effect A phenomenon in which a person who witnesses another in need is less likely to help when there are other bystanders present to witness the event.

To see how this works, put yourself in the shoes of one of Darley and Latané's (1968) participants. You think you are going to be having a conversation over an intercom system about the challenges of being at college. You learn that it will just be you and another student, or that you will be part of a group of either three or six. To protect everyone's privacy, you are each in your own room, only able to hear the others over the intercom. As the discussion gets under way, one of the other participants discloses his history of having seizures and talks about how disruptive and stressful it can be. You are also asked to share something about your experience, as are the other participants if you are part of a group. After another round of sharing, the student who had complained of seizures seems to be having one. The transcript of what people actually heard included:

> I-er-um-I think I-I need-er-if-if could-er-er-somebody er-er-er-er-er-er-er give me a little-er-give me a little help here because-er-I-er-I'm-er-er—having a-a-a real problem-er-right now and I-er-if somebody could help me out it would-it would-er-er s-s-sure be-sure be good . . . (p. 379).

Clearly, this person is having a hard time and is explicitly asking for help. If you were like the students who participated in this study over 40 years ago, you probably would get up to find the experimenter if you thought you had been having a private conversation with this person. Every single participant in that condition got up to help, and 85% of them did so within a minute and before the victim's apparent seizure had ended. When participants believed instead that four other people were listening, only 31% tried to help by the time the seizure had ended.

In another study (Latané & Darley, 1968), participants completed questionnaires in a waiting room, either alone or with two others who were sometimes confederates of the study or sometimes other naive participants. As they dutifully answered surveys, smoke began to stream into the room through a wall vent. In the group condition, the two confederates both looked up at the smoke briefly and then went back to their questionnaires. If participants were alone, 75% of them got up and alerted the experimenters to the smoke. But this dropped to less than 40% when three naive participants were in the room, and only 10% if the participant sat alongside confederates who remained inactive.

A recent meta-analysis of 50 years of research shows the bystander effect to be a reliable phenomenon (Fischer et al., 2011). A tendency toward inaction even increases as the number of bystanders gets larger. Interestingly, despite the many documented cases of inaction in high danger situations, the bystander effect is generally more likely to occur when the situation seems less dangerous. Although people clearly fail to act sometimes when the victim is in great peril, they are even less likely to act if the need for help is minor and others might be expected to intervene (Fischer et al., 2011). The bystander effect also is more likely to occur among strangers than among friends. But even if we are with strangers, the mere expectation that later we will be working alongside these people increases our tendency to provide help to someone, even in the presence of other observers (Gottlieb & Carver, 1980). Feeling a sense of connection to those around you can turn a mere collection of inactive individuals into a powerful collective. Even learning about the bystander effect, as you are right now, can prompt people into action when they face a crisis in the midst of a crowd (Beaman et al., 1978). A little knowledge can be empowering!

Steps to Helping—or Not!—in an Emergency

What is it about being in a group that immobilizes us? When we break down an event into its component parts, we can see that the decision to provide help in an emergency situation requires several steps. As a result, there are several places and

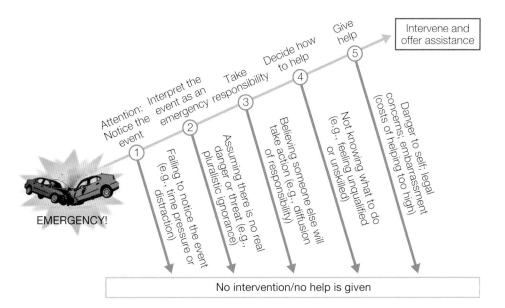

Figure 13.2

Steps to Helping . . . or Not

When encountering a potential emergency situation, people must take multiple steps in deciding whether to offer help. At each step, we can make a judgment about ourselves or the situation that prevents us from helping.

several reasons that people don't always get the help they need. **FIGURE 13.2** presents several steps leading to helping behavior. At each step, something in the situation can waylay the process, causing us to keep walking and ignore others in need.

Step 1: Notice the situation. The first step on the path to helping is to notice that something is amiss and that help might be needed. Although the seizure study clearly was designed to make the victim's plight quite obvious, in the real world we often go about our day immersed in our egocentric bubble and somewhat oblivious to the needs of those around us. We don't like to think that something as simple as being rushed for time would prevent us from offering assistance to someone in need. But this is exactly what Darley and Batson (1973) found in one intriguing experiment that was designed to provide the strongest test that situational factors can prevent people from acting on their moral values. For their study, the researchers recruited people they thought surely would be the most compassionate folks around—theology students at Princeton University. They even put half the participants in a frame of mind that should have brought compassionate values to the fore by having them prepare to give a sermon on the parable of the Good Samaritan. In this biblical story, a Jewish man is attacked by robbers and lies, injured and suffering, on the side of the road. Several high-status individuals pass by, ignoring him. Only a low-status Samaritan stops to help, an act that is particularly significant, given the long-standing hostility between the Jews and the Samaritans.

After rehearsing this story of goodwill and compassion, these practiced preachers were sent to another building where they would give their sermons. The experimenter explained either that they had plenty of time to get there or that they were running late. As these unwitting participants followed a map to the assigned location, they passed a person hunched over and moaning in a doorway. In other words, these ministers in training encountered a modern-day version of the very parable they were about to preach on! Surely every single one of them would stop to help this poor man in pain. Alas, that was not what happened. Of those participants who were in a rush, only 10% stopped to provide help, compared with 63% of those on a leisurely stroll. Not only did simply being in a hurry prevent these men from taking the time to help, but many of them in this condition seemed not to have noticed passing a person who needed help. Leading a moral life involves stopping to notice when others need help as well as stopping to smell the roses.

Pluralistic ignorance A situation in which individuals rely on others to identify a norm but falsely interpret others' beliefs and feelings, resulting in inaction.

Diffusion of responsibility A situation in which the presence of others prevents any one person from taking responsibility (e.g., for helping).

Step 2: Interpret the situation as an emergency. Assuming that you notice that something is not quite right, stepping in to provide help requires you to interpret the event as one in which help is needed. In the Kitty Genovese case, a dozen people reported hearing yelling, but most of them actually interpreted it as a lover's quarrel rather than a murderous attack. Likewise, if you were in the study where smoke started wafting through an air vent, you would also probably feel uncertain of whether this was cause for alarm. So what does this have to do with the bystander effect? If you recall our discussion of *informational social influence* in chapter 7, you'll remember that when situations are ambiguous, we take our cues from other people. If they aren't taking any action, we take that to mean that there is no cause for alarm. So when two confederates look at the smoke and then turn back to their questionnaires, it is not too surprising that only 10% of people bother to go alert the experimenter to the growing haze in the room. Even when the situation includes other naive bystanders like yourself, if you are all glancing at each other trying to decide whether there is anything to be worried about, then no one is actually doing anything. What occurs in this situation is known as **pluralistic ignorance**. The inaction of all the members of the group can itself contribute to a collective ignorance that anything is wrong. In such situations, when bystanders are instead able and encouraged to communicate with one another, they are not paralyzed by pluralistic ignorance (Darley et al., 1973). So if you're in a group and think something is wrong but are not sure, communicate with others about it!

Step 3: Take responsibility. In some of our examples, bystanders should sail through these first two steps. When you hear someone tell you outright that they need help after just informing you of her tendency toward seizures, it is a bit hard to imagine that you wouldn't notice or be aware that she was in trouble. Nevertheless, the presence of others can prevent us from helping. This is because of another powerful effect that groups can have on us, known as **diffusion of responsibility**. For a victim to receive help, someone needs to decide that it will be his or her responsibility to act. When you are responsible, the moral thing to do is to help. When you are the only witness, the burden clearly rests on your shoulders. But when others are present, it is easy to imagine that someone else should or has already taken action. In fact, even being primed to think about being part of a group can make people feel less personally accountable and less likely to donate money or stay to help out the experimenter (Garcia et al., 2002). If you ever need help and there are multiple witnesses, you can solve the problem of diffusion of responsibility by picking out—talking or pointing to—a specific individual and asking that person to help. That puts the responsibility squarely on that one person.

Step 4: Decide how to help. In this day and age, many people can help by using their cellphones to call 911 instead of making a video of the emergency as it unfolds. But in some situations, a specific kind of help is needed. If you feel that you lack the expertise, it is particularly easy to imagine that someone else might be better qualified to give help. A student having a seizure might need someone with medical training, so a witness in the presence of others could hope that someone else is more knowledgeable than he or she would be. In the subway collapse study we talked about earlier, the researchers actually had to exclude two trials that they conducted when a nurse was on the train. In those cases, the nurse immediately rushed to help. When people are trained to handle emergency situations, they are more likely to burst the bubble of inaction and rush to the aid of a person in need even as others stand by and watch (Pantin & Carver, 1982).

Step 5: Decide whether to give help. You've noticed the event, interpreted it as an emergency, and taken responsibility, and you know what needs to be done. At this point, the only thing that might still prevent you from providing help is a quick calculation of the risks and other costs involved. When people witness a violent attack, they might be afraid to intervene for fear of getting hurt themselves.

When someone has collapsed and needs CPR, witnesses might be worried that they could injure the person when performing chest compressions or otherwise make the situation worse and get sued. To counter these concerns, all 50 states and all the Canadian provinces have enacted "Good Samaritan" laws that protect people from liability for any harm they cause when they act in good faith to save another person.

Population Density

Social psychologists most often concern themselves with the effects of immediate situations on our behavior. But broader social contexts also can influence how we act. Think about where you live. Is it a small rural community, a large urban area, a suburban neighborhood? If you fall and break your leg, are you more likely to get help depending on the city where you take your tumble? We tend to assume that smaller communities are friendlier places and that large cities bring an inevitable sense of anonymity and indifference to others' needs (Simmel, 1903/2005). But is that the case?

Think
ABOUT

[Michael Shake/Shutterstock]

[AMzPhoto/Shutterstock]

In a unique study, Levine and colleagues (2008) traveled to 24 different U.S. cities and staged the following three helping opportunities. In one situation, a research assistant dropped a pen and acted as though he or she did not notice. In a second, he or she appeared to have an injured leg and struggled to pick up a pile of dropped magazines. In a third situation, the assistant approached people and asked if they could provide change for a quarter. The cities they chose varied from small (Chattanooga, Tennessee, population 486,000), medium (Providence, Rhode Island, population 1,623,000), to large (New York, New York, population 18,641,000). Across the cities, the researchers consistently found that they received less help in larger, denser cities (**FIGURE 13.3**). For example, the correlation between the population density of the city and likelihood of receiving help was -0.55 when the assistant dropped the pen, -0.54 when the assistant needed help picking up magazines,

Figure 13.3

Where's the Help?

Do many hands mean people are less likely to lend a hand? Studies of helping suggest that strangers receive more help in smaller cities than in larger ones.

[Data source: Levine et al. (2008)]

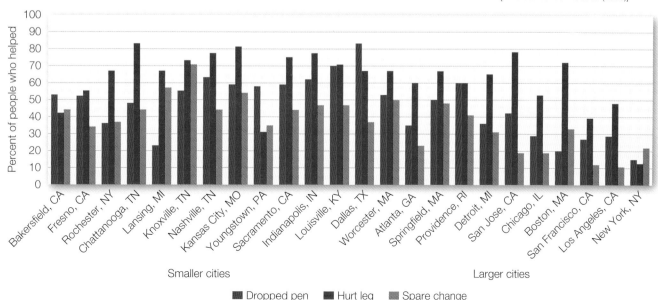

Smaller cities   Larger cities

■ Dropped pen   ■ Hurt leg   ■ Spare change

and −0.47 when the assistant was trying to make change for a quarter. Notice that those correlations are negative, meaning that the bigger the city, the less likely people were to help. There is a kernel of truth to the stereotypical image of small-town friendliness.

One caveat, however, is that it is always a bit difficult to know what to make of correlations. Do these patterns tell us something about the personalities of the people living in these different parts of the country or about local cultural norms? Are New Yorkers unhelpful contrarians? Or does living in an urban environment like New York work against whatever help-giving tendencies you might have? The jury is still out on that one. At least some research suggests that where you currently live better predicts how helpful you are than where you were born and raised (Korte, 1980). But this could mean either that the local norms of a culture change our behavior or that people choose to live in places that best reflect their personalities.

Urban overload hypothesis
The idea that city dwellers avoid being overwhelmed by stimulation by narrowing their attention, making it more likely that they overlook legitimate situations where help is needed.

Milgram (1970) speculated that living in a dense urban area exposes people to greater stimulation, or noise pollution. Living in a city apartment, you get used to the sounds of sirens, crying babies, car alarms, late-night partiers, and impatient drivers honking their horns. To deal with the din that comes with population density, people might learn to cope by shutting out these sounds. If this **urban overload hypothesis** is true, then city dwellers might sometimes find it difficult to distinguish between real cries of help and a normal night in the city.

SECTION review | Why Do People Fail to Help?

Although people are capable of empathy and compassion, their current situation powerfully influences their decision whether to help or not.

The bystander effect	Helping—or not—in an emergency	Population density
The greater the number of witnesses to a situation requiring help, the less likely any one of them will help.	Helping behavior results from several steps in sequence: • attending to and interpreting the situation as an emergency. • taking responsibility for helping. • deciding how to help. • cost-benefit analysis. At any step, some aspect of the situation (e.g., the presence of others) can short-circuit helping.	In bigger cities, despite a denser population, people tend to be less willing to help strangers.

Who Is Most Likely to Help?

The study of human virtue is as old as history itself. The ancient Greek philosopher Aristotle stated, "We do not act rightly because we have virtue or excellence, but we rather have those because we have acted rightly." On the other side of the globe, 200 years earlier, Confucius remarked, "The superior man thinks always of virtue; the common man thinks of comfort." Both of these great thinkers were commenting on the variability among people in our tendency to be virtuous, moral, and prosocial. People have for centuries used these words of wisdom as touchstones for how to become more virtuous and compassionate. Fast forward well over two millennia. What has modern research taught us about the moral heroes who live among us? How do we identify those individuals who stop to help the person in need even though they are running late for a meeting, those who jump into the raging river to save a perfect stranger from drowning, or those who devote their lives to helping people with terminal illness despite how emotionally draining such hospice care can be? A fair amount of research illuminates the qualities of moral individuals.

An Altruistic Personality?

On the one hand, some of the social psychological factors that prevent us from helping seem to question the very notion of a moral character. If seminary students rush by a moaning person as they prepare a sermon on the Good Samaritan, what hope do any of the rest of us have in following the advice of Confucius and Aristotle? Other research, however, suggests that we can measure meaningful individual differences in what is known as the altruistic personality. For example, one such measure assesses the frequency with which people engage in helpful acts such as giving someone directions, donating blood, or offering a seat on the bus (Rushton et al., 1981). Others have emphasized more specific characteristics of the altruistic personality, such as the tendency to take another person's perspective, a tendency to experience empathy, and a tendency to take personal responsibility for the welfare of others (Eisenberg et al., 1989). When it comes to pinpointing traits relevant to prosocial behavior, we do find evidence that the ability to empathize acts like a trait. Teenagers who score higher in empathy when they are 13 still view themselves as prosocially oriented a decade later, when they are young adults (Eisenberg et al., 2002). Even their moms agree: Those teens who later scored highest in prosociality in their early 20s tended to be seen as pretty helpful kids by their moms a decade earlier. Chances are that the college friend of yours most likely to volunteer for the local soup kitchen was out there raising money for a local charity before he even hit puberty.

Furthermore, although strong situational forces can constrain people's behavior, keeping them from acting in line with their underlying values and traits, personality characteristics shine through when situations are more ambiguous. Remember the "trading places" study we described earlier, in which participants decided whether to switch places with a confederate and receive mild shocks instead of watching the electricity-phobic Elaine suffer? In a different version of that study, participants could choose to trade places with a woman who was visibly upset about having to read about a physical assault as part of a study procedure (Carlo et al., 1991). Just as Batson had shown previously, people were more likely to schedule an appointment to take her place if they would otherwise have to watch her suffer than if they were free to leave. When the situation was relatively easy to escape, people tended to take that option. But it was in this easy-to-escape condition that moral character mattered. Those who scored highest on a measure of altruism were more likely to take the other person's place. Similar effects have been found for the other variables that make up the altruistic personality, such as taking responsibility for others' well-being, the ability to take another's perspective, the tendency to experience empathy or sympathy, and overall agreeableness (Eisenberg et al., 1989; Graziano et al., 2007).

Even relatively young children show evidence of helping that is predicted by personality. In one study with grade-school children, those who generally reported feeling sorry for others who are sad or in pain were more likely to donate money to a burn unit after watching a video about a young burn victim (Knight et al., 1994). Of course, donating money in this kind of scenario actually requires other skills that not all young children (or adults, for that matter) might have: being able to perceive accurately that someone is feeling sad and understanding the value of money. Children who possess all three of these qualities (empathy, perceiving emotions accurately, and understanding money) were the most likely to donate. In a

The ancient philosopher Aristotle (shown to the right of his mentor, Plato) stated, "We do not act rightly because we have virtue or excellence, but we rather have those because we have acted rightly."

[APIC/Hulton Archive/Getty Images]

Altruistic personality
A collection of personality traits, such as empathy, that render some people more helpful than others.

more dramatic example of personality predicting altruism, research has shown that those who risked their lives to save others during the Holocaust can be distinguished from those who did nothing by a constellation of relevant traits such as strong moral reasoning, a sense of social responsibility, and empathy (Midlarsky et al., 2005). Together, these research results describe a profile of more specific traits that likely combine to making some of us more altruistic than others.

Individual Differences in Motivations for Helping

Some research has tackled the question of who is most likely to help by examining the motivations people generally have for helping. For example, people who score high on a measure of trait agreeableness are thought to be motivated by prosocial concerns (Graziano et al., 2007). They are sensitive to the needs of others and motivated to adapt their behavior to meet those needs. Graziano and colleagues (2007) have found that agreeableness is a good predictor of people's general willingness to help out, but particularly in those contexts in which helping is not necessarily expected. When it comes to helping family or group members, our dispositional agreeableness doesn't predict whether we help. But it is a useful predictor of who will help a stranger or a member of a social outgroup. The motivation to act prosocially seems to broaden our scope of social connection.

But saying that someone is motivated to act prosocially could itself be understood in different ways. When you see a child share a toy with a classmate who is feeling sad, is he being helpful because this is merely what he has been told to do, or because he knows he might be praised for being such a helpful little boy, or because he truly wants to make his friend feel better? Research inspired by self-determination theory (see chapter 6) shows that these different possibilities fall on a continuum from completely external ("I help because others tell me to") to completely internal ("I help because I think it is important to"). Those who say they help for more intrinsic reasons also show higher levels of empathy and report feeling a stronger connection to others (Ryan & Connell, 1989). In fact, because helping others can satisfy a basic need to feel connected to others, helping for these intrinsic reasons seems to have the most emotional benefits for both the giver and the receiver of help (Weinstein & Ryan, 2010).

All this talk of intrinsic motivations brings up the idea that those who are helpful are more likely to see themselves as helpful people. In other words, some people stake their sense of identity on being moral (Aquino & Reed II, 2002), a finding that fits research conclusions regarding the Nazi-era rescuers we described earlier. If you have a strong moral identity, you are better able to bring to mind examples of moral goodness and to feel uplifted by other people's benevolence (Aquino et al., 2011). In addition, in experimental situations intended to prime helpful behavior, people who say that being a moral, helpful person is central to their sense of identity respond by being more helpful than those who don't define themselves along these prosocial lines (Aquino et al., 2009).

Being oriented toward others, and incorporating that role into one's sense of identity, also bodes well for sustaining prosocial behavior over time. People who are more oriented toward others and better at taking their perspective tend to volunteer more and also are better able to sustain such volunteer activity over longer stretches of time. For example, in one study the best predictor of whether people volunteered for AIDS organizations was the extent to which they were motivated toward others, rather than toward the self (Omoto et al., 2010). Of course, they can't do or sustain it alone, that is, only on the basis of their own motivation. Levels of social support for the volunteer experience, and the satisfaction they get from the experience itself, also contribute to whether they keep at it (Kiviniemi et al., 2002; Omoto & Snyder, 2002; Penner & Finkelstein, 1998). In fact, when these experiences are positive and rewarding, the role of volunteering is more likely to

When you see a child share a toy with a classmate who is feeling sad, is he being helpful because this is merely what he has been told to do, or because he knows he might be praised for being such a helpful little boy, or because he truly wants to make his friend feel better? People have both internal and external reasons for being helpful.

[Dave Clark Digital Photo/Shutterstock]

become incorporated into one's identity. The more helping is part of one's identity, the more likely one is to sustain an investment in these kinds of prosocial activities (Piliavin et al., 2002).

The Role of Political Values

We've seen that morality clearly plays a role in helping, but at least in the United States, different moral domains are important to people, depending on their political orientation. In American political culture, liberals are sometimes seen as "bleeding hearts," but what is the evidence that people's political leanings predict a more prosocial orientation? One way to answer this question is to look at how people's ideologies relate to the kinds of policies they support. True to the "bleeding heart" label, when it comes to providing assistance to people who are poor, sick, homeless, or unemployed, liberals more than conservatives vote in favor of such social programs (Kluegel & Smith, 1986). Whereas conservatives are more likely to withhold public assistance to people whom they view as responsible for their own predicament, liberals tend to support providing assistance to people regardless of how they got there (Skitka & Tetlock, 1992; Skitka et al., 1991; Skitka, 1999; Weiner et al., 2011). But this liberal generosity only extends so far. If resources are scarce and belts need to be tightened, both liberals and conservatives choose to help those who are least to blame for being in a bind.

What accounts for these differences in political proclivities of helpfulness? Are liberals more empathic and less inclined to make "us versus them" distinctions? Are conservatives simply savvier in making financial investments that pay off for society as a whole? Some evidence points to the different motivations of liberals and conservatives in making policy decisions (Skitka & Tetlock, 1993). Conservatives are more motivated to maintain traditional values and norms. When they see people violating those norms, there are more inclined to punish than to help them. Liberals, on the other hand, are more motivated by egalitarian values and don't like to see a price tag put to anyone's pain and suffering.

We can also gain insight into the role of political ideology in moral reasoning by turning to research on moral foundation theory, which we introduced back in chapter 2 (e.g., Graham et al., 2009). This work finds that people take into account five guiding principles when they prioritize whom and when to help or how to be virtuous: preventing harm to others, ensuring fair treatment to all, being loyal to one's group, respecting authority, and maintaining purity in one's actions (Haidt & Joseph, 2007).

In **FIGURE 13.4**, you can see that across the political spectrum, Americans generally make moral decisions with an eye toward avoiding harm and maintaining

Figure 13.4

Political Differences in Moral Foundations

Although Americans generally place the highest value on being fair and doing no harm, conservatives also base their moral decisions on ingroup loyalty, respect for authority, and purity, whereas liberals want to help those who are suffering unnecessarily.

[Data source: Graham et al. (2009)]

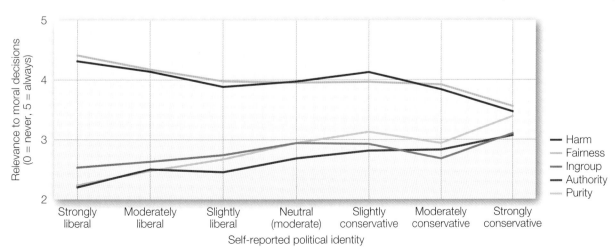

fairness (Graham et al., 2009). The graph also shows that conservatives prioritize respecting authority, maintaining purity, and protecting the ingroup—but liberals do not. These different moral foundations suggest that liberals will tend to reach out primarily to those who seem to be suffering unnecessarily or as a result of unfair disadvantage, whereas conservatives will be more likely to help individuals and groups they see as conforming to traditional moral and religious norms and values and generally upholding the social order.

The Role of Gender

> What are little boys made of?
> Snips and snails and puppy dogs tails,
> That's what little boys are made of.
> What are little girls made of?
> Sugar and spice and everything nice,
> That's what little girls are made of.
>
> —Traditional nursery rhyme

We've all heard this nursery rhyme and its chipper little message about sex differences. This cultural clipping reflects an assumption that boys are rough and tumble, girls sweet and good. Although discussions of sex differences and stereotypes often turn on ways in which women are thought to be weaker, more submissive, and less competent than their male peers, prosocial behavior is one arena in which women usually are thought to reign victorious. For example, in 2012, women made up more than 70% of those working in professions such as counseling (70%), social work (81%), teaching (74%), nursing (91%), medical assistance (94%), legal assistance (86%), administrative support (73%), restaurant host- or hostessing (82%), and cleaning (88%) (U.S. Bureau of Labor Statistics, n.d). But are women in fact more helpful than men, as stereotypes and career choices would suggest? The answer to this question is not so straightforward, so let's take a look at it from a few different angles.

First, we can ask whether any sex differences in personality traits are associated with a prosocial orientation. Women often score higher than men on measures of agreeableness (Feingold, 1994) and empathy (Baron-Cohen & Wheelwright, 2004). They also are better at decoding people's emotions (McClure, 2000). Furthermore, research often identifies two fundamental dimensions of identity: agency (being assertive, confident, and active) and communion (being oriented toward others, caring, and compassionate) (Bakan, 1966; McAdams, 1988). In findings consistent with the common stereotypes of men and women, women often score higher in communion than do men. These difference are found across many cultures (Costa et al., 2001; Schwartz & Rubel, 2005).

One problem with focusing on gender differences in personality, however, is that personality is most often measured with surveys. This means that what we really learn is whether women *think about themselves* as being more helpful and prosocial compared with how men think of themselves. We might ask ourselves whether these gender differences in self-perceptions are backed up by actual behavior. As you have gathered from reading through this chapter so far, a fair amount of research has been devoted to setting up experimental tests of helping behavior both in the laboratory and in the field. When it comes to helping someone pick up a spilled pile of pencils, staying late to work on an experimental task, or trading places with another student who is upset, are women more likely to help? A meta-analysis of such studies conducted back in the heyday of helping research suggested that there is a reliable gender difference in a tendency to provide help, but it's not the difference you might have expected. In 62% of the studies that Eagly and Crowley analyzed, men were more likely to help than were women (Eagly & Crowley, 1986). For example, recall the studies in which someone collapsed on a subway. In those field experiments, men

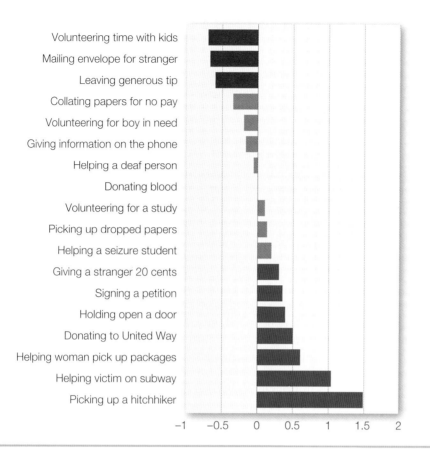

Volunteering time with kids
Mailing envelope for stranger
Leaving generous tip
Collating papers for no pay
Volunteering for boy in need
Giving information on the phone
Helping a deaf person
Donating blood
Volunteering for a study
Picking up dropped papers
Helping a seizure student
Giving a stranger 20 cents
Signing a petition
Holding open a door
Donating to United Way
Helping woman pick up packages
Helping victim on subway
Picking up a hitchhiker

−1   −0.5   0   0.5   1   1.5   2

Figure 13.5

Gender Differences in How We Help

A review of studies on helping reveals that men and women help in different ways. Women are more likely to volunteer time, sometimes on an ongoing basis, to provide care for others (red bars), whereas men are more likely to help in potentially dangerous situations or when norms for chivalry are present (blue bars).

[Data source: Eagly & Crowley (1986)]

were more likely than women to step in and assist the collapsed stranger (Piliavin et al., 1975).

Before we draw broad conclusions about gender and prosocial tendencies on the basis of this result, let's take a closer look at some of the studies reviewed in the meta-analysis. **FIGURE 13.5** shows approximately every sixth study reported in the meta-analysis, rank ordered by the size of the effect. Positive effect sizes indicate that men were more likely to help than were women; effects shown in blue were statistically significant. Negative effect sizes mean that women were more likely to help than were men; effects shown in red were examples of significantly greater prosocial behavior from women. Studies shown in green did not find significant sex differences between men and women. Notice any patterns?

Eagly and Crowley coded these studies for various characteristics and noted that men are more likely to help in those situations that call for chivalrous behavior or taking action in spite of possible danger. Men are more likely to help a woman with heavy packages, hold a door open (especially for a woman), or be willing to take the risk of picking up a hitchhiker or letting a stranger in to their home. Men are also more likely to help when others will *know* that they have helped, suggesting that men more than women might act prosocially as a way to boost their own social status. They might be smart to do this: It turns out that women report being more attracted to men who behave prosocially (Jensen-Campbell et al., 1995).

Women, on the other hand, are more likely to volunteer their time for others or go out of their way to mail a letter that has been left behind. In other words, both men and women are prosocially oriented in some ways, but gender roles suggest who should help in which kinds of situations. Underscoring these conclusions from research, more men than women have received the Carnegie Hero Fund Award (given for heroic acts), whereas more women than men have received the Caring Canadian Award (which rewards volunteerism).

If there are some average differences in prosocial orientation between men and women, are these differences really a function of "what little boys and girls are made of," as the poem would suggest? Or are they passed along from one generation to the next through such poetry? As in most nature versus nurture disputes, both elements likely factor in. On the side of biology, Shelly Taylor and her colleagues have argued that in addition to the typical fight-or-flight response to acutely stressful situations, women might also exhibit a "tend-and-befriend" response to stressors (Taylor et al., 2000). In other words, in stressful situations, a suite of hormonal responses, including increases in oxytocin, spur women to seek safety and comfort for both themselves and close others, especially their offspring, and to build social networks. From this perspective, evolved biological differences in hormonal responses might lead women more than men to reach out to others and offer a helping hand.

Developmental and comparative studies also provide compelling evidence for sex differences. In babies who are less than a year old, boys look longer at a truck than at a doll, whereas girls look longer at a doll than a truck (Alexander et al., 2009; Ruble et al., 2006). Because these same sex-typed preferences show up in nonhuman primates (Alexander & Hines, 2002; Hassett et al., 2008), some researchers have argued that females have an inherent preference for people over things, whereas males show interest in things before people (Lippa, 1998). These biologically based differences might set the stage for girls and women to be more prosocially attuned than boys and men and to help out of a concern for alleviating the suffering of others.

Other perspectives layer on top of these initial differences the role of socialization and cultural influences in magnifying gendered behavior (Bussey & Bandura, 2004). From Eagly and Crowley's perspective, because we so often see women in caregiving, communal roles, little girls grow up to be better able to envision themselves in those roles. Those communal personality traits might also be shaped partly by our environment. For example, grade-school girls score higher than boys in empathy (Eisenberg et al., 1991; Knight et al., 1994), but parents are also more likely to talk about emotional reactions and behave in more emotionally warm ways with their daughters than with their sons (Eisenberg et al., 1991; Leaper et al., 1998). Even if girls show some greater preference for attending to people rather than to things, it seems that parents also provide a richer education to their daughters on how to attend to, interpret, and respond to what other people need. In this way, cultural forces help to amplify and reinforce what might begin as smaller, biologically disposed differences between the sexes.

Even among the most aggressive nonhuman primates, some evidence indicates that sex differences in more communal or affiliative behaviors can be reduced by cultural changes. For example, baboons are thought to be one of the most aggressive primate species. Like most female primates, female baboons are more affiliative than the males, spending more of their time grooming each other and caring for offspring. The male baboons are much more aggressive and combative, fighting with competing troops and establishing a hierarchy of dominance. In the 1980s, the primatologist Robert Sapolsky observed a troop of baboons in East Africa whose behavior changed entirely when the most dominant males in their hierarchy suddenly died of tuberculosis. Without these alpha males around, the remaining males in the troop began to engage in more affiliative grooming behavior—grooming both females and

[John Fedele/Blend Images/Getty Images]

Think
ABOUT

other males alike, a behavior that was nearly unprecedented. More amazing, six years later Sapolsky discovered that the troop had maintained this new norm of prosociability. By that time, new adolescent males had joined the troop but apparently had learned to adopt this kinder, gentler lifestyle (Sapolsky & Share, 2004). Even among baboons, changes in social dynamics can narrow the gap between the sexes in prosocial tendencies.

Think about your own experiences. In what ways do you feel culture has influenced the ways that you help others?

SECTION review | Who Is Most Likely to Help?

Although situations matter, there are meaningful individual differences in prosocial tendencies.

Altruism	Individual differences	Political values	Gender
Personality traits such as moral reasoning, sense of social responsibility, and empathy predict altruism.	People who identify themselves as being moral and helpful generally are more prosocial.	Political conservatives and liberals endorse different moral foundations, making them more or less likely to help depending on their moral interpretation of the situation.	Women are generally seen as being more prosocial, but in some situations men are more willing to help.

APPLICATION
Toward a More Prosocial Society

Our tour through the research on prosocial behavior has taught us that humans, along with many other social species, have an innate capacity for helping. It is important to note, however, that there is also variation in this tendency and the degree to which we act on it. It might not even be realistic to expect individuals to engage in prosocial behavior all the time. As a New York teenager, living in Queens and attending a high school in Manhattan, one of your authors had to take an hour subway ride to school every day. A thought he had numerous times during that commute was that if he had stopped to help every person in need he saw during that morning journey, he never would have made it to school on the average day. People have to take care of their own needs and responsibilities. Fortunately, their efforts to become secure and fully developed adults make it more likely that they will then be better able to contribute to society in small and sometimes big ways throughout their lives. As in the advice given during the safety instructions before a flight, you might have to put on your own oxygen mask before you can properly help someone else put on theirs.

Having acknowledged that, we also can acknowledge that there is undoubtedly room for most if not all of us, in one way or another, to be a little more giving and helpful to each other. This chapter offers a useful blueprint for creating a more prosocially oriented society. In a nutshell, it looks something like this: Raise our children to be adults who have a great capacity for empathy and a strong moral identity. Model how to show warmth and take the perspective of others, especially of those others who seem most different from ourselves. Teach children to view various forms of prosocial behavior as an important basis for being a good, valued person in the world; this can help them become adults who strongly value their identity as generous, helpful people. Parents, teachers, and peers all can enact these changes. Through television shows, movies, and video games, the mass media also can facilitate them by depicting more prosocial role models. It would help further if these media resources reinforced the rewarding nature of prosocial behavior. These changes will be more likely the more we foster a communal orientation in how we think about our families, friends, communities, culture, humanity, and even perhaps all living things. ✒

CONNECT ONLINE:

Check out our videos and additional resources located at:
www.macmillanhighered.com/launchpad/greenberg1e

Interpersonal Attraction

[alex grabchilev/evgeniya bakanova/Getty Images]

You wake up one morning, and things are surprisingly quiet. The low murmur of accelerating traffic that usually hums just outside your window cannot be heard. You check your phone. "That's strange," you think to yourself, "no new texts or e-mails." Walking around campus, you don't see a single soul. As the day goes on, the bizarre truth dawns on you: You are completely, utterly alone.

This scenario—with slight variations—has been the plot of numerous science fiction novels, television shows, and movies, most recently *I Am Legend*, starring Will Smith (Goldsman et al., 2007). Why are so many people fascinated by the idea of an individual coming to terms with being the only person left on the planet? Perhaps it allows us to indulge vicariously in the feeling of complete freedom from the constraints and demands imposed on us by others. With everyone else wiped out by a virus or nuclear war, nothing would stop you from sleeping in every morning, availing yourself of the finest consumer goods, and enjoying some peace and quiet.

No, the real reason we watch is that we know, deep down, that complete isolation would be a horrible fate, and we wonder how Will Smith or anyone else could survive it. The fact is that we need intimate contact with other people. Our relationships with family members, friends, and romantic partners are central and indispensable parts of our lives. We spend a great deal of time and energy seeking out new relationships and working to maintain and improve the ones we have. What's more, our close relationships can be a source of great joy when they go well but a source of misery and frustration when they don't.

Will Smith stars in the movie *I Am Legend*, based on Richard Matheson's science fiction novel about how a man comes to terms with being the last living person on Earth. Why are we so intrigued by this plot, and what does that tell us about our need for other people?

[Warner Bros. Pictures/Photofest]

This and the next, final chapter are devoted to the many discoveries that social psychologists have made regarding interpersonal attraction and close relationships—our liking and loving of other people. In this first chapter, we will begin by considering why we humans need to form and sustain social relationships. Then we will focus on the factors that determine who is attracted to, and forms relationships with, whom. We will take a close look at physical attractiveness and conclude by considering sex differences in sexual attitudes and behavior, and jealousy. In our second chapter we will focus on the nature and functioning of close relationships.

The Need to Belong

The desire to form social relationships is a fundamental part of human nature. We *need* to be part of stable, healthy bonds with family members, romantic partners, and friends in order to function normally. In fact, this very idea is central to why a subfield of psychology called *social* psychology first was developed.

Do We Really Need to Belong?

It may seem obvious that people need other people, but appreciate that although we use the word *need* loosely in everyday language, in psychology the stakes are higher when we claim that something is a **psychological need**. It could be that close relationships are just nice, not necessary. (Consider: People may seek frequent, pleasant interactions with their computers, but they don't *need* them.) What evidence is there that the motive to belong is inherent to our nature?

Psychological need A mechanism for regulating behavior to acquire the tangible or intangible resources necessarily for survival and well-being.

The Need to Belong Is Satiable

Biologically based needs work on the principle of homeostasis: You experience a deficiency (e.g., you're hungry) that motivates thoughts and behaviors (you eat) until the need is satisfied (you're full, stop eating). The same principle applies to close relationships. People do not need hundreds of relationships, just a few that are lasting and caring, and when they have them they are less motivated to form additional relationships. For example, although most college students have over 300 "friends" on Facebook, only a fraction of these are close friends or family (Manago et al., 2012). Intimate, face-to-face interactions might take place with only about six people (Wheeler & Nezlek, 1977).

The need to belong also resembles biologically based needs in that it can be satisfied in flexible ways. If your late-night hunger pangs motivate you to get up and search for cereal, and you discover that you are out of milk, you'll find something else to eat. Similarly, when people are unable to satisfy their need to belong in their existing relationships, they turn to other relationships. For example, people in prison cope with the stressful separation from their biological family by forming substitute "families" with other prisoners (Burkhart, 1973).

All genetically inherited traits vary from person to person, and the need to belong is no different. People have different levels of this need and so differ in how many social relationships they want and how intimate they want them to be. Measures of need for affiliation (McAdams, 1989), need for intimacy (McAdams, 1980), need to belong (Leary et al., 2013), and attachment style (Hazan & Shaver, 1987) have been developed to capture this variability.

When the Need to Belong Is Satisfied, People Thrive

When people receive proper nutrition, shelter, sleep, and so on, they feel good psychologically and physically. In the same way, feeling connected to others promotes an individual's mental and physical health. Compared with people who live more isolated lives, people who have pleasant interactions with a network of close friends, lovers, family members, and coworkers have higher self-esteem (Denissen et al., 2008; Leary & Baumeister, 2000), feel happier and more satisfied with their lives (Diener et al., 1999), and have better mental health (Kim & McKenry, 2002). Across different cultures, people who marry and stay married are happier overall than are those who are less committed to an intimate partnership (Diener et al., 2000). With regard to physical health, people who feel socially connected have stronger cardiovascular, immune, and endocrine systems, and they are less likely to die a premature death (Cacioppo & Patrick, 2008; House et al., 1988; Uchino, 2006; Uchino et al., 1996).

When the Need to Belong Is Chronically Unmet, Mental and Physical Health Decline

A hallmark of a need is that if it goes unsatisfied for a long time, people suffer negative consequences. It is in this respect that we see perhaps the strongest evidence for the claim that the need to belong qualifies as a true need. Hundreds of studies support the overall conclusion that when people are isolated for long periods of time, their mental and physical health deteriorates.

Many of these studies look at the experience of **loneliness**, or the feeling that one is deprived of human social connections (Cacioppo & Patrick, 2008). People find it very stressful to be entirely alone for a long period of time (Schachter, 1959). In fact, people claim to feel more fulfilled in an *unhappy* relationship than they do when in no relationship at all (Kamp Dush & Amato, 2005). Loneliness is such a miserable state that people often try to numb their pain by turning to alcohol or drugs (Rook, 1984). Over time, loneliness contributes to a range of mental health complications, including depression, eating disorders, and schizophrenia (Cacioppo et al., 2006; Segrin, 1998).

Loneliness also can take a toll on physical health. During times of loneliness, college students have weaker immune systems, making them more vulnerable to catching a cold or flu (Pressman et al., 2005). Looking across the life span, we see that people who have few friends or lovers are likely to die at a younger age than those who are happily connected to others. In one study, people who lacked close social bonds were two to three times more likely to die over a nine-year span (Berkman & Glass, 2000). In fact, when it comes to predicting people's physical health, loneliness is as significant a risk factor as smoking and obesity (Hawkley et al., 2009).

Aside from feeling lonely, the experience of being rejected outright or pushed away by close others takes a serious toll on mental and physical health (Cohen, 2004; Ryff & Singer, 2000). When people are rejected or stigmatized, they report feeling very distressed (Leary, 2001; Smart Richman & Leary, 2009; Williams, 2007). They also have a great deal of difficulty concentrating on tasks (Baumeister et al., 2002). The effects of divorce provide another way to look at the consequences of separation and rejection. Compared with people who are happily married, those who just got divorced are much more likely to be admitted to hospitals for psychological problems (Bloom et al., 1979). After a divorce, people's blood pressure increases, and their immune systems become weaker (Kiecolt-Glaser & Newton, 2001), and they are more likely to die an early death than individuals in long-term unions (Sbarra et al., 2011).

Evolution and Belonging

We hope you're convinced by now that social relationships are essential for a good, long life. But an important question remains unanswered: Where did this need come from? Why do virtually all of us care so much about forming and maintaining

Companionship and Support
Video on LaunchPad

Loneliness The feeling that one is deprived of human social connections.

Feelings of loneliness take a toll on mental and physical health, providing evidence that humans need to feel a sense of belonging.
[Ju Fumero/Moment Open/Getty Images]

relationships? A good answer is provided by considering how our species evolved its social needs.

From an evolutionary perspective, early humans who successfully formed close social bonds were more likely to survive and reproduce than were the loners, outcasts, and misanthropes. As a result, more and more people were born with gregariousness built into their genes. In this way, over thousands of generations, the need to belong came to be a basic characteristic of our species (Baumeister & Leary, 1995; Buss & Schmitt, 1993; Simpson & Kenrick, 1997).

What made it advantageous for our ancestors to form and maintain social relationships? To answer this question, try to envision yourself in the environments of our hominid ancestors—environments very different from the ones we live in today. You are in a desert or forested area, and every day you're scrambling to find food (no pizza delivery), looking out for dangerous predators, and protecting yourself from illness and harsh climates.

In those environments, being embedded in a network of social relationships helped people survive and have children who would grow to maturity and also reproduce. Most obviously, heterosexual relationship bonds provide the opportunity to have sex, which obviously increases chances of reproduction. Also, hominid infants were especially vulnerable and dependent for many years after birth. Thus, infants with a tendency to form close attachments to their parents would have been more likely than aloof offspring to receive the care and protection they needed to survive until they could function on their own (Bowlby, 1969, 1973, 1980; Buss, 1994). Also, friendships were a means for non-kin to cooperate in finding food, build shelters, and explore the environment. They also helped people avoid the costs of competition and aggression (Fehr, 1996; Trivers, 1971). Such friendships might also have contributed to survival by improving individuals' ability to defend against predators' attacks.

In short, those early ancestors disposed to join in, lend a hand, listen to others, care, and be interdependent were more likely to enjoy all of the benefits of stable, affectionate connections to others. As a result, they were more likely to have offspring and to raise those offspring to maturity so that they could reproduce as well.

Although this evolutionary explanation for a need to belong makes sense, it relies on speculative assumptions about the primeval social environment in which our ancestors lived. Therefore, it is important to consider the evidence that the need to establish and maintain intimate bonds with others has an evolutionary basis. Here are four pieces of evidence:

- *The motive to belong is universal.* In every culture that has been examined, people care deeply about forming and maintaining romantic bonds, parent-offspring attachments, and close relations with siblings, friends, and group members (e.g., Eibl-Eibesfeldt, 1989).
- *Innate affiliation behaviors.* Soon after human infants exit the womb, they instinctively engage with other people (Murray & Trevarthen, 1986). They pay special attention to other people's faces, and they delight in mimicking others' facial expressions (Meltzoff & Moore, 1977). They also pay particular attention to human voices, especially when others use baby talk (Cooper & Aslin, 1990). These tendencies are seen in children born all over the world, and they are not seen in other species.
- *Rejection hurts—literally.* Earlier we noted that the experience of social rejection causes a great deal of subjective distress. Here we add that the human nervous system responds to rejection with a stress response similar to our response to physical pain. Even minor forms of rejection—such as hearing someone spread unkind gossip about oneself—increases stress-related cardiovascular arousal and a flood of the stress hormone cortisol. Similarly, as we noted in chapter 6,

when people experience rejection (for example, when they are playing an interactive computer game with others and they are ignored), they show increased activation of the anterior cingulate cortex, a region of the brain that processes physically painful stimuli (Eisenberger et al., 2003).

According to MacDonald and Leary (2005), the similarity of the stress responses to physical pain and social rejection makes perfect sense if we think about the need to belong as an evolved tendency. Those individuals who felt horrible pain when they were rejected were presumably more motivated to alleviate that pain by repairing their relationships, thereby increasing their chances of producing offspring who would survive and thrive. Those who were less rattled by social rejection simply may have gone off on their own, but such people would be less likely to survive and continue to contribute to the human gene pool. However, people who are too afraid of rejection—that is, high in **rejection sensitivity**—may avoid seeking social relationships so much that they become dysfunctional. Indeed, people especially high in sensitivity to rejection do not function well socially (Downey & Feldman, 1996).

- *Reproductive success.* Adults who form stable close relationships are more likely to reproduce than those who fail to form them. Long-term relationships tend to increase the chances that the offspring will survive and reach maturity (Buss & Schmitt, 1993).

Rejection sensitivity A dispositional tendency to have an especially strong fear of being rejected or evaluated negatively by others.

SECTION review | The Need to Belong

The desire to form social relationships is a fundamental part of human nature.

Evidence of a fundamental need to belong	Evidence that the need to belong has an evolutionary basis
• Like hunger, the need to belong can be satisfied. • Belonging promotes mental and physical health. • Loneliness takes a toll on mental and physical health.	• People of all cultures share the need to belong. • Newborn infants instinctively engage other people. • Social rejection activates the same stress responses as physical pain. • Long-term relationships promote successful procreation and raising of offspring.

The Basics of Interpersonal Attraction

Now that we have established the importance to people of forming social relationships, we can address how people choose others with whom to develop such relationships. Note that for the most part we'll be focusing on social relationships, which include friendships as well as both opposite-sex and same-sex romantic connections, although the research on this topic has tended to focus primarily on heterosexual attraction and relationships.

Proximity: Like the One You're With

One simple determinant of social relationships is known as the **propinquity effect**, *propinquity* meaning closeness in space. The original idea was that you can't form a relationship with someone unless you meet them, and the closer you are physically to someone else, the more likely you are to meet and therefore form a relationship with him or her.

With the proliferation of Internet technology in many contemporary cultures, this is not so true anymore. Facebook, Twitter, blogs, message boards, and other

Propinquity effect The increased likelihood of forming relationships with people who are physically close by.

apps make it more and more possible to form relationships with people we rarely, if ever, actually meet. This includes people from around the globe and in cyberspace with whom we share an interest. Before the Internet, people sometimes developed relationships with "pen pals," friends known only through an exchange of letters. So for a long time, physical propinquity has not been necessary for developing a social relationship; nevertheless, it's less important, at least for casual relationships, than ever before. At the same time, face-to-face social interactions are more important and beneficial to mental health and life satisfaction than cyber socializing (Green et al., 2005; Kraut et al., 1998; Latané et al., 1995).

With these caveats in mind, it's still worth considering the role of proximity. The first empirical breakthrough in examining this factor was a study by Festinger and colleagues (1950). They interviewed residents in a new apartment complex. As in most apartment complexes, the apartment manager had placed residents in their particular apartments in an essentially random fashion. Festinger and colleagues saw this as a natural experiment that gave them the opportunity to study whether and how proximity influences friendship formation. They found that the physical location of one's apartment within the complex had a large impact on who made friends with whom and on how many friendships one formed within the complex. For example, people were nearly twice as likely to form a friendship with the person in the next-door apartment as they were to form a friendship with the person who lived two doors away. In a similar study of classroom friendships, students were more likely to get to know a classmate who sat next to them than those who sat just a few seats away (Byrne, 1961). Many of us like to think we choose our friends carefully on the basis of their unique attributes, but these findings suggest that some of our choices are based largely on who happens to be next door or seated next to us in a class.

Festinger and his colleagues also found that among people who lived in first-floor apartments, those next to stairwells made more friends on the second floor, presumably because they were more likely to run into second-floor residents. Moreover, in a neighboring housing project, people whose houses faced the street made fewer friends in the area than people whose houses faced a common courtyard. This set of findings suggests that sometimes loneliness may develop not because of an individual's attributes but simply because of the physical isolation inherent in where an individual lives or works.

A number of explanations have been offered for the surprising impact of physical location. One is based on familiarity. As you may recall from chapter 8, evidence supporting the mere exposure effect shows that we tend to like novel stimuli better the more we are exposed to them (Zajonc, 1968). The unfamiliar makes most people initially wary or even anxious. As a stimulus becomes more familiar, people feel more at ease, and that positive feeling becomes associated with the stimulus. In the case of interpersonal interactions, the more you see a new person, the more positive you are likely to feel about that person. Because you'll see your next-door neighbor more often than the person a few doors down, the mere exposure effect works to the benefit of that nearest neighbor.

The power of proximity. In many contexts, such as apartment complexes, you are randomly placed near some people and far from others. Nevertheless, physical location powerfully predicts who you are attracted to and form relationships with.

[Lisa Werner/Alamy]

An Oregon State speech professor demonstrated the benefits of familiarity by having someone come to his class every day in a big black bag (Rubin, 1973). At first, the students were wary of the human black bag and sat as far away as possible. However, by the end of the course, the students were very friendly with the black bag and treated it like a beloved class mascot. Moreland and Beach (1992) assessed this phenomenon more systematically. They had typical college-age female confederates of similar appearance attend a class 0, 5, 10, or 15 times during a semester—without ever speaking to anyone in the class. At the end of the semester, they showed photos of each confederate to the students in the class and asked them to evaluate each confederate on dimensions such as honesty, popularity, and likeability. The more the confederate attended the class, the more positively she was rated. So we tend to like people who are more familiar.

More recently, Reis and colleagues (2011) systematically varied how many chats, ranging from 1 to 8, participants had with a same-sex fellow student. Generally, the more chats, the more the participants liked the other person. Additional measures in the studies showed that more conversation led to more liking because it increased comfort and satisfaction with the other person and a sense that the other person was responsive to them. These findings fit the mere exposure notion that by increasing familiarity, proximity leads to greater comfort and attraction. It also suggests another explanation for the proximity-liking effect: that the more interactions we have with people close by, the more attentive to us they seem. And it may not be just our perceptions of responsiveness that are influenced by repeated interaction. Chances are that the more we see people, the more they actually do respond to us and our needs.

A related explanation for the proximity effect is that, in general, casual interactions with other people are mildly pleasant. You exchange greetings, perhaps commiserate about the weather, or discuss the fortunes of the local sports teams. The more mildly pleasant conversations you have, the more positive feelings you will associate with the person with whom you are conversing.

Of course, there are important exceptions to the proximity effect—the roommates who grate on each other, the annoying neighbor, the cultural groups that share a border and can't get along. Indeed, research has found that the mere exposure effect does not occur if the stimulus is initially disliked or is associated with negative outcomes (e.g., Brickman et al., 1972; Swap, 1977). If repeated exposure to others due to close proximity only reminds people of ways that they differ from one another, they can like others less rather than more (Norton et al., 2007). This brings us to our first broad theory of attraction, often known as the reward model of liking.

The Reward Model of Liking

The core idea of the **reward model of liking** is simple: We like people we associate with positive feelings and dislike people we associate with negative feelings (e.g., Byrne & Clore, 1970; Lott & Lott, 1974). It is basically a classical conditioning model of liking, similar to the influences on persuasion we talked about in chapter 8. Recall that advertisers often will pair their product with an uplifting jingle or cute scene, trying to foster a positive association with the product. In the reward model, a new person begins as a relatively neutral stimulus. If exposure to the person is temporally linked to a second stimulus you already like, the positive feelings evoked by the second stimulus start to become evoked by the person. Conversely, if the second stimulus evokes negative feelings in you, some of those negative feelings start to become linked to the person. This raises the question, What are these second stimuli that influence our liking for others?

When we think of why we like someone, we usually talk about that person's attributes, and that is certainly part of the total picture. But the reward model suggests that we could come to like (or dislike) someone not because of any attribute they have or behavior they engage in, but simply because they happened to be around when we were feeling good (or bad). The idea seems to fit the rather unfair practice of ancient Roman rulers who sometimes would kill messengers who brought bad news (prompting the old expression "Don't kill the messenger").

One early test of this idea had participants simply sit in a room for 45 minutes and fill out some questionnaires. One of the questionnaires described a stranger's attitudes on various issues. The experimenter varied the temperature in the room so that it was either comfortable or unpleasantly hot. Participants were then asked to

Reward model of liking
Proposes that people like other people whom they associate with positive stimuli and dislike people whom they associate with negative stimuli.

This messenger might be a jerk, but the reward model suggests that this woman will like him if she associates him with the positive feelings evoked by the package.

[Tyler Olson/Shutterstock]

indicate how they felt about the stranger. As the reward model predicts, participants liked the stranger better if the room was comfortable than if it was not (Griffitt, 1970). Researchers have used a variety of other methods to make the same point. For example, one study had participants overhear bad or good news on a radio broadcast and then evaluate a stranger (Veitch & Griffitt, 1976). They liked the stranger better if the radio broadcast good rather than bad news. So sometimes, we may like or dislike someone because they just happen to be there when something pleasant or unpleasant happens to occur.

We probably overlook these sorts of influences most of the time in thinking about why we like or dislike someone, because we focus on that person's attributes. On the other hand, most of us also probably have some intuition that feelings created by things we don't cause can rub off on how people feel about us. For example, if you are going on a first date with someone—let's say dinner and a movie—you probably hope the weather is nice, the food at the restaurant is good, and the movie is enjoyable, even though you have little or no control over those outcomes. Research suggests that intuition is correct: All else being equal, you will be better liked, and also like the other person better, if it's a lovely evening, the food is delicious, and the movie is delightful. Of course, we often use this intuition to plan a date or meeting to our advantage. On their first date, one of your authors took his salsa-loving future wife to a salsa festival in the Southwest. Suffice it to say, the evening went quite well.

Others' Attributes Can Be Rewarding

Having acknowledged the role of situational factors, we next ask, What attributes of people themselves evoke the positive feelings that increase our attraction to them? Most of the research on interpersonal attraction addresses this question in one way or another.

Transference

Transference A tendency to map on, or transfer, feelings for a person who is known onto someone new who resembles that person in some way.

First, some attributes may evoke positive feelings because we associate them with people we like or positive experiences we had in the past. For example, Collins and Read (1990) found that people are often drawn to romantic partners who have a caregiving style similar to that of their opposite-sex parent. More generally, in a finding consistent with the Freudian concept of **transference** (Freud, 1912/1958), Susan Andersen and colleagues discovered that if a newly encountered individual resembles a significant other in your life whom you like or dislike, you will carry over those feelings to the new person (Andersen & Baum, 1994; Andersen et al., 1996). Often these associations can even be fairly subtle, such as sharing the same birthday or wearing a similar style of eyeglasses.

"I LIKE YOU, YOU REMIND ME OF SOMEONE"

[RGJ—Richard Jolley/Cartoonstock]

Culturally Valued Attributes

As cultural animals, we also are drawn to people who have talents or have achieved things that our culture values (e.g., Fletcher et al., 2000). Celebrities are an extreme example. Many if not most people are fascinated by celebrities because the culture has deemed them to be of great value—that's what makes them celebrities. Even if the more cynical and reserved of us happen to run into Will Smith or Jennifer Lawrence at a bar in Los Angeles, we would be star struck. If we were lucky enough to have a conversation with them, undoubtedly we would tell virtually everyone we know about it. Why? Think back to BIRGing—basking in reflected glory (Cialdini et al., 1976). Being connected to, or simply being near, another person with culturally valued attributes can enhance our own self-esteem.

This form of attraction extends not only to the extremes of celebrity but also to any attributes highly valued. In the United States, these include such things as wealth, beauty, musical or athletic talent, and so forth. Acquiring a so-called trophy wife gives a sense of self-worth (a trophy) to an older, rich man who has a beautiful young wife by his side. In a less clichéd example, one of your authors had a roommate in college who was brilliantly talented in music. He read symphony scores for fun and on hearing a song once could play it on the piano. Your author recalls taking great pride in his friend's ability, even though he himself entirely lacked that ability! This connects with our discussion of Tesser's (1988) self-evaluation model in chapter 6: When someone else is talented in a domain that you don't claim for yourself, it is easy to identify with him or her and gain self-worth from doing so.

Personality Traits

Next, let's consider personality traits. Across a wide range of studies, people generally report preferring certain traits in their partners and friends. Not surprisingly, these include friendliness, honesty, warmth, kindness, intelligence, a good sense of humor, emotional stability, reliability, ambition, openness, and extraversion (e.g., Sprecher & Regan, 2002). The culture promotes the valuing of these traits. In addition, it's easy to imagine how people with any of these desirable traits could evoke positive feelings in us, and, by the same token, how people with the opposite traits might evoke negative feelings in us. Which traits people desire in others depends to some extent on their relationship with the other person. For example, people report that agreeableness and emotional stability are more valued in a close friend than in a study group partner, whereas intelligence is reported to be more valued for a study group partner than for a close friend (Cottrell et al., 2007).

Although research on the traits we like in an ideal partner is valuable, we should note that the vast majority of this work assesses what traits people *report* or *think* they like, not those that they actually like (Eastwick et al., 2013). This is because the best test of what attributes people actually like would be very difficult, if not impossible, to conduct. You would have to assign people randomly and have them get to know other people who systematically vary in these traits to really sort out what attributes people like and dislike in others.

We make this point because the cultural worldview we learn as children teaches us that kindness, intelligence, honesty, and so forth are good qualities. Thus, our self-reports are likely to mimic these teachings. In fact, when we examine what traits people in different cultures claim they like, the traits they value mirror aspects of the culture. This was observed in a large Internet survey of participants from 53 nations. When they were asked to rate the importance of various attributes of a romantic partner, participants from modern, individualistic nations rated humor and kindness higher, and dependability and intelligence lower, than did participants from more traditional collectivistic nations (Lippa, 2007). Perhaps individuals in different cultures really do find different attributes attractive. But we can also interpret these findings to show that culture influences what qualities people *think* that they should like in others.

One method that tries to tease apart reported and actual preferences is to create a situation that resembles speed dating. In one set of studies, Eastwick and colleagues (Eastwick, Eagly et al., 2011; Eastwick, Finkel et al., 2011) had male and female participants sit at individual tables as a parade of potential partners (or "dates") rotated through, spending about 4 minutes with each participant. Later, the participants were asked whom they would have liked to see again. The researchers found that the traits the participants reported caring about in a prospective romantic partner *failed* to predict how interested they were in others who had or did not have those qualities when they met them face to face.

Each of these people likely came into the speed-dating context with an idea of what qualities they like in a partner. Turns out, however, that those preferences tell us little about who they end up being attracted to.

[CB2/ZOB/Supplied by WENN.com/Newscom]

Of course, speed-dating studies have their own limitations. One is that they don't tell us which traits people like in others whom they have known for a long time. In fact, one study of middle-aged participants currently in relationships showed that the match between their reported ideal traits in a romantic partner and their perceptions of their current partners was in fact a good predictor of how positively they viewed their partner and the relationship (Eastwick, Finkel et al., 2011).

Once we acknowledge these caveats, Eastwick and colleagues' findings may help explain why finding a date or friend online might not work (Finkel et al., 2012). You get all sorts of information about what the person is like before you even meet. It seems very handy. But this research suggests what we *think* we like doesn't necessarily predict whether things will go smoothly when we meet that person face-to-face and learn more about each other. For example, you may think you'd like someone who is extraverted, the life of the party, and open to experiences, but on meeting such a person face to face, you may find him or her to be obnoxious or exhausting.

Attraction to Those Who Fulfill Needs

Beyond having talents, achievements, and desirable traits, people also can be attractive to us because they help to satisfy our psychological needs. One is the need to sustain faith in a worldview that gives meaning to life. Another is to maintain a strong sense of self-esteem. We like people who help validate these psychological resources. These include people who seem similar to us, who like us, and who flatter us. Let's look closer at each.

Similarity in Attitudes

One of the strongest determinants of attraction is perceived similarity. As the old saying goes, "Birds of a feather flock together." Similarity on several dimensions matters. People who become friends, lovers, and spouses tend to be similar in socio-economic status, age, geographical location, ethnic identity, looks, and personality (Byrne et al., 1966; Caspi & Herbener, 1990; Hinsz, 1989). But particularly powerful is similarity in attitudes and overall worldview. Imagine Lana, a Republican Christian young woman who is against abortion and is a supporter of low taxes, a strong military, and gun rights. She likes country music and soft rock, skiing, tennis, action movies, designer clothes, fine wine, and Italian food. She meets Rosa and Erica at a party. Rosa is a Republican Christian who supports the same issues, who likes country music, tennis, action movies, fine clothes, and (OMG) Italian food. Erica is a Democratic agnostic who is prochoice and antigun, and likes hip-hop and metal, basketball, independent art movies, beer, and gluten-free vegan cuisine. Whom is Lana going to like better, and perhaps see as a potential new friend to hang out with?

Rosa, of course. She validates Lana's beliefs about the way the world works, what good music sounds like, what makes for a good meal, and so forth. In having similar beliefs and preferences, she bolsters Lana's worldview and self-esteem. Erica, in contrast, challenges the validity of Lana's beliefs and preferences, threatening her worldview and self-esteem. In addition, Lana can imagine having good times shopping, eating, and going to concerts with Rosa; with Erica, not so much. Support for these intuitions comes from many studies showing that people with similar attitudes are more likely to be liked, become friends, and become romantic partners (Byrne, 1971; Griffitt & Veitch, 1974; Newcomb, 1956). In one early study, Newcomb (1956) examined attitudes of transfer students moving into a college dorm. When he tracked liking among those in the dorm, as more time passed, sharing similar attitudes became an increasingly

We like to be around people who share our attitudes and interests because it validates our view of the world.

[From left to right: © Tommy (Louth)/Alamy; Roger Cracknell16/Glastonbury/Alamy; Mark Ralston/AFP/Getty Images]

stronger predictor of liking. Also, people who marry are likely to have more satisfying, longer-lasting marriages to the extent they perceive their attitudes to be similar (Bentler & Newcomb, 1978; Cattell & Nesselroade, 1967; Houts et al., 1996).

It is interesting to note that the causal arrow works both ways. Just as perceived similarity increases attraction, attraction increases perceived similarity. If we like someone, we also tend to assume he or she has similar attitudes (Miller & Marks, 1982). In addition, couples tend to think their attitudes are more similar than they actually are (Kenny & Acitelli, 2001; Murray et al., 2002).

Perceived Versus Actual Similarity

Several studies show that what is important for attraction and relationship commitment is how much people *perceive* that they are similar to another, and not necessarily how similar they are from an objective point of view (Montoya et al., 2008). For example, people's initial attraction in a speed-dating context, and their satisfaction in long-term relationships, are better predicted by perceived similarity than actual similarity (Dyrenforth et al., 2010; Tidwell et al., 2013).

Why is actual personality similarity not very predictive of attraction and relationship satisfaction, whereas perceived similarity is? Perhaps the answer lies in that old trope that "opposites attract." This idea has some intuitive appeal. Shouldn't someone who likes to make decisions get along with someone who doesn't? Shouldn't someone given to emotional ups and downs fit with someone very stable and consistent? In other words, shouldn't people who have complementary qualities get along (Winch, 1958)? Of course, dissimilar people sometimes will hit it off as friends or romantic partners, but most evidence suggests this is more the exception rather than the rule.

However, a few studies show ways in which opposites may attract. One way is that highly masculine men tend to be attracted to highly feminine women (Orlofsky, 1982). In addition, Dryer and Horowitz (1997) found in two studies that after a brief interaction, female students high in dominance preferred a submissive partner, and females high in submissiveness preferred a dominant partner. So it appears that for the traits of dominance and submission, complementarity contributes to attraction. The same applies to fiscal habits: People who tend to scrimp and save often marry people who like to spend. Still, their different spending styles contribute to conflicts over finances, which reduce marital well-being (Rick et al., 2011). Other studies show that people partner up with a dissimilar other if they are looking for a short-term, low-commitment relationship, presumably because they find their differences to be novel and exciting (Amodio & Showers, 2005).

Tesser's (1988) self-evaluation maintenance model (described in chapter 6) suggests another way that dissimilarity can help a relationship. If friends or partners are both strong in the same domains of abilities and accomplishments, it can lead to threatening social comparisons and friction. This implies that people will get along if they are good at different things—if, for example, one person is great at math and the other is a great writer. That way, each person can take pride in the other's accomplishments rather than experiencing self-esteem threat from them (Pilkington et al., 1991). To test this idea, Tesser (1980) studied the biographies of famous male scientists. He found that the scientists had had better relationships with their sons if the sons went into a field different from their own.

Similarity in Perceptions

So far, we've been talking about similarity (perceived or actual) in personality traits, demographic characteristics, behavioral preferences, or attitudes. These are all features of the self that William James called the "Me." But recall that James distinguished what the self is in terms of the content of who we are (the Me) from our subjective point of view on the world around us (the I). According to Liz Pinel and colleagues (Pinel et al., 2004), we "Me-share" with others when we feel that we are the same kind of person, but we "I-share" with others when we believe that our subjective experiences of the world are the same, even if our respective "Me's" seem very different.

By way of example, your current author once joined a crew tasked with painting the interior of non-air-conditioned dorms in one blazingly hot summer in Dallas, Texas. Being an introverted liberal from New York, he developed a strong dislike for a boisterous, politically conservative crew member from Georgia. However, about two weeks into the job, this odd couple came to realize that they shared a rare love of Italian Opera. They spent the rest of their time as fast friends, joyfully singing tunes from Verdi's *Aida* while painting, probably high on paint fumes.

I-sharing can indeed create strong feelings of connection. In fact, as the paint crew story suggested, it can even lead people to look past the objective differences that normally keep them separated. In one study (Pinel & Long, 2012), heterosexual men were shown nonsensical associations between famous people and objects (e.g., "If Oprah Winfrey were a plant, what would she be?") and four possible responses (in this case: Dried flower, Venus fly trap, Kudzu, or Red rose). They were instructed to "go with their gut" and select the response that made sense to them. Immediately after making their response, they learned how two other participants—one straight, one gay—responded to the same association. In truth, there were no other participants. The feedback was set up to make it appear that one of the two others I-shared with the participant, picking the same responses nearly every time. Finally, they were asked which other participant they wanted to interact with. Attesting to the power of I-sharing to bolster liking, heterosexual men preferred to interact with a gay man with whom they I-shared rather than another heterosexual man with whom they did not I-share.

If You Like Me, I'll Like You!

Other people, particularly those we respect or care about, can bolster or threaten our self-esteem by liking or rejecting us. As we've discussed, social rejection and ostracism can be extremely distressing experiences. On the other hand, it's hard not to feel a little better about someone who feeds your need for self-esteem by approving of and warmly embracing you.

In chapter 13 we discussed the norm of reciprocity. This idea extends to liking. All else being equal, if you find out that someone else likes you (more than he or she likes others), it makes you more likely to like them too (Condon & Crano, 1988; Curtis & Miller, 1986; Eastwick et al., 2007). In one study, people's reports of how they fell in love or formed a friendship with a person indicated that a key factor was realizing that the other person liked them (Aron et al., 1989). In fact, when compared with attitude similarity, being liked by another is a stronger initial factor in attraction (Condon & Crano, 1988; Curtis & Miller, 1986). One obvious explanation for the reciprocity of liking effect is based on self-esteem. Our self-esteem benefits when others like us (Becker, 1962; James, 1890; Leary et al., 1995), so we like those who enhance our self-esteem. Another plausible explanation is that we expect someone who likes us to treat us well, so the anticipation of rewards enhances our liking for that person (Montoya & Insko, 2008).

Flattery

It's no surprise that we also like people who compliment us, even to the point of flattery. Studies show that the more nice things someone says about us, the more we like them (Gordon, 1996; Jones, 1990). The benefits of flattery even extend to computers. When participants received randomly generated positive performance evaluations from a computer, they liked the computer better—even if they knew the positive evaluations were randomly generated and not contingent on their performance (Fogg & Nass, 1997)!

Flattery doesn't always work, however. If it is clear the flatterer has an ulterior motive, the compliments are not quite so effective (Gordon, 1996; Matsumura & Ohtsubo, 2012). Still, we generally prefer someone who says nice things about us (even if that person's motives are suspect) to someone who doesn't have anything nice to say at all (Drachman et al., 1978). This is because any compliment will still make us feel good (Chan & Sengupta, 2010). We usually are more motivated to embrace positive feedback than to question its validity (Jones, 1964, 1990; Vonk, 2002).

Aronson and Linder's **gain-loss theory** (1965) adds an interesting complexity to our tendency to like those who flatter us. They noted that in some contexts, a compliment from a stranger, or someone you know but never has complimented you, is more potent than a compliment from a friend or spouse. They proposed that this is because we have a long history of being complimented by a friend or romantic partner, so one additional compliment is expected and doesn't affect us much: You already know the person likes you. But the unexpected compliment from a stranger or an acquaintance who has not expressed liking for you before is more unexpected and fresher, and thus may have a bigger impact on your self-esteem and your liking for the complimenter. On the flip side of the same coin, a criticism will have more impact if it comes from a friend or romantic partner because they usually say positive things to you.

Aronson and Linder tested this hypothesis by having participants overhear a series of evaluations of them by a discussion partner who was a confederate of the experimenter. There were four patterns of evaluations: consistently positive, consistently negative, initially negative and then becoming positive (gain), and initially positive and becoming negative (loss). The participants liked the confederate best in the gain condition, second best in the consistently positive condition, even less in the consistently negative condition, and least in the loss condition. Positive judgments from someone who was initially negative and negative judgments from someone who was initially positive polarized people's attitudes for the evaluator. Aronson and Linder noted that this phenomenon may put a long-term spouse at a disadvantage relative to new people the spouse meets: The spouse's compliments will have less impact, and his or her criticisms will have more impact. Married 10 years, Rondae may compliment his wife, Renée, on how nice she looks to little apparent effect as they head to a party, and then observe that she is quite overtly pleased when someone at the party says the same thing.

What other aspects of the person giving us compliments affect how much we like him or her? One saying floating around in our culture is that "playing hard to get" can increase one's attractiveness. Evidence doesn't generally support that idea, but it does support the idea that people are more attractive if they seem hard *for others* to "get" (Eastwick et al., 2007; Wright & Contrada, 1986). Some people are very free with compliments and seem to like everybody. Other people are very discriminating, doling out compliments only to the lucky few. Compliments and liking increase attraction more if the person giving them out seems discriminating rather than giving out compliments freely or seeming to like virtually everyone.

Gain-loss theory A theory of attraction that posits that liking is highest for others when they increase their positivity toward you over time.

Several factors affect how we choose others with whom we form close relationships.

Proximity	Reward model	Attributes of the person	Our psychological needs
Physical proximity is an important factor in developing relationships, although its importance is tempered by social media.	People like others whom they associate with positive feelings and dislike those associated with negative feelings.	• People like those who remind them of others they like. • People like those with culturally desirable attributes. • Self-reports of traits that people prefer often don't predict their liking of people they meet who have those traits.	People tend to like others who fulfill their needs for meaning and self-esteem. Specifically, those who: • are perceived as similar to the self. • reciprocate liking. • flatter them.

Physical Attractiveness

In 2010, the CNN correspondent and blogger Jack Cafferty posed the following question "What does it mean that despite the worst recession since the Great Depression, Americans spent more than $10 billion on cosmetic procedures last year?" Although many Americans worried about health care costs, employment, and the like, they still managed to spend what money they had on tucking their tummies, enlarging their breasts, and chiseling their cheekbones—in short, making themselves appear more physically attractive. In fact, Americans collectively spent the same amount that some economists estimate it would cost to provide universal schooling. So to answer Cafferty's question: Clearly, physical attractiveness is important to people.

The Importance of Physical Attractiveness

But just how important is physical attractiveness to liking someone? Is it important enough to influence who we decide to put in charge of leading our country? Todorov and colleagues (2005) showed students photographs of two of the major political candidates from each of 95 different Senate races and 600 different races for the House of Representatives in the United States. Simply by viewing these candidates' pictures and judging their physical attractiveness, students correctly guessed the winner of each contest in 72% of the Senate and 67% of the House races.

If physical attractiveness can have such a potent influence on political decisions, just imagine how important it is for our interpersonal decisions. As you probably would guess, people who are more physically attractive are also more popular and date more frequently (Berscheid et al., 1971; Reis et al., 1980). But is physical attractiveness more important than other factors in determining whether a relationship gets off the ground? The short answer, at least in terms of the spark that gets the relationship going, is yes. For most people heading off to a blind date, the physical attractiveness of their partner is going to be the most important factor influencing whether they want to have a second date. Although as we will see later in our discussion, after we meet and get to know another person, attractiveness matters less for sustaining our interest over time.

Why Is Physical Attractiveness Important?

Physical attractiveness is important for a variety of reasons. Seen from the perspective of the reward model, it obviously contributes to sexual appeal. But sex aside, it also simply may be more pleasant to look at attractive (rather than unattractive) babies, kids, and adults. In fact, even infants gaze more at attractive adult faces

(Langlois et al., 1990). Physical appearance is also typically the first attribute we come to know about a person. It takes much less time to assess someone's looks than his or her honesty, intelligence, and other qualities; some evidence suggests it takes as little as 0.15 seconds (Zajonc, 1998). So when you meet someone, the very first impression you form will be based on his or her looks.

Physical attractiveness also may be important in many cultures because the hotter the person we're with, the more we can BIRG (bask in their reflected glory). Consider a study by Sigall and Landy from 1973. As a participant in this study, you show up at the lab and find two other people in the waiting room. These two people are actually confederates. One is an average-looking guy, and the other is a naturally good-looking woman. For half of the participants, her appearance accentuates her attractiveness. She wears makeup and is tastefully dressed. But for the other half of the participants, she wears an unflattering wig, no makeup, and unbecoming clothes to mask her attractiveness. After a few minutes, an experimenter enters and asks the other people if they are here for a study on perception. Half the time the woman holds the man's hand and says, "No, I'm just waiting with my boyfriend." This leads you to infer that she is in a relationship with the man. The other half of the time she does not hold the other confederate's hand and replies, "No, I'm just waiting for Dr. X." Subsequently both you (the participant) and the man are led to different rooms, and under the pretext of a person-perception study, you're asked to give your impressions of him.

What did the researchers find? As you can see in **FIGURE 14.1**, participants formed more positive impressions of the man when he was the boyfriend of the attractive woman (the condition labeled Associated) than when he was unassociated with the attractive woman. They formed the least positive impressions when he was the boyfriend of the unattractive woman. This shows how our impressions of people are influenced by the attractiveness of those with whom they are associated. When we date attractive people, other people see us more positively than if we dated unattractive people. What is more, people anticipate that an attractive partner can have this effect! In a second study, Sigall and Landy (1973) created a similar scenario, but asked male participants to pretend to be either the boyfriend of an attractive or unattractive confederate and then to guess how other people would rate him. Sure enough, guys thought they would be evaluated more positively when they were seen as having a relationship with an attractive woman. So part of the reason we like to be with attractive people is that we know that this will lead others to think better of us.

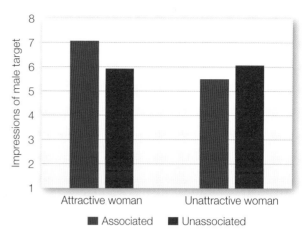

Figure 14.1

Basking in the Glow of Attractive Others

People's impressions of a man were more positive when he was seen in the presence of an attractive rather than an unattractive woman, but only if he seemed to be dating her (i.e., was associated with her).

[Data source: Sigall & Landy (1973)]

The Physical Attractiveness Stereotype, AKA the Halo Effect

Another reason we might care about someone's attractiveness is that we assume it will mean that they have other positive characteristics. Despite the cultural maxims to "never judge a book by its cover" or that "beauty is only skin deep," in Western cultures people see beautiful people (compared with those of average attractiveness) as happier, warmer, more dominant, mature, mentally healthy, and more outgoing, intelligent, sensitive, confident, and successful—though not more honest, concerned for others, or modest (e.g., Eagly et al., 1991; Feingold, 1992b; Langlois et al., 2000). This tendency to see attractive people as having positive traits, to see beautiful as good in a global sense, is referred to as a *physical attractiveness stereotype*, or halo effect (Dion et al., 1972). The effects of a physical attractiveness stereotype have been shown in a number of studies, many of which simply asked people to judge others, or work attributed to them, on the basis of only a photograph (Anderson & Nida, 1978; Cash & Trimer, 1984). For example, people evaluated an essay supposedly written by an attractive person more positively than that very same essay when it was supposedly written by an unattractive person (Landy & Sigall, 1974).

Halo effect A tendency to assume that people with one positive attribute (e.g., who are physically attractive) also have other positive traits.

Lest you be tempted to think that folks simply judge more positively those people with whom they want to hook up, note that halo effects occur throughout the life span in many contexts in which sexual arousal or interest is not involved. In one alarming study, cuter premature infants were treated better in hospitals and consequently fared better than their less cute fellow preemies (Badr & Abdallah, 2001). Young children show preferences for other attractive children (Dion & Berscheid, 1974). Attractive babies get more attention from parents and staff even before leaving the hospital (Langlois et al., 1995). Halo effects continue to occur in nursery school, with attractive children being more popular (Dion, 1973). But maybe it weakens by the time children get to elementary school? No—attractiveness biases occur there as well. Clifford and Walster (1973), for example, gave fifth-grade teachers identical information about a boy or a girl but manipulated whether the information was paired with an attractive or unattractive photograph. When asked how intelligent the student was and how successful the student was likely to be in school, teachers saw the attractive child as both more intelligent and more likely to be successful.

In some ways, though, at least with predicted success, the teachers may not have been entirely inaccurate. The benefits of physical attractiveness continue into adulthood, with implications for several positive outcomes. For example, for each point increase on a 1 (homely) to 5 (strikingly attractive) scale of attractiveness, people are likely to earn an average of about $2,000 more a year (Frieze et al., 1991; Roszell et al., 1989). Other life domains are affected as well. For instance, attractive defendants are less likely than unattractive defendants to be found guilty when accused of a crime (Efran, 1974), and when they are found guilty, they are given lighter sentences (Stewart, 1980). This bias in the legal domain is strongest in jurors who rely on their emotions and gut-level reactions in their decision making (Gunnell & Ceci, 2010).

These kinds of outcomes raise important questions about whether or not there is truth to the stereotype. The answer is somewhat complex. Attractive people are generally more outgoing, popular, and socially skilled (Feingold, 1992b; Langlois et al., 2000), but they are not higher in self-esteem, life satisfaction, mental health, sensitivity, or intelligence (Diener et al., 1995; Feingold, 1992b; Sparacino & Hansell, 1979; Major et al., 1984).

Given how favorably people react to those who are highly attractive, it's a bit surprising that physical attractiveness is not more of a psychological boon than it actually is. Research suggests two reasons the benefits are limited. First, it turns out that people are often mistaken in their perceptions of how physically attractive other people think they are (Feingold, 1992b). So some people think they are less physically attractive than they really are. Second, no one wants to be valued only because of their looks or any other single characteristic. Highly attractive people may sometimes wonder if that's the only reason people compliment them or care for them (Major et al., 1984).

Nevertheless, although the stereotype paints a much more positive picture than the reality, it does have some validity in the domain of social skills. For example, when researchers conduct phone interviews with attractive versus unattractive people, more attractive people are rated by interviewers (who don't know what they look like) as more likable and socially skilled (Goldman & Lewis, 1977).

But then the next important question to ask is why? Is it because more attractive people are in fact naturally more socially skilled? Or might it have something to do with the way they have been treated throughout their lives? Take a moment and think back to our discussion in chapter 3 of self-fulfilling prophecies and how they might operate in this context. When we see an attractive person, we assume all kinds of good things and become motivated to impress him. As a consequence, we are likely to be more pleasant and charming with him. Because we treat him in a more accepting and encouraging manner, he is likely to respond in kind. In the television show *30 Rock*, the TV writer Liz Lemon (Tina Fey) begins dating a super handsome man (played by John Hamm) and is awed and dismayed at the special treatment he receives (Fey & Brock, 2009):

> Liz (telling her boss, Jack, about her new boyfriend): He's a doctor who doesn't know the Heimlich maneuver. He can't play tennis. He can't cook. He's as bad at sex as I am. But he has no idea!
>
> Jack: That is the danger of being super handsome. When you are in the bubble, no one tells you the truth.

So do beautiful people really get special treatment that then makes them more socially skilled? Snyder and colleagues (1977) set up a study to test this idea. They had a male and female participant show up (separately) to their lab and escorted them to separate cubicles such that they never saw each other. The male participant was told to interview the female through a microphone setup, and their conversation was recorded. In a critical step, before the interview, the male participant was given some information about the participant, including a photograph. The photograph either depicted a very attractive or a rather unattractive woman. Thus, the male participant thought he knew what the person he was talking to looked like, but in actuality, the photograph was of a different person. Later, independent judges who did not know what the study was about rated the female participants on various characteristics only on the basis of listening to the tape-recorded interview. What do you think happened?

In an episode of the television show *30 Rock*, Liz Lemon learns that her very attractive boyfriend is treated differently by others because of his good looks. For example, no one has ever told him that he doesn't speak fluent French.
[NBC/Photofest]

When the male participant thought he was talking to an attractive woman, the independent judges actually rated her more positively (e.g., friendlier and more open). Thinking that he was talking to an attractive woman, the male participant was more pleasant, and elicited pleasantness in return. This effect occurred when women conversed with men they thought were attractive or unattractive (Andersen & Bem, 1981). Indeed, meta-analyses have found that people are equally positive in their treatment of attractive men and women (Eagly et al., 1991; Feingold, 1992b; Langlois et al., 2000).

Where does this stereotype come from? Partly it comes from our own motivations. We generally want to bond with attractive people, so on seeing them—whether in photographs, as romantic partners, or as friends—we very quickly make a judgment of desirability (Lemay et al., 2010). We then project onto them other positive characteristics that fit this judgment. But as we noted earlier, these halo effects occur even when we are judging young children. Thus, such motivations for bonding are likely only part of the story.

Think
ABOUT

A major source of these stereotypes is the culture in which we live (Dion et al., 1972). Pretty much as soon as we pop out of the womb, we are bombarded with images, stories, and fairytales that convey a clear and simple message: Good people are good looking; bad people are ugly. Cultures probably promote this stereotype because, after all, wouldn't life be simpler and better if the people we find physically attractive are also great in

[RKO Radio Pictures/Photofest]

other ways, and the people we think are great were also physically attractive? Think **about your favorite childhood movie or fairytale book. How were the principal characters portrayed?**

Overwhelmingly the good princess is beautiful and the hero handsome, whereas the evil witch and villain are ugly. When Anakin Skywalker chooses the dark side of the force, his good looks are masked in robotic, menacing armor. From Cinderella, Sleeping

Beauty, and Princess Leia (and their accompanying saviors) to stepsisters, wicked witches (with crooked noses complete with bulging warts), and Darth Vader, all of them convey pretty consistent messages.

Supporting this cultural media explanation, Smith and colleagues (1999) found that in popular Hollywood movies, there was a positive correlation between how physically attractive the main character was and how virtuous and successful the character was in the film. In a second study, they showed college students a film reinforcing the beautiful-is-good stereotype. Subsequently, the students were asked to give their impression of two people they thought were applicants to graduate school. They thought more highly of the physically attractive applicant than the less attractive applicant, even though the two applicants had similar academic credentials.

If the physical attractiveness stereotype is at least partly a product of our culture, then we should expect it to vary along cultural lines. And to a certain extent it does. People tend to associate beauty with those traits that their culture generally defines as positive and valuable. So in the United States and other Western cultures, this means seeing beautiful people as friendly, independent, and assertive. But when researchers gave Korean students pictures of attractive Koreans, they did not see them as having characteristics such as potency, which Americans value (Wheeler & Kim, 1997). Rather, Korean students judged attractive Koreans as being more honest and concerned for others, precisely the traits that are valued in that culture and less so than in the United States.

Common Denominators of Attractive Faces

"Beauty is in the eye of the beholder." This popular saying suggests that people have very different notions of who is physically attractive. There are indeed important differences among individuals, cultures, and historical periods in assessments of what is attractive (Darwin, 1872; Landau, 1989; Newman, 2000; Wiggins et al., 1968). In recent years, teenage *Twilight* film fans have debated the merits of Jacob versus Edward. Magazines such as *People* and *Maxim* have yearly issues on the most attractive celebrity men and women; the rankings change substantially from year to year. People's tastes in food, music, and clothes vary; surely their tastes in whom they find attractive also vary, both within and across cultures.

But research shows that people actually agree about who is (and isn't) physically attractive much more than they disagree (Langlois et al., 2000; Marcus & Miller, 2003). Within and across cultures, the consensus as to who is and who is not attractive is generally strong. For example, when Latino, Asian, Black, and White men rated the attractiveness of different women in pictures, there was some variability in preferred body shape, but in general, the correlations across the groups exceeded 0.90 (Cunningham et al., 1995). This indicates strong agreement in perceptions of who is hot and who is not. What's more, newborn infants—too young to be aware of their culture's local beauty standards—prefer to gaze longer at the faces that adults find attractive than at those adults find unattractive (Langlois et al., 1987; Langlois et al., 1991; Slater et al., 2000). But what exactly makes those faces so lovely?

The Averageness Effect

Beautiful faces seem to stand out from the crowd, so we might infer that attractive faces have unique features. Think again. To be attractive is actually to have quite average facial features. Researchers studying attraction have used computer-imaging software to superimpose images of faces on top of each other, thus creating composite faces that represent the digital "average" of the individual faces (see **FIGURE 14.2**).

Figure 14.2

The Allure of "Average" Faces

If you digitally average original photos of faces, the result is a composite face. The more real faces that are used to create the composite face, the more attractive the composite face is deemed to be. Evolutionary psychologists argue that we are attracted to these "average" faces because they signal good health and thus good mating potential.

[Research from: Langlois & Roggman (1990). Photos courtesy of Dr. Marin Gruendl, www.beautycheck.de]

Original photo A   Original photo B   Composite

Both men and women rate these composite faces as more attractive than nearly all of the individual faces that make them up, leading to what is known as the **averageness effect** (Langlois & Roggman, 1990; Rubenstein et al., 2002). And the more faces that are combined to create a composite face, the more attractive that face is perceived to be. However, it's also the case that composites of sets of faces that are attractive to begin with are viewed as more attractive than composites of nonselective samples of faces.

Do these averaging effects mean that to be attractive is to have bland, ordinary looks? Not at all. These composite faces are actually quite unusual (that's why we put "average" in quotes): They are mean composites, not modal or common faces. Their features are all proportional to one another; no nose is remarkably big or small; no cheeks are puffy or sunken. In short, nothing about these composite faces is exaggerated, underdeveloped, or odd.

Symmetry

Another feature of faces that both men and women find attractive is bilateral symmetry (Thornhill & Gangestad, 1993). Symmetry occurs when the two sides of the face are mirror images of one another (**FIGURE 14.3**). You might think that you have a symmetrical face; after all, you probably have one eye on the right side of your face and another eye on the left. Yes, but look closer (perhaps with the help of a computer, as researchers have done) and you will find numerous asymmetries: Your eyes are slightly different in shape, size, and position on your face, your cheekbones are at slightly different angles, and, if you are like the current author, one of your nostrils has a bigger circumference than the other. All things being equal, the more symmetrical a face, the more people find it attractive.

It is interesting to note that symmetry and "averageness" each make a unique contribution to facial beauty. Composite faces made by the digital averaging process we just mentioned tend to be more symmetrical than the individual faces making them up (Rhodes, 2006). This is to be expected: When you combine faces, each face's unique asymmetries become less noticeable. But facial symmetry is attractive in its own right, whether or not a face is "average" (Fink et al., 2006). Among symmetrical faces, those that average together the features of many individual faces are seen as the most attractive (Rhodes et al., 1999).

The preference for "average" and symmetrical faces is universal. Men and women from all over the world—in the United States, China, Nigeria, India, and Japan—agree that "average," symmetrical faces are more attractive than faces with exaggerated features or asymmetries (Rhodes et al., 2002). Why do we see widespread agreement that these features are attractive?

Why Are "Average," Symmetrical Faces Attractive?

One influential answer comes from evolutionary psychology. It seems plausible that a big challenge to successful reproduction was—and continues to be—finding a healthy person to mate with. Because diseases and developmental disorders can be passed on genetically, our ancestors who mated with healthy partners were more likely to have healthy offspring, who themselves went on to reproduce, than were those who mated with unhealthy partners.

But how can we tell whether or not a potential mate is in good health? One indicator may be facial features. When people are developing *in utero* (in the womb) before birth, their genes are normally set up to create a symmetrical face and body, with no skeletal feature badly out of proportion. Yet if they are exposed to pathogens, parasites, or viruses during development, the result can be irregular and asymmetric features of the face and body. For example, the more infectious diseases experienced by a mother during pregnancy, the more likely her infant is to show departures from perfect facial and bodily symmetry (Livshits & Kobyliansky, 1991).

Averageness effect The tendency to perceive a composite image of multiple faces that have been photographically averaged as more attractive than any individual face included in that composite.

Figure 14.3

The Importance of Symmetry

Which of these faces do you find most attractive? People tend to rate more symmetrical faces as more attractive. Some psychologists say that this preference stems from an innate tendency to search for healthy mates.

[Research from: Rhodes et al. (1999)]

  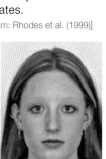

Asymmetrical   Original   Symmetrical

Indeed, some research shows that men and women with more symmetrical faces are healthier than are people whose faces have odd proportions. For example, studies have found that symmetrical-faced individuals tend to have fewer respiratory and intestinal infections than less symmetrical individuals (Thornhill & Gangestad, 2006) and have higher potential fertility (Jasienska et al., 2006; Soler et al., 2003).

Although this evolutionary perspective on the allure of averageness and symmetry has some appeal, another explanation is that more average-appearing and symmetrical faces simply seem more familiar and are thus easier for us to process as faces. Research has not always supported the idea that facial averageness and symmetry are indicators of physical health (e.g., Kalick et al., 1998; Rhodes et al., 2001). But other evidence shows that people like faces more to the extent that they look like very familiar faces—their own (Little & Perrett, 2002)! Also spouses, siblings, and close friends, who tend to stay near each other, agree more in their ratings of facial attractiveness than pairs of strangers do (Bronstad & Russell, 2007). Such evidence has led some researchers to argue that the preference for averageness may be a byproduct of liking for familiarity and stimuli that are easily processed rather than the legacy of an evolved mechanism to read these cues as signals of health.

Sexual Orientation and Attraction

I met Thea at the Portofino, a restaurant in the West Village. There was a place near it called the Bagatelle, over on University Place, and I used to go there five nights a week. I would read the *Saturday Review of Literature*; I would have my coffee there—me and a bunch of buddies. I thought she was sensational, and mostly she was a great dancer. And we really danced. And then we met over the next two years. We always danced together. But it wouldn't have occurred to me to make any moves on someone who was with someone. And she was always with someone. And then one summer she was not with someone. I knew she had a place in the Hamptons, so I wrangled an invitation through a friend. I was wild for her. I don't know how to describe it. It was everything. It was just more so. We were profoundly in love and stayed that way. Many, many years later, I said to her, "When did you really start to deeply love me?" And she said, "Mrs. Fordham's house," which is the house we rented one summer in the Hamptons. We had very different passions, but we both had enormous love for each other's passions. She played the violin. She played golf. And she did them both obsessively. With golf I had to make certain rules, because if she came home talking her head off about every shot, I would say, "The idea is for you to go and enjoy it and discuss it completely and *then* come home" (Hicklin, 2011).

Edith Windsor provides this account of her long-time relationship with Thea Spyer. In 2007, they were married in Canada, which recognizes same-sex marriages. They lived in New York City. (New York State also recognizes same-sex marriages.) When Thea died of multiple sclerosis in 2009, she left her estate to Edith. Edith, who was denied the federal inheritance-tax exceptions typically afforded for heterosexual marriages, was the plaintiff in a landmark lawsuit that ultimately led to the repeal of the Defense of Marriage Act (*United States v. Windsor*, 2013).

Edith's description of how her relationship with Thea unfolded reveals many of the same factors that influence heterosexual attraction. In fact, the factors that predict attraction in gay and lesbian relationships are quite similar to those that predict attraction in heterosexual relationships. People, whether they are gay, straight, or bisexual, generally are attracted to people who provide affection, are dependable, and have shared interests (Peplau & Fingerhut, 2007).

Edith Windsor (left) and her wife, Thea Spyer.
[© Neville Elder/Corbis]

Gender Differences in What Is Attractive

Now you might wonder if there are differences in what men and women find attractive. Research into such differences covers two distinct questions. One is whether men and women differ in the kinds of physical attributes they think make a person physically attractive. The second, somewhat related question is whether men place more importance on physical attractiveness and whether women prioritize signs of social status.

We preface this section by acknowledging a few points. One is that research on this question can sometime be controversial, invoking a common nature versus nurture debate that we'll return to later. The second is that any evidence of mean differences between men's and women's preferences does not preclude the possibility of a wide range of individual variation within each sex, which we will also discuss. Finally, it's also worth acknowledging that most of the research in this area has focused on attraction to members of the opposite sex, but we will also highlight the emerging interest in studying patterns of attraction among same-sex couples. This topic is the focus of the *Social Psych out in the World* section.

From this brief snapshot of Edith and Thea's relationship, we can see that an initial shared interest, in dancing for example, was an important bond that fueled attraction. But they are different in many ways, consistent with some evidence that suggests less prevalence of matching on attractiveness, education, and other variables in gay than in straight relationships (Kurdek, 1995).

The overall similarity between same-sex and opposite-sex attraction is evident in other ways as well. Whereas men, regardless of sexual orientation, are prone to report emphasizing physical attractiveness, women, regardless of sexual orientation, are more prone to report emphasizing personality characteristics (Peplau & Spalding, 2000). This gender difference notwithstanding, there are some interesting nuances in what gay men and lesbians consider most attractive. Studies of personal ads reveal that many gay men look for masculine traits and partners who adopt what are typically masculine roles (Bailey et al., 1997). For gay men, physical appearance (in particular, a lean, muscular build) is especially important when evaluating prospects for short-term as opposed to long-term relationships (Varangis et al., 2012).

In contrast, whereas lesbians look for partners with feminine characteristics, they don't necessarily want partners who assume what are typically feminine roles (Bailey et al., 1997). Indeed, perhaps because lesbians eschew typical gender roles, the physique they report as being most attractive is less close to the thin ideal promoted by the mass media and often preferred by heterosexual men (Swami & Tovee, 2006).

Overall, such differences are broadly consistent with the notion that women's views on what is physically attractive about a partner of either sex are more complex and flexible than men's views. For example, men's sexual orientation tends to be much more fixed as being attracted either to women or to men. And men with higher sex drives are even more attracted to whichever sex is their preference. But for women, the patterns are more complex. Although heterosexual women are generally more attracted to men than to women, those with a higher sex drive are more sexually attracted to both men and women (Lippa, 2006, 2007). Yet for lesbians, a higher sex drive only predicts attraction to other women and not to men.

What happens with gay and lesbian relationships over time? In chapter 15 we will explore the challenges of maintaining close relationships over the long haul, so we won't delve into that here. But generally, as with initial attraction, the important factors for relationships, regardless of someone's sexual orientation, are more similar than they are different (Peplau & Fingerhut, 2007).

Edith Windsor speaks to press after winning landmark gay rights lawsuit.

[Bryan Smith/Zumapress.com/Alamy]

What Attributes Do Men and Women Find Attractive?

Although both men and women prefer "average" and symmetrical faces, heterosexual men and women differ somewhat in the physical features they find attractive in someone of the opposite sex. Here an evolutionary perspective might shed some light. Over the course of evolutionary history, men and women both were motivated to reproduce, but they faced different reproductive challenges. As a result, men and women evolved to have different, specialized preferences in their mates that favor the conception, birth, and survival of their offspring (Buss & Schmitt, 1993; Gangestad & Simpson, 2000; Geary, 2010; Trivers, 1972). Let's look at the features that men and women each consider attractive in a potential mate, and then think back to our deep evolutionary past to see why evolution may have favored different preferences in men and women.

For Men, Signs of Fertility

The psychologist David Buss (1989) asked thousands of men and women in 37 cultures what they found attractive in a romantic partner. Across these cultures, men and women judged the attractiveness of the opposite sex on the basis of many common attributes. Both men and women gave their highest rating—and equally high ratings—to kindness, dependability, a good sense of humor, and a pleasant disposition. But women and men differ in some ways as well. One gender difference concerned preferred age. Across many cultures, men universally prefer their sexual partners to be younger than themselves. It is no surprise that men report a preference for female features that signal a potential mate's youth. For example, men like facial features that resemble to some extent those of a baby: large eyes, a small nose, a small chin, and full lips (Jones, 1995). But, in fact, men are most attracted to women whose "baby-faced" features are combined with features that signal maturity, such as prominent cheekbones and a broad smile (Cunningham et al., 2002).

How can we account for these universal patterns in the preferences men report? An evolutionary perspective suggests that the challenge men face when attempting to reproduce is finding a mate who is *fertile*—put simply, capable of producing offspring. But how can men deduce a potential mate's fertility level? One useful clue is a woman's age. Women are not fertile until puberty, and their fertility ends after they reach menopause around age 50. As our species evolved, men who were attracted to features of women's faces and bodies that signal that they are young (but not too young) were more likely to find a fertile mate and successfully reproduce. Those attracted to women with other features were less successful in populating the gene pool. As a result, those preferences may be built into modern men's genetic inheritance (Buss, 2003).

Another physical feature linked to fertility in women is waist-to-hip ratio (**FIGURE 14.4**). If you measure the circumference of your waist at its narrowest point, and divide that by the circumference of your hips at your broadest point (including your butt), the number you get is your waist-to-hip ratio. Men are most attracted to women's bodies with a waist-to-hip ratio of 0.7—a very curvy "hourglass" figure in which the waist is 30% narrower than the hips (Furnham et al., 2005; Singh, 1993).

Interestingly, even though men in different cultures and historical periods are attracted to varying levels of plumpness, they all agree on the appeal of a 0.7 waist-to-hip ratio. For example, in the United States, Black men prefer women with heavier physiques than do White men, and yet both Black and White men prefer the same curvaceous 0.7 waist-to-hip ratio

Figure 14.4

Waist-to-hip Ratio

When people are asked to judge which of these women is most attractive, the average preference is usually a woman with a 0.7 ratio of waist to hip.

[Copyright © 1993 by the American Psychological Association. Reproduced with permission. Singh, D., Adaptive significance of female physical attractiveness: Role of waist-to-hip ratio. 1993, *Journal of Personality and Social Psychology* 65:293–307. The use of APA information does not imply endorsement by APA.]

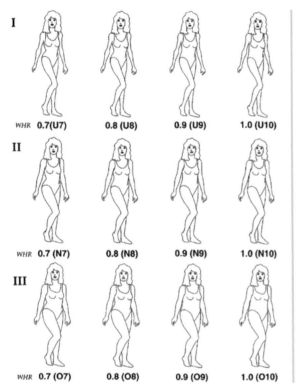

I			
WHR 0.7(U7)	0.8 (U8)	0.9 (U9)	1.0 (U10)
II			
WHR 0.7 (N7)	0.8 (N8)	0.9 (N9)	1.0 (N10)
III			
WHR 0.7 (O7)	0.8 (O8)	0.9 (O9)	1.0 (O10)

Over time, standards of attractiveness for the overall size of women's bodies have changed, but the ideal of a 0.7 waist-to-hip ratio has remained fairly constant. Today, films like *Into the Blue* (2005) try to draw large audiences by featuring actresses like Jessica Alba wearing outfits that highlight this ideal waist-to-hip ratio.

[From left to right: Alftredo Dagli Orti/The Art Archive/Corbis; Hulton Archive/Getty Images; Columbia Pictures/Eccles, Andrew/Album/Newscom]

(Singh & Luis, 1995). Similarly, a quick glance at Renaissance paintings or the pin-up girls popular in the United States in the 1940s and 1950s reveals that women considered to be consummately sexy during those periods in history look rather voluptuous by today's standards (Pettijohn & Jungeberg, 2004; Silverstein et al., 1986; Wiseman et al., 1992). Yet all those women who were considered attractive have the same curvaceous 0.7 waist-to-hip ratio. For example, even though there are clear differences in the body masses of Marilyn Monroe and Jessica Alba, two women deemed by their respective times to be very attractive, they share similar waist-to-hip ratios (0.63 for Marilyn and 0.7 for Jessica).

A person's waist-to-hip ratio is largely determined by the distribution of fat on his or her body, which is determined by hormones. Women with a waist-to-hip ratio near the attractiveness norm of 0.7 have a particular mix of hormones (estradiol and progesterone) that allows them to become pregnant more easily and to enjoy better physical health than do women with fewer curves (Lassek & Gaulin, 2008). So there is some evidence that the physical attributes that appeal to men around the world are signs of women's fertility. In the past, men who were not sensitive to such cues, or who didn't care enough to respond to them by seeking out sexual partners with certain features, presumably left fewer copies of their genes in the gene pool over the millennia.

For Women, Signs of Masculinity and Power

From an evolutionary perspective, women did not need to be so concerned as men with finding a youthful partner, because men's fertility is less bound to their age. In theory, men can continue to reproduce until they die (although sperm motility does decrease, and chromosomal mutations do increase, with age). Consistent with these factors, women generally prefer their mates to be the same age as themselves or older (Buss, 1989). But consider what made it challenging for women to reproduce successfully in the primeval social environment. During the many months of pregnancy, it was more difficult for them to go out on their own to forage for food, build shelters, and fend off saber-toothed tigers. What's more, they had to nurse the child and stay by its side to ensure that it didn't die.

Given these challenges to survival and reproduction, what features do you suppose women looked for when evaluating potential mates? They might have pursued men whose physical features they associated with masculinity, virility, and social power, as well as men who could be counted on to invest resources in protecting and providing for them and their offspring. For example, women find most attractive those men who have a waist-to-hip ratio around 0.9, yielding a V shape that signals more muscle than fat (Singh, 1995). Height is also important in standards of male attractiveness. Taller men tend to be seen as more attractive, and it's especially important that a man be at least somewhat taller than the woman who is considering dating him (Shepperd & Strathman, 1989). Other signs of masculinity are seen in a man's face. Preferences run to prominent cheekbones and a large chin (e.g., Cunningham et al., 1990).

When women are at their peak fertility, they are more attracted to men with very masculine features (such as George Clooney) than to men with baby-faced features (such as Tobey McGuire).

[Left: Elisabetta A. Villa/WireImage/Getty Images; right: Jean-Paul Aussenard/WireImage/Getty Images]

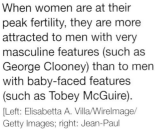

To demonstrate a role for women's evolved preferences for more masculine-looking men, the evolutionary perspective must be able to account for patterns of attraction that are not easily explained by a sociocultural perspective. The strongest evidence of the evolutionary perspective can be found in studies on women's mate preferences at different times of their monthly menstrual cycle. Women are fertile for only a few days preceding ovulation each month. This is the time when they are most likely to conceive if they have sex (of course, this all changes with the Pill or other forms of contraception), and so it also is the time when issues of genetic transmission are most relevant. During this stage of the menstrual cycle, some research suggests that women report preferring more masculine faces, that is, faces with strong jaws and broad foreheads (think George Clooney) rather than youthful boyishness (think Tobey Maguire) (Penton-Voak et al., 1999).

In addition, during the ovulatory phase of the menstrual cycle, women seem to prefer men who have deeper, more masculine voices (Puts, 2005) and who present themselves as more assertive, confident, and dominant (Gangestad et al., 2004; Gangestad et al., 2007; Macrae et al., 2002). Thus, during the fertile phase of the menstrual cycle (as opposed to the nonfertile phase), when the probability of conception is relatively high, women might become more attracted to men who show signs of power and dominance. Presumably, over the millennia, women genetically prone to mate with more dominant men were more likely to have their genes live on in future generations. In a related study, female strippers reported earning higher tips for lap dances during high-fertility phases (Miller et al., 2007), suggesting that women may appear more sexually appealing or behave in more appealing ways to men during fertile phases.

Men also seem to pick up on women's fertility unconsciously and play the part of the dominant man. Men who sniffed T-shirts worn by women who were in the fertile phase of their cycle showed a bigger spike in their testosterone levels than did men who sniffed T-shirts worn by women who were not fertile (Miller & Maner, 2010). Testosterone plays a role in dominant behavior, aggressiveness, and risk taking. These results suggest that men's hormonal reactions increase their chances of appearing attractive to fertile women and thus mating with them.

Do findings like this mean that there are fundamental, built-in, or hard-wired differences between men and women? Not necessarily. This is a very strong claim, and you might not be surprised to hear that it has sparked controversy. Scientists are not currently in agreement about whether women's mate preferences vary by ovulatory cycle. In 2014, two different meta-analyses were published drawing quite different interpretations about the strength of the evidence for these effects (Gildersleeve et al., 2014; Wood et al., 2014). This debate reminds us that it is important to keep a couple points in mind whenever we come across research that asserts a biologically innate mechanism. First, most of these studies have been conducted only with participants from Western cultures, and it's difficult to tease apart how culture might inform what is considered to be attractive. Before jumping to conclusions about innate differences, we need to see whether the findings we're discussing (e.g., women's preferences during specific phases of their menstrual cycle) replicate across non-Western cultures. Second, even if there are some biologically driven components to attraction that differentiate the sexes, it's also important to remember that men and women are far more similar than they are different in terms of the traits they rate as highly preferable in a romantic partner. If we focus solely on the differences, we risk losing the broader perspective on human attraction.

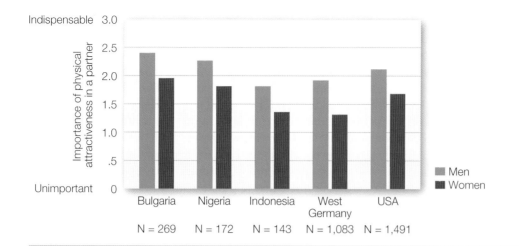

Figure 14.5

Gender Differences in Desire for Physically Attractive Partners

Across 37 cultures, men reported desiring physical attractiveness in a romantic partner more than women did.

[Data source: Buss & Schmitt (1993)]

Do Men Prefer Beauty? Do Women Prefer Status?

The evidence reviewed above largely supports an evolutionary perspective for why men and women consider different physical attributes attractive. However, another controversial question is whether men more than women care about physical attractiveness in the first place, whereas women more than men care about evidence of financial status and resources. Certainly some of the evidence fits our stereotype that men care about a woman's beauty, whereas women care more about a man's social status.

For example, Buss's (1989) initial research suggested that these gender differences exist across the 37 countries he assessed (see **FIGURE 14.5**) (Buss, 2008; Buss & Schmitt, 1993; Feingold, 1992a; Geary, 2010). And when given pictures and background information of potential dating partners, men were more likely than women to base their preferences on appearance, selecting the more attractive women (Feingold, 1990). In contrast, the better predictor of women's interest in a man was his income (see **FIGURE 14.6**). In studies of online dating, wealthier guys get more e-mails from the ladies (Hitsch et al., 2010). Such evidence seems to support our stereotypes about what men and women want.

However, other researchers suggest that these results are limited. For example, note that in these studies participants are indicating only whom they *think* they want to go out with. Studies that examine what happens when people actually meet and interact reveal a different picture. As far back as 1966, Walster and colleagues recruited students for a "welcome dance" at the University of Minnesota. They measured the students' personality traits, rated their physical attractiveness, and then later randomly matched men and women up for the evening. What was the best predictor of whether the students wanted to see their partners again after the dance? For men and women equally, it was the physical attractiveness of the partner.

Interpersonal Attraction: Clothes That Make the Man Video on LaunchPad

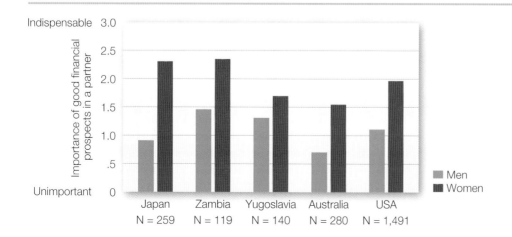

Figure 14.6

Gender Differences in Desire for Partners With Good Financial Prospects

Across cultures, women were more likely than men to say that they look for romantic partners with financial status and resources.

[Data source: Buss & Schmitt (1993)]

Eastwick and Finkel (2008) got the same results from their speed-dating paradigm. Men more than women self-reported valuing physical attractiveness, but when it came to choosing a live dating partner, both sexes were equally influenced by physical attractiveness. In fact, a recent meta-analysis confirms that across many studies, once live interaction occurs with a potential romantic partner, physical attractiveness is equally predictive of liking and interest for men and women (Eastwick et al., 2013).

The same is true for the gender difference in focus on wealth and status. Once live interaction with a potential partner occurs, the wealth and status of a potential partner are only slightly influential and equally so for both women and men (Eastwick et al., 2014). As we've seen throughout this textbook, we don't always know what it is we really want. So one caveat to this discussion of physical attractiveness is that what we *think* we will be attracted to often is wrong once we are face to face with a real person.

To understand why women say they prefer men of higher status, when their actual behavior doesn't follow these same trends, let's turn to a more sociocultural account. Although it historically has been the case that men have had disproportionate if not exclusive control over material resources and economic and political power, women have gained greater access to equal opportunities in recent decades. Women's preference for higher-status men makes rational sense in a historic or cultural context in which women rely on men for protection and support (Eagly & Wood, 1999; Wood & Eagly, 2002, 2007). But this sociocultural perspective suggests that in societies with greater gender equality—that is, societies in which women's occupation of powerful positions and their earning capacity are similar to men's—the greater female emphasis on finding a mate with status and economic resources should be reduced, and in fact it is (Eagly & Diekman, 2003; Wood & Eagly, 2002; Zentner & Mitura, 2012).

Because women in more egalitarian societies do not need to depend on their partners' earning capacity, they tend to report placing more value on the physical attractiveness of a potential mate. If we look at the distribution of wealth in each of the countries in Buss's (1989) study of mate preferences, we find that the more women had direct access to economic power, the more they reported that physical attractiveness mattered to them in selecting a long-term mate (Eagly & Wood, 1999; Gangestad, 1993). Also, when they are looking for a short-term fling, women prefer physically attractive mates as much as men do (Li & Kenrick, 2006). Because women in gender-egalitarian societies also tend to enjoy more sexual freedom, any gender differences in using physical attractiveness as a cue will be reduced. Finally, women who are higher in intelligence also indicate less emphasis on the status of potential male partners (Stanik & Ellsworth, 2010). This evidence cannot be explained by the evolutionary account, which points to innate preferences that evolved over thousands of years. It seems instead that women report caring more than men do about pursuing desirable resources through their partners when they expect to have relatively lower social and economic status.

Evolution in Context

Evolutionary psychology offers a provocative perspective on what characteristics men and women initially seek in partners. However, the evolutionary perspective on mate preferences also has sparked considerable controversy as researchers debate the role of innate mechanisms and sociocultural inputs. The current evidence seems to support a role for both sets of factors.

For example, according to evolutionary psychology, both sexes are most attracted to physical features that signal the highest likelihood of good health in the other sex, but the case for this explanation as opposed to one based on familiarity is inconclusive at this point. Furthermore, although men more than women report a greater interest in physically attractive mates, whereas women report a greater interest in mates with higher status, these gender differences in stated preferences are not found in studies of actual evaluation and dating patterns and are reduced in countries with greater gender equality. Thus, sociocultural influences seem to play a role in shaping women's changing prioritization of attractiveness and status in a mate.

However, evolutionary psychologists further posit that men and women are attracted to different physical attributes that helped them to solve sex-specific challenges to successful reproduction. And the current evidence does suggest that modern men have inherited a preference for youthfully mature, low-waist-to-hip-ratio partners, because these partners are most likely to be fertile. But researchers continue to debate whether during times of peak fertility, women have an increased preference for men with physical attributes that suggest dominance.

Finally, as we noted earlier, the sex differences we've discussed are small compared with the similarities between men and women. In every culture, both sexes look for partners who offer warmth and loyalty, which are always rated above physical attractiveness and status (Buss, 1989; Tran et al., 2008). Everyone, it seems, desires a partner who is agreeable, loving, and kind.

The broader point is this: The study of gender differences in attraction is addressed by some researchers from an evolutionary perspective and by others from a sociocultural perspective. The truth might lie somewhat in the middle. The most important thing to keep in mind is that much like other forms of human behavior, attraction stems from an intricate web of influences derived from each person's biology, culture, and immediate social context.

Cultural and Situational Influences on Attractiveness

Despite the cross-cultural consistency in what people find physically attractive, there is also plenty of variability. As you've likely noticed from your own travels or even just from looking at issues of *National Geographic*, from nose rings to filed teeth to hairstyles to body weight and even neck stretching, there are often considerable cultural and subcultural differences in what people find fetching (e.g., Darwin, 1872; Fallon, 1990; Ford & Beach, 1951; Hebl & Heatherton, 1998). Moreover, people in different cultures are attracted to those who exemplify the traits that their culture values (Wheeler & Kim, 1997).

In addition, within cultures, standards of beauty often vary over time. For example, a study of female models appearing in women's magazines from 1901 to 1981 found that bust-to-waist ratios varied over time, with a more slender look becoming popular more recently. Similarly, a study of *Playboy* centerfolds from 1953 to 2001 also showed a trend toward thinner figures and a lower bust-to-waist ratio (Voracek & Fisher, 2002). It is impossible to explain such cultural trends with confidence, but a plausible speculation is that with increases in women's rights and power in the United States has come a shift toward a more athletic, health-conscious ideal for women.

Cultures vary in the kind of ornamentation people use to enhance their attractiveness.

[From left to right: © Nigel Pavitt/JAI/Corbis; Angelo Giampiccolo/Shutterstock; Dan Kitwood/Getty Images; © Blend Images/Alamy]

Status and Access to Scarce Resources

One approach to understanding cultural variations in preferences is to note that attributes that are associated with having high status in a given culture are often seen as more attractive. Consider the current preference for tanning among Caucasian Americans. In days gone by, those lower in socioeconomic status worked outside as manual laborers. As a result, they tended to be more tanned than their financially well-off counterparts, and it seems, at least for the upper class, pale skin tones were culturally valued and considered attractive. But the Industrial Revolution and the consequent proliferation of factories changed those standards by moving many low-paying jobs indoors.

Think
ABOUT

[Alberto Zornetta/Shutterstock]

The result? Take a look at the two images of the young woman and think about which one you find more attractive. If you're like most people, you picked the one on the right.

Most people judging Caucasian individuals now consider tanned skin more attractive. This is what Chung and colleagues (2010) discovered when they manipulated the skin tones of women on the web site hotornot.com and had people rate the attractiveness of different faces. What about for judgments of African Americans? Evidence shows that lighter skin tones are considered more attractive than darker complexions (Frisby, 2006). This may help to explain why Caucasians frequent tanning salons as well as the push for skin-lightening products among darker-skinned minority groups.

And it's not just skin tone. Body size and weight are similarly influenced by cultural trends and values. In cultures and societies in which resources such as food are scarce, men tend to prefer heavier women, but in cultures and societies with an abundance of resources, men prefer thinner women (Anderson et al., 1992; Sobal & Stunkard, 1989). Conditions of scarcity or plenty thus influence what is desired.

Nelson and Morrison (2005) took the analysis one step further. They reasoned that not only would cultural and temporal trends in scarcity influence perceptions of attractiveness, but these influences might also operate differently depending on the situations people are in. To test this hypothesis, they asked people how much money they currently had in their pocket and later asked them to estimate the ideal body weight of an attractive opposite-sex person. When men had more cash on hand and they were reminded to make an estimate, they suggested that a really attractive woman would weigh about 125 pounds. But when they had less cash on hand and were reminded to make an estimate, they said she would weigh about 127 pounds. In a clever follow-up study, Nelson and Morrison interviewed participants either before they entered, or after they came out of, the dining hall at their university. Walking into the cafeteria and presumably hungry, men preferred women who weighed approximately 125.5 pounds. But after they had chowed down and were no longer hungry, their preferences were more in the ballpark of 123 pounds. So we see that for men, the current motivational state of having or not having resources influences what they consider an attractive body weight for women. This could reflect men's wanting what for the moment seems scarcer, or men's feeling more able to shoot for the thinner cultural ideal when they feel they have more resources.

One interesting finding was that across all of Nelson and Morrison's (2005) studies, women were not influenced by their own resources when judging the attractiveness of men. This might be because body weight is a less critical aspect of how women perceive male physical attractiveness, or because women are less influenced by situational factors when judging attractiveness.

Media Effects

Certainly the most ubiquitous situational influences on perceptions of attractiveness come from the mass media. Billboards, television shows, movies, magazines, and the Internet all routinely expose us to a seemingly endless parade of images of attractive people, especially women. In an interesting twist, women are less likely to be represented in some mass media such as feature films and television, but when they are, they are more likely to be physically attractive and dressed in revealing clothing (e.g., Smith et al., 2013). This leads to critical questions about what kinds of effects such exposure has both on how we view others and on how we view ourselves.

Back in 1980, people had no cable or satellite television or hundreds of channels, no DVRs, no shows streaming over the Internet—let alone handheld devices to watch them on. (Yes, it was a bleak time.) You watched what was on one of the three or four channels you could tune in. In 1980, one of the most popular TV shows was *Charlie's Angels*, which centered on the adventures of three very attractive, crime-solving women. It also formed the basis for a naturalistic study by Kenrick and Gutierres (1980). The researchers sent two confederates to the common TV areas in dorms (no, practically nobody had their own TVs in their rooms; as we said, a bleak time) either just before the show was scheduled to start or while the episode was on the air. Check out **FIGURE 14.7** for a transcript of what the confederates said to the groups of people who either were or were not watching *Charlie's Angels*. The short of it is that they had students rate the attractiveness of a purported blind date for one of their friends while those students were watching *Charlie's Angels* or while they were not watching the show. In what they coined "the Farrah factor" (after the most famous of the "angels," Farrah Fawcett), the researchers found that those watching *Charlie's Angels* rated the blind date as less physically attractive than did those not watching the show. Although this study was methodologically limited (note that participants were not randomly assigned to conditions of watching the show or not), subsequent studies using more tightly controlled laboratory procedures have replicated this effect (Kenrick et al., 1989).

Confederate A: Listen, could I just interrupt you guys for 30 seconds? We're having a major philosophical dispute here and we need to do an informal survey to resolve the question. You see, we have a friend coming to town this week and we want to fix him up with a date, but we can't decide whether to fix him up with her or not, so we decided to conduct a survey.

Confederate B: You see, I don't think she looks very good.

Confederate A: But I think she looks pretty good. At any rate, we want you to give us your vote on how attractive you think she is. (Confederate A begins to hold up the picture, but is faced away from the subjects so they can't see it).

Confederate B: Right, on a scale of 1 to 7, with 1 being very unattractive, 4 being exactly average, and 7 being beautiful.

Confederate A: (turns over photo) Now, nobody say anything until everyone makes up his own mind, and be honest—give your honest opinion.

Confederate B: Remember, 1 is very unattractive, 4 is right in the middle, and 7 is very attractive.

Figure 14.7

Angels?

When college students were asked to rate an average-looking woman, they rated her as less attractive if they had just been watching a television show featuring extremely attractive women.

[Research from: Kenrick et al. (1989)]

APPLICATION

Living Up to Unrealistic Ideals

The findings just mentioned imply that when we see mass media depictions of beauty, the people we encounter in everyday life can suffer by comparison. Indeed, after men looked at *Playboy* centerfolds, they tended to see typical women and even their own wives as less attractive (Kenrick et al., 1989). And it is not only men's perceptions that are affected; women's own self-perceived attractiveness also suffers (Thornton & Maurice, 1997). Mass media can be downright harmful to women's self-images.

The media's powerful effect on women's self-perceptions has spawned considerable research on the unhealthy consequences. A recent meta-analysis documented that at least 144 studies showed that media depictions of women—often falling under the rubric of the modern thin ideal we noted earlier—do indeed cause women to have problems coming to terms with their own body shapes and sizes, sometimes contributing to the development of serious eating disorders such as anorexia and bulimia (Grabe et al., 2008).

The emphasis on the thin ideal is one facet of the broader tendency to objectify women, which we discussed in chapter 11 (Fredrickson & Roberts, 1997). As part of the objectification of women—whereby women are socialized to see themselves as objects of often sexual utility—they are held to a ridiculously unrealistic standard of what constitutes beauty. Physical attractiveness, both in body shape and facial features, becomes equated with a woman's value as a person.

We refer to these standards as ridiculously unrealistic because even the people whose faces and figures appear on billboards, magazines, and movies cannot actually meet the standards of their media-fostered images. Widely used processes, such as body or body-part doubles in films, Photoshop manipulation, and graphical rearrangements, make even the "beautiful people" look more "beautiful" than they actually are. In 1990, Michelle Pfeiffer's face appeared on the cover of *Esquire* with the caption "What Michelle Pfeiffer needs . . . is absolutely nothing." It turned out that *Esquire* apparently felt that she needed over a thousand dollars' worth of photo alterations to make her image acceptably beautiful (DeVoss & Platt, n.d). Reports suggest that more recent subjects of elaborate Photoshopping include Jessica Alba, Mischa Barton, Anne Hathaway, Kiera Knightly, Kate Middleton, Katy Perry, Andy Roddick, Britney Spears, and Kate Winslet (Weber, n.d). Dove Soap's *Evolution* campaign video made the public aware that beauty standards are often unattainable fabrications (Dove, 2007). Check out the images in **FIGURE 14.8**. They reveal that not only are the model's hair and makeup meticulously styled but also that photo-editing software was used to raise her cheekbones, enlarge her eyes, and align her nose and ears to enhance her facial symmetry. Until young girls are no longer bombarded with extremely thin and otherwise unrealistic images of "beauty," the media will continue to contribute to body-image issues and the psychological and physical problems that result from them.

We can be thankful that some contemporary celebrities are beginning to resist these trends. Lena Dunham, Natalie Portman, Kelly Clarkson, Tyra Banks, Amy Poehler, Tina Fey, and Jennifer Lawrence are just a few of the famous women who

Figure 14.8

Evolution

Notice the progression in the model's unrealistic attractiveness as makeup and then various computer enhancements are applied.

[Dove (2007). *Evolution* (Television commercial). Toronto: Ogilvy & Mather]

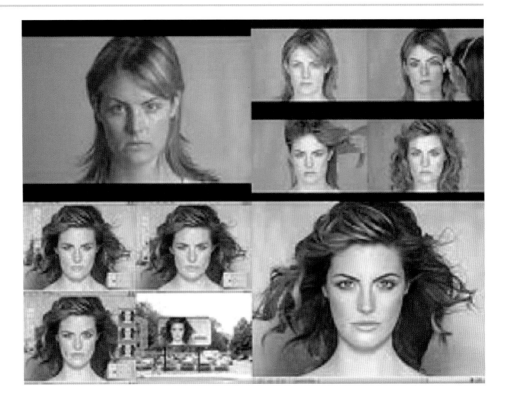

have spoken out against public and professional pressures to present an unrealistic ideal of women's bodies. Some organizations are putting these principles into policy. In France, Great Britain, and Norway, for example, proposals are being considered to label any image that has been digitally altered (Lohr, 2011).

Is Appearance Destiny?

Over 2,000 years ago, the Roman statesman Cicero (45 BC/1883) advised, "The final good and supreme duty of the wise person is to resist appearance." If that is so, wisdom has come to our species rather slowly if at all. So far in this chapter we have dwelled on the fact that physical attractiveness is a major factor in how people evaluate potential mates. However, despite certain universal standards and the genetic basis of many of our physical features, people's perceived attractiveness is not locked in stone at birth. Standards of physical beauty change over time and place. In addition, people often become more or less attractive as they age. Indeed, some research suggests that someone's perceived attractiveness at age 17 does not predict the same person's perceived attractiveness at ages 30 and 50 (Zebrowitz, 1997).

Finally, even though some physical attributes are considered universally attractive, experience with a person can also elevate his or her beauty. Research clearly shows that people who are viewed positively or as familiar and who are liked or loved are all rated by perceivers to be more physically attractive (e.g., Gross & Crofton, 1977; Lewandowski et al., 2007; Price & Vandenberg, 1979). And the happier a couple is with their relationship, the more physically attractive they view each other as being (Murray & Holmes, 1997).

SECTION review | Physical Attractiveness

Research reveals the importance of physical attractiveness, what people find physically attractive (and why), and the consequences for relationships.

The importance of physical attractiveness	Common denominators of attractive faces	Gender differences in what is attractive	Cultural and situational factors	Is appearance destiny?
• Sexual and aesthetic appeal do predict liking. • Association with attractive people can bolster self-esteem. • Attractive people are stereotyped to have positive traits.	Composite and symmetrical faces are rated as more attractive, perhaps as a reflection of good health or because they seem familiar.	• Men universally prefer a waist-to-hip ratio that suggests fertility. • At times of peak fertility, women seem to be more attracted to more masculine faces. • Men report an ideal preference for attractiveness and women an ideal preference for social and financial status. • In actual relationships, men and women are equally influenced by physical attractiveness and, to a lesser extent, partner status. • Women's stated preference for higher-status men might also be changing as women achieve greater equality. • Both men and women rank warmth and loyalty above all other factors.	• Standards of beauty vary across cultures and over time. • Scarcity and status influence trends. • Mass media have been influential in creating impossible standards of beauty that may be hurtful to self-image, especially for women.	• Attractiveness can change across time and place. • People can control their perceived attractiveness by being positive in expression and behavior.

The following scene from the movie *Annie Hall* (Joffe et al., 1977) satirizes how men and women can view sex differently.

[*Alvy and Annie are seeing their therapists at the same time on a split screen*]

Alvy Singer's Therapist: How often do you sleep together?

Annie Hall's Therapist: Do you have sex often?

Alvy Singer [*lamenting*]: Hardly ever. Maybe three times a week.

Annie Hall [*annoyed*]: Constantly. I'd say three times a week.

[United Artists/Photofest]

Gender Differences in Sexual Attitudes and Behaviors

We've seen how men and women sometimes differ in what they find attractive. It turns out they differ in attitudes and behavior regarding sex as well. Most of us are familiar with the common stereotypes: Men, it is often said, want sex all the time, whereas women typically play the role of gatekeeper, deciding if and when sex begins in a relationship. Is there some truth to these stereotypes? Although there is important variation within each gender, many findings support the idea that, compared with women, men have more permissive attitudes about sexuality in and out of relationships:

- Men are much more likely than women to say that they would enjoy casual sex outside the context of a committed relationship, whereas women prefer to engage in sexual activities as part of an emotionally intimate relationship (Hendrick et al., 2006; Oliver & Hyde, 1993; Ostovich & Sabini, 2004).

- If you ask teenagers how they feel about having sex for the first time, most of the young men cannot wait to lose their virginity, and only one third of them view the prospect with a mix of positive and negative feelings. Young women have a different view: Most are ambivalent about having sex, some are opposed, and only a third of them are looking forward to their first experience of sex (Abma et al., 2004).

- If you went on a date with someone and *didn't* have sex, would you regret it? Men report regretting not pursuing a sexual opportunity much more often than women do (Roese et al., 2006).

- Once in a romantic relationship, men want to begin having sex sooner than women do, they want sex more often, and they are more likely to express dissatisfaction with the amount of sex they have (Sprecher, 2002).

The differences between men and women go beyond what they say. When we look at what people are actually doing, men on average have higher sex drives than women do:

- Men experience sexual desire more frequently and intensely than do women, and they are more motivated to seek out sexual activity (Vohs et al., 2004). Young men experience sexual desire on average 37 times per week, whereas women experience sexual desire only about 9 times per week (Regan & Atkins, 2006). Men also spend more time fantasizing about sex than women do: Sex crosses men's minds about 60 times per week; for women, only about 15 times (Leitenberg & Henning, 1995; Regan & Atkins, 2006).

- Men spend more money on sex. Not only do men spend a lot of money on sexual toys and pornography (Laumann et al., 2004), men are much more likely than women to pay for sex. One study found that, among Australians, 23 percent of men said that they paid for sex at least once, but almost none of the women had (Pitts et al., 2004).

- Men masturbate more frequently than women do (Oliver & Hyde, 1993). Among people who have a regular sexual partner, about half of the men still masturbate more than once a week, whereas only 16 percent of women pleasure themselves as frequently (Klusmann, 2002).

- Men are more likely to be sexually unfaithful to their romantic partners. Although most husbands and wives never have sex with someone other than their partner after they marry, about one out of every three husbands, compared with only one out of five wives, has an extramarital affair (Tafoya & Spitzberg, 2007).

- Where polygamy is practiced, such as in some African cultures, it is almost always men who have the multiple spouses (Zeitzen, 2008).

These and other facts paint a pretty clear picture: On average, men are more sex driven than women, and are interested in more frequent sex with more partners. A big question, of course, is why these differences exist.

An Evolutionary Perspective

Evolutionary psychology gives us one way to understand these sex differences. Robert Trivers (1972) proposed that reproductive success means different things to men and women because the sexes differ in their inherent **parental investment**, that is, the time and effort that they necessarily have to invest in each child they produce. Men's parental investment can be relatively low. If a man has sex with 100 different women in a year, he can, in theory, father as many as 100 children with little more time and effort than it takes to ejaculate. Women have a much higher level of parental investment. The number of children they can bear and raise in a lifetime is limited, and they have to commit enormous time and energy to each child lest it die before reaching maturity.

Trivers argued that because men and women differ in the necessity of their parental investment, they evolved to have different **mating strategies**, or overall approaches to mating, that helped them to reproduce successfully (Buss, 2003; Geary, 2010). For men, there may be some benefit to a mating strategy of pursuing every available sexual opportunity and to focus more on a *short-term mating strategy*. If a man mates with as many women as possible in short-term relationships, he probably won't be able to provide high-quality parenting to every child he fathers, and so many of those children will not thrive as well as they would with high investment from both parents (Allen & Daly, 2007). But what a man lacks in parental quality he might make up in sheer quantity: Chances are that at least some of those children will survive to propagate the man's genes.

Women, in contrast, would get no reproductive benefit from being highly promiscuous. If they flitted from partner to partner, mating indiscriminately, they would not be able to produce any more children than they would by having sex with only one fertile man for a lifetime. Instead, women would benefit from a mating strategy of choosing their mates carefully, seeking out partners with good genes who would contribute resources to protect and feed their offspring. In other words, women might prefer a *long-term mating strategy*.

This evolutionary perspective could explain many of the systematic gender differences in sexual attitudes and behavior that we listed above. Given the evolutionary explanation, it is not surprising that men all over the world show a greater desire than women for brief affairs with a variety of partners, and that when they enter a new romantic relationship, they are more eager than women to jump in the sack (Schmitt, 2005). What's more, women are indeed more careful and deliberate than men in their choice of sexual partners. They are less interested than men are in casual, uncommitted sex (Gangestad & Simpson, 1990). They will not have sex with a partner unless he meets a fairly high bar of intelligence, friendliness, prestige, and emotional security, whereas men set the bar much lower for the personal qualities they demand in a potential sexual partner (Kenrick et al., 1990).

It is important to note, however, that the evolutionary perspective does not imply that men and women employ a single mating strategy across all situations and periods in their lives, or, for that matter, that all men and women will employ the same strategy. For one thing, the mating strategies that men and women adopt depend on whether they are looking for a short-term fling or a long-term partnership (Buss & Schmitt, 1993). For example, when men are in the market for a short-term partner—someone with whom to have a casual sexual encounter—they adjust their radar to look for women who appear sexually available, or "easy" (Schmitt et al., 2001). But men do not always act like dogs on the hunt for promiscuous women. When they are looking for a longer, more committed relationship, they seek out women who appear chaste (Buss, 2000).

It is also important to emphasize that any strategy has its costs and benefits. The social, cultural, and physical environment can alter the way these balance out (Geary, 2010). Some of these trade-offs are listed in Table 14.1.

Parental investment The time and effort that parents must invest in each child they produce.

Mating strategies Approaches to mating that help people reproduce successfully. People prefer different mating strategies depending on whether they are thinking about a short-term pairing or a long-term commitment.

Evolutionary Psychology
Video on LaunchPad

Table 14.1 **Examples of Costs and Benefits of Short-Term and Long-Term Sexual Relationships**

Costs	Benefits
Women's short-term mating	
Risk of disease Risk of pregnancy Reduced value as a long-term mate	Some resources from mate Good genes from mate
Women's long-term mating	
Restricted sexual opportunity Sexual obligation to mate	Significant resources from mate Paternal investment
Men's short-term mating	
Risk of disease Some resource investment	Potential to reproduce No parental investment
Men's long-term mating	
Restricted sexual opportunity Heavy parental investment Heavy relationship investment	Increased paternal certainty Higher-quality children Sexual and social companionship

[Research from: Geary (2010)]

Thus, even if certain mating strategies were adaptive in our distant evolutionary past, they should not be viewed as natural or preferable ways to act. For example, although mating with as many women as possible brings a man some elements of advantage, it also brings potential costs: conflict with and violent reactions by other men in the man's vicinity; development of a negative reputation among women in the vicinity; and lack of contribution to the survival of the children he does father. All of these factors would favor a more monogamous approach. In certain contexts, then—such as where the sex ratio is male dominated, or where infant mortality is a particular concern—men may benefit more from greater monogamy and parental investment (e.g., Pollet & Nettle, 2008). Thus, David Geary (2010) suggests that one way to think about it is that biology and evolutionary pressures may create an ideal preference (i.e., for men to have sex with as many attractive women as possible and for women to selectively choose high-investment men), but the actual strategy is informed by cultural and social contexts. The challenge for research, then, is to be able to specify which social and cultural factors interact with generalized preferences for evolved mating strategies.

Consider today's modern world. Do you think these strategies would be advantageous in the contemporary mating landscape? In the modern environment we inhabit now, male promiscuity and female chastity might not necessarily help people reproduce more effectively. For one thing, many women now use birth control to prevent fertility. Also, many casual sexual encounters involve the use of prophylactics to prevent the spread of sexually transmitted diseases (as well as pregnancy). In fact, in this environment, men might be able to reproduce more successfully if, instead of pursuing multiple partners, they consistently showed love and commitment to one partner and increased their parental investment. Geary (2010) notes, for example, that humans are quite different from nearly all other mammals in the relatively high degree of involvement that fathers have in child rearing. Furthermore, as women gain more equal footing with men in terms of economic and social power, and because technology has potentially reduced the burdens of infant care (e.g., formula as a substitute for breast milk, the ability to pump and store breast milk), women may benefit from a less selective approach (Schmitt, 2005). These are just a few of the cultural factors influencing people's views of sex and their sexual behavior. Next we briefly consider additional factors that play a role in sexual attitudes and behavior.

Cultural Influences

It is important to recognize that although sex obviously serves the biological function of reproduction, many psychological motives influence people's decisions to have sex. When college students were asked to list all of the reasons why they or someone they know had recently engaged in sexual intercourse, they mentioned 237 reasons (Meston & Buss, 2007). Most of these reasons had to do with seeking positive states such as pleasure, affection, love, emotional closeness, adventure, and excitement. Students also mentioned more calculating and callous reasons, albeit less frequently. Some used sex as a way to aggress against someone ("I was mad at my partner, so I had sex with someone else"), to gain some advantage ("I wanted a raise"), or to enhance their social status ("I wanted to impress my friends").

Lynne Cooper and colleagues (1998) have shown that many of these reasons for sex boil down to five core motives. Specifically, she finds that the among both college-student and community samples, the most frequently endorsed motives for sex are (in descending order) to enhance physical or emotional pleasure, to foster intimacy, to affirm one's sense of self-worth, to cope with negative emotions, and to gain partner or peer approval. A number of factors can influence which motive tends to affect sexual behavior.

Whether a person has sex is influenced by the prevailing cultural norms about what is and what is not permissible. Whether you are a man or a woman, you probably are more accepting of premarital sexual intercourse than your grandparents were. Sixty or so years ago, most Americans disapproved of sex before marriage; these days, fewer than a third of Americans think that premarital sex is wrong (Wells & Twenge, 2005; Willetts et al., 2004). At the same time, most people generally disapprove of sex between unmarried partners who are not emotionally committed to each other, and they look more favorably on sexually active partners who are in a "serious" rather than a "casual" relationship (Bettor et al., 1995; Willetts et al., 2004). In short, although people today generally are not expected to "save themselves for marriage" in the same way that your grandparents were expected to do, most of us still believe that sex outside of marriage is more acceptable if it occurs in the context of a committed, affectionate relationship (Sprecher et al., 2006).

These changes in norms over the past few decades are also reflected in people's sexual behavior. In today's United States, by the age of 44, almost everyone—95 percent of the population—has had sexual intercourse before marriage (Finer, 2007). Although on average American men and women do not marry until their mid- to late 20s, they usually have sex for the first time around the age of 17. In fact, by the time Americans reach 20 years of age, only 15 percent have not yet had sex (Fryar et al., 2007). These are very different patterns than those researchers see in the first half of the twentieth century. Most people back then waited two to three years longer to begin having sex (Wells & Twenge, 2005).

Cultural norms influence not only whether people engage in sex, but how comfortable they feel about *reporting* permissive sexual attitudes and behavior. Consider this puzzle: The average middle-aged man reports that he has had seven sexual partners during his lifetime, whereas the average woman has had only four (Fryar et al., 2007). Shouldn't these numbers be the same (given the survey's focus on heterosexual encounters)? If a partner is required for sex, it would seem that each time a man engages in heterosexual sex, his female partner does, too. There are several possible explanations for this common sex difference. For example, men are more likely than women to have sex with prostitutes, but prostitutes rarely respond to these surveys. Also, men and women tend to hold different definitions of what constitutes "sex." For example, in heterosexual couples, men are more likely than women to say that oral sex qualifies as sex (Sanders & Reinisch, 1999).

But another explanation is that men tend to exaggerate the number of partners they've been with, whereas women tend to minimize that number (Willetts et al., 2004). When men are asked about their number of partners, they tend to estimate the number rather than counting diligently, and when in doubt, they round up. As a result, they almost always report round numbers, such as 10 or 30, and almost never provide seemingly exact counts such as 14 or 27 (Brown & Sinclair, 1999). Women, on the other hand, respond to researchers' inquiries into their sex lives by counting their partners more accurately and then fudging by subtracting a partner or two from their reported total (Wiederman, 2004).

How do we know that norms play a role in men's and women's biased reporting? You might expect that if, for impression-management purposes, men exaggerate their numbers to appear like studs, and women downplay their numbers to appear chaste, then the difference between men and women would be especially pronounced if men and women were told that an experimenter would view their responses. That is exactly what a study by Alexander and Fisher (2003) found. But this study produced an even more interesting result: If men and women were put into a "bogus pipeline" condition in which they were led to believe that lying could be detected, sex differences in reported sexual behavior were almost nonexistent. So here we clearly see that cultural gender norms influence not only people's sexual behavior but also their willingness to report on it.

More generally, cultures vary in the permissiveness of their attitudes regarding sex, presumably as a result of particular historical, political, and religious influences. Americans have more conservative sexual attitudes than people in many other technologically advanced countries (Widmer et al., 1998). For example, when asked about their attitudes about sex before marriage, sex before age 16, extramarital sex, and same-sex relations, Americans are stricter than respondents in a variety of other countries, as Table 14.2 shows.

One general point to take from all this is that although some of the reasons people pursue sex certainly involve biological tendencies toward pleasure seeking and reproduction, many others reflect how a person is shaped by, and interacts with, his or her social and cultural environment.

Your Cheating Heart: Reactions to Infidelity

Let's do a little thought experiment, shall we? Imagine you are in a committed relationship with someone whom you love very deeply. If you are lucky, maybe you already are there, and not much imagination is required. Now imagine that you learn that your partner has been carrying on secretly with another person. In one version of this dark scenario, you learn that the affair is about wild, passionate sex. In an alternative version, it is about a deep emotional attachment. If you were forced to choose between these two tragic turns in your relationship, which would seem to be the lesser of two evils?

Early Research

When researchers first examined how people react to infidelity, they found evidence of a significant difference between men and women. In an early set of studies, 49% of men but only 19% of women said they would be more upset if they caught their partner sleeping around than if their partner had fallen for another person (Buss et al., 1992). Of course, this means that 81% of women, compared with only 51% of men, said they would be more bothered by learning that their partner had fallen in love with someone else. Do men and women really have such different views of disloyalty? If so, why? The next two decades of research sought to answer these two questions.

Table 14.2 **Attitudes Toward Various Sexual Practices by Country**

| Countries | Percentage of Respondents Who Felt This Type of Sex Was Always Wrong | | | |
	Sex before marriage	Sex before Age 16	Extramarital sex	Same-sex relations
Australia	13%	61%	59%	55%
Canada	12	55	68	39
Germany	5	34	55	42
Great Britain	12	67	67	58
Israel	19	67	73	57
Japan	19	60	58	65
Netherlands	7	45	63	19
Russia	13	45	36	57
Spain	20	59	76	45
Sweden	4	32	68	56
USA	29	71	80	70

[Data source: Widmer et al. (1998)]

Despite humans' monogamous tendencies, cases of infidelity in committed couples do occur with some frequency, as previously noted (Tafoya & Spitzberg, 2007). From an evolutionary standpoint, people have a lot to lose from their partner's extrarelational affairs. The emotion of jealousy might have evolved to be an affective warning light signaling our partner's real or imagined indiscretions. Jealousy might cue us to be alert to possible rivals who could catch our partner's eye and woo him or her away (Buss, 2000). But an evolutionary perspective claims that infidelity carries different meanings for men and women because it differentially affected their ability to reproduce.

Of course, marriages do happen and men stay around to change diapers, attend dance recitals, and coach little Susie's soccer league. These monogamous tendencies are thought to have evolved, and led to cultural rituals that sanction them, because there was an adaptive advantage to having the proud papa available to provide resources, protection, and a role model for developing kids (Geary, 2010). Romantic attachments provide the emotional glue to bond couples together. From this theory of evolved cost-benefit analysis, women could have evolved a greater sensitivity than men to any suggestion of that emotional bond's dissipating, and their partners' leaving them with the burden of child rearing. For a man, **mate guarding** would have served the propagation of his genes by keeping his mate from cheating on him, leading to a situation in which he expended a lot of resources raising some other man's offspring. Thus women may have evolved to experience jealousy primarily in response to emotional infidelity, whereas men may have evolved to experience jealousy primarily in response to sexual infidelity.

Mate guarding The process of preventing others from mating with one's partner in order to avoid the costs of rearing offspring that do not help to propagate one's genes.

Modern Perspectives

This evolutionary argument for gender differences in jealousy fits the findings of those early studies, but theorists soon raised questions both about the data themselves as well as the conclusions that might be drawn from them. Some research fits the original view. Some does not.

First, following up on Buss's original research, studies have replicated his pattern of sex differences. Men's greater worry over sexual infidelity and women's greater concern with emotional infidelity have been found across cultures (Buss et al., 1999; Buunk et al., 1996; Geary et al., 1995) and also show up when people consider online relationships (Groothof et al., 2009). A meta-analysis of studies that have presented participants with the choice between sexual and emotional infidelity shows this sex difference to be of moderate size, although stronger among college-age, heterosexual participants (Harris, 2003). The sex difference goes beyond what people say. When male and female college students imagined these two types of infidelity, their bodies reacted somewhat differently

Human Attraction in *Best in Show*

At first glance, the movie *Best in Show* (2000) might seem like an odd choice for a discussion of human attraction. What does a mockumentary about a dog show have to do with how people partner up? But on closer inspection, it provides the perfect satirical account of the various factors that attract people to one another. The movie (directed by Christopher Guest) follows the trials and tribulations of several dogs on their journey toward the title Best in Show at the annual Mayflower Kennel Club Dog Show. But the movie really centers around the owners of these dogs and their quirky personalities and relationships.

As the movie begins, we get to know each set of dog owners in an interview-type format typical of true documentaries. Many of these introductions involve a brief retelling of how the couple met, and it is in these brief scenes that we see various patterns of attraction on display. The couples are as different as the breeds of dogs represented in the show, and their stories reflect many of the themes discussed throughout this chapter.

One couple's story shows the importance of *propinquity*. Hamilton and Meg Swan met at Starbucks. Not at the same Starbucks, mind you, but at two different Starbucks that were just across the street from each other. After noticing each other, they soon realized that their shared yuppie interests extended far beyond soy chai lattes to Apple computers and J. Crew. Clearly these two thirtysomethings are meant for each other! Or at least, they have similar attitudes. Unfortunately, as we get to know Hamilton and Meg a bit more, we learn that they also

share a tendency to crack under pressure. One gets the sense that this shared disposition for being hot tempered is bound to do this couple in eventually. When their Weimeraner's favorite squeaky toy goes missing, their frantic search for it leads to an early disqualification from the competition.

Another couple, Leslie and Sherri Ann Cabot, pushes evolutionary theorizing on sex differences in *mating strategies* to its limits. Leslie is ancient but very wealthy. Sherri Ann is much younger and obviously spends a lot of time on her appearance. But in their interview (during which he merely blankly gums his dentureless mouth), she insists that what really makes their relationship work is his very high sex drive and all the interests they have in common: "We both love soup. We love the outdoors. We love snow peas. And, uh, talking and not talking. We could not talk or talk forever and still find things to not talk about."

But as the movie continues, it's clear that their relationship contains no true attraction. Instead, Sherri Ann is having an affair with her dog's handler, Christy. When Sherri Ann and Christy discuss their relationship to each other and to their poodle, Rhapsody in White, we see that they are attracted by complementary characteristics—reflecting the idea that "opposites attract" (see text for more discussion). Sherri Ann, who generally seems to need someone else to be in charge, describes Christy as the disciplinarian. Christy, on the other hand, values Sherri Ann's tendency to provide unconditional love, just as her mother had (note the effect of *transference*).

The one couple whose source of attraction to each other is the most difficult to identify is Jerry and Cookie Fleck. Cookie is an energetic and not unattractive middle-aged woman who spent the earlier years of her adult life pursing what we've labeled a short-term mating strategy of having many, many one-night stands. Throughout the movie, she repeatedly runs depending on their gender. Male participants imagining their partners sexually cheating on them had elevated skin conductance, indicative of an increased sympathetic response of the fight-or-flight type. Women showed higher levels of skin conductance when imagining that their partners had become emotionally attached to someone else (Buss et al., 1992).

The story might have ended here, with the field concluding that we have an evolved tendency to feel jealous and that these mental modules of jealousy are distinct for men and women. However, other researchers have had problems with this interpretation and the data on which it has relied. One argument is that the existence of these sex differences actually has been overstated (Harris, 2003). Forcing people to choose between a love affair and a lustful liaison is a rather contrived scenario, a bit like asking whether someone would prefer a kick in the head or a punch in the stomach. Neither is particularly desirable, and by focusing on sex differences in preferring one choice over the other, we might be ignoring a rather obvious but important point: that both sexes would experience jealousy in either

into old flames, which only ignites feelings of jealousy in her husband, Jerry. And Jerry, it must be said, is neither highly attractive nor financially secure. In fact, he literally has two left feet, a cinematic device that could hardly scream "Hey, I'm asymmetrical" any louder. So what does this woman who had "hundreds of boyfriends" in her past see in this man, whose nickname used to be Loopy because his two left feet made him always walk in circles? It can only be their shared love for their pooch, little Winky, who is the underdog (no pun intended) contender for the title of Best in Show.

It's unclear whether Christopher Guest and Eugene Levy, who cowrote the screenplay, intended to convey any broad messages about human attraction. But somehow each of these couples found each other, partnered up, and have remained together through various hardships. One does get the sense, however, that it might be the shared love of dogs and the dog-show lifestyle that really sustains these relationships, whereas other sources of attraction were only fleeting factors that initially brought them together. Dog shows themselves feature a rather odd obsession with finding the dog that is the best genetic specimen of its breed. But although no one in this quirky cast of characters fits anyone's ideal notion of a partner, they all manage in the end to find some degree of happiness with each other.

[Warner Bros./Photofest]

[Warner Bros./Photofest]

case. When people are asked about each kind of infidelity independently rather than being forced to choose between one or the other, the normally observed sex difference seems to disappear (DeSteno & Salovey, 1996; Harris, 2003; Sagarin et al., 2003).

Other methodological aspects of the original studies have been questioned. For example, studies of actual infidelity rather than imagined infidelity sometimes replicate the sex difference, but not always (Edlund et al., 2006; Harris, 2002). It also might be difficult to draw conclusions about the greater sympathetic activation when men imagine sexual versus emotional infidelity. It turns out that men generally show greater sympathetic activation when imagining their partner having sex instead of becoming emotionally attached, regardless of whether this imagined relationship is actually with themselves instead of with someone else (Harris, 2000). These critiques of the methods used in the original studies have led some researchers to question how large or meaningful this purported sex difference really is.

If we do accept that men tend to bristle at a wife's one-night stand, whereas women fret that a husband is confiding his deepest feelings to a secret pen pal, controversy also arises over how to explain this difference. Perhaps these differences are more a function of cultural learning than evolved propensities. For example, women tend to assume that a man in love will also be having sex, whereas men assume that a woman having sex will also be in love (DeSteno & Salovey, 1996; Harris & Christenfeld, 1996). So women might be more bothered than men by emotional infidelity because they are more likely to assume that their partner has or is very likely to consummate the affair (DeSteno et al., 2002).

Another culturally based argument is that men derive more self-esteem from their sex lives than women do, whereas women derive more self-esteem from being emotionally bonded to a partner than men do (Goldenberg et al., 2003). Therefore, it's no surprise that a partner's emotional disloyalty would trigger greater self-esteem concerns for women, whereas a partner's sexual disloyalty would trigger greater self-esteem concerns for men. For example, when participants are asked to think about death, a condition known to elevate efforts to defend self-esteem, men become even more threatened by imagining their partner sleeping with someone else, whereas women become even more threatened by imagining their partner falling in love with someone else. In further support of a self-esteem-based argument, research that actually induces jealousy in the laboratory (as opposed to measuring it by having participants imagine hypothetical scenarios) finds that situations that increase jealousy do so by threatening self-esteem (DeSteno et al., 2006). For example, seeing a desirable person choose to work with someone else decreases a person's self-esteem. This decrease in self-esteem fuels increases in jealousy.

A third critique is that certain aspects of the data just don't seem to fit with an evolutionary account. For example, if differences in jealous reactions truly are sex linked, then gay men should show the same patterns of response found in straight men—they simply desire partners of their same sex (Symons, 1979). This does not appear to be the case. In a study of both gay and straight men and women, straight men reported greater relative concern about sexual than about emotional infidelity, but gay men did not. In addition, every group reported greater concerns about emotional infidelity. When asked to recollect a time when a partner actually cheated on them, people were more upset about the emotional rather than the sexual aspects of the affair (Harris, 2002). In fact, most studies using the "choose your infidelity" method find that the percentage of men (typically straight) who say they would be more bothered by sexual infidelity is at or near 50%. If a sex-specific mechanism had evolved such that men could detect and react to sexual infidelity in their mates, perhaps we would expect men's aversion to sexual infidelity to be stronger than a coin toss (DeSteno & Salovey, 1996).

Final Thoughts

In sum, the evolutionary account offers a provocative explanation of gender differences in jealousy, but different studies point to other explanations for when and why men and women feel jealous. As scientists continue to examine these processes, we think it is important to get some perspective on these debates. On the one hand, there is general agreement that our current psychology is influenced by our evolutionary past, but that rarely if ever means any particular propensity is rigidly determined by it. If you think about the differences between men and women as a pie, one slice of that pie is our evolved tendencies. Another slice might be cultural upbringing. Yet other slices might be gender differences in other relevant personality traits or the person's experiences in the immediate social context. The argument about men's and women's jealousies might be framed better as what kinds of explanations are the bigger pieces of the pie, not whether the entire pie belongs to evolution or to culture. Maybe the biggest lesson we learn from this line of research is that even scientists get jealous if they worry that a single explanation is getting more than its fair share of attention.

Regarding the sex-difference issue, it is also worth noting that research finds that both men and women report feeling angry when they think about a partner sleeping with someone else, but feel sad and hurt if they imagine their partner having an emotional connection with someone else (Green & Sabini, 2006; Sabini & Green, 2004). One explanation for these reactions is that we all get angry when someone fails to control his or her impulses, but we feel a sense of loss if we imagine that our partner could leave us for another.

SECTION review | Gender Differences in Sexual Attitudes and Behaviors

Men and women differ in behavior and attitudes toward sex. Explaining those differences requires a diversity of perspectives.

The evolutionary perspective	Cultural influences	Men, women, and infidelity
Men's attitudes reflect the reproductive advantages of mating with multiple women, while women's attitudes reflect the need to find one mate to help support child rearing.	Cultural norms also affect attitudes, as evidenced by the change in acceptance of premarital sex across generations as well as among cultures.	• There is some evidence that men and women view infidelity from different perspectives. • Researchers debate the relative role of evolution and culture in creating these differences.

CONNECT ONLINE:

Macmillan Education
LaunchPad

Check out our videos and additional resources located at:
www.macmillanhighered.com/launchpad/greenberg1e

Close Relationships

TOPIC OVERVIEW

Relationships come in all shapes and sizes, including casual acquaintanceships, life partners, and what can only be described using the label "It's complicated," popularized by Facebook. This chapter focuses on the world of close relationships: friendships, romantic relationships, love, sex, and marriage. We will first consider the value of close relationships. Then we will examine the nature and functions of love and consider basic models of romantic relationships and the roles of interdependency and commitment in both romantic relationships and friendships. We will then conclude this chapter, and indeed this book, by considering the time course of romantic relationships, sources of problems in romantic relationships, relationship dissolution, and strategies for optimizing satisfaction and longevity in relationships.

What Makes Close Relationships Special

We all have a sense that close relationships are different from our casual interactions with strangers and acquaintances, but what exactly makes them special? According to both scholars and laypersons, closeness involves six components: *knowledge,*

[Ira Block/National Geographic/Getty Images]

caring, interdependence, mutuality, trust, and *commitment* (Laurenceau et al., 2004; Marston et al., 1998; Parks & Floyd, 1996). Let's look at each of these.

People in close relationships *know* a lot about each other, and they are comfortable sharing intimate, often confidential, information about their personal histories, feelings, and desires that they do not typically share with casual acquaintances. They also feel more *care* or affection for one another than they do for most others. The closer people are, the more they experience **interdependence**: What each person does significantly influences what the other person does over long periods of time (Berscheid et al., 2004). Close relationships are also characterized by a high degree of **mutuality**: Partners acknowledge that their lives are intertwined, and they think of themselves as a couple ("us") instead of two separate individuals ("me" and "you") (Fitzsimons & Kay, 2004; Levinger & Snoek, 1972). People in close relationships also *trust* each other, meaning that they expect their partners to treat them with fairness, to be responsive to their needs, and not to cause them unnecessary harm (Reis et al., 2004; Simpson, 2007). Finally, closeness is defined by a high degree of **commitment**, meaning that partners invest time, effort, and resources in their relationship with the expectation that it will continue indefinitely.

Relationships that include all six of these components are the most satisfying and feel the closest to us. Nevertheless, closeness can exist to varying degrees when only some of these components are present. For instance, roommates who frequently influence each other (interdependence) and treat each other fairly (trust) are likely to feel closer to each other than they do to acquaintances, but not as close as they feel in relationships that include more components.

Parasocial Relationships

Breaking down closeness into these components helps us to understand a curious but common phenomenon: People can feel surprisingly close to others whom they've never met face to face, and even to others who do not exist outside the world of fiction. We're referring, of course, to people's relationships with those in the media: celebrities, television characters, talk-show hosts, athletes, and fictional characters in soap operas and novels. These are called **parasocial relationships** (Horton & Wohl, 1956). Unlike real close relationships with people we know personally, parasocial relationships lack interdependency: Media personalities influence fans' lives, but fans do not normally influence the personalities' lives (aside from funding their commercial projects). Nevertheless, parasocial relationships usually include three components of closeness: Fans believe that they *know* the media personalities, they *care* what happens to them, and they are *committed* to following and supporting them.

Because parasocial relationships involve some components of closeness, we can understand why they are so important and satisfying for many people. In fact, people report turning to their favorite television programs when they feel lonely. Merely bringing to mind a favorite television program buffers people from feeling rejected when their real relationships are threatened (Derrick et al., 2009). What's more, a parasocial breakup, such as when a favorite television character is killed off or otherwise taken off the air, can be as emotionally distressing as that of a real relationship (Cohen, 2004; Giles, 2002).

And as some celebrities know too well, parasocial relationships have led some mentally unstable fans to stalking and even worse. For example, in chapter 12, we described how John Hinckley, Jr. became obsessed with and a stalker of Jodie Foster.

Of course, despite the importance that some people place on parasocial relationships, most close relationships involve real people interacting with each other. And so it is not surprising that theory and research in social psychology focus on real close relationships.

Interdependence Situation in which what each person does significantly influences what the partner does over long periods of time.

Mutuality Partners' acknowledgment that their lives are intertwined and that they think of themselves as a couple ("us") instead of as two separate individuals ("me" and "you").

Commitment Partners' investment of time, effort, and resources in their relationship with the expectation that it will continue indefinitely.

Parasocial relationships Individuals' relationships with people in the media: celebrities, television characters, and athletes.

Parasocial relationships with celebrities such as Angelina Jolie can include some core components of closeness, but usually lack interdependence.

[Yoshikazu Tsuno/AFP/Getty Images]

Why Are Close Relationships So Important?

Because close relationships involve a high degree of care, interdependency, and commitment, they can be very demanding. Your friends, family members, and romantic partners all expect you to respond to their needs in various ways, and often that means sacrificing your desires, your freedom, and even some of your aspirations. Also, as we all know, close relationships can be the source of extreme stress, frustration, and emotional pain. So why bother with them? To put the question another way: Why do people care so deeply about forming and maintaining close relationships, given how costly they can be?

One rather obvious answer to this question is that, despite their potential costs, close relationships have many *practical benefits*, meaning that they facilitate our day-to-day activities. They allow us to pool resources and share labor. For example, while your current author sits at home writing this chapter, my partner is braving the snow to pick up groceries, thus saving me time and effort and bringing me food: Relationships *rule*! Also, when we are distressed because we face a problem that is difficult to understand, others can provide much-needed advice and consolation. Indeed, when people are in situations in which something threatening is about to happen (e.g., electric shocks), they are especially desirous of contact with others, particularly those who are facing a similar threat (Schachter, 1959) or, even more so, who have already dealt with it (Kulik et al., 1994).

But pointing out practical benefits takes us only so far in explaining why people care about their close relationships. To see why, imagine that a devious genie appears and offers you a team of personal assistants devoted to satisfying all your tangible needs—the kind of care you currently get from your friends, family members, and romantic partners. *But* this will happen only on the condition that for the rest of your life you will never have a close, intimate connection with someone. Would you accept the offer? Most of us wouldn't choose such a carefree but solitary life. People want—indeed *need*—love in their lives. Why is that?

SECTION review | What Makes Close Relationships Special

Closeness in relationships involves knowledge, caring, interdependence, mutuality, trust, and commitment.

Closeness in relationships	Parasocial relationships	The importance of close relationships
Relationships feel the closest when they include all six components, but they can exist to varying degrees when only some are in place.	Parasocial relationships are those in which, for example, fans feel close to a fictional character or media personality.	• Relationships have practical benefits, such as sharing responsibilities. • They also are the basis of emotional support.

This Thing Called Love

To this crib I always took my doll; human beings must love something, and, in the dearth of worthier objects of affection, I contrived to find a pleasure in loving and cherishing a faded graven image, shabby as a miniature scarecrow.

—Charlotte Brontë, *Jane Eyre* (1847/1992, p. 27)

The British novelist Charlotte Brontë captured a basic truth not only about humans but about other primates as well. Over a hundred years later, the comparative psychologist Harry Harlow discovered that when he separated infant monkeys from their moms and put them in cages by themselves, they became intensely attached to cheesecloth baby blankets he included in their cages; when the blankets were removed for laundering, the poor little monkeys became distressed (Harlow, 1959).

In its most general sense, love is a strong, positive feeling we have toward someone or some thing we care deeply about (e.g., Berscheid, 2006). The object of our love is of great value to us. We feel possessive toward it, and if it is a living being, we usually want the love object to love us back. Indeed, in the romantic context, unrequited love causes damage to self-esteem and hostility in the rebuffed lover and guilt in the nonreciprocating beloved (Baumeister et al., 1993). We typically love our parents, our children, our siblings, our pets, and our romantic partners. We also may love other relatives, friends, our car, our flat-screen TV, our hometown, and our country. Although all of these forms of love can be important, social psychologists have focused primarily on love between adults, which includes sexual attraction and which is commonly referred to as romantic love.

Romantic Love

Attesting to the importance of romantic love, studies have found that when asked to name the person they felt closest to, the most popular choice was one's romantic partner (e.g., Berscheid et al., 1989). Many people have made valuable observations about love, including ancient philosophers, poets, and storytellers; Renaissance writers such as Shakespeare; 19th-century poets such as Keats and Shelley, and novelists such as Austen and Brontë; early psychologists such as Freud and Karen Horney; and present-day poets, songwriters, and novelists. Homer's great epic *The Odyssey* is fundamentally a love story. Shakespeare's *Romeo and Juliet* is perhaps the most famous love story of all. Romantic love is often portrayed as inspiring great feelings of joy and wholeness (e.g., Pope, 1980). At the same time, romantic love has also been described as a madness or a disease and a cause of great suffering, pain, and discord (Pope, 1980). Consider this anonymous poem by a Kwakiutl Indian of Alaska, transcribed in 1896 (Fisher, 2004, from Hamill, 1996):

> I am torn by your love for me
> Pain and more pain
> Where are you going with my love?
> I'm told you will go from here
> I am told you will leave me here
> My body is numb with grief
> Remember what I've said, my love
> Goodbye, my love, goodbye.

And indeed, when love is unrequited or romantic relationships don't work out, it can lead to stalking, abuse, murder, and suicide (e.g., Daly & Wilson, 1988; Fisher, 2004).

Social psychologists began focusing on love with Zick Rubin's seminal 1973 book *Liking and Loving*. Rubin developed scales to distinguish feelings of liking, which characterize many types of relationships, from feelings of love, which characterize romantic relationships. As the sample questionnaire items in **FIGURE 15.1** show, Rubin assessed positive evaluations of, and perceived similarity to, another person as the core of liking, but attachment, caring, and intimacy as the key aspects of romantic love. In support of the validity of his love scale, Rubin found that the higher people scored on love, the more they thought marriage to their partner was likely, the more eye contact they made when with their romantic partner, and the more the relationship had progressed in intensity six months later (Rubin, 1973). Since the development of Rubin's

Figure 15.1

Sample Items from Rubin's Liking and Love Scales

Rubin's liking and love scales were among the first to assess two different kinds of attraction: romantic love and liking.

[Research from: Rubin (1973)]

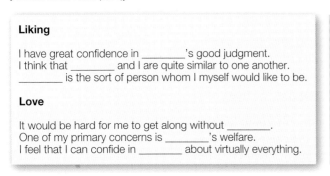

Liking

I have great confidence in _____'s good judgment.
I think that _____ and I are quite similar to one another.
_____ is the sort of person whom I myself would like to be.

Love

It would be hard for me to get along without _____.
One of my primary concerns is _____'s welfare.
I feel that I can confide in _____ about virtually everything.

scale, researchers have developed a variety of other love scales, often tapping particular types or aspects of romantic love (e.g., Hatfield & Sprecher, 1986; Hendrick & Hendrick, 1986).

The culture theorist Kenneth Pope (1980, p. 4) described the subjective experience of romantic love this way, consistent with Rubin's scale:

> A preoccupation with another person. A deeply felt desire to be with the loved one. A feeling of incompleteness without him or her. Thinking of the loved one often, whether together or apart. Separation frequently provokes feelings of genuine despair or else tantalizing anticipation of reuniting. Reunion is seen as bringing feelings of euphoric ecstasy or peace and fulfillment.

This description captures what researchers have found out about people who are in the throes of love. After conducting a survey of people's thoughts about romantic love that she administered in the United States and Japan, the anthropologist Helen Fisher (2004) noted some recurring themes:

> The beloved is idealized and becomes a center of attention, intrusive thoughts, emotion, energy, sexual desire, and a special source of meaning and value. The feeling is associated with mood swings from ecstasy to despair, and proneness to feelings of jealousy.

Consistent with the energy, desire, and ecstasy that accompanies love, when people in love contemplate their beloved, there is increased activation of the dopamine-rich ventral tegmental area and the caudate nucleus, two areas of the brain associated with reward, motivation, and pleasure (e.g., Aron et al., 2005; Fisher, 2004).

Of course, love may not be experienced in this way (or at all) by all people or in all cultures. Some people and cultures may see this kind of love as too dramatic or reflecting codependency, but evidence suggests both that when one falls in love and when one is in a love relationship for a decade or more, emotional dependence is pretty likely. This is why people sometimes resort to violence when they perceive a threat to their relationship, or if it is ended (e.g., Fisher, 2004), and why people mourn, often to the point of depressive symptoms, when they lose a romantic partner (e.g., Bowlby, 1980).

We can consider such a high level of emotional investment healthy or unhealthy, but evidence suggests it occurs in many, if not the majority of, committed romantic relationships. From this perspective, love is a leap, a risk, with the individual investing his or her happiness partly on the partner and the relationship. If you love someone—this can be just as true of love for a parent, child, friend, or pet as of love for a romantic partner—you care about the loved one's fortunes as well as your own. So your emotions are partly dependent on how the loved one is feeling and what is happening to him or her. If you don't want to risk that, don't love someone else. That way, your emotions will be based only on your own fortunes. Yet most people do take those risks, as children, parents, friends, pet owners, and lovers. Of these loves, romantic love is probably the most unstable and the most likely to lead to heartache. Most of us take the plunge anyway, often multiple times. Let's consider some informative perspectives on this fascinating phenomenon.

Culture and Love

Romantic love is partly a cultural creation. The culture we are raised in tells us what love is like, whom we should love and when, and what we should do about love (e.g., Hatfield & Rapson, 1996; Landis & O'Shea, 2000; Rubin, 1973). To gain insight into how the nature of love is articulated, researchers examined the use of words and songs to express love in the United States and China. Although they found similar levels of passion expressed, the Chinese were more likely to incorporate suffering and sadness

This painting by Eduard Ille, based on a medieval poem called "Underneath the Linden Tree," is one of many depicting conceptions of romantic love during the Middle Ages.

[Alfredo Dagli Orti/Art Resource, NY]

as part of the love experience (Rothbaum & Tsang, 1998; Shaver et al., 1992). Regarding what to do about love, many contemporary cultures, such as the United States and Japan, consider love a primary basis for deciding whom to marry. But in some cultures, such as those prevalent in many parts of India and Pakistan, marriages are arranged; in fact, basing a marriage on love is considered inappropriate and foolhardy (Levine et al., 1995). Even in European cultures, until well into the 19th century, love generally was not considered a basis for marriage (e.g., Coontz, 2005; Finkel et al., 2014). Rather, marriage was a pragmatic arrangement that served social and economic goals of the bride's and groom's families. Rubin (1973) noted that many Western ideas about romantic love developed out of medieval concepts of courtly love. This kind of love was considered likely only between people who weren't married, often between a man and a woman who became his mistress.

In many stories, such as *Romeo and Juliet*, love emerges in opposition to cultural forces that control who marries whom. The very well-known Chinese story of the Butterfly Lovers is over a thousand years old (Idema, 2010). The young lovers are blocked from marrying by their society. As a result, the man eventually pines away and dies, and the woman subsequently commits suicide by throwing herself into his grave. The good news is that they re-emerge as butterflies. Stories such as *Romeo and Juliet*, *The Butterfly Lovers*, and countless others dating back over 4,000 years (Fisher, 2006; Wolkstein, 1991) attest to the universality of romantic love and to the fact that it often persists despite cultural pressures.

Research shows that although specific conceptions of love vary somewhat from culture to culture, love seems to exist in the vast majority of cultures, and perhaps all of them. In a survey of cultures around the globe, anthropologists found clear evidence of romantic love in 147 out of 166 cultures (Jankowiak & Fischer, 1992). What about the 19 cultures without evidence of romantic love? In these cultures, this aspect of people's lives was not necessarily absent but had not been studied (Fisher, 2006).

Theories of Romantic Love

We've seen that culture shapes some features of romantic love, but what explains the widespread existence of the phenomenon and the power it often holds over people? Let's consider three broad theoretical perspectives that help clarify the nature and importance of romantic love and relationships.

Attachment Theory: Love's Foundation

From an evolutionary perspective, love may be advantageous because it generally helps us focus on courting and mating with a single individual at a time. This focus conserves energy and motivates lengthy pair bonding, which aids a couple's effective raising of their offspring (e.g., Fisher, 2004). However, evolutionary adaptations don't spring out of nowhere; they build on preexisting tendencies and structures. Any compelling theory of love must combine insights from human evolution, human development, and adult psychological functioning. Attachment theory provides just such an integrative perspective on love.

The Basics of Attachment: Infancy and Childhood

Attachment theory is rooted in the ideas of psychologists such as Otto Rank, Karen Horney, and Melanie Klein, but was formally developed by the British psychoanalyst John Bowlby in his three-volume classic *Attachment and Loss* (1969; 1973; 1980).

His attachment theory combines insights from the Freudian psychoanalytic tradition, studies of primate evolution, developmental psychology, and Bowlby's own clinical experiences with children separated from their parents (Mikulincer & Shaver, 2007). Attachment theory posits that the prototypic experience of love is the young child's bond with the primary caretaker, typically the child's mother.

The importance of this bond is rooted in our primate heritage. But it is particularly essential for humans, whose newborns are the most helpless and dependent of all mammalian species and need the longest period of care before reaching adulthood. Human newborns lack the capacity to roll over, let alone move on their own, find food, feed themselves, or defend themselves against predators. How do they survive long enough to reach some degree of independence? They rely on close attachments to parental figures who can provide care and protection. In fact, infants come into the world with a number of evolved techniques for assuring proximity to attachment figures. For one, their cries guarantee that no one (their parents or anyone else!) can ignore them in times of need. Add those heart-warming smiles that start by about 6 weeks of age, and you generally have caregivers who are very attentive to the child's well-being (Berry & McArthur, 1986; McArthur & Baron, 1983).

Infants lack the physical and cognitive abilities to survive in the world on their own. But they have a number of characteristics that we adults seem to find irresistible. These characteristics help to ensure that grown-ups will attend to and care for them.

[Anneka/Shutterstock]

When infants feel close to an available and responsive attachment figure, they feel comfort and reassurance. Bowlby proposed that when parents are responsive and supportive, they provide a safe haven when the child is fearful and a secure base from which the child can venture forth, explore, and grow.

The developmental psychologist Mary Ainsworth studied attachment before and independent of Bowlby. However, after working with Bowlby, she became the primary researcher to study infant attachment systematically. Along with naturalistic observation of infants and their mothers in their homes, she developed a set of *strange situation tests* to examine the early attachment bond between mothers and their children (Ainsworth & Bell, 1970). Through this research, Ainsworth and colleagues were able to demonstrate the role of attachment in providing young children with psychological security. They were also able to establish three major forms of attachment that are associated with particular patterns of child-maternal interaction (Ainsworth et al., 1978).

- *Secure attachment style.* In the initial version of the strange situation test, a mother and her nearly one-year-old child enter an unfamiliar room with toys and chairs. After a short time, a female stranger enters the room and sits down. The mother eventually leaves for a few minutes, and then returns. In the typical case, the child is attentive to her mother but then happily turns to exploring the toys. When the stranger enters, the child exhibits distress and relieves that distress by returning to her mother. When the mother leaves, distress returns. When the mother returns, the child greets her, becomes relaxed, and resumes exploring the toys. The mother is a secure base for the child's explorations and play. About 60% of the children displayed this form of secure attachment.

    The other 40% of the children were split about evenly between two insecure attachment styles.

- *Anxious-ambivalent attachment style.* Children who exhibit the anxious-ambivalent attachment style are overly clingy while the mom is there, but they do explore the toys. When the mom leaves the room, they cry and protest. When she returns, they seem angry and resistant (ambivalent) and have difficulty calming down and returning to play with the toys. Parents of these anxious-ambivalent children tend to be very inconsistent, fluctuating between unresponsive and overly intrusive.

• *Avoidant attachment style.* Children who exhibit the avoidant attachment style are not very affectionate with the mom there. They play with the toys but not very enthusiastically. When the mother leaves, they show little distress, and when she returns, they often turn away or avoid her. Parents of avoidant children tend to reject or deflect the child's bids for comfort and closeness.

Subsequent research has confirmed this general distribution of what now are known as attachment styles. For example, Campos and colleagues (1983) found that among American samples, 62% of infants were secure, 23% were avoidant, and 15% were anxious-ambivalent.

The Enduring Influence of Attachment: Adult Romantic Relationships

So what does attachment have to do with adult romantic relationships? The nature of this initial love relationship influences the close relationships individuals have over the course of their lives, including adult love relationships. Just as attachment to the parents is central to a child's psychological security, attachment to the romantic partner is central to psychological security for most adults (e.g., Mikulincer, 2006; Simpson et al., 1992). Attachment theorists explain that these childhood experiences result in working models of relationships—that is, global feelings about the nature and worth of close relationships and other people's trustworthiness and ability to provide warmth and security (Baldwin et al., 1996; Collins & Read, 1994; Pietromonaco & Barrett, 2000). These working models of relationships, which originate early in life, become our style of attachment, stable patterns in the way we think about and behave in our adult relationships (Hazan & Shaver, 1987; Shaver & Hazan, 1993).

Working models of relationships Global feelings about the nature and worth of close relationships and other people's trustworthiness.

Cindy Hazan and Phil Shaver (1987) conducted the first studies providing evidence that these attachment styles relate to adult romantic relationships. They recruited community participants of various ages in their first study and college students in their second study. They created three descriptions of how people think and feel about getting close to others that corresponded to the secure, anxious-ambivalent, and avoidant attachment styles established by Ainsworth. These are depicted in **FIGURE 15.2**. Take a look and, as the participants did in the study, pick which of the three best characterizes how you relate to other people. Hazan and Shaver hypothesized that if attachment theory applies to adult relationships, the percentages of people who picked one of the three different paragraphs should be similar to the percentages that Ainsworth and colleagues found with very young children. And indeed it was: Across the two studies, roughly 56% reported the secure style, 24% the avoidant style, and 20% the anxious-ambivalent style. Subsequent studies have found similar frequencies of these attachment styles (Mickelson et al., 1997).

A. I am somewhat uncomfortable being close to others; I find it difficult to trust them completely, difficult to allow myself to depend on them. I am nervous when anyone gets too close, and often, others want me to be more intimate than I feel comfortable being.

B. I find it relatively easy to get close to others and am comfortable depending on them and having them depend on me. I don't worry about being abandoned or about someone getting too close to me.

C. I find that others are reluctant to get as close as I would like. I often worry that my partner doesn't really love me or won't want to stay with me. I want to get very close to my partner, and this sometimes scares people away.

Figure 15.2

Attachment Style Questionnaire

Hazan and Shaver developed these descriptions to capture three basic attachment styles. Which one best fits your view of close relationships?

[Research from: Hazan & Shaver (1987)]

Over the years researchers have specified two dimensions of attachment feelings that underlie these styles of attachment (Bartholomew & Horowitz, 1991; Brennan et al., 1998). One dimension is referred to as attachment-related *anxiety*. When someone is high in attachment anxiety, he or she is overly concerned with whether the partner is attentive and responsive. The other dimension is labeled attachment-related *avoidance* and refers to a reluctance to depend on others. People can be high or low in either or both dimensions. As shown in **FIGURE 15.3**, this yields what many researchers now recognize as four possibilities. Research using this dimensional approach provides further insight into how people's attachment feelings relate to the nature of their most important romantic relationship, their views of romantic love, their approach to sex, and their reports of how their parents raised them.

Low Avoidance/Low Anxiety: Securely Attached Adults

Participants who are **securely attached** are low in both attachment anxiety and attachment avoidance. They tend to report the longest-lasting, most satisfying romantic relationships. They believe that love can endure, and they tend to be self-confident and trusting of others. They recall having warm relationships with both of their parents while growing up. Moreover, securely attached people are generally psychologically well adjusted (Mikulincer & Shaver, 2007). When their relationship partners need care or comfort, they are very responsive in providing it. Also, securely attached people react less negatively than insecurely attached people to unflattering feedback from their partners (Collins & Feeney, 2004).

Those with a more secure attachment style are also more comfortable with their sexuality and generally enjoy sex (Tracy et al., 2003). But this does not mean they will jump into the sack with anybody and at any opportunity. They are also more likely to have sex within a committed relationship (Feeney et al., 1993) and to see sex as a way to enhance intimacy in the relationship and express their love for their partners (Cooper et al., 2006).

Low Avoidance/High Anxiety: Anxious-ambivalent Adults

Anxious-ambivalent (or preoccupied) individuals tend to have a negative view of themselves (i.e., low self-esteem) but a positive view of others. They have short, intense relationships but with many emotional highs and lows (Hazan & Shaver, 1987), featuring frequent feelings of passion, jealousy, anger, and smothering (e.g., Davis et al., 2004; Shaver et al., 2005). They tend to fall in love very easily but at the same time are skeptical of how long love can last, and are dissatisfied with the attentiveness of romantic partners. They give affection according to their own needs as opposed to being responsive to the needs of their relationship partners.

Not surprisingly, they also use and see sex differently. Like many aspects of relationships for these individuals, sex can become riddled with anxiety. The more attachment anxiety men have, the older they are when they first have sex, and they have less frequent intercourse and fewer partners (Feeney et al., 1993; Gentzler & Kerns, 2004). But among anxious-ambivalent women, greater attachment anxiety predicts higher likelihood of having sex, earlier age at first intercourse, and less exclusivity in partners (Cooper et al., 1998). In part this is because such women succumb to pressures to have sex (Gentzler & Kerns, 2004) and use sex to avoid partner disapproval and to reassure themselves of their self-worth (Cooper et al., 2006).

High Avoidance/High or Low Anxiety: Avoidantly Attached Adults

Participants who report higher levels of avoidance tend to have shorter relationships that lack intimacy (Hazan & Shaver, 1987). They don't believe love endures, are fearful of closeness, and lack trust in romantic partners. They seem not to want to get much from their romantic relationships, are emotionally distant, and tend to ignore their partners' needs for care and intimacy (e.g., Collins & Feeney, 2000). They recall their mothers as being cold and rejecting.

People who are high in attachment avoidance show yet another profile of sexual behavior. They are more likely to delay having sex, and when they do, they do so in contexts that limit intimacy, such as having more casual as well as solitary sex (Cooper et al., 1998). This is partly because avoidant people tend to use sex to affirm their desirability and to cope with negative emotions, rather than to seek pleasure or enhance intimacy.

Avoidant styles can come in one of two forms (Bartholomew & Horowitz, 1990). High levels of avoidance can be paired with high levels of anxiety (i.e., a fearful

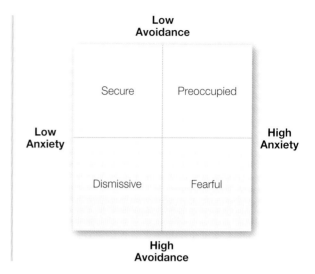

Figure 15.3

Attachment Dimensions

Expanding on the categorical approach of distinct attachment styles, research uncovered two attachment dimensions. People can be high or low on attachment avoidance and attachment anxiety, which when crossed yield four attachment styles.
[Research from: Brennan et al. (1998)]

Securely attached An attachment style characterized by a positive view of the self and others, low anxiety and avoidance, and satisfying, stable relationships.

Anxious-ambivalent An attachment style characterized by a negative view of the self but a positive view of others, high anxiety, low avoidance, and intense but unstable relationships.

Fearfully avoidant An avoidant attachment style characterized by a negative view of both self and others, high anxiety and avoidance, and distant relationships, in which the person doesn't feel worthy, doesn't trust others, and fears rejection.

Dismissive avoidant An avoidant attachment style characterized by a negative view of others but a positive view of the self, high anxiety and avoidance, and distant relationships.

avoidant style) and reflect negative views of both self and of others. So the **fearfully avoidant** person doesn't feel worthy, doesn't trust others, and fears rejection. High levels of avoidance can also be paired with low levels of anxiety. Those with this **dismissive avoidant** attachment style tend to show a positive view of the self but a negative view of others. Dismissive avoidant people are more self-satisfied and appear not to need closeness with others. They hide their vulnerability, deny their desire for intimacy, and tend to be sexually promiscuous (Gjerde et al., 2004; Mikulincer et al., 2004).

Combinations of Attachment Styles and Long-term Relationships

Clearly the best bet for a stable and satisfying long-term relationship is for both members of a couple to have a secure attachment style (e.g., Kane et al., 2007; Senchak & Leonard, 1992; Shaver & Mikulincer, 2010; Simpson, 1990). Other combinations of attachment styles yield less mutual satisfaction and stability, with one interesting exception. Over a four-year period, Kirkpatrick and Davis (1994) found that anxious women and avoidant men had relationships as stable as those of secure couples, although far less satisfying. Kirkpatrick and Davis suggested that this is because women who are highly invested in relationships and men who are distant and less invested fit the prevailing gender stereotypes. In these relationships, the women put up with the men and vice versa, even though neither of them is very satisfied. In fact, some studies of heterosexual couples have found that women's dissatisfaction increases the more avoidant their male partners are, whereas men's dissatisfaction increases the more anxious their female partners are (e.g., Collins & Read, 1990; Kane et al., 2007).

Attachment Style, Genes, and Parental Caregiving

Research on attachment theory raises a number of questions. One issue concerns the extent to which a child's temperament and genetic inheritance contribute to the attachment style he or she develops (Kagan, 1994). Research findings on this issue are mixed. Some studies have found that genes have a negligible influence (e.g., Bokhorst et al., 2003). Other research suggests that DNA associated with low dopamine levels is linked to high levels of attachment anxiety, and DNA associated with low serotonin levels is linked to high levels of attachment avoidance (Gillath et al., 2008). This latter work suggests that about 20% of variability in attachment anxiety and attachment avoidance may result from genetic factors.

Clearly, though, as attachment theory proposes, the primary determinant of attachment style is how attachment figures interact with the child (e.g., Fraley, 2002; Main, 1995; Waller & Shaver, 1994). In one particularly ambitious study, Dymphna van den Boom (1994) showed that when a random half of mothers of temperamentally difficult 6-month-old infants were trained for three months in sensitive responding to the child, by 12 months of age, 62% of the infants were securely attached, whereas only 22% of the children whose parents weren't so trained exhibited secure attachment. And a follow-up study found that the children whose mothers had received training were still benefiting from it at age 3 (van den Boom, 1995).

Stability of Attachment Style

Another issue concerns stability of attachment style over time. Although the Hazan and Shaver study suggested that early childhood attachment style relates to adult attachment style, the best way to test this stability is with a longitudinal study in which parent-child attachment style is assessed in young children and then again when the same children are adults. Such time-consuming studies have been conducted, and they generally suggest considerable stability of attachment style from infancy to adulthood (Fraley, 2002; Simpson et al., 2007).

However, early attachment style is not set in stone. As Bowlby (1980) proposed, experiences with attachment figures throughout one's life can alter one's predominant working model of attachment. A horrible relationship, full of betrayal, could make a securely attached person insecure; a happy, stable relationship might shift an insecure person toward a secure style. Indeed, in a four-year longitudinal study of adults, Kirkpatrick and Hazan (1994) found that overall, 30% of the adults in the study changed their attachment style. Secures were more stable, with 17% changing. In other words, the anxious and avoidant attached adults were more likely to change styles over the four years (also see Baldwin & Fehr, 1995).

Love, the Ultimate Security Blanket

As we wrap up our discussion of attachment theory and research, we want to close by reiterating this theory's central insight regarding love. From the perspective of attachment theory, we seek and maintain love for significant others to garner a sense of support, comfort, relief, trust, and security, particularly when we are confronted with threats from the outside world or distressing thoughts and emotions (e.g., Mikulincer et al., 2001). The sense of warmth and physical protection that we experience as infants when we are close to a responsive caregiver lays the foundation for the comforting experience we have as adults when we feel a secure bond with our romantic partners.

Love and Death

> Unable are the Loved to die
> For Love is Immortality
>
> —Emily Dickinson (1864/1960, p. 394)

In the weeks following the terrorist attacks of September 11, 2001, Americans showed an increased tendency to solidify their close relationships, express more commitment, spend more time with family and friends, and seek more intimate sexual encounters with their romantic partners (e.g., Ai et al., 2009). Various newspapers and magazines such as *Newsweek* also reported similar trends in the wake of the Oklahoma City bombing in 1995 and Hurricane Katrina in 2005, as well as among military units facing more combat and higher levels of violence (e.g., Mitchell, 2009). Why?

One answer comes from the existential perspective offered by terror management theory. Terror management theory is highly compatible with attachment theory in its focus on how children develop security and how that sets the stage for adults' bases of psychological security. From this theoretical perspective, romantic partners help each other manage the threat of mortality by giving life meaning and reinforcing self-worth (Kosloff et al., 2010; Solomon et al., 1991). Thus, even in situations in which a person faces no immediate threat to her survival, the knowledge that life is fragile and destined to end—a fact made salient, for example, by media reports of the attacks of September 11—helps fuel feelings of love by driving people to cling to close relationships for security.

According to Otto Rank (1936a), as Western societies became more secular during the 20th century, romantic relationships largely replaced religion as the primary source of meaning and value, which in turn provide a sense of transcendence of death. Rank suggested that as this occurred in Western cultures, the romantic relationship became viewed increasingly as a magical, eternal bond of love with a cosmically designated soul mate. Thus, romantic relationships became a central basis of feeling that one's life is meaningful and enduringly significant. You know you are valued because you are loved. A life partner knows your life story and cares about the minute details of your life, thus bearing witness to and validating your existence and its value. Though perhaps particularly prevalent in modern Western societies, this idea has been around for many centuries and has been expressed in many cultures. A Hindu song put it this way: "My lover is like God: if he accepts me my existence is utilized" (Becker, 1973, p. 161). Eli Finkel and colleagues (2014) have recently made similar observations, suggesting that people in North America increasingly view romantic relationships as a way to meet the needs for self-esteem and self-actualization.

Studies have supported the idea that romantic partners enhance people's self-worth and validate their worldviews. Aron and colleagues (1995) tracked people who did and did not fall in love over time. One of their findings was that people who fell in love showed an increase in self-esteem. And even more directly, studies show that thinking of our mortality leads us to be more committed to lovers who positively regard us and make us feel good about ourselves. In addition, when participants were reminded of death, the more highly committed they were to the relationship, the more positively they viewed their romantic partners, and the more positively they felt that their romantic partners viewed them (Cox & Arndt, 2012).

Further support for the role of romantic relationships in terror management has been provided by a series of studies conducted in Israel by Mario Mikulincer and colleagues, who noted that such relationships may be especially important for managing fear of death because they provide the same type of physical and emotional closeness we all relied on as children when scared (see Mikulincer et al., 2003). They have found that for people in committed relationships, threats to the relationship or thoughts of being away from their partners increase the accessibility of death-related thought. In addition, reminders of mortality increase the desire for closeness in the romantic relationship. In people lacking a romantic relationship, they increase the desire to have one. Finally, thinking about a current romantic partner reduces the need for defensiveness after a reminder of death, but only for people who are securely attached. This suggests that romantic relationships help securely attached people manage their concerns about mortality, but they don't do so for those who are insecurely attached. Additional evidence suggests that insecurely attached young adults, at least, still rely on their parents, rather than their romantic partners, for existential security (Cox et al., 2008).

Terror management theory also contributes to understanding the desire for and love of one's children, as children can be one way to feel that a part of the self lives on beyond one's own death. In line with this account, research shows that death reminders increase desire for offspring among Dutch, German, and Chinese individuals (Fritsche et al., 2007; Wisman & Goldenberg, 2005; Zhou et al., 2008). Furthermore, for young married adults without children, death reminders increase positive thoughts of parenthood, and thinking about becoming parents reduces the accessibility of death-related thoughts (Yaakobi et al., 2014). Taken together, this work suggests that the idea of having children, and thereby continuing to live on in some way, helps to quell concerns about personal mortality.

WHAT'S THE POINT OF LIVING THROUGH YOU IF YOU'RE GOING TO KEEP COMING IN SECOND?

[© Nick Galofianakis]

Self-expansion model of relationships The idea that romantic relationships serve the desire to expand the self and grow.

The Self-expansion Model: Love as a Basis of Growth

So far we've been focusing on theories that portray love primarily as a basis for feeling safe and secure in the world. But this is undoubtedly an incomplete picture of why we pursue love relationships. You'll remember from chapter 6 that humanistic psychology and self-determination theory emphasize the person's potential to grow and change. These theories view the person as inherently motivated to cultivate her inner potentialities, seek out optimal challenges, and master and integrate new experiences.

According to Art Aron's **self-expansion model of relationships**, one way that people satisfy this motive is through romantic relationships. The self-expansion model proposes that a central human motive is the desire to expand the self and that loving another person is an important way to do so (Aron et al., 2001). From this perspective, the romantic partner becomes incorporated as part of the self, thus helping to expand the self, making the self more complex. When you fall in love, you start to care about the things your partner cares about. You may start doing different

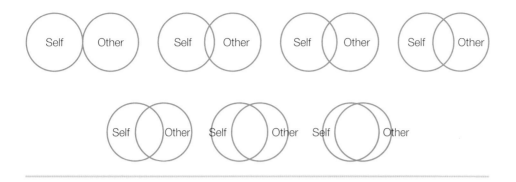

Figure 15.4

The Inclusion of Other in the Self Scale

How much mutuality do people feel in a relationship? Asking people to choose the pair of overlapping circles that best portrays their relationship with their partner provides a measure of the closeness they feel.

[Research from: Aron et al. (1992)]

activities, eating different foods, listening to different music, reading different books, and so forth. In this way, love can enhance growth. In support of this idea, Aron and colleagues (1995) found that when people fell in love, their self-concept did indeed become more complex.

To assess the idea that people incorporate their partners partly into the self, Aron and colleagues (1992) developed the Inclusion of Other in the Self (IOS) Scale. As depicted in **FIGURE 15.4**, the scale consists of seven pairs of circles that represent varying degrees of overlap between self and partner. Individuals are asked to select the pair that best describes their relationship with their partners. This simple, one-item scale has proven very useful for assessing relationship closeness (Agnew et al., 2004).

People who chose more overlapping circles have more satisfying relationships and use more plural pronouns in describing their relationship. They are also more likely to blur the line between their sense of who they are and who their partner is. After rating some traits for self and other traits for their partners, they were more likely to mistake traits they rated for self for those they rated for others (Aron & Fraley, 1999).

The self-expansion model also posits that the experience of self-expanding in relationships adds pleasure and excitement to relationships (Aron & Aron, 2006). On the basis of this idea, Aron and colleagues proposed that early in relationships, during the "honeymoon period," people are getting to know each other. This stimulates a great deal of rapid self-expansion and consequent exhilaration. Over time, however, the self-expanding aspect of a relationship tends to slow down as the relationship falls into routine. The challenge then is to keep the process of mutual self-expansion going over the long haul, an idea we will return to later in this chapter.

Models of the Nature of Love

Attachment theory, terror management theory, and the self-expansion model help explain why love is a virtually universal and very important aspect of human experience. Other social psychological models of love provide insights into the subjective experience of love and the various forms romantic love can take.

Schachter's Two Factor Theory: Love as an Emotion

Love is often a lasting feeling toward another person, but people also have intense feelings of falling in love and being in love. Where do these feelings come from? Berscheid and Walster (1974) applied Schachter's (1964) two factor theory of emotion to understanding love as a felt emotion. As you'll recall from chapter 5, Schachter's theory proposed that emotions partly consist of physiological arousal and a label for that arousal based on cues present when the arousal is being felt. As applied to love (and lust), this theory suggests that when an individual is aroused, in the presence of a member of the appropriate sex, and in a context that cultural learning suggests is romantic, the individual may very well label that arousal as love. One interesting implication of the two factor theory is that cultures direct when and with whom the label *love* is most likely to be applied to arousal that occurs in the presence of another person.

A second interesting implication of this approach is that the real source of the arousal doesn't always matter, as long as it is labeled *attraction* or *love*. One set of studies supporting this idea was conducted by Dutton and Aron (1974). In one of their studies, adult males were interviewed on one of two bridges over the Capilano River in British Columbia by an attractive female interviewer or a male interviewer. One bridge was a very wide, safe bridge, only 10 feet over a small rivulet. The other bridge was a wobbly, narrow 450-foot suspension bridge over a 230-foot gorge, with shallow rapids below. Dutton and Aron assumed that the narrow bridge over the deep drop would generate some physiological arousal because of the possibility of danger (and perhaps also the spectacular setting), whereas the small footbridge would not. Applying the two factor theory, they thus proposed that men interviewed over the scary bridge by the female interviewer would attribute some of their arousal to their feelings of attraction to and perhaps romantic interest in her. They therefore predicted that men would be more attracted to the female interviewer if the setting was the scary bridge than if it was the safe bridge.

Don't look down! But if you do, do you think the emotions you experience might influence your affection for an attractive person you meet on the bridge? When Dutton and Aron (1974) interviewed people on this bridge over the Capilano River in British Columbia, they found that the answer is yes.

[Bob Stelko/Getty Images]

Dutton and Aron used two clever dependent variables to test this idea. First, while on the bridge, the interviewer showed the interviewees an ambiguous picture of a young woman covering her face with one hand and reaching out with the other and asked them to write a brief story about it. Dutton and Aron had the stories coded for sexual content. They expected more sexual content in the stories by the men who were interviewed by the female over the scary bridge. Second, they had the interviewer give the interviewees her phone number in case they wanted to learn more about the study. Dutton and Aron figured that if the scary bridge interviewees were more attracted to the female interviewer, they would be more likely to call her. Both hypotheses were supported. The scary bridge interviewees made more calls and wrote more sexual stories. For example, 50% of these interviewees called, whereas only about 20% called in the other three conditions (male interviewer, safe bridge).

The idea that love and attraction can be fueled by extraneous sources of arousal has been supported in other ways as well (e.g., Valins, 1966; White et al., 1981; White & Kight, 1984). For example, working with the excitation transfer paradigm developed by Zillmann (1971) and described in chapter 5, White and colleagues (1981) showed that arousal from both exercise and funny or disturbing audiotapes subsequently increased male romantic attraction to a physically attractive female confederate. In a study conducted at an amusement park, individuals found a photographed member of the opposite sex more desirable as a date after exiting a roller coaster than before getting on the roller coaster—unless they were with a romantic partner on the roller coaster (Meston & Frohlich, 2003). Some additional research suggests that arousal intensifies attraction in part because, as you may recall from chapter 9, arousal intensifies dominant responses. The dominant response when viewing or in the presence of a physically attractive member of the appropriate sex may be romantic interest (Foster et al., 1998).

How much of our attraction to, and even love for, a romantic partner may have been fueled or intensified by extrapersonal sources of arousal? It is hard to say in any specific case. But the research supporting the two factor theory suggests that initial attraction to or feelings of love for a romantic partner may indeed be affected by extrapersonal sources of arousal. And if you think of what people do when they date others they are interested in, they often do exciting, physiologically arousing things: They go dancing, watch exciting or scary movies, go on amusement-park rides or hikes, play sports or watch sporting events, or visit exciting places. Coincidence?

Sternberg's Triangular Model of Love

There are a variety of models that describe different types of romantic love. Perhaps the most basic distinction is between passionate love and companionate love (e.g., Hatfield, 1988). Passionate love involves an emotionally intense and erotic desire to be absorbed in another person. Companionate love is believed to better character-ize older couples who have been together a long time. There is still great affection, trust, and a sense that the relationship is important, but passion is much diminished or absent.

Robert Sternberg's triangular model of love relationships (depicted in **FIGURE 15.5**) rather elegantly captures not only these two kinds of love but five others as well. The model posits three basic components of love relationships that in different combinations describe different kinds of relationships. The components are passion, intimacy, and com-mitment. Passion is the excitement about, sex-ual attraction to, and longing for the partner. Intimacy involves liking, sharing, knowing, and emotional support of the partner. Com-mitment is the extent to which the individual is invested in maintaining the relationship. Sternberg proposes that the ideal roman-tic relationship has a high level of all three components. He refers to this as consummate

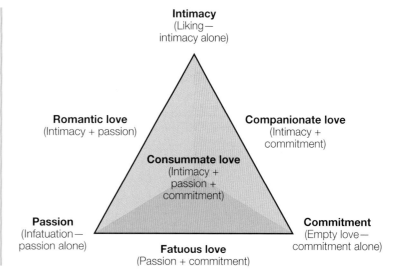

love. Research supports his model by showing that almost all aspects of relationships seem to fit under one of the three factors (Aron & Westbay, 1996) and that people view the ideal lover as someone high in all three factors (Sternberg, 1997).

Many other kinds of relationships lack one or more component, but can still be meaningfully experienced as love. A relationship with only passion is an infatuation; there is strong attraction and arousal, but the partner is not well known and there is no commitment to a relationship. Intimacy alone can characterize a close acquain-tanceship or friendship. Commitment alone is labeled by Sternberg as empty love. There is investment in maintaining the relationship, but there is no sharing and no passion. This sometimes occurs in older couples for whom the passion and even the sense of liking for the partner is no longer there, but out of habit, familiarity, or fear of being alone, commitment persists. The relationship still helps the individual feel secure, but there is no growth or stimulation.

The combination of passion and intimacy is labeled romantic, or passionate, love. People are in love and share knowledge of each other but haven't made a real commitment to sustaining the relationship over time. Romantic love often is a step toward consummate love, but in some cases that commitment is never made. The combination of passion and commitment is called fatuous love and is exemplified by young adults who have developed a strong infatuation and jump to the commitment of marriage before they really know each other well. These kinds of relationships often don't turn out well because, lacking intimacy, partners don't know what they are getting into. Each partner will tend to idealize the other, but over time they may encounter less-than-ideal surprises as they get to know each other better.

Finally, the combination of intimacy and commitment without passion is compan-ionate love, a kind of love not uncommon in very long-term romantic relationships. Stimulation and sexual attraction have died out, but the positive feelings, sharing,

Figure 15.5

Triangular Model of Love Relationship

Robert Sternberg proposes that we can break love down into three main facets, which when combined with one another yield seven different types of love. Think about where some of the most important close relationships in your life fit within this triangle.

[Research from: Sternberg (1997) © 1997 John Wiley & Sons, Inc. Reprinted by permission.]

and commitment have remained strong. Though passion in relationships does tend to diminish somewhat in intensity over time, it still can be found in many long-standing relationships (Acevedo & Aron, 2009; Acker & Davis, 1992). If consummate love is the ideal, keeping passion alive over the long haul is one of the biggest challenges of long-term relationships, and something we will address later in the chapter.

SECTION review | This Thing Called Love

Social scientists have focused research primarily on romantic love.

Romantic love	Culture and love	Theories of why love exists	Models define the experience of love
• Early research distinguished between liking and loving. • Loving typically involves intense caring, intimacy, and a deep emotional investment.	• The experience of romantic love is partly shaped by culture. • But it is a basic, likely universal aspect of human experience.	• Attachment theory proposes that most people seek security from their romantic relationships much as they once did from their parents. • The nature of that original child-parent bond affects the nature of subsequent adult close relationships. • Terror management theory suggests that love and close relationships help us to buffer the dread of being aware of our mortality. • The self-expansion model of relationships suggests that love relationships often are valuable paths to personal growth.	• The two factor theory posits that love is partly a label we apply to feelings of arousal on the basis of contextual cues. • The triangular model of love suggests that love is based on combinations of three basic components: passion, intimacy, and commitment.

The social exchange model takes an economic perspective on relationships in which prospective and actual partners are assessed on the basis of costs and benefits.
[IPGGutenbergUKLtd/iStock/360/ Getty Images]

Social exchange model
An economic perspective that assumes that people approach relationships with an underlying motivation of self-interest.

Cost-benefit Perspectives on Relationships

No doubt you have heard people refer to the dating scene as a meat market. This rather blunt expression is a nod to the ways in which romantic relationships are like commodities to be negotiated and bartered on the open market. We bring certain strengths to the table, try to tuck our baggage under our chair, and look to make a good deal with a partner. With the advent of online and searchable dating sites such as Match.com and eHarmony, this shopping metaphor has taken on an even more literal dimension. When we take this market-driven approach to studying how people form relationships, we are applying social exchange theory.

The Social Exchange Model

The social exchange model (Thibaut & Kelley, 1959) takes an economic perspective and assumes that people approach relationships with the underlying motivation of self-interest. Just as two businesses enter into a corporate merger only if the CEOs of both expect a higher return from combining forces than from staying in competition, relationships have value when both people perceive that they have more to gain than to lose from being in a partnership. The benefits of a relationship can be financial, emotional, sexual, and social. But entering into any relationship also carries certain costs that need to be negotiated along the way.

Clearly, this is not the most romantic view of love. But a social exchange approach to relationships does make intuitive sense. Every relationship has its ups and downs, but so long as the ups outnumber the downs, the outcome of the relationship is generally positive. Several studies have confirmed that people are more satisfied in a relationship to the extent that they see the benefits as outweighing the costs (Duffy & Rusbult, 1986; Rusbult, 1980, 1983; Rusbult et al., 1986; Rusbult & Martz, 1995).

But not everyone is equally happy with the same relationship outcome. If you were brought up in a harmonious, two-parent home, watched a steady diet of Disney movies, or paid a lot of attention to online matchmaking sites advertising the importance of finding your soul mate (Finkel et al., 2012), you might have internalized ideals of happily ever after and one true love. These cultural standards can set a high **comparison level**, your expectation of how rewarding a relationship should be. A relationship that merely delivers more benefits than costs might not quite live up to the ideal of finding your soul mate. On the other extreme, if you were raised in a home full of marital strife and domestic violence, your comparison level for a satisfying relationship would likely be much lower and thus more easily met or exceeded. A relationship with a given set of rewards and costs would seem much more satisfying to the person with the very low comparison level than to the person with the very high one (Rusbult, 1983). In fact, those who believe in the idea of a soul mate are satisfied in their relationship only to the extent that they see the partner as an ideal mate (Franiuk et al., 2002, 2004; Knee, 1998). Using the logic of the social exchange model, we can describe people's satisfaction with their current relationship in a formal equation:

> SATISFACTION = (REWARDS − COSTS) − COMPARISON LEVEL

From the perspective of the social exchange model, we should always be looking to maximize benefits for ourselves—assuming that more is always better. For something as deeply emotional and prosocial as our close, intimate relationships, is it fair to say that these self-interested concerns are the only driving force in how we form and maintain strong bonds with each other? Critics of the social exchange model have said, "No!" They point out that the social exchange model does not explain the sense of fairness that is so important in our relationships (Clark & Mills, 1979; Fiske, 1991). We generally don't keep a ledger of who contributes what to the relationship, and we generally don't try to maximize our own outcomes at the expense of our partner—at least not if we want the relationship to last!

Equity Theory

Equity theory addresses these critiques of the social exchange model. According to equity theory, people are motivated to maintain a sense of fairness or equity, where both partners feel that the proportion of rewards or outcomes (benefits) to inputs (costs) that each receives is roughly equal (Adams, 1963; Hatfield et al., 1978). The equity formula looks like this, with "O" standing for outcomes and "I" standing for inputs:

> O/I FOR SELF = O/I FOR PARTNER

When we feel that our partner is getting a higher proportion of outcomes relative to inputs than we are, we feel angry and resentful. But the partner who feels unfairly advantaged in a relationship also can feel a sense of guilt that can motivate effort to balance the scales (Sprecher, 1986, 1992). How is equity restored? You can either increase the inputs or decrease the outcomes for yourself or your partner. Alternatively, you can decrease the inputs or increase the outcomes of the person who is disadvantaged. You can also make these adjustments to objective contributions (e.g., the amount of work done) and payouts (e.g., benefits received) or to your *subjective* perception of these factors.

Comparison level
The expectation of how rewarding a relationship should be.

Equity theory The idea that people are motivated to maintain a sense of fairness or equity, whereby both partners feel that the proportion of outcomes (rewards) to inputs (costs) that each receives is roughly equal.

The TV show *Modern Family* depicts some of the dynamics of maintaining close relationships. In one episode, Cameron and Mitchell make adjustments to try and maintain equitable contributions to their relationship.

[ABC-TV/The Kobal Collection]

Assortative mating The idea that people are attracted to others who are similar to them in some kind of social hierarchy.

Matching phenomenon The idea that people seek romantic relationships with others who are similar to them in physical attractiveness.

The matching phenomenon describes how relationships maintain an equitable balance. Often this is in the same domain, such as appearance, but at other times the balance can exist across different domains, such as appearance and status. This may help to explain the striking age difference between the Playboy mogul Hugh Hefner and his girlfriends.

[David Livingston/Getty Images]

To see how equity works, let's consider an example from a popular television show. In the sitcom *Modern Family*, the clean freak Mitchell works full time as an attorney. He resists the urge to clean up the house in order to send a message to his stay-at-home, less tidy husband, Cameron, that perhaps he should help with the housework (Wrubel et al., 2011). In this example, the overburdened Mitchell has reduced his cleaning inputs to try to restore a sense of equity. At the same time, he hopes that this reduction in input—his no longer cleaning up the mess—will prompt Cameron to increase his input. These two strategies are adjustments to inputs, but adjustments also can be made to outcomes. The overworked partner might withhold other, you know, "benefits" of the relationship. Or the person doing less housework might surprise his or her partner with a weekend trip to a spa.

These little adjustments in relationships happen all the time as partners try to maintain a sense of equity. Even when equity isn't achieved objectively, just *feeling* as if things are equitable can make a difference. In the *Modern Family* example, we imagine that Cameron might not permanently change his sloppier habits, but maybe he'll make up for his low inputs in cleaning by being especially appreciative of the hard work that Mitchell puts into the house. Gratitude actually can go a long way toward making the scales seem more balanced.

The motivation for fairness in our relationships helps to explain **assortative mating**, people's tendency to seek relationships with others who are similar to them in some kind of social hierarchy. Of course, we've already noted that similarity is a key component of attraction and liking. But pairing up with those who are similar to you in social value also helps to equate partners on what rewards or resources they bring to the relationship (Hatfield & Rapson, 1993). For example, on the web site hotornot.com, people can post pictures of themselves to be rated by others on attractiveness, but they can also use this web site to contact other people to strike up conversations. Although there is strong agreement in who is rated as most attractive—and we know how much people value physical attractiveness in potential relationship partners—people still generally contact others who are similar to them in attractiveness (Lee et al., 2008), those in their own league, so to speak. Not-so-hot people try to connect with other not-so-hot people. This is known as the **matching phenomenon**. It helps to ensure a certain balance of outcomes in the relationship. People generally seek and end up in romantic relationships with someone similar to them in physical attractiveness (Feingold, 1988). Granted, the exchange of relationship rewards can cross currencies: One person (more often a woman) might trade on her youth and good looks to attract a mate who can provide financial resources and security (Baumeister & Vohs, 2004). For example, Hugh Hefner, the famed and wealthy impresario of all things Playboy, has had a string of beautiful girlfriends decades younger than himself.

The preference for equity in close relationships appears to be a cross-cultural universal, although the degree to which equity is achieved might vary a great deal (Aumer-Ryan et al., 2007). When people feel that the proportion of costs to benefits is roughly equivalent for both themselves and their partners, they are more likely to have sex, fall in love, commit to a long-term relationship, and be satisfied in that relationship (Buunk & van Yperen, 1989; Sprecher, 1998; van Yperen & Buunk, 1990).

SECTION
review | Cost-benefit Perspectives on Relationships

People evaluate relationships according to the costs and benefits to themselves and their partners.

Social exchange model	**Equity theory**
The social exchange model is based on the idea that relationship satisfaction depends on both the rewards received minus the costs, and expectations about the relationship (comparison level).	• Equity theory is based on the idea that partners look for fairness within a relationship both for themselves and for their partners. • This desire for a fair relationship may help account for people's tendency to form relationships with others of similar perceived social value.

Cultural and Historical Perspectives on Relationships

Suppose that a man (woman) had all the qualities you desired in a partner. Think about it. Would you marry this person if you were not in love with him (her)? Chances are that you answered "no." In today's Western world, love typically is viewed as the *raison d'être* for getting hitched and for staying committed to the relationship. We're bombarded with stories and songs that exalt love as the glue that binds people together and lead us into the happily ever after (Jackson et al., 2006). It is part of our cultural fabric. In fact, when American students were asked this question in 1995, only 3.5% of men and women said "yes" to the prospect of a loveless but otherwise satisfying marriage (Levine et al., 1995). But it's not just Americans who are romantics. As **FIGURE 15.6** shows, respondents from only two of 11 countries were fine with choosing to marry without love—India and Pakistan, where arranged marriages have remained common. Research shows that love and romance are shared around the world. But love has not always played so central a role in marriage even in the United States, and certainly does not always capture what draws many people across the world to a long-term commitment to another person. When the same question was presented to American students in 1967, only 65% of men and 24% of women said "no" (Kephart, 1967). Such studies tell us that in different eras and countries, people have been more receptive to entering into, and staying in, a marriage for reasons other than being in love. Let's take a look at this cross-cultural variability.

Think
ABOUT

[Robyn Beck/AFP/ Getty Images]

Responses:	**Yes**	**No**	**Undecided**
India	49.0%	24.0%	26.9%
Pakistan	50.4%	39.1%	10.4%
Thailand	18.8%	33.8%	47.5%
United States	3.5%	85.9%	10.6%
England	7.3%	83.6%	9.1%
Japan	2.3%	62.0%	35.7%
Philippines	11.4%	63.6%	25.0%
Mexico	10.2%	80.5%	9.3%
Brazil	4.3%	85.7%	10.0%
Hong Kong	5.8%	77.6%	16.7%
Australia	4.8%	80.0%	15.2%

FIGURE 15.6

Love and Marriage in Different Countries

Responses to the question, If a man (woman) had all the other qualities you desired, would you marry this person if you were not in love with him (her)?

[Data source: Levine et al. (1995) © 1995 SAGE. Reprinted by permission.]

Cross-cultural Differences in Romantic Commitment

Differences between individualistic and collectivistic cultures shape the way people view intimate commitments. In collectivistic cultures, family considerations and opinion have a much stronger influence than they do in individualistic cultures in determining whom people decide to marry, as well as whether or not they stay in the relationship (Dion & Dion, 1996).

Take China as an example. In Chinese culture, two fundamental values are *xiao* (loosely translated as filial piety—respect for and devotion to family) and *guanxi*

Different cultures, different customs. Marriage and weddings are often construed very differently in different cultures. The relatively collectivistic culture of China prescribes different norms and expectations for both entering into and staying committed to a close relationship.

[Oliver Strewe/Lonely Planet Images/Getty Images]

(network, referring to broader social interdependence). Both strongly drive decisions about intimate relationships. Chinese students are more likely to report family disapproval as an obstacle to marriage than are U.S. students. In China, judgments about whether the partner will support one's parents are more important factors in decisions to marry and stay together than in the United States (Zhang & Kline, 2009).

The fairy-tale themes of romantic bliss that pervade the Western conception of a lifelong commitment to another are much less prevalent in Chinese culture (Jackson et al., 2006). If the basis of commitment to another person is not one's own personal fulfillment, then one's own satisfaction, or lack thereof, in a relationship is not a compelling reason to get divorced. In collectivistic cultures, as long as the relationship fulfills the cultural expectation of maintaining communal cohesion and family unity, it is more likely to be maintained. This is partly how cultural psychologists explain the negative correlation between collectivism and divorce rates (**FIGURE 15.7**). In fact, this correlation appears even among U.S. states as well as among countries (Toth & Kemmelmeier, 2009; Vandello & Cohen, 1999). In India, where arranged marriages are the cultural norm, the divorce rate is around 5%, compared with the over 50% rate observed in many individualistic cultures, such as the United States.

Does this mean that people are more happily married in India or other countries where arranged marriages are prevalent? Not necessarily: Evidence suggests it can go either way. In China and Turkey, for example, partner-selected marriages appear to be happier both initially and over the long term than arranged marriages (e.g., Demir

Historical Differences in Long-term Commitment

Like the study of cross-cultural differences in intimate commitment, the historical record reveals the powerful influence of cultural expectation and norms. You live in a very different world than did your grandparents. Marriage, and staying in that marriage, is now much more of a choice than it used to be.

People hook up more frequently without any expectation of a long-term commitment (Paul et al., 2000). Fewer people are getting married than ever before, and those who do wait longer to marry (Popenoe & Whitehead, 2007). More and more couples are living together, even when they're not married (Bramlett & Mosher, 2002). People are increasingly having or adopting babies out of wedlock (Popenoe & Whitehead, 2007). In fact, after steadily rising for five decades, the number of children born to unmarried women has crossed a critical threshold: More than half of births to American women under 30 occur outside of marriage. This is especially true for those who don't go to college and among African Americans: 73% of Black children are

born outside marriage, compared with 53% of Latino children and 29% of White children. In the United States, relationships in which couples have children are more than twice as likely to dissolve if they are not married than if they are. In one study, two thirds of cohabiting couples split up by the time their child turned 10 years old (Smock & Greenland, 2010).

Thus, what was once viewed as deviant and illegitimate is now becoming more commonplace and turning into a cultural norm. These changes are important because we rely on cultural norms to interpret what is normal and how we should conduct a relationship. But some of the changing norms can lead to erroneous expectations about relationships. For example, high school seniors now believe that it is a good idea for a couple to cohabit for a while before marriage. Yet research shows that cohabitation does not make it more likely that a subsequent marriage will be successful. If anything, cohabitation prior to marriage is associated with a greater likelihood of divorce, although the reasons for this remain unclear (Dush et al., 2003; McGinnis, 2003).

Of course, cultural change does not occur in isolation but in the context of, and in part because of, changes in the economic,

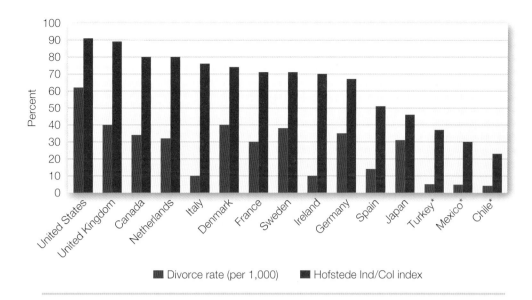

Figure 15.7

Divorce Rates in Different Countries

Why do different countries have different rates of divorce? Some research suggests that a critical factor is the level of individualism or collectivism of a culture. Individualistic cultures, such as the United States, tend to have higher divorce rates than more collectivistic cultures, such as Mexico. Note: Divorce rate is per 1,000. In the Hofstede Individualism/ Collectivism Index, higher numbers indicate more individualistic countries.

[Data sources: Divorce rate: Data from U.S. Census Bureau, Statistical Abstract of the United States, 2011, International Statistics, Table 1336, Marriage and Divorce Rates by Country: 1980 to 2008, U.S. Census Bureau (2012), retrieved from http://www.census.gov/compendia/statab/2011/tables/11s1335.pdf; for Turkey, Mexico, and Chile: Data from Top Ten Countries with Lowest Divorce Rate, Maps of the World, www.mapsofworld.com. Hofstede Individualism/collectivism index: Data from the Hofstede Centre, http://geert-hofstede.com/countries.html.]

& Fisiloglu, 1999). In contrast, partner-selected marriages in India are often happier initially, whereas arranged marriages grow happier as the years go by (e.g., Yelsma & Athappilly, 1988). Researchers speculate that these differences may reflect different cultural expectations for marital satisfaction. As Bradbury and Karney (2010) explain, given the typically more formalized structure of arranged marriages in India, spouses may expect it to take time for intimacy and satisfaction to develop, so they nurture these qualities over the years. But those in partner-selected marriages may be surprised and unprepared when their initial passion fades over the years.

technological, and population landscape. For example, whereas marriage traditionally was fueled in part by economic concerns, this is now less the case. Women's role in the workplace is changing the relationship context, with women becoming less reliant on a husband's financial contributions. Indeed, nations tend to tolerate more divorces as those countries become more industrialized and there are fewer gender disparities in the workplace. For example, as China has moved toward a market economy, the divorce rate has steadily risen (Wang, 2001).

Cultural, economic, and technological changes have contributed to what Finkel and colleagues (2014) characterize as three dominant models of marriage. They argue that from the late 1700s to the mid-1800s, marriage was geared primarily toward resolving practical concerns and meeting pragmatic goals, such as economic self-sufficiency. They refer to this model as practical marriage. From the mid-1800s to the mid-1960s, the breadwinner model dominated. During this time, a wife's labor became less essential to the household's economic self-sufficiency, and consistent with Rank's (1936a) idea that romantic love became more important in the 20th century, marriages focused more on love, passion,

and intimacy. Finkel and colleagues suggest that from the mid-1960s to the present time, marriages increasingly have become a forum for trying to experience a greater sense of satisfaction from life and self-growth and actualization. This self-expressive model can put a lot of pressure on the relationship if it is not built to support those kinds of goals. In fact, Finkel and colleagues use the metaphor that such a reliance often sets people up to climb Mount Maslow (referring to the famous psychologist who introduced the concept of self-actualization; see chapter 6) without enough oxygen.

[Blazej Lyjak/Shutterstock]

Culture and Similarity in Friendship

Think

ABOUT

[Monkey Business Images/Shutterstock]

Think about what it is to be friends with someone. Do you prefer your friends to be similar to you, sharing your religious beliefs, political views, and lifestyle? As you'll remember, individuals are attracted to others with similar attributes to their own. To be sure, people from cultures all over the world are more attracted to similar than to dissimilar others. It is interesting to note, however, that the degree of similarity between friendship partners tends to be lower in East Asian societies, such as Japan, Korea, and Taiwan, than it is in North American settings (Igarashi et al., 2008; Kashima et al., 1995; Uleman et al., 2000). This is true of both actual levels of similarity and perceptions of similarity. What's more, whereas similarity plays a major role in determining relationship quality in the United States, it is much less tied to relationship quality in East Asian countries (Heine & Renshaw, 2002; Lee & Bond, 1998).

The distinction between individualist and collectivist cultures helps explain these differing views on the importance of similarity. If you view yourself as independent and thus free to make friends with whomever you want, then why not pursue others who like what you like, validate your beliefs, and share your lifestyle? If you find that they are not quite similar enough, that's no problem: You have hundreds of other people to choose from. In contrast, individuals in collectivist cultures experience the self as constrained by norms and obligations imposed by family and society as a whole. They do not feel so free to create friendships and are less likely to enter into friendships that are based solely on similarity. As a result, friends in these cultures may be more dissimilar.

SECTION review | Cultural and Historical Perspectives on Relationships

Differences in romantic commitment

- Historical differences in the United States and cultural differences across the world suggest that love is not always the central basis of marriage.
- In collectivist cultures, family considerations have more influence on choice of marriage partners than in individualist cultures.

Culture and similarity in friendship

- Differences in individualist and collectivist cultures affect whether or not similarity is important in a friendship.
- People in collectivist cultures may be constrained by norms and obligations, feeling less free to form friendships, and so are less likely to rely on similarity.

The Time Course of Romantic Relationships

Although romantic relationships progress in a variety of ways, some theories and research programs illuminate certain commonalities in how relationships change over time. As we have done throughout this chapter, we will generally discuss these issues without focusing on the sexual orientation of the partners in the relationship. To be sure, the vast majority of relationship research has been conducted with heterosexual couples, and this can be an important factor to keep in mind. At the same time, however, the factors that influence relational commitment and satisfaction have generally been found to be similar among same-sex and heterosexual couples (e.g., Balsam et al., 2008; Ducharme & Kollar, 2012; Kurdek, 2004; Roisman et al., 2008).

Self-disclosure

Imagine two people meeting for the first time. During this initial stage of a relationship, people engage in varying degrees of **self-disclosure**, sharing information about themselves. Self-disclosure plays a key role in the formation and maintenance of close relationships and in the intimacy developed between two people. When people first meet, they usually engage in *small talk*, superficial forms of self-disclosure that generally go no deeper than the weather or where they are from. If both find these initial encounters rewarding, they tend to open up, communicating about a broader range of topics and revealing deeper, more intimate information about themselves (Altman & Taylor, 1973). Typically, smooth, enjoyable conversations in early stages tend to involve exchanges of self-disclosure at the same depth. Too much self-discourse too soon is viewed as bizarre and off putting (think of the colloquial abbreviation TMI–too much information); too little self-disclosure can interfere with the progress of trust and intimacy.

> **Self-disclosure** The sharing of information about oneself.

It turns out that relationship partners share different types of information about themselves at different stages of the relationship. According to Bernard Murstein's (1987) *stimulus-value-role theory* (**FIGURE 15.8**), when partners first meet, their attraction to each other is primarily based on *stimulus* information— conspicuous attributes such as age and physical appearance.

If the relationship progresses beyond these first impressions, partners enter the *value* stage, in which they share their attitudes and beliefs (about religion and sex, for example). This stage helps them to decide whether they are sufficiently compatible to continue the relationship. It is generally only later, after partners have been committed to each other for a while, that they begin communicating about their roles, meaning their attitudes and plans when it comes to major life tasks such as parenting and establishing a career.

Research suggests that these stages are not really that discrete or orderly (e.g., Brehm, 1992). Some couples get into values and roles early in the relationship; some may discuss roles before getting to know their values. However, Murstein's model is useful when we think about how relationships progress and the types of shared knowledge that matter. One consequence of sharing different types of information at different stages of the relationship is that partners may not be aware of differences that can create problems down the road. In the budding stages of a new relationship, during the value stage, people learn about each other's likes and dislikes. Having found someone who shares their interests in cuisine, entertainment, and politics, they may believe that they have finally found *the* one. It may not be until they are together for a long time that they learn of incompatibilities in, for example, role expectations. Of course, for some couples this can be a time when partners discover how truly compatible they are and that they share a foundation from which their relationship can grow.

Rose-colored Lenses?

Another reason that people in a new romantic relationship often believe that they have found the perfect partner is that they perceive their new partner through rose-colored lenses. People all over the world want to have a romantic partner who is warm and trustworthy, loyal and passionate, attractive and exciting, and smart and competent (Tran et al., 2008). What we usually end up with, however,

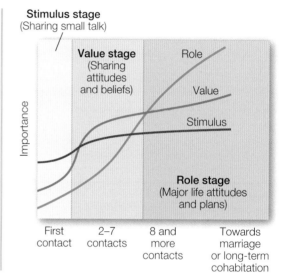

Figure 15.8

Self-disclosing Different Types of Personal Information at Three Different Phases of Relationship Development

Murstein's stimulus-value-role theory suggests that as time goes by and romantic partners continue to self-disclose, they share three types of information that influence the relationship. However, it is not until late in the developing relationship—in some cases, after marriage—that partners learn about their role (in)compatibility.

[Data source: Murstein (1987) © 1987 Blackwell Publishing Inc. Reprinted by permission.]

is someone with less than the total package. How is it, then, that we can be satisfied with the partner we're with? As you'll remember from our discussion of cognitive dissonance theory (chapter 6), after a person has made a choice between alternatives that are similar in attractiveness, the nagging doubt that she made the wrong choice creates an uncomfortable feeling of dissonance. To reduce dissonance, people often exaggerate the positive qualities of the alternative they chose and, at the same time, exaggerate the negative qualities of the alternative they did not choose.

In a similar manner, people show a powerful tendency—at least, early in a relationship—to construct idealized perceptions of their romantic partners that highlight their positive qualities and downplay their faults. These idealized perceptions are called positive illusions (Murray et al., 1996). They are not full-blown illusions in the sense that partners are completely blind to the truth about each other's virtues and faults. Rather, they are illusions in the sense that individuals interpret facts about their partners in a more benevolent fashion than other people would (Gagné & Lydon, 2004).

To illustrate, in one line of studies people wrote about their partner's greatest fault (Murray & Holmes, 1993, 1999). People judged their partner's faults to be less important than outside observers judged them to be. Also, they focused on the bright side of their partner's faults. For example, a woman might write that although her boyfriend got upset easily, that behavior reflected his exceptionally passionate and vivacious personality. Similarly, people offered "yes, but" interpretations of their partner's faults—that is, they recognized their partner's faults but focused on the positive repercussions. For example, a man might write that, *yes*, his fiancée does not help with household chores, *but* at least that gives her more time to pursue her yoga career, which is probably more important. Related research shows that people perceive their partner's faults as affecting the relationship less than the partner's many positive qualities (Neff & Karney, 2003).

Positive illusions Idealized perceptions of romantic partners that highlight their positive qualities and downplay their faults.

"I don't care if she is a tape dispenser. I love her."

[Sam Gross/The New Yorker Collection/ The Cartoon Bank]

You might be asking yourself, Is it really such a good idea to put our lovers up on a pedestal? Aren't we setting ourselves up for crushing disappointment when our partners inevitably fail to live up to our idealized perceptions of them? The answer hinges on just how removed from reality people's positive illusions are (Neff & Karney, 2005). If people are projecting positive qualities onto their partners that they simply don't have, then they likely are setting themselves up for disappointment (Miller, 1997).

On the other hand, if people are aware of their partner's positive and negative qualities but interpret them positively, such illusions can benefit the relationship. Sandra Murray and her colleagues have shown that people who idealize their romantic partners are more satisfied and feel stronger love and trust (Murray & Holmes, 1993, 1997; Murray et al., 2000; Neff & Karney, 2002). In one study (Murray et al., 1996), married couples and dating partners were asked to rate themselves and their partners on their positive and negative qualities. They also were asked to indicate how satisfied they were in the relationship. Idealization was measured by the participants' tendency to overestimate their partner's positive qualities and underestimate their faults, compared with the partner's ratings of him- or herself. The more participants idealized their romantic partners, the more satisfied they were in the relationship.

By idealizing our partner, we are likely to view his or her qualities and behaviors as all the more rewarding—so much so, in fact, that it seems inconceivable that someone else out there could provide us with the same rewards. Although perhaps illusory, such perceptions have the beneficial consequence of strengthening commitment.

Furthermore, these positive perceptions also can motivate people to reach for the ideal with which they are perceived, and thus grow and develop in ways that are appreciated by their partners. When Murray and colleagues (1996) followed couples over time, they found that in more satisfied relationships, the partners came to perceive themselves more as they initially were idealized to be. This may partly reflect the operation of self-fulfilling prophecies, which we discussed in chapters 3 and 11. When people hold expectations of us, we often come to act in a way that confirms those expectations. Such findings led Murray and colleagues to suggest that these illusions can be more prescient than blind.

Adjusting to Interdependency

So far, we have seen that early in the relationship, partners disclose in a way that obscures potential incompatibilities, and they view each other through the rose-colored lenses of positive illusions. As a result of these (and other) processes, romantic relationships usually start off with a rapid increase in satisfaction as partners are overtaken with the excitement and passion of new love. But soon after this initial state of bliss, most dating relationships—even those that eventually result in marriage—hit a plateau in which satisfaction levels off for a while (Eidelson, 1980) (see **FIGURE 15.9**).

Why? According to the model of relational turbulence proposed by Solomon and Knobloch (2004) (**FIGURE 15.10**), in the early stage of a relationship there is little conflict, largely because partners are relatively independent and thus do not interfere with each other's routines or goals. But as partners make the transition from casual

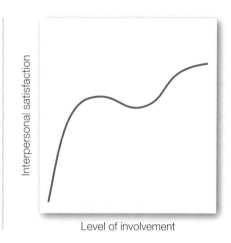

Level of involvement

Figure 15.9

Relationship Satisfaction Changes With Level of Involvement

The beginning of a romantic relationship typically is marked by a rapid rise in satisfaction. Soon after, though, satisfaction levels off, most likely because the partners are adjusting to their increasing interdependence. If the relationship survives this turbulent period and the partners accommodate to each other's needs and lives, the couple enjoys even more satisfaction, albeit at a more gradual rate.

[Data source: Eidelson (1980)]

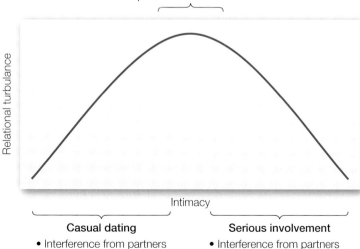

Transition from casual dating to serious involvement
• Interference from partners is high because partners are influencing each other's routines without expertise.

Intimacy

Casual dating
• Interference from partners is low because individuals are autonomous.

Serious involvement
• Interference from partners is low because partners are skilled at helping each other accomplish goals.

FIGURE 15.10

The Relational Turbulence Model

The level of turbulence in a new relationship increases as the partners become more interdependent, spending more time together and interfering with each other's routines. If the partners stay together and negotiate how to facilitate each other's goals, then turbulence declines.

[Data source: Knobloch & Donovan-Kicken (2006) © 2006 John Wiley & Sons, Inc. Reprinted by permission.]

Model of relational turbulence The idea that as partners make the transition from casual dating to more serious involvement in the relationship, they go through a turbulent period of adjustment.

dating to more serious involvement in the relationship, they go through a turbulent period of adjustment and turmoil (Knobloch & Donovan-Kicken, 2006; Knobloch et al., 2007). As they spend more time together and become dependent on each other, they can start to feel that the partner is restricting their freedom and demanding too much of them. Partners start to interfere with each other's daily routines, which take up the time the partners previously devoted to the activities they enjoyed before the relationship began. For example, perhaps Jane had plans to hang out with her friends this weekend, but her long-term boyfriend assumed that she was going to hang out with him, and now she is stressed out by the competing demands on her time.

If the partners stay together and learn how to adjust to their increasing interdependency, coordinating their routines and accommodating each other's personal needs and plans, the period of turmoil quiets down. ("Honey, let's agree that Friday is my 'friend night.'") This can result in another, albeit subtler, increase in satisfaction (see Figure 15.9).

This model helps to explain why conflict in romantic relationships is particularly high during the period of young adulthood. As you can see in **FIGURE 15.11**, the frequency of conflict increases as people go from their late teens to their mid-20s. Things become more peaceful after that (Chen et al., 2006).

This pattern occurs most likely due to the fact that, during their mid-20s, many people are starting romantic relationships while simultaneously choosing what occupational role to pursue and making plans to get their careers off the ground. As we discussed earlier in this chapter (see also chapter 6), individuals raised in Western cultures derive a sense of self-esteem from choosing their life path and making a unique mark on the world. But this motive of asserting individuality can conflict with relationship demands. If individuals invest their resources into a romantic relationship, they may be held back from pursuing other personal goals. At the same time, if they focus too much on making their unique mark, they will likely create tension in the relationship (Baxter, 2004). After their mid-20s, many people have a firmer footing in their professional careers, so they experience less conflict between their desires for attachment and intimacy and their desires for independence and achievement, allowing them to get along better with their partners.

Let's say a couple has made it through the turbulence caused by adjusting to interdependency, and they have struck a workable balance between their motives for independence and belonging. They decide to get married, pledging to spend the rest of their lives together. We can now expect that they will live happily ever after, enjoying the same or even higher levels of satisfaction. *Right?*

Marital Satisfaction?

Unfortunately, research shows that, in most cases and even despite the partners' good intentions, the prognosis for the course of the marital relationship is not so blissful as most couples expect it will be when they tie the knot. In one of the more comprehensive studies of marital satisfaction, Huston and colleagues (2001) followed dozens of spouses who married in 1981. Relationship satisfaction steadily declined for both husbands and wives as the years ticked by (see **FIGURE 15.12**). It's unlikely that the married couples in this study were particularly hard to please: Other studies show a similar overall decline in ratings of marital quality (Karney & Bradbury, 2000; Kurdek, 1999). Of course, not all couples experience the same rate of decline, but most do (Kurdek, 2005).

Marital satisfaction tends to take a particularly steep dive at two points (Kurdek, 1999). The first drop occurs within the first year of marriage; the second

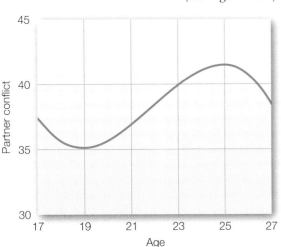

Figure 15.11

Romantic Conflict in Young Adulthood

Many people begin romantic relationships in their mid-20s, but this is also a time when people typically struggle to establish their careers and pursue their personal goals. As a result, conflict in romantic relationships tends to spike. After a while, though, perhaps because people feel more secure in their careers, conflict gradually diminishes.

[Data source: Chen et al. (2006) © 2006 John Wiley & Sons, Inc. Reprinted by permission.]

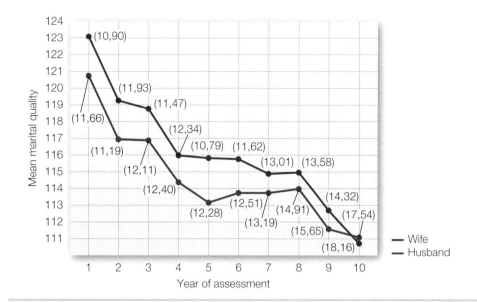

Figure 15.12

The Trajectory of Marital Satisfaction

Most newlyweds presume that their marriages will become more and more satisfying over time, but statistics suggest that on average, satisfaction actually tends to decline over time.

[Data source: Kurdek (1999)]

occurs at about the eighth year of marriage (Kovacs, 1983). The big question, of course, is what causes the decline in marital satisfaction once the honeymoon is over. Although many important factors are involved, let's focus on six important ones.

Slacking Off

When two people start dating, they go to a lot of trouble to be—or at least appear to be—polite and thoughtful. They suppress their burps, hold the door open, and put on makeup. But once this initial courtship phase has passed and the ink on the marriage certificate is dry, people may stop trying so hard to be consistently courteous and charming (Miller, 2001). One study showed that acts of kindness and expressions of affection dropped by half within the first two years of marriage (Huston et al., 2001). Remember how we said that relationship satisfaction is largely a function of rewards? Well, soon after the marriage vows, spouses start getting fewer rewards, due in large part to a lack of effort.

Small Issues Get Magnified

Interdependency acts like a magnifying glass, exaggerating conflicts that do not exist in more casual relationships. Why? Because we spend so much time with our romantic partners and depend so heavily on them for unique and valuable rewards, they have the power to cause us more pain and frustration than anyone else can. Indeed, spouses can stress each other out even if they do not intend to do so. For example, people are more negatively affected by their intimate partner's cranky moods (Caughlin et al., 2000) and work-related stress (Lavee & Ben-Ari, 2007) than they are by the similar tribulations of their friends or of strangers. Another consequence of spending so much time together is that trivial annoyances can, through sheer repetition, add up to significant frustration. Just as the light tapping of a dripping faucet can drive you insane after a couple days, frequent interaction means that a partner's grating quirks gradually build up to real annoyance (Cunningham et al., 2005).

Sore Spots are Revealed

As we mentioned, increasing levels of intimacy are closely associated with self-disclosure. As the relationship grows, partners reveal more and more of themselves to each other. Although opening up to another person can be very exciting (Archer & Cook, 1986; Taylor et al., 1981), it also means that partners know a lot of not-so-pleasant information about each other, including their secrets, foibles, and weaknesses. This means that when conflict occurs, our romantic partners have at their disposal an entire arsenal of emotional weaponry that they can use to tease us, wound us, and threaten us in ways others can't. In fact, even if partners do not intend to cause each other harm, their access to this sensitive information suggests that they can, sooner or later, accidently reveal our secrets (Petronio et al., 1989), hurt our feelings (Kowalski, 2003), or embarrass us in public (Miller, 1996).

Unwelcome Surprises Appear

Although couples might recognize their incompatibilities when they choose to get married, it's often the surprises down the road that dampen marital satisfaction. These surprises tend to fall into two general categories. First, we can be surprised to learn the truth about things we thought we knew. One clear example of this is what are called *fatal attractions* (Felmlee, 2001). Qualities that we initially found attractive in the other person gradually become irritating or disappointing. Although, as we mentioned, newlyweds initially idealize each other (Murray et al., 1996), positive illusions usually wear off over time. For instance, at first you liked the fact that your partner was spontaneous and fun, but now he seems irresponsible, flaky, and childish. Or perhaps you initially celebrated your partner's high level of attention and devotion, but after a couple years you come to resent the same behavior when it seems overly possessive and clingy. It's not that partners are unaware of each other's fatal qualities when they choose to marry. Rather, they fail to appreciate how their attitudes toward those qualities will change after a few years. Needless to say, these unexpected shifts in attitudes can take a bite out of marital satisfaction (Watson & Humrichouse, 2006).

A second category of unwelcome surprises occurs when married couples discover things that they did not know or expect at all. A good example is offered by the realities of parenthood, which, along with money, is the biggest source of marital conflict (Stanley et al., 2002). Most newlyweds, if they plan to have children, presume that parenthood will be enjoyable and bring them closer to each other. But most soon discover that parenthood, though wonderful at times, takes a significant toll on their marital satisfaction. Parents often underestimate how much time their children will demand, and therefore how little time they will have to enjoy each other's company (Claxton & Perry-Jenkins, 2008). The arrival of babies increases stress, robs people of sleep, and introduces new responsibilities, thereby heightening conflict and, in turn, decreasing how satisfied partners are and even how much they love each other (Lawrence et al., 2008).

How do we know that this decline in satisfaction is related to the stress of having and raising children? For one, cohabitating couples without children do not show the same dip in satisfaction as their heterosexual, child-raising counterparts (Kurdek, 2008). In fact, same-sex couples who have children also report a decline in relationship satisfaction (Ducharme & Kollar, 2012). Second, parents report a small but reliable increase in marital satisfaction once their children have grown up and left the nest (Gorchoff et al., 2008). And you thought your parents were devastated when you went away to college!

Partners Have Unrealistic Expectations

Good relationships demand a great deal more work and sacrifice than is typically portrayed in movies and on greeting cards. If a couple weds with unrealistically high expectations about the magic of marriage, they can feel cheated and disappointed later on, even if their relationship is healthy according to objective criteria (Amato et al., 2007). As we mentioned when discussing social exchange, satisfaction in close relationships depends on how well the partners' current outcomes match their comparison level—the outcomes they expected to have when they married.

Passionate Love Loses Steam

A final reason satisfaction declines during the first years of marriage is that passionate love—that burning desire for each other that makes life so blissful and exciting—tends to diminish over time (Sprecher & Regan, 1998; Tucker & Aron, 1993). Whereas early on husbands and wives claim that they feel an urgent longing

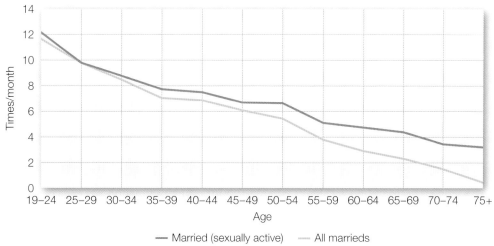

Figure 15.13

Frequency of Sexual Intercourse Over the Course of Marriages in the United States

As the years tick by in a marriage, the frequency with which the partners have sex tends to decline.

[Data source: Call et al. (1995) © 1995 John Wiley & Sons, Inc. Reprinted by permission.]

for each other and that they melt when they look into each other's eyes, pretty soon the intensity dissipates. Indeed, the decrease in a couple's romantic love can happen rapidly. Only two years after tying the knot, spouses express affection about half as often as they did when they first wed (Huston & Chorost, 1994). This may be one reason that, across the globe, divorces occur most frequently in the fourth year of marriage, when married couples complain that the "magic" has died (Fisher, 1995).

Part of the reason for this dwindling of romance is that, over time, what was novel becomes less so. The sheer novelty of new love makes the partners especially arousing and exciting (Foster et al., 1998). Partners may continue to view each other with affection and sexual interest but the intensity of the arousal—a principal ingredient in passionate love—inevitably diminishes somewhat (Acker & Davis, 1992). **FIGURE 15.13** displays some of the results from a broad survey of American sexuality.

Here we see that the average couple has intercourse less and less frequently over the course of their marriage. In fact, some married couples have so little sex after age 50 that the researchers made a separate line just for married couples who have sex at least once a month (Call et al., 1995). Couldn't this decline occur simply because the spouses are getting older? Although advancing age is indeed a factor, evidence also shows that people who remarry (and thus experience the novelty of a new partner) increase their frequency of intercourse, at least for a while (Call et al., 1995).

When the Party's Over . . . The Breakup

For these and many other reasons, relationships often do end. As we will see later in this chapter, some estimates place the U.S. divorce rate near 50%. A much higher percentage of even serious dating relationships will ultimately come to a close. What are some of the consequences of the breakup for the individual? Even for the "dumper" as opposed to the "dumpee," a breakup often exacts a severe toll on overall well-being (Sbarra, 2006).

The two major emotions that people experience in the face of a breakup are anger and sadness. Anger typically is pretty strong at first but diminishes somewhat quickly, whereas sadness may not be so severe initially but will diminish more slowly. Of course, the strength of these emotions depends on the importance of the relationship, the circumstances of the breakup, and how quickly the individual can accept it. Those who maintain love for the partner and are unable to accept the dissolution of the relationship recover much more slowly from these negative emotions (Sbarra, 2006). Recall our discussion of self-regulatory perseveration from chapter 5. When people stay invested in a goal, such as being with another person, that is unattainable, this perpetuates a cycle of negativity (Pyszczynski & Greenberg, 1987a). They continually confront their failed aspirations.

Who is best able to come to terms with the dissolution of a relationship? A person's level of attachment security plays a pivotal role. Those who are higher in attachment anxiety cling more tightly to the relationship. The hope of rekindling the extinguished flame allows the negative emotions to persist. In contrast, more securely attached people generally are better able to accept the breakup and so recover from sadness more quickly (Mikulincer & Shaver, 2007).

Perhaps when getting dumped by an ex, you've heard the line that your now ex-partner would rather "just be friends." Do you think this is a good idea? For the person whose love has dissipated, it may not be that bad, but for the person who just got jilted, it can be difficult. Indeed, in one study that followed college students for a month after they broke up, recurring contact with an ex was associated with persisting love and sadness (Sbarra & Emery, 2005). After a breakup, absence makes the heart grow less fond, and that might be exactly what you need to move on with your life. Investing in alternative pursuits, such as other relationships or challenges at school or work, can be precisely the catalyst that helps people to disengage from the failed relationship (Pyszczynski & Greenberg, 1987a).

In addition to causing an emotional upheaval, a breakup can also jar our sense of who we are, blurring our sense of self and ultimately instigating a redefinition of our self-concept. Research by Slotter and colleagues (2010) found that when people recalled or imagined a breakup, they reported changes in their self-concept and reduced self-concept clarity. This is reflected in the language that people use to talk about breakups. One study, for example, examined what people wrote in their online diaries and blogs. Unlike with other life disruptions such as a career change, those who experienced a breakup used more words connoting confusion ("bewildered," "uncertain") when describing how they thought of themselves. This lack of self-concept clarity plays a key role in the reduced well-being that people experience after a breakup. Over a six-month window, the more self-concept confusion people experienced, the more distress they experienced (Mason et al., 2012). This kind of dynamic occurs, for example, when the person reflects back and says something such as "Now that I'm not with Carol, I just don't know who I am anymore."

So what can you do to facilitate the recovery process? We previously mentioned that recurring contact with the ex probably is not a good idea, but that engaging in alternative activities and investments is. In addition, research suggests that you also should strive to have compassion for yourself, that is, to love and appreciate yourself and be aware of your place in a shared humanity. When Dave Sbarra and colleagues (2012) studied divorcing couples, they audiotaped the participants talking about the divorce for four minutes, and later had judges rate the participants' level of self-compassion. Even this short snippet of observation was informative. The more self-compassion judges saw in the participants, the better the participants' emotional recovery in the nine months following the divorce.

Are We All Doomed, Then?

All of this can seem depressing, but it shouldn't be. The processes we've described—the trials and tribulations, the inevitable decline in novelty, and so on—are normal and probably will happen to most married couples. But people can mitigate the negative impact of these processes simply by being informed of what to expect as marriage develops over time. Studies show that spouses who began their marriages with unrealistically positive expectations of marital bliss are the least satisfied with their marriages as the years tick on. Conversely, after four years of marriage, the happiest couples are those who started out with realistic outlooks about what married life would be like (McNulty & Karney, 2004). Simply by being aware of these processes and starting marriage with reasonable expectations, couples can still enjoy their relationships long after the honeymoon is over (Srivastava et al., 2006).

Of course, some committed romantic relationships end in a few years, some last but become less and less satisfying, and others remain satisfying and passionate for a lifetime. Even in marriages where the passion has dwindled, older couples sometimes continue to express deep companionate love for each other that can keep them genuinely happy (Hecht et al., 1994; Lauer & Lauer, 1985). Next, we'll take a close look at factors that contribute to romantic relationships that dissolve and those that thrive.

SECTION review | The Time Course of Romantic Relationships

Relationships change over time in common ways.

Self-disclosure	Rose-colored lenses?	Adjusting to interdependency	Marital satisfaction?	The breakup	Doomed or not?
Partners share information about themselves gradually, so it may take a long time for some fundamental differences to emerge.	• Early on, the romantic partner may be idealized. • This may lead to disappointment unless one is aware of—and interprets positively—all the partner's range of qualities.	• As independence evolves into interdependence, conflict may arise. • Adjusting to interdependence creates a firmer footing for the relationship.	On average, marital satisfaction tends to decrease over time, especially after the first year and after the eighth year of marriage.	Breakups result in anger and sadness, best healed by alternative investments and self-compassion.	The happiest couples start out with realistic outlooks about married life.

Long-term Relationships: Understanding Those That Dissolve and Those That Thrive

First let me state to you, Alfred, and to you, Patricia, that of the 200 marriages that I have performed, all but seven have failed. So the odds are not good. We don't like to admit it, especially at the wedding ceremony, but it's in the back of all our minds, isn't it? How long will it last?

—Reverend Dupas (played by Donald Sutherland), in the movie *Little Murders* (Brodsky et al., 1971)

Most estimates put the divorce rate in the United States at nearly 50%, meaning that almost half of all marriages don't last "so long as you both shall live." Depending on the source, this divorce rate is at, or at least near, the highest of most industrialized countries. Moreover, the estimate climbs to between 65% and 75% for second marriages and even higher for third marriages.

These figures are troubling, given that stable and fulfilling marriages are associated with better physical and mental health, better educational attainment, and economic achievement for both parents and children (Kiecolt-Glaser & Newton, 2001). This is also true of same-sex marriages (Ducharme & Kollar, 2012). Divorce, on the other hand, is linked to a number of negative outcomes, not the least of which is risk of early death. Divorced people are at a 23% greater risk for all causes of mortality (Sbarra et al., 2011), though it is important to note that these data do not permit a causal inference that divorce causes death. It may be that people who are likely to get divorced also have some characteristic that is likely to contribute to their dying earlier.

Celebrity couple Gwyneth Paltrow and Chris Martin announced their plan to divorce in 2014, a fate shared by approximately 50% of American marriages.

[Kevin Mazur/Getty Images for J/P Haitian Relief Organization]

Given the benefits of a good long-term relationship, it would be useful to know how to identify when a marriage might find itself on the rocks and how to steer it back to safer waters. On the high seas of marriage, two parts of the journey seem to be most treacherous: the first seven years and midlife (around 14 to 16 years), typically when couples are dealing with the stress of teenage children. By observing conversations early in marriage, Gottman and Levenson (2000) have been able to forecast when these storms will hit. They observed the conversations of newlywed couples and then tracked them over years. During the initial interview, they videotaped the couples having conversations about different topics, from a mundane catch-up on the day's events to a discussion about something good in the relationship to a discussion about a recurring issue or problem.

On the basis of observations of thousands of couples discussing sources of marital conflict, Gottman pinpointed a cascading process in which *criticism* (telling the partner his or her faults) by one partner leads to *contempt* (making sarcastic comments about the partner or rolling one's eyes), which in turn leads to *defensiveness* (denying responsibility), which in turn leads to *stonewalling* (withdrawing or avoiding).

Gottman refers to these stages as the four horsemen of the (relational) apocalypse, because their appearance strongly foreshadows the dissolution of a relationship. Fortunately, as we will see, there are ways of overcoming this cycle of relational doom.

Not a good sign: According to John Gottman's research, eye-rolling is one telltale sign of communication patterns that could forecast an early demise to a relationship.

[cstar55/E+/Getty Images]

Gottman (1993) found that by looking at patterns of negative affect and contempt when discussing problems, he could predict which couples were likely to divorce in the first few years and which were more likely to divorce after about 14 years. A high level of negativity—those four horsemen—portends early divorce. In contrast, a lack of strong positive affect in couple conversations predicts divorce in the second decade of marriage. One way to account for these patterns is to think about the security and growth functions of relationships. The early divorces may be predicted by high negative affect, which disrupts the sense of security people seek from romantic relationships. A roller coaster of a relationship, one characterized by intense positivity but also intense negativity, is unlikely to provide much security, so it tends to fail in the first few years. In contrast, a lack of strong positive affect early on may lead to boredom over the long haul. Relationships lacking strong positive affect may provide little growth and stimulation after a decade of marriage.

Interdependence theory
The idea that satisfaction, investments, and perceived alternatives are critical in determining commitment to a particular relationship.

Should I Stay or Should I Go?

Think about one of the romantic relationships that you've had. Did you stick with it? Or did you head for the door? Why? Your initial response may be that it depended on how satisfied you were with the relationship. The less satisfied you were, the more likely you were to get out the dump truck. But this is likely only part of the story.

Recall that the social exchange model takes an economic perspective on relationships and posits that rewards, costs, and comparison level determine relationship satisfaction. Caryl Rusbult's (1983) interdependence theory expanded on the social exchange model to understand relationship commitment. This theory proposes that satisfaction is only one of three critical factors that determine commitment to a particular relationship. Check out **FIGURE 15.14**. In addition to the person's satisfaction with the relationship (which is influenced by rewards, costs, and comparison levels), Rusbult argues that we also need to consider the person's *investments* in the relationship and the alternatives that the person sees out there in the field.

Think
ABOUT

[Yaromir/Shutterstock]

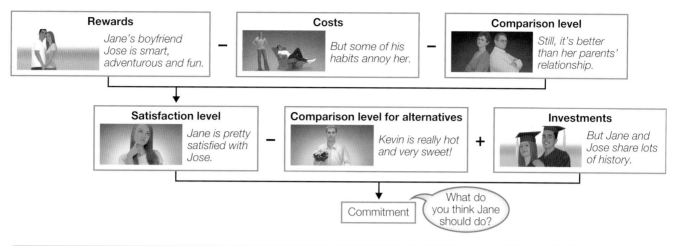

Rewards		Costs		Comparison level
Jane's boyfriend Jose is smart, adventurous and fun.	−	*But some of his habits annoy her.*	−	*Still, it's better than her parents' relationship.*

Satisfaction level		Comparison level for alternatives		Investments
Jane is pretty satisfied with Jose.	−	*Kevin is really hot and very sweet!*	+	*But Jane and Jose share lots of history.*

Commitment   What do you think Jane should do?

Figure 15.14

Rusbult's Interdependence Model

According to Rusbult, the commitment to a relationship is influenced not just by a person's satisfaction with that relationship, but also by how much the person has invested and the quality of the alternatives the person thinks are elsewhere. When satisfaction and investment are high, and the quality of alternatives is low, stronger commitment and relationship maintenance generally follow.

[Research from: Rusbult (1983)]

Part of what keeps people committed to a relationship is the investment of time and resources they have put into building a life together. In the short term, spending even a few weeks dating someone, getting to know him and his friends, giving up other activities to be with him, all contribute to a sense of having invested in the relationship. The greater the sense of investment, the harder it is to give up and walk away on what you have begun to build together. Once you have held an extravagant wedding ceremony, combined financial accounts, signed your names on a mortgage, raised children, and melded your social networks and sense of family, it's not exactly easy to disentangle two individual lives from the partnership that has developed. Costs might need to really start outweighing not just current benefits but the sum total of what you've put in to the relationship. For example, among same-sex couples, those who had a civil union were less likely to end the relationship than those who did not go through this legal process, even though before doing so there was no difference in relationship satisfaction between the groups (Balsam et al., 2004). In fact, despite often reporting less heated debates and conflict in their relationships than do heterosexuals, same-sex couples who don't go through the process of legalizing their union tend to break up more frequently (Kurdek, 2004). This is likely because without a legal commitment to the relationship, they face fewer barriers in ending that relationship when times get tough.

In addition to satisfaction and investment, the third factor that can contribute to your overall commitment is an assessment of the options available to you. When you apply the comparison level for alternatives, you are assessing whether you have other, better options than your current relationship. People may remain committed to or dependent on a dysfunctional or devolving relationship if they cannot imagine a better alternative. Current outcomes might seem bad, but perhaps being alone seems even worse. When your comparison level for alternatives is low, your commitment remains high. This relationship is consistent for both men and women (Bui et al., 1996; Le & Agnew, 2003). In light of the comparison level for alternatives, it's not too surprising that over a third of marriages that end in divorce involve at least one partner having an extramarital affair (South & Lloyd, 1995). Many people don't think about leaving their current relationship until they have a glimpse of what life could be like in another. Of course, once a partner has been unfaithful, the likelihood of divorce increases (Previti & Amato, 2004).

One of the interesting aspects of the interdependence theory of relationship commitment is that it highlights how an individual can be relatively satisfied in a relationship and invest a great deal in it but still decide to leave if he or she suspects there are better alternatives. For example, perhaps Brad Pitt was satisfied with Jennifer Aniston but left because he thought Angelina Jolie was that much more appealing. Conversely, some individuals might decide to stay in a relationship, not

Comparison level for alternatives The perceived quality of alternatives to the current relationship.

because they are especially satisfied, but because they don't see any other better options out there. This helps to explain why people will sometimes stay in relationships that to any outside observer look rather bleak and may even involve abuse. Research has supported this explanation. For example, a study by Rusbult (1983) that followed couples over a seven-month period found that those who stayed together experienced increased costs (e.g., time, effort, loss of freedom) but increased rewards as well (e.g., satisfaction, pleasure). But for couples who broke up, the rewards did not increase as much as the costs did, the alternatives became more appealing, and so commitment declined.

The decision to stick with a relationship also is influenced by how well the relationship meets our psychological needs. As we discussed in chapter 6, self-determination theory argues that people need a basic sense not just of relatedness but also of autonomy and competence. A sense of competence makes us feel secure and valued; a sense of autonomy—feeling that we're taking ownership of what we do—contributes to our growth. And when a relationship doesn't provide a sense of competence and autonomy, and thus doesn't meet these core psychological needs, it is less satisfying, and our commitment wanes (Drigotas & Rusbult, 1992; La Guardia et al., 2000).

Sometimes the decision to break up, though obviously destructive to the relationship, is ultimately good for one or both of the individuals. We all know people—and maybe we've been those people ourselves—who stay in a relationship that is not really in their best interests. It's not meeting our needs and is not especially satisfying, but we think we have no other options and so try to stick it out. Who is most likely to be in this situation? Those who are prone to anxious attachments (i.e., have high attachment anxiety) often think they are unworthy of being in a good relationship but are especially dependent on what relationships they do have and will try to maintain them at all costs (Davila & Bradbury, 2001; Mikulincer & Shaver, 2007). Research by Slotter and Finkel (2009) confirms this reasoning. They followed couples over six months and found that when people were low in attachment anxiety, they were more likely to break up when their needs were not being met. But people high in attachment anxiety were more likely to cling to a sinking ship, maintaining the relationship even when it did not meet their needs.

The longitudinal aspect of this study is powerful because it reveals how, in this case, attachment anxiety and need satisfaction influence behavior over time. However, all study designs have their weaknesses, and here the weakness is that we can't be sure that attachment anxiety was really the important factor. This is because it was just measured, not manipulated. Some other variable associated with attachment anxiety might be influencing relationship commitment.

To address this issue, in a second study, Slotter and Finkel (2009) took advantage of the strengths of the experimental method, reasoning that anyone can feel more or less secure in their relationships at various times. Think about those times when you've eagerly monitored your partner for signs, such as smiling or holding your hand, that he or she is in fact really into the relationship, but at other times you wonder if perhaps he or she has tired of you. Because most people have a mix of good and bad memories, the researchers manipulated whether participants brought to mind ideas related to relational security or insecurity. They first measured how much participants regarded the relationship as meeting psychological needs, and then randomly assigned participants to unscramble various words to form a sentence. The list contained either words such as *was, reliable, the, mother* or words such as *was, unreliable, the, mother.* Thus, participants were making sentences that got them thinking about either relational security (e.g., *the mother was reliable)* or insecurity (e.g., *the mother was unreliable).* The results were similar to those in Study 1. When participants did not see the relationship as meeting their psychological needs and were primed with insecurity, they expressed greater levels of commitment to the relationship. But when primed with security, they expressed less commitment to the relationship when it was not meeting their needs.

In short, more securely attached people are more likely to bolt from a relationship that they do not see as sufficiently fulfilling their psychological needs. Without a strong sense of commitment, such individuals are unlikely to engage in behaviors that help to maintain the relationship, such as making sacrifices for the relationship and responding to betrayals or problems with forgiveness (Finkel et al., 2002).

APPLICATION

One Day at a Time: Dealing With Daily Hassles

Infidelity and emotional and physical abuse are common and rather dramatic causes of relationship problems and breakups. But all long-term relationships, if they are to endure, must also overcome the day-to-day hassles that inevitably occur. Your partner is late getting home from work, fails to notice something that is important to you, or commits to going to dinner with a group of people you find dreadfully boring. Or maybe your partner leaves dirty clothes lying around or hogs all the blankets on the bed. How do such events affect your relationship? All relationships involve disagreements, irritations, and the like, from both inside and outside. The cumulative impact of these hassles can contribute to the dissolution of a long-term relationship (Bolger et al., 1989). Thus, a big challenge to maintaining a successful relationship is how the couple deals with the daily events that are a part of life.

"It's a major fixer-upper. How's your marriage?"

[David Sipress/The New Yorker Collection/The Cartoon Bank]

Maintaining a satisfying long-term relationship requires that we both come to terms with our partner's strengths and weaknesses and that we learn to weight them accordingly. Recall from cognitive dissonance theory (see chapter 6) that people are motivated to maintain consistency among their cognitions. Those who have the most successful relationships develop a priority structure that downplays the importance of their partner's faults and allows them to maintain a positive view of their partner (Neff & Karney, 2003).

Another factor is how relationship partners interpret the variability—the ups and downs—of the day-to-day events they confront (Jacobson et al., 1982; McNulty & Karney, 2001). When a partner's global perception of the relationship rises and falls with every daily event, the relationship can become more precarious and vulnerable to decline and dissolution (e.g., Arriaga, 2001). It's not good if on Wednesday your partner ticks you off and you think this relationship is in trouble, but then on Thursday your partner impresses you and you think this is your match made in heaven. Being so reactive to daily events generally is likely to send a marriage into a tailspin. Instead, separating overall judgment of the quality of the relationship from immediate events can lead to more consistent satisfaction (McNulty & Karney, 2001).

How do people separate their overall evaluation of the relationship from the immediate events that they are experiencing? It depends in large part on the attributions that they make for the recent event. People who are in happier relationships tend to attribute their partner's irritating actions to external factors. So if the partner fails to call to let them know that he or she will be late, the happily married person tends to attribute that faux pas to a busy time at work rather than being inconsiderate. This helps to protect the relationship and maintain a measure of positivity. In contrast, spouses who make internal attributions and blame the other person tend to have unhappier marriages (Bradbury & Fincham, 1990). The moral here is, Don't sweat the small stuff.

Obviously, letting daily hassles roll off your back will make for a happier relationship both in the short run and over time (McNulty et al., 2008). But what if your partner really is being inconsiderate? The tricky part of relationships is that some of the small stuff really is small, but some of it can be signs of something larger. (Remember those eye rolls that can signal contempt?) Couples who ignore the big issues, or issues for which they are unable to come up with external attributions, are likely to report lower marital satisfaction as time goes by. So the key, then, is to pick your battles wisely: to recognize what are the little things you can let slide and attribute to external factors, and what are the bigger issues that you need to address more candidly. Indeed, research shows that when the problem is not a major one that will fester, avoiding conflict over it can be the best strategy (Cahn, 1992; Canary et al., 1995).

As you probably know from your own experience, distinguishing little and big issues can be challenging to pull off. Often it's easier early in the relationship, when the novelty of the person casts a more positive glow on your interactions. But as times goes by, and the hassles of life crash the party, the partners' personality characteristics and elements of their situation can push them toward maladaptive relationship cognitions. Benjamin Karney and colleagues' (e.g., Karney & Bradbury, 1995) *vulnerability stress adaption model* of relationships provides a framework with which to understand how these challenges operate. The model in **FIGURE 15.15** highlights two key factors that contribute to marital dissolution. First, in any intimate relationship some people bring with them vulnerabilities (e.g., personality traits) that dispose them to have less adaptive relationship cognitions. For example, people with low self-esteem (Murray et al., 2002), as well as those with anxious attachment styles (Campbell et al., 2005), tend to be uncertain of their partner's feelings for them and so search for signs of validation. This leads them to put undue weight on daily events. So on days when they perceive more conflict, they feel less close and less optimistic about the relationship. Someone without these vulnerabilities might more easily recognize the small stuff as just small stuff.

But dealing with enduring vulnerabilities is only part of the issue. The second key factor is external situations that put more strain on the relationship. Imagine a person in sales who faces added work pressure as the economy plummets. As a result, she spends less time at home and is worn out when she does. So she shows less affection to her boyfriend and shares in fewer mutual activities. This adds stress directly to the relationship (Neff & Karney, 2004). But this stress can also affect the relationship indirectly. Recall from chapter 5 our discussion of ego depletion. This work taught us that our ability to regulate our behavior effectively toward desired goals is undermined when we are burdened with additional demands. It requires effort to engage in adaptive relationship cognitions, to realize for example, that your partner's not complimenting you on your surprise cleanup of the house is the product of her work distractions and not her general lack of appreciation for you. Thus, when people encounter outside stress, it can consume the cognitive resources that they would otherwise use to support their relationships. For example, satisfied couples make allowances for a partner's bad behavior and attribute it to external causes (Bradbury & Fincham, 1992), but when under stress, they shift to a more maladaptive attributional pattern (Neff & Karney, 2009).

Figure 15.15

Vulnerability Stress Adaptation Model

When does a relationship dissolve? Karney and colleagues' vulnerability stress adaptation model of relationships proposes that the answer depends on how situational stressors interact with personality traits (or vulnerabilities) to create unproductive processes. For example, being insecure and facing stress at work could lead a person to have more maladaptive thoughts about the relationship, which can contribute to dissolution.

[Research from: Karney et al. (1995)]

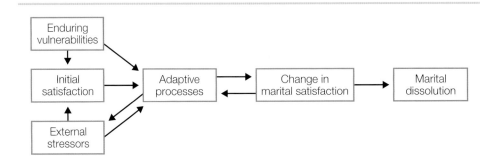

And in the Red Corner: Managing Conflict

As if day-to-day stressors and irritations are not enough, all intimate relationships will also face a certain amount of actual conflict. The noted marital researcher John Gottman (1993) points out that it's not conflict that is bad for a relationship. How the couple manages that conflict will determine their enduring satisfaction and likelihood of staying together (see also Canary et al., 1995). Gottman's research identifies different types of couples. For example, *volatile* couples have a short fuse and seem to argue about everything. *Conflict-avoiding* couples have almost no fuse and seem to avoid all disagreements. One type is not necessarily better than the other. Both can have stable relationships as long as the partners' styles match.

All couples, however, will need to confront conflict at least some of the time. Indeed, it is healthy for the relationship for this to happen (Cahn, 1992; Cloven & Roloff, 1991; Rusbult, 1987). Disagreements will happen: There is no perfect partner who will agree with you about everything. Your expectations have to be realistic. Your partner may prefer different types of movies to see or music to listen to. You may disagree about who should take out the garbage, cook, do the laundry. Partners may have different preferences in terms of sexual activity. They may have different ideas about where to vacation or how to spend disposable income. Issues may arise regarding whether to have children and when, and if so, how to raise them. Resolving such disagreements involves communication and compromise. So what separates happy from distressed couples in how they with deal with such problems?

Let's take a closer look at some of the strategies people apply when conflicts come up. We can divide them along two dimensions (Rusbult et al., 1982). Along one dimension are responses ranging from active (e.g., barraging your partner with a list of reasons that what she did was wrong) to passive (e.g., sitting quietly and seething). Along the other dimension are responses ranging from constructive (e.g., sticking by your partner and hoping things will get better) to destructive (e.g., smashing the headlights out of your partner's new car). When we cross these two dimensions with one another (see **FIGURE 15.16**), we see four different types of responses.

An *exit* response is active but destructive to the relationship. It involves separating or threatening to leave. An example of an exit response is "I told him I couldn't take it anymore and it was over." A *voice* response is similarly active but more constructive to the relationship. It involves discussing problems, seeking solutions and help, and attempting to change. For example, with a voice response, one might say, "We talked things over and worked things out."

But not all responses take this active approach. Partners also can respond constructively but in a more passive way. *Loyalty* entails hoping for improvement, supporting a partner, sticking with it, and continuing to wear relationship symbols (such

Figure 15.16

Managing Conflict: The EVLN Model

Carol Rusbult's work on managing conflict suggests that people can do so in active or passive and constructive or destructive ways. When we combine these two dimensions, we get four kinds of responses. Your best bet if you want to nurture your relationship: Try for the voice response, which is both active and constructive!

[Research from: Rusbult et al. (1982)]

as rings): "I just waited to see if things would get better." Although loyalty is generally considered a constructive response, it can be relatively ineffective, because it may be difficult for the other partner to notice and pick up on it (Drigotas et al., 1995). And if it does go unnoticed, it is not likely to help the relationship. Finally, a person may respond both passively and destructively with *neglect*, letting things fall apart, and ignoring a partner or drifting away from him or her: "Mostly my response was silence to anything he said."

In asking people to recall a time when they had conflicts with their partner, Rusbult's work finds that people in satisfied and committed relationships are more likely to use constructive responses such as voice and loyalty and less likely to turn to exit and neglect responses. So it's not that good relationships don't involve conflict but that they deal with it more positively, primarily with voice. People in good relationships are also more likely to accommodate a partner's initially destructive response and respond constructively to it. So what do you do when your partner comes home from a long day, you're excitedly telling him about your day, and he responds, "Just be quiet for a moment"? Whereas some people's first response might be a similarly caustic and disparaging comment—which of course would only further escalate negativity in the relationship—those for whom the relationship is more important will try to inhibit that tit-for-tat strategy and respond constructively (Rusbult et al., 1991). Securely attached people are most likely to rise above and respond well to less-than-constructive remarks from a partner (Collins & Feeney, 2004).

Another characteristic that facilitates more productive accommodation is taking the partner's perspective. The more we can put ourselves in our partner's shoes and see that perhaps a frustrating day at work led her to act that way, the better off our relationship is. Indeed, among both dating and married couples, preexisting tendencies for perspective taking and being induced to take the other's perspective led to more positive emotional reactions and relationship-enhancing attributions (Arriaga & Rusbult, 1998).

Given that voice is the best response to serious or recurring relationship problems, it may be worth considering two primary reasons that it isn't always how people respond. The first reason is that people often avoid conflict. They are afraid to bring up issues because they don't "want to get into it" or have it "blow up." So instead, they often complain to friends or relatives about what's bothering them. This approach doesn't give the other person a chance to step up and help make things better.

The second reason is that people often approach communicating about problems in the wrong way. Canary and colleagues (Canary & Cupach, 1988; Canary & Spitzberg, 1987) proposed that there are three strategies for conflict management: integrative strategies, distributive strategies, and avoidant strategies. As we noted earlier, avoidance can be best when the problem is relatively minor and we can mentally or behaviorally adjust to it. But if it's a problem that must be addressed through some kind of compromise, then it's a matter of how you do it.

An *integrative* strategy works best. You present the problem as a challenge to shared relational goals, as *our* problem, something we have to solve together. You raise your concern while seeking areas of agreement, express trust and positive regard, and negotiate alternative solutions through frank and positive discussions (Masuda & Duck, 2002). Recently Eli Finkel and colleagues (2013) showed that having couples take about 20 minutes to learn to think about resolving their disagreements in an integrative way improved marital satisfaction over a two-year period.

In contrast, a *distributive* strategy is competitive, emphasizes individual goals, assigns blame, and often devolves into insults and hostility (Masuda & Duck, 2002): "I have a problem with your behavior. You need to change. My needs are not being met." If you are defensive or insecure, or if you've "bitten your lip" for a long time and so are very frustrated, you are more likely to express your concerns in this distributive, accusatory fashion—and your partner is more likely to respond defensively in kind. Try to think about and express problems integratively, as "ours," not distributively as "yours." And don't apply an *avoidance* strategy by ignoring a problem until you have brooded so long about it that you have lost your sense of positive regard for your partner (Masuda & Duck, 2002).

Booster Shots: Keeping the Relationship and Passion Alive

Managing conflicts and dealing productively with day-to-day hassles can make the relationship more secure, which is critical for the growth of the individual. When one partner provides a secure base (e.g., is available when needed), this enables the other partner to explore, grow, and discover new things about himself (Feeney, 2007). Individuals who view their relationship partner as providing a more secure base spend more time and show greater interest in novel and enriching challenges (Feeney & Thrush, 2010).

Love as Flow

Security is wonderful, and the longer one is with a partner, the more familiar and comfortable a relationship is likely to feel. But a big issue in long-term relationships is how to keep the excitement, fun, stimulation, and passion alive. Csiksentmihalyi (1980) provided some useful insight into this problem by applying his *flow* analysis (introduced in chapter 6) to love relationships. Love relationships are best when people are in flow, when the challenges of a relationship partner are commensurate with one's relationship-related abilities. Early in a relationship, the other person is new, and so there are many challenges that keep things interesting.

If the challenges of satisfying your partner are more than you can handle and it is too difficult to keep your partner satisfied, you experience stress, and the relationship is likely to flame out early. However, if you're in a relationship for a long time, you learn a lot about your partner. It becomes easier to know his or her likes and dislikes, to predict his or her actions, and so forth. The challenge tends to diminish over time even as your skills increase. But if the challenges become insufficient, flow is impeded, and boredom is likely to set in. This suggests that the prospects for long-term bliss are rather dim. Luckily, Csiksentmihalyi (1980) offered a solution. A partner will become boring if he or she doesn't change. A stagnant partner means a stagnant relationship. So the trick to keeping a long-term relationship alive is for both partners to continue to grow and change so they remain stimulating to each other. One way to accomplish this is for the partners to continue to support each other's growth. Encourage each other to do new things and take on new challenges, both together and separately. Then you are always with someone who is challenging and vibrant. These kinds of efforts can also help remove some of the pressure that occurs when being with the partner is the only way in which the other gets his or her growth needs met (Finkel et al., 2014).

The prospect of change can be scary, though: The same old same old is comfortable and easy. And it's a hassle to support your partner's personal growth; it's easier to maintain the status quo. Thus people are often tempted to squelch their partner's efforts to grow and change. For example, some years back, one of your author's wives, who had been working part time ever since they got married and had children, raised the idea of going back to school to get a PhD. He instantly realized this would mean loss of income and years of stress for her (and him); pushing through the challenges of advanced education, such as writer's block; and so on. But his wife was bored with her work and needed this growth experience to meet her professional goals, and so he supported it. By supporting her growth, he gained a more stimulating, fulfilled partner, which served both his wife and their relationship well. Research supports this example. One partner's helping the other achieve his or her own self-improvement goals is associated with greater relationship satisfaction (e.g., Drigotas et al., 1999; Overall et al., 2010).

Emotional Support

Being a responsive partner is not limited to supporting big-time self-improvement goals such as career changes. It also involves interjecting positivity and support into the little things. When a partner shares positive news about his or her day, for example, an active, encouraging, and enthusiastic response is associated with better relationship quality over time (Gable et al., 2004). Even the seemingly mundane things that elicit gratitude, such as taking on more routine household chores during a partner's stressful period, enhance relationship quality (Algoe et al., 2010). Overall, mutually responsive partners who offer emotional support and active interest will enhance the relationship for each other (Iida et al., 2008; Lemay & Clark, 2008; Reis et al., 2004).

Keeping the Home Fires Burning

Of course, a big part of nourishing a relationship is keeping passion alive. This can be tough. One of the chief complaints about long-term relationships is a decline in sexual desire (Sprecher & Cate, 2004). What can one do to keep fanning the flames? Research suggests a few strategies that can help. Adopting approach goals can help keep partners turned on. Although there can be a variety

Husbands and Wives

Although many feature films focus on romantic relationships, the emphasis usually is on the early stages and rarely on the challenges of maintaining a satisfying marriage over the long haul. One exception is the Woody Allen film *Husbands and Wives* (Greenhut et al., 1992), which focuses, almost in documentary style, on two long-married, middle-aged couples having problems: Jack (Sydney Pollack) and Sally (Judy Davis), and Gabe (Woody Allen) and Judy (Mia Farrow). As the film opens, Jack and Sally, married over 20 years, rather causally and apparently amicably announce to their good friends Gabe and Judy that they are getting a divorce.

As the film unfolds we learn why. These reasons, and the dynamics they lead to, reflect many of the ideas discussed throughout this chapter. Jack becomes dissatisfied with his and Sally's sexual relationship and also feels judged and stifled by Sally. He senses a lack of stimulation and growth. They have intimacy and commitment but little passion. He begins engaging the services of a high-priced prostitute. Eventually Sally finds out he is having some sort of affair. Instead of confronting Jack, she keeps quiet about it, an avoidant strategy. Instead of applying the more productive conflict management response of voice, she becomes increasingly neglectful of the relationship. Infidelity is not the kind of small stuff one can easily let go, so she gets more

and more bitter. This contributes to her increasingly negative view of Jack and of even small additional problems that arise. Their discussions of their problems become distributive (assigning blame) rather than integrative. All of these issues culminate in their mutual decision to divorce, although we later find out Jack was already seeing Sam (Lysette Anthony), an aerobics instructor who is into astrology. She is considerably younger than Sally and is more open and less judgmental, so when Jack considered the comparison level of the alternatives to his wife Sally, this further eroded his commitment to the marriage.

[TriStar Pictures/Photofest]

of motives involved in having sex (Cooper et al., 1998), seeking pleasure is one of the most powerful. Because we're generally motivated to approach pleasure, those who adopt more general approach relationship goals may better stimulate sexual desire and avoid declines in their libido. In support of this point, Impett and colleagues (2008) found that people who endorsed more approach than avoidant relationship goals, such as trying to deepen their relationship with their partner as opposed to avoiding disagreements, reported greater sexual desire. Such goals also buffered against declines in sexual desire six months into the relationship.

One of the aspects of approach goals that may facilitate desire is that they lead people to more arousing and exciting activities. Such activities can help to restore the stimulation and novelty of a relationship that typically wanes over time (Aron et al., 2000). There are a number of reasons why novel and arousing activities might help to do this. As Aron and colleagues point out, such activities are often intrinsically enjoyable. When they are shared, this enjoyment becomes associated with the relationship. Such activities can also generally increase positive mood, which in turn, can be a booster shot making life, and perhaps the relationship, seem more meaningful (King et al., 2006).

Once Jack and Sally break up, Jack is better able to grow in his relationship with Sam. He starts eating right and exercising and can enjoy sports events and movies, activities that would have met with Sally's disapproval. Judy sets Sally up with Michael (Liam Neeson), who is handsome, charming, romantic, and younger. But Sally can't really give him a chance, partly because of the anger she still feels toward Jack. But it's also because she misses the deep sense of psychological security she derived from her marriage and her sense of the investment she had put into it. Eventually, Jack finds out that Sally has begun dating, which makes him jealous. He starts seeing the younger and less sophisticated Sam through the eyes of his friends as an embarrassment that is hurting his stature and self-worth, thereby undermining his own sense of security. Eventually he returns to Sally, and she takes him back. Ultimately they choose the psychological security of their shared life and self-worth from being "Jack and Sally" while recognizing that passion, stimulation, and growth will not be part of their marriage, and that rocky times may lie ahead.

Gabe and Judy seem solid as the film opens, but Judy becomes particularly upset when Sally and Jack announce their divorce. It strikes a nerve. Judy begins to reexamine whether she is happy in her marriage, and as she does, we start to see its shortcomings. Meanwhile, Gabe, a professor of English and an accomplished fiction writer, becomes attracted to and interested in one of his much younger students, Rainer (Juliette Lewis). She is a big fan of his work and reciprocates the interest.

It turns out that Judy doesn't feel valued or emotionally supported by Gabe. He dismisses her feedback on his new novel while being intrigued by Rainer's feedback about it. Judy becomes attracted to Michael even though she sets him up with Sally. She shows Michael poems she has written. When Gabe finds out, he asks her why she didn't show him the poems. She says that she wanted some supportive feedback, not the kind of objective critique that Gabe would have offered. Gabe likes the security he gets from his marriage, but a lot of his self-worth and consequent security and all of his growth really seem to come from his career and his budding platonic relationship with Rainer.

After Sally dumps Michael to return to Jack, Judy, seeing a better alternative, ends her marriage and starts seeing Michael. Eventually Judy and Michael marry. Toward the film's conclusion, Gabe rejects a romantic advance from the much younger Rainer, sensing that it would not work out in the long run, and expresses regret that he took Judy for granted. In an interesting twist, soon after this movie came out, Woody Allen, then 56, became committed to a much younger woman, Soon-Yi Previn, 21, the adopted daughter of his then girlfriend, the actress Mia Farrow (OTRC: Woody Allen on marriage to Soon-Yi, 2011). Woody and Soon-yi married in 1997, and as of this writing, are still together.

During the film, we learn about Gabe's new novel, which discusses Nap and Pepkin, men who live on the same floor of an apartment building. Summing up a major theme of the movie, Gabe writes: "Pepkin married and raised a family. He led a warm domestic life, placid but dull. Nap was a swinger. He eschewed nuptial ties and bedded five different women a week. . . . Pepkin, from the calm of his fidelity, envied Nap; Nap, lonely beyond belief, envied Pepkin." *Husbands and Wives* thus offers insights into a variety of relationship processes, including how people try to balance the desires for security and for stimulation and growth.

Furthermore, as the two factor theory of love and related research demonstrates, arousal from exciting activities also can be transferred to feelings of lust and love for the partner. A similar process even seems to hold for nonhuman animals, who exhibit what has come to be known as the Coolidge effect. There is a tendency, first observed in rats but subsequently in all mammals studied, for animals initially to have repeated intercourse with an available mate. The animals will lose interest over time, but then have repeated intercourse again when introduced to new sexual partners (Beach & Jordan, 1956; Dewsbury, 1981). This phenomenon is named after former American President Calvin Coolidge. Apparently when Mrs. Coolidge was touring a farm, she was impressed with the vigorous sexual activity of a particular rooster. When she asked the attendant how often it happened and was told "Dozens of times each day," Mrs. Coolidge suggested, "Tell that to the president when he comes by." On hearing this, the president asked, "Same hen every time?" The reply was, "Oh, no, Mr. President, a different hen every time," to which the president responded, "Tell that to Mrs. Coolidge."

Now, we are by no means advocating the introduction of sexual promiscuity if a long-term, satisfying, monogamous relationship is the goal. But one of the more interesting demonstrations related to the Coolidge effect was that, though even a bull's sexual appetite might wane after repeated copulation with the same receptive cow, when the pair was taken to a new enclosure and given a change of scenery, the formerly tired bull's interest was reengaged, and the vigorous sexual activity resumed (Dewsbury, 1981). The lesson here is that interjecting novelty, excitement, and change into a relationship, perhaps by taking a trip and experiencing new settings, can bring new life to a relationship.

Early in relationships, couples do a lot of stimulating, fun things together. One key for couples to maintain passion over the long haul is to keep doing such activities.

[Cultura RM/JAG Images/Getty Images]

Doing novel, fun, exciting things together in new places sounds like a no-lose proposition: Who wouldn't want to do that? However, over the long haul, couples often lose sight of this aspect of their relationship. In early courtship, having fun together is a central focus—restaurants, dancing, concerts, movies, travel. But when you move in together, take on more and more career responsibilities, and then add pets, kids, financial pressures, and the health issues that come with aging, the partners increasingly focus on just getting through each day. So the trick is to continue to make time to spend alone together doing enjoyable, stimulating things.

To explore the potential benefits of such self-expanding novel engagement, Aron and colleagues (2000) first conducted some survey studies and found that the more couples reported doing arousing and novel activities together, the more relationship satisfaction they reported. But does navigating through novelty *causally* increase relational satisfaction? To find out, Aron and colleagues (Aron et al., 2000; Lewandowski & Aron, 2004) conducted a series of experiments in which couples were brought into a lab and engaged either in challenging, novel tasks, which should be self-expanding, or in mundane ones. In these studies, when couples first arrived at the lab, they completed measures assessing relationship quality and satisfaction. Then each couple was asked to do either novel physical tasks or more mundane tasks. In one set of studies, the novel, self-expanding task involved the couple's being Velcroed together at the wrists and ankles. They had a limited amount of time to seek a prize by successfully crawling 12 meters over a barrier and pushing a foam cylinder with their heads. In a number of such studies, the couples who combined forces to do challenging and nutty things later reported greater relationship satisfaction than those who did the mundane tasks. These effects were not limited to what the couples reported. Coders who rated videotapes of their interactions for signs of hostility and support observed these benefits as well.

Maintaining passion and enhancing relational satisfaction takes effort, but it is effort that we can all put in if we're motivated to do so and keep some basic ideas in mind. Approaching the relationship positively and not just seeking to keep it afloat, mutually supporting growth goals, preserving quality time alone together, and interjecting arousal and novelty are all strategies that pay off. We hope they do for those of you seeking an enriching long-term relationship, now or in the future.

SECTION review | Long-term Relationships: Understanding Those That Dissolve and Those That Thrive

Stay or go?	Daily hassles	Conflict	Home fires burning
• The interdependence theory proposes three factors that determine commitment: satisfaction level, quality of alternatives, and investment. • Decisions are also based on whether the relationship meets psychological needs. • Securely attached people are more likely to leave an unsatisfying relationship.	• The ability to let daily hassles roll off one's back makes for a happier relationship. • Predisposed vulnerabilities and external stress make this harder to do.	• Conflict is inevitable. • The partner's ability to use voice constructively facilitates optimal compromise solutions.	• Maintaining a healthy relationship depends on a secure base and mutual support of growth. • Emotional support also is important, as is sharing novel and enjoyable experiences together.

CONNECT ONLINE:

Check out our videos and additional resources located at:
www.macmillanhighered.com/launchpad/greenberg1e

GLOSSARY

A priori causal theories Preexisting theories, acquired from culture or factors that are particularly prominent in conscious attention at the moment.

Accessibility The ease with which people can bring an idea into consciousness and use it in thinking.

Acculturation The process whereby individuals adapt their behavior in response to exposure to a new culture.

Action identification theory The theory that explains how people conceive of action—their own or others'—in ways that range from very concrete to very abstract.

Actor-observer effect The tendency to make internal attributions for the behavior of others and external attributions for our own behavior.

Adaptations Attributes that improve an individual's prospects for survival and reproduction.

Affective aggression Harm done to another person that is elicited in response to some negative emotion.

Affective forecasting Predicting what one's emotional reactions to potential future events will be.

Aggression Any physical or verbal behavior that is intended to harm another person or persons (or any living thing).

Altruism The desire to help another purely for his or her own sake, regardless of whether we derive any benefit.

Altruistic personality A collection of personality traits, such as empathy, that renders some people more helpful than others.

Ambivalent racism The influence on White Americans' racial attitudes of two clashing sets of values: a belief in individualism and a belief in egalitarianism.

Anxiety-buffer The idea that self-esteem allows people to face threats with their anxiety minimized.

Anxious-ambivalent Describes an attachment style characterized by a negative view of the self but a positive view of others, high anxiety, low avoidance, and intense but unstable relationships.

Appraisals What other people think about us.

Argument The true merits of the person, object, or position being advocated in the message.

Assimilation effects Occur when priming a schema (e.g., reckless) changes a person's thinking in the direction of the primed idea (e.g., perceiving others as more reckless).

Assimilation The process whereby people gradually shift almost entirely from their former culture to the beliefs and ways of the new culture.

Associative networks Models for how pieces of information are linked together and stored in memory.

Assortative mating The idea that people are attracted to others who are similar to them in some kind of social hierarchy.

Attitude Evaluation of a stimulus; can range from positive to negative.

Attribution theory The view that people act as intuitive scientists when they observe other people's behavior and infer explanations as to why those people acted the way they did.

Attributional ambiguity A phenomenon whereby members of stigmatized groups often can be uncertain whether negative experiences are based on their own actions and abilities or are the result of prejudice.

Audience The person or group receiving the message.

Authoritarian personality A complex of personality traits, including uncritical acceptance of authority, preference for well-defined power arrangements in society, adherence to conventional values and moral codes, and black-and-white thinking. Predicts prejudice toward out-groups in general.

Automatic processes Human thoughts or actions that occur quickly, often without the aid of conscious awareness.

Availability heuristic The tendency to assume that information that comes easily to mind (or is readily available) is more frequent or common.

Averageness effect The tendency to perceive a composite image of multiple faces that have been photographically averaged as more attractive than any individual face included in that composite.

Aversive racism Conflicting, often nonconscious, negative feelings about African Americans that Americans may have, even though most do in fact support principles of racial equality and do not knowingly discriminate.

Balance theory Theory proposing that the motivation to maintain consistency among one's thoughts colors how people form new attitudes and can also drive them to change existing attitudes.

Basking in reflected glory Associating oneself with successful others to help bolster one's own self-esteem.

Better than average effect The tendency to rank oneself higher than most people on positive attributes.

Bystander effect A phenomenon in which many people witness a need for help, and the knowledge that there are other witnesses makes it less likely that each particular witness will do anything to help.

Categories Mental "containers" in which people place things that are similar to each other.

Causal attribution The explanation that people use for what caused a particular event or behavior.

Central route to persuasion A style of processing a persuasive message by a person who has both the ability and the motivation to think carefully about the message's argument. Attitude change depends on the strength of the argument.

Chameleon effect The tendency to mimic unconsciously the nonverbal mannerisms of someone with whom you are interacting.

Charismatic leader An individual in a leadership role who exhibits boldness and self-confidence and emphasizes the greatness of the in-group.

Chronically accessible schemas Schemas that are easily brought to mind because they are personally important and used frequently.

Cognitive appraisal theory The idea that our subjective experience of emotions is determined by a two-step process involving a primary appraisal of benefit or harm, and a secondary appraisal providing a more differentiated emotional experience.

Cognitive dissonance theory The idea that people have such distaste for perceiving inconsistencies in their beliefs, attitudes, and behavior that they will bias their own attitudes and beliefs to try to deny inconsistencies.

Cognitive misers A term that conveys the human tendency to avoid expending effort and cognitive resources when thinking and to prefer seizing on quick and easy answers to questions.

Cognitive reappraisal The cognitive reframing of a situation to minimize one's emotional reaction to it.

Cognitive response approach to persuasion Occurs when people's attitude is influenced not only by *what* they think about the message but also by their confidence in those thoughts and beliefs.

Cognitive system A conscious, rational, and controlled system of thinking.

Collectivistic culture A culture in which the emphasis is on interdependence, cooperation, and the welfare of the group over that of the individual.

Colorblind ideology The idea that group identities should be ignored and that people should be judged solely on their individual merits, thereby avoiding any judgment based on group membership.

Commitment Partners' investment of time, effort, and resources in their relationship with the expectation that it will continue indefinitely.

Common ingroup identity A recategorizing of members of two or more distinct groups into a single, overarching group.

Communal orientation Situation in which people don't distinguish between what's yours and what's mine.

Comparison level for alternatives The perceived quality of alternatives to the current relationship.

Comparison level The expectation of how rewarding a relationship should be.

Compensation After a blow to self-esteem in one domain, people often shore up their overall sense of self-worth by bolstering how they think of themselves in an unrelated domain.

Complementary stereotypes Both positive and negative stereotypes that are ascribed to a group as a way of justifying the status quo.

Conceptual replication The repetition of a study with different operationalizations of the crucial variables but yielding similar results.

Confederate A supposed participant in a research study who actually is working with experimenters, unknown to the real participants.

Confirmation bias The tendency to view events and people in ways that fit how we want and expect them to be.

Conformity The phenomenon whereby an individual alters his or her beliefs, attitudes, or behavior to bring them in accordance with those of a majority.

Confound A variable other than the conceptual variable intended to be manipulated that may be responsible for the effect on the dependent variable, making alternative explanations possible.

Construal level theory The theory that people focus more on concrete details when thinking about the near future, but focus more on abstract meaning when thinking about the distant future.

Construct validity The degree to which the dependent measure assesses what it intends to assess or the manipulation manipulates what it intends to manipulate.

Contrast effects Occur when priming a schema (e.g., reckless) changes a person's thinking in the opposite direction of the primed idea (e.g., perceiving others as less reckless).

Controlled processes Human thoughts or actions that occur more slowly and deliberatively, and are motivated by some goal that is often consciously recognized.

Conversion theory The explanation that people are influenced by a minority because the minority's distinctive position better captures their attention.

Correlation coefficient A positive or negative numerical value that shows the direction and the strength of a relationship between two variables.

Correlational method Research in which two or more variables are measured and compared to determine to what extent if any they are associated.

Correspondent inference The tendency to attribute to the actor an attitude, desire, or trait that corresponds to the action.

Covariation principle The tendency to see a causal relationship between an event and an outcome when they happen at the same time.

Cover story An explanation of the purpose of the study that is different from the true purpose.

Cultural animals Humans are animals who view reality through a set of symbols provided by the culture in which they are raised.

Cultural diffusion The transfer of inventions, knowledge, and ideas from one culture to another.

Cultural evolution The process whereby cultures develop and propagate according to systems of belief or behavior that contribute to the success of a society.

Cultural knowledge A vast store of information, accumulated within a culture, that explains how the world works and why things happen as they do.

Cultural perspective A view that focuses on the influence of culture on thought, feeling, and behavior.

Cultural transmission The process whereby members of a culture learn explicitly or implicitly to imitate the beliefs and behaviors of others in that culture.

Cultural traumas Tragic historical examples of cultural disruptions, some of which have led to complete cultural disintegration.

Cultural worldview Human-constructed shared symbolic conception of reality that imbues life with meaning, order, and permanence.

Culture A set of beliefs, attitudes, values, norms, morals, customs, roles, statuses, symbols, and rituals shared by a self-identified group, a group whose members think of themselves as a group.

Debriefing At the end of a study, the procedure in which participants are assessed for suspicion and then receive a gentle explanation of the true nature of the study in a manner that counteracts any negative effects of the study experience.

Dehumanization The tendency to hold stereotypic views of outgroup members as animals rather than humans.

Deindividuation A tendency to lose one's sense of individuality when in a group or crowd.

Demand characteristics Aspects of a study that give away its purpose or communicate how the participant is expected to behave.

Descriptive norm A belief about what most people typically do.

Diffusion of responsibility A situation in which the presence of others prevents any one person from taking responsibility (e.g., for helping).

Discounting principle The tendency to reduce the importance of any potential cause of another's behavior to the extent that other potential causes exist.

Discrimination Negative behavior toward an individual solely on the basis of that person's membership in a particular group.

Disidentification The process of disinvesting in any area in which one's group traditionally has been underrepresented or negatively stereotyped.

Dismissive avoidant Describes an avoidant attachment style characterized by a negative view of both self and others, high anxiety and avoidance, and distant relationships.

Displaced aggression Aggression directed to a target other than the source of one's frustration.

Dispositions Consistent preferences, ways of thinking, and behavioral tendencies that manifest across varying situations and over time.

Domain-general adaptations Attributes that are useful for dealing with various challenges across different areas of life.

Domain-specific adaptations Attributes that evolved to meet a particular challenge but that are not particularly useful when dealing with other types of challenges.

Door-in-the-face effect Phenomenon whereby people are more likely to comply with a moderate request after they have first been presented with and refused to agree to a much larger request.

Downward comparison Comparing oneself with those who are worse off.

Downward counterfactuals Imagined worse alternative outcomes to something that actually happened.

Dramaturgical perspective Using the theater as a metaphor, the idea that people, like actors, perform according to a script. If we all know the script and play our parts well, then like a successful play, our social interactions flow smoothly and seem meaningful, and each actor benefits.

Dual process theories Theories that are used to explain a wide range of phenomena by positing two ways of processing information.

Ease of retrieval effect Process whereby people judge how frequently an event occurs on the basis of how easily they can retrieve examples of that event.

Effort justification The phenomenon whereby people reduce dissonance by convincing themselves that what they suffered for is actually quite valuable.

Ego depletion The idea that ego strength becomes depleted by extended bouts of self-control.

Ego The aspect of self that directs your thoughts and actions.

Elaboration likelihood model A theory of persuasion that proposes that persuasive messages can influence attitudes by two different routes, central or peripheral.

Empathy gap The underestimation of other people's experience of physical pain as well as the pain of social rejection.

Empathy-altruism model The idea that people provide help to others to get certain psychological payoffs.

Entitativity The degree to which a collection of people feels like a cohesive group.

Equity theory The idea that people are motivated to maintain a sense of fairness or equity, whereby both partners feel that the proportion of outcomes (rewards) to inputs (costs) that each receives is roughly equal.

Eros Freud's term for what he proposed is the human inborn instinct to seek pleasure and to create.

Ethnocentrism Viewing the world through our own cultural value system and thereby judging actions and people based on our own culture's views of right and wrong and good and bad.

Evolution The concept that different species are descended from common ancestors but have evolved over time, acquiring different genetic characteristics as a function of different environmental demands.

Evolutionary perspective A view that humans are a species of animal and that their social behavior is a consequence of particular evolved adaptations.

Excitation transfer theory The idea that leftover arousal caused by an initial event can intensify emotional reactions to a second event.

Existential perspective A view that focuses on the cognitive, affective, and behavioral consequences of basic aspects of the human condition such as the knowledge of mortality, the desire for meaning, and the precarious nature of identity.

Expectancy-value theory The theory that effort is based on the value or desirability of the goal, multiplied by the person's assessment of how likely it is that she will be able to attain the goal.

Experiential associations Mental links between two concepts that are experienced close together in time or space.

Experiential system An unconscious, intuitive, and automatic system of thinking.

The experimental method A study in which a researcher manipulates a variable, referred to as the independent variable, measures possible effects on another variable, referred to as the dependent variable, and tries to hold all other variables constant.

Experimenter bias The possibility that the experimenter's knowledge of the condition a particular participant is in could affect her behavior toward the participant and thereby introduce a confounding variable to the independent variable manipulation.

Explicit attitudes Attitudes people are consciously aware of through the cognitive system.

External validity The judgment that a research finding can be generalized to other people, in other settings, at other times.

Facial feedback hypothesis The idea that changes in facial expression elicit emotions associated with those expressions.

False consensus A general tendency to assume that other people share our own attitudes, opinions, and preferences.

Fearfully avoidant Describes an avoidant attachment style characterized by a negative view of both self and others, high anxiety and avoidance, and distant relationships, in which the person doesn't feel worthy, doesn't trust others, and fears rejection.

Field research Research that occurs outside the laboratory, for example, in schools, office buildings, medical clinics, football games, or even in shopping malls or on street corners.

Flow The feeling of being completely absorbed in an activity that is appropriately challenging to one's skills.

Foot-in-the-door effect Phenomenon whereby people are more likely to comply with a moderate request after having initially complied with a smaller request.

Free choice paradigm A laboratory situation in which people make a choice between two alternatives, and after they do, attraction to the alternatives is assessed.

Frustration-aggression hypothesis Originally the idea that aggression is always preceded by frustration and that frustration inevitably leads to aggression. Revised to suggest that frustration produces an emotional readiness to aggress.

Fundamental attribution error (FAE) The tendency to attribute behavior to internal or dispositional qualities of the actor and consequently underestimate the causal role of situational factors.

Fusiform face area A region in the temporal lobe of the brain that helps us recognize the people we know.

Gain-loss theory A theory of attraction that posits that liking is highest for others when they increase their positivity toward you over time.

Goals Cognitions that represent outcomes that we strive for in order to meet our needs and desires.

Group polarization A tendency for group discussion to shift group members toward an extreme position.

Groupthink A tendency toward flawed group decision making when group members are so intent on preserving group harmony that they fail to analyze a problem completely.

Halo effect A tendency to assume that people with one positive attribute (e.g., who are physically attractive) also have other positive traits.

Hedonism The human preference for pleasure over pain.

Heuristics Mental short cuts, or rules of thumb, that are used for making judgments and decisions.

Hierarchy of goals The idea that goals are organized hierarchically from very abstract goals to very concrete goals, with the latter serving the former.

Hostile attribution bias The tendency to attribute hostile intent to others' actions, even when others' intentions are innocent.

Hypothesis An "if-then" statement that follows logically from a theory and specifies how certain variables should be related to each other if the theory is correct.

Illusion of transparency The tendency to overestimate another's ability to know our internal thoughts and feelings.

Illusory correlation A tendency to assume an association between two rare occurrences, such as being in a minority group and performing negative actions.

Implementation-intentions Mental rules that link particular situational cues to goal-directed behaviors.

Implicit attitudes Automatic associations based on previous learning through the experiential system.

Implicit prejudice Negative attitudes or affective reactions associated with an outgroup, for which the individual has little or no conscious awareness and which can be automatically activated in intergroup encounters.

Impressions Schemas people have about other individuals.

Independent self-construal Viewing self as a unique active agent serving one's own goals.

Individualistic culture A culture in which the emphasis is on individual initiative, achievement, and creativity over maintenance of social cohesion.

Induced compliance paradigm A laboratory situation in which participants are induced to engage in a behavior that runs counter to their true attitudes.

Induced hypocrisy paradigm A laboratory situation in which participants are asked to advocate for an opinion they already believe in, but then are reminded about a time when their actions ran counter to that opinion, thereby arousing dissonance.

Informational influence Occurs when we use others as a source of information about the world.

Infrahumanization The perception that outgroup members lack qualities viewed as unique to human beings, such as language, rational intelligence, and complex social emotions.

Ingroup bias A tendency to favor groups we belong to more than those that we don't.

Injunctive norm A belief about what behaviors are generally approved of or disapproved of in one's culture.

Institutional discrimination Unfair restrictions on opportunities for certain groups of people through institutional policies, structural power relations, and formal laws.

Instrumental aggression Harm done to another person that serves some other goal.

Integration The process whereby people retain aspects of their former culture while internalizing aspects of a new host culture.

Interaction A pattern of results in which the effect of one independent variable on the dependent variable depends on the level of a second independent variable.

Interdependence theory The idea that satisfaction, investments, and perceived alternatives are critical in determining commitment to a particular relationship.

Interdependence Situation in which what each person does significantly influences what the partner does over long periods of time.

Interdependent self-construal Viewing self primarily in terms of how one relates to others and contributes to the greater whole.

Intergroup anxiety theory Theory proposing that intergroup prejudice leads individuals to experience anxiety when they think of or interact with members of an outgroup.

Internal validity The judgment that for a particular experiment it is possible to conclude that the manipulated independent variable caused the change in the measured dependent variable.

Ironic processing The idea that the more we try not to think about something, the more those thoughts enter our mind and distract us from other things.

Just world beliefs The idea that good things will happen to the worthy and bad things will happen to the unworthy.

Justification suppression model The idea that people endorse and freely express stereotypes in part to justify their own negative affective reactions to outgroup members.

Kin selection The idea that natural selection led to greater tendencies to help close kin than to help those with whom we have little genetic relation.

Linguistic intergroup bias A tendency to describe stereotypic behaviors (positive ingroup and negative outgroup) in abstract terms while describing counterstereotypic behaviors (negative ingroup and positive outgroup) in concrete terms.

Literal immortality A culturally shared belief that there is some form of life after death for those who are worthy.

Locus of causality Attribution of behavior to either an aspect of the actor (internal) or to some aspect of the situation (external).

Longitudinal studies Studies in which variables are measured in the same individuals over two or more periods of time, typically over months or years.

Long-term memory Information from past experience that may or may not be currently activated.

Looking glass self The idea that significant people in our lives reflect back to us (much like a looking glass, or mirror) who we are by how they behave toward us.

Lowballing Occurs when after agreeing to an offer, people find it hard to break that commitment even if they later learn of some extra cost to the deal.

Matching phenomenon The idea that people seek romantic relationships with others who are similar to them in physical attractiveness.

Mate guarding The process of preventing others from mating with one's partner in order to avoid the costs of rearing offspring that do not help to propagate one's genes.

Mating strategies Approaches to mating that help people reproduce successfully. People prefer different mating strategies depending on whether they are thinking about a short-term pairing or a long-term commitment.

Melting pot An ideological view holding that diverse peoples within a society should converge toward the mainstream culture.

Mere exposure effect Occurs when people hold a positive attitude toward a stimulus simply because they have been exposed to it repeatedly.

Metaphor A cognitive tool that allows people to understand an abstract concept in terms of a dissimilar, concrete concept.

Mindfulness The state of being and acting fully in the current moment.

Minimal deterrence Use of the minimal level of external justification necessary to deter unwanted behavior.

Minority influence The process by which dissenters (or numerical minorities) produce attitude change within a group, despite the extraordinary risk of social rejection and disturbance of the status quo.

Minority slowness effect Occurs when people who hold the minority position take longer to express their opinions.

Mirror neurons Certain neurons that are activated both when one performs an action oneself and when one simply observes another person perform that action.

Misattribution of arousal Ascribing arousal resulting from one source to a different source.

Misinformation effect The process by which cues that are given after an event can plant false information into memory.

Model of relational turbulence The idea that as partners make the transition from casual dating to more serious involvement in the relationship, they go through a turbulent period of adjustment.

Monitor The mental process that is on the lookout for signs of unwanted thoughts.

Mortality salience The state of being reminded of one's mortality.

Motivation The process of generating and expending energy toward achieving or avoiding some outcome.

Multicultural ideology A worldview in which different cultural identities and viewpoints are acknowledged and appreciated.

Multiculturalism (cultural pluralism) An ideological view holding that cultural diversity is valued and that diverse peoples within a society should retain aspects of their traditional culture while adapting to the host culture.

Mutuality Partners' acknowledgment that their lives are intertwined and that they think of themselves as a couple ("us") instead of as two separate individuals ("me" and "you").

Natural selection The process by which certain attributes are more successful in a particular environment and therefore become more represented in future generations.

Naturalistic fallacy A bias toward believing that biological adaptations are inherently good or desirable.

Need for cognition Differences between people in their need to think about things critically and analytically.

Need for structured knowledge A personality trait defined as a general preference for thinking about things in simple, clear-cut ways.

Needs Internal states that drive action that is necessary to survive or thrive.

Negative state relief hypothesis The idea that people help in order to reduce their own distress.

Neuroscience perspective The study of the neural processes that occur during social judgment and behavior. Neuroscience involves assessments of brain waves, brain imaging, and cardiovascular functioning.

Norm for social commitment Belief whereby once we make a public agreement, we tend to stick to it even if circumstances change.

Norm of reciprocity An explanation for why we give help: if I help you today, you might be more likely to help me tomorrow.

Normative influence Occurs when we use others to know how to fit in.

Obedience Any action engaged in to fulfill the direct order or command of another person.

Objectification theory Theory proposing that the cultural value placed on women's appearance leads people to view women more as objects and less as full human beings.

Operational definition A specific, concrete method of measuring or manipulating a conceptual variable.

Operator The mental process that actively pushes any signs of the unwanted thoughts out of consciousness.

Outgroup homogeneity effect The tendency to view individuals in outgroups as more similar to each other than they really are.

Overjustification effect The tendency for salient rewards or threats to lead people to attribute the reason, or justification, for engaging in an activity to an external factor, which thereby undermines their intrinsic motivation for and enjoyment of the activity.

Parasocial relationships Individuals' relationships with people in the media: celebrities, television characters, and athletes.

Parental investment The time and effort that parents must invest in each child they produce.

Peripheral cues Aspects of the communication that are irrelevant (that is, peripheral) to the true merits of the person, object, or position advocated in the message (e.g., a speaker's physical attractiveness when attractiveness is irrelevant to the position).

Peripheral route to persuasion A style of processing a persuasive message by a person who is not willing or able to put effort into thinking carefully about the message's argument. Attitude change depends on the presence of peripheral cues.

Person-group discrimination discrepancy The tendency for people to estimate that they personally experience less discrimination than is faced by the average member of their group.

Persuasion Intentional effort to change other people's attitudes in order to change their behavior.

Pluralistic ignorance A situation in which all bystanders glance at each other as they try to decide whether there is anything to be worried about, but no one actually does anything.

Positive illusions Idealized perceptions of romantic partners that highlight their positive qualities and downplay their faults.

Possible selves Images of what the self might become in the future.

Prefrontal cortex The region of the brain that regulates impulsive behavior.

Prejudice A negative attitude toward an individual solely on the basis of that person's presumed membership in a particular group.

Prevention focus People's general tendency to think and act in ways oriented toward the avoidance of negative outcomes.

Primacy effect The idea that initially encountered information has a disproportionate influence on attitudes (e.g., the first speaker in a policy debate influences the audience's policy approval).

Priming The process by which exposure to a stimulus in the environment increases the salience of a schema.

Private acceptance Conforming by altering private beliefs as well as public behavior.

Projection Assigning to others those traits that people fear they possess themselves.

Promotion focus People's general tendency to think and act in ways oriented toward the approach of positive outcomes.

Propinquity effect The increased likelihood of forming relationships with people who are physically close by.

Prosocial behavior An action by an individual that is intended to benefit another individual or set of individuals.

Prosopagnosia The inability to recognize familiar faces.

Prototype/willingness model of health behavior The idea that willingness refers specifically to a person's openness to being influenced by social circumstances, so that when it comes to opportunistic behaviors, one's willingness is the best predictor of behavior.

Psychological need A mechanism for regulating behavior to acquire the tangible or intangible resources necessarily for survival and well-being.

Psychological reactance theory Theory proposing that people value thinking and acting freely. Therefore, situations that threaten their freedom arouse discomfort and prompt efforts to restore freedom.

Public compliance Conforming only outwardly to fit in with a group without changing private beliefs.

Quasi-experimental designs Type of research in which groups of participants are compared on some dependent variable, but for practical or ethical reasons, the groups are not formed on the basis of random assignment.

Random assignment A procedure in which participants are assigned to conditions in such a way that each person has an equal chance of being in any condition of an experiment.

Realistic group conflict theory asserts that the initial negative feelings between groups are often based on a real conflict or competition regarding scarce resources.

Recency effect Occurs when recently encountered information primarily influences attitudes (e.g., a commercial viewed just before shopping influences a shopper's choices).

Reference group A group with which an individual strongly identifies.

Reflected appraisals What we think other people think about us.

Rejection identification theory The idea that people can offset the negative consequences of being targeted by discrimination by feeling a strong sense of identification with their stigmatized group.

Representativeness heuristic The tendency to overestimate the likelihood that a target is part of a larger category if it has features that seem representative of that category.

Research The process whereby scientists observe events, look for patterns, and evaluate theories proposed to explain those patterns.

Reverse causality problem A correlation between variables x and y may occur because one causes the other, but it is often impossible to determine if x causes y or y causes x.

Reward model of liking Proposes that people like other people whom they associate with positive stimuli and dislike people whom they associate with negative stimuli.

Salience The aspect of a schema that is active in one's mind and, consciously or not, colors perceptions and behavior.

Schema A mental structure, stored in memory, that is based on prior knowledge.

Scientific method The process of developing, testing, and refining theories to understand the determinants of social behavior.

Scripts Schemas about an event that specify the typical sequence of actions that take place.

Securely attached Describes an attachment style characterized by a positive view of the self and others, low anxiety and avoidance, and satisfying, stable relationships.

Self-affirmation theory The idea that people respond less defensively to threats to one aspect of themselves if they think about another valued aspect of themselves.

Self-awareness theory The theory that aspects of the self—one's attitudes, values, and goals—will be most likely to influence behavior when attention is focused on the self.

Self-compassion Being kind to ourselves when we suffer, fail, or feel inadequate, recognizing that imperfection is part of the human condition, and accepting rather than denying negative feelings about ourselves.

Self-complexity The extent to which an individual's self-concept consists of many different aspects.

Self-concept A person's knowledge about him- or herself, including one's own traits, social identities, and experiences.

Self-concept clarity A clearly defined, internally consistent, and temporally stable self-concept.

Self-determination theory The idea that people function best when they feel that their actions stem from their own desires rather than from external forces.

Self-disclosure The sharing of information about oneself.

Self-discrepancy theory The theory that people feel anxiety when they fall short of how they ought to be, but feel sad when they fall short of how they ideally want to be.

Self-esteem A person's evaluation of his of her value or self-worth.

Self-evaluation maintenance model The idea that people adjust their perceived similarity to successful others to minimize threatening comparisons and maximize self-esteem-supporting identifications.

Self-expansion model of relationships The idea that romantic relationships serve the desire to expand the self and grow.

Self-fulfilling prophecy The phenomenon whereby initially false expectations cause the fulfillment of those expectations.

Self-handicapping Placing obstacles in the way of one's own success to protect self-esteem from a possible future failure.

Self-monitoring An individual difference in people's desire and ability to adjust their self-presentations for different audiences.

Self-narrative A coherent life story that connects one's past, present, and possible future.

Self-objectification A phenomenon whereby intense cultural scrutiny of the female body leads many girls and women to view themselves as objects to be looked at and judged.

Self-perception theory The theory that people sometimes infer their attitudes and attributes by observing their behavior and the situation in which it occurs.

Self-regulation The process of guiding one's thoughts, feelings, and behavior to reach desired goals.

Self-regulatory perseveration theory of depression The theory that one way in which people can fall into depression is by persistent self-focus on an unattainable goal.

Self-schema An integrated set of memories, beliefs, and generalizations about an attribute that is part of one's self-concept.

Self-verification Seeking out other people and social situations that support the way one views oneself in order to sustain a consistent and clear self-concept.

Semantic associations Mental links between two concepts that are similar in meaning or that are parts of the same category.

Serotonin A neurotransmitter that regulates our experience of negative affect.

Sexual objectification The tendency to think about women in a narrow way as objects rather than full humans, as if their physical appearance is all that matters.

Short-term memory Information and input that is currently activated.

Sleeper effect The phenomenon whereby people can remember a message but forget where it came from; thus, source credibility has a diminishing effect on attitudes over time.

Social cognition The way an individual understands his or her own social world.

Social cognition perspective A view that focuses on how people perceive, remember, and interpret events and individuals, including themselves, in their social world.

Social comparison theory The theory that people come to understand themselves partly by comparing themselves with similar others.

Social contagion The phenomenon whereby ideas, feelings, and behaviors seem to spread across people like wildfire.

Social exchange model An economic perspective that assumes that people approach relationships with an underlying motivation of self-interest.

Social facilitation theory The theory that the presence of others increases a person's dominant response in a performance situation, the response that is most likely for that person for that particular task.

Social identity theory The theory that people define and value themselves largely in terms of the social groups with which they identify.

Social influence The effects of other people on an individual's beliefs, attitudes, values, or behavior.

Social learning The capacity to learn from observing others.

Social loafing A tendency to exert less effort when performing as part of a collective or group than when performing as an individual.

Social proof A tendency to conform to what we believe respected others think and do.

Social psychology The scientific study of the causes and consequences of people's thoughts, feelings, and actions regarding themselves and other people.

Social role theory The theory that gender differences in behavior, personality, and self-definition arise because of a long history of role distribution between the sexes.

Socialization Learning from parents and others what is desirable and undesirable conduct in a particular culture.

Sociometer model The idea that a basic function of self-esteem is to indicate to the individual how much he or she is accepted by other people.

Solo status A sense that one is unique in some specific manner in relation to other people in the current environment.

Somatic marker hypothesis The idea that changes in the body, experienced as emotion, guide decision making.

Source credibility The degree to which the audience perceives a message's source as expert and trustworthy.

Source The person or group communicating the message.

Spotlight effect The belief that others are more focused on us than they actually are.

Stereotype threat The concern that one might do something to confirm a negative stereotype about one's group either in one's own eyes or the eyes of someone else.

Stereotypes Overgeneralized beliefs about the traits and attributes of members of a particular group.

Superordinate goal A common problem or shared goal that groups work together to solve or achieve.

Symbolic immortality A culturally shared belief that, by being part of something greater and more enduring than our individual selves, some part of us will live on after we die.

Symbolic interactionism The perspective that people use their understanding of how significant people in their lives view them as the primary basis for knowing and evaluating themselves.

Symbolic racism A tendency to express negative biases held about a racial outgroup not at the group directly, but at social policies seen as benefiting that group.

System justification theory The theory that negative stereotypes get attached to groups partly because they help to explain and justify why some individuals are more advantaged than others.

Target empowerment model A model suggesting that targets of bias can employ strategies that deflect discrimination, as long as those methods aren't perceived as confrontational.

Terror management theory To minimize fear of mortality, humans strive to sustain faith that they are enduringly valued contributors to a meaningful world and therefore transcend their physical death.

Thanatos Freud's term for what he proposed is the human inborn instinct to aggress and to destroy.

Theory of planned behavior Theory proposing that attitudes, subjective norms, and perceived behavioral control interact to shape people's behavioral intentions.

Theory of symbolic self-completion The idea that when people perceive that a self-defining aspect is threatened, they feel incomplete, and then try to compensate by acquiring and displaying symbols that support their desired self-definition.

Theory An explanation for how and why variables are related to each other.

Third variable problem The possibility that two variables may be correlated but do not exert a causal influence on one another; rather, both are caused by some additional variable.

Transference A tendency to map on, or transfer, feelings for a person who is known onto someone new who resembles that person in some way.

Two-factor theory of emotion The theory that people's emotions are the product of both their arousal level and how they interpret that arousal.

Ultimate attribution error The tendency to believe that bad actions by outgroup members occur because of their internal dispositions and good actions by them occur because of the situation, while believing the reverse for ingroup members.

Uncertainty-identity theory The theory that people join and identify with groups in order to reduce negative feelings of uncertainty about themselves and others.

Upward comparison Comparing oneself with those who are better off.

Upward counterfactuals Imagined alternative where the outcome is better than what actually happened.

Urban overload hypothesis The idea that city dwellers learn to cope with the sounds that arise from population density by shutting out these sounds.

Weapons effect The tendency for the presence of firearms to increase the likelihood of aggression, especially when people are frustrated.

Working models of relationships Global feelings about the nature and worth of close relationships and other people's trustworthiness.

Working self-concept The portion of one's self-schema that is currently activated and strongly influences thoughts, feelings, and actions.

Worldview defense The tendency to derogate those who violate important cultural ideals and to venerate those who uphold them.

Aarts, H., & Dijksterhuis, A. (2003). The silence of the library: Environment, situational norm, and social behavior. *Journal of Personality and Social Psychology, 84*(1), 18–28.

Aarts, H., Dijksterhuis, A., & Custers, R. (2003). Automatic normative behavior in environments: The moderating role of conformity in activating situational norms. *Social Cognition, 21*(6), 447–464.

Aarts, H., Gollwitzer, P. M., & Hassin, R. R. (2004). Goal contagion: Perceiving is for pursuing. *Journal of Personality and Social Psychology, 87*(1), 23–37.

Abdel-Khalek, A. M. (1998). The structure and measurement of death obsession. *Personality and Individual Differences, 24*(2), 159–165.

Abma, J. C., Martinez, G. M., Mosher, W. D., & Dawson, B. S. (2004). *Teenagers in the United States: Sexual activity, contraceptive use, and childbearing, 2002. National Center for Health Statistics: Vital and Health Statistics, 23*(24). Washington, DC: U.S. Department of Health and Human Services, Centers for Disease Control and Prevention, National Center for Health Statistics. Retrieved from http://www.cdc.gov/nchs/data/series/sr_23/sr23_024.pdf

Aboud, F. (1988). *Children and prejudice*. New York: Basil Blackwell.

Acevedo, B. P., & Aron, A. (2009). Does a long-term relationship kill romantic love? *Review of General Psychology, 13*(1), 59–65.

Acker, M., & Davis, M. H. (1992). Intimacy, passion and commitment in adult romantic relationships: A test of the triangular theory of love. *Journal of Social and Personal Relationships, 9*(1), 21–50.

Adams, J. S. (1963). Towards an understanding of inequity. *Journal of Abnormal and Social Psychology, 67*(5), 422–436.

Adler, A. (1964). *Individual Psychology of Alfred Adler*. New York: HarperCollins.

Adler, L. L., & Adler, H. E. (1977). Ontogeny of observational learning in the dog (*Canis familiaris*). *Developmental Psychobiology, 10*(3), 267–271.

Adorno, T. W., Frenkel-Brunswik, E., Levinson, D. J., & Sanford, R. N. (1950). *The authoritarian personality*. Oxford: Harpers.

Agnew, C. R., Loving, T. J., Le, B., & Goodfriend, W. (2004). Thinking close: Measuring relational closeness as perceived self-other inclusion. In D. J. Mashek & A. Aron (Eds.), *Handbook of closeness and intimacy* (pp. 103–115). Mahwah, NJ: Erlbaum.

Ai, A. L., Tice, T. N., & Kelsey, C. L. (2009). Coping after 9/11: Deep interconnectedness and struggle in posttraumatic stress and growth. In M. Morgan (Ed.), *The impact of 9/11 on psychology and education: The day that changed everything?* (pp. 115–138). New York: Palgrave Macmillan.

Ainsworth, M. D. S., & Bell, S. M. (1970). Attachment, exploration, and separation: Illustrated by the behavior of one-year-olds in a strange situation. *Child Development, 41*(1), 49–67.

Ainsworth, M. D. S., Blehar, M. C., Waters, E., & Wall, S. (1978). *Patterns of attachment: A psychological study of the strange situation*. Oxford: Erlbaum.

Ajzen, I. (1985). From intentions to actions: A theory of planned behavior. In J. Kuhl & J. Beckman (Eds.), *Action-control: From cognition to behavior* (pp. 11–39). Heidelberg, Germany: Springer.

Aknin, L. B., Sandstrom, G. M., Dunn, E. W., & Norton, M. I. (2011). It's the recipient that counts: Spending money on strong social ties leads to greater happiness than spending on weak social ties. *PloS ONE, 6*(2), e17018.

Albarracín, D., Johnson, B. T., Fishbein, M., & Muellerleile, P. A. (2001). Theories of reasoned action and planned behavior as models of condom use: A meta-analysis. *Psychological Bulletin, 127*(1), 142–161.

Alexander, G. M., & Hines, M. (2002). Sex differences in response to children's toys in nonhuman primates (*Cercopithecus aethiops sabaeus*). *Evolution and Human Behavior, 23*(6), 467–479.

Alexander, G. M., Wilcox, T., & Woods, R. (2009). Sex differences in infants' visual interest in toys. *Archives of Sexual Behavior, 38*(3), 427–433.

Alexander, M. G., & Fisher, T. D. (2003). Truth and consequences: Using the bogus pipeline to examine sex differences in self-reported sexuality. *Journal of Sex Research, 40*(1), 27–35.

Algoe, S. B., Gable, S. L., & Maisel, N. C. (2010). It's the little things: Everyday gratitude as a booster shot for romantic relationships. *Personal Relationships, 17*(2), 217–233.

Alicke, M. D. (1985). Global self-evaluation as determined by the desirability and controllability of trait adjectives. *Journal of Personality and Social Psychology, 49*(6), 1621–1630.

Alksnis, C., Desmarais, S., & Curtis, J. (2008). Workforce segregation and the gender wage gap: Is "women's" work valued as highly as "men's"? *Journal of Applied Social Psychology, 38*(6), 1416–1441.

Allen, S., & Daly, K. (2007). The effects of father involvement: An updated research summary of the evidence inventory. Guelph, ON: Centre for Families, Work & Well-Being, University of Guelph. Retrieved from: http://www.fira.ca/cms/documents/29/Effects_of_Father_Involvement.pdf

Allen, V. L., & Levine, J. M. (1968). Social support, dissent and conformity. *Sociometry, 31*(2), 138–149.

Allen, V. L., & Levine, J. M. (1969). Consensus and conformity. *Journal of Experimental Social Psychology, 5*(4), 389–399.

Allison, S. T., Messick, D. M., & Goethals, G. R. (1989). On being better but not smarter than others: The Muhammad Ali effect. *Social Cognition, 7*(3), 275–295.

Alloy, L. B., & Abramson, L. Y. (1979). Judgment of contingency in depressed and nondepressed students: Sadder but wiser? *Journal of Experimental Psychology: General, 108*(4), 441–485.

Allport, F. H. (1924). *Social psychology*. Boston: Houghton Mifflin.

Allport, G. W. (1937). *Personality: A psychological interpretation*. Oxford: Holt.

Allport, G. W. (1954). *The nature of prejudice*. Cambridge, MA: Addison-Wesley.

Allport, G. W., & Postman, L. J. (1947). *The psychology of rumor*. Oxford: Henry Holt.

Altemeyer, B. (1981). *Right-wing authoritarianism*. Winnipeg: University of Manitoba Press.

Altemeyer, B. (1998). The other "authoritarian personality." In M. P. Zanna (Ed.), *Advances in experimental social psychology* (Vol. 30, pp. 47–92). San Diego: Academic Press.

Altman, I., & Taylor, D. A. (1973). *Social penetration: The development of interpersonal relationships*. Oxford: Holt, Rinehart & Winston.

Amato, P. R., Booth, A., Johnson, D. R., & Rogers, S. J. (2007). *Alone together: How marriage in America is changing*. Cambridge, MA: Harvard University Press.

Ambady, N., & Rosenthal, R. (1992). Thin slices of expressive behavior as predictors of interpersonal consequences: A meta-analysis. *Psychological Bulletin, 111*(2), 256–274.

Amodio, D. M., & Devine, P. G. (2006). Stereotyping and evaluation in implicit race bias: Evidence for independent constructs and unique effects on behavior. *Journal of Personality and Social Psychology, 91*(4), 652–661.

Amodio, D. M., & Showers, C. J. (2005). 'Similarity breeds liking' revisited: The moderating role of commitment. *Journal of Social and Personal Relationships, 22*(6), 817–836.

Andersen, S. M., & Baum, A. (1994). Transference in interpersonal relations: Inferences and affect based on significant other representations. *Journal of Personality, 62*(4), 459–497.

Andersen, S. M., & Bem, S. L. (1981). Sex typing and androgyny in dyadic interaction: Individual differences in responsiveness to physical attractiveness. *Journal of Personality and Social Psychology, 41*(1), 74–86.

Andersen, S. M., Reznik, I., & Manzella, L. M. (1996). Eliciting facial affect, motivation, and expectancies in transference: Significant-other representations in social relations. *Journal of Personality and Social Psychology, 71*(6), 1108–1129.

Anderson, C. A. (1989). Temperature and aggression: Ubiquitous effects of heat on occurrence of human violence. *Psychological Bulletin, 106*(1), 74–96.

Anderson, C. A., Anderson, K. B., & Deuser, W. E. (1996). Examining an affective aggression framework: Weapon and temperature effects on aggressive thoughts, affect, and attitudes. *Personality and Social Psychology Bulletin, 22*(4), 366–376.

Anderson, C. A., Bushman, B. J., & Groom, R. W. (1997). Hot years and serious and deadly assault: Empirical tests of the heat hypothesis. *Journal of Personality and Social Psychology, 73*(6), 1213–1223.

Anderson, C. A., & Dill, K. E. (2000). Video games and aggressive thoughts, feelings, and behavior in the laboratory and in life. *Journal of Personality and Social Psychology, 78*(4), 772–790.

Anderson, C. A., Sakamoto, A., Gentile, D. A., Ihori, N., Shibuya, A., Yukawa, S., . . . & Kobayashi, K. (2008). Longitudinal effects of violent video games on aggression in Japan and the United States. *Pediatrics, 122*(5), e1067–e1072.

Anderson, E. (2000). *Code of the street: Decency, violence and the moral life of the inner city*. New York: W. W. Norton.

Anderson, J. L., Crawford, C. B., Nadeau, J., & Lindberg, T. (1992). Was the Duchess of Windsor right? A cross-cultural review of the socioecology of ideals of female body shape. *Ethology and Sociobiology, 13*(3), 197–227.

Anderson, J. R. (1996). *The architecture of cognition*. Mahwah, NJ: Erlbaum.

Anderson, N. B., & Armstead, C. A. (1995). Toward understanding the association of socioeconomic status and health: A new challenge for the biopsychosocial approach. *Psychosomatic Medicine*, 57(3), 213–225. Retrieved from http://www.psychosomaticmedicine.org/content/57/3/213.short

Anderson, N. H. (1974). Cognitive algebra: Integration theory applied to social attribution. In L. Berkowitz (Ed.), *Advances in experimental social psychology* (Vol. 7, pp. 1–101). New York: Academic Press.

Anderson, R., & Nida, S. A. (1978). Effect of physical attractiveness on opposite- and same-sex evaluations. *Journal of Personality*, 46(3), 401–413.

Anderson, S. C., & Lauderdale, M. L. (1982). Characteristics of abusive parents: A look at self-esteem. *Child Abuse & Neglect*, 6(3), 285–293.

Andreychik, M. R., & Gill, M. J. (2012). Do negative implicit associations indicate negative attitudes? Social explanations moderate whether ostensible "negative" associations are prejudice-based or empathy-based. *Journal of Experimental Social Psychology*, 48(5), 1082–1093.

Ansfield, M. E., Wegner, D. M., & Bowser, R. (1996). Ironic effects of sleep urgency. *Behaviour Research and Therapy*, 34(7), 523–531.

Apfelbaum, E. P., Sommers, S. R., & Norton, M. I. (2008). Seeing race and seeming racist? Evaluating strategic colorblindness in social interaction. *Journal of Personality and Social Psychology*, 95(4), 918–932.

Aquino, K., Freeman, D., Reed II, A., Lim, V. K., & Felps, W. (2009). Testing a social-cognitive model of moral behavior: The interactive influence of situations and moral identity centrality. *Journal of Personality and Social Psychology*, 97(1), 123–141.

Aquino, K., McFerran, B., & Laven, M. (2011). Moral identity and the experience of moral elevation in response to acts of uncommon goodness. *Journal of Personality and Social Psychology*, 100(4), 703–718.

Aquino, K., & Reed II, A. (2002). The self-importance of moral identity. *Journal of Personality and Social Psychology*, 83(6), 1423–1440.

Archer, D., & Gartner, R. (1984). *Violence and crime in cross-national perspective*. New Haven: Yale University Press.

Archer, D., & McDaniel, P. (1995). Violence and gender: Differences and similarities across societies. In R. B. Ruback & N. A. Weiner (Eds.), *Interpersonal violent behaviors: Social and cultural aspects* (pp. 63–87). New York: Springer.

Archer, J. (1994). *Male violence*. New York: Routledge.

Archer, J. (2004). Sex differences in aggression in real-world settings: A meta-analytic review. *Review of General Psychology*, 8(4), 291–322.

Archer, R. L., & Cook, C. E. (1986). Personalistic self-disclosure and attraction: Basis for relationship or scarce resource. *Social Psychology Quarterly*, 49(3), 268–272.

Arndt, J., & Goldenberg, J. L. (2011). When self-enhancement drives health decisions: Insights from a terror management health model. In M. D. Alicke & C. Sedikides (Eds.), *The handbook of self enhancement and self protection* (pp. 380–398). New York: Guilford Press.

Arndt, J., & Greenberg, J. (1999). The effects of a self-esteem boost and mortality salience on responses to boost relevant and irrelevant worldview threats. *Personality and Social Psychology Bulletin*, 25(11), 1331–1341.

Arndt, J., Greenberg, J., Schimel, J., Pyszczynski, T., & Solomon, S. (2002). To belong or not to belong, that is the question: Terror management and identification with gender and ethnicity. *Journal of Personality and Social Psychology*, 83(1), 26–43.

Arndt, J., Schimel, J., Greenberg, J., & Pyszczynski, T. (2002). The intrinsic self and defensiveness: Evidence that activating the intrinsic self reduces self-handicapping and conformity. *Personality and Social Psychology Bulletin*, 28(5), 671–683.

Aron, A., & Aron, E. N. (2006). Romantic relationships from the perspectives of the self-expansion model and attachment theory. In M. Mikulincer & G. S. Goodman (Eds.), *Dynamics of romantic love: Attachment, caregiving, and sex* (pp. 359–382). New York: Guilford Press.

Aron, A., Aron, E. N., & Norman, C. (2001). Self-expansion model of motivation and cognition in close relationships and beyond. In G. J. O. Fletcher & M. S. Clark (Eds.), *Blackwell handbook of social psychology: Interpersonal processes* (pp. 478–501). Malden, MA: Blackwell Publishers Ltd.

Aron, A., Aron, E. N., & Smollan, D. (1992). Inclusion of other in the self scale and the structure of interpersonal closeness. *Journal of Personality and Social Psychology*, 63(4), 596–612.

Aron, A., Dutton, D. G., Aron, E. N., & Iverson, A. (1989). Experiences of falling in love. *Journal of Social and Personal Relationships*, 6(3), 243–257.

Aron, A., Fisher, H., Mashek, D. J., Strong, G., Li, H., & Brown, L. L. (2005). Reward, motivation, and emotion systems associated with early-stage intense romantic love. *Journal of Neurophysiology*, 94(1), 327–337.

Aron, A., & Fraley, B. (1999). Relationship closeness as including other in the self: Cognitive underpinnings and measures. *Social Cognition*, 17(2), 140–160.

Aron, A., Norman, C. C., Aron, E. N., McKenna, C., & Heyman, R. E. (2000). Couples' shared participation in novel and arousing activities and experienced relationship quality. *Journal of Personality and Social Psychology*, 78(2), 273–284.

Aron, A., Paris, M., & Aron, E. N. (1995). Falling in love: Prospective studies of self-concept change. *Journal of Personality and Social Psychology*, 69(6), 1102–1112.

Aron, A., & Westbay, L. (1996). Dimensions of the prototype of love. *Journal of Personality and Social Psychology*, 70(3), 535–551.

Aronson, E., Blaney, N., Stephin, C., Sikes, J., & Snapp, M. (1978). *The jigsaw classroom*. Beverly Hills: Sage.

Aronson, E., & Carlsmith, J. M. (1963). Effect of the severity of threat on the devaluation of forbidden behavior. *Journal of Abnormal and Social Psychology*, 66(6), 584–588.

Aronson, E., & Linder, D. (1965). Gain and loss of esteem as determinants of interpersonal attractiveness. *Journal of Experimental Social Psychology*, 1(2), 156–171.

Aronson, E., & Mills, J. (1959). The effect of severity of initiation on liking for a group. *Journal of Abnormal and Social Psychology*, 59(2), 177–181.

Aronson, E., Turner, J. A., & Carlsmith, J. M. (1963). Communicator credibility and communication discrepancy as determinants of opinion change. *Journal of Abnormal and Social Psychology*, 67(1), 31–36.

Arriaga, X. B. (2001). The ups and downs of dating: Fluctuations in satisfaction in newly formed romantic relationships. *Journal of Personality and Social Psychology*, 80(5), 754–765.

Arriaga, X. B., & Rusbult, C. E. (1998). Standing in my partner's shoes: Partner perspective taking and reactions to accommodative dilemmas. *Personality and Social Psychology Bulletin*, 24(9), 927–948.

Asch, S. E. (1946). Forming impressions of personality. *Journal of Abnormal and Social Psychology*, 41(3), 258–290.

Asch, S. E. (1955). Opinions and social pressure. *Scientific American*, 193(5), 31–35.

Asch, S. E. (1956). Studies of independence and conformity: I. A minority of one against a unanimous majority. *Psychological Monographs: General and Applied*, 70(9), 1–70.

Asch, S. E., & Zukier, H. (1984). Thinking about persons. *Journal of Personality and Social Psychology*, 46(6), 1230–1240.

Ashe, A., & Rampersad, A. (1994). *Days of grace: A memoir*. New York: Ballantine Books.

Ashman, H., Musker, J. (Producers), Clements, R., & Musker, J. (Directors) (1989). *The little mermaid* [Motion picture]. United States: Walt Disney Pictures in association with Silver Screen Partners IV.

Aubrey, J. S. (2007). The impact of sexually objectifying media exposure on negative body emotions and sexual self-perceptions: Investigating the mediating role of body self-consciousness. *Mass Communication & Society*, 10(1), 1–23.

Auden, W. H. (1950). *Collected shorter poems: 1930–1944*. London: Faber & Faber.

Aumer-Ryan, K., Hatfield, E., & Frey, R. (2007). Examining equity theory across cultures. *Interpersona*, 1(1), 61–75.

Averill, J. R. (1982). *Anger and aggression: An essay on emotion*. New York: Springer-Verlag.

Avnet, J., Tisch, S., Schreder, C., Goldemberg, R. L. (Producers), & Greenwald, R. (Director) (1984). *The burning bed* [Motion picture]. United States: Tisch/Avnet Productions Inc.

Ayduk, Ö., Gyurak, A., & Luerssen, A. (2008). Individual differences in the rejection–aggression link in the hot sauce paradigm: The case of rejection sensitivity. *Journal of Experimental Social Psychology*, 44(3), 775–782.

Ayduk, O., Mendoza-Denton, R., Mischel, W., Downey, G., Peake, P. K., & Rodriguez, M. (2000). Regulating the interpersonal self: Strategic self-regulation for coping with rejection sensitivity. *Journal of Personality and Social Psychology*, 79(5), 776–792.

Azar, S. T., & Rohrbeck, C. A. (1986). Child abuse and unrealistic expectations: Further validation of the Parent Opinion Questionnaire. *Journal of Consulting and Clinical Psychology*, 54(6), 867–868.

Badr, L. K., & Abdallah, B. (2001). Physical attractiveness of premature infants affects outcome at discharge from the NICU. *Infant Behavior and Development*, 24(1), 129–133.

Bailey, M.J., Kim, P.Y., Hills, A., & Linsenmeier, J.A.W. (1997). Butch, femme, or straight acting? Partner preferences of gay men and lesbians. *Journal of Personality and Social Psychology*, 73(5), 960–973.

Bakan, D. (1966). *The duality of human existence: Isolation and communion in Western man*. Chicago: Rand McNally.

Baldwin, J. (1963). *The fire next time*. New York: Dial Press.

Baldwin, M. W., Carrell, S. E., & Lopez, D. F. (1990). Priming relationship schemas: My advisor and the Pope are watching me from the back of my mind. *Journal of Experimental Social Psychology*, 26(5), 435–454.

Baldwin, M. W., & Fehr, B. (1995). On the instability of attachment style ratings. *Personal Relationships, 2*(3), 247–261.

Baldwin, M. W., Keelan, J. P. R., Fehr, B., Enns, V., & Koh-Rangarajoo, E. (1996). Social-cognitive conceptualization of attachment working models: Availability and accessibility effects. *Journal of Personality and Social Psychology, 71*(1), 94–109.

Balsam, K. F., Beauchaine, T. P., Rothblum, E. D., & Solomon, S. E. (2008). Three-year follow-up of same-sex couples who had civil unions in Vermont, same-sex couples not in civil unions, and heterosexual married couples. *Developmental Psychology, 44*(1), 102–116.

Bandura, A. (1965). Influence of models' reinforcement contingencies on the acquisition of imitative responses. *Journal of Personality and Social Psychology, 1*(6), 589–595.

Bandura, A. (1973). *Aggression: A social learning analysis.* Englewood Cliffs, NJ: Prentice-Hall.

Bandura, A., Ross, D., & Ross, S. A. (1961). Transmission of aggression through imitation of aggressive models. *Journal of Abnormal and Social Psychology, 63*(3), 575–582.

Bandura, A., Ross, D., & Ross, S. A. (1963a). Imitation of film-mediated aggressive models. *Journal of Abnormal and Social Psychology, 66*(1), 3–11.

Bandura, A., Ross, D., & Ross, S. A. (1963b). Vicarious reinforcement and imitative learning. *Journal of Abnormal and Social Psychology, 67*(6), 601–607.

Bandura, A., Underwood, B., & Fromson, M. E. (1975). Disinhibition of aggression through diffusion of responsibility and dehumanization of victims. *Journal of Research in Personality, 9*(4), 253–269.

Banerjee, S. C., & Greene, K. (2007). Antismoking initiatives: Effects of analysis versus production media literacy interventions on smoking-related attitude, norm, and behavioral intention. *Health Communication, 22*(1), 37–48.

Banfield, J. F., Wyland, C. L., Macrae, C. N., Munte, T. F., & Heatherton, T. F. (2004). The cognitive neuroscience of self-regulation. In R. F. Baumeister & K. D. Vohs (Eds.), *Handbook of self-regulation: Research, theory, and applications* (pp. 62–83). New York: Guilford Press.

Banks, S. M., Salovey, P., Greener, S., Rothman, A. J., Moyer, A., Beauvais, J., & Epel, E. (1995). The effects of message framing on mammography utilization. *Health Psychology, 14*(2), 178–184.

Bar-Tal, D. (1976). *Prosocial behavior: Theory and research.* Washington, DC: Hemisphere Publishing Corp.

Barbaree, H. E., & Marshall, W. L. (1991). The role of male sexual arousal in rape: Six models. *Journal of Consulting and Clinical Psychology, 59*(5), 621–630.

Barber, N. (2006). Why is violent crime so common in the Americas? *Aggressive Behavior, 32*(5), 442–450.

Bargh, J. A., Bond, R. N., Lombardi, W. J., & Tota, M. E. (1986). The additive nature of chronic and temporary sources of construct accessibility. *Journal of Personality and Social Psychology, 50*(5), 869–878.

Bargh, J. A., Chen, M., & Burrows, L. (1996). Automaticity of social behavior: Direct effects of trait construct and stereotype activation on action. *Journal of Personality and Social Psychology, 71*(2), 230–244.

Bargh, J. A., & Pietromonaco, P. (1982). Automatic information processing and social perception: The influence of trait information presented outside of conscious awareness on impression formation. *Journal of Personality and Social Psychology, 43*(3), 437–449.

Bargh, J. A., Raymond, P., Pryor, J. B., & Strack, F. (1995). Attractiveness of the underling: An automatic power → sex association and its consequences for sexual harassment and aggression. *Journal of Personality and Social Psychology, 68*(5), 768–781.

Barkow, J. H. (1989). *Darwin, sex, and status: Biological approaches to mind and culture.* Toronto: University of Toronto Press.

Barkow, J. H., Cosmides, L. E., & Tooby, J. E. (Eds.). (1992). *The adapted mind: Evolutionary psychology and the generation of culture.* New York: Oxford University Press.

Barnett, P. A., & Gotlib, I. H. (1988). Psychosocial functioning and depression: Distinguishing among antecedents, concomitants, and consequences. *Psychological Bulletin, 104*(1), 97–126.

Baron-Cohen, S., & Wheelwright, S. (2004). The empathy quotient: An investigation of adults with Asperger syndrome or high functioning autism, and normal sex differences. *Journal of Autism and Developmental Disorders, 34*(2), 163–175.

Baron-Cohen, S., Wheelwright, S., Hill, J., Raste, Y., & Plumb, I. (2001). The "Reading the mind in the eyes" test revised version: A study with normal adults, and adults with Asperger syndrome or high-functioning autism. *Journal of Child Psychology and Psychiatry, 42*(2), 241–251.

Baron-Cohen, S. E., Tager-Flusberg, H. E., & Cohen, D. J. (2000). *Understanding other minds: Perspectives from developmental cognitive neuroscience.* New York: Oxford University Press.

Baron, R. A. (1977). *Human aggression.* New York: Plenum.

Baron, R. S. (1986). Distraction-conflict theory: Progress and problems. In L. Berkowitz (Ed.), *Advances in experimental social psychology* (Vol. 19, pp. 1–40). New York: Academic Press.

Baron, R. S. (2005). So right it's wrong: Groupthink and the ubiquitous nature of polarized group decision making. In M. P. Zanna (Ed.), *Advances in experimental social psychology* (Vol. 37, pp. 219–253). San Diego: Elsevier Academic Press.

Baron, R. S., David, J. P., Brunsman, B. M., & Inman, M. (1997). Why listeners hear less than they are told: Attentional load and the teller–listener extremity effect. *Journal of Personality and Social Psychology, 72*(4), 826–838.

Barratt, E. S. (1994). Impulsiveness and aggression. In J. Monahan & H. J. Steadman (Eds.), *Violence and mental disorder: Developments in risk assessment* (pp. 61–78). Chicago: University of Chicago Press.

Barrett, L. F., Mesquita, B., Ochsner, K. N., & Gross, J. J. (2007). The experience of emotion. *Annual Review of Psychology, 58*, 373.

Barry, D. (1996, March 30). Chipping away those "V" words on TV. *The Free Lance-Star.* Retrieved from http://news.google.com/newspapers?nid=1298&dat=19960330&id=nuoyAAAAIBAJ&sjid=zQcGAAAAIBAJ&pg=3089,5944603

Bartal, I. B. A., Decety, J., & Mason, P. (2011). Empathy and pro-social behavior in rats. *Science, 334*(6061), 1427–1430.

Bartholomew, K., & Horowitz, L. M. (1991). Attachment styles among young adults: A test of a four-category model. *Journal of Personality and Social Psychology, 61*(2), 226–244.

Bartholow, B. D. (2010). Event-related brain potentials and social cognition: On using physiological information to constrain social cognitive theories. *Social Cognition, 28*(6), 723–747.

Bartholow, B. D., Anderson, C. A., Carnagey, N. L., & Benjamin, Jr., A. J. (2005). Interactive effects of life experience and situational cues on aggression: The weapons priming effect in hunters and nonhunters. *Journal of Experimental Social Psychology, 41*(1), 48–60.

Bartholow, B. D., Dickter, C. L., & Sestir, M. A. (2006). Stereotype activation and control of race bias: Cognitive control of inhibition and its impairment by alcohol. *Journal of Personality and Social Psychology, 90*(2), 272–287.

Bartholow, B. D., Fabiani, M., Gratton, G., & Bettencourt, B. A. (2001). A psychophysiological examination of cognitive processing of and affective responses to social expectancy violations. *Psychological Science, 12*(3), 197–204.

Bartholow, B. D., & Heinz, A. (2006). Alcohol and aggression without consumption: Alcohol cues, aggressive thoughts, and hostile perception bias. *Psychological Science, 17*(1), 30–37.

Bartholow, B. D., Henry, E. A., Lust, S. A., Saults, J. S., & Wood, P. K. (2012). Alcohol effects on performance monitoring and adjustment: Affect modulation and impairment of evaluative cognitive control. *Journal of Abnormal Psychology, 121*(1), 173–186.

Bartholow, B. D., Pearson, M. A., Gratton, G., & Fabiani, M. (2003). Effects of alcohol on person perception: A social cognitive neuroscience approach. *Journal of Personality and Social Psychology, 85*(4), 627–638.

Bartlett, M. Y., & DeSteno, D. (2006). Gratitude and prosocial behavior: Helping when it costs you. *Psychological Science, 17*(4), 319–325.

Bass, B. M. (1985). *Leadership and performance beyond expectations.* New York: Free Press.

Bassili, J. N. (2003). The minority slowness effect: Subtle inhibitions in the expression of views not shared by others. *Journal of Personality and Social Psychology, 84*(2), 261–276.

Batson, C. D. (1991). *The altruism question: Toward a social-psychological answer.* Hillsdale, NJ: Erlbaum.

Batson, C. D. (2011). *Altruism in humans.* New York: Oxford University Press.

Batson, C. D., Batson, J. G., Griffitt, C. A., Barrientos, S., Brandt, J. R., Sprengelmeyer, P., & Bayly, M. J. (1989). Negative-state relief and the empathy—altruism hypothesis. *Journal of Personality and Social Psychology, 56*(6), 922–933.

Batson, C. D., Chang, J., Orr, R., & Rowland, J. (2002). Empathy, attitudes, and action: Can feeling for a member of a stigmatized group motivate one to help the group? *Personality and Social Psychology Bulletin, 28*(12), 1656–1666.

Batson, C. D., Duncan, B. D., Ackerman, P., Buckley, T., & Birch, K. (1981). Is empathic emotion a source of altruistic motivation? *Journal of Personality and Social Psychology, 40*(2), 290–302.

Batson, C. D., Eklund, J. H., Chermok, V. L., Hoyt, J. L., & Ortiz, B. G. (2007). An additional antecedent of empathic concern: Valuing the welfare of the person in need. *Journal of Personality and Social Psychology, 93*(1), 65–74.

Batson, C. D., Polycarpou, M. P., Harmon-Jones, E., Imhoff, H. J., Mitchener, E. C., Bednar, L. L., . . . & Highberger, L. (1997). Empathy and attitudes: Can feeling for a member of a stigmatized group improve feelings toward the group? *Journal of Personality and Social Psychology, 72*(1), 105–118.

Batson, C. D., Schoenrade, P., & Ventis, W. L. (1993). *Religion and the individual: A social-psychological perspective.* New York: Oxford University Press.

Baum, S. K, Cohen, F., and Jacobs, S. L. (Eds.) (in press). *Antisemitism in North America: Theory, research and methodology*. Boston: Brill.

Baumeister, R. F., & Jones, E. E. (1978). When self-presentation is constrained by the target's knowledge: Consistency and compensation. *Journal of Personality and Social Psychology, 36*(6), 608–618.

Baumeister, R. F., & Leary, M. R. (1995). The need to belong: Desire for interpersonal attachments as a fundamental human motivation. *Psychological Bulletin, 117*(3), 497–529.

Baumeister, R. F., Smart, L., & Boden, J. M. (1996). Relation of threatened egotism to violence and aggression: The dark side of high self-esteem. *Psychological Review, 103*(1), 5–33.

Baumeister, R. F., Stillwell, A. M., & Heatherton, T. F. (1994). Guilt: An interpersonal approach. *Psychological Bulletin, 115*(2), 243–267.

Baumeister, R. F., Twenge, J. M., & Nuss, C. K. (2002). Effects of social exclusion on cognitive processes: Anticipated aloneness reduces intelligent thought. *Journal of Personality and Social Psychology, 83*(4), 817–827.

Baumeister, R. F., & Vohs, K. D. (2004). Sexual economics: Sex as female resource for social exchange in heterosexual interactions. *Personality and Social Psychology Review, 8*(4), 339–363.

Baumeister, R. F., Wotman, S. R., & Stillwell, A. M. (1993). Unrequited love: On heartbreak, anger, guilt, scriptlessness, and humiliation. *Journal of Personality and Social Psychology, 64*(3), 377–394.

Baumrind, D. (1964). Some thoughts on ethics of research: After reading Milgram's "Behavioral study of obedience." *American Psychologist, 19*(6), 421–423.

Baxter, L. A. (2004). Relationships as dialogues. *Personal Relationships, 11*(1), 1–22.

Beach, F. A., Jordan, L., 1956. Sexual exhaustion and recovery in the male rat. *Quarterly Journal of Experimental Psychology, 8*, 121–133.

Beaman, A. L., Barnes, P. J., Klentz, B., & McQuirk, B. (1978). Increasing helping rates through information dissemination: Teaching pays. *Personality and Social Psychology Bulletin, 4*(3), 406–411.

Beaman, A. L., Klentz, B., Diener, E., & Svanum, S. (1979). Self-awareness and transgression in children: Two field studies. *Journal of Personality and Social Psychology, 37*(10), 1835–1846.

Beauvais, F. (2000). Indian adolescence: Opportunity and challenge. In R. Montemayor, G. R. Adams, & T. P. Gullotta (Eds.), *Adolescent diversity in ethnic, economic, and cultural contexts* (Vol. 1, pp. 110–140). Thousand Oaks, CA: Sage.

Bechara, A., Damasio, H., Tranel, D., & Damasio, A. R. (1997). Deciding advantageously before knowing the advantageous strategy. *Science, 275*(5304), 1293–1295.

Bechara, A., Tranel, D., Damasio, H., & Damasio, A. R. (1996). Failure to respond autonomically to anticipated future outcomes following damage to prefrontal cortex. *Cerebral Cortex, 6*(2), 215–225.

Beck, A., & Heinz, A. (2013). Alcohol-related aggression: Social and neurobiological factors. *Deutsches Ärzteblatt International, 110*(42), 711–715.

Becker, E. (1962). *The birth and death of meaning*. New York: Free Press.

Becker, E. (1971). *The birth and death of meaning: An interdisciplinary perspective on the problem of man* (2nd ed.). Harmondsworth: Penguin.

Becker, E. (1973). *The denial of death*. New York: Free Press.

Becker, E. (1975). *Escape from evil*. New York: Free Press.

Becker, J. C., & Wright, S. C. (2011). Yet another dark side of chivalry: Benevolent sexism undermines and hostile sexism motivates collective action for social change. *Journal of Personality and Social Psychology, 101*(1), 62–77.

Beer, C. (1984). Fearful curiosity in animals. In J. A. Crook, J. B. Haskins, & P. G. Ashton (Eds.), *Morbid curiosity and the mass media: Proceedings of a symposium*. Knoxville: University of Tennessee and the Gannett Foundation.

Beer, J. S. (2002). Implicit self-theories of shyness. *Journal of Personality and Social Psychology, 83*(4), 1009–1024.

Beer, J. S., Heerey, E. A., Keltner, D., Scabini, D., & Knight, R. T. (2003). The regulatory function of self-conscious emotion: Insights from patients with orbitofrontal damage. *Journal of Personality and Social Psychology, 85*(4), 594–604.

Beilock, S. (2011). *Choke: What the secrets of the brain reveal about getting it right when you have to*. New York: Free Press.

Beilock, S. L., & Carr, T. H. (2001). On the fragility of skilled performance: What governs choking under pressure? *Journal of Experimental Psychology: General, 130*(4), 701–725.

Beilock, S. L., Kulp, C. A., Holt, L. E., & Carr, T. H. (2004). More on the fragility of performance: Choking under pressure in mathematical problem solving. *Journal of Experimental Psychology: General, 133*(4), 584–600.

Bell, J. (2009). Why embarrassment inhibits the acquisition and use of condoms: A qualitative approach to understanding risky sexual behaviour. *Journal of Adolescence, 32*(2), 379–391.

Bem, D. J. (1965). An experimental analysis of self-persuasion. *Journal of Experimental Social Psychology, 1*(3), 199–218.

Bem, D. J. (1967). Self-perception: An alternative interpretation of cognitive dissonance phenomena. *Psychological Review, 74*(3), 183–200.

Ben-Ari, O. T., Florian, V., & Mikulincer, M. (1999). The impact of mortality salience on reckless driving: A test of terror management mechanisms. *Journal of Personality and Social Psychology, 76*(1), 35–45.

Bentler, P. M., & Newcomb, M. D. (1978). Longitudinal study of marital success and failure. *Journal of Consulting and Clinical Psychology, 46*(5), 1053–1070.

Bergen, R. (1991). *Beliefs about intelligence and achievement-related behaviors* (Unpublished doctoral dissertation). University of Illinois, Urbana-Champaign.

Berger, J. (1972). *Ways of seeing*. London: Penguin.

Berger, J. (1994, February 12). Shattering the Silence of Autism. *The New York Times*, pp. 21, 27. Retrieved from http://www.nytimes.com/1994/02/12/nyregion/shattering-silence-autism-new-communication-method-hailed-miracle-derided.html

Berger, P. L., & Luckmann, T. (1967). *The social construction of reality: A treatise in the sociology of knowledge*. New York: Doubleday Anchor.

Berglas, S., & Jones, E. E. (1978). Drug choice as a self-handicapping strategy in response to noncontingent success. *Journal of Personality and Social Psychology, 36*(4), 405–417.

Bergsieker, H. B., Shelton, J. N., & Richeson, J. A. (2010). To be liked versus respected: Divergent goals in interracial interactions. *Journal of Personality and Social Psychology, 99*(2), 248–264.

Berkman, L. F., & Glass, T. A. (2000). Social integration, social networks, asocial support and health. In L. F. Berkman & I. Kawachi (Eds.), *Social epidemiology* (pp. 137–174). New York: Oxford University Press.

Berkowitz, L. (1965). Some aspects of observed aggression. *Journal of Personality and Social Psychology, 2*(3), 359–369.

Berkowitz, L. (1968). Impulse, aggression and the gun. *Psychology Today, 2*(4), 18–22.

Berkowitz, L. (1989). Frustration-aggression hypothesis: Examination and reformulation. *Psychological Bulletin, 106*(1), 59–73.

Berkowitz, L. (1993). *Aggression: Its causes, consequences, and control*. New York: McGraw-Hill.

Berkowitz, L., Cochran, S. T., & Embree, M. C. (1981). Physical pain and the goal of aversively stimulated aggression. *Journal of Personality and Social Psychology, 40*(4), 687–700.

Berkowitz, L., & Geen, R. G. (1967). Stimulus qualities of the target of aggression: A further study. *Journal of Personality and Social Psychology, 5*(3), 364–368.

Berkowitz, L., & LePage, A. (1967). Weapons as aggression-eliciting stimuli. *Journal of Personality and Social Psychology, 7*(2, Pt.1), 202–207.

Berkowitz, L., & Troccoli, B. T. (1990). Feelings, direction of attention, and expressed evaluations of others. *Cognition and Emotion, 4*(4), 305–325.

Berman, M., Gladue, B., & Taylor, S. (1993). The effects of hormones, type A behavior pattern, and provocation on aggression in men. *Motivation and Emotion, 17*(2), 125–138.

Berman, M. E., McCloskey, M. S., Fanning, J. R., Schumacher, J. A., & Coccaro, E. F. (2009). Serotonin augmentation reduces response to attack in aggressive individuals. *Psychological Science, 20*(6), 714–720.

Bernard, M. M., Maio, G. R., & Olson, J. M. (2003). The vulnerability of values to attack: Inoculation of values and value-relevant attitudes. *Personality and Social Psychology Bulletin, 29*(1), 63–75.

Berns, G. S., Chappelow, J., Zink, C. F., Pagnoni, G., Martin-Skurski, M. E., & Richards, J. (2005). Neurobiological correlates of social conformity and independence during mental rotation. *Biological Psychology, 58*(3), 245–253.

Berry, D. S., & McArthur, L. Z. (1986). Perceiving character in faces: The impact of age-related craniofacial changes on social perception. *Psychological Bulletin, 100*(1), 3–18.

Berry, J. W. (1966). Temne and Eskimo perceptual skills. *International Journal of Psychology, 1*(3), 207–229.

Berry, J. W. (1997). *Immigration, acculturation, and adaption*. Hove: Psychology Press.

Berry, J. W. (2001). A psychology of immigration. *Journal of Social Issues, 57*(3), 615–631.

Berry, J. W. (2006). Stress perspectives on acculturation. In D. L. Sam & J. W. Berry (Eds.), *The Cambridge handbook of acculturation psychology* (pp. 43–57). Cambridge: Cambridge University Press.

Berscheid, E. (2006). Searching for the meaning of "love." In R. J. Sternberg & K. Weis (Eds.), *The new psychology of love* (pp. 171–183). New Haven: Yale University Press.

Berscheid, E., Dion, K., Walster, E., & Walster, G. W. (1971). Physical attractiveness and dating choice: A test of the matching hypothesis. *Journal of Experimental Social Psychology, 7*(2), 173–189.

Berscheid, E., Snyder, M., & Omoto, A. M. (1989). The Relationship Closeness Inventory: Assessing the closeness of interpersonal relationships. *Journal of Personality and Social Psychology, 57*(5), 792–807.

Berscheid, E., Snyder, M., & Omoto, A. M. (2004). Measuring Closeness: The Relationship Closeness Inventory (RCI) revisited. In D. J. Mashek & A. Aron (Eds.), *Handbook of closeness and intimacy* (pp. 81–101). Mahwah, NJ: Erlbaum.

Berscheid, E., & Walster, E. (1974). A little bit about love. In T. Huston (Ed.), *Foundations of interpersonal attraction* (pp. 356–379). New York: Academic Press.

Betsch, T., & Dickenberger, D. (1993). Why do aggressive movies make people aggressive? An attempt to explain short-term effects of the depiction of violence on the observer. *Aggressive Behavior*, 19(2), 137–149.

Bettencourt, B. A., & Miller, N. (1996). Gender differences in aggression as a function of provocation: A meta-analysis. *Psychological Bulletin*, 119(3), 422–447.

Bettencourt, B. A., Talley, A., Benjamin, A. J., & Valentine, J. (2006). Personality and aggressive behavior under provoking and neutral conditions: A meta-analytic review. *Psychological Bulletin*, 132(5), 751–777.

Bettor, L., Hendrick, S. S., & Hendrick, C. (1995). Gender and sexual standards in dating relationships. *Personal Relationships*, 2(4), 359–369.

Björkqvist, K., Österman, K., & Kaukiainen, A. (1992). The development of direct and indirect aggressive strategies in males and females. In K. Björkqvist & P. Niemelä (Eds.), *Of mice and women: Aspects of female aggression* (pp. 51–64). San Diego: Academic Press.

Björkqvist, K., Österman, K., & Lagerspetz, K. M. J. (1994). Sex differences in covert aggression among adults. *Aggressive Behavior*, 20(1), 27–33.

Blair, I. V., Judd, C. M., & Chapleau, K. M. (2004). The influence of Afrocentric facial features in criminal sentencing. *Psychological Science*, 15(10), 674–679.

Blair, I. V., Ma, J. E., & Lenton, A. P. (2001). Imagining stereotypes away: The moderation of implicit stereotypes through mental imagery. *Journal of Personality and Social Psychology*, 81(5), 828–841.

Blakeslee, S. (January 10, 2006). Cells that read minds. *The New York Times*, 10, 1. Retrieved from: http://www.nytimes.com/2006/01/10/science/10mirr.html?pagewanted=all&_r=0

Blaney, N. T., Stephan, C., Rosenfield, D., Aronson, E., & Sikes, J. (1977). Interdependence in the classroom: A field study. *Journal of Educational Psychology*, 69(2), 121–128.

Blanton, H., & Jaccard, J. (2006). Arbitrary metrics in psychology. *American Psychologist*, 61(1), 27–41.

Blanton, H., Jaccard, J., Gonzales, P. M., & Christie, C. (2006). Decoding the implicit association test: Implications for criterion prediction. *Journal of Experimental Social Psychology*, 42(2), 192–212.

Blascovich, J., & Mendes, W. B. (2000). Challenge and threat appraisals: The role of affective cues. In J. Forgas (Ed.), *Feeling and thinking: The role of affect in social cognition* (pp. 59–82). Paris: Cambridge University Press.

Blascovich, J., Mendes, W. B., Hunter, S. B., & Salomon, K. (1999). Social "facilitation" as challenge and threat. *Journal of Personality and Social Psychology*, 77(1), 68–77.

Blascovich, J., Seery, M. D., Mugridge, C. A., Norris, R. K., & Weisbuch, M. (2004). Predicting athletic performance from cardiovascular indexes of challenge and threat. *Journal of Experimental Social Psychology*, 40(5), 683–688.

Blascovich, J., & Tomaka, J. (1996). The biopsychosocial model of arousal regulation. In M. P. Zanna (Ed.), *Advances in experimental social psychology* (Vol. 28, pp. 1 51). San Diego: Academic Press.

Blascovich, J., Wyer, N. A., Swart, L. A., & Kibler, J. L. (1997). Racism and racial categorization. *Journal of Personality and Social Psychology*, 72(6), 1364–1372.

Blass, T. (Ed.). (2000). *Obedience to authority: Current perspectives on the Milgram paradigm*. Mahwah, NJ: Erlbaum.

Bless, H., Bohner, G., Schwarz, N., & Strack, F. (1990). Mood and persuasion: A cognitive response analysis. *Personality and Social Psychology Bulletin*, 16(2), 331–345.

Bless, H., Clore, G. L., Schwarz, N., Golisano, V., Rabe, C., & Wölk, M. (1996). Mood and the use of scripts: Does a happy mood really lead to mindlessness? *Journal of Personality and Social Psychology*, 71(4), 665–679.

Bloom, B. L., White, S. W., & Asher, S. J. (1979). Marital disruption as a stressful life event. In G. Levinger & O. C. Moles (Eds.), *Divorce and separation: Context, causes, and consequences* (pp. 184–200). New York: Basic Books.

Bodenhausen, G. V. (1990). Stereotypes as judgmental heuristics: Evidence of circadian variations in discrimination. *Psychological Science*, 1(5), 319–322.

Bodenhausen, G. V., Kramer, G. P., & Süsser, K. (1994). Happiness and stereotypic thinking in social judgment. *Journal of Personality and Social Psychology*, 66(4), 621–632.

Boehm, C. (1999). The natural selection of altruistic traits. *Human Nature*, 10(3), 205–252.

Bokhorst, C. L., Bakermans-Kranenburg, M. J., Fonagy, P., & Schuengel, C. (2003). The importance of shared environment in mother–infant attachment security: A behavioral genetic study. *Child Development*, 74(6), 1769–1782.

Bolger, N., DeLongis, A., Kessler, R. C., & Wethington, E. (1989). The contagion of stress across multiple roles. *Journal of Marriage and the Family*, 51(1)175–183. Stable URL: http://www.jstor.org/stable/352378

Bond, R., & Smith, P. B. (1996). Culture and conformity: A meta-analysis of studies using Asch's (1952b, 1956) line judgment task. *Psychological Bulletin*, 119(1), 111–137.

Borduin, C. M., Schaeffer, C. M., & Heiblum, N. (2009). A randomized clinical trial of multisystemic therapy with juvenile sexual offenders: Effects on youth social ecology and criminal activity. *Journal of Consulting and Clinical Psychology*, 77(1), 26–37.

Borgida, E., & Brekke, N. (1985). Psycholegal research on rape trials. In A. Burgess (Ed.), *Research handbook on rape and sexual assault* (pp. 313–342). New York: Garland.

Born, M., Chevalier, V., & Humblet, I. (1997). Resilience, desistance and delinquent career of adolescent offenders. *Journal of Adolescence*, 20(6), 679–694.

Bornstein, R. F. (1989). Exposure and affect: Overview and meta-analysis of research, 1968–1987. *Psychological Bulletin*, 106(2), 265–289.

Bosson, J. K., Haymovitz, E. L., & Pinel, E. C. (2004). When saying and doing diverge: The effects of stereotype threat on self-reported versus non-verbal anxiety. *Journal of Experimental Social Psychology*, 40(2), 247–255.

Bosson, J. K., Swann, W. B., & Pennebaker, J. W. (2000). Stalking the perfect measure of implicit self-esteem: The blind men and the elephant revisited? *Journal of Personality and Social Psychology*, 79(4), 631–643.

Boster, F., Fediuk, T., & Kotowski, M. R. (2001). The effectiveness of an altruistic appeal in the presence and absence of favors. *Communication Monographs*, 68(4), 340–346.

Bower, G. H., & Forgas, J. P. (2000). Affect, memory, and social cognition. In E. Eich, J. F. Kihlstrom, G. H. Bower, J. P. Forgas, & P. M. Niedenthal (Eds.), *Cognition and emotion* (pp. 87–168). New York: Oxford University Press.

Bowlby, J. (1969). *Attachment and loss, Vol. 1: Attachment*. New York: Basic Books.

Bowlby, J. (1973). *Attachment and loss, Vol. 2: Separation, anxiety and anger*. New York: Basic Books.

Bowlby, J. (1980). *Attachment and loss, Vol. 3: Loss: Sadness and depression*. New York: Basic Books.

Box Office Mojo. (2014, July 2). All Time Box Office. Retrieved from http://boxofficemojo.com/alltime/world/

Brach, T. (2003). *Radical acceptance*. New York: Bantam Books.

Bradbury, T. N., & Fincham, F. D. (1990). Attributions in marriage: Review and critique. *Psychological Bulletin*, 107(1), 3–33.

Bradbury, T. N., Fincham, F. D., & Beach, S. R. (2000). Research on the nature and determinants of marital satisfaction: A decade in review. *Journal of Marriage and Family*, 62(4), 964–980.

Bradbury, T. N., & Karney, B. R. (2010). *Intimate relationships*. New York: W. W. Norton.

Bramlett, M. D., & Mosher, W. D. (2002). *Cohabitation, marriage, divorce and remarriage in the United States*. U. S. Department of Health and Human Services, Centers for Disease Control and Prevention, National Center for Health Statistics, Vital Health Statistics, 23(22). Retrieved from http://www.cdc.gov/nchs/data/series/sr_23/sr23_022.pdf

Brandt, M. J., & Reyna, C. (2011). The chain of being: A hierarchy of morality. *Perspectives on Psychological Science*, 6(5), 428–446.

Branscombe, N. R., Schmitt, M. T., & Harvey, R. D. (1999). Perceiving pervasive discrimination among African Americans: Implications for group identification and well-being. *Journal of Personality and Social Psychology*, 77(1), 135–149.

Bransford, J. D., & Johnson, M. K. (1973). Considerations of some problems of comprehension. In W. G. Chase (Ed.), *Visual information processing* (pp. 383–438). New York: Academic Press.

Braver, S. L., Linder, D. E., Corwin, T. T., & Cialdini, R. B. (1977). Some conditions that affect admissions of attitude change. *Journal of Experimental Social Psychology*, 13(6), 565–576.

Brehm, J. W. (1956). Postdecision changes in the desirability of alternatives. *Journal of Abnormal and Social Psychology*, 52(3), 384–389.

Brehm, J. W. (1966). *A theory of psychological reactance*. New York: Academic Press.

Brehm, J. W., & Cohen, A. R. (1962). *Explorations in cognitive dissonance*. Hoboken, NJ: Wiley.

Brehm, J. W., & Self, E. A. (1989). The intensity of motivation. *Annual Review of Psychology*, 40(1), 109–131.

Brehm, J. W., Stires, L. K., Sensenig, J., & Shaban, J. (1966). The attractiveness of an eliminated choice alternative. *Journal of Experimental Social Psychology*, 2(3), 301–313.

Brehm, S. S. (1992). *Intimate relationships* (2nd ed.). New York: McGraw-Hill.

Brehm, S. S., & Brehm, J. W. (1981). *Psychological reactance: A theory of freedom and control*. New York: Academic Press.

Brennan, K. A., Clark, C. L., & Shaver, P. R. (1998). Self-report measurement of adult attachment: An integrative overview. In J. A. Simpson & W. S. Rholes (Eds.), *Attachment theory and close relationships* (pp. 46–76). New York: Guilford Press.

Brewer, M. B. (1979). In-group bias in the minimal intergroup situation: A cognitive-motivational analysis. *Psychological Bulletin, 86*(2), 307–324.

Brewer, M. B. (1991). The social self: On being the same and different at the same time. *Personality and Social Psychology Bulletin, 17*(5), 475–482.

Brewer, M. B., & Caporael, L. R. (2006). An evolutionary perspective on social identity: Revisiting groups. In M. Schaller, J. Simpson, & D. Kenrick (Eds.), *Evolution and social psychology* (pp. 143–161). New York: Psychology Press.

Brickman, P., Redfield, J., Harrison, A. A., & Crandall, R. (1972). Drive and predisposition as factors in the attitudinal effects of mere exposure. *Journal of Experimental Social Psychology, 8*(1), 31–44.

Brickner, M. A., Harkins, S. G., & Ostrom, T. M. (1986). Effects of personal involvement: Thought-provoking implications for social loafing. *Journal of Personality and Social Psychology, 51*(4), 763–769.

Briñol, P., & Petty, R. E. (2003). Overt head movements and persuasion: A self-validation analysis. *Journal of Personality and Social Psychology, 84*(6), 1123–1139.

Brock, T. C., & Brannon, L. A. (1992). Liberalization of commodity theory. *Basic and Applied Social Psychology, 13*(1), 135–144.

Brock, T. C., & Buss, A. H. (1964). Effects of justification for aggression and communication with the victim on postaggression dissonance. *Journal of Abnormal and Social Psychology, 68*(4), 403–412.

Brock, T. C., & Mazzocco, P. J. (2004) Responses to scarcity: A commodity theory perspective on reactance and rumination. In R. A. Wright, J. Greenberg, & S. S. Brehm (Eds.), *Motivational analyses of social behavior: Building on Jack Brehm's contributions to psychology* (pp. 129–148). Mahwah, NJ: Erlbaum.

Brockner, J., Ackerman, G., Greenberg, J., Gelfand, M. J., Francesco, A. M., Chen, Z. X., . . . & Shapiro, D. (2001). Culture and procedural justice: The influence of power distance on reactions to voice. *Journal of Experimental Social Psychology, 37*(4), 300–315.

Brodsky, J., & Harris, B. (Producers), & Arkin, A. (Director). (1971). *Little murders* [Motion picture]. United States: 20th Century Fox.

Bronstad, P. M., & Russell, R. (2007). Beauty is in the 'we' of the beholder: Greater agreement on facial attractiveness among close relations. *Perception, 36*(11), 1674–1681.

Brontë, C. (1992). *Jane Eyre*. Ware: Wordsworth Classics. (Original work published 1847)

Brophy, I. N. (1946). The luxury of anti-Negro prejudice. *Public Opinion Quarterly, 9*(4), 456–466.

Brosnan, S. F., & de Waal, F. B. (2002). A proximate perspective on reciprocal altruism. *Human Nature, 13*(1), 129–152.

Brown v. Board of Education of Topeka, 347 U.S. 483. (1954). Retrieved from http://www.sbdp.org.br/arquivos/material/98_Brown%20v%20Board%20 of%20Education%20e%20Plessy%20v%20Ferguson.pdf

Brown, B. R. (1968). The effects of need to maintain face on interpersonal bargaining. *Journal of Experimental Social Psychology, 4*(1), 107–122.

Brown, J. C., & Strickland, B. R. (1972). Belief in internal-external control of reinforcement and participation in college activities. *Journal of Consulting and Clinical Psychology, 38*(1), 148.

Brown, K. W., Ryan, R. M., & Creswell, J. D. (2007). Mindfulness: Theoretical foundations and evidence for its salutary effects. *Psychological Inquiry, 18*(4), 211–237.

Brown, M. F. (1986). *Tsewa's gift: Magic and meaning in an Amazonian society*. Tuscaloosa: University of Alabama Press.

Brown, M. G., Rosenthal, J., Misher, K., Mann, M. (Producers), & Mann, M. (Director) (2009). *Public enemies* [Motion picture]. United States: Universal Pictures, Forward Pass, & Misher Films, in association with Relativity Media, Tribeca Productions, Appian Way, & Dentsu.

Brown, N. R., & Sinclair, R. C. (1999). Estimating number of lifetime sexual partners: Men and women do it differently. *Journal of Sex Research, 36*(3), 292–297.

Brown, R., González, R., Zagefka, H., Manzi, J., & Čehajić, S. (2008). Nuestra culpa: Collective guilt and shame as predictors of reparation for historical wrongdoing. *Journal of Personality and Social Psychology, 94*(1), 75–90.

Brown, R., & Hewstone, M. (2005). An integrative theory of intergroup contact. In M.P. Zanna (Ed.), *Advances in experimental social psychology* (Vol. 37, pp. 255–343). San Diego: Academic Press.

Brown, R., Vivian, J., & Hewstone, M. (1999). Changing attitudes through intergroup contact: The effects of group membership salience. *European Journal of Social Psychology, 29*(56), 741–764.

Brownmiller, S. (1975). *Against our will: Men, women and rape*. New York: Simon & Schuster.

Brownstein, R. J., & Katzev, R. D. (1985). The relative effectiveness of three compliance techniques in eliciting donations to a cultural organization. *Journal of Applied Social Psychology, 15*(6), 564–574.

Bruckheimer, J. (Producer) & Yakin, B. (Director). (2000). *Remember the Titans* [Motion picture]. United States: Walt Disney Pictures, Jerry Bruckheimer Films, Technical Black, & Run It Up Productions Inc.

Bruner, J. S. (1957). Going beyond the information given. In J. S. Bruner, E. Brunswik, L. Festinger, F. Heider, K. F. Muenzinger, C. E., Osgood, & D. Rapaport (Eds.), *Contemporary approaches to cognition* (pp. 41–69). Cambridge, MA: Harvard University Press.

Bruner, J. S. (1990). *Acts of meaning*. Cambridge, MA: Harvard University Press.

Brunner, H. G., Nelen, M., Breakefield, X. O., & Ropers, H. H. (1993). Abnormal behavior associated with a point mutation in the structural gene for monoamine oxidase A. *Science, 262*(5133), 578–580.

Bui, K. V. T., Peplau, L. A., & Hill, C. T. (1996). Testing the Rusbult model of relationship commitment and stability in a 15-year study of heterosexual couples. *Personality and Social Psychology Bulletin, 22*(12), 1244–1257.

Burdett, K., & Jensen, L. C. (1983). The self-concept and aggressive behavior among elementary school children from two socioeconomic areas and two grade levels. *Psychology in the Schools, 20*, 370–375.

Bureau of Justice Statistics (n.d.). Recidivism. Retrieved from http://www.bjs.gov/index.cfm?ty=tp&tid=17

Burger, J. M. (2009). Replicating Milgram: Would people still obey today? *American Psychologist, 64*(1), 1–11.

Burger, J. M., & Caldwell, D. F. (2003). The effects of monetary incentives and labeling on the foot-in-the-door effect: Evidence for a self-perception process. *Basic and Applied Social Psychology, 25*(3), 235–241.

Burger, J. M., Hornisher, J., Martin, V. E., Newman, G., & Pringle, S. (2007). The pique technique: Overcoming mindlessness or shifting heuristics? *Journal of Applied Social Psychology, 37*(9), 2086–2096.

Burger, J. M., & Petty, R. E. (1981). The low-ball compliance technique: Task or person commitment? *Journal of Personality and Social Psychology, 40*(3), 492–500.

Burke, B. L., Martens, A., & Faucher, E. H. (2010). Two decades of terror management theory: A meta-analysis of mortality salience research. *Personality and Social Psychology Review, 14*(2), 155–195.

Burkhart, K. W. (1973). *Women in prison*. New York: Doubleday.

Burkley, E. (2008). The role of self-control in resistance to persuasion. *Personality and Social Psychology Bulletin, 34*(3), 419–431.

Burnette, J. L., O'Boyle, E. H., VanEpps, E. M., Pollack, J. M., & Finkel, E. J. (2012). Mind-sets matter: A meta-analytic review of implicit theories and self-regulation. *Psychological Bulletin, 139*(3), 655–701.

Burnstein, E., Crandall, C., & Kitayama, S. (1994). Some neo-Darwinian decision rules for altruism: Weighing cues for inclusive fitness as a function of the biological importance of the decision. *Journal of Personality and Social Psychology, 67*(5), 773–789.

Burnstein, E., & Vinokur, A. (1977). Persuasive argumentation and social comparison as determinants of attitude polarization. *Journal of Experimental Social Psychology, 13*(4), 315–332.

Burnstein, E., Vinokur, A., & Trope, Y. (1973). Interpersonal comparison versus persuasive argumentation: A more direct test of alternative explanations for group-induced shifts in individual choice. *Journal of Experimental Social Psychology, 9*(3), 236–245.

Burt, M. R. (1980). Cultural myths and supports for rape. *Journal of Personality and Social Psychology, 38*(2), 217–230.

Burton, C. M., & King, L. A. (2004). The health benefits of writing about intensely positive experiences. *Journal of Research in Personality, 38*(2), 150–163.

Bush, G., Luu, P., & Posner, M. I. (2000). Cognitive and emotional influences in anterior cingulate cortex. *Trends in Cognitive Sciences, 4*(6), 215–222.

Bushman, B. J. (1995). Moderating role of trait aggressiveness in the effects of violent media on aggression. *Journal of Personality and Social Psychology, 69*(5), 950–960.

Bushman, B. J. (1998). Priming effects of media violence on the accessibility of aggressive constructs in memory. *Personality and Social Psychology Bulletin, 24*(5), 537–545.

Bushman, B. J., & Anderson, C. A. (2001). Media violence and the American public: Scientific facts versus media misinformation. *American Psychologist, 56*(6–7), 477–489.

Bushman, B. J., & Baumeister, R. F. (1998). Threatened egotism, narcissism, self-esteem, and direct and displaced aggression: Does self-love or self-hate lead to violence? *Journal of Personality and Social Psychology, 75*(1), 219–229.

Bushman, B. J., Bonacci, A. M., Pedersen, W. C., Vasquez, E. A., & Miller, N. (2005). Chewing on it can chew you up: Effects of rumination on triggered displaced aggression. *Journal of Personality and Social Psychology, 88*(6), 969–983.

Bushman, B. J., & Cooper, H. M. (1990). Effects of alcohol on human aggression: An integrative research review. *Psychological Bulletin, 107*(3), 341–354.

Bushman, B. J., & Geen, R. G. (1990). Role of cognitive-emotional mediators and individual differences in the effects of media violence on aggression. *Journal of Personality and Social Psychology, 58*(1), 156–163.

Bushman, B. J., & Huesmann, L. R. (2006). Short-term and long-term effects of violent media on aggression in children and adults. *Archives of Pediatrics & Adolescent Medicine, 160*(4), 348–352.

Bushman, B. J., & Huesmann, L. R. (2010). Aggression. In S. T. Fiske, D. T. Gilbert, & G. Lindzey (Eds.), *Handbook of social psychology* (5th ed., Vol. 2, pp. 833–863). Hoboken, NJ: Wiley.

Bushman, B. J., Jamieson, P. E., Weitz, I., & Romer, D. (2013). Gun violence trends in movies. *Pediatrics, 132*(6), 1014–1018.

Bushman, B. J., Wang, M. C., & Anderson, C. A. (2005). Is the curve relating temperature to aggression linear or curvilinear? Assaults and temperature in Minneapolis reexamined. *Journal of Personality and Social Psychology, 89*(1), 62–66.

Buss, A. H. (1961). *The psychology of aggression.* Hoboken, NJ: Wiley.

Buss, A. H. (1963). Physical aggression in relation to different frustrations. *Journal of Abnormal and Social Psychology, 67*(1), 1–7.

Buss, A. H., & Perry, M. (1992). The aggression questionnaire. *Journal of Personality and Social Psychology, 63*(3), 452–459.

Buss, D. M. (1989). Sex differences in human mate preferences: Evolutionary hypotheses tested in 37 cultures. *Behavioral and Brain Sciences, 12*(1), 1–49.

Buss, D. M. (1994). The strategies of human mating. *American Scientist, 82*(3), 238–249. Stable URL: http://www.jstor.org/stable/29775193

Buss, D. M. (2000). *The dangerous passion: Why jealousy is as necessary as love and sex.* New York: Free Press.

Buss, D. M. (2003). *The evolution of desire: Strategies of human mating.* New York: Basic Books.

Buss, D. M. (2008). *Evolutionary psychology: The new science of the mind* (3rd ed.). Boston: Allyn and Bacon.

Buss, D. M., Larsen, R. J., Westen, D., & Semmelroth, J. (1992). Sex differences in jealousy: Evolution, physiology, and psychology. *Psychological Science, 3*(4), 251–255.

Buss, D. M., & Malamuth, N. M. (Eds.) (1996). *Sex, power, conflict: Evolutionary and feminist perspectives.* New York: Oxford University Press.

Buss, D. M., & Schmitt, D. P. (1993). Sexual strategies theory: An evolutionary perspective on human mating. *Psychological Review, 100*(2), 204–232.

Buss, D. M., Shackelford, T. K., Kirkpatrick, L. A., Choe, J. C., Lim, H. K., Hasegawa, M., & . . . Bennett, K. (1999). Jealousy and the nature of beliefs about infidelity: Tests of competing hypotheses about sex differences in the United States, Korea, and Japan. *Personal Relationships, 6*(1), 125–150.

Bussey, K., & Bandura, A. (1999). Social cognitive theory of gender development and differentiation. *Psychological Review, 106*(4), 676–713.

Bussey, K. & Bandura, A. (2004). Social cognitive theory of gender development and functioning. In A. H. Eagly, A. E. Beall, & R. J. Sternberg (Eds.), *The psychology of gender* (2nd ed., pp. 92–119). New York: Guilford Press.

Buunk, B. P., Angleitner, A., Oubaid, V., & Buss, D. M. (1996). Sex differences in jealousy in evolutionary and cultural perspective: Tests from the Netherlands, Germany, and the United States. *Psychological Science, 7*(6), 359–363.

Buunk, B. P., & VanYperen, N. W. (1989). Social comparison, equality, and relationship satisfaction: Gender differences over a ten-year period. *Social Justice Research, 3*(2), 157–180.

Byrne, D. (1961). Interpersonal attraction and attitude similarity. *Journal of Abnormal and Social Psychology, 62*(3), 713–715.

Byrne, D. (1971). *The attraction paradigm.* New York: Academic Press.

Byrne, D., & Clore, G. L. (1970). A reinforcement model of evaluative responses. *Personality: An International Journal, 1*(2), 103–128.

Byrne, D., Clore, G. L., & Worchel, P. (1966). Effect of economic similarity-dissimilarity on interpersonal attraction. *Journal of Personality and Social Psychology, 4*(2), 220–224.

Byrne, S. (2009). Media literacy interventions: What makes them boom or boomerang? *Communication Education, 58*(1), 1–14.

Cacioppo, J. T., Hughes, M. E., Waite, L. J., Hawkley, L. C., & Thisted, R. A. (2006). Loneliness as a specific risk factor for depressive symptoms: Cross-sectional and longitudinal analyses. *Psychology and Aging, 21*(1), 140–151.

Cacioppo, J. T., & Patrick, W. (2008). *Loneliness: Human nature and the need for social connection.* New York: W. W. Norton.

Cacioppo, J. T., & Petty, R. E. (1979). Effects of message repetition and position on cognitive response, recall, and persuasion. *Journal of Personality and Social Psychology, 37*(1), 97–109.

Cacioppo, J. T., & Petty, R. E. (1982). The need for cognition. *Journal of Personality and Social Psychology, 42*(1), 116–131.

Cacioppo, J. T., Petty, R. E., & Morris, K. J. (1983). Effects of need for cognition on message evaluation, recall, and persuasion. *Journal of Personality and Social Psychology, 45*(4), 805–818.

Cadinu, M., Maass, A., Rosabianca, A., & Kiesner, J. (2005). Why do women underperform under stereotype threat? Evidence for the role of negative thinking. *Psychological Science, 16*(7), 572–578.

Cadinu, M. R., & Kiesner, J. (2000). Children's development of a theory of mind. *European Journal of Psychology of Education, 15*(2), 93–111.

Cafferty, J. (2010, March 10). $10 billion spent on cosmetic procedures despite recession [Web log comment]. CNN. Retrieved from http://caffertyfile.blogs.cnn.com/2010/03/10/10-billion-spent-on-cosmetic-procedures-despite-recession/

Cahn, D. D. (1992). *Conflict in intimate relationships.* New York: Guilford Press.

Calder, B. J., Insko, C. A., & Yandell, B. (1974). The relation of cognitive and memorial processes to persuasion in a simulated jury trial. *Journal of Applied Social Psychology, 4*(1), 62–93.

Call, V., Sprecher, S., & Schwartz, P. (1995). The incidence and frequency of marital sex in a national sample. *Journal of Marriage & the Family, 57*(3), 639–652.

Calogero, R. M. (2004). A test of objectification theory: The effect of the male gaze on appearance concerns in college women. *Psychology of Women Quarterly, 28*(1), 16–21.

Camerer, C. (2003). *Behavioral game theory: Experiments in strategic interaction.* Princeton, NJ: Princeton University Press.

Cameron, C. D., & Payne, B. K. (2011). Escaping affect: How motivated emotion regulation creates insensitivity to mass suffering. *Journal of Personality and Social Psychology, 100*(1), 1–15.

Campbell, D. T. (1958). Common fate, similarity, and other indices of the status of aggregates of persons as social entities. *Behavioral Science, 3*(1), 14–25.

Campbell, J. D. (1986). Similarity and uniqueness: The effects of attribute type, relevance, and individual differences in self-esteem and depression. *Journal of Personality and Social Psychology, 50*(2), 281–294.

Campbell, J. D. (1990). Self-esteem and clarity of the self-concept. *Journal of Personality and Social Psychology, 59*(3), 538–549.

Campbell, L., Simpson, J. A., Boldry, J., & Kashy, D. A. (2005). Perceptions of conflict and support in romantic relationships: The role of attachment anxiety. *Journal of Personality and Social Psychology, 88*(3), 510–531.

Campbell, W. K., & Sedikides, C. (1999). Self-threat magnifies the self-serving bias: A meta-analytic integration. *Review of General Psychology, 3*(1), 23–43.

Campos, J. J., Barrett, K. C., Lamb, M. E., Goldsmith, H. H., & Stenberg, C. (1983). Socioemotional development. In M. M. Haith & J. J. Campos (Eds.), *Handbook of child psychology, Vol. 2: Infancy and developmental psychobiology* (4th ed., pp. 783–915). New York: Wiley.

Canary, D. J., & Cupach, W. R. (1988). Relational and episodic characteristics associated with conflict tactics. *Journal of Social and Personal Relationships, 5*(3), 305–325.

Canary, D. J., Cupach, W. R., & Messman, S. J. (1995). *Relationship conflict: Conflict in parent-child, friendship, and romantic relationships.* Thousand Oaks, CA: SAGE Publications, Inc.

Canary, D. J., & Spitzberg, B. H. (1987). Appropriateness and effectiveness perceptions of conflict strategies. *Human Communication Research, 14*(1), 93–120.

Cantor, J. (1998). Children's attraction to television programming. In J. H. Goldstein (Ed.), *Why we watch: The attractions of violent entertainment* (pp. 88–115). New York: Oxford University Press.

Cantor, J. R., Bryant, J., & Zillmann, D. (1974). Enhancement of humor appreciation by transferred excitation. *Journal of Personality and Social Psychology, 30*(6), 812–821.

Cantor, J. R., & Zillmann, D. (1973). The effect of affective state and emotional arousal on music appreciation. *Journal of General Psychology, 89* (1), 79–108.

Capaldi, D. M., Pears, K. C., Patterson, G. R., & Owen, L. D. (2003). Continuity of parenting practices across generations in an at-risk sample: A prospective comparison of direct and mediated associations. *Journal of Abnormal Child Psychology, 31*(2), 127–142.

Caplan, N. (1970). The new ghetto man: A review of recent empirical studies. *Journal of Social Issues, 26*(1), 59–73.

Caprara, G. V., Regalia, C., & Bandura, A. (2002). Longitudinal impact of perceived self-regulatory efficacy on violent conduct. *European Psychologist, 7*(1), 63–69.

Card, N. A., Stucky, B. D., Sawalani, G. M., & Little, T. D. (2008). Direct and indirect aggression during childhood and adolescence: A meta-analytic review of gender differences, intercorrelations, and relations to maladjustment. *Child Development, 79*(5), 1185–1229.

Carlo, G., Eisenberg, N., Troyer, D., Switzer, G., & Speer, A. L. (1991). The altruistic personality: In what contexts is it apparent? *Journal of Personality and Social Psychology, 61*(3), 450–458.

Carlson, E. N., Vazire, S., & Furr, R. M. (2011). Meta-insight: Do people really know how others see them? *Journal of Personality and Social Psychology, 101*(4), 831–846.

Carlson, M., Charlin, V., & Miller, N. (1988). Positive mood and helping behavior: A test of six hypotheses. *Journal of Personality and Social Psychology, 55*(2), 211–229.

Carlson, M., & Miller, N. (1987). Explanation of the relation between negative mood and helping. *Psychological Bulletin, 102*(1), 91–108.

Carney, D. R., Cuddy, A. J., & Yap, A. J. (2010). Power posing: Brief nonverbal displays affect neuroendocrine levels and risk tolerance. *Psychological Science, 21*(10), 1363–1368.

Carrillo, M., Ricci, L. A., Coppersmith, G. A., & Melloni, R. H. (2009). The effect of increased serotonergic neurotransmission on aggression: A critical meta-analytical review of preclinical studies. *Psychopharmacology, 205*(3), 349–368.

Carroll, J. (2007, August 16). Most Americans approve of interracial marriages. Gallup News Service. Retrieved from http://www.gallup.com/poll/28417/most-americans-approve-interracial-marriages.aspx

Carron, A. V., Coleman, M. M., Wheeler, J., & Stevens, D. (2002). Cohesion and performance in sport: A meta analysis. *Journal of Sport and Exercise Psychology, 24*(2), 168–188. Retrieved from http://journals.humankinetics.com/jsep-back-issues/JSEPVolume24Issue2June/CohesionandPerformanceinSportAMetaAnalysis

Carstensen, L. L. (2009). *A long bright future: An action plan for a lifetime of happiness, health, and financial security.* New York: Broadway Books.

Carstensen, L. L., Isaacowitz, D. M., & Charles, S. T. (1999). Taking time seriously: A theory of socioemotional selectivity. *American Psychologist, 54*(3), 165–181.

Cartwright, D. (1971). Risk taking by individuals and groups: An assessment of research employing choice dilemmas. *Journal of Personality and Social Psychology, 20*(3), 361–378.

Cartwright, D., & Zander, A. (1960). Group cohesiveness: Introduction. In D. Cartwright & A. Zander (Eds.), *Group dynamics: Research and theory* (2nd ed., pp. 69–94). Evanston, IL: Row, Peterson.

Carver, C. S. (1975). Physical aggression as a function of objective self-awareness and attitudes toward punishment. *Journal of Experimental Social Psychology, 11*(6), 510–519.

Carver, C. S., Blaney, P. H., & Scheier, M. F. (1979). Reassertion and giving up: The interactive role of self-directed attention and outcome expectancy. *Journal of Personality and Social Psychology, 37*(10), 1859–1870.

Cash Cash, Phillip. (2006). *The ecology of Nez Perce names.* Paper presented at the Plateau Conference, Plateau Center for American Indian Studies, Washington State University, Pullman, Washington.

Cash, T. F., & Trimer, C. A. (1984). Sexism and beautyism in women's evaluations of peer performance. *Sex Roles, 10*(1–2), 87–98.

Caspi, A., & Herbener, E. S. (1990). Continuity and change: Assortative marriage and the consistency of personality in adulthood. *Journal of Personality and Social Psychology, 58*(2), 250–258.

Caspi, A., McClay, J., Moffitt, T. E., Mill, J., Martin, J., Craig, I. W., . . . & Poulton, R. (2002). Role of genotype in the cycle of violence in maltreated children. *Science, 297*(5582), 851–854.

Castano, E., & Dechesne, M. (2005). On defeating death: Group reification and social identification as immortality strategies. *European Review of Social Psychology, 16*(1), 221–255.

Castano, E., & Giner-Sorolla, R. (2006). Not quite human: Infrahumanization in response to collective responsibility for intergroup killing. *Journal of Personality and Social Psychology, 90*(5), 804–818.

Castano, E., Yzerbyt, V., Paladino, M. P., & Sacchi, S. (2002). I belong, therefore, I exist: Ingroup identification, ingroup entitativity, and ingroup bias. *Personality and Social Psychology Bulletin, 28*(2), 135–143.

Catanese, K. (2007). Date rape. In R. Baumeister & K. Vohs (Eds.), *Encyclopedia of social psychology* (pp. 217–219). Thousand Oaks, CA: Sage.

Cattell, R. B. (1971). *Abilities: Their growth, structure, and action.* Boston: Houghton Mifflin.

Cattell, R. B., & Nesselroade, J. R. (1967). Likeness and completeness theories examined by sixteen personality factor measures on stably and unstably married couples. *Journal of Personality and Social Psychology, 7*(4, Pt. 1), 351–361.

Caughlin, J. P., Huston, T. L., & Houts, R. M. (2000). How does personality matter in marriage? An examination of trait anxiety, interpersonal negativity, and marital satisfaction. *Journal of Personality and Social Psychology, 78*(2), 326–336.

CBS News/New York Times. (2006, February 5). A woman for president. Retrieved from http://www.cbsnews.com/htdocs/pdf/020306woman.pdf

Cesario, J., Grant, H., & Higgins, E. T. (2004). Regulatory fit and persuasion: Transfer from "feeling right." *Journal of Personality and Social Psychology, 86*(3), 388–404.

Cesario, J., Plaks, J. E., Hagiwara, N., Navarrete, C. D., & Higgins, E. T. (2010). The ecology of automaticity: How situational contingencies shape action semantics and social behavior. *Psychological Science, 21*(9), 1311–1317.

Cesario, J., Plaks, J. E., & Higgins, E. T. (2006). Automatic social behavior as motivated preparation to interact. *Journal of Personality and Social Psychology, 90*(6), 893–910.

Chaiken, S. (1979). Communicator physical attractiveness and persuasion. *Journal of Personality and Social Psychology, 37*(8), 1387–1397.

Chaiken, S. (1980). Heuristic versus systematic information processing and the use of source versus message cues in persuasion. *Journal of Personality and Social Psychology, 39*(5), 752–766.

Chaiken, S. (1987). The heuristic model of persuasion. In M. Zanna, J. Olson, & C. Herman (Eds.), *Social influence: The Ontario Symposium* (Vol. 5, pp. 3–39). Hillsdale, NJ: Erlbaum.

Chan, E., & Sengupta, J. (2010). Insincere flattery actually works: A dual attitudes perspective. *Journal of Marketing Research, 47*(1), 122–133.

Chapman, H. A., Kim, D. A., Susskind, J. M., & Anderson, A. K. (2009). In bad taste: Evidence for the oral origins of moral disgust. *Science, 323*(5918), 1222–1226.

Chapman, L. J., & Chapman, J. P. (1967). Genesis of popular but erroneous psychodiagnostic observations. *Journal of Abnormal Psychology, 72*(3), 193–204.

Chapman, L. J., & Chapman, J. P. (1969). Illusory correlation as an obstacle to the use of valid psychodiagnostic signs. *Journal of Abnormal Psychology, 74*(3), 271–280.

Chartrand, T. L., & Bargh, J. A. (1999). The chameleon effect: The perception–behavior link and social interaction. *Journal of Personality and Social Psychology, 76*(6), 893–910.

Chartrand, T. L., & Bargh, J. A. (2002). Nonconscious motivations: Their activation, operation, and consequences. In A. Tesser, D. A. Stapel, & J. V. Wood (Eds.), *Self and motivation: Emerging psychological perspectives* (pp. 13–41). Washington, DC: American Psychological Association.

Chasteen, A. L., Bhattacharyya, S., Horhota, M., Tam, R., & Hasher, L. (2005). How feelings of stereotype threat influence older adults' memory performance. *Experimental Aging Research, 31*(3), 235–260.

Chemers, M. M., Watson, C. B., & May, S. T. (2000). Dispositional affect and leadership effectiveness: A comparison of self-esteem, optimism, and efficacy. *Personality and Social Psychology Bulletin, 26*(3), 267–277.

Chen, D. H. C. (2004). *Gender equality and economic development: The role for information and communication technologies* (World Bank Policy Research Working Paper 3285). Retrieved from http://info.worldbank.org/etools/docs/library/117321/35079_wps3285.pdf

Chen, H., Cohen, P., Kasen, S., Johnson, J. G., Ehrensaft, M., & Gordon, K. (2006). Predicting conflict within romantic relationships during the transition to adulthood. *Personal Relationships, 13*(4), 411–427.

Chen, J., Chiu, C. Y., & Chan, S. F. (2009). The cultural effects of job mobility and the belief in a fixed world: Evidence from performance forecast. *Journal of Personality and Social Psychology, 97*(5), 851–865.

Chen, S. (2009, October 30). Gang rape raises questions about bystanders' role. CNN. Retrieved from http://www.cnn.com/2009/CRIME/10/28/california.gang.rape.bystander/index.html?_s=PM:CRIME

Cheng, C. M., & Chartrand, T. L. (2003). Self-monitoring without awareness: Using mimicry as a nonconscious affiliation strategy. *Journal of Personality and Social Psychology, 85*(6), 1170–1179.

Chenier, T., & Winkielman, P. (2007). Mere exposure effect. In R. Baumeister & K. Vohs (Eds.), *Encyclopedia of social psychology* (Vol. 2, pp. 556–558). Thousand Oaks, CA: Sage.

Chermack, S. T., & Giancola, P. R. (1997). The relation between alcohol and aggression: An integrated biopsychosocial conceptualization. *Clinical Psychology Review, 17*(6), 621–649.

Cheryan, S., & Bodenhausen, G. V. (2000). When positive stereotypes threaten intellectual performance: The psychological hazards of "model minority" status. *Psychological Science, 11*(5), 399–402.

Cheryan, S., Plaut, V. C., Davies, P., & Steele, C. M. (2009). Ambient belonging: How stereotypical environments impact gender participation in computer science. *Journal of Personality and Social Psychology, 97*(6), 1045–1060.

Choi, I., & Nisbett, R. E. (1998). Situational salience and cultural differences in the correspondence bias and actor-observer bias. *Personality and Social Psychology Bulletin, 24*(9), 949–960.

Christakis, N. A., & Fowler, J. H. (2007). The spread of obesity in a large social network over 32 years. *New England Journal of Medicine, 357*(4), 370–379.

Chua-Eoan, H. (2007, March 1). Columbine massacre, 1999. *Time.* Retrieved from http://content.time.com/time/specials/packages/article/0,28804,1937349_1937350_1937526,00.html

Chung, V. Q., Gordon, J. S., Veledar, E., & Chen, S. C. (2010). Hot or not—evaluating the effect of artificial tanning on the public's perception of attractiveness. *Dermatologic Surgery, 36*(11), 1651–1655.

Church, A. T. (1982). Sojourner adjustment. *Psychological Bulletin, 91*(3), 540–572.

Cialdini, R. B. (1987). Compliance principles of compliance professionals: Psychologists of necessity. In M. P. Zanna, M. Olson, & C. P. Herman (Eds.), *Social influence: The Ontario symposium* (Vol. 5, pp. 165–184). Hillsdale, NJ: Erlbaum.

Cialdini, R. B. (2003). Crafting normative messages to protect the environment. *Current Directions in Psychological Science*, 12(4), 105–109.

Cialdini, R. B. (2006). *Influence: The psychology of persuasion*. New York: HarperCollins.

Cialdini, R. B., Baumann, D. J., & Kenrick, D. T. (1981). Insights from sadness: A three-step model of the development of altruism as hedonism. *Developmental Review*, 1(3), 207–223.

Cialdini, R. B., Borden, R. J., Thorne, A., Walker, M. R., Freeman, S., & Sloan, L. R. (1976). Basking in reflected glory: Three (football) field studies. *Journal of Personality and Social Psychology*, 34(3), 366–375.

Cialdini, R. B., Brown, S. L., Lewis, B. P., Luce, C., & Neuberg, S. L. (1997). Reinterpreting the empathy–altruism relationship: When one into one equals oneness. *Journal of Personality and Social Psychology*, 73(3), 481–494.

Cialdini, R. B., Cacioppo, J. T., Bassett, R., & Miller, J. A. (1978). Low-ball procedure for producing compliance: Commitment then cost. *Journal of Personality and Social Psychology*, 36(5), 463–476.

Cialdini, R. B., Demaine, L. J., Sagarin, B. J., Barrett, D. W., Rhoads, K., & Winter, P. L. (2006). Managing social norms for persuasive impact. *Social Influence*, 1(1), 3–15.

Cialdini, R. B., & Goldstein, N. J. (2004). Social influence: Compliance and conformity. *Annual Review of Psychology*, 55, 591–621.

Cialdini, R. B., Schaller, M., Houlihan, D., Arps, K., Fultz, J., & Beaman, A. L. (1987). Empathy-based helping: Is it selflessly or selfishly motivated? *Journal of Personality and Social Psychology*, 52(4), 749–758.

Cialdini, R. B., Vincent, J. E., Lewis, S. K., Catalan, J., Wheeler, D., & Darby, B. L. (1975). Reciprocal concessions procedure for inducing compliance: The door-in-the-face technique. *Journal of Personality and Social Psychology*, 31(2), 206–215.

Cialdini, R. B., Wosinska, W., Barrett, D. W., Butner, J., & Gornik-Durose, M. (1999). Compliance with a request in two cultures: The differential influence of social proof and commitment/consistency on collectivists and individualists. *Personality and Social Psychology Bulletin*, 25(10), 1242–1253.

Cicero, M. T. (1883). De finibus bonorum et malorum |On the ends of good and evil] (J. S. Reid, Trans.). Cambridge: Cambridge University Press. (Original work published 45 BC).

Cikara, M., Eberhardt, J. L., & Fiske, S. T. (2011). From agents to objects: Sexist attitudes and neural responses to sexualized targets. *Journal of Cognitive Neuroscience*, 23(3), 540–551.

Cimino, M., Deeley, M., Peverall, J., Spikings, B. (Producers), & Cimino, M. (Director) (1978). *The deer hunter* [Motion picture]. United States/United Kingdom: EMI films & Universal Pictures.

Clark, M. S., & Mills, J. (1979). Interpersonal attraction in exchange and communal relationships. *Journal of Personality and Social Psychology*, 37(1), 12–24.

Clark, M. S., Mills, J., & Powell, M. C. (1986). Keeping track of needs in communal and exchange relationships. *Journal of Personality and Social Psychology*, 51(2), 333–338.

Clark, M. S., Oullette, R., Powell, M. C., & Milberg, S. (1987). Recipient's mood, relationship type, and helping. *Journal of Personality and Social Psychology*, 53(1), 94–103.

Claxton, A., & Perry-Jenkins, M. (2008). No fun anymore: Leisure and marital quality across the transition to parenthood. *Journal of Marriage and Family*, 70(1), 28–43.

Cleare, A. J., & Bond, A. J. (1995). The effect of tryptophan depletion and enhancement on subjective and behavioural aggression in normal male subjects. *Psychopharmacology*, 118(1), 72–81.

Clifford, M. M., & Walster, E. (1973). The effect of physical attractiveness on teacher expectations. *Sociology of Education*, 46(2), 248–258.

Cloven, D. H., & Roloff, M. E. (1991). Sense-making activities and interpersonal conflict: Communicative cures for the mulling blues. *Western Journal of Communication*, 55(2), 134–158.

Clutton-Brock, T. H., & Parker, G. A. (1995). Punishment in animal societies. *Nature*, 373(6511), 209–216.

CNN Political Unit (2012, June 6). CNN Poll: Americans' attitudes toward gay community changing. CNN Politics. Retrieved from http://politicalticker.blogs.cnn.com/2012/06/06/cnn-poll-americans-attitudes-toward-gay-community-changing/

Coan, R. W. (1977). *Hero, artist, sage, or saint?* New York: Columbia University Press.

Cohen, C. E. (1981). Person categories and social perception: Testing some boundaries of the processing effect of prior knowledge. *Journal of Personality and Social Psychology*, 40(3), 441–452.

Cohen, D., & Nisbett, R. E. (1994). Self-protection and the culture of honor: Explaining southern violence. *Personality and Social Psychology Bulletin*, 20(5), 551–567.

Cohen, D., & Nisbett, R. E. (1997). Field experiments examining the culture of honor: The role of institutions in perpetuating norms about violence. *Personality and Social Psychology Bulletin*, 23(11), 1188–1199.

Cohen, D., Nisbett, R. E., Bowdle, B. F., & Schwarz, N. (1996). Insult, aggression, and the southern culture of honor: An "experimental ethnography." *Journal of Personality and Social Psychology*, 70(5), 945–960.

Cohen, F., Solomon, S., Maxfield, M., Pyszczynski, T., & Greenberg, J. (2004). Fatal attraction: The effects of mortality salience on evaluations of charismatic, task-oriented, and relationship-oriented leaders. *Psychological Science*, 15(12), 846–851.

Cohen, G. L., Garcia, J., Apfel, N., & Master, A. (2006). Reducing the racial achievement gap: A social-psychological intervention. *Science*, 313(5791), 1307–1310.

Cohen, G. L., Garcia, J., Purdie-Vaughns, V., Apfel, N., & Brzustoski, P. (2009). Recursive processes in self-affirmation: Intervening to close the minority achievement gap. *Science*, 324(5925), 400–403.

Cohen, J. (2004). Parasocial break-up from favorite television characters: The role of attachment styles and relationship intensity. *Journal of Social and Personal Relationships*, 21(2), 187–202.

Cohen, S. (2004). Social relationships and health. *American Psychologist*, 59(8), 676–684.

Coke, J. S., Batson, C. D., & McDavis, K. (1978). Empathic mediation of helping: A two-stage model. *Journal of Personality and Social Psychology*, 36(7), 752–766.

Coker, A. L., Davis, K. E., Arias, I., Desai, S., Sanderson, M., Brandt, H. M., & Smith, P. H. (2002). Physical and mental health effects of intimate partner violence for men and women. *American Journal of Preventive Medicine*, 23(4), 260–268.

Cole, S. W., Kemeny, M. E., & Taylor, S. E. (1997). Social identity and physical health: Accelerated HIV progression in rejection-sensitive gay men. *Journal of Personality and Social Psychology*, 72(2), 320–335.

Coleridge, S. T., & Fenby, T. (1877). *Aids to reflection in the formation of a manly character on the several grounds of prudence, morality and religion* (Rev. ed.). Liverpool: Edward Howell. (Original work published 1825)

Colligan, M., Pennebaker, J., & Murphy, P. (Eds.) (1982). *Mass psychogenic illness: A social psychological analysis*. Hillsdale, NJ: Erlbaum.

Collins, A. M., & Loftus, E. F. (1975). A spreading-activation theory of semantic processing. *Psychological Review*, 82(6), 407–428.

Collins, J., & Lidz, F., (2013, May 6). Why NBA center Jason Collins is coming out now. *Sports Illustrated*. Retrieved from http://sportsillustrated.cnn.com/magazine/news/20130429/jason-collins-gay-nba-player/#all

Collins, N. L., & Feeney, B. C. (2000). A safe haven: An attachment theory perspective on support seeking and caregiving in intimate relationships. *Journal of Personality and Social Psychology*, 78(6), 1053–1073.

Collins, N. L., & Feeney, B. C. (2004). Working models of attachment shape perceptions of social support: Evidence from experimental and observational studies. *Journal of Personality and Social Psychology*, 87(3), 363–383.

Collins, N. L., & Read, S. J. (1990). Adult attachment, working models, and relationship quality in dating couples. *Journal of Personality and Social Psychology*, 58(4), 644–663.

Collins, N. L., & Read, S. J. (1994). Cognitive representations of attachment: The structure and function of working models. In K. Bartholomew & D. Perlman (Eds.), *Advances in personal relationships, Vol. 5: Attachment processes in adulthood* (pp. 53–90). London: Jessica Kingsley.

Collins, S. (2008). *The hunger games*. New York: Scholastic, Inc.

Collins, S., Kilik, J., Jacobson, N. (Producers), & Ross, G. (Director) (2012). *The hunger games* [Motion picture]. United States: Lionsgate & Color Force.

Columb, C., & Plant, E. A. (2011). Revisiting the Obama Effect: Exposure to Obama reduces implicit prejudice. *Journal of Experimental Social Psychology*, 47(2), 499–501.

Condon, J. W., & Crano, W. D. (1988). Inferred evaluation and the relation between attitude similarity and interpersonal attraction. *Journal of Personality and Social Psychology*, 54(5), 789–797.

Conger, R. D., Neppl, T., Kim, K. J., & Scaramella, L. (2003). Angry and aggressive behavior across three generations: A prospective, longitudinal study of parents and children. *Journal of Abnormal Child Psychology*, 31(2), 143–160.

Contrada, R. J., Ashmore, R. D., Gary, M. L., Coups, E., Egeth, J. D., Sewell, A., . . . & Chasse, V. (2000). Ethnicity-related sources of stress and their effects on well-being. *Current Directions in Psychological Science*, 9(4), 136–139.

Cooley, C. H. (1902). *Human nature and the social order*. New York: Charles Scribner's Sons.

Coontz, S. (2005). *Marriage, a history: From obedience to intimacy, or how love conquered marriage*. New York: Viking.

Cooper, J. (1980). Reducing fears and increasing assertiveness: The role of dissonance reduction. *Journal of Experimental Social Psychology*, 16(3), 199–213.

Cooper, J., & Fazio, R. H. (1984). A new look at dissonance theory. In L. Berkowitz (Ed.), *Advances in experimental social psychology* (Vol. 17, pp. 229–266). New York: Academic Press.

Cooper, J., & Jones, E. E. (1969). Opinion divergence as a strategy to avoid being miscast. *Journal of Personality and Social Psychology*, 13(1), 23–30.

Cooper, M. L., Pioli, M., Levitt, A., Talley, A. E., Micheas, L., & Collins, N. L. (2006). Attachment styles, sex motives, and sexual behavior: Evidence for gender-specific expressions of attachment dynamics. In M. Mikulincer & G. S. Goodman (Eds.), *Dynamics of romantic love: Attachment, caregiving, and sex* (pp. 243–274). New York: Guilford Press.

Cooper, M. L., Shapiro, C. M., & Powers, A. M. (1998). Motivations for sex and risky sexual behavior among adolescents and young adults: A functional perspective. *Journal of Personality and Social Psychology*, 75(6), 1528–1558.

Cooper, M. L., Shaver, P. R., & Collins, N. L. (1998). Attachment styles, emotion regulation, and adjustment in adolescence. *Journal of Personality and Social Psychology*, 74(5), 1380–1397.

Cooper, R. P., & Aslin, R. N. (1990). Preference for infant-directed speech in the first month after birth. *Child Development*, 61(5), 1584–1595.

Coopersmith, S. (1967). *The antecedents of self-esteem*. San Francisco: W. H. Freeman.

Correll, J., Park, B., Judd, C. M., Wittenbrink, B., Sadler, M. S., & Keesee, T. (2007). Across the thin blue line: Police officers and racial bias in the decision to shoot. *Journal of Personality and Social Psychology*, 92(6), 1006–1023.

Correll, J., Wittenbrink, B., Park, B., Judd, C. M., & Goyle, A. (2011). Dangerous enough: Moderating racial bias with contextual threat cues. *Journal of Experimental Social Psychology*, 47(1), 184–189.

Costa, P., Jr., Terracciano, A., & McCrae, R. R. (2001). Gender differences in personality traits across cultures: Robust and surprising findings. *Journal of Personality and Social Psychology*, 81(2), 322–331.

Costa, P. T., Jr., & McCrae, R. R. (1994). Stability and change in personality from adolescence through adulthood. In C. F. Halverson, Jr., G. A. Kohnstamm, & R. P. Martin (Eds.), *The developing structure of temperament and personality from infancy to adulthood* (pp. 139–150). Hillsdale, NJ: Erlbaum.

Cottrell, C. A., Neuberg, S. L., & Li, N. P. (2007). What do people desire in others? A sociofunctional perspective on the importance of different valued characteristics. *Journal of Personality and Social Psychology*, 92(2), 208–231.

Cox, C. R., & Arndt, J. (2012). How sweet it is to be loved by you: The role of perceived regard in the terror management of close relationships. *Journal of Personality and Social Psychology*, 102(3), 616–632.

Cox, C. R., Arndt, J., Pyszczynski, T., Greenberg, J., Abdollahi, A., & Solomon, S. (2008). Terror management and adults' attachment to their parents: The safe haven remains. *Journal of Personality and Social Psychology*, 94(4), 696–717.

Cox, C. R., Goldenberg, J. L., Arndt, J., & Pyszczynski, T. (2007). Mother's milk: An existential perspective on negative reactions to breast-feeding. *Personality and Social Psychology Bulletin*, 33(1), 110–122.

Crandall, C. S. (1991). Do heavy-weight students have more difficulty paying for college? *Personality and Social Psychology Bulletin*, 17(6), 606–611.

Crandall, C. S. (1994). Prejudice against fat people: Ideology and self-interest. *Journal of Personality and Social Psychology*, 66(5), 882–894.

Crandall, C. S., Bahns, A. J., Warner, R., & Schaller, M. (2011). Stereotypes as justifications of prejudice. *Personality and Social Psychology Bulletin*, 37(11), 1488–1498.

Crandall, C. S., & Eshleman, A. (2003). A justification-suppression model of the expression and experience of prejudice. *Psychological Bulletin*, 129(3), 414–446.

Crandall, C. S., Eshleman, A., & O'Brien, L. (2002). Social norms and the expression and suppression of prejudice: The struggle for internalization. *Journal of Personality and Social Psychology*, 82(3), 359–378.

Crano, W. D., & Chen, X. (1998). The leniency contract and persistence of majority and minority influence. *Journal of Personality and Social Psychology*, 74(6), 1437–1450.

Crick, N. R., & Dodge, K. A. (1994). A review and reformulation of social information-processing mechanisms in children's social adjustment. *Psychological Bulletin*, 115(1), 74–101.

Crick, N. R., & Grotpeter, J. K. (1995). Relational aggression, gender, and social-psychological adjustment. *Child Development*, 66(3), 710–722.

Crick, N. R., & Grotpeter, J. K. (1996). Children's treatment by peers: Victims of relational and overt aggression. *Development and Psychopathology*, 8(2), 367–380.

Crocker, J. (2011). Safety in numbers: Shifting from egosystem to ecosystem. *Psychological Inquiry*, 22(4), 259–264.

Crocker, J., Canevello, A., Breines, J. G., & Flynn, H. (2010). Interpersonal goals and change in anxiety and dysphoria in first-semester college students. *Journal of Personality and Social Psychology*, 98(6), 1009–1024.

Crocker, J., Cornwell, B., & Major, B. (1993). The stigma of overweight: Affective consequences of attributional ambiguity. *Journal of Personality and Social Psychology*, 64(1), 60–70.

Crocker, J., & Major, B. (1989). Social stigma and self-esteem: The self-protective properties of stigma. *Psychological Review*, 96(4), 608–630.

Crocker, J., & Park, L. E. (2004). The costly pursuit of self-esteem. *Psychological Bulletin*, 130(3), 392–414.

Crocker, J., Voelkl, K., Testa, M., & Major, B. (1991). Social stigma: The affective consequences of attributional ambiguity. *Journal of Personality and Social Psychology*, 60(2), 218–228.

Crocker, J., & Wolfe, C. T. (2001). Contingencies of self-worth. *Psychological Review*, 108(3), 593–623.

Crockett, M. J., Clark, L., Tabibnia, G., Lieberman, M. D., & Robbins, T. W. (2008). Serotonin modulates behavioral reactions to unfairness. *Science*, 320(5884), 1739–1739.

Croizet, J. C., & Claire, T. (1998). Extending the concept of stereotype threat to social class: The intellectual underperformance of students from low socioeconomic backgrounds. *Personality and Social Psychology Bulletin*, 24(6), 588–594.

Cross, K. P. (1977). Not can, but will college teaching be improved? *New Directions for Higher Education*, 1977(17), 1–15.

Cross, S. E., Hardin, E. E., & Gercek-Swing, B. (2010). The what, how, why, and where of self-construal. *Personality and Social Psychology Review*, 15(2), 142–179.

Crutchfield, R. S. (1955). Conformity and character. *American Psychologist*, 10(5), 191–198.

Csikszentmihalyi, M. (1980). Love and the dynamics of personal growth. In K. S. Pope (Ed.), *On love and loving* (pp. 306–326). San Francisco: Jossey-Bass.

Csikszentmihalyi, M. (1990). *Flow: The psychology of optimal experience*. New York: Harper & Row.

Csikszentmihalyi, M. (1996). *Creativity: Flow and the psychology of discovery and invention*. New York: HarperCollins.

Cuddy, A. J., Fiske, S. T., & Glick, P. (2007). The BIAS map: Behaviors from intergroup affect and stereotypes. *Journal of Personality and Social Psychology*, 92(4), 631–648.

Cuddy, A. J., Fiske, S. T., & Glick, P. (2008). Warmth and competence as universal dimensions of social perception: The stereotype content model and the BIAS map. In M. P. Zanna (Ed.), *Advances in experimental social psychology* (Vol. 40, pp. 61–149). San Diego: Academic Press.

Cuddy, A. J., Rock, M. S., & Norton, M. I. (2007). Aid in the aftermath of Hurricane Katrina: Inferences of secondary emotions and intergroup helping. *Group Processes & Intergroup Relations*, 10(1), 107–118.

Cummings, E. M., Iannotti, R. J., & Zahn-Waxler, C. (1985). Influence of conflict between adults on the emotions and aggression of young children. *Developmental Psychology*, 21(3), 495–507.

Cummings, E. M., Zahn-Waxler, C., & Radke-Yarrow, M. (1981). Young children's responses to expressions of anger and affection by others in the family. *Child Development*, 52(4), 1274–1282. Stable URL: http://www.jstor.org/stable/1129516

Cunningham, M. R., Barbee, A. P., & Philhower, C. L. (2002). Dimensions of facial physical attractiveness: The intersection of biology and culture. In G. Rhodes & L. A. Zebrowitz (Eds.), *Facial attractiveness: Evolutionary, cognitive, and social perspectives* (pp. 193–238). Westport, CT: Ablex.

Cunningham, M. R., Barbee, A. P., & Pike, C. L. (1990). What do women want? Facial metric assessment of multiple motives in the perception of male facial physical attractiveness. *Journal of Personality and Social Psychology*, 59(1), 61–72.

Cunningham, M. R., Roberts, A. R., Barbee, A. P., Druen, P. B., & Wu, C. H. (1995). "Their ideas of beauty are, on the whole, the same as ours": Consistency and variability in the cross-cultural perception of female physical attractiveness. *Journal of Personality and Social Psychology*, 68(2), 261–279.

Cunningham, M. R., Shamblen, S. R., Barbee, A. P., & Ault, L. K. (2005). Social allergies in romantic relationships: Behavioral repetition, emotional sensitization, and dissatisfaction in dating couples. *Personal Relationships*, 12(2), 273–295.

Cunningham, M. R., Steinberg, J., & Grev, R. (1980). Wanting to and having to help: Separate motivations for positive mood and guilt-induced helping. *Journal of Personality and Social Psychology*, 38(2), 181–192.

Cunningham, W. A., Johnson, M. K., Raye, C. L., Gatenby, J. C., Gore, J. C., & Banaji, M. R. (2004). Separable neural components in the processing of Black and White faces. *Psychological Science*, 15(12), 806–813.

Cunningham, W. A., Nezlek, J. B., & Banaji, M. R. (2004). Implicit and explicit ethnocentrism: Revisiting the ideologies of prejudice. *Personality and Social Psychology Bulletin*, 30(10), 1332–1346.

Curtis, M. (Writer), & Jensen, S. (Director). (1998, October 18). The one where Phoebe hates PBS [Television series episode]. In D. Crane,

M. Kauffman, K. Bright, A. Chase, G. Malins, . . . & M. Curtis (Producers), *Friends*. Burbank, CA: Bright/Kauffman/Crane Productions, & Warner Bros. Television.

Curtis, R. C., & Miller, K. (1986). Believing another likes or dislikes you: Behaviors making the beliefs come true. *Journal of Personality and Social Psychology*, 51(2), 284–290.

Czopp, A. M., Monteith, M. J., & Mark, A. Y. (2006). Standing up for a change: Reducing bias through interpersonal confrontation. *Journal of Personality and Social Psychology*, 90(5), 784–803.

Dabbs, J. M., Carr, T. S., Frady, R. L., & Riad, J. K. (1995). Testosterone, crime, and misbehavior among 692 male prison inmates. *Personality and Individual Differences*, 18(5), 627–633.

Dabbs, J. M., Frady, R. L., Carr, T. S., & Besch, N. F. (1987). Saliva testosterone and criminal violence in young adult prison inmates. *Psychosomatic Medicine*, 49(2), 174–182. Retrieved from http://www.psychosomaticmedicine.org/content/49/2/174.short

Dabbs, J. M., & Hargrove, M. F. (1997). Age, testosterone, and behavior among female prison inmates. *Psychosomatic Medicine*, 59(5), 477–480. Retrieved from http://www.psychosomaticmedicine.org/content/59/5/477.short

DaGloria, J. (1984). Frustration, aggression, and the sense of justice. In A. Mummendey (Ed.), *Social psychology of aggression: From individual behavior to social interaction* (pp. 127–141). New York: Springer.

Dal Cin, S., Gibson, B., Zanna, M. P., Shumate, R., & Fong, G. T. (2007). Smoking in movies, implicit associations of smoking with the self, and intentions to smoke. *Psychological Science*, 18(7), 559–563.

Daly, M., & Wilson, M. (1988a). Evolutionary social psychology and family homicide. *Science*, 242(4878), 519–524.

Daly, M., & Wilson, M. (1988b). *Homicide*. New York: Aldine de Gruyter.

Damasio, A. (1994). *Descartes' error: Emotion, reason, and the human brain*. New York: Grosset/Putnam.

Damasio, A. (1999). *The feeling of what happens: Body and emotion in the making of consciousness*. Fort Worth: Harcourt College Publishers.

Damasio, A. R. (2001). Fundamental feelings. *Nature*, 413(6858), 781–782.

Damasio, H., Grabowski, T., Frank, R., Galaburda, A. M., & Damasio, A. R. (1994). The return of Phineas Gage: Clues about the brain from the skull of a famous patient. *Science*, 264(5162), 1102–1105.

Darley, J. M., & Batson, C. D. (1973). "From Jerusalem to Jericho": A study of situational and dispositional variables in helping behavior. *Journal of Personality and Social Psychology*, 27(1), 100–108.

Darley, J. M., & Gross, P. H. (1983). A hypothesis-confirming bias in labeling effects. *Journal of Personality and Social Psychology*, 44(1), 20–33.

Darley, J. M., & Latané, B. (1968). Bystander intervention in emergencies: Diffusion of responsibility. *Journal of Personality and Social Psychology*, 8(4, Pt. 1), 377–383.

Darley, J. M., Teger, A. I., & Lewis, L. D. (1973). Do groups always inhibit individuals' responses to potential emergencies? *Journal of Personality and Social Psychology*, 26(3), 395–399.

Darwin, C. (1860). *On the origin of species by means of natural selection: Or the preservation of the favoured races in the struggle for life*. London: John Murray.

Darwin, C. (1872). *The expression of the emotions in man and animals*. London: John Murray.

Dasen, P. (1994). Culture and cognitive development from a Piagetian perspective. In W. J. Lonner & R. S. Malpass (Eds.), *Psychology and culture*. Boston: Allyn and Bacon.

Dasgupta, N., & Asgari, S. (2004). Seeing is believing: Exposure to counterstereotypic women leaders and its effect on the malleability of automatic gender stereotyping. *Journal of Experimental Social Psychology*, 40(5), 642–658.

Dasgupta, N., & Greenwald, A. G. (2001). On the malleability of automatic attitudes: Combating automatic prejudice with images of admired and disliked individuals. *Journal of Personality and Social Psychology*, 81(5), 800–814.

Davidson, A. R., & Jaccard, J. J. (1979). Variables that moderate the attitude–behavior relation: Results of a longitudinal survey. *Journal of Personality and Social Psychology*, 37(8), 1364–1376.

Davidson, R. J., Kabat-Zinn, J., Schumacher, J., Rosenkranz, M., Muller, D., Santorelli, S. F., & Sheridan, J. F. (2003). Alterations in brain and immune function produced by mindfulness meditation. *Psychosomatic Medicine*, 65(4), 564–570.

Davidson, R. J., Putnam, K. M., & Larson, C. L. (2000). Dysfunction in the neural circuitry of emotion regulation—A possible prelude to violence. *Science*, 289(5479), 591–594.

Davila, J., & Bradbury, T. N. (2001). Attachment insecurity and the distinction between unhappy spouses who do and do not divorce. *Journal of Family Psychology*, 15(3), 371–393.

Davis, B. P., & Knowles, E. S. (1999). A disrupt-then-reframe technique of social influence. *Journal of Personality and Social Psychology*, 76(2), 192–199.

Davis, C. G., Lehman, D. R., Wortman, C. B., Silver, R. C., & Thompson, S. C. (1995). The undoing of traumatic life events. *Personality and Social Psychology Bulletin*, 21(2), 109–124.

Davis, D., Shaver, P. R., & Vernon, M. L. (2004). Attachment style and subjective motivations for sex. *Personality and Social Psychology Bulletin*, 30(8), 1076–1090.

Davis, K. E., & Jones, E. E. (1960). Changes in interpersonal perception as a means of reducing cognitive dissonance. *Journal of Abnormal and Social Psychology*, 61(3), 402–410.

Davis, L. V., & Carlson, B. E. (1987). Observation of spouse abuse: What happens to the children? *Journal of Interpersonal Violence*, 2(3), 278–291.

de Castro, B. O., Bosch, J. D., Veerman, J. W., & Koops, W. (2003). The effects of emotion regulation, attribution, and delay prompts on aggressive boys' social problem solving. *Cognitive Therapy and Research*, 27(2), 153–166.

De Dreu, C. K. W., & De Vries, N. K. (1993). Numerical support, information processing, and attitude change. *European Journal of Social Psychology*, 23(6), 647–663.

De Fina, B. (Producer), & Scorsese, M. (Director). (1995). *Casino* [Motion picture]. United States/France: Universal Pictures, Syalis DA, Légende Entreprises, & De Fina-Cappa.

de Vignemont, F., & Singer, T. (2006). The empathic brain: How, when and why? *Trends in Cognitive Sciences*, 10(10), 435–441.

De Vries, M., Fagerlin, A., Witteman, H., & Scherer, L. D. (2013). Combining deliberation and intuition in patient decision support. *Patient Education and Counseling*, 91(2), 154–160.

de Waal, F. B. (1996). *Good natured: The origins of right and wrong in humans and other animals*. Cambridge, MA: Harvard University Press.

Dearing, R. L., Stuewig, J., & Tangney, J. P. (2005). On the importance of distinguishing shame from guilt: Relations to problematic alcohol and drug use. *Addictive Behaviors*, 30(7), 1392–1404.

Deaux, K. (1984). From individual differences to social categories: Analysis of a decade's research on gender. *American Psychologist*, 39(2), 105–116.

Dechesne, M., Janssen, J., & van Knippenberg, A. (2000). Derogation and distancing as terror management strategies: The moderating role of need for closure and permeability of group boundaries. *Journal of Personality and Social Psychology*, 79(6), 923–932.

Deci, E. L., & Ryan, R. M. (1995). Human autonomy: The basis for true self-esteem. In M. Kernis (Ed.), *Efficacy, agency, and self-esteem* (pp. 31–49). New York: Plenum.

Deci, E. L., & Ryan, R. M. (2000). The "what" and "why" of goal pursuits: Human needs and the self-determination of behavior. *Psychological Inquiry*, 11(4), 227–268.

Deci, E. L., & Ryan, R. M. (Eds.). (2002). *Handbook of self-determination research*. Rochester, NY: University of Rochester Press.

Decker, S. H., & Lauritsen, J. L. (2002). Breaking the bonds of membership: Leaving the gang. In C. R. Huff (Ed.), *Gangs in America III* (pp. 103–122). Thousand Oaks, CA: Sage.

Decker, S. H., & Van Winkle, B. (1996). *Life in the gang: Family, friends, and violence*. New York: Cambridge University Press.

Dellarocas, C. (2006). Strategic manipulation of Internet opinion forums: Implications for consumers and firms. *Management Science*, 52(10), 1577–1593.

Delton, A. W., Krasnow, M. M., Cosmides, L., & Tooby, J. (2011). Evolution of direct reciprocity under uncertainty can explain human generosity in one-shot encounters. *Proceedings of the National Academy of Sciences*, 108(32), 13335–13340.

Demir, A., & Fişiloğlu, H. (1999). Loneliness and marital adjustment of Turkish couples. *Journal of Psychology*, 133(2), 230–240.

Dengerink, H. A., & Covey, M. K. (1983). Implications of an escape-avoidance theory of aggressive responses to attack. In R. G. Geen & E. I. Donnerstein (Eds.), *Aggression: Theoretical and empirical reviews* (Vol. 1, pp. 163–188). New York: Academic Press.

Denissen, J. J., Penke, L., Schmitt, D. P., & van Aken, M. A. (2008). Self-esteem reactions to social interactions: Evidence for sociometer mechanisms across days, people, and nations. *Journal of Personality and Social Psychology*, 95(1), 181–196.

Denson, T. F., Pedersen, W. C., Ronquillo, J., & Nandy, A. S. (2009). The angry brain: Neural correlates of anger, angry rumination, and aggressive personality. *Journal of Cognitive Neuroscience*, 21(4), 734–744.

DePaulo, B. M., & Kashy, D. A. (1998). Everyday lies in close and casual relationships. *Journal of Personality and Social Psychology*, 74(1), 63–79.

DePaulo, B. M., Kashy, D. A., Kirkendol, S. E., Wyer, M. M., & Epstein, J. A. (1996). Lying in everyday life. *Journal of Personality and Social Psychology*, 70(5), 979–995.

Derrick, J. L., Gabriel, S., & Hugenberg, K. (2009). Social surrogacy: How favored television programs provide the experience of belonging. *Journal of Experimental Social Psychology, 45*(2), 352–362.

Derryberry, D., & Tucker, D. M. (1994). Motivating the focus of attention. In P. M. Niedenthal & S. Kitayama (Eds.), *The heart's eye: Emotional influences in perception and attention* (pp. 167–196). San Diego: Academic Press.

DeSteno, D., Bartlett, M. Y., Braverman, J., & Salovey, P. (2002). Sex differences in jealousy: Evolutionary mechanism or artifact of measurement? *Journal of Personality and Social Psychology, 83*(5), 1103–1116.

DeSteno, D., Bartlett, M. Y., & Salovey, P. (2006). Constraining accommodative homunculi in evolutionary explorations of jealousy: A reply to Barrett et al. (2006). *Journal of Personality and Social Psychology, 91*(3), 519–523.

DeSteno, D. A., & Salovey, P. (1996). Jealousy and the characteristics of one's rival: A self-evaluation maintenance perspective. *Personality and Social Psychology Bulletin, 22*(9), 920–932.

Deutsch, M., & Gerard, H. B. (1955). A study of normative and informational social influences upon individual judgment. *Journal of Abnormal and Social Psychology, 51*(3), 629–636.

Devine, P. G. (1989). Stereotypes and prejudice: Their automatic and controlled components. *Journal of Personality and Social Psychology, 56*(1), 5–18.

DeVoss, D. N., & Platt, J. (n.d). Image manipulation and ethics in a digital-visual world [Weblog post]. Retrieved from http://www2.bgsu.edu/departments/english/cconline/ethics_special_issue/DEVOSS_PLATT

DeWeerd, M., & Klandermans, B. (1999). Group identification and political protest: Farmers' protest in the Netherlands. *European Journal of Social Psychology, 29*(8), 1073–1095.

Dewey, J. (1922). *Human nature and conduct: An introduction to social psychology.* New York: Carlton House.

Dewsbury, D. A. (1981). Effects of novelty of copulatory behavior: The Coolidge effect and related phenomena. *Psychological Bulletin, 89*(3), 464–482.

Diamond, J., & Bellwood, P. (2003). Farmers and their languages: The first expansions. *Science, 300*(5619), 597–603.

Dickens, C. (1950). *A Christmas Carol in prose: Being a ghost story of Christmas.* San Francisco: Grabhorn Press // Ransohoffs. (Original work published 1843)

Dickerson, C. A., Thibodeau, R., Aronson, E., & Miller, D. (1992). Using cognitive dissonance to encourage water conservation. *Journal of Applied Social Psychology, 22*(11), 841–854.

Dickerson, S. S., & Kemeny, M. E. (2004). Acute stressors and cortisol responses: A theoretical integration and synthesis of laboratory research. *Psychological Bulletin, 130*(3), 355–391.

Dickerson, S. S., Mycek, P. J., & Zaldivar, F. (2008). Negative social evaluation, but not mere social presence, elicits cortisol responses to a laboratory stressor task. *Health Psychology, 27*(1), 116–121.

Dickinson, E. (1864/1960). *The complete poems of Emily Dickinson.* (T. H. Johnson, Ed.) Boston: Little, Brown. (Original work published 1864)

Dickter, C. L., & Bartholow, B. D. (2007). Racial ingroup and outgroup attention biases revealed by event-related brain potentials. *Social Cognitive and Affective Neuroscience, 2*(3), 189–198.

Diekelmann, S., & Born, J. (2010). The memory function of sleep. *Nature Reviews: Neuroscience, 11*(2), 114–126.

Diener, E., Gohm, C. L., Suh, E., & Oishi, S. (2000). Similarity of the relations between marital status and subjective well-being across cultures. *Journal of Cross-Cultural Psychology, 31*(4), 419–436.

Diener, E., Suh, E. M., Lucas, R. E., & Smith, H. L. (1999). Subjective well-being: Three decades of progress. *Psychological Bulletin, 125*(2), 276–302.

Diener, E., & Wallbom, M. (1976). Effects of self-awareness on antinormative behavior. *Journal of Research in Personality, 10*(1), 107–111.

Diener, E., Wolsic, B., & Fujita, F. (1995). Physical attractiveness and subjective well-being. *Journal of Personality and Social Psychology, 69*(1), 120–129.

Dienstbier, R. A., Kahle, L. R., Willis, K. A., & Tunnell, G. B. (1980). The impact of moral theories on cheating. *Motivation and Emotion, 4*(3), 193–216.

Dijksterhuis, A., Spears, R., Postmes, T., Stapel, D. A., Koomen, W., van Knippenberg, A., & Scheepers, D. (1998). Seeing one thing and doing another: Contrast effects in automatic behavior. *Journal of Personality and Social Psychology, 75*, 862–871.

Dikeos, T. (2009, July 23). Teen's death highlights cyber bullying trend. ABC News. Retrieved from http://www.abc.net.au/news/2009-07-23/teens-death-highlights-cyber-bullying-trend/1363362

Dion, K. K. (1973). Young children's stereotyping of facial attractiveness. *Developmental Psychology, 9*(2), 183–188.

Dion, K. K., & Berscheid, E. (1974). Physical attractiveness and peer perception among children. *Sociometry, 37*(1), 1–12.

Dion, K., Berscheid, E., & Walster, E. (1972). What is beautiful is good. *Journal of Personality and Social Psychology, 24*(3), 285–290.

Dion, K. K., & Dion, K. L. (1996). Cultural perspectives on romantic love. *Personal Relationships, 3*(1), 5–17.

Dishion, T. J., Patterson, G. R., & Griesler, P. C. (1994). Peer adaptations in the development of antisocial behavior: A confluence model. In L. R. Huesmann (Ed.), *Aggressive behavior: Current perspectives* (pp. 61–95). New York: Plenum Press.

Disney, W. (Producer), & Geronimi, C. (Director) (1959). *Sleeping beauty* [Motion picture]. United States: Walt Disney Pictures.

Disney, W. (Producer), & Geronimi, C., Luske, H., & Jackson, W. (Directors). (1950). *Cinderella* [Motion picture]. United States: Walt Disney Pictures.

Disney, W. (Producer), & Hand, D. (Director). (1937). *Snow White and the seven dwarfs* [Motion picture]. United States: Walt Disney Pictures.

Dixon, T. L. (2008a). Crime news and racialized beliefs: Understanding the relationship between local news viewing and perceptions of African Americans and crime. *Journal of Communication, 58*(1), 106–125.

Dixon, T. L. (2008b). Network news and racial beliefs: Exploring the connection between national television news exposure and stereotypical perceptions of African Americans. *Journal of Communication, 58*(2), 321–337.

Dixon, T. L., & Linz, D. (2000). Overrepresentation and underrepresentation of African Americans and Latinos as lawbreakers on television news. *Journal of Communication, 50*(2), 131–154.

Dodge, K. A. (1980). Social cognition and children's aggressive behavior. *Child Development, 51*(1), 162–170.

Dodge, K. A. (1983). Behavioral antecedents of peer social status. *Child Development, 54*(6), 1386–1399.

Dodge, K. A., Bates, J. E., & Pettit, G. S. (1990). Mechanisms in the cycle of violence. *Science, 250*(4988), 1678–1683.

Dodge, K. A., & Coie, J. D. (1987). Social-information-processing factors in reactive and proactive aggression in children's peer groups. *Journal of Personality and Social Psychology, 53*(6), 1146–1158.

Dodge, K. A., Price, J. M., Bachorowski, J. A., & Newman, J. P. (1990). Hostile attributional biases in severely aggressive adolescents. *Journal of Abnormal Psychology, 99*(4), 385–392.

Dodson, C. S., Darragh, J., & Williams, A. (2008). Stereotypes and retrieval-provoked illusory source recollections. *Journal of Experimental Psychology: Learning, Memory, and Cognition, 34*(3), 460–477.

Dollard, J. (1938). Hostility and fear in social life. *Social Forces, 17*(1), 15–26. Stable URL: http://www.jstor.org/stable/2571143

Dollard, J., Miller, N. E., Doob, L. W., Mowrer, O. H., & Sears, R. R. (1939). *Frustration and aggression.* New Haven: Yale University Press.

Donnerstein, E. (2011). The media and aggression: From TV to the Internet. In J. P. Forgas & A. W. Kruglanski (Eds.), *The psychology of social conflict and aggression* (pp. 267–284). New York: Psychology Press.

Donnerstein, E., Linz, D., & Penrod, S. (1987). *The question of pornography: Research findings and policy implications.* New York: Free Press.

Dove (2007). Evolution [Television commercial]. Toronto: Ogilvy & Mather. Retrieved from http://www.dove.ca/en/Tips-Topics-And-Tools/Videos/default.aspx

Dovidio, J. F., Allen, J. L., & Schroeder, D. A. (1990). Specificity of empathy-induced helping: Evidence for altruistic motivation. *Journal of Personality and Social Psychology, 59*(2), 249–260.

Dovidio, J. F., Brigham, J. C., Johnson, B. T., & Gaertner, S. L. (1996). Stereotyping, prejudice, and discrimination: Another look. In C. N. Macrae, C. Stangor, & M. Hewstone (Eds.), *Stereotypes and stereotyping* (pp. 276–322). New York: Guilford Press.

Dovidio, J., Kawakami, K., & Beach, K. (2001). Implicit and explicit attitudes: Examination of the relationship between measures of intergroup bias. In R. Brown & S. L. Gaertner (Eds.), *Blackwell handbook of social psychology* (Vol. 4, pp. 175–197). Oxford: Blackwell.

Dovidio, J. F., Kawakami, K., & Gaertner, S. L. (2002). Implicit and explicit prejudice and interracial interaction. *Journal of Personality and Social Psychology, 82*(1), 62–68.

Dovidio, J. F., ten Vergert, M., Stewart, T. L., Gaertner, S. L., Johnson, J. D., Esses, V. M., . . . & Pearson, A. R. (2004). Perspective and prejudice: Antecedents and mediating mechanisms. *Personality and Social Psychology Bulletin, 30*(12), 1537–1549.

Downey, G., & Feldman, S. I. (1996). Implications of rejection sensitivity for intimate relationships. *Journal of Personality and Social Psychology, 70*(6), 1327–1343.

Drabman, R. S., & Thomas, M. H. (1974). Does media violence increase children's toleration of real-life aggression? *Developmental Psychology, 10*(3), 418–421.

Drachman, D., DeCarufel, A., & Insko, C. A. (1978). The extra credit effect in interpersonal attraction. *Journal of Experimental Social Psychology, 14*(5), 458–465.

Drigotas, S. M., & Rusbult, C. E. (1992). Should I stay or should I go? A dependence model of breakups. *Journal of Personality and Social Psychology, 62*(1), 62–87.

Drigotas, S. M., Rusbult, C. E., Wieselquist, J., & Whitton, S. W. (1999). Close partner as sculptor of the ideal self: Behavioral affirmation and the

Michelangelo phenomenon. *Journal of Personality and Social Psychology, 77*(2), 293–323.

Drigotas, S. M., Whitney, G. A., & Rusbult, C. E. (1995). On the peculiarities of loyalty: A diary study of responses to dissatisfaction in everyday life. *Personality and Social Psychology Bulletin, 21*(6), 596–609.

Driscoll, R., Davis, K. E., & Lipetz, M. E. (1972). Parental interference and romantic love: The Romeo and Juliet effect. *Journal of Personality and Social Psychology, 24*(1), 1–10.

Dryer, D. C., & Horowitz, L. M. (1997). When do opposites attract? Interpersonal complementarity versus similarity. *Journal of Personality and Social Psychology, 72*(3), 592–603.

D'Silva, K., & Duggan, C. (2010). Revisiting the overcontrolled–undercontrolled typology of violent offenders. *Personality and Mental Health, 4*(3), 193–205.

Du Toit, L., & Duckitt, J. (1990). Psychological characteristics of over- and undercontrolled violent offenders. *Journal of Psychology, 124*(2), 125–141.

Ducharme, J. K., & Kollar, M. M. (2012). Does the "marriage benefit" extend to same-sex union? Evidence from a sample of married lesbian couples in Massachusetts. *Journal of Homosexuality, 59*(4), 580–591.

Duckitt, J. (2001). A dual process cognitive-motivational theory of ideology and prejudice. In M. P. Zanna (Ed.), *Advances in experimental social psychology* (Vol. 33, pp. 41–113). San Diego: Academic Press.

Duckitt, J. (2006). Differential effects of right wing authoritarianism and social dominance orientation on outgroup attitudes and their mediation by threat from and competitiveness to outgroups. *Personality and Social Psychology Bulletin, 32*(5), 684–696.

Duckitt, J., & Sibley, C. G. (2007). Right wing authoritarianism, social dominance orientation and the dimensions of generalized prejudice. *European Journal of Personality, 21*(2), 113–130.

Duffy, S. M., & Rusbult, C. E. (1986). Satisfaction and commitment in homosexual and heterosexual relationships. *Journal of Homosexuality, 12*(2), 1–23.

Duncan, B. L. (1976). Differential social perception and attribution of intergroup violence: Testing the lower limits of stereotyping of Blacks. *Journal of Personality and Social Psychology, 34*(4), 590–598.

Duncker, K. (1945). On problem-solving. (L. S. Lees, Trans.) *Psychological Monographs, 58*(5), i–113.

Dunfield, K. A., & Kuhlmeier, V. A. (2010). Intention-mediated selective helping in infancy. *Psychological Science, 21*(4), 523–527.

Dunn, E. W., Aknin, L. B., & Norton, M. I. (2008). Spending money on others promotes happiness. *Science, 319*(5870), 1687–1688.

Dunn, E. W., Wilson, T. D., & Gilbert D. T. (2003). Location, location, location: The misprediction of satisfaction in housing lotteries. *Personality and Social Psychology Bulletin, 29*,1421–1432.

Dunning, D., Johnson, K., Ehrlinger, J., & Kruger, J. (2003). Why people fail to recognize their own incompetence. *Current Directions in Psychological Science, 12*(3), 83–87.

Dunning, D., & Sherman, D. A. (1997). Stereotypes and tacit inference. *Journal of Personality and Social Psychology, 73*(3), 459–471.

Dunning, J. (July 16, 1997). Eating disorders haunt ballerinas. *The New York Times.* Retrieved from http://www.nytimes.com/1997/07/16/arts/eating-disorders-haunt-ballerinas.html?pagewanted=all&src=pm

Dush, C. M. K., Cohan, C. L., & Amato, P. R. (2003). The relationship between cohabitation and marital quality and stability: Change across cohorts? *Journal of Marriage and Family, 65*(3), 539–549.

Dutton, D. G. (1998). *The abusive personality: Violence and control in intimate relationships.* New York: Guilford Press.

Dutton, D. G. (2002). Personality dynamics of intimate abusiveness. *Journal of Psychiatric Practice, 8*(4), 216–228.

Dutton, D. G., & Aron, A. P. (1974). Some evidence for heightened sexual attraction under conditions of high anxiety. *Journal of Personality and Social Psychology, 30*(4), 510–517.

Dutton, D. G., & Lennox, V. L. (1974). Effect of prior "token" compliance on subsequent interracial behavior. *Journal of Personality and Social Psychology, 29*(1), 65–71.

Duval, S., & Wicklund, R. A. (1972). *A theory of objective self awareness.* Oxford: Academic Press.

Dweck, C. S. (1975). The role of expectations and attributions in the alleviation of learned helplessness. *Journal of Personality and Social Psychology, 31*(4), 674–685.

Dweck, C. S. (2012). Implicit theories. In P. A. M. Van Lange, A. W. Kruglanski, & E. T. Higgins (Eds.), *Handbook of theories in social psychology* (Vol. 2, pp. 43–61). Thousand Oaks, CA: Sage.

Dweck, C. S., Davidson, W., Nelson, S., & Enna, B. (1978). Sex differences in learned helplessness: II. The contingencies of evaluative feedback in the classroom and III. An experimental analysis. *Developmental Psychology, 14*(3), 268–276.

Dyrenforth, P. S., Kashy, D. A., Donnellan, M. B., & Lucas, R. E. (2010). Predicting relationship and life satisfaction from personality in nationally representative samples from three countries: The relative importance of actor, partner, and similarity effects. *Journal of Personality and Social Psychology, 99*(4), 690–702.

Eagly, A. H. (1974). Comprehensibility of persuasive arguments as a determinant of opinion change. *Journal of Personality and Social Psychology, 29*(6), 758–773.

Eagly, A. H. (1987). *Sex differences in social behavior: A social role interpretation.* Hillsdale, NJ: Erlbaum.

Eagly, A. H. (2007). Female leadership advantage and disadvantage: Resolving the contradictions. *Psychology of Women Quarterly, 31*(1), 1–12.

Eagly, A. H., Ashmore, R. D., Makhijani, M. G., & Longo, L. C. (1991). What is beautiful is good, but . . . : A meta-analytic review of research on the physical attractiveness stereotype. *Psychological Bulletin, 110*(1), 109–128.

Eagly, A. H., & Carli, L. L. (1981). Sex of researchers and sex-typed communications as determinants of sex differences in influenceability: A meta-analysis of social influence studies. *Psychological Bulletin, 90*(1), 1–20.

Eagly, A. H., & Carli, L. L. (2007). *Through the labyrinth: The truth about how women become leaders.* Boston: Harvard Business School Press.

Eagly, A. H., & Crowley, M. (1986). Gender and helping behavior: A meta-analytic review of the social psychological literature. *Psychological Bulletin, 100*(3), 283–308.

Eagly, A. H., & Diekman, A. B. (2003). The malleability of sex differences in response to changing social roles. In L. G. Aspinwall & U. M. Staudinger (Eds.), *A psychology of human strengths: Fundamental questions and future directions for a positive psychology* (pp. 103–115). Washington, DC: American Psychological Association.

Eagly, A. H., & Steffen, V. J. (1984). Gender stereotypes stem from the distribution of women and men into social roles. *Journal of Personality and Social Psychology, 46*(4), 735–754.

Eagly, A. H., & Steffen, V. J. (1986). Gender and aggressive behavior: A meta-analytic review of the social psychological literature. *Psychological Bulletin, 100*(3), 309–330.

Eagly, A. H., & Wood, W. (1999). The origins of sex differences in human behavior: Evolved dispositions versus social roles. *American Psychologist, 54*(6), 408–423.

Eastwick, P. W., Eagly, A. H., Finkel, E. J., & Johnson, S. E. (2011). Implicit and explicit preferences for physical attractiveness in a romantic partner: A double dissociation in predictive validity. *Journal of Personality and Social Psychology, 101*(5), 993–1011.

Eastwick, P. W., & Finkel, E. J. (2008). Sex differences in mate preferences revisited: Do people know what they initially desire in a romantic partner? *Journal of Personality and Social Psychology, 94*(2), 245–264.

Eastwick, P. W., Finkel, E. J., & Eagly, A. H. (2011). When and why do ideal partner preferences affect the process of initiating and maintaining romantic relationships? *Journal of Personality and Social Psychology, 101*(5), 1012–1032.

Eastwick, P. W., Finkel, E. J., Mochon, D., & Ariely, D. (2007). Selective versus unselective romantic desire: Not all reciprocity is created equal. *Psychological Science, 18*(4), 317–319.

Eastwick, P. W., Luchies, L. B., Finkel, E. J., & Hunt, L. L. (2014). The predictive validity of ideal partner preferences: A review and meta-analysis. *Psychological Bulletin, 140*(3), 623–665.

Eaton, D. K., Kann, L., Kinchen, S., Ross, J., Hawkins, J., Harris, W. A., & Wechsler, H. (2006). Youth risk behavior surveillance—United States, 2005. *Journal of School Health, 76*(7), 353–372.

Eberhardt, J. L., Davies, P. G., Purdie-Vaughns, V. J., & Johnson, S. L. (2006). Looking deathworthy: Perceived stereotypicality of black defendants predicts capital-sentencing outcomes. *Psychological Science, 17*(5), 383–386.

Eberhardt, J. L., Goff, P. A., Purdie, V. J., & Davies, P. G. (2004). Seeing Black: Race, crime, and visual processing. *Journal of Personality and Social Psychology, 87*(6), 876–893.

Eberts, J., Héroux, D., Moore, B. (Producers), & Beresford, B. (Director). (1991). *Black Robe* [Motion picture]. Canada/Australia/United States: Alliance Communications Corporation, Samson Productions, Téléfilm Canada, First Choice Canadian Communication Corporation, Rogers Telefund, Australian Film Finance Corporation, & Goldwyn Pictures Corporation.

Eden, D. (1990). Pygmalion without interpersonal contrast effects: Whole groups gain from raising manager expectations. *Journal of Applied Psychology, 75*(4), 394–398.

Edlund, J. E., Heider, J. D., Scherer, C. R., Fare, M., & Sagarin, B. J. (2006). Sex differences in jealousy in response to actual infidelity. *Evolutionary Psychology, 4*, 462–470.

Effron, D. A., Cameron, J. S., & Monin, B. (2009). Endorsing Obama licenses favoring whites. *Journal of Experimental Social Psychology, 45*(3), 590–593.

Efran, M. G. (1974). The effect of physical appearance on the judgment of guilt, interpersonal attraction, and severity of recommended punishment in a simulated jury task. *Journal of Research in Personality, 8*(1), 45–54.

Ehrhart, M. G., & Klein, K. J. (2001). Predicting followers' preferences for charismatic leadership: The influence of follower values and personality. *Leadership Quarterly, 12*(2), 153–179.

Ehrlinger, J., Johnson, K., Banner, M., Dunning, D., & Kruger, J. (2008). Why the unskilled are unaware: Further explorations of (absent) self-insight among the incompetent. *Organizational Behavior and Human Decision Processes, 105*(1), 98–121.

Eibl-Eibesfeldt, I. (1989). *Human ethology.* Hawthorne, NY: Aldine de Gruyter.

Eid, M., & Diener, E. (2001). Norms for experiencing emotions in different cultures: Inter- and intranational differences. *Journal of Personality and Social Psychology, 81*(5), 869–885.

Eidelman, S., & Biernat, M. (2003). Derogating black sheep: Individual or group protection? *Journal of Experimental Social Psychology, 39*(6), 602–609.

Eidelson, R. J. (1980). Interpersonal satisfaction and level of involvement: A curvilinear relationship. *Journal of Personality and Social Psychology, 39*(3), 460–470.

Einhorn, H. J., & Hogarth, R. M. (1986). Judging probable cause. *Psychological Bulletin, 99*(1), 3–19.

Eisenberg, N., Cialdini, R. B., McCreath, H., & Shell, R. (1987). Consistency-based compliance: When and why do children become vulnerable? *Journal of Personality and Social Psychology, 52*(6), 1174–1181.

Eisenberg, N., Guthrie, I. K., Cumberland, A., Murphy, B. C., Shepard, S. A., Zhou, Q., & Carlo, G. (2002). Prosocial development in early adulthood: A longitudinal study. *Journal of Personality and Social Psychology, 82*(6), 993–1006.

Eisenberg, N., Miller, P. A., Schaller, M., Fabes, R. A., Fultz, J., Shell, R., & Shea, C. L. (1989). The role of sympathy and altruistic personality traits in helping: A reexamination. *Journal of Personality, 57*(1), 41–67.

Eisenberg, N., Miller, P. A., Shell, R., McNalley, S., & Shea, C. (1991). Prosocial development in adolescence: A longitudinal study. *Developmental Psychology, 27*(5), 849–857.

Eisenberg, N., & Mussen, P. H. (Eds.). (1989). *The roots of prosocial behavior in children.* New York: Cambridge University Press.

Eisenberger, N. I., & Lieberman, M. D. (2004). Why rejection hurts: A common neural alarm system for physical and social pain. *Trends in Cognitive Sciences, 8*(7), 294–300.

Eisenberger, N. I., Lieberman, M. D., & Williams, K. D. (2003). Does rejection hurt? An fMRI study of social exclusion. *Science, 302*(5643), 290–292.

Eisenberger, R., & Armeli, S. (1997). Can salient reward increase creative performance without reducing intrinsic creative interest? *Journal of Personality and Social Psychology, 72*(3), 652–663.

Ekman, P. (1980). *The face of man: Expressions of universal emotions in a New Guinea village.* New York: Garland STPM Press.

Ekman, P., & Cordaro, D. (2011). What is meant by calling emotions basic. *Emotion Review, 3*(4), 364–370.

Ekman, P., Friesen, W. V., & Ellsworth, P. (1972). *Emotion in the human face: Guidelines for research and an integration of findings.* New York: Pergamon Press.

Eley, T. C., Lichtenstein, P., & Moffitt, T. E. (2003). A longitudinal behavioral genetic analysis of the etiology of aggressive and nonaggressive antisocial behavior. *Development and Psychopathology, 15*(2), 383–402.

Eliade, M. (1959). *Cosmos and history: The myth of the eternal return.* New York: Harper.

Eliezer, D., Major, B., & Mendes, W. B. (2010). The costs of caring: Gender identification increases threat following exposure to sexism. *Journal of Experimental Social Psychology, 46*(1), 159–165.

Eliot, T. S. (1964). *T. S. Eliot: Selected Poems.* New York: Harcourt, Brace & World. (Original work published 1917)

Ellemers, N., van Knippenberg, A., De Vries, N., & Wilke, H. (1988). Social identification and permeability of group boundaries. *European Journal of Social Psychology, 18*(6), 497–513.

Elliot, A. J., & Devine, P. G. (1994). On the motivational nature of cognitive dissonance: Dissonance as psychological discomfort. *Journal of Personality and Social Psychology, 67*(3), 382–394.

Elshinnawi, M. (2010, October 8). Arab-Americans favor Democrats in new poll [Web log post]. NC Rumors. Retrieved from http://www.ncrumors.com/?p=2346

Emmons, R. A., & McCullough, M. E. (2003). Counting blessings versus burdens: An experimental investigation of gratitude and subjective well-being in daily life. *Journal of Personality and Social Psychology, 84*(2), 377–389.

Emswiller, T., Deaux, K., & Willits, J. E. (1971). Similarity, sex, and requests for small favors. *Journal of Applied Social Psychology, 1*(3), 284–291.

Encyclopedia of Children's Health. (n.d). Gender identity [online article]. Illinois: Advameg, Inc. Retrieved from http://www.healthofchildren.com/G-H/Gender-Identity.html

Engelhardt, C. R., Bartholow, B. D., Kerr, G. T., & Bushman, B. J. (2011). This is your brain on violent video games: Neural desensitization to violence predicts increased aggression following violent video game exposure. *Journal of Experimental Social Psychology, 47*(5), 1033–1036.

Enquist, M., & Leimar, O. (1983). Evolution of fighting behaviour: Decision rules and assessment of relative strength. *Journal of Theoretical Biology, 102*(3), 387–410.

Epley, N., & Dunning, D. (2000). Feeling "holier than thou": Are self-serving assessments produced by errors in self- or social prediction? *Journal of Personality and Social Psychology, 79*(6), 861–875.

Epley, N., & Gilovich, T. (1999). Just going along: Nonconscious priming and conformity to social pressure. *Journal of Experimental Social Psychology, 35*(6), 578–589.

Epstein, S. (1980). The self-concept: A review and the proposal of an integrated theory of personality. In E. Staub (Ed.), *Personality: Basic issues and current research.* Englewood Cliffs, NJ: Prentice-Hall.

Epstein, S. (1990). Cognitive-experiential Self-theory. In L. Pervin (Ed.), *Handbook of personality: Theory and research* (2nd ed., pp. 165–192). New York: Guilford Press.

Epstein, S. (1994). Integration of the cognitive and the psychodynamic unconscious. *American Psychologist, 49*(8), 709–724.

Epstein, S. (2013). Cognitive-experiential self-theory: An integrative theory of personality. In H. Tennen, J. Suls, & I. B. Weiner (Eds.), *Handbook of psychology, Vol. 5: Personality and social psychology* (2nd edition, pp. 93–118). Hoboken, NJ: Wiley.

Epstude, K., & Roese, N. J. (2008). The functional theory of counterfactual thinking. *Personality and Social Psychology Review, 12*(2), 168–192.

Erickson, B., Lind, E. A., Johnson, B. C., & O'Barr, W. M. (1978). Speech style and impression formation in a court setting: The effects of "powerful" and "powerless" speech. *Journal of Experimental Social Psychology, 14*(3), 266–279.

Erikson, E. H. (1959). *Identity and the life cycle.* New York: W. W. Norton.

Erikson, E. H. (1963). *Childhood and society.* New York: W. W. Norton.

Erikson, E. H. (1968). *Identity: Youth and crisis.* New York: W. W. Norton.

Eron, L. D., Huesmann, L. R., & Zelli, A. (1991). The role of parental variables in the learning of aggression. In D. J. Pepler & K. H. Rubin (Eds.), *The development and treatment of childhood aggression* (pp. 169–188). Hillsdale, NJ: Erlbaum.

ESPN News Services (2011, May 18). Charles Barkley: I had gay teammates [online article]. Retrieved from http://sports.espn.go.com/nba/news/story?id=6563128

Esser, J. K., & Lindoerfer, J. S. (1989). Groupthink and the space shuttle Challenger accident: Toward a quantitative case analysis. *Journal of Behavioral Decision Making, 2*(3), 167–177.

Esses, V. M., Haddock, G., & Zanna, M. P. (1993). Values, stereotypes, and emotions as determinants of intergroup attitudes. In D. M. Mackie & D. L. Hamilton (Eds.), *Affect, cognition, and stereotyping: Interactive processes in group perception* (pp. 137–166). San Diego: Academic Press.

Evans, L. (2010, January 14). Haiti earthquake aid. *The Guardian.* Retrieved from http://www.theguardian.com/news/datablog/2010/jan/14/haiti-quake-aid-pledges-country-donations

Fallon, A. (1990). Culture in the mirror: Sociocultural determinants of body image. In T. Cash & T. Pruzinsky (Eds.), *Body images: Development, deviance, and change* (pp. 80–109). New York: Guilford Press.

Farber, P. D., Khavari, K. A., & Douglass, F. M. (1980). A factor analytic study of reasons for drinking: Empirical validation of positive and negative reinforcement dimensions. *Journal of Consulting and Clinical Psychology, 48*(6), 780–781.

Faulkner, J., Schaller, M., Park, J. H., & Duncan, L. A. (2004). Evolved disease-avoidance mechanisms and contemporary xenophobic attitudes. *Group Processes & Intergroup Relations, 7*(4), 333–353.

Fazio, R. H. (1990). Multiple processes by which attitudes guide behavior: The MODE model as an integrative framework. In M. P. Zanna (Ed.), *Advances in experimental social psychology* (Vol. 23, pp. 75–109). New York: Academic Press.

Fazio, R. H., Jackson, J. R., Dunton, B. C., & Williams, C. J. (1995). Variability in automatic activation as an unobtrusive measure of racial attitudes: A bona fide pipeline? *Journal of Personality and Social Psychology, 69*(6), 1013–1027.

Fazio, R. H., & Williams, C. J. (1986). Attitude accessibility as a moderator of the attitude-perception and attitude-behavior relations: An investigation of the 1984 presidential election. *Journal of Personality and Social Psychology, 51*(3), 505–514.

Feather, N. T. (1982). *Expectations and actions: Expectancy-value models in psychology.* Hillsdale, NJ: Erlbaum.

Federal Bureau of Investigation (2009). 2008 Crime in the United States. Retrieved from http://www2.fbi.gov/ucr/cius2008/offenses/violent_crime/murder_homicide.html

Federal Bureau of Investigation (2010). Expanded homicide data. Retrieved from http://www.fbi.gov/about-us/cjis/ucr/crime-in-the-u.s/2010/crime-in-the-u.s.-2010/offenses-known-to-law-enforcement/expanded/expandhomicidemain

Federal Bureau of Investigation (2011). 2011 National gang threat assessment – Emerging trends. Retrieved from http://www.fbi.gov/stats-services/publications/2011-national-gang-threat-assessment

Federal Bureau of Investigations (2012, December 10). Hate Crimes Accounting: Annual Report Released. Washington, DC: FBI National Press Office. Retrieved from http://www.fbi.gov/news/stories/2012/december/annual-hate-crimes-report-released/annual-hate-crimes-report-released

Feeney, B. C. (2007). The dependency paradox in close relationships: Accepting dependence promotes independence. *Journal of Personality and Social Psychology*, 92(2), 268–285.

Feeney, B. C., & Thrush, R. L. (2010). Relationship influences on exploration in adulthood: The characteristics and function of a secure base. *Journal of Personality and Social Psychology*, 98(1), 57–76.

Feeney, J. A., Noller, P., & Patty, J. (1993). Adolescents' interactions with the opposite sex: Influence of attachment style and gender. *Journal of Adolescence*, 16(2), 169–186.

Fehr, B. (1996). *Friendship processes*. Thousand Oaks, CA: Sage.

Fehr, E., & Gächter, S. (1998). Reciprocity and economics: The economic implications of *Homo Reciprocans*. *European Economic Review*, 42(3), 845–859.

Fein, S., & Spencer, S. J. (1997). Prejudice as self-image maintenance: Affirming the self through derogating others. *Journal of Personality and Social Psychology*, 73(1), 31–44.

Feingold, A. (1988). Matching for attractiveness in romantic partners and same-sex friends: A meta-analysis and theoretical critique. *Psychological Bulletin*, 104(2), 226–235.

Feingold, A. (1990). Gender differences in effects of physical attractiveness on romantic attraction: A comparison across five research paradigms. *Journal of Personality and Social Psychology*, 59(5), 981–993.

Feingold, A. (1992a). Gender differences in mate selection preferences: A test of the parental investment model. *Psychological Bulletin*, 112(1), 125–139.

Feingold, A. (1992b). Good-looking people are not what we think. *Psychological Bulletin*, 111(2), 304–341.

Feingold, A. (1994). Gender differences in personality: A meta-analysis. *Psychological Bulletin*, 116(3), 429–456.

Feldman, R. S., & Prohaska, T. (1979). The student as Pygmalion: Effect of student expectation on the teacher. *Journal of Educational Psychology*, 71(4), 485–493.

Felmlee, D. H. (2001). From appealing to appalling: Disenchantment with a romantic partner. *Sociological Perspectives*, 44(3), 263–280.

Felson, R. B. (1982). Impression management and the escalation of aggression and violence. *Social Psychology Quarterly*, 45(4), 245–254.

Felson, R. B., & Tedeschi, J. T. (Eds.) (1993). *Aggression and violence: Social interactionist perspectives*. Washington, DC: American Psychological Association.

Fenigstein, A., Scheier, M. F., & Buss, A. H. (1975). Public and private self-consciousness: Assessment and theory. *Journal of Consulting and Clinical Psychology*, 43(4), 522–527.

Fernández, S., Branscombe, N. R., Gómez, Á., & Morales, J. (2012). Influence of the social context on use of surgical-lengthening and group-empowering coping strategies among people with dwarfism. *Rehabilitation Psychology*, 57(3), 224–235.

Ferris, C. F., Melloni Jr., R. H., Koppel, G., Perry, K. W., Fuller, R. W., & Delville, Y. (1997). Vasopressin/serotonin interactions in the anterior hypothalamus control aggressive behavior in golden hamsters. *Journal of Neuroscience*, 17(11), 4331–4340. Retrieved from http://www.jneurosci.org/content/17/11/4331.short

Festinger, L. (1954). A theory of social comparison processes. *Human Relations*, 7(2), 117–140.

Festinger, L. (1957). *A theory of cognitive dissonance*. Stanford: Stanford University Press.

Festinger, L., & Carlsmith, J. M. (1959). Cognitive consequences of forced compliance. *Journal of Abnormal and Social Psychology*, 58(2), 203–210.

Festinger, L., Schachter, S., & Back, K. (1950). *Social pressures in informal groups: A study of human factors in housing*. Oxford: Harper.

Fey, T. (Writer), & Brock, T. (Director). (2009, March 19). The bubble [Television series episode]. In A. Baldwin, J. Kupfer, & D. Scardino, D. (Producers), *30 Rock*. New York: Broadway Video, Little Stranger, & Universal Media Studios.

Fiedler, F. E. (1967). *A theory of leadership effectiveness*. New York: McGraw-Hill.

Finer, L. B. (2007). *Trends in premarital sex in the United States, 1954–2003*. Public Health Reports, 122(1), 73–78. Retrieved from http://www.ncbi.nlm.nih.gov/pmc/articles/PMC1802108/

Fink, B., Neave, N., Manning, J. T., & Grammer, K. (2006). Facial symmetry and judgments of attractiveness, health and personality. *Personality and Individual Differences*, 41(3), 491–499.

Finkel, E. J., DeWall, C. N., Slotter, E. B., Oaten, M., & Foshee, V. A. (2009). Self-regulatory failure and intimate partner violence perpetration. *Journal of Personality and Social Psychology*, 97(3), 483–499.

Finkel, E. J., Eastwick, P. W., Karney, B. R., Reis, H. T., & Sprecher, S. (2012). Online dating: A critical analysis from the perspective of psychological science. *Psychological Science in the Public Interest*, 13(1), 3–66.

Finkel, E. J., Hui, C. M., Carswell, K. L., & Larson, G. M. (2014). The suffocation of marriage: Climbing Mount Maslow without enough oxygen. *Psychological Inquiry*, 25, 1–41.

Finkel, E. J., Rusbult, C. E., Kumashiro, M., & Hannon, P. A. (2002). Dealing with betrayal in close relationships: Does commitment promote forgiveness? *Journal of Personality and Social Psychology*, 82(6), 956–974.

Finkel, E. J., Slotter, E. B., Luchies, L. B., Walton, G. M., & Gross, J. J. (2013). A brief intervention to promote conflict reappraisal preserves marital quality over time. *Psychological Science*, 24(8), 1595–1601.

Fiorito, G., & Scotto, P. (1992). Observational learning in *Octopus vulgaris*. *Science*, 256(5056), 545–547.

Fischer, P., Krueger, J. I., Greitemeyer, T., Vogrincic, C., Kastenmüller, A., Frey, D., . . . & Kainbacher, M. (2011). The bystander-effect: A meta-analytic review on bystander intervention in dangerous and non-dangerous emergencies. *Psychological Bulletin*, 137(4), 517–537.

Fishbein, M., & Ajzen, I. (1975). *Belief, attitude, intention, and behavior: An introduction to theory and research*. Reading, MA: Addison-Wesley.

Fisher, H. (1995). The nature and evolution of romantic love. In W. Jankowiak (Ed.), *Romantic passion: A universal experience?* (pp. 23–41). New York: Columbia University Press.

Fisher, H. (2004). *Why we love: The nature and chemistry of romantic love*. New York: Henry Holt.

Fisher, H. (2006). The drive to love: The neural mechanism for mate selection. In R. J. Sternberg & K. Weis (Eds.), *The new psychology of love* (pp. 87–115). New Haven: Yale University Press.

Fishman, C. G. (1965). Need for approval and the expression of aggression under varying conditions of frustration. *Journal of Personality and Social Psychology*, 2(6), 809–816.

Fiske, A. P. (1990). Relativity within Moose ("Mossi") culture: Four incommensurable models for social relationships. *Ethos*, 18(2), 180–204.

Fiske, A. P. (1991). *Structures of social life: The four elementary forms of human relations; Communal sharing, authority ranking, equality matching, market pricing*. New York: Free Press.

Fiske, S. T. (1998). Stereotyping, prejudice, and discrimination. In D. T. Gilbert, S. T. Fiske, & G. Lindzey (Eds.), *The handbook of social psychology* (4th ed., Vol. 2, pp. 357–411). New York: McGraw-Hill.

Fiske, S. T., Cuddy, A. J. C., & Glick, P. (2007). Universal dimensions of social perception: Warmth and competence. *Trends in Cognitive Science*, 11(2), 77–83.

Fiske, S. T., Cuddy, A. J., Glick, P., & Xu, J. (2002). A model of (often mixed) stereotype content: Competence and warmth respectively follow from perceived status and competition. *Journal of Personality and Social Psychology*, 82(6), 878–902.

Fiske, S. T., & Neuberg, S. L. (1990). A continuum model of impression formation, from category based to individuating processes: Influence of information and motivation on attention and interpretation. In M. P. Zanna (Ed.), *Advances in experimental social psychology* (Vol. 23, pp. 1–74). New York: Academic Press.

Fiske, S. T., & Taylor, S. E. (2008). *Social cognition: From brains to culture*. New York: McGraw-Hill.

Fitz, D. (1976). A renewed look at Miller's conflict theory of aggression displacement. *Journal of Personality and Social Psychology*, 33(6), 725–732.

Fitzsimons, G. M., & Bargh, J. A. (2003). Thinking of you: Nonconscious pursuit of interpersonal goals associated with relationship partners. *Journal of Personality and Social Psychology*, 84(1), 148–164.

Fitzsimons, G. M., & Kay, A. C. (2004). Language and interpersonal cognition: Causal effects of variations in pronoun usage on perceptions of closeness. *Personality and Social Psychology Bulletin*, 30(5), 547–557.

Flannery, D. J., Vazsonyi, A. T., & Waldman, I. D. (2007). *The Cambridge handbook of violent behavior and aggression*. New York: Cambridge University Press.

Fleischman, J. (2002). *Phineas Gage: A gruesome but true story about brain science*. Boston: Houghton Mifflin.

Fleming, J. H., Darley, J. M., Hilton, J. L., & Kojetin, B. A. (1990). Multiple audience problem: A strategic communication perspective on social perception. *Journal of Personality and Social Psychology*, 58(4), 593–609.

Fleming, J. H., & Rudman, L. A. (1993). Between a rock and a hard place: Self-concept regulating and communicative properties of distancing behaviors. *Journal of Personality and Social Psychology*, 64(1), 44–59.

Fletcher, G. J., Simpson, J. A., & Thomas, G. (2000). Ideals, perceptions, and evaluations in early relationship development. *Journal of Personality and Social Psychology*, 79(6), 933–940.

Florence, W., Summers, I., & Allchin, M. (2008). Kiss with a Fist [Recorded by Florence and the Machine]. *On Lungs* [LP / CD]. United Kingdom: Universal International (2009).

Florian, V., & Mikulincer, M. (1998). Symbolic immortality and the management of the terror of death: The moderating role of attachment style. *Journal of Personality and Social Psychology*, 74(3), 725–734.

Foderaro, L. W. (2010, September 29). Private moment made public, then a fatal jump. *The New York Times*. Retrieved from http://www.nytimes.com/2010/09/30/nyregion/30suicide.html?_r=0

Fogelman, E., & Wiener, V. L. (1985). The few, the brave, the noble. *Psychology Today*, 19(8), 60–65.

Fogg, B. J., & Nass, C. (1997). Silicon sycophants: The effects of computers that flatter. *International Journal of Human-Computer Studies*, 46(5), 551–561.

Fointiat, V. (2004). "I know what I have to do, but . . ." When hypocrisy leads to behavioral change. *Social Behavior and Personality*, 32(8), 741–746. Stable URL: http://www.sbpjournal.com/index.php/sbp/article/view/1366

Follenfant, A., & Ric, F. (2010). Behavioral rebound following stereotype suppression. *European Journal of Social Psychology*, 40(5), 774–782.

Fonda, H., Justin, J., Rose, R. (Producers), & Lumet, S. (Director) (1957). *12 Angry Men* [Motion picture]. United States, New York: Orion-Nova Productions.

Forbes, C. E., Cox, C. L., Schmader, T., & Ryan, L. (2012). Negative stereotype activation alters interaction between neural correlates of arousal, inhibition, and cognitive control. *Social Cognitive and Affective Neuroscience*, 7(7), 771–781.

Forbes, C. E., & Schmader, T. (2010). Retraining attitudes and stereotypes to affect motivation and cognitive capacity under stereotype threat. *Journal of Personality and Social Psychology*, 99(5), 740–754.

Forbes, G., Zhang, X., Doroszewicz, K., & Haas, K. (2009). Relationships between individualism–collectivism, gender, and direct or indirect aggression: A study in China, Poland, and the US. *Aggressive Behavior*, 35(1), 24–30.

Ford, C. S., & Beach, F. A. (1951). *Patterns of sexual behavior*. New York: Harper & Row.

Fordham, S., & Ogbu, J. U. (1986). Black students' school success: Coping with the "burden of 'acting white.'" *Urban Review*, 18(3), 176–206.

Forgas, J. P. (1995). Mood and judgment: The affect infusion model (AIM). *Psychological Bulletin*, 117(1), 39–66.

Forgas, J. P. (1998). On feeling good and getting your way: Mood effects on negotiator cognition and bargaining strategies. *Journal of Personality and Social Psychology*, 74(3), 565–577.

Forgas, J. P., Laham, S. M., & Vargas, P. T. (2005). Mood effects on eyewitness memory: Affective influences on susceptibility to misinformation. *Journal of Experimental Social Psychology*, 41, 574–588.

Foster, C. A., Witcher, B. S., Campbell, W. K., & Green, J. D. (1998). Arousal and attraction: Evidence for automatic and controlled processes. *Journal of Personality and Social Psychology*, 74(1), 86–101.

Frable, D. E., Blackstone, T., & Scherbaum, C. (1990). Marginal and mindful: Deviants in social interactions. *Journal of Personality and Social Psychology*, 59(1), 140–149.

Fraley, R. C. (2002). Attachment stability from infancy to adulthood: Meta-analysis and dynamic modeling of developmental mechanisms. *Personality and Social Psychology Review*, 6(2), 123–151.

Franiuk, R., Cohen, D., & Pomerantz, E. M. (2002). Implicit theories of relationships: Implications for relationship satisfaction and longevity. *Personal Relationships*, 9(4), 345–367.

Franiuk, R., Pomerantz, E. M., & Cohen, D. (2004). The causal role of theories of relationships: Consequences for satisfaction and cognitive strategies. *Personality and Social Psychology Bulletin*, 30(11), 1494–1507.

Frantz, C. M., Cuddy, A. J., Burnett, M., Ray, H., & Hart, A. (2004). A threat in the computer: The race implicit association test as a stereotype threat experience. *Personality and Social Psychology Bulletin*, 30(12), 1611–1624.

Frawley, T. J. (2008). Gender schema and prejudicial recall: How children misremember, fabricate, and distort gendered picture book information. *Journal of Research in Childhood Education*, 22(3), 291–303.

Fredrickson, B. L. (2001). The role of positive emotions in positive psychology: The broaden-and-build theory of positive emotions. *American Psychologist*, 56(3), 218–226.

Fredrickson, B. L., & Branigan, C. (2005). Positive emotions broaden the scope of attention and thought-action repertoires. *Cognition & Emotion*, 19(3), 313–332.

Fredrickson, B. L., & Roberts, T.-A. (1997). Objectification theory. *Psychology of Women Quarterly*, 21(2), 173–206.

Fredrickson, B. L., Roberts, T.-A., Noll, S. M., Quinn, D. M., & Twenge, J. M. (1998). That swimsuit becomes you: Sex differences in self-objectification, restrained eating, and math performance. *Journal of Personality and Social Psychology*, 75(1), 269–284.

Freedman, J. L. (1965). Long-term behavioral effects of cognitive dissonance. *Journal of Experimental Social Psychology*, 1(2), 145–155.

Freedman, J. L., & Fraser, S. C. (1966). Compliance without pressure: The foot-in-the-door technique. *Journal of Personality and Social Psychology*, 4(2), 195–202.

Freeman, J. B., & Ambady, N. (2011). A dynamic interactive theory of person construal. *Psychological Review*, 118(2), 247–279.

French, J., & Raven, B. H. (1959). The bases of social power. In D. Cartwright (Ed.), *Studies in social power* (pp. 150–167). Ann Arbor: Institute for Social Research.

Freud, A. (1966). *The ego and the mechanisms of defense* (C. Baines, Trans.). London: Hogarth Press (Original work published 1936)

Freud, S. (1950). *Totem and taboo*. (J. Strachey, Trans.) London: Routledge. (Original work published 1913)

Freud, S. (1955). *Group psychology and the analysis of the ego*. In J. Strachey (Ed. and Trans.), *The standard edition of the complete psychological works of Sigmund Freud* (Vol. 18, pp. 67–143). London: Hogarth Press. (Original work published 1921)

Freud, S. (1958). *The dynamics of transference*. In J. Strachey (Ed. and Trans.), *The standard edition of the complete psychological works of Sigmund Freud* (Vol. 12, pp. 97–108). London: Hogarth Press. (Original work published 1912)

Freud, S. (1960). *Three essays on the theory of sexuality*. In J. Strachey (Ed. & Trans.), *The standard edition of the complete psychological works of Sigmund Freud* (Vol. 7, pp. 123–246). London: Hogarth Press. (Original work published 1905)

Freud, S. (1961a). *Beyond the pleasure principle* (J. Strachey, Ed. and Trans). New York: W. W. Norton (Original work published 1920)

Freud, S. (1961b). *The Ego and the Id* (J. Strachey, Ed. and Trans.). New York: W. W. Norton (Original work published 1923)

Frey, D. (1982). Different levels of cognitive dissonance, information seeking, and information avoidance. *Journal of Personality and Social Psychology*, 43(6), 1175–1183.

Fried, C. B., & Aronson, E. (1995). Hypocrisy, misattribution, and dissonance reduction. *Personality and Social Psychology Bulletin*, 21(9), 925–933.

Friedman, R. S., McCarthy, D. M., Bartholow, B. D., & Hicks, J. A. (2007). Interactive effects of alcohol outcome expectancies and alcohol cues on nonconsumptive behavior. *Experimental and Clinical Psychopharmacology*, 15(1), 102–114.

Fries, A., & Frey, D. (1980). Misattribution of arousal and the effects of self-threatening information. *Journal of Experimental Social Psychology*, 16(5), 405–416.

Frieze, I. H., Olson, J. E., & Russell, J. (1991). Attractiveness and income for men and women in management. *Journal of Applied Social Psychology*, 21(13), 1039–1057.

Frisby, C. M. (2006). "Shades of beauty": Examining the relationship of skin color to perceptions of physical attractiveness. *Facial Plastic Surgery*, 22(3), 175–179.

Frith, C. D., & Frith, U. (1999). Interacting minds—a biological basis. *Science*, 286(5445), 1692–1695.

Fritsche, I., Jonas, E., Fischer, P., Koranyi, N., Berger, N., & Fleischmann, B. (2007). Mortality salience and the desire for offspring. *Journal of Experimental Social Psychology*, 43(5), 753–762.

Fromm, E. (1941). *Escape from freedom*. New York: Holt, Rinehart and Winston.

Fryar, C. D., Hirsch, R., Porter, K. S., Kottiri, B., Brody, D. J., & Louis, T. (2007, June 28). Drug use and sexual behaviors reported by adults: United States, 1999–2002 [Data file]. Advance Data from Vital Health and Statistics 384. Retrieved from http://www.cdc.gov/nchs/data/ad/ad384.pdf

Fryberg, S. A., Markus, H. R., Oyserman, D., & Stone, J. M. (2008). Of warrior chiefs and Indian princesses: The psychological consequences of American Indian mascots. *Basic and Applied Social Psychology*, 30(3), 208–218.

Fuglestad, P. T., Rothman, A. J., & Jeffery, R. W. (2008). Getting there and hanging on: The effect of regulatory focus on performance in smoking and weight loss interventions. *Health Psychology*, 27(3S), S260–S270.

Furnham, A., & Bochner, S. (1986). *Culture shock: Psychological reactions to unfamiliar environments*. London: Methuen.

Furnham, A., & Gunter, B. (1984). Just world beliefs and attitudes towards the poor. *British Journal of Social Psychology*, 23(3), 265–269.

Furnham, A., Petrides, K. V., & Constantinides, A. (2005). The effects of body mass index and waist-to-hip ratio on ratings of female attractiveness, fecundity, and health. *Personality and Individual Differences*, 38(8), 1823–1834.

Gable, S. L., Reis, H. T., Impett, E. A., & Asher, E. R. (2004). What do you do when things go right? The intrapersonal and interpersonal benefits of sharing positive events. *Journal of Personality and Social Psychology*, 87(2), 228–245.

Gaertner, S. L. (1973). Helping behavior and racial discrimination among liberals and conservatives. *Journal of Personality and Social Psychology*, 25(3), 335–341.

Gaertner, S. L., & Dovidio, J. F. (1977). The subtlety of White racism, arousal, and helping behavior. *Journal of Personality and Social Psychology, 35*(10), 691–707.

Gaertner, S. L., & Dovidio, J. F. (1986). The aversive form of racism. In J. F. Dovidio & S. L. Gaertner (Eds.), *Prejudice, discrimination, and racism*. Orlando: Academic Press.

Gaertner, S. L., & Dovidio, J. F. (2000). *Reducing intergroup bias: The common ingroup identity model*. Philadelphia: Psychology Press.

Gagné, F. M., & Lydon, J. E. (2004). Bias and accuracy in close relationships: An integrative review. *Personality and Social Psychology Review, 8*(4), 322–338.

Gagné, M., & Deci, E. L. (2005). Self-determination theory and work motivation. *Journal of Organizational Behavior, 26*(4), 331–362.

Gailliot, M. T., & Baumeister, R. F. (2007). The physiology of willpower: Linking blood glucose to self-control. *Personality and Social Psychology Review, 11*(4), 303–327.

Gailliot, M. T., Baumeister, R. F., DeWall, C. N., Maner, J. K., Plant, E. A., Tice, D. M., Brewer, L. E., & Schmeichel, B. J. (2007). Self-control relies on glucose as a limited energy source: Willpower is more than a metaphor. *Journal of Personality and Social Psychology, 92*(2), 325–336.

Gailliot, M. T., Stillman, T. F., Schmeichel, B. J., Maner, J. K., & Plant, E. A. (2008). Mortality salience increases adherence to salient norms and values. *Personality and Social Psychology Bulletin, 34*(7), 993–1003.

Galdi, S., Arcuri, L., & Gawronski, B. (2008). Automatic mental associations predict future choices of undecided decision-makers. *Science, 321*(5892), 1100–1102.

Galinsky, A. D., Magee, J. C., Inesi, M. E., & Gruenfeld, D. H. (2006). Power and perspectives not taken. *Psychological Science, 17*(12), 1068–1074.

Galinsky, A. D., & Moskowitz, G. B. (2000). Perspective-taking: Decreasing stereotype expression, stereotype accessibility, and in-group favoritism. *Journal of Personality and Social Psychology, 78*(4), 708–724.

Gallup Center for Muslim Studies (2010, January 21). In U.S., religious prejudice stronger against Muslims. Gallup Well-Being. Retrieved from http://www.gallup.com/poll/125312/religious-prejudice-stronger-against-muslims.aspx

Gangestad, S. W. (1993). Sexual selection and physical attractiveness. *Human Nature, 4*(3), 205–235.

Gangestad, S. W., Garver-Apgar, C. E., Simpson, J. A., & Cousins, A. J. (2007). Changes in women's mate preferences across the ovulatory cycle. *Journal of Personality and Social Psychology, 92*(1), 151–163.

Gangestad, S. W., & Simpson, J. A. (1990). Toward an evolutionary history of female sociosexual variation. *Journal of Personality, 58*(1), 69–96.

Gangestad, S. W., & Simpson, J. A. (2000). The evolution of human mating: Trade-offs and strategic pluralism. *Behavioral and Brain Sciences, 23*(4), 573–644.

Gangestad, S. W., Simpson, J. A., Cousins, A. J., Garver-Apgar, C. E., & Christensen, P. N. (2004). Women's preferences for male behavioral displays change across the menstrual cycle. *Psychological Science, 15*(3), 203–206.

Gannon, T. A., Keown, K., & Polaschek, D. L. (2007). Increasing honest responding on cognitive distortions in child molesters: The bogus pipeline revisited. *Sexual Abuse: A Journal of Research and Treatment, 19*(1), 5–22.

Gansberg, M. (1964, March 27). Thirty-eight who saw murder didn't call the police. *The New York Times*, 1, 38. Retrieved from http://www.nytimes.com/1964/03/27/37-who-saw-murder-didnt-call-the-police.html?_r=0

Gapinski, K. D., Brownell, K. D., & LaFrance, M. (2003). Body objectification and "fat talk": Effects on emotion, motivation, and cognitive performance. *Sex Roles, 48*(9–10), 377–388.

Garcia, D. M., Reser, A. H., Amo, R. B., Redersdorff, S., & Branscombe, N. R. (2005). Perceivers' responses to in-group and out-group members who blame a negative outcome on discrimination. *Personality and Social Psychology Bulletin, 31*(6), 769–780.

Garcia, S. M., Weaver, K., Moskowitz, G. B., & Darley, J. M. (2002). Crowded minds: The implicit bystander effect. *Journal of Personality and Social Psychology, 83*(4), 843–853.

Gardner, W. L., Gabriel, S., & Dean, K. K. (2004). The individual as "melting pot": The flexibility of bicultural self-construals. *Cahiers de Psychologie Cognitive / Current Psychology of Cognition, 22*, 181–201.

Gardner, W. L., Gabriel, S., & Lee, A. Y. (1999). "I" value freedom, but "we" value relationships: Self-construal priming mirrors cultural differences in judgment. *Psychological Science, 10*(2), 321–326.

Gasper, K., & Clore, G. L. (2002). Attending to the big picture: Mood and global versus local processing of visual information. *Psychological Science, 13*(1), 34–40.

Gaunt, R., Leyens, J. P., & Demoulin, S. (2002). Intergroup relations and the attribution of emotions: Control over memory for secondary emotions associated with the ingroup and outgroup. *Journal of Experimental Social Psychology, 38*(5), 508–514.

Gawronski, B., & Bodenhausen, G. V. (2006). Associative and propositional processes in evaluation: An integrative review of implicit and explicit attitude change. *Psychological Bulletin, 132*(5), 692–731.

Geary, D. C. (2010). *Male, female: The evolution of human sex differences* (2nd ed.). Washington, DC: American Psychological Association.

Geary, D. C., Rumsey, M., Bow-Thomas, C., & Hoard, M. K. (1995). Sexual jealousy as a facultative trait: Evidence from the pattern of sex differences in adults from China and the United States. *Ethology & Sociobiology, 16*(5), 355–383.

Geen, R. G. (1968). Effects of frustration, attack, and prior training in aggressiveness upon aggressive behavior. *Journal of Personality and Social Psychology, 9*(4), 316–321.

Geen, R. G. (1998). Aggression and antisocial behavior. In D. T. Gilbert, S. T. Fiske, & G. Lindzey (Eds.), *The handbook of social psychology* (4th ed., Vol. 2, pp. 317–356). New York: McGraw-Hill.

Geen, R. G. (2001). *Human aggression* (2nd ed.). Philadelphia: Open University Press.

Geen, R. G., & Berkowitz, L. (1966). Name-mediated aggressive cue properties. *Journal of Personality, 34*(3), 456–465.

Geen, R. G., & Pigg, R. (1970). Acquisition of an aggressive response and its generalization to verbal behavior. *Journal of Personality and Social Psychology, 15*(2), 165–170.

Geen, R. G., & Stonner, D. (1971). Effects of aggressiveness habit strength on behavior in the presence of aggression-related stimuli. *Journal of Personality and Social Psychology, 17*(2), 149–153.

Geen, R. G., & Stonner, D. (1972). The context of observed violence: Inhibition of aggression through displays of unsuccessful retaliation. *Psychonomic Science, 27*(6), 342–344.

Geen, R. G., & Stonner, D. (1973). Context effects in observed violence. *Journal of Personality and Social Psychology, 25*(1), 145–150.

Geller, J., Johnston, C., Madsen, K., Goldner, E. M., Remick, R. A., & Birmingham, C. L. (1998). Shape- and weight-based self-esteem and the eating disorders. *International Journal of Eating Disorders, 24*(3), 285–298.

Gelles, R. J. (2007). The politics of research: The use, abuse, and misuse of social science data—The cases of intimate partner violence. *Family Court Review, 45*(1), 42–51.

Gentile, D. A., Anderson, C. A., Yukawa, S., Ihori, N., Saleem, M., Ming, L. K., . . . & Sakamoto, A. (2009). The effects of prosocial video games on prosocial behaviors: International evidence from correlational, longitudinal, and experimental studies. *Personality and Social Psychology Bulletin, 35*(6), 752–763.

Gentzler, A. L., & Kerns, K. A. (2004). Associations between insecure attachment and sexual experiences. *Personal Relationships, 11*(2), 249–265.

Gerbner, G., Gross, L., Morgan, M., & Signorielli, N. (1980). The "mainstreaming" of America: Violence profile no. 11. *Journal of Communication, 30*(3), 10–29.

Gerbner, G., Gross, L., Morgan, M., & Signorielli, N. (1982). Charting the mainstream: Television's contributions to political orientations. *Journal of Communication, 32*(2), 100–127.

Gergen, K. J., & Gergen, M. M. (1988). Narrative and the self as relationship. In L. Berkowitz (Ed.), *Advances in experimental social psychology* (Vol. 21, pp. 17–56). San Diego: Academic Press.

Gerrard, M., Gibbons, F. X., Houlihan, A., Stock, M. L., & Pomery, E. A. (2008). A dual-process approach to health risk decision making: The prototype willingness model. *Developmental Review, 28*(1), 29–61.

Gerrard, M., Gibbons, F. X., Stock, M. I., Vande Lune, L. S. & Cleveland, M. J. (2005). Images of smokers and willingness to smoke among African American pre-adolescents: An application of the prototype/willingness model of adolescent health risk behavior to smoking initiation. *Pediatric Psychology, 30*, 305–318.

Gershoff, E. T. (2002). Corporal punishment by parents and associated child behaviors and experiences: A meta-analytic and theoretical review. *Psychological Bulletin, 128*(4), 539–579.

Gervais, W. M., & Norenzayan, A. (2012). Like a camera in the sky? Thinking about God increases public self-awareness and socially desirable responding. *Journal of Experimental Social Psychology, 48*(1), 298–302.

Gibbons, F. X., & Gerrard, M. (1997). Health images and their effects on health behavior. In B. P. Buunk & F. X. Gibbons (Eds.), *Health, coping, and well-being: Perspectives from social comparison theory* (pp. 63–94). Mahwah, NJ: Erlbaum.

Gibbons, F. X., Gerrard, M., Reimer, R. A., & Pomery, E. A. (2006). Unintentional behavior: A subrational approach to health risk. In D. T. M. de Ridder & J. B. F. de Wit (Eds.), *Self-regulation in health behavior* (pp. 45–70). Chichester: John Wiley & Sons Ltd.

Gilbert, D. T., & Malone, P. S. (1995). The correspondence bias. *Psychological Bulletin, 117*(1), 21–38.

Gilbert, D. T., Morewedge, C. K., Risen, J. L., & Wilson, T. D. (2004). Looking forward to looking backward: The misprediction of regret. *Psychological Science, 15*(5), 346–350.

Gilbert, D. T., Pelham, B. W., & Krull, D. S. (1988). On cognitive busyness: When person perceivers meet persons perceived. *Journal of Personality and Social Psychology*, *54*(5), 733–740.

Gildersleeve, K., Haselton, M. G., & Fales, M. R. (2014). Do women's mate preferences change across the ovulatory cycle? A meta-analytic review. *Psychological Bulletin*, *140*(5), 1205–1259.

Giles, D. C. (2002). Parasocial interaction: A review of the literature and a model for future research. *Media Psychology*, *4*(3), 279–305.

Gillath, O., Shaver, P. R., Baek, J. M., & Chun, D. S. (2008). Genetic correlates of adult attachment style. *Personality and Social Psychology Bulletin*, *34*(10), 1396–1405.

Gilovich, T. (1987). Secondhand information and social judgment. *Journal of Experimental Social Psychology*, *23*(1), 59–74.

Gilovich, T., Kerr, M., & Medvec, V. H. (1993). Effect of temporal perspective on subjective confidence. *Journal of Personality and Social Psychology*, *64*(4), 552.

Gilovich, T., & Medvec, V. H. (1994). The temporal pattern to the experience of regret. *Journal of Personality and Social Psychology*, *67*(3), 357–365.

Gilovich, T., Medvec, V. H., & Savitsky, K. (2000). The spotlight effect in social judgment: An egocentric bias in estimates of the salience of one's own actions and appearance. *Journal of Personality and Social Psychology*, *78*(2), 211–222.

Gilovich, T., Savitsky, K., & Medvec, V. H. (1998). The illusion of transparency: Biased assessments of others' ability to read one's emotional states. *Journal of Personality and Social Psychology*, *75*(2), 332–346.

Gjerde, P. F., Onishi, M., & Carlson, K. S. (2004). Personality characteristics associated with romantic attachment: A comparison of interview and self-report methodologies. *Personality and Social Psychology Bulletin*, *30*(11), 1402–1415.

Glasman, L. R., & Albarracín, D. (2006). Forming attitudes that predict future behavior: A meta-analysis of the attitude-behavior relation. *Psychological Bulletin*, *132*(5), 778–822.

Glass, I. (Host). (2009, March 27). Scenes from a recession [Radio broadcast]. In I. Glass (Producer), *This American life*. Chicago: Chicago Public Media & Ira Glass. Available at http://www.thisamericanlife.org/radio-archives/episode/377/transcript

Glass, I. (Host). (2013, February, 22). 488: Harper high school, part two [Radio broadcast]. In I. Glass (Producer). *This American life*. Illinois, Chicago: Chicago Public Media & Ira Glass. Retrieved from http://www.thisamericanlife.org/radio-archives/episode/488/transcript

Glass, I. (Host). (2013, April 12). Dr. Gilmer & Mr. Hyde [Radio broadcast]. In I. Glass (Producer), *This American life*. Chicago: Chicago Public Media & Ira Glass. Retrieved from http://www.thisamericanlife.org/radio-archives/episode/492/dr-gilmer-and-mr-hyde

Gleitman, H. (1981). *Psychology*. New York: W. W. Norton.

Glick, P., Diebold, J., Bailey-Werner, B., & Zhu, L. (1997). The two faces of Adam: Ambivalent sexism and polarized attitudes toward women. *Personality and Social Psychology Bulletin*, *23*(12), 1323–1334.

Glick, P., & Fiske, S. T. (1996). The ambivalent sexism inventory: Differentiating hostile and benevolent sexism. *Journal of Personality and Social Psychology*, *70*(3), 491–512.

Glynn, S. A., Busch, M. P., Schreiber, G. B., Murphy, E. L., Wright, D. J., Tu, Y., & Kleinman, S. H. (2003). Effect of a national disaster on blood supply and safety. *JAMA: The Journal of the American Medical Association*, *289*(17), 2246–2253.

Goethals, G. R., & Nelson, R. E. (1973). Similarity in the influence process: The belief-value distinction. *Journal of Personality and Social Psychology*, *25*(1), 117–122.

Goff, P. A., Eberhardt, J. L., Williams, M. J., & Jackson, M. C. (2008). Not yet human: Implicit knowledge, historical dehumanization, and contemporary consequences. *Journal of Personality and Social Psychology*, *94*(2), 292–306.

Goffman, E. (1959). *The presentation of self in everyday life*. New York: Doubleday.

Goffman, E. (1963). *Stigma: Notes on the management of spoiled identity*. Englewood Cliffs, NJ: Prentice-Hall.

Goldenberg, J., Heflick, N., Vaes, J., Motyl, M., & Greenberg, J. (2009). Of mice and men, and objectified women: A terror management account of infrahumanization. *Group Processes & Intergroup Relations*, *12*(6), 763–776.

Goldenberg, J. L. (2013). Black Swan/White Swan: On female objectification, creatureliness, and death denial. In D. Sullivan & J. Greenberg (Eds.), *Death in classic and contemporary film: Fade to black* (pp. 105–118). New York: Palgrave Macmillan.

Goldenberg, J. L., & Arndt, J. (2008). The implications of death for health: A terror management health model for behavioral health promotion. *Psychological Review*, *115*(4), 1032–1053.

Goldenberg, J. L., Landau, M. J., Pyszczynski, T., Cox, C. R., Greenberg, J., Solomon, S., & Dunnam, H. (2003). Gender-typical responses to sexual and emotional infidelity as a function of mortality salience induced self-esteem striving. *Personality and Social Psychology Bulletin*, *29*(12), 1585–1595.

Goldin, P. R., McRae, K., Ramel, W., & Gross, J. J. (2008). The neural bases of emotion regulation: Reappraisal and suppression of negative emotion. *Biological Psychiatry*, *63*(6), 577–586.

Goldman, W., & Lewis, P. (1977). Beautiful is good: Evidence that the physically attractive are more socially skillful. *Journal of Experimental Social Psychology*, *13*(2), 125–130.

Goldschmidt, W. R. (1990). *The human career: The self in the symbolic world*. Cambridge, MA: B. Blackwell.

Goldsman, A., Lassiter, J., Heyman, D., Moritz, N. H. (Producers), & Lawrence, F. (Director) (2007). *I am legend* [Motion picture]. USA: Warner Bros, in association with Village Roadshow Pictures, Weed Road, Overbrook Entertainment, 3 Arts Entertainment, Heyday Films, & Original Film.

Goldstein, A. P. (1994). Delinquent gangs. In L. R. Huesman (Ed.), *Aggressive behavior: Current perspectives* (pp. 255–273). New York: Plenum Press.

Goldstein, A. P., Glick, B. & Gibbs, J. C. (1998). *Aggression replacement training: A comprehensive intervention for aggressive youth* (Rev. ed.). Champaign, IL: Research Press.

Goldstein, D., & Rosenbaum, A. (1985). An evaluation of the self-esteem of maritally violent men. *Family Relations*, *34*(3), 425–428. Stable URL: http://www.jstor.org/stable/583583

Goldstein, J. H. (1986). *Aggression and crimes of violence*. New York: Oxford University Press.

Goldstein, J. H. (Ed.) (1998). *Why we watch: The attractions of violent entertainment*. New York: Oxford University Press.

Goldwyn, S., Jr., Henderson D., Rothman, T. (Producers), & Ward, D. S. (Director) (1993). *The program* [Motion picture]. United States: Samuel Goldwyn Company & Touchstone Pictures.

Gollwitzer, P. M. (1999). Implementation intentions: Strong effects of simple plans. *American Psychologist*, *54*(7), 493–503.

Gollwitzer, P. M., & Bargh, J. A. (2005). Automaticity in goal pursuit. In A. J. Elliot & C. S. Dweck (Eds.), *Handbook of competence and motivation* (pp. 624–646). New York: Guilford Press.

Gollwitzer, P. M., Marquardt, M. K., Scherer, M., & Fujita, K. (2013). Identity-goal threats: Engaging in distinct compensatory efforts. *Social Psychological and Personality Science*, *4*(5), 555–562.

Gollwitzer, P. M., Sheeran, P., Michalski, V., & Seifert, A. E. (2009). When intentions go public: Does social reality widen the intention-behavior gap? *Psychological Science*, *20*(5), 612–618.

Gollwitzer, P. M., & Wicklund, R. A. (1985). Self-symbolizing and the neglect of others' perspectives. *Journal of Personality and Social Psychology*, *48*(3), 702–715.

Gollwitzer, P. M., Wicklund, R. A., & Hilton, J. L. (1982). Admission of failure and symbolic self-completion: Extending Lewinian theory. *Journal of Personality and Social Psychology*, *43*(2), 358–371.

Goode, W. J. (1960). A theory of role strain. *American Sociological Review*, *25*(4), 483–496.

Goodwin, S. A., Gubin, A., Fiske, S. T., & Yzerbyt, V. Y. (2000). Power can bias impression processes: Stereotyping subordinates by default and by design. *Group Processes & Intergroup Relations*, *3*(3), 227–256.

Gorchoff, S. M., John, O. P., & Helson, R. (2008). Contextualizing change in marital satisfaction during middle age: An 18-year longitudinal study. *Psychological Science*, *19*(11), 1194–1200.

Gordijn, E. H., Hindriks, I., Koomen, W., Dijksterhuis, A., & Van Knippenberg, A. (2004). Consequences of stereotype suppression and internal suppression motivation: A self-regulation approach. *Personality and Social Psychology Bulletin*, *30*(2), 212–224.

Gordon, R. A. (1996). Impact of ingratiation on judgments and evaluations: A meta-analytic investigation. *Journal of Personality and Social Psychology*, *71*(1), 54–70.

Gorman, B. J. (1999). Facilitated communication: Rejected in science, accepted in court—A case study and analysis of the use of FC evidence under *Frye* and *Daubert*. *Behavioral Sciences & the Law*, *17*(4), 517–541.

Gosling, S. D., Ko, S. J., Mannarelli, T., & Morris, M. E. (2002). A room with a cue: Personality judgments based on offices and bedrooms. *Journal of Personality and Social Psychology*, *82*(3), 379–398.

Gottlieb, J., & Carver, C. S. (1980). Anticipation of future interaction and the bystander effect. *Journal of Experimental Social Psychology*, *16*(3), 253–260.

Gottman, J. M. (1993). The roles of conflict engagement, escalation, and avoidance in marital interaction: A longitudinal view of five types of couples. *Journal of Consulting and Clinical Psychology*, *61*(1), 6–15.

Gottman, J. M., & Levenson, R. W. (2000). The timing of divorce: Predicting when a couple will divorce over a 14-year period. *Journal of Marriage and Family*, *62*(3), 737–745.

Grabe, S., Ward, L. M., & Hyde, J. S. (2008). The role of the media in body image concerns among women: A meta-analysis of experimental and correlational studies. *Psychological Bulletin*, *134*(3), 460–476.

Graddy, K. (1997). Do fast-food chains price discriminate on the race and income characteristics of an area? *Journal of Business & Economic Statistics, 15*(4), 391–401.

Grafman, J., Schwab, K., Warden, D., Pridgen, A., Brown, H. R., & Salazar, A. M. (1996). Frontal lobe injuries, violence, and aggression: A report of the Vietnam Head Injury Study. *Neurology, 46*(5), 1231–1238.

Graham, J., Haidt, J., & Nosek, B. A. (2009). Liberals and conservatives rely on different sets of moral foundations. *Journal of Personality and Social Psychology, 96*(5), 1029–1046.

Graham, S., & Lowery, B. S. (2004). Priming unconscious racial stereotypes about adolescent offenders. *Law and Human Behavior, 28*(5), 483–504.

Grant, A. M., & Gino, F. (2010). A little thanks goes a long way: Explaining why gratitude expressions motivate prosocial behavior. *Journal of Personality and Social Psychology, 98*(6), 946–955.

Graziano, W. G., Habashi, M. M., Sheese, B. E., & Tobin, R. M. (2007). Agreeableness, empathy, and helping: A person × situation perspective. *Journal of Personality and Social Psychology, 93*(4), 583–599.

Green, A. H. (1998). Factors contributing to the generational transmission of child maltreatment. *Journal of the American Academy of Child & Adolescent Psychiatry, 37*(12), 1334–1336.

Green, E. G. T., Staerkle, C., & Sears, D. O. (2006). Symbolic racism and whites' attitudes towards punitive and preventive crime policies. *Law and Human Behavior, 30*(4), 435–454.

Green, J. D., & Campbell, W. K. (2000). Attachment and exploration in adults: Chronic and contextual accessibility. *Personality and Social Psychology Bulletin, 26*(4), 452–461.

Green, M. C., Hilken, J., Friedman, H., Grossman, K., Gasiewskj, J., Adler, R., & Sabini, J. (2005). Communication via instant messenger: Short- and long-term effects. *Journal of Applied Social Psychology, 35*(3), 445–462.

Green, M. C., & Sabini, J. (2006). Gender, socioeconomic status, age, and jealousy: Emotional responses to infidelity in a national sample. *Emotion, 6*(2), 330–334.

Greenberg, J., & Arndt, J. (2012). Terror management theory. In P. A. M. Van Lange, A. Kruglanski, & E. T. Higgins (Eds.), *Handbook of theories of social psychology* (Vol. 1, pp. 398–415). London: Sage.

Greenberg, J., Landau, M. J., Kosloff, S., Soenke, M., & Solomon, S. (2009). How our means for feeling transcendent of death foster prejudice, stereotyping, and intergroup conflict. In T. D. Nelson (Ed.), *Handbook of Prejudice, Stereotyping, and Discrimination* (2nd ed.). New York: Psychology Press.

Greenberg, J., Porteus, J., Simon, L., Pyszczynski, T., & Solomon, S. (1995). Evidence of a terror management function of cultural icons: The effects of mortality salience on the inappropriate use of cherished cultural symbols. *Personality and Social Psychology Bulletin, 21*(11), 1221–1228.

Greenberg, J., & Pyszczynski, T. (1985a). Compensatory self-inflation: A response to the threat to self-regard of public failure. *Journal of Personality and Social Psychology, 49*(1), 273–280.

Greenberg, J., & Pyszczynski, T. (1985b). The effect of an overheard ethnic slur on evaluations of the target: How to spread a social disease. *Journal of Experimental Social Psychology, 21*(1), 61–72.

Greenberg, J., Pyszczynski, T., & Paisley, C. (1984). Effect of extrinsic incentives on use of test anxiety as an anticipatory attributional defense: Playing it cool when the stakes are high. *Journal of Personality and Social Psychology, 47*(5), 1136–1145.

Greenberg, J., Pyszczynski, T., & Solomon, S. (1986). The causes and consequences of a need for self-esteem: A terror management theory. In R. F. Baumeister (Ed.), *Public self and private self* (pp. 189–212). New York: Springer-Verlag.

Greenberg, J., Pyszczynski, T., Solomon, S., Rosenblatt, A., Veeder, M., Kirkland, S., & Lyon, D. (1990). Evidence for terror management theory II: The effects of mortality salience on reactions to those who threaten or bolster the cultural worldview. *Journal of Personality and Social Psychology, 58*(2), 308–318.

Greenberg, J., & Rosenfield, D. (1979). Whites' ethnocentrism and their attributions for the behavior of blacks: A motivational bias. *Journal of Personality, 47*(4), 643–657.

Greenberg, J., Simon, L., Solomon, S., Chatel, D., & Pyszczynski, T. (1992). Terror management and tolerance: Does mortality salience always intensify negative reactions to others who threaten one's cultural worldview? *Journal of Personality and Social Psychology, 63*(2), 212–220.

Greenberg, J., Solomon, S., & Arndt, J. (2008). A basic but uniquely human motivation: Terror management. In J. Y. Shah & W. L. Gardner (Eds.), *Handbook of motivation science* (pp. 114–134). New York: Guilford Press.

Greenberg, J., Solomon, S., Pyszczynski, T., Rosenblatt, A., Burling, J., Lyon, D., & Pinel, E. (1992). Why do people need self-esteem? Converging evidence that self-esteem serves an anxiety-buffering function. *Journal of Personality and Social Psychology, 63*(6), 913–922.

Greenhut R., Joffe, C. H., Rollins, J. (Producers), & Allen, W. (Writer & Director). *Husbands and wives* (1992). United States: TriStar Pictures.

Greenwald, A. G. (1968). Cognitive learning, cognitive response to persuasion, and attitude change. In A. G. Greenwald, T. C. Brock, and T. M. Ostrom (Eds.), *Psychological foundations of attitudes* (pp. 147–170). New York: Academic Press.

Greenwald, A. G., McGhee, D. E., & Schwartz, J. L. (1998). Measuring individual differences in implicit cognition: The implicit association test. *Journal of Personality and Social Psychology, 74*(6), 1464–1480.

Greenwald, A. G., Poehlman, T. A., Uhlmann, E. L., & Banaji, M. R. (2009). Understanding and using the Implicit Association Test: III. Meta-analysis of predictive validity. *Journal of Personality and Social Psychology, 97*(1), 17–41.

Greenwald, A. G., Smith, C. T., Sriram, N., Bar-Anan, Y., & Nosek, B. A. (2009). Implicit race attitudes predicted vote in the 2008 U.S. presidential election. *Analyses of Social Issues and Public Policy, 9*(1), 241–253.

Greenwald, A. G., Spangenberg, E. R., Pratkanis, A. R., & Eskenazi, J. (1991). Double-blind tests of subliminal self-help audiotapes. *Psychological Science, 2*(2), 119–122.

Gregory, R. L. (1966). *Eye and brain: The psychology of seeing.* New York: McGraw-Hill.

Gregory, R. L. (1968). Visual illusions. *Scientific American, 219*(5), 66–76.

Greitemeyer, T. (2011a). Effects of prosocial media on social behavior: When and why does media exposure affect helping and aggression? *Current Directions in Psychological Science, 20*(4), 251–255.

Greitemeyer, T. (2011b). Exposure to music with prosocial lyrics reduces aggression: First evidence and test of the underlying mechanism. *Journal of Experimental Social Psychology, 47*(1), 28–36.

Greitemeyer, T., & Osswald, S. (2009). Prosocial video games reduce aggressive cognitions. *Journal of Experimental Social Psychology, 45*(4), 896–900.

Greitemeyer, T., & Osswald, S. (2010). Effects of prosocial video games on prosocial behavior. *Journal of Personality and Social Psychology, 98*(2), 211–221.

Griffitt, W. (1970). Environmental effects on interpersonal affective behavior: Ambient effective temperature and attraction. *Journal of Personality and Social Psychology, 15*(3), 240–244.

Griffitt, W., & Veitch, R. (1974). Preacquaintance attitude similarity and attraction revisited: Ten days in a fall-out shelter. *Sociometry, 37*(2), 163–173. Stable URL: http://www.jstor.org/stable/2786373

Groothof, H. K., Dijkstra, P., & Barelds, D. H. (2009). Sex differences in jealousy: The case of Internet infidelity. *Journal of Social and Personal Relationships, 26*(8), 1119–1129.

Gross, A. E., & Crofton, C. (1977). What is good is beautiful. *Sociometry, 40*(1), 85–90. Stable URL: http://www.jstor.org/stable/3033549

Gross, J. J. (1998). Antecedent- and response-focused emotion regulation: Divergent consequences for experience, expression, and physiology. *Journal of Personality and Social Psychology, 74*(1), 224–237.

Gross, J. J. (2001). Emotion regulation in adulthood: Timing is everything. *Current Directions in Psychological Science, 10*(6), 214–219.

Gross, J. J. (2002). Emotion regulation: Affective, cognitive, and social consequences. *Psychophysiology, 39*(3), 281–291.

Guendelman, M. D., Cheryan, S., & Monin, B. (2011). Fitting in but getting fat: Identity threat and dietary choices among U.S. immigrant groups. *Psychological Science, 22*(7), 959–967.

Guerra, N. G., Nucci, L., & Huesmann, L. R. (1994). Moral cognition and childhood aggression. In L. R. Huesmann (Ed.), *Aggressive behavior: Current perspectives* (pp. 13–33). New York: Plenum Press.

Guinote, A. (2007). Power and goal pursuit. *Personality and Social Psychology Bulletin, 33*(8), 1076–1087.

Guinote, A., Willis, G. B., & Martellotta, C. (2010). Social power increases implicit prejudice. *Journal of Experimental Social Psychology, 46*(2), 299–307.

Gunn, G. R., & Wilson, A. E. (2011). Acknowledging the skeletons in our closet: The effect of group affirmation on collective guilt, collective shame, and reparatory attitudes. *Personality and Social Psychology Bulletin, 37*(11), 1474–1487.

Gunnell, J. J., & Ceci, S. J. (2010). When emotionality trumps reason: A study of individual processing style and juror bias. *Behavioral Sciences & the Law, 28*(6), 850–877.

Guyll, M., Matthews, K. A., & Bromberger, J. T. (2001). Discrimination and unfair treatment: Relationship to cardiovascular reactivity among African American and European American women. *Health Psychology, 20*(5), 315–325.

Gwinn, J. D., Judd, C. M., & Park, B. (2013). Less power = less human? Effects of power differentials on dehumanization. *Journal of Experimental Social Psychology, 49*(3), 464–470.

Hafer, C. L., & Bègue, L. (2005). Experimental research on just-world theory: Problems, developments, and future challenges. *Psychological Bulletin, 131*(1), 128–167.

Haidt, J., & Joseph, C. (2007). The moral mind: How 5 sets of innate moral intuitions guide the development of many culture-specific virtues, and perhaps even modules. In P. Carruthers, S. Laurence, & S. Stich (Eds.), *The innate mind* (Vol. 3, pp. 367–391). New York: Oxford University Press.

Haidt, J., & Kesebir, S. (2010). Morality. In S. T. Fiske, D. T. Gilbert, & G. Lindzey (Eds.), *Handbook of social psychology* (5th ed., pp. 797–832). Hoboken, NJ: Wiley.

Halberstadt, J., Sherman, S. J., & Sherman, J. W. (2011). Why Barack Obama is Black: A cognitive account of hypodescent. *Psychological Science, 22*(1), 29–33.

Hald, G. M., Malamuth, N. M., & Yuen, C. (2010). Pornography and attitudes supporting violence against women: Revisiting the relationship in nonexperimental studies. *Aggressive Behavior, 36*(1), 14–20.

Hall, H. V. (1999). *Lethal violence: A sourcebook on fatal domestic, acquaintance and stranger violence.* Boca Raton: CRC Press.

Hamberger, L. K., & Hastings, J. E. (1991). Personality correlates of men who batter and nonviolent men: Some continuities and discontinuities. *Journal of Family Violence, 6*(2), 131–147.

Hamill, R., Wilson, T. D., & Nisbett, R. E. (1980). Insensitivity to sample bias: Generalizing from atypical cases. *Journal of Personality and Social Psychology, 39*(4), 578–589.

Hamill, S. (ed.) (1996). *The erotic spirit: An anthology of poems of sensuality, love and longing.* Boston: Shambhala.

Hamilton, D. L., Driscoll, D. M., & Worth, L. T. (1989). Cognitive organization of impressions: Effects of incongruency in complex representations. *Journal of Personality and Social Psychology, 57*(6), 925–939.

Hamilton, D. L., Dugan, P. M., & Trolier, T. K. (1985). The formation of stereotypic beliefs: Further evidence for distinctiveness-based illusory correlations. *Journal of Personality and Social Psychology, 48*(1), 5–17.

Hamilton, D. L., & Sherman, J. W. (1994). Stereotypes. In J. R. S. Wyer & T. K. Srull (Eds.), *Handbook of social cognition* (2nd ed., Vol. 2, pp. 1–68). Hillsdale, NJ: Erlbaum.

Hamilton, D. L., & Sherman, S. J. (1989). Illusory correlations: Implications for stereotype theory and research. In D. Bar-Tal, C. F. Graumann, A. W. Kruglanski, & W. Stroebe (Eds.), *Stereotypes and prejudice: Changing conceptions* (pp. 59–82). New York: Springer-Verlag.

Hamilton, R., Hong, J., & Chernev, A. (2007). Perceptual focus effects in choice. *Journal of Consumer Research, 34*(2), 187–199. Stable URL: http://www.jstor.org/stable/10.1086/519147

Hamilton, W. D. (1964). The genetical evolution of social behaviour. II. *Journal of Theoretical Biology, 7*(1), 17–52.

Hamlin, J. K., & Wynn, K. (2011). Young infants prefer prosocial to antisocial others. *Cognitive Development, 26*(1), 30–39.

Hamlin, J. K., Wynn, K., & Bloom, P. (2007). Social evaluation by preverbal infants. *Nature, 450*(7169), 557–559.

Hamlin, J. K., Wynn, K., & Bloom, P. (2010). Three-month-olds show a negativity bias in social evaluation. *Developmental Science, 13*(6), 923–939.

Haney, C., Banks, C., & Zimbardo, P. (1973). Interpersonal dynamics in a simulated prison. *International Journal of Criminology and Penology, 1*(1), 69–97.

Hänze, M., & Berger, R. (2007). Cooperative learning, motivational effects, and student characteristics: An experimental study comparing cooperative learning and direct instruction in 12th grade physics classes. *Learning and Instruction, 17*(1), 29–41.

Hardin, G. (1968). The tragedy of the commons. *Science, 162*(3859), 1243–1248.

Harkins, S. G., & Petty, R. E. (1987). Information utility and the multiple source effect. *Journal of Personality and Social Psychology, 52*(2), 260–268.

Harkins, S. G., & Szymanski, K. (1988). Social loafing and self-evaluation with an objective standard. *Journal of Experimental Social Psychology, 24*(4), 354–365.

Harlow, H. F. (1959). Love in infant monkeys. *Scientific American, 200*(6), 68–86.

Harmon-Jones, E. (2003). Clarifying the emotive functions of asymmetrical frontal cortical activity. *Psychophysiology, 40*(6), 838–848.

Harmon-Jones, E., & Allen, J. J. B. (1998). Anger and frontal brain activity: EEG asymmetry consistent with approach motivation despite negative affective valence. *Journal of Personality and Social Psychology, 74*(5), 1310–1316.

Harmon-Jones, E., Brehm, J. W., Greenberg, J., Simon, L., & Nelson, D. E. (1996). Evidence that the production of aversive consequences is not necessary to create cognitive dissonance. *Journal of Personality and Social Psychology, 70*(1), 5–16.

Harmon-Jones, E., Harmon-Jones, C., & Amodio, D. M. (2012). A neuroscientific perspective on dissonance, guided by the action-based model. In B. Gawronski & F. Strack (Eds.), *Cognitive consistency: A fundamental principle in social cognition* (pp. 47–65). New York: Guilford Press.

Harmon-Jones, E., & Sigelman, J. (2001). State anger and prefrontal brain activity: Evidence that insult-related relative left-prefrontal activation is associated with experienced anger and aggression. *Journal of Personality and Social Psychology, 80*(5), 797–803.

Harmon-Jones, E., Simon, L., Greenberg, J., Pyszczynski, T., Solomon, S., & McGregor, H. (1997). Terror management theory and self-esteem: Evidence that increased self-esteem reduced mortality salience effects. *Journal of Personality and Social Psychology, 72*(1), 24–36.

Harris, C. R. (2000). Psychophysiological responses to imagined infidelity: The specific innate modular view of jealousy reconsidered. *Journal of Personality and Social Psychology, 78*(6), 1082–1091.

Harris, C. R. (2002). Sexual and romantic jealousy in heterosexual and homosexual adults. *Psychological Science, 13*(1), 7–12.

Harris, C. R. (2003). A review of sex differences in sexual jealousy, including self-report data, psychophysiological responses, interpersonal violence, and morbid jealousy. *Personality and Social Psychology Review, 7*(2), 102–128.

Harris, C. R., & Christenfeld, N. (1996). Gender, jealousy, and reason. *Psychological Science, 7*(6), 364–366.

Harris, L. T., & Fiske, S. T. (2006). Dehumanizing the lowest of the low: Neuroimaging responses to extreme out-groups. *Psychological Science, 17*(10), 847–853.

Harris, M. (1979). *Cultural materialism: The struggle for a science of culture.* New York: Random House.

Harris, M. B. (1974). Mediators between frustration and aggression in a field experiment. *Journal of Experimental Social Psychology, 10*(6), 561–571.

Harris, M. J., & Rosenthal, R. (1985). Mediation of interpersonal expectancy effects: 31 meta-analyses. *Psychological Bulletin, 97*(3), 363–386.

Harris, P. R., Mayle, K., Mabbott, L., & Napper, L. (2007). Self-affirmation reduces smokers' defensiveness to graphic on-pack cigarette warning labels. *Health Psychology, 26*(4), 437–446.

Harter, S. (1998). The development of self-representations. In W. Damon & N. Eisenberg (Eds.), *Handbook of child psychology* (5th ed., Vol. 3, pp. 553–617). Hoboken, NJ: Wiley.

Harvey, O. J., White, B. J., Hood, W. R., & Sherif, C. W. (1961). *Intergroup conflict and cooperation: The Robbers Cave experiment.* Norman, OK: University Book Exchange.

Harwood, J. (2009, January 7). John Harwood interviews Barack Obama. *The New York Times.* Retrieved from: http://www.nytimes.com/2009/01/07/us/politics/07text-harwood.html?pagewanted=all&_r=0

Hassett, J. M., Siebert, E. R., & Wallen, K. (2008). Sex differences in rhesus monkey toy preferences parallel those of children. *Hormones and Behavior, 54*(3), 359–364.

Hastie, R., & Kumar, P. A. (1979). Person memory: Personality traits as organizing principles in memory for behaviors. *Journal of Personality and Social Psychology, 37*(1), 25–38.

Hastorf, A. H., & Cantril, H. (1954). They saw a game: A case study. *Journal of Abnormal and Social Psychology, 49*(1), 129–134.

Hatfield, E. (1988). Passionate and companionate love. In R. Sternberg & M. L. Barnes (Eds.), *The psychology of love* (pp. 191–217). New Haven: Yale University Press.

Hatfield, E., Cacioppo, J. T., & Rapson, R. L. (1993). Emotional contagion. *Current Directions in Psychological Science, 2*(3), 96–99. Stable URL: http://www.jstor.org/stable/20182211

Hatfield, E., & Rapson, R. L. (1993). *Love, sex, and intimacy: Their psychology, biology, and history.* New York: HarperCollins College Publishers.

Hatfield, E., & Sprecher, S. (1986). Measuring passionate love in intimate relationships. *Journal of Adolescence, 9*(4), 383–410.

Hatfield, E., & Walster, G. W. (1978). *A new look at love.* Reading, MA: Addison-Wesley.

Hatfield, E., Walster, G. W., & Berscheid, E. (1978). *Equity: Theory and research.* Boston: Allyn & Bacon.

Hawkley, L. C., Thisted, R. A., & Cacioppo, J. T. (2009). Loneliness predicts reduced physical activity: Cross-sectional & longitudinal analyses. *Health Psychology, 28*(3), 354–363.

Hayes, J., Schimel, J., Arndt, J., & Faucher, E. H. (2010) A theoretical and empirical review of the death-thought accessibility concept in terror management research. *Psychological Bulletin, 136*(5), 699–739.

Hayes, J., Schimel, J., Faucher, E. H., & Williams, T. J. (2008). Evidence for the DTA hypothesis II: Threatening self-esteem increases death-thought accessibility. *Journal of Experimental Social Psychology, 44*(3), 600–613.

Hayes, J., Schimel, J., & Williams, T. J. (2008). Fighting death with death: The buffering effects of learning that worldview violators have died. *Psychological Science, 19*(5), 501–507.

Hazan, C., & Shaver, P. (1987). Romantic love conceptualized as an attachment process. *Journal of Personality and Social Psychology, 52*(3), 511–524.

Heatherton, T. F., & Baumeister, R. F. (1991). Binge eating as escape from self-awareness. *Psychological Bulletin, 110*(1), 86–108.

Hebl, M. R., & Heatherton, T. F. (1998). The stigma of obesity in women: The difference is black and white. *Personality and Social Psychology Bulletin, 24*(4), 417–426.

Hecht, M. L., Marston, P. J., & Larkey, L. K. (1994). Love ways and relationship quality in heterosexual relationships. *Journal of Social and Personal Relationships*, 11(1), 25–43.

Heflick, N. A., & Goldenberg, J. L. (2009). Objectifying Sarah Palin: Evidence that objectification causes women to be perceived as less competent and less fully human. *Journal of Experimental Social Psychology*, 45(3), 598–601.

Heflick, N. A., Goldenberg, J. L., Cooper, D. P., & Puvia, E. (2011). From women to objects: Appearance focus, target gender, and perceptions of warmth, morality and competence. *Journal of Experimental Social Psychology*, 47(3), 572–581.

Heider, F. (1946). Attitudes and cognitive organisations. *Journal of Psychology*, 21, 107–112.

Heider, F. (1958). *The psychology of interpersonal relations*. New York: Wiley.

Heider, F., & Simmel, M. (1944). An experimental study of apparent behavior. *American Journal of Psychology*, 57(2), 243–259.

Heine, S. J., Proulx, T., & Vohs, K. D. (2006). The meaning maintenance model: On the coherence of social motivations. *Personality and Social Psychology Review*, 10(2), 88–110.

Heine, S. J., & Renshaw, K. (2002). Interjudge agreement, self-enhancement, and liking: Cross-cultural divergences. *Personality and Social Psychology Bulletin*, 28(5), 578–587.

Hendrick, C., & Hendrick, S. (1986). A theory and method of love. *Journal of Personality and Social Psychology*, 50(2), 392–402.

Hendrick, C., Hendrick, S. S., & Reich, D. A. (2006). The brief sexual attitudes scale. *Journal of Sex Research*, 43(1), 76–86.

Henggeler, S. W., Schoenwald, S. K., Borduin, C. M., Rowland, M. D., & Cunningham, P. B. (1998). *Multisystemic treatment of antisocial behavior in children and adolescents: Treatment manuals for practitioners*. New York: Guilford Press.

Henrich, J., Heine, S. J., & Norenzayan, A. (2010). The weirdest people in the world. *Behavioral and Brain Sciences*, 33(2–3), 61–83.

Henrich, N., & Henrich, J. (2007). *Why humans cooperate: A cultural and evolutionary explanation*. Oxford: Oxford University Press.

Henry, P. B., & Miller, C. (2009). Institutions vs. policies: A tale of two islands. NBER Working Paper 14604. *American Economic Review*, 99(2), 261–267. Retrieved from http://www.nber.org/papers/w14604

Henry, P. J. (2009). Low-status compensation: A theory for understanding the role of status in cultures of honor. *Journal of Personality and Social Psychology*, 97(3), 451–466.

Hepworth, J. T., & West, S. G. (1988). Lynchings and the economy: A time-series reanalysis of Hovland and Sears (1940). *Journal of Personality and Social Psychology*, 55(2), 239–247.

Herold, E. S. (1981). Contraceptive embarrassment and contraceptive behavior among young single women. *Journal of Youth and Adolescence*, 10(3), 233–242.

Herr, P. M. (1986). Consequences of priming: Judgment and behavior. *Journal of Personality and Social Psychology*, 51(6), 1106–1115.

Herrett-Skjellum, J., & Allen, M. (1996). Television programming and sex stereotyping: A meta-analysis. *Communication Yearbook*, 19, 157–186.

Heslin, P. A., & Vandewalle, D. (2008). Managers' implicit assumptions about personnel. *Current Directions in Psychological Science*, 17(3), 219–223.

Heslov, G., Affleck, B., Clooney, G. (Producers), & Affleck, B. (Director) (2012). *Argo* [Motion picture]. United States: Warner Bros. & Smokehouse Pictures, in association with G. K. Films.

Hewstone, M. (1990). The 'ultimate attribution error'? A review of the literature on intergroup causal attribution. *European Journal of Social Psychology*, 20(4), 311–335.

Hicklin, A. (2011, January 9). Edie Windsor and Thea Spyer: When Edie met Thea. *Out*. Retrieved from http://www.out.com/entertainment/2011/01/09/edie-windsor-and-thea-spyer-when-edie-met-thea?page=0,1

Higgins, E. T. (1989). Self-discrepancy theory: What patterns of self-beliefs cause people to suffer? In L. Berkowitz (Ed.), *Advances in experimental social psychology* (Vol. 22, pp. 93–136). New York: Academic Press.

Higgins, E. T. (1996). Knowledge activation: Accessibility, applicability, and salience. In E. T. Higgins & A. W. Kruglanski, (Eds.), *Social psychology: Handbook of basic principles* (pp. 133–168). New York: Guilford Press.

Higgins, E. T. (2012). Accessibility theory. In P. A. M. Van Lange, A. W. Kruglanski, & E. T. Higgins (Eds.), *Handbook of theories of social psychology* (Vol. 1, pp. 75–96). Thousand Oaks, CA: Sage.

Higgins, E. T., & Brendl, C. M. (1995). Accessibility and applicability: Some "activation rules" influencing judgment. *Journal of Experimental Social Psychology*, 31(3), 218–243.

Higgins, E. T., King, G. A., & Mavin, G. H. (1982). Individual construct accessibility and subjective impressions and recall. *Journal of Personality and Social Psychology*, 43(1), 35–47.

Higgins, E. T., Rhodewalt, F., & Zanna, M. P. (1979). Dissonance motivation: Its nature, persistence, and reinstatement. *Journal of Experimental Social Psychology*, 15(1), 16–34.

Higgins, E. T., Rholes, W. S., & Jones, C. R. (1977). Category accessibility and impression formation. *Journal of Experimental Social Psychology*, 13(2), 141–154.

High school classmates say gunman was bullied (2007, April 19). NBC, msnbc.com and News Services. Retrieved from http://www.nbcnews.com/id/18169776/

Higley, J. D., Linnoila, M., & Suomi, S. J. (1994). Ethological contributions. In M. Hersen, R. T. Ammennan & L. A. Sisson (Eds.), *Handbook of aggressive and destructive behavior in psychiatric patients* (pp. 17–32). New York: Plenum Press.

Hill, J., & Nathan, R. (2008). Childhood antecedents of serious violence in adult male offenders. *Aggressive Behavior*, 34(3), 329–338.

Hilton, J. L., & Darley, J. M. (1985). Constructing other persons: A limit on the effect. *Journal of Experimental Social Psychology*, 21(1), 1–18.

Hilton, J. L., & Von Hippel, W. (1996). Stereotypes. *Annual Review of Psychology*, 47(1), 237–271.

Hinsz, V. B. (1989). Facial resemblance in engaged and married couples. *Journal of Social and Personal Relationships*, 6(2), 223–229.

Hirschberger, G., Ein-Dor, T., & Almakias, S. (2008). The self-protective altruist: Terror management and the ambivalent nature of prosocial behavior. *Personality and Social Psychology Bulletin*, 34(5), 666–678.

Hirschberger, G., Florian, V., & Mikulincer, M. (2005). Fear and compassion: A terror management analysis of emotional reactions to physical disability. *Rehabilitation Psychology*, 50(3), 246–257.

Hirsh, J. B., Galinsky, A. D., & Zhong, C. B. (2011). Drunk, powerful, and in the dark: How general processes of disinhibition produce both prosocial and antisocial behavior. *Perspectives on Psychological Science*, 6(5), 415–427.

Hitsch, G. J., Hortaçsu, A., & Ariely, D. (2010). What makes you click?—Mate preferences in online dating. *Quantitative Marketing and Economics*, 8(4), 393–427.

Ho, A. K., Sidanius, J., Levin, D. T., & Banaji, M. R. (2011). Evidence for hypodescent and racial hierarchy in the categorization and perception of biracial individuals. *Journal of Personality and Social Psychology*, 100(3), 492–506.

Hobson, P. (2004). Symbol minded. *Nature*, 431(7005), 127–128.

Hodges, B. H., & Geyer, A. L. (2006). A nonconformist account of the Asch experiments: Values, pragmatics, and moral dilemmas. *Personality and Social Psychology Review*, 10(1), 2–19.

Hodson, G., Dovidio, J. F., & Gaertner, S. L. (2002). Processes in racial discrimination: Differential weighting of conflicting information. *Personality and Social Psychology Bulletin*, 28(4), 460–471.

Hoffman, E., McCabe, K. A., & Smith, V. L. (1998). Behavioral foundations of reciprocity: Experimental economics and evolutionary psychology. *Economic Inquiry*, 36(3), 335–352.

Hoffman, M. L. (1981). Is altruism part of human nature? *Journal of Personality and Social Psychology*, 40(1), 121–137.

Hofling, C. K., Brotzman, E., Dalrymple, S., Graves, N., & Pierce, C. M. (1966). An experimental study in nurse-physician relationships. *Journal of Nervous and Mental Disease*, 143(2), 171–180.

Hofmann, W., Gawronski, B., Gschwendner, T., Le, H., & Schmitt, M. (2005). A meta-analysis on the correlation between the implicit association test and explicit self-report measures. *Personality and Social Psychology Bulletin*, 31(10), 1369–1385.

Hofstede, G., & Bond, M. H. (1984). Hofstede's culture dimensions: An independent validation using Rokeach's value survey. *Journal of Cross-Cultural Psychology*, 15(4), 417–433.

Hofstede, G., Hofstede, G. J., & Minkov, M. (2010). *Cultures and organizations: Software of the mind* (3rd ed). New York: McGraw-Hill.

Hogg, M. A. (2006). Social identity theory. In P. J. Burke (Ed.), *Contemporary social psychological theories* (pp. 111–136). Palo Alto: Stanford University Press.

Hogg, M. A. (2007). Uncertainty-identity theory. In M. P. Zanna (Ed.), *Advances in experimental social psychology* (Vol. 39, pp. 69–126). San Diego: Academic Press.

Hogg, M. A. (2010). Influence and leadership. In S. T. Fiske, D. T. Gilbert & Lindzey, G. (Eds.), *Handbook of Social Psychology* (5th ed., Vol. 2, pp. 1166–1207). Hoboken, NJ: Wiley.

Hogg, M. A., Sherman, D. K., Dierselhuis, J., Maitner, A. T., & Moffitt, G. (2007). Uncertainty, entitativity, and group identification. *Journal of Experimental Social Psychology*, 43(1), 135–142.

Holbrook, M. B. (1993). Nostalgia and consumption preferences: Some emerging patterns of consumer tastes. *Journal of Consumer Research*, 20(2), 245–256. Stable URL: http://www.jstor.org/stable/2489272

Hollis-Walker, L., & Colosimo, K. (2011). Mindfulness, self-compassion, and happiness in nonmeditators: A theoretical and empirical examination. *Personality and Individual Differences*, 50(2), 222–227.

Holm, O. (1983). Four factors affecting perceived aggressiveness. *Journal of Psychology*, 114(2), 227–234.

Hong, Y. Y., Chiu, C., & Dweck, C. S. (1995). Implicit theories of intelligence: Reconsidering the role of confidence in achievement motivation. In M. H. Kernis (Ed.), *Efficacy, agency, and self-esteem. Plenum Series in Social/Clinical Psychology* (pp. 197–216). New York: Plenum Press.

Hong, Y.Y., Chiu, C., Dweck, C. S., Lin, D., & Wan, W. (1999) Implicit theories, attributions, and coping: A meaning system approach. *Journal of Personality and Social Psychology*, 77(3), 588–599.

Hong, Y. Y., Chiu, C. Y., & Kung, T. M. (1997). Bringing culture out in front: Effects of cultural meaning system activation on social cognition. In K. Leung, Y. Kashima, U. Kim, S. Yamaguchi, & Y. Kashima (Eds.), *Progress in Asian social psychology* (Vol. 1, pp. 135–146). Singapore: Wiley.

Hops, H., Davis, B., Leve, C., & Sheeber, L. (2003). Cross-generational transmission of aggressive parent behavior: A prospective, mediational examination. *Journal of Abnormal Child Psychology*, 31(2), 161–169.

Horney, K. (1937). *The neurotic personality of our time.* New York: W. W. Norton.

Horton, D., & Wohl, R. R. (1956). Mass communication and para-social interaction: Observations on intimacy at a distance. *Psychiatry*, 19(3), 215–229.

Horton, R. (1967). African traditional thought and Western science. *Africa*, 37, 155–187. Stable URL: http://www.jstor.org/stable/1158253

Hotaling, G. T., & Sugarman, D. B. (1990). A risk marker analysis of assaulted wives. *Journal of Family Violence*, 5(1), 1–13.

Houben, K., & Wiers, R. W. (2007). Personalizing the alcohol-IAT with individualized stimuli: Relationship with drinking behavior and drinking-related problems. *Addictive Behaviors*, 32(12), 2852–2864.

Houlette, M. A., Gaertner, S. L., Johnson, K. M., Banker, B. S., Riek, B. M., & Dovidio, J. F. (2004). Developing a more inclusive social identity: An elementary school intervention. *Journal of Social Issues*, 60(1), 35–55.

House, J. S., Landis, K. R., & Umberson, D. (1988). Social relationships and health. *Science*, 241(4865), 540–545.

Houts, R. M., Robins, E., & Huston, T. L. (1996). Compatibility and the development of premarital relationships. *Journal of Marriage and the Family*, 58(1), 7–20. Stable URL: http://www.jstor.org/stable/353373

Hovland, C. I., Harvey, O. J., & Sherif, M. (1957). Assimilation and contrast effects in reactions to communication and attitude change. *Journal of Abnormal and Social Psychology*, 55(2), 244–252.

Hovland, C. I., Lumsdain, A. A., & Sheffield, F. D. (1949). *Experiments in mass communication.* Princeton, NJ: Princeton University Press.

Hovland, C. I., & Sears, R. R. (1940). Minor studies of aggression: VI. Correlation of lynchings with economic indices. *Journal of Psychology*, 9(2), 301–310.

Hovland, C. I., & Weiss, W. (1951). The influence of source credibility on communication effectiveness. *Public Opinion Quarterly*, 15(4), 635–650.

Hudley, C., & Graham, S. (1993). An attributional intervention to reduce peer-directed aggression among African-American boys. *Child Development*, 64(1), 124–138.

Huesmann, L. R. (1988). An information processing model for the development of aggression. *Aggressive Behavior*, 14(1), 13–24.

Huesmann, L. R., Dubow, E. F., & Boxer, P. (2009). Continuity of aggression from childhood to early adulthood as a predictor of life outcomes: Implications for the adolescent-limited and life-course-persistent models. *Aggressive Behavior*, 35(2), 136–149.

Huesmann, L. R., & Eron, L. D. (1984). Cognitive processes and the persistence of aggressive behavior. *Aggressive Behavior*, 10(3), 243–251.

Huesmann, L. R., Eron, L. D., Lefkowitz, M. M., & Walder, L. O. (1984). Stability of aggression over time and generations. *Developmental Psychology*, 20(6), 1120–1134.

Huesmann, L. R., Lagerspetz, K., & Eron, L. D. (1984). Intervening variables in the TV violence-aggression relation: Evidence from two countries. *Developmental Psychology*, 20(5), 746–775.

Huesmann, L. R., Moise-Titus, J., Podolski, C. L., & Eron, L. D. (2003). Longitudinal relations between children's exposure to TV violence and their aggressive and violent behavior in young adulthood: 1977–1992. *Developmental Psychology*, 39(2), 201–221.

Hugenberg, K., & Bodenhausen, G. V. (2003). Facing prejudice: Implicit prejudice and the perception of facial threat. *Psychological Science*, 14(6), 640–643.

Hughes, R. (1929). *A high wind in Jamaica.* London: Chatto & Windus.

Hull, J. G., Levenson, R. W., Young, R. D., & Sher, K. J. (1983). Self-awareness-reducing effects of alcohol consumption. *Journal of Personality and Social Psychology*, 44(3), 461–473.

Hull, J. G., & Slone, L. B. (2004). Alcohol and self-regulation. In R. F. Baumeister & K. D. Vohs (Eds.), *Handbook of self-regulation: Research, theory, and applications* (pp. 466–491). New York: Guilford Press.

Hull, J. G., & Young, R. D. (1983). Self-consciousness, self-esteem, and success–failure as determinants of alcohol consumption in male social drinkers. *Journal of Personality and Social Psychology*, 44(6), 1097–1109.

Hull, J. G., Young, R. D., & Jouriles, E. (1986). Applications of the self-awareness model of alcohol consumption: Predicting patterns of use and abuse. *Journal of Personality and Social Psychology*, 51(4), 790–796.

Huston, T. L., Caughlin, J. P., Houts, R. M., Smith, S. E., & George, L. J. (2001). The connubial crucible: Newlywed years as predictors of marital delight, distress, and divorce. *Journal of Personality and Social Psychology*, 80(2), 237–252.

Huston, T. L., & Chorost, A. F. (1994). Behavioral buffers on the effect of negativity on marital satisfaction: A longitudinal study. *Personal Relationships*, 1(3), 223–239.

Hyde, J. S. (2005). The gender similarities hypothesis. *American Psychologist*, 60(6), 581–592.

Hynan, D. J., & Grush, J. E. (1986). Effects of impulsivity, depression, provocation, and time on aggressive behavior. *Journal of Research in Personality*, 20(2), 158–171.

Iacoboni, M. (2009). Imitation, empathy, and mirror neurons. *Annual Review of Psychology*, 60, 653–670.

Ichiyama, M. A. (1993). The reflected appraisal process in small-group interaction. *Social Psychology Quarterly*, 56(2), 87–99.

Idema, W. L. (Ed. and Trans.) (2010). *The butterfly lovers: The Legend of Liang Shanbo and Zhu Yingtai: Four versions, with related texts.* Indianapolis: Hackett Publishing Company.

Igarashi, T., Kashima, Y., Kashima, E. S., Farsides, T., Kim, U., Strack, F., . . . & Yuki, M. (2008). Culture, trust, and social networks. *Asian Journal of Social Psychology*, 11(1), 88–101.

Iida, M., Seidman, G., Shrout, P. E., Fujita, K., & Bolger, N. (2008). Modeling support provision in intimate relationships. *Journal of Personality and Social Psychology*, 94(3), 460–478.

Impett, E. A., Strachman, A., Finkel, E. J., & Gable, S. L. (2008). Maintaining sexual desire in intimate relationships: The importance of approach goals. *Journal of Personality and Social Psychology*, 94(5), 808–823.

Inzlicht, M., & Gutsell, J. N. (2007). Running on empty: Neural signals for self-control failure. *Psychological Science*, 18(11), 933–937.

Inzlicht, M., Kaiser, C. R., & Major, B. (2008). The face of chauvinism: How prejudice expectations shape perceptions of facial affect. *Journal of Experimental Social Psychology*, 44(3), 758–766.

Inzlicht, M., McKay, L., & Aronson, J. (2006). Stigma as ego depletion: How being the target of prejudice affects self-control. *Psychological Science*, 17(3), 262–269.

Inzlicht, M., & Schmeichel, B. J. (2012). What is ego depletion? Toward a mechanistic revision of the resource model of self-control. *Perspectives on Psychological Science*, 7(5), 450–463.

Ip, G. W. M., Chiu, C. Y., & Wan, C. (2006). Birds of a feather and birds flocking together: Physical versus behavioral cues may lead to trait- versus goal-based group perception. *Journal of Personality and Social Psychology*, 90(3), 368–381.

Ipsos/Reuters (April 25, 2011). Ipsos global @dvisory: Supreme being(s), the afterlife and evolution. Retrieved from http://www.ipsos-na.com/download/pr.aspx?id=10670

Isen, A. M. (1970). Success, failure, attention, and reaction to others: The warm glow of success. *Journal of Personality and Social Psychology*, 15(4), 294–301.

Isen, A. M. (1987). Positive affect, cognitive processes, and social behavior. In L. Berkowitz (Ed.), *Advances in experimental social psychology* (Vol. 20, pp. 203–253). San Diego: Academic Press.

Isen, A. M., Clark, M., & Schwartz, M. F. (1976). Duration of the effect of good mood on helping: "Footprints on the sands of time." *Journal of Personality and Social Psychology*, 34(3), 385–393.

Isen, A. M., Daubman, K. A., & Nowicki, G. P. (1987). Positive affect facilitates creative problem solving. *Journal of Personality and Social Psychology*, 52(6), 1122–1131.

Isen, A. M., & Levin, P. F. (1972). Effect of feeling good on helping: Cookies and kindness. *Journal of Personality and Social Psychology*, 21(3), 384–388.

Isen, A. M., Shalker, T. E., Clark, M., & Karp, L. (1978). Affect, accessibility of material in memory, and behavior: A cognitive loop? *Journal of Personality and Social Psychology*, 36(1), 1–12.

Isenberg, D. J. (1986). Group polarization: A critical review and meta-analysis. *Journal of Personality and Social Psychology*, 50(6), 1141–1151.

Ismail, I., Martens, A., Landau, M. J., Greenberg, J., & Weise, D. R. (2012). Exploring the effects of the naturalistic fallacy: Evidence that genetic explanations increase the acceptability of killing and male promiscuity. *Journal of Applied Social Psychology*, 42(3), 735–750.

Ito, T. A., & Bartholow, B. D. (2009). The neural correlates of race. *Trends in Cognitive Sciences*, 13(12), 524–531.

Ito, T. A., Larsen, J. T., Smith, N. K., & Cacioppo, J. T. (1998). Negative information weighs more heavily on the brain: The negativity bias in evaluative categorizations. *Journal of Personality and Social Psychology*, 75(4), 887–900.

Ito, T. A., Miller, N., & Pollock, V. E. (1996). Alcohol and aggression: A meta-analysis on the moderating effects of inhibitory cues, triggering events, and self-focused attention. *Psychological Bulletin, 120*(1), 60–82.

Iyer, A., Leach, C. W., & Crosby, F. J. (2003). White guilt and racial compensation: The benefits and limits of self-focus. *Personality and Social Psychology Bulletin, 29*(1), 117–129.

Iyer, A., Schmader, T., & Lickel, B. (2007). Why individuals protest the perceived transgressions of their country: The role of anger, shame, and guilt. *Personality and Social Psychology Bulletin, 33*(3), 572–587.

Izard, C. E. (1977). *Human emotions.* New York: Plenum Press.

Jackson, J. M., & Harkins, S. G. (1985). Equity in effort: An explanation of the social loafing effect. *Journal of Personality and Social Psychology, 49*(5), 1199–1206.

Jackson, L. M., & Esses, V. M. (1997). Of scripture and ascription: The relation between religious fundamentalism and intergroup helping. *Personality and Social Psychology Bulletin, 23*(8), 893–906.

Jackson, T., Chen, H., Guo, C., & Gao, X. (2006). Stories we love by: Conceptions of love among couples from the People's Republic of China and the United States. *Journal of Cross-Cultural Psychology, 37*(4), 446–464.

Jacobs, R. C., & Campbell, D. T. (1961). The perpetuation of an arbitrary tradition through several generations of a laboratory microculture. *Journal of Abnormal and Social Psychology, 62*(3), 649–658.

Jacobson, N. S., Follette, W. C., & McDonald, D. W. (1982). Reactivity to positive and negative behavior in distressed and nondistressed married couples. *Journal of Consulting and Clinical Psychology, 50*(5), 706–714.

Jacobson, W. [Host] (2012, September 27). "Killing is the solution," gang member tells Walter Jacobson. CBS Chicago. Retrieved from http://chicago.cbslocal.com/2012/09/27/killing-is-the-solution-gang-member-tells-walter-jacobson/

James, W. (1890). *The principles of psychology.* New York: Henry Holt and Company.

James, W. (1906). The moral equivalent of war. Address to Stanford University. Retrieved from http://www.constitution.org/wj/meow.htm

Jamieson, D. W., & Zanna, M. P. (1989). Need for structure in attitude formation and expression. In A. R. Pratkanis, S. J. Breckler, & A. G. Greenwald (Eds.), *Attitude structure and function* (pp. 383–406). Hillsdale, NJ: Erlbaum.

Jamieson, J. P., & Harkins, S. G. (2007). Mere effort and stereotype threat performance effects. *Journal of Personality and Social Psychology, 93*(4), 544–564.

Jamieson, J. P., Mendes, W. B., Blackstock, E., & Schmader, T. (2010). Turning the knots in your stomach into bows: Reappraising arousal improves performance on the GRE. *Journal of Experimental Social Psychology, 46*(1), 208–212.

Janis, I. L. (1982). *Groupthink: Psychological studies of policy decisions and fiascoes.* Boston: Houghton Mifflin.

Janis, I. L., & Feshbach, S. (1953). Effects of fear-arousing communications. *Journal of Abnormal and Social Psychology, 48*(1), 78–92.

Janis, I. L., Kaye, D., & Kirschner, P. (1965). Facilitating effects of "eating-while-reading" on responsiveness to persuasive communications. *Journal of Personality and Social Psychology, 1*(2), 181–186.

Jankowiak, W. R., & Fischer, E. F. (1992). A cross-cultural perspective on romantic love. *Ethnology, 31*(2), 149–155. Stable URL: http://www.jstor.org/stable/3773618

Janoff-Bulman, R., & Yopyk, D. J. (2004). Random outcomes and valued commitments: Existential dilemmas and the paradox of meaning. In J. Greenberg, S. L. Koole, & T. Pyszczynski (Eds.), *Handbook of experimental existential psychology* (pp. 122–138). New York: Guilford Press.

Jasienska, G., Lipson, S. F., Ellison, P. T., Thune, I., & Ziomkiewicz, A. (2006). Symmetrical women have higher potential fertility. *Evolution and Human Behavior, 27*(5), 390–400.

Jaynes, J. (1976). *The origin of consciousness in the breakdown of the bicameral mind.* Boston: Houghton Mifflin.

Jensen-Campbell, L. A., Graziano, W. G., & West, S. G. (1995). Dominance, prosocial orientation, and female preferences: Do nice guys really finish last? *Journal of Personality and Social Psychology, 68*(3), 427–440.

Jessop, D. C., & Wade, J. (2008). Fear appeals and binge drinking: A terror management theory perspective. *British Journal of Health Psychology, 13*(4), 773–788.

Ji, L. J., Zhang, Z., & Nisbett, R. E. (2004). Is it culture or is it language? Examination of language effects in cross-cultural research on categorization. *Journal of Personality and Social Psychology, 87*(1), 57–65.

Jinks, D., Cohen, B. (Producers), & Van Sant, G. (Director) (2008). *Milk* [Motion picture]. United States: Focus Features, Jinks/Cohen Company, Groundswell Productions & Cinema Vehicle Services, in association with Axon Films.

Job, V., Dweck, C., & Walton, G. (2010). Ego depletion: Is it all in your head? Implicit theories about willpower affect self-regulation. *Psychological Science, 21*(11), 1686–1693.

Joffe, C. H., Rollins, J., Greenhut, R. (Producers), & Allen, W. (Writer & Director) (1977). *Annie Hall* [Motion picture]. USA: Rollins-Joffe Productions.

Joffe-Walt, C. (2010, October 4). How fake money saved Brazil. [Radio broadcast]. In A. Blumberg & A. Davidson, *All things considered: Planet money.* Washington, DC: National Public Radio. Retrieved from: http://www.npr.org/blogs/money/2010/10/04/130329523/how-fake-money-saved-brazil

Johns, M., Inzlicht, M., & Schmader, T. (2008). Stereotype threat and executive resource depletion: Examining the influence of emotion regulation. *Journal of Experimental Psychology: General, 137*(4), 691–705.

Johns, M., Schmader, T., & Martens, A. (2005). Knowing is half the battle: Teaching stereotype threat as a means of improving women's math performance. *Psychological Science, 16*(3), 175–179.

Johnson, A. L., Crawford, M. T., Sherman, S. J., Rutchick, A. M., Hamilton, D. L., Ferreira, M. B., & Petrocelli, J. V. (2006). A functional perspective on group memberships: Differential need fulfillment in a group typology. *Journal of Experimental Social Psychology, 42*(6), 707–719.

Johnson, C. A. (2009, February, 11). Cutting through advertising clutter. CBS News. Retrieved from http://www.cbsnews.com/8301-3445_162-2015684.html

Johnson, D. J., Cheung, F., & Donnellan, M. B. (2014). Does cleanliness influence moral judgments? A direct replication of Schnall, Benton, and Harvey (2008). *Social Psychology, 45*(3), 209–215.

Johnson, K. L., Gill, S., Reichman, V., & Tassinary, L. G. (2007). Swagger, sway, and sexuality: Judging sexual orientation from body motion and morphology. *Journal of Personality and Social Psychology, 93*(3), 321–334.

Johnson, K. L., & Tassinary, L. G. (2005). Perceiving sex directly and indirectly: Meaning in motion and morphology. *Psychological Science, 16*(11), 890–897.

Johnson, R. D., & Downing, L. L. (1979). Deindividuation and valence of cues: Effects on prosocial and antisocial behavior. *Journal of Personality and Social Psychology, 37*(9), 1532–1538.

Jonas, E., Fritsche, I., & Greenberg, J. (2005). Currencies as cultural symbols—An existential psychological perspective on reactions of Germans toward the Euro. *Journal of Economic Psychology, 26*(1), 129–146.

Jonas, E., Graupmann, V., Kayser, D. N., Zanna, M., Traut-Mattausch, E., & Frey, D. (2009). Culture, self, and the emergence of reactance: Is there a "universal" freedom? *Journal of Experimental Social Psychology, 45*(5), 1068–1080.

Jonas, E., Martens, A., Niesta Kayser, D., Fritsche, I., Sullivan, D., & Greenberg, J. (2008). Focus theory of normative conduct and terror-management theory: The interactive impact of mortality salience and norm salience on social judgment. *Journal of Personality and Social Psychology, 95*(6), 1239–1251.

Jonas, E., Schimel, J., Greenberg, J., & Pyszczynski, T. (2002). The Scrooge effect: Evidence that mortality salience increases prosocial attitudes and behavior. *Personality and Social Psychology Bulletin, 28*(10), 1342–1353.

Jonas, E., Sullivan, D., & Greenberg, J. (2013). Generosity, greed, norms, and death—Differential effects of mortality salience on charitable behavior. *Journal of Economic Psychology, 35,* 47–57:

Jones, D. (1995). Sexual selection, physical attractiveness, and facial neoteny: Cross-cultural evidence and implications. *Current Anthropology, 36*(5), 723–748.

Jones, E. E. (1964). *Ingratiation.* East Norwalk, CT: Appleton-Century-Crofts.

Jones, E. E. (1990). *Interpersonal perception.* New York: W. H. Freeman.

Jones, E. E., & Davis, K. E. (1965). A theory of correspondent inferences: From acts to dispositions. In L. Berkowitz (Ed.), *Advances in experimental social psychology* (Vol. 2, pp. 219–266). San Diego: Academic Press.

Jones, E. E., & Harris, V. A. (1967). The attribution of attitudes. *Journal of Experimental Social Psychology, 3*(1), 1–24.

Jones, E. E., Jones, R.G., & Gergen, K. J. (1963). Some conditions affecting the evaluation of a conformist. *Journal of Personality, 31*(2), 270–288.

Jones, E. E., & Nisbett, R. E. (1971). *The actor and the observer: Divergent perceptions of the causes of behavior.* New York: General Learning Press.

Jones, E. E., & Pittman, T. S. (1982). Toward a general theory of strategic self-presentation. In J. Suls (Ed.), *Psychological perspectives on the self* (Vol. 1, pp. 231–262). Hillsdale, NJ: Erlbaum.

Jones, E. E., & Sigall, H. (1971). The bogus pipeline: A new paradigm for measuring affect and attitude. *Psychological Bulletin, 76*(5), 349–364.

Jones, E. E., & Wortman, C. B. (1973). *Ingratiation: An attributional approach.* Morristown, NJ: General Learning Press.

Jones, J. H. (1981). *Bad blood: The Tuskegee syphilis experiment.* New York: Free Press.

Jones, T. F., Craig, A. S., Hoy, D., Gunter, E. W., Ashley, D. L., Barr, D. B., . . . & Schaffner, W. (2000). Mass psychogenic illness attributed to toxic exposure at a high school. *New England Journal of Medicine, 342*(2), 96–100.

Jordan, C. H., Spencer, S. J., Zanna, M. P., Hoshino-Browne, E., & Correll, J. (2003). Secure and defensive high self-esteem. *Journal of Personality and Social Psychology, 85*(5), 969–978.

Josephs, R. A., Sellers, J. G., Newman, M. L., & Mehta, P. H. (2006). The mismatch effect: When testosterone and status are at odds. *Journal of Personality and Social Psychology, 90*(6), 999–1013.

Josephson, W. L. (1987). Television violence and children's aggression: Testing the priming, social script, and disinhibition predictions. *Journal of Personality and Social Psychology*, 53(5), 882–890.

Jost, J. T., & Banaji, M. R. (1994). The role of stereotyping in system-justification and the production of false consciousness. *British Journal of Social Psychology*, 33(1), 1–27.

Jost, J. T., Glaser, J., Kruglanski, A. W., & Sulloway, F. J. (2003). Political conservatism as motivated social cognition. *Psychological Bulletin*, 129(3), 339–375.

Jost, J. T., Kivetz, Y., Rubini, M., Guermandi, G., & Mosso, C. (2005). System-justifying functions of complementary regional and ethnic stereotypes: Cross-national evidence. *Social Justice Research*, 18(3), 305–333.

Joyce, J. (1961). *Ulysses*. New York: Random House.

Judge, T. A., Bono, J. E., Ilies, R., & Gerhardt, M. W. (2002). Personality and leadership: A qualitative and quantitative review. *Journal of Applied Psychology*, 87(4), 765–780.

Jung, C. G. (1970). *After the catastrophe*. In G. Adler & R. F. C. Hull (Eds. and Trans.), *Collected works of C. G. Jung: Vol. 10. Civilization in transition*. Princeton, NJ: Princeton University Press. (Original work published 1945)

Jung, C. G., & von Franz, M. L. (Eds.) (1968). *Man and his symbols*. New York: Random House.

Jussim, L. (1986). Self-fulfilling prophecies: A theoretical and integrative review. *Psychological Review*, 93(4), 429–445.

Jussim, L., Cain, T. R., Crawford, J. T., Harber, K., & Cohen, F. (2009). The unbearable accuracy of stereotypes. In T. D. Nelson (Ed.), *Handbook of prejudice, stereotyping and discrimination* (pp. 199–227). New York: Psychology Press.

Kabat-Zinn, J. (1990). *Full catastrophe living: Using the wisdom of your body and mind to face stress, pain, and illness*. New York: Delacorte.

Kagan, J. (1994). *Galen's prophecy: Temperament in human nature*. New York: Basic Books.

Kahneman, D. (2011). *Thinking, fast and slow*. New York: Farrar, Straus and Giroux.

Kahneman, D., & Tversky, A. (1982). The simulation heuristic. In D. Kahneman, P. Slovic, & A. Tversky (Eds.), *Judgment under uncertainty: Heuristics and biases* (pp. 201–208). New York: Cambridge University Press.

Kaiser, C. R., Drury, B. J., Spalding, K. E., Cheryan, S., & O'Brien, L. T. (2009). The ironic consequences of Obama's election: Decreased support for social justice. *Journal of Experimental Social Psychology*, 45(3), 556–559.

Kaiser, C. R., & Miller, C. T. (2001). Stop complaining! The social costs of making attributions to discrimination. *Personality and Social Psychology Bulletin*, 27(2), 254–263.

Kaiser, C. R., Vick, S. B., & Major, B. (2006). Prejudice expectations moderate preconscious attention to cues that are threatening to social identity. *Psychological Science*, 17(4), 332–338.

Kalick, S. M., Zebrowitz, L. A., Langlois, J. H., & Johnson, R. M. (1998). Does human facial attractiveness honestly advertise health? Longitudinal data on an evolutionary question. *Psychological Science*, 9(1), 8–13.

Kamp Dush, C. M., & Amato, P. R. (2005). Consequences of relationship status and quality for subjective well-being. *Journal of Social and Personal Relationships*, 22(5), 607–627.

Kane, H. S., Jaremka, L. M., Guichard, A. C., Ford, M. B., Collins, N. L., & Feeney, B. C. (2007). Feeling supported and feeling satisfied: How one partner's attachment style predicts the other partner's relationship experiences. *Journal of Social and Personal Relationships*, 24(4), 535–555.

Kantola, S. J., Syme, G. J., & Campbell, N. A. (1984). Cognitive dissonance and energy conservation. *Journal of Applied Psychology*, 69(3), 416–421.

Kanwisher, N., McDermott, J., & Chun, M. M. (1997). The fusiform face area: A module in human extrastriate cortex specialized for face perception. *Journal of Neuroscience*, 17(11), 4302–4311.

Karau, S. J., & Williams, K. D. (1993). Social loafing: A meta-analytic review and theoretical integration. *Journal of Personality and Social Psychology*, 65(4), 681–706.

Karau, S. J., & Williams, K. D. (1997). The effects of group cohesiveness on social loafing and social compensation. *Group Dynamics: Theory, Research, and Practice*, 1(2), 156–168.

Karney, B. R., & Bradbury, T. N. (1995). The longitudinal course of marital quality and stability: A review of theory, methods, and research. *Psychological Bulletin*, 118(1), 3–34.

Karney, B. R., & Bradbury, T. N. (2000). Attributions in marriage: State or trait? A growth curve analysis. *Journal of Personality and Social Psychology*, 78(2), 295–309.

Karsten, R. (1935). *The head-hunters of western Amazonus*. Helsingfors: Societas Scientiarum Fennica.

Kashima, Y., Yamaguchi, S., Kim, U., Choi, S. C., Gelfand, M. J., & Yuki, M. (1995). Culture, gender, and self: A perspective from individualism-collectivism research. *Journal of Personality and Social Psychology*, 69(5), 925–937.

Kasser, T., & Ryan, R. M. (1993). A dark side of the American dream: Correlates of financial success as a central life aspiration. *Journal of Personality and Social Psychology*, 65(2), 410–422.

Katz, I., & Hass, R. G. (1988). Racial ambivalence and American value conflict: Correlational and priming studies of dual cognitive structures. *Journal of Personality and Social Psychology*, 55(6), 893–905.

Kaufman, J., & Zigler, E. (1987). Do abused children become abusive parents? *American Journal of Orthopsychiatry*, 57(2), 186–192.

Kawakami, K., Dovidio, J. F., Moll, J., Hermsen, S., & Russin, A. (2000). Just say no (to stereotyping): Effects of training in the negation of stereotypic associations on stereotype activation. *Journal of Personality and Social Psychology*, 78(5), 871–888.

Kawakami, K., Dunn, E., Karmali, F., & Dovidio, J. F. (2009). Mispredicting affective and behavioral responses to racism. *Science*, 323(5911), 276–278.

Kawakami, K., Phills, C. E., Steele, J. R., & Dovidio, J. F. (2007). (Close) distance makes the heart grow fonder: Improving implicit racial attitudes and interracial interactions through approach behaviors. *Journal of Personality and Social Psychology*, 92(6), 957–971.

Kay, A. C., & Jost, J. T. (2003). Complementary justice: Effects of "poor but happy" and "poor but honest" stereotype exemplars on system justification and implicit activation of the justice motive. *Journal of Personality and Social Psychology*, 85(5), 823–837.

Kay, A. C., Jost, J. T., Mandisodza, A. N., Sherman, S. J., Petrocelli, J. V., & Johnson, A. L. (2007). Panglossian ideology in the service of system justification: How complementary stereotypes help us to rationalize inequality. In M. P. Zanna (Ed.), *Advances in experimental social psychology* (Vol. 39, pp. 305–358). San Diego: Academic Press.

Keane, T. M., Litz, B. T., & Blake, D. D. (1990). Post-traumatic stress disorder in adulthood. In M. Hersen & C. G. Last (Eds.), *Handbook of child and adult psychopathology: A longitudinal perspective*. Elmsford, NY: Pergamon Press.

Keinan, G. (1994). The effects of stress and tolerance of ambiguity on magical thinking. *Journal of Personality and Social Psychology*, 67(1), 48–55.

Keinan, G. (2002). The effects of stress and desire for control on superstitious behavior. *Personality and Social Psychology Bulletin*, 28(1), 102–108.

Keller, J., & Bless, H. (2008). Flow and regulatory compatibility: An experimental approach to the flow model of intrinsic motivation. *Personality and Social Psychology Bulletin*, 34(2), 196–209.

Kellermann, A. L., Rivara, F. P., Rushforth, N. B., Banton, J. G., Reay, D. T., Francisco, J. T., . . . & Somes, G. (1993). Gun ownership as a risk factor for homicide in the home. *New England Journal of Medicine*, 329(15), 1084–1091.

Kelley, D. E. (Writer), & D'Elia, B. (Director). (2008). Tabloid nation [Television series episode]. In D. E. Kelley (Producer), *Boston legal*. Manhattan Beach, CA: David E. Kelley Productions & 20th Century Fox Television.

Kelley, H. H. (1967). Attribution theory in social psychology. *Nebraska Symposium on Motivation*, 17, 192–238.

Kelley, H. H. (1971). *Attribution in social interaction*. New York: General Learning Press.

Kelley, H. H. (1973). The processes of causal attribution. *American Psychologist*, 28(2), 107–128.

Kelly, M. H. (1999). Regional naming patterns and the culture of honor. *Names: A Journal of Onomastics*, 47(1), 3–20. Retrieved from: http://cogprints.org/1315/1/warPeace.html

Kelman, H. C. (1976). Violence without restraint: Reflections on the dehumanization of victims and victimizers. In G. M. Kren & L. H. Rappoport (Eds.), *Varieties of psychohistory* (pp. 282–314). New York: Springer.

Keltner, D., Gruenfeld, D. H., & Anderson, C. (2003). Power, approach, and inhibition. *Psychological Review*, 110(2), 265–284.

Keltner, D., Young, R. C., Heerey, E. A., Oemig, C., & Monarch, N. D. (1998). Teasing in hierarchical and intimate relations. *Journal of Personality and Social Psychology*, 75(5), 1231–1247.

Kenny, D. A., & Acitelli, L. K. (2001). Accuracy and bias in the perception of the partner in a close relationship. *Journal of Personality and Social Psychology*, 80(3), 439–448.

Kenrick, D. T., & Gutierres, S. E. (1980). Contrast effects and judgments of physical attractiveness: When beauty becomes a social problem. *Journal of Personality and Social Psychology*, 38(1), 131–140.

Kenrick, D. T., Gutierres, S. E., & Goldberg, L. L. (1989). Influence of popular erotica on judgments of strangers and mates. *Journal of Experimental Social Psychology*, 25(2), 159–167.

Kenrick, D. T., & MacFarlane, S. W. (1986). Ambient temperature and horn honking: A field study of the heat/aggression relationship. *Environment and Behavior*, 18(2), 179–191.

Kenrick, D. T., Sadalla, E. K., Groth, G., & Trost, M. R. (1990). Evolution, traits, and the stages of human courtship: Qualifying the parental investment model. *Journal of Personality*, 58(1), 97–116.

Kenworthy, J. B., Hewstone, M., Levine, J. M., Martin, R., & Willis, H. (2008). The phenomenology of minority–majority status: Effects on innovation in argument generation. *European Journal of Social Psychology*, 38(4), 624–636.

Kephart, W. M. (1967). Some correlates of romantic love. *Journal of Marriage and the Family*, 29(3), 470–474. Stable URL: http://www.jstor.org/stable/349585

Kernis, M. H., Grannemann, B. D., & Barclay, L. C. (1989). Stability and level of self-esteem as predictors of anger arousal and hostility. *Journal of Personality and Social Psychology*, 56(6), 1013–1022.

Kernis, M. H., & Waschull, S. B. (1995). The interactive roles of stability and level of self-esteem: Research and theory. In M. P. Zanna (Ed.), *Advances in experimental social psychology* (Vol. 27, pp. 93–141). San Diego: Academic Press.

Kernis, M. H., Whisenhunt, C. R., Waschull, S. B., Greenier, K. D., Berry, A. J., Herlocker, C. E., & Anderson, C. A. (1998). Multiple facets of self-esteem and their relations to depressive symptoms. *Personality and Social Psychology Bulletin*, 24(6), 657–668.

Kerr, N. L., & Bruun, S. E. (1983). Dispensability of member effort and group motivation losses: Free-rider effects. *Journal of Personality and Social Psychology*, 44(1), 78–94.

Kessler, R. C., Mickelson, K. D., & Williams, D. R. (1999). The prevalence, distribution, and mental health correlates of perceived discrimination in the United States. *Journal of Health and Social Behavior*, 40(3), 208–230.

Kids Count (2013). Children in single-parent families by race. Kids Count Data Center. Retrieved from http://datacenter.kidscount.org/data/acrossstates/Rankings.aspx?ind=107

Kiecolt-Glaser, J. K., & Newton, T. L. (2001). Marriage and health: His and hers. *Psychological Bulletin*, 127(4), 472–503.

Kierkegaard, S. (1980). *The concept of anxiety* (Trans. R. Thomte). Princeton, NJ: Princeton University Press. (Original work published 1844)

Kihlstrom, J. F. (1994). Hypnosis, delayed recall, and the principles of memory. *International Journal of Clinical and Experimental Hypnosis*, 42(4), 337–345.

Kim, H. K., & McKenry, P. C. (2002). The relationship between marriage and psychological well-being: A longitudinal analysis. *Journal of Family Issues*, 23(8), 885–911.

Kim, S. H., Smith, R. H., & Brigham, N. L. (1998). Effects of power imbalance and the presence of third parties on reactions to harm: Upward and downward revenge. *Personality and Social Psychology Bulletin*, 24(4), 353–361.

Kimball, M. M. (1986). Television and sex-role attitudes. In T. M. Williams (Ed.), *The impact of television: A natural experiment in three communities* (pp. 265–301). Orlando: Academic Press.

Kimble, C. E., & Hirt, E. R. (2005). Self-focus, gender, and habitual self-handicapping: Do they make a difference in behavioral self-handicapping? *Social Behavior and Personality: An International Journal*, 33(1), 43–56.

Kim-Cohen, J., Caspi, A., Taylor, A., Williams, B., Newcombe, R., Craig, I. W., & Moffitt, T. E. (2006). MAOA, maltreatment, and gene-environment interaction predicting children's mental health: New evidence and a meta-analysis. *Molecular Psychiatry*, 11(10), 903–913.

King, L. A., Hicks, J. A., Krull, J. L., & Del Gaiso, A. K. (2006). Positive affect and the experience of meaning in life. *Journal of Personality and Social Psychology*, 90(1), 179–196.

King, M. L., Jr. (1992). I have a dream. In J. M. Washington (Ed.), *I have a dream: Writings and speeches that changed the world* (pp. 101–106). San Francisco: HarperSanFrancisco. (Original speech given 1963)

Kingdon, J. (1993). *Self-made man: Human evolution from Eden to extinction?* New York: Wiley.

Kipnis, D. (1972). Does power corrupt? *Journal of Personality and Social Psychology*, 24(1), 33–41.

Kirkpatrick, L. A., & Davis, K. E. (1994). Attachment style, gender, and relationship stability: A longitudinal analysis. *Journal of Personality and Social Psychology*, 66(3), 502–512.

Kirkpatrick, L. A., & Epstein, S. (1992). Cognitive-experiential self-theory and subjective probability: Further evidence for two conceptual systems. *Journal of Personality and Social Psychology*, 63(4), 534–544.

Kirkpatrick, L. A., & Hazan, C. (1994). Attachment styles and close relationships: A four-year prospective study. *Personal Relationships*, 1(2), 123–142.

Kirsch, I. (2010). *The emperor's new drugs: Exploding the antidepressant myth.* New York: Basic Books.

Kirschbaum, C., Pirke, K. M., & Hellhammer, D. H. (1993). The 'Trier Social Stress Test'—A tool for investigating psychobiological stress responses in a laboratory setting. *Neuropsychobiology*, 28(1–2), 76–81.

Kitayama, S., & Markus, H. R. (2000). The pursuit of happiness and the realization of sympathy: Cultural patterns of self, social relations, and well-being. In E. Diener & E. Suh (Eds.), *Subjective well-being across cultures* (pp. 113–161). Cambridge, MA: MIT Press.

Kitayama, S., Snibbe, A. C., Markus, H. R., & Suzuki, T. (2004). Is there any "free" choice? Self and dissonance in two cultures. *Psychological Science*, 15(8), 527–533.

Kiviniemi, M. T., Snyder, M., & Omoto, A. M. (2002). Too many of a good thing? The effects of multiple motivations on stress, cost, fulfillment, and satisfaction. *Personality and Social Psychology Bulletin*, 28(6), 732–743.

Klandermans, B., Werner, M., & Van Doorn, M. (2008). Redeeming apartheid's legacy: Collective guilt, political ideology, and compensation. *Political Psychology*, 29(3), 331–349.

Klauer, K. C., & Wegener, I. (1998). Unraveling social categorization in the "Who said what?" paradigm. *Journal of Personality and Social Psychology*, 75(5), 1155–1178.

Klein, R. G., & Edgar, B. (2002). *The dawn of human culture*. New York: Wiley.

Klein, S. B., Sherman, J. W., & Loftus, J. (1996). The role of episodic and semantic memory in the development of trait self-knowledge. *Social Cognition*, 14(4), 277–291.

Kleinfeld, J. S. (1971). *Some instructional strategies for the cross-cultural classroom.* Juneau: Alaska State Department of Education.

Klinesmith, J., Kasser, T., & McAndrew, F. T. (2006). Guns, testosterone, and aggression: An experimental test of a mediational hypothesis. *Psychological Science*, 17(7), 568–571.

Klonoff, E. A., Landrine, H., & Ullman, J. B. (1999). Racial discrimination and psychiatric symptoms among Blacks. *Cultural Diversity and Ethnic Minority Psychology*, 5(4), 329–339.

Klucharev, V., Hytönen, K., Rijpkema, M., Smidts, A., & Fernández, G. (2009). Reinforcement learning signal predicts social conformity. *Neuron*, 61(1), 140–151.

Kluegel, J. R., & Smith, E. R. (1986). *Beliefs about inequality: Americans' views of what is and what ought to be.* Hawthorne, NY: Aldine de Gruyter.

Klusmann, D. (2002). Sexual motivation and the duration of partnership. *Archives of Sexual Behavior*, 31(3), 275–287.

Knafo, A., Israel, S., & Ebstein, R. P. (2011). Heritability of children's prosocial behavior and differential susceptibility to parenting by variation in the dopamine receptor D4 gene. *Development and Psychopathology*, 23(1), 53–67.

Knafo, A., & Plomin, R. (2006). Prosocial behavior from early to middle childhood: Genetic and environmental influences on stability and change. *Developmental Psychology*, 42(5), 771–786.

Knee, C. R. (1998). Implicit theories of relationships: Assessment and prediction of romantic relationship initiation, coping, and longevity. *Journal of Personality and Social Psychology*, 74(2), 360–370.

Knight, G. P., Johnson, L. G., Carlo, G., & Eisenberg, N. (1994). A multiplicative model of the dispositional antecedents of a prosocial behavior: Predicting more of the people more of the time. *Journal of Personality and Social Psychology*, 66(1), 178–183.

Knobloch, L. K., & Donovan-Kicken, E. (2006). Perceived involvement of network members in courtships: A test of the relational turbulence model. *Personal Relationships*, 13(3), 281–302.

Knobloch, L. K., Miller, L. E., & Carpenter, K. E. (2007). Using the relational turbulence model to understand negative emotion within courtship. *Personal Relationships*, 14(1), 91–112.

Knoch, D., Pascual-Leone, A., Meyer, K., Treyer, V., & Fehr, E. (2006). Diminishing reciprocal fairness by disrupting the right prefrontal cortex. *Science*, 314(5800), 829–832.

Knox, R. E., & Inkster, J. A. (1968). Postdecision dissonance at post time. *Journal of Personality and Social Psychology*, 8(4, Pt. 1), 319–323.

Koenig, L. B., McGue, M., & Iacono, W. G. (2008). Stability and change in religiousness during emerging adulthood. *Developmental Psychology*, 44(2), 532–543.

Koestler, A. (1978). *Janus: A summing up.* London: Hutchinson.

Konijn, E. A., Nije Bijvank, M., & Bushman, B. J. (2007). I wish I were a warrior: The role of wishful identification in the effects of violent video games on aggression in adolescent boys. *Developmental Psychology*, 43(4), 1038–1044.

Koppel, N. (2011, August 24). "Hot sauce" mom convicted of child abuse. *The Wall Street Journal*. Retrieved from http://blogs.wsj.com/law/2011/08/24/hot-sauce-mom-convicted-of-child-abuse/

Korte, C. (1980). Urban-nonurban differences in social behavior and social psychological models of urban impact. *Journal of Social Issues*, 36(3), 29–51.

Kosfeld, M., Heinrichs, M., Zak, P. J., Fischbacher, U., & Fehr, E. (2005). Oxytocin increases trust in humans. *Nature*, 435(7042), 673–676.

Kosloff, S., & Greenberg, J. (2009). Pearls in the desert: The proximal and distal effects of mortality salience on the appeal of extrinsic goals. *Journal of Experimental Social Psychology*, 45(1), 197–203.

Kosloff, S., Greenberg, J., & Solomon, S. (2010). The effects of mortality salience on political preferences: The roles of charisma and political orientation. *Journal of Experimental Social Psychology*, 46(1), 139–145.

Kosloff, S., Greenberg, J., Sullivan, D., & Weise, D. (2010). Of trophies and pillars: Exploring the terror management functions of short-term and long-term relationship partners. *Personality and Social Psychology Bulletin*, 36(8), 1037–1051.

Kovacs, L. (1983). A conceptualization of marital development. *Family Therapy*, 10(3), 183–210.

Kövecses, Z. (2010). *Metaphor: A practical introduction*. New York: Oxford University Press.

Kowalski, R. M. (2003). *Complaining, teasing, and other annoying behaviors*. New Haven: Yale University Press.

Krämer, U. M., Jansma, H., Tempelmann, C., & Münte, T. F. (2007). Tit-for-tat: The neural basis of reactive aggression. *Neuroimage*, 38(1), 203–211.

Kraus, M. W., Piff, P. K., Mendoza-Denton, R., Rheinschmidt, M. R., & Keltner, D. (2012). Social class, solipsism, and contextualism: How the rich are different from the poor. *Psychological Review*, 119(3): 546–572.

Kraut, R., Patterson, M., Lundmark, V., Kiesler, S., Mukophadhyay, T., & Scherlis, W. (1998). Internet paradox: A social technology that reduces social involvement and psychological well-being? *American Psychologist*, 53(9), 1017–1031.

Kraut, R. E., & Johnston, R. E. (1979). Social and emotional messages of smiling: An ethological approach. *Journal of Personality and Social Psychology*, 37(9), 1539–1553.

Kray, L. J., & Haselhuhn, M. P. (2007). Implicit negotiation beliefs and performance: Experimental and longitudinal evidence. *Journal of Personality and Social Psychology*, 93(1), 49–64.

Kray, L. J., Thompson, L., & Galinsky, A. (2001). Battle of the sexes: Gender stereotype confirmation and reactance in negotiations. *Journal of Personality and Social Psychology*, 80(6), 942–958.

Krebs, D. (1975). Empathy and altruism. *Journal of Personality and Social Psychology*, 32(6), 1134–1146.

Kressel, N. J. (1996). *Mass hate: The global rise of genocide and terror*. New York: Plenum Press.

Kretschmar, J. M., & Flannery, D. J. (2007). Substance use and violent behavior. In D. J. Flannery, A. T. Vazsonyi, & I. D. Waldman (Eds.), *The Cambridge handbook of violent behavior and aggression* (pp. 647–663). New York: Cambridge University Press.

Kroon, M. B., Hart, P. T., & Van Kreveld, D. (1991). Managing group decision making processes: Individual versus collective accountability and groupthink. *International Journal of Conflict Management*, 2(2), 91–115.

Krosnick, J. A. (1988). The role of attitude importance in social evaluation: A study of policy preferences, presidential candidate evaluations, and voting behavior. *Journal of Personality and Social Psychology*, 55(2), 196–210.

Krosnick, J. A., & Alwin, D. F. (1989). Aging and susceptibility to attitude change. *Journal of Personality and Social Psychology*, 57(3), 416–425.

Krueger, J., & Zeiger, J. S. (1993). Social categorization and the truly false consensus effect. *Journal of Personality and Social Psychology*, 65(4), 670–680.

Kruesi, M. J. (2007). Psychopharmacology of violence. In D. J. Flannery, A. T. Vazsonyi, & I. D. Waldman (Eds), *The Cambridge handbook of violent behavior and aggression* (pp. 618–635). New York: Cambridge University Press.

Kruger, J., & Dunning, D. (1999). Unskilled and unaware of it: How difficulties in recognizing one's own incompetence lead to inflated self-assessments. *Journal of Personality and Social Psychology*, 77(6), 1121–1134.

Kruglanski, A. W. (1980). Lay epistemo-logic—process and contents: Another look at attribution theory. *Psychological Review*, 87(1), 70.

Kruglanski, A. W. (1989). *Lay epistemics and human knowledge: Cognitive and motivational bases*. New York: Plenum Press.

Kruglanski, A. W. (1996). Motivated social cognition: Principles of the interface. In E. T. Higgins & A. W. Kruglanski, (Eds.), *Social psychology: Handbook of basic principles* (pp. 133–168). New York: Guilford Press.

Kruglanski, A. W. (2004). *The psychology of closed mindedness*. New York: Psychology Press.

Kruglanski, A. W., & Freund, T. (1983). The freezing and unfreezing of lay-inferences: Effects on impressional primacy, ethnic stereotyping, and numerical anchoring. *Journal of Experimental Social Psychology*, 19(5), 448–468.

Kruglanski, A. W., Schwartz, J. M., Maides, S., & Hamel, I. Z. (1978). Covariation, discounting, and augmentation: Towards a clarification of attributional principles. *Journal of Personality*, 46(1), 176–189.

Kruglanski, A. W., & Webster, D. M. (1996). Motivated closing of the mind: "Seizing" and "freezing." *Psychological Review*, 103(2), 263–283.

Krull, D. S., Loy, M. H. M., Lin, J., Wang, C. F., Chen, S., & Zhao, X. (1999). The fundamental fundamental attribution error: Correspondence bias in individualist and collectivist cultures. *Personality and Social Psychology Bulletin*, 25(10), 1208–1219.

Kubrick, S., Litvinoff, S., Raab, M. L., (Producers), & Kubrick, S., (Director) (1971). *A clockwork orange* [Motion picture]. United Kingdom: Warner Bros. & Hawk Films.

Kuhlman, D. M., & Marshello, A. F. (1975). Individual differences in game motivation as moderators of preprogrammed strategy effects in prisoner's dilemma. *Journal of Personality and Social Psychology*, 32(5), 922–931.

Kulik, J. A., Mahler, H. I., & Earnest, A. (1994). Social comparison and affiliation under threat: Going beyond the affiliate-choice paradigm. *Journal of Personality and Social Psychology*, 66(2), 301–309.

Kunda, Z. (1990). The case for motivated reasoning. *Psychological Bulletin*, 108(3), 480–498.

Kunda, Z. (1999). *Social cognition: Making sense of people*. Cambridge, MA: MIT press.

Kunda, Z., Davies, P. G., Adams, B. D., & Spencer, S. J. (2002). The dynamic time course of stereotype activation: Activation, dissipation, and resurrection. *Journal of Personality and Social Psychology*, 82(3), 283–299.

Kunda, Z., & Thagard, P. (1996). Forming impressions from stereotypes, traits, and behaviors: A parallel-constraint-satisfaction theory. *Psychological Review*, 103(2), 284–308.

Kunstman, J. W., & Plant, E. A. (2008). Racing to help: Racial bias in high emergency helping situations. *Journal of Personality and Social Psychology*, 95(6), 1499–1510.

Kurdek, L. A. (1995). Lesbian and gay couples. In A. R. D'Augelli & C. J. Patterson (Eds.), *Lesbian, gay, and bisexual identities over the lifespan: Psychological perspectives* (pp. 243–261). New York: Oxford University Press.

Kurdek, L. A. (1999). The nature and predictors of the trajectory of change in marital quality for husbands and wives over the first 10 years of marriage. *Developmental Psychology*, 35(5), 1283–1296.

Kurdek, L. A. (2004). Are gay and lesbian cohabiting couples really different from heterosexual married couples? *Journal of Marriage and Family*, 66(4), 880–900.

Kurdek, L. A. (2005). Gender and marital satisfaction early in marriage: A growth curve approach. *Journal of Marriage and Family*, 67(1), 68–84.

Kurdek, L. A. (2008). Change in relationship quality for partners from lesbian, gay male, and heterosexual couples. *Journal of Family Psychology*, 22(5), 701–711.

Kurzban, R., & Neuberg, S. (2005). Managing ingroup and outgroup relationships. In D. M. Buss (Ed.), *The handbook of evolutionary psychology* (pp. 653–675). Hoboken, NJ: Wiley.

Kurzban, R., Tooby, J., & Cosmides, L. (2001). Can race be erased? Coalitional computation and social categorization. *Proceedings of the National Academy of Sciences*, 98(26), 15387–15392.

La Barre, W. (1954). *The human animal*. Chicago: University of Chicago Press.

La Guardia, J. G. (2009). Developing who I am: A self-determination theory approach to the establishment of healthy identities. *Educational Psychologist*, 44(2), 90–104.

La Guardia, J. G., Ryan, R. M., Couchman, C. E., & Deci, E. L. (2000). Within-person variation in security of attachment: A self-determination theory perspective on attachment, need fulfillment, and well-being. *Journal of Personality and Social Psychology*, 79(3), 367–384.

Lagerspetz, K. M. J., & Björkqvist, K. (1994). Indirect aggression in boys and girls. In L. R. Huesmann (Ed.), *Aggressive behavior: Current perspectives* (pp. 131–150). New York: Plenum.

Lagerspetz, K. M. J., Björkqvist, K., & Peltonen, T. (1988). Is indirect aggression typical of females? Gender differences in aggressiveness in 11- to 12-year-old children. *Aggressive Behavior*, 14(6), 403–414.

Laird, J. D. (1974). Self-attribution of emotion: The effects of expressive behavior on the quality of emotional experience. *Journal of Personality and Social Psychology*, 29(4), 475–486.

Lakin, J. L., & Chartrand, T. L. (2003). Using nonconscious behavioral mimicry to create affiliation and rapport. *Psychological Science*, 14(4), 334–339.

Lakoff, G., & Johnson, M. (1980). *Metaphors we live by*. Chicago: University of Chicago Press.

Lamm, C., Batson, C. D., & Decety, J. (2007). The neural substrate of human empathy: Effects of perspective-taking and cognitive appraisal. *Journal of Cognitive Neuroscience*, 19(1), 42–58.

Lamm, H. (1967). Will an observer advise higher risk taking after hearing a discussion of the decision problem? *Journal of Personality and Social Psychology*, 6(4, Pt. 1), 467–471.

Lamm, H., Myers, D., & Ochsmann, R. (1976). On predicting group-induced shifts toward risk or caution: A second look at some experiments. *Psychologische Beitrage*, 18(3), 288–296.

Landau, M. J., Goldenberg, J. L., Greenberg, J., Gillath, O., Solomon, S., Cox, C., . . . & Pyszczynski, T. (2006). The siren's call: Terror management and the threat of men's sexual attraction to women. *Journal of Personality and Social Psychology*, 90(1), 129–146.

Landau, M. J., Greenberg, J., Sullivan, D., Routledge, C., & Arndt, J. (2009). The protective identity: Evidence that mortality salience heightens the clarity and coherence of the self-concept. *Journal of Experimental Social Psychology*, 45(4), 796–807.

Landau, M. J., Johns, M., Greenberg, J., Pyszczynski, T., Martens, A., Goldenberg, J. L., & Solomon, S. (2004). A function of form: Terror management and structuring the social world. *Journal of Personality and Social Psychology*, 87(2), 190–210.

Landau, M. J., Kosloff, S., & Schmeichel, B. J. (2011). Imbuing everyday actions with meaning in response to existential threat. *Self and Identity*, 10(1), 64–76.

Landau, M. J., Meier, B. P., & Keefer, L. A. (2010). A metaphor-enriched social cognition. *Psychological Bulletin*, 136(6), 1045–1067.

Landau, M. J., Robinson, M., & Meier, B. (Eds.) (2013). *The power of metaphor: Examining its influence on social life*. Washington, DC: American Psychological Association.

Landau, M. J., Solomon, S., Greenberg, J., Cohen, F., Pyszczynski, T., Arndt, J., . . . & Cook, A. (2004). Deliver us from evil: The effects of mortality salience and reminders of 9/11 on support for President George W. Bush. *Personality and Social Psychology Bulletin*, 30(9), 1136–1150.

Landau, M. J., Sullivan, D., Rothschild, Z. K., & Keefer, L. A. (2012). Deriving solace from a nemesis: Having scapegoats and enemies buffers the threat of meaninglessness. In P. R. Shaver & M. Mikulincer (Eds.), *Meaning, mortality, and choice: The social psychology of existential concerns* (pp. 183–202). Washington, DC: American Psychological Association.

Landau, T. (1989). *About faces: The evolution of the human face*. New York: Anchor Books.

Landis, D., & O'Shea, W. A. (2000). Cross-cultural aspects of passionate love: An individual differences analysis. *Journal of Cross-Cultural Psychology*, 31(6), 752–777.

Landy, D., & Sigall, H. (1974). Beauty is talent: Task evaluation as a function of the performer's physical attractiveness. *Journal of Personality and Social Psychology*, 29(3), 299–304.

Langer, E. J. (1975). The illusion of control. *Journal of Personality and Social Psychology*, 32(2), 311–328.

Langer, E. J. (1989). *Mindfulness*. Reading, MA: Addison-Wesley.

Langer, E. J., & Abelson, R. P. (1974). A patient by any other name. . . : Clinician group difference in labeling bias. *Journal of Consulting and Clinical Psychology*, 42(1), 4–9.

Langer, E. J., Blank, A., & Chanowitz, B. (1978). The mindlessness of ostensibly thoughtful action: The role of "placebic" information in interpersonal interaction. *Journal of Personality and Social Psychology*, 36(6), 635–642.

Langer, E. J., & Moldoveanu, M. (2000). The construct of mindfulness. *Journal of Social Issues*, 56(1), 1–9.

Langer, S. K. (1967, 1972, 1982). *Mind: An essay on human feeling* (3 vols.). Baltimore: Johns Hopkins University Press.

Langlois, J. H., Kalakanis, L., Rubenstein, A. J., Larson, A., Hallam, M., & Smoot, M. (2000). Maxims or myths of beauty? A meta-analytic and theoretical review. *Psychological Bulletin*, 126(3), 390–423.

Langlois, J. H., Ritter, J. M., Casey, R. J., & Sawin, D. B. (1995). Infant attractiveness predicts maternal behaviors and attitudes. *Developmental Psychology*, 31(3), 464–472.

Langlois, J. H., Ritter, J. M., Roggman, L. A., & Vaughn, L. S. (1991). Facial diversity and infant preferences for attractive faces. *Developmental Psychology*, 27(1), 79–84.

Langlois, J. H., & Roggman, L. A. (1990). Attractive faces are only average. *Psychological Science*, 1(2), 115–121.

Langlois, J. H., Roggman, L. A., Casey, R. J., Ritter, J. M., Rieser-Danner, L. A., & Jenkins, V. Y. (1987). Infant preferences for attractive faces: Rudiments of a stereotype? *Developmental Psychology*, 23(3), 363–369.

LaPiere, R. T. (1934). Attitudes vs. actions. *Social Forces*, 13(2), 230–237. Stable URL: http://www.jstor.org/stable/2570339

Larrick, R. P., Timmerman, T. A., Carton, A. M., & Abrevaya, J. (2011). Temper, temperature, and temptation: Heat-related retaliation in baseball. *Psychological Science*, 22(4), 423–428.

Lassek, W. D., & Gaulin, S. J. (2008). Waist-hip ratio and cognitive ability: Is gluteofemoral fat a privileged store of neurodevelopmental resources? *Evolution and Human Behavior*, 29(1), 26–34.

Latané, B., & Darley, J. M. (1968). Group inhibition of bystander intervention in emergencies. *Journal of Personality and Social Psychology*, 10(3), 215–221.

Latané, B., Liu, J. H., Nowak, A., Bonevento, M., & Zheng, L. (1995). Distance matters: Physical space and social impact. *Personality and Social Psychology Bulletin*, 21(8), 795–805.

Latané, B., Williams, K., & Harkins, S. (1979). Many hands make light the work: The causes and consequences of social loafing. *Journal of Personality and Social Psychology*, 37(6), 822–832.

Lau, M. A., Pihl, R. O., & Peterson, J. B. (1995). Provocation, acute alcohol intoxication, cognitive performance, and aggression. *Journal of Abnormal Psychology*, 104(1), 150–155.

Lauer, J., & Lauer, R. (1985, June). Marriages made to last. *Psychology Today*, 19(6), 22–26.

Laughlin, P. R., Zander, M. L., Knievel, E. M., & Tan, T. K. (2003). Groups perform better than the best individuals on letters-to-numbers problems:

Informative equations and effective strategies. *Journal of Personality and Social Psychology*, 85(4), 684–694.

Laumann, E. O., Ellingson, S., Mahay, J., Paik, A., & Youm, Y. (Eds.) (2004). *The sexual organization of the city*. Chicago: University of Chicago Press.

Laurenceau, J. P., Rivera, L. M., Schaffer, A. R., & Pietromonaco, P. R. (2004). Intimacy as an interpersonal process: Current status and future directions. In D. J. Mashek & A. Aron (Eds.), *Handbook of closeness and intimacy* (pp. 61–78). Mahwah, NJ: Erlbaum.

Lavee, Y., & Ben-Ari, A. (2007). Relationship of dyadic closeness with work-related stress: A daily diary study. *Journal of Marriage and Family*, 69(4), 1021–1035.

Lawrence, E., Rothman, A. D., Cobb, R. J., Rothman, M. T., & Bradbury, T. N. (2008). Marital satisfaction across the transition to parenthood. *Journal of Family Psychology*, 22(1), 41–50.

Lazarus, R. S. (1991). *Emotion and adaptation*. New York: Oxford University Press.

Lazarus, R. S., & Folkman, S. (1984). *Stress, appraisal, and coping*. New York: Springer-Verlag.

Le, B., & Agnew, C. R. (2003). Commitment and its theorized determinants: A meta–analysis of the Investment Model. *Personal Relationships*, 10(1), 37–57.

Leaper, C., Anderson, K. J., & Sanders, P. (1998). Moderators of gender effects on parents' talk to their children: A meta-analysis. *Developmental Psychology*, 34(1), 3–27.

Leary, M. R. (Ed.) (2001). *Interpersonal rejection*. New York: Oxford University Press.

Leary, M. R., & Baumeister, R. F. (2000). The nature and function of self-esteem: Sociometer theory. In M. P. Zanna (Ed.), *Advances in experimental social psychology* (Vol. 32, pp. 1–62). San Diego: Academic Press.

Leary, M. R., & Jones, J. L. (1993). The social psychology of tanning and sunscreen use: Self-presentational motives as a predictor of health risk. *Journal of Applied Social Psychology*, 23(17), 1390–1406.

Leary, M. R., Kelly, K. M., Cottrell, C. A., & Schreindorfer, L. S. (2013). Construct validity of the need to belong scale: Mapping the nomological network. *Journal of Personality Assessment*, 95(6), 610–624.

Leary, M. R., Kowalski, R. M., Smith, L., & Phillips, S. (2003). Teasing, rejection, and violence: Case studies of the school shootings. *Aggressive Behavior*, 29(3), 202–214.

Leary, M. R., Tambor, E. S., Terdal, S. K., & Downs, D. L. (1995). Self-esteem as an interpersonal monitor: The sociometer hypothesis. *Journal of Personality and Social Psychology*, 68(3), 518–530.

Leary, M. R., Tate, E. B., Adams, C. E., Batts Allen, A., Hancock, J. (2007). Self-compassion and reactions to unpleasant self-relevant events: The implications of treating oneself kindly. *Journal of Personality and Social Psychology*, 92(5), 887–904.

Leary, M. R., Tchividjian, L. R., & Kraxberger, B. E. (1994). Self-presentation can be hazardous to your health: Impression management and health risk. *Health Psychology*, 13(6), 461–470.

Leary, M. R., Twenge, J. M., & Quinlivan, E. (2006). Interpersonal rejection as a determinant of anger and aggression. *Personality and Social Psychology Review*, 10(2), 111–132.

LeBel, E. P., & Paunonen, S. V. (2011). Sexy but often unreliable: The impact of unreliability on the replicability of experimental findings with implicit measures. *Personality and Social Psychology Bulletin*, 37(4), 570–583.

Le Bon, G. (1897). *The crowd: A study of the popular mind*. New York: Macmillan.

LeDoux, J. E. (1996) *The emotional brain*. New York: Simon & Schuster.

Lee, E. J. (2007). Deindividuation effects on group polarization in computer-mediated communication: The role of group identification, public-self-awareness, and perceived argument quality. *Journal of Communication*, 57(2), 385–403.

Lee, F. R. (1993, September 20). New York trend: Young urban volunteers. *The New York Times*. Retrieved from http://www.nytimes.com/1993/09/20/nyregion/new-york-trend-young-urban-volunteers.html

Lee, L., Loewenstein, G., Ariely, D., Hong, J., & Young, J. (2008). If I'm not hot, are you hot or not? Physical-attractiveness evaluations and dating preferences as a function of one's own attractiveness. *Psychological Science*, 19(7), 669–677.

Lee, R. Y. P., & Bond, M. H. (1998). Personality and roommate friendship in Chinese culture. *Asian Journal of Social Psychology*, 1(2), 179–190.

Leeming, D. A., & Leeming, M. A. (1994). *A dictionary of creation myths*. Oxford: Oxford University Press.

Lefcourt, H. M. (Ed.) (1981). *Research with the locus of control construct: Vol. 1. Assessment methods*. San Diego: Academic Press.

Lefcourt, H. M. (1992). Durability and impact of the locus of control construct. *Psychological Bulletin*, 112(3), 411–414.

Lefkowitz, M. M., Eron, L. D., Walder, L. O., & Huesmann, L. R. (1977). *Growing up to be violent: A longitudinal study of the development of aggression*. New York: Pergamon.

Lefkowitz, M. M., Huesmann, L. R., & Eron, L. D. (1978). Parental punishment: A longitudinal analysis of effects. *Archives of General Psychiatry*, 35(2), 186–191.

Lehman, D. R., & Taylor, S. E. (1987). Date with an earthquake: Coping with a probable, unpredictable disaster. *Personality and Social Psychology Bulletin*, 13(4), 546–555.

Lehmiller, J. J., Law, A. T., & Tormala, T. T. (2010). The effect of self-affirmation on sexual prejudice. *Journal of Experimental Social Psychology*, 46(2), 276–285.

Leitenberg, H., & Henning, K. (1995). Sexual fantasy. *Psychological Bulletin*, 117(3), 469–496.

Lemay, E. P., Jr., & Clark, M. S. (2008). How the head liberates the heart: Projection of communal responsiveness guides relationship promotion. *Journal of Personality and Social Psychology*, 94(4), 647–671.

Lemay, E. P., Jr., Clark, M. S., & Greenberg, A. (2010). What is beautiful is good because what is beautiful is desired: Physical attractiveness stereotyping as projection of interpersonal goals. *Personality and Social Psychology Bulletin*, 36(3), 339–353.

Lepore, L., & Brown, R. (1997). Category and stereotype activation: Is prejudice inevitable? *Journal of Personality and Social Psychology*, 72(2), 275–287.

Lepper, M. R., Greene, D., & Nisbett, R. E. (1973). Undermining children's intrinsic interest with extrinsic reward: A test of the "overjustification" hypothesis. *Journal of Personality and Social Psychology*, 28(1), 129–137.

Lerner, M. (1980). *The belief in a just world: A fundamental delusion*. New York: Plenum.

Lerner, M. J., & Simmons, C. H. (1966). Observers' reaction to the "innocent victim": Compassion or rejection? *Journal of Personality and Social Psychology*, 4(2), 203–210.

Leung, A. K. Y., & Chiu, C. Y. (2010). Multicultural experience, idea receptiveness, and creativity. *Journal of Cross-Cultural Psychology*, 41(5–6), 723–741.

Leung, K. (1988). Some determinants of conflict avoidance. *Journal of Cross-Cultural Psychology*, 19(1), 125–136.

Leventhal, H. (1970). Findings and theory in the study of fear communications. *Advances in Experimental Social Psychology*, 5, 119–186.

Leventhal, H., Singer, R., & Jones, S. (1965). Effects of fear and specificity of recommendation upon attitudes and behavior. *Journal of Personality and Social Psychology*, 2(1), 20–29.

Levin, P. F., & Isen, A. M. (1975). Further studies on the effect of feeling good on helping. *Sociometry*, 38(1), 141–147. Stable URL: http://www.jstor.org/stable/2786238

Levin, S., Federico, C. M., Sidanius, J., & Rabinowitz, J. L. (2002). Social dominance orientation and intergroup bias: The legitimation of favoritism for high-status groups. *Personality and Social Psychology Bulletin*, 28(2), 144–157.

Levine, R., Sato, S., Hashimoto, T., & Verma, J. (1995). Love and marriage in eleven cultures. *Journal of Cross-Cultural Psychology*, 26(5), 554–571.

Levine, R. A., & Campbell, D. T. (1972). *Ethnocentrism: Theories of conflict, ethnic attitudes and group behavior*. New York: Wiley.

Levine, R. V., Reysen, S., & Ganz, E. (2008). The kindness of strangers revisited: A comparison of 24 US cities. *Social Indicators Research*, 85(3), 461–481.

Levine, S. V. (1981). Cults and mental health: Clinical conclusions. *Canadian Journal of Psychiatry / La Revue canadienne de psychiatrie*, 26(8), 534–539.

Levinger, G. K., & Snoek, J. D. (1972). *Attraction in relationship: A new look at interpersonal attraction*. New York: General Learning Press.

Lewandowski, G. W., & Aron, A. P. (2004). Distinguishing arousal from novelty and challenge in initial romantic attraction between strangers. *Social Behavior and Personality: An International Journal*, 32(4), 361–372.

Lewandowski, G. W., Aron, A., & Gee, J. (2007). Personality goes a long way: The malleability of opposite-sex physical attractiveness. *Personal Relationships*, 14(4), 571–585.

Lewin, K. (1927). Investigations on the psychology of action and affection. III. The memory of completed and uncompleted actions. *Psychologische Forschung*, 9, 1–85.

Lewin, K. (1935). *A dynamic theory of personality*. New York: McGraw-Hill.

Lewin, K. (1936). *Principles of topographical psychology*. New York: McGraw-Hill.

Lewin, K. (1952). *Field theory in social science: Selected theoretical papers*. (D. Cartwright, Ed.). London: Tavistock.

Lewis, T. T., Everson-Rose, S. A., Powell, L. H., Matthews, K. A., Brown, C., Karavolos, K., . . . & Wesley, D. (2006). Chronic exposure to everyday discrimination and coronary artery calcification in African-American women: The SWAN Heart Study. *Psychosomatic Medicine*, 68(3), 362–368.

Leyens, J. P., Camino, L., Parke, R. D., & Berkowitz, L. (1975). Effects of movie violence on aggression in a field setting as a function of group dominance and cohesion. *Journal of Personality and Social Psychology*, 32(2), 346–360.

Leyens, J. P., Désert, M., Croizet, J. C., & Darcis, C. (2000). Stereotype threat: Are lower status and history of stigmatization preconditions of stereotype threat? *Personality and Social Psychology Bulletin*, 26(10), 1189–1199.

Leyens, J. P., Paladino, P. M., Rodriguez-Torres, R., Vaes, J., Demoulin, S., Rodriguez-Perez, A., & Gaunt, R. (2000). The emotional side of prejudice: The attribution of secondary emotions to ingroups and outgroups. *Personality and Social Psychology Review*, 4(2), 186–197.

Leyens, J. P., Rodriguez-Perez, A., Rodriguez-Torres, R., Gaunt, R., Paladino, M. P., Vaes, J., & Demoulin, S. (2001). Psychological essentialism and the differential attribution of uniquely human emotions to ingroups and outgroups. *European Journal of Social Psychology*, 31(4), 395–411.

Li, N. P., & Kenrick, D. T. (2006). Sex similarities and differences in preferences for short-term mates: What, whether, and why. *Journal of Personality and Social Psychology*, 90(3), 468–489.

Li, Y. J., Johnson, K. A., Cohen, A. B., Williams, M. J., Knowles, E. D., & Chen, Z. (2012). Fundamental(ist) attribution error: Protestants are dispositionally focused. *Journal of Personality and Social Psychology*, 102(2), 281–290.

Liberman, N., & Trope, Y. (1998). The role of feasibility and desirability considerations in near and distant future decisions: A test of temporal construal theory. *Journal of Personality and Social Psychology*, 75(1), 5–18.

Liberman, V., Samuels, S. M., & Ross, L. (2004). The name of the game: Predictive power of reputations versus situational labels in determining prisoner's dilemma game moves. *Personality and Social Psychology Bulletin*, 30(9), 1175–1185.

Licata, A., Taylor, S., Berman, M., & Cranston, J. (1993). Effects of cocaine on human aggression. *Pharmacology Biochemistry and Behavior*, 45(3), 549–552.

Lickel, B., Hamilton, D. L., & Sherman, S. J. (2001). Elements of a lay theory of groups: Types of groups, relational styles, and the perception of group entitativity. *Personality and Social Psychology Review*, 5(2), 129–140.

Lickel, B., Hamilton, D. L., Wieczorkowska, G., Lewis, A., Sherman, S. J., & Uhles, A. N. (2000). Varieties of groups and the perception of group entitativity. *Journal of Personality and Social Psychology*, 78(2), 223–246.

Lickel, B., Miller, N., Stenstrom, D. M., Denson, T. F., & Schmader, T. (2006). Vicarious retribution: The role of collective blame in intergroup aggression. *Personality and Social Psychology Review*, 10(4), 372–390.

Lieberman, D., Oum, R., & Kurzban, R. (2008). The family of fundamental social categories includes kinship: Evidence from the memory confusion paradigm. *European Journal of Social Psychology*, 38(6), 998–1012.

Lieberman, J. D., & Arndt, J. (2000). Understanding the limits of limiting instructions: Social psychological explanations for the failures of instructions to disregard pretrial publicity and other inadmissible evidence. *Psychology, Public Policy, and Law*, 6(3), 677–711.

Lieberman, J. D., Solomon, S., Greenberg, J., & McGregor, H. A. (1999). A hot new way to measure aggression: Hot sauce allocation. *Aggressive Behavior*, 25(5), 331–348.

Lieberman, M. D., Gaunt, R., Gilbert, D. T., & Trope, Y. (2002). Reflexion and reflection: A social cognitive neuroscience approach to attributional inference. In M. P. Zanna (Ed.), *Advances in experimental social psychology* (Vol. 34, pp. 199–249). San Diego: Academic Press.

Lifton, R. J. (1979). *The broken connection: On death and the continuity of life*. New York: Basic Books.

Lifton, R. J. (1986). *The Nazi doctors: Medical killing and the psychology of genocide*. New York: Basic Books.

Liljenquist, K., Zhong, C. B., & Galinsky, A. D. (2010). The smell of virtue: Clean scents promote reciprocity and charity. *Psychological Science*, 21(3), 381–383.

Linder, D. E., Cooper, J., & Jones, E. E. (1967). Decision freedom as a determinant of the role of incentive magnitude in attitude change. *Journal of Personality and Social Psychology*, 6(3), 245–254.

Lindquist, C. U., Lindsay, J. S., & White, G. D. (1979). Assessment of assertiveness in drug abusers. *Journal of Clinical Psychology*, 35(3), 676–679.

Lindquist, K. A., Wager, T. D., Kober, H., Bliss-Moreau, E., & Barrett, L. F. (2012). The brain basis of emotion: A meta-analytic review. *Behavioral and Brain Sciences*, 35(3), 121–143.

Linton, R. (1936). *The study of man: An introduction*. New York: Appleton-Century.

Linville, P. W. (1985). Self-complexity and affective extremity: Don't put all of your eggs in one cognitive basket. *Social Cognition*, 3(1), 94–120.

Linville, P. W., Fischer, G. W., & Salovey, P. (1989). Perceived distributions of the characteristics of in-group and out-group members: Empirical evidence and a computer simulation. *Journal of Personality and Social Psychology*, 57(2), 165–188.

Linz, D., Donnerstein, E., & Adams, S. M. (1989). Physiological desensitization and judgments about female victims of violence. *Human Communication Research*, 15(4), 509–522.

Lippa, R. (1998). Gender-related individual differences and the structure of vocational interests: The importance of the people–things dimension. *Journal of Personality and Social Psychology*, 74(4), 996–1009.

Lippa, R. A. (2006). Is high sex drive associated with increased sexual attraction to both sexes? It depends on whether you are male or female. *Psychological Science*, 17(1), 46–52.

Lippa, R. A. (2007). The preferred traits of mates in a cross-national study of heterosexual and homosexual men and women: An examination of biological and cultural influences. *Archives of Sexual Behavior, 36*(2), 193–208.

Little, A. C., & Perrett, D. I. (2002). Putting beauty back in the eye of the beholder. *Psychologist, 15*(1), 28–32.

Liu, J. H., & Latané, B. (1998). Extremitization of attitudes: Does thought- and discussion-induced polarization cumulate? *Basic and Applied Social Psychology, 20*(2), 103–110.

Livshits, G., & Kobyliansky, E. (1991). Fluctuating asymmetry as a possible measure of developmental homeostasis in humans: A review. *Human Biology, 66*(4), 441–466. Stable URL: http://www.jstor.org/stable/41464192

Loeber, R., & Dishion, T. J. (1984). Boys who fight at home and school: Family conditions influencing cross-setting consistency. *Journal of Consulting and Clinical Psychology, 52*(5), 759–768.

Loew, C. A. (1967). Acquisition of a hostile attitude and its relationship to aggressive behavior. *Journal of Personality and Social Psychology, 5*(3), 335–341.

Loewenstein, G. (2005). Hot-cold empathy gaps and medical decision making. *Health Psychology, 24*(4S), S49–S56.

Loffreda, B. (2000). *Losing Matt Shepard.* New York: Columbia University Press.

Loftus, E. F. (2013). Eyewitness testimony in the Lockerbie bombing case. *Memory, 21*(5), 584–590.

Loftus, E. F., Miller, D. G., & Burns, H. J. (1978). Semantic integration of verbal information into a visual memory. *Journal of Experimental Psychology: Human Learning and Memory, 4*(1), 19–31.

Logel, C., Walton, G. M., Spencer, S. J., Iserman, E. C., von Hippel, W., & Bell, A. E. (2009). Interacting with sexist men triggers social identity threat among female engineers. *Journal of Personality and Social Psychology, 96*(6), 1089–1103.

Lohr, S. (2011, November 28). Photoshopped or not? A tool to tell. *The New York Times.* Retrieved from http://www.nytimes.com/2011/11/29/technology/software-to-rate-how-drastically-photos-are-retouched.html?_r=0

Lombardi, W. J., Higgins, E. T., & Bargh, J. A. (1987). The role of consciousness in priming effects on categorization: Assimilation versus contrast as a function of awareness of the priming task. *Personality and Social Psychology Bulletin, 13*(3), 411–429.

Loo, R. (1984). Personality correlates of the fear of death and dying scale. *Journal of Clinical Psychology, 40*(1), 120–122.

Lord, C. G., Ross, L., & Lepper, M. R. (1979). Biased assimilation and attitude polarization: The effects of prior theories on subsequently considered evidence. *Journal of Personality and Social Psychology, 37*(11), 2098–2109.

Lorenz, K. (1966). *On aggression.* New York: Harcourt, Brace & World.

Lott, A. J., & Lott, B. E. (1974). The role of reward in the formation of positive interpersonal attitudes. In T. Huston (Ed.), *Foundations of interpersonal attraction* (pp. 171–192). New York: Academic Press.

Lykken, D. T. (2000). The causes and costs of crime and a controversial cure. *Journal of Personality, 68*(3), 559–605.

Lyubomirsky, S., King, L., & Diener, E. (2005). The benefits of frequent positive affect: Does happiness lead to success? *Psychological Bulletin, 131*(6), 803–855.

Ma, D. S., & Correll, J. (2011). Target prototypicality moderates racial bias in the decision to shoot. *Journal of Experimental Social Psychology, 47*(2), 391–396.

Maass, A., Ceccarelli, R., & Rudin, S. (1996). Linguistic intergroup bias: Evidence for in-group-protective motivation. *Journal of Personality and Social Psychology, 71*(3), 512–526.

Maass, A., & Clark, R. D. (1983). Internalization versus compliance: Differential processes underlying minority influence and conformity. *European Journal of Social Psychology, 13*(3), 197–215.

Maass, A., & Clark, R. D. (1984). Hidden impact of minorities: Fifteen years of minority influence research. *Psychological Bulletin, 95*(3), 428–450.

Maass, A., Volpato, C., & Mucchi-Faina, A. (1996). Social influence and the verifiability of the issue under discussion: Attitudinal versus objective items. *British Journal of Social Psychology, 35*(1), 15–26.

MacBeth, A., & Gumley, A. (2012). Exploring compassion: A meta-analysis of the association between self-compassion and psychopathology. *Clinical Psychology Review, 32,* 545–552.

Maccoby, E. E., & Jacklin, C. N. (1974). *The psychology of sex differences.* Stanford: Stanford University Press.

MacDonald, G., & Leary, M. R. (2005). Why does social exclusion hurt? The relationship between social and physical pain. *Psychological Bulletin, 131*(2), 202–223.

MacEwen, K. E., & Barling, J. (1988). Multiple stressors, violence in the family of origin, and marital aggression: A longitudinal investigation. *Journal of Family Violence, 3*(1), 73–87.

Mackie, D. M., & Worth, L. T. (1989). Processing deficits and the mediation of positive affect in persuasion. *Journal of Personality and Social Psychology, 57*(1), 27–40.

Mackie, D. M., Worth, L. T., & Asuncion, A. G. (1990). Processing of persuasive in-group messages. *Journal of Personality and Social Psychology, 58*(5), 812–822.

Macrae, C. N., Alnwick, K. A., Milne, A. B., & Schloerscheidt, A. M. (2002). Person perception across the menstrual cycle: Hormonal influences on social-cognitive functioning. *Psychological Science, 13*(6), 532–536.

Macrae, C. N., Bodenhausen, G. V., Milne, A. B., & Jetten, J. (1994). Out of mind but back in sight: Stereotypes on the rebound. *Journal of Personality and Social Psychology, 67*(5), 808–817.

Macrae, C. N., Hewstone, M., & Griffiths, R. J. (1993). Processing load and memory for stereotype-based information. *European Journal of Social Psychology, 23*(1), 77–87.

Macrae, C. N., Milne, A. B., & Bodenhausen, G. V. (1994). Stereotypes as energy-saving devices: A peek inside the cognitive toolbox. *Journal of Personality and Social Psychology, 66*(1), 37–47.

Madsen, E.A., Tunney, R. J., Fieldman, G., Plotkin, H. C., Dunbar, R. I. M., Richardson, J., & McFarland, D. (2007). Kinship and altruism: A cross-cultural experimental study. *British Journal of Psychology, 98*(2), 339–359.

Mahler, H. I., Kulik, J. A., Gerrard, M., & Gibbons, F. X. (2007). Long-term effects of appearance-based interventions on sun protection behaviors. *Health Psychology, 26*(3), 350–360.

Main, M. (1995). Recent studies in attachment: overview, with selected implications for clinical work. In S. Goldberg, R. Muir, & J. Kerr (Eds.), *Attachment theory: Social, developmental and clinical perspectives* (pp. 407–474). Hillsdale, NJ: Analytic Press.

Major, B., Carrington, P. I., & Carnevale, P. J. (1984). Physical attractiveness and self-esteem: Attributions for praise from an other-sex evaluator. *Personality and Social Psychology Bulletin, 10*(1), 43–50.

Major, B., Gramzow, R. H., McCoy, S. K., Levin, S., Schmader, T., & Sidanius, J. (2002). Perceiving personal discrimination: The role of group status and legitimizing ideology. *Journal of Personality and Social Psychology, 82*(3), 269–282.

Major, B., Quinton, W. J., & Schmader, T. (2003). Attributions to discrimination and self-esteem: Impact of group identification and situational ambiguity. *Journal of Experimental Social Psychology, 39*(3), 220–231.

Major, B., & Schmader, T. (1998). Coping with stigma through psychological disengagement. In J. K. Swim & C. Stangor (Eds.), *Prejudice: The target's perspective* (pp. 219–241). San Diego: Academic Press.

Ma-Kellams, C., & Blascovich, J. (2012). Enjoying life in the face of death: East–West differences in responses to mortality salience. *Journal of Personality and Social Psychology, 103*(5), 773–786.

Mala, E., & Goodman, J. D. (2011, July 22). At least 80 dead in Norway shooting. *The New York Times.* Retrieved from http://www.nytimes.com/2011/07/23/world/europe/23oslo.html?pagewanted=all&_r=0

Malamuth, N. M. (1981). Rape proclivity among males. *Journal of Social Issues, 37*(4), 138–157.

Malamuth, N. M. (2007). Hostile masculinity syndrome. In R. Baumeister & K. Vohs (Eds.), *Encyclopedia of social psychology* (p. 448). Thousand Oaks, CA: Sage.

Malamuth, N. M., & Check, J. V. (1981). The effects of mass media exposure on acceptance of violence against women: A field experiment. *Journal of Research in Personality, 15*(4), 436–446.

Malamuth, N., & Huppin, M. (2007). Rape. In R. Baumeister, & K. Vohs (Eds.), *Encyclopedia of social psychology* (pp. 723–724). Thousand Oaks, CA: Sage.

Malka, A., Soto, C. J., Cohen, A. B., & Miller, D. T. (2011). Religiosity and social welfare: Competing influences of cultural conservatism and prosocial value orientation. *Journal of Personality, 79*(4), 763–792.

Malle, B. F. (2006). The actor-observer asymmetry in attribution: A (surprising) meta-analysis. *Psychological Bulletin, 132*(6), 895–919.

Malle, B. F., & Hodges, S. D. (Eds.). (2005). *Other minds: How humans bridge the divide between self and others.* New York: Guilford Press.

Malle, B. F., Knobe, J. M., & Nelson, S. E. (2007). Actor-observer asymmetries in explanations of behavior: New answers to an old question. *Journal of Personality and Social Psychology, 93*(4), 491–514.

Manago, A. M., Taylor, T., & Greenfield, P. M. (2012). Me and my 400 friends: The anatomy of college students' Facebook networks, their communication patterns, and well-being. *Developmental Psychology, 48*(2), 369–380.

Mandler, G. (1984). *Mind and body: Psychology of emotion and stress.* New York: W. W. Norton.

Mandler, J. (2004). *The foundations of mind: Origins of conceptual thoughts.* New York: Oxford University Press.

Mann, L. (1981). The baiting crowd in episodes of threatened suicide. *Journal of Personality and Social Psychology, 41*(4), 703–709.

Manning, R., Levine, M., & Collins, A. (2007). The Kitty Genovese murder and the social psychology of helping: The parable of the 38 witnesses. *American Psychologist, 62*(6), 555–562.

Mansouri, F. A., Tanaka, K., & Buckley, M. J. (2009). Conflict-induced behavioural adjustment: a clue to the executive functions of the prefrontal cortex. *Nature Reviews Neuroscience, 10*(2), 141–152.

Mantell, D. M. (1971). The potential for violence in Germany. *Journal of Social Issues*, 27(4), 101–112.

Marcus, D. K., & Miller, R. S. (2003). Sex differences in judgments of physical attractiveness: A social relations analysis. *Personality and Social Psychology Bulletin*, 29(3), 325–335.

Marcus-Newhall, A., Pedersen, W. C., Carlson, M., & Miller, N. (2000). Displaced aggression is alive and well: A meta-analytic review. *Journal of Personality and Social Psychology*, 78(4), 670–689.

Markman, K. D., & Miller, A. K. (2006). Depression, control, and counterfactual thinking: Functional for whom? *Journal of Social and Clinical Psychology*, 25(2), 210–227.

Marks, G., & Miller, N. (1987). Ten years of research on the false-consensus effect: An empirical and theoretical review. *Psychological Bulletin*, 102(1), 72–90.

Markus, H. (1977). Self-schemata and processing information about the self. *Journal of Personality and Social Psychology*, 35(2), 63–78.

Markus, H. R., & Kitayama, S. (1991). Culture and the self: Implications for cognition, emotion, and motivation. *Psychological Review*, 98(2), 224–253.

Markus, H., & Kunda, Z. (1986). Stability and malleability of the self-concept. *Journal of Personality and Social Psychology*, 51(4), 858–866.

Markus, H., & Nurius, P. (1986). Possible selves. *American Psychologist*, 41(9), 954–969.

Marston, P. J., Hecht, M. L., Manke, M. L., McDaniel, S., & Reeder, H. (1998). The subjective experience of intimacy, passion, and commitment in heterosexual loving relationships. *Personal Relationships*, 5(1), 15–30.

Martens, A., Greenberg, J., & Allen, J. B. (2008). Self-esteem and autonomic physiology: Parallels between self-esteem and cardiac vagal tone as buffers of threat. *Personality and Social Psychology Review*, 12(4), 370–389.

Martens, A., Kosloff, S., Greenberg, J., Landau, M. J., & Schmader, T. (2007). Killing begets killing: Evidence from a bug-killing paradigm that initial killing fuels subsequent killing. *Personality and Social Psychology Bulletin*, 33(9), 1251–1264.

Martin, C. L., Eisenbud, L., & Rose, H. (1995). Children's gender-based reasoning about toys. *Child Development*, 66(5), 1453–1471.

Martin, L. L. (1986). Set/reset: The use and disuse of concepts in impression formation. *Journal of Personality and Social Psychology*, 51(3), 493–504.

Martin, R., Martin, P. Y., Smith, J. R., & Hewstone, M. (2007). Majority versus minority influence and prediction of behavioral intentions and behavior. *Journal of Experimental Social Psychology*, 43(5), 763–771.

Marx, D. M., & Roman, J. S. (2002). Female role models: Protecting women's math test performance. *Personality and Social Psychology Bulletin*, 28(9), 1183–1193.

Marx, G. (1959). *Groucho and me*. New York: Bernard Geis Associates.

Marx, K. (1847). Wage labor and capital (F. Engels, Trans.) [On-line document]. Marx/Engels Internet Archive (http://www.marxists.org). Retrieved from http://www.marxists.org/archive/marx/works/1847/wage-labour/ch06.htm

Maslow, A. (1964). *Religion, values and peak experiences*. New York: Viking.

Maslow, A. H., Frager, R., & Fadiman, J. (1970). *Motivation and personality* (Vol. 2). New York: Harper & Row.

Mason, A. E., Law, R., Bryan, A. E. B., Portley, R., & Sbarra, D. A. (2012). Facing a breakup: Electromyographic responses moderate self-concept recovery following a romantic separation. *Personal Relationships*, 19(3), 551–568.

Mastro, D. E. (2003). A social identity approach to understanding the impact of television messages. *Communication Monographs*, 70(2), 98–113.

Masuda, M., & Duck, S. (2002). Issues in ebb and flow: Management and maintenance of relationships as a skilled activity. In J. H. Harvey & A. Wenzel (Eds.), *A clinician's guide to maintaining and enhancing close relationships* (pp. 13–41). Mahwah, NJ: Erlbaum.

Matsumura, A., & Ohtsubo, Y. (2012). Praise is reciprocated with tangible benefits: Social exchange between symbolic resources and concrete resources. *Social Psychological and Personality Science*, 3(2), 250–256.

McAdams, D. P. (1980). A thematic coding system for the intimacy motive. *Journal of Research in Personality*, 14(4), 413–432.

McAdams, D. P. (1988). Personal needs and personal relationships. In S. Duck (Ed.), *Handbook of personal relationships: Theory, research, and interventions* (pp. 7–22). New York: Wiley.

McAdams, D. P. (1989). *Intimacy: The need to be close*. New York: Doubleday.

McAdams, D. P. (1993). *The stories we live by: Personal myths and the making of the self*. New York: William Morrow.

McAdams, D. P. (2001). The psychology of life stories. *Review of General Psychology*, 5(2), 100–122.

McAdams, D. P. (2006). *The redemptive self*. New York: Oxford University Press.

McArthur, L. A. (1972). The how and what of why: Some determinants and consequences of causal attribution. *Journal of Personality and Social Psychology*, 22(2), 171–193.

McArthur, L. Z., & Baron, R. M. (1983). Toward an ecological theory of social perception. *Psychological Review*, 90(3), 215–238.

McArthur, L. Z., & Post, D. L. (1977). Figural emphasis and person perception. *Journal of Experimental Social Psychology*, 13(6), 520–535.

McCarrey, M., Edwards, H. P., & Rozario, W. (1982). Ego-relevant feedback, affect, and self-serving attributional bias. *Personality and Social Psychology Bulletin*, 8(2), 189–194.

McCauley, C. (1998). When screen violence is not attractive. In J. H. Goldstein (Ed.), *Why we watch: The attractions of violent entertainment* (pp. 144–162). New York: Oxford University Press.

McClelland, D. C., Atkinson, J. W., Clark, R. A., & Lowell, E. L. (1953). *The achievement motive*. New York: Appleton-Century-Crofts.

McClure, E. B. (2000). A meta-analytic review of sex differences in facial expression processing and their development in infants, children, and adolescents. *Psychological Bulletin*, 126(3), 424–453.

McConnell, A. R., & Leibold, J. M. (2001). Relations among the Implicit Association Test, discriminatory behavior, and explicit measures of racial attitudes. *Journal of Experimental Social Psychology*, 37(5), 435–442.

McConnell, A. R., Renaud, J. M., Dean, K. K., Green, S. P., Lamoreaux, M. J., Hall, C. E., & Rydell, R. J. (2005). Whose self is it anyway? Self-aspect control moderates the relation between self-complexity and well-being. *Journal of Experimental Social Psychology*, 41(1), 1–18.

McCord, J. (1983). A longitudinal study of aggression and antisocial behavior. In K. T. van Dusen & S. A. Mednick (Eds.), *Prospective studies of crime and delinquency* (pp. 269–275). Boston: Kluwer-Nijhoff Publishing Company.

McCoy, S. K., & Major, B. (2003). Group identification moderates emotional responses to perceived prejudice. *Personality and Social Psychology Bulletin*, 29(8), 1005–1017.

McCrea, S. M., Hirt, E. R., & Milner, B. J. (2008). She works hard for the money: Valuing effort underlies gender differences in behavioral self-handicapping. *Journal of Experimental Social Psychology*, 44(2), 292–311.

McCullough, M. E. (2008). *Beyond revenge: The evolution of the forgiveness instinct*. San Francisco: Jossey-Bass.

McCullough, M. E., Emmons, R. A., & Tsang, J. A. (2002). The grateful disposition: A conceptual and empirical topography. *Journal of Personality and Social Psychology*, 82(1), 112–127.

McDermott, R., Tingley, D., Cowden, J., Frazzetto, G., & Johnson, D. D. (2009). Monoamine oxidase A gene (MAOA) predicts behavioral aggression following provocation. *Proceedings of the National Academy of Sciences*, 106(7), 2118–2123.

McDougall, W. (1908). *An introduction to social psychology*. London: Methuen.

McDougall, W. (1923). *An outline of psychology*. London: Methuen.

McFarland, C., & Ross, M. (1987). The relation between current impressions and memories of self and dating partners. *Personality and Social Psychology Bulletin*, 13(2), 228–238.

McGinnis, S. L. (2003). Cohabitating, dating, and perceived costs of marriage: A model of marriage entry. *Journal of Marriage and the Family*, 65(1), 105–116.

McGuire, W. J. (1964). Inducing resistance to persuasion: Some contemporary approaches. In L. Berkowitz (Ed.), *Advances in experimental social psychology* (Vol. 1, pp. 191–229). New York: Academic Press.

McGuire, W. J. (1968). Personality and attitude change: An information-processing theory. In A. G. Greenwald, T. C. Brock, & T. A. Ostrom (Eds.), *Psychological foundations of attitudes* (pp. 171–196). San Diego: Academic Press.

McGuire, W. J., & Papageorgis, D. (1961). The relative efficacy of various types of prior belief-defense in producing immunity against persuasion. *Journal of Abnormal and Social Psychology*, 62(2), 327–337.

McGuire, W. J., McGuire, C. V., Child, P., & Fujioka, T. (1978). Salience of ethnicity in the spontaneous self-concept as a function of one's ethnic distinctiveness in the social environment. *Journal of Personality and Social Psychology*, 36(5), 511–520.

McIntyre, R. B., Paulson, R. M., & Lord, C. G. (2003). Alleviating women's mathematics stereotype threat through salience of group achievements. *Journal of Experimental Social Psychology*, 39(1), 83–90.

McKenna, T. (1993). *True hallucinations: Being an account of the author's extraordinary adventures in the devil's paradise*. New York: HarperCollins.

McNulty, J. K., & Karney, B. R. (2001). Attributions in marriage: Integrating specific and global evaluations of a relationship. *Personality and Social Psychology Bulletin*, 27(8), 943–955.

McNulty, J. K., & Karney, B. R. (2004). Positive expectations in the early years of marriage: Should couples expect the best or brace for the worst? *Journal of Personality and Social Psychology*, 86(5), 729–743.

McNulty, J. K., O'Mara, E. M., & Karney, B. R. (2008). Benevolent cognitions as a strategy of relationship maintenance: "Don't sweat the small stuff" . . . . But it is not all small stuff. *Journal of Personality and Social Psychology*, 94(4), 631–646.

McPherson, S., & Joireman, J. (2009). Death in groups: Mortality salience and the interindividual-intergroup discontinuity effect. *Group Processes & Intergroup Relations*, 12(4), 419–429.

Mead, G. H. (1934). *Mind, self, and society*. Chicago: University of Chicago Press.

Medavoy, M., Messer, A. W., Oliver B., Franklin, S., (Producers), & Aronofsky, D., (Director). (2010). *Black Swan* [Motion picture]. United States: Fox Searchlight Pictures, Protozoa Pictures, & Phoenix Pictures, in association with Cross Creek Pictures & Dune Entertainment.

Medvec, V. H., Madey, S. F., & Gilovich, T. (1995). When less is more: Counterfactual thinking and satisfaction among Olympic medalists. *Journal of Personality and Social Psychology, 69*(4), 603–610.

Meeus, W. H. J., & Raaijmakers, Q. A. W. (1995). Obedience in modern society: The Utrecht studies. *Journal of Social Issues, 51*(3), 155–176.

Megargee, E. I. (1966). Undercontrolled and overcontrolled personality types in extreme antisocial aggression. *Psychological Monographs: General and Applied, 80*(3), 1–29.

Mehl, M. R., Vazire, S., Ramírez-Esparza, N., Slatcher, R. B., & Pennebaker, J. W. (2007). Are women really more talkative than men? *Science, 317*(5834), 82.

Meltzoff, A. N., & Moore, M. K. (1977). Imitation of facial and manual gestures by human neonates. *Science, 198*(4312), 75–78.

Menaker, E. (1982). *Otto Rank: A rediscovered legacy*. New York: Columbia University Press.

Mendes, W. B., Blascovich, J., Lickel, B., & Hunter, S. (2002). Challenge and threat during social interactions with White and Black men. *Personality and Social Psychology Bulletin, 28*(7), 939–952.

Merton, R. K. (1948). The self-fulfilling prophecy. *Antioch Review, 8*(2), 193–210. Stable URL: http://www.jstor.org/stable/4609267

Merwin, W. S. (1970). *The carrier of ladders*. New York: Atheneum.

Mesquita, B., & Frijda, N. H. (1992). Cultural variations in emotions: A review. *Psychological Bulletin, 112*(2), 179–204.

Messick, D. M., & Mackie, D. M. (1989). Intergroup relations. *Annual Review of Psychology, 40*, 45–81.

Meston, C. M., & Buss, D. M. (2007). Why humans have sex. *Archives of Sexual Behavior, 36*(4), 477–507.

Meston, C. M., & Frohlich, P. F. (2003). Love at first fright: Partner salience moderates roller-coaster-induced excitation transfer. *Archives of Sexual Behavior, 32*(6), 537–544.

Metcalfe, J., & Mischel, W. (1999). A hot/cool-system analysis of delay of gratification: Dynamics of willpower. *Psychological Review, 106*(1), 3–19.

Meyer, I. H. (2003). Prejudice, social stress, and mental health in lesbian, gay, and bisexual populations: Conceptual issues and research evidence. *Psychological Bulletin, 129*(5), 674–697.

Meyer-Lindenberg, A., Buckholtz, J. W., Kolachana, B., Hariri, A. R., Pezawas, L., Blasi, G., . . . & Weinberger, D. R. (2006). Neural mechanisms of genetic risk for impulsivity and violence in humans. *Proceedings of the National Academy of Sciences, 103*(16), 6269–6274.

Michotte, A. (1963). *The perception of causality*. Oxford: Basic Books.

Mickelson, K. D., Kessler, R. C., & Shaver, P. R. (1997). Adult attachment in a nationally representative sample. *Journal of Personality and Social Psychology, 73*(5), 1092–1106.

Midlarsky, E., Fagin Jones, S., & Corley, R. P. (2005). Personality correlates of heroic rescue during the Holocaust. *Journal of Personality, 73*(4), 907–934.

Mikolajczak, M., Gross, J. J., Lane, A., Corneille, O., de Timary, P., & Luminet, O. (2010). Oxytocin makes people trusting, not gullible. *Psychological Science, 21*(8), 1072–1074.

Mikulincer, M. (1997). Adult attachment style and information processing: Individual differences in curiosity and cognitive closure. *Journal of Personality and Social Psychology, 72*(5), 1217–1230.

Mikulincer, M. (2006). Attachment, caregiving, and sex within romantic relationships: A behavioral systems perspective. In M. Mikulincer & G. S. Goodman (Eds.), *Dynamics of romantic love* (pp. 23–44). New York: Guilford Press.

Mikulincer, M., Dolev, T., & Shaver, P. R. (2004). Attachment-related strategies during thought suppression: Ironic rebounds and vulnerable self-representations. *Journal of Personality and Social Psychology, 87*(6), 940–956.

Mikulincer, M., Florian, V., & Hirschberger, G. (2003). The existential function of close relationships: Introducing death into the science of love. *Personality and Social Psychology Review, 7*(1), 20–40.

Mikulincer, M., Gillath, O., Halevy, V., Avihou, N., Avidan, S., & Eshkoli, N. (2001). Attachment theory and reactions to others' needs: Evidence that activation of the sense of attachment security promotes empathic responses. *Journal of Personality and Social Psychology, 81*(6), 1205–1224.

Mikulincer, M., & Shaver, P. R. (2007). *Attachment in adulthood: Structure, dynamics, and change*. New York: Guilford Press.

Mikulincer, M., Shaver, P. R., Gillath, O., & Nitzberg, R. A. (2005). Attachment, caregiving, and altruism: Boosting attachment security increases compassion and helping. *Journal of Personality and Social Psychology, 89*(5), 817–839.

Miles, D. R., & Carey, G. (1997). Genetic and environmental architecture on human aggression. *Journal of Personality and Social Psychology, 72*(1), 207–217.

Milgram, S. (1963). Behavioral study of obedience. *Journal of Abnormal and Social Psychology, 67*(4), 371–378.

Milgram, S. (1970). The experience of living in cities. *Science, 167*(3924), 1461–1468.

Milgram, S. (1974). *Obedience to authority: An experimental view*. New York: Harper & Row.

Milgram, S., Bickman, L., & Berkowitz, L. (1969). Note on the drawing power of crowds of different size. *Journal of Personality and Social Psychology, 13*(2), 79–82.

Miller, C. T., Rothblum, E. D., Felicio, D., & Brand, P. (1995). Compensating for stigma: Obese and nonobese women's reactions to being visible. *Personality and Social Psychology Bulletin, 21*(10), 1093–1106.

Miller, D. T., & McFarland, C. (1986). Counterfactual thinking and victim compensation: A test of norm theory. *Personality and Social Psychology Bulletin, 12*(4), 513–519.

Miller, D. T., Norman, S. A., & Wright, E. (1978). Distortion in person perception as a consequence of the need for effective control. *Journal of Personality and Social Psychology, 36*(6), 598–607.

Miller, G., Tybur, J. M., & Jordan, B. D. (2007). Ovulatory cycle effects on tip earnings by lap dancers: Economic evidence for human estrus? *Evolution and Human Behavior, 28*(6), 375–381.

Miller, J. G. (1984). Culture and the development of everyday social explanation. *Journal of Personality and Social Psychology, 46*(5), 961–978.

Miller, N., & Campbell, D. T. (1959). Recency and primacy in persuasion as a function of the timing of speeches and measurements. *Journal of Abnormal and Social Psychology, 59*(1), 1–9.

Miller, N., & Carlson, M. (1990). Valid theory-testing meta-analyses further question the negative state relief model of helping. *Psychological Bulletin, 107*(2), 215–225.

Miller, N., & Marks, G. (1982). Assumed similarity between self and other: Effect of expectation of future interaction with that other. *Social Psychology Quarterly, 45*(2), 100–105. Stable URL: http://www.jstor.org/stable/3033932

Miller, N., Maruyama, G., Beaber, R. J., & Valone, K. (1976). Speed of speech and persuasion. *Journal of Personality and Social Psychology, 34*(4), 615–624.

Miller, N., Pedersen, W. C., Earleywine, M., & Pollock, V. E. (2003). A theoretical model of triggered displaced aggression. *Personality and Social Psychology Review, 7*(1), 75–97.

Miller, N. E., & Bugelski, R. (1948). Minor studies of aggression: II. The influence of frustrations imposed by the in-group on attitudes expressed toward out-groups. *Journal of Psychology, 25*(2), 437–442.

Miller, R. S. (1996). *Embarrassment: Poise and peril in everyday life*. New York: Guilford Press.

Miller, R. S. (1997). We always hurt the ones we love: Aversive interpersonal interactions in close relationships. In R. M. Kowalski (Ed.), *Aversive interpersonal behaviors* (pp. 11–29). New York: Plenum Press.

Miller, R. S. (2001). *Behaving badly: Aversive behaviors in interpersonal relationships*. Washington, DC: American Psychological Association.

Miller, S. L., & Maner, J. K. (2010). Scent of a woman: Men's testosterone responses to olfactory ovulation cues. *Psychological Science, 21*(2), 276–283.

Mills, J., & Aronson, E. (1965). Opinion change as a function of the communicator's attractiveness and desire to influence. *Journal of Personality and Social Psychology, 1*(2), 173–177.

Milne, S., Orbell, S., & Sheeran, P. (2002). Combining motivational and volitional interventions to promote exercise participation: Protection motivation theory and implementation intentions. *British Journal of Health Psychology, 7*(2), 163–184.

Miroff, N., & Booth, W. (2010, July 27). Mexican drug cartels bring violence with them in move to Central America. *The Washington Post*. Retrieved from http://www.washingtonpost.com/wp-dyn/content/article/2010/07/26/AR2010072605661.html

Miron, A. M., Branscombe, N. R., & Schmitt, M. T. (2006). Collective guilt as distress over illegitimate intergroup inequality. *Group Processes & Intergroup Relations, 9*(2), 163–180.

Mischel, W. (1977). The interaction of person and situation. In D. Magnusson & N. S. Endler (Eds.), *Personality at the crossroads: Current issues in interactional psychology* (pp. 333–352). Hillsdale, NJ: Erlbaum.

Mischel, W., & Ayduk, O. (2002). Self-regulation in a cognitive-affective personality system: Attentional control in the service of the self. *Self and Identity, 1*(2), 113–120.

Mischel, W., & Ayduk, O. (2004). Willpower in a cognitive-affective processing system: The dynamics of delay of gratification. In R. F. Baumeister & K. D. Vohs (Eds.), *Handbook of self-regulation: Research, theory, and applications* (pp. 99–129). New York: Guilford Press.

Mischel, W., & Ebbesen, E. B. (1970). Attention in delay of gratification. *Journal of Personality and Social Psychology, 16*(2), 329–337.

Mischel, W., & Peake, P. K. (1982). Beyond déjà vu in the search for cross-situational consistency. *Psychological Review, 89*(6), 730–755.

Mitchell, B. (2009, June 30). Troops find love in war on web. Military.com. Retrieved from http://www.military.com/cs/Satellite?c=maArticle&cid=1199422038952&pagename=News%2FnwsLayout

Mitchell, T. R., Thompson, L., Peterson, E., & Cronk, R. (1997). Temporal adjustments in the evaluation of events: The "rosy view." *Journal of Experimental Social Psychology, 33*(4), 421–448.

Mithen, S. (1996). *The prehistory of the mind: A search for the origins of art, religion, and science.* London: Thames and Hudson.

Mithen, S. (Ed.). (1998). *Creativity in human evolution and prehistory.* London: Routledge.

Miyake, A., Kost-Smith, L. E., Finkelstein, N. D., Pollock, S. J., Cohen, G. L., & Ito, T. A. (2010). Reducing the gender achievement gap in college science: A classroom study of values affirmation. *Science, 330*(6008), 1234–1237.

Moghaddam, F. M. (1988). Individualistic and collective integration strategies among immigrants. In J. W. Berry & R. C. Annis (Eds.), *Ethnic psychology* (pp. 69–79). Amsterdam: Swets & Zeitlinger.

Molloy, M., & Bowden, C. (Eds.). (2011). *El sicario: The autobiography of a Mexican assassin.* New York: Nation Books.

Montoya, R. M., Horton, R. S., & Kirchner, J. (2008). Is actual similarity necessary for attraction? A meta-analysis of actual and perceived similarity. *Journal of Social and Personal Relationships, 25*(6), 889–922.

Montoya, R. M., & Insko, C. A. (2008). Toward a more complete understanding of the reciprocity of liking effect. *European Journal of Social Psychology, 38*(3), 477–498.

Moore, L. V., & Diez Roux, A. V. (2006). Associations of neighborhood characteristics with the location and type of food stores. *American Journal of Public Health, 96*(2), 325–331.

Moreland, R. L., & Beach, S. R. (1992). Exposure effects in the classroom: The development of affinity among students. *Journal of Experimental Social Psychology, 28*(3), 255–276.

Morelli, G. A., & Rothbaum, F. (2007). Situating the child in context: Attachment relationships and self-regulation in different cultures. In S. Kitayama & D. Cohen (Eds.) *Handbook of cultural psychology* (pp. 500–527). New York: Guilford Press.

Mori, D., Chaiken, S., & Pliner, P. (1987). "Eating lightly" and the self-presentation of femininity. *Journal of Personality and Social Psychology, 53*(4), 693–702.

Morris, M. W., & Peng, K. (1994). Culture and cause: American and Chinese attributions for social and physical events. *Journal of Personality and Social Psychology, 67*(6), 949–971.

Morrison, M., & Roese, N. J. (2011). Regrets of the typical American: Findings from a nationally representative sample. *Social Psychological and Personality Science, 2*(6), 576–583.

Morse, S., & Gergen, K. J. (1970). Social comparison, self-consistency, and the concept of self. *Journal of Personality and Social Psychology, 16*(1), 148–156.

Moscovici, S. (1980). Toward a theory of conversion behavior. In L. Berkowitz (Ed.), *Advances in experimental social psychology* (Vol. 13, pp. 209–239). New York: Academic Press.

Moscovici, S., Lage, S., & Naffrechoux, M. (1969). Influence of a consistent minority on the responses of a majority in a color perception task. *Sociometry, 32*(4), 365–380. Stable URL: http://www.jstor.org/stable/2786541

Moscovici, S., Mungy, G., & Van Avermaet, E. (Eds.) (1985). *Perspectives on minority influence.* Cambridge: Cambridge University Press.

Moscovici, S., & Zavalloni, M. (1969). The group as a polarizer of attitudes. *Journal of Personality and Social Psychology, 12*(2), 125–35.

Moskalenko, S., & Heine, S. J. (2003). Watching your troubles away: Television viewing as a stimulus for subjective self-awareness. *Personality and Social Psychology Bulletin, 29*(1), 76–85.

Moskowitz, G. (2005). *Social cognition.* New York: Guilford Press.

Moskowitz, G. B. (2010). On the control over stereotype activation and stereotype inhibition. *Social and Personality Psychology Compass, 4*(2), 140–158.

Moskowitz, G. B., & Li, P. (2011). Egalitarian goals trigger stereotype inhibition: A proactive form of stereotype control. *Journal of Experimental Social Psychology, 47*(1), 103–116.

Motyl, M., Hart, J., Pyszczynski, T., Weise, D., Maxfield, M., & Siedel, A. (2011). Subtle priming of shared human experiences eliminates threat-induced negativity toward Arabs, immigrants, and peace-making. *Journal of Experimental Social Psychology, 47*(6), 1179–1184.

Mountain, M. (2012, February 21). Big step forward for rights of dolphins and whales [Web log post]. Earth in Transition. Retrieved from http://www.earthintransition.org/2012/02/big-step-forward-for-rights-of-dolphins-and-whales/

Mucchi-Faina, A., Maass, A., & Volpato, C. (1991). Social influence: The role of originality. *European Journal of Social Psychology, 21*(3), 183–197.

Mueller, C. W., & Donnerstein, E. (1981). Film-facilitated arousal and prosocial behavior. *Journal of Experimental Social Psychology, 17* (3), l–41.

Mullen, B. (1986). Atrocity as a function of lynch mob composition: A self-attention perspective. *Personality and Social Psychology Bulletin, 12*(2), 187–197.

Mullen, B., Atkins, J. L., Champion, D. S., Edwards, C., Hardy, D., Story, J. E., & Vanderklok, M. (1985). The false consensus effect: A meta-analysis of 115 hypothesis tests. *Journal of Experimental Social Psychology, 21*(3), 262–283.

Munafò, M. R., Clark, T. G., Moore, L. R., Payne, E., Walton, R., & Flint, J. (2003). Genetic polymorphisms and personality in healthy adults: A systematic review and meta-analysis. *Molecular Psychiatry, 8*(5), 471–484.

Muraven, M., Baumeister, R. F., & Tice, D. M. (1999). Longitudinal improvement of self-regulation through practice: Building self-control strength through repeated exercise. *Journal of Social Psychology, 139*(4), 446–457.

Muraven, M., Collins, R. L., & Neinhaus, K. (2002). Self-control and alcohol restraint: An initial application of the self-control strength model. *Psychology of Addictive Behaviors, 16*(2), 113–120.

Muraven, M., Tice, D. M., & Baumeister, R. F. (1998). Self-control as a limited resource: Regulatory depletion patterns. *Journal of Personality and Social Psychology, 74*(3), 774–789.

Murphy, F. C., Nimmo-Smith, I., & Lawrence, A. D. (2003). Functional neuroanatomy of emotions: A meta-analysis. *Cognitive, Affective & Behavioral Neuroscience, 3*(3), 207–233.

Murphy, G., Murphy, L. B., & Newcomb, T. M. (1937). *Experimental social psychology* (Rev. ed.). New York: Harper.

Murphy, W. D., Coleman, E. M., & Haynes, M. R. (1986). Factors related to coercive sexual behavior in a nonclinical sample of males. *Violence and Victims, 1*(4), 255–278.

Murray, L., & Trevarthen, C. (1986). The infant's role in mother-infant communications. *Journal of Child Language, 13*(1), 15–29.

Murray, S. L., & Holmes, J. G. (1993). Seeing virtues in faults: Negativity and the transformation of interpersonal narratives in close relationships. *Journal of Personality and Social Psychology, 65*(4), 707–722.

Murray, S. L., & Holmes, J. G. (1997). A leap of faith? Positive illusions in romantic relationships. *Personality and Social Psychology Bulletin, 23*(6), 586–604.

Murray, S. L., & Holmes, J. G. (1999). The (mental) ties that bind: Cognitive structures that predict relationship resilience. *Journal of Personality and Social Psychology, 77*(6), 1228–1244.

Murray, S. L., Holmes, J. G., Bellavia, G., Griffin, D. W., & Dolderman, D. (2002). Kindred spirits? The benefits of egocentrism in close relationships. *Journal of Personality and Social Psychology, 82*(4), 563–581.

Murray, S. L., Holmes, J. G., Dolderman, D., & Griffin, D. W. (2000). What the motivated mind sees: Comparing friends' perspectives to married partners' views of each other. *Journal of Experimental Social Psychology, 36*(6), 600–620.

Murray, S. L., Holmes, J. G., & Griffin, D. W. (1996). The benefits of positive illusions: Idealization and the construction of satisfaction in close relationships. *Journal of Personality and Social Psychology, 70*(1), 79–98.

Murray, S. L., Rose, P., Bellavia, G. M., Holmes, J. G., & Kusche, A. G. (2002). When rejection stings: How self-esteem constrains relationship-enhancement processes. *Journal of Personality and Social Psychology, 83*(3), 556–573.

Murstein, B. I. (1987). A clarification and extension of the SVR theory of dyadic pairing. *Journal of Marriage and Family, 49*(4), 929–933. Stable URL: http://www.jstor.org/stable/351985

Myers, D. G. (1975). Discussion-induced attitude polarization. *Human Relations, 28*(8), 699–714.

Myers, D. G. (1982). Polarization effects of social interaction. In H. Brandstatter, J. H. Davis, & G. Stocher-Kreichgauer (Eds.), *Contemporary problems in group decision-making* (pp. 125–161). New York: Academic Press.

Myers, D. G., & Bishop, G. D. (1970). Discussion effects on racial attitudes. *Science, 169*(3947), 778–779.

Myers, D. G., Bruggink, J. B., Kersting, R. C., & Schlosser, B. A. (1980). Does learning others' opinions change one's opinions? *Personality and Social Psychology Bulletin, 6*(2), 253–260.

Myers, D. G., & Lamm, H. (1976). The group polarization phenomenon. *Psychological Bulletin, 83*(4), 602–627.

Nadler, A., Goldberg, M., & Jaffe, Y. (1982). Effect of self-differentiation and anonymity in group on deindividuation. *Journal of Personality and Social Psychology, 42*(6), 1127–1136.

Nasby, W., Hayden, B., & DePaulo, B. M. (1980). Attributional bias among aggressive boys to interpret unambiguous social stimuli as displays of hostility. *Journal of Abnormal Psychology, 89*(3), 459–468.

National Gang Center (2011). National youth gang survey analysis. Retrieved from https://www.nationalgangcenter.gov/Survey-Analysis/Demographics#anchorregm

National Safety Council (2013). *Injury Facts 2014 edition.* Itasca, IL: National Safety Council.

Neff, K. D. (2011). *Self-compassion.* New York: William Morrow.

Neff, K. D., & Vonk, R. (2009). Self-compassion versus global self-esteem: Two different ways of relating to oneself. *Journal of Personality, 77*(1), 23–50.

Neff, L. A., & Karney, B. R. (2002). Judgments of a relationship partner: Specific accuracy but global enhancement. *Journal of Personality, 70*(6), 1079–1112.

Neff, L. A., & Karney, B. R. (2003). The dynamic structure of relationship perceptions: Differential importance as a strategy of relationship maintenance. *Personality and Social Psychology Bulletin, 29*(11), 1433–1446.

Neff, L. A., & Karney, B. R. (2004). How does context affect intimate relationships? Linking external stress and cognitive processes within marriage. *Personality and Social Psychology Bulletin, 30*(2), 134–148.

Neff, L. A., & Karney, B. R. (2005). To know you is to love you: The implications of global adoration and specific accuracy for marital relationships. *Journal of Personality and Social Psychology, 88*(3), 480–497.

Neff, L. A., & Karney, B. R. (2009). Stress and reactivity to daily relationship experiences: How stress hinders adaptive processes in marriage. *Journal of Personality and Social Psychology, 97*(3), 435–450.

Neiss, M. B., Sedikides, C., & Stevenson, J. (2002). Self-esteem: A behavioural genetic perspective. *European Journal of Personality, 16*(5), 351–367.

Nelson, L. D., & Morrison, E. L. (2005). The symptoms of resource scarcity: Judgments of food and finances influence preferences for potential partners. *Psychological Science, 16*(2), 167–173.

Nelson, R. 1969. *Hunters of the northern ice.* Chicago: Aldine.

Nelson, T. D. (Ed.) (2009). *Handbook of prejudice, stereotyping and discrimination.* New York: Psychology Press.

Nemeth, C. (1979). The role of an active minority in intergroup relations. In W. G. Austin & S. Worchel (Eds.), *The social psychology of intergroup relations.* Monterey, CA: Brooks/Cole.

Nemeth, C., Brown, K., & Rogers, J. (2001). Devil's advocate versus authentic dissent: Stimulating quantity and quality. *European Journal of Social Psychology, 31*(6), 707–720.

Nemeth, C., & Wachtler, J. (1974). Creating the perceptions of consistency and confidence: A necessary condition for minority influence. *Sociometry, 37*(4), 529–540.

Nemeth, C. J. (1986). Differential contributions of majority and minority influence. *Psychological Review, 93*(1), 23–32.

Nemeth, C. J., Connell, J. B., Rogers, J. D., & Brown, K. S. (2001). Improving decision making by means of dissent. *Journal of Applied Social Psychology, 31*(1), 48–58.

Nemeth, C. J., & Kwan, J. L. (1987). Minority influence, divergent thinking and detection of correct solutions. *Journal of Applied Social Psychology, 17*(9), 788–799.

Nemeth, C. J., & Ormiston, M. (2007). Creative idea generation: Harmony versus stimulation. *European Journal of Social Psychology, 37*(3), 524–535.

Neuberg, S. L. (1988). Behavioral implications of information presented outside of conscious awareness: The effect of subliminal presentation of trait information on behavior in the Prisoner's Dilemma Game. *Social Cognition, 6*(3), 207–230.

Neuberg, S. L., & Fiske, S. T. (1987). Motivational influences on impression formation: Outcome dependency, accuracy-driven attention, and individuating processes. *Journal of Personality and Social Psychology, 53*(3), 431–444.

Neuberg, S. L., Kenrick, D. T., & Schaller, M. (2010). Evolutionary social psychology. In S. T. Fiske, D. T. Gilbert, & G. Lindzey (Eds.), *Handbook of social psychology* (5th ed., pp. 761–796). New York: Wiley.

Neuberg, S. L., & Newsom, J. T. (1993). Personal need for structure: Individual differences in the desire for simpler structure. *Journal of Personality and Social Psychology, 65*(1), 113–131.

Neumann, R., & Strack, F. (2000). "Mood contagion": The automatic transfer of mood between persons. *Journal of Personality and Social Psychology, 79*(2), 211–223.

Newby-Clark, I. R., McGregor, I., & Zanna, M. P. (2002). Thinking and caring about cognitive inconsistency: When and for whom does attitudinal ambivalence feel uncomfortable? *Journal of Personality and Social Psychology, 82*(2), 157–166.

Newcomb, T. M. (1943). *Personality and social change: Attitude formation in a student community.* New York: Dryden Press.

Newcomb, T. M. (1956). The prediction of interpersonal attraction. *American Psychologist, 11*(11), 575–586.

Newcomb, T., Koenig, K. E., Flacks, R., & Warwick, D. P. (1967). *Persistence and change: Bennington College and its students after twenty-five years.* New York: Wiley.

Newman, C. (2000, January). The enigma of beauty. *National Geographic,* pp. 94–121. Retrieved from http://science.nationalgeographic.com/science/health-and-human-body/human-body/enigma-beauty.html#page=1

Nieuwenhuis, S., Aston-Jones, G., & Cohen, J. D. (2005). Decision making, the P3, and the locus coeruleus–norepinephrine system. *Psychological Bulletin, 131*(4), 510–532.

Nisbett, R. E. (1993). Violence and US regional culture. *American Psychologist, 48*(4), 441–449.

Nisbett, R. E. (2003). *The geography of thought: How Asians and Westerners think differently—And why.* New York: Free Press.

Nisbett, R. E. (2009). *Intelligence and how to get it: Why schools and cultures count.* New York: W. W. Norton.

Nisbett, R. E., Caputo, C., Legant, P., & Marecek, J. (1973). Behavior as seen by the actor and as seen by the observer. *Journal of Personality and Social Psychology, 27*(2), 154–164.

Nisbett, R. E., & Cohen, D. (1996). *Culture of honor: The psychology of violence in the South.* Boulder, CO: Westview Press.

Nisbett, R. E., Peng, K., Choi, I., & Norenzayan, A. (2001). Culture and systems of thought: Holistic versus analytic cognition. *Psychological Review, 108*(2), 291–310.

Nisbett, R. E., & Schachter, S. (1966). Cognitive manipulation of pain. *Journal of Experimental Social Psychology, 2*(3), 227–236.

Nisbett, R. E., & Wilson, T. D. (1977a). The halo effect: Evidence for unconscious alteration of judgments. *Journal of Personality and Social Psychology, 35*(4), 250–256.

Nisbett, R. E., & Wilson, T. D. (1977b). Telling more than we can know: Verbal reports on mental processes. *Psychological Review, 84*(3), 231–259.

Nordgren, L. F., Banas, K., & MacDonald, G. (2011). Empathy gaps for social pain: Why people underestimate the pain of social suffering. *Journal of Personality and Social Psychology, 100*(1), 120–128.

Nordgren, L. F., Bos, M. W., & Dijksterhuis, A. (2011). The best of both worlds: Integrating conscious and unconscious thought best solves complex decisions. *Journal of Experimental Social Psychology, 47*(2), 509–511.

Norenzayan, A., & Shariff, A. F. (2008). The origin and evolution of religious prosociality. *Science, 322*(5898), 58–62.

Norton, M. I., Frost, J. H., & Ariely, D. (2007). Less is more: The lure of ambiguity, or why familiarity breeds contempt. *Journal of Personality and Social Psychology, 92*(1), 97–105.

Norton, M. I., & Sommers, S. R. (2011). Whites see racism as a zero-sum game that they are now losing. *Perspectives on Psychological Science, 6*(3), 215–218.

Norton, M. I., Sommers, S. R., Apfelbaum, E. P., Pura, N., & Ariely, D. (2006). Color blindness and interracial interaction: Playing the political correctness game. *Psychological Science, 17*(11), 949–953.

Nosek, B. A. (2005). Moderators of the relationship between implicit and explicit evaluation. *Journal of Experimental Psychology: General, 134*(4), 565–584.

Nosek, B. A. (2007). Implicit–explicit relations. *Current Directions in Psychological Science, 16*(2), 65–69.

Nosek, B. A., Hawkins, C. B., & Frazier, R. S. (2011). Implicit social cognition: From measures to mechanisms. *Trends in Cognitive Sciences, 15*(4), 152–159.

Nowak, M., & Sigmund, K. (1993). A strategy of win-stay, lose-shift that outperforms tit-for-tat in the Prisoner's Dilemma game. *Nature, 364*(6432), 56–58.

Nunn, N. (2008). The long-term effects of Africa's slave trades. *Quarterly Journal of Economics, 123*(1), 139–176.

Nunn, N., & Wantchekon, L. (2011). The slave trade and the origins of mistrust in Africa. *American Economic Review, 101*(7), 3221–3252.

O'Connor, B. P., & Dyce, J. (1993). Appraisals of musical ability in bar bands: Identifying the weak link in the looking-glass self chain. *Basic and Applied Social Psychology, 14*(1), 69–86.

Ogbu, J. U., & Simons, H. D. (1998). Voluntary and involuntary minorities: A cultural-ecological theory of school performance with some implications for education. *Anthropology & Education Quarterly, 29*(2), 155–188.

Ohbuchi, K. (1982). Aggressive reaction to arbitrary frustration as a function of causal information. *Japanese Journal of Criminal Psychology, 19*(1–2), 11–20.

Öhman, A., & Mineka, S. (2003). The malicious serpent: Snakes as a prototypical stimulus for an evolved module of fear. *Current Directions in Psychological Science, 12*(1), 5–9.

Oishi, S. (2010). The psychology of residential mobility: Implications for the self, social relationships, and well-being. *Perspectives on Psychological Science, 5*(1), 5–21.

Oishi, S., Ishii, K., & Lun, J. (2009). Residential mobility and conditionality of group identification. *Journal of Experimental Social Psychology, 45*(4), 913–919.

Oishi, S., & Kisling, J. (2009). The mutual constitution of residential mobility and individualism. In R. S. Wyer, C. Chiu, & Y. Hong (Eds.), *Understanding culture: Theory, research, and application* (pp. 223–238). New York: Psychology Press.

Oishi, S., Lun, J., & Sherman, G. D. (2007). Residential mobility, self-concept, and positive affect in social interactions. *Journal of Personality and Social Psychology, 93*(1), 131–141.

Oishi, S., Rothman, A. J., Snyder, M., Su, J., Zehm, K., Hertel, A. W., Gonzales, M. H., & Sherman, G. D. (2007). The socioecological model of procommunity action: The benefits of residential stability. *Journal of Personality and Social Psychology, 93*(5), 831–844.

O'Leary, K. D., & Vivian, D. (1990). Physical aggression in marriage. In F. D. Fincham & T. N. Bradbury (Eds.), *The psychology of marriage* (pp. 323–348). New York: Guilford Press.

Oliver, M. B., & Hyde, J. S. (1993). Gender differences in sexuality: A meta-analysis. *Psychological Bulletin, 114*(1), 29–51.

Olson, K. R., Dunham, Y., Dweck, C. S., Spelke, E. S., & Banaji, M. R. (2008). Judgments of the lucky across development and culture. *Journal of Personality and Social Psychology, 94*(5), 757–776.

Olson, M. A., & Fazio, R. H. (2004). Reducing the influence of extrapersonal associations on the Implicit Association Test: Personalizing the IAT. *Journal of Personality and Social Psychology, 86*(5), 653–667.

Olweus, D. (1979). Stability of aggressive reaction patterns in males: A review. *Psychological Bulletin, 86*(4), 852–875.

Olweus, D. (1995). Bullying or peer abuse at school: Facts and intervention. *Current Directions in Psychological Science, 4*(6), 196–200. Stable URL: http://www.jstor.org/stable/20182370

Olweus, D., Mattsson, Å., Schalling, D., & Löw, H. (1980). Testosterone, aggression, physical, and personality dimensions in normal adolescent males. *Psychosomatic Medicine, 42*(2), 253–269. Retrieved from http://www.psychosomaticmedicine.org/content/42/2/253.short

Omoto, A. M., & Snyder, M. (2002). Considerations of community: The context and process of volunteerism. *American Behavioral Scientist, 45*(5), 846–867.

Omoto, A. M., Snyder, M., & Hackett, J. D. (2010). Personality and motivational antecedents of activism and civic engagement. *Journal of Personality, 78*(6), 1703–1734.

Operario, D., & Fiske, S. T. (2001). Ethnic identity moderates perceptions of prejudice: Judgments of personal versus group discrimination and subtle versus blatant bias. *Personality and Social Psychology Bulletin, 27*(5), 550–561.

Opotow, S. (1990). Moral exclusion and injustice: An introduction. *Journal of Social Issues, 46*(1), 1–20.

Orlofsky, J. L. (1982). Psychological androgyny, sex-typing, and sex-role ideology as predictors of male-female interpersonal attraction. *Sex Roles, 8*(10), 1057–1073.

Orne, M. T. (1962). On the social psychology of the psychological experiment: With particular reference to demand characteristics and their implications. *American Psychologist, 17*, 776–783.

Orwell, G. (1949). *1984.* New York: Harcourt.

Ostovich, J. M., & Sabini, J. (2004). How are sociosexuality, sex drive, and lifetime number of sexual partners related? *Personality and Social Psychology Bulletin, 30*(10), 1255–1266.

OTRC: Woody Allen on marriage to Soon-Yi: "What was the scandal?" (2011, June 23). [Online journal]. OnTheRedCarpet.com. Retrieved from http://abc7.com/archive/8209443/

Over, H., & Carpenter, M. (2009). Eighteen-month-old infants show increased helping following priming with affiliation. *Psychological Science, 20*(10), 1189–1193.

Overall, N. C., Fletcher, G. J., & Simpson, J. A. (2010). Helping each other grow: Romantic partner support, self-improvement, and relationship quality. *Personality and Social Psychology Bulletin, 36*(11), 1496–1513.

Overbeck, J. R., & Park, B. (2001). When power does not corrupt: Superior individuation processes among powerful perceivers. *Journal of Personality and Social Psychology, 81*(4), 549–565.

Oyserman, D., Bybee, D., & Terry, K. (2006). Possible selves and academic outcomes: How and when possible selves impel action. *Journal of Personality and Social Psychology, 91*(1), 188–204.

Packer, D. J. (2009). Avoiding groupthink: Whereas weakly identified members remain silent, strongly identified members dissent about collective problems. *Psychological Science, 20*(5), 546–548.

Page, S. E. (2007). *The difference: How the power of diversity creates better groups, firms, schools, and societies.* Princeton, NJ: Princeton University Press.

Pager, D., & Shepherd, H. (2008). The sociology of discrimination: Racial discrimination in employment, housing, credit, and consumer markets. *Annual Review of Sociology, 34*, 181–209.

Paloutzian, R. F. (1981). Purpose in life and value changes following conversion. *Journal of Personality and Social Psychology, 41*(6), 1153–1160.

Paluck, E. L. (2009). Reducing intergroup prejudice and conflict using the media: A field experiment in Rwanda. *Journal of Personality and Social Psychology, 96*(3), 574–587.

Panati, C. (1996). *Sacred origins of profound things: The stories behind the rites and rituals of the world's religions.* New York: Penguin Books.

Pantin, H. M., & Carver, C. S. (1982). Induced competence and the bystander effect. *Journal of Applied Social Psychology, 12*(1), 100–111.

Park, B., & Rothbart, M. (1982). Perception of out-group homogeneity and levels of social categorization: Memory for the subordinate attributes of in-group and out-group members. *Journal of Personality and Social Psychology, 42*(6), 1051–1068.

Park, J. H., Faulkner, J., & Schaller, M. (2003). Evolved disease-avoidance processes and contemporary anti-social behavior: Prejudicial attitudes and avoidance of people with physical disabilities. *Journal of Nonverbal Behavior, 27*(2), 65–87.

Parkes, C. M., & Weiss, R. S. (1983). *Recovery from bereavement.* New York: Basic Books.

Parks, M. R., & Floyd, K. (1996). Meanings for closeness and intimacy in friendship. *Journal of Social and Personal Relationships, 13*(1), 85–107.

Pastore, N. (1952). The role of arbitrariness in the frustration-aggression hypothesis. *Journal of Abnormal and Social Psychology, 47*(3), 728–731.

Patterson, G. R., Chamberlain, P., & Reid, J. B. (1982). A comparative evaluation of a parent-training program. *Behavior Therapy, 13*(5), 638–650.

Paul, E. L., McManus, B., & Hayes, K. A. (2000). "Hookups": Characteristics and correlates of college students' spontaneous and anonymous sexual experiences. *Journal of Sex Research, 37*(1), 76–88.

Pavlov, I. (1927). *Conditioned reflexes.* New York: Oxford University Press.

Payne, B. K. (2001). Prejudice and perception: The role of automatic and controlled processes in misperceiving a weapon. *Journal of Personality and Social Psychology, 81*(2), 181–192.

Payne, D. L., Lonsway, K. A., & Fitzgerald, L. F. (1999). Rape myth acceptance: Exploration of its structure and its measurement using the Illinois Rape Myth Acceptance Scale. *Journal of Research in Personality, 33*(1), 27–68.

Peck, T. C., Seinfeld, S., Aglioti, S.M., & Slater, M. (2013). Putting yourself in the skin of a black avatar reduces implicit racial bias. *Consciousness and Cognition, 22*, 779–787.

Pedersen, W. C., Bushman, B. J., Vasquez, E. A., & Miller, N. (2008). Kicking the (barking) dog effect: The moderating role of target attributes on triggered displaced aggression. *Personality and Social Psychology Bulletin, 34*(10), 1382–1395.

Pedersen, W. C., Gonzales, C., & Miller, N. (2000). The moderating effect of trivial triggering provocation on displaced aggression. *Journal of Personality and Social Psychology, 78*(5), 913–927.

Peng, K., & Nisbett, R. E. (1999). Culture, dialectics, and reasoning about contradiction. *American Psychologist, 54*(9), 741–754.

Pennebaker, J. W., & Beall, S. K. (1986). Confronting a traumatic event: Toward an understanding of inhibition and disease. *Journal of Abnormal Psychology, 95*(3), 274–281.

Pennebaker, J. W., Mayne, T. J., & Francis, M. E. (1997). Linguistic predictors of adaptive bereavement. *Journal of Personality and Social Psychology, 72*(4), 863–871.

Penner, L., Brannick, M. T., Webb, S., & Connell, P. (2005). Effects on volunteering of the September 11, 2001, attacks: An archival analysis. *Journal of Applied Social Psychology, 35*(7), 1333–1360.

Penner, L. A., & Finkelstein, M. A. (1998). Dispositional and structural determinants of volunteerism. *Journal of Personality and Social Psychology, 74*(2), 525–537.

Penton-Voak, I. S., Perrett, D. I., Castles, D. L., Kobayashi, T., Burt, D. M., Murray, L. K., & Minamisawa, R. (1999). Menstrual cycle alters face preference. *Nature, 399*(6738), 741–742.

Peplau, L.A., & Fingerhut, A.W. (2007). The close relationships of lesbians and gay men. *Annual Review of Psychology, 58*, 405–424.

Peplau, L. A., & Spalding, L. R. (2000). The close relationships of lesbians, gay men and bisexuals. In C. Hendrick & S. S. Hendrick (Eds.), *Close relationships: A sourcebook* (pp. 111–124). Thousand Oaks, CA: Sage.

Pepler, D. J., King, G., Craig, W., Byrd, B., & Bream, L. (1995). The development and evaluation of a multisystem social skills group training program for aggressive children. *Child and Youth Care Forum, 24*(5), 297–313.

Perdue, C. W., Dovidio, J. F., Gurtman, M. B., & Tyler, R. B. (1990). Us and them: Social categorization and the process of intergroup bias. *Journal of Personality and Social Psychology, 59*(3), 475–486.

Perry, D. G., & Bussey, K. (1979). The social learning theory of sex differences: Imitation is alive and well. *Journal of Personality and Social Psychology, 37*(10), 1699–1712.

Perry, D. G., & Perry, L. C. (1976). Identification with film characters, covert aggressive verbalization, and reactions to film violence. *Journal of Research in Personality, 10*(4), 399–409.

Peters, W. (1987). *A class divided: Then and now.* New Haven: Yale University Press.

Peters, W., (Writer, Producer and Director), & Cobb, C., (Writer). (1985, March 26). A Class Divided [Television series episode]. In D. Fanning & M. Kirk (Producers), *Frontline.* Arlington, VA: PBS. Retrieved from http://www.pbs.org/wgbh/pages/frontline/shows/divided/etc/view.html

Peterson, D., Taylor, T. J., & Esbensen, F. (2004). Gang membership and violent victimization. *Justice Quarterly, 21*(4), 794–815.

Peterson, L., & Brown, D. (1994). Integrating child injury and abuse/neglect research: Common histories, etiologies, and solutions. *Psychological Bulletin, 116*(2), 293–315.

Petronio, S., Olson, C., & Dollar, N. (1989). Privacy issues in relational embarrassment: Impact on relational quality and communication satisfaction. *Communication Research Reports, 6*(1), 21–27.

Pettigrew, T. F. (1958). Personality and sociocultural factors in intergroup attitudes: A cross-national comparison. *Journal of Conflict Resolution*, 2(1), 29–42. Stable URL: http://www.jstor.org/stable/172842

Pettigrew, T. F. (1959). Regional differences in anti-Negro prejudice. *Journal of Abnormal and Social Psychology*, 59(1), 28–36.

Pettigrew, T. F. (1961). Social psychology and desegregation research. *American Psychologist*, 16(3), 105–112.

Pettigrew, T. F. (1979). The ultimate attribution error: Extending Allport's cognitive analysis of prejudice. *Personality and Social Psychology Bulletin*, 5(4), 461–476.

Pettigrew, T. F. (1998). Intergroup contact theory. *Annual Review of Psychology*, 49, 65–85.

Pettigrew, T. F., & Tropp, L. R. (2006). A meta-analytic test of intergroup contact theory. *Journal of Personality and Social Psychology*, 90(5), 751–783.

Pettijohn, T. F., & Jungeberg, B. J. (2004). Playboy Playmate curves: Changes in facial and body feature preferences across social and economic conditions. *Personality and Social Psychology Bulletin*, 30(9), 1186–1197.

Petty, R. E., Briñol, P., & Tormala, Z. L. (2002). Thought confidence as a determinant of persuasion: The self-validation hypothesis. *Journal of Personality and Social Psychology*, 82(5), 722–741.

Petty, R. E., & Cacioppo, J. T. (1979). Issue involvement can increase or decrease persuasion by enhancing message-relevant cognitive responses. *Journal of Personality and Social Psychology*, 37(10), 1915–1926.

Petty, R. E., & Cacioppo, J. T. (1984). The effects of involvement on responses to argument quantity and quality: Central and peripheral routes to persuasion. *Journal of Personality and Social Psychology*, 46(1), 69–81.

Petty, R. E., & Cacioppo, J. T. (1986). *Communication and persuasion: Central and peripheral routes to attitude change*. New York: Springer-Verlag.

Petty, R. E., Cacioppo, J. T., & Schumann, D. (1983). Central and peripheral routes to advertising effectiveness: The moderating role of involvement. *Journal of Consumer Research*, 10(2), 135–146.

Petty, R. E., & Krosnick, J. A. (Eds.) (1995). *Attitude strength: Antecedents and consequences*. Mahwah, NJ: Erlbaum.

Petty, R. E., Wells, G. L., & Brock, T. C. (1976). Distraction can enhance or reduce yielding to propaganda: Thought disruption versus effort justification. *Journal of Personality and Social Psychology*, 34(5), 874–884.

Pew Research Center. (2007, November 13). Blacks see growing values gap between poor and middle class: Optimism about black progress declines. Washington, DC:. Pew Research Center. Retrieved from http://www.pewsocialtrends.org/2007/11/13/blacks-see-growing-values-gap-between-poor-and-middle-class/

Pew Research Center (2013, August 22). King's dream remains an elusive goal: Many Americans see racial disparities. Washington, DC: Pew Research Center. Retrieved from http://www.pewsocialtrends.org/files/2013/08/final_full_report_racial_disparities.pdf

Pezawas, L., Meyer-Lindenberg, A., Drabant, E. M., Verchinski, B. A., Munoz, K. E., Kolachana, B. S., . . . & Weinberger, D. R. (2005). 5-HTTLPR polymorphism impacts human cingulate-amygdala interactions: A genetic susceptibility mechanism for depression. *Nature Neuroscience*, 8(6), 828–834.

Pfau, M., Roskos-Ewoldsen, D., Wood, M., Yin, S., Cho, J., Lu, K. H., & Shen, L. (2003). Attitude accessibility as an alternative explanation for how inoculation confers resistance. *Communication Monographs*, 70(1), 39–51.

Phelps, E. A., O'Connor, K. J., Cunningham, W. A., Funayama, E. S., Gatenby, J. C., Gore, J. C., & Banaji, M. R. (2000). Performance on indirect measures of race evaluation predicts amygdala activation. *Journal of Cognitive Neuroscience*, 12(5), 729–738.

Phillips, D. P. (1974). The influence of suggestion on suicide: Substantive and theoretical implications of the Werther effect. *American Sociological Review*, 39(3), 340–354.

Phillips, D. P. (1979). Suicide, motor vehicle fatalities, and the mass media: Evidence toward a theory of suggestion. *American Journal of Sociology*, 84(5), 1150–1174. Stable URL: http://www.jstor.org/stable/2778220

Phillips, D. P. (1982). The impact of fictional television stories on U.S. adult fatalities. *American Journal of Sociology*, 87(6), 1340–1359. Stable URL: http://www.jstor.org/stable/2779364

Phillips, D. P. (1983). The impact of mass media violence on U.S. homicides. *American Sociological Review*, 48(4), 560–568. Stable URL: http://www.jstor.org/stable

Phillips, D. P., & Hensley, J. E. (1984). When violence is rewarded or punished: The impact of mass media stories on homicide. *Journal of Communication*, 34(3), 101–116.

Phillips, M., Phillips, J., Goldfarb, P. M. (Producers), Schrader, P. (Writer), & Scorsese, M. (Director) (1976). *Taxi driver* [Motion picture]. United States: Columbia Pictures, Bill/Phillips, and Italo/Judeo Productions.

Pierro, A., Mannetti, L., Kruglanski, A. W., Klein, K., & Orehek, E. (2012). Persistence of attitude change and attitude–behavior correspondence based on extensive processing of source information. *European Journal of Social Psychology*, 42(1), 103–111.

Pietromonaco, P. R., & Barrett, L. F. (2000). The internal working models concept: What do we really know about the self in relation to others? *Review of General Psychology*, 4(2), 155–175.

Piff, P. K., Kraus, M. W., Côté, S., Cheng, B. H., & Keltner, D. (2010). Having less, giving more: The influence of social class on prosocial behavior. *Journal of Personality and Social Psychology*, 99(5), 771–784.

Piliavin, I. M., Piliavin, J. A., & Rodin, J. (1975). Costs, diffusion, and the stigmatized victim. *Journal of Personality and Social Psychology*, 32(3), 429–438.

Piliavin, I. M., Rodin, J., & Piliavin, J. A. (1969). Good samaritanism: An underground phenomenon? *Journal of Personality and Social Psychology*, 13(4), 289–299.

Piliavin, J. A., Grube, J. A., & Callero, P. L. (2002). Role as resource for action in public service. *Journal of Social Issues*, 58(3), 469–485.

Piliavin, J. A., & Piliavin, I. M. (1972). Effect of blood on reactions to a victim. *Journal of Personality and Social Psychology*, 23(3), 353–361.

Pilkington, C. J., Tesser, A., & Stephens, D. (1991). Complementarity in romantic relationships: A self-evaluation maintenance perspective. *Journal of Social and Personal Relationships*, 8(4), 481–504.

Pinel, E. C. (1999). Stigma consciousness: The psychological legacy of social stereotypes. *Journal of Personality and Social Psychology*, 76(1), 114–128.

Pinel, E. C. (2002). Stigma consciousness in intergroup contexts: The power of conviction. *Journal of Experimental Social Psychology*, 38(2), 178–185.

Pinel, E. C., & Long, A. E. (2012). When I's meet: Sharing subjective experience with a member of the outgroup. *Personality and Social Psychology Bulletin*, 38(3), 296–307.

Pinel, E. C., Long, A. E., Landau, M., & Pyszczynski, T. (2004). I-sharing, the problem of existential isolation, and their implications for interpersonal and intergroup phenomena. In J. Greenberg, S. Koole, & T. Pyszczynski (Eds.), *Handbook of experimental existential psychology* (pp. 352–368). New York: Guilford Press.

Pinel, E. C., Warner, L. R., & Chua, P. P. (2005). Getting there is only half the battle: Stigma consciousness and maintaining diversity in higher education. *Journal of Social Issues*, 61(3), 481–506.

Pinhey, T. K., Rubinstein, D. H., & Colfax, R. S. (1997). Overweight and happiness: The reflected self-appraisal hypothesis reconsidered: Consequences of obesity. *Social Science Quarterly*, 78(3), 747–755. Stable URL: http://www.jstor.org/stable/42863565

Pinker, S. (2003). *The blank slate: The modern denial of human nature*. New York: Penguin.

Pitkanen-Pulkinen, L. (1979). Self-control as a prerequisite for constructive behavior. In S. Feshbach and A. Fraczek (Eds.), *Aggression and behavior change: Biological and social process* (pp. 250–270). New York: Praeger.

Pitts, M. K., Smith, A. M., Grierson, J., O'Brien, M., & Misson, S. (2004). Who pays for sex and why? An analysis of social and motivational factors associated with male clients of sex workers. *Archives of Sexual Behavior*, 33(4), 353–358.

Plant, E. A., & Devine, P. G. (1998). Internal and external motivation to respond without prejudice. *Journal of Personality and Social Psychology*, 75(3), 811–832.

Plant, E. A., & Devine, P. G. (2001). Responses to other-imposed pro-Black pressure: Acceptance or backlash? *Journal of Experimental Social Psychology*, 37(6), 486–501.

Plant, E. A., & Devine, P. G. (2009). The active control of prejudice: Unpacking the intentions guiding control efforts. *Journal of Personality and Social Psychology*, 96(3), 640–652.

Plant, E. A., Devine, P. G., Cox, W. T., Columb, C., Miller, S. L., Goplen, J., & Peruche, B. M. (2009). The Obama effect: Decreasing implicit prejudice and stereotyping. *Journal of Experimental Social Psychology*, 45(4), 961–964.

Planty, M., & Truman, J. L. (2013, May 7). Special report: Firearm violence, 1993–2011. U.S. Department of Justice, Office of Justice Programs, Bureau of Justice Statistics. Retrieved from http://www.bjs.gov/content/pub/pdf/fv9311.pdf

Plaut, V. C., Thomas, K. M., & Goren, M. J. (2009). Is multiculturalism or color blindness better for minorities? *Psychological Science*, 20(4), 444–446.

Pliner, P., & Chaiken, S. (1990). Eating, social motives, and self-presentation in women and men. *Journal of Experimental Social Psychology*, 26(3), 240–254.

Plomin, R., Chipuer, H. M., & Loehlin, J. C. (1990). Behavioral genetics and personality. In L. A. Pervin (Ed.), *Handbook of personality: Theory and research* (pp. 225–243). New York: Guilford Press.

Pollet, T. V., & Nettle, D. (2008). Driving a hard bargain: Sex ratio and male marriage success in a historical US population. *Biology Letters*, 4(1), 31–33.

Polo, M. (2007). *The travels of Marco Polo*. New York: Cosimo Classics.

Pope, A. (1903). An essay on man. in H. W. Boynton (Ed.), *The complete poetical works of Alexander Pope*. Boston: Houghton Mifflin. (Original works published in 1732–1744). Also available online at: https://notes.utk.edu/Bio/

greenberg.nsf/11b7b90a9fa8e19585256c76000ed30a/a41ea6f017abe5b4852 56db100676048?OpenDocument

Pope, K. S. (1980). *On love and loving*. San Francisco: Jossey-Bass.

Popenoe, D., & Whitehead, B. D. (2007). *The state of our unions, 2007: The social health of marriage in America*. Piscataway, NJ: National Marriage Project.

Porges, S. W. (1998). Love: An emergent property of the mammalian autonomic nervous system. *Psychoneuroendocrinology, 23*(8), 837–861.

Pornpitakpan, C. (2004). The persuasiveness of source credibility: A critical review of five decades' evidence. *Journal of Applied Social Psychology, 34*(2), 243–281.

Postmes, T., & Branscombe, N. R. (2002). Influence of long-term racial environmental composition on subjective well-being in African Americans. *Journal of Personality and Social Psychology, 83*(3), 735–751.

Postmes, T., & Spears, R. (1998). Deindividuation and antinormative behavior: A meta-analysis. *Psychological Bulletin, 123*(3), 238–259.

Postmes, T., Spears, R., & Cihangir, S. (2001). Quality of decision making and group norms. *Journal of Personality and Social Psychology, 80*(6), 918–930.

Powers, W. T. (1973). *Behavior: The control of perception*. Chicago: Aldine.

Pratkanis, A. (2007). Sleeper effect. In R. Baumeister, & K. Vohs (Eds.), *Encyclopedia of social psychology* (pp. 879–881). Thousand Oaks, CA: Sage.

Pratt, T. C., & Cullen, F. T. (2000). The empirical status of Gottfredson and Hirschi's general theory of crime: A meta-analysis. *Criminology, 38*(3), 931–964.

Pratto, F., & John, O. P. (1991). Automatic vigilance: The attention-grabbing power of negative social information. *Journal of Personality and Social Psychology, 61*(3), 380–391.

Pratto, F., Sidanius, J., Stallworth, L. M., & Malle, B. F. (1994). Social dominance orientation: A personality variable predicting social and political attitudes. *Journal of Personality and Social Psychology, 67*(4), 741–763.

Prentice, D. A., Miller, D. T., & Lightdale, J. R. (1994). Asymmetries in attachments to groups and to their members: Distinguishing between common-identity and common-bond groups. *Personality and Social Psychology Bulletin, 20*(5), 484–493.

Pressman, S. D., Cohen, S., Miller, G. E., Barkin, A., Rabin, B. S., & Treanor, J. J. (2005). Loneliness, social network size, and immune response to influenza vaccination in college freshmen. *Health Psychology, 24*(3), 297–306.

Preston, S. D., & de Waal, F. (2002). Empathy: Its ultimate and proximate bases. *Behavioral and Brain Sciences, 25*(01), 1–20.

Previti, D., & Amato, P. R. (2004). Is infidelity a cause or a consequence of poor marital quality? *Journal of Social and Personal Relationships, 21*(2), 217–230.

Price, R. A., & Vandenberg, S. G. (1979). Matching for physical attractiveness in married couples. *Personality and Social Psychology Bulletin, 5*(3), 398–400.

Prinstein, M. J., & Wang, S. S. (2005). False consensus and adolescent peer contagion: Examining discrepancies between perceptions and actual reported levels of friends' deviant and health risk behaviors. *Journal of Abnormal Child Psychology, 33*(3), 293–306.

Proctor, D., Williamson, R. A., de Waal, F. B., & Brosnan, S. F. (2013). Chimpanzees play the ultimatum game. *Proceedings of the National Academy of Sciences, 110*(6), 2070–2075.

Pronin, E., Steele, C. M., & Ross, L. (2004). Identity bifurcation in response to stereotype threat: Women and mathematics. *Journal of Experimental Social Psychology, 40*(2), 152–168.

Pronin, E., Wegner, D. M., McCarthy, K., & Rodriguez, S. (2006). Everyday magical powers: The role of apparent mental causation in the overestimation of personal influence. *Journal of Personality and Social Psychology, 91*(2), 218–231.

Prot, S., Gentile, D. A., Anderson, C. A., Suzuki, K., Swing, E., Lim, K. M., . . . & Lam, B. C. P. (2013). Long-term relations among prosocial-media use, empathy, and prosocial behavior. *Psychological Science, 25*(2), 358–368.

Proulx, T., & Heine, S. J. (2008). The case of the transmogrifying experimenter: Affirmation of a moral schema following implicit change detection. *Psychological Science, 19*(12), 1294–1300.

Proulx, T., & Heine, S. J. (2009). Connections from Kafka: Exposure to meaning threats improves implicit learning of an artificial grammar. *Psychological Science, 20*(9), 1125–1131.

Provine, R. R. (2004). Laughing, tickling, and the evolution of speech and self. *Current Directions in Psychological Science, 13*(6), 215–218.

Public Broadcasting Service. Biography: John Hinckley, Jr. (n.d). *The American Experience*. Retrieved from http://www.pbs.org/wgbh/americanexperience/features/biography/reagan-hinckley/

Puts, D. A. (2005). Mating context and menstrual phase affect women's preferences for male voice pitch. *Evolution and Human Behavior, 26*(5), 388–397.

Pyszczynski, T., Abdollahi, A., Solomon, S., Greenberg, J., Cohen, F., & Weise, D. (2006). Mortality salience, martyrdom, and military might: The great Satan versus the axis of evil. *Personality and Social Psychology Bulletin, 32*(4), 525–537.

Pyszczynski, T., & Greenberg, J. (1987a). Self-regulatory perseveration and the depressive self-focusing style: A self-awareness theory of reactive depression. *Psychological Bulletin, 102*(1), 122–138.

Pyszczynski, T., & Greenberg, J. (1987b). Toward an integration of cognitive and motivational perspectives on social inference: A biased hypothesis-testing model. In L. Berkowitz (Ed.), *Advances in experimental social psychology* (Vol. 20, pp. 297–340). New York: Academic Press.

Pyszczynski, T., Greenberg, J., & LaPrelle, J. (1985). Social comparison after success and failure: Biased search for information consistent with a self-serving conclusion. *Journal of Experimental Social Psychology, 21*(2), 195–211.

Pyszczynski, T., Greenberg, J., Solomon, S., Arndt, J., & Schimel, J. (2004). Why do people need self-esteem? A theoretical and empirical review. *Psychological Bulletin, 130*(3), 435–468.

Pyszczynski, T., LaPrelle, J., & Greenberg, J. (1987). Encoding and retrieval effects of general person characterizations on memory for incongruent and congruent information. *Personality and Social Psychology Bulletin, 13*(4), 556–567.

Pyszczynski, T., Motyl, M., Vail, K., Hirschberger, G., Arndt, J., & Kesebir, P. (2012). A collateral advantage of drawing attention to global climate change: Increased support for peace-making and decreased support for war. *Journal of Peace Psychology, 18*(4), 354–368.

Pyszczynski, T., Solomon, S., & Greenberg, J. (2003). *In the wake of 9/11: The psychology of terror*. Washington, DC: American Psychological Association.

Pyszczynski, T. A., & Greenberg, J. (1981). Role of disconfirmed expectancies in the instigation of attributional processing. *Journal of Personality and Social Psychology, 40*(1), 31–38.

Pyszczynski, T. A., & Greenberg, J. (1992). *Hanging on and letting go: Understanding the onset, progression, and remission of depression*. New York: Springer-Verlag.

Quattrone, G. A. (1986). On the perception of a group's variability. In S. Worchel & W. G. Austin (Eds.), *Psychology of intergroup relations* (2nd ed., pp. 25–48). Chicago: Nelson-Hall.

Quattrone, G. A., & Jones, E. E. (1980). The perception of variability within in-groups and out-groups: Implications for the law of small numbers. *Journal of Personality and Social Psychology, 38*(1), 141–152.

Rabbie, J. M., & Horwitz, M. (1988). Categories versus groups as explanatory concepts in intergroup relations. *European Journal of Social Psychology, 18*(2), 117–123.

Raghubir, P., & Menon, G. (1998). AIDS and me, never the twain shall meet: The effects of information accessibility on judgments of risk and advertising effectiveness. *Journal of Consumer Research, 25*(1), 52–63.

Raine, A. (2008). From genes to brain to antisocial behavior. *Current Directions in Psychological Science, 17*(5), 323–328.

Raine, A., Buchsbaum, M., & LaCasse, L. (1997). Brain abnormalities in murderers indicated by positron emission tomography. *Biological Psychiatry, 42*(6), 495–508.

Raine, A., Lencz, T., Bihrle, S., LaCasse, L., & Colletti, P. (2000). Reduced prefrontal gray matter volume and reduced autonomic activity in antisocial personality disorder. *Archives of General Psychiatry, 57*(2), 119–127.

Randles, D., Proulx, T., & Heine, S. J. (2011). Turn-frogs and careful-sweaters: Non-conscious perception of incongruous word pairings provokes fluid compensation. *Journal of Experimental Social Psychology, 47*(1), 246–249.

Rank, O. (1989). *Art and artist: Creative urge and personality development* (C. F. Atkinson, Trans.). New York: W. W. Norton. (Original work published 1932)

Rank, O. (1936a). *Truth and reality: A life history of the human will*. New York: Knopf.

Rank, O. (1936b). *Will therapy: An analysis of the therapeutic process in terms of relationship*. New York: Knopf.

Rank, O. (1998). *Psychology and the soul: A study of the origin, conceptual evolution, and nature of the soul* (G. C. Richter & E. J. Lieberman, Trans.). Baltimore: Johns Hopkins University Press. (Original work published 1930)

Rapp-Paglicci, L. A., Roberts, A. R., & Wodarski, J. S. (2002). *Handbook of violence*. New York: Wiley.

Razran, G. H. S. (1940). Conditioned response changes in rating and appraising sociopolitical slogans. *Psychological Bulletin, 37*(1), 481–493.

Read, S. J., Cesa, I. L., Jones, D. K., & Collins, N. L. (1990). When is the federal budget like a baby? Metaphor in political rhetoric. *Metaphor and Symbolic Activity, 5*(3), 125–149.

Regan, D. T. (1971). Effects of a favor and liking on compliance. *Journal of Experimental Social Psychology, 7*(6), 627–639.

Regan, D. T., & Fazio, R. H. (1977). On the consistency between attitudes and behavior: Look to the method of attitude formation. *Journal of Experimental Social Psychology, 13*(1), 28–45.

Regan, D. T., Williams, M., & Sparling, S. (1972). Voluntary expiation of guilt: A field experiment. *Journal of Personality and Social Psychology, 24*(1), 42–45.

Regan, J. W. (1971). Guilt, perceived injustice, and altruistic behavior. *Journal of Personality and Social Psychology, 18*(1), 124–132.

Regan, P. C., & Atkins, L. (2006). Sex differences and similarities in frequency and intensity of sexual desire. *Social Behavior and Personality: An International Journal, 34*(1), 95–102.

Reifman, A. S., Larrick, R. P., & Fein, S. (1991). Temper and temperature on the diamond: The heat-aggression relationship in major league baseball. *Personality and Social Psychology Bulletin, 17*(5), 580–585.

Reilly, R. (2003, July 02). No ordinary Joe: Remembering a heroic act that ended in tragedy. *Sports Illustrated*. Retrieved from http://sportsillustrated.cnn.com/vault/2003/07/07/345894/no-ordinary-joe

Reis, H. T., Clark, M. S., & Holmes, J. G. (2004). Perceived partner responsiveness as an organizing construct in the study of intimacy and closeness. In D. J. Mashek & A. Aron (Eds.), *Handbook of closeness and intimacy* (pp. 201–225). Mahwah, NJ: Erlbaum.

Reis, H. T., Maniaci, M. R., Caprariello, P. A., Eastwick, P. W., & Finkel, E. J. (2011). Familiarity does indeed promote attraction in live interaction. *Journal of Personality and Social Psychology, 101*(3), 557–570.

Reis, H. T., Nezlek, J., & Wheeler, L. (1980). Physical attractiveness in social interaction. *Journal of Personality and Social Psychology, 38*(4), 604–617.

Reisenzein, R. (1983). The Schachter theory of emotion: Two decades later. *Psychological Bulletin, 94*(2), 239–264.

Reisenzein, R. (1986). A structural equation analysis of Weiner's attribution–affect model of helping behavior. *Journal of Personality and Social Psychology, 50*(6), 1123–1133.

Reisenzein, R., & Gattinger, E. (1982). Salience of arousal as a mediator of misattribution of transferred excitation. *Motivation and Emotion, 6*(4), 315–328.

Rentfrow, P. J., & Gosling, S. D. (2006). Message in a ballad: The role of music preferences in interpersonal perception. *Psychological Science, 17*(3), 236–242.

Rhee, S. H., & Waldman, I. D. (2002). Genetic and environmental influences on antisocial behavior: A meta-analysis of twin and adoption studies. *Psychological Bulletin, 128*(3), 490–529.

Rhodes, G. (2006). The evolutionary psychology of facial beauty. *Annual Review of Psychology, 57*, 199–226.

Rhodes, G., Harwood, K., Yoshikawa, S., Nishitani, M., & McLean, I. (2002). The attractiveness of average faces: Cross-cultural evidence and possible biological basis. In G. Rhodes & L. A. Zebrowitz (Eds.), *Facial attractiveness: Evolutionary, cognitive, and social perspectives* (pp. 35–58). Westport, CT: Ablex.

Rhodes, G., Sumich, A., & Byatt, G. (1999). Are average facial configurations attractive only because of their symmetry? *Psychological Science, 10*(1), 52–58.

Rhodes, G., Zebrowitz, L. A., Clark, A., Kalick, S. M., Hightower, A., & McKay, R. (2001). Do facial averageness and symmetry signal health? *Evolution and Human Behavior, 22*(1), 31–46.

Riach, P., & Rich, J. (2004). Fishing for discrimination. *Review of Social Economy, 62*(4), 465–486.

Richards, J. M., & Gross, J. J. (2000). Emotion regulation and memory: The cognitive costs of keeping one's cool. *Journal of Personality and Social Psychology, 79*(3), 410–424.

Richardson, D. R., Hammock, G. S., Smith, S. M., Gardner, W., & Signo, M. (1994). Empathy as a cognitive inhibitor of interpersonal aggression. *Aggressive Behavior, 20*(4), 275–289.

Richer, S. F., & Vallerand, R. J. (1995). Supervisors' interactional styles and subordinates' intrinsic and extrinsic motivation. *Journal of Social Psychology, 135*(6), 707–722.

Richeson, J. A., Baird, A. A., Gordon, H. L., Heatherton, T. F., Wyland, C. L., Trawalter, S., & Shelton, J. N. (2003). An fMRI investigation of the impact of interracial contact on executive function. *Nature Neuroscience, 6*(12), 1323–1328.

Richeson, J. A., & Shelton, J. N. (2003). When prejudice does not pay: Effects of interracial contact on executive function. *Psychological Science, 14*(3), 287–290.

Richeson, J. A., & Trawalter, S. (2005). Why do interracial interactions impair executive function? A resource depletion account. *Journal of Personality and Social Psychology, 88*(6), 934–947.

Rick, S. I., Small, D. A., & Finkel, E. J. (2011). Fatal (fiscal) attraction: Spendthrifts and tightwads in marriage. *Journal of Marketing Research, 48*(2), 228–237.

Rising, M. (2013, November 6). Swedish cinemas launch feminist movie rating. Associated Press, as reported in *USA Today*. Retrieved from http://www.usatoday.com/story/news/world/2013/11/06/sweden-cinema-feminist-rating/3451431/

Roberts, T. A., & Gettman, J. Y. (2004). Mere exposure: Gender differences in the negative effects of priming a state of self-objectification. *Sex Roles, 51*(1–2), 17–27.

Rodin, J., & Langer, E. J. (1977). Long-term effects of a control-relevant intervention with the institutionalized aged. *Journal of Personality and Social Psychology, 35*(12), 897–902.

Roese, N. J. (1994). The functional basis of counterfactual thinking. *Journal of Personality and Social Psychology, 66*(5), 805–818.

Roese, N. J., Pennington, G. L., Coleman, J., Janicki, M., Li, N. P., & Kenrick, D. T. (2006). Sex differences in regret: All for love or some for lust? *Personality and Social Psychology Bulletin, 32*(6), 770–780.

Rogers, C. R. (1961). *On becoming a person: A psychotherapist's view of psychotherapy*. Oxford: Houghton Mifflin.

Rogers, R. W., & Prentice-Dunn, S. (1981). Deindividuation and anger-mediated interracial aggression: Unmasking regressive racism. *Journal of Personality and Social Psychology, 41*(1), 63–73.

Rogers, R. W., & Prentice-Dunn, S. (1997). Protection motivation theory. In D. S. Gochman (Ed.), *Handbook of health behavior research* (Vol. 1, pp. 113–132). New York: Plenum.

Rohner, R. P. (1975). *They love me, they love me not: A worldwide study of the effects of parental acceptance and rejection*. New Haven: HRAF Press.

Rohrer, J. H., Baron, S. H., Hoffman, E. L., & Swander, D. V. (1954). The stability of autokinetic judgments. *Journal of Abnormal and Social Psychology, 49*(4, Pt.1), 595–597.

Rohsenow, D. J., & Bachorowski, J. A. (1984). Effects of alcohol and expectancies on verbal aggression in men and women. *Journal of Abnormal Psychology, 93*(4), 418–432.

Roisman, G. I., Clausell, E., Holland, A., Fortuna, K., & Elieff, C. (2008). Adult romantic relationships as contexts of human development: A multimethod comparison of same-sex couples with opposite-sex dating, engaged, and married dyads. *Developmental Psychology, 44*(1), 91–101.

Rook, K. S. (1984). Interventions for loneliness: A review and analysis. In L. A. Peplau & S. E. Goldston (Eds.), *Preventing the harmful consequences of severe and persistent loneliness* (pp. 47–79). Rockville, MD: National Institute of Mental Health.

Rosen, W., & Weil, A. (2004). *From chocolate to morphine: Everything you need to know about mind-altering drugs* (Rev. ed.). New York: Houghton Mifflin.

Rosenberg, M. (1965). *Society and the adolescent self-image*. Princeton, NJ: Princeton University Press.

Rosenblatt, A., Greenberg, J., Solomon, S., Pyszczynski, T., & Lyon, D. (1989). Evidence for terror management theory: I. The effects of mortality salience on reactions to those who violate or uphold cultural values. *Journal of Personality and Social Psychology, 57*(4), 681–690.

Rosenfield, D., Greenberg, J., Folger, R., & Borys, R. (1982). Effect of an encounter with a Black panhandler on subsequent helping for Blacks: Tokenism or confirming a negative stereotype? *Personality and Social Psychology Bulletin, 8*(4), 664–671.

Rosenhan, D. L. (1973). On being sane in insane places. *Science, 179*(4070), 250–258.

Rosenkoetter, L. I., Rosenkoetter, S. E., & Acock, A. C. (2009). Television violence: An intervention to reduce its impact on children. *Journal of Applied Developmental Psychology, 30*(4), 381–397.

Rosenthal, R. (2002). Covert communication in classrooms, clinics, courtrooms, and cubicles. *American Psychologist, 57*(11), 839–849.

Rosenthal, R., & Jacobson, L. (1968). *Pygmalion in the classroom: Teacher expectation and pupils' intellectual development*. New York: Holt, Rinehart and Winston.

Ross, L., Greene, D., & House, P. (1977). The "false consensus effect": An egocentric bias in social perception and attribution processes. *Journal of Experimental Social Psychology, 13*(3), 279–301.

Ross, L. D., Amabile, T. M., & Steinmetz, J. L. (1977). Social roles, social control, and biases in social-perception processes. *Journal of Personality and Social Psychology, 35*(7), 485–494.

Roszell, P., Kennedy, D., & Grabb, E. (1989). Physical attractiveness and income attainment among Canadians. *Journal of Psychology, 123*(6), 547–559.

Roth, J. A. (1994). Psychoactive substances and violence. Washington, DC: U.S. Department of Justice, Office of Justice Programs, National Institute of Justice.

Rothbart, M. (1981). Memory processes and social beliefs. In D. L. Hamilton (Ed.), *Cognitive processes in stereotyping and intergroup behavior* (pp. 145–181). Hillsdale, NJ: Erlbaum.

Rothbart, M. K., Ellis, L. K., & Posner, M. I. (2004). Temperament and self-regulation. In R. F. Baumeister & K. D. Vohs (Eds.), *Handbook of self-regulation: Research, theory, and applications* (pp. 357–370). New York: Guilford Press.

Rothbaum, F., & Tsang, B. Y. P. (1998). Lovesongs in the United States and China on the nature of romantic love. *Journal of Cross-Cultural Psychology, 29*(2), 306–319.

Rothman, A. J. (2000). Toward a theory-based analysis of behavioral maintenance. *Health Psychology, 19*(1S), 64–69.

Rothman, A. J., & Salovey, P. (1997). Shaping perceptions to motivate healthy behavior: The role of message framing. *Psychological Bulletin, 121*(1), 3–19.

Rothman, A. J., & Schwarz, N. (1998). Constructing perceptions of vulnerability: Personal relevance and the use of experiential information in health judgments. *Personality and Social Psychology Bulletin, 24*(10), 1053–1064.

Rothschild, Z. K., Abdollahi, A., & Pyszczynski, T. (2009). Does peace have a prayer? The effect of mortality salience, compassionate values, and religious fundamentalism on hostility toward out-groups. *Journal of Experimental Social Psychology, 45*(4), 816–827.

Rothschild, Z. K., Landau, M. J., Sullivan, D., & Keefer, L. A. (2012). A dual-motive model of scapegoating: Displacing blame to reduce guilt or increase control. *Journal of Personality and Social Psychology, 102*(6), 1148–1163.

Rotter, J. B. (1954). *Social learning and clinical psychology.* Englewood Cliffs, NJ: Prentice-Hall.

Routledge, C., Arndt, J., & Goldenberg, J. L. (2004). A time to tan: Proximal and distal effects of mortality salience on sun exposure intentions. *Personality and Social Psychology Bulletin, 30*(10), 1347–1358.

Routledge, C., Arndt, J., Sedikides, C., & Wildschut, T. (2008). A blast from the past: The terror management function of nostalgia. *Journal of Experimental Social Psychology, 44*(1), 132–140.

Routledge, C., Arndt, J., Wildschut, T., Sedikides, C., Hart, C. M., Juhl, J., Vingerhoets, A. J. J. M., & Schlotz, W. (2011). The past makes the present meaningful: Nostalgia as an existential resource. *Journal of Personality and Social Psychology, 101*(3), 638–652.

Rozin, P., & Fallon, A. E. (1987). A perspective on disgust. *Psychological Review, 94*(1), 23–41.

Rozin, P., Haidt, J., McCauley, C., Dunlop, L., & Ashmore, M. (1999). Individual differences in disgust sensitivity: Comparisons and evaluations of paper-and-pencil versus behavioral measures. *Journal of Research in Personality, 33*(3), 330–351.

Rozin, P., Lowery, L., Imada, S., & Haidt, J. (1999). The CAD triad hypothesis: a mapping between three moral emotions (contempt, anger, disgust) and three moral codes (community, autonomy, divinity). *Journal of Personality and Social Psychology, 76*(4), 574–586.

Rubenstein, A. J., Langlois, J. H., & Roggman, L. A. (2002). What makes a face attractive and why: The role of averageness in defining facial beauty. In G. Rhodes & L. A. Zebrowitz, (Eds.), *Facial attractiveness: Evolutionary, cognitive, and social perspectives* (pp. 1–33). Westport, CT: Ablex.

Rubin, Z. (1973). *Liking and loving: An invitation to social psychology.* Oxford: Holt, Rinehart & Winston.

Ruble, D. N., Martin, C. L., & Berenbaum, S. A. (2006). Gender development. In *Handbook of child psychology.* Wiley Online Library.

Ruby, M. B., & Heine, S. J. (2012). Too close to home: Factors predicting meat avoidance. *Appetite, 59*(1), 47–52.

Rudman, L. A. (1998). Self-promotion as a risk factor for women: The costs and benefits of counterstereotypical impression management. *Journal of Personality and Social Psychology, 74*(3), 629–645.

Rusbult, C. E. (1980). Commitment and satisfaction in romantic associations: A test of the investment model. *Journal of Experimental Social Psychology, 16*(2), 172–186.

Rusbult, C. E. (1983). A longitudinal test of the investment model: The development (and deterioration) of satisfaction and commitment in heterosexual involvements. *Journal of Personality and Social Psychology, 45*(1), 101–117.

Rusbult, C. E. (1987). Responses to dissatisfaction in close relationships: The exit-voice-loyalty-neglect model. In D. Perlman & S. Duck (Eds.), *Intimate relationships: Development, dynamics, and deterioration* (pp. 209–237). Thousand Oaks, CA: Sage.

Rusbult, C. E., Johnson, D. J., & Morrow, G. D. (1986). Predicting satisfaction and commitment in adult romantic involvements: An assessment of the generalizability of the investment model. *Social Psychology Quarterly, 49*(1), 81–89. Stable URL: http://www.jstor.org/stable/2786859

Rusbult, C. E., & Martz, J. M. (1995). Remaining in an abusive relationship: An investment model analysis of nonvoluntary dependence. *Personality and Social Psychology Bulletin, 21*(6), 558–571.

Rusbult, C. E., Verette, J., Whitney, G. A., Slovik, L. F., & Lipkus, I. (1991). Accommodation processes in close relationships: Theory and preliminary empirical evidence. *Journal of Personality and Social Psychology, 60*(1), 53–78.

Rusbult, C. E., Zembrodt, I. M., & Gunn, L. K. (1982). Exit, voice, loyalty, and neglect: Responses to dissatisfaction in romantic involvements. *Journal of Personality and Social Psychology, 43*(6), 1230–1242.

Rushton, J. P., Chrisjohn, R. D., & Fekken, G. C. (1981). The altruistic personality and the Self-Report Altruism Scale. *Personality and Individual Differences, 2*(4), 293–302.

Rushton, J. P., Fulker, D. W., Neale, M. C., Nias, D. K. B., & Eysenck, H. J. (1986). Altruism and aggression: The heritability of individual differences. *Journal of Personality and Social Psychology, 50*(6), 1192–1198.

Russell, S. T., & Toomey, R. B. (2012). Men's sexual orientation and suicide: Evidence for US adolescent-specific risk. *Social Science & Medicine, 74*(4), 523–529.

Rutherford, M. D., Baron-Cohen, S., & Wheelwright, S. (2002). Reading the mind in the voice: A study with normal adults and adults with Asperger syndrome and high functioning autism. *Journal of Autism and Developmental Disorders, 32*(3), 189–194.

Ryan, R. M., & Connell, J. P. (1989). Perceived locus of causality and internalization: Examining reasons for acting in two domains. *Journal of Personality and Social Psychology, 57*(5), 749–761.

Rydell, R. J., & McConnell, A. R. (2006). Understanding implicit and explicit attitude change: A systems of reasoning analysis. *Journal of Personality and Social Psychology, 91*(6), 995–1008.

Rydell, R. J., McConnell, A. R., & Beilock, S. L. (2009). Multiple social identities and stereotype threat: Imbalance, accessibility, and working memory. *Journal of Personality and Social Psychology, 96*(5), 949–966.

Ryff, C. D., & Singer, B. (2000). Interpersonal flourishing: A positive health agenda for the new millennium. *Personality and Social Psychology Review, 4*(1), 30–44.

Saad, L. (2011, November 28). To lose weight, Americans rely more on dieting than exercise. Gallup News Service. Retrieved from http://www.gallup.com/poll/150986/Lose-Weight-Americans-Rely-Dieting-Exercise.aspx

Sabini, J., & Green, M. C. (2004). Emotional responses to sexual and emotional infidelity: Constants and differences across genders, samples, and methods. *Personality and Social Psychology Bulletin, 30*(11), 1375–1388.

Sagarin, B. J., Becker, D., Guadagno, R. E., Nicastle, L. D., & Millevoi, A. (2003). Sex differences (and similarities) in jealousy: The moderating influence of infidelity experience and sexual orientation of the infidelity. *Evolution and Human Behavior, 24*(1), 17–23.

Sagarin, B. J., Cialdini, R. B., Rice, W. E., & Serna, S. B. (2002). Dispelling the illusion of invulnerability: The motivations and mechanisms of resistance to persuasion. *Journal of Personality and Social Psychology, 83*(3), 526–541.

Salmivalli, C., Kaukiainen, A., Kaistaniemi, L., & Lagerspetz, K. M. (1999). Self-evaluated self-esteem, peer-evaluated self-esteem, and defensive egotism as predictors of adolescents' participation in bullying situations. *Personality and Social Psychology Bulletin, 25*(10), 1268–1278.

Salzman, M. B. (2001). Cultural trauma and recovery: Perspectives from terror management theory. *Trauma, Violence, & Abuse, 2*(2), 172–191.

Salzman, M. B., & Halloran, M. J. (2004). Cultural trauma and recovery: Cultural meaning, self-esteem, and the reconstruction of the cultural anxiety buffer. In J. Greenberg, S. Koole, & T. Pyszczynski (Eds.), *Handbook of experimental existential psychology* (pp. 231–246). New York: Guilford Press.

Sanders, G. S., & Baron, R. S. (1975). The motivating effects of distraction on task performance. *Journal of Personality and Social Psychology, 32*(6), 956–963.

Sanders, S. A., & Reinisch, J. M. (1999). Would you say you "had sex" if . . . ? *JAMA: The Journal of the American Medical Association, 281*(3), 275–277.

Sanfey, A. G., Rilling, J. K., Aronson, J. A., Nystrom, L. E., & Cohen, J. D. (2003). The neural basis of economic decision-making in the ultimatum game. *Science, 300*(5626), 1755–1758.

Sani, F., Herrera, M., & Bowe, M. (2009). Perceived collective continuity and ingroup identification as defence against death awareness. *Journal of Experimental Social Psychology, 45*(1), 242–245.

Sani, F., & Todman, J. (2002). Should we stay or should we go? A social psychological model of schisms in groups. *Personality and Social Psychology Bulletin, 28*(12), 1647–1655.

Santee, R. T., & Maslach, C. (1982). To agree or not to agree: Personal dissent amid social pressure to conform. *Journal of Personality and Social Psychology, 42*(4), 690–700.

Santos, M. D., Leve, C., & Pratkanis, A. R. (1994). Hey buddy, can you spare seventeen cents? Mindful persuasion and the pique technique. *Journal of Applied Social Psychology, 24*(9), 755–764.

Sapolsky, R. M. (1998). *The trouble with testosterone: And other essays on the biology of the human predicament.* New York: Simon & Schuster.

Sapolsky, R. M., & Share, L. J. (2004). A pacific culture among wild baboons: Its emergence and transmission. *PLoS Biology, 2*(4), e106.

Sargent, F. (Ed.). (1974). *Human ecology.* New York: American Elsevier.

Sargent, J. D., Dalton, M. A., Beach, M. L., Mott, L. A., Tickle, J. J., Ahrens, M. B., & Heatherton, T. F. (2002). Viewing tobacco use in movies: Does it shape attitudes that mediate adolescent smoking? *American Journal of Preventive Medicine, 22*(3), 137–145.

Sassenberg, K., & Moskowitz, G. B. (2005). Don't stereotype, think different! Overcoming automatic stereotype activation by mindset priming. *Journal of Experimental Social Psychology, 41*(5), 506–514.

Saucier, D. A., Miller, C. T., & Doucet, N. (2005). Differences in helping Whites and Blacks: A meta-analysis. *Personality and Social Psychology Review, 9*(1), 2–16.

Savitsky, K., & Gilovich, T. (2003). The illusion of transparency and the alleviation of speech anxiety. *Journal of Experimental Social Psychology, 39*(6), 618–625.

Sbarra, D. A. (2006). Predicting the onset of emotional recovery following nonmarital relationship dissolution: Survival analyses of sadness and anger. *Personality and Social Psychology Bulletin, 32*(3), 298–312.

Sbarra, D. A., & Emery, R. E. (2005). The emotional sequelae of nonmarital relationship dissolution: Analysis of change and intraindividual variability over time. *Personal Relationships, 12*(2), 213–232.

Sbarra, D. A., Law, R. W., & Portley, R. M. (2011). Divorce and death: A meta-analysis and research agenda for clinical, social, and health psychology. *Perspectives on Psychological Science, 6*(5), 454–474.

Sbarra, D. A., Smith, H. L., & Mehl, M. R. (2012). When leaving your ex, love yourself: Observational ratings of self-compassion predict the course of emotional recovery following marital separation. *Psychological Science, 23*(3), 261–269.

Schachter, S. (1951). Deviation, rejection, and communication. *Journal of Abnormal and Social Psychology, 46*(2), 190–207.

Schachter, S. (1959). *The psychology of affiliation: Experimental studies of the sources of gregariousness.* Palo Alto: Stanford University Press.

Schachter, S. (1964). The interaction of cognitive and physiological determinants of emotional state. In L. Berkowitz (Ed.), *Advances in experimental social psychology* (Vol. 1, pp. 48–81). New York: Academic Press.

Schachter, S., & Singer, J. (1962). Cognitive, social, and physiological determinants of emotional state. *Psychological Review, 69*(5), 379–399.

Schacter, D. L. (1996). *Searching for memory: The brain, the mind, and the past.* New York: Basic Books.

Schaller, M., Miller, G. E., Gervais, W. M., Yager, S., & Chen, E. (2010). Mere visual perception of other people's disease symptoms facilitates a more aggressive immune response. *Psychological Science, 21*(5), 649–652.

Schimel, J., Arndt, J., Pyszczynski, T., & Greenberg, J. (2001). Being accepted for who we are: Evidence that social validation of the intrinsic self reduces general defensiveness. *Journal of Personality and Social Psychology, 80*(1), 35–52.

Schimel, J., Greenberg, J., & Martens, A. (2003). Evidence that projection of a feared trait can serve a defensive function. *Personality and Social Psychology Bulletin, 29*(8), 969–979.

Schimel, J., Simon, L., Greenberg, J., Pyszczynski, T., Solomon, S., Waxmonsky, J., & Arndt, J. (1999). Stereotypes and terror management: Evidence that mortality salience enhances stereotypic thinking and preferences. *Journal of Personality and Social Psychology, 77*(5), 905–926.

Schkade, D. A., & Kahneman, D. (1998). Does living in California make people happy? A focusing illusion in judgments of life satisfaction. *Psychological Science, 9*(5), 340–346.

Schkade, D. A., & Sunstein, C. R. (2003, June 11). Judging by where you sit. *The New York Times.* Retrieved from http://www.nytimes.com/2003/06/11/opinion/judging-by-where-you-sit.html

Schlenker, B. R., & Forsyth, D. R. (1977). On the ethics of psychological research. *Journal of Experimental Social Psychology, 13*(4), 369–396.

Schmader, T., & Beilock, S. L. (2011). An integration of processes that underlie stereotype threat. In M. Inzlicht & T. Schmader & (Eds.), *Stereotype threat: Theory, process, and application* (pp. 34–50). New York: Oxford University Press.

Schmader, T., Johns, M., & Forbes, C. (2008). An integrated process model of stereotype threat effects on performance. *Psychological Review, 115*(2), 336–356.

Schmader, T., & Major, B. (1999). The impact of ingroup vs outgroup performance on personal values. *Journal of Experimental Social Psychology, 35*(1), 47–67.

Schmader, T., Major, B., Eccleston, C. P., & McCoy, S. K. (2001). Devaluing domains in response to threatening intergroup comparisons: Perceived legitimacy and the status value asymmetry. *Journal of Personality and Social Psychology, 80*(5), 782–796.

Schmader, T., Major, B., & Gramzow, R. H. (2001). Coping with ethnic stereotypes in the academic domain: Perceived injustice and psychological disengagement. *Journal of Social Issues, 57*(1), 93–111.

Schmeichel, B. J., Gailliot, M. T., Filardo, E. A., McGregor, I., Gitter, S., & Baumeister, R. F. (2009). Terror management theory and self-esteem revisited: The roles of implicit and explicit self-esteem in mortality salience effects. *Journal of Personality and Social Psychology, 96*(5), 1077–1087.

Schmeichel, B. J., & Vohs, K. D. (2009). Self-affirmation and self-control: Affirming core values counteracts ego depletion. *Journal of Personality and Social Psychology, 96*(4), 770–782.

Schmitt, D. P. (2005). Sociosexuality from Argentina to Zimbabwe: A 48-nation study of sex, culture, and strategies of human mating. *Behavioral and Brain Sciences, 28*(2), 247–274.

Schmitt, D. P., Couden, A., & Baker, M. (2001). The effects of sex and temporal context on feelings of romantic desire: An experimental evaluation of sexual strategies theory. *Personality and Social Psychology Bulletin, 27*(7), 833–847.

Schmitt, M. T., Branscombe, N. R., & Postmes, T. (2003). Women's emotional responses to the pervasiveness of gender discrimination. *European Journal of Social Psychology, 33*(3), 297–312.

Schmitt, M. T., Branscombe, N. R., Postmes, T., & Garcia, A. (2014). The consequences of perceived discrimination for psychological well-being: A meta-analytic review. *Psychological Bulletin, 140*(4), 921–948.

Schnall, S., Haidt, J., Clore, G. L., & Jordan, A. H. (2008). Disgust as embodied moral judgment. *Personality and Social Psychology Bulletin, 34*(8), 1096–1109.

Scholer, A. A., & Higgins, E. T. (2013). Dodging monsters and dancing with dreams: Success and failure at different levels of approach and avoidance. *Emotion Review, 5*(3), 254–258.

Schriesheim, C. A., Tepper, B. J., & Tetrault, L. A. (1994). Least preferred co-worker score, situational control, and leadership effectiveness: A meta-analysis of contingency model performance predictions. *Journal of Applied Psychology, 79*(4), 561–573.

Schultz, R. T. (2005). Developmental deficits in social perception in autism: The role of the amygdala and fusiform face area. *International Journal of Developmental Neuroscience, 23*(2), 125–141.

Schwartz, S. H. (1992). Universals in the content and structure of values: Theoretical advances and empirical tests in 20 countries. In M. P. Zanna (Ed.), *Advances in experimental social psychology* (Vol. 25, pp. 1–65). New York: Academic Press.

Schwartz, S. H., & Bardi, A. (2001). Value hierarchies across cultures: Taking a similarities perspective. *Journal of Cross-Cultural Psychology, 32*(3), 270–275.

Schwartz, S. H., Caprara, G. V., Vecchione, M., Bain, P., Bianchi, G., Caprara, M. G., . . . & Zaleski, Z. (2013). Basic personal values underlie and give coherence to political values: A cross national study in 15 countries. *Political Behavior, 36*(4), 1–32.

Schwartz, S. H., & Rubel, T. (2005). Sex differences in value priorities: Cross-cultural and multimethod studies. *Journal of Personality and Social Psychology, 89*(6), 1010–1028.

Schwartz, S. H., & Sagie, G. (2000). Value consensus and importance: A cross-national study. *Journal of Cross-Cultural Psychology, 31*(4), 465–497.

Schwarz, N., & Bless, H. (1992). Constructing reality and its alternatives: An inclusion/exclusion model of assimilation and contrast effects in social judgment. In L. L. Martin & A. Tesser (Eds.), *The construction of social judgments* (pp. 217–245). Hillsdale, NJ: Erlbaum.

Schwarz, N., Bless, H., & Bohner, G. (1991). Mood and persuasion: Affective states influence the processing of persuasive communications. In M. P. Zanna (Ed.), *Advances in experimental social psychology* (pp. 161–199). San Diego: Academic Press.

Schwarz, N., Bless, H., Strack, F., Klumpp, G., Rittenauer-Schatka, H., & Simons, A. (1991). Ease of retrieval as information: Another look at the availability heuristic. *Journal of Personality and Social Psychology, 61*(2), 195–202.

Schwarz, N., & Clore, G. L. (1983). Mood, misattribution, and judgments of well-being: Informative and directive functions of affective states. *Journal of Personality and Social Psychology, 45*(3), 513–523.

Schwarz, N., & Clore, G. L. (2003). Mood as information: 20 years later. *Psychological Inquiry, 14*(3-4), 296–303.

Schwirtz, M., & Saltmarsh, M. (2011, July 24). Oslo Suspect Cultivated Parallel Life to Disguise "Martyrdom Operation." *The New York Times.* Retrieved from http://www.nytimes.com/2011/07/25/world/europe/25breivik.html?pagewanted=all&_r=0

Sears, D. O., & Henry, P. J. (2005). Over thirty years later: A contemporary look at symbolic racism. *Advances in Experimental Social Psychology, 37*, 95–150.

Sears, D. O., & Kinder, D. R. (1971). Racial tensions and voting in Los Angeles. In W. Z. Hirsch (Ed.), *Los Angeles: Viability and prospects for metropolitan leadership* (pp. 51–88). New York: Praeger.

Sedikides, C., Gaertner, L., & Toguchi, Y. (2003). Pancultural self-enhancement. *Journal of Personality and Social Psychology, 84*(1), 60–79.

Sedikides, C., Gaertner, L., & Vevea, J. L. (2005). Pancultural self-enhancement reloaded: A meta-analytic reply to Heine (2005). *Journal of Personality and Social Psychology, 89*(4), 539–551.

Sedikides, C., Meek, R., Alicke, M. D., & Taylor, S. (2014). Behind bars but above the bar: Prisoners consider themselves more pro-social than non-prisoners. *British Journal of Social Psychology, 53*(2), 396–403.

Sedikides, C., & Strube, M. J. (1997). Self-evaluation: To thine own self be good, to thine own self be sure, to thine own self be true, and to thine own self be better. *Advances in Experimental Social Psychology, 29*, 209–269.

Sedikides, C., Wildschut, T., Gaertner, L., Routledge, C., & Arndt, J. (2008). Nostalgia as enabler of self-continuity. In F. Sani (Ed.), *Self-continuity: Individual and collective perspectives* (pp. 227–239). New York: Psychology Press.

Segall, M. H., Campbell, D. T., & Herskovits, M. J. (1963). Cultural differences in the perception of geometric illusions. *Science, 139*(3556), 769–771.

Segrin, C. (1998). Disrupted interpersonal relationships and mental health problems. In B. H. Spitzberg & W. R. Cupach (Eds.), *The dark side of close relationships* (pp. 327–365). Mahwah, NJ: Erlbaum.

Sell, A. (2011). Applying adaptationism to human anger: The recalibrational theory. In P. R. Shaver & M. Mikulincer (Eds.), *Human aggression and violence: Causes, manifestations, and consequences* (pp. 53–70). Washington, DC: American Psychological Association.

Semega, J. (2009). Men's and women's earnings by state: 2008 American community survey. Washington, DC: Department of Commerce, Economics and Statistics Administration, U.S. Census Bureau. Retrieved from http://www.census.gov/library/publications/2009/acs/acsbr08-3.html

Senchak, M., & Leonard, K. E. (1992). Attachment styles and marital adjustment among newlywed couples. *Journal of Social and Personal Relationships, 9*(1), 51–64.

Sethi, A., Mischel, W., Aber, J. L., Shoda, Y., & Rodriguez, M. L. (2000). The role of strategic attention deployment in development of self-regulation: Predicting preschoolers' delay of gratification from mother–toddler interactions. *Developmental Psychology, 36*(6), 767–777.

Shah, J. (2003). The motivational looking glass: How significant others implicitly affect goal appraisals. *Journal of Personality and Social Psychology, 85*(3), 424–439.

Shakespeare, W. (1869). *Macbeth* (2nd ed., ed. W. G. Clark & W. A. Wright). Oxford: Clarendon Press. (Original work published 1606)

Shallice, T. I. M., & Burgess, P. W. (1991). Deficits in strategy application following frontal lobe damage in man. *Brain, 114*(2), 727–741.

Shanab, M. E., & Yahya, K. A. (1978). A cross-cultural study of obedience. *Bulletin of the Psychonomic Society, 11*(4), 267–269.

Shanahan, J., & Morgan, M. (1999). *Television and its viewers: Cultivation theory and research.* Cambridge: Cambridge University Press.

Shapira, L. B., & Mongrain, M. (2010). The benefits of self-compassion and optimism exercises for individuals vulnerable to depression. *Journal of Positive Psychology, 5*(5), 377–389.

Shapiro, S. L., Schwartz, G. E., & Bonner, G. (1998). Effects of mindfulness-based stress reduction on medical and premedical students. *Journal of Behavioral Medicine, 21*(6), 581–599.

Shariff, A. F., & Norenzayan, A. (2007). God is watching you: Priming God concepts increases prosocial behavior in an anonymous economic game. *Psychological Science, 18*(9), 803–809.

Shariff, A. F., Norenzayan, A., & Henrich, J. (2010). The birth of high gods: How the cultural evolution of supernatural policing influenced the emergence of complex, cooperative human societies, paving the way for civilization. In M. Schaller, A. Norenzayan, S. J., Heine, T. Yamagishi, & T. Kameda (Eds.), *Evolution, culture, and the human mind* (pp. 119–136). New York: Psychology Press.

Shariff, A. F., & Tracy, J. L. (2011). What are emotion expressions for? *Current Directions in Psychological Science, 20*(6), 395–399.

Sharpe, D., & Faye, C. (2009). A second look at debriefing practices: Madness in our method? *Ethics & Behavior, 19*(5), 432–447.

Shaver, P. R., & Hazan, C. (1993). Adult romantic attachment: Theory and evidence. In D. Perlman & W. Jones (Eds.), *Advances in personal relationships* (Vol. 4, pp. 29–70). London: Jessica Kingsley.

Shaver, P. R., & Mikulincer, M. (2010). New directions in attachment theory and research. *Journal of Social and Personal Relationships, 27*(2), 163–172.

Shaver, P. R., & Mikulincer, M. (2012). Attachment theory. In P. M. Van Lange, A. W. Kruglanski, & E. Higgins (Eds.), *Handbook of theories of social psychology* (Vol. 2, pp. 160–179). Thousand Oaks, CA: Sage.

Shaver, P. R., Schachner, D. A., & Mikulincer, M. (2005). Attachment style, excessive reassurance seeking, relationship processes, and depression. *Personality and Social Psychology Bulletin, 31*(3), 343–359.

Shaver, P. R., Wu, S., & Schwartz, J. C. (1992). Cross-cultural similarities and differences in emotion and its representation. In M. S. Clark (Ed.), *Emotion: Review of personality and social psychology* (Vol. 13, pp. 175–212). Thousand Oaks, CA: Sage.

Shavitt, S., Swan, S., Lowrey, T. M., & Wänke, M. (1994). The interaction of endorser attractiveness and involvement in persuasion depends on the goal that guides message processing. *Journal of Consumer Psychology, 3*(2), 137–162.

Shaw, L. L., Batson, C. D., & Todd, R. M. (1994). Empathy avoidance: Forestalling feeling for another in order to escape the motivational consequences. *Journal of Personality and Social Psychology, 67*(5), 879–887.

Shaw, M. E. (1981). *Group dynamics: The psychology of small group behavior.* New York: McGraw-Hill.

Sheeran, P., & Orbell, S. (2000). Using implementation intentions to increase attendance for cervical cancer screening. *Health Psychology, 19*(3), 283–289.

Sheeran, P., & Taylor, S. (1999). Predicting intentions to use condoms: A meta-analysis and comparison of the theories of reasoned action and planned behavior. *Journal of Applied Social Psychology, 29*(8), 1624–1675.

Sheldon, K. M., & Elliot, A. J. (1999). Goal striving, need satisfaction, and longitudinal well-being: The self-concordance model. *Journal of Personality and Social Psychology, 76*(3), 482–497.

Sheldon, K. M., & Krieger, L. S. (2007). Understanding the negative effects of legal education on law students: A longitudinal test of self-determination theory. *Personality and Social Psychology Bulletin, 33*(6), 883–897.

Sheldon, K. M., Ryan, R. M., Deci, E. L., & Kasser, T. (2004). The independent effects of goal contents and motives on well-being: It's both what you pursue and why you pursue it. *Personality and Social Psychology Bulletin, 30*(4), 475–486.

Shelton, J. N., & Richeson, J. A. (2006). Interracial interactions: A relational approach. In M. P. Zanna, (Ed.), *Advances in experimental social psychology* (Vol. 38, pp. 121–181). San Diego: Elsevier Academic Press.

Shelton, J. N., Richeson, J. A., & Salvatore, J. (2005). Expecting to be the target of prejudice: Implications for interethnic interactions. *Personality and Social Psychology Bulletin, 31*(9), 1189–1202.

Shepperd, J. A., & Strathman, A. J. (1989). Attractiveness and height: The role of stature in dating preference, frequency of dating, and perceptions of attractiveness. *Personality and Social Psychology Bulletin, 15*(4), 617–627.

Sherif, M. (1936). *The psychology of social norms.* New York: Harper.

Sherif, M. (1966). *In common predicament: Social psychology of intergroup conflict and cooperation.* Boston: Houghton Mifflin.

Sherif, M., Harvey, O. J., White, B. J., Hood, W. R., & Sherif, C. W. (1961). *Intergroup conflict and cooperation: The Robbers Cave experiment.* Norman, OK: University Book Exchange.

Sherif, M., & Sherif, C. (1969). *Social Psychology.* New York: Harper & Row.

Sherman, D. K., & Cohen, G. L. (2006). The psychology of self-defense: Self-affirmation theory. In M. P. Zanna (Ed.), *Advances in experimental social psychology* (Vol. 38, pp. 183–242). San Diego, CA: Elsevier Academic Press.

Sherman, D. K., Kinias, Z., Major, B., Kim, H. S., & Prenovost, M. (2007). The group as a resource: Reducing biased attributions for group success and failure via group affirmation. *Personality and Social Psychology Bulletin, 33*(8), 1100–1112.

Sherman, S. J., Chassin, L., Presson, C., Seo, D. C., & Macy, J. T. (2009). The intergenerational transmission of implicit and explicit attitudes toward smoking: Predicting adolescent smoking initiation. *Journal of Experimental Social Psychology, 45*(2), 313–319.

Sherman, S. J., Presson, C. C., & Chassin, L. (1984). Mechanisms underlying the false consensus effect: The special role of threats to the self. *Personality and Social Psychology Bulletin, 10*(1), 127–138.

Shih, M., Ambady, N., Richeson, J. A., Fujita, K., & Gray, H. M. (2002). Stereotype performance boosts: The impact of self-relevance and the manner of stereotype activation. *Journal of Personality and Social Psychology, 83*(3), 638–647.

Shoda, Y., Mischel, W., & Peake, P. K. (1990). Predicting adolescent cognitive and self-regulatory competencies from preschool delay of gratification: Identifying diagnostic conditions. *Developmental Psychology, 26*(6), 978–986.

Shoham, V., & Rohrbaugh, M. (1997). Interrupting ironic processes. *Psychological Science, 8*(3), 151–153.

Short, J. F. (1997). *Poverty, ethnicity, and violent crime.* Boulder, CO: Westview Press.

Shrauger, J. S., & Schoeneman, T. J. (1979). Symbolic interactionist view of self-concept: Through the looking glass darkly. *Psychological Bulletin, 86*(3), 549–573.

Shreve, J. (1997, September 25). Dissing Disney [Online article]. Metroactive. Retrieved from http://www.metroactive.com/papers/metro/09.25.97/disney-9739.html

Shupe, L. M. (1954). Alcohol and crime: A study of the urine alcohol concentration found in 882 persons arrested during or immediately after the commission of a felony. *Journal of Criminal Law, Criminology, and Police Science, 44*(5), 661–664. Stable URL: http://www.jstor.org/stable/1139637

Shweder, R. A., Much, N. C., Mahapatra, M., & Park, L. (1997). The "big three" of morality (autonomy, community, and divinity), and the "big three" explanations of suffering. In A. Brandt & P. Rozin (Eds.), *Morality and health* (pp. 119–169). New York: Routledge.

Sidanius, J., Levin, S., Federico, C. M., & Pratto, F. (2001). Legitimizing ideologies: The social dominance approach. In J. T. Jost & B. Major (Eds.), *The psychology of legitimacy: Emerging perspectives on ideology, justice, and intergroup relations* (pp. 307–331). New York: Cambridge University Press.

Sidanius, J., Liu, J. H., Shaw, J. S., & Pratto, F. (1994). Social dominance orientation, hierarchy attenuators and hierarchy enhancers: Social dominance theory and the criminal justice system. *Journal of Applied Social Psychology, 24*(4), 338–366.

Sidanius, J., & Pratto, F. (1999). *Social dominance: An intergroup theory of social hierarchy and oppression.* New York: Cambridge University Press.

Siever, L. J. (2008). Neurobiology of aggression and violence. *American Journal of Psychiatry, 165*(4), 429–442.

Sigall, H., & Landy, D. (1973). Radiating beauty: Effects of having a physically attractive partner on person perception. *Journal of Personality and Social Psychology, 28*(2), 218–224.

Silver, J., & Cracchiolo, D. (Producers), Wachowski, A., & Wachowski, L. (Producers, Writers, & Directors) (1999). *The matrix* [Motion picture]. United

States: Warner Bros & Silver Pictures, in association with Village Roadshow Pictures & Groucho II Film Partnership.

Silverstein, B. (1992). The psychology of enemy images. In S. Staub & P. Green (Eds.), *Psychology and social responsibility* (pp. 145–164). New York: New York University Press.

Silverstein, B., Peterson, B., & Perdue, L. (1986). Some correlates of the thin standard of bodily attractiveness for women. *International Journal of Eating Disorders, 5*(5), 895–905.

Silvia, P. J. (2005). Deflecting reactance: The role of similarity in increasing compliance and reducing resistance. *Basic and Applied Social Psychology, 27*(3), 277–284.

Simmel, G. (2005). The metropolis and mental life. In J. Lin & C. Mele (Eds.), *The urban sociology reader* (pp. 23–31). New York: Routledge. (Original work published 1903)

Simon, L., Greenberg, J., & Brehm, J. (1995). Trivialization: The forgotten mode of dissonance reduction. *Journal of Personality and Social Psychology, 68*(2), 247.

Simonton, D. (1987). *Why presidents succeed: A political psychology of leadership.* New Haven: Yale University Press.

Simpson, J. A. (1990). Influence of attachment styles on romantic relationships. *Journal of Personality and Social Psychology, 59*(5), 971–980.

Simpson, J. A. (2007). Psychological foundations of trust. *Current Directions in Psychological Science, 16*(5), 264–268.

Simpson, J. A., Collins, W. A., Tran, S., & Haydon, K. C. (2007). Attachment and the experience and expression of emotions in romantic relationships: A developmental perspective. *Journal of Personality and Social Psychology, 92*(2), 355–367.

Simpson, J. A., & Kenrick, D. T. (Eds.). (1997). *Evolutionary social psychology.* Mahwah, NJ: Erlbaum.

Simpson, J. A., Rholes, W. S., & Nelligan, J. S. (1992). Support seeking and support giving within couples in an anxiety-provoking situation: The role of attachment styles. *Journal of Personality and Social Psychology, 62*(3), 434–446.

Sinclair, L., & Kunda, Z. (1999). Reactions to a Black professional: Motivated inhibition and activation of conflicting stereotypes. *Journal of Personality and Social Psychology, 77*(5), 885–904.

Sinclair, L., & Kunda, Z. (2000). Motivated stereotyping of women: She's fine if she praised me but incompetent if she criticized me. *Personality and Social Psychology Bulletin, 26*(11), 1329–1342.

Sinclair, S., Huntsinger, J., Skorinko, J., & Hardin, C.D. (2005). Social tuning of the self: Consequences for the self-evaluations of stereotype targets. *Journal of Personality and Social Psychology, 89*(2), 160–175.

Sinclair, S., Lowery, B. S., Hardin, C. D., & Colangelo, A. (2005). Social tuning of automatic racial attitudes: The role of affiliative motivation. *Journal of Personality and Social Psychology, 89*(4), 583–592.

Singelis, T. M., Triandis, H. C., Bhawuk, D. P., & Gelfand, M. J. (1995). Horizontal and vertical dimensions of individualism and collectivism: A theoretical and measurement refinement. *Cross-Cultural Research, 29*(3), 240–275.

Singer, J. L., & Singer, D. G. (1981). *Television, imagination and aggression: A study of preschoolers.* Hillsdale, NJ: Erlbaum.

Singh, D. (1993). Adaptive significance of female physical attractiveness: Role of waist-to-hip ratio. *Journal of Personality and Social Psychology, 65*(2), 293–307.

Singh, D. (1995). Female judgment of male attractiveness and desirability for relationships: Role of waist-to-hip ratio and financial status. *Journal of Personality and Social Psychology, 69*(6), 1089–1101.

Singh, D., & Luis, S. (1995). Ethnic and gender consensus for the effect of waist-to-hip ratio on judgment of women's attractiveness. *Human Nature, 6*(1), 51–65.

Sirois, F. (1982). Perspective on epidemic hysteria. In M. Colligan, J. Pennebaker, & P. Murphy (Eds.), *Mass psychogenic illness: A social psychological analysis* (pp. 217–236). Hillsdale, NJ: Erlbaum.

Sivacek, J., & Crano, W. D. (1982). Vested interest as a moderator of attitude–behavior consistency. *Journal of Personality and Social Psychology, 43*(2), 210–221.

Skitka, L. J. (1999). Ideological and attributional boundaries on public compassion: Reactions to individuals and communities affected by a natural disaster. *Personality and Social Psychology Bulletin, 25*(7), 793–808.

Skitka, L. J., McMurray, P. J., & Burroughs, T. E. (1991). Willingness to provide post-war aid to Iraq and Kuwait: An application of the contingency model of distributive justice. *Contemporary Social Psychology, 15*(4), 179–188.

Skitka, L. J., Mullen, E., Griffin, T., Hutchinson, S., & Chamberlin, B. (2002). Dispositions, scripts, or motivated correction? Understanding ideological differences in explanations for social problems. *Journal of Personality and Social Psychology, 83*(2), 470–487.

Skitka, L. J., & Tetlock, P. E. (1992). Allocating scarce resources: A contingency model of distributive justice. *Journal of Experimental Social Psychology, 28*(6), 491–522.

Skitka, L. J., & Tetlock, P. E. (1993). Providing public assistance: Cognitive and motivational processes underlying liberal and conservative policy preferences. *Journal of Personality and Social Psychology, 65*(6), 1205–1223.

Sklansky, D. A. (1995). Cocaine, race, and equal protection. *Stanford Law Review, 47*(6), 1283–1322. Stable URL: http://www.jstor.org/stable/1229193

Slaby, R. G., & Guerra, N. G. (1988). Cognitive mediators of aggression in adolescent offenders: I. Assessment. *Developmental Psychology, 24*(4), 580–588.

Slater, A., Bremner, G., Johnson, S. P., Sherwood, P., Hayes, R., & Brown, E. (2000). Newborn infants' preference for attractive faces: The role of internal and external facial features. *Infancy, 1*(2), 265–274.

Slavin, R. E. (2012). Classroom applications of cooperative learning. In K. R. Harris, S. Graham, T. Urdan, A. G. Bus, S. Major & H. Swanson (Eds.), *APA educational psychology handbook* (Vol. 3, pp. 359–378). Washington, DC: American Psychological Association.

Sloman, S. A. (1996). The empirical case for two systems of reasoning. *Psychological Bulletin, 119*(1), 3–22.

Slotter, E. B., & Finkel, E. J. (2009). The strange case of sustained dedication to an unfulfilling relationship: Predicting commitment and breakup from attachment anxiety and need fulfillment within relationships. *Personality and Social Psychology Bulletin, 35*(1), 85–100.

Slotter, E. B., Gardner, W. L., & Finkel, E. J. (2010). Who am I without you? The influence of romantic breakup on the self-concept. *Personality and Social Psychology Bulletin, 36*(2), 147–160.

Smart, L., & Wegner, D. M. (1999). Covering up what can't be seen: Concealable stigma and mental control. *Journal of Personality and Social Psychology, 77*(3), 474–486.

Smart Richman, L., & Leary, M. R. (2009). Reactions to discrimination, stigmatization, ostracism, and other forms of interpersonal rejection: A multimotive model. *Psychological Review, 116*(2), 365–383.

Smith, E. R., & Henry, S. (1996). An in-group becomes part of the self: Response time evidence. *Personality and Social Psychology Bulletin, 22*(6), 635–642.

Smith, P. K., Jostmann, N. B., Galinsky, A. D., & van Dijk, W. W. (2008). Lacking power impairs executive functions. *Psychological Science, 19*(5), 441–447.

Smith, P. K., & Trope, Y. (2006). You focus on the forest when you're in charge of the trees: Power priming and abstract information processing. *Journal of Personality and Social Psychology, 90*(4), 578–596.

Smith, S. L., & Choueiti, M. (n.d.) Gender disparity on screen and behind the camera in family films: The executive report. University of Southern California. Retrieved from http://thegeenadavisinstitute.net/downloads/FullStudy_GenderDisparityFamilyFilms.pdf

Smith, S. L., Choueiti, M., Scofield, E., & Pieper, K. (2013). Gender inequality in 500 popular films: Examining on-screen portrayals and behind-the-scenes employment patterns in motion pictures released between 2007–2012. Unpublished manuscript, Annenberg School for Communication & Journalism, University of Southern California. Retrieved from http://annenberg.usc.edu/Faculty/Communication%20and%20Journalism/~/media/A41FBC3E62084AC8A8C047A9D4A54033.ashx

Smith, S. L., Pieper, K. M., Granados, A., & Choueiti, M. (2010). Assessing gender-related portrayals in top-grossing G-rated films. *Sex Roles, 62*(11–12), 774–786.

Smith, S. M., McIntosh, W. D., & Bazzini, D. G. (1999). Are the beautiful good in Hollywood? An investigation of the beauty-and-goodness stereotype on film. *Basic and Applied Social Psychology, 21*(1), 69–80.

Smith, T. W., & Greenberg, J. (1981). Depression and self-focused attention. *Motivation and Emotion, 5*(4), 323–331.

Smock, P. J., & Greenland, F. R. (2010). Diversity in pathways to parenthood: Patterns, implications, and emerging research directions. *Journal of Marriage and Family, 72*(3), 576–593.

Snyder, C. R., Lassegard, M., & Ford, C. E. (1986). Distancing after group success and failure: Basking in reflected glory and cutting off reflected failure. *Journal of Personality and Social Psychology, 51*(2), 382–388.

Snyder, H. N., & Sickmund, M. (2006). Juvenile offenders and victims: 2006 national report. Washington, DC: U.S. Department of Justice, Office of Justice Programs, Office of Juvenile Justice and Delinquency Prevention. Retrieved from http://eric.ed.gov/?id=ED495786

Snyder, M. (1974). Self-monitoring of expressive behavior. *Journal of Personality and Social Psychology, 30*(4), 526–537.

Snyder, M., & DeBono, K. G. (1985). Appeals to image and claims about quality: Understanding the psychology of advertising. *Journal of Personality and Social Psychology, 49*(3), 586–597.

Snyder, M., & Gangestad, S. (1986). On the nature of self-monitoring: Matters of assessment, matters of validity. *Journal of Personality and Social Psychology, 51*(1), 125–139.

Snyder, M., & Kendzierski, D. (1982). Acting on one's attitudes: Procedures for linking attitude and behavior. *Journal of Experimental Social Psychology, 18*(2), 165–183.

Snyder, M., & Swann, W. B. (1978). Hypothesis-testing processes in social interaction. *Journal of Personality and Social Psychology, 36*(11), 1202.

Snyder, M., Tanke, E. D., & Berscheid, E. (1977). Social perception and interpersonal behavior: On the self-fulfilling nature of social stereotypes. *Journal of Personality and Social Psychology, 35*(9), 656–666.

Snyder, M. L., & Frankel, A. (1976). Observer bias: A stringent test of behavior engulfing the field. *Journal of Personality and Social Psychology, 34*(5), 857–864.

Snyder, M. L., Smoller, B., Strenta, A., & Frankel, A. (1981). A comparison of egotism, negativity, and learned helplessness as explanations for poor performance after unsolvable problems. *Journal of Personality and Social Psychology, 40*(1), 24–30.

Snyder, M. L., Stephan, W. G., & Rosenfield, D. (1976). Egotism and attribution. *Journal of Personality and Social Psychology, 33*(4), 435–441.

Sobal, J., & Stunkard, A. J. (1989). Socioeconomic status and obesity: A review of the literature. *Psychological Bulletin, 105*(2), 260–275.

Soler, C., Nuñez, M., Gutierrez, R., Nuñez, J., Medina, P., Sancho, M., . . . & Nuñez, A. (2003). Facial attractiveness in men provides clues to semen quality. *Evolution and Human Behavior, 24*(3), 199–207.

Solomon, D. H., & Knobloch, L. K. (2004). A model of relational turbulence: The role of intimacy, relational uncertainty, and interference from partners in appraisals of irritations. *Journal of Social and Personal Relationships, 21*(6), 795–816.

Solomon, S., Greenberg, J., & Pyszczynski, T. (1991). A terror management theory of social behavior: On the psychological functions of self-esteem and cultural worldviews. In M. P. Zanna (Ed.), *Advances in Experimental Social Psychology* (Vol. 24, pp. 93–159). San Diego: Academic Press.

Solomon, S., Greenberg, J., & Pyszczynski, T. (in press). *The worm at the core: On the role of death in life*. New York: Random House.

Sommers, S. R. (2006). On racial diversity and group decision making: Identifying multiple effects of racial composition on jury deliberations. *Journal of Personality and Social Psychology, 90*(4), 597–612.

Sommers, S. R., Warp, L. S., & Mahoney, C. C. (2008). Cognitive effects of racial diversity: White individuals' information processing in heterogeneous groups. *Journal of Experimental Social Psychology, 44*(4), 1129–1136.

Soubrié, P. (1986). Reconciling the role of central serotonin neurons in human and animal behavior. *Behavioral and Brain Sciences, 9*(2), 319–335.

South, S. J., & Lloyd, K. M. (1995). Spousal alternatives and marital dissolution. *American Sociological Review, 60*(1), 21–35. Stable URL: http://www.jstor.org/stable/2096343

Spalding, L. R., & Hardin, C. D. (1999). Unconscious unease and self-handicapping: Behavioral consequences of individual differences in implicit and explicit self-esteem. *Psychological Science, 10*(6), 535–539.

Sparacino, J., & Hansell, S. (1979). Physical attractiveness and academic performance: Beauty is not always talent. *Journal of Personality, 47*(3), 449–469.

Spears, R., Lea, M., & Lee, S. (1990). De-individuation and group polarization in computer-mediated communication. *British Journal of Social Psychology, 29*(2), 121–134.

Spencer, H. (1855). *The principles of psychology*. London: Longman, Brown, Green and Longmans.

Spencer, S. J., Fein, S., Wolfe, C. T., Fong, C., & Duinn, M. A. (1998). Automatic activation of stereotypes: The role of self-image threat. *Personality and Social Psychology Bulletin, 24*(11), 1139–1152.

Spencer, S. J., Steele, C. M., & Quinn, D. M. (1999). Stereotype threat and women's math performance. *Journal of Experimental Social Psychology, 35*(1), 4–28.

Spencer-Rodgers, J., Boucher, H. C., Mori, S. C., Wang, L., & Peng, K. (2009). The dialectical self-concept: Contradiction, change, and holism in East Asian cultures. *Personality and Social Psychology Bulletin, 35*(1), 29–44.

Spencer-Rodgers, J., Williams, M. J., & Peng, K. (2010). Cultural differences in expectations of change and tolerance for contradiction: A decade of empirical research. *Personality and Social Psychology Review, 14*(3), 296–312.

Spiegel, I. (2006, December 15). Shouting across the divide [Radio broadcast]. In I. Glass (Producer). *This American life*. Illinois, Chicago: Chicago Public Media & Ira Glass. Retrieved from http://www.thisamericanlife.org/radio-archives/episode/322/shouting-across-the-divide

Spiegel, I. (2011, September 9). Ten years in [Radio broadcast]. In I. Glass (Producer). *This American life*. Illinois, Chicago: Chicago Public Media & Ira Glass. Retrieved from http://www.thisamericanlife.org/radio-archives/episode/445/transcript

Spielberg, S., Kennedy, K., (Producers), & Spielberg, S., (Director) (1982). *E.T.: The extra terrestrial* [Motion picture]. United States: Universal Pictures.

Sprecher, S. (1986). The relation between inequity and emotions in close relationships. *Social Psychology Quarterly, 49*(4), 309–321. Stable URL: http://www.jstor.org/stable/2786770

Sprecher, S. (1992). How men and women expect to feel and behave in response to inequity in close relationships. *Social Psychology Quarterly, 55*(1), 57–69. Stable URL: http://www.jstor.org/stable/2786686

Sprecher, S. (1998). Social exchange theories and sexuality. *Journal of Sex Research, 35*(1), 32–43.

Sprecher, S. (2002). Sexual satisfaction in premarital relationships: Associations with satisfaction, love, commitment, and stability. *Journal of Sex Research, 39*(3), 190–196.

Sprecher, S., & Cate, R. M. (2004). Sexual satisfaction and sexual expression as predictors of relationship satisfaction and stability. In J. H. Harvey, A. Wenzel, & S. Sprecher (Eds.), *The handbook of sexuality in close relationships* (pp. 235–256). Mahwah, NJ: Erlbaum.

Sprecher, S., Christopher, F. S., & Cate, R. (2006). Sexuality in close relationships. In A. L. Vangelisti & D. Perlman (Eds.), *The Cambridge handbook of personal relationships* (pp. 463–482). New York: Cambridge University Press.

Sprecher, S., & Regan, P. C. (1998). Passionate and companionate love in courting and young married couples. *Sociological Inquiry, 68*(2), 163–185.

Sprecher, S., & Regan, P. C. (2002). Liking some things (in some people) more than others: Partner preferences in romantic relationships and friendships. *Journal of Social and Personal Relationships, 19*(4), 436–481.

Srivastava, S., McGonigal, K. M., Richards, J. M., Butler, E. A., & Gross, J. J. (2006). Optimism in close relationships: How seeing things in a positive light makes them so. *Journal of Personality and Social Psychology, 91*(1), 143–153.

Staats, A. W., & Staats, C. K. (1958). Attitudes established by classical conditioning. *Journal of Abnormal and Social Psychology, 57*(1), 37–40.

Stangor, C. (2009). The study of stereotyping, prejudice, and discrimination within social psychology: A quick history of theory and research. In T. D. Nelson (Ed.), *Handbook of prejudice, stereotyping and discrimination* (pp. 1–22). New York: Psychology Press.

Stanik, C. E., & Ellsworth, P. C. (2010). Who cares about marrying a rich man? Intelligence and variation in women's mate preferences. *Human Nature, 21*(2), 203–217.

Stanley, S. M., Markman, H. J., & Whitton, S. W. (2002). Communication, conflict and commitment: Insights on the foundations of relationship success from a national survey. *Family Process, 41*(4), 659–675.

Staub, E. (1989). *The roots of evil: The psychological and cultural origins of genocide and other forms of group violence*. Cambridge: Cambridge University Press.

Staub, E. (1996). Cultural-societal roots of violence: The examples of genocidal violence and of contemporary youth violence in the United States. *American Psychologist, 51*(2), 117–132.

Staw, B. M. (1974). Attitudinal and behavioral consequences of changing a major organizational reward: A natural field experiment. *Journal of Personality and Social Psychology, 29*(6), 742–751.

Steele, C. M. (1988). The psychology of self-affirmation: Sustaining the integrity of the self. In L. Berkowitz (Ed.), *Advances in experimental social psychology* (Vol. 21, pp. 261–302). New York: Academic Press.

Steele, C. M. (1997). A threat in the air: How stereotypes shape intellectual identity and performance. *American Psychologist, 52*(6), 613–629.

Steele, C. M., & Aronson, J. (1995). Stereotype threat and the intellectual test performance of African Americans. *Journal of Personality and Social Psychology, 69*(5), 797–811.

Steele, C. M., & Josephs, R. A. (1990). Alcohol myopia: Its prized and dangerous effects. *American Psychologist, 45*(8), 921–933.

Steele, C. M., Spencer, S. J., & Aronson, J. (2002). Contending with group image: The psychology of stereotype and social identity threat. In M. P. Zanna (Ed.), *Advances in experimental social psychology* (Vol. 34, pp. 379–440). San Diego: Academic Press.

Steenbarger, B. N., & Aderman, D. (1979). Objective self-awareness as a nonaversive state: Effect of anticipating discrepancy reduction. *Journal of Personality, 47*(2), 330–339.

Stephan, W. G. (1978). School desegregation: An evaluation of predictions made in Brown v. Board of Education. *Psychological Bulletin, 85*(2), 217–238.

Stephan, W. G., & Stephan, C. W. (1985). Intergroup anxiety. *Journal of Social Issues, 41*(3), 157–175.

Sternberg, R. J. (1997). Construct validation of a triangular love scale. *European Journal of Social Psychology, 27*(3), 313–335.

Stevens, D. (2010, December 3). Nutcracked: Natalie Portman as an unstable dancer in the inert *Black Swan. Slate*. Retrieved from http://www.slate.com/articles/arts/movies/2010/12/nutcracked.html

Stewart, J. E. (1980). Defendant's attractiveness as a factor in the outcome of criminal trials: An observational study. *Journal of Applied Social Psychology, 10*(4), 348–361.

Stewart, V. M. (1973). Tests of the "carpentered world" hypothesis by race and environment in America and Zambia. *International Journal of Psychology, 8*(2), 83–94.

Stith, S. M., & Farley, S. C. (1993). A predictive model of male spousal violence. *Journal of Family Violence, 8*(2), 183–201.

Stone, A. A., Hedges, S. M., Neale, J. M., & Satin, M. S. (1985). Prospective and cross-sectional mood reports offer no evidence of a "blue Monday" phenomenon. *Journal of Personality and Social Psychology, 49*(1), 129–134.

Stone, J., Aronson, E., Crain, A. L., Winslow, M. P., & Fried, C. B. (1994). Inducing hypocrisy as a means of encouraging young adults to use condoms. *Personality and Social Psychology Bulletin*, 20(1), 116–128.

Stone, J., Chalabaev, A., & Harrison, C. K. (2012). Stereotype threat in sports. In M. Inzlicht & T. Schmader (Eds.), *Stereotype threat: Theory, process, and application* (pp. 217–230). New York: Oxford University Press.

Stone, J., & Fernandez, N. C. (2008). To practice what we preach: The use of hypocrisy and cognitive dissonance to motivate behavior change. *Social and Personality Psychology Compass*, 2(2), 1024–1051.

Stone, J., Lynch, C. I., Sjomeling, M., & Darley, J. M. (1999). Stereotype threat effects on Black and White athletic performance. *Journal of Personality and Social Psychology*, 77(6), 1213–1227.

Stone, J., Whitehead, J., Schmader, T., & Focella, E. (2011). Thanks for asking: Self-affirming questions reduce backlash when stigmatized targets confront prejudice. *Journal of Experimental Social Psychology*, 47(3), 589–598.

Stoner, J. A. F. (1961). A comparison of individual and group decisions involving risk (Unpublished master's thesis). Massachusetts Institute of Technology, Sloan School of Management.

Storms, M. D. (1973). Videotape and the attribution process: Reversing actors' and observers' points of view. *Journal of Personality and Social Psychology*, 27(2), 165–175.

Storms, M. D., & Nisbett, R. E. (1970). Insomnia and the attribution process. *Journal of Personality and Social Psychology*, 16(2), 319–328.

Stouffer, S. A., Schuman, E. A., DeVinney, L. C., Star, S. A., & Williams, R. B. (1949). *The American soldier: Adjustment during army life*, Vol. 1. Oxford: Princeton University Press.

Stout, J. G., Dasgupta, N., Hunsinger, M., & McManus, M. A. (2011). STEMing the tide: Using ingroup experts to inoculate women's self-concept in science, technology, engineering, and mathematics (STEM). *Journal of Personality and Social Psychology*, 100(2), 255–270.

Strack, F., Martin, L. L., & Stepper, S. (1988). Inhibiting and facilitating conditions of the human smile: A nonobtrusive test of the facial feedback hypothesis. *Journal of Personality and Social Psychology*, 54(5), 768–777.

Strahan, E. J., Spencer, S. J., & Zanna, M. P. (2002). Subliminal priming and persuasion: Striking while the iron is hot. *Journal of Experimental Social Psychology*, 38(6), 556–568.

Strange, J. J., & Leung, C. C. (1999). How anecdotal accounts in news and in fiction can influence judgments of a social problem's urgency, causes, and cures. *Personality and Social Psychology Bulletin*, 25(4), 436–449.

Strasburger, V. C. (2007). Go ahead punk, make my day: It's time for pediatricians to take action against media violence. *Pediatrics*, 119(6), e1398–e1399.

Straus, M. A. (2000). Corporal punishment and primary prevention of physical abuse. *Child Abuse & Neglect*, 24(9), 1109–1114.

Straus, M. A. (2005). Women's violence toward men is a serious social problem. In D. R. Loseke, R. J. Gelles, & M. M. Cavanaugh (Eds.), *Current controversies on family violence* (2nd ed., pp. 55–77). Thousand Oaks, CA: Sage.

Straus, M. A., Gelles, R. J., & Steinmetz, S. K. (1980). *Behind closed doors: Violence in the American family*. Garden City, NY: Doubleday.

Strube, M. J., & Roemmele, L. A. (1985). Self-enhancement, self-assessment, and self-evaluative task choice. *Journal of Personality and Social Psychology*, 49(4), 981–993.

Stucky, T. D. (2012). The conditional effects of race and politics on social control: Black violent crime arrests in large cities, 1970 to 1990. *Journal of Research in Crime and Delinquency*, 49(1), 3–30.

Suarez, E. C., & Krishnan, K. R. R. (2006). The relation of free plasma tryptophan to anger, hostility, and aggression in a nonpatient sample of adult men and women. *Annals of Behavioral Medicine*, 31(3), 254–260.

Suh, E. M. (2002). Culture, identity consistency, and subjective well-being. *Journal of Personality and Social Psychology*, 83(6), 1378–1391.

Sullivan, D., Landau, M. J., & Rothschild, Z. K. (2010). An existential function of enemyship: Evidence that people attribute influence to personal and political enemies to compensate for threats to control. *Journal of Personality and Social Psychology*, 98(3), 434–449.

Summers, G., & Feldman, N. S. (1984). Blaming the victim versus blaming the perpetrator: An attributional analysis of spouse abuse. *Journal of Social and Clinical Psychology*, 2(4), 339–347.

Sumner, W. G. (1906). *Folkways: A study of the sociological importance of usages, manners, customs, mores, and morals*. New York: Ginn and Co.

Support Our Law Enforcement and Safe Neighborhood Act, Arizona Senate Bill 1070 (2010). Retrieved from http://www.azleg.gov/legtext/49leg/2r/bills/sb1070s.pdf

Surowiecki, J., (2004). *The wisdom of crowds*. New York: Doubleday.

Swami, V., & Tovee, M. J. (2006). The influence of body mass index on the physical attractiveness preferences of feminist and nonfeminist heterosexual women and lesbians. *Psychology of Women Quarterly*, 30(3), 252–257.

Swann, W. B., & Pittman, T. S. (1975). Salience of initial ratings and attitude change in the "forbidden toy" paradigm. *Personality and Social Psychology Bulletin*, 1(3), 493–496.

Swann, W. B., Wenzlaff, R. M., & Tafarodi, R. W. (1992). Depression and the search for negative evaluations: More evidence of the role of self-verification strivings. *Journal of Abnormal Psychology*, 101(2), 314–317.

Swann, W. B. Jr. (1983). Self-verification: Bringing social reality into harmony with the self. In J. Suls & A. G. Greenwald (Eds.), *Social psychological perspectives on the self* (Vol. 2, pp. 33–66). Hillsdale, NJ: Erlbaum.

Swap, W. C. (1977). Interpersonal attraction and repeated exposure to rewarders and punishers. *Personality and Social Psychology Bulletin*, 3(2), 248–251.

Swendsen, J. D., & Merikangas, K. R. (2000). The comorbidity of depression and substance abuse disorders. *Clinical Psychology Review*, 20(2), 173–189.

Swift, J. (2001). *Gulliver's travels*. New York: W. W. Norton (Original work published 1726)

Swim, J. K., & Hyers, L. L. (1999). Excuse me—What did you just say?! Women's public and private responses to sexist remarks. *Journal of Experimental Social Psychology*, 35(1), 68–88.

Symons, D. (1979). *The evolution of human sexuality*. New York: Oxford University Press.

Szymanski, K., & Harkins, S. G. (1987). Social loafing and self-evaluation with a social standard. *Journal of Personality and Social Psychology*, 53(5), 891–897.

Tafoya, M. A., & Spitzberg, B. H. (2007). The dark side of infidelity: Its nature, prevalence, and communicative functions. In B. H. Spitzberg & W. R. Cupach (Eds.), *The dark side of interpersonal communication* (2nd ed., pp. 201–242). Mahwah, NJ: Erlbaum.

Tajfel, H., Billig, M. G., Bundy, R. P., & Flament, C. (1971). Social categorization and intergroup behaviour. *European Journal of Social Psychology*, 1(2), 149–178.

Tajfel, H., & Turner, J. C. (1979). An integrative theory of intergroup conflict. In W. G. Austin & S. Worchel (Eds.), *The social psychology of intergroup relations* (pp. 33–47). Monterey, CA: Brooks/Cole.

Tajfel, H., & Turner, J. C. (1986). The social identity theory of intergroup behavior. In S. Worchel & W. G. Austin (Eds.), *Psychology of intergroup relations* (pp. 7–24). Chicago: Nelson-Hall.

Tamborini, R., & Stiff, J. (1987). Predictors of horror film attendance and appeal: An analysis of the audience for frightening films. *Communication Research*, 14(4), 415–436.

Tangney, J. P. (1991). Moral affect: The good, the bad, and the ugly. *Journal of Personality and Social Psychology*, 61(4), 598–607.

Tangney, J. P., & Dearing, R. L. (2002). *Shame and guilt*. New York: Guilford Press.

Tangney, J. P., Miller, R. S., Flicker, L., & Barlow, D. H. (1996). Are shame, guilt, and embarrassment distinct emotions? *Journal of Personality and Social Psychology*, 70(6), 1256–1269.

Tangney, J. P., Stuewig, J., Mashek, D., & Hastings, M. (2011). Assessing jail inmates' proneness to shame and guilt: Feeling bad about the behavior or the self? *Criminal Justice and Behavior*, 38(7), 710–734.

Tangney, J. P., Wagner, P., Fletcher, C., & Gramzow, R. (1992). Shamed into anger? The relation of shame and guilt to anger and self-reported aggression. *Journal of Personality and Social Psychology*, 62(4), 669–675.

Tangney, J. P., Wagner, P., & Gramzow, R. (1992). Proneness to shame, proneness to guilt, and psychopathology. *Journal of Abnormal Psychology*, 101(3), 469–478.

Tangney, J. P., Wagner, P. E., Hill-Barlow, D., Marschall, D. E., & Gramzow, R. (1996). Relation of shame and guilt to constructive versus destructive responses to anger across the lifespan. *Journal of Personality and Social Psychology*, 70(4), 797–809.

Tattersall, I. (1998). *Becoming human: Evolution and human uniqueness*. New York: Harcourt Brace.

Taylor, D. A., Gould, R. J., & Brounstein, P. J. (1981). Effects of personalistic self-disclosure. *Personality and Social Psychology Bulletin*, 7(3), 487–492.

Taylor, D. M., Wright, S. C., Moghaddam, F. M., & Lalonde, R. N. (1990). The personal/group discrimination discrepancy: Perceiving my group, but not myself, to be a target for discrimination. *Personality and Social Psychology Bulletin*, 16(2), 254–262.

Taylor, D. M., Wright, S. C., & Porter, L. E. (1994). Dimensions of perceived discrimination: The personal/group discrimination discrepancy. In M. P. Zanna & J. M. Olson (Eds.), *The psychology of prejudice: The Ontario Symposium* (Vol. 7, pp. 233–255). Hillsdale, NJ: Erlbaum.

Taylor, S. E. (1981). A categorization approach to stereotyping. In D. L. Hamilton (Ed.), *Cognitive processes in stereotyping and intergroup behavior* (pp. 83–114). Hillsdale, NJ: Erlbaum.

Taylor, S. E., & Brown, J. D. (1988). Illusion and well-being: A social psychological perspective on mental health. *Psychological Bulletin*, 103(2), 193–210.

Taylor, S. E., & Fiske, S. T. (1975). Point of view and perceptions of causality. *Journal of Personality and Social Psychology*, 32(3), 439–445.

Taylor, S. E., Fiske, S. T., Etcoff, N. L., & Ruderman, A. J. (1978). Categorical and contextual bases of person memory and stereotyping. *Journal of Personality and Social Psychology, 36*(7), 778–793.

Taylor, S. E., Klein, L. C., Lewis, B. P., Gruenewald, T. L., Gurung, R. A., & Updegraff, J. A. (2000). Biobehavioral responses to stress in females: Tend-and-befriend, not fight-or-flight. *Psychological Review, 107*(3), 411–429.

Taylor, S. P. & Leonard, K. E. (1983). Alcohol and human physical aggression. In R. G. Green & E. I. Donnerstein (Eds.), *Aggression: Theoretical and empirical reviews* (Vol. 2, pp. 77–101). New York: Academic Press.

Tedeschi, R. G., & Calhoun, L. G. (2004). Posttraumatic growth: Conceptual foundations and empirical evidence. *Psychological Inquiry, 15*(1), 1–18.

Tenenbaum, H. R., & Leaper, C. (2002). Are parents' gender schemas related to their children's gender-related cognitions? A meta-analysis. *Developmental Psychology, 38*(4), 615–630.

Terracciano, A., Abdel-Khalek, A. M., Adam, N., Adamovova, L., Ahn, C. K., Ahn, H. N.,...& McCrae, R. R. (2005). National character does not reflect mean personality trait levels in 49 cultures. *Science, 310*(5745), 96–100.

Tesser, A. (1980). Self-esteem maintenance in family dynamics. *Journal of Personality and Social Psychology, 39*(1), 77–91.

Tesser, A. (1988). Toward a self-evaluation maintenance model of social behavior. In L. Berkowitz (Ed.), *Advances in experimental social psychology* (Vol. 21, pp. 181–228). San Diego: Academic Press.

Tesser, A., & Conlee, M. C. (1975). Some effects of time and thought on attitude polarization. *Journal of Personality and Social Psychology, 31*(2), 262–270.

Thibaut, J. W., & Kelley, H. H. (1959). *The social psychology of groups.* Oxford: Wiley.

Thibodeau, P. H., & Boroditsky, L. (2011). Metaphors we think with: The role of metaphor in reasoning. *PLoS One, 6*(2), e16782.

Thomaes, S., & Bushman, B. J. (2011). Mirror, mirror, on the wall, who's the most aggressive of them all? Narcissism, self-esteem, and aggression. In P. R. Shaver & M. Mikulincer (Eds.), *Human aggression and violence: Causes, manifestations, and consequences* (pp. 203–219). Washington, DC: American Psychological Association.

Thomas, M. H., Horton, R. W., Lippincott, E. C., & Drabman, R. S. (1977). Desensitization to portrayals of real-life aggression as a function of television violence. *Journal of Personality and Social Psychology, 35*(6), 450–458.

Thompson, M. M., Naccarato, M. E., Parker, K. C., & Moskowitz, G. B. (2001). The personal need for structure and personal fear of invalidity measures: Historical perspectives, current applications, and future directions. In G. B. Moskowitz (Ed.), *Cognitive social psychology: The Princeton Symposium on the Legacy and Future of Social Cognition* (pp. 19–39). Mahwah, NJ: Erlbaum.

Thomsen, L., Green, E. T., Ho, A. K., Levin, S., van Laar, C., Sinclair, S., & Sidanius, J. (2010). Wolves in sheep's clothing: SDO asymmetrically predicts perceived ethnic victimization among White and Latino students across three years. *Personality and Social Psychology Bulletin, 36*(2), 225–238.

Thornberry, T. P., Freeman-Gallant, A., Lizotte, A. J., Krohn, M. D., & Smith, C. A. (2003). Linked lives: The intergenerational transmission of antisocial behavior. *Journal of Abnormal Child Psychology, 31*(2), 171–184.

Thornberry, T. P., Huizinga, D., & Loeber, R. (2004). The causes and correlates studies: Findings and policy implications. *Juvenile Justice, 9*(1), 3–19. Retrieved from https://www.ncjrs.gov/html/ojjdp/203555/jj2.html

Thorndike, E. L. (1920). A constant error in psychological ratings. *Journal of Applied Psychology, 4*(1), 25–29.

Thornhill, R., & Gangestad, S. W. (1993). Human facial beauty. *Human Nature, 4*(3), 237–269.

Thornhill, R., & Gangestad, S. W. (2006). Facial sexual dimorphism, developmental stability, and susceptibility to disease in men and women. *Evolution and Human Behavior, 27*(2), 131–144.

Thornhill, R., & Thornhill, N. W. (1992). The evolutionary psychology of men's coercive sexuality. *Behavioral and Brain Sciences, 15*(02), 363–375.

Thornton, B., & Maurice, J. (1997). Physique contrast effect: Adverse impact of idealized body images for women. *Sex Roles, 37*(5–6), 433–439.

Tidwell, N. D., Eastwick, P. W., & Finkel, E. J. (2013). Perceived, not actual, similarity predicts initial attraction in a live romantic context: Evidence from the speed-dating paradigm. *Personal Relationships, 20*(2), 199–215.

Toch, H. (1969). *Violent men.* Chicago: Aldine.

Todd, A. R., Bodenhausen, G. V., Richeson, J. A., & Galinsky, A. D. (2011). Perspective taking combats automatic expressions of racial bias. *Journal of Personality and Social Psychology, 100*(6), 1027–1042.

Todorov, A., & Bargh, J. A. (2002). Automatic sources of aggression. *Aggression and Violent Behavior, 7*(1), 53–68.

Todorov, A., Mandisodza, A. N., Goren, A., & Hall, C. C. (2005). Inferences of competence from faces predict election outcomes. *Science, 308*(5728), 1623–1626.

Topolinski, S., & Strack, F. (2009). The architecture of intuition: Fluency and affect determine intuitive judgments of semantic and visual coherence and judgments of grammaticality in artificial grammar learning. *Journal of Experimental Psychology: General, 138*(1), 3–63.

Tormala, Z. L., Petty, R. E., & Briñol, P. (2002). Ease of retrieval effects in persuasion: A self-validation analysis. *Personality and Social Psychology Bulletin, 28*(12), 1700–1712.

Toth, K., & Kemmelmeier, M. (2009). Divorce attitudes around the world: Distinguishing the impact of culture on evaluations and attitude structure. *Cross-Cultural Research, 43*(3), 280–297.

Townsend, S. S., Major, B., Gangi, C. E., & Mendes, W. B. (2011). From "in the air" to "under the skin": Cortisol responses to social identity threat. *Personality and Social Psychology Bulletin, 37*(2), 151–164.

Townsend, S. S., Major, B., Sawyer, P. J., & Mendes, W. B. (2010). Can the absence of prejudice be more threatening than its presence? It depends on one's worldview. *Journal of Personality and Social Psychology, 99*(6), 933–947.

Tracy, J. L., & Robins, R. W. (2004). Show your pride: Evidence for a discrete emotion expression. *Psychological Science, 15*(3), 194–197.

Tracy, J. L., Shaver, P. R., Albino, A. W., & Cooper, M. L. (2003). Attachment styles and adolescent sexuality. In P. Florsheim (Ed.), *Adolescent romance and sexual behavior: Theory, research, and practical implications* (pp.137–159). Mahwah, NJ: Erlbaum.

Tran, S., Simpson, J. A., & Fletcher, G. J. O. (2008). The role of ideal standards in relationship initiation processes. In S. Sprecher, A. Wenzel & J. Harvey (Eds.), *The handbook of relationship initiation* (pp. 487–498). New York: Psychology Press.

Travis, A. (1999, September 10). Retake on Kubrick film ban: Family may release A Clockwork Orange as classification board reassesses banned movies for video. *The Guardian.* Retrieved from http://www.theguardian.com/uk/1999/sep/11/alantravis

Trawalter, S., & Richeson, J. A. (2006). Regulatory focus and executive function after interracial interactions. *Journal of Experimental Social Psychology, 42*(3), 406–412.

Tremblay, R. E. (2000). The development of aggressive behaviour during childhood: What have we learned in the past century? *International Journal of Behavioral Development, 24*(2), 129–141.

Triandis, H. C. (1989). The self and social behavior in differing cultural contexts. *Psychological Review, 96*(3), 506–520.

Triandis, H. C. (1994). *Culture and social behavior.* New York: McGraw-Hill.

Triplett, N. (1898). The dynamogenic factors in pacemaking and competition. *American Journal of Psychology, 9*(4), 507–533.

Trivers, R. L. (1971). The evolution of reciprocal altruism. *Quarterly Review of Biology, 46*(1), 35–57. Stable URL: http://www.jstor.org/stable/2822435

Trivers, R. L. (1972). Parental investment and sexual selection. In B. Campbell (Ed.), *Sexual selection and the descent of man: 1871–1971* (pp. 136–179). Chicago: Aldine.

Trope, Y. (1986). Self-enhancement and self-assessment in achievement behavior. In R. M. Sorrentrino & E. T. Higgins (Eds.), *Handbook of motivation and cognition: Foundations of social behavior* (pp. 350–378). New York: Guilford Press.

Trope, Y., & Liberman, A. (1996). Social hypothesis-testing: Cognitive and motivational mechanisms. In E. T. Higgins & A. W. Kruglanski (Eds.), *Social psychology: Handbook of basic principles* (pp. 239–270). New York: Guilford Press.

Trope, Y., & Liberman, N. (2003). Temporal construal. *Psychological Review, 110*(3), 403–421.

Tropp, L. R. (2003). The psychological impact of prejudice: Implications for intergroup contact. *Group Processes & Intergroup Relations, 6*(2), 131–149.

Tropp, L. R., & Pettigrew, T. F. (2005). Relationships between intergroup contact and prejudice among minority and majority status groups. *Psychological Science, 16*(12), 951–957.

Tropp, L. R., & Wright, S. C. (2001). Ingroup identification as the inclusion of ingroup in the self. *Personality and Social Psychology Bulletin, 27*(5), 585–600.

Troxel, W. M., Matthews, K. A., Bromberger, J. T., & Sutton-Tyrrell, K. (2003). Chronic stress burden, discrimination, and subclinical carotid artery disease in African American and Caucasian women. *Health Psychology, 22*(3), 300–309.

Trzesniewski, K. H., Donnellan, M. B., & Robins, R. W. (2003). Stability of self-esteem across the life span. *Journal of Personality and Social Psychology, 84*(1), 205.

Tsai, J. L. (2007). Ideal affect: Cultural causes and behavioral consequences. *Perspectives on Psychological Science, 2*(3), 242–259.

Tucker, P., & Aron, A. (1993). Passionate love and marital satisfaction at key transition points in the family life cycle. *Journal of Social and Clinical Psychology, 12*(2), 135–147.

Turner, C. W., & Berkowitz, L. (1972). Identification with film aggressor (covert role taking) and reactions to film violence. *Journal of Personality and Social Psychology, 21*(2), 256–264.

Turner, C. W., Layton, J. F., & Simons, L. S. (1975). Naturalistic studies of aggressive behavior: Aggressive stimuli, victim visibility, and horn honking. *Journal of Personality and Social Psychology, 31*(6), 1098–1107.

Turner, J. C. (1991). *Social influence.* Belmont, CA: Brooks/Cole.

Turner, J. C., Hogg, M. A., Oakes, P. J., Reicher, S. D., & Wetherell, M. S. (1987). *Rediscovering the social group: A self-categorization theory.* Oxford: Blackwell.

Turner, J. C., & Oakes, P. J. (1989). Self-categorization theory and social influence. In P. B. Paulus (Ed.), *The psychology of group influence* (2nd ed., pp. 233–275). Hillsdale, NJ: Erlbaum.

Tversky, A., & Kahneman, D. (1973). Availability: A heuristic for judging frequency and probability. *Cognitive Psychology, 5*(2), 207–232.

Tversky, A., & Kahneman, D. (1981). The framing of decisions and the psychology of choice. *Science, 211*(4481), 453–458.

Twain, M. (1902). Does the race of man love a lord? *North American Review, 174,* 433–444.

Twenge, J. M., Baumeister, R. F., DeWall, C. N., Ciarocco, N. J., & Bartels, J. M. (2007). Social exclusion decreases prosocial behavior. *Journal of Personality and Social Psychology, 92*(1), 56–66.

Twenge, J. M., Baumeister, R. F., Tice, D. M., & Stucke, T. S. (2001). If you can't join them, beat them: Effects of social exclusion on aggressive behavior. *Journal of Personality and Social Psychology, 81*(6), 1058–1069.

Twenge, J. M., Campbell, W. K., & Gentile, B. (2013). Changes in pronoun use in American books and the rise of individualism, 196–008. *Journal of Cross-Cultural Psychology, 44*(3), 406–415.

U.S. Bureau of Labor Statistics (n.d). Labor force statistics from the Current Population Survey. Household data, 2013 annual averages [data file]. Retrieved from http://www.bls.gov/cps/cpsaat11.pdf

U. S. Department of Health and Human Services, Centers for Disease Control and Prevention (2011). National Youth Risk Behavior Surveillance. Retrieved from http://www.cdc.gov/mmwr/pdf/ss/ss6104.pdf

U.S. Department of Labor, Bureau of Labor Statistics (2009). Highlights of Women's Earnings in 2008. Report 1017 (July). Retrieved from http://www.bls.gov/cps/cpswom2008.pdf

Uchino, B. N. (2006). Social support and health: A review of physiological processes potentially underlying links to disease outcomes. *Journal of Behavioral Medicine, 29*(4), 377–387.

Uchino, B. N., Cacioppo, J. T., & Kiecolt-Glaser, J. K. (1996). The relationship between social support and physiological processes: A review with emphasis on underlying mechanisms and implications for health. *Psychological Bulletin, 119*(3), 488–531.

Uddin, L. Q., Iacoboni, M., Lange, C., & Keenan, J. P. (2007). The self and social cognition: The role of cortical midline structures and mirror neurons. *Trends in Cognitive Sciences, 11*(4), 153–157.

Uleman, J. S., Rhee, E., Bardoliwalla, N., Semin, G., & Toyama, M. (2000). The relational self: Closeness to ingroups depends on who they are, culture, and the type of closeness. *Asian Journal of Social Psychology, 3*(1), 1–17.

Ullman, C. (1982). Cognitive and emotional antecedents of religious conversion. *Journal of Personality and Social Psychology, 43*(1), 183–192.

United Nations Office on Drugs and Crime (2013). Global study on homicide. Homicide statistics 2013. Retrieved from http://www.unodc.org/gsh/en/data.html

United States v. Windsor, Executor of the estate of Spyer et al., 570 U.S. 12 (2013). Retrieved from http://www.supremecourt.gov/opinions/12pdf/12-307_6j37.pdf

US: Federal statistics show widespread prison rape (2007, December 16). Human Rights Watch. Retrieved from http://www.hrw.org/news/2007/12/15/us-federal-statistics-show-widespread-prison-rape

Vaden-Kiernan, N., Ialongo, N. S., Pearson, J., & Kellam, S. (1995). Household family structure and children's aggressive behavior: A longitudinal study of urban elementary school children. *Journal of Abnormal Child Psychology, 23*(5), 553–568.

Vail, K. E., Juhl, J., Arndt, J., Vess, M., Routledge, C., & Rutjens, B. T. (2012). When death is good for life: Considering the positive trajectories of terror management. *Personality and Social Psychology Review, 16*(4), 303–329.

Valins, S. (1966). Cognitive effects of false heart-rate feedback. *Journal of Personality and Social Psychology, 4*(4), 400–408.

Vallacher, R. R., & Wegner, D. M. (1987). What do people think they're doing? Action identification and human behavior. *Psychological Review, 94*(1), 3–15.

Van Boven, L., Kruger, J., Savitsky, K., & Gilovich, T. (2000). When social worlds collide: Overconfidence in the multiple audience problem. *Personality and Social Psychology Bulletin, 26*(5), 619–628.

van den Boom, D. C. (1994). The influence of temperament and mothering on attachment and exploration: An experimental manipulation of sensitive responsiveness among lower-class mothers with irritable infants. *Child Development, 65*(5), 1457–1477.

van den Boom, D. C. (1995). Do first-year intervention effects endure? Follow-up during toddlerhood of a sample of Dutch irritable infants. *Child Development, 66*(6), 1798–1816.

Van Goozen, S. H. M., Cohen-Kettenis, P. T., Gooren, L. J. G., & Frijda, N. H. (1995). Gender differences in behaviour: Activating effects of cross-sex hormones. *Psychoneuroendocrinology, 20*(4), 343–363.

van Kleef, G. A., Oveis, C., Van der Löwe, I., LuoKogan, A., Goetz, J., & Keltner, D. (2008). Power, distress, and compassion: Turning a blind eye to the suffering of others. *Psychological Science, 19*(12), 1315–1322.

Van Knippenberg, A. D., & Dijksterhuis, A. (2000). Social categorization and stereotyping: A functional perspective. *European Review of Social Psychology, 11*(1), 105–144.

van Lange, P. A., De Bruin, E., Otten, W., & Joireman, J. A. (1997). Development of prosocial, individualistic, and competitive orientations: Theory and preliminary evidence. *Journal of Personality and Social Psychology, 73*(4), 733–746.

van Lange, P. A., Rusbult, C. E., Drigotas, S. M., Arriaga, X. B., Witcher, B. S., & Cox, C. L. (1997). Willingness to sacrifice in close relationships. *Journal of Personality and Social Psychology, 72*(6), 1373–1395.

Van Swol, L. M. (2009). Extreme members and group polarization. *Social Influence, 4*(3), 185–199.

van Yperen, N. W., & Buunk, B. P. (1990). A longitudinal study of equity and satisfaction in intimate relationships. *European Journal of Social Psychology, 20*(4), 287–309.

Vandello, J. A., & Cohen, D. (1999). Patterns of individualism and collectivism across the United States. *Journal of Personality and Social Psychology, 77*(2), 279–292.

Vandello, J. A., & Cohen, D. (2003). Male honor and female fidelity: Implicit cultural scripts that perpetuate domestic violence. *Journal of Personality and Social Psychology, 84*(5), 997–1010.

Vandello, J. A., Cohen, D., Grandon, R., & Franiuk, R. (2009). Stand by your man: Indirect prescriptions for honorable violence and feminine loyalty in Canada, Chile, and the United States. *Journal of Cross-Cultural Psychology, 40*(1), 81–104.

Vandello, J. A., Cohen, D., & Ransom, S. (2008). US southern and northern differences in perceptions of norms about aggression: Mechanisms for the perpetuation of a culture of honor. *Journal of Cross-Cultural Psychology, 39*(2), 162–177.

Vanman, E. J., Saltz, J. L., Nathan, L. R., & Warren, J. A. (2004). Racial discrimination by low-prejudiced Whites: Facial movements as implicit measures of attitudes related to behavior. *Psychological Science, 15*(11), 711–714.

Varangis, E., Lanzieri, N., Hildebrandt, T., & Feldman, M. (2012). Gay male attraction toward muscular men: Does mating context matter? *Body Image, 9*(2), 270–278.

Vargas, T. (2014, June 18). Federal agency cancels Redskins trademark registration, says name is disparaging. *Washington Post.* Retrieved from http://www.washingtonpost.com/local/us-patent-office-cancels-redskins-trademark-registration-says-name-is-disparaging/2014/06/18/e7737bb8-f6ee-11e3-8aa9-dad2ec039789_story.html

Varnum, M. E. W., Na, J., Murata, A., & Kitayama, S. (2011). Social class differences in N400 indicate differences in spontaneous trait inference. *Journal of Experimental Psychology: General, 141*(3), 518–526.

Vaughan, D. (1996). *The Challenger launch decision: Risky technology, culture, and deviance at NASA.* Chicago: University of Chicago Press.

Vazire, S., & Gosling, S. D. (2004). e-Perceptions: Personality impressions based on personal websites. *Journal of Personality and Social Psychology, 87*(1), 123–132.

Vázquez, C. A. (1994). A multitask controlled evaluation of facilitated communication. *Journal of Autism and Developmental Disorders, 24*(3), 369–379.

Vega, V., & Malamuth, N. M. (2007). Predicting sexual aggression: The role of pornography in the context of general and specific risk factors. *Aggressive Behavior, 33*(2), 104–117.

Veitch, R., & Griffitt, W. (1976). Good news-bad news: Affective and interpersonal effects. *Journal of Applied Social Psychology, 6*(1), 69–75.

Vescio, T. K., & Biernat, M. (2003). Family values and antipathy toward gay men. *Journal of Applied Social Psychology, 33*(4), 833–847.

Vescio, T. K., Sechrist, G. B., & Paolucci, M. P. (2003). Perspective taking and prejudice reduction: The mediational role of empathy arousal and situational attributions. *European Journal of Social Psychology, 33*(4), 455–472.

Vohs, K. D., Catanese, K. R., & Baumeister, R. F. (2004). Sex in "his" versus "her" relationships. In J. H. Harvey, A. Wenzel & S. Sprecher (Eds.), *The handbook of sexuality in close relationships* (pp. 455–474). Mahwah, NJ: Erlbaum.

von Hippel, C., Walsh, A. M., & Zouroudis, A. (2011). Identity separation in response to stereotype threat. *Social Psychological and Personality Science, 2*(3), 317–324.

Vonk, J., Brosnan, S. F., Silk, J. B., Henrich, J., Richardson, A. S., Lambeth, S. P., . . . & Povinelli, D. J. (2008). Chimpanzees do not take advantage of very low cost opportunities to deliver food to unrelated group members. *Animal Behaviour*, 75(5), 1757–1770.

Vonk, R. (2002). Self-serving interpretations of flattery: Why ingratiation works. *Journal of Personality and Social Psychology*, 82(4), 515–526.

Voracek, M., & Fisher, M. L. (2002). Shapely centrefolds? Temporal change in body measures: trend analysis. *BMJ: British Medical Journal*, 325(7378), 1447–1448. Retrieved from http://www.ncbi.nlm.nih.gov/pmc/articles/PMC139033/

Vorauer, J. D., Main, K. J., & O'Connell, G. B. (1998). How do individuals expect to be viewed by members of lower status groups? Content and implications of meta-stereotypes. *Journal of Personality and Social Psychology*, 75(4), 917–937.

Vorauer, J. D., & Sasaki, S. J. (2009). Helpful only in the abstract? Ironic effects of empathy in intergroup interaction. *Psychological Science*, 20(2), 191–197.

Walker, L. E. (1979). *The battered woman*. New York: Harper & Row.

Wallas, G. (1926). *The art of thought*. New York: Harcourt-Brace.

Waller, N. G., & Shaver, P. R. (1994). The importance of nongenetic influences on romantic love styles: A twin-family study. *Psychological Science*, 5(5), 268–274.

Wallis, H. B. (Producer), & Curtiz, M. (Director). (1942). *Casablanca* [Motion picture]. United States: Warner Bros. Pictures, Inc.Walster, E., Aronson, E., & Abrahams, D. (1966). On increasing the persuasiveness of a low prestige communicator. *Journal of Experimental Social Psychology*, 2(4), 325–342.

Walster, E., Aronson, V., Abrahams, D., & Rottman, L. (1966). Importance of physical attractiveness in dating behavior. *Journal of Personality and Social Psychology*, 4(5), 508–516.

Walster, E., & Festinger, L. (1962). The effectiveness of "overheard" persuasive communications. *Journal of Abnormal and Social Psychology*, 65(6), 395–402.

Walton, G. M., & Cohen, G. L. (2003). Stereotype lift. *Journal of Experimental Social Psychology*, 39(5), 456–467.

Walton, G. M., & Cohen, G. L. (2007). A question of belonging: Race, social fit, and achievement. *Journal of Personality and Social Psychology*, 92(1), 82–96.

Walton, G. M., & Cohen, G. L. (2011). A brief social-belonging intervention improves academic and health outcomes of minority students. *Science*, 331(6023), 1447–1451.

Walton, G. M., & Spencer, S. J. (2009). Latent ability grades and test scores systematically underestimate the intellectual ability of negatively stereotyped students. *Psychological Science*, 20(9), 1132–1139.

Wan, H.-H., & Pfau, M. (2004). The relative effectiveness of inoculation, bolstering, and combined approaches in crisis communication. *Journal of Public Relations Research*, 16(3), 301–328.

Wang, Q. (2001). China's divorce trends in the transition toward a market economy. *Journal of Divorce & Remarriage*, 35(1–2), 173–189.

Warneken, F., & Tomasello, M. (2006). Altruistic helping in human infants and young chimpanzees. *Science*, 311(5765), 1301–1303.

Warner, W. L. (1959). *The living and the dead: A study of the symbolic life of Americans*. New Haven: Yale University Press.

Watson, D. (1982). The actor and the observer: How are their perceptions of causality divergent? *Psychological Bulletin*, 92(3), 682–700.

Watson, D., & Humrichouse, J. (2006). Personality development in emerging adulthood: Integrating evidence from self-ratings and spouse ratings. *Journal of Personality and Social Psychology*, 91(5), 959–974.

Watson, E. (Producer), & Aronofsky, D. (Director). (1998). *Pi* [Motion picture]. United States: Harvest Film Works, Truth and Soul Pictures, Plantain Films, & Protozoa Pictures.

Watson, J. (1973). Investigation into deindividuation using a cross-cultural survey technique. *Journal of Personality and Social Psychology*, 25(3), 342–345.

Watson, J. B. (1930). *Behaviorism* (Rev. ed.). New York: Norton.

Weary, G., Rich, M. C., Harvey, J. H., & Ickes, W. J. (1980). Heider's formulation of social perception and attributional processes: Toward further clarification. *Personality and Social Psychology Bulletin*, 6(1), 37–43.

Weber, F. (n.d). Is seeing believing? [Web log post]. Retrieved from http://www.frankwbaker.com/isbmag.htm

Wegener, D. T., & Petty, R. E. (1995). Flexible correction processes in social judgment: The role of naive theories in corrections for perceived bias. *Journal of Personality and Social Psychology*, 68(1), 36–51.

Wegner, D. M. (1994). Ironic processes of mental control. *Psychological Review*, 101(1), 34–52.

Wegner, D. M., Connally, D., Shearer, D., & Vallacher, R. R. (1983). Disruption and identifications of the act of eating. Unpublished research data. In R. R. Vallacher & D. M. Wegner (1985), *A theory of action identification*. Hillsdale, NJ: Erlbaum.

Wegner, D. M., Erber, R., & Zanakos, S. (1993). Ironic processes in the mental control of mood and mood-related thought. *Journal of Personality and Social Psychology*, 65(6), 1093–1104.

Wegner, D. M., Richard, M., & Vallacher, R. R. (1982). [Identifications of the act of rearing a child]. Unpublished research data. In R. R. Vallacher & D. M. Wegner (1985), *A theory of action identification*. Hillsdale, NJ: Erlbaum.

Wegner, D. M., Vallacher, R. R., Kiersted, G. W., & Dizadji, D. (1986). Action identification in the emergence of social behavior. *Social Cognition*, 4(1), 18–38.

Wegner, D. M., Wenzlaff, R. M., & Kozak, M. (2004). Dream rebound: The return of suppressed thoughts in dreams. *Psychological Science*, 15(4), 232–236.

Weigel, R. H., & Newman, L. S. (1976). Increasing attitude-behavior correspondence by broadening the scope of the behavioral measure. *Journal of Personality and Social Psychology*, 33(6), 793–802.

Weil, A. (1972). *The natural mind: A new way of looking at drugs and the higher consciousness*. Boston: Houghton Mifflin.

Weiner, B. (1980). A cognitive (attribution)-emotion-action model of motivated behavior: An analysis of judgments of help-giving. *Journal of Personality and Social Psychology*, 39(2), 186–200.

Weiner, B., Osborne, D., & Rudolph, U. (2011). An attributional analysis of reactions to poverty: The political ideology of the giver and the perceived morality of the receiver. *Personality and Social Psychology Review*, 15(2), 199–213.

Weiner, B., Perry, R. P., & Magnusson, J. (1988). An attributional analysis of reactions to stigmas. *Journal of Personality and Social Psychology*, 55(5), 738–748.

Weingarten, G. (2007, April 8). Pearls before breakfast. Can one of the nation's great musicians cut through the fog of a D.C. rush hour? Let's find out. *The Washington Post*, 13–28. Retrieved from http://www.washingtonpost.com/lifestyle/magazine/pearls-before-breakfast-can-one-of-the-nations-great-musicians-cut-through-the-fog-of-a-dc-rush-hour-lets-find-out/2014/09/23/8a6d46da-4331-11e4-b47c-f5889e061e5f_story.html

Weinstein, N., & Ryan, R. M. (2010). When helping helps: Autonomous motivation for prosocial behavior and its influence on well-being for the helper and recipient. *Journal of Personality and Social Psychology*, 98(2), 222–244.

Weiss, B., Dodge, K. A., Bates, J. E., & Pettit, G. S. (1992). Some consequences of early harsh discipline: Child aggression and a maladaptive social information processing style. *Child Development*, 63(6), 1321–1335.

Wells, B. E., & Twenge, J. M. (2005). Changes in young people's sexual behavior and attitudes, 1943–1999: A cross-temporal meta-analysis. *Review of General Psychology*, 9(3), 249–261.

Wells, G. L., Memon, A., & Penrod, S. D. (2006). Eyewitness evidence: Improving its probative value. *Psychological Science in the Public Interest*, 7(2), 45–75.

Wells, G. L., & Petty, R. E. (1980). The effects of overt head movements on persuasion: Compatibility and incompatibility of responses. *Basic and Applied Social Psychology*, 1(3), 219–230.

Wendorf, F. (1968). *The prehistory of Nubia*. Dallas: Fort Burgwin Research Center and Southern Methodist University Press.

West, S. G. (1975). Increasing the attractiveness of college cafeteria food: A reactance theory perspective. *Journal of Applied Psychology*, 60(5), 656–658.

Wheeler, L., & Kim, Y. (1997). What is beautiful is culturally good: The physical attractiveness stereotype has different content in collectivistic cultures. *Personality and Social Psychology Bulletin*, 23(8), 795–800.

Wheeler, L., & Nezlek, J. (1977). Sex differences in social participation. *Journal of Personality and Social Psychology*, 35(10), 742–754.

Wheelis, A. (1980). *The scheme of things*. New York: Harcourt Brace Jovanovich.

White, G. L., Fishbein, S., & Rutsein, J. (1981). Passionate love and the misattribution of arousal. *Journal of Personality and Social Psychology*, 41(1), 56–62.

White, G. L., & Kight, T. D. (1984). Misattribution of arousal and attraction: Effects of salience of explanations for arousal. *Journal of Experimental Social Psychology*, 20(1), 55–64.

Whitman, W. (2001). *Leaves of grass*. New York: Random House (Original work published 1855)

Whitman, W. (2003). *The portable Walt Whitman* (Michael Warner, Ed.). New York: Penguin Classics.

Whitson, J. A., Liljenquist, K. A., Galinsky, A. D., Magee, J. C., Gruenfeld, D. H., & Cadena, B. (2013). The blind leading: Power reduces awareness of constraints. *Journal of Experimental Social Psychology*, 49(3), 579–582.

Whittler, T. E., & Spira, J. (2002). Model's race: A peripheral cue in advertising messages? *Journal of Consumer Psychology*, 12(4), 291–301.

Wicker, A. W. (1969). Attitudes versus actions: The relationship of verbal and overt behavioral responses to attitude objects. *Journal of Social Issues*, 25(4), 41–78.

Wicklund, R. A., & Gollwitzer, P. M. (1982). *Symbolic self-completion*. Hillsdale, NJ: Erlbaum.

Widmer, E. D., Treas, J., & Newcomb, R. (1998). Attitudes toward nonmarital sex in 24 countries. *Journal of Sex Research*, 35(4), 349–358.

Widom, C. S. (1989). Does violence beget violence? A critical examination of the literature. *Psychological Bulletin*, 106(1), 3–28.

Wiebe, D. J. (2003). Firearms in US homes as a risk factor for unintentional gunshot fatality. *Accident Analysis & Prevention*, 35(5), 711–716.

Wiederman, M. W. (2004). Self-control and sexual behavior. In R. F. Baumeister & K. D. Vohs (Eds.), *Handbook of self-regulation: Research, theory, and applications* (pp. 525–536). New York: Guilford Press.

Wiggins, J. S., Wiggins, N., & Conger, J. C. (1968). Correlates of heterosexual somatic preference. *Journal of Personality and Social Psychology*, 10(1), 82–90.

Wildschut, T., Sedikides, C., Arndt, J., & Routledge, C. (2006). Nostalgia: Content, triggers, functions. *Journal of Personality and Social Psychology*, 91(5), 975–993.

Wilkinson, G. S. (1990). Food sharing in vampire bats. *Scientific American*, 262(2), 76–82.

Willetts, M. C., Sprecher, S., & Beck, F. D. (2004). Overview of sexual practices and attitudes within relational contexts. In J. H. Harvey, A. Wenzel & S. Sprecher (Eds.), *The handbook of sexuality in close relationships* (pp. 57–85). Mahwah, NJ: Erlbaum.

Williams, D. R. (1999). Race, socioeconomic status, and health: The added effects of racism and discrimination. *Annals of the New York Academy of Sciences*, 896(1), 173–188.

Williams, D. R., Spencer, M. S., & Jackson, J. S. (1999). Race, stress, and physical health. In R. J. Contrada & R. D. Ashmore (Eds.), *Self, social identity, and physical health: Interdisciplinary explorations* (Vol. 2, pp. 71–100). New York: Oxford University Press.

Williams, J. E., Best, D. L., & Boswell, D. A. (1975). The measurement of children's racial attitudes in the early school years. *Child Development*, 46(2), 494–500. Stable URL: http://www.jstor.org/stable/1128147

Williams, K., Harkins, S. G., & Latané, B. (1981). Identifiability as a deterrent to social loafing: Two cheering experiments. *Journal of Personality and Social Psychology*, 40(2), 303–311.

Williams, K. D. (2007). Ostracism. *Annual Review of Psychology*, 58(1), 425–452.

Williams, K. D., & Zadro, L. (2001). Ostracism: On being ignored, excluded, and rejected. In M. R. Leary (Ed.), *Interpersonal rejection* (pp. 21–53). New York: Oxford University Press.

Williams, L. E., & Bargh, J. A. (2008). Experiencing physical warmth influences interpersonal warmth. *Science*, 322(5901), 606–607.

Williams, L. E., Huang, J. Y., & Bargh, J. A. (2009). The scaffolded mind: Higher mental processes are grounded in early experience of the physical world. *European Journal of Social Psychology*, 39(7), 1257–1267.

Williamson, G. M., & Clark, M. S. (1989). Providing help and desired relationship type as determinants of changes in moods and self-evaluations. *Journal of Personality and Social Psychology*, 56(5), 722–734.

Williamson, G. M., & Clark, M. S. (1992). Impact of desired relationship type on affective reactions to choosing and being required to help. *Personality and Social Psychology Bulletin*, 18(1), 10–18.

Wills, T. A. (1981). Downward comparison principles in social psychology. *Psychological Bulletin*, 90(2), 245–271.

Wills, T. A., Sargent, J. D., Stoolmiller, M., Gibbons, F. X., & Gerrard, M. (2008). Movie smoking exposure and smoking onset: A longitudinal study of mediation processes in a representative sample of U.S. adolescents. *Psychology of Addictive Behaviors*, 22(2), 269–277.

Wilson, A. E., & Ross, M. (2001). From chump to champ: People's appraisals of their earlier and present selves. *Journal of Personality and Social Psychology*, 80(4), 572–584.

Wilson, J. P. (1976). Motivation, modeling, and altruism: A Person × Situation analysis. *Journal of Personality and Social Psychology*, 34(6), 1078–1086.

Wilson, T. D. (2002). *Strangers to ourselves: Discovering the adaptive unconscious*. Cambridge, MA: Harvard University Press.

Wilson, T. D., Dunn, D. S., Kraft, D., & Lisle, D. J. (1989). Introspection, attitude change, and attitude-behavior consistency: The disruptive effects of explaining why we feel the way we do. In L. Berkowitz (Ed.), *Advances in experimental social psychology* (Vol. 19, pp. 123–205). Orlando: Academic Press.

Wilson, T. D., & Gilbert, D. T. (2005). Affective forecasting: Knowing what to want. *Current Directions in Psychological Science*, 14(3), 131–134.

Wilson, T. D., & Kraft, D. (1993). Why do I love thee? Effects of repeated introspections about a dating relationship on attitudes toward the relationship. *Personality and Social Psychology Bulletin*, 19(4), 409–418.

Wilson, T. D., Laser, P. S., & Stone, J. I. (1982). Judging the predictors of one's own mood: Accuracy and the use of shared theories. *Journal of Experimental Social Psychology*, 18(6), 537–556.

Wilson, T. D., Wheatley, T., Meyers, J. M., Gilbert, D. T., & Axsom, D. (2000). Focalism: A source of durability bias in affective forecasting. *Journal of Personality and Social Psychology*, 78(5), 821–836.

Winch, R. F. (1958). *Mate-selection: A study of complementary needs*. Oxford: Harper.

Winkel, F. W., & Denkers, A. (1995). Crime victims and their social network: A field study on the cognitive effects of victimisation, attributional responses and the victim-blaming model. *International Review of Victimology*, 3(4), 309–322.

Winkielman, P., & Cacioppo, J. T. (2001). Mind at ease puts a smile on the face: Psychophysiological evidence that processing facilitation elicits positive affect. *Journal of Personality and Social Psychology*, 81(6), 989–1000.

Winkielman, P., Knutson, B., Paulus, M., & Trujillo, J. L. (2007). Affective influence on judgments and decisions: Moving towards core mechanisms. *Review of General Psychology*, 11(2), 179–192.

Winkler-Rhoades, N., Medin, D., Waxman, S. R., Woodring, J., & Ross, N. O. (2010). Naming the animals that come to mind: Effects of culture and experience on category fluency. *Journal of Cognition and Culture*, 10(1–2), 1–2.

Wiseman, C. V., Gray, J. J., Mosimann, J. E., & Ahrens, A. H. (1992). Cultural expectations of thinness in women: An update. *International Journal of Eating Disorders*, 11(1), 85–89.

Wisman, A., & Goldenberg, J. L. (2005). From the grave to the cradle: Evidence that mortality salience engenders a desire for offspring. *Journal of Personality and Social Psychology*, 89(1), 46–61.

Witte, K., & Allen, M. (2000). A meta-analysis of fear appeals: Implications for effective public health campaigns. *Health Education & Behavior*, 27(5), 591–615.

Wolf, S., & Montgomery, D. A. (1977). Effects of inadmissible evidence and level of judicial admonishment to disregard on the judgments of mock jurors. *Journal of Applied Social Psychology*, 7(3), 205–219.

Wolfgang, M. E., & Ferracuti, F. (1967). *The subculture of violence: Towards an integrated theory in criminology*. London: Tavistock Publications.

Wolkstein, D. (1991). *The first love stories: From Isis and Osiris to Tristan and Iseult*. New York: HarperCollins.

Wong, P. T., & Weiner, B. (1981). When people ask "why" questions, and the heuristics of attributional search. *Journal of Personality and Social Psychology*, 40(4), 650–663.

Wong, R. Y. M., & Hong, Y. Y. (2005). Dynamic influences of culture on cooperation in the prisoner's dilemma. *Psychological Science*, 16(6), 429–434.

Wood, W., & Eagly, A. H. (2002). A cross-cultural analysis of the behavior of women and men: Implications for the origins of sex differences. *Psychological Bulletin*, 128(5), 699–727.

Wood, W., & Eagly, A. H. (2007). Social structural origins of sex differences in human mating. In S. W. Gangestad & J. A. Simpson (Eds.), *The evolution of mind: Fundamental questions and controversies* (pp. 383–390). New York: Guilford Press.

Wood, W., Kallgren, C. A., & Preisler, R. M. (1985). Access to attitude-relevant information in memory as a determinant of persuasion: The role of message attributes. *Journal of Experimental Social Psychology*, 21(1), 73–85.

Wood, W., Kressel, L., Joshi, P. D., & Louie, B. (2014). Meta-analysis of menstrual cycle effects on women's mate preferences. *Emotion Review*, 6(3), 229–249.

Wood, W., Lundgren, S., Ouellette, J. A., Busceme, S., & Blackstone, T. (1994). Minority influence: A meta-analytic review of social influence processes. *Psychological Bulletin*, 115(3), 323–345.

Wood, W., & Neal, D. T. (2007). A new look at habits and the habit-goal interface. *Psychological Review*, 114(4), 843–863.

Wood, W., & Stagner, B. (1994). Why are some people easier to influence than others? In S. Shavitt & T. Brock (Eds.), *Persuasion: Psychological insights and perspectives* (pp. 149–174). Boston: Allyn & Bacon.

Worchel, S., & Teddie, C. (1976). The experience of crowding: A two-factor theory. *Journal of Personality and Social Psychology*, 34(1), 30–40.

Word, C. O., Zanna, M. P., & Cooper, J. (1974). The nonverbal mediation of self-fulfilling prophecies in interracial interaction. *Journal of Experimental Social Psychology*, 10(2), 109–120.

World's tallest man meets world's shortest man (2007, July 13). Metro. Retrieved from http://metro.co.uk/2007/07/13/worlds-tallest-man-bao-xishun-meets-worlds-shortest-man-he-pingping-539537/

Wosinska, W., Dabul, A. J., Whetstone-Dion, R., & Cialdini, R. B. (1996). Self-presentational responses to success in the organization: Costs and benefits of modesty. *Basic and Applied Social Psychology*, 18(2), 229–242.

Wright, R. A., & Contrada, R. J. (1986). Dating selectivity and interpersonal attraction: Toward a better understanding of the elusive phenomenon. *Journal of Social and Personal Relationships*, 3(2), 131–148.

Wrubel, B., Lloyd, C., Levitan, S. (Writers), & Koch, C. (Director). (2011, October 5). Door to door [Television series episode]. In C. Lloyd, P. S. Levitan, P. Corrigan, A. Higginbotham, D. O'Shannon,...& B. Wrubel (Producers), *Modern family*. Los Angeles: Levitan / Lloyd & 20th Century Fox Television.

Wyer, R. S., Weatherley, D. A., & Terrell, G. (1965). Social role, aggression, and academic achievement. *Journal of Personality and Social Psychology*, 1(6), 645–649.

Yaakobi, E., Mikulincer, M., & Shaver, P. (2014). Parenthood as a terror management mechanism: The moderating role of attachment orientations. *Personality and Social Psychology Bulletin*, 40(6), 762–774.

Yang, X. G., Li, Y. P., Ma, G. S., Hu, X. Q., Wang, J. Z., Cui, Z. H., . . . & Zhai, F. Y. (2005). [Study on weight and height of the Chinese people and the differences between 1992 and 2002] (in Chinese). *Zhonghua Liu Xing Bing Xue Za Zhi*, *26*(7), 489–493. PMID: 16334998.

Yang, Y. (2008). Social inequalities in happiness in the United States, 1972 to 2004: An age-period-cohort analysis. *American Sociological Review*, *73*(2), 204–226.

Yelsma, P., & Athappilly, K. (1988). Marital satisfaction and communication practices: Comparisons among Indian and American couples. *Journal of Comparative Family Studies*, *19*(1), 37–54. Stable URL: http://www.jstor.org/stable/41601406

Yeung, N. C. J., & von Hippel, C. (2008). Stereotype threat increases the likelihood that female drivers in a simulator run over jaywalkers. *Accident Analysis & Prevention*, *40*(2), 667–674.

York, A. (2001, April 26). The product placement monster that E.T. spawned. Salon [Online journal]. Retrieved from http://dir.salon.com/tech/feature/2001/04/26/product_placement/index.html.

Yum, Y. O., & Schenck-Hamlin, W. (2005). Reactions to 9/11 as a function of terror management and perspective taking. *Journal of Social Psychology*, *145*(3), 265–286.

Zaccaro, S. J. (1984). Social loafing: The role of task attractiveness. *Personality and Social Psychology Bulletin*, *10*(1), 99–106.

Zadro, L., Williams, K. D., & Richardson, R. (2004). How low can you go? Ostracism by a computer is sufficient to lower self-reported levels of belonging, control, self-esteem, and meaningful existence. *Journal of Experimental Social Psychology*, *40*(4), 560–567.

Zajonc, R. B. (1965). Social facilitation. *Science*, *149*(3681), 269–274.

Zajonc, R. B. (1968). Attitudinal effects of mere exposure. *Journal of Personality and Social Psychology*, *9*(2, Pt. 2), 1–27.

Zajonc, R. B. (1980). Feeling and thinking: Preferences need no inferences. *American Psychologist*, *35*(2), 151–175.

Zajonc, R. B. (1998). Emotions. In D. T. Gilbert, S. T. Fiske, & G. Lindzey (Eds.), *The handbook of social psychology* (4th ed., Vol. 1, pp. 591–632). Boston: McGraw-Hill.

Zajonc, R. B., Heingartner, A., & Herman, E. M. (1969). Social enhancement and impairment of performance in the cockroach. *Journal of Personality and Social Psychology*, *13*(2), 83–92.

Zak, P. J., Kurzban, R., & Matzner, W. T. (2005). Oxytocin is associated with human trustworthiness. *Hormones and Behavior*, *48*(5), 522–527.

Zanna, M. P., & Cooper, J. (1974). Dissonance and the pill: An attribution approach to studying the arousal properties of dissonance. *Journal of Personality and Social Psychology*, *29*(5), 703–709.

Zanna, M. P., Lepper, M. R., & Abelson, R. P. (1973). Attentional mechanisms in children's devaluation of a forbidden activity in a forced-compliance situation. *Journal of Personality and Social Psychology*, *28*(3), 355–359.

Zebrowitz, L. A. (1997). *Reading faces: Window to the soul?* Boulder, CO: Westview Press.

Zeigarnik, B. (1938). On finished and unfinished tasks. In W. D. Ellis (Ed.), *A sourcebook of Gestalt psychology* (pp. 300–314). New York: Harcourt.

Zeitzen, M. K. (2008). *Polygamy: A cross-cultural analysis*. Oxford: Berg.

Zell, E. & Alicke, M. D. (2010). The local dominance effect in self-evaluation: Evidence and explanations. *Personality and Social Psychology Review*, *14*(4), 368–384.

Zellner, M. (1970). Self-esteem, reception, and influenceability. *Journal of Personality and Social Psychology*, *15*(1), 87–93.

Zenger, T. R. (1992). Why do employers only reward extreme performance? Examining the relationships among performance, pay, and turnover. *Administrative Science Quarterly*, *37*(2), 198–219.

Zentner, M., & Mitura, K. (2012). Stepping out of the caveman's shadow: Nations' gender gap predicts degree of sex differentiation in mate preferences. *Psychological Science*, *23*(10), 1176–1185.

Zhang, S., & Kline, S. L. (2009). Can I make my own decisions? A cross-cultural study of perceived social network influence in mate selection. *Journal of Cross-Cultural Psychology*, *40*(1), 3–23.

Zhong, C., & House, J. (2013). Dirt, pollution, and purity: A metaphorical perspective on morality. In M. J. Landau, M. D. Robinson, & B. P. Meier (Eds.), *The power of metaphor: Examining its influence on social life*. Washington, DC: American Psychological Associaton.

Zhou, Q., Eisenberg, N., Losoya, S. H., Fabes, R. A., Reiser, M., Guthrie, I. K., . . . & Shepard, S. A. (2002). The relations of parental warmth and positive expressiveness to children's empathy-related responding and social functioning: A longitudinal study. *Child Development*, *73*(3), 893–915.

Zhou, X., Liu, J., Chen, C., & Yu, Z. (2008). Do children transcend death? An examination of the terror management function of offspring. *Scandinavian Journal of Psychology*, *49*(5), 413–418.

Zillmann, D. (1971). Excitation transfer in communication-mediated aggressive behavior. *Journal of Experimental Social Psychology*, *7*(4), 419–434.

Zillmann, D. (1978). Attribution and misattribution of excitatory reactions. In J. H. Harvey, W. J. Ickes, & R. F. Kidd (Eds.), *New directions in attribution research* (Vol. 2, pp. 335–368). Hillsdale, NJ: Erlbaum.

Zillmann, D. (1979). *Hostility and aggression*. Hillsdale, NJ: Erlbaum.

Zillmann, D. (1998). The psychology of the appeal of portrayals of violence. In J. H. Goldstein (Ed.), *Why we watch: The attractions of violent entertainment* (pp. 179–211). New York: Oxford University Press.

Zillmann, D. (2003). Theory of affective dynamics: Emotions and moods. In J. Bryant, D. Roskos-Ewoldsen, & J. Cantor (Eds.), *Communication and emotion: Essays in honor of Dolf Zillmann* (pp. 533–567). Mahwah, NJ: Erlbaum.

Zillman, D. & Bryant, J. (1974). Effect of residual excitation on the emotional response to provocation and delayed aggressive behavior. *Journal of Personality and Social Psychology*, *30*(6), 782–791.

Zillmann, D., Bryant, J., Cantor, J. R., & Day, K. D. (1975). Irrelevance of mitigating circumstances in retaliatory behavior at high levels of excitation. *Journal of Research in Personality*, *9*(4), 282–293.

Zillmann, D., & Cantor, J. R. (1976). Effect of timing of information about mitigating circumstances on emotional responses to provocation and retaliatory behavior. *Journal of Experimental Social Psychology*, *12*(1), 38–55.

Zillmann, D., Jennings, B., Cantor, J. R., & Day, K. D. (1975). Irrelevance of mitigating circumstances in retaliatory behavior at high levels of excitation. *Journal of Research in Personality*, *9*(4), 282–293.

Zillmann, D., Katcher, A. H., & Milavsky, B. (1972). Excitation transfer from physical exercise to subsequent aggressive behavior. *Journal of Experimental Social Psychology*, *8*(3), 247–259.

Zimbardo, P. (2007). *The Lucifer effect: Understanding how good people turn evil*. New York: Random House.

Zimbardo, P. G. (1960). Involvement and communication discrepancy as determinants of opinion conformity. *Journal of Abnormal and Social Psychology*, *60*(1), 86–94.

Zimbardo, P. G. (1970). The human choice: Individuation, reason and order versus deindividuation, impulse, and chaos. In W. J. Arnold & D. Levine (Eds.), *Nebraska symposium on motivation* (Vol. 18, pp. 237–307). Lincoln: University of Nebraska Press.

Zurbriggen, E. L. (2000). Social motives and cognitive power–sex associations: Predictors of aggressive sexual behavior. *Journal of Personality and Social Psychology*, *78*(3), 559–581.

Note: Page numbers followed by f indicate illustrations; those followed by t indicate tables.

Note: Page numbers followed by f indicate figures; those followed by t indicate tables.